# Principles of Insurance Law

# Principles of Insurance Law

## FIFTH EDITION

**Jeffrey W. Stempel**

DORIS S. & THEODORE B. LEE PROFESSOR OF LAW
WILLIAM S. BOYD SCHOOL OF LAW
UNIVERSITY OF NEVADA, LAS VEGAS

**Erik S. Knutsen**

PROFESSOR AND ASSOCIATE DEAN (ACADEMIC)
QUEEN'S UNIVERSITY FACULTY OF LAW
KINGSTON, ONTARIO, CANADA

**The Late Peter N. Swisher**

T. C. WILLIAMS SCHOOL OF LAW
UNIVERSITY OF RICHMOND

CAROLINA ACADEMIC PRESS
Durham, North Carolina

ISBN     978-1-5310-0740-9
eISBN   978-1-5310-0741-6
LCCN    2019957153

Carolina Academic Press
700 Kent Street
Durham, North Carolina 27701
Telephone (919) 489-7486
Fax (919) 493-5668
www.cap-press.com

Printed in the United States of America

*For Ann, Ryan, Shanen, and Reed*

*For Wenjue, Kai, and Landon*

*To Karen and Stephanie — For all your love and support*

# Contents

# Table of Cases

# Preface

Our Fifth Edition of *Principles of Insurance Law* has been substantially revised, re-organized and updated in order to create the best teaching and learning tool about insurance law that we can. Our aim is to make the book both instructor and learner friendly. To that end, we re-envisioned the book to make it as "ready to teach" as possible, with the busy practitioner-instructor in mind. It is our hope that this book can be easily picked up and used with a minimum of preparation by the sessional instructor as easily as the lifelong academic scholar of insurance. Coupled with our Teacher's Manual, we expect the practitioner-instructor will find a user-friendly text that will allow them to easily plan their course syllabus and choose those topics that best play to their strengths.

In this casebook, we aim to offer the insurance law student and practitioner a broad perspective of both traditional insurance law concepts and cutting-edge legal issues affecting contemporary insurance law theory and practice. We strive to make the content both reflective and practical, maintaining a realistic balance between insurance law theory and practice.

We have also re-designed the book to best fit with how instructors would organize a typical insurance course (especially that busy sessional instructor in full-time insurance law practice or that first-time insurance law instructor whose main area of teaching may not be insurance). To that end, we have adopted a modular approach to the chapter divisions within the book, so instructors can select the modules that best suit them depending on the type of class taught. Because the modules (or chapters, as we call them) can be addressed standalone in the classroom, this should allow instructors to build a syllabus that plays to their strengths in insurance law while also being mindful of the time allowed in a course to cover (or not) particular topics.

The book itself has been substantially compressed, with targeted material in each chapter. Some of the material that has been removed from the prior version has been ported to the Teacher's Manual, if historical adopters wish to continue to use those materials.

One important innovation for the insurance law teacher and learner is the incorporation of practical Problems within each chapter. These Problems often draw on actual case examples and allow for opportunities to apply one's cumulative knowledge of insurance law topics to "real life" situations and legal disputes, and to make the type of difficult decisions with which a practicing attorney or judge would be faced. These Problems are designed to draw out the controversies and challenges that make insurance law such a fascinating field, while also giving the new student to insurance a taste of how a typical insurance law problem may arrive at a practitioner's door.

The new edition further includes new and expanded treatment of important insurance law developments that have taken place since the prior edition:

- inclusion, where appropriate, of how the new *Restatement of the Law of Liability Insurance* relates to a variety of insurance fundamentals (including specific analysis of key elements of the RLLI in the Liability Insurance chapter);

- discussion of the continued fallout from the wranglings and controversies with the Affordable Care Act ("Obamacare");

- a discussion of the corpus linguistics movement, which posits that the use of massive textual databases or even consumer surveys can aid in interpreting insurance policies (somehow);

- the drama from *Henkel* and *Fluor:* the California Supreme Court's flip-flop cases about anti-assignment clauses in insurance policies;

- new cases on cyber-insurance, insurable interest in property, and consequences of breach of duty to defend;

- new commentary and discussion on recoupment of defense costs, bad faith, and underlying insurance issues; and,

- a new section on reinsurance.

Between the Fourth and Fifth Edition, we were saddened to lose our co-author and friend, Professor Peter Nash Swisher. Peter very sadly passed away in 2016, leaving a large hole in the scholarly insurance law firmament. His important contributions to this book through a number of editions are gratefully acknowledged. He was a fond adopter of the formalist-functionalist modality, which we use as a key explanatory tool in the text.

Thanks also to our long-suffering families and to our respective colleagues at UNLV and Queen's, all of whom are probably more than a bit puzzled at our constant fascination with insurance—an interest we hope students will grow to appreciate as they read the materials in this casebook. Special thanks to UNLV Wiener-Rogers Law Library Director Jeanne Price and Assistant Director David McClure.

Insurance is often regarded as a topic that induces a feeling of "stirring cement with my eyelids" (to use Oliver Wendell Holmes's memorable description of first-year law school), even as compared to other parts of the law school curriculum. We beg to differ. Insurance involves many of the most intellectually interesting issues in modern law as well as topics central to modern human existence: life; death; greed; money; property; business; cars; homes; family; lawsuits; deals made and broken; steadfastness; and sharp dealing. It's all there in insurance law. We hope we have captured some significant part of this rich picture in *Principles of Insurance Law*.

Welcome to the fascinating and challenging world of insurance law!

Jeffrey W. Stempel
Erik S. Knutsen
April 2020

# Principles of Insurance Law

# Chapter 1

# Insurance History and Fundamental Concepts

## § 1.01. Introduction

Insurance has historically been something of a Rodney Dangerfield of the law. To put it in the famous[1] comedian's vernacular, insurance "don't get no respect"—at least not compared to constitutional law, anti-discrimination, legal theory, jurisprudence, and the various "isms" and "law ands" that often captivate both students and faculty in the academy.[2] One leading academic expert on insurance even includes in his treatise a self-deprecating story of being introduced at a social gathering as "boring" solely on the basis of his vocation.[3] If lawyers and teachers cannot embrace insurance

---

1. At least for folks as old as the authors, the late Rodney Dangerfield (1921–2004) qualifies as a famous, or at least well-known, comic. For the benefit of younger readers, we simply note that Dangerfield was primarily a standup comic who appeared in some movies (perhaps most notably *Caddyshack*) and that his standard comic pose is one of a loser who (you guessed it) "don't get no respect," as evidenced by the self-deprecating stories he proceeded to tell during his routine.

2. In separate writings, we have quoted with a mixture of approval and bemusement the observations of Seventh Circuit Judge Richard Posner, who once stated:

> Disinterested legal-doctrinal analysis of the traditional kind remains the indispensable core of legal thought, and there is no surfeit of such analysis today. I daresay that many legal scholars who today are breathing the heady fumes of deconstruction, structuralism, moral philosophy, and the theory of the second best would be better employed studying the origins of the *Enlow-Ettleson* doctrine or *synthesizing the law of insurance.*

See Richard A. Posner, *The Decline of Law as an Autonomous Discipline: 1962–1987*, 100 Harv. L. Rev. 761, 777 (1987), quoted in Jeffrey W. Stempel & Erik S. Knutsen, Stempel & Knutsen on Insurance Coverage (4th ed. 2016); Peter Nash Swisher, *Judicial Rationales in Insurance Law: Dusting Off the Formal for the Function*, 52 Ohio St. L.J. 1037 (1990). Although we agree with the sentiment that insurance law should get more attention in the academy, we also want to make it clear that insurance law, like any other legal topic, can often be better understood and implemented through application of learning from other realms of the law or fields other than law.

3. *See* Robert H. Jerry, II and Douglas R. Richmond, Understanding Insurance Law § 1, at 3, n.7 (6th ed. 2016). Notwithstanding that he is the co-author of a competing casebook (Christopher C. French & Robert H. Jerry, II, Insurance Law and Practice: Cases, Materials, and Exercises (2018)), we find Prof. Jerry an interesting, even scintillating colleague. There is solidarity among the fraternity of the disrespected.

In the same vein, students may note that our text liberally cites the works of other insurance authors, including those who disagree with us on a number of issues, which may be a departure from the custom in some areas of law where there is disinclination to even acknowledge "the competition." We reject such

as an appealing subject, it should come as no surprise that most laypersons think of insurance as boring.[4]

At the risk of sounding defensive, we contend insurance is not boring. Since no law school has yet been possessed of the wisdom to make insurance a required course, we (along with your classroom instructor) will have to convince you. Insurance is of prime importance to modern economies that depend on effective risk management as well as upon production, transportation, sales, service, and technology. It is a practical necessity of conducting business, at least for industrialized nations. Insurance is also one of the leading sources of capital formation and investment (insurers have to do something with all the premiums we pay).

Even those who maintain that insurance is boring must nonetheless concede it is important. "If insurance was a country, it would have the third biggest economy in the world." *See* Aaron Doyle & Richard Erichson, *Five Ironies of Insurance, in* The Appeal of Insurance 226 (Geoffrey Clark, Gregory Anderson, Christian Thomann & J. Matthias Graf von der Schulenburg, eds. 2010) (citing Evan Mills, *Insurance in a Climate of Change*, Science, Aug. 12, 2005, at 1040–44). "The insurance policy is created and designed to play a particular role in social and economic activity" and operate as key components in the operation of everyday life as well as the economic consequences of activity. *See* Jeffrey W. Stempel, *The Insurance Policy as Social Instrument and Social Institution*, 51 Wm. & Mary L. Rev. 1489, 1495–513 (2010). The ability of insurance to affect conduct is so great that it has been compared to governments not only in sheer size but also in its practical power. *See* Richard Ericson, Aaron Doyle & Dean Barry, Insurance As Governance (2003). The author of the promotional material for one excellent collection of essays on insurance was not exaggerating:

> [I]nsurance is a global economic colossus and a fixture in the developed countries of the world. But neither the financial clout of the insurance industry nor its ubiquity conveys the full measure of its social and political influence. The insurance industry has in fact become a primary agent of discipline and control over public and private behaviours by imposing upon them the criterion of insurability. By tracing the boundaries of acceptable (and compensated) from unacceptable (and uncompensated) risk, insurers directly or indirectly govern people, products, and markets, and by this process become one of the most powerful and pervasive agents of social and economic control.

*See* Book Jacket Description to The Appeal of Insurance, *supra*.

---

an approach and are at least attempting to provide readers not only with our assessment of insurance issues but also a full range of analyses as well as referrals to additional sources of information.

4. Popular business writer Andrew Tobias, author of the best-selling *The Only Investment Guide You'll Ever Need* and a most readable but now out-of-print book for laypersons about insurance (*The Invisible Bankers* (1982)), notes that when a friend found out that Tobias's next project was a book about insurance, the friend screamed at him: "Insurance? Insurance is boring." With friends like these....

Sometimes the necessity of insurance is legally imposed. For example, the financial responsibility laws of every state require automobile insurance as a condition of owning and driving a car (unless the auto owner is able to post a bond, something both more expensive and less protective than an insurance policy).[5] Similarly, banks will not lend money for a home purchase unless the property is insured—both against physical perils such as fire and against defects in the title to the property. Major construction projects usually will not receive the required government permits without proof of insurance, including a surety's performance and payment bonds to protect against contractor failure or delays in completion.[6]

In other instances, the law may not directly require insurance, but the legal, social, and business framework makes it a practical necessity. No responsible business can operate without some form of risk management and protection against property loss or liability claims. Large businesses may be able to do this through "self-insurance" but most commercial entities need to buy conventional insurance for their possessions and liability insurance to protect them from potentially crippling lawsuits.[7] Insurance even touches the realm of popular culture in that sports franchises and entertainment companies routinely have substantial life and disability insurance on star players or performers.[8] New insurance products designed to fill particular niches emerge almost

---

5. A bond guarantees the availability of a certain amount of money for payment of obligations. The typical auto insurance policy not only provides this (up to the policy limits) but also ordinarily requires the insurer to defend the policyholder against claims of alleged auto accident victims, with the defense expenditures being in addition to the policy limits available for victim compensation. Because litigation costs can often be substantial and even exceed damages awarded (which is always the case where there is a defense verdict), the duty to defend "outside limits" is a particularly valuable feature of both automobile policies and general liability insurance policies.

6. Technically, suretyship (the promise to respond to the obligation of another) is not insurance. At least that has been the historical conventional wisdom in the law. However, the modern trend is to treat suretyship as the equivalent of insurance for purposes of regulation and contract enforcement. Chapter 9, *infra*, discusses suretyship in general while Chapter 12 discusses the current status of the application of bad faith liability to sureties and insurers.

7. This includes not only the traditional tort liability that may attach from slip-and-fall problems on the policyholder's premise and auto accidents involving a company driver, but also statutory liability such as discrimination claims as well as liability for defective products, corporate mismanagement, and mass tort claims such as, most famously, asbestos-related liability.

It is important to remember, however, that although virtually all risks are insurable, different risks are subject to different insurance products. For example, a business auto policy does not protect the company from product liability claims while a general liability policy does not cover motor vehicle claims.

8. *See* David Wharton & Lisa Dillman, *At Today's Salaries, It's Tough to Risk It; Stratospheric Contracts Are Convincing More Teams to Pay Big Money to Cover the Possible Loss of Elite Players*, L.A. Times, Aug. 5, 1999, at D1; *Jolie's 'Salt' Wins Insurer's Award for Riskiest Film of 2010*, www.advisen. com, Feb. 11, 2011 (originally reported by Dow Jones Newswires) (actress Angelina Jolie's "decision to do her own stunts earned her movie the dubious honor, since an injury to a star can force a halt in production and cost $250,000 a day or more"). In addition, Fireman's Fund, which "insures four of every five movies to come out of Hollywood" frequently had a representative on the scene monitoring the stunts—which illustrates another important role of insurance in addition to defending and paying claims. Insurers often actively attempt to prevent or at least reduce claims by recommending or even imposing safety obligations upon policyholders.

daily. *See, e.g.*, Rachel M. Zahorsky, *Policy Matter: Firm Plans Insurance Against Evidence Loss*, A.B.A. J., Mar. 2011, at 31 (noting that insurer "plans to offer extended policies to guard against spoliation tort claims against clients that are often entrusted with property that can affect the outcome of a court case." Currently, nine states "recognize spoliation tort claims for the destruction of or failure to preserve evidence that is necessary to litigation.").

Many of the most important government programs consuming much of state and federal budgets are in essence insurance programs of a sort: social security; medicare; medicaid. Chapter 3 discusses regulation of insurance as insurance and also touches upon the intersection of private insurance and public legislation.

In short, insurance runs over, under, behind, and through most everything in modern industrial society, particularly in the United States, which shows a fondness for insurance that outpaces even that of Western Europe, Japan and, increasingly, China.[9] In addition to the mainstream, relatively standard insurance products discussed at length in this casebook, there is a plethora of specialized insurance products for specialized submarkets, which can include insurance for product recall, political risk, contract, risk, and even consequences of divorce.

As with any other activity, the result of insurance initiatives can sometimes be unintended consequences. "For instance, insurers insisted that a guard dog be hired to protect a collection of hundreds of rare teddy bears in Somerset, England. Unfortunately, the Doberman Pinscher recommended by the insurers went on a rampage and shredded dozens of the teddy bears he was supposed to protect." *See* Doyle, *Five Ironies of Insurance, supra* (footnoted omitted). Where insurance is unavailable, the consequences can be significant.[10]

For example, insurance was an important legal aspect of the terrorist attacks of September 11, 2001. In the aftermath of the fall of the World Trade Center towers arose a major dispute between the policyholder landlord[11] and property insurers re-

---

9. China, for example, has seen total insurance premiums triple during the past 20 years and may surpass the United States in total premiums by 2040. As national economic activity increases, insurance tends to grow correspondingly. Even though many commercial entities are large enough and wealthy enough to self-insure, they nonetheless tend to purchase insurance. *See* Victor P. Goldberg, *The Devil Made Me Do It: The Corporate Purchase of Insurance*, 5 Rev. L. & Econ. 541 (2009) (noting that in addition to seeking protection and managing cash flow through insurance, companies may find that "their contractual counterparties — buyers, lessors, and lenders — require that they carry insurance") (italics of abstract removed). Because of their extensive involvement in all aspects of social and economic life, insurers are often in the forefront of emerging issues. *See, e.g.*, Swiss Re, *Weathering Climate Change: Insurance Solutions for More Resilient Communities* (2010) (major insurer materials addressing issues of climate change). The pervasive presence of insurance also creates a situation in which insurers may become participants in larger tort law and policy issues.

10. *See Firefighters Let Home Burn; Owner Didn't Pay Fee*, www.advisen.com, Oct. 5, 2010 (homeowner's failure to pay locality's $75 fire protection fee, a form of insurance, results in fire department refusing to suppress home fire, leading to loss of home).

11. New York real estate mogul Larry Silverstein, who held a long-term lease on the property. The Port Authority of New York and New Jersey is the entity that actually "owns" the World Trade Center site.

garding the value of the destroyed property and whether the incident was one occurrence (due to one terrorist plot) or two occurrences (due to two separate airplane strikes felling two separate buildings).[12] Because insurance on the property was written in an amount of $3.6 billion per occurrence, the answer to this "boring" question of insurance law is worth more than the gross national product of many nations.[13]

In addition, the September 11 tragedy served as a wake-up call for the insurance industry as well as for the nation as a whole. Prior to September 11, property and liability insurance did not exclude coverage for terrorist acts although, as discussed at greater length below, exclusion of war-related risks was a standard provision of most standard policies. After September 11, billionaire Warren Buffett, reputedly the world's second-richest person and the effective controlling owner of one of the world's largest reinsurers (a reinsurer is a company that insures insurers against loss; *see* Chapter 13)[14] publicly lamented that his company and other insurers had been foolish to fail to exclude terrorism risks without at least demanding a higher premium in return for terrorism coverage. And remember — there was a frighteningly destructive terrorist attack on the World Trade Center in 1993 and yet insurers generally continued

---

12. *See* Jeffrey W. Stempel, *The Insurance Aftermath of September 11: Myriad Claims, Multiple Lines, Arguments over Occurrence Counting, War Risk Exclusions, the Future of Terrorism Coverage, and New Issues of Government Role*, 37 Tort & Ins. L.J. 817 (2002) (reviewing insurance issues arising in wake of September 11 terrorism and specifically addressing World Trade Towers dispute, concluding that two insured occurrences took place). The trial court in the matter found one occurrence (under particular language found in some of the policies at issue), but refused insurer motions for summary judgment where policy language was viewed as less clear and unable to foreclose the possibility that a reasonable factfinder would deem the two air attacks as two occurrences. *Compare SR Int'l Bus. Ins. Co. v. World Trade Ctr. Props. LLC*, 222 F. Supp. 2d 385 (S.D.N.Y. 2002) (holding as a matter of law that policy with language defining occurrence as "all losses or damages that are attributable directly or indirectly to one cause or to one series of similar causes "defines September 11 damage to WTC Towers as one occurrence), *with SR Int'l Bus. Ins. Co. v. World Trade Ctr. Props. LLC*, 2003 U.S. Dist. LEXIS 1103 (S.D.N.Y. Jan. 29, 2003) (policy ambiguous as to meaning of occurrence when policy speaks of a "series of losses ... arising out of one event"); *SR Int'l Bus. Ins. Co., Ltd. v. World Trade Center Properties LLC*, 222 F. Supp. 2d 385 (S.D.N.Y. 2002) (policy ambiguous where referring to merely an "occurrence"). Eventually, a jury found two occurrences for insurance policies where the "batching" language was absent. The battle over insurance coverage continued for years. *See WTC's Silverstein Fights $1.2 Billion Settlement in Sept. 11 Property Damage Case*, www.advisen.com, Oct. 21, 2010 (developer challenges apparent settlement "over concern that it could exhaust coverage limits before his own company's related claims are addressed.").

13. In addition to the discussion of fortuity in this Chapter, Chapter 6 discusses in more detail the concept of an insured "occurrence" or event and the tendency of the law to look more at the "causes" of a loss rather than the "effects" of the loss.

14. As discussed more fully in Chapter 13, *infra*, reinsurance is insurance purchased by front line insurers so that the initial insurer has some sharing of the risk with other insurers, particularly if covered losses are larger than anticipated. For very large or less predictable risks, reinsurance (or its rough equivalent such as a catastrophe bond) is considered a practical necessity for most insurers. Even though insurance companies are essentially amalgamations of money, only the largest insurers are thought capable of taking on very large or dangerous risk without reinsurance in place to support it if disaster strikes. The law generally recognizes this. For example, even in states that restrict an insurer's right to cancel an insurance policy, the insurer is often permitted to cancel if it loses its reinsurance and thus is no longer comfortable with the risk exposure.

to write coverage—even on landmark properties—without a specific terrorism exclusion and without an increase in premium. Some insurers or counsel have argued that excluding coverage for acts of war also excludes coverage for terrorist acts. But, as we shall see below, courts have almost uniformly rejected such arguments well before September 11, so much so that leading insurance executives such as Buffett and Maurice "Hank" Greenberg, former CEO of the mammoth American International Group ("AIG," which acquired some infamy when its loss with "credit default swaps" helped to trigger the Great Recession of 2008),[15] publicly ridiculed the idea that a war risk exclusion could also function as a terrorism exclusion.[16] But after September 11, insurers were not inclined (at they might have been prior to that date) to simply charge an additional premium to allow them to invest funds for possible payout later on terrorism claims.

The magnitude of the September 11 claims prompted the industry to demand government backing of terrorism insurance. Insurers achieved their goal in part when Congress enacted the Terrorism Risk Insurance Act of 2002, signed into law on November 26, 2002. Subsequent extensions of and revisions to the Act are discussed in Chapter 3 regarding insurance regulation.

Although September 11 "hardened" the insurance market, at least temporarily, and made coverage more expensive and less available generally, insurers and policyholders continued to do business, with a considerable amount of terrorism coverage still in force. Insurers responded to the new uncertainty over "mega" or "ultra-destructive" terrorism by raising prices, putting limits on the amount of terrorism risk insured, and excluding terrorism outright where the risk is seen as too great. Although some policyholders are undoubtedly upset about these developments, few appear to have constricted their activities or closed their doors due to this new problem of in-

---

15. Outside the United States, the Recession is perhaps more commonly referred to as the "Global Economic Crisis." Although others disagree, we regard a Credit Default Swap ("CDS") as a form of insurance. In a CDS, the seller agrees to compensate the buyer in the event that there is a default by the debtor (which could be a large loss and looks to us suspiciously like an insured event similar to a house fire, a hurricane, or a judgment resulting from a lawsuit). In return, the CDS seller is paid a fee for the "guaranty" of payment in the event of default, which looks to us a lot like a premium. The buyer incurs a relatively small but certain loss in return for a promise of protection in the event a contingent/uncertain loss (nonpayment to the creditor by the debtor). Notwithstanding that CDS contracts operate much like insurance, they have typically not been as extensively regulated as insurance.

AIG's more typical or ordinary insurance business was historically quite profitable and has returned to profitability in the years since the Great Recession. Its foray into CDS instruments was initially also quite profitable, because debtors seldom defaulted during the economic boom of the early 2000s. But when the economy soured in 2007–2008, defaults soared, leaving AIG and other CDS sellers unable to make good on their promises of compensation for creditors holding the promissory notes that were in default. It was akin to a "run on the bank" in which all the depositors wanted to withdraw funds and close accounts on the same day, a problem made worse because the pool of CDS investments was not sufficiently diversified.

16. *See* Stempel, *Insurance Aftermath of September 11, supra*, at 843–65 (reviewing history and rationale of war risk exclusion, case law of exclusion, and concluding war exclusion would not apply to claims arising out of September 11 terrorism).

surability and risk management. In the meantime, insurers have been attempting to increase their ability to predict and spread terrorism risk in accordance with historical risk distribution principles discussed below.

On a more mundane, less tragic, and occasionally almost comical level, insurance also frequently involves a gallery of rogues attempting to perpetrate scams in order to collect insurance benefits. One "high-end" example (if that's not an oxymoron) is Martin Frankel, described in the popular press as something of a nerd who perpetrated a multi-million scam of international proportion (and also found that he no longer had trouble getting dates after he became rich by misappropriating other people's money).[17] More pedestrian perhaps was Rev. Roland Gray, a Harvey, Illinois Baptist minister, who was sentenced to four and one-half years in prison for "faking at least 14 auto accidents to defraud insurance companies of more than $450,000." Arguably less reverent was Andrea Cabiale of Turin, Italy, who was charged with "arranging at least 500 bump-and-stop car accidents involving young female drivers, in largely unsuccessful attempts to date them." Found in Cabiale's apartment were "2,159 photographs of female car owners and their damaged vehicles."

Although insurance, like any area of the law, has its "dog bite cases," these too can be pretty interesting. Certainly, insurance can be exotic or even glitzy. Insurers have covered "Betty Grable's legs and Bruce Springsteen's voice, both of which proved to be good bets." *See* Michael D. Goldhaber, *The Flop! A Nightmare on Court Street*, Am. Law., May 2003, at 91 (describing some not-so-good bets made by insurers in selling coverage for financially unsuccessful movies or "flop insurance").

In light of all this, how can anyone say insurance is boring? Even if insurance lacks the drama of presidential impeachment or constitutional equal protection, it is sufficiently pervasive and important that lawyers should have a basic understanding of its operation and legal framework.

A basic orientation to insurance—its history, its function, its typical operation, its key concepts, and its standard policies—is an essential first step in studying insurance. This chapter attempts to set forth these basic concepts in the operation of insurance.

## § 1.02. The Historical Background and Nature of Insurance

Insurance in some form has existed for centuries. Insurance broadly defined is simply a form of risk shifting and risk spreading among persons. When prehistoric tribes hunted dangerous prey in packs or divided precious goods among several members for safe keeping, these cooperative ventures also acted to spread the risk of injury or loss among the tribe and to shift the risk of loss from the individual to the group.

---

17. *See* Ellen Joan Pollock, The Pretender (2002); Ellen Joan Pollock, *The Pretender: A Look at the Strange World of Martin Frankel*, Wall St. J., Jan. 7, 2002, at C1, C10 ("Gawky, with a deathly pallor, [Frankel] was not a looker. But he attracted women by appearing to absorb himself in their problems and needs. And, of course, there was the money.").

As society became more organized and mercantile, this sort of "insurance-in-kind" became more express. For example, trade caravans and Phoenician and Greek merchants (circa 300 B.C.) expressly divided their goods among different carriers and agreed to jointly share losses if the caravan was attacked or a ship lost in a storm.[18] Some authorities trace marine and casualty insurance to the Babylonian Code of Hammurabi (circa 2250 B.C.). In the merchant city-states of the Venice, Genoa, and Florence (circa 1300–1700), insurance became a more detailed and monetary industry, with financiers expressly receiving money in exchange for a promise for reimburse possible losses befalling a trade shipment.

By 1400, there were statutes regulating insurance in these cities. The Italian custom of making written contracts of insurance spread throughout Europe, in part because of the commerce of the Hanseatic League (circa 1300–1500). The modern term insurance "policy" is derived from the Italian word "poliza," which means a "folded writing." Barcelona appears to have had a reasonably well-established market for life insurance by the 15th century as well. *See* Geoffrey Clark, *The Slave's Appeal: Insurance and the Rise of Commercial Property*, *in* The Appeal of Insurance 57–58 & nn.25–27 (Geoffrey Clark et al. eds. 2010).[19] *See also* Geoffrey Clark, Betting on Lives (1999) (expansive tracing of rise of life insurance, with focus on England).

The earliest record of an insurance contract in England appears to be the opinion in a 1545 admiralty case. At the opening of the first Elizabethan Parliament in 1558, the Lord Keeper of the Great Seal stated the essence of insurance risk spreading and suggested that insurance had indeed arrived in England by stating "Doth not the wise merchant in every adventure of danger give part to have the rest assured?"

The birth of modern insurance, at least from the Anglo-American perspective, occurred in the 1600s in a now-famous coffeehouse near the docks of London. Proprietor Edward Lloyd permitted the merchants who gathered there for coffee and tea[20] to collectively agree to share risks on shipping ventures, often by posting a notice of the voyage and cargo and inviting other patrons to subscribe to a portion of the risk. In-

---

18. For a brief but lively review of insurance history, *see* Andrew Tobias, The Invisible Bankers (1982). For more extensive historical background, *see* Anthony Brown, Lloyd's of London (1975). For an updated but slightly polemical look at Lloyd's and its reaction to the "asbestos coverage crisis" of the 1980s and internal strive at Lloyd's, *see* Adam Raphael, Ultimate Risk (1995). Several successful suits by Lloyd's passive investors alleged mismanagement, favoritism, or occasionally even fraud by the active managers of certain Lloyd's syndicates.

19. A depressing, scandalous aspect of the rise of insurance practice included insurance on slaves shipped across the Mediterranean and the Atlantic, a practice that when highlighted in the infamous case of the *Zong* (a ship on which the captain threw injured and sick slaves overboard in 1781 as part of what appears to have been an insurance scam) helped to fuel abolitionist public sentiment in England. *See* Clark, *The Slave's Appeal*, *supra*.

20. Although, in contrast to current stereotypes about the British affection for tea, coffee was the more popular drink of the time. *See* Tom Standage, A History of the World in 6 Glasses (2005) (tracing historical popularity of wine, beer, coffee, tea, cocktails, and soda as reflections on economics, culture, and society).

terested merchants wrote beneath the description of their willingness to be part of these informal insuring syndicates, a practice that gave rise to the term "underwriter."

The merchants at Lloyd's of London agreed to share a percentage of the risk of loss of the cargo in transit. If the voyage went well, they received a portion of the profit. If the cargo was lost, the syndicate reimbursed the shipper for its loss. Obviously, it was not a coffee shop diversion for the faint of heart. Many underwriters, including *Robinson Crusoe* author Daniel Defoe, were driven to bankruptcy by ships that never reached their destination. Nonetheless, the potential profits of and business need for insurance spurred continued growth of the practice.[21]

By 1779, the "Lloyd's policy" became a standard form of marine insurance. In 1795, it was made the standard form policy by act of Parliament. By the late 18th century, insurance was established enough in England to merit legal treatise treatment. *See* Samuel Marshall, A Treatise On The Law of Insurance (1802); John Millar, Elements of The Law Relating to Insurances (1787); James Allan Park, A System of The Law of Marine Insurances (1787).

Today Lloyd's has become the well-known modern and professional insurance exchange, a development reflected in the growth of non-Lloyd's insurers during this same time period. As in the past, Lloyd's continues to operate in a sort of open market fashion. Various brokers representing applicants for insurance approach representatives of syndicates (groups of insurer investors) to seek the syndicates' commitment to provide insurance for a manufacturer or a voyage, or reinsurance of an American company's portfolio of life insurance policies, and so on. Computers have replaced Edward Lloyd's posted list, but there remains a town square atmosphere where personal contact and relationships continue to be key to transacting business. Huge risks are routinely undertaken quickly and with a minimum of paperwork.

Insurance, like any industry, has its highs, lows, and periods of scandal. In 1666, the Great London Fire devastated the city. But 15 years later, fire insurance was in wide use. The oldest fire insurance company, the Sun Fire Office, was established in 1710. English life and burial insurance contracts appeared in the early 1700s. The Equitable Life Assurance Company was established in 1762. Accident insurance came on to the scene in the early 1800s in response to the disturbing number of British steam locomotives that were blowing up, killing or injuring passengers. The industrialization of the United States created a similar perceived need for insurance that eventually led to the growth of life insurance, accident insurance, and our current system of workers' compensation.[22]

---

21. Lloyd's itself describes its origins as arising as merchants having met in coffee houses to discuss managing risk in the aftermath of the 1666 fire that ravaged London and notes that the first mention of Edward Lloyd's Coffee House in the press appears to have been a 1688 article in the London Gazette. *See* Lloyd's Pocket Guide.

22. *See* John Fabian Witt, *Toward a New History of American Accident Law: Classical Tort Law and the Cooperative First-Party Insurance Movement*, 114 Harv. L. Rev. 690 (2001), which provides an excellent review of the social and legal ferment surrounding the workplace in late 19th century America.

In 18th century England, insurance was for a time disturbingly used as a form of wagering by many Britons. Syndicates were formed and policies written regarding contingent events in which the policyholders had no personal stake or where the policyholder had an unusual degree of control over the "risk." For example, some insurers took a premium and promised to pay should public events such as a coronation be canceled. Other policies offered benefits to the family of the policyholder should he die of drinking too much on a gin binge. In reaction to the rampant use of insurance as a form of gambling, more conservative underwriters formed a new Lloyd's in 1771 that has been largely intact since.

In the United States, notions of insurance were largely imported wholesale from England but without the prominence of a central clearinghouse such as Lloyd's, although a similar group operated in Philadelphia as the "London Coffee House" for a time. As early as 1735, a fire insurance company appears to have been formed in South Carolina, although a Philadelphia company begun in 1752 is usually listed as the first American fire insurer. Benjamin Franklin was a director.

The first American life insurance mutual benefit associations were founded in 1759 to insure Presbyterian ministers. Such "discrimination" in the operation of insurance was not unusual in the 18th and 19th centuries. Many of the life insurance arrangements of the time were the product of what sales and marketing consultants now call an "affinity group"—the entire insurance product was designed for some subgroup of society as a means by which these groups could pool their resources in order to protect others in the "extended family" from unfortunate events. Thus, much of pre-20th century insurance was based on marketing to a particular religious group, work group, or social group.

Even today, some insurance products are available only to applicants who are members of the target group, but such restrictions are generally fading. For example, purchase of insurance from Aid Association for Lutherans was initially restricted to members of the Missouri Synod of the Lutheran Church, then expanded to all Lutherans. Lutheran Brotherhood was an insurer for another branch of the Lutheran Church. After the two companies merged into Thrivent Financial for Lutherans, sales were opened to all Christians and the company became just Thrivent Financial. GEICO (which stands for Government Employees Insurance Company), started out limiting sales to government employees and their families but now sells to the general public with sufficient zeal that you may have received a direct mail overture from them or seen one of the television ads with the famous Gecko. San Antonio-based USAA historically required a requisite connection to the U.S. Military (as a soldier, veteran, child of a veteran, etc.), relaxed the requirement for several years to include the FBI, Secret Service, and Foreign Service, but now appears to be more exclusively focused on customers with a military connection.

This shift from "fraternal society" or "affinity group" insurance to general sales to the general public reflects the modern trend of insurance. The business today is too competitive for most major companies to consider losing sales by limiting eligibility.

This is not to say, however, that persons from certain groups might more easily obtain insurance than other persons. For example, Presbyterian ministers are probably still a good bet for a life insurer. The parson is unlikely to live a reckless or self-destructive lifestyle and by definition tends to have indoor duties that do not involve grave physical danger (even with the most difficult congregation). By contrast, a life insurer may be unwilling to cover a high steel construction worker or NASCAR driver at standard rates. Life insurance did not cover military personnel until the federal government created a program in which the government was willing to back the insurers in the event that combat-related deaths required more death benefit payments than actuarially predicted.

In 1792, the Insurance Company of North America (INA) received its charter as the first stockholder-owned insurer in the United States.[23] Life insurance in general did not become widespread in the United States until after the Civil War. Until that time, life insurance was regarded with suspicion as a form of wagering. One American case (*Lord v. Dall*, 12 Mass 115 [1815]) questioned whether life insurance contracts were valid in America. They were acceptable in England, but the Revolution had severed America's legal ties from those of England. France at the time treated life insurance as illegal (a position that persisted until 1820).

Faced with the issue, the Massachusetts high court upheld the life insurance policy. The blood of ethnicity was thicker than the water of politics (remember, by this point, the U.S. and Britain had fought two fierce wars and the English had burned the White House): the Court rejected the French rationale that insurance "indecorous[ly]" put a price on the life of a free person, whose life should be "above all price." According to the perhaps Francophobe Massachusetts court, "freedom has never been known to exist" in France (not a misquote — that's an American court saying this) while England has "for several centuries" been "the country of established and regulated liberty." This is an odd assessment in light of France's role as an ally in the American Revolution and the role of the French Revolution (1789–1799) in limiting the powers of monarchy and expanding democracy, albeit with some rough years during the Reign of Terror (1793–94) when overzealous revolutionaries found the guillotine or the noose to be a convenient way of eliminating the politically incorrect.

But notwithstanding the ethnic bias and Anglo-jingoism of the *Lord v. Dall* court, the decision made several other rulings still relevant today. It found that decedent Lord's sister had an "insurable interest" (*see* Ch. 5) in her brother's life, that the $5,000 policy limit (a pretty reasonable/low $83,000 in 2019 dollars) was not so high as to

---

23. *See generally* John A. Bogardus Jr. with Robert H. Moore, Spreading the Risks: Insuring the American Experience (2003); William H.A. Carr, Perils Named and Unnamed: The Story of the Insurance Company of North America (1966). INA subsequently merged with CIGNA Insurance in 1982 and was acquired by ACE Limited in 1999 (subsequently renamed Chubb Limited when ACE acquired Chubb in 2016 and chose to use the Chubb name, which had an excellent reputation). As in many other industries, mergers, acquisitions, and rebranding that includes name changes is relatively frequent for insurers.

invalidate the contract (*see* Ch. 12),[24] that the decedent's arguable involvement in the slave trade at time of death did not invalidate the contract (*see* § 2.13 regarding public policy arguments for and against coverage) both because of unclear facts and because his sister was what today would be called an "innocent" beneficiary with no role in her brother's work; and that (upholding a jury's verdict), the decedent did not improperly conceal from the insurer plans to travel to Africa (see Chs. 4 & 6 regarding insurance contract formation and rescission defenses).

Although insurance can have the unseemly appearance of putting a price on things many regard as priceless, a bit of less emotional reflection makes it clear that life and death have dramatic economic consequences that can be priced, at least roughly. A reasonable basketball fan can debate the precise worth of various star players (e.g., LeBron James versus Kevin Durant), but without doubt, any team that loses a player of this caliber will likely suffer economic loss through a weaker record, declining attendance, reduced television revenue, truncated playoff rewards, etc. While it is true that there is some aspect of gambling when one insures anything, this "bet" on the someone's life will probably not lead to skullduggery or recklessness so long as the person buying the insurance (e.g., the basketball team) has an "insurable interest" in the life[25] and the player is not overinsured.

In early America, as now, each state was largely responsible for regulating insurance, a task largely accomplished through detailed charters giving long lists of express powers and limitations on the insurer. In the mid-1800s, states began to establish insurance departments, including the single insurance commissioner model of regulation that began in New York and remains the typical model of state regulation. A more complete history of the origins of insurance can be found in Vance On Insurance 7–35 (3d ed. 1951).

For years, the conventional legal wisdom held that insurance was not a part of "commerce" and that the federal government thus lacked power to regulate it under

---

24. In general, courts will not revise life insurance policy limits even if the size of the policy seems inapt relative to the economic value of the decedent's continued living activity. No one forces the life insurer to sell a policy. If it is willing to sell a $10 million policy on the life of a retail clerk, it cannot, absent fraud (e.g., claiming that the retail clerk was an investment banker), reduce its coverage commitment. In practice, life insurers have guidelines that often place some restrictions on policy limits based on income or other factors.

25. The insurable interest concept, which applies to property insurance as well as to life insurance, is discussed in Chapter 5, *infra*. A person with an insurable interest has something to lose if the life or property insured is destroyed. Consequently, the policyholder with an insurable interest will be unlikely to injure person or property just to collect the insurance because the insurance, if not written in excessive amounts, will do no more than put the policyholder in its original position. But where an entity without a proper stake in the life or property insured is allowed to procure insurance, there may then be some real risk of arson or murder designed to collect insurance benefits. Even with an insurable interest, property insurers will not issue a policy in an amount larger than the replacement cost of the property (except when there is a "blanket" policy covering several different structures or locations). Life insurers may also determine maximum limits by a formula linked to the income or wealth of the person whose life is insured.

the Commerce Clause of the Constitution. *See Paul v. Virginia*, 19 L. Ed. 357, 8 Wall. (75 U.S.) 168 (1869), and Ch. 3, *infra*. However, changing judicial views of the Commerce Clause and the appropriate mix of federal and state authority led to a change in the Supreme Court's perspective, briefly making insurance law subject to federal regulation, particularly antitrust suits, since so many insurers expressly cooperated in sharing data and setting premium rates and policy packages.[26] The insurance industry and state regulators quickly prevailed upon Congress to pass the McCarran-Ferguson Act,[27] which returned regulatory authority to the states.

In modern times, insurance contracts have become standardized, often written on an industry-wide basis. Today in the United States and throughout the world, the insurance industry writes billions of dollars in coverage, covering life, health, property, casualty, and general liability insurance as well as other types of risks. Most drivers carry automobile insurance, which is compulsory in most states. More than 90 percent of American homeowners and 30 percent of renters are insured. There exists a wide range of basic policies and special provisions which can be purchased by policyholders. Thousands of insurance companies compete for business, charging premiums that are viewed by the industry as too low and by many consumers as too high. The amount of premiums paid by Americans is staggering. Estimated total premium payments to U.S. insurers exceed $1 trillion per year. More than $7 trillion of life insurance is in force upon American lives. At the same time, however, nearly 30 million Americans have no medical expense insurance.[28]

Insurance can be broadly classified among several important dimensions. First, the insurance world tends to be divided into property/casualty insurance and life/health insurance (which includes disability, nursing home care, and the like). The division is widely followed throughout the industry. For example, major insurance publishers such as *National Underwriter* and *Best*'s have separate periodicals for the two branches of the industry.

---

26. *See United States v. South-Eastern Underwriters Ass'n*, 322 U.S. 533 (1944).

27. 15 U.S.C. § 1011 *et seq. These developments are discussed at greater length in Chapter 3 concerning the regulation of insurance.*

28. And this does not count the number of American with bare bones medical insurance that is probably inadequate for their needs. Although, like everyone else, we will lapse into calling medical expense coverage "health insurance," the former term is more accurate. This type of insurance provides for payment of medical bills. It does not in any way guarantee health, although better medical insurance programs promote health through wellness programs and paying for regular preventive care.

As to the number of uninsured Americans, one encouraging development in the years between this edition of this coursebook and its predecessor is that the number of uninsured Americans declined because the Affordable Care Act of 2009 took effect. Unfortunately, political resistance to the Act in some states prompted some loss of initial progress. The Act remains politically disputed, and one can certainly debate the merits of various health care policies (ranging from no government involvement to employer-provided benefits plans to Obamacare/Romneycare/Switzerland systems to German, French, Canadian systems, Medicare for all to the English system of medical care not only financed but operated by government). But it is beyond debate that the Affordable Care Act has reduced the number of uninsured in the United States.

Second, insurance can be classified as "first-party" insurance and "third-party" insurance. First-party insurance is that designed to provide coverage for the policyholder's own loss of property, life, or the incursion of medical and related costs. The parties to the contract and the claim are the policyholder (the first party) and the insurer (the second party). Third-party insurance provides the policyholder with protection against the claims brought by third parties against the policyholder, which generally means providing a defense to the third-party's claims and paying if a claim is covered and results in a judgment against the policyholder or an agreed settlement of the claim.

*Types of insurance* widely offered include: marine and inland marine; life (including whole life, term, group, and universal life policies); fire; wind; rain; riot; explosion; earthquake; renter's; homeowner's; general property; business interruption (also called business income); product recall; health; accident; casualty; mortgage; general liability; automobile; aircraft; product liability; professional malpractice; burglary and theft; workers' compensation; employer's liability; employment practices liability; professional liability; directors' & officers' liability; fidelity and surety; credit and title; industrial; personal injury; pollution coverage; and excess and umbrella policies (which begin covering risks where the loss or liability exceeds the amount of primary insurance). In addition, one may purchase (at a price, of course) specialized risk insurance that covers: lightning; insects; blight; earthquake; volcano; civil war and insurrection; nationalization of private property or other takings; animals; glass; water damage; floods; drought; elevators; reputational damage; and identity theft as well as steam boiler and numerous other targeted risks.[29]

In addition, all of the above forms of insurance may be the subject of "reinsurance"—which is essentially insurance bought by the insurance company to protect it by providing payment should the insurer be required to pay a sufficient amount of claims under its policies.[30]

Irrespective of social and political debate surrounding insurance, the basic transaction remains the same: the policyholder pays a premium and in return the insurer promises to indemnify the policyholder should he or she[31] suffer one of the losses for which the policy provides coverage. When a policyholder buys insurance, she purchases a product ("coverage") but the precise contours of coverage can become disputed after a loss occurs.

---

29. Insurance may also be classified according to whether the insurer is owned by investors (a stock company) or is instead owned jointly by the policyholders (a mutual company).

30. Chapter 13, *infra*, discusses reinsurance in more detail.

31. In the remainder of this book, masculine and feminine pronouns are used interchangeably in order to avoid both the additional verbiage of "he or she" constructions as well as wordy, passive voice explanations (e.g., "should a loss be incurred by the policyholder"). Unless otherwise indicated, use of either a masculine or feminine pronoun is not intended to restrict the illustration to only men or only women.

# § 1.03. Risk Distribution and Pooling — Defining Insurance

The very reason for having insurance is to spread risk. People or businesses purchase insurance as a way of spreading risk among a wide group of similarly situated policyholders.[32] By doing this, the policyholder agrees to accept a certain loss (the payment of the premium) in return for obtaining protection should it experience a large but unpredictable loss such as a fire, hurricane damage, or burglary. Of course, the losses covered by an insurance policy may not occur. If covered events were certain to occur, no sane insurer could offer coverage except at astronomical premiums sufficient to establish a fund to be drawn upon when the inevitable catastrophe occurs. Faced with such hypothetically large premiums, a rational policyholder would probably forgo or discontinue insurance and simply save its own money in anticipation of the coming loss.

Thus, the nature of insurance realistically requires that the happening of insured events — or at least their severity and time of occurrence — be contingent rather than certain in order to create an environment in which private insurers will want to operate and in which other entities will want to purchase insurance. This is true for life insurance as well even though, as the famous economist John Maynard Keynes once quipped, "In the long run, we're all dead." True, but the length of individual lives varies dramatically, meaning that life insurance covers a contingency (the time of death) rather than a certainty. Consequently, insurers can make actuarial calculations and charge appropriate premiums that permit them to make a profit. Policy language excludes potential sources of mass death (e.g., war) that might ruin the actuarial assumptions of the insurer. Thus, despite the certainty of death, life insurance is generally considered one of the more reliably profitable lines of insurance (remember, the insurer also earns money from investing premium dollars during the decades of human lives insured).

The ability to give up a comparatively small amount of certain loss (the premium) in return for a large amount of protection (payment for loss or liability by the insurer, up to the policy limits as necessary) (and always policy limits for life insurance) should a large loss occur makes insurance an attractive concept. Insurers are able to offer this product by virtue of spreading the risk of the contingent loss (e.g., fire, hurricane, flood) among a large group of policyholders. More important, the group (or "risk pool") of policyholders must be sufficiently large and variegated that the pool of policyholders as a whole is not too greatly damaged by any one incident or series of related incidents.

---

32. Risk management also entails effort at loss reduction other than the purchase of insurance. For an informative historical discussion of the concept of risk and human efforts to tame it, *see* PETER L. BERNSTEIN, AGAINST THE GODS: THE REMARKABLE STORY OF RISK (1996).

Insurers seek to cover "uncorrelated" risk and avoid "correlated" risk. For example, providing homeowner's insurance to more than a million policyholders randomly distributed across the continental United States provides a risk pool upon which a property insurer can profitably operate provided it charges adequate premiums and otherwise engages in sound underwriting. A property insurer who wrote coverage for a million homes all located in South Florida might make handsome profits for several years but would likely be devastated by a large hurricane, such as Hurricane Andrew, which struck Florida in August 1992. In this example, the risk assumed by the Florida-only insurer is simply too closely correlated to permit safe operation of a property insurance business. The carrier would likely fail at some point. Worse yet, it would lack sufficient funds to indemnify policyholders for their losses.

Because risk distribution and pooling is so central to insurance, the underwriting process seeks to achieve a large but sound and uncorrelated pool of policyholders. As a result, insurance underwriting is designed to avoid issuing policies that will work against this goal. As discussed more fully in the following chapters, insurers attempt to avoid issuing policies to persons who lack an insurable interest in the subject of the insurance (Chapter 5) or where issuing the policy will give rise to problems of adverse selection or moral hazard (§ 1.05[B] & [C]). In addition, insurance policies are written to provide defenses to coverage and grounds for rescission (Chapter 4) should the policyholder's conduct tend to undermine maintenance of a sound risk pool. For example, a typical insurance policy provides that an insurer may rescind the policy if the policyholder made misrepresentations during the application process or made false statements in connection with filing a claim (Chapter 4).

Where a particular risk becomes too difficult to calculate or presents too large a cluster of concentrated risk, coverage may be difficult or even impossible to obtain. After Hurricane Andrew hit South Florida in 1992, many insurers refused to issue windstorm coverage in the state. Florida responded with a state-administered pool that provided windstorm coverage to homeowners who were unable to purchase such coverage from private insurers. The plan was that over time, the windstorm pool has been depopulated as increasing numbers of private insurers have been willing to return to writing wind coverage or new insurers have stepped in to fill the coverage void left by Hurricane Andrew. But critics have argued that the government program has gained too much market share, creating a risk of major problems should there be another bad hurricane year in Florida, as took place in 2005 when four major storms ravaged the state. Flood and earthquake insurance have presented similar problems that have required similar government-backed solutions to either provide insurance or spur the private sector to offer coverage.

Sometimes the emergence of a new risk leads to exclusions, at least for a time because of uncertainty. This appears to be the case regarding terrorism coverage, as discussed above. Insurers may also respond to increased risk not by barring coverage altogether but by charging a higher premium, requiring the policyholder to share more risk (through a deductible or self-insured retention or through express pro-rata risk sharing), or imposing sub-limits on the amount of coverage for the difficult risk. For example, an insurer might be willing to underwrite $1 million of terrorism coverage, which would probably provide coverage against "lone wolf" acts of terrorism but be unwilling to write the higher amounts that would be implicated and perhaps exhausted or exceed by major events such as 9/11 or the 2004 Madrid train station bombing.[33]

One often sees a pattern where insurers are reluctant to insure some difficult risks at all and then progress to being willing to offer limited coverage. As the amount of coverage in force increases, the risk pool expands, and more and better data about the risk emerges. As a result, coverage for the risk often becomes easier and cheaper to obtain. For example, Employment Practices Insurance, which began to be offered extensively in the 1990s, was initially quite expensive per $1,000 of coverage (a common insurance metric) and available only in low policy limits. Over time, premium rates have declined, and coverage has become more available with higher policy limits.

A less dramatic example of a hardening market than terrorism is mold in homes. Mold claims grew like—well, like fungus—during the 1990s,[34] creating a new area of substantial exposure that could tend to be area-wide rather than confined to an individual house. When mold strikes, it may be common throughout a region. By contrast, when lightning strikes, it is unlikely to hit more than a few houses in the affected area. Insurers paid a lot for mold damage claims ($1.3 billion during 2001) even though many insurer lawyers disputed the propriety of coverage under the applicable policies.[35] Many insurers simply excluded altogether any homeowner's coverage for "mold, fungus, wet rot, dry rot or bacteria" unless the problem is a symptom from some other risk already covered under the policy.[36] In similar fashion, some homeowners insurers have restricted the liability coverage provided in a typical policy if the policyholder has a pet dog from a breed thought to be particularly dangerous.

---

33. The several coordinated bombings at several Madrid train stations on March 11, 2004, killed 193 people and injured 2,000 more, causing an estimated $300 million in economic damage.

34. The upsurge in mold claims may have been the result of better detection, and probably in part resulted from more erratic quality control in home building in fast-growing areas (California, Texas, and Nevada were growth centers for mold and other construction defect claims) as well as increased awareness and more litigious homeowners (for property insurers). In addition, many of the problems were alleged to be common to an entire building or neighborhood developed by a single builder, effectively converting such claims into a "mini-mass tort" (for liability insurers) if a neighborhood association sponsored the suit or a sufficient number of residents joined in.

35. *See* Christopher Oster, *Insurance Companies Just Say "No" to Covering Mold*, Wall St. J., Aug. 8, 2002, at D1, col. 2; Walter J. Andrews, Lon A. Berk & Michael S. Levine, *Mold-Related Property Damage; Is It Really Covered Under First Party Property Insurance?*, 11 Coverage No. 5, Sept./Oct. 2001, at 1.

36. *See* Oster, *supra*, at D1. For example, if a showerhead bursts, sprays the bathroom wall, and begets a mold infestation, this will generally remain covered despite the general mold exclusion if the precipitating event is promptly reported to the homeowner's insurer.

Where the policy language is silent or open-ended, courts may provide some protection to insurers through common law doctrines or favorable interpretation of the policy. For example, courts usually will accept an insurer's invitation to void coverage where the policyholder lacks an insurable interest even though the policy text itself and the application do not expressly establish this requirement (*see* Ch. 5). In some instances, doctrines favorable to insurers are codified in state statutes and thus may provide protection to the insurer even if the policy language is silent. Proper application of many of the common defenses to a coverage claim are justified at least as much by a perceived need to protect the integrity of insurance risk pools as by bilateral contract principles. Conversely, as discussed in Chapter 2, many judge-made doctrines and statutes are designed to protect policyholders in the case of ambiguity or silence in the policy language. More detailed discussion of risk distribution and the nature of insurance is readily found in broad-based insurance law treatises or business course texts on insurance.[37]

## [A] What Is Insurance — And What Is Not?

U.S. Supreme Court Justice Potter Stewart once wrote that pornography resisted a precise definition but "I know it when I see it."[38] As most of us know from both an ensuing three decades of litigation on the topic and the often very different opinions of family, friends, and neighbors, not everyone appears to see the same thing when trying to determine what is obscene. As you read the following cases, ask yourself whether there is any greater legal consensus as to what constitutes insurance. Also ask yourself why it matters if a product or service is classified as insurance.

> [**Author's Note:** In editing cases for publication, we have attempted to condense cases to the maximum extent possible in order to cover more territory in this book. Where substantial citations or substantive text have been excised from a case report, this is indicated through ellipses or similar devices but minor condensations may not be obviously marked and we have taken some liberties to break up long, difficult-to-read paragraphs used in some opinions. We have also condensed or eliminated citations when not necessary to the meaning of the case. Where only minor verbiage such as "*id.*" or "*ibid*" have been eliminated, these have simply been excised from the edited case report.]

---

37. *See, e.g.*, Robert H. Jerry, II, Understanding Insurance Law (6th ed. 2018); George E. Rejda & Michael J. McNamara, Principles of Risk Management and Insurance (13th ed. 2017); Emmet J. Vaughn & Therese M. Vaughan, Fundamentals of Risk and Insurance (11th ed. 2014); Mark S. Dorfman & David A. Cather, Introduction to Risk Management & Insurance (10th ed. 2013); Robert E. Keeton & Alan I. Widiss, Insurance Law (2d ed. 1988); Kenneth S. Abraham, Distributing Risk (1986).

38. *See Jacobellis v. Ohio*, 378 U.S. 184, 197 (1964) (Stewart, J., concurring). Often forgotten in the historical hubbub of Stewart's provocative comment is the entirety of his statement ("and the motion picture involved in this case is not that" he continued, referring to the French film *Les Amants* ("The Lovers")).

# Griffin Systems, Inc. v. Washburn

Appellate Court of Illinois, First District, Fourth Division
153 Ill. App. 3d 113, 106 Ill. Dec. 330, 505 N.E.2d 1121 (1987)

**Linn, J.**

Appellant, Griffin Systems, Inc. (Griffin), brings this appeal seeking reversal of a cease and desist order issued by the Illinois Department of Insurance (the Department), and affirmed after review by the trial court. The trial court agreed with the Department's finding that Griffin was engaged in the selling of insurance without a certificate of authority.

The Department's cease and desist order prohibits Griffin from distributing its "Vehicle Protection Plan" (plan). Griffin was marketing the plan to Illinois residents who had recently purchased new automobiles. Under the plan, consumers pay a yearly fee in exchange for Griffin's promise to pay for the repair or replacement of certain automobile parts should those parts break down or fail to operate during a specified coverage period.

After a hearing on the matter, the Department ruled that the plan constituted an insurance policy and entered a cease and desist order against Griffin. Griffin appealed the Department's ruling to the trial court which, after holding its own hearing, agreed with the Department's findings.

Griffin now appeals contending: (1) that the trial court erred in ruling that the plan constitutes an insurance policy rather than a service contract; (2) that the Department's cease and desist order is not supported by the evidence; and (3) that the trial court erred in failing to find that the plan, because it is a service contract, is governed by Federal law and is therefore exempt from State regulation. We affirm.

The facts of this case are not in dispute. Griffin is an Ohio corporation which began marketing the plan in Illinois in early 1984. Griffin sent a sales brochure and a sales agreement to Illinois residents who had recently purchased new automobiles. The brochure describes the plan as "a mechanical service contract." Under the plan, Griffin agrees to repair or replace any of the specific automobile parts covered by the plan should those parts break down or fail during the coverage period.

The plan provides for a $25 deductible per part. When a customer needs mechanical service, he contacts Griffin, which then forwards the claim request to Great Plains Insurance, Inc. Only upon approval by Great Plains adjusters will a repair be covered by the plan's provisions. A customer can bring his vehicle into any facility the customer selects. Griffin itself, however, does not perform any of the repair services. The customer is permitted to select one of four different policies. The policies differ in their length of time and with respect to the number of parts covered. The policies also contain certain exclusions, limitations, and conditions.

The Department determined that under Illinois common law the plan indemnified customers against possible future losses and, as a result, the plan constituted an insurance policy. The trial court subsequently agreed with the Department's ruling, prompting Griffin to bring this appeal.

The central issue in this appeal is whether Griffin engages in the business of selling insurance when it offers the plan to Illinois residents. In reviewing the Department's decision, our function is to determine whether the Department's finding that the plan constitutes an insurance policy was clearly against the manifest weight of the evidence.... The Illinois Insurance Code (Ill. Rev. Stat. 1983, ch. 73, par. 733) fails to define the term "insurance." Nevertheless, a definition is provided by the Illinois common law. One Illinois court, for example, defined "insurance" as:

> "[A]n agreement by which the insurer, for a consideration, agrees to indemnify the insured against loss, damage, or prejudice to certain property described in the agreement, for a specified period, by reason of specified perils." (*Barnes v. People ex rel. Moloney* (1897), 168 Ill. 425, 429, 48 N.E. 91.)

Insurance has also been described as:

> "[A] contract of indemnity by which the insurer * * * undertakes to indemnify the insured against pecuniary loss arising from the destruction of, or injury to, the insured's property * * *. The essence of the contract is indemnity against loss." ...

Thus, it appears that "insurance" can be characterized as involving: (1) a contract or agreement between an insurer and an insured which exists for a specific period of time; (2) an insurable interest (usually property) possessed by the insured; (3) consideration in the form of a premium paid by the insured to the insurer; and (4) the assumption of risk by the insurer whereby the insurer agrees to indemnify the insured for potential pecuniary loss to the insured's property resulting from certain specified perils.

In the present case, Griffin's plan contains each of the four elements set forth above.

First, the "Mechanical Service Contract" is clearly an agreement between Griffin and a customer which lasts for a specified period of time. The exact length of the time period varies and depends upon which of the four policies the customer purchases.

Second, there is an insurable interest involved, namely, the mechanical parts of the customer's vehicle which are covered by the plan.

Third, under the plan, the customer is obligated to pay a premium in return for Griffin's promise to reimburse the customer for the repair or replacement of certain automobile parts.

And fourth, Griffin agrees to indemnify the customer for a potential future loss; specifically, the costs involved in the repair or replacement of certain automobile parts.

Hence, we agree with the Department and the trial court that Griffin's plan contains all of the elements contained within the common law definition of insurance. The essence of the plan is to indemnify the customer; to reimburse the customer for a possible future loss to a specified piece of property caused by a specified peril, namely, mechanical failure. Consequently, the plan constitutes insurance and properly falls within the authority of the Department.

The plan is not, as Griffin contends, merely a "service contract," nor does it fall within the purview of a "warranty."

An example of a "service contract" can be found in the case of *Rayos v. Chrysler Credit Corp.*, 683 S.W.2d 546 (Tex. App. 1985). In *Rayos*, the court reviewed a 5-year/50,000-mile owner protection plan issued by Chrysler. Under the Chrysler plan, Chrysler agreed to repair or replace certain parts should those parts fail or break down within the specified period (5 years or 50,000 miles). The court in *Rayos* noted, however, that the Chrysler plan included a requirement that the customer bring his vehicle into a Chrysler Corporation dealer for any of the covered repairs. Because Chrysler built the vehicle to which it was going to make repairs, the *Rayos* court properly determined that the plan issued by Chrysler amounted to a service contract rather than an insurance policy.

A "warranty," on the other hand, was found to exist in *GAF Corp. v. County School Board* (4th Cir. 1980), 629 F.2d 981. There, a company agreed to repair or replace a roof it had sold to a customer should the roof ever leak in the future. However, the company which agreed to perform the repairs was the same company that had sold the roof. Consequently, because the company promising to make the repairs was the same company that had sold the roof, the *GAF* court found that the agreement to repair or replace constituted a warranty rather than an insurance policy.

An analysis of the cases set forth above reveals that a warranty and a service contract have many of the same features. Nonetheless, the distinguishing feature which sets them apart from an insurance policy is the fact that the respective companies *manufacture or sell the products which they agreed to repair or replace*. No third parties are involved, nor is there a risk accepted which the company, because of its expertise, is unaware of. Through a warranty or service contract, a company simply guarantees that its own product will perform adequately for a period of time.

Insurance policies, on the other hand, are generally issued by third parties and are based on a theory of distributing a particular risk among many customers. The case of *Guaranteed Warranty Corp., Inc. v. State ex rel. Humphrey* (1975), 23 Ariz. App. 327, 533 P.2d 87, is a prime example of a company's selling an insurance policy rather than a warranty or a service contract.

In *Guaranteed*, a company was in the business of selling contracts which provided that the company would replace the customer's television picture tube should the tube ever fail as a result of a manufacturing defect. The company, however, did not manufacture, nor did it sell, television sets or television tubes. Instead, the company merely marketed the tube replacement contracts. Because the company did not manufacture or sell the television tubes, the *Guaranteed* court found that the tube replacement contracts were, in reality, promises to indemnify the customer for a potential future loss. The tube replacement contracts were not merely a method to guarantee the performance of the company's product, for the company did not manufacture or sell the tubes in question. That being the case, the *Guaranteed* court found that the tube replacement contracts constituted insurance policies.

Likewise, in the case at bar, it is significant to note that Griffin itself does not perform any of the repairs or replacements covered by the plan. Nor does Griffin manufacture or sell automobiles or automobile parts. Instead, Griffin merely sells a plan which promises to indemnify the customer for any losses he may suffer through the breakdown or failure of certain mechanical parts in his automobile. In this respect, Griffin's plan is analogous to that which was found to constitute an insurance policy by the *Guaranteed* court.

The procedure employed by Griffin also suggests that the plan amounts to an insurance policy rather than a warranty or service contract. The plan requires a customer who needs a repair to first obtain an estimate from an independent automobile service center. The estimate is then reviewed by a claims adjuster with the Great Plains Insurance Company. Upon receiving approval by the adjuster, the customer authorizes the independent service center to perform the work.

Under the plan, the customer is obligated to pay a $25 deductible for each repair performed. Griffin thereafter pays the service center the balance due. Furthermore, like an insurance policy, the plan involves exclusions and limitations as to Griffin's liability.

We believe that based on these facts, the evidence supports the Department's decision that Griffin's plan constitutes an insurance policy. It is clearly not a warranty such as that present in *GAF*, nor is it a service agreement like that existing in *Rayos*. Instead, the plan issued by Griffin is an indemnity agreement whereby Griffin agrees to indemnify its insured for potential losses arising from the mechanical breakdown of the insured's vehicle. That being the case, Griffin is engaged in the business of selling insurance and is therefore subject to the Department's rules and regulations. Accord, *Guaranteed Warranty Corp., Inc. v. State ex rel. Humphrey* (1975), 23 Ariz. App. 327, 533 P.2d 87.

We also find that the facts of the instant case are clearly distinguishable from those present in *Vredenburgh v. Physicians Defense Co.* (1906). In *Vredenburgh*, a group of attorneys agreed to represent several physicians in any malpractice claims that might be brought against the physicians. The agreement contained an attorney fee cap at which point the attorney's obligation under the agreement ceased. However, as the *Vredenburgh* court found, such an arrangement involves no indemnity for losses; instead it was merely a commonplace attorney-retainer agreement. Unlike the employer-employee relationship existing in *Vredenburgh*, Griffin's plan includes an element of indemnity and is therefore more properly considered to be an insurance policy.

The remaining arguments raised by Griffin must fail as a result of the discussion presented above. Griffin first argues that the Department's original cease and desist order was unsupported by the evidence. As set forth previously, however, our function is to determine whether the Department's decision was contrary to the manifest weight of the evidence. (*Anzinger v. O'Connor* (1982), 109 Ill. App. 3d 550, 440 N.E.2d 981.) In the present case, Griffin submitted all of its sales literature, a copy of the plan, and a copy of the mechanical service contract. These are the documents which contain the details of Griffin's business. Because these documents form the heart of the dispute, they are, in this instance, sufficient evidence to support the Department's decision. Consequently, Griffin's assertion that the Department's original decision was unsupported by the evidence is rejected.

Griffin's claim that its plan is governed exclusively by Federal law is also in error. Individual States clearly have the right to regulate the business of insurance and, in light of our finding that Griffin's plan constitutes an insurance policy, no Federal preemption exists.

## Griffin Systems, Inc. v. Ohio Dept. of Insurance

Supreme Court of Ohio
61 Ohio St. 3d 552, 575 N.E.2d 803 (1991)

**Sweeney, J.**

The determinative issue presented in this appeal is whether appellant's vehicle protection plans are contracts "substantially amounting to insurance" within the meaning of R.C. 3905.42. For the reasons that follow, we answer such inquiry in the negative, and therefore reverse the judgment of the court of appeals and reinstate the trial court's judgment.

R.C. 3905.42 provides as follows:

> "No company, corporation, or association, whether organized in this state or elsewhere, shall engage either directly or indirectly in this state in the business of insurance, or enter into any contracts substantially amounting to insurance, * * * unless it is expressly authorized by the laws of this state, and the laws regulating it and applicable thereto, have been complied with."

Appellee ODI argues that the vehicle protection plans offered and sold by appellant are "contracts substantially amounting to insurance," and, thus, should be subject to the full array of insurance regulations within R.C. Title 39. ODI contends, and the court of appeals below agreed, that the key element that subjects appellant's protection plans to insurance laws and regulations is that appellant is neither the seller nor the manufacturer of the product it purports to warrant. ODI essentially asserts that extended warranties offered by sellers and manufacturers are part of the inducement process of making the product more desirable to the prospective buyer. Since appellant is an independent third party to the transaction, ODI submits that the claimed warranty appellant offers and sells is in reality a contract "substantially amounting to insurance."

The appellant, on the other hand, citing *State, ex rel. Duffy, v. Western Auto Supply Co.* (1938) and *State, ex rel. Herbert, v. Standard Oil Co.* (1941), contends that since its vehicle protection plans cover only those repairs necessitated by mechanical breakdown of defective parts, the protection plans constitute warranties and not contracts of insurance. Appellant relies on *Duffy* and argues that the instant vehicle protection plans limit reimbursement to loss due to defects in the product, and do not promise to reimburse loss or damage resulting from perils outside of and unrelated to defects in the product itself. Appellant submits that the issue of whether the seller or manufacturer (as opposed to an independent third party) offers or sells the type of contract in issue is wholly irrelevant.

In *Duffy, supra,* this court was asked to determine whether written guarantees issued by Western Auto covering tires it sold constituted contracts "substantially amounting to insurance." The language of one of the Western Auto guarantees stated that it protected the tires " 'against blowouts, cuts, bruises, rim-cuts, under-inflation, wheels out of alignment, faulty brakes or other road hazards that may render the tire unfit for further service (except fire and theft).' It then provided that 'In the event that the tire becomes unserviceable from the above conditions, we will (at our option) repair it free of charge, or replace it with a new tire of the same make at any of our stores, charging __th of our current price for each month which has elapsed since the date of purchase. The new tire will be fully covered by our regular guarantee in effect at time of adjustment. Furthermore: every tire is guaranteed against defects in material or workmanship without limit as to time, mileage or service.' "

In finding that the Western Auto guarantees were contracts substantially amounting to insurance, this court held in *Duffy, supra,* at paragraphs three and four of the syllabus:

> "A warranty promises indemnity against defects in an article sold, while insurance indemnifies against loss or damage resulting from perils outside of and unrelated to defects in the article itself.

> "A contract whereby the vendor of automobile tires undertakes to guarantee the tires sold against defects in material or workmanship without limit as to time, mileage or service, and further expressly guarantees them for a specified period against 'blowouts, cuts, bruises, rim-cuts, under-inflation, wheels out of alignment, faulty brakes or other road hazards that may render the tire unfit for further service (except fire or theft),' or contracts to indemnify the purchaser 'should the tire fail within the replacement period' specified, without limitation as to cause of such 'failure,' is a contract 'substantially amounting to insurance' within the provisions of Section 665, General Code, which requires such guarantor or insurer to comply with the laws of the state authorizing and regulating the business of insurance."

The foregoing syllabus language clearly indicates that the "guarantees" in *Duffy* were found to be contracts substantially amounting to insurance because such guarantees promised to indemnify for losses or damages to the product outside of and unrelated to defects inherent in the product itself.

Several years later, in *Herbert, supra,* this court was faced with another tire warranty/guarantee that was challenged by the Attorney General of Ohio. Therein, the tire warranty offered by Standard Oil promised repair or replacement for a limited period under certain conditions and provided in pertinent part:

> " 'This Warranty and Adjustment Agreement does not cover punctures, tires ruined in running flat, tires injured or destroyed by fire, wrecks or collisions,

tires cut by chains, or by obstruction on vehicle, theft, clincher tires, tubes used in any form, or tires used in taxicab or common carrier bus service.

"'This Warranty and Adjustment Agreement does not cover consequential damages.'" 35 N.E.2d at 439.

In finding that the Standard Oil tire warranty was indeed a warranty, and not a contract substantially amounting to insurance, this court held in paragraphs four and five of the syllabus as follows:

"A warranty or guaranty issued to a purchaser in connection with the sale of goods containing an agreement to indemnify against loss or damage resulting from perils outside of and unrelated to inherent weaknesses in the goods themselves, constitutes a contract substantially amounting to insurance within the purview of Section 665, General Code. (*State, ex rel. Duffy, Atty. Genl., v. Western Auto Supply Co.*, 134 Ohio St., 163 [11 O.O. 583, 16 N.E.2d 256], followed.)

"A written warranty delivered to a purchaser, representing that the articles sold are so well and carefully manufactured that they will give satisfactory service under ordinary usage for a specified length of time, and providing for an adjustment in the event of failure from faulty construction or materials, but expressly excluding happenings not connected with imperfections in the articles themselves, is not a contract substantially amounting to insurance within the meaning of Section 665, General Code."

In summarizing the law enunciated in both *Duffy* and *Herbert* it is readily apparent that a contract "substantially amounting to insurance" in this context is one that promises to cover losses or damages over and above, or unrelated to, defects within the product itself.

A careful review of the instant vehicle protection plans indicates that losses or damages sustained by the purchaser of the product which are unrelated to defects within the product itself are specifically excluded from coverage. Thus, it would appear that under both *Duffy* and *Herbert*, the instant vehicle protection plans are indeed warranties, and are not contracts substantially amounting to insurance.

However, as mentioned before, ODI asserts that the crucial distinction, as noted by the court of appeals below, is that warranties not sold by either the vendor or manufacturer of the product are not made to induce a purchase of the product, and therefore constitute contracts substantially amounting to insurance. While the foregoing assertion may appear to be facially valid, we find it to be unpersuasive. Obviously, the distinction made in this vein was of no apparent consequence in *Duffy* inasmuch as it was the *seller* of the product therein who issued the "warranty" that this court found to be a contract substantially amounting to insurance.

In our view, the crucial factor in determining whether a contract is a warranty or something substantially amounting to insurance is not the status of the party offering or selling the warranty, but rather the type of coverage promised within the four corners of the contract itself. Under the rule of law announced in both *Duffy* and *Herbert*, it is clear that warranties that cover only defects within the product itself are properly characterized as warranties (as was the case in *Herbert*), whereas warranties promising to cover damages or losses unrelated to defects within the product itself are, by definition, contracts substantially amounting to insurance (as was the case in *Duffy*).

The fact that appellant herein is not the manufacturer, supplier, or seller of the products it purports to warrant is, in our view, of little or no consequence in determining whether its protection plans are [insurance]. Common experience in today's marketplace indicates that a large number of consumer products carry a short-term warranty, but that agreements that extend the warranty beyond the period of time offered by the manufacturer may often be purchased for additional consideration. Certainly, it can be safely surmised that most people are not induced to buy a specific product based upon an extended warranty agreement that may be purchased at an extra cost.

Carrying ODI's arguments to their logical extreme, however, a seller of consumer products can offer such extended warranties to cover losses or damages, while independent third parties would be subject to insurance regulations even if the extended warranties specifically exclude losses or damages unrelated to defects in the product. Under such circumstances, we reject the status-determinative approach urged by ODI and adopted by the appellate court below, in favor of the substance-of-the-contract approach urged by appellant. Such a substance-of-the-contract approach was implemented by the court in *Mein v. United States Car Testing Co.* (1961), 115 Ohio App. 145, 20 O.O.2d 242, 184 N.E.2d 489, and is abundantly more consonant with the law and analysis set forth in both *Duffy* and *Herbert*.

Therefore, based on all the foregoing, we hold that a motor vehicle service agreement which promises to compensate the promisee for repairs necessitated by mechanical breakdown resulting exclusively from failure due to defects in the motor vehicle parts does not constitute a contract "substantially amounting to insurance" * * *

**Wright, J.,** dissenting.

This case evolved out of a number of complaints against Griffin Systems, Inc. ("Griffin") concerning fraud in the inducement and failure to pay claims, filed directly with the Ohio Department of Insurance ("ODI") and out of an investigation instigated by ODI, with the assistance of the Cleveland Better Business Bureau and others. A full-scale hearing was held by ODI covering these matters. Thereafter, the Superintendent of Insurance ordered Griffin to "cease and desist from violating R.C. 3901.20 by advertising, soliciting, selling or underwriting the Vehicle Protection Plan without authorization from the Department of Insurance; from placing before the public advertising which contains untrue, deceptive or misleading assertions and representations; and from entering into contracts with the public that substantially amount to the business of insurance * * *."

During the last twenty years, factory and dealer warranties on various consumer goods have proliferated, particularly in the automobile business. In recent years, a much more comprehensive warranty has been offered by various dealers covering almost every aspect of the future functioning of the automobiles sold and the component parts thereof. This sort of warranty has proved attractive to the buyer and highly profitable to the dealer.

In this instance, Griffin had no relationship with the consumer whatsoever until after the consumer had purchased the automobile, at which point Griffin directly solicited the consumer by mail for sale of its VPP. Having signed up the consumer, Griffin reinsured its business with the Great Plains Insurance Company, a Nebraska corporation, which is a wholly owned subsidiary of Griffin and is unlicensed to sell insurance in the state of Ohio. Therefore, without considering whether the VPPs before us here insure against contingencies other than product defects, we have a contract that is totally distinguishable from the warranty we found in *Herbert.*

It is perfectly apparent that the VPP is not a warranty proposed by a manufacturer-seller *and* used for the purpose of inducing or increasing sales of the product in question. In a word, we have a case of first impression here which is certainly not controlled by either *Herbert* or *State, ex rel. Duffy, v. Western Auto Supply Co.* (1938).

Here, Griffin is not the warrantor of a product it has manufactured or sold but is rather the insurer of the performance of component parts in a product manufactured and sold by a third party. The *Herbert* case certainly did not exclude all warranties or guarantees from control by ODI but only those warranties guaranteeing "satisfactory service under ordinary usage" of products being sold to a purchaser by the manufacturer or seller of that product.

The appellee herein cites Vance, The Law of Insurance (3 Ed.1951) 2, Section 1, which lists the following five elements as distinguishing characteristics of insurance: (1) the insured possesses an insurable interest; (2) the insured is subject to loss through the destruction or impairment of that interest by the happening of some designated peril; (3) the insurer assumes the risk of loss; (4) such assumption is part of the general scheme to distribute actual losses among a large group of persons bearing similar risks; and (5) the insured pays a premium as consideration for the promise. There is no question that each of the above-described elements is present under Griffin's VPP.

As further evidence that Griffin's VPP is insurance and not a warranty, appellee cites a Federal Trade Commission ("F.T.C.") regulation, Section 700.11, Title 16, C.F.R., promulgated pursuant to the authority granted to the F.T.C. to enact rules implementing the Magnuson-Moss Warranty Act, Sections 2301 *et seq.*, Title 15, U.S.Code. See Sections 2309 and 2312(c), Title 15, U.S.Code. The rule is relevant to the issue before us today in that it determines that VPPs such as the ones offered by Griffin are policies of insurance. Part (a) of the rule reads as follows:

"The [Magnuson-Moss Warranty] Act recognizes two types of agreements which may provide similar coverage of consumer products, the written warranty, and the service contract. In addition, other agreements may meet the statutory definitions of either 'written warranty' or 'service contract,' but are sold and regulated under state law as contracts of insurance. One example is the *automobile breakdown insurance policies* sold in many jurisdictions and regulated by the state as a form of casualty insurance. The McCarran-Ferguson Act, 15 U.S.C. 1011 et seq., precludes jurisdiction under federal law over 'the business of insurance' to the extent an agreement is regulated by state law as insurance. Thus, such agreements are subject to the Magnuson-Moss Warranty Act only to the extent they are not regulated in a particular state as the business of insurance." (Emphasis added.) Thus, the F.T.C. considers such contracts ripe for insurance regulation.

Griffin urges this court to focus on whether it would "make sense" to apply the insurance statutes and regulations to its VPPs. The real issue, however, is whether each VPP contains the requisite elements of insurance such that it is a contract that "substantially amount[s] to insurance." See *Mein v. United States Car Testing Co.*, 184 N.E.2d 489 (Ohio 1961). As shown above, Griffin's VPP contains those elements and is, therefore, insurance. Because it is insurance, under R.C. 3905.42, ODI has the authority to regulate it.

## *Notes and Questions*

1. After now having masochistically read these two "what is insurance" cases that involve the same product but reach opposite results, are you still satisfied with the definition of insurance put forth at the beginning of this section?

(a) What exactly, in a nutshell, is the definition this casebook has implicitly put forth?

(b) Are the cases consistent with the definition? Explain.

(c) Would a different or revised definition better fit the cases?

2. Which court do you think is correct about the Griffin Systems operation — Illinois or Ohio? Explain.

3. What factors may influence judicial decisions in this area?

4. Are both *Griffin Systems* decisions arguably too formalist in that they focus on the identity of repair providers and undertake relatively little analysis of important public policy factors such as the goal of insurance regulation and whether that goal is furthered or inhibited by classifying the Griffin plans as insurance? In addition, the Ohio Supreme Court majority focuses on whether the damage to a vehicle is "internal" failure or "external" injury as a formalist bright line.

Instead of simply classifying according to the identity of the repair provider or the source of the equipment failure/injury, one might ask: (1) is the consumer at greater risk if a vehicle is subject to a manufacturer's warranty or the Griffin Systems protection plan? (2) Are these greater risks, if any, better mitigated by classifying the Griffin plans as insurance or as warranties (or at least something other than insurance)?

5. Why is Griffin fighting so hard not to be classified as an insurer? What is the downside for the company? Conversely, what is the upside for the state or "the public interest" (assuming we can agree on what constitutes the public interest) in classifying

Griffin as an insurer? Should the courts be asking these questions? Why or why not? Do courts implicitly ask these questions but refrain from discussing them explicitly in opinions? If so, why?

6. *See also* Bobby L. Dexter, *Rethinking "Insurance," Especially After AIG*, 87 Denv. U. L. Rev. 59 (2009) (noting that because of the advent of sophisticated financial products designed to deal with risk (famously unsuccessfully in the case of AIG's now infamous credit default swaps),[39] standard conceptions of insurance and breadth of "insurance" regulation may need rethinking). *But see* M. Todd Henderson, *Credit Derivatives Are Not "Insurance,"* 16 Conn. Ins. L.J. 1 (2009). *See also* Jonathan Simmons & Akif Siddiqui, *Canada: "Takaful"—Islamic Insurance*, Mondaq.com, Feb.

---

39. As briefly noted in an earlier footnote, a credit default swap or "CDS," is an agreement in which the seller of the CDS agrees to compensate the buyer in the event that a financial product purchased by the buyer should default on its obligation to pay the holder of the instrument as promised. For example, if Jack has a bond with AcmeCo but is worried that AcmeCo may default on its obligation to pay Jack, he may buy a CDS from Jill. In return for Jack's purchase price of the CDS—which is always far less than the potential loss from default of the bond—the CDS seller promises to pay Jack what he would have received from the bond in the absence of the default. Jill can sell this product for an affordable price because—if she is doing the job right—she has a large and varied pool of bonds presenting uncorrelated risk on which she has issued CDS contracts. The bonds are unlikely to all default at once. If Jill's investigation (oh, heck, let's just call it underwriting just like we should call Jack's payment a premium) and business judgment is good (she doesn't have to sell to every Jack who knocks on her office door), the risk may be minimal because the bonds are all solid (but if they are so very solid, Jack is probably wasting his money buying a CDS).

If all this sounds like insurance to you, you are on our side of the debate about whether a CDS contract is insurance. But even if it is not, it presents comparable risks in that the CDS business model depends on a relatively small, manageable number of defaults that do not happen all at once and follow relatively predictable but random patterns (we don't know which bonds will default, but we know that in an average year, three percent of bonds will default). But 2008—the year of the "Great Recession"—was no average year. There was a spike in bond defaults, mortgage defaults, contract breaches, insolvencies, etc. This cascade of economic distress in turn prompted a wave of CDS payment claims to AIG, which had sold thousands of CDS contracts on financial risks that were not sufficiently diversified (perhaps because its employees had too much incentive to sell the product and earn commission). In addition, AIG was issuing CDS contracts on a substantial number of its own financial products. This would be a bit like State Farm issuing insurance or similar financial protection products on itself and its own business risks—there simply is not much diversification if something goes wrong. And because so many of the financial products subject to an AIG CDS were AIG products, it mattered a lot when AIG's credit rating went down, which by the terms of many of the CDS contracts triggered an obligation to pay, which in turn generated a "run on the bank" that outstripped even AIG's substantial liquidity.

When the "Black Swan" event, such as the unexpected and unexpectedly massive economic decline of 2008 took place, AIG simply could not make good on its promised payments, which in turn prompted government assistance to avoid collapse. This "bailout" was and remains politically controversial (we support it, because it helped to prevent the economic turmoil from becoming worse, even though it is a little galling to have government subsidize businesses in a way that it seldom subsidizes individuals who get in over their head financially), but the core of the company was stabilized ("saved" if you will), and the stock the government took in exchange for assistance was later resold at a profit for the government. The question remains: would we be better off if CDS contracts were treated like insurance and regulated like insurance? And should such regulation be done by states (as is the case with ordinary insurance) or by the national government?

14, 2011 (describing Muslim variant of insurance designed to avoid certain religious limitations on lending and financial activity). *See also* Kenneth E. Spahn, *Service Warranty Associations: Regulating Service Contracts as "Insurance" Under Florida's Chapter 634*, 25 STETSON L. REV. 597 (1996) (arguing that such plans should be subject to insurance regulation and providing list of helpful considerations for classification as well as a list of the costs and benefits of such regulation).

7. In case you're considering buying a Griffin Systems plan, forget it. The company is now out of business, according to the Better Business Bureau, which appears never to have "accredited" it. However. such plans are available (you may have even received a solicitation). *See, e.g.*, Fidelity Warranty Services, Inc., Vehicle Protection Plan www.fidelitywarrantyservices.com/products/vehicle-protection (visited July 23, 2019) (describing three levels of plan with long list of exclusions and no information regarding price or deductibles, presumably not an oversight but an incentive to call company's toll-free number for further information).

8. Insurance regulators are relatively overworked and understaffed. Absent special circumstances (such as the Commissioner receiving a solicitation in the mail and wondering "why aren't these guys licensed?") regulators are unlikely to target a provider for insurance regulation except in response to consumer complaints.

## PROBLEM ONE

Petra lands in Las Vegas at the conveniently close-to-town McCarran Airport and then, after an inconvenient shuttle to the Car Rental Center, rents a Mercedes convertible from Bunker Hill Rent-a-Car as part of planned touring. The car rental agent suggests she purchase a Collision Damage Waiver ("CDW") which will provide "full coverage" in the event the vehicle is in an accident for the low, low cost of $29.50 per day (it is, after all, a Mercedes), and she agrees.

Sure enough, Petra is pinched between two trucks on the winding roads leading to the Grand Canyon. The rental car is a total loss. Petra makes a claim, which Bunker Hill processes—and then tells her it can't pay. It seems the rental agreement (unread by either Petra or the agent) states that the CDW is backed by Bermuda Risk, a specialized company that is an independent contractor with Bunker Hill for purposes of its CDW program. Bermuda Risk has just been looted by one of its shadowy founders, and the company is now insolvent and in receivership. There is a moratorium on claims payments. According to business press coverage of the matter, there is some chance that Bermuda will make some proportional claims payments from what assets the company can muster after the receivership is sorted out. But for now, Petra is out of luck.

She complains to Bunker Hill, but Bunker Hill maintains it is not liable—her CDW contract was with Bermuda Risk, and Bunker Hill is but a conduit. She complains to the state Insurance Commissioner, who informs her that, influenced by the Ohio Supreme Court's decision, the state has never tried to regulate CDWs as insurance. The Commissioner, however, is moved by Petra's plight and seeks to have CDWs classified as insurance beginning with the next calendar year. Rental car companies and CDW providers predictably oppose the measure.

- What should a court decide?

- Why?

- What additional facts would be helpful for the decision?

- Or is this a case where the mode of analysis chosen (e.g., the Illinois approach versus the Ohio approach) is the determinative factor?

- What benefits would you posit from regulating the CDW as insurance?

- What costs or negative effects might there be?

### PROBLEM TWO

Bunker Hill sues Petra for the cost of the Mercedes, which has been totaled by the collision and is beyond repair. The rental agreement, Paragraph 21, states that "Renter is responsible for any physical injury to the Rented Vehicle unless CDW coverage has been purchased, in which case financial responsibility is governed by the terms of the CDW."

Petra refuses to pay and retains counsel, who argues that as the owner of the Mercedes and the party that chose Bermuda Risk as its CDW vender, Bunker Hill is financially responsible for damage to the Mercedes. Bunker Hill moves for summary judgment based on its Rental Agreement.

- What is the most likely ruling on the motion?

- Can Petra avoid or at least delay summary judgment by arguing for additional discovery?

- What additional discovery, if any, may be necessary?

## [B] Examples of Exclusions Designed to Avoid Coverage for Large or Excessively Correlated Risk

As discussed above, insurers usually retain the option of excluding a risk altogether if it appears to threaten the soundness of the risk pool. Because intensely destructive terrorist acts such as the September 11 suicide hijackings tend to injure a wide swath of persons and property, insurers may henceforth treat terrorism as akin to war in writing policies. However, we think that the two are distinct yet related in ways that will permit continued underwriting of terror risks, but that war risk will always be excluded. What is the rationale for our view? Do you agree or disagree?

*War and Force Majeure*

A commonly used commercial property insurance form lists as a covered cause of loss "Riot or Civil Commotion, including: (1) Acts of striking employees while occupying the described premises; and (2) Looting occurring at the time and place of a riot or civil commotion."[40] Fire damage, of course, is also covered, so long as it was neither expected nor intended from the standpoint of the policyholder (this policy form does exclude losses resulting from war or revolution, an exclusion discussed below). Many policies, however, contain exclusions for riot or looting damage.

However, the basic commercial property policy, even one that covers riot and looting losses, usually excludes losses for:

(1) War, including undeclared or civil war;

(2) Warlike action by a military force, including action in hindering or defending against an actual or expected attack, by any government, sovereign or other authority using military personnel or other agents; or

(3) Insurrection, rebellion, revolution, usurped power, or action taken by governmental authority in hindering or defending against any of these.[41]

Liability policies typically contain a similar exclusion but often provide that the exclusion "applies only to liability assumed under a contract or agreement."

The purpose of these exclusions is to prevent the insurer from becoming responsible for the coverage of a large and correlated risk. If war comes to Elm City, it will bring area-wide property damage, destroying the risk spreading and law of averages used by insurers to make money. Even a bad hailstorm or tornado will usually have only confined or episodic damage. By contrast, a peril such as war tends to bring widespread damage to all policyholders in a region.

Two interesting and notable riot exclusion cases involved policies issued in connection with famed stuntman Evil Knievel's 1974 attempted motorcycle jump of the

---

40. *See* Insurance Services Office, Commercial Property Policy No. CP 10 20 06 95 (1994), *reprinted in* Alliance of American Insurers, The Insurance Professionals' Policy Kit: A Collection Of Sample Insurance Forms 174 (1997–98 Edition). A common homeowners policy excludes coverage for "Riot or Civil Commotion" but does not define the term. *See* ISO Form HO 00 03 05 11 (2010) (this is the "HO-3" form that is perhaps the most common homeowners insurance policy in the U.S.).

For the convenience of the reader and to conserve print, future citations to sample forms will identify the Insurance Services Office as "ISO" and the Alliance of American Insurers compendium of policies as the "*Policy Kit*." The *Policy Kit*, which the Alliance of American Insurers ceased publishing after 2003, remains a useful source for reference to common insurance policy language. It contains a variety of forms for different lines of insurance and common endorsements. Another good reference source for policy forms and language is The CPCU Handbook Of Insurance Policies published by the American Institute of Chartered Property Casualty Underwriters and the Insurance Institute of America. The *Handbook* may be ordered from the Institutes at 720 Providence Road, P.O. Box 3016, Malvern, PA 19355-0716, (610) 644-2100. In addition, persons with access to libraries or other organizations belonging to the Insurance Services Office (ISO) may obtain form policies and endorsement language from ISO. Life and Health policy language is less standardized, but examples of common policy forms are found in the on-line Appendix to this treatise and the appendices of treatises and casebooks cited throughout this book.

41. *See* ISO CGL Form CG 00 01 04 13 (2012). The term "war" is not, however, defined in the policy's Definitions section.

Snake River Canyon near distinctive Twin Falls, Idaho. *See Foremost Ins. Co. v. Putzier*, 606 P.2d 987 (Idaho1980); *Foremost Ins. Co. v. Putzier*, 627 P.2d 317 (Idaho 1981). As a condition of issuing a permit for the event,[42] local authorities required that Knievel and the event sponsors obtain liability insurance. Sure enough, some of the 10,000–15,000 people who assembled for the jump got a little inebriated and restless waiting for the action and caused damage to vendors at the site.

The vendors whose equipment had been sacked sued Knievel and the promoter seeking compensation. When they tendered the defense to the insurer, it refused based on language in a separate endorsement that stated that the policy did not apply to injuries "arising out of riot, civil commotion or mob action or out of any act or omission in connection with the prevention or suppression of any of the foregoing." *See* 606 P.2d at 990. The court had little trouble concluding that a riot had occurred and upheld the insurer's refusal to provide coverage.[43]

However, Antonio Guanche, a vendor at the event, had more success in his case seeking first-party property damage coverage when his concession stand was looted by hungry attendees-cum-rioters. There — in contrast to the liability insurance case involving the famed motorcycle stuntman — the Idaho Supreme Court found coverage, noting that Mr. Guanche, who had difficulty speaking English, had never been given a copy of the policy nor had its limitations explained. Hence, the court refused to apply the riot/civil commotion exclusion that it applied in the related case. *See* 627 P.2d at 322–24.[44]

Liability insurance policies tend to exclude coverage for riot-related injuries, because the risk is difficult to calculate and may be far-flung. For example, the Knievel insurer

---

42. Or, as it turned out, non-event. Knievel's motorcycle malfunctioned and he never really became airborne.

43. However, in another case arising out of the disastrous venture, the court refused to enforce the exclusion against an unsophisticated vendor who made a first-party property claim based on his payment of a premium to the insurer, whose agent did not provide the vendor with a written policy but told him he was "covered." *See Foremost Ins. Co. v. Putzier*, 102 Idaho 138, 627 P.2d 317 (1981). The differences between these two case outcomes can be characterized as stemming from the estoppel that bound the Antonio Guanche insurer or as resulting from a more result-oriented judicial desire to aid the unsophisticated vendor who otherwise would have been wiped out by the riot.

44. In the 1980 liability insurance case, the Idaho Supreme Court took pains to note that, as expressed in then-recent precedent, it did not follow the "reasonable expectations" approach to insurance policy construction and hence had no trouble enforcing the policy exclusion, which it regarded as clearly written even if perhaps disappointingly surprising to Knievel. However, in the 1981 property insurance case, the court — despite citing the same anti-reasonable expectations precedent — relied on other precedent favoring policyholders where there was unequal bargaining power and circumstances suggesting that full application of an exclusion would be unfair. In particular, Mr. Gaunche testified that the insurance agent told him that he was "covered," which he assumed mean fully covered without exclusion, a belief that, although perhaps not objectively reasonable, was credited by the court.

Cynics might argue — persuasively in our view — that the court applied different lines of precedent to cut a break for "little guy" Antonio Gaunche in the second case. But is that necessarily bad? Ordinary policyholders, unaware of the importance to insurers of avoiding correlated risk, may in fact be objectively reasonable to assume that a property insurance policy covers losses from riot just as it usually covers losses from burglary or vandalism.

did not want to be responsible for any mass craziness that might be associated with the Canyon jump under circumstances where the promoters could not eliminate this danger absent massive security expenses. In addition, the amount of potential liability is hard to calculate. What if a group of motorcycle thugs at the Knievel jump beats a busload of investment bankers to a vegetative pulp? The potential tort damages could be astronomic. Property insurers are more willing to cover riot-related damages, because the amount of possible loss is more confined to the value of the insured property. In addition, many property owners, particularly urban businesses, want such coverage and will pay for it. Homeowners have less interest in such insurance (to the extent they think about it consciously at all), because a riot resulting in looting or vandalism of a home in a residential area is far less likely than a protest riot at a business (think Sal's Pizzeria in Spike Lee's 1989 film *Do the Right Thing*)[45] or looting of a business after a power outage or hurricane. Neither a liability nor a property policy is required to include or exclude riot or war coverage, although it is hard to imagine a policy without a war exclusion. Life insurance policies, for example, exclude war as a cause of death so that they are not faced with an avalanche of claims should the population be mobilized.

### PROBLEM THREE

Same facts as Problems 1 and 2 except that Bermuda Risk is not in receivership and Petra has been hurt in the collision of her rented Mercedes with the trucks—badly enough to incur $15,000 in medical bills and miss two weeks of work. She seeks coverage for both the medical bills and lost wages under the CDW, arguing that the rental agent's promise of "full coverage" makes this a reasonable expectation on her part.

• What result? (Think of this as a preview for § 2.12 regarding the reasonable expectations approach.)

Courts enforce well-drafted riot or war exclusions where the insurer has been careful not to mislead the policyholder or where the policyholder is reasonably sophisticated. Because most courts look for the cause nearest the loss or most dominant in bringing a loss about to determine if coverage exists, policyholder counsel may be able to turn the confusion of riot-related or perhaps even war-related destruction to their advantage by arguing that the real cause of the loss was something other than war or riot (*see* Chapter 6 regarding causation). The following case illustrates the

---

45. Realizing that this movie predates the birth of many users of this coursebook, we direct readers to https://en.wikipedia.org/wiki/Do_the_Right_Thing for a quick synopsis that squares with our recollection of the movie.

Although one needs to exercise some caution in assessing information sources on the internet, we find Wikipedia extremely useful, particularly where precision is not at a premium, because of its accessibility and conciseness as well as its being essentially and consistently accurate. One may, for example, use Wikipedia to refresh one's memory about films in which Kevin Bacon has appeared and not be too worried if one is overlooked or attributed to the wrong year. But if the question involves the first date a manufacturer became aware of a product defect, a more dependable source is required.

conflicting factors at work when the insurer asserts a "war, riot, or insurrection" exclusion under atypical circumstances.

## Pan American World Airways v. Aetna Casualty and Surety Co.

United States Court of Appeals, Second Circuit
505 F.2d 989 (1974)

**Hays, Circuit Judge.**

On September 6, 1970, Pan American Flight 083, while on a regularly scheduled flight from Brussels to New York, was hijacked in the sky over London about 45 minutes after it had taken off from an intermediate stop in Amsterdam. Two men, Diop and Gueye, acting for the Popular Front for the Liberation of Palestine [the "PFLP"], forced the crew of the aircraft to fly to Beirut, where a demolitions expert and explosives were put on board. The aircraft, a Boeing 747, was then flown to Egypt still under PFLP control. In Cairo, after the passengers were evacuated, the aircraft was totally destroyed.

We are asked on this appeal to determine which of the various underwriters that insured the aircraft must bear the cost of the loss. This determination depends on whether the September 6 hijacking was proximately caused by an agency fairly described, for insurance purposes, by any of the exclusions contained in a group of identical all risk aviation policies—policies which, if not for the exclusions, would cover the loss. The district court held that the all risk policies covered the loss.

The aircraft in question was covered by "a more or less seamless mosaic" of insurance policies, distributing among three classes of insurers, the risk of loss depending on the proximate cause of the damage.

Members of the first class of insurers wrote identical aviation all risk policies. These policies indemnified Pan American against "all physical loss of or damage to the aircraft," except for any loss "due to or resulting from" certain specified exclusions. The exclusions in the all risk policies, insofar as they are relevant here, read as follows:

"34. LOSS OR DAMAGE NOT COVERED

1. capture, seizure, arrest, restraint or detention or the consequences thereof or of any attempt threat, or any taking of the property insured or damage to or destruction thereof by any Government or governmental authority or agent (whether secret or otherwise) or by any military, naval or usurped power, whether any of the foregoing be done by way of requisition or otherwise and whether in time of peace or war and whether lawful or unlawful (this subdivision 1. shall not apply, however, to any such action by a foreign government or foreign governmental authority follow—the forceful diversion to a foreign country by any person not in lawful possession or custody of such insured aircraft and who is not an agent or representative, secret or

otherwise, of any foreign government or governmental authority) [hereinafter "clause 1"];

2. war, invasion, civil war, revolution, rebellion, insurrection or warlike operations, whether there be a declaration of war or not [hereinafter "clause 2"];

3. strikes, riots, civil commotion [hereinafter "clause 3"].

## II. The District Court Proceeding

\* \* \*

At the trial, the all risk insurers put in an immense amount of evidence relating to the history of war and political tension in the Middle East, and to the climate of political unrest in Jordan. They undertook to show that the hijacking was caused by PFLP or Palestinian Arab "military ... or usurped power," by offering evidence that these groups operated as paramilitary quasi-governments in parts of Jordan, independently of King Hussein's authority. They relied on the same kind of evidence and an asserted PFLP intent to overthrow King Hussein, to establish that the loss of the 747 was caused by an "insurrection" in Jordan. With regard to the applicability of these two exclusions, they claimed that various "Fedayeen," organizations of Palestinian refugees seeking to return Israel to Arab control, had power over substantial territory from which they excluded government functionaries, and that the Fedayeen engaged in violent clashes with the Jordanian Army, culminating in a 10-day "civil war" following the September 1970 hijacking. The all risk insurers also attempted to bring the loss within the scope of the term "war" and "warlike operations" by showing that the PFLP engaged in "guerilla warfare." Finally, they sought to connect the Pan American hijacking with other hijackings committed on the same day, arguing that all of the hijackings together constituted a single "civil commotion."

\* \* \* The district court made detailed findings as to the goals and structure of the Fedayeen in general and the PFLP in particular. It found that the PFLP was a militant Marxist-Leninist-Maoist organization, which received financial support and arms from China and North Korea. The PFLP had approximately 600 to 1200 members, 150 of whom constituted a permanent core. Though the PFLP's primary enemy was Israel, it also condemned "reactionary" Arab regimes, "universal capitalism" and the United States as its enemies, and it was hostile toward the other, generally more moderate, Fedayeen groups.

[T]he district court found that under governing New York law an ambiguity in a term of exclusion will be resolved in the manner least favorable to the insurer. It held that "war" means a conflict between governments, not political groups like the PFLP. It further held that the loss was not due to a PFLP "warlike operation" because that term does not include the inflicting of damage on the civilian property of non-belligerents by political groups far from the site of warfare, particularly when the purpose is propaganda. *Id.*

The district court also held that the loss was not due to the acts of the PFLP as a "military or usurped power." First, the PFLP did not qualify as such a power since it held territory only at the sufferance of the Jordanian government, the de jure sovereign. Second, even if the PFLP was a "power" in Jordan, it did not act as such when it hijacked a plane over London. In addition, the court held that the PFLP activity was not part of an "insurrection" since there was insufficient evidence that an insurrection against the Jordanian government was in progress at that time, and even if there was an insurrection, the hijacking in question was not primarily caused by it. The loss was not due to "riot" because the hijacking was not accompanied by the sort of uproar or disorder that riot connotes in current usage. Finally, the district court held that the phrase "civil commotion" comprehends a local disorder rather than a hijacking occurring in the skies over two continents.

In short, the district court held that the all risk insurers failed to meet their burden of proving that the cause of the loss was fairly within the intended scope of any of the exclusions. It found that the ancient marine insurance terms selected by the all risk insurers simply do not describe a violent and senseless intercontinental hijacking carried out by an isolated band of political terrorists.

The all risk insurers appeal, assailing the district court's findings of fact as to the size, power, organization, intent and purpose of the Fedayeen and the PFLP, and as to the lack of connection between the hijacking and the larger Middle Eastern events. They attack the district court's interpretations of the contract clauses, claiming that these interpretations are not supported by the weight of authority, particularly the authorities founded on the law of England. Pan American and the government cross-appeal. We affirm.

* * *

IV. Preliminary Legal Issues

The all risk insurers, if they were to prevail, had the burden of proving that the proximate cause of the loss of the 747 was included within one of the terms of exclusion. The all risk insurers' task is made even more difficult by the rule that exclusions will be given the interpretation which is most beneficial to the insured. The maxim contra proferentem receives added force in this case because the all risk insurers knew that their exclusions were ambiguous in the context of a political hijacking, and they knew of but did not employ exclusionary terms used by other all risk insurers which would have clarified the ambiguity. Finally on this appeal, the all risk insurers have the burden of demonstrating that the trial judge's findings of fact adverse to them were clearly erroneous.

### A. Burden of Proof.

In the district court the insured had the burden of proving the existence of the all risk policies, and the loss of the covered property. Neither of these elements is disputed. Thus Pan American began the action with a prima facie case for recovery which the all risk insurers could meet only by proving that the cause of the loss came under one of the terms of exclusion.

### B. Contra Proferentem.

The loss in this case is covered by the all risk policies if Pan American or the war risk insurers can formulate a reasonable interpretation of the terms of exclusion to permit coverage. On the other hand, it is not sufficient for the all risk insurers' case for them to offer a reasonable interpretation under which the loss is excluded; they must demonstrate that an interpretation favoring them is the only reasonable reading of at least one of the relevant terms of exclusion. Contra proferentem has special relevance as a rule of construction when an insurer fails to use apt words to exclude a known risk.

The evidence indicates that the risk of a hijacking was well known to the all risk insurers. Between 1960 and 1970 over 200 commercial aircraft were hijacked, eight of which belonged to Pan American.... In August, 1969, the PFLP hijacked a Trans World Airlines 707 to Damascus and seriously damaged it through the use of explosives. * * * The present all risk insurers took no steps to clarify their exclusions even after the Damascus loss made it clear that the London market did not consider the PFLP hijackings to be within the terms of the all risk exclusions.

Various exclusionary terms in use [by insurers] or being considered for use [by insurrers] prior to the present loss would have excluded the loss had they been employed. For example, in 1969 underwriters in the London all risk aviation market began to consider various alternative wordings for a hijacking exclusion. In November, 1969, an organization of such underwriters adopted the text of an exclusion called "AV-48," which excluded the following:

> "(f) Unlawful seizure or wrongful exercise of control of the Aircraft or crew in flight (including any attempt at such seizure or control) made by any person or persons on board the Aircraft acting without the consent of the Insured."

The text of AV-48 was known [to insurers] by June, 1969. Had AV-48 been employed by the present all risk insurers, they might well have avoided liability for the loss of the 747.

On September 12, 1969, the London all risk market revised AV-48 to make it even more specific. The revised exclusion, AV-48A, includes the following language:

> "This Policy does not cover claims directly or indirectly occasioned by, happening through or in consequences of: —
>
> ....
>
> "(d) Any act of one or more persons, whether or not agents of a sovereign Power, for political or terrorist purposes and whether the loss or damage resulting therefrom is accidental or intentional.
>
> "(e) Any malicious act or act of sabotage.
>
> ....
>
> "(g) Hi-jacking or any unlawful seizure or wrongful exercise of control of the Aircraft or crew in flight...."

Any of these three AV-48A clauses, if employed by the appellant all risk insurers, might well have excluded the present loss.

* * * When the all risk insurers failed to exclude "political risks in words descriptive of today's world events," they acted at their own peril.

* * *

## B. Proximate Cause.

The all risk policies exclude "loss or damage due to or resulting from" the various enumerated perils, a phrase that clearly refers to the proximate cause of the loss. Remote causes of causes are not relevant to the characterization of an insurance loss. In the context of this commercial litigation, the causation inquiry stops at the efficient physical cause of the loss; it does not trace events back to their metaphysical beginnings. The words "due to or resulting from" limit the inquiry to the facts immediately surrounding the loss. Thus, in *Queen Insurance Co. v. Globe & Rutgers Fire Insurance Co.*, 263 U.S. 487 (1924), Mr. Justice Holmes wrote:

> "The common understanding is that in construing these policies we are not to take broad views but generally are to stop our inquiries with the cause nearest to the loss. This is a settled rule of construction, and if it is understood, does not deserve much criticism, since theoretically at least the parties can shape their contract as they like."

New York courts give especially limited scope to the causation inquiry. The leading case is *Bird v. St. Paul Fire & Marine Insurance Co.*, 120 N.E. 86 (N.Y. 1918) (Cardozo, J.). In *Bird*, the insured vessel was damaged by a concussion caused by an explosion in a freight yard about a thousand yards from the vessel. The explosion came about when a fire set off a stock of explosives. The insured sued on an insurance policy covering losses caused by "fire." The Court of Appeals held that the loss was not caused by fire. It ascertained that the scope of causation relevant to the insurance nature of a loss is largely a question of fact depending on the reasonable expectations of businessmen:

> "The question is not what men ought to think of as a cause. The question is what they do think of as a cause. We must put ourselves in the place of the average owner whose boat or building is damaged by the concussion of a distant explosion, let us say a mile away. Some glassware in his pantry is thrown down and broken. It would probably never occur to him that within the meaning of his policy of insurance, he had suffered loss by fire. A philosopher or a lawyer might persuade him that he had, but he would not believe it until they told him. He would expect indemnity, of course, if the fire reached the thing insured. He would expect indemnity, very likely, if the fire was near at hand, if his boat or his building was within the danger zone of ordinary experience, if damage of some sort, whether from ignition or from the indirect consequences of fire, might fairly be said to be within the range of normal apprehension."

*Britain S.S. Co. v. The King*, [1919] 2 K.B. 670, illustrates how this principle has been applied by the English courts in the context of war-related losses. While on a voyage from England to Alexandria in the company and under the orders of a British escort, the Matiana went aground and was lost, because the convoy had taken a more northerly route than usual to avoid German submarines. The Court of Appeals held that the loss was due to a marine peril, running aground, rather than to a "warlike operation." It held that the warlike activity of the escorts did not proximately cause the loss: The Crown's naval authorities ordered the ship to take a general course fraught with maritime perils, but they did not actually order the Matiana aground. The House of Lords agreed.

Decisions in a variety of other jurisdictions follow the same approach. When the Linwood went aground as a result of the Confederates putting out the Hatteras light, the loss was a "consequence" of a marine peril, rather than "hostilities." *Ionides v. Universal Marine Insurance Co.*, 143 Eng. Rep. 445, 456 (C.P. 1863) (per Erle, C.J.). When the John Worthington collided with a minesweeper that was clearing the channel approaches to New York harbor in 1942, the loss was due to the collision, a marine peril, rather than the warlike reason for the minesweeper's presence in the harbor. *Standard Oil v. United States*, 340 U.S. 54 (1950). When the Napoli was lost in a head-on collision with another ship because it was sailing without running lights under British order, the loss was due to a marine peril, the collision. *Queen Insurance Co. v. Globe & Rutgers Fire Insurance Co.*, 282 F. 976 (2d Cir. 1922), *aff'd*, 263 U.S. 487 (1924). When an insured aircraft was lost over Vietnam in a collision with a military aircraft, the loss was due to an aviation peril, notwithstanding that the two aircraft were flying over Vietnam only because there was a war. *Airlift International, Inc. v. United States*, 335 F. Supp. 442, 449 (S.D. Fla. 1971), *aff'd*, 460 F.2d 1065 (5th Cir. 1972) (mem.).

These cases establish a mechanical test of proximate causation for insurance cases, a test that looks only to the "causes nearest to the loss." *Queen Insurance Co. v. Globe & Rutgers Fire Insurance Co.*, *supra* at 492. This rule is adumbrated by the maxim contra proferentem: if the insurer desires to have more remote causes determine the scope of exclusion, he may draft language to effectuate that desire. *Id.*; *Feeney & Meyers v. Empire State Insurance Co.*, 228 F.2d 770, 771 (10th Cir. 1955). In the present case, events drawn from the general history of unrest in the Middle East did not proximately cause the destruction of the 747. Of course, in some attenuated "cause of causes" sense, the loss may have resulted from the Fedayeen or PFLP pattern of military operations against Israel, from the domestic unrest in Jordan, or from the most recent of the three wars which prior to 1970 had convulsed the Middle East. But for insurance purposes, the mechanical cause of the present loss was two men, who by force of arms, diverted Flight 093 from its intended destination.

The principle that the taking characterizes the loss has been applied by at least one court to an aircraft hijacking. In *Sunny South Aircraft Service, Inc. v. American Fire & Casualty Co.*, 140 So. 2d 78 (Fla. Dist. Ct. App. 1962), *aff'd*, 151 So. 2d 276 (Fla. 1973), the insured aircraft was covered for theft excluding losses "due to war ... rebellion or revolution." The airplane was hijacked in the United States and taken to Cuba where it was damaged by a Cuban military plane. The court found that the loss was proximately caused by theft rather than by warlike activity, and accordingly held that the loss was not excluded. If events following a hijacking were permitted to control the insurance nature of the loss, the outcome in any case would vary according to the whim of the hijacker. In the present case the 747 might well have been destroyed in the air over London by two hijackers, rather than in Cairo by a larger group. The parties cannot have intended that the caprice of the hijackers would control the insurance consequences of the loss. It is not relevant in this case that after the aircraft was hijacked by two actors, a third came aboard, or that extensive civil disorders broke out in Jordan nine days after the hijacking.

* * * We hold that in order to constitute a military or usurped power the power must be at least that of a de facto government. On the facts of this case, the PFLP was not a de facto government in the sky over London when the 747 was taken. Thus the loss was not "due to or resulting from" a "military ... or usurped power."

The words military or usurped power have a long history of inclusion in insurance policies, but they have received only scant judicial attention, presumably because the events necessary to bring them into play are extraordinary. They have been considered in the context of the Irish rebellion, the American Civil War, and, hypothetically, in the context of the invasion of England by Charles Edward Stuart. The insurance meaning of military or usurped power was first considered in *Drinkwater v. The Corporation of the London Assurance*, 95 Eng. Rep. 863 (C.P. 1767). In 1766, Drinkwater's malting house at Norwich was burned by a mob which "arose ... upon account of the high price of provisions." The building was insured by a fire policy excluding fires caused by "any military or usurped power whatsoever." Common Pleas held that the loss was not excluded by the phrase. Mr. Justice Bathurst, in an opinion that has not gone unnoticed by American authorities, see *City Fire Insurance Co. v. J.&H.P. Corlies*, 21 Wend. 367, 370 (N.Y. 1839), said that military or usurped power can "only mean an invasion of the kingdom by foreign enemies ... or an internal armed force in rebellion assuming the power of government, by making laws, and punishing for not obeying those laws...." Considering the events closest to the present loss, the events mechanically causing the loss, the 747 hijacking comes within no fair reading of Drinkwater.

Thirteen years after *Drinkwater* was decided, Lord Mansfield charged a jury as to the insurance meaning of military or usurped power in *Langdale v. Mason*, 1 Bennett's Fire Ins. Cas. 16 (K.B. 1780). A distillery owned by Langdale, a Catholic, was set on fire by a mob in London during the "no popery" riot led by Lord Gordon in 1780. The distillery was covered by a fire policy issued by the Sun Fire Office, which policy excluded losses caused by "civil commotion" and "military or usurped power." Lord Mansfield instructed the jury as follows:

> "The words military or usurped power ... must mean rebellion conducted by authority, as in the year 1745, when the rebels [led by Charles Edward Stuart] came to Derby; and if they had ordered any part of the town, or a single house to be set on fire, that would have been by authority of a rebellion.... Usurped power takes in rebellion, acting under usurped authority."
> *Id.* at 17.

Taking an unduly broad view of proximate cause and considering the events in Jordan and Lebanon as bearing on the insurance nature of a loss that occurred over London, the PFLP did not have sufficient incidents of a de facto government in those countries to constitute a military or usurped power. The all risk insurers have marshalled the evidence favoring their view that the PFLP was a de facto government, but that body of evidence is so unimpressive that it is clear that the district court was not in error in holding that it was a mere political group.

The fact that [King] Hussein negotiated with the PFLP for the release of hostages does not establish that the PFLP was being dealt with as a government. Officials may negotiate with individuals who hold hostages without according such individuals governmental status. The only power that these events reflect is the power of the PFLP to hold hostages, which, though the very essence of hijacking is surely not an incident of "quasi-government."

The cases establish that war is a course of hostility engaged in by entities that have at least significant attributes of sovereignty. Under international law war is waged by states or state-like entities. Lauterpacht defines war as a "contention between two or more States through their armed forces...." 2 L. Oppenheim, International Law 202 (H. Lauterpacht, 7th ed. 1952). War is "that state in which a nation prosecutes its right by force." The Brig Amy Warwick (The Prize Cases), 67 U.S. (2 Black) 635, 666, 17 L. Ed. 459 (1862); see also *Bas v. Tingy (The Eliza)*, 4 U.S. (4 Dall.) 37, 1 L. Ed. 731 (1800).

English and American cases dealing with the insurance meaning of "war" have defined it in accordance with the ancient international law definition: war refers to and includes only hostilities carried on by entities that constitute governments at least de facto in character. In the present case, the loss of the Pan American 747 was in no sense proximately caused by any "war" being waged by or between recognized states. The PFLP has never claimed to be a state. The PFLP could not have been acting on behalf of any of the states in which it existed when it hijacked the 747, since those states uniformly opposed hijacking.

## A. Civil Commotion.

For the proposition that the loss of the 747 was due to civil commotion the all risk insurers have offered no argument or authority which was not duly considered and rejected by the district court. The district court clearly applied the correct rule of law: civil commotion does not comprehend a loss occurring in the skies over two continents.... For there to be a civil commotion, the agents causing the disorder must gather together and cause a disturbance and tumult. * * *

## B. Riots.

Leaving aside the issue of causation, the authority as to the insurance meaning of "riot" is in some disarray. There is one body of authority that at least nominally supports the all risk non-availing technical definition of riot. But there is a second body of authority that a common law riot must be accompanied by a tumult or commotion, a rule under which the taking of the 747 would not be a riot since there was no tumult at the time of the taking. And there is a third, also respectable, body of authority that in insurance the term "riot" takes its meaning from common speech, namely a tumultuous assembly of a multitude of people. In that sense, the sense adopted by the district court, the loss of the 747 was surely not caused by a riot.

We would be hard pressed to choose between these three formulations were we required to do so. But recalling that the insured has the benefit of contra proferentem, the all risk insurers have the burden of showing that their definition is the only reasonable formulation. They have not discharged this burden. The war risk insurers have clearly established that the two definitions requiring tumult are at least reasonable.

## Notes and Questions

1. In *Pan American World Airways v. Aetna Casualty and Surety Co.*, the Second Circuit found the policy's version of the war exclusion—which included riot and civil commotion—inapplicable. The court reasoned that the exclusion, although lengthy, was ambiguous regarding the appropriate characterization of this event: whether the two gun-toting plane thieves were garden variety hijackers, soldiers in an ongoing war of liberation, or something else. Faced with the uncertainty, the court applied the ambiguity principle to find for the policyholder. In addition, the availability of specific hijacking exclusions used by insurers prompted the court to make the negative inference that the standard war exclusion was therefore not a hijacking exclusion unless the plane was taken by uniformed army personnel or a more obviously paramilitary group for a purpose resembling more traditional warfare activity.

Whatever the rationale, the *Pan Am v. Aetna* holding seems correct. The purpose of the war exclusion is to prevent insurers from being wiped out by correlated claims (those emanating from one source or affecting a discreet group rather than a cross-section or large population) that inflict abnormal losses throughout society.

The War Exclusion did not carry the day for the all-risk (we prefer the term with a hyphen, notwithstanding the court's preference) insurers. And—in case it was insufficiently clear from the court's opinion—an all-risk property insurer is in a more vulnerable position that specified risk insurers, because the all-risk insuring agreement provides a broad grant of coverage while a specified risk policy promises more targeted coverage by (you guessed it) specifying or listing the risks covered. In practice, a policy with a long list of specified risks may not look much different than an all-risk policy. But as you will seek in Ch. 2, exclusions are narrowly construed against insurers in a stronger version of the ambiguity rule enunciated in *Pan Am*. In addition, while the policyholder has the burden of making an initial or prima facie case for coverage (easily done when the policy has a broad all-risk insuring agreement), once that burden is met, the insurer bears the burden to establish the applicability of an asserted exclusion.

2. The court in *Universal Cable Productions v. Atlantic Specialty Ins.* 929 F.3d 1143 (9th Cir. 2019), made extensive use of the *Pan Am* case, as well as the *Holiday Inn*

case noted in Problem 4 below, in interpreting similarly worded war exclusions in a television production insurance policy. Universal Cable Productions moved production of the television series *Dig* out of Jerusalem after Hamas fired rockets from Gaza into Israel. Atlantic refused to cover Universal Cable's production costs under the television production insurance policy because it asserted that Hamas' conduct was "war" and "warlike action by a military force." The court relied on section 1644 of the California Civil Code to hold that both terms should be ascribed special meaning unique to the insurance context (as opposed to merely colloquial meaning). To that end, for coverage to attach, the court found that hostilities had to be between sovereigns, and Hamas was not such an organization. Thus, the court held that the two exclusions were inapplicable. (The question of whether or not Hamas' activities triggered the exclusion for "insurrection, rebellion, or revolution" was remanded to the district court.)

## PROBLEM FOUR

Lebanon was a hotbed of unrest and sectarian violence during the 1980s. Armed groups (described in much of the popular press as "militias") of Muslims fought Christian counterparts in Beirut, once perceived as the "Paris of the Middle East." The Holiday Inn Beirut became subject to a turf battle as both groups sought to occupy the hotel to use its vantage points for sniper and mortar fire. Occupation of the hotel seesawed between the groups. As a result, the hotel was trashed in ways that not even Joe Walsh could imagine.

The hotel seeks coverage pursuant to its property insurance policy. The insurer invokes a war exclusion similar to that in the Pan Am policy.

• What result?[46]

• Do you find the following assessment persuasive?

The risk pool maintenance function of the exclusion is not imperiled when it does not bar coverage for what is essentially an isolated crime, albeit one with political overtones. When in doubt, courts dealing with either the war or riot exclusions should take a functional approach rather than a hypertextual one, asking whether granting the coverage claim would defeat the purpose of the exclusions and expose the insurer to dangerous losses outside the contemplation of the parties to the policy.

• If so, does such an approach auger in favor or against coverage for the hotel?

---

46. Spoiler alert (of sorts): *See Holiday Inns, Inc. v. Aetna Ins. Co.*, 571 F. Supp. 1460 (S.D.N.Y. 1983) (finding coverage for damage to hotel that changed hands repeatedly in 1975 and 1976 during Lebanon conflict and was even used as a paramilitary headquarters and sniper's roost). But the exclusion in that case was somewhat narrowly focused on "war." Would an exclusion for riot, civil commotion, or usurped power change the result? Unquestionably, Lebanon was eventually engulfed in civil war. The court, however, found that the state of misery in Lebanon did not reach the level of war until sometime after the fall of the Holiday Inn Beirut. *See also* Stempel, *Insurance Aftermath of September 11, supra*, 37 Tort & Ins. L.J. at 852–55.

## PROBLEM FIVE

Mark Brushman—a Wall Street billionaire who thinks the Democrats are too far left and the Republicans are too far right—runs for President as an Independent. His campaign computers are hacked and used to produce a string of outrageous emails and texts designed to make Brushman look egomaniacally sexist, racist, homophobic and just plain creepy. Then the campaign's voter registration information becomes subject to ransomware.

Brushman immediately alerts Denial Mutual, his (and the campaign's) cyber insurer, which sold a policy that promises crisis management, hardware and software repair, as well as indemnification for losses and payment of ransom money if "such payment will cost less than the value to the policy-holder of the impounded information."

Denial's investigation quickly finds clear proof that an elite cyber unit of the Red [Russian for readers who are too young to remember this once-common nickname] Army is responsible for the hack.

Denial asserts that the policy's War Exclusion (similar to that in *Pan Am*) bars coverage and refuses to pay any ransom. Billionaire that he is, Brushman purchases new voter registration data from the political parties at a cost of $10 million. But tainted by the bogus emails, his once-promising candidacy sinks in the polls and he eventually withdraws from the race, buys an island in the Pacific, and enters into a sulking retirement.

- Would a court make a ruling similar to *Pan Am*?

- Or is this situation sufficiently different to enable the insurer to prevail?

- What are the best arguments for and against coverage?

- If the court finds that Denial should have paid the ransom, is its liability limited to $10 million?

- Or is Denial also responsible for the collapse of the Brushman Campaign (assuming a monetary value can be placed on dashed presidential aspirations)?

### *Nuclear Incident Exclusions*

Another example of an exclusion designed to further the insurer's goal of covering varied and uncorrelated risk is the nuclear disaster. This exclusion is usually made part of insurance policies by endorsement and is found in both property and liability policies. In liability policies, a common means of accomplishing this is through the "Nuclear Energy Liability Exclusion," which provides that the insurance does not apply to any loss resulting from "nuclear material." Neither first-party property nor liability insurers want to be holding a big tab if the Elm City Atomic Generating Plant melts down.

As a result of this prohibition in most policies, a separate market for nuclear incident insurance has arisen. *See* Brad Kane, *Glastonbury Insurer of Nuclear Plants Sees No Exposure in Japan Tragedy*, Hartford Business, Mar. 21, 2011 (describing American Nuclear Insurers, a specialty insurance company comprised of participating insurers, that covers half of the world's 451 nuclear power plants, including all those in the U.S.) ("We fill the gap of the nuclear exclusion in other policies," noted a spokesperson.).

Under the Price-Anderson Act designed to foster nuclear power, American reactors enjoy some limitations on liability and are insured for $375 million by a government program, with policyholders paying an average of roughly $1 million per year to obtain additional excess coverage, available up to a maximum limit of $12.6 billion per incident. For perspective, consider the 1979 Three Mile Island accident resulted in $71 million in claims payments (finally finalized in 2003).

Even mega-risks are usually insurable if the policyholder is willing to pay a high enough premium. But the full extent of damage limits have yet to be explored, a situation that may change in light of the March 2011 earthquake and tsunami-related nuclear incident in Japan. American Nuclear was relaxed not because the incident was minor but rather because, in spite of its large market share, it insured no Japanese reactors. The incident at Chernobyl in the former Soviet Union caused even more damage, but lack of transparency by the [now Russian] government has prevented calculation or even knowledge of the amount of insurance claims that may have resulted.

*Miscellaneous Additional Examples*

Property insurers typically exclude coverage for flooding or "earth movement" (a/k/a earthquakes or mudslides) for reasons of protecting the risk pool. Specific flood policies are available from the federal government[47] and earth movement coverage may be obtained by endorsement or through government-supported earthquake insurance. The additional coverage is available at an additional premium and is made feasible by the wide-spread risk underwriting made possible by the government or an alliance of insurers.

In addition, insurers, particularly liability insurers, may exclude certain risks not so much because they are universal in scope when they take place but because they occur with sufficient frequency and severity so as to make underwriting and pricing very difficult. For example, the standard commercial general liability (CGL) policy discussed in Chapter 9 excludes coverage for pollution liability and often excludes asbestos-related claims. Pollution and asbestos claims swamped the courts and insurers during the 1980s and caused significantly subpar economic performance for many insurers.

Some exclusions are broad but are included not because of the correlation of risk but because the nature of the risk differs significantly from the basic thrust of the policy. For example, the standard CGL typically excludes coverage for employment-related liability and for liquor liability. The latter is specifically insurable however under liquor liability or "dram shop" policies sold to bars, restaurants, and liquor

---

47. *See* National Flood Insurance Act of 1968, 42 U.S.C. §§ 4011–4128.

stores (at substantial premiums) while coverage for the former is available through purchase of an employment practices liability (EPL) policy. These additional coverages beyond basic general liability of course require an additional premium.

In this manner, exclusions operate not only to limit the scope of a particular insurance policy but also to define the contours of particular insurance products. For example, typical general liability policies contain an automobile liability exclusion. If you want auto insurance, you need to buy auto insurance. And general liability is distinguished from professional liability, worker's compensation liability, environmental liability, directors & officers (D&O) liability, and so on.

An effective risk manager not only attempts to minimize risk through safety precautions but also through purchase of a cluster of insurance products appropriate to the risks faced by a business. For example, the construction of a large commercial building will typically involve a surety bond for protection against faulty construction or delays, a builder's risk policy that covers the property until completion (with property insurance after that), a general liability policy, an architect's professional liability policy, D&O insurance for the owning company and the contracting company and finally workers compensation coverage. In addition, subcontractors on the project are typically required to purchase a minimum amount of insurance and to name the general contractor and the owner as "additional insureds" to the subcontractor policies. Premiums for such policies may be millions of dollars in order to secure tens of millions in coverage.

On a less grand (and expensive) level, average families act as their own de facto risk managers by purchasing homeowners' insurance (which includes property insurance on the dwelling and liability insurance should persons be injured on premises), auto insurance for each household vehicle, disability and life insurance for the parents (and perhaps the children as well), medical insurance (usually as part of an employer-sponsored group plan) and, for higher income families with more assets to protect, "umbrella" insurance that provides additional or "excess" liability coverage (*see* Ch. 13) should a really serious injury spur a lawsuit against a member of the family.

Boring or not—insurance is everywhere.

# § 1.04. The Indemnity Principle

Insurance exists not to prevent losses or to improve the financial situation of policyholders but only to repay them for incurred losses covered by insurance. In other words, insurance exists to "pay back" or "indemnify" policyholders for what they have lost. Losses are usually measured in strictly monetary terms. To some extent, life insurance is different in that it operates both as an investment vehicle and because life insurers do not attempt to value the worth of an insured life with fine-tuned accuracy.[48]

---

48. Life insurance, like all forms of insurance, is written in rough denominations. However, after a fire destroys a $75,000 home covered by a $100,000 policy, the policyholder may collect only a maximum of $75,000 whereas a $100,000 life insurance policy pays $100,000 to the beneficiary even if the decedent's living economic value to the beneficiary could never approach that amount.

This indemnity principle behind insurance explains what might otherwise seem grudging decisions limiting funds for policyholders, particularly in cases focusing on the calculation of the "actual cash value" of a loss (*see* Chapter 6). Because ordinarily, under the indemnity concept, policyholders are to receive insurance proceeds equal only to the amount of their financial losses, the amounts due after a loss may at first disappoint the policyholder.

For example, the owner of the hypothetical $75,000 house burned to ashes may feel an emotional loss far beyond the fair market value of the home. Furthermore, the policyholder faces the problem of buying equivalently satisfactory housing, which may require more than $75,000 depending upon the local real estate market, the effect of modern building costs, the number of homes available in the policyholder's price range, and so on. Although these and similar factors have real consequences for the policyholder, they do not change the basic nature of property insurance: the policyholder is able to collect funds only to the extent of a tangible economic loss unless it has purchased or the law requires a "valued policy" that pays to the victim the full policy limits.

The indemnity principle helps to explain several aspects of the typical valuation of loss such as considerations of depreciation and market values of property. It also explains part of the reason underlying the insurable interest requirement and the importance of fortuity, adverse selection, and moral hazard considerations in underwriting, which in turn undergird specific contract language or legal doctrines such as the intentional act exclusion. The indemnity principle also provides a rationale for subrogation actions. A subrogation action is one in which the insurer, after paying a claim, acquires a policyholder's claim for relief against a third party that caused the insured loss. Unless subrogation is permitted to the insurer, the policyholder whose loss results from the misconduct of others could potentially obtain double recovery by both collecting insurance proceeds for the loss and also successfully suing the tortfeasor over that same loss.[49]

But, as the example of life insurance illustrates, not all insurance policies completely comport with the indemnity principle. For example, many property insurers offer

---

49. We find it odd, however, that insurance policies do not bar coverage if the policyholder has entered into a contract with a vendor that waives the insurer's rights of subrogation should the vendor's negligence cause injury to insured property of the policyholder/customer.

First, it is not at all clear to us that the policyholder has the authority to restrict the insurer's rights, particularly when it is clear that the property policy in question contains a subrogation clause.

Second, a policyholder's waiver of subrogation undermines the public policy of requiring wrongdoers to pay for or "internalize" (as an economist might say) the costs of the wrongdoing. Subrogation provides incentive for vendors to be more careful. Even if an individual insured lacks incentive to sue after having the bulk of loss compensated by its insurer, the insurer that paid for the bulk of the loss may very well pursue the negligent vendor which should, at least in theory, provide additional incentive for the vendor to be more careful in its work.

Nonetheless, insurers typically do not forbid policyholders from entering into contracts waiving subrogation and do not have exclusions or other limits in their policies for insureds that waive subrogation.

"valued policies" which stipulate to the amount paid for a total loss irrespective of other indices (e.g., purchase price, resale market) of the value of the property. These policyholders may on occasion actually make money after a loss if the property's actual cash value falls below the amount of the policy. Although valued policies are consequently criticized by some as creating incentives toward moral hazard, they nonetheless enjoy substantial popularity and are mandated by statute in some states. We think that valued policies create only modest moral hazard and in return provide greater protection and streamline the claims process in cases of catastrophic loss, with the attendant virtue of reducing an insurer's ability to "nickel-and-dime" a policyholder in the wake of a catastrophic loss.

In similar fashion, many property policies, particularly homeowner's and renter's insurance, offer "replacement value" coverage that provides payment equal to the cost of replacing the lost structure. Technically, these policies violate the indemnity principle. For example, the policyholder in the house fire hypothetical did not lose a brand new three-bedroom/two-bath home but in fact lost an older three-bedroom/two-bath home, perhaps one not only showing wear-and-tear but also needing major repairs. Nonetheless, the holder of a valued policy receives the pre-determined amount while the replacement value policyholder is awarded the cost of new construction even though what it lost was old construction.[50]

However, this departure from strict compliance with the indemnity principle does not open the gates to moral hazard because the increased costs of building (since the house was originally built) both justify the increased protection for the homeowner and make it unlikely that a policyholder will neglect or intentionally destroy a home simply to get a modern rebuild. The hassle of being displaced, dealing with contractors, etc. is simply too much for a sane person. Actual fraudsters and arsonists do not want to rebuild. They want the insurance money for absconding, paying gambling (oops, we mean "gaming") debts, etc.

## PROBLEM SIX

Financial author Andrew Tobias in his book about insurers (THE INVISIBLE BANKERS (1982)) suggested requiring rebuilding as an anti-fraud device. Insurers have not followed this advice.

• Should they?

• If you think not, is this because you think Tobias is wrong?

---

50. This will perhaps initially sound wrong to readers. Everyone knows that home prices generally rise rather than fall, right? True. But property insurance coverage applies to only the building in question and does not insure the value of the underlying land. Real estate values go up over time primarily if not exclusively because available dwellings in good neighborhoods become comparatively rarer as population and wealth increases. Supply and demand and all that. And, to be sure, the cost of new construction rises as materials and labor cost more. But a 40-year-old three bedroom/two bath structure is like any other physical asset in that it degrades over time, requires ongoing repair, and is worth comparatively less than when first built.

- The detrimental effects of the proposal outweigh the benefit of deterring fraud?

- What detrimental effects do you posit?

- Would a ban on valued policies and replacement cost policies be a better deterrent to fraud?

- What drawbacks would accompany such proposals?

The indemnity principle should be distinguished from an "indemnity policy." A true indemnity policy provides payment to the policyholder of an amount the policyholder has already paid out in satisfaction of a covered claim. For example, the policyholder may lose a house in a tornado and pay a contractor to replace the structure. If the insurer does not pay until the policyholder has paid, this is true indemnity under an indemnity policy. Similarly, the policyholder may be sued for an automobile accident. Under an indemnity policy, the insurer will not pay until the third-party claimant has obtained a judgment or settlement actually paid by the policyholder.

By contrast, under a "liability policy," the insurer is obligated to pay the amount of coverage as soon as the policyholder's liability or loss becomes fixed. For example, the homeowner needing to rebuild ordinarily arranges for the insurer to pay the contractor or obtains insurance proceeds in time to pay for replacement construction. Similarly, the auto insurer normally pays for a settlement or judgment rather than first insisting that the policyholder pay and then seek reimbursement.

Most insurance today is written on a "liability" or loss basis rather than an "indemnity" basis, because insurers normally have greater liquidity for paying claims than do their policyholders. This is particularly true for personal lines. But liability basis or fixed obligation coverage does not violate the indemnity principle. The policyholder still only obtains insurance proceeds equal to the value of its loss. Modern policies have moved far enough away from requiring pure "reimbursement-style" indemnity. For example, as noted above, most homeowner's or auto collision policies do not require the policyholder to repair or rebuild. Absent specific terms to the contrary in the policy, the policyholder may accept a check and then sell the burned home or the mangled car.

Other aspects of modern insurance practice vary from a pure traditional concept of indemnity as reimbursement for out-of-pocket outlays. For example, a standard liability policy provides a legal defense for the policyholder sued by a third party. Where the defense is provided by counsel who bills the insurer directly (in lieu of having the insurer reimburse the policyholder for previously paid legal fees), this is not indemnity per se. However, this type of defense arrangement is not a material departure from standard indemnity. Rather, it is more of a pre-emptive strike in which the insurer provides counsel in order to avoid getting potentially controversial legal bills (which may be contested based on rates or time expended on the defense) from the policyholder later in the litigation. In a similar vein, health insurers often pay medical providers directly rather than requiring policyholders to pay physicians and then seek reimbursement.

Notwithstanding the exceptions, the indemnity principle remains a rule of both persuasive and explanatory force. For example, even pro-policyholder contract interpretation doctrines such as construing ambiguities against the drafter (Ch. 2), waiver and estoppel (Ch. 4), and the reasonable expectations approach (Ch. 2), seldom violate the indemnity principle. These doctrines may result in decisions imposing a type of coverage the insurer denied or require a loss calculation formula more favorable to the policyholder, but they rarely if ever result in the policyholder receiving funds exceeding the actual amount of the policyholder's economic loss.

# § 1.05. Fortuity, Adverse Selection and Moral Hazard

In addition to the basic insurance concepts previously discussed, the concepts of randomness and chance are important to a properly functioning insurance market. Fortuity, adverse selection, and moral hazard are additional key concepts related to ensuring randomness in underwriting losses.

## [A] Fortuity Generally

Although it is often erroneously used as a synonym for fortunate, "fortuity" simply means by chance. A fortuitous circumstance may sometimes be lucky and sometimes will be disastrous, but it will always occur by chance. Insurers will usually be successful only if they are writing coverage for fortuitous events. For example, if they write property insurance that provides indemnity for hurricane damage, they are well within the zone of fortuity: no one can predict a specific hurricane and its destination more than a few days in advance, let alone cause or direct a hurricane. Although one can be confident that at least some hurricanes will occur in some regions of the world during certain times of the year, the inability to control or foretell such events means that policyholders have no control over the matter. There is little any policyholder can do to influence the risk that her property insurer underwrites.

Even after a serious loss event, the damages resulting from the event may be sufficiently uncertain to satisfy the fortuity concept and permit the sale of insurance. For example, after the horrific 1980 fire at the MGM Grand Hotel in Las Vegas, MGM was able to purchase general liability insurance on the risk. *See In re MGM Grand Hotel Fire Litigation*, 570 F. Supp. 913, 928–29 (D. Nev. 1983). Although the fire had obviously already taken place, there still remained uncertainty as to the resolution of the pending or expected claims arising out of the event. There was sufficient fortuity to make the matter insurable and to create a market in which an insurer was willing to sell coverage to the prospective policyholder, who was already a defendant in litigation (undoubtedly at a far larger premium than would be required for ordinary liability coverage in the absence of the fire).

For insurers, fortuity or its absence can make the difference between success and failure. If an insurer is providing coverage only for random losses, it can make rough actuarial calculations as to the risk of loss based on past claims experience. If it takes advantage of sound underwriting practice through the law of large numbers (the larger the sample, the closer its experience will parallel reality) by writing policies for a large uncorrelated risk pool, the insurer can profit. If the insurer provides coverage for non-fortuitous events, an intended or nonrandom set of losses could ripple through its entire risk pool.

Since insurance exists to provide indemnity for fortuitous losses only, insurers would logically seek to reduce the chances that they would be inadvertently required to pay a policyholder for non-fortuitous losses. Most commonly, insurers seek to accomplish this by inserting into their policies an exclusion from coverage for losses that were "expected or intended from the standpoint of the insured," better known as the "intentional act exclusion" discussed in § 1.04[A][1]. By definition, losses intended or surely expected by the policyholder are not the result of chance. This applies with equal force irrespective of whether the policyholder intentionally damages property on which he has insurance or injures a third party who subsequently makes a liability claim.

As discussed in the previous section, the concept of fortuity and accident are important to insurance theory. Insurance is available to protect against the losses that may occur by chance—so-called "fortuitous" losses—and should not be available to provide payment for things that are certain to happen or are within the effective control of the policyholder. Life insurance fits the model because there is risk and uncertainty about the length of life even though death itself is inexorable.

The notion that losses must take place inadvertently because of oversight, chance, or bad luck rather than intent dominates judicial concepts of what constitutes a covered loss for purposes of property insurance (Ch. 8) or an "occurrence" for purpose of liability insurance (see Ch. 9). Courts get this concept wrong with surprising frequency and may apply 20-20 hindsight to label a loss non-fortuitous or intentional even when the requisite intent to bring about harm or loss is lacking. For example, some courts have found even negligent misrepresentations not to be accidents or occurrences because the person making the representation intended to induce reliance. See, e.g., Green v. State Farm Fire & Cas. Co., 127 P.3d 1279 (Utah Ct. App. 2005). The problem with this line of thought is that it confuses volitional conduct (which takes place constantly in life and business) with intent to injure, which is thankfully relatively rare. See, e.g., Aetna Cas. & Sur. Co. v. Metropolitan Baptist Church, 967 F. Supp. 217 (S.D. Tex. 1996) (negligent representation an "occurrence"); Sheets v. Brethren Mut. Ins. Co., 342 Md. 634, 679 A.2d 540 (1996) (misrepresentation without intent to injure can still be covered accident or occurrence).

The same analysis applies to questions of whether liability insurance provides coverage for foolishly reckless acts. See, e.g., Metro. Prop. & Cas. Ins. Co. v. Pittington, 841 N.E.2d 413 (Ill. Ct. App. 2005) (shooting incident may be sufficiently accidental and fortuitous for potential coverage even where policyholder was criminally convicted for reckless conduct in connection with deadly shooting; court reasons that policyholder may have behaved abominably but injury may not have been intentional or practically certain to take place); *Cumberland Mut. Fire Ins. Co. v. Murphy*, 183 N.J. 344, 873 A.2d 534 (2005) (injuries caused by teenagers shooting BB gun at cars sufficiently accidental because insureds did not expect or intend injury but were negligent in use of gun); *Allstate Ins. Co. v. McCarn*, 683 N.W.2d 656 (Mich. 2004) (same).

The requisite degree of fortuity or "accidentalness" may exist for some persons insured under a policy even if others are engaging in intentional destruction. *See, e.g., Ill. Farmers Ins. Co. v. Kure*, 846 N.E.2d 644 (Ill. App. Ct. 2006) (allegations of negligent supervision by parents sufficient to come within potential coverage even where child intentionally caused injury). *But see Am. Family Mut. Ins. Co. v. Corrigan*, 697 N.W.2d 108 (Iowa 2005) (criminal act exclusion in homeowner policy precludes coverage where innocent parents were negligent in supervising their child, who was subsequently convicted of endangering another child).[51]

Staged or fraudulent claims, of course, clearly are not accidental and do not satisfy the fortuity concept. Unfortunately, they abound in spite of serious insurer and government efforts against them. *See, e.g., Insurance Scam Plotted by Mich. Prison Inmates Takes Fatal Twist*, Ins. J., Apr. 28, 2006 (describing scam in which prisoners created phony business and then insured one another as business partners; original plan to mutually stage fake deaths went awry when one prisoner killed co-conspirator in effort to take sole possession of fraudulently obtained payments).

### ILLUSTRATION ONE: THE MYSTERIOUS COLONEL

A particularly memorable, tragi-comic case involving the issue of whether a loss (in this case a self-inflicted loss) was sufficiently unintended to be adequately fortuitous for insurance purposes is *Fed. Ins. Co. v. Ace Prop. & Cas. Co.*, 429 F.3d 120 (5th Cir. 2005) (applying Texas law). Electronic Data Systems (EDS), perhaps best known as the computer company started by the late billionaire (and 1992 presidential candidate) Ross Perot, was approached by a man identifying himself only as "Colonel West," purporting to be a representative of NATO (the North Atlantic Treaty Organization) and expressing interest in perhaps contracting with EDS as general contractor for a covert operation requiring purchase of electronic goods. Eager for the business, EDS induced two prospective subcontractors to provide "Colonel West" with exemplary equipment worth millions of dollars as part of EDS's effort to land the job.

"Colonel West" turned out to be a con man and the equipment was never seen again. The subcontractors sued EDS for the cost of the lost equipment. EDS sought insurance coverage for its potential liability to the subcontractors.

---

51. For an extensive discussion of the concept of an "accident" in the context of accidental death insurance, *see* Adam F. Scales, *Man, God and the Serbonian Bog: The Evolution of Accidental Death Insurance*, 86 Iowa L. Rev. 173 (2000).

The court denied coverage, ruling that there was nothing accidental about these events (in spite of the story's film noir/O. Henry-style ending) because EDS and the subcontractors always intended that the equipment be given to the mysterious colonel in hopes that this would induce future business worth much more than the electronic products given as "samples." Those hopes were dashed when the colonel turned out to be an imposter, but the court treated the matter as an intentional loss rather than an accidental loss or "occurrence" within the meaning of the EDS liability policy.

And some people say insurance is boring. More important for our purposes, the case illustrates the sometimes murky boundaries of fortuity and insurability. On one hand, as the court noted, EDS and the prospective subcontractors intended to give the equipment to the mysterious Colonel West.

- But was the loss of the equipment intended?

- Even if EDS et al. were not assured of future business from the faux Colonel, can it not be said that the subcontractors lost their equipment because of an EDS negligent misrepresentation about the bona fides of Colonel West?

- Even if the subcontractors were willing to use the equipment as a loss leader, could they not have changed their minds and sought its return from a legitimate business?

This last avenue was foreclosed due to the alleged negligence of EDS in implicitly vouching for Colonel West even though he proved to be just a Matchstick Man in a uniform. Now you see why courts divide on insurance issues.

The correct outcome of the EDS case, in our view, turns on the factual context. If the subcontractors completely parted with their expensive equipment with no expectations of its return in the absence of landing a contract with the Cardboard Cut-Out Colonel, then the court's decision is right. EDS and the putative subs would then only have been engaging in the type of ordinary loss leader business practices that are not insurable events.

For example, a fast food restaurant may, for a time, sell its hamburgers at "1960s prices," hoping that the losses on each hamburger sale will be more than made up for by increased consumer traffic that includes purchase of other items on which the company earns good profits. If the restaurant guesses wrong, it loses money, but this is not "accidental" within the meaning of insurance.

On the other hand, if a vendor lends equipment for a customer "tryout" and expects to get the equipment back in the absence of purchase, then there has been a fortuitous loss if the customer skips town with the vendor's property (without paying). Ordinarily, the vendor would sue the customer (which was foreclosed in the EDS case), but the event could still be fortuitous under the right set of facts.

Also, of course, fortuity and liability should be distinguished. Even if the loss is accidental because a vendor and EDS both expected to have the equipment returned if there was no purchase, EDS may or may not have said or done things to make it legally responsible for the vendor's loss. On one hand, EDS could have said, "We have a really good shot at landing this military contract," which arguably implies that it is vouching for Colonel West, or it could have said, "We're not sure about this outfit, but we're willing to gamble, are you?" The latter presentation would seem not to create any misrepresentation or similar liability.

As we will learn in Chs. 7 and 9, liability insurance exists to defend claims against the policyholder even when the claim lacks merit. Why? Because part of the purpose of liability insurance is to provide "litigation insurance" and remove from the policyholder the albatross of defending and resolving claims (some valid, some meritless). Absent collusion, the existence of a claim by a third party is almost always fortuitous. Even the most careful of policyholders cannot prevent others from suing.

### [1] The "Intentional Act" or "Expected or Intended" Exclusion

A basic aspect of insurance is that it provides indemnity for unexpected or fortuitous events. It would defeat the purpose of insurance and encourage "moral hazard" if policyholders could be compensated for losses they intentionally bring about by their own acts. Likewise, indemnity for clearly anticipated losses would encourage "adverse selection," the other twin evil feared by insurers, because policyholders could go shopping for coverage for a pending loss that has yet to fully materialize. Insuring these sorts of situations would permit unscrupulous or antisocial policyholders to have their blameworthy acts subsidized by innocent policyholders or society generally.

In response to this concern, insurance policies typically contain an exclusion for injury that is "expected or intended from the standpoint of the insured." To state an obvious example, the policyholder cannot set fire to his own house and expect the insurer to provide payment. Similarly, the policyholder cannot shoot a disliked neighbor and then, when facing civil suit from the neighbor, expect the insurer to provide defense or indemnity.

In the jargon of the trade, this exclusion is often referred to as the "intentional act" exclusion, although the term is not strictly accurate and may even be misleading. A policyholder does not lose coverage for intentional acts (e.g., manufacturing a product) that leads to surprisingly adverse results (e.g., a product defect injuring someone). If this was the case, the promised liability insurance coverage would be illusory. Only if the manufacturer wanted to cause injury (e.g., selling a known defective product to a rival business in hopes that it would malfunction and cause production losses to the rival) is the exclusion met. And, to reiterate from the *Pan-Am* case, the insurer has the burden to demonstrate the applicability of an exclusion, with ambiguous language construed against the insurer as drafter of the policy.

But that said, the fortuity principle is strong and may be a factor in coverage decisions apart from any intentional act exclusion. Liability insurance policies, for example, provide coverage for "accidents" and "occurrences," which must be sufficiently fortuitous to fall within coverage.

The public policy against indemnification of the intended loss is so strong that courts will in some circumstances forbid payment of benefits even if the insurance contract is silent on the point. However, the states differ markedly on type of conduct that is sufficiently volitional to bar coverage. Public policy defenses to payment are often made by insurers to attempt to save themselves from poor policy drafting. In addition, the relevant state law (statutory or common) regarding indemnity for intentional acts may affect the court's interpretation of policy language as the court attempts to give the policy a legal rather than illegal interpretation.

## ILLUSTRATION TWO:
## OBJECTIVE VS. SUBJECTIVE INTENT

Courts divide somewhat over whether to apply a subjective or objective standard in applying the exclusion, with some courts seeking to determine whether a reasonable person would expect a loss to result from the conduct in question. Most courts appear to gauge intent according to the subjective view of the policyholder—which we find to be the clearly correct answer. *See* Erik S. Knutsen, *Fortuity Victims and the Compensation Gap: Re-envisioning Liability Insurance Coverage for Intentional and Criminal Conduct,* 21 CONN. INS. L. REV. 209 (2014). If insurance covered only objectively reasonable acts, it would not cover negligence (which is typically defined as a violation of the duty of objectively reasonable care), and the policy would be close to worthless. This aspect of insurance coverage focuses not on the degree to which an "act" was voluntary but on the degree to which injury or damage was intended or expected.

In an important opinion in massive insurance coverage litigation related to asbestos claims, a California court reviewed the law of the expected or intended defense and concluded that the phrase should be given its "plain meaning" and construed to mean that the policyholder had "an actual awareness that harm was practically certain even though harm was not intended."[52] The court reviewed jurisdictions using subjective and objective approaches to the intentional act exclusion.

Under an objective approach to the exclusion, the policyholder may be denied coverage where the court finds that a reasonable policyholder "should have known" that its conduct would bring about injury to a third party. Under a subjective approach, the inquiry centers around whether the policyholder in question in fact knew that injury was virtually certain to occur. Courts that reject the objective approach reason that its application would in effect deprive policyholders of coverage for mere negligence—the very protection the policyholder attempts to acquire through purchase

---

52. *Armstrong World Indus. v. Aetna Cas. & Sur. Co.,* 45 Cal. App. 4th 1, 52 Cal. Rptr. 2d 690, 718 (1996).

of an insurance policy. Other courts have rejected an objective standard on textual grounds because the typical policy speaks of the expectations of *the* insured, not those of *a reasonable person.* In the *Armstrong* case noted above, the court concluded that the exclusion would apply if the policyholder "knew of the hazards of asbestos and was aware of the substantial probability of harm from its manufacture and sale."

At one time, a significant number of courts and commentators thought that intentional acts by a perpetrator barred insurance coverage. Insurers have since clarified that intent or expectation is to be measured "from the standpoint" of the policyholder. Most recently, in an effort to cover innocent co-insureds, insurers have begun to use language that states the exclusion as applying whenever there is expected injury inflicted by "an insured" or "any insured" rather than "the insured." *See* RANDY J. MANILOFF & JEFFREY STEMPEL, COMMERCIAL GENERAL LIABILITY INSURANCE COVERAGE: KEY ISSUES IN EVERY STATE Ch. 10 (4th ed. 2018) (50-state survey suggest that this change in language has been effective in permitting insurers to deny coverage to an innocent co-insured for losses intentionally caused by another co-insured). Liability policies also provide related exclusions for acts such as assault and battery or criminal violations.

The line separating intentional and fortuitous conduct is sometimes blurred, prompting courts to treat some unwise behavior as the equivalent of an intentional act. Generally, however, where the policyholder has only been foolish, even very foolish, the purposes of insurance would tend to support a finding of coverage. Where a claim against the policyholder alleged both intentional harm and other theories of liability, a liability insurer is ordinarily required to provide a defense of the entire action even though indemnity will not lie if a final judgment against the policyholder results from a determination that the liability-creating damage was expected or intended.

Courts have taken different views in the application of the intentional act exclusion and may roughly be classified as:

> (1) *Pro-insurer:* these courts take the broadest view of the scope of the exclusion and consequently the narrowed view of coverage, holding that claims stemming from the natural and probable results of the policyholder's act are sufficiently expected or intended to preclude coverage.[53] Fortunately, there are relatively few courts that are this severe because this approach could eviscerate much of the policy protection that a reasonable policyholder seeks to purchase.[54] If carried to extremes, as in the manufacturing examples above, this approach

---

53. *See, e.g., Farmers Ins. Co. v. Vagnozzi,* 138 Ariz. 443, 675 P.2d 703 (1983) (no coverage for injuries incurred when policyholder threw an elbow in roughly played pickup basketball game); *Hins v. Heer,* 259 N.W.2d 38 (N.D. 1977).

54. The pro-insurer view has been specifically rejected by many courts (*see, e.g., Rajspic v. Nationwide Mut. Ins. Co.,* 110 Idaho 729, 718 P.2d 1167 (1986); *Continental Western Ins. Co. v. Toal,* 309 Minn. 169, 244 N.W.2d 121 (1976). In at least one instance, a state statute overruled a judicial line of cases broadly applying the exclusion. *See Estabrook v. American Hoist & Derrick,* 127 N.H. 162, 498 A.2d 741 (1985) (noting legislative overruling of *Vittum v. New Hampshire Ins. Co.,* 117 N.H. 1, 369 A.2d 184 (1977)).

would essentially preclude coverage for any policyholder activity that is risky. And virtually all activities, especially commercial activities, entail some risk.

(2) *Moderate:* this is the approach followed by a majority of courts and requires that the policyholder both have intended the conduct in question and have intended or expected some type of damage to result from the activity in question.[55] This approach deserves its majority status because it prevents coverage for acts amounting to moral hazard or that otherwise undermine effective functioning of the insurance market[56] while permitting policyholders to conduct their affairs without undue fear that resulting losses will not be covered. Courts applying this approach tend also to correctly confine their inquiry to the particular activity of the policyholder that occasioned the claim. For example, courts would focus upon the policyholder's immediate decision rather than asking if the policyholder generally expected some liability claims as a result of its ongoing activity.

(3) *Pro-policyholder:* this approach gives the exclusion a narrow construction, resulting in broader policy coverage generally. The exclusion applies only if the policyholder has a specific intent to cause the particular sort of injury giving rise to the third-party claim.

The specific intent view errs too greatly in favor of the policyholder by insulating him or her from the financial consequences of antisocial conduct. For example, in *Farmers Insurance Group v. Hastings,*[57] the policyholder "bushwhacked" a friend, hit him, and caused permanent eye injury out of anger over an altercation at a party (in which the friend had tried to intercede to keep peace). In *Earl Mutual Insurance v. Burkholder Estate,*[58] the policyholder shot at his wife and accidently killed his daughter.

With friends and family like this, the victims hardly needed enemies. They did, however, want compensation, which propels some courts toward the "specific intent" view of the exclusion. But the inevitable consequence of this approach is less incentive for policyholders like Messrs. Hastings or Burkholder to control their drinking and treat their loved ones and others with care and respect. The two major values of tort and insurance law—compensation and deterrence—are thus often in stark conflict in intentional act cases. The moderate approach is preferred because it strikes a reasonable balance of these concerns by making compensation widely available except where society's interest in deterring the policyholder's conduct is quite strong. But

---

55. *See, e.g., Universal Underwriters Ins. Co. v. Stokes Chevrolet, Inc.,* 990 F.2d 598 (11th Cir. 1993) (applying Alabama law). *Farmer in the Dell Enterprises, Inc. v. Farmers Mut. Ins. Co.,* 514 A.2d 1097 (Del. 1986); *Mutual Serv. Casualty Ins. Co. v. McGehee,* 711 P.2d 826 (Mont. 1985); *Pachucki v. Republic Ins. Co.,* 89 Wis. 2d 703, 278 N.W.2d 898 (1979).

56. *See, e.g., Unigard Mut. Ins. Co. v. Argonaut Ins. Co.,* 20 Wash. App. 261, 579 P.2d 1015 (1978) (damage from uncontrolled fire at school resulting from 11-year-old's vandalism is excluded notwithstanding that he intended to keep the fire contained; however, his parents were covered as innocent co-policyholders).

57. *Farmers Ins. Group v. Hastings,* 358 N.W.2d 473 (Minn. Ct. App. 1984) (taking pro-policyholder approach), *rev'd,* 366 N.W.2d 293 (1985).

58. 1984–85 Fire & Ins. Cases (CCH) at 1386 (Pa. Ct. Com. Pleas 1984).

where a volitional act is inherently wrongful and automatically injurious, no coverage is available regardless of the policyholder's beliefs as to whether injury would result.

Notwithstanding the sometimes thorny questions of compensation and fairness or the rights of victims versus society's interest in deterring misconduct, application of the exclusion is in many cases relatively straightforward. For example, if the policyholder has done something with the specific intent of causing damage or where the conduct is inherently condemnable, even pro-policyholder courts will generally apply the exclusion to bar coverage.

In interpreting the exclusion, courts usually focus exclusively on the act in question and its degree of voluntariness and are not concerned with whether the policyholder thought that it was immune from liability for the conduct in question. For example, a policyholder's liability for improper repossession of trucks has been held to be sufficiently expected by the policyholder as not to be an "accident" subject to coverage under a CGL policy that defines an "occurrence" as an "accident." The key was the policyholder's volitional intent to inflict a loss on the debtor. The mere fact that the policyholder miscalculated its legal rights did not make its repossession of the trucks any less intentional.[59] In addition, this sort of loss intentionally inflicted on entities with which one does business is often excluded from liability coverage as a business risk outside the scope of liability insurance, which is generally aimed at providing coverage for tort claims.[60] *See* Ch. 9, *infra*.

Where the conduct giving rise to a liability claim cannot be shown to be specifically directed, policyholders have a much better chance of obtaining coverage. Even some pretty reckless conduct has been held to be outside of the intentional act exclusion. The policyholder must face more than the mere probability (even high probability) of loss but must show sufficient conscious desire for the result to make it properly viewed as intentional. To be "expected," the general rule is that the loss must be *substantially certain to occur* from the insured's subjective perspective. Although knowing and certain acts trigger the exclusion, reckless or stupid ones ordinarily do not so long as the intent is not clearly and purposefully to impose a loss.

Where intent and stupidity merge, however, courts often divide on whether to enforce the intentional act exclusion. A number of reported cases deal with injury claims resulting from "pranks" in which the policyholder intentionally did something that brought about the harm in question but intended only to "play a joke" rather than cause serious injury. Whether such claims are covered under a liability policy varies from state to state and depends on the court's approach. Pro-policyholder courts find coverage because there was no specific intent to injure. Pro-insurer courts would tend to exclude coverage where the volitional conduct was likely to lead to injury, al-

---

59. *See, e.g., Red Ball Leasing, Inc. v. Hartford Acci. & Indem. Co.*, 915 F.2d 306 (7th Cir. 1990) (applying Indiana law).

60. At least, the "bodily injury" portion of the CGL is aimed primarily at tort claims based on negligence. The "personal injury" and "advertising injury" portions of the CGL cover certain claims usually classified as intentional torts, such as defamation and copyright infringement.

though really odd injuries resulting from generally benign pranks may still be covered. Moderate jurisdictions tend to find coverage unless the prank was highly dangerous.

Another unfortunately recurring case is one involving claims against the policyholder for sexual molestation of children. Policyholder perpetrators usually claim they meant no harm. Some may even have the chutzpah to argue that they intended to give pleasure to the children. Although a few courts might find coverage on reasoning similar to those finding coverage in the prank cases, the reported cases indicate that all jurisdictions are likely to exclude coverage because the likelihood of injury to the child victim is inescapably apparent.

An important entry into the field is *Minkler v. Safeco Ins. Co. of America*, 232 P.3d 612 (Cal. 2010). The case involved alleged molestation of a neighbor child by the son of the named policyholder, with the victim alleging that the perpetrator's mother knew about the problem but negligently failed to stop their son's conduct (he was the little league coach of the victim). The policy in question contained an exclusion stating that coverage was not available where injury was expected or intended by "an" insured. Nonetheless, the *Minkler* court found coverage due to a severability of interests clause in the "Conditions" section of the liability policy at issue, stating that the "insurance applies separately to each insured."

In the court's view, this gave the defendant's policyholder parent a reasonable expectation of coverage so long as she was not intentionally injuring a third party. Further, it was "unlikely Betty [Schwartz, the mother of defendant David Schwartz] understood that by allowing David to reside in her home, and thus to become an additional insured on her homeowners policies," she was narrowing her coverage should David commit any intentionally or expectedly injurious acts. At a minimum, there was "ambiguity [that] must be resolved in the [policyholder's] favor." *See* 232 P.3d at 618–19. In *Safeco Insurance Co. of Am. v. White*, 913 N.E.2d 426 (Ohio 2009), which also involved the situation of negligent supervision of a child of the household (a 17-year-old who "attacked and repeatedly stabbed" a 13-year-old), the Ohio Supreme Court found coverage.

Nothing prevents an insurer from using a more specific exclusion to reach the sort of conduct for which it wishes to avoid coverage under the intentional act exclusion. For example, a liability insurer may exclude coverage for injuries caused by conduct deemed to violate the law, thereby sidestepping the question of whether the damage committed during the course of the crime was actually expected by the policyholders. But the mere fact that a violation of law is alleged does not make the intentional act exclusion applicable.[61]

A particular focus of litigation and public concern as well as underwriter's fears has concerned child abuse claims directed at policyholders who operate child care

---

61. *State Farm Mut. Auto. Ins. Co. v. Martinez-Lozano*, 916 F. Supp. 996 (E.D. Cal. 1996) (claim alleging violation of Migrant and Seasonal Agricultural Workers Protection Act (29 U.S.C. § 1801) does not allege intentional act precluding coverage).

facilities. In some states, for example, proof that a day care employee touched a child in the genital or anal area may raise a presumption of intent to harm or willful molestation, but most states do not hold the presumption to be conclusive. Rather, the issue of the employee's intent is one of fact. This makes sense because unwanted touching can be purely accidental or misinterpreted by the claimant.

One suspects that courts harbor a more severe attitude about deviant sexual practices than other misconduct. For example, the courts are split on whether death by autoerotic hanging, where the victim is a consenting adult injured by a self-inflicted mishap, is death by "accident."[62] Courts may find such conduct intentional as well where an intentional act life insurance exclusion is involved.[63] Presumably, a similar view would prevail where a third-party liability claim arose from erotic behavior that results in injury or death. In resolving any such claims, courts should, if not blinded by distaste for the activity or the participants, focus on the degree of danger in the activity. Ordinarily benign if offbeat activity that results in injury should ordinarily be covered, but activity that inevitably involves harm to another should ordinarily be excluded from coverage as expected injury and a nonfortuitous loss.

Another area of recurring difficulty involves conduct by a policyholder with impaired mental capacity. In assessing causation in cases presenting intentional act defenses, courts follow the normal insurance contract rule of efficient proximate cause. The cause nearest in time or most dominant in bringing about the loss thus is classified as the cause of the loss for insurance purposes. Although courts are occasionally presented with claims that intentional acts causing loss were in fact mere ripples of nonintentional causes, they seldom accept such creative causation theories. For example, in a life insurance case, a widow unsuccessfully argued that her husband's death from a self-inflicted gunshot wound really resulted from depression caused by a recent auto accident and was unintentional because he was intoxicated at the time.[64]

---

62. *Compare International Underwriters, Inc. v. Home Ins. Co.*, 662 F.2d 1084 (4th Cir. 1981) (applying Virginia law) (no additional coverage in life policy because autoerotic death not an "accident"), *with Kennedy v. Washington Nat'l Ins. Co.*, 136 Wis. 2d 425, 401 N.W.2d 842, 846 (Ct. App. 1987) (death was accidental because procedure was not intended to result in death, only stimulation). *See* Alan Stephens, Annot., *Accident or Life Insurance: Death by Autoerotic Asphyxiation as Accidental*, 62 A.L.R.4th 823 (1988). Yes, there is an entire ALR Annotation devoted to the subject. Insurance, boring? Ha!

63. *See, e.g., Sims v. Monumental Gen. Ins. Co.*, 960 F.2d 478 (5th Cir. 1992) (autoerotic asphyxiation is intentional injury within meaning of life insurance policy). *But see Todd v. AIG Life Ins. Co.*, 47 F.3d 1448 (5th Cir. 1995), which rejected an intentional act defense to a life insurance claim where the CQV died when the release on his autoerotic noose malfunctioned. The two cases can be distinguished because *Todd* involved an ERISA benefit plan (*see* Chapter 3, regarding the ERISA statute, which is interpreted according to federal common law, even as to insurance coverage aspects of an ERISA employee welfare benefit plan), which *Sims* did not (the *Sims* court apparently applied Texas law, although it was not explicit). The *Todd* decision, written by the late Supreme Court Justice Byron White, is well reasoned and probably represents the emerging majority view on this topic.

64. *See Meusy v. Montgomery Ward Life Ins. Co.*, 943 F.2d 1097 (9th Cir. 1991) (applying Washington law); *accord Mutual Fire Ins. Co. v. Hancock*, 634 A.2d 1312 (Me. 1993) (systematic, brutal beating and rape is intentional act as a matter of law precluding coverage under liability provisions of homeowner's policy despite policyholder perpetrator's claim that he lacked intent due to alcoholic blackout).

In other life insurance cases, policyholders or their beneficiaries have recovered where the seemingly intentional act was viewed as the result of an irresistible impulse or where a prior injury dramatically altered the policyholder's cognitive process. As in the life insurance cases, liability cases can present a compelling case for finding coverage in order to give compensation to innocent third parties. Consequently, diminished mental capacity usually negates the intent or expectation required to invoke the exclusion. Courts are somewhat less sympathetic to policyholder arguments that intoxication negated their intent but often find coverage in favor of the inebriated policyholder who injures unless there is a specific intoxication exclusion or criminal acts exclusion that encompasses drunken driving or the like.

The deterrence prong of the debate suggests that policyholders afflicted by mental illness should be accorded more sympathy than those whose judgment is merely warped by alcohol that they chose to ingest. The compensation prong argues for finding coverage. The victim of a policyholder's actions cares not at all whether he or she has been attacked by a deranged policyholder or a drunken policyholder. On balance, however, since the average aggressive drunk (even an alcoholic) may be motivated to control himself by the threat of personal liability, the case for coverage is weaker.

Self-defense issues also recur with some frequency. Where nothing is stated in the text of the policy, courts have split on the question. Although excluding coverage can be justified by a hyper-literal reading of a liability policy, a sensible construction would exclude coverage only when the policyholder has used excessive force or intentionally inflicted injury when he was no longer in danger and controlled the situation. Many policies now specifically provide that the intentional act exclusion does not apply where the claimant's injury results "from the use of reasonable force to protect persons or property."

In a particularly unusual case involving intentional conduct, a CGL policy issued to a political organization was found to provide coverage for liability arising from settlement of a suit alleging conscious attempts to intimidate minority voters notwithstanding that these civil rights violations raise the possibility of the intentional act defense.[65] The court reasoned that the policy should cover volitional civil rights violations since it already had an endorsement covering intentional torts such as false arrest, detention, malicious prosecution, defamation, and advertising injury. Although the state law in question prohibited as a matter of public policy insurance of criminal, malicious, or outrageous conduct, state law also provided that policies be interpreted according to the reasonable expectations of the policyholder. Thus, so long as the conduct alleged by the third party was not adjudicated as criminal, malicious, or outrageous, its volitional quality did not bar coverage in view of the other intentional acts expressly insured under the policy.

Intentional act questions are, of course, not confined to liability policies. However, they are generally less problematic in the context of life, health, and accident policies

---

65. *See Vargas v. Hudson County Bd. of Elections*, 949 F.2d 665, 671–72 (3d Cir. 1991) (applying New Jersey law).

because the conduct in question is often more obviously focused and specifically intended. By contrast, the conduct giving rise to injuries to third parties and resulting liability claims can often be characterized as intentional, reckless, or grossly negligent. Also, the policyholder in a health or accidental injury case is usually his or her own victim. Consequently, the court is not faced with the tough choice of limiting compensation to an innocent party in order to promote deterrence of antisocial conduct. Where, however, the claimant in a first-party insurance case is an innocent co-insured or beneficiary, the legal and policy issues often mirror those of liability coverage cases. Nonetheless, courts may even then be somewhat less solicitous of such co-insureds or beneficiaries than of true third-party claimants because first-party insurance presents more direct opportunities for fraud, collusion, moral hazard, and adverse selection.

## PROBLEM SEVEN

(based on *Automobile Ins. Co. of Hartford v. Cook*,
850 N.E.2d 1152 (N.Y. 2006))

Alfred Cook shot Richard Barber. The two men became involved in a business dispute. Barber weighed 360 pounds (Cook almost two-thirds smaller at 135 pounds) and had previously attacked Cook, injuring Cook's leg. Barber had also thrown things at Cook's house. Later that same day, Barber returned with two men. As Cook saw them approaching, he locked the door and retrieved a .25 caliber hand gun from his bedroom. Barber and his group broke into Cook's home. The men gathered in the kitchen. Barber began demanding money from Cook, pounding his fists on the kitchen table. Cook drew his gun and demanded that they leave. Barber laughed at the small size of the pistol, at which point Cook withdrew to his bedroom for a larger weapon. He picked up a loaded, 12-gauge shotgun and ordered them to leave the house. Barber started to head toward the door with his companions, telling them to take anything of value and that he would meet them outside because he had some business to attend to. Barber started advancing toward Cook. Cook warned him that he would shoot if he came any closer. Cook aimed his gun toward the lowest part of Barber's body that was not obscured by furniture—Barber's navel. When Barber was about one step away from the barrel of the gun, Cook fired a shot into Barber's abdomen. Barber died later that day at a hospital.

Cook was indicted for intentional and depraved indifference murder. At trial he raised a justification defense. A jury acquitted him of both murder counts and of the lesser included offenses of manslaughter in the first and second degrees. The administrator of Barber's estate commenced a wrongful death action against Cook. The first cause of action alleged that "injury to the decedent and the decedent's death were caused by the negligence of the defendant, Alfred S. Cook." In a separate cause of action, the complaint alleges that Cook intentionally shot Barber causing Barber's death.

Cook sought homeowner's personal liability coverage from his insurer, which denied coverage, stating that Barber's death was not an accidental occurrence and that Cook's shooting Barber caused injury "expected or intended" by Cook.

- How do you think the court responded to these defenses to coverage?

- What other facts, if any, might be important?

- The liability portion of Cook's homeowner's policy contained a "duty to defend" provision (a topic addressed in more detail in Ch. 7). Under prevailing law, this insurer duty is triggered if there is a "potential for coverage" based on the allegations of the complaint, which are assumed to be true. Does this change your analysis?

- Also, remember (if you can) Fed. R. Civ. P. 8(d)(3) and similar state pleading rules. Does that affect your analysis?

## Minnesota Fire and Casualty Company v. Greenfield

855 A.2d 854 (Pa. 2004)

**Madame Justice Newman.**

We must decide today whether an insurance company owes a duty to defend or indemnify a homeowner for the wrongful death of his houseguest occasioned by his selling heroin to her. For the reasons that follow, we affirm the holding of the Superior Court, albeit on different grounds, that no such obligation exists.

At 8 p.m. on February 9, 1998, eighteen-year-old Angela Smith (Smith) arrived at the home of Michael J. Greenfield (Greenfield) at 600 North Third Street, in Wormleysburg, hoping to obtain some heroin from him. Another young woman, Brook Broadwater (Broadwater), was with Smith. When they arrived, Greenfield had been drinking Mad Dog beer and was under the influence of marijuana and heroin. * * * Greenfield was no stranger to the use of heroin, having lost consciousness three times from it in the past. He was using heroin on a daily basis. He had used heroin with Smith before, and she, too, had become unconscious twice from it. Greenfield had sold heroin to Smith on other occasions and was arrested in 1995 for possession of marijuana. Greenfield acknowledged that he sold drugs out of his house "occasionally;" for the most part, he sold "mostly just weed" and "didn't really sell heroin to too many people."

In exchange for some marijuana and a small sum of money, Greenfield provided Smith with a bag of heroin, which was labeled "Suicide." At approximately 8:20 p.m., Smith voluntarily injected herself with the heroin. From that time until 10 p.m., Smith lay in a chair and communicated only when directly addressed. Greenfield put out some blankets for her, and she went to sleep on the floor. Greenfield left with Broadwater, returning to the house approximately 10:45 p.m. Smith remained in the residence, and when Greenfield awoke around 6:30 a.m., he found Smith still on the floor. When he left for work, he told Smith to lock the door if she left, and Smith groggily responded.

When Greenfield came home from work later that day, he found Smith dead on the floor where he had left her that morning. Greenfield knew that she was dead because "she was pale and not breathing." Autopsy results showed that Smith died from a heroin overdose. Greenfield called a friend, Robert Rollins (Rollins), who came to his residence. Wearing gloves because he "didn't want to touch" Smith's dead body, Greenfield [and Rollins] took the body and put it in a vehicle owned by Greenfield. They drove around the area, and then dumped the body in York County near the Yellow Breeches Creek. Greenfield then contacted the police and concocted a story to the effect that he had simply found a body near the creek. Rollins initially told the same story, but recanted and told the truth. The men were arrested later that same day.

Greenfield was charged criminally for the outcome of the death of Smith; he pled guilty and was sentenced on counts of involuntary manslaughter, abuse of a corpse, and unlawful delivery of heroin. * * * Greenfield [had] obtained a homeowner's policy (the Policy) from Minnesota Fire and Casualty Company (Insurance Company) when he purchased his residence. This was the Policy in place when Smith died.... The Policy defines "occurrence" as "an **accident**, including exposure to conditions, **which results**, during the policy period, **in: a. bodily injury**; or b. property damage. "Bodily injury" is "bodily harm, sickness or disease, including required care, loss of services and death that result." However, **the Policy excludes coverage for bodily injury** "which is expected or intended by the insured." Bodily injury "arising out of business pursuits of an insured" is also excluded. "Business" is defined as a "trade, profession or occupation." [Boldface is the Court's.]

On June 10, 1999, Sharon L. Smith and Arlin C. Smith, the parents of Smith, filed wrongful death and survival actions against Greenfield in the Court of Common Pleas of Cumberland County (trial court), individually and on behalf of all the other beneficiaries of the Estate of Angela C. Smith, as administrators of that Estate. They alleged, *inter alia*, that: (1) Greenfield had sold heroin to Smith; (2) he knew of, or should have foreseen, the harmful and dangerous consequences of selling heroin to Smith; (3) he made no attempts to check on her condition during the evening of February 8, 1998, and the following morning; and (4) he made no attempt to revive her, instead, leaving her and going to work. * * * The Insurance Company filed a Declaratory Judgment Action in the trial court, claiming, *inter alia* that [Greenfield's actions] "do not constitute 'an occurrence,' i.e., an accidental event; rather the allegations are premised solely upon the intentional and criminal act of the insured of selling heroin, a controlled substance."

The Insurance Company further alleged that it had no legal obligation to defend or indemnify Greenfield on the ground that public policy bars the insurance coverage asserted.

The [trial] court found that the record "does not, as a matter of law, show that the Smiths' claim is excluded under Minnesota's policy." The trial court, however, did not grant the Smiths' Motion for Summary Judgment on the issue of indemnification, finding that the Insurance Company was required to defend Greenfield until the claim could be confined to a recovery that was not within the scope of the Policy. * * * The Superior Court reversed and determined that two factors precluded coverage: (1) its expanded doctrine of "inferred intent," which had been applied previously in Pennsylvania only to cases involving child abuse. The court noted "compelling public policy reasons" to deny coverage, for, "in effect, the courts are being asked to help provide insurance for heroin dealers.... The legislature ... has already determined the inherent danger of heroin.... It should not be the public policy ... to insure the sale of such a ... dangerous and illegal narcotic...."

[T]he Superior Court in the instant matter stated that "inferred intent results when there is an intentional act on the part of the insured and it is inherent in that act that harm will occur. In child abuse cases, the actor's abuse will frequently cause long-term harm to the child." Reasoning that it was frequently certain that harm would occur to the buyer of heroin, the Superior Court extended the doctrine of inferred intent....

[W]e determine that although the Superior Court erred in expanding the inferred intent doctrine, it reached the correct result in determining that public policy precludes the Insurance Company from any duty to defend or indemnify Greenfield.

The interpretation of an insurance contract regarding the existence or non-existence of coverage is "generally performed by the court." "Where a provision of a policy is ambiguous, the policy provision is to be construed in favor of the insured and against the insurer.... Where, however, the language of the contract is clear and unambiguous, a court is required to give effect to that language." In light of the fact that the appropriate construction of the Policy poses a question of law, our standard of review is plenary.

The Superior Court and the Insurance Company focused their analyses on that part of the Policy that excludes coverage for injuries that are "expected or intended by the insured." The question concerning whether Greenfield "expected or intended" Smith to die when he provided her with heroin is certainly difficult to answer, as reflected by the fact that the trial court and the Superior Court came to opposite conclusions. The trial court found that the averred facts support that the death of Smith was caused by the **negligence** of Greenfield; and the Superior Court inferred that "an intent to cause injury existed as a matter of law due to ... Greenfield's providing Angela Smith with what ... all too predictably, proved to be a fatal dose of heroin."

When this Court first considered the effect of a similar exclusionary clause in a homeowner's policy, we stated that "the vast majority of courts which have considered such a provision [an exclusionary clause] have reached the conclusion that before the insurer may validly disclaim liability, it must be shown that the insured intended by his act to produce the damage which did in fact occur." We emphasized in that case the difference between intending an **act** and intending a **result**. [W]e [have] held that the exclusionary clause did not preclude coverage for damages caused by a house fire during the course of a burglary. Further, we found that although the perpetrators intended to burglarize the house, they did not anticipate or plan the resulting house fire occasioned by their use of matches to light their way in the dark.

The trial court found that "the facts averred support Smiths' allegation that the death of Angela Smith was caused by Greenfield's negligence." It is in the context of this jurisprudential background that the Superior Court extended and applied the doctrine of **inferred** intent, presumably for the reason that it was unable to establish **actual** intent, given the absence of allegations that Greenfield expected or intended Smith to lose consciousness or die. * * * The Superior Court stated that "the notion of inferred intent is accepted in Pennsylvania," however, the concept has not been extended beyond child sexual abuse cases. In adjudicating general liability insurance cases, as opposed to those **exceptional** cases involving child sexual abuse, Pennsylvania courts presently follow the view that precedent has stated the very narrow applicability of inferred intent, and stated that "in cases that do not involve child sexual abuse, Pennsylvania has adopted a general liability standard for determining the existence of this specific intent that looks to the insured's actual subjective intent."

Jurisprudence in Pennsylvania does not support the extension of inferred intent to cases other than exceptional ones involving child sexual abuse. Although this Court is not bound by the precedent established in a subsequent diversity case based on the law of Pennsylvania, we note that the Third Circuit has refused to extend the doctrine of inferred intent to preclude coverage for harm suffered by a female college student after a sexual assault by the homeowner's son.

We cannot know with certainty what Greenfield's state of mind was, a fact neither necessary to nor dispositive of our decision. We do ratify existing principles of our jurisprudence and, by doing so, we reject the Superior Court's extension of inferred intent, which established, as a matter of law, that Greenfield intended the harm that befell Smith. Having said that, however, the Superior Court's determination that the Insurance Company is not required to defend or indemnify under the Policy is correct. In addition to applying an expanded inferred intent doctrine, the court based its determination on the "compelling public policy reasons for denying a claim such as this where, in effect, the courts are being asked to help provide insurance for heroin dealers." * * * In [a prior case], we rejected an argument that allowing recovery pursuant to an insurance policy where property damage arose out of the commission of a crime by the insured would contravene public policy. We did so for two reasons: (1) the insurance contract itself did not contain a "violation of law" clause; and (2) our analysis that "under the facts of this case, we are not confronted with any overriding public policy which would preclude recovery." Our decision in that case determined that an insurance company was required to indemnify against losses caused by a carelessly lit match that was dropped when teenagers were burglarizing a home. We supported our holding on two bases: (1) the widely accepted principle that "before the insurer may validly disclaim liability, it must be shown that the insured intended by his act to produce the damage which did in fact occur[;]" and (2) the absence of any "overriding public policy" to preclude recovery.

[By contrast, in this case,] Our Commonwealth, from the legislature to the Secretary of Health, has made its policy on the illegality of heroin abundantly clear: "heroin has a high potential for abuse, has no accepted medical use within the United States, and … is unsafe for use even under medical supervision." Given this clear enunciation of public policy regarding Schedule I controlled substances, we find that the Insurance Company is not required to defend or indemnify against damages arising out of its insured's criminal acts where the voluntary participation of the victim in an illegal heroin-transaction caused her death. * * *

**CONCURRING OPINION (Mr. Justice Castille).**

I concur in the result of the lead opinion, but not in its reasoning. I do not seriously doubt that considerations of public policy would warrant denying coverage here, where liability would be premised upon the putative insured's deliberate criminal conduct in selling heroin. In my view, however, this case is resolvable, and the result is the same, by resort to bedrock principles of contract construction. Specifically, I would find that the deliberate conduct here, which would form the basis for homeowners' insurance liability, did not constitute an "accidental occurrence" which would trigger coverage under the plain language of the policy. * * * As the lead opinion notes, the homeowners' policy at issue here promises personal liability coverage for, *inter alia*, bodily injuries which are caused by a covered "occurrence." The policy then unambiguously defines an occurrence as "an accident" which results in bodily injury or property damage.

The unfortunate teenage victim in this case, Angela Smith, did not trip down the stairs in Michael Greenfield's home, or fall upon a knife, or die in a fire. Rather, Smith and Greenfield engaged in a common, commercial transaction of a criminal nature, which just happened to occur in the home: Greenfield delivered heroin to Smith in exchange for a quantity of marijuana and, possibly, a small amount of cash. Smith then voluntarily injected herself with the heroin, thereby causing her own death from heroin intoxication. Greenfield did not inject Smith with the drug; instead, the basis for his liability was premised upon the simple fact of his delivering the narcotic to Smith, and her later dying from it while still in Greenfield's home.

Whatever else Greenfield's delivery to Smith may have been, it was not an accident. Smith wanted heroin; Greenfield accommodated and delivered it to her. Smith's decision to inject herself with the heroin, as she had done in the past, likewise was not an "accident" for that act, too, was deliberate and voluntary. Following upon the heels of the intentional and illegal activities of both Greenfield and Smith, the fortuity of the fatal overdose, while tragic, can hardly fall into the category of a covered "accident." As appellants themselves note:

> "Accident" has been defined in the context of insurance contracts as "an event or happening without human agency or, if happening through such agency, an event which, under circumstances, is unusual and not expected by the person to whom it happens." Black's Law Dictionary (6th ed. 1990). "Accident" has also been defined as an "unintended and unforeseen injurious occurrence." Black's Law Dictionary (7th ed. 1999). The Superior Court has defined an accident as an "untoward or unexpected happening."

The overdose here plainly resulted from human agency. Moreover, the prospect of heroin intoxication, including death from heroin intoxication, was no less plainly foreseeable. Although the overwhelming majority of heroin users do not die from a single injection of the narcotic, it nevertheless is an inherently dangerous drug and the risk of such a lethal result certainly is foreseeable. * * * There having been no "accident," there was no covered occurrence. I therefore agree with the plurality's determination to affirm the Superior Court's holding that Minnesota Fire does not have a duty to defend or indemnify Greenfield, albeit I concur only in the result because I arrive at that conclusion as a matter of contract construction, rather than resorting to an external ground for decision, such as public policy.

## CONCURRING OPINION (Mr. Justice Saylor).

[P]revailing Pennsylvania law establishes that "an insured intends an injury if he desired to cause the consequences of his act or if he acted knowing that such consequences were substantially certain to result." Appellee's concession that "the prospect of a fatal overdose may be statistically remote as a function of the number of regular heroin users on a national basis," thus answers the contractual coverage question under the law as it presently stands. * * *

## DISSENTING OPINION (Mr. Chief Justice Cappy).

Because I cannot agree with the majority's decision to rewrite the insurance policy at issue, I must respectfully dissent. * * * We are not here confronted with the question of whether an insurer may enforce an exclusion which excludes from coverage damages arising out of the sale of heroin or any other illegal drug. Rather, at issue is whether this court may insert, via the invocation of public policy, such an exclusion into an insurance policy. The majority finds that this court may rewrite the contract on the basis that an insured should be precluded from receiving coverage where damages result from the insured's criminal act.

In my opinion, this court should not rewrite the contract for the insurance company. The [insurer] drafted the insurance policy. It is beyond cavil that it was capable of writing an exclusion which would exempt from coverage damages arising out of the sale of illegal narcotics, and yet it did not do so. Arguably, this was a failing on the part of the insurance company. Yet, is it the role of this court to act as super-scrivener, correcting the apparent errors in business judgment committed by insurers? With all due respect to the majority, I submit that this is not a proper role for this body.

Furthermore, I am concerned about the potential sweeping reach of the majority's decision and have grave concerns about its application to future cases. While the majority purports to limit its public policy exception to situations in which an insured engages in illegal activity regarding Schedule I controlled substances, its underlying rationale for creating that limited exception could easily be extended to create exceptions for other illegal acts. Indeed, the majority suggests in a footnote that this court should not require an insurance company to reimburse a policyholder for damages arising from any "conduct ... that our legislature has defined as illegal." I am uneasy about this court issuing such a broad and amorphous pronouncement.... Mr. Justice Nigro joins this dissenting opinion.

## Notes and Questions

1. *Minnesota Fire v. Greenfield* is arguably too pro-insurer. It engages in two judicial pronouncements that should make even the most activist judge wince a bit. One, the court seems to find that heroin sale makes death by the user an "expected occurrence," concluding in effect that death to a third party was practically certain to occur from sale by the insured. Two, the court finds a public policy bar to insuring against liability from illicit drug sales.

The first rationale is at odds with basic insurance principles in that liability insurance normally provides coverage even where the liability-creating conduct was foolish, socially undesirable, or even callous. The usual inquiry focuses on whether the insured had a subjective intent to inflict injury or cause the harm in question. Drug use is not a wise thing for the health-conscious. But it is not inevitably fatal. If it were, the Rolling Stones, Aerosmith, and numerous other rock bands would no longer be with us. Although heroin does kill on occasion (e.g., Jimi Hendrix, Janice Joplin), so too does alcohol (e.g., Jim Morrison). If Greenfield gave a visitor too much to drink and she died by falling down the front steps of the house, no serious court would find the death uncovered absent a clear and specific alcohol or intoxication exclusion.

The second rationale is also troubling, in that it has the court "making" law rather than applying it. Rather than construing the insurance policy, the court in this phase of the case is simply decreeing that deaths incident to illegal drug use are not covered under a standard liability policy. (The liability section of a homeowner's policy operates in essentially the same manner as a general liability policy or an automobile liability policy.) The prevailing American view is that judges' views of public policy or justice should not be used to alter contractual agreements. One can of course question whether an insurance policy is better viewed as a contractual agreement or a risk management product and whether policy text should be viewed as conclusive. But without doubt, the text of the policy at issue in *Greenfield* says nothing about excluding coverage for claims arising out of drug deals or other criminal activity. The insurer when writing the policy chose to exclude only expected or intended injury or non-fortuitous events (the insurer's "not an accident or occurrence" argument). Is it really fair to say Smith's death was not unexpected or an accidental consequence of a socially taboo activity?

2. Michael Greenfield is not a very likeable policyholder. After his customer used the heroin he sold, he neglected her and then attempted to cover up the death out of fear that he would be busted. As the court noted with some understatement, "there is not one scintilla of evidence to suggest that Greenfield felt remorse or personal responsibility for the death of Smith. He seems to have little conscience or regret for what transpired." From this, the court concluded that his indifference combined with the dangers of heroin to make Smith's death a sufficient certainty to preclude coverage.

But this is strained reasoning. Greenfield was no prince, but what was the court expecting: the Mr. Rogers of drug dealers? If Greenfield were a well-adjusted, empathetic human being, perhaps he would be engaged in more socially useful activity.

But the fact remains that Minnesota Fire sold him an insurance policy that provided coverage for his negligent, reckless, stupid, callous, and even sociopathic and remorseless acts—so long as he did not subjectively intend to injure anyone or the activity was not otherwise specifically excluded by the policy language.

If one could look into Greenfield's presumably dark soul, one would probably find a drug seller who did not want Smith to die and did not expect Smith to die. Rather, he almost certainly expected Smith to live to purchase and shoot up again, all to Greenfield's profit. The question is not whether Greenfield is a good guy or bad guy. The question is whether Greenfield intended to injure or kill Smith. Also, Greenfield pled guilty to involuntary manslaughter and lesser crimes. As the name of the crime implies—and as the *Cook* decision implicitly found—"involuntary" manslaughter is not expected or intended. The "accident" or occurrence in question is not the sale of the heroin, which of course was volitional, but its impact on the victim. Angela Smith took the heroin to get high, not to die. Her adverse reaction to the drug and death was the accident.

3. The second reason for the decision—a public policy against illegal drugs—is understandable but overreaching. Although insurance should not encourage misconduct, neither should insurance coverage litigation be a podium for the court's expression of moral outrage. Sure, illegal drugs are a bad thing. But if the insurer wanted nothing to do with drug-related injury, it could have included specific language in the policy. If the court in fact fears that insurance coverage for drug-related death creates problems of moral hazard or adverse selection, the court would presumably want to encourage the use of clear and specific exclusions of this type in liability policies. A judicially created unwritten exclusion does not properly put policyholders on notice and does not encourage insurers to write clearer policies that adequately inform policyholders of the contours of coverage. Is there not a public policy problem with that?

4. In reaching its decision barring coverage and its enthusiasm for a public policy against drug abuse, the Pennsylvania Supreme Court also gave insufficient consideration to the important insurance public policy of compensation. It also arguably erred regarding the deterrence issues in the case. First, the matter of compensation. Angela Smith is dead and no amount of money will bring her back. But her parents are entitled to whatever compensation the law of wrongful death provides. Why should they be deprived of a source of funds when facing a perhaps judgment proof defendant who had insurance? More particularly, why should the state supreme court rewrite the defendant's insurance policy to absolve the insurer from keeping its contract commitment? Then there is the matter of deterrence. Greenfield will presumably pay his debt to society through the criminal justice system. Will Greenfield (when he gets out of prison) and others like him be deterred from selling drugs because they cannot get insurance for the liability? Not likely. Denying insurance to his victim hardly serves any reasonable deterrence goal in cases like this.

5. The battle over coverage, fortuity, and intentional injury is also often fought over the issue of whether an event is sufficiently "accidental" rather than whether

the resulting injuries were accidental, particularly in liability insurance cases, because "accident" is part of the definition of a covered "occurrence" under a liability policy. *See, e.g., Delgado v. Interinsurance Exchange of Automobile Club of Southern California,* 211 P.3d 1083 (Cal. 2009) (claim alleging assault and battery by policyholder defendant not an "accident" and hence no potential for coverage even if defendant did not intend victim's injuries). *Delgado* specifically rejected the policyholder's argument that he had negligently acted in self-defense. No matter, said the unanimous court, the fact remained that the conduct alleged was not accidental, however justified it might have been.

In this sense, *Delgado* is troubling (as well as adding some confusion rather than clarity to California law) because most liability policies contain an express self-defense exception to the intentional injury requirement. Consequently, it would appear that the liability insurance community expected to provide coverage in cases of self-defense even if it wanted to avoid coverage when the policyholder was the perpetrator of intentional injury. Even without an express self-defense exception to the intentional injury exclusion, one can make a strong case that such a mitigation of the exclusion is implied by common sense. Is the policyholder supposed to be a punching bag for third parties in order to preserve his or her liability insurance coverage?

Subsequently, the California Supreme Court issued a ruling more favorable to policyholders in these matters. In *Liberty Surplus Ins. Corp. v. Ledesma & Meyer Construction Co.,* 418 P.3d 400 (Cal. 2018), the court ruled that a liability insurer must defend a builder in a case where an employee was accused of sexually abusing a 13-year-old student at the school where the company was working. Plaintiff counsel, undoubtedly aware of typical insurance exclusions, alleged liability of the company based on negligent hiring, retention, and supervision of the offending employee. The insurer argued that the claim nonetheless was not covered because it did not stem from an "accident."[66] A federal trial court agreed and granted summary judgment for the insurer. When plaintiff appealed to the Ninth Circuit, the appeals court sought guidance from the California Supreme Court,[67] which found the complaint sufficiently alleging accidental error to require the insurer to defend the claim.[68] Summarizing California law and distinguishing *Delgado,* the *Ledesma* Court stated:

---

66. The insurer did defend the policyholder while filing a separate lawsuit seeking a declaratory judgment of no coverage. As addressed in Chs. 7 and 9, insurers frequently do this to avoid being estopped to deny coverage should they be held to have breached the duty to defend as well as to avoid an undefended policyholder allowing a default judgment or settling the case in a manner disadvantageous to an insurer that later is required to provide coverage for the resulting settlement or default judgment—which may be especially large if the claim is undefended.

67. Where permitted by the state that provides the controlling law on a matter, a federal court hearing a diversity jurisdiction case may certify questions of state law to the relevant state supreme court.

68. As also discussed in Chs. 7 and 9, most primary general liability policies obligate the insurer to defend claims where there is a potential for coverage based on the allegations of the complaint, assuming the allegations are correct. This is why the duty to defend is said to be "broader" than an insurer's duty to pay claims, which will hinge on facts determined at trial rather than facts merely alleged.

Under the principles discussed [in prior cases, the employee's] molestation of [plaintiff victim] Doe may be deemed an unexpected consequence of [the policyholder's] independently tortious acts of negligence....

We recognize society's interest in providing an incentive for employers to take precautions against sexual abuse by their employees. However, the threat of liability for negligent hiring, retention, and supervision is a significant deterrent even when insurance coverage is available. We also acknowledge that insurance does not generally cover intentionally inflicted injuries. But as noted ... "the public policy against insurance for one's own intentional sexual misconduct does not bar liability coverage for others whose mere negligence contributed in some way to the acts of abuse. In such cases ... there is no overriding policy reason why a person injured by sexual abuse should be denied compensation for the harm from insurance coverage purchased by the negligent facilitator."

418 P.3d at 408–09 (quoting *Minkler v. Safeco Ins. Co. of America*, 232 P.3d 612 (Cal. 2010).

In *Safeco Ins. Co. of Am. v. White*, 913 N.E.2d 426 (Ohio 2009), which involved situation of negligent supervision of a child of the household (a 17-year-old who "attacked and repeatedly stabbed" a 13-year-old), the court found coverage. The court held

that when a liability insurance policy defines an "occurrence" as an "accident," a negligent act committed by an insured that is predicated on the commission of an intentional tort by another person, e.g., negligent hiring or negligent supervision, qualifies as an "occurrence." In this case, neither [of the policyholder parents] injured [the claimant]. From their perspective, the injury was accidental, and thus the act that caused her injury constitutes an "occurrence" as defined in the policies they purchased form Safeco.

913 N.E.2d at 432. *Safeco v. White* has factual similarity with *Minkler v. Safeco Ins. Co. of America*, 49 Cal. 4th 315, 110 Cal. Rptr. 3d 612 (Cal. 2010), discussed above, suggesting perhaps that courts may be more receptive to negligent supervision claims than to self-defense claims by insureds who were directly involved in seeming wrongdoing. It may also be that Ohio's high court is simply less receptive to fortuity-based defenses to coverage than is California's, at least as reflected in *Delgado*. See *Allstate Ins. Co. v. Campbell*, 128 Ohio St. 3d 186, 2010-Ohio-6312, 942 N.E.2d 1090 (rejecting doctrine of inferred intent, discussed in *Greenfield*, *supra*, in case where injuries resulted from "misguided teenage prank"); *Elevators Mutual Ins. Co. v. J. Patrick O'Flaherty's, Inc.*, 928 N.E.2d 685 (Ohio 2010) (policyholder's no contest pleas and subsequent criminal convictions for arson and insurance fraud were not admissible to aid insurer in its declaratory judgment action seeking finding of no coverage).

6. At the duty to defend stage, as discussed in *Cook*, *supra*, the issue is not whether there ultimately will be indemnity coverage but only whether there is a potential for coverage. Until facts are developed through discovery or trial, it would logically seem that in all but the clearest cases, the liability insurer must at least defend the physical

altercation case. This was the approach in *Automobile Insurance Co. of Hartford v. Cook* (on which Problem 7 is based) and appears to be the dominant approach of most courts.[69]

7. Occasionally, a court produces unfortunately incorrect or misleading discussion in a fortuity/accident case, as did the Indiana Supreme Court in *Tri-Etch, Inc. v. Cincinnati Ins. Co.* 909 N.E.2d 997 (Ind. 2009). In *Tri-Etch*, a liquor store employee was tragically robbed, mugged, and tied to a tree, receiving no medical treatment until discovered the next morning. The policyholder, an alarm company, was supposed to check on the store if the night alarm was not set within 15 minutes of the store's closing. Because of the alarm company's error, it was sued by the victim's family and eventually sought coverage from its liability insurer. Shockingly, the court held that the alarm company's failure to properly render its alarm monitoring services was not an "accident" and therefore could not be a covered "occurrence" under the liability policy. *See* 909 N.E.2d at 1001.

The case contains a generally accurate discussion of the concept of an accident and then abruptly concludes that the policyholder's tragic error was (as a matter of law, no less) not an accident. Reading this portion of the opinion is a little like seeing 2 + 2 added up to make 5.

Ironically, the opinion as a whole probably is correct because the general liability policy at issue contained a specific exclusion for liability arising out of alarm monitoring services. In addition, the policyholder also had a professional negligence (errors and omissions) policy with another insurer that defended the case for years, with the general liability umbrella insurer's participation being sought rather late in the proceedings because of the large exposure presented by the claim.

Nonetheless, the Indiana Supreme Court was incorrect in concluding that because the professional liability policy was closer to the risk than the general liability policy that failure to monitor could not be an "accident" as the term is properly understood. Under apt circumstances, a liability-producing incident can be both an instance of professional failure and an accidental oversight in a policyholder's general business operations.

---

69. *See, e.g., Copp v. Nationwide Mut. Ins. Co.*, 692 S.E.2d 220 (Va. 2010) (altercation among college students stemming from beer pong game subject to liability insurer's duty to defend even though policyholder defendant pled no contest to assault and battery charge); *Pekin Ins. Co. v. Wilson*, 930 N.E.2d 1011 (Ill. 2010) (insurer has duty to defend where policyholder hit claimant with pipe, allegedly because he was intimidated by larger claimant; policyholder argues self-defense and wins (at least at the duty to defend stage), unlike *Delgado* case in California); *Alfa Mut. Ins. Co. v. Bone*, 13 So. 3d 369 (Ala. 2009) (claimant ex-husband injured by gun discharge of policyholder current husband claimed to be unintentional; insurer must defend pending resolution of factual uncertainty at trial); *Tanner v. Nationwide Mut. Fire Ins. Co.* 289 S.W.3d 828 (Tex. 2009) (intentional injury exclusion not applicable merely because policyholder defendant's act leading to injury was volitional; policyholder must have intended injury or known it was substantially certain to take place before coverage lost; injury to claimant resulted from policyholder fleeing police pursuit). *But see Safeco Ins. Co. of Am. v. Vecsey*, 2010 U.S. Dist. LEXIS 103503 (D. Conn. Sept. 30, 2010) ("abuse" exclusion applicable in wife's suit against husband claiming serious eye injuries after being allegedly struck by carrot thrown as part of domestic dispute; court expresses thinly veiled skepticism as to whether airborne carrot could have inflicted such serious injury).

## PROBLEM EIGHT

Since *Greenfield* was decided, the extent of the destruction wrought by over-prescribed painkillers such as OxyContin has become apparent. Manufacturers such as Purdue Pharmaceuticals and even its main owners, the Sackler Family, have been sued and (as this edition of *Principles* goes to press) paid hundreds of millions in settlement with litigation still ongoing. *See generally* Hilary Tuttle, *New Opioid Lawsuits Hold Executives Liable*, Risk Management (June 2019) at p. 4 (summarizing opioid crisis and ensuing litigation). It has been alleged that the manufacturers of the painkillers were actually or constructively aware of the drugs' addictive power yet continued to sell them (some might even call it pushing) anyway without sufficient warning, in order to make higher profits.

DefendCo, the liability insurer for DrugCo, files suit in Pennsylvania seeking a declaration that it has no duty to provide coverage for DrugCo based on the "expected or intended injury" exclusion and overarching principles of public policy.

- How will the court rule?

- What are the strongest arguments for DefendCo?

- And the strongest arguments for DrugCo?

- If DrugCo obtains coverage, does this effectively mean that Pennsylvania bars coverage for illegal drugs that kill people but is just fine with prescription drugs that kill people?

- And if so, is that distinction (even if unspoken) necessarily irrational or bad?

## *[2] The Known Loss Doctrine*

A variant of the fortuity/intentional act concept is the "known loss" doctrine, which provides that a policyholder may not obtain coverage for a loss or liability that it knows has already taken place or is substantially certain to occur in the near future. Surprisingly, this phrase—"known loss"—has only appeared in the case law in recent times. However, the concept has implicitly existed for a long time. For example, if one has an auto accident and then buys an insurance policy, the insurer will have no trouble rescinding the policy (*see* Ch. 4). But, as this example shows, in practice insurers refuse to pay for "known losses" through a variety of means other than invoking the known loss doctrine to deny a particular claim. Rescinding the entire policy on grounds of fraud or misrepresentation is probably the most common.

When addressed on its own terms, the known loss doctrine is in essence simply a name for a subset of non-fortuitous losses in which the claim or damage is largely expected by the policyholder. The phrase "known loss" is generally associated with liability insurance while the phenomenon in property insurance is commonly referred to as a "loss-in-progress" and is discussed in the ensuring subsection. *See generally* Matt W. Holley, *The "Fortuity Doctrine": Misapplying the Known Loss Rule to Liability Insurance Policies*, 41 Tex. Tech L. Rev. 529 (2008) (suggesting that courts have mistakenly applied the known loss concept due to a misunderstanding of the relationship of fortuity to insurance). For example, if a manufacturer knows that it has just shipped 800,000 cans of contaminated soup and then obtains insurance coverage, the insurer may invoke the known loss doctrine when consumers become ill, file claims, and the policyholder tenders claims to the insurer.

The difficulty in applying the known loss concept is doing so in a manner that ensures that only fortuitous losses are covered but that does not bar coverage for risky, negligent, or even stupid policyholder behavior conduct that gives rise to liability claims.[70] Insurance exists to spread the risk of risky or boneheaded behavior among a pool of policyholders. Only knowing attempts to obtain insurance coverage for losses that have already occurred should be precluded under the known loss concept. Thus, if the soup manufacturer purchases insurance after realizing that the former third-shift foreman was incompetent and is worried about the quality of product produced under his watch, this sort of appreciation of risk does not rise to the level of a known loss as in the previous example.

## [3] Loss-in-Progress

In property insurance, the fortuity, expected injury, and known loss concepts are often encompassed in the loss-in-progress. This doctrine provides that a property policyholder may not obtain coverage after the time property damage has become manifest or apparent.[71] The doctrine may be applied to bar coverage even when the damage was not known to the policyholder on the theory that regardless of knowledge, the loss was no longer contingent once set in motion, even if the damage grew progressively worse during the policy period.

However, some courts carry this concept too far and preclude coverage merely because the policyholder was aware of a threat of loss. Unless the threat of loss is a virtual certainty, mere awareness of risk should not preclude insurability or coverage. For example, if an earthquake has occurred and a house sits precariously on a precipice as a result, the likely future damage to the house when it tips down the ravine is probably a virtual certainty and the loss would be viewed as a loss-in-progress. But if the house is merely located in an avalanche zone or in a region prone

---

70. *See Johnstown v. Bankers Standard Ins. Co.*, 877 F.2d 1146, 1153 (2d Cir. 1989) (applying New York law) (known risk is not the same thing as a known loss; policyholders may insure for and obtain coverage for known risks where loss has not already occurred); *Montrose Chem. Corp. v. Admiral Ins. Co.*, 10 Cal. 4th 645, 42 Cal. Rptr. 2d 324, 913 P.2d 878 (1995) (where contingency of risk exists, known loss doctrine not applicable). The *City of Johnstown* opinion provides a particular well-reasoned and articulated assessment of the issue.

71. *See Prudential-LMI Com. Ins. v. Superior Court*, 51 Cal. 3d 674, 699, 274 Cal. Rptr. 387, 403–04, 798 P.2d 1230, 1246–47 (1990); *Sentinel Ins. Co. v. First Ins. Co.*, 76 Haw. 277, 302–03, 875 P.2d 894, 919–20, *amended on reconsideration*, 76 Haw. 453, 879 P.2d 558 (1994).

to earthquakes, this is not sufficient certainty to preclude coverage. Because the known loss and loss-in-progress concepts are so similar, courts tend to conflate or even confuse them, or at least to talk about them with less clarity than precedent-loving attorneys would prefer. In addition, perhaps courts invoke these doctrines when others would provide a more effective or intellectually precise means of resolving coverage questions.

The known loss/loss-in-progress situation gets more complicated when a hypothetical policyholder is genuinely unaware of a liability-creating event or an unusually threatening deterioration of property. On one hand, the policyholder in such a situation is blameless and not purchasing insurance because of the adverse selection motivation. On the other hand, the situation arguably presents a greater-than-ordinary risk to the insurer because the impending loss is already "in the pipeline." Courts are divided on the issue. *Compare Inland Waters Pollution Control v. Insurance Co.*, 997 F.2d 172, 176 (6th Cir. 1993) (applying Michigan law) (loss-in-progress/known loss doctrine applicable either where policyholder is actually aware of loss or when there is "immediate threat of loss" sufficient to be "tantamount to foreknowledge" by the policyholder), *with Montrose Chem. Corp. v. Admiral Ins. Co.*, 35 Cal. App. 4th 335, 5 Cal. Rptr. 2d 358 (1992) (policyholder must be subjectively aware of substantial certainty of liability claim rather than merely potential for liability claims).

In practice, most cases in which either doctrine is applied will satisfy both standards. But in some circumstances, an innocent but unobservant or undiscerning policyholder may simply have failed to appreciate the loss potential of a situation. In ensuing litigation, the availability of coverage may differ among courts. In general, however, the known loss or loss-in-progress concepts, like the general concept of fortuity and the intentional injury concept, all express the same theme: insurance is only available where there is a risk of loss rather than when the loss is certain. Now, if the courts could only stick to a consistent terminology for the concept.

One possible means of improving judicial assessments in this area is to focus on the application and underwriting process as the gatekeeper rather than having coverage turn on post-hoc attempts to discern a policyholder's subjective anticipation of claims on the basis of often conflicting, usually circumstantial evidence. Regarding direct evidence, a policyholder will almost always testify that although it may have known it had significant exposure, it was not subjectively certain that its actions would cause injury, or that it would be sued or that it did not know that a claimant was practically certain to win. Insurers will then marshal available circumstantial evidence to suggest that the policyholder must have known that claims or losses of particular magnitude were practically certain to take place.

This type of "swearing match" can result in extensive litigation and debatable outcomes, depending on whether one thinks a court or jury has correctly assessed credibility and weighed the evidence. However, if these issues are addressed primarily as misrepresentation and concealment matters, the judicial inquiry may be more clearcut and the results more consistent.

## [4] Pre-Existing Conditions

In health and disability insurance, the fortuity concept is largely litigated under the rubric of pre-existing condition. Unless prohibited by government regulation, medical expense and disability policies routinely provide that they will not provide coverage where the illness or disability results from a condition already present at the time the insurance was procured — at least not until the insured has been with the health plan a requisite amount of time. Insurers may, however, agree to cover future losses related to such pre-existing conditions with an endorsement and additional premium, depending on the risk and severity of the pre-existing condition. For example, health insurers will probably not agree to insure an applicant with AIDS but might for a higher premium agree to provide coverage for an applicant with high blood pressure. In health insurance coverage litigation, a common battle is one over whether the source of a current claim is a pre-existing condition.[72] Similarly, a health insurer may attempt to rescind coverage on grounds of misrepresentation when a policyholder makes a claim related to a pre-existing condition that was not disclosed at the time of application.

Generally, however, the insurer is better off making the policy contingent on the lack of a pre-existing condition rather than seeking a representation that the applicant has no pre-existing conditions. *See, e.g., Green v. Life & Health of Am.*, 704 So. 2d 1386 (Fla. 1998) (where insurance application asked whether applicant had knowledge of previous pre-existing conditions, insurer could void coverage only for fraud and not from mere presence of one of the listed pre-existing conditions).

Because of protections implemented in the Affordable Care Act, which prohibits exclusion of coverage for pre-existing conditions (*see* Ch. 10, *infra*), the number of such policies and cases has drastically declined. However, there continue to be efforts to roll back or abolish the Act, which may produce a renewal of such disputes.

## [5] Implied Exceptions to Coverage

Notwithstanding the large volume of text surrounding insurance transactions, there also exist a number of implied exceptions to coverage that result not so much from any specific contractual provision as from the courts' construction of the nature of the insurance arrangement. These implied exceptions support the function of insurance and prevent coverage from being unduly expanded to cover risks the policy was not reasonably intended to protect.

This process might also be termed invocation of public policy to prohibit inequitable recoveries by the policyholder. When courts render pro-policyholder con-

---

72. *See, e.g., Estate of Doe v. Paul Revere Ins. Group*, 86 Haw. 262, 948 P.2d 1103 (1997) (medical maladies that in hindsight appear to have been associated with onset of AIDS insufficient to make AIDS a pre-existing condition where treating physician and other medical professionals failed to diagnose earlier problems as AIDS). *See also Amex Life Assurance Co. v. Superior Court*, 14 Cal. 4th 1231, 60 Cal. Rptr. 2d 898, 930 P.2d 1264 (1997) (coverage available because of incontestability clause even though policyholder with AIDS defrauded the insurer by having a stand-in take his blood test).

structions in the face of seemingly contrary policy language, they implicitly treat insurance as a product that must be minimally adequate to the needs of the policyholder. By contrast, with implied exceptions to coverage, courts are accepting that insurers must be permitted to protect the actuarial integrity of their businesses even where the policy language is silent, vague, or even unfavorable concerning this point.

Common instances of implied exceptions include the fortuity-based losses discussed above. Another example is loss incurred through the ordinary "wear and tear" of the policyholder's regular activity or product use. Uncovered wear and tear losses are just that: if machinery at the Acme Sewing Company that malfunctions or stops altogether due to old age, the policyholder does not have a valid claim for property damage or business interruption loss. To "compensate" itself from the inevitable demise of machinery businesses and consumers alike "insure" by saving to buy new equipment when the old stuff wears out. Under normal circumstances, policyholders would not purchase express insurance on normal wear and tear: it is simply too expensive for consumers or unprofitable for insurers because the risk of loss would be 100 percent (everything wears out eventually). Consequently, courts are unsympathetic to a policyholder claiming coverage for normal wear and tear losses typical of its ordinary activity.

Public policy concerns often result in implied exceptions to coverage. For example, jurisdictions that forbid the insurability of punitive damages implicitly rewrite otherwise open insurance policy language to exclude such damages, an exception discussed at greater length below. A particularly chilling example of an implied public policy exception to coverage is the prevailing rule that a life insurance beneficiary cannot collect when he has murdered the insured. Another example is the traditional doctrine that life insurance does not cover death resulting from execution by the state, although the more modern decisions seem to have moved away from this position. In addition, death resulting from injury incurred while engaging in illegal activity often prevents coverage.

Some jurisdictions have included suicide by the life policyholder as well, although most states will not imply a suicide exclusion, although they will enforce one written into the policy (which is now standard). In general, traditional public policy prohibitions against recovery by an "innocent" beneficiary have gradually relaxed during the 20th century, but, as previously noted, insurers have often revised policy language to bar coverage whenever "any" insured expects or intends injury. Because the conduct of a life insurance beneficiary or policyholder in these situations is frequently specific and focused, these sorts of implied exceptions are often analyzed by courts and commentators under the rubric of intentional conduct rather than implied exceptions flowing from the nature and function of insurance.

A nonobvious implied exception frequently found in marine insurance is one for "inherent vice," which means, in landlubber's terms, the natural wear and tear deterioration of goods or a vessel or property's self-destruction due to an inherent defect that made the loss inevitable since this sort of loss does not stem from the perils of the sea. However, where a loss is traceable to sea perils rather than spoilation, marine insurance would ordinarily cover the loss.

## [a] The "Friendly Fire" Implied Exception

Perhaps the best known implied exception to coverage is the "friendly fire" rule of property insurance. Even though not found in the text of the policy, the friendly fire rule has existed for most of the 19th and 20th centuries. It had its official birth in *Austin v. Drew*, 171 Eng. Rpt. 115 (1815), an English case involving a sugar manufacturer. An employee failed to open the register at the top of a chimney and heat from the sugar plant built up tremendously, spreading heat, smoke, and sparks through the plant. Two workers suffocated. The flew was opened before the fire caused the building itself to burn. The court held that the damages resulting to the equipment, loss of materials, and personal injury were not covered because the fire had never left the confines where it ordinarily stood during normal business operations. Being so confined, the court saw the fire as "friendly," just as a crackling fire that stays in the fireplace is friendly to incoming skiers.

So defined, the friendly fire rule makes sense in that it prevents fire coverage from becoming general accident coverage for ordinary household or business activity. The friendly fire rule flows not so much from any public policy but rather results because friendly fires, however damaging, resemble normal wear and tear. Invocation of the defense thus prevents indemnity from events that, although not inevitable, are common occurrences from the policyholder's daily activities and are not well within the focus of fire insurance, the purpose of which is to indemnify for structural losses caused by raging and uncontrolled fires. In effect, the friendly fire rule tells policyholders to purchase liability or errors and omissions coverage to supplement fire insurance and prevents first-party property insurance from becoming product liability, product longevity, or liability insurance.

There are, however, ways of confining the exception so that it does not swallow the "rule" of fire indemnity. For example, if a fire develops in the chimney of the house, courts have held it to be "unfriendly" since fires should stay confined to the fireplace. Similarly, cigarettes or matches that are negligently left where they can start fires have ceased to be friendly. Perhaps the most significant American expansion of the strict English version of the friendly fire rule as articulated in *Austin v. Drew* is the willingness of American courts to find coverage for soot, smoke, and heat damage that stems from a fire where flame alone has not left its intended friendly confines. These courts reason that smoke outside the fireplace in significant amount to damage the curtains, the rug, etc., has ceased to be friendly within any reasonable meaning of the word. *See also* Ch. 8, *infra*, regarding Property Insurance.

## [b] Punitive Damages as an Implied Exception

In liability insurance policies, coverage is often provided for "all sums" or "such sums" which the insured shall become legally obligated to pay. *Query*: Does this mean the insurer is liable for punitive damages as well as compensatory damages? Since punitive damages have the function of punishing the defendant, and deterring others from like conduct, a number of courts have held that insurance against liability for punitive damages would violate public policy and is therefore invalid. Other courts, however, have held that an insurer's liability for punitive damages would not violate public policy and is therefore valid.

This conflict over punitive damages insurability may be the hottest dispute over implied exceptions, particularly the question of whether indemnity of a policyholder's liability for punitive damages violates public policy. The jurisdictions are currently roughly split between those which permit insurance coverage for punitive damages and those which find it to violate public policy. It appears that all states prohibit indemnity for intentional torts. Jurisdictions banning insurability of punitive damages have generally reasoned that punitive liability connotes an intentional act or similarly blame-worthy conduct. These courts usually also suggest that allowing insurance for punitive damages will reduce the incentive of policyholders to exercise due care since they will not completely bear the cost of a punitive damages judgment.

Other jurisdictions have found nothing amiss about liability insurance that covers punitive damages. These courts usually find that punitive damages may be assessed for a host of activities that fall short of satisfying the criteria for the intentional act clause or the public policy prohibition of intentional torts. These courts further tend to suggest that policyholders have plenty of incentive for due care because of the risk of excess judgments, future premium increases, future uninsurability, and uncovered losses should they be on the receiving end of a large judgment including punitive damages.

Some jurisdictions are a hybrid, generally disallowing insurance for punitive damages unless the punitive liability is vicarious or imposed for activity that falls comfortably short of an intentional tort. The modern trend appears to be in favor of allowing punitive damages to be insured. According to one source, a slight majority of states that have considered the issue have permitted insurability even for directly assessed punitive damages. When the issue is whether punitive damages imposed through vicarious liability are insurable, nearly all states permit insurability.

Commentators appear to decidedly oppose any restriction on insurability. Where state law or public policy permits an award of punitive damages, the issue remains: does the policy relevant to the instant dispute encompass punitive awards? Most courts, unhindered by public policy constraints, apply ambiguity analysis to find that terms such as "damages" or "amount required to be paid" include punitive awards and that standard CGL policy language thus provides coverage. There is a clear split of authority on whether or not liability insurance policies ought to provide coverage for punitive damages to third-party plaintiffs. *See generally* Randy Maniloff & Jeffrey Stempel, General Liability Insurance Coverage: Key Issues In Every State, Ch. 19 (4th ed. 2018); Richard L. Blatt, Robert W. Hammesfahr & Lori S. Nugent, Punitive Damages: A State-By-State Guide to Law and Practice (2009 ed.).

Although it can be dangerous to characterize jurisdictions too formally, the synopsis of one state supreme court justice provides a good summary:

> The cases defy easy categorization but it appears that 19 states generally permit coverage of punitive damages; 8 states would permit coverage of puni-

nesses acquire as a result of contractual dealings such as agreeing to indemnify business partners for tortious conduct. But this type of coverage sounds more in tort than contract. Less common, specialty insurance products may also specifically cover commercial risk.

For the most part, however, insurance does not provide compensation to the policyholder who purchases an inferior product, invests in a bad mutual fund, botches a task sufficiently that the customer demands it be redone; drives away customers with poor service, and the like. Viewed broadly, all of these sorts of noncoverage can be seen as a part of the fortuity concept. If Acme Plumbing "fixes" a faucet but it continues to leak and Acme refuses to make good on the work, Acme is not covered if the customer sues and cannot obtain "bad debt" coverage if the customer refuses to pay.

### [6] The Limits of Fortuity as a Defense to Coverage

Although fortuity is an important concept undergirding insurance, the concept should not be so broadly interpreted or rigorously incorporated into the policy so as to create a "phantom exclusion" from coverage. Insurers should not generally be able to invoke fortuity as a defense unless the nature of the loss to the policyholder or the claim against the policyholder clearly falls within the zone of uninsurable non-fortuitous conduct. Insurers should not be able to invoke 20-20 hindsight to second guess policyholder conduct to defeat coverage unless the coverage dispute falls clearly outside the text and scope of the insuring agreement or clearly violates the fortuity principle.

For example, a policyholder may decide to build a manufacturing plant in a corrupt third world country. The manufacturer is then saddled with frivolous but successful product liability claims set up by local organized crime, resulting in judgments entered by the local corrupt bench. Bowing to reality, the policyholder settles these claims as prudently as possible while extracting its assets from the country. When the policyholder seeks coverage for these bogus (but costly) suits, the insurer cannot avoid coverage by characterizing the policyholder's venture as a dumb business move or the result of commercial error.

These hypothetical suits still are liability claims against the policyholder and are covered. The losses are still "fortuitous" from the standpoint of the policyholder in that they were unexpected, unintended, and outside the control of the insured once the foreign operation was commenced. The intent of the local criminals is irrelevant. But if the policyholder decided to head off the suits by bribing the local mafia or bribing the judges not to find for the claimants, this policyholder activity is not fortuitous and is therefore outside coverage, even if it might be understandable under the circumstances and cheaper in the long run.

In short, the fortuity concept should not be extended to allow insurers to agree to cover the claims of only prudent policyholders. The standard insurance policies cover even gross negligence, recklessness, and stupidity. Thus, the homeowner who leaves the stove on is covered when the house burns even though a third-party observer might at first want to characterize this as something other than an accident. The manufacturer of a dangerous child's toy (remember metal-spiked lawn darts, since banned or withdrawn from the market?) is covered even though most observers could have seen this liability problem a mile away. Insurance exists to cover losses occurring by chance. The fact that some policyholders may be less adept at predicting risk than others does not negate fortuity.

## [B] Adverse Selection

Adverse selection and moral hazard by applicants or policyholders provides perhaps the greatest threat to fortuitous underwriting by the insurer. Adverse selection is the tendency of persons who are more likely to suffer a loss to purchase insurance on such risks. At its worst, adverse selection can mean an insurance applicant seeking a policy that will cover a loss he knows is certain to occur. For example, an applicant who is HIV-positive could obtain insurance knowing this and hoping that the insurer does not discover the illness, which will eventually result in full-blown AIDS and death absent discovery of a miracle cure. In fact, this sort of nearly absolute adverse selection probably did occur to some degree until life and health insurers began insisting on blood tests for all insurance applicants.

At a less extreme level, some insurance applicants present greater risk of future loss than do "average" or "normal" applicants. For example, an applicant may be a skydiver or a member of a street gang, or have some other hobby or habit that increases his or her risk of loss. When persons in these groups seek insurance, particularly substantial amounts of insurance, adverse selection is occurring. When these applicants know about their higher-risk status but insurers do not, such applicants present a major threat to the insurer because the unwitting insurer may charge them standard premium rates when it should have either declined to issue a policy or charged far higher premiums.

Insurers generally try to homogenize the relative knowledge of policyholder and insurer by asking the applicant a substantial number of questions designed to identify the applicant's potential for presenting a high risk. If it successfully obtains this information, the insurer can either decline the risk or "rate" the policy by charging higher premiums. In addition to requiring blood tests or medical examinations to test for the physiologically risky, insurers attempt to enhance screening of applicants and also often specify that any misrepresentations by the applicant will provide grounds for rescission of the policy (*see* Ch. 4). Insurers also reserve the right to cancel a policy or decline to renew it (insurance policies are usually written for one year) to provide an escape hatch should they discover adverse selection.

## [C] Moral Hazard

Related to adverse selection is the concept of moral hazard, which at the extreme can mean a policyholder's intent to incur a loss in order to collect insurance proceeds through outright fraud or its equivalent. In the broader and usual sense in which the term is used, moral hazard means the tendency of a policyholder to be less careful in avoiding loss because she will be indemnified if the loss occurs. In addition to exclusionary language and underwriting practices, insurers attempt to reduce the risk of both adverse selection and moral hazard by engaging in experience rating, i.e., setting premiums based on the policyholder's previous claim experience, and also by means of deductibles and co-insurance.

Despite various underwriting and claims defense practices, moral hazard has a substantial impact on the insurance markets. For example, arson is a substantial risk in the United States, notwithstanding deductibles and co-insurance. In life insurance, moral hazard is reduced because the purchaser of the policy is usually the life-insured, also known in insurance jargon as the CQV, who presumably is unlikely to commit suicide, or a close relative (who presumably is unlikely to kill the CQV for insurance benefits). In medical and disability insurance, although the policyholder is unlikely to maim himself to collect benefits, the small risk of this and the greater risk of garden-variety hypochondria have made deductibles and co-insurance a major feature of such policies. As the examples of arson and theft by the policyholder show, moral hazard in the more depersonalized context of property is of substantial concern to insurers.

## § 1.06. A Note on Insurer Operations

As previously discussed, insurance involves incurring the small loss of premium payment in return for protection against larger but contingent losses—with risks shifted from the policyholder to the insurer, which then distributes its risk across a pool of policyholders. To work effectively, it depends on pooling of uncorrelated risk.

To measure their underwriting effectiveness and administrative efficiency, insurers normally pay considerable attention to the company loss ratio and the company combined ratio. The loss ratio, expressed as a fraction, involves the company's claims payments divided by its premium receipts. If the loss ratio is greater than one (1), the company is paying more in claims than it receives in premium payments. Conversely, a loss ratio of less than one (1) means the company has an underwriting profit.

Perhaps more important is the combined ratio of a company. For this measure, the numerator of the ratio is the combination of company claims payments plus administrative costs such as paying workers, renting space or paying a mortgage on company HQ. If the combined ratio exceeds one (1), the company is losing money on underwriting and operations. If the combined ratio is less than one (1), the company is making money on its underwriting and operations.

Because insurers receive premiums and earn investment income on those funds before they must pay claims, an insurer can be profitable even if it is operating with a combined ratio of less than one, particularly if the investment climate is good. In some years, for example, an insurer may have a combined ratio as high as 1.5 and still remain solvent.[73] Many well-known insurers regularly have combined ratios above

---

73. As discussed in Ch. 3, insurance is comparatively highly regulated as compared to most businesses. And a primary focus of insurance regulation is insurance solvency. In addition to following a company's combined ratio, regulators regularly monitor the amount of capital reserves held by an

one and operate at an underwriting loss. But if an insurer can regularly have a combined ratio below one, it will not only survive but thrive. It is then making money on underwriting alone—and adding to that money earned through investment of premiums received.

In addition, insurers generally pay claims in currency that has become less valuable per unit due to inflation, which provides another economic advantage for the insurer. Liability insurers in particular may benefit from inflation, particularly for claims with delayed onset in which claims against the policyholder emerge years or even decades after a policyholder may have exposed a bystander to chemicals or delivered substandard surgery or construction services.

By contrast, property and medical insurers have considerably less ability to profit from inflation. People will tend to need medical services nearly every year, although they may not need major surgery for many years after paying premiums. Property insurers may be subject to an onslaught of claims after a catastrophic event such as a hurricane. But absent such events, all insurers will tend to have some delay between premium receipt and claims payment, but with the typical delay varying by type of insurance product.

Because the business model of insurance is so centered on profiting from investment, insurers may be tempted to accept poor risks or charge unduly low prices simply to capture premium dollars for investment. This is commonly described as a "soft" market in which coverage is easy to obtain at low prices with little hassle.

This type of behavior may seem like a good idea during times of investment boom, particularly if interest rates on relatively safe bonds or deposit certificates are high, real estate prices are rising or the stock market is strong.[74] But investment climates change, which can leave the insurer with a lower return on investment and some bad risks or policies sold too cheaply that now face substantial claims.

This scenario takes place with sufficient frequency that it is referred to as the insurance underwriting "cycle" in which insurers, even if they should know better, chase premium revenue without sufficient underwriting and pricing discipline. When the investment bubble bursts or claims come on policies that perhaps should not

---

insurer as well as its reinsurance protection. If the company lacks sufficient solvency, regulators may step in to require business adjustments or, in extreme cases, may even place the company in receivership or "run-off" in which it is not allowed to accept new business but pays claims as they emerge from the company's existing "book" of business.

74. Regulations in all states place some limits on insurer investment portfolios. For example, an insurer would not be able to invest all premium dollars in stocks, must less only one or two stocks. Instead, diversification is forced, with percentage limits on insurer investment in stocks, corporate bonds, government bonds, "junk" (high risk but higher yielding) bonds, real estate, savings accounts, and the like. A greater percentage of investment is permitted in comparatively "safe" investments such as bank certificates of deposit or money market funds. But even this less volatile type of investment will fluctuate. For example, in the high inflation period of the late 1970s and early 1980s, money market funds were commonly paying double-digit annual interest. Today, corresponding interest rates are two percent or less.

have been issued (or only issued at higher prices), the insurer normally must contract operations to survive. This produces a "hard" insurance market in which premiums rise, underwriting standards stiffen, and coverage is hard to obtain.

In reaction to hardening insurance markets, business may form "captive" insurers of their own or "risk retention groups." A captive insurer is an entity created and owned by a non-insurer in order to provide the non-insurer with coverage more advantageous (in terms of scope, cost, or both) than the non-insurer can obtain in the insurance marketplace. If the company's loss experience is better than anticipated, this "profit" is retained by the company, which also typically enjoys some savings in that its payments to the captive are generally less than premium payments for corresponding coverage. If this were not the case, it would be hard to justify the time, effort, and distraction required for a company to established and maintain a captive insurer.

While obviously similar to self-insurance (simply going without insurance and counting on company wealth to be sufficient to process and pay liability or loss claims), captive insurance is different in the degree to which the captive will collect and marshal funds to create reserves sufficient to pay claims. Captives also may purchase reinsurance for financial backing. Like ordinary insurers, captives can experience difficulty if they miscalculate the payments required, the ability to earn investment income, or the chances and severity of losses or claims.

A risk retention group involves a group of non-insurers (usually in the same type of industry) banding together to establish what amounts to their own self-insurance or captive insurance program. But this is done pursuant to the federal Liability Risk Retention Act, which permits some arrangements so long as the Group forms as an insurer pursuant to state law and meets regulatory requirements. In a manner similar to captives, the Group, which usually buys reinsurance as well, seeks to pay less for coverage than the premium prices available and distributes profits as dividends to the members where there is good loss experience.

Non-insurers engaging in these activities typically contract with a vendor to establish the captive or group or hire employees with experience in the insurance industry.

# § 1.07. Becoming Better
# Informed about Insurance

If one wants to be a better insurance student—and certainly if one wants to be a better insurance lawyer—it helps to stay informed not only about recent cases and evolving legal doctrine but also about insurance operations and trends in the business of insurance. Helpful sources include but are not limited to the following. Not all of these are affordable on a student budget but some are relatively inexpensive or even free—while many will (or should) be in your school's law library.

*Textbooks*

GEORGE E. REJDA & MICHAEL J. MCNAMARA, PRINCIPLES OF RISK MANAGE-MENT AND INSURANCE (13th ed. 2017)—a classic popular textbook used for undergraduate and graduate courses in insurance.

EMMETT J. VAUGHAN & THERESE M. VAUGHAN, FUNDAMENTALS OF RISK AND INSURANCE (11th Ed. 2014)—another classic popular textbook.

MARKS S. DORFMAN & DAVID A. CATHER, INTRODUCTION TO RISK MANAGE-MENT & INSURANCE (10th ed. 2012)—another popular textbook.

*Treatises*

JEFFREY W. STEMPEL & ERIK S. KNUTSEN, STEMPEL & KNUTSEN ON INSURANCE COVERAGE (4th ed. 2018)—a two-volume treatise providing an overview of insurance concepts, products, and legal doctrine.

RANDY MANILOFF & JEFFREY STEMPEL, COMMERCIAL GENERAL LIABILITY INSURANCE COVERAGE: KEY ISSUES IN EVERY STATE (4th ed. 2018)—contains more than twenty 50-state surveys on important and recurring insurance controversies.

ROBERT H. JERRY, II & DOUGLAS R. RICHMOND, UNDERSTANDING INSURANCE LAW (6th ed. 2018)—a one-volume treatise designed for students that can provide additional orientation and reference.

BARRY R. OSTRAGER & THOMAS R. NEWMAN, HANDBOOK OF INSURANCE COVERAGE DISPUTES (16th ed. 2014).

EUGENE R. ANDERSON, LORELIE S. MASTERS & JORDAN STANZLER, INSURANCE COVERAGE, ETC. (2d ed. 2000) (with annual updates).

APPLEMAN ON INSURANCE AND NEW APPLEMAN ON INSURANCE—a multi-volume treatise what also includes supplements with articles discussing emerging insurance issues.

COUCH ON INSURANCE—another classic multi-volume treatise.

FIDELITY CASUALTY & SURETY (FC&S) BULLETINS—a newsletter/treatise service of National Underwriter Company, which covers insurance products and coverage issues in eight volumes addressing several lines of insurance: Fire & Marine; Personal Lines; Casualty & Surety; Umbrella; and Directors & Officers Liability (as well as publishing a guide to policies and a guide to various companies and their policies).

NATIONAL UNDERWRITER COVERAGE GUIDES—separate volumes that each provide an overview to separate common insurance products like homeowners insurance, auto insurance, or general liability insurance. Unlike the more costly FC&S Bulletins or other treatises designed for practitioners, these mini-treatises sell for roughly $50 each.

*Newsletters, Periodicals, and Other Services*

INSURANCE JOURNAL—an emailed newsletter of the field that canvases the nation by region and includes tort and litigation news as well as insurance information per se. Subscriptions are free and it is possible to receive a number of related or affiliated insurance information services such as CLAIMS JOURNAL (which will have substantial overlap) and Carrier Management.

COVERAGE OPINIONS—an emailed newsletter authored by noted insurance attorney Randy Maniloff that follows current case law developments as well as providing interviews with noted legal figures. Subscription is free.

BEST'S INSURANCE REVIEW—a monthly magazine (published in Property/Casualty and Life/Health editions) addressing current news and industry trends.

NATIONAL UNDERWRITER—another monthly published in both a Property/Casualty and a Life/Health edition.

BUSINESS INSURANCE—a weekly newspaper reporting on the economics of the insurance industry and other developments.

MONDAQ—an emailed newsletter about insurance, business and litigation centered in the UK but covering topics globally. Subscription is free.

ADVISEN PROFESSIONAL FRONT PAGE NEWS—a comprehensive newsletter that brings news (including international news) of litigation, transport, and regulation—as well as about insurance. Requires a fee.

MY NEW MARKETS—an emailed newsletter that advertises and discusses insurance products as well as containing articles about insurance and brokerage. It can be obtained through the Risk Insurance Management Society (RIMS).

The Insurance Risk Management Institute (IRMI) produces many authoritative publications regarding the meaning of particular insurance policies.

# Chapter 2

# The Construction of the Insurance Policy

## § 2.01. A Brief Review of Contract Law

"It is well-settled that an insurance policy is a contract and that the relationship between the insured and the insurer is purely contractual in nature."[1] This statement, although basically correct, glosses over a host of complexities of both insurance and contract. One might question whether any legal controversy can be decided "purely" upon a single subset of the law.

For example, insurance policies can be considered products as well in that the policyholder purchases insurance, usually with an "off-the-rack" standardized policy that is designed to protect it from particular risks. *See* Jeffrey W. Stempel, *The Insurance Policy as Thing*, 44 TORT TRIAL & INS. PRAC. L.J. 813 (2009); Daniel Schwarcz, *A Products Liability Theory for the Judicial Regulation of Insurance Policies*, 48 WM. & MARY L. REV. 1389 (2007).

Further, because much of the standardization of insurance policies takes place through industry collaboration, insurance has characteristics similar to private legislation. *See* Jeffrey W. Stempel, *The Insurance Policy as Statute*, 41 MCGEORGE L. REV. 203 (2010).

In addition, because insurance plays a key role in risk management and as a practical matter is a prerequisite to commerce and other activity, one might deem it a social instrument or social institution. *See* Jeffrey W Stempel, *The Insurance Policy as Social Instrument and Social Institution*, 51 WM. & MARY L. REV. 1489 (2010). Consideration of these various perspectives can have implications for the application of various insurance law doctrines and resolution of insurance coverage disputes.

But the primary characterization of insurance as contract is well-entrenched, even to the point where mainstream insurance scholars have criticized courts for taking too superficial and formalistic a view of insurance policies as contracts that ignores the heavy regulation of insurance (addressed in Ch. 3) and the adhesive nature of insurance policies. *See e.g.* Susan Randall, *Freedom of Contract in Insurance*, 14 CONN.

---

1. *See Good v. Krohn*, 786 N.E.2d 480, 485 (Ohio Ct. App. 2002), *citing Nationwide Mut. Ins. Co. v. Marsh*, 15 Ohio St. 3d 107, 109, 472 N.E.2d 1061 (1984).

INS. L.J. 107 (2007). An adhesion contract is one offered on a take-it-or-leave-it basis with no bargaining over terms. *See* Friedrich Kessler, *Contracts of Adhesion—Some Thoughts About Freedom of Contract*, 43 COLUM. L. REV. 629, 630–31 (1943); Edwin Patterson, *The Delivery of a Life Insurance Policy*, 33 HARV. L. REV. 198, 222 & n.106 (1919). *But see* Leo P. Martinez, *A Unified Theory of Insurance Risk,* 74 U PITTSBURGH L. REV. 713 (2014) (arguing that insurance policies remain best understood as contracts but that nature of insurance contracting differs from other contracting in the quality and degree of risk assignment and spreading).

As students learn during the first year of law school, a contract is an agreement which the law will enforce. To be valid and enforceable, the contract must be properly formed with an offer, acceptance of the offer, and giving of consideration. In the insurance context, the choreography of contract formation is a bit different than the standard sale of goods. Chapter 4 discusses the formation, operation, and termination of insurance policies in detail. Suffice it to say here that insurance policies, like other contracts, must be a product of offer and acceptance and be supported by consideration. If a policy is obtained by or issued pursuant to fraud, it is not enforceable (provided the reviewing court sees the situation as one of fraud).

After formation, a contract can nonetheless be void if it is for an illegal purpose or otherwise violates public policy. For example, the "contracts" placed on criminal competitors or troublesome witnesses by mob kingpins are not enforceable contracts (at least not legally enforceable) and are void at the inception. Contracts for slavery or some other prohibited transaction would also be legal nullities. In the law of insurance, one seldom finds insurance policies ruled void. The insurance policies may, however, contain unconscionable terms that a court refuses to enforce or that the court reforms through construction so that a term no longer brings an unconscionable result. "Public policy" and unconscionability as bases for insurance contract interpretation are discussed at greater length later in this chapter.

In addition, a contract may be unenforceable—or at least voidable at the option of one party—due to lack of capacity. For example, contracts made by insane persons or minors (persons under age 18) are considered voidable. The insane party (or its representative) or the underage person may either comply with the contract, sue to have it set aside, or simply defend against a contractual enforcement action by the other party. This part of contract doctrine has some exceptions. For example, a contract by a minor for "necessaries" such as food, clothing, or shelter is enforceable so that (a) minors are able to obtain necessities and (b) merchants do not get unfairly "stiffed" by child purchasers of these items. Imagine McDonald's or Old Navy operating without this exception to the capacity rule, although many of these transactions are cash-and-carry consumption exchanges.

As a practical matter, capacity rules of contract formation seldom affect insurance law. Usually only sane adults are interested in purchasing insurance which, as discussed in Chapter 1, by definition involves some tradeoff of long-term planning for contingencies and short-term payment for this planning. When children are insured, they are usually insured not because they are an active contracting party but because they are considered "an insured" under a policy purchased by an adult. This is the case with automobile, homeowner's, and health insurance (where the purchase is usually by the adult parent's employer as a group health policy rather than by the parent individually). Although a child may be the life insured in a life insurance policy, these policies are of course usually purchased by parents during the child's minority as investment vehicles or to protect against the child later becoming uninsurable as an adult.

Under standard contract law, the remedy for a breach of contract is usually determined by an "expectations" approach to damages: what would the victimized party have received had the contract not been breached? *See generally* E. ALAN FARNSWORTH, CONTRACTS § 12.9 (4th ed. 2004) (discussing the "benefit of the bargain" approach to damages as variations on this approach). The general measure of damages in contract law is the loss in value suffered from breach of contract added to other loss occasioned by the breach (for example, a party may have been forced to obtain substitute goods at a higher "short notice" price) minus any cost or loss avoided by the breach. Applied to insurance, the measure of damages for breach ordinarily is payment of the benefits owed under the policy, which ordinarily includes the amount of the insured loss that was improperly denied by the insurer (it could be a partial denial based on a property valuation dispute rather than a total denial of the claim). For liability insurance, the policyholder may also be entitled to reimbursement of costs of defending a claim if the policy included a duty to defend.

Insurance law works a lot like "regular" contract law regarding damages—but there are some important differences. The breach of a noninsurance contract is normally treated as (what else?) a breach of contract; the victimized party may not obtain any extra-contractual damages no matter how intentional and mean-spirited the other party's failure to perform so long as the breaching party's conduct does not rise to the level of an independent tort such as fraud, conversion, or defamation.

However, because of the reliance of policyholders upon insurance, many states treat the bad faith breach of an insurance policy as an independent tort, permitting the wronged policyholder to perhaps obtain noneconomic damages (e.g., pain and suffering) and even punitive damages. Other jurisdictions may stop short of treating bad faith breach as a distinct tort but recognize it as a separate contract-based cause of action with an expanded range of damages.[2] As one might expect, policyholders and their counsel tend to prefer a legal regime in which bad faith is a tort creating the additional leverage provided by the possibility of a large punitive damages award, while insurers tend to prefer a bad faith regime that treats insurer bad faith as a "mere" breach of contract for which punitive damages are not available. Chapter 14 discusses bad faith in detail.

---

2. *See E.I. DuPont de Nemours & Co. v. Pressman*, 679 A.2d 436, 447 (Del. 1996) (confining recovery for bad faith breach to insurance policies because, "Insurance is different. Once an insured files a claim, the insurer has a strong incentive to conserve its financial resources balanced against the effect on its reputation of a 'hard-ball' approach.").

This chapter, however, deals not with the remedies available when insurers or policyholders breach contract terms but rather with the methods by which the legal system assesses the meaning of insurance policies and determines coverage. Although the focus is necessarily on contested matters (we would have a pretty thin "casebook" if we didn't take this approach), it is important to remember that the prevailing ground rules of insurance law and norms of policy interpretation govern insurance coverage on a daily basis. Litigation is but a subset of the system. Every day, policyholders are deciding whether to make a claim for insurance coverage as well as the amount of the claim. This may be with or without the advice of counsel. In response, agents, brokers, and claims adjusters take positions reacting to the claims.[3] Insurer representatives above the claims adjuster may become involved for uncertain, difficult, large, or contested claims.

The opinions and decisions of these actors are of course influenced by their views of insurance law and policy construction (although it may be the understanding of an intelligent layperson and not that of a lawyer or the understanding of a lawyer who subscribes to a particular philosophy of contract interpretation discussed in this chapter). Lawyers may enter the process for either side at various junctures. Even when a dispute is pronounced, it may be resolved through negotiation, arbitration, mediation, or appraisal without resort to the courts. Nonetheless, judicial pronouncements may have substantial impact on these nonjudicial resolutions. In that regard, insurance is no different than any other area of legal rights, where well over 90% of the issues are resolved through means other than a final judgment. As with other areas of law and life, negotiated resolution is common and may result in better outcomes for all concerned. But the parties will tend to bargain "in the shadow of the law" based on their understanding of what range of results would likely obtain after full-dress litigation.[4]

A word of caution is in order about excessively myopic focus on the text of the insurance policy alone. Despite the long-standing rule that party intent is the touchstone of contract meaning, attorneys and courts sometimes focus so intently on the words of the writing that they lose sight of this larger picture. But the words on paper are more properly viewed as "contract documents" than the "contract" itself. Although

---

3. Chapters 1 and 4 both discuss the role these actors and the law of insurance agency and brokerage. Generally, agents are representatives of the insurer although, as we know from watching the plethora of heartwarming television commercials put forth by insurers, the agent also has a relationship with the policyholder. Although agents are unlikely to forget for whom they work (the insurance company), the agent will also want to keep the policyholder customer happy if possible and may offer her opinion as to coverage and how best to prosecute the claim or value the loss to maximize the chance of a cooperative claims process. Brokers are the representatives of the policyholder (commercial policyholders are far more likely than individuals to use a broker for procuring insurance) and typically agree with the policyholder on coverage matters. But like agents, brokers can be subject to competing forces of loyalty. In order to do business with an insurer in the future, it is not helpful for the broker to be perceived as so slavishly loyal to the policyholder that she supports weak or inflated claims.

4. The phrase "in the shadow of the law" is a widely established term for the manner in which potential legal outcomes effect settlement behavior and appears to have been coined in Robert Mnookin & Lewis Kornhauser, *Bargaining in the Shadow of Law: The Case of Divorce*, 88 YALE L.J. 950 (1980).

the text of a written contract is of course important for determining contract meaning, the words on a piece of paper—and certainly not a few isolated words in one part of the policy form—are not themselves "the contract." Rather, the written document functions as a memorialization of the parties' intent and agreement. That agreement is "the contract." As one contract law casebook observes:

> People often use the word "contract" to refer to the writing that embodies an agreement or deal.... But the piece of paper is not a contract.... At most, that piece of paper is a memorialization of the contract.... [A] contract is a promise or set of promises that the law will enforce.... That is the contract.
>
> [T]here is a tendency to confuse the written paper signed by the parties with the contract that binds them. It is an easy mistake to make; everyone calls the signed paper "the contract." But that paper is, at best, only *evidence* of the contract. That is, the contract is represented by that paper; it is not that paper.

See David G. Epstein, Bruce A. Markell & Lawrence Ponoroff, Making And Doing Deals: Contracts In Context 13, 465 (5th ed. 2018) (emphasis in original).

This perspective squares with the reality of much of humanity's daily "contracting." *See, e.g.,* Debra Cassens Weiss, *Chief Justice [John] Roberts Admits He Doesn't Read the Computer Fine Print*, A.B.A.J., Oct. 20, 2010, *available at* http://www.abajournal. com (also describing Chief Justice's admission that he does not read the package insert literature and warnings that accompany medications because it has "the smallest type you can imagine and you unfold it like a map"); Debra Cassens Weiss, *Judge [Richard] Posner Admits He Didn't Read Boilerplate for Home Equity Loan*, A.B.A.J., June 23, 2010, *available at* http://www.abajournal.com (also noting that prominent lawyers appearing at NYU Law School program all signed school's liability release form without scrutiny of the form). If guys like these are not going to hang on every word of the text of the document memorializing an agreement or transaction, why should any of us (or courts reviewing and construing these "contract documents," a/ k/a "contracts")?

# § 2.02. The Nature of an Insurance Policy

It is a conventional wisdom of the law that judicial interpretations of insurance contract disputes are often confusing and inconsistent. But there is a logical explanation for these apparent judicial inconsistencies in insurance law decisions if one keeps in mind several explanatory factors:

- The perceived inconsistency may be exaggerated. It may not be that the courts are as inconsistent as the cases are different. Also, standardization does not mean complete uniformity. Policy language may be basically the same across the country but differ in specific ways that become important in a particular coverage controversy. Differing case outcomes may be the result of these distinctions rather than different interpretative approaches.

- Insurance is a heavily regulated industry. Some differences in case outcomes stem from the regulatory directives of the applicable regulator or may be influenced by the general activity of the regulator. For example, if a state insurance commissioner (perhaps one that wants to run for governor) is conducting a high-profile publicity campaign in support of finding a certain sort of coverage in a homeowner's policy, this may influence the judiciary notwithstanding the standard nostrums about judicial independence.

- Regulation of insurance is state-centered. In fact (as discussed in Chapter 3), there is federal law (the McCarran-Ferguson Act) that removes the federal government from most insurance regulation so long as the state has a regulatory apparatus (which every state has in order to take advantage of this federal law).

- In addition to having different regulation by the executive branch of state government via an executive agency, states will have different statutes about insurance. For example, approximately 20 states have "valued policy" statutes that require payment of the full policy limits on property that is a "total loss" while other states permit the insurer to argue that even a totally destroyed home was worth less than the policy limits.

- Different case outcomes may reflect differential quality of advocacy.

- Insurance case outcomes may be inconsistent but no more inconsistent than outcomes in any other area of law. It may be that insurance jurisprudence has gotten a "bum rap" for inconsistencies that are inevitable.

Beyond these observations, however, insurance law is a bit different than regular contract law. As discussed above, insurance policies can almost as readily be characterized as products, statutes, or socioeconomic instruments and social institutions. But the differences between insurance policies and "regular" contracts does not mean that insurance law jurisprudence is inferior to "regular" contract jurisprudence either due to inconsistency or perceived favoritism toward policyholders. Rather, the nature of the insurance relationship may require different contract construction outcomes in the context of various disputes. Some of the ways in which insurance law may legitimately be different than regular contract law include:

- The insurance policy is an aleatory contract that involves an intrinsically uncertain exchange. *See* EDWIN W. PATTERSON, ESSENTIALS OF INSURANCE LAW 62 (2d ed. 1957).[5] Buying insurance is quite a bit different than a trip to the

---

5. Professor Patterson probably would agree with those who find insurance law more result-oriented than we perceive it to be. Shortly after noting the aleatory nature of the insurance policy, he also wrote:

> [T]he insured, because of his indifference to an event that will probably never happen, and because of his inability to understand the technical conditions imposed by the insurer, needs guidance and protection to a greater extent than in most of the other business deals in which he engages. The general law of contracts has been considerably distorted by American courts in applying it to insurance controversies, because they have sought to protect the insured.

*Id.* at 62.

grocery store. At the grocer, one pays a dollar and receives a loaf of bread that can be physically evaluated at the store (e.g., does the bread look fresh, feel fresh, appear appetizing?) and completely tested minutes after purchase (e.g., how does the bread taste, does it toast well, can butter be spread on it without tearing it apart?).[6] By contrast (as discussed in more detail in Chapter 4 regarding the making of the insurance contract), the policyholder may not even have a copy of the insurance policy to read for weeks after making the purchase.

• The policyholder is in an extremely vulnerable position vis-a-vis the insurer. The policyholder by definition has already paid a premium and parted with funds. Further, the policyholder has incurred an event that it regards as a loss and for which it is seeking indemnification. Because the loss has already occurred, it cannot be insured against (that would violate the fortuity principle). Thus, if the policyholder is to obtain any coverage, it must be from a particular insurer. The policyholder is dependent on the insurer's payment of the claim or loss. Prof. Baker has analogized this aspect of insurance to Shakespeare's famous play King Lear, in which the aged king gives all of his wealth to his daughters before death and is therefore dependent upon them for support. For students who have not seen the play, we remind you it is one of Shakespeare's tragedies, largely because at least two of the daughters do not fulfill their part of the bargain.[7]

• In addition, the claim or loss facing the policyholder may be looming immediately before the policyholder. The insurer, however, may see no particular urgency about paying the claim. The insurer collected the premium long ago. It will get no additional funds from the policyholder save for perhaps a deductible. The insurer's incentive will be to "play the float" and continue to earn interest on the premium as long as possible. Such an incentive may prompt

---

6. In economic terms, there are considerable "information costs" associated with understanding an insurance policy, while many common products have far lower information costs. In addition, consumer products like bread have "inspection qualities" or "search qualities" that make it possible to immediately evaluate the product in more effective manner. The "use qualities" of the loaf of bread permit rapid knowledge through the experience of using the product. *See* Bailey Kuklin & Jeffrey W. Stempel, Foundations Of The Law: An Interdisciplinary And Jurisprudential Primer 42 (1994). In contrast, insurance may be in place for years before it can be evaluated. Prior to a claim, laypersons are generally not in a good position to inspect the product and assess it because of the complexity and legal implications of the language. However, the buyer of insurance is able to tell the difference in cost between insurance policies. Perhaps this accounts for the seemingly irrational behavior of some consumers continuing to purchase insurance from carriers with whom they have had a bad experience — they may price shop when they would be better off shopping for quality or coverage better suited to the risks they face.

7. *See* Tom Baker, *Constructing the Insurance Relationship: Sales Stories, Claims Stories, and Insurance Contract Damages*, 72 Tex. L. Rev. 1429 (1994). Professor Baker also provided a Shakespearean analogy of the problem facing insurers: Richard III. King Richard, with the battle lost and desirous of escape, utters the famous line: "My Kingdom for a horse." Professor Baker sees this as reflecting the tendency of some policyholders to set unrealistic prices on the amount of a loss or the value of a pending claim which the policyholder would like to have the insurer settle and eliminate.

an insurer to see an inordinate number of claims as doubtful or even bogus. This financial differential also helps to explain the growth of insurance contract law in ways that benefit the policyholder in close cases and also helps to explain the availability of bad faith remedies against insurers (*see* Chapter 14) as a means of equalizing the insurers' incentives of self-interest and duty to the policyholder.

• Minimal competition regarding policy cost. Most of us simply lack the stamina to hunt high and low for the best premium value. Although the Internet and some disclosure initiatives by state regulators may be changing this, it remains much more difficult to price shop for insurance than to price shop for gasoline or other products.[8]

• Minimal competition regarding policy terms. The consumer must largely take the initiative if she is to discover the actual contours of coverage purchased. At most, insurers may volunteer that the policy is a "replacement cost" policy or includes wind-driven rain coverage at no additional charge, but this is comparatively rare. Of course, part of the reason that insurers tend not to compete on the basis of coverage provided is due to the standardization of policies and available endorsements.[9] One can customize insurance coverage to an extent, but this tends to happen only for more sophisticated policyholders who utilize the expertise of a commercial insurance broker. As a result, the consumer is again vulnerable in that there may be few choices if he is to obtain insurance at all.

• Insurers are immune from much federal regulation because of the McCarran-Ferguson Act (discussed in detail in Chapter 3). At a minimum, insurers are outside the reach of the antitrust laws, enabling them to act jointly regarding coverage offered, rate-setting, and other matters. This of course accentuates the lack of price and coverage competition noted above.

• Unlike most parties in a "regular" contract setting, insurers have enhanced responsibilities toward the policyholder.

---

8. Put another way, when was the last time you saw an insurer advertise its premium prices? Most insurer advertisements are image-building advertisements. There is little in the way of specifics that can facilitate consumer choice. We're not necessarily blaming insurers for this state of affairs. The nature of the product may make it inevitable. However, the fact remains that insurance is a hard product for which to shop, at least for the average person.

9. Professor Schwarcz, after studying homeowner's policies sold in the field, found that policy term vary much more substantially than commonly supposed and that "different carriers' homeowners policies differ radically with respect to numerous important coverage provisions," with most constricting coverage. *See* Daniel Schwarcz, *Reevaluating Standardized Insurance Policies*, 78 U. Chi. L. Rev. 1263 (2011). However, this variegation hardly means that insurers are competing regarding policy terms or scope of coverage. On the contrary, policyholders usually only see policy several weeks after purchase when it is eventually mailed to them by the insurers.

Although the relationship between insurer and policyholder is not fiduciary, it is fiduciary in nature. *See* Jeffrey W. Stempel & Erik S. Knutsen, Knutsen & Stempel on Insurance Coverage § 10.01 (4th ed. 2016). Some decisions in fact describe the relationship as a fiduciary one, particularly regarding liability insurance when the insurer has control of the defense of claims against the policyholder. *Compare* William Shernoff, Sanford Gage & Harvey Levine, Insurance Bad Faith Litigation § 1.05 (rev. ed. 1997) (policyholder counsel conclude that insurer is a fiduciary), *with* William Barker, Paul Glad & Steven Levy, *Is an Insurer a Fiduciary to Its Insurers?*, 25 Tort & Ins. L.J. 1 (1989) (insurer counsel conclude that insurer is not a fiduciary).

Although the insurer (at least outside the context of control of the defense of litigation against the policyholder) does not have the same responsibilities as a true fiduciary such as a lawyer, doctor, or investment advisor, the insurer cannot engage in sharp practices or take unfair advantage of the policyholder. This may preclude the insurer from taking positions on the meaning of a contract term that would be available in an ordinary commercial setting between two vendors dealing at arm's length. Similarly, an insurer is saddled with a tension of sorts between duty to its shareholders or other investors (to make money) and duty to its policyholders (to pay money).

In short, in addition to the ordinary forces that may make contract litigation inconsistent or difficult to categorize, insurance policies are subject to special forces that differentiate insurance law from regular contract law in several respects, although perhaps not so dramatically as is sometimes asserted by critics of insurance law decisions.

There is also a vigorous debate among legal scholars as to whether insurance policies are unilateral or bilateral contracts. The traditional view, most prominently associated with Professor Joseph Perillo, is that insurance policies are unilateral or, more specifically, "reverse-unilateral" contracts because the policyholder fully performs by paying the premium before receiving anything from the insurer. *See* Joseph M. Perillo, Calamari And Perillo On Contracts § 2.10, at 58 (6th ed. 2009). *Accord* Mark S. Dorfman, Introduction To Risk Management And Insurance 151 (8th ed. 2005); Edwin W. Patterson, Essentials Of Insurance Law § 11, at 65 (2d ed. 1957).

> [W]here only one party to a contract promises and the other performs, historically the contract has been deemed unilateral. For the typical unilateral contract, an offer or conditional promise is first made (e.g., "I'll pay you $100 if you walk across the Brooklyn Bridge"). The offer is accepted and is completed by performance following the offer (e.g., the offeree walks across the bridge, hopefully before any revocation by the offeror).
>
> In contrast to typical unilateral formation, in an insurance policy, the policyholder often makes payment (performance) prior to receiving promises by the insurer such as indemnity for loss and defense of liability claims.... When payment by the policyholder precedes the insurer's promise to insure,

the resulting contract is a reverse-unilateral contract and the policyholder is the offeror according to Professor Perillo.

*See* Hazel Beh & Jeffrey W. Stempel, *Misclassifying the Insurance Policy: The Unforced Errors of Unilateral Contract Characterization*, 32 Cardozo L. Rev. 85, 100 (2010).

As the title of their article implies, Professors Beh and Stempel disagree, concluding that insurance policies are better characterized as bilateral because the insurer-policyholder arrangement contains a number of promises on both sides and because the nature of the transaction and arrangement is considerably more complicated, ongoing, and relational than the types of walking-across-the-Brooklyn-Bridge or climbing-a-flagpole hypothetical that dominate unilateral contract literature. Other scholars, principally Dean Jerry, take a similar view. *See* Robert H. Jerry, II & Douglas R. Richmond, Understanding Insurance Law § 31[a] (6th ed. 2018); Beh & Stempel, *supra*, at 102, n.83 (reproducing email exchange between Professor Jerry and Professor Perillo on this point).

Contracts scholars generally have sought to confine or modify unilateral contract doctrine, which was in its heyday in the late 19th and early 20th Centuries, because of its potential for mischief and unfairness, *see* Samuel J. Stoljar, *The False Distinction Between Bilateral and Unilateral Contracts*, 64 Yale L.J. 515, 524 (1955); Karl Llewellyn, *Our Case-Law of Contract: Offer and Acceptance, II*, 48 Yale L.J. 779 (1939). *See also Davis v. Jacoby*, 34 P.2d 1026 (Cal. 1934) (noting this preference for bilateral characterization by courts and commentators, including *Williston on Contracts*). For the most part, courts appear to have held fast to the traditional view of insurance policies as unilateral contracts notwithstanding the now 80-year-old general preference in contract law for characterizing contracts as bilateral.

Although the distinction may be of only academic interest in most situations, Professors Beh & Stempel conclude that unilateral characterization generally leads to sub-par coverage decisions because unilateral characterization pushes courts to give inordinate importance to purported "conditions" (e.g., giving timely notice, providing adequate proof of loss, cooperating with the insurer, maintaining certain protocols) that must be satisfied in order to obtain coverage, when what in fact has occurred is an exchange of promises, any breach of which is better analyzed according to whether the breach is material. *See* Beh & Stempel, 32 Cardozo L. Rev. at 135–156. In particular, treating insurance policies as unilateral contracts has led some courts to deny to policyholders a right to proceed against the insurer on a theory of anticipatory repudiation after a denial of the first benefit payment, forcing the policyholder to sue seriatim and unfairly increasing the transaction costs of enforcing a contract that was supposed to provide financial security and peace of mind. *Id.* at 150–55.

The assignability of insurance policies can also present issues. Generally, contract rights are considered assignable and contract duties delegable as long as delegation does not materially increase the risk of non-performance for the party holding a right of performance. *See* DAVID G. EPSTEIN, BRUCE A. MARKELL & LAWRENCE PONOROFF, MAKING AND DOING DEALS: CONTRACTS IN CONTEXT 1005–1018 (5th ed. 2018); AMERICAN LAW INSTITUTE, RESTATEMENT (SECOND) CONTRACTS §318 (1981); E. ALLAN FARNSWORTH, CONTRACTS, Ch. 11 (4th ed. 2004).

Insurance policies usually, however, contain a clause restricting assignment without the insurer's consent and include such clauses in order to prevent assignment of the policy to a person or entity that poses greater risk of loss. This type of clause effectively prohibits a policyholder from assigning the policy to another entity prior to a loss or liability-creating occurrence. But anti-assignment clauses are not effective to prevent the assignment of the right to coverage under a policy after a liability-creating incident has already taken place.

> A non-assignment provision generally does not prohibit the assignment of rights accrued under an insurance policy after the occurrence of a loss. Thus, once an insured event has occurred, the insured should be able to assign its right to recover the proceeds of a policy without the insurer's consent, even though the policy prohibits assignments of the policy itself. The non-assignment provision is not applicable because, in this type of transaction, the insured is not assigning the policy itself, but rather the insured's right to recover money from the insurer, i.e., it's "chose in action." Moreover, the purpose of the non-assignment provision — protecting an insurer from an increased risk or hazard — is not implicated by the assignment of an accrued claim. This general rule applies equally to losses under property policies. Moreover, some courts have suggested that a restriction in an insurance policy against the assignment of an insured's rights after a loss would be violative of public policy and invalid.

PETER J. KALIS ET AL., POLICYHOLDER'S GUIDE TO THE LAW OF INSURANCE COVERAGE §21.02[A], [B] (1997 & Supp. 2001). Case law is pretty overwhelmingly clear on this point. *See, e.g., Maneikis v. St. Paul Ins. Co.*, 655 F.2d 818 (7th Cir. 1981) (holding that assignment after loss does not operate to increase risk of loss and therefore may be assignable); *Ocean Accident & Guarantee Corp. v. Southwestern Bell Tel. Co.*, 100 F.2d 441 (8th Cir.), *cert. denied*, 306 U.S. 658 (1939) (same; perhaps the leading classic case of this type).

Notwithstanding this seemingly well-accepted and logical view that post-loss assignment is not prohibited by a general anti-assignment clause, the California Supreme Court took a dozen year wrong turn on the issue in *Henkel Corp. v. Hartford Accident & Indemnity Co.*, 62 P.3d 69 (Cal. 2003), enforcing such a clause to deprive a successor company of the insurance policies it had acquired as part of a company acquisition in matters involving events that predated the acquisition that gave rise to claims. *Henkel* was reversed in *Fluor Corporation v. Superior Court*, 354 P.3d 302 (Cal. 2015), restoring California to the mainstream. *See also* 62 P.3d at 81–84 (discussing *Ocean Accident* at length and approvingly).

# § 2.03. Interpreting Insurance Policies: Legal Formalism versus Legal Functionalism

Different views of insurance policy construction (and contract interpretation generally) can be explained in substantial part by the presence of at least two major competing "schools" of American jurisprudence and their effect on judicial interpretations of insurance contracts.

## [A] Legal Formalism

The first school of American jurisprudence has variously been labeled as "Legal Formalism," or the "traditional" school of American legal thought. Under this formalist view, correct legal decisions are determined by pre-existing ground rules, usually as expressed in legislation and judicial precedents setting forth rules of legal doctrine. A formalist court faced with interpretative issues attempts to reach its decision solely by logical deduction, applying pre-existing legal rules to the facts of a particular case. From the general rule, the formalist reaches a specific resolution of the case before it. Under this formalistic theory, the law is viewed as a complete and autonomous system of logical principles and rules, where the judge applies the law and remains socially neutral. Formalists view this approach as a matter of logical necessity rather than a matter of choice.

Although formalism is not necessarily textualism, formalist judges generally look at the "four corners" of an insurance contract and interpret the insurance contract by applying rules applicable to all contracts in general, with the exception of various insurance forms and procedures that are regulated by statute. *See* 7 SAMUEL WILLISTON, A TREATISE ON THE LAW OF CONTRACTS 900 (1963) ("Unless contrary to statute or public policy, a contract of insurance will be enforced according to its terms.").

## [B] Legal Functionalism

In contrast to Legal Formalism, there is a countervailing school of American jurisprudence variously referred to as "Legal Functionalism," "Instrumentalism," "Legal Realism," or "Legal Pragmatism." According to this second school of thought, the traditional Formalistic view of logical "certainty" and "predictability" is rarely attainable, and perhaps undesirable, in a changing society. The paramount concern for legal functionalists therefore is not logical consistency, as the formalists seek, but desirable consequences for society and the legal system.

Put another way, where legal formalism emphasizes logic, precedent and text, legal functionalism emphasizes sociology, party intent, and contract purpose as well as social and individual expectations. Legal functionalism is also often viewed as result-oriented in that it may lead judges to select the contract construction that most accords with the court's sense of justice or fairness. Consequently, functionalist judges are more apt be accused of being "judicial activists." However, a formalist judge may also be activist and result-oriented but the imposition of personal preferences may be harder to detect because the formalist judge can pursue these ends subtly through the selection of the primary rule or precedent to guide the decision or by giving text a particular meaning even though other meanings are available.[10] Generally, however, because functionalist judges tend to be more open about their use of interpretative techniques that are not strictly rule-based or text-driven, they tend to be viewed by the public and the academy as more activist.

Wrapped in this issue as well are differing judicial views regarding separation of powers. A formalist judge is more likely to express a formalist view of the judicial function and to distrust any interpretative technique that looks like a substitution of the judge's personal preferences for those of the legislature (if a statute arguably applies), the executive (if insurance department regulation applies) or the parties (who presumably have expressed their views in the text of the policy). Most formalist judges also tend to see less encroachment upon other branches if the judge's focus is on statutory or contract text rather than other factors that could bear on construction of a statute or contract.

A functionalist judge is more likely to be seen as operating from a philosophy in which the court is legislatively and administratively co-equal, one with perhaps more institutional competence over some issues because of judicial structure (e.g., independence from partisan pressures). As to text as an expression of party intent, a formalist is likely to praise the view that contract text is an adequate, even sublime expression of party intent while a functionalist is likely to minimize the veracity of text as an indication of intent by emphasizing the standardized nature of the insurance policy as a contract of adhesion. Mass-marketed form contracts may not reflect the insurer's intent particularly well and may even be at odds with the policyholder's intent, or at least her expectations. In an insurance law context, many functionalist courts stress that insurance law contracts are not the same as other contracts. They are, rather, contracts of adhesion and "complex instruments, unilaterally prepared [by the insurer], and seldom understood by the insured." *Prudential Ins. Co. v. Lamme*, 83 Nev. 146, 425 P.2d 346, 347 (1967).

---

10. If you don't believe us, look in any dictionary. Words usually have more than one meaning, which will often turn on context. Although many words have a clearly primary meaning, many do not. In addition, many dictionary users appear not to realize that most dictionaries list word meanings in the order in which they came into usage. Thus, the first meaning of a word in most dictionaries is not the most popular meaning but the oldest. This, in turn, means that a court looking only at the dictionary could easily mistake an outdated meaning as the dominant meaning of a word.

One of the many ironies of the insurance coverage battles over pollution liability (discussed in Chapter 9) is that it was the more "liberal" and pro-policyholder judges who tended to seize on a dictionary definition, which is more commonly a tactic of "conservative" or pro-insurer judges. The word in question was "sudden," and its meaning of "unexpected" was seized upon by some because this made it more likely that the policyholder would receive coverage. Another definition of "sudden" of course, probably the connotatively more common meaning, is "swift" or "fast" or "abrupt."

The two styles of jurisprudence wax and wane in popularity. In the aftermath of the legal realism movement, legal functionalism was considered the dominant legal theory of American law until the 1970s. Since then, formalism and textualism have been in ascendancy, a trend that may accelerate due to the 100-plus judicial appointments of President Donald Trump, who has largely made nominations supported by (or even determined by) the Federalist Society. Particularly influential in this swing of the pendulum was the late Supreme Court Justice Antonin Scalia, who is a self-avowed textualist and formalist who has carried the standard for this school of thought both in his judicial opinions and his scholarly writings.[11]

Legal formalism, exemplified by a traditional contractual interpretation of insurance contracts, co-exists with legal functionalism, exemplified by the insurance law doctrine of "reasonable expectations." These alternatives may be in tension or even outright conflict, but both are clearly part of the fabric of insurance policy interpretation. It is not enough, therefore, to understand insurance law "in the books" and insurance law "in action." One must also know the judge, and understand the jurisprudential philosophy of each particular court. *See* Peter Nash Swisher, *Judicial Rationales in Insurance Law: Dusting Off the Formal for the Function*, 52 Ohio St. L.J. 1037 (1991).

# § 2.04. Mainstream Approaches to Contract Construction

Mainstream contract jurisprudence embraces as legitimate a number of different considerations for use in construing contracts. All of these factors for determining contract meaning may be used, alone or in combination, by courts. Crudely summarized, courts consider the following factors in adjudicating contract disputes, including insurance coverage disputes:

> *Text*—Almost all courts consider the language of the contract to be important in resolving insurance coverage and other contract disputes. Some courts are more avowedly "textualist" and may be extremely reluctant and even unwilling to consider other indicia of meaning where policy language is sufficiently clear to enable the court to reach a reasonable resolution of the dispute.

> *Party Intent*—Party intent is the specific intent of the parties and the conscious design of the parties in entering the contract. For example, a widget manufacturer may have purchased property insurance with business interruption coverage and with a specific intent (hopefully one shared by the insurer) that it would be compensated for any decline in sales after a fire until such time as the facility is restored to full capacity.

---

11. *See, e.g.*, Antonin Scalia, *The Rule of Law as a Law of Rules*, 56 U. Chi. L. Rev. 1175 (1989); Antonin Scalia & Bryan A. Garner, Reading Law: The Interpretation of Legal Texts (2012) (advocating textualism and use of canons of construction rather than examination of drafter intent, purpose, or situational context). *See also* Frederick Schauer, Playing by The Rules: A Defense of Formalism (1992).

*Purpose of the Agreement*—Purpose is similar to intent but is a broader concept that goes beyond the specific intent or expectations of the parties and focuses more on the general objectives of the insuring arrangement. For example, a policy may be procured to protect a driver from automobile liability. Neither the driver nor the insurer may have specifically had a conscious thought as to whether the policy covers claims brought about when the policyholder drives negligently because he has first negligently failed to get adequate sleep or negligently has had more alcohol to drink than his digestive system can safely absorb. However, the purpose of the insuring agreement—protecting the policyholder from claims due to his negligence—suggests that there should be coverage and that ordinarily such claims will not be excluded on intentional act grounds.

*Reasonable Expectations*—Party expectations are a cousin of party intent. In contract law generally, courts frequently consider the expectations of the parties in determining contract meaning where the text of the contract is insufficiently clear. For insurance policies, the expectations issue has taken on additional importance, perhaps because the widely standardized insurance policy language often does not speak sufficiently to the dispute before the court.

*Unconscionability and Public Policy*—Courts also frequently consider whether a policy term is unconscionable or violates public policy. If so, the court may either modify the meaning or force of the term or strike it from the contract altogether. At a minimum, most courts will refuse to enforce a provision that is unconscionable or violative of public policy. Unconscionability is generally defined as a term that is unreasonably favorable to one party.

Some commentators further divide the field into procedural unconscionability and substantive unconscionability. *See, e.g.,* Arthur A. Leff, *Unconscionability and the Code: The Emperor's New Clause,* 115 U. Pa. L. Rev. 485 (1967) (arguably defining this dichotomy for classifying unconscionability). Procedural unconscionability, or "bargaining naughtiness" (Leff's phrase) is what might be called "dirty tricks" of contracting: misrepresentation, misleading the other party, hiding certain terms in the fine print or in a section of the contract where one would not expect it (e.g., placing exclusionary language in the "Conditions" section of a policy), pressuring the other party into hasty agreement, duress, coercion, and the like. Substantive unconscionability occurs when the contract provision (no matter how clear, prominent, and even voluntary at the time of contracting) is simply too unreasonably favorable for one party and/or too unreasonably detrimental for another. For example, a wager about the sun rising tomorrow with 10:1 odds in favor of the party betting on another day to come is simply too unfavorable, even in the most uncertain and troubled times.

When courts and commentators refer to "unconscionability" they usually mean substantive unconscionability rather than procedural unconscionability, although some elements of both are usually required before a court will deem a contract term unconscionable.

The doctrine has two elements: one procedural and the other substantive.

Procedural unconscionability looks to the circumstances surrounding contract formation. Its definition varies among jurisdictions from the bare fact that a seller offered a standard form on a take-it-or-leave-it-basis, to unequal bargaining power plus an inability to obtain the goods or services elsewhere, to a holistic evaluation of the parties' standing in life and the disputed clause's font size. Substantive unconscionability focuses on what the clause at issue accomplishes. It applies to grossly unfair clauses....

*See* David Horton, *Unconscionability in the Law of Trusts*, 84 Notre Dame L. Rev. 1675 (2009).

Many types of procedural unconscionability are better known by another name such as fraud, misrepresentation, duress, or coercion. However, a number of insurance unconscionability cases (and reasonable expectations cases as well) could be characterized as procedural unconscionability cases when the court attempts to protect the policyholder from hidden or misleading contract terms woven into a long, complex, standardized insurance policy.

# § 2.05. The Ambiguity Factor

In addition, courts frequently apply the "ambiguity rule" of construing unclear policy language against the drafter and also utilize a number of canons of construction (discussed at greater length below) as a means of aiding their interpretation of contract text. As discussed below, courts vary to degree in the zeal with which they apply the ambiguity canon or rule of *contra proferentem* (a Latin term meaning "against the drafter").[12] Some invoke the canon almost as soon as finding the policy text unclear[13] while most tend to use the canon as a tiebreaker to guide decision when the textual ambiguity cannot be resolved by resort to nontextual factors.[14]

---

12. The term contra proferentem is often spelled "contra proferentum." Casebook authors are in some dispute over the preferred spelling but will attempt to consistently used "contra proferentem" throughout this casebook. We will also refrain from italicizing the term except when quoting from an original source that placed the term in italics.

13. *See, e.g., Eli Lilly & Co. v. Home Ins. Co.*, 482 N.E.2d 467 (Ind. 1985), *cert. denied*, 479 U.S. 1060 (1987) (holding that under Indiana law, contra proferentem canon is to be invoked upon a finding of textual ambiguity and resisting arguments to consider extrinsic evidence prior to utilizing ambiguity principle). *Accord Vlastos v. Sumitomo Marine & Fire Ins. Co.*, 707 F.2d 775 (3rd Cir. 1983) (applying Pennsylvania law) (finding term "occupied as a janitor's residence" sufficiently ambiguous that policyholder did not lose coverage when the third floor was also home to a massage parlor; court gives little attention to extrinsic evidence but does appear to consider whether purpose of policy provision (safety) was served if janitor stayed on the third floor at least some amount of time).

14. *See, e.g., Myers v. Merrimack Mut. Fire Ins. Co*, 788 F. 2d 468 (7th Cir. 1986) (applying Illinois law) (finding phrase "in the process of construction" unambiguous); *Deni Assocs. v. State Farm Fire & Cas. Ins. Co.*, 711 So. 2d 1135 (1998) (finding absolute pollution exclusion language unambiguous as a matter of law when applied to accidental ammonia spill while moving blueprint machine). *See also Goldman v. Metro. Life Ins. Co.*, 5 N.Y.3d 561, 841 N.E.2d 742 (2005) (no ambiguity in use of word "annual" to describe premium payments).

Most courts do agree on the basic definition of ambiguity: a term is ambiguous if it is reasonably susceptible to two or more reasonable constructions. *See* JEFFREY W. STEMPEL & ERIK S. KNUTSEN, STEMPEL & KNUTSEN ON INSURANCE COVERAGE § 4.08[b] (4th ed. 2016); BARRY R. OSTRAGER & THOMAS R. NEWMAN, HANDBOOK ON INSURANCE COVERAGE DISPUTES § 1.02 (16th ed. 2016). Note that the specter of the law student's first year—the "reasonable person"—once again rears his moderate and mainstream head. For a term to be ambiguous, the party arguing this position must be able to articulate an objectively reasonable interpretation that augers in its favor and do this without going through unreasonable linguistic gymnastics. Courts frequently state that they will not "torture" or "distort" contract language in order to create an ambiguity.

Despite wide acceptance of these general ground rules, actual application by the courts leads to different views concerning what constitutes ambiguity. *See, e.g., Northwest Airlines, Inc. v. Globe Indem. Co.*, 303 Minn. 16, 26, 225 N.W.2d 831, 837 (1975) (finding that "the very fact that [the parties to the contract take views] so contrary" indicates ambiguity); *Alliance Life Ins. Co. v. Ulysses Volunteer Fireman's Relief Ass'n*, 215 Kan. 937, 948, 529 P.2d 171, 180 (1974) (conflicting case precedent attaching different meaning to term is conclusive proof of ambiguity); *Metropolitan Property & Liability Ins. Co. v. Finlayson*, 751 P.2d 254, 257 (Utah Ct. App. 1988), *vacated*, 766 P.2d 437 (Utah Ct. App. 1989) (differing precedents not conclusive but strongly suggest ambiguity); *Cody v. Remington Electric Shavers, Div. of Sperry Rand Corp.*, 179 Conn. 494, 427 A.2d 810, 812 (1980) (irrespective of variant precedent, reviewing court must be convinced that proffered alternative interpretation is objectively reasonable).

One need not be a cynic to conclude that the simple truth is that contract language is ambiguous if counsel can convince the court that it is ambiguous. In general, however, courts have rejected the view that a word or term is ambiguous if it has been assigned different meanings by the courts. Frankly, we disagree. Judges are assumed to be reasonable people, which by definition means that different conclusions as to the meaning of words like "accident" and "occurrence" strongly suggest the word is unclear. But in many cases, the ambiguity can be resolved through consultation of other evidence so that the drafter of the contract (almost always the insurer) is not reflexively punished by application of the rule of contra proferentem. But judges, particularly textualist judges, are reluctant to take this fork in the road and instead prefer to find (we would say "pretend") that judicial divergence is not indicative of ambiguity.

Beyond the simplicity of defining ambiguity and the unpredictability of an individual judge's view of the clarity of contract language in a particular context, one can also analyze contract language according to the types of uncertainty that may be created by the contract language. Perhaps the most widely accepted subdivision in this regard has been provided by Professor E. Allan Farnsworth, first in a law review article[15] and then in his prominent treatise.[16]

---

15. *See* E. Allan Farnsworth, *"Meaning" in the Law of Contracts*, 76 YALE L.J. 939 (1967).

16. *See* E. ALLAN FARNSWORTH, CONTRACTS (4th ed. 2004). Prof. Farnsworth was a Reporter for the American Law Institute's *Restatement (Second) of Contracts*, which in our view makes him a pretty mainstream figure in American contracts jurisprudence. Farnsworth and the rest of the modern legal

A contract provision is *vague* when it fails to set forth a concept into a clearly bound class but rather sets forth a general norm over which there can be a considerable range of variation. A classic illustration is the word "green" which although perhaps not unclear to the average person is vague in that it can be almost yellow in one application and nearly blue at the other end of the continuum surrounding the word.[17]

The ambiguity in a contract provision may be *ambiguity of term* where the same word is capable of more than one meaning. This concept is illustrated by the two ships named *Peerless* in the famous case *Raffles v. Wichelhaus*, 159 Eng. Rep. 375 (Ex. 1864).

The ambiguity may, however, be *ambiguity of syntax*, in which the arrangement of the words in the contract create uncertainty for the reader. For example, does an exclusion in a health insurance policy referring to any "disease of organs of the body not common to both sexes" bar coverage for a fibroid tumor (capable of afflicting either gender) in the uterus (an organ found only in women)?[18] The uncertainty comes not so much from the multiple meanings of any particular word but from the organization of the words,

---

profession obviously built upon the monumental contract studies of Corbin and Williston, who used different terminology and emphasis but touched upon the issue of the different causes of lack of clarity in contract text. *See generally* ARTHUR L. CORBIN, CONTRACTS (1960); SAMUEL WILLISTON, CONTRACTS (1st ed. 1920).

17. *See* FARNSWORTH, CONTRACTS § 7.8, at 454 (citation omitted).

18. *See* FARNSWORTH, CONTRACTS § 7.8, at 455. Examples of ambiguity of syntax abound. Common sources are toy or other assembly instructions and the *Federal Register*. Even well-edited newspapers and periodicals can produce some passages where, quite literally, one guess is as good as another regarding meaning. Consider the following example from the front-page news summary of the *Wall Street Journal*: "Women run a higher risk of breast cancer after taking estrogen-only pills for at least 15 years, says a study overseen by Harvard-affiliated researchers." *See What's News*, WALL ST. J., May 9, 2006, at A1, col. 3. Do women who take estrogen pills face an increased risk of breast cancer for 15 years thereafter or do women only face this increased risk should they consume the estrogen pills for some 15 years? The bare text quoted above would permit either interpretation. Or, put another way, either interpretation would seem reasonable. A reader may have a preferred interpretation. For example, we think the news item more likely was intended to mean that women must be taking the estrogen pill for 15 years or more to face the increased risk. But although this is our preferred interpretation, we would be hard-pressed to refute the contrary construction of the new item. The text supports either interpretation and it cannot be definitively said that one interpretation is clearly correct or that the other is unreasonable.

Fortunately, there are usually means of resolving such a dispute rather than reflexively ruling against the drafter of the problematic language. For example, a look at the full Harvard study would probably reveal quite quickly the study's actual posited relationship between breast cancer and estrogen pills. Applied to contract disputes and insurance coverage questions, this usually means that the information other than simply the specific written term in dispute can be used to resolve the dispute. However, as discussed below, if there are no additional indicia of meaning, the ambiguity is resolved against the drafter of the problematic language.

which make it uncertain whether the thing that must not be the exclusive affliction of any one gender is the disease (tumor) or the organ (uterus). As we can see, it makes a difference.

A contract may also have *contextual ambiguity* in that it uses words inconsistently throughout the document or on its face contains conflicting terms that cannot be reconciled. In such a case, the instrument is unclear even if a particular term in isolation would be clear.[19]

The type of ambiguity may exert at least a subtle pull on judicial interpretation. For example, if an asserted uncertainty in a contract is vagueness, the problem may perhaps be easily resolved through extrinsic evidence and leave no remaining linguistic uncertainty for the court. Ambiguity of term may similarly be dispelled upon consideration of the common understanding of a term in the relevant field in which the insurance is written. However, where the asserted ambiguity is based on context or syntax, the tension may not be easily resolved based on other evidence of contract meaning. In these types of cases, the contra proferentem canon may be more likely to be the basis for decision. But, of course, no one can be certain of that without conducting painstaking empirical analysis of a very large sum of court decisions.

Courts and commentators have divided to some extent on the wisdom and benefits of the rule. Some have embraced fairly aggressive use of contra proferentem in order streamline decision making or level the playing field between policyholders and insurers.

A supporting rationale is that insurers tend to have more extensive experience and expertise that permits them to "draft around" anticipated contract disputes to the disadvantage of policyholders, who might even think they have coverage despite reading the complex language of insurance policies. From the perspective of these observers, insurers are entitled to enjoy the fruits of the written contract but must earn those benefits through sufficiently clear and careful drafting that there is no room for serious doubt as to the meaning of the policy text. If the insurer falls short of this desired level of draftsmanship, the policyholder "deserves" to win these close cases.[20]

Other commentators take almost the opposite view and would like to see the contra proferentem principle banished forever as unfairly slanted toward the policyholder.

---

19. *See* FARNSWORTH, CONTRACTS § 7.8, at 456; ROBERT H. JERRY, II AND DOUGLAS R. RICHMOND, UNDERSTANDING INSURANCE LAW § 25A[a] (6th ed. 2018). *See, e.g., Rice v. Shelter Mut. Ins. Co.*, 301 S.W.3d 43, 49 (Mo. 2009) ("inconsistent and irreconcilable provisions in an insurance policy create an ambiguity that will be resolved in favor of the insured").

20. *See George Backer Management Corp. v. Acme Quilting Co.*, 385 N.E.2d 1062, 1065 (N.Y. 1978) (permissible to resolve dispute against drafter of contract because drafter could have selected words that clearly set forth the drafter's current preferred reading of the instrument).

We tend to regard the assault on the ambiguity doctrine as overdone. In the first place, contra proferentem is not peculiar to insurance law. It is a part of plain vanilla contract law. *See* E. Allan Farnsworth, Contracts §§ 7.7–7.10 (4th ed. 2004). However, the ambiguity canon probably is more actively invoked for insurance cases.[21] We are in sympathy with the critics' view that courts should not resort too quickly to the ambiguity tiebreaker in order to decide cases. However, if ambiguity analysis and the contra proferentem canon is employed with restraint and used more as a tiebreaker of last resort rather than an "insurer loses" canon, we believe the ambiguity principle has an important and legitimate role to play in the determination of insurance coverage disputes. *See* Stempel & Knutsen, *supra*, § 4.08 (defending restrained use of ambiguity analysis and finding criticisms of contra proferentem exaggerated); Peter Nash Swisher, *Judicial Interpretation of Insurance Contract Disputes: Toward a Realistic Middle Ground Approach*, 57 Ohio St. L.J. 543 (1996) (concluding that limited role for ambiguity canon is apt as part of comprehensive approach to determining insurance policy meaning).

One commentator has suggested that "[i]f an insurer uses consumer research to test policy language before adopting it, the insurer can present the results of the research to rebut a finding of ambiguity." *See* Michelle Boardman, *Insuring Understanding: The Tested Language Defense*, 95 Iowa L. Rev. 1075 (2010) (italics removed from original). Another scholar has suggested placing the ambiguity tiebreaker further back in the queue of techniques for assessing policy meaning. Under this methodology,

> [c]ourts ought to [first] discern the "subjective purpose" of the insurance contract, namely the joint subjective intent of the parties. Second, in those cases where subjective intent cannot be inferred by the court, it should resort to the objective purpose of the contract by employing the reasonable expectations test. Third, and finally, when courts cannot identify the objective purpose of the contract, they ought to use the interpretation against the drafter rule.

Dudi Schwartz, *Interpretation and Disclosure in Insurance Contracts*, 21 Loyola Consumer L. Rev. 105 (2008) (italics removed from original).

## § 2.06. The Hierarchy and Coordination of Mainstream Contract Interpretation Factors

In some instances, a court or judicial system (e.g., a particular state) emphasizes one or more approaches to the derision of others. In most cases, however, all of the following approaches or factors discussed below may permissibly be used to resolve

---

21. *See Gaunt v. John Hancock Mut. Life Ins. Co.*, 160 F.2d 599 (2d Cir. 1954) (per Learned Hand, J.) (applying Connecticut law) (contra proferentem invoked more frequently for insurance disputes than other cases).

contract interpretation disputes—but there is normally a hierarchy in the court's invocation of and preference for the various approaches. For example, some supreme courts have self-consciously laid out a rank ordering of the priority of the mainstream approaches and a process of applying them.[22]

Most commonly, a court will first look at the language of the insurance policy or other contract. If the language is clear, the court will resolve the dispute based on its view of the linguistic meaning of the text. If the text is unclear, a court generally then considers non-textual evidence of meaning, although individual courts may differ in the relative weight of the non-textual factors, which include any specific intent of the parties, the purpose of the contract, and the expectations of the parties. At this juncture, a court may consider "extrinsic" evidence outside the four corners of the face of the contract. This extrinsic evidence can take the form of other documents reflecting contract meaning such as a letter of understanding or notes of a meeting, or they may involve testimony as to oral statements of the parties of their agents. If none of these interpretative tools produces a conclusive construction of the disputed policy term, the court then invokes the ambiguity principle and rules against the drafter of the unclear term.

## § 2.07. Attitudes toward Extrinsic Evidence

Alumni of first-year Contracts undoubtedly remember that most courts put strictures on the receipt of extrinsic evidence. Prominent among these is the Parol Evidence Rule, which provides that where there is a written "integrated" agreement, courts should not consider extrinsic evidence that contradicts the text of the writing. As you might remember from Contracts class, the parol evidence rule is often construed to bar consideration only of pre-contract negotiations rather than all extrinsic evidence, although many courts (incorrectly in our view) apply the rule broadly as a bar to all extrinsic evidence. Courts also divide over the degree to which a recital in the document indicating its integrated status is conclusive or whether the court may hear extrinsic evidence as to whether the document was intended to be a full and final memorialization of the agreement (the latter approach is the majority view, but not overwhelmingly).

As you also remember from Contracts, the parol evidence rule does not apply to agreements made after the memorialization of the integrated contract document. Further, a party's reasonable detrimental reliance may supersede the parol evidence rule.

---

22. *See, e.g., Bank of the West v. Superior Court*, 2 Cal. 4th 1254, 10 Cal. Rptr. 2d 538, 833 P.2d 545 (1992) (setting forth hierarchy of factors and order of their application to determine contract meaning); *Smith v. Melson, Inc.*, 135 Ariz. 119, 659 P.2d 1264 (1983) (same, but with somewhat different approach and emphasis). In *Minkler v. Safeco Ins. Co. of America*, 232 P.3d 612, 616 (Cal. 2010), the California Supreme Court reiterated its support for this hierarchy of factors.

Consistent with our concerns about excessive textualism in contract construction, we are not fans of the parol evidence rule. It was born out of the suspicion that lay juries and even judges would be misled by smooth-talking litigants. Therefore, like Ulysses chaining himself to the mast to avoid succumbing to the Sirens' song, judges operating under the rule refuse to consider anything but the written contract document before the court, which keeps jurors from seeing or hearing other evidence. But this public policy rationale for the parol evidence rule ignores that a smooth talking litigant has as good or a better chance of deceiving the adjudicator about the meaning of text as about what was said at a meeting or whether there the parties had an implicit understanding regarding performance. The feared mythical charismatic distorter can persuasively argue for an interpretation of isolated text that may in fact not represent the actual agreement of the parties, let alone the overall objective and purpose of the contract. Arguably, this distorter has less freedom to distort when confronted with actual facts, which may be less malleable than the range of word meanings.

Comparative law analysis lends support to our view. The parol evidence rule is a creature of Anglo-American law. EU countries do not follow it. *See* UNIDROIT PRINCIPLES OF EUROPEAN CONTRACT LAW ART. 1.2 (2016) ("Nothing in these Principles requires a contact, statement or any other act to be made in or evidenced by a particular form. It may be proved by any means, including witnesses."). Insurance is big business throughout Europe, with Germany (e.g., Munich Re, Hanover) and Switzerland (e.g., Zurich, Swiss Re) home to some of the largest insurers in the world. They do business perfectly well without the parol evidence rule and find it head-scratchingly curious that Americans seem so committed to it. Some European lawyers argue that the rule has more potential for mischief than accuracy, pointing out that even among insurance professionals, it is common for persons to accept or even sign written contract documents that do not reflect or that even contradict specific understandings of the parties made in reaching the agreement.

But in the U.S., most courts will not consider extrinsic evidence if the court's initial examination of the document does not reveal any uncertainty as to meaning. However, some jurisdictions are willing to consider extrinsic information at the outset of the examination of the contract in order to better understand the written text and determine if the asserted meanings of the disputed text are plausible. *See, e.g., Pacific Gas & Electric Co. v. G. W. Thomas Drayage & Rigging Co.*, 69 Cal. 2d 33, 38–40, 69 Cal. Rptr. 561, 564–566, 442 P.2d 641, 644–46 (1968); *Berg v. Hudesman*, 801 P.2d 222, 230 (Wash. 1990). *See also Trident Ctr. v. Connecticut Gen. Life Ins. Co.*, 847 F.2d 564, 567–69 (9th Cir. 1988) (Kosinski, J., dissenting) (criticizing this approach but finding it firmly rooted in California law).

In our view, most courts first look at policy text and attempt to determine if the contract text standing alone is sufficiently clear to enable the court to adjudicate the dispute. If it is, the court will resist examining extrinsic information, even as a check on its accuracy of hermeneutic interpretation, unless there are compelling circumstances. But where counsel can make the case that there is more to the agreement than its bare text, courts generally are willing to hear additional evidence even if the text initially seemed clear.

For example, a party may be able to show that a seemingly clear term (e.g., "chicken") has a specific meaning in a given industry. *See* E. ALLAN FARNSWORTH, CONTRACTS § 7.9 (3d ed. 1999); *Frigaliment Importing Co. v. B.N.S. International Sales Corp.*, 190 F. Supp. 116, 121 (S.D.N.Y. 1960) (dispute between the parties as to whether "chicken" meant chicken suitable for stewing and processing or meant that chicken must be broiler quality; court ruled that industry understanding was satisfied by stewing chicken but that buyer claiming right to broiler quality chicken could prevail if it carried the burden of persuasion to show that the parties intended the narrower meaning of broiler quality chicken; finding burden unsatisfied, court ruled for seller). As students surely remember from first-year contracts, even a proper name can be the subject of a dispute that cannot be resolved solely through examination of contract text. *See Raffles v. Wichelhaus*, 159 Eng. Rep. 375 (Ex. 1964) (two ships named "Peerless"; court finds mutual mistake preventing formation of contract).

### Extrinsic Evidence as Distinguished from the Parol Evidence Rule

A court's use of extrinsic evidence should be distinguished from the parol evidence rule. Although courts often mistakenly use the terms interchangeably, they are distinct concepts. The parol evidence rule refers to evidence of pre-contract negotiation and generally bars reference to such evidence unless the contract is ambiguous on its face. Courts facing such situations are self-consciously concerned that one party may attempt to rewrite the actual written contract by falsely claiming an earlier oral understanding that was subsumed in the written contract.

Extrinsic evidence can include information about pre-contract oral statements by the parties but also refers to a range of information that may shed light on contract meaning. Extrinsic evidence includes not only other documents and statements surrounding the contract but the course of dealing of the parties and the customs and practices in the particular field that is the subject of the contract (a concept often referred to as "usage in trade"). Extrinsic evidence can also include the commercial, legal, social, or historical backdrop upon which the contract was created. For example, if a contract is made during wartime, this may have implications for the understanding and reasonable expectations of the parties to the contract.

If, after applying the hierarchy of these interpretative factors, a court continues to find the mater uncertain, the court will usually apply contra proferentem as tiebreaker or determinative factor of last resort. However, as discussed above, some courts will deploy the ambiguity canon sooner in the analysis, perhaps in lieu of considering extrinsic evidence of meaning.

Courts also vary considerably in their fondness for consideration of public policy and fairness in construing a contract. However, where the court employs unconscionability or public policy analysis, this usually occurs near the end of the process, although perhaps before invocation of the ambiguity principle. As a practical matter, it is difficult for a court to determine whether a contract provision is unconscionable or violative of public policy until the court determines what the provision means. The Court may modify or refuse to enforce a provision that is unconscionable or violative of public policy.

### The ALI Approach to Insurance Policy Interpretation

In its *Restatement of the Law, Liability Insurance*, approved at its May 2018 Annual Meeting, the American Law Institute endorsed an approach to policy construction that expressly supports a textualist approach but one with reasonably broad support for consideration of contextual factors. The "RLLI,"[23] as it has come to be called, provides that:

> The plain meaning of an insurance policy term is the single meaning to which the language of the term is reasonably susceptible when applied to the facts of the claim at issue in the context of an entire insurance policy.

> If the insurance policy term has a plain meaning when applied to the facts of the claim at issue, the term is interpreted according to that meaning.

> An insurance policy is ambiguous if there is more than one meaning to which the language of the term is reasonably susceptible when applied to the facts of the claim at issue in the context of the entire insurance policy. An ambiguous term is interpreted as specified in § 4.[24]

The RLLI argues that its proposed plain meaning approach "promotes consistency of interpretation of insurance policies using the same language in similar contests, giving the parties to standardized insurance policies greater confidence that they will be uniformly enforced."[25]

Notwithstanding that the RLLI endorses a plain meaning textual approach, which is generally preferred by insurers—and commercial entities in general—to more contextual approaches,[26] this portion of the RLLI received substantial insurance in-

---

23. Because the RLLI, as its name implies, focuses on liability insurance, it will generally be discussed in Chapter 9. However, because its provisions regarding interpretation will presumably impact other types of insurance, we address them in this chapter regarding insurance policy construction.

24. AMERICAN LAW INSTITUTE, RESTATEMENT OF THE LAW OF LIABILITY INSURANCE § 3 (Revised Proposed Final Draft No. 2, September 7, 2018) (approved at May 2018 ALI Annual Meeting; published in 2019) ("RLLI"). Comment f. to § 3 defines an ambiguous term as one "that has at least two interpretations to which the language of the term is reasonably susceptible when applied to the facts of the claim in question." Section 4 sets forth the widely accepted rule that an ambiguous term is "interpreted against the party that supplied the term" but adds that this is not the case if the party authoring the unclear language "persuades the court that a reasonable person in the policyholder's position would not give the term that interpretation." *See* RLLI § 4.

25. RLLI § 3, *Comment a.* Although criticism of the plain meaning rule itself is beyond the scope of this book, it should be noted that this justification for a more exclusively textual approach is not particularly persuasive in a world where different courts each purport to find insurance policy language clear but construe exactly the same language to mean different things. *Compare, e.g., Hazen Paper Co. v. U.S. Fidelity & Guar. Co.*, 555 N.E.2d 576 (Mass. 1990) (administrative proceeding seeking environmental remediation a "suit" within the meaning of CGL policy) *with Foster-Gardner, Inc. v. National Union Fire Ins. Co.*, 959 P.2d 265 (Cal. 1998) (government action seeking remediation not a "suit" under CGL policy).

dustry criticism, albeit primarily directed toward earlier drafts that gave less emphasis to text and exhibited greater receptiveness to extrinsic evidence.[27] Insurer opposition to § 3 (and to the RLLI generally) has continued, perhaps because the comments to the section continue to exhibit more receptiveness to extrinsic evidence than one would expect from the black letter of the Section.

> Generally accepted sources that courts consult when determining the plain meaning of an insurance policy term include: dictionaries, court decisions, statutes and regulations, and secondary legal authority such as treatises and law review articles. Such sources of meaning are not "extrinsic evidence" under any definition of that term. Rather, they are legal authorities that courts consult when determining the plain meaning of an insurance policy term, which is a legal question.[28]

The RLLI notes that "[m]any courts that follow a strict plain-meaning rule also consider custom, practice, and usage when determining the plain meaning of insurance policies" where this is "between parties who can reasonably be expected to have transacted with knowledge of that custom, practice, or usage."[29] Although this might sound like use of extrinsic evidence to a reasonable person, the RLLI finds this sufficiently within the plain meaning approach so long as "such sources of meaning can be discerned from public sources" through only "limited discovery."[30]

The RLLI notes that "[c]onsideration of custom, practice, and usage at the plain-meaning stage does not open the door to extrinsic evidence such as drafting history, course of dealing, or precontractual negotiations."[31] The comment adds that "it is important to note that the term 'extrinsic evidence' does not include all sources of meaning that are extrinsic to the policy. [For example, the] facts of the claim at issue are extrinsic to the policy [but] all courts that follow the plain meaning rule permit consideration of claim facts and many of those courts also permit consideration of trade custom, practice, and usage when determining whether the term has a plain meaning and, if so, what that meaning is."[32]

The RLLI will not, of course, end debate about what constitutes extrinsic evidence. For example, lawyers and judges appear to divide on the question of whether use of a dictionary is use of extrinsic evidence. The literal answer must be "yes," in that the dictionary is evidence of word meaning outside the four corners of the insurance

---

26. *See* Geoffrey Miller, *Bargains Bicoastal: New Light on Contract Theory*, 31 Cardozo L. Rev. 1475 (2010).

27. *See* ALI Website, ali.org, Comments submitted regarding RLLI.

28. RLLI § 3, *Comment b.*

29. RLLI § 3, *Comment c.*

30. RLLI § 3, *Comment c. Comment c* uses as an example of limited discovery proof "through an affidavit of an expert in the trade or business, who is subject to deposition, but without the need for extensive document requests." *Id.*

31. RLLI § 3, *Comment c.*

32. RLLI § 3, *Comment b.*

policy itself (whereas a resort to the Definitions section of a policy would not be use of extrinsic evidence, but merely part of the process of construing the policy as a whole).[33] In practice, however, many if not most courts appear not to regard consulting a dictionary as the use of extrinsic evidence.[34]

Notwithstanding that insurers have been the primary critics of the RLLI, including § 3, this Section is arguably a victory for insurers in that it expressly rejects decisions receptive to receipt of a wide variety of extrinsic evidence in all cases and also disputes the contextualist approach of the *Second Restatement of Contracts*. As policyholder counsel have pointed out, it is a bit jarring to have the same organization (ALI) endorse a contextualist approach for all contracts in 1981 and then reject it in favor of a more textual (albeit not strictly textual) approach for the particular contracts of insurance policies in 2018. Most policyholder lawyers would have preferred that the RLLI say nothing about contract interpretation per se.

The official ALI answer is that the bulk of case law regarding insurance supports the modified but not hypertextual approach of § 3. And it is correct that during the 40 years between the two *Restatements*, formalism and textualism have experienced a resurgence, with many states failing to follow the more contextualist contours of the *Contracts Restatement*. But support for a "plain meaning" textualist approach, although the majority rule, is not so lopsided as to preclude the RLLI from having favored a more contextual approach if that was deemed the better approach. The ALI position on *Restatements* is that they generally adopt the majority rule but are not bound to do so if the minority rule is regarded as better.

But the contract interpretation scorecard is not as lopsided as some would suggest. Classifying jurisdictions can be difficult because of variations in opinion writing, changes in precedent over time, differing case facts, lack of clarity in opinions, and individual variance among judges—variance that in our view often is greater than any doctrinal variation between jurisdictions. But one can reasonably deem as many as 14 states "contextualist" in their contract jurisprudence (California and its cousins) with 19 states (New York and its cousins) as textualist with the others resisting classification. Against this backdrop, the RLLI surely had sufficient leeway to adopt a broader approach to extrinsic evidence. That said, the RLLI version of plain meaning nonetheless permits ample judicial consideration of contextual factors even if it is not a fully contextualist approach.

---

33. Relatedly, one might ask: "If one needs a dictionary to be sure of the meaning of words in a contract document, then the text of the document is by definition insufficiently plain on its face."

34. *See, e.g., Hartford Fire Ins. Co. v. T.A. Loving Co.*, 1995 U.S. Dist. LEXIS 13598, at *7–8 (E.D.N.C. Aug. 29, 1995) (referring to definitions of "waterborne" in *Webster's Third New International Dictionary*; noting multiple definitions and selecting the definition more favorable to policyholder "in the context of this case"); *Martin v. Allianz Life Ins. Co.*, 573 N.W.2d 823, 825–26 (N.D. 1998) (giving literal enforcement to accident policy provision that loss of limb covered only if limb is "severed" within 90 days of event giving rise to injury and citing *American Heritage College Dictionary*).

# § 2.08. The Kinship between Contract Interpretation and Statutory Interpretation

Students who have worked in government or taken a legislation and statutory interpretation course will probably recognize the contract interpretation factors and hierarchy as similar to that governing the law of statutory interpretation. When interpreting statutes, courts deploy statutory text (which is analogous to contract text, particularly where the contract is standardized); legislative history (which is analogous to party intent or expectations); statutory purpose (which is similar to contract purpose) and may utilize particular sorts of extrinsic information, either from the legislative history, the application of the statute by administrative agencies, or commentary about the law. This is similar to the extrinsic information that may be considered by courts in a contract dispute.

Because insurance policies tend to be standardized and drafted through a collaborative process for many insurance products, insurance has aspects of private ordering akin to the rules and regulations of parts of the private sector such as a stock exchange or a commodity exchange. Courts and commentators have even begun to refer to the legislative history or "drafting history" of some insurance policy provisions. As with statutory interpretation, individual judges may differ in their views regarding contract interpretation. *See generally* Stempel, *The Insurance Policy as Statute*, 41 McGeorge L. Rev. 203 (2010); Jonathan R. Siegel, *The Inexorable Radicalization of Textualism*, 158 U. Pa. L. Rev. 117 (2009); Jonathan T. Molot, *The Rise and Fall of Textualism*, 106 Colum. L. Rev. 1 (2006); John F. Manning, *What Divides Textualists from Purposivists*, 106 Colum. L. Rev. 70 (2006).

The great insurance scholar Edwin Patterson touched on this in his classic article *The Interpretation and Construction of Contracts*, 65 Colum. L. Rev. 833 (1964). He listed the following maxims of interpretation (that today appear to be more commonly deployed by courts in statutory interpretation cases) as relevant to contract construction in general and insurance policy interpretation in particular.

*Noscitur a sociis.* The meaning of a word in a series is affected by others in the same series; or, a word may be affected by its immediate context....

*Ejusdem generis.* A general term joined with a specific one will be deemed to include only things that are like (of the same genus) as the specific one. This one if applied usually leads to a restrictive interpretation. *E.g.* S Contracts to sell R his farm together with the "cattle, hogs, and other animals." This would probably not include S's favorite house-dog, but might include a few sheep that S was rising for the market.

*Expressio unius exclusio alterius.* If one or more specific items are listed, without any more general or inclusive terms, other items although similar in kind are excluded. *E.g.*, S contracts to sell R his farm together with "the cattle and hogs on the farm." This language would be interpreted to exclude the sheep and S's favorite house-dog.

*Ut magis valeat quam pereat.* An interpretation that makes the contract valid is preferred to one that makes it invalid [a cousin to the principle that "law abhors a forfeiture].

*Omnia praesumuntur contra proferentem* [a/k/a the ambiguity doctrine].

*Id.* at 852–54 (also noting general rule of interpreting the contract as a whole, giving life to the purpose of the parties; that specific contract provisions normally control general provisions; that handwritten terms normally control over pre-printed terms; and that the public interest is preferred when construing a contract).

## § 2.09. The Role of Reasonable Expectations and the Semi-Controversial Reasonable Expectations "Doctrine"

Judge [then a professor] Robert Keeton in an influential 1970 Harvard Law Review article propounded a "reasonable expectations" test for determining coverage:

The objectively reasonable expectations of the [insurance] applicants and intended beneficiaries regarding the terms of insurance contracts [should] be honored even though painstaking study of the policy provisions would have negated those expectations.

Robert E. Keeton, *Insurance Law Rights at Variance with Policy Provisions (Part I)*, 83 Harv. L. Rev. 961, 963–64 (1970).

The Keeton test is what might be termed a "strong" form of the reasonable expectations formula in which the objectively reasonable expectations of the policyholder can trump even clear policy language to the contrary. Few jurisdictions embrace the reasonable expectations doctrine in this form. Even in cases where expectations are found to overcome clear language to the contrary, there are often additional interpretative or contextual factors favoring the policyholder. For example, there may be extrinsic evidence tending to establish coverage or the insurer may have engaged in deceptive conduct.

A far more common version of the reasonable expectations approach looks to policyholder expectations in cases where the policy language itself is ambiguous or insufficiently clear to establish a resolution of the dispute. In fact, this version of the reasonable expectations doctrine is the law in most states. *See* Stempel & Knutsen, *supra*, § 4.09 (noting different versions of reasonable expectations approach, giving illustrations, and noting factors that may affect strength of the doctrine).

The policyholder's expectations must be "objectively reasonable" if there is to be coverage based on those expectations. That is, they must be the type of expectations for coverage that could be held by a reasonable policyholder under the circumstances. Purely subjective of idiosyncratic expectations of coverage are not sufficient to bring coverage (although they will not preclude coverage if other contextual factors or interpretative ground rules auger in favor of coverage). Properly understood, reasonable expectations analysis should not be available to the policyholder where the expectations are outlandish.

Perhaps some of the resistance to expectations analysis by some judges and practically all insurers stems from the fact that it appears to be a one-way street in that the concept focuses on policyholder expectations and is normally articulated as focusing only on policyholder expectations. However, the concept could apply to all parties to an insuring arrangement (or any contract), including insurers, and could be used to inform the court as to the likely meaning of a doubtful contract provision. *See* Jeffrey W. Stempel, *Unmet Expectations: Undue Restriction of the Reasonable Expectations Approach and the Misleading Mythology of Judicial Role*, 5 CONN. INS. L.J. 181 (1998–1999).

For example, consistent with the fortuity concept discussed in Chapter 1, an insurer may reasonably believe that the liability policy it issued is not a "performance bond" and thus does not provide defense or indemnity to the contractor who is accused of shoddy work by a customer. *See, e.g., Weedo v. Stone-E-Brick, Inc.,* 81 N.J. 233, 405 A.2d 788 (1979) (making this very point in just such language in ruling that a standard liability policy does not provide coverage for a claim of unattractive, pitted stucco application by a builder). As the *Weedo* example suggests, courts may in fact actually be taking insurer expectations into account when rendering decisions but simply not using reasonable expectations language to describe their analysis. More likely, a court that is solicitous of insurer expectations as well as policyholder expectations will discuss the issue using terms like fortuity, the purpose of the insuring agreement, the understanding of the parties, or similar words that do not make reference to the reasonable expectations doctrine.

As the discerning reader has probably concluded by now, the reasonable expectations approach fits more comfortably under the tent of legal functionalism and tends to be less well-liked by legal formalists. A review of these articles and relevant sections of the major insurance law treatises will equip a lawyer to consider the potential utility of the approach in his or her own pending cases and will provide both citations to precedent in various jurisdictions as well as critical commentary on the doctrine. Today, the reasonable expectations approach, at least in modified form, is firmly established as part of the legal landscape but remains subject to disagreement and even controversy.

Despite the ongoing debate, expectations analysis in some form is found in many, perhaps most insurance law decisions. But, like the legal functionalism from which it is derived, the reasonable expectations doctrine both has majority status while continuing to face substantial criticism from formalist sources. The primary and most sustained criticism has been directed at the strong version of the concept expressed by Professor Keeton's "reasonable expectations" test, which can be read as suggesting that the insurance contract need not be read at all, nor interpreted by its plain and explicit language. This is anathema to a formalist theory of insurance contract interpretation and to formalism and formalists generally. Not surprisingly, they have attacked Keeton-style reasonable expectations with considerable vigor over the years.

Although several jurisdictions have become reasonable expectations jurisdictions a considerable time after the initial emergence of the doctrine during the 1970s, these courts have done so only to the extent of adopting the weaker or more moderate version of the doctrine that will not overcome clear policy language but is used only when policy language is insufficiently clear. *See, e.g., Max True Plastering Co. v. United States Fidelity & Guar. Co.*, 912 P.2d 861, 863–64, n.5 (Okla. 1996). There are also states that have rather emphatically rejected any role for expectations analysis. *See, e.g., Deni Assocs. v. State Farm Fire & Cas. Ins. Co.*, 711 So. 2d 1135 (Fla. 1998) (rejecting doctrine as too pro-policyholder and unnecessary because of other contract construction canons); *Allen v. Prudential Property & Casualty Ins. Co.*, 839 P.2d 798 (Utah 1992) (rejecting doctrine as attempt to rewrite contracts and suggesting that this would be illegitimate judicial activism because insurance policy language was approved by regulators from executive agency, the insurance department).[35]

Today, the reasonable expectations concept is well-established as (1) an aid to interpreting policy language generally and (2) a means of resolving ambiguity in policy terms absent other indicia of meaning. *See* Randy Maniloff & Jeffrey Stempel, General Liability Insurance Coverage: Key Issues in Every State, Ch. 20 (4th ed. 2018). A weak or moderate version of reasonable expectations analysis that proceeds in this manner is applicable in almost all states, although eight states (Florida, Illinois, Michigan, North Dakota, Ohio, South Carolina, South Dakota, and Utah) purport to reject at least the doctrine, if not the concept. A strong Keetonesque version of reasonable expectations analysis may be applicable in perhaps four states, depending on the continued strength of older precedent.

As with so many insurance issues, clear categorization is difficult. For example, Iowa continues to have as good law the strong version reasonable expectations precedent of *Rodman v. State Farm Mut. Auto. Ins.*, 208 N.W. 2d 903, 906 (Iowa 1973). However, the Iowa Supreme Court more recently found that the pollution exclusion in a general liability policy applied to bar coverage when a company was sued for the wrongful death of a worker overcome by carbon monoxide fumes while using the bathroom at the policyholder's plant (in which there was a flaw in the heating system)—a decision that, regardless of whether or not correct, would appear to violate the objectively reasonable expectations of a commercial policyholder (that when business invitees are hurt or killed on the premise due to alleged company negligence, the company's liability insurer will provide coverage). *See Bituminous Cas. Corp. v. Sand Livestock Sys.*, 728 N.W.2d 216, 222 (Iowa 2007). *See also Postell v. American Family Mut. Ins. Co.*, 823 N.W.2d 35, 48 (Iowa 2012) ("We have only applied the reasonable expectations doctrine to 'representations made by the insurer at the time of

---

35. We have been critical of this aspect of the *Allen* decision as reflecting an inaccurately crude misunderstanding of separation of powers principles. *See* Stempel & Knutsen, § 4.09[d]; Stempel, *Unmet Expectations: Undue Restriction of the Reasonable Expectations Approach and the Misleading Mythology of Judicial Role*, 5 Conn. Ins. L.J. 181 (1998–99).

policy negotiation and issuance'[.] ... However, we have recognized that there may be 'other circumstances attributable to the insurer' which could create such expectations.") (citations omitted).

# § 2.10. General Canons of Construction and Other Ground Rules of Contract Interpretation

In addition to various factors for consideration in construing contracts and a relative hierarchy for the use of these factors, courts have also established several axioms that govern the contract interpretation process.

*First*, contract interpretation is considered a *matter of law for the court to decide* rather than a question of fact for jury consideration. Certainly, the threshold question of whether a contract provision is ambiguous is considered a matter of law that the judge must decide. Consequently, insurance coverage disputes, like other contract cases, may be more susceptible to summary judgment than other cases that more frequently turn upon unavoidable factual disputes (e.g., tort cases where the issue is excessive speed or the color of a traffic light at time of impact). If the court finds the contested language unambiguous it may adjudicate the meaning of the contract provision as a matter of law without trial.

Because interpretation of an insurance policy is a question of law, appellate review of insurance policy construction is de novo, without the deference accorded trial courts under the clearly erroneous or abuse-of-discretion standards of review. Considering contract construction as a matter of law means that the judge(s) will determine the meaning of a contract, but disputed facts that may bear on contract construction are decided by the jury.

However, there will frequently be fact questions, the resolution of which will have implications for the court's determination of contract meaning. This is certainly true where the court's initial view was that the policy language was unclear absent resolution of fact issues in the case (e.g., Did the insurer promise that a given endorsement would not affect coverage? Did the policyholder know he had terminal cancer at the time he applied for the life insurance policy?). In addition, even where some aspects of coverage are determined as a matter of law by the court, there may be additional factual issues in the case concerning other policy terms, compliance with reporting requirements, the amount of loss, whether either party acted in bad faith, and so on.

*Second*, in interpreting insurance policies, courts seek to read the words as would an ordinary layperson viewing the document. Unless there are extenuating circumstances, the "plain meaning" assigned to a contract is the meaning it would receive from the mythical average person.

*Third*, and related to this, is the principle that words used in a contract are to be given their ordinary meaning rather than any specialized meaning.

*Fourth*—and in arguable tension with the previous canon—where the contract or insurance policy is specialized and peculiar to a given industry, the words will be given the technical or specialized meaning common for the words in that industry. This can include both technical terminology and usage in trade concepts.

*Fifth*, any course of dealing between the parties will usually be considered (although some courts will refuse to hear such evidence if they find the face of the contract unambiguous). In many interpretative hierarchies, any prior course of dealing between the parties is accorded more weight than the general understanding of a given industry. This concept is more apparent in the seemingly endless hypotheticals first-year law students receive about sales of widgets (and is codified for sale of goods transactions in UCC § 1-205). If the buyer has been accepting widgets with flat paint for five years, the court is unlikely to be moved by the buyer's argument that the last shipment was in breach because it was covered in flat paint rather than semi-gloss paint, even if the general industry standard for such widgets calls for semi-gloss paint.

Applied to insurance, an analogous example might be the regular receipt of late payments by the insurer or the insurer's historical acceptance of a very vaguely completed renewal questionnaire from the policyholder (designed to update the insurer on risks presented). If a loss occurs and a dispute arises, the insurer will probably not get very far arguing that the industry standard requires prompt payment or a very detailed renewal questionnaire. In the absence of such a course of dealing, however, the common understandings of the industry for this sort of policy can often influence the court's adjudication of what the insurance policy or the insurer-policyholder relationship may require.

Commentators also may distinguish between *course of dealing* (which relates to a series of separate contracts between the parties over time) and *course of performance* (which relates to the parties' prior activity in connection with the single contract currently in dispute). The principle underlying both is the same, but most observers would argue that course of performance takes precedence over course of dealing to the extent they are inconsistent with one another.

*Sixth*, in assessing the meaning of contract language, courts construe the entire contract and are not to focus myopically on a single word, phrase, or provision in isolation.

*Seventh*, courts strive to give effect to all terms and provisions of a contract and to render an interpretation that does not nullify any one contract provision through the meaning accorded to another part of the contract. Alternatively, the court may use other canons or sub-canons of construction such as: treating customized language as controlling over standardized language or treating a policy endorsement (a separate clause added to a standardized insurance policy) as controlling over contrary language in the policy either because it is

> more recent in time (many policies are changed by endorsement added to the main policy at the time of annual renewal or where the insurer wishes

to add an exclusion due to unforeseen circumstances; for example, many homeowner's insurers added exclusions eliminating coverage for toxic mold damage during the early 21st Century unless the damage was linked to another coverage even such as a burst pipe) or

more specific to the issue in question or

more customized than the standard, even "boilerplate," language of the body of the insuring agreement. Endorsements may or may not be themselves standardized. For example, the Insurance Services Office (ISO), which drafts policy provisions for insurers, publishes hundreds of specialized endorsements that may be used by insurers in "mix-and-match" fashion to establish the scope of an insuring agreement. In some cases, however, particularly where the risk insured is large and the participants sophisticated, the endorsement language may have been drafted by one of the parties or its agents specifically for the transaction at issue. This "ultra-customized" policy language is usually given the greatest precedence over other language and other factors bearing on contract meaning.

*Eighth*, courts will not interpret contract language in a manner that produces an "absurd result." Even if the language is clear on its face, it will not be enforced if the literal meaning of the words would produce an absurdity. For example, an insurance policy might in its insuring agreement state "insurer agrees to indemnify policyholder for covered loss, unless the CEO of insurer determines that it will adversely affect her stock option." Although the language is quite clear and gives the insurer substantial discretion to deny a covered claim, no court in the world (we hope) would ever apply the language literally. To do so would be too inconsistent with the purpose of insurance and the general contract norm of making mutually binding promises that expose the parties to mutual detriment, which would make literal application of this clear provision "absurd."

The absurd result canon (which is also a part of statutory interpretation) is not particularly well defined by the courts and has a certain "I know it when I see it" quality when used by judges. Similarly, when advocates argue for and against the absurd result canon, they tend to argue in generalities and platitudes rather than stating with precision the reasons why literal application of a clear term would produce an absurdity. This makes absurd result jurisprudence hard to classify and evaluate.

In addition, advocates, courts, and commentators may discuss a contract controversy in term of absurd result when other terminology, such as unconscionability or public policy, might better capture the concept. Thus, when the judicial system finds something to be an "absurd" result, the term may cover a wide range of possible reasons why contract language cannot be interpreted literally or why one linguistically possible construction of a contract is not a legally permissible construction of the term.

*Ninth*, although the insuring agreement of a policy is given its ordinary meaning, an insurer's attempt to rely on an exclusion negating coverage is given much closer scrutiny. Once the policyholder has met its burden of showing that it has experienced a loss within coverage (or faces a claim within coverage or potential within coverage regarding the liability insurer's duty to defend), a purportedly applicable exclusion will be narrowly construed and strictly construed against the insurer, with the insurer bearing the burden of persuasion to clearly demonstrate that the exclusion applies. In close cases, this assignment of the burden of persuasion can be determinative.

*Tenth*, where a policy provision is ambiguous, it will be construed against the drafter unless the ambiguity can be resolved by resort to other interpretative factors. A policy provision is considered ambiguous if it is subject to more than one objectively reasonable interpretation.

*Eleventh*, policy terms are to be interpreted in light of their purpose in the context of the entire policy and surrounding circumstances.

Despite this long list of factors, courts often tend to emphasize policy text and often read it broadly and very literally, sometimes in isolation, sometimes without regard to problems such as confirmation bias (reading a text to confirm a pre-existing view rather than with neutrality), false consensus bias (assuming that there is wide agreement with one's preferred reading of a text even though there is substantial difference of opinion) and to read broad language broadly.

## § 2.11. The Organization of the Insurance Policy and Insurance Policy Construction Canons

In addition, there are some maxims of construction that are particular to insurance policies. But in order to appreciate these special "insurance canons" one needs to appreciate the typical organization and architecture of an insurance policy. Although the following delineation of insurance policy organization is largely based on a standard general liability policy, other forms of insurance are not greatly disparate in organizational form.

*The Declarations Page*—The "dec sheet" as it is often called, summarizes the policy. It sets forth the identity of the policyholder or "named insured" and the insurer and also usually includes information such as the location and contract data of the parties, including any agents or brokers involved in the transaction. The dec sheet also will set forth the type of coverage purchased, the policy limits, the premium charged, and the policy period and effective dates. Where the policy limits differ according particular coverages provided in the policy, the separate limits are usually set forth. The dec sheet also will contain the policy number and list all endorsements that are part of the policy (or at least it should). Also included are the names of other insureds such as a mortgagee, loss payee, or additional insured. Along with the policy limits, any applicable deductible or self-insured retention will be set forth. In a property policy, the dec sheet also usually gives the physical location and description of any covered property or operations. If the policy is one of excess insurance, it will usually state the "attachment point" at which the excess insurance takes over after the exhaustion of underlying primary insurance.

The policy limits are always set forth by "loss," "occurrence," or "claim" covered (more on that in a minute). Modern policies also usually contain an "aggregate limit" that caps the insurer's responsibility at a certain amount, no matter how many losses (for property insurance), occurrences (for liability insurance), or claims (for liability insurance) may take place during the policy period. Life and health policies are a bit different. Because health policies are usually written on a group basis, they tend to be more like a private regulatory regime for the group covered. But there are also aggregate limits in these areas. The life insurance policy pays a set amount per life, and death comes but once. Health policies typically also contain an ultimate cap on the insurer's liability. Consequently, an insured afflicted with more than one catastrophic illness in a lifetime may run out of health insurance.

Insurance policies are often written on an annual basis, but the effective dates frequently do not begin or end on a calendar year basis. Policies are also frequently written for a multi-year period, although a policy period of more than three years is unusual. The dec sheet and policy can be strikingly vague as to whether limits stated in the policy apply to the entire multi-year period or are per annum limits. Where the policy is not specific, the aggregate limits are generally regarded as per annum limits.

A policy is usually written for and purchased by a named insured. When we use the term "policyholder" in this casebook, we are usually referring to the named insured but may also use the term to refer to any entity that is covered under the policy. Strictly speaking, the policy itself will usually refer to a "named insured" or an "insured" and will define who is an "insured" under the policy. For example, the named insured may be a corporate policyholder is an artificial entity that acts through human agents, who are "insureds" when acting within the scope of their employment. It would be impossible to conceive of insurance for a corporation without treating as "insureds" the corporate agents acting within their scope of employment. Policies may also specifically add on "additional insureds" who are not obviously part of the named insured's organization but are logically connected to the policyholder's activities and the nature of the coverage sought. For example, subcontractors for a housing contractor are often additional insureds under the contractor's general liability policy.

*The Insuring Agreement*—This is the portion of the policy that sets forth in fairly succinct detail the scope of coverage and describes what is insured under the policy. The insuring agreement generally states that it will provide coverage for certain events in return for premium paid as more precisely defined in the policy as a whole. For example, a standard property insurance policy provides coverage for losses resulting from physical injury to the insured property. A standard liability policy provides coverage for amounts for which the policyholder becomes liable through judgment or settlement if the claim arises out of a covered "occurrence," which is usually defined to exclude intentionally inflicted injury. The liability policy commonly also obligates the insurer to provide a defense to the claim.

*Exclusions*—After the insuring agreement sets forth the basic boundaries of coverage, a standard policy then usually contains a section of exclusions that remove coverage for certain items that might otherwise fall within the insuring agreement. For example, a commercial general liability policy typically provides a broad grant of coverage for all claims against the company but the exclusions section of the policy usually contains an exclusion for pollution liability claims.

> The insurer bears the burden of persuasion to show the applicability of an exclusion and the exclusion is usually narrowly construed, particularly where there is any ambiguity in policy language.

> Basic coverage provisions are construed broadly in favor of affording protection, but clauses setting forth specific exclusions from coverage are interpreted narrowly against the insurer. The insured has the burden of establishing that a claim, unless specifically excluded, is within basic coverage, while the insurer has the burden of establishing that a specific exclusion applies.

See *Minkler v. Safeco Ins. Co. of America*, 232 P.3d 612, 616 (Cal. 2010).

Sometimes, the exclusion contains an exception to the exclusion that, if satisfied, nullifies the exclusion and brings the incident in question back within coverage. When an exclusion has been shown to be applicable, the policyholder invoking an exception to the exclusion bears the burden of persuasion. For example, prior to 1986, most commercial general liability policies (which then even had the more coverage-suggesting title of "*comprehensive* general liability" policies) contained a so-called "qualified" pollution exclusion. The exclusion stated that pollution liability claims did not come within the broad insuring agreement grant of coverage (the exclusionary part of the exclusion) unless the pollution resulted from a discharge that was "sudden and accidental" (the exception to the exclusion). Thus, although a pollution claim would at first blush appear to be outside coverage, the policyholder might obtain coverage by showing that the pollution resulted from a sudden and accidental release of alleged pollutants, thereby meeting the exception to the qualified pollution exclusion.

*Conditions*—The conditions section of a policy sets forth certain prerequisites to coverage and also tends to establish the relative rights and responsibilities of the policyholder and insurer. For example, a common condition imposed by the insurer is that the policyholder must give prompt notice of a loss event or claim (or possibly an occurrence that may give rise to a claim). The presence of this condition is understandable. The insurer wants prompt notice in order to better evaluate the situation as to coverage and to have the opportunity to resolve the problem (e.g., by settlement of a liability claim or repair of a property claim) before the situation gets worse. If a condition such as this is not satisfied, the insurer may be able to successfully deny coverage.

Because the conditions section of a policy tends to impose additional burdens on the policyholder rather than the insurer (after all, the insurers write the policies), some conditions in a policy may operate more in the nature of exclusions. If so, courts sometimes treat these conditions as exclusions for purpose of determining coverage. In addition, because law abhors a forfeiture (or at least a *disproportionate* forfeiture of contract rights) and because insurance policies are (in our view) better viewed as bilateral contracts rather than unilateral contracts, courts should generally look to see if conditions are substantially complied with or whether there has been a material breach of a condition in determining whether coverage is available. *See* Hazel Beh & Jeffrey W. Stempel, *Misclassifying the Insurance Policy: The Unforced Errors of Unilateral Contract Characterization*, 32 CARDOZO L. REV. 85, 135–50 (2010).

Although the *RESTATEMENT (SECOND) OF CONTRACTS* (1981) officially ended the distinction between conditions precedent and conditions subsequent, the distinction lives on in practice, particularly regarding insurance policies. As one court described the distinction,

> [i]n an insurance policy, "[c]onditions precedent are those which relate to the attachment of the risk," meaning whether the agreement is effective. Examples include conditions that applicant satisfy the requirement of insurability, be in good health for life and health policies, and pay the required premium. In addition, an applicant must "answer all questions in the application to the best of the applicant's knowledge and belief." In contrast, conditions subsequent in an insurance policy are those which pertain to the contract of insurance after the risk has attached and during the existence thereof; that is, those conditions which must be maintained or met after the risk has commenced, in order that the contract may remain in full force and effect. Clauses which provide that a policy shall become void or its operation defeated or suspended, or the insurer relieved wholly or partially from liability upon the happening of some event, or the doing or omission to do some act, are not conditions precedent but are conditions subsequent and are matters of defense to be pleaded and proved by the insurer.

*D & S Realty, Inc. v. Markel Ins. Co.*, 789 N.W.2d 1, 11 (Neb. 2010) (footnotes omitted; citing and quoting 6 LEE R. RUSS & THOMAS F. SEGALLA, COUCH ON INSURANCE 3D §§ 81:19, 81:20 (2006)). Under this type of analysis, the satisfaction of conditions precedent must be pleaded and proved by the policyholder in order to obtain coverage.

*Definitions* — This section of the policy defines certain terms found in the policy. Frequently, defined terms in a policy are indicated in boldface type, capital letters, italics, or quotation marks. This alerts the reader that the term in question is defined in the definitions section of the policy so that the reader may consult that section and find out if there is a particular or problematic definition used in the policy. In the definitions section of a policy, the insurer attempts to control its risk by confining the reach of key terms that might otherwise be susceptible to broad construction.

*Endorsements* — These are the provisions of an insurance policy that are separately set forth after presentation of the main or standard policy. The additional language is "endorsed upon" the policy (although laypersons might think of endorsement as a fancy term for stapling). The endorsement is in effect a modification or clarification of the main policy. Endorsements commonly adjust policy length or limits or establish a special sublimit for certain types of losses. Endorsements may also simply be separately attached exclusions—or grants of additional coverage. For a more detailed discussion of the insurance policy organization, see STEMPEL & KNUTSEN ON INSURANCE COVERAGE, *supra*, § 2.06. What, if anything, matters about where policy language is located in a policy? It can matter for purposes of the special insurance policy canons of construction, to wit:

- A policyholder bears the burden of persuasion to show that a matter falls within coverage, which normally means showing that a loss or claim falls within the insuring agreement. If the policyholder fails to sustain this burden, the insurer may succeed in defeating the claim as a matter of law via summary judgment.

- Once the policyholder satisfied the burden of bringing the claim within coverage, the insurer may rely on an exclusion to defeat coverage by showing that the claim in question falls within the exclusion and is removed from the scope of the insuring agreement. However, when relying on an exclusion the insurer bears the burden of persuasion. Furthermore, the language of the exclusion will be strictly construed against the insurer and in favor of the policyholder.

- If the insurer carries its burden regarding applicability of an exclusion, the policyholder may be able to yet obtain coverage by demonstrating that an exception to the exclusion applies and restores coverage. The policyholder will have the burden of persuasion as to the applicability of the exception, which is the flip side of the insurer having the burden as to the applicability of the exclusion in the first place.

# § 2.12. Contract Construction Theory and Doctrine in Practice

Some courts have been rather hard on insurance companies with their often unreadable "legalese" and "boiler plate" policy provisions:

> Unfortunately, the insurance industry has become addicted to the practice of building into policies one condition or exception upon another, in the shape of a linguistic Tower of Babel. We join other courts in decrying a trend which both plunges the insured into a state of uncertainty and burdens the judiciary with the task of resolving it. We reiterate our plea for clarity and simplicity in policies that fulfill so important a public service.

*See Insurance Co. of North America v. Electronic Purification Co.*, 67 Cal. 2d 679, 63 Cal. Rptr. 382, 433 P.2d 174 (1967). For a different view, see *Grandpre v. Northwestern Nat'l Life Ins. Co.*, 261 N.W.2d 804 (S.D. 1977): "The insurance company is a risk industry ... [and] the conditions must be met to attain insurance coverage. We cannot expect the insurers to write their contracts in the language of children's primers 'see the dog run, run dog run' style."

*Query*: Which rationale is more persuasive? What if a confusing "boiler plate" policy was mandated by state statute, as many fire insurance policies are? What if a "Plain English" insurance policy is mandated by state statute?

Under a general rule of insurance contract interpretation, whenever an insurance policy is susceptible to two or more reasonable interpretations so that an ambiguity exists, under the doctrine of contra proferentem, the insurance policy will be strictly construed against the insurer who drafted the contract, and the policy will be liberally construed in favor of the insured who was the non-drafting party. On this general rule of insurance contract interpretation, both the Formalist courts and the Functionalist courts can readily agree.

In order to protect the insured—normally the unversed layman or "common man in the marketplace"—from the confusing complexities of insurance contracts, many courts interpret the meaning of an insurance contract by giving effect to the policy language as it would be construed and interpreted by the untrained mind—a "common man" or "common woman" standard rather than being interpreted in a strictly legal or technical sense.

Where sophisticated parties are involved in the insurance contract dispute, some courts utilize the *contra proferentem* rule only when the intent of the parties cannot be determined by the use of extrinsic evidence.

## PROBLEM ONE

Should a "sophisticated policyholder" such as a reinsurance or excess insurance company contracting with a primary insurance company, or a large commercial policyholder with ready access to legal and technical assistance in procuring and understanding its insurance coverage, be entitled to this same interpretive rule as the untrained policyholder or the "common man or woman in the marketplace"?

- Why or why not?
- What constitutes a "sophisticated policyholder"?
- Every large commercial or corporate policyholder?
- A businessman with an MBA degree?
- Your insurance law professor?
- Your insurance law classmates (after reading this note)?
- What realistic test for a "sophisticated policyholder" would you propose?

*See generally* Jeffrey Stempel, *Reassessing the "Sophisticated" Policyholder Defense in Insurance Coverage Litigation*, 42 Drake L. Rev. 807, 849–857 (1993); Hazel Glenn Beh, *Reassessing the Sophisticated Insured Exception*, 39 Tort Trial & Ins. Prac. L.J. 85, 85 (2003) ("The sophisticated insured exception to contra proferentem continues to percolate in insurance law; however, the parameters of the exception have proved difficult to define.") (footnotes omitted).

A "Middle Ground" Interpretive Approach to Insurance Contract Disputes. As discussed above, a majority of American courts have not yet explicitly adopted, nor explicitly rejected, the Keeton Functionalist doctrine of "reasonable expectations" in the interpretation of insurance policies. A majority of American courts therefore arguably apply a "middle ground" approach to the interpretation of insurance policy disputes: somewhere between a traditional (Williston) contractual formalistic approach and a modern functionalistic (Corbin and Keeton) "reasonable expectations" approach. This "middle ground" approach to the interpretation of insurance policies may be summarized as follows:

> Generally speaking, insurance contracts will be construed according to general principles of contract law, unless modified or regulated by state statute, or judicial interpretation. However, since insurance contracts are not ordinary contracts, and are often contracts of adhesion, and since the reasonable expectations of the insured should be honored when appropriate, insurance contracts are subject to the following additional interpretive rules:
>
> (1) Insurance contracts should be construed and interpreted in their ordinary sense, rather than in a purely technical or legal sense, from the viewpoint of the untrained mind, or the "common man or woman in the marketplace."
>
> (2) If the insurance contract is susceptible to two or more reasonable interpretations, then it will be construed liberally in favor of the non-drafting party (the insured), and it will be strictly construed against the drafting party (the insurer). This rule, however, is subject to extrinsic evidence to determine the parties' intent, and subject to the "sophisticated policyholder" defense.
>
> (3) If an insurance contract or provision is unconscionable and against state public policy, a court may refuse to enforce that contract, or may enforce the remainder of the insurance contract without the unconscionable term.
>
> (4) Based on the acts and representations made by the insurer and its agents, the legal doctrines of waiver, estoppel, election, and reformation of contract are available to the insured, and should be liberally construed to validate the insured's objective reasonable expectation to coverage.
>
> (5) In order to further validate the reasonable expectations of the insured to coverage, any exclusion, exception, or limitation to coverage must be clearly, expressly, and unambiguously stated in the insurance contract.

*See* Peter Nash Swisher, *Judicial Interpretations of Insurance Contract Disputes: Toward a Realistic Middle Ground Approach*, 57 Ohio St. L.J. 543 (1996); Peter Nash Swisher, *A Realistic Consensus Approach to the Insurance Law Doctrine of Reasonable Expectations*, 35 Tort & Ins. L.J. 729 (2000).

## PROBLEM TWO

Consider one prominent scholar's summary of the contract jurisprudence of two states.

> The differences between New York and California contract law turn out to align with the formalist-contextualist distinction in contract theory. New York judges are formalists. Especially in commercial cases, they have little tolerance for attempts to re-write contracts to make them fairer or more equitable, and they look to the written agreement as the definitive source of interpretation. California judges, on the other hand, more willingly reform or reject contracts in the service of morality or public policy; they place less emphasis on the written agreement of the parties and seek instead to identify the contours of their commercial relationship within a broader context framed by principles of reason, equity, and substantial justice.

Geoffrey P. Miller, *Bargains Bicoastal: New Light on Contract Theory*, 31 CAR-DOZO L. REV. 1475, 1478 (2010) (Professor Miller also positing that the more formal and textual New York approach is significantly more popular with business, as reflected in the comparatively larger number of contracts containing New York choice of law clauses).

- Does this metric make sense?
- Does it necessarily mean that the formalist approach is better for society?
- Why or why not?
- And how are you defining "better" for "society"?

## PROBLEM THREE

Classify the following case excerpts as representing: (1) a formalist ("traditional") approach; (2) a "middle ground" approach; or (3) functionalist approach to insurance contract interpretation; (4) mainstream with differential emphases on the interpretative factors we have discussed in this Chapter:

(a) "The insurance contract's language must be construed according to its plain and ordinary meaning. It does not permit the court to make a forced construction or a new contract for the parties."

(b) "The reasonable expectation of the insured is the focal point of the insurance transaction.... Courts should be concerned with assuring that the insurance purchasing public's reasonable expectations are fulfilled."

(c) "The problem in deciding an insurance claim seems no longer to be one of ascertaining what the contract as written means, but of somehow divining the 'reasonable expectation' of the insured as to what the contract should mean."

(d) "Where the language of an insurance policy is plain, unambiguous, and susceptible to only one reasonable construction, the courts must enforce that contract according to its terms."

## [A] Additional Aspects of the Formal-Functional Tension of Insurance Law

There *is* a logical explanation for these apparent inconsistencies in insurance coverage disputes if one keeps in mind the two competing "schools" of Formalism and Functionalism and what Professor Robert Jerry believes is a "continuing battle for the heart and soul of insurance contract law":

> On one side are the formalists or classicists, whose champions are Professor [Samuel] Williston and the first *Restatement of Contracts.* The formalists care mightily about texts and the four corners of documents. They believe that words often have a plain meaning that exists independently of any sense in which the speaker or writer may intend the words. They insist that a court or a party can discern the meaning of contractual language without asking about the intentions or [reasonable] expectations of the parties.... In the world of the formalists, an insurer that drafts a clear form should be entitled to rely on that form in setting rates without worrying that a court will disregard the finely tuned, clear language....
>
> The other contestants in the battle for the soul of contract law are the functionalists, who are sometimes also labeled as the progressives, the realists, or the post-classicists. The champions of this side are Professor [Arthur] Corbin and the *Restatement (Second) of Contracts.* The functionalists care less about the text of contracts, believing it to be most useful as an articulation of the objective manifestations of the contracting parties and as a means to understanding their intentions and [reasonable] expectations.... Where a form is standardized, the functionalists substitute objectively reasonable expectations for whatever the particular recipient of the form understood, given that the recipient has less reason to know what the drafter means, while the drafter has insights into what the ordinary, reasonable recipient of the form is likely to understand.

Robert Jerry, II, *Insurance, Contract, and the Doctrine of Reasonable Expectation*, 5 CONN. INS. L.J. 21, 55–56 (1998–99).

### An Interpretative Checklist

Accordingly, in reading and analyzing the following cases discussing the formation, operation, and termination of an insurance contract within this chapter, ask yourself the following interpretive questions that a judge and jury must also decide in resolving many insurance coverage disputes:

(1) Is the policy language within an insurance contract susceptible to *two or more reasonable interpretations* such that an *ambiguity* exists? If so, then under the doctrine of contra proferentem such ambiguous policy language will be strictly construed against the insurer who drafted the contract, and the language will be liberally construed in favor of the insured who was the non-drafting party.

(2) If the insurance policy language *is* clear and unambiguous, is the insurance contract nevertheless unconscionable and unenforceable based upon public policy grounds? *See generally* RESTATEMENT (SECOND) OF CONTRACTS § 208 (1981):

> If a contract or term thereof is unconscionable at the time the contract is made a court may refuse to enforce the contract, or may enforce the remainder of the contract without the unconscionable term, or may so limit the application of an unconscionable term as to avoid any unconscionable result. *Id.*

(3) If the insured has breached a warranty (or a condition of coverage) in the insurance policy, or if the insured has made a material misrepresentation or concealment in the insurance application, has the insurance company waived such noncompliance, or should it be estopped to deny coverage? *See generally* Ch. 4, *infra.*

## [B] Text versus Context and Expectation (Formalism and Functionalism: The Battle Continues)

### Atwater Creamery Co. v. Western National Mut. Ins. Co.

Supreme Court of Minnesota
366 N.W.2d 271 (1985)

**Wahl, Justice.**

Atwater Creamery Company (Atwater) sought a declaratory judgment against its insurer, Western National Mutual Insurance Company (Western), seeking coverage for losses sustained during a burglary of the creamery's storage building. Atwater joined Strehlow Insurance Agency and Charles Strehlow (Strehlow), its agent, as defendants, seeking damages in the alternative due to Strehlow's alleged negligence and misrepresentation. The Kandiyohi County District Court granted a directed verdict for Strehlow because Atwater failed to establish an insurance agent's standard of care by expert testimony. The trial court then dismissed the jury for lack of disputed issues of fact and ordered judgment in favor of the insurer, concluding that the burglary insurance policy in effect defined burglary so as to exclude coverage of this burglary. We affirm the directed verdict for Strehlow but reverse as to the policy coverage.

Atwater does business as a creamery and as a supplier of farm chemicals in Atwater, Minnesota. It was insured during the time in question against burglary, up to a ceiling of $20,000, by Western under Merchantile Open Stock Burglary Policy SC10-1010-12, which contained an "evidence of forcible entry" requirement in its definition of burglary. The creamery had recovered small amounts under this policy for two separate burglaries prior to the events in this case.

Atwater built a separate facility, called the Soil Center, a few blocks away from its main plant in 1975 for the purpose of storing and selling chemicals. The Soil Center is a large rectangular building with two regular doors along the north side and two large, sliding doors, one each on the east and west sides. There are no other entrances or exits to or from the building itself. One of the doors on the north side leads into the office in the northwest corner of the building. It is secured by a regular dead bolt lock, opened with a key. There is no access into the main portion of the building from the office. Persons entering the main area must use the other door on the north side which is secured by a padlock after hours. The large sliding doors on the east and west are secured by large hasps on each side of each door which are held tight by turnbuckles that must be loosened before the doors can be opened.

Inside the main area of the building, along the north wall, is a large storage bin with three separate doors, each of which is secured by a padlock. Between the storage bin and the office is an "alleyway," entered through the large sliding doors, which runs east and west the length of the building. Trucks are stored in the alleyway when not in use.

Sometime between 9:30 p.m., Saturday, April 9, and 6 a.m., Monday, April 11, 1977, one or more persons made unauthorized entry into the building, took chemicals worth $15,587.40, apparently loading them on the truck that had been parked inside and driving away after loosening the turnbuckles on the east door and closing it. The truck was later found parked near the town dump, with the key still in the ignition.

Larry Poe, the plant manager at the Soil Center, had left at 9:30 p.m. on Saturday, after making sure everything was properly secured. On Monday morning, the north side doors were locked securely, but two of the three doors to the storage bin were ajar. Their padlocks were gone and never found. The turnbuckles had been loosened on the east sliding door so that it could be easily opened or closed.

An investigation by the local police, the Kandiyohi County Sheriff's Department, and the Minnesota Bureau of Criminal Investigation determined that no Atwater Creamery employees, past or present, were involved in the burglary. Suspicion settled on persons wholly unconnected with the creamery or even with the local area, but no one has been apprehended or charged with the crime.

Atwater filed a claim with Western under the burglary policy. Western denied coverage because there were no visible marks of physical damage to the exterior at the point of entrance or to the interior at the point of exit, as required by the definition of burglary in the policy. The creamery then brought suit against Western for the $15,587.40 loss, $7,500 in other directly related business losses and costs, disbursements and reasonable attorney fees.

Charles H. Strehlow, the owner of the Strehlow Insurance Agency in Willmar, Minnesota, and Western's agent, testified that he is certain he mentioned the evidence-of-forcible-entry requirement to Poe and members of the Atwater Board of Directors but was unable to say when the discussion occurred. Poe and the board members examined do not remember any such discussion. None of the board members had read the policy, which is kept in the safe at the main plant, and Poe had not read it in its entirety. He stated that he started to read it but gave up because he could not understand it.

\* \* \*

## 2. APPLICATION OF THE POLICY DEFINITION OF BURGLARY.

The definition of burglary in this policy is one used generally in burglary insurance. Courts have construed it in different ways. It has been held ambiguous and construed in favor of coverage in the absence of visible marks of forceable entry or exit. *United States Fidelity & Guaranty Co. v. Woodward, 118 Ga. App. 591, 164 S.E.2d 878 (1968).* We reject this analysis because we view the definition in the policy as clear and precise. It is not ambiguous.

In determining the intent of the parties to the insurance contract, courts have looked to the purpose of the visible-marks-of-forcible-entry requirement. These purposes are two: to protect insurance companies from fraud by way of "inside jobs" and to encourage insureds to reasonably secure the premises. As long as the theft involved clearly neither an inside job nor the result of a lack of secured premises, some courts have simply held that the definition does not apply. *Limberis v. Aetna Casualty & Surety Co.*, 263 A.2d 83 (Me. 1970); *Kretschmer's House of Appliances, Inc. v. United States Fidelity & Guaranty Co.*, 410 S.W.2d 617 (Ky. 1966).

In the instant case, there is no dispute as to whether Atwater is attempting to defraud Western or whether the Soil Center was properly secured. The trial court found that the premises were secured before the robbery and that the law enforcement investigators had determined that it was not an "inside job." To enforce the burglary definition literally against the creamery will in no way effectuate either purpose behind the restrictive definition. We are uncomfortable, however, with this analysis given the right of an insurer to limit the risk against which it will indemnify insureds.

At least three state courts have held that the definition merely provides for one form of evidence which may be used to prove a burglary and that, consequently, other evidence of a burglary will suffice to provide coverage. *Ferguson v. Phoenix Assurance Co. of New York*, 370 P.2d 379 (Kan. 1962); *National Surety Co. v. Silberberg Bros.*, 176 S.W. 97 (Tex. Civ. App. 1915); *Rosenthal v. American Bonding Co. of Baltimore*, 124 N.Y.S. 905 (N.Y. Sup. Ct. 1910). The Nebraska Supreme Court recently rejected this argument in *Cochran v. MFA Mutual Insurance Co.*, 271 N.W.2d 331 (Neb. 1978). The *Cochran* court held that the definition is not a rule of evidence but is a limit on liability, is unambiguous and is applied literally to the facts of the case at hand. We, too, reject this view of the definition as merely a form of evidence. The policy attempts to comprehensively define burglaries that are covered by it. In essence, this approach ignores the policy definition altogether and substitutes the court's or the statute's definition of burglary. This we decline to do, either via the conformity clause or by calling the policy definition merely one form of evidence of a burglary.

Some courts and commentators have recognized that the burglary definition at issue in this case constitutes a rather hidden exclusion from coverage. Exclusions in insurance contracts are read narrowly against the insurer. Running through the many court opinions refusing to literally enforce this burglary definition is the concept that the definition is surprisingly restrictive, that no one purchasing something called burglary insurance would expect coverage to exclude skilled burglaries that leave no visible marks of forcible entry or exit. Professor Robert E. Keeton, in analyzing these and other insurance cases where the results often do not follow from the rules stated, found there to be two general principles underlying many decisions. These principles are the reasonable expectations of the insured and the unconscionability of the clause itself or as applied to the facts of a specific case. Keeton, *Insurance Law Rights at Variance with Policy Provisions*, 83 Harv. L. Rev. 961 (1970). Keeton's article and subsequent book, *Basic Text on Insurance Law*, (1971), have had significant impact on the construction of insurance contracts.

The doctrine of protecting the reasonable expectations of the insured is closely related to the doctrine of contracts of adhesion. Where there is unequal bargaining power between the parties so that one party controls all of the terms and offers the contract on a take-it-or-leave-it basis, the contract will be strictly construed against the party who drafted it. Most courts recognize the great disparity in bargaining power between insurance companies and those who seek insurance. Further, they recognize that, in the majority of cases, a lay person lacks the necessary skills to read and understand insurance policies, which are typically long, set out in very small type and written from a legalistic or insurance expert's perspective. Finally, courts recognize that people purchase insurance relying on others, the agent or company, to provide a policy that meets their needs. The result of the lack of insurance expertise on the part of insureds and the recognized marketing techniques of insurance companies is that "the objectively reasonable expectations of applicants and intended beneficiaries regarding the terms of insurance contracts will be honored even though painstaking study of the policy provisions would have negated those expectations." Keeton, 83 Harv. L. Rev. at 967.

The traditional approach to construction of insurance contracts is to require some kind of ambiguity in the policy before applying the doctrine of reasonable expectations. Several courts, however, have adopted Keeton's view that ambiguity ought not be a condition precedent to the application of the reasonable-expectations doctrine.

The burglary definition is a classic example of a policy provision that should be, and has been, interpreted according to the reasonable expectations of the insured. *C & J Fertilizer, Inc. v. Allied Mutual Insurance Co.*, 227 N.W.2d 169 (Iowa 1975). *C & J Fertilizer* involved a burglary definition almost exactly like the one in the instant case as well as a burglary very similar to the Atwater burglary. The court applied the reasonable-expectations-regardless-of-ambiguity doctrine, noting that "the most plaintiff might have reasonably anticipated was a policy requirement of visual evidence (abundant here) indicating the burglary was an 'outside' not an 'inside' job. The exclusion in issue, masking as a definition, makes insurer's obligation to pay turn on the skill of the burglar, not on the event the parties bargained for: a bona fide third party burglary resulting in loss of plaintiff's chemicals and equipment." *Id.* at 177.

The burglary in *C & J Fertilizer* left no visible marks on the exterior of the building, but an interior door was damaged. In the instant case, the facts are very similar except that there was no damage to the interior doors; their padlocks were simply gone. In *C & J Fertilizer*, the police concluded that an "outside" burglary had occurred. The same is true here.

Atwater had a burglary policy with Western for more than 30 years. The creamery relied on Charles Strehlow to procure for it insurance suitable for its needs. There is some factual dispute as to whether Strehlow ever told Poe about the "exclusion," as Strehlow called it. Even if he had said that there was a visible-marks-of-forcible-entry requirement, Poe could reasonably have thought that it meant that there must be clear evidence of a burglary. There are, of course, fidelity bonds which cover employee theft. The creamery had such a policy covering director and manager theft. The fidelity company, however, does not undertake to insure against the risk of third-party burglaries. A business that requests and purchases burglary insurance reasonably is seeking coverage for loss from third-party burglaries whether a break-in is accomplished by an inept burglar or by a highly skilled burglar. Two other burglaries had occurred at the Soil Center, for which Atwater had received insurance proceeds under the policy. Poe and the board of the creamery could reasonably have expected the burglary policy to cover this burglary where the police, as well as the trial court, found that it was an "outside job."

The reasonable-expectations doctrine gives the court a standard by which to construe insurance contracts without having to rely on arbitrary rules which do not reflect real-life situations and without having to bend and stretch those rules to do justice in individual cases. As Professor Keeton points out, ambiguity in the language of the contract is not irrelevant under this standard but becomes a factor in determining the reasonable expectations of the insured, along with such factors as whether the insured was told of important, but obscure, conditions or exclusions and whether the particular provision in the contract at issue is an item known by the public generally. The doctrine does not automatically remove from the insured a responsibility to read the policy. It does, however, recognize that in certain instances, such as where major exclusions are hidden in the definitions section, the insured should be held only to reasonable knowledge of the literal terms and conditions. The insured may show what actual expectations he or she had, but the factfinder should determine whether those expectations were reasonable under the circumstances.

We have used the reasonable-expectations-of-the-insured analysis to provide coverage where the actual language interpreted as the insurance company intended would have proscribed coverage. *Canadian Universal Insurance Co. v. Fire Watch, Inc.*, 258 N.W.2d 570 (Minn. 1977).[36] Western correctly points out that the issue there concerned a special endorsement issued subsequent to the policy which reduced coverage without

---

36. [*Fire Watch* held that when an insurer renews insurance coverage but changes policy language in a way that reduces the coverage available in the prior policy form, the insurer must provide notice

notice to the insured. While the issue is somewhat different in the instant case, it is not so different that the general concept is made inapplicable.

In our view, the reasonable-expectations doctrine does not automatically mandate either pro-insurer or pro-insured results. It does place a burden on insurance companies to communicate coverage and exclusions of policies accurately and clearly. It does require that expectations of coverage by the insured be reasonable under the circumstances. Neither of those requirements seems overly burdensome. Properly used, the doctrine will result in coverage in some cases and in no coverage in others.

We hold that where the technical definition of burglary in a burglary insurance policy is, in effect, an exclusion from coverage, it will not be interpreted so as to defeat the reasonable expectations of the purchaser of the policy. Under the facts and circumstances of this case, Atwater reasonably expected that its burglary insurance policy with Western would cover the burglary that occurred. Our holding requires reversal as to policy coverage.

---

## Limitations on Reasonable Expectations — Even in a Reasonable Expectations State

In *Board of Regents of the University of Minnesota v. Royal Insurance Co.*, 517 N.W.2d 888 (Minn. 1994), the Minnesota Supreme Court distinguished *Atwater Creamery*, agreeing with the insurer that a pollution exclusion precluded coverage for asbestos claims. In doing so, the court distinguished an intermediate court of appeals opinion cited by the Regents, *Grinnell Mutual Reinsurance Co. v. Wasmuth*, 432 N.W.2d 495 (Minn. App. 1988), *pet. for rev. denied* (Minn., Feb. 10, 1989), with a somewhat similar fact situation. There, the insured's insulation material, when installed in a home, emitted formaldehyde fumes. The court of appeals found insurance coverage, holding that an insured would not reasonably have expected its comprehensive general liability policy to exclude coverage for "unexpected damage due to installation of building materials in a home." 432 N.W.2d at 499.

> The reasonable expectations test of *Atwater Creamery Co. v. Western National Mutual Insurance Co.*, 366 N.W.2d 271 (Minn. 1985), however, has no place here, and the contrary ruling of Grinnell is overruled. In Atwater, we held that "where major exclusions are hidden in the definitions section, the insured should be held only to reasonable knowledge of the literal terms

---

of the change. The rationale for this rule, followed in most states, is that that this information — which a policyholder would otherwise probably overlook (because policyholders seldom read the policy) — allows the policyholder to decide whether to shop around for better coverage from another insurer or to otherwise adjust to the reduced coverage by exercising greater caution, building a contingent loss fund, etc. — Eds.]

and conditions." 366 N.W.2d at 278. In the comprehensive general liability policy involved in this case, the pollution exclusion is plainly designated as such; consequently, the wording of the exclusion should be construed, if a claim of ambiguity is raised, in accordance with the usual rules of interpretation governing insurance contracts. The reasonable expectation test is not a license to ignore the pollution exclusion in this case nor to rewrite the exclusion solely to conform to a result that the insured might prefer.

The court added in a footnote:

> *Atwater Creamery* presented a unique situation. Under the policy definition, there was no "burglary" on the insured's premises, even though admittedly a burglary had occurred and even though the policy was a "Mercantile Open Stock Burglary Policy." 366 N.W.2d at 274–75. For there to be a burglary, the policy definition required that there be a burglar who left visible marks of a forcible entry or exit. If, as was the case in Atwater, the burglar is skillful enough to leave no marks, there is no "burglary." This "visible marks" qualification, we said in Atwater, was really a "hidden" or masked exclusion, impermissibly disguised within the definition section of the policy. *Id.* at 276–78. The Iowa Supreme Court, it is interesting to note, has limited the application of its reasonable expectations doctrine to egregious situations similar to that in Atwater. See *AID (Mut.) Ins. v. Steffen*, 423 N.W.2d 189, 192 (Iowa 1988).

## *Note*

For an example of a different, textualist/formalist view, see *Charania v. Travelers Indemnity Co. of Canada*, 47 O.R. (2d) 705 (Ontario Court of Appeal 1984). A jewelry store had its locks picked, as evidenced by marks inside the cylinder of the picked lock. The insurer denied coverage, invoking a policy definition of burglary that required felonious entry "by actual force and violence, of which force and violence there are visible marks made by tools, explosives, electricity or chemicals upon, or physical damage to the exterior of the Premises at the place of such entry." The court agreed with the insurer, because the physical evidence of lock-picking, being inside the cylinder of the lock, was not visible on the "exterior" of the premises.

Realizing that Knutsen has plenty of retaliatory material, Stempel regards this as further evidence of the general superiority of Minnesota over Ontario (notwithstanding the *Board of Regents v. Royal* retreat from *Atwater Creamery*). The *Charania* decision is astonishingly narrow in focusing only on the words of the definition (and arguably fails at that, as well, in that a fairly strong ambiguity argument can be made based on the totality of the rather involved definition).

The court gives no consideration of the purpose and function of a burglary policy and the practical impact of the court's decision, which does not encourage greater security or discourage "inside jobs" (and there appears to be no suggestion that the court suspected an inside job).

The decision merely deprives an apparently innocent policyholder of coverage and sends a clear message to policyholders who might be planning insurance fraud: be sure to break a window on the way out.[37] This from a country that gave the world Gordon Lightfoot, Wayne Gretzky, Jim Carrey, Celine Dion, Bryan Adams, Ryan Reynolds, Ellen Page, Drake, Tim Horton's Donuts and (gulp) Justin Bieber.

## [C] The Sophisticated Policyholder Concept

As noted above, insurer counsel have argued with some success that commercial policyholders, who often have risk management specialists, brokers, and counsel assisting them, know enough about insurance that these policyholders should not be entitled to the benefits of certain portions of the body of insurance coverage law. In particular, argue insurers, it is unfair to them when large commercial policyholders are protected by the reasonable expectations doctrine (in even moderate form when a court deems policy language ambiguous) and the ambiguity approach construing uncertain policy language against the insurer. *See* OSTRAGER & NEWMAN, *supra*, § 1.03 (11th ed. 2002) (describing the issue and expressing sympathy for insurer position); STEMPEL & KNUTSEN, *supra*, § 4.11 (describing issue with less sympathy for insurer position but arguing that policyholder sophistication may be considered not to eliminate the contra proferentem principle but as a means of ascertaining the range of reasonable expectations). *Compare Shell Oil Co. v. Winterthur Swiss Ins. Co.*, 12 Cal. App. 4th 715, 15 Cal. Rptr.2d 815 (1993) (read by some as suggesting that large commercial policyholder could not use ambiguity principle alone to prevail), *with A.I.U. Ins. Co. v. Superior Court*, 51 Cal.3d 807, 274 Cal. Rptr. 820, 799 P.2d 1253 (1990) (rejecting view that large commercial policyholders may not invoke contra proferentem maxim). The case traditionally seen as the historical "birth" of the sophisticated policyholder concept is *Eagle Leasing Corp. v. Hartford Fire Ins. Co.*, 540 F.2d 1257 (5th Cir. 1976) (applying Missouri law), in which prominent Judge John Minor Wisdom suggested that the ambiguity principle had less force where the policyholder was a sophisticated commercial entity and the policy was a non-standard or "manuscript" policy that resulted from negotiation between insurer and policyholder.

Policyholder counsel counter that the insurer remains the typical drafter of the insurance policy and should be held accountable through the contra proferentem principle if the language is not sufficiently clear. Commercial policyholders also argue

---

37. To be fair, one could perhaps make a case that the visible marks requirement may, at the margin, make fraudsters who have read the *Charania* opinion (or its U.S. counterparts; not every state follows the *Atwater Creamery* approach on this issue) more likely to be apprehended in that this amount of physical force is more likely to trigger alarms, witnesses, or other scrutiny. Perhaps. But as we suggest, the clever fraudster who reads coverage opinions like *Charania* will be sure to create visible exterior marks of forced entry after having stealthily entered and removed valuable items, making a relatively clean getaway likely.

that they are as entitled to considerations of their expectations as any other policy-holders and that insurers frequently receive similar treatment, albeit pursuant to other doctrines or aspects of insurance law. In addition to making these "equal protection" sorts of arguments, policyholders also argue that it is too great an administrative and jurisprudential nightmare to have differing contract interpretation ground rules that vary with the identity of the policyholder.

One commentator has suggested that the sophistication of a policyholder should not dramatically alter the ground rules for insurance policy construction but that sophistication and related concepts may have a legitimate role to play by suggesting that courts consider the following factors particularly carefully when assessing a dispute involving a large commercial policyholder.

1. The actual identity of the drafter of the insurance policy.

2. Broker presence and activity.

3. Attorney presence and activity.

4. The degree of negotiation surrounding the policy and whether it is fairly characterized as "customized" rather than standardized insurance.

5. Whether, regardless of the drafter's identity, the term in dispute is really ambiguous if examined in light of the parties and the facts regarding their intent and the purpose of the policy.

6. The understandings conveyed by the oral and written conduct of the parties surrounding the negotiation, finalization, and implementation of the policy.

7. The presence of an objectively reasonable expectation or reasonable reliance upon coverage due to no fault of the policyholder and where the insurer, if it took a different view of the term in dispute, could have corrected the policyholder's view.

8. The presence of a genuine contractual relationship between the disputants and the length and character of the relationship, which may include inquiry into course of performance, course of dealing, and specialized understanding of policy terms.

9. The presence and character of extrinsic evidence.

10. Whether, in the absence of more probative evidence of contract meaning, it is fundamentally fair to apply contra proferentem against the insurer in light of the conduct of both parties to the policy.

*See* Jeffrey W. Stempel, *Reassessing the "Sophisticated" Policyholder Defense in Insurance Coverage Litigation*, 42 DRAKE L. REV. 807 (1993). *See also Travelers Indem. Co. v. United States*, 543 F.2d 71 (9th Cir. 1976) (applying Oregon law) (contra proferentem inapplicable where policyholder or its agents supplied policy language in dispute); *Fireman's Fund Ins. Co. v. Fibreboard Corp.*, 182 Cal. App. 3d 462, 227 Cal. Rtpr. 203 (1986) (finding that insurer and policyholder co-drafted policy, making ambiguity canon inapt).

# § 2.13. The Role of Unconscionability and Public Policy in Construing Insurance Policies

*Unconscionability.* As discussed above, standard contract law provides that an unconscionable contract term will be set aside or unenforced. An unconscionable term is defined as one that is unreasonably favorable to one of the contracting parties or one that is onerous if enforced. Where a contract is unreasonably unfair, it is connotatively thought to be defective and that the law should not enforce the agreement, even if the agreement was voluntarily entered into without fraud.

*Public Policy.* Public policy is the general set of norms that a society adopts or fosters. For example, as a general rule, we want people to pay their debts, we want to encourage the free exchange of goods, we want to avoid invidious discrimination, we want business and government to operate efficiently, we value consent, but we also want exchange to be fair, and so on. These public policy goals are somewhat less powerful than unconscionability.

For example, in the case of automobile insurance, the public policy of most states (often reflected on the face of insurance codes passed by the legislature) is to provide broad coverage for members of the public who are injured in motor vehicle accidents. This is true even though the insurance company may be unwilling to provide coverage to drivers who are deemed "poor" risks. In such situations, it is well settled that a state legislature has the power to compel private insurance companies to assume this unwanted risk distribution, and that, in any conflict between the insurer's policy terms and state public policy, the state's statutory mandate will prevail. *See, e.g., California State Auto. Ass'n Inter-Insurance Bureau v. Maloney*, 341 U.S. 105, 71 S. Ct. 601, 95 L. Ed. 788 (1951). *See also* Spencer Kimball, *The Purpose of Insurance Regulation: A Preliminary Inquiry in the Theory of Insurance Law*, 45 Minn. L. Rev. 471 (1961).

An inordinate share of the insurance coverage cases decided on public policy grounds appear to involve automobile insurance, which is both heavily regulated by the states and mandated (at least to a statutory minimum) as a way of protecting auto accident victims. Although courts perhaps police restrictions on automobile coverage more than limitations on coverage in other policies, many auto policy restrictions withstand such challenges. Notwithstanding judicial policing, problematic terms continue to keep cropping up in both insurance policies and other contracts. *See* Charles A. Sullivan, *The Puzzling Persistence of Unenforceable Contract Terms*, 70 Ohio St. L.J. 1127 (2009); Robert L. Tucker, *Disappearing Ink: The Emerging Duty to Remove Invalid Policy Provisions*, 42 Akron L. Rev. 519 (2009).

In the following case, the question arises as to which branch of government should decide a state's public policy in an insurance contract dispute—a state court, or the state legislature through its duly appointed administrative agency, the state insurance commissioner or director?

## Karl v. New York Life Insurance Co.

Superior Court of New Jersey
353 A.2d 564 (N.J. Super. Ct. 1976),
*aff'd*, 381 A.2d 62 (N.J. Super. 1977)

This is an action to recover under the accidental death benefit (double indemnity) provisions of two life insurance policies. Defendant insurance company has refused to pay these benefits on the ground that the insured died 11 months after the accident which allegedly caused his death, whereas the two policies in question provided that death must occur within 90 days or 120 days of the accident for accidental death benefits to be payable.

There is no reported New Jersey decision on point. The rule in almost every jurisdiction which has considered the question is that the time limitations set forth in the policy are controlling and that recovery must be denied in a case such as the present one. *See* Appleman, *Insurance Law and Practice* (2d ed. 1963)....

Edward J. Karl suffered severe brain and skull injuries in a criminal assault made upon him in Madison, New Jersey, on January 6, 1969. Without ever having regained anything remotely approaching normal physical or mental functioning, he died in Morristown Memorial Hospital, Morristown, New Jersey on December 6, 1969. At the time of his death Karl was covered by two life insurance policies issued by defendant New York Life Insurance Company which contained accidental death benefits in addition to ordinary death benefits. One of the policies had been issued in 1955, the other in 1963.

The insured's wife, plaintiff Rosemary M. Karl, was the beneficiary under each policy. Defendant insurance company has paid the $10,000 face amount of each policy to the beneficiary, but has refused to pay the accidental death benefit. Its refusal is based primarily upon the time limitation for the period between date of accident and date of death in each policy. The limitation is 90 days for the 1955 policy and 120 days for the 1963 policy. The refusal to pay is also grounded upon a secondary factual argument that death was not caused solely by the accident but was also partially the result of an intervening lung infection.

The 1955 policy provided in pertinent part that

> The Company will pay to the beneficiary ... an additional amount (the Double Indemnity Benefit) equal to the face amount of this policy upon receipt of due proof that the Insured's death resulted directly, and independently of all other causes, from accidental bodily injury and that such death occurred within 90 days of such injury....

The 1963 policy provided in pertinent part that

> ... the Company will pay the Accidental Death Benefit, as part of the policy's death benefit proceeds, upon due proof that the Insured's death resulted directly, and independently of all other causes, from accidental bodily injury and that such death occurred within 120 days after such injury ...

The insured suffered severe brain and skull injuries when he was criminally as-saulted in the early evening of January 6, 1969. He was admitted promptly to Mor-ristown Memorial Hospital. Within hours after his admission to the hospital, he underwent drastic brain surgery. Four additional surgical procedures were performed on the insured between the date of his admission and April 22, 1969. Karl remained in Morristown Memorial Hospital until June 13, 1969, when he was transferred to the Morristown Rehabilitation Center, a nursing home. He remained at the Reha-bilitation Center until August 13, when he was readmitted to Morristown Memorial Hospital. He died in the hospital on December 6, 1969.

From the date of the accident to the date of his death Karl was totally paralyzed, except that he occasionally was able to squeeze with one hand in response to command or by way of primitive communication. A tracheotomy was necessary to permit breathing. The insured never was able to speak. He could never feed himself and, indeed, could never eat anything approaching a normal diet. So far as could be ob-served, the insured never achieved anything approaching full consciousness or normal intellectual functioning....

Having reviewed the medical testimony in this case, I am satisfied that it has been clearly and convincingly established that Karl died on December 6, 1969 as the direct result, independently of all other causes, from accidental bodily injury received by him on January 6, 1969. I am equally satisfied that the infection existing at the time of Karl's death was a normal part of the pathology resulting from the massive traumatic brain damage and does not amount in any legally significant sense to an independent cause of death. Hence, there has been an accidental death within the meaning of both policies upon Mr. Karl's life.

We turn now to the time limitations upon recovery for accidental death imposed by the policies. As a matter of fair linguistic analysis, there is no ambiguity about the time limitations imposed by these policies. The clear, unequivocal thrust of the lan-guage in both policies is to exclude coverage where death does not occur either 90 days or 120 days after the date of accident. Read in a literal and straightforward way, the policies would exclude recovery in this case.

The vast majority of courts construing time limitations such as the ones contained in the present policies have enforced the policies as written and have denied recovery where death did not occur within the time period set forth in the policy. *See* Appleman [on Insurance] § 612. They have done so because such a result is clearly called for by the language of the applicable policy, and because, as a matter of basic legal philosophy, there is a great deal to be said for giving straightforward effect to clear contractual language. Nevertheless, the fair application and development of law is more than a matter of good linguistic analysis, and a legal result should not be accepted merely because it is called for by contractual language. This fundamental proposition was recognized by the Pennsylvania Supreme Court in *Burne v. Franklin Life Ins. Co.*, [451 Pa. 218, 301 A.2d 799 (1973)].

In *Burne*, the court held that time limitations such as these are unenforceable be-cause they violate public policy in that they introduce into the agonizing, difficult and delicate deliberations of the treating physicians and family of a mortally injured person a potentially sinister economic factor suggesting non-treatment. The problem is that as the patient's life is prolonged by treatment, insurance death benefits to his family may be decreased. Although there may be many cases where simple love for the patient and the underlying medical realities and expectations may suggest that certain forms of treatment not be undertaken, or that they be abandoned at some point after they have been started, this most difficult of human decisions should not be influenced by the crass thought that death benefits will be reduced if the patient lives beyond a certain number of days. This is the public policy foundation of the Pennsylvania Supreme Court's decision.

The court also noted in *Burne* that the time limitations in policies such as the one before us were developed in an age when medicine was much less advanced than it is today and when causation was much less traceable than it is today. Also, the development of these time conditions predated the present ability of medicine to prolong life. The Pennsylvania court viewed the purpose of this time condition as being the elimination of doubt as to the cause of death. Where the cause of death is clear, there is no reason for the condition, and the condition should simply be dropped from the policy. As the court said:

> Under the life insurance contract the specific hazard indemnified is premature death resulting from an accident. Recovery for that loss should not be forfeited by the arbitrary and unreasonable condition that payment will be made only if the accident victim dies within ninety days but not if he survives beyond that point. On this record it is obvious that to enforce the ninety day condition would serve only "as a trap to the assured or as a means of escape for the company in case of loss." [451 Pa. at 226, 301 A.2d 799 at 803.]

I am persuaded that the public policy position of the Pennsylvania court in *Burne* is sound. I also believe that in a case such as the present one where the cause of death is clear, the enforcement of a 90-day or 120-day time limitation would be arbitrary and unreasonable.

There is another, perhaps more basic, reason for allowing recovery in this case. It is a reason which I have not seen enunciated in any decision dealing with the interpretation of an insurance policy, but it is a reason which underlies much of the judicial approach to the whole problem of insurance coverage. That reason is founded upon the recognition of the enormous social utility of having losses covered by insurance. Because of the enormous social utility of insurance coverage, whenever there is a reasonable coverage, the court should find coverage if the terms of the policy (read broadly in light of the general social and economic factors surrounding the policy) afford any fair and reasonable basis for finding coverage. In short, as a matter of basic public policy, courts should find coverage wherever it is possible to do so on a fair basis. Such an approach would lead to the conclusion that time conditions contained in an insurance policy should be read in terms of broad purpose and function in cases in which a literal reading would defeat coverage.

It should be noted that I am not suggesting that all time terms in an insurance policy are to be read in a broad functional sense. Surely, some time terms must be read literally. For example, the time terms setting forth the period during which the policy is in force would almost always have to be read literally because any other reading of them would destroy any fair and reasonable basis for defining and limiting the period of coverage.

## *Notes and Questions*

1. The appellate court affirmed the trial court decision in *Karl* except for legal fees:

> The policy behind [the statute awarding legal fees] is to discourage groundless disclaimers made in bad faith by insurance carriers so as to escape a duty to defend their insureds. We do not believe the rule can be interpreted to impose counsel fees upon an insurer which defends in good faith an action upon an accidental death provision of a life insurance policy by its insured, particularly where, as here, there is no controlling precedent in New Jersey and the great weight of authority throughout the country supports the position of the carrier.

*Karl v. New York Life Ins. Co.*, 381 A.2d 62 (N.J. Super. 1977).

2. The *Burne* decision, relied upon by *Karl*, was a then-radical departure from the traditional rule upholding the contractual agreement of the time limitation period for double indemnity liability. Today, the approach of the *Karl* court appears to have substantial support. However, not all courts have been quick to adopt the *Burne* rule.

　• Which approach is preferable?

　• Why?

3. An insurance policy that is contrary to state public policy, no matter how clear and unambiguous, may be illegal and void. The test of whether or not an insurance policy is void as against state public policy is whether it is injurious to the public or contravenes some important, established social interest, or when its purpose is to promote, effect, or encourage a violation of the law. *See, e.g., L'Orange v. Medical Protective Co.*, 394 F.2d 57 (6th Cir. 1968) (applying Ohio law) (cancellation of physician's medical malpractice coverage because he gave testimony adverse to another doctor insured by the company violates public policy in that insurers and other contracting parties should not attempt to chill or restrict the testimony of a witness at trial).

On other occasions, a policy provision may not be obviously illegal or clearly promoting illegal behavior but may constitute a more subtle violation of public policy in that it encourages antisocial or undesirable behavior that stops short of being illegal. The degree of antisocial cum illegal consequences required is another continuum upon which courts differ when interpreting contracts. Some courts are unwilling to modify or strike down a clear policy term unless the term crosses the line of illegality. Other courts are willing to invoke public policy to countermand a policy term when the result is merely antithetical to widely held public values rather than outright illegal. *See* E. ALLAN FARNSWORTH, CONTRACTS, Ch. 5 (3d ed. 1999) (characterizing much judicial activity in this area as "policing the agreement").

4. Traditionally, state public policy is normally expressed through the state legislature and through the legislature's duly authorized administrative agency, the state insurance commission, since a state has a valid legal right to regulate and control the business of insurance and to approve or disapprove insurance policies contracted within that state — for the public good. The majority approach to use of public policy concerns in contract construction and enforcement, particularly in the federal courts, is to require that the public policy be clearly discernable from state statutes or the constitution or a similar policy of the executive branch, including administrative agencies.

Various courts, however, have held that an insurance policy may also be void because it violates not only statutorily declared public policy, but also because it violates a public policy that the courts would enforce in the absence of any statutory authority. But if not relying on statute or executive pronouncement, from what sources might a court legitimately discern applicable public policy? Courts taking a broad approach to use of the public policy factor have suggested that public policy can be discerned from the overall legal and social topography as well as from examination of specific legislation and administrative regulation.

In effect, courts making more aggressive use of public policy engage in something akin to judicial notice (*see* Fed. R. Evid. 201), only instead of taking judicial notice of an adjudicative fact, the accuracy of which cannot reasonably be questioned, the court is drawing from similarly unquestioned or weighty sources, including common law precedent, the public policy consensus as to preferred values in law and society. Examples are the recognized public policies against restraint of trade and against impairment of family relations.

To some extent, the dichotomy between public policy grounded in positive law and public policy derived from indicators of public sentiment may be exaggerated. In the examples above, for instance, one can discern that restraint of trade is disfavored not only because of common law norms and general social attitudes (as empirically verified by the circulation of business magazines), but also because we have antitrust laws on the books as part of the United States Code and state statutory law as well. The policy against impairment of family relations, although appearing to be firmly rooted in the common law, also is reflected in modern statutes protective of the family.

Thus, public policy can legitimately be seen as derived from a wide variety of sources that may be part of society's positive law (constitution, statute, common law, or administrative regulations and precedent). Public policy concerns may also be reflected in the leading nonlegal texts and in the actions and attitudes of various social institutions and the public at large. However, these types of indicators of public policy are inherently less objectively verifiable than positive law or legal precedent. Hence, their use will continue to be more controversial as a matter of jurisprudential propriety.

A legal realist would perhaps regard this concern as flowing more from mythology and form than the substance of adjudicating cases. For example, there may be a long line of common law precedent expressing a state's public policy. However, that lineage may have all begun with one case in which a single judge announced the public policy base on personal preference.

There is a difference, however, in that a line of common law cases stands as a row of potential targets for legislative correction since case holdings may be overturned by new legislation. When the legislature has failed to act to alter a common law result, American jurisprudence tends to regard the non-interference as either tacit approval or at least apathy, which at least suggests the case holding is not at odds with widely held attitudes of policymakers. Consequently, discerning public policy from nonlegal or informal legal sources appears as a general rule to be a riskier course. Again, however, a legal realist might respond that infirmities in the political system mean that legislative or executive action (or inaction) may not reflect widespread social beliefs. Rather, they may instead reflect interest group power, idiosyncrasies of those bodies, or electoral imperfections.

Whatever the lurking issues and continuum of judicial attitudes, public policy factors are frequently used as an aid in contract construction. Not surprisingly, formalist and functionalist judges appear to reflect different views regarding the appropriate use of public policy for insurance policy construction.

# § 2.14. "Reformation" of the Insurance Contract

Under general contract law principles, a policyholder is bound by all the provisions in the insurance policy, whether or not the policyholder has read them. But what happens if the insurance agent makes an innocent — or fraudulent — representation to the policyholder about policy coverage. Does the policyholder have any legal recourse? Under these circumstances, the policyholder may proceed in equity for a reformation of the insurance policy based on a mutual mistake of the parties, or based upon mistaken or fraudulent representations or conduct of the insurer or its agent who issues the policy.

According to traditional contract law principles, reformation must be proved by clear and convincing evidence, although some insurance cases have required less proof. The policyholder may show by parol evidence that the parties' intent was different from the terms of the insurance policy and may, in some jurisdictions, also present evidence that the policyholder had not read the policy to support the policyholder's allegations that he or she had a mistaken understanding of its terms.

## Notes and Questions

1. Some courts still hold under traditional principles of contract law that the policyholder *is* held to the duty of reading his or her insurance policy, and that failure to read the policy will bar the policyholder from having the policy reformed. But what if the policyholder did not have an adequate opportunity to read the policy before the loss occurred?

2. Other courts, however, have held that the failure of the policyholder to read his or her policy will not per se constitute negligence or laches to deprive the policyholder of the remedy of reformation. What is the rationale behind this non-traditional rule?

## PROBLEM FOUR

The policyholder, who was in the business of installing swimming pools, asked his general agent to provide products liability insurance coverage in his general comprehensive liability insurance policy. The agent told the policyholder that it was "no problem" and that the policyholder had such coverage. In fact, the policyholder's policy excluded products liability coverage in clear and unambiguous language on page three of the policy. Another provision in the insurance policy (on page four) stated "no agent has any authority to change this policy." At the top of the policy were the words in bold capital letters "READ YOUR POLICY."

The policyholder argued that contract reformation was appropriate in this case since the agent's assertion that the policyholder had products liability coverage negated his duty to read the policy, and the agent's assertion of coverage should estop the insurer from denying coverage. How should the court rule in this case?

## PROBLEM FIVE

The policyholder, who owned a liquor store, wanted to obtain an "all risk" liability insurance policy for his place of business. The insurer's general agent, who had not read the particular "all risk" policy and who was not familiar with its contents, promised the policyholder that he would have a comprehensive "all risk" policy covering "everything you need for your business," and the promotional brochure published by the insurer promised that "This Broad Plan offers protection against all perils of your business except those excluded in the policy."

In fact, when the insurance policy was delivered to the policyholder, there was a clear and unambiguous policy exclusion for "personal injury resulting from the selling or serving of any alcoholic beverage to a minor." The policyholder did not read his policy.

Later the policyholder sold liquor to a minor without asking for or obtaining proof of the purchaser's age. The minor, while intoxicated, was badly injured in an automobile accident. The policyholder now demands reformation of his policy based on the agent's conduct and representations. How should the court rule in this case?

• Which case presents a better chance of coverage for the policyholder: Problem 4 or Problem 5?

# § 2.15. Must the Policy Coverage Be Explained to the Policyholder?

In the case of standardized insurance policies, exceptions and limitations on coverage that the policyholder could not "*reasonably expect, ... must be called to his attention, clearly and plainly*, before the exclusions will be interpreted to relieve the insurer of liability or performance." *Logan v. John Hancock Mut. Life Ins. Co.*, 41 Cal. App. 3d 988, 995, 116 Cal. Rptr. 528, 532 (1974). (Emphasis in the original.)

This is very helpful language for policyholders. But it is found in comparatively few judicial decisions. Rather, most courts do not impose a duty of explanation and stop at requiring that insurers avoid misleading customers during sales.

Further, even in a "duty to explain" jurisdiction (if one can be found; not every California case reads like *Logan v. John Hancock*), what happens when there is no live human intermediary, or even a website, to present or clarify coverage? What approach should the court take regarding the interpretation of language, particularly if the language is arguably specialized? The following case, although focused on the "vending machine" aspect of the insurance, also contains extensive interpretative analysis.

## Lachs v. Fidelity & Casualty Co. of New York

New York Court of Appeals
118 N.E.2d 555 (N.Y. 1954)

**Conway, J.**

This is a motion by defendant insurance company for summary judgment in an action by the daughter beneficiary named in an airplane trip insurance contract....

There are some undisputed facts. Thus, it is clear that the day before her death, the decedent, a resident of New York City, visited a tourist agency in New York City and made arrangements to fly on the following day to Miami, Florida. She received an "exchange order" which she brought to Newark Airport at 8:00 A.M. on the following morning. She purchased "AIRLINE TRIP INSURANCE" in the sum of $25,000 from an automatic vending machine. She then went to the Consolidated Air Service counter and completed her flight arrangements, with one McManus of the agency, to fly to Miami on a Miami Airline, Inc., plane and mentioned to him her purchase of the insurance and her hopes for a good flight. She later entered the plane, after a delay, the reason for which is not disclosed in the record, and in less than an hour was dead as the result of a crash.

Plaintiff claims that the vending machine was situated in front of the Consolidated Air Service counter at which decedent obtained her transportation ticket. Pictures of the machine and affidavits indicate that in letters ten times larger than any other words on the machine and in prominent lighting, appeared the words "AIRLINE TRIP INSURANCE". Over those words was a well-illuminated display of airplanes flying round and round, and in large characters appeared the words and numerals

"25 For Each $5,000 Maximum $25,000". Below that on a placard, in letters *many times* the size of the other words thereon, we find:

> " 'DOMESTIC' AIRLINE TRIP INSURANCE 25 FOR EACH $5,000 MAXIMUM $25,000".

Below in *much smaller print* on the same placard appears:

> "Covers first one-way flight shown on application (also return flight if round trip airline ticket purchased) completed in 12 months within or between United States, Alaska, Hawaii or Canada or between any point therein and any point in Mexico, Bermuda or West Indies on any scheduled airline. Policy void outside above limits. For 'international' coverage see airline agent."

The application mentioned on the placard is obtained by inserting 25 cents in a slot for each $5,000 of insurance desired. Upon such insertion, a small slot of approximately one inch opens and the application for insurance is presented. It reads as follows:

> "I hereby apply to Company named below for Airline Trip Insurance to insure me on one Airline trip between: Point of Departure? ... Destination? ... And return ... Beneficiary's home? ... Beneficiary's Street Address? ... Beneficiary's City? ... Beneficiary's State? ... Name of Applicant (please print) Signature of Applicant".

Upon completion of the application, the applicant presses a button and there comes from the machine a policy of insurance. The policy is approximately eleven inches in height and is printed on both sides—thus there are twenty-two inches of printed matter. However, the purchaser does find across the front of the policy in type *many times larger* than all the other printing on the page and obliterating some words of the policy: "THIS POLICY IS LIMITED TO AIRCRAFT ACCIDENTS READ IT CAREFULLY". There is also an envelope in the machine to mail to the beneficiary, for the insured is not expected to read the policy on the plane. The envelope has printed on it: "AIRLINE TRIP INSURANCE".

Plaintiff says that some but not all machines have a specimen policy attached and that it has not been established that the machine from which decedent purchased her policy had a specimen attached. Be that as it may, the defendant has presented as an exhibit a specimen policy and the words quoted *(supra)*: "THIS POLICY IS LIMITED TO AIRCRAFT ACCIDENTS READ IT CAREFULLY" obliterate the words: "Civilian Scheduled Airline" in the coverage clause so that they cannot be read.

This was the "coverage" clause in the policy on page 1: "This insurance shall apply only to such injuries sustained following the purchase by or for the Insured of a transportation ticket from ... a Scheduled Airline during any portion of the first one way or round airline trip covered by such transportation ticket ... in consequence of: (a) boarding, riding as a passenger in, alighting from or coming in contact with any aircraft operated on a regular or special or chartered flight by a Civilian Scheduled Airline maintaining regular, published schedules and licensed for interstate, intrastate or international transportation of passengers by the Governmental Authority having jurisdiction over Civil Aviation....'

Defendant on its part points to the fact that there was hanging on the wall at the right hand end of the counter where decedent picked up her ticket, a fairly large sign — approximately three feet by four feet — bearing the caption in large size capital letters:

"NON SCHEDULED AIR CARRIERS AUTHORIZED TO CONDUCT BUSI-NESS IN THIS TERMINAL"

and that there followed a list of ten carriers, among which was included on a separate line,

"MIAMI AIRLINE".

In answer, the plaintiff has presented an affidavit from McManus, the representative of the tourist agency at the Consolidated Air Service counter, that the sign was on one wall of a waiting room near the counter and not at the counter. Plaintiff claims that the sign was on a wall of a public waiting room at an extreme end of the Newark Air Terminal, at an *exit* where persons *leaving* the airport obtain taxis. Plaintiff further claims that to get to the Consolidated counter, the decedent had to enter through the main entrance of the airport hundreds of feet away from the waiting room. There is, of course, no proof that decedent ever saw the sign.

Little, if anything, turns on the sign or what it said or where it was, for applicants for insurance are not affected with notice by reason of wall signs nor do they incorporate words or definitions from wall signs into their insurance contracts. It does serve the purpose of showing that the parties here are in disagreement on nearly everything except a few undisputed facts.

What contract of insurance, then, did the decedent purchase? She intended to buy coverage for her flight to Miami. The defendant says it did not intend to cover her on that flight. We all know that a contract of insurance, drawn by the insurer, must be read through the eyes of the average man on the street or the average housewife who purchases it. Neither of them is expected to carry the Civil Aeronautics Act or the Code of Federal Regulations when taking a plane. We have never departed from our statement in *Kenyon v. Knights Templar & Masonic Mut. Aid Assn.* (122 N.Y. 247, 254): "It may preliminarily be observed that, as a general rule, the construction of a written instrument is a question of law for the court to determine, but when the language employed is not free from ambiguity, or when it is equivocal and its interpretation depends upon the sense in which the words were used, in view of the subject to which they relate, the relation of the parties and the surrounding circumstances properly applicable to it, the intent of the parties becomes a matter of inquiry, and the interpretation of the language used by them is a mixed question of law and fact." [Additional citations omitted.]

Was the decedent entitled to believe that she had purchased "AIRLINE TRIP IN-SURANCE" through a policy "LIMITED TO AIRCRAFT ACCIDENTS"? It seems to us that a jury could find that when decedent purchased her policy on an application for "AIRLINE TRIP INSURANCE" from a machine having in prominent lighting those same three words, before obtaining her ticket *from a counter in front of which the machine stood*, she was covered on her flight, since the minds of the decedent and the company had met on that basis. In other words, since defendant put one of its automatic vending machines in front of the ticket counter of the Consolidated Air Service which, according to an affidavit submitted by defendant, "was utilized by all non-scheduled airlines operating out of the Newark Airport, as a processing point for their passengers, and before any passenger on a non-scheduled airline could receive his ticket he was required to present his 'exchange order' at said counter" we think a jury might find that the defendant was inviting those passengers to insure themselves by its "AIRLINE TRIP INSURANCE".

Decedent was invited to purchase "AIRLINE TRIP INSURANCE"; she applied for "AIRLINE TRIP INSURANCE"; on the envelope to carry the policy to her daughter beneficiary was "AIRLINE TRIP INSURANCE" but defendant says that was not what decedent purchased. Shall the defendant, which wrote the policy, be permitted to say that "AIRLINE TRIP INSURANCE" "means just what I choose it to mean" and therefore means that a flight on a "non-scheduled" airline is not covered by the policy? Defendant concedes that the "action is brought by the plaintiff to recover upon defendant's Airline Trip Insurance policy" but "defendant contends that the policy did not cover the alleged loss of life of the said Sadie Bernstein because she lost her life in the crash of an aircraft which was not a flight operated *by* a Civilian *Scheduled* Airline." (Emphasis by defendant.) That draws the line of construction very finely.

Plaintiff claims that Miami Airline, Inc., maintained regular, published schedules of fares and schedules showing passenger mile rates and that it held itself out as maintaining regular schedules of flights and tickets were sold for stated hours of departure and that it was licensed by the Civil Aeronautics Board to carry passengers and freight with large aircraft in interstate, overseas and foreign air transportation.

We think there is a question of fact presented. [T]he burden in such a case as this is on the defendant to establish that the words and expressions used not only are susceptible of the construction sought by defendant but that it is the only construction which may fairly be placed on them. The defendant in its large illuminated lettering and in its application could have added proper, unambiguous words or a definition or could have avoided allowing its vending machine to be placed in front of the ticket counter "utilized by all non-scheduled airlines operating out of the Newark Airport", thus removing the ambiguity or equivocal character of the invitation to insure, of the application for insurance and the contract of insurance itself.

Perhaps we should point out here that even that might not have helped, for if decedent had engaged a lawyer to examine the Civil Aeronautics Act of 1938 as amended and the Code of Federal Regulations before purchasing her policy, she would have learned, and the defendant concedes, that the term "Civilian Scheduled Airline" cannot be found in them and there is no such terminology used. There is also no reference to nor mention of the words "Scheduled Airline" in the Code of Federal Regulations. There is no definition of "Scheduled Airline" or of "Non-scheduled Airline" in the Civil Aeronautics Act of 1938 as amended.

No doubt it is advisable, if not indeed necessary, as a matter of business competition to sell insurance policies from automatic vending machines. It may save money to have a number of machines instead of a salesman. It may be wise because people hurrying to planes will not wait on a line to buy insurance. However, there must be a meeting of minds achieved between the applicant and the company through an application and signs and lettering, for while the applicant has a mind the machine has none and cannot answer questions.

If the defendant had paid for a living salesman, the decedent would not have purchased the insurance if it did not cover her trip or she might have purchased it and changed her plane. So there must be additional care taken. While all this makes it more difficult for the insurance company, there is another side to the question. If the rule here was not made strict when machines are utilized it would mean that in this large terminal *all* persons who put money into the machines there and then, thinking they were insured, went off on one of the ten so-called "non-scheduled air carriers," would have no insurance for their beneficiaries and the company would be in receipt of contributions for which no service was ever rendered.

It is urged upon us that the term "scheduled airline" has gained such wide and general currency that it has become part of the speech of the average man even though it is not defined in any statute. That may or may not be so as to [frequent] air-travelers but we do not know whether the decedent had ever been on a plane before. At any rate this court has no power to make findings here. Even the definition suggested by defendant in its brief seems to require more knowledge than the average layman has. According to defendant a "Civilian Scheduled Airline" is an "air carrier which obtains a certificate of public convenience and necessity as provided in Section 401 of the Civil Aeronautics Act."

It should be noted that the defense is not that a particular flight is not scheduled but that the airline is not a civilian scheduled one. The attempt of defendant to establish that the term "Civilian Scheduled Airline" has a clear and definite meaning has caused it to bring forward and present an enormous amount of proof extrinsic to the policy including a statute, regulations, newspaper and magazine articles, etc. By this mountain of work it seems to us that defendant has established that "Civilian Scheduled Airline" is not at all free from ambiguity and vagueness — if it were not so the contract of insurance itself would disclose within its four corners the intent of the parties in entering into it.

**Fuld, J.,** dissenting.

In Alice's Wonderland, a word, said Humpty Dumpty, "means just what I choose it to mean." But, in a jurisdiction more mundane, I do not perceive how we may say that the word "scheduled" can mean "non-scheduled," nor do I see how we may tell a jury that it can say that an insurance policy which in express terms applies "only" to "scheduled airlines" can cover flights by an airline listed and self-described as "non-scheduled".

The policy, on its first page, in clear and legible type, states in so many words that it is limited to flights by "Scheduled Airlines"; the provision reads, in part, as follows:

"This insurance shall apply *only* to such injuries sustained following the purchase by or for the Insured of a transportation ticket from ... *a Scheduled Airline* during any portion of the first one way or round airline trip covered by such transportation ticket ... between the Point of Departure and the Destination shown above, in consequence of: (a) boarding, riding as a passenger in, alighting from ... any aircraft operated on a regular or special or chartered flight by a *Civilian Scheduled Airline* maintaining regular, published schedules and licensed for interstate, intrastate or international transportation of passengers by the Governmental Authority having jurisdiction over Civil Aviation". (Emphasis supplied.)

And, at the bottom of that same page, in larger letters, appears the further legend,

"THIS LIMITED POLICY PROVIDES PAYMENT FOR LOSS OF LIFE, LIMB OR SIGHT AND OTHER SPECIFIED LOSSES BY ACCIDENTAL BODILY INJURY WHILE A PASSENGER ON CIVILIAN SCHEDULED AIRLINES".

A specimen policy, identical with that issued, was attached to the vending machine for inspection by any person desiring to obtain one of the policies. And, in addition, a large placard on the face of the machine—following the caption "'Domestic' Airline Trip Insurance"—also gave notice that the insurance "COVERS * * * FLIGHT * * * ON ANY SCHEDULED AIRLINE."

While it might have been sufficient to show that there are two separate and distinct classes of airlines, the "scheduled" and the "nonscheduled", the insurer went far beyond that in this case. Recognizing, perhaps, the inconspicuousness of the obvious, defendant has marshaled a veritable mountain of material—contained in statute and regulations, in opinions and reports, in newspapers and magazines—to demonstrate that the term "scheduled airline" has gained a wide and general currency, and that it is a term of clear and precise meaning, which has become part and parcel of the ordinary person's everyday vocabulary. Defined by any standard and from any point of view, and compressed into a sentence, it simply and solely denotes a common carrier permitted to operate, or to hold out to the public that it operates, one or more airplanes between designated points regularly, or with a reasonable degree of regularity, in accordance with a previously announced schedule.

Its origin is in the Civil Aeronautics Act and the pertinent regulations issued by the Civil Aeronautics Board. By subdivision (a) of section 401 of the Act, no citizen is authorized to engage in interstate, overseas or foreign air transportation, unless he first obtains a certificate of public convenience and necessity from the Board.... The Board, however, is empowered to exempt from the requirement of certification any class of air carrier, including those "*not engaged in scheduled air transportation*".... And, pursuant to the authority thus granted, the Board in 1938 provided that "every air carrier which engages solely in *non-scheduled operations* shall be exempt" from the statute's certification provisions....

The controversies involving the nonscheduled airlines, the endeavor to provide greater safety to the public traveling those lines, are reflected in the Board's reports.

Those matters do not, as such, concern us, and we refer to them only for the purpose of demonstrating that the distinction, between "an air carrier engaged in scheduled air transportation" and a carrier not so engaged, has been consistently maintained. In the investigations carried on over the years, the meaning of the term, "scheduled airline" or "scheduled air carrier," was crucial and vital. In its *Investigation of Non-scheduled Air Services....* for instance, the Board declared: "The scheduled air carrier operates pursuant to a scheme or plan under which, within the physical limitations of equipment and facilities, a definite quantum of service is constantly available to the traveling public, and is held out as such through course of conduct in maintaining reasonably regular service, filing of schedules and tariffs, advertisements, etc.... It therefore becomes apparent that 'nonscheduled' has a far more restrictive meaning than the mere absence of a published timetable." And similar definitions are contained in an almost endless number of other opinions by the Board....

* * *

In point of fact, we might well have taken judicial notice of the term and its meaning, had the record not been as replete as it is with illustrations from the daily press and from popular magazines and books with large nationwide circulations. For instance, the president of a firm leasing planes to a non-scheduled carrier wrote in *Fortune* Magazine for August, 1949: "It is now only a year ago that my air-freight line, California Eastern Airways, Inc., leased one of its DC-4 ships to a 'large irregular' or non-scheduled carrier, popularly known as a nonsked.... *Non-scheduled airlines* use the same well-proved planes used by all airlines. But Douglas DC-3's of the *scheduled airlines* carry twenty-one seats; those of the nonskeds, twenty-eight. Most of the DC-4's of the scheduled lines contain forty-four seats; we now have sixty-seven in ours" (pp. 51–52). A feature article in the March, 1951, issue of *Cosmopolitan* Magazine captioned, "Don't Fly the Unscheduled Air Lines!", takes for granted the classification of, and the distinction between, scheduled and nonscheduled carriers (p. 66). And in *Harper's* Magazine for May, 1949, we find this discussion of scheduled airlines and nonscheduled flights (p. 67): "Including taxes, you would pay $113 for a *non-scheduled flight* from New York to Los Angeles, as against $181 on a *scheduled airline.* These carriers are non-scheduled in the sense that they are not permitted by the Civil Aeronautics Board to fly more than a limited number of trips between any two cities each month, and because they cannot, therefore, represent themselves to the public as running on regular time-tables."

It is thus made evident that the general public encountered the term "scheduled airline" in the course of its normal and ordinary reading of newspapers and magazines, and the context in which the term appeared demonstrates that to the average person it had the same clear and definite meaning as it had for the federal agency which originally used it.

That being so, it follows, almost as a matter of course, that the fatal flight upon which plaintiff's insured had embarked was not covered by the policy. The Letter of Registration, which Miami Airline had received from the Civil Aeronautics Board, classified and described it as a "Non-certificated Irregular Air Carrier"—the equivalent of a Nonscheduled Airline....— and its status as such finds indisputable confirmation in Miami's Tariff, which specifies, on its title page, that it "contains local rates and rules.... Applicable For *Non-Scheduled* [passenger and freight] *Service.*" ...

### *Notes and Questions*

1. Which opinion do you find more persuasive in *Lachs*: the majority or the dissent?

2. Is the majority opinion in *Lachs* based solely on the use of the vending machine to sell the policy at issue? What other factors were important to the Majority? What factor or factors were most important to the dissenters?

3. Is the *Lachs* decision based on: Mode of sale? Policyholder expectations? Contra proferentem? Public policy? Unconscionability (procedural or substantive)? All of the above? Something else?

4. For further commentary on *Lachs, see* Jeffrey W. Stempel, Lachs v. Fidelity & Casualty Co. of New York: *Timeless and Ahead of Its Time*, 2 Nev. L.J. 319 (2002), and *Favorite Insurance Cases Symposium*, 2 Nev. L.J. 287 (2002).

5. Has modern technology solved the problem in *Lachs*? In particular, does online booking eliminate the risk of ambiguity, confusion, or misplaced reliance by someone purchasing airfare? Should it make a difference if the decedent had bought the flight insurance (a) two months before the flight on her home desktop computer? (b) two weeks before the flight on her laptop during a particularly dull part of a corporate meeting? (c) on her smartphone while going through security minutes before takeoff?

# § 2.16. Policy Language and Big Data: Promise or Peril?

Today, talk of a "scheduled" or "non-scheduled" airline most likely brings puzzled expression to the face of readers. But perhaps this was not the case during the 1950s (when every cool cat or daddy-o had it made in the shade and was on Cloud 9 or otherwise in Fat City in the era preceding "fab" and "groovy" developments). Judge Fuld's dissent marshals information suggesting that even laypersons understood that a non-schedule airline was not a major air carrier and hence posed greater risk. Although his dissent strikes us as too technical and we still agree with the majority that the limits of coverage are just not sufficiently clear in light of not only policy text but also the context and environment surrounding the sale, we could be wrong. Perhaps talking of scheduled and non-scheduled airlines during the 1950s was the equivalent of discussing Mac and PC computers or Apple and Samsung phones today.

But how can one be sure? One possibility is to examine not just the materials to which Judge Fuld referred in dissent but to survey a massive base of writings from the era to see how terms were used and with what frequency. This is in essence the enterprise of the corpus linguistics movement. As described by one of its leading scholars:

corpus linguistics may be thought of as a linguistic methodology that analyses language function and use by means of an electronic database called a corpus.

* * *

The data in the corpus are considered "natural" because they were not elicited for the purpose of study. That is, generally no one asks the speakers or writers whose words are represented in the corpus to speak or write for the purpose of subjecting their words to linguistic scrutiny. Instead, the architect of the corpus assembles her collection of speech and writing samples after the fact, from newspapers, books, transcripts of conversations, or interviews, etc.

Stephen C. Mouritsen, *The Dictionary Is Not a Fortress: Definitional Fallacies and a Corpus-Based Approach to Plain Meaning*, 2010 BYU L. Rev. 1915, 1954–55.

One prominent linguist has posited four unifying traits of the corpus methodology, in particular that it: (1) is empirical and looks at patterns of use of natural text; (2) from a large and fairly assembled collection of natural texts (the "corpus"); (3) uses computer technology extensively, both to gather data and to interact with it; and (4) uses quantitative and qualitative techniques of data analysis. *See* Douglas Biber, *Corpus-Based and Corpus-Driven Analyses of Language Variation and Use, in* The Oxford Handbook of Linguistic Analysis 159 (2009) (Bernd Heine & Heiko Narrog, eds.). *Accord*, Paul Baker et al., A Glossary of Corpus Linguistics (2006) ("In linguistics, empiricism is the idea that the best way to find out about how language works is by analyzing real examples of language as it is actually used. Corpus Linguistics is therefore a sternly empirical methodology."). *See also* Mourtisen, 2010 BYU L. Rev. at 1954–1966 (explaining mechanics and technique of corpus linguistics research). Other writings in the area include Douglas Biber & Randi Reppen, The Cambridge Handbook of English Corpus Linguistics (2015); Tony McEnery & Andrew Hardie, Corpus Linguistics: Method, Theory and Practice (2012); Tony McEnery & Andrew Wilson, Corpus Linguistics: An Introduction (2d ed. 2001); Thomas R. Lee & Stephen C. Mouritsen, *Judging Ordinary Meaning*, 127 Yale L.J. 788 (2018).

Several databases have been assembled containing millions or even billions of entries from newspapers, books, periodicals, broadcast transcripts and the like. *See, e.g.,* Corpus of Historical American English ("COHA"). Brigham Young University, http://corpus.byu.edu/coha; Corpus of Contemporary American English ("COHA"). Brigham Young University, http://corpus.byu.edu/coha. One might run the terms "scheduled airline" and "non-scheduled" airline through either corpus and collate examples of the use of the term, which would presumably shine at least some light on the manner in which the terms were understood at the time of the *Lachs v. Fidelity* decision as well as the evolution of the terms. The use of the terms during the 1950s would, of course, be the more relevant inquiry even if both are interesting.

But empirical data — even if based on millions of documents — remains just data. An advocate or adjudicator still has to do something with it. If the understanding of the terms as set forth in the dissent was reflected in a corpus linguistics examination, the insurer would presumably argue that it was the beneficiary of a clearly written, widely understood limitation on coverage that precluded any judicial consideration of contextual factors or the policyholder's own understanding or reliance. Conversely, if the big data was inconclusive, the estate of the policyholder would argue that the policy was ambiguous on its face, opening the door to receipt of the extrinsic evidence favoring the decedent policyholder or triggering contra proferentem in her favor (or both).

But if the big data supported the dissent, would the policyholder's estate still have an argument that the circumstances surrounding the sale of the flight insurance precluded avoiding coverage through policy text? Would it be appropriate for a court to deem the sale price misleading or the arrangement unconscionable or violative of public policy?

And just because the data is big, does not necessarily make it Delphic (as in the all-seeing Delphi Oracle).[38] What if the database is not sufficiently broad? Or if the search strategy yielding the numbers is flawed? More important, does the use of a large corpus simply substitute a computer database for a shelf of dictionaries without addressing the problems of excessive focus on documentary text?

For a friendly but thoughtful cautionary critique of the corpus linguistics approach, see Lawrence M. Solan & Tammy Gales, *Corpus Linguistics as a Tool in Legal Interpretation*, 2017 BYU L. Rev. 1311. *See also* Lee & Mouritsen, 127 Yale L.J. at 865–76 (recognizing and responding to criticisms of corpus linguistics approach based on lack of "proficiency" of lawyers and judges with the tool, "propriety" of judicial research in databases, "practicality" concerns that assessing meaning via corpus linguistics will require inordinate investment of judicial resources; limitations on the observed data; and prospect of political opportunism.

In general, we find the use of a corpus as a guide to word meaning promising—particularly when dealing with historical searches for word meaning. Although one can do this with an older dictionary as well, we in general prefer more information to less information. And in a given personal or commercial context, the manner in which society uses words in that context may well be a more accurate guide than the definitions assigned by professional lexicographers.

Consequently, we regard corpus linguistics as a promising tool, but only a tool, for adjudication rather than a substitute for the adjudicatory process. As elaborated more in the following section, we are skeptical of interpretative approaches that are too fundamentalist in their focus on text. As noted in a passage earlier in this Chapter, the "contract" is the agreement between the parties. The written expression of the agreement is just that—an expression. It is not "the contract" but is the documen-

---

38. The continued cachet of the Oracle led social scientists in the 1960s to develop the "Delphi Method" of problem solving through systemic surveying of experts in particular field. *See* Juan Batalier-Grau, Elies Segue-Mas, Javier Vercher-Moll & Jeffrey W. Stempel, *Constructing More Reliable Law and Policy: The Potential Benefits of the Underused Delphi Method*, 87 UMKC L. Rev. 919 (2019).

tation of the contract, a "contract document," if you will. And there may be several "contract documents" of relevance in resolving a contract dispute, even in cases where the contract document purports to be a final and full expression of the agreement and is subject to the parol evidence rule.

We are concerned that advocates of the corpus linguistics approach may be simply using a bigger dictionary without thinking sufficiently about the task of contract construction. Despite its big data, the corpus linguistics movement remains a text-focused movement. Although this places the movement squarely within the legal mainstream of focus on contract document text, it is a focus we find myopic (more on that in the next section) in that it assumes (wrongly) that contract document text is all there is to a contract and that the judicial role is confined to only linguistic analysis of the face of a contract document.

For example, one prominent jurist stated at a program during the 2019 AALS (Association of American Law Schools) Meeting that he was "paid to disambiguate language." We understand that in context the statement was not a comprehensive job description but nonetheless find it concerning in that this statement, like undue enthusiasm for corpus linguistics, reflects undue preoccupation with the written word and insufficient attention to a more comprehensive assessment of contractual undertakings and disputes generally.

Judges are not scholars of sacred scripts. They are, in our view, paid not to "disambiguate" language but to adjudicate disputes.[39] When those disputes involve contract disputes, the job description of the judge is to resolve them consistent with

---

39. We realize that this assessment will grate against the prevailing views of many readers and arguably runs counter to the conventional wisdom of the judicial role, in which court nominees often sift through confirmation by maintaining that all they do is "apply" the law, a perspective that in extreme cases reduces the richness of the common law to a caricature.

Although modern law (at least in Western democracies) is secular, many of its roots are religious. The great religions of the world place a primacy on text, e.g.: The Old Testament and the Talmud for Judaism; the entire Bible for Christianity; the Koran for Islam. The constant study and assessment of these sacred texts is at the heart of these religions. The leaders of the religions are viewed as experts in the text and are usually formally trained in the "correct" interpretation of the text, with the rank and file or "flock" of the religion receiving training-cum-indoctrination in the text at an early age as part of being received into adult membership in the religion.

Most members of the legal profession grew up in this tradition. For example, the current U.S. Supreme Court is comprised of five Roman Catholics (Justices Roberts, Thomas, Alito, Sotomayor and Kavanaugh), an Episcopalian (Justice Gorsuch), and three Jews (Justices Ginsburg, Breyer and Kagan). It is no accident that American lawyers and judges bring with them this socio-religious background that places primacy on sacred texts.

American constitutional law is particularly associated with this perspective, with constitutional discourse often discussing the text of the document as if discussing stone tablets brought down from Mount Sinai. The authors of the Constitution are commonly referred to as the "Founders" or the more gendered "Founding Fathers" as if deities. Perhaps not God, Yahweh or Allah, but at least Zeus or Athena. Constitutional originalists are extreme in this view, taking the position that the document must in 2020 be construed as understood by property-owning (including slaves in some cases) white men who, despite their wisdom, could never have envisioned air travel, the internet, social media, smart phones, Russian troll farms, nuclear weapons, or that California would eventually be not only a state but the nation's largest state. (cont'd on next page)

the context of the dispute in light of the intent of the parties and the purpose of the agreement in light of the legal infrastructure, which, where apt, may include consideration of unconscionability, illegality, public policy, custom, practice, and reasonable expectation.

For courts overly focused on text, corpus linguistics allows them to retain an excessive textual focus but claim to have the support of society as reflected by social use of words in dispute. By appearing to be — and in all likelihood actually being — more reliable than an individual judge's internal understanding of language or a dictionary definition, corpus linguistics discourages judges from considering other indicia of contract meaning.

In that sense, it has kinship with the modern judicial preference for deciding cases pursuant to Rule 12 motions or summary judgment motions. The judge remains in chambers focusing on documents or, in the case of corpus linguistics, a database. In doing so, the judge invests time, probably more time than appreciated, that could have been spent actually investigating the surrounding circumstances of the dispute rather than exercising a tunnel vision focus on text alone. The same time devoted toward understanding an industry, party relations, the goal of the arrangement, the negotiations, and the behaviors of the parties as well as the dispute itself would in our view lead to more accurate resolution of disputes, perhaps in less time than is required for constructing and assessing a corpus language search.

### Layperson Surveys

Related to but distinct from the corpus linguistics approach is the use of survey research specifically directed at eliciting layperson meaning of a contractual provision, which may be seen as a variant of use of surveys in trademark/antitrust/consumer confusion cases. *See, e.g*, Omri Ben-Shahar & Lior Strahilevitz, *Interpreting Contracts via Surveys and Experiments*, 92 N.Y.U. L. Rev. 1753 (2017). It differs in that it does not attempt to catch laypersons speaking "naturally" but instead asks them to interpret

---

Statutory interpretation is similarly afflicted with the perspective, particularly in the jurisprudence of extreme textualists such as the late Justice Scalia, who refused to even consider legislative history when construing statutes (or at least professed that view). His rationale was that only the language of the statute was the positive law of the sovereign — the sacred text, if you will — and that additional information bearing on meaning was only gloss. The proper judicial role therefore was to construe the text according to the judge's best hermeneutic efforts, employing canons of construction as necessary. For example, Scalia & Garner, Reading Law (2012), collects and discusses hundreds of canons of construction.

The flaws of the Scalia approach in our view are two-fold. One, it falsely presumes that text in isolation is capable of accurate construction. Context is essential, and legislative history provides particularly valuable context. To be sure, it must be assessed prudently. The isolated floor statement of Senator Foghorn Leghorn (who may have opposed the bill) may be misleading. But does that mean courts should ignore the Committee Report about the legislation that was issued without even a dissent? Second, Scalia and other advocates of strict textualism contradict themselves when they use not only canons of word meaning (such as those discussed earlier in this chapter) but also canons of substantive law or policy such as the canon that a law should be construed as constitutional if possible. It's not a bad canon — but it is one silently considering context and public policy, something textualists claim not to be doing when rendering decisions.

or construe terms. Respondents are presented with particular contract language and asked whether it does or does not have a particular meaning or compel a particular result.

We find this approach far less promising than corpus linguistics and even potentially pernicious to the extent it is used as anything other than a rough guide to lay perception of words in dispute in a given case. And even then, to what value is an untrained random mall-wanderer's opinion about the interpretation of an insurance policy? As we know, most have never even read their own policy. Most would certainly have no training in risk principles of insurance, or underwriting, or even basic law, let alone have any inkling as to the just result in an insurance coverage dispute.

We are all for courts considering contextual information to aid in interpreting insurance policies. But we do have a basic assumption that that contextual information have at least a modicum of helpful value to it. In short, the information needs to be relevant to context. Interrupting people shopping for shoes and asking them what "flood" means and if they think they would be covered if faced with a "water" exclusion in a homeowners policy does nothing at all to add to interpretive context. We would not value such disambiguated input in a murder case (i.e., "guilty or innocent—what do you think?") or even a motor vehicle accident case (i.e., "did the driver breach the standard of care?"). So how does doing it in a case where peoples' entire financial universe depends on the answer make it relevant? In short, this sort of data does nothing to improve the "justness" of the outcome of an insurance policy coverage dispute.

## § 2.17. Evaluating Contract Construction Approaches and Considering Alternative Conceptions of the Insurance Policy

By now it is pretty obvious that we are not textualists regarding insurance policy interpretation or contract construction generally.[40] But neither are we anti-text. Rather, we regard text as an important element of resolving contract and insurance disputes. In most cases, it will probably be the predominant resolution factor. Over time, most language in common insurance policies has come to have sufficiently understood meanings that a court's initial reading of an insurance policy is unlikely to be changed by consideration of other information. Sometimes, there is little or no additional in-

---

40. Although it has fallen into relative disuse, there has historically been a distinction between "interpretation" and "construction." Interpretation, strictly speaking, is a court's assessment of the meaning of a text or the "discovery of communicative content," while construction involves the "determination of legal effect" of a text (we borrow the quoted phrases from Prof. Lawrence Solum). Seen in this light, some factors extrinsic to document text are clearly matters of construction rather than interpretation, e.g.: illegality; unconscionability; public policy. However, extrinsic evidence about technical meaning of a term or party understanding regarding the connotation of words used in a written instrument appear to us to bear upon interpretation.

formation relevant to a contract but the text (although this should not preclude consideration of other factors such as public policy or effective risk management).

Our point is simply that courts should generally not refuse proffers of non-textual evidence purportedly bearing on meaning when such information is available. Rather, courts should consider the proffered information and determine whether it is sufficiently reliable, germane, or weighty to affect the court's reading of policy text.

In other words, courts should be willing to make a comprehensive assessment of a disputed insurance policy or other salient document in an insurance dispute. Refusal to do so makes too much ride on the judge's reading of text alone. Consideration of the additional material can serve as a check on erroneous textual construction. Even if the judges correctly read insurance policies or other contract documents 80 percent of the time, there is still an unacceptably high error rate that can be reduced by consideration of additional information.[41] In many cases, non-textual information (even if proffered by an attorney disputing the apparent meaning of text) merely buttresses the court's initial reading of policy text. But where this is not the case, the court (and the parties and the judicial system) are saved from the consequences of an erroneous reading of text in isolation.

Textualists argue that consideration of non-textual information squanders judicial resources. First, we think the argument is, if not empirically wrong, overstated. Reading and interpreting takes time. Considering non-textual information may take somewhat more time but in our view is not a daunting task, particularly when one considers that time spent considering additional evidence may well reduce the time a judge needs to ponder text in isolation. And, if there are the better results we posit from a more comprehensive approach, judicial resources will be saved because there will be fewer reversals on appeal and fewer second and third rounds of pretrial litigation and trial. Justice is improved.

Second, if the error rate of text-only analysis is anything more than miniscule, a full and fair cost-benefit analysis is likely to weigh on the side of a more comprehensive approach. Judicial costs and benefits are not the only things that count. Costs and benefits to society count. There are hundreds of thousands of contract disputes in the courts, and at least tens of thousands of insurance disputes. This means even a modest improvement in the accuracy of contract adjudication outcomes—which we posit comes if the court considers more things (e.g., party intent, contract purpose, custom, practice, course of dealing/performance, extrinsic evidence, contracting context) rather than fewer things (e.g., text alone or text in conjunction with dictionaries and canons of construction)—will produce significant social benefits.

---

41. Because of the cognitive trait of "false consensus bias," judges, like everyone else, are prone to inaccurately predicting that most everyone reads a document in accordance with the judge's reading. But there is substantially more variation in textual interpretation than readers realize. *See* Lawrence Solan, et al., *False Consensus Bias in Contract Interpretation*, 108 COLUM. L. REV. 1268 (2008). *See also* Dan Kahan, et al., *Whose Eyes Are You Going to Believe? Scott v. Harris and the Perils of Cognitive Illiberalism*, 122 HARV. L. REV. 837 (2009) (noting degree of variation in perception of a videotaped car chase deemed absolutely conclusive by eight of nine U.S. Supreme Court justices).

The benefits of a more comprehensive approach to contract construction will come at the price of some marginal increase in expenditure of judicial resources. But we think that (a) the marginal increase will not be particularly great and certainly not prohibitively expensive; and (b) the increase will be outweighed by the net social benefit of more consistently accurate and/or fair[42] resolution of contract disputes. Again, justice is improved. Is justice not supposed to be the very aim of the court system?

It should be remembered that the American judicial system is "adversarial" and not "inquisitorial" as are the European legal systems. Although calling something "inquisitorial" has a negative connotation, a la Edgar Allen Poe's *The Pit and the Pendulum*, it really means nothing more than that, in European countries, judges are charged with more development of the facts in adjudicating a dispute. By contrast, Anglo-American judges have the facts developed and presented to them by counsel to a greater degree than in continental countries.

This means that if an insurance litigant or other contract disputant wants the court to consider something other than just the text of an insurance policy or contract document, the party's counsel must place before the judge the additional information

---

42. In some cases, the result we favor will be at odds with an arguably or even concededly better reading of policy text but will be the "fairer" or "better" result because it was commanded by factors of preventing fraud, avoiding unfair surprise or oppression, or furthering the apt function of insurance markets or society. Although the notion of a fair result surmounting policy text is generally thought to benefit policyholders, we think a more comprehensive approach has bilateral benefits and would equally assist insurers. After all, if a court considers underwriting evidence, that would assist insurers in being "truer" to the risk insured.

For example, policyholders have at times attempted to achieve pollution liability coverage through the portion of the standard general liability policy that covers claims for "trespass," arguing that pollution incursion constitutes a trespass. Most courts rejected this view based on their understanding of the term "trespass." But those courts would be on solider ground by also considering that this portion of the policy is intended only to cover certain types of "personal injury" claims rather than the "bodily injury" claims covered under another portion of the policy that contains and explicit pollution exclusion.

As another example of a comprehensive approach reaching a pro-insurer but socially correct result, consider a bar that buys a standard general liability insurance policy, as addressed in Problem 5 of this Chapter. The policy has a liquor liability exclusion, so a purely textual approach would find no coverage if the bar is sued by a drunken patron who collides with a tree on his way home after closing time. But one can make a good case that the bar owner policyholder had an objectively reasonable expectation of coverage because the insurer knew he was operating a bar when the policy was sold. However, if one considers the purpose, function, history, and risk management objectives of insurance, enforcing the liquor liability exclusion makes sense.

General liability policies are designed to cover general liability risks such as clients slipping, falling, getting food poisoning and the like. Liquor liability risks, like pollution risks or professional liability risks, have long been viewed as presenting a separate set of challenges that require underwriting and coverage through separately purchased liquor liability, pollution, and professional liability policies, which are all available for purchase in the open market.

Although it is in some sense unfair to the bar owner who was blindsided by lack of coverage, this is the better result in light of the comprehensive set of concerns. In addition, the unfairness can be mitigated in that the bar owner probably has a claim for professional negligence against the insurance agent that sold the bar a general liability policy without also procuring a liquor liability policy.

that purportedly illuminates the meaning of policy or other documentary text. In other words, the party arguing for something other than the most natural reading of text must "put up or shut up." A litigant and counsel will not waste resources or invite sanctions by proffering obviously inapt information.

Consequently, comprehensive, non-textual information will flow to the court only in instances where litigants and counsel have made a considered decision that the information either buttresses a seemingly favorable text or negates a seemingly unfavorable text. The former (piling extrinsic evidence on top of seemingly favorable text) will be comparatively rarer, because counsel may perceive a danger in bringing in additional information if counsel sees the text as favorable, particularly in jurisdictions that are resistant to extrinsic evidence. Litigants and counsel are unlikely to invest their own personal resources in perceived futile battles once aware that a court is leaning against it on a question of textual interpretation. This will mean less demand on judicial resources than feared by critics of extrinsic evidence.

Under these circumstances, we posit that when parties seek to add extra-textual information to the record, it will either (a) be important and have a reasonable chance of affecting the court's assessment of policy text or (b) be so tangential or unimportant that judges can dispense with it quickly without much investment of judicial resources. To be sure, even weak arguments that are quickly dismissed can become a drag on the judiciary if they appear in sufficient volume. An extremely permissive attitude with introduction of extrinsic evidence holds some risk of "death by a thousand cuts." But we think the risk is minimal and likely to be far outweighed by improvement in the overall quality and improved socioeconomic results of a more comprehensive approach to determining contract meaning.

In addition to taking a broad approach to assessing contract meaning or giving significant weight to contract purpose and the reasonable expectations of the parties, one might look at insurance policies not so much as contracts but as products. *See* Jeffrey W. Stempel, *The Insurance Policy as Thing*, 44 Trial & Ins. L.J. 813 (2009); Daniel Schwarcz, *A Product Liability Theory of Insurance*, 48 Wm. & Mary L. Rev. 1389 (2007). Or as statutes or private legislation. *See* Jeffrey W. Stempel, *The Insurance Policy as Statute*, 41 McGeorge L. Rev. 203 (2010). Or as a social institution serving particular functions. *See* Jeffrey W. Stempel, *The Insurance Policy as Social Instrument and Social Institution*, 51 Wm. & Mary L. Rev. 1489 (2010) (Winner, 2009 Liberty Mutual Insurance Prize). Or as a regulated industry such as a utility. *See* Kenneth S. Abraham, *Four Conceptions of Insurance*, 161 U. Pa. L. Rev. 653 (2013); Erik S. Knutsen, *Auto Insurance as Social Contract: Solving Automobile Insurance Coverage Disputes Through a Public Regulatory Framework*, 48 Alberta L. Rev. 715 (2011).

Although none of these alternative views of the insurance policy are likely to displace the contract paradigm—at least regarding articulated doctrine—consideration of these alternative "identities" of the insurance policy would help courts in deciphering problematic policy language and resolving coverage disputes and disputes involving conduct in the administration of an insurance policy such as allegations of bad faith claims-handling (*see* Ch. 12).

For example, thinking of an insurance policy as a product serves as a means of making sure that isolated, unclear, problematic text neither negates the basic value and purpose of the policy or unduly extends it beyond insuring intent. Considering the policy as a statute permits consideration of potentially helpful approaches to statutory construction, including judicious and cost-effective examination of the background and development of particular coverages and coverage limitations, which may include more searching examination of drafting history. Seeing insurance policies as social instruments or important regulated industries with network effects helps inform the public policy choices courts may need to make about how insurance operates as the financial backbone of the compensatory system in society, as well as application of doctrines such as unconscionability or fortuity.

A common thread connecting these alternative viewpoints is their greater kinship with contextual approaches to policy interpretation and to the view that insurance policies generally should operate as reasonably expected by policyholders and insurers. An approach to resolving disputes over insurance policy meaning that vindicates the purposes and objectives of the policy, effective risk management, and social concerns such as victim compensation, policyholder protection, and optimal distribution of losses should be preferred to one excessively focused on words alone.

## PROBLEM SIX

*Version One:* Neighbor is visiting Typical Family. While Neighbor is leaving, she gets hit by a go-cart being driven in the driveway by 8-year-old Son and suffers a broken ankle. Despite the risk to the social fabric of the block, Neighbor sues Family for negligent supervision and Boy (as an insured under the Family homeowners policy) for negligent "driving."

Family and Boy tender defense of the claim to Insurer. Insurer denies coverage, invoking the following provisions of the policy:

> you are not insured for claims made against you arising from ... the ownership, use or operation of any motorized land vehicle, trailer, or watercraft, except those for which coverage is shown in this policy, and motorized land vehicles in dead storage on the premises.

Family counters by noting additional policy language that provides exceptions to these exclusions for "ownership, use or operation" of:

> lawn mowers, snow blowers, garden-type tractors, or implements used or operated mainly on your premises provided they are not used for compensation or hire;
>
> motorized golf carts while in use on a golf course; and
>
> motorized wheelchairs and their trailers [and further]

> you are insured against claims arising out of your use or operation of any self-propelled land vehicle, amphibious vehicle or air cushion vehicle, including their trailers, which you do not own provided:

the vehicle is designed primarily for use off public roads; and you are not using it for business or organized racing [however] you are not insured for damage to the vehicle itself.

Insurer moves for summary judgment.

 • What is the likely ruling?

 • Are there additional facts that should be developed?

 • Will it vary according to interpretative approach?

*Version Two:* Same visit from Neighbor and same insurance policy language, but Neighbor breaks her ankle stepping on and tripping over Boy's motorized Tonka Truck powered by four "D" batteries.

 • Same likely result?

 • Does the change in facts change the relative merits of different contract construction factors?

# § 2.18. Conflict of Laws

In insurance policy problems where the laws of two or more jurisdictions are involved, the conflict of laws question under the traditional view has been resolved in favor of applying the law of the place where the contract was in fact made or finally executed. Commonly, this is the state where the insurance policy is delivered to the policyholder.

When following this approach, the applicable law is clear when the policy application, premium payments, and delivery of the policy all occurred in the same state. But all these acts are not always performed in the same state. When various events happen in different jurisdictions, the traditional view is that an insurance policy is deemed to be executed at the place where the last significant act is done to complete the transaction and bind both the parties.

With the adoption of the *Restatement (Second) of Conflict of Laws* by a majority of states, the traditional approach has been replaced in many jurisdictions in favor of applying the law of the state with the "most significant relationship" to the insurance policy. Under the *Second Restatement* approach, for example, the principal location of the insured risk, or the parties' domicile, constitutes an adequate relationship for that state's law to apply. RESTATEMENT (SECOND) OF CONFLICT OF LAWS §§ 191–193 (1971). *Restatement* § 6(2) provides that the following seven factors are relevant in conducting a choice of law inquiry:

 (a) the needs of the interstate and international systems;

 (b) the relevant policies of the forum;

 (c) the relevant policies of other interested states and the relative interests of those states in the determination of the particular issue;

 (d) the protection of justified expectations;

(e) the basic policies underlying the particular field of law;

(f) certainty, predictability and uniformity of result; and

(g) ease in the determination and application of the law to be applied.

Section 145(2) also instructs that when applying the §6 factors, courts should take into account the following four contacts:

(a) the place where the injury occurred;

(b) the place where the conduct causing the injury occurred;

(c) the domicile, residence, nationality, place of incorporation and place of business of the parties; and

(d) the place where the relationship, if any, between the parties is centered.

Finally, § 146 provides that the law of the state where the injury occurred should apply "unless, with respect to the particular issue, some other state has a more significant relationship under the principles stated in § 6 to the occurrence and the parties."

Although choice of law questions can be complex and time-consuming to resolve, in the majority of cases, they are not. As one treatise summarized:

> [I]f the policy declarations show an address for the named insured and the broker in one state, the person seeking coverage is the named insured (or some other entity in that same state), and the claim arose and the underlying lawsuit are pending in that same state, then that state's law should control absent some unusual circumstance.

*See* RANDY MANILOFF & JEFFREY STEMPEL, GENERAL LIABILITY INSURANCE COVERAGE: KEY ISSUES IN EVERY STATE Ch. 18 (4th ed. 2018) (chapter authored by Stephen Klepper, Esq.) (chapter also provides survey of aspects of state approaches to choice of law).

Insurance disputes can present a different aspect of choice of law in that some courts have applied a "site of the insured risk" analysis in lieu of a pure *Restatement* or place-of-contract-formation analysis. By contrast, commercial liability and property policies are often sold to policyholders who own property and do business (thereby risking litigation) throughout the United States or even the world. For example, a manufacturer of widgets may have processing plants, distribution centers, and sales in all 50 states.

When these policyholders are sued in all 50 states, should a court select a single applicable state law or look to the law of the place where the underlying event gave rise to a coverage dispute? In these situations, the question arises as to whether courts should attempt to select the law of a single jurisdiction with the most significant relationship to the entire insurer-policyholder relationship or should instead select differing state law depending on where the policy was sold or delivered or where the particular risk at issue in the case may be located. Under the site-of-the-risk analysis the court applies the law of the state in which the events take place that give rise to the insurance coverage dispute.

Although the "site specific" or site-of-the-insured-risk or particular-place-of-policy-delivery approaches have significant support, it appears that the so-called "uniform" approach is gaining ground in modern cases. *See Nat'l Union Fire Ins. Co. v. Std. Fusee Corp.*, 940 N.E.2d 810 (Ind. 2010) (opting for uniform approach and finding Maryland law applicable rather than Indiana or California law) ("[a]lthough none of the [*Restatement*] factors are determinative, 'the overall number and quality of contacts' favor Maryland over Indiana") (California law would have applied only if the court would have followed a site-specific approach). Describing the distinction in approaches, the *Standard Fusee* court stated that

> the uniform-contract-interpretation approach applies the law of a single state to the whole contract even though it covers multiple risks in multiple states; the site-specific approach applies the law of the state or states where the insured risks are located, unless another state has a more significant relationship to the particular issue.

*See id.* at 812. The Indiana Supreme Court noted that its precedents had "not allowed for *depecage*, or 'the process of analyzing different issues within the same case separately under the laws of different states'" and that the "general development of Indiana's choice-of-law rules leads us to conclude that the uniform-contract-interpretation approach is more consistent with our jurisprudence, as it applies a single state's law to the entire contract." *Id.* at 815 (citation omitted).

"[I]f the substantive law is the same in all jurisdictions whose law could possibly apply, there is no need to undertake a choice-of-law analysis." MANILOFF & STEMPEL, *supra*, at 19. The choice between two jurisdictions with the same rule of law is usually termed a "false conflict," although "no conflict" would probably be a more accurate term. The party seeking to invoke state law other than that of the forum state generally has the burden to establish a material difference between the law of the two states. *See, e.g., Excess Underwriters at Lloyd's v. Frank's Casing Crew & Rental Tools, Inc.*, 246 S.W.3d 42, 53 (Tex. 2008).

Students will remember from Civil Procedure class that federal courts hearing cases where subject matter jurisdiction is founded on diversity must under the *Erie* doctrine usually apply state law rather than any general federal common law. A corollary of this is that the federal court must apply the choice of law methodology of the state in which the federal court sits so that choice of law in a given dispute would be the same in either federal or state court. *See Klaxon Co. v. Stentor Electric Mfg. Co.*, 313 U.S. 487, 496 (1941).

Judges tend to apply forum state law absent compelling factors to the contrary. Despite the command of the Constitution's Full Faith and Credit Clause that the laws of one state be respected by other courts, courts as a constitutional matter have broad discretion regarding choice of law so long as the court's decision is "neither arbitrary nor fundamentally unfair." *See Allstate Ins. Co. v. Hague*, 449 U.S. 302, 312–13 (1981). In practice, this means that it will be difficult to overturn more trial court decisions on choice of law.

One means of minimizing court discretion and obtaining greater certainty as to the applicable law is use of a choice of law clause in the insurance policy in order to designate a particular state's (or country's) law as applicable. Although the applicable law is a default rule that can be changed by the contracting parties, courts generally place some limits on enforceability of choice of law clauses, requiring that the state or country chosen have a sufficient relationship to the parties or the transaction (or the risk).

Choice of law clauses should be distinguished from choice of forum clauses. For example, many of the high limit excess liability insurance policies sold by Bermuda-based insurers provide that disputes will be arbitrated in London pursuant to the procedural rules of the English Arbitration Act. However, these policies also typically provide that New York substantive law will apply. But just to make it complex, these clauses also commonly state that the arbitrators are to apply New York law shorn of the part of the state's contract and insurance law that considers the objectively reasonable expectations of the parties and resolves ambiguous language against the drafter, at least as a tie-breaker. Arguably such clauses are better described as customization of law clauses rather than choice of law clauses — and they have been challenged by policyholders on that basis. But to our knowledge, such challenges have generally been rejected and, much to the consternation of policyholders, the arbitrators have endeavored to apply New York law stripped of two important pro-policyholder provisions.

Although not everyday happenings, cases involving serious choice of law issues emerge with some frequency. In the case that follows, consider whether the majority has correctly applied the American Law Institute's *Restatement (Second) of the Conflict of Laws* or whether, as the dissent asserts, the majority erred by failing to consider the applicable underlying tort law of the state in which the accident occurred.

- In addressing choice of law issues, students should ask themselves:
  - What are the arguable benefits and detriments of the different approaches?
  - Which makes more sense in a world of multi-national policyholders and insurers?
  - Does the presumed efficiency of a uniform approach pose significant risk to the public policy goals of states whose laws would apply under a site-specific approach but are disregarded under the uniform approach?

## Krauss v. Manhattan Life Insurance Co. of New York

United States Court of Appeals, Second Circuit
643 F.2d 98 (1981)

### Lumbard, Circuit Judge.

Frances Krauss is the beneficiary under a group life insurance policy held by her deceased husband, Hyman Krauss. At all times relevant to this action, the Krausses were Illinois domiciliaries. Hyman Krauss, an attorney and member of the Illinois bar, was a part-time officer of Lettercraft, Inc., an Illinois corporation based in Chicago which has since changed its name to Chicago Aligraphy and Lithography.

Lettercraft was and is a member of the Master Printers Management Group Life Insurance Trust Fund (Trust Fund) which has its principal place of business in Buffalo, New York. The Trust Fund provides group life insurance to the employees of its members and has members in virtually every state. On December 21, 1960, Manhattan Life issued and delivered a group life insurance policy (the master policy) to the Trust Fund in Buffalo. Manhattan Life is a New York corporation, licensed to do business in every state, with its principal offices in New York City. The master policy contained no choice-of-law provision.

Manhattan Life issued certificate number 1196 to Hyman Krauss, effective September 14, 1966, for $50,000 coverage of term life insurance, which was increased to $100,000 on December 18, 1967. From 1966 until Hyman Krauss's death, Lettercraft paid Krauss's insurance premiums to the Trust Fund administrator in Los Angeles who collected all premium payments from members and forwarded a single check to Manhattan Life. Under the master policy, the premiums increased for each $1,000 of insurance coverage obtained, and thus Lettercraft paid four times as much for $100,000 coverage as it would have for $25,000 coverage.

The master policy, however, did not provide $100,000 coverage for part-time employees such as Hyman Krauss. Manhattan Life asserts that the group policy allowed only $25,000 for part-time employees, while Frances Krauss asserts $40,000 as the correct figure. In any event, due to his part-time status, Hyman Krauss was ineligible under the group policy for $100,000 in coverage. Neither on the application form nor at any time before Hyman Krauss's death did Manhattan Life inquire as to whether he was a full-or part-time employee of Lettercraft, how many hours a week he worked there, or whether that work constituted his primary business activity. On the other hand, Lettercraft paid the premiums even though the master policy clearly excluded part-time employees from that coverage; and, when Hyman Krauss applied for an increase in coverage from $50,000 to $100,000 on December 1, 1967, he stated that he had no other occupation although in fact he was practicing law in Chicago.

Hyman Krauss died of leukemia on April 18, 1977. Frances Krauss filed an application for payment of $100,000, plus interest, under her husband's certificate on May 18, 1977. Manhattan Life paid her $25,000, plus interest, which it stated was the maximum coverage under the policy for part-time employees. Since the master policy was issued and delivered in New York State, section 161(1)(a) of the New York Insurance Law required the policy to include an incontestability clause. That clause provides that the "validity of this Policy shall not be contested, except for nonpayment of premiums, after it has been in force for two years from its date of issue." Illinois and New York differ regarding the effect of such an incontestability clause where, as here, an insurance company seeks to defend against liability on grounds that the insured was not eligible for insurance under the group policy.

Under New York law, as established in *Simpson v. Phoenix Mutual Life Insurance Co.*, 24 N.Y.2d 262, 299 N.Y.S.2d 835, 247 N.E.2d 655 (1969), Manhattan Life cannot raise Hyman Krauss's ineligibility as a defense and would hence be liable for the entire $100,000. Under Illinois law, as established in *Crawford v. Equitable Life Assurance*

*Society of the United States*, 56 Ill. 2d 41, 305 N.E.2d 144 (1973), Manhattan Life can raise Hyman Krauss's ineligibility as a defense. Contrary to the conclusions of the district court, we believe that, because Illinois is the only state with an enunciated interest in this dispute, Illinois law should apply. Accordingly, despite the incontestability clause, Manhattan Life can assert Hyman Krauss's ineligibility as a defense.

Under the principles of *Erie Railroad Co. v. Tompkins*, 304 U.S. 64 (1938), a federal court in a diversity case must apply the substantive law of the forum state, including its choice-of-law rules. Thus, as recognized by the district court, New York choice-of-law rules govern this case. In *Dym v. Gordon*, 209 N.E.2d 792, 794 (N.Y. 1965), the Court of Appeals outlined those rules as a three-step analysis. First, the court must isolate the issue on which the laws conflict. Second, it must identify the purposes of the conflicting state laws to determine whether a genuine conflict exists. Third, it must examine the contacts of the interested jurisdictions to ascertain which has the closer connection with the facts of the case and thus has the superior interest in seeing its law applied.

The first step in the New York choice-of-law analysis is determining the issue in dispute: here, the issue on which Illinois and New York law differ is the interpretation of the incontestability clause, not the requirement that it be included in the policy. The statutes of both New York, N.Y. Ins. L. § 161(1)(a), and Illinois, Ill. Ins. Code § 231, require that an incontestability clause be placed in any group insurance policy issued or delivered in the respective state. The two states differ, however, on whether the clause precludes challenges to the insured's eligibility.

We next identify the policies of New York and Illinois that are promoted by the conflicting state rules, the second step in the New York choice-of-law analysis.

Illinois law would allow Manhattan Life to raise Hyman Krauss's ineligibility as a defense while New York would not. The district court determined that Illinois's interest in that approach was the protection of Illinois insurance companies, and it therefore held that Illinois had no interest in the application of its law to this case because a New York insurer was involved. We disagree.

The Illinois Supreme Court in *Crawford, supra*, expressly based its decision on a policy of protecting Illinois residents who held group insurance certificates against a rate increase that would occur if insurance companies had to investigate each insured's eligibility. 56 Ill. 2d at 52, 305 N.E.2d at 151. Moreover, *Crawford*, like this case, involved an Illinois insured suing a New York insurance company. There can be no doubt that the Illinois Supreme Court intended to benefit Illinois certificate-holders who are fully eligible at the expense of those who, like Hyman Krauss, are ineligible; the location of the insurance company is irrelevant. Thus, were the courts of Illinois to address this case, they would advance Illinois's interest in keeping group insurance rates lower by permitting Manhattan Life to contest eligibility.

New York, on the other hand, would allow Frances Krauss to recover if she were a New York domiciliary, but it has expressed no interest in allowing recovery by nondomiciliaries. As aptly summarized by the district court, the New York Court of Appeals's motivation in *Simpson, supra,* was to allow New York residents greater security in planning their estates by freeing them from the risks of posthumous life insurance disputes. 24 N.Y.2d at 266, 299 N.Y.S.2d at 839, 247 N.E.2d at 657. Nothing in *Simpson* suggests that the court was concerned with making New York a more desirable place to obtain insurance or that an altruistic concern for citizens of other states was involved.

Thus the interests of only one state, Illinois, would be advanced by applying its law to the facts of this case. New York has expressed no interest in protecting non-domiciliaries with its restriction on insurance companies' available defenses, but Illinois's concern for Illinois group insurance holders would be advanced—precisely as it was in *Crawford*—by allowing Manhattan Life to raise the eligibility defense.

The choice of Illinois law is also buttressed by the third consideration of the New York choice-of-law analysis—evaluating the grouping of contacts between the competing jurisdictions on the facts of the case. The district court, relying on its interpretation of Illinois's and New York's interests in the dispute, held that New York was the "center of gravity" of the transaction. We disagree. We have found no New York choice-of-law case that has applied New York law upon such limited contacts with the state. Lettercraft was a Chicago-based, Illinois corporation. All of its employees, including Hyman Krauss, worked in that state. The Krausses were Illinois domiciliaries. The certificate of insurance evidencing Hyman Krauss's coverage was delivered in Illinois. Manhattan Life was licensed to do business in Illinois. The only New York contacts were the issuance and delivery of the master policy.

In light of Illinois being the only jurisdiction with an interest in having its law applied, those two events in New York are insufficient to establish that New York has superior contacts with this case. The plaintiff relies, as did the district court, on § 192, comment h, of the *Restatement (Second) of Conflict of Laws* (1971). Comment h provides that, under group insurance contracts, "the rights against the insurer are usually governed by the law which governs the master policy," and the parties agree that New York law would govern the master policy here. Mrs. Krauss argues that New York courts have adopted comment h as law. Although several New York holdings are consistent with the outcomes comment h would dictate, no New York court has wholly adopted the comment as law.

Because certificate holders in other states under the same master policy are apt to be governed by other states' laws, we recognize that the rule formulated by the *Second Restatement* might offer greater uniformity than the interest-analysis and center-of-gravity approach used by the New York courts. This does not, however, compel a different result. Uniformity and predictability were undeniably compromised when the classical territorial approach to choice-of-law problems was abandoned in [*Dym v. Gordon* and other modern New York cases]. The compromise was performed, however, to obtain a less rigid, more rational system. Under the principles of *Erie, supra,* it is not our role to question the policy choices of states whose law we apply. Moreover, this outcome retains substantial uniformity as to Lettercraft, all of whose employees are in Illinois.

Illinois law, therefore, should govern the interpretation of the incontestability clause. We accordingly reverse and remand for further proceedings consistent with this opinion.

## PROBLEM SEVEN

Should the rights of the insured employee be determined by:

• the law of the state where the "master policy" is located?

• or the law of the state where the insured employee's individual certificate is issued?

## PROBLEM EIGHT

For marine insurance controversies, which law should apply:

• The law of the country where the vessel was registered, or the law of the place of contracting?

• Should federal admiralty law apply in such matters, or state insurance law?

## PROBLEM NINE

A group credit life insurance policy was issued by an insurance company through a Kansas car dealer to a Missouri resident who bought his Dodge automobile from the car dealer. The master policy was delivered in Kansas, and the automobile was sold in Kansas, along with the credit life insurance policy.

In the policy was a provision, lawful under Kansas law, excluding suicide from coverage, but a Missouri statute barred suicide as an exclusion to coverage. A relevant clause in the insurance policy read: "Conformity with State Statutes: Any provision of this policy which is in conflict with the statutes of the state [in] which the Insured resides . . . is hereby amended to conform to the minimum requirements of such statutes."

When the insured committed suicide, his wife as beneficiary argued that since her husband resided in Missouri, Missouri law should apply. However, the insurer argued that the master policy was in Kansas, the insurance contract was executed in Kansas, and the dealer rather than the buyer was in fact the insured under the group policy.

How should the court rule in this case?

# Chapter 3

# Regulation of Insurance

## § 3.01. Insurance Regulation at the State and Federal Levels

Insurance is predominantly a state-regulated field, with a few notable exceptions. Under the U.S. Constitution's Commerce Clause, courts initially took the position that Congress has no authority to regulate the field of insurance. In 1905, the New York Armstrong Investigation uncovered major ethical issues in the life insurance industry. The state of New York's response was to increase regulation of that industry with greater controls. Since that time, the insurance business has been a heavily regulated industry with the dual purpose of promoting fair business practices and maintaining insurer solvency. The McCarran-Ferguson Act, 15 U.S.C. §§ 1011–1015 enshrined the interests of the states. Insurance law is thus a hybrid mixture of private contractual law and state statutory law which seeks to control the substantive terms of the insurance policy so that the insured may enter into a fair and equitable contract. *See, e.g.*, Spencer Kimball, *The Purpose of Insurance Regulation: A Preliminary Inquiry in the Theory of Insurance Law*, 45 Minn. L. Rev. 471, 490–91 (1961).

Accordingly, various "standard" statutory policy forms have been enacted at the insistence of the National Association of Insurance Commissioners (NAIC) in an attempt to bring certainty and uniformity into state statutory and regulatory practices. Efforts towards standardization have been successful to the extent that "standard" fire insurance policies and "standard" accident and sickness insurance policies in most states are now wholly mandated by statute. Life insurance and automobile liability insurance provisions are also largely controlled by state statutory law. If any conflict exists between the contractual provisions in an insurance policy and state statutory requirements, the statute prevails.

In fact, state regulation of the insurance business is so well established that in *California State Auto. Ass'n Inter-Ins. Bureau v. Maloney*, 341 U.S. 105 (1951), the United States Supreme Court held that the individual states could arguably take over the entire insurance business, leaving no part to private insurance companies. Moreover, after the passage in 1947 of Section 2(b) of the McCarran-Ferguson Act [15 U.S.C. § 1101], which mandates that federal regulation "shall be applicable to the business of insurance to the extent that such business is not regulated by State law," the insurance industry appears more willing to be subject to existing state regulation rather than to face the possibility of greater federal control.

Within this state statutory framework, domestic, foreign [sister state], and alien [foreign country] insurance companies are also administratively regulated by state insurance departments through their insurance commissioners or superintendents by virtue of authority delegated by the state legislature. Such departments are responsible for licensing or delicensing insurance companies and their agents, approving or disapproving insurance policy forms and rates, and periodically examining the insurers to ensure solvency and compliance with applicable state law. Part of the state regulatory scheme governing the insurance business is to regulate insurance rates to maintain a competitive level within the industry and to avoid rates that are excessive, inadequate, or unfairly discriminatory.

But an insurance commissioner is a ministerial officer, and possesses only such powers as state statute confers upon him or her. This chapter presents selected examples of governmental control over the insurance industry, and demonstrates how the private contractual relationship between the policyholder and the insurer is often largely controlled and regulated by public statutory and administrative law.

What is "insurance," for regulatory purposes? An activity classified as insurance must ordinarily have both risk transfer and risk distribution. Cases diverge over whether the peril insured must be external as well. As reflected in the different opinions in the *Griffin Systems* cases in Chapter 1, regulators view economic activity with an eye to classifying it as "insurance" if they believe that regulation is required by the public interest due to concerns over solvency of the vendor or the risk of harm through purchase of inadequate or defective agreements by consumers. The primary concern of most regulators is that the insurer be sufficiently financially sound to pay claims. *See, e.g., United Healthcare Benefits Trust v. Insurance Comm'r of Pa.*, 620 A.2d 81 (Pa. 1993).

# § 3.02. State Regulatory Powers over Insurance

## [A] Power to License Insurance Companies, Agents, and Brokers

States have the power to license insurance companies. *See, e.g., Fairmont Ins. Co. v. Commonwealth, Ins. Dep't*, 481 A.2d 696 (Pa. Commw. Ct. 1984). In addition to the power to license insurance companies, the *Fairmont* case demonstrates that the state insurance department may also refuse to renew an insurer's license if the insurance commissioner or superintendent no longer considers the company to be safe, reliable, or entitled to public confidence. However, the notice and opportunity for a hearing required by due process must be provided. *See, e.g., Bell v. Burson*, 402 U.S. 535 (1971); *Union Fidelity Life Ins. Co. v. Whaland*, 330 A.2d 782 (N.H. 1974).

In addition to licensing insurance companies, state legislatures also have the power to license insurance agents and brokers in order to protect the public in the purchase and sale of insurance policies. *See, e.g., Massachusetts Indem. & Life Ins. Co. v. Texas State Bd. of Ins.*, 685 S.W.2d 104 (Tex. App. 1985). The primary purpose of state statutes enumerating situations which justify the revocation or suspension of an insurance agent's license is to protect the public, and not to punish licensees or applicants. Therefore, any agent or applicant who practiced or aided in the practice of fraud, forgery, deception, collusion, or conspiracy in connection with any insurance transaction may be denied a license, or have his or her license suspended or revoked. It has also been held that the criminal defense of entrapment would not be available to an applicant, and that taped conversations between an applicant and undercover police officers could be admissible at an administrative hearing held by the state insurance commission. *See, e.g., Ballew v. Ainsworth*, 670 S.W.2d 94 (Mo. Ct. App. 1984). An applicant's or agent's criminal record or felony conviction may also be taken into account in deciding whether to grant, revoke, or suspend his license. *See, e.g., Appeal of Dillinger*, 26 Pa. Commw. 494, 364 A.2d 757 (1976); *Beck v. Ins. Comm'r & Treasurer*, 405 So. 2d 466 (Fla. Dist. Ct. App. 1981).

An insurance agent's or broker's license may also be suspended or revoked based on evidence of her "untrustworthiness," applied broadly as a term of art. *See, e.g., Bowley Associates, Ltd. v. State Ins. Dep't*, 98 A.D.2d 521, 471 N.Y.S.2d 585, aff'd, 63 N.Y.2d 982, 483 N.Y.S.2d 1011, 473 N.E.2d 261 (1984). For example, in Florida, an insurance agent's license was revoked after he pled guilty to conspiracy to distribute marijuana. This was a sufficient basis for the Insurance Department's findings that the agent demonstrated a lack of fitness or trustworthiness to engage in the business of insurance. *See Natelson v. Dep't of Ins.*, 454 So. 2d 31 (Fla. Dist. Ct. App. 1984), *review denied*, 461 So. 2d 115 (Fla. 1985).

## [B] Power to Prescribe Forms

State insurance regulation also typically provides that the state insurance commissioner has power to approve or disapprove the insurers' policy forms. The commissioner typically approves most forms submitted by insurers because there is nothing unusual about them. However, certain provisions deemed confusing, deceptive, or excessively favorable to the insurer may be disallowed. Under ordinary circumstances, the insurer whose form is rejected simply returns to the drafting table, revises the policy to meet regulator objections, and resubmits the form for approval.

But what if an insurer does business on an unapproved or disapproved form? The problematic provisions of such forms are generally unenforceable. *See, e.g., Minnehoma Ins. Co. v. Oklahoma State Bd. for Property & Casualty Rates*, 562 P.2d 1152 (Okla. 1977). A proposed insurance policy can be disapproved by the state insurance department if the policy: (1) does not comply with the state insurance code, or (2) if it contains ambiguous or misleading clauses, provisions, or titles. On the other hand, an insurance department cannot validly approve an insurance policy form or a rider which contravenes state insurance statutes. *See, e.g., Margolin v. Public Mut. Fire Ins.*

*Co.*, 281 N.E.2d 728 (Ill. App. Ct. 1972) (approval of a notice of cancellation policy endorsement in violation of state statutory requirements).

Assuming the insurer fails to secure proper approval of its insurance policy from the state insurance department, is the policy valid or invalid? *Compare Graf v. Employers' Liability Assurance Corp.*, 180 N.W. 297 (Iowa. 1920) (failure to file policy form with state regulator does not void policy provisions, in this case warranty of accuracy of application information, absent bad faith by insurer), *and Hill v. Nationwide Mut. Ins. Co.*, 535 S.W.2d 327 (Tenn. 1976) (properly filed policy language is implicitly approved by the state; enforcement of such language does not violate public policy), *with Commercial Union Assurance Co. v. Preston*, 282 S.W. 563 (Tex. 1926) (endorsement exempting certain property from coverage unenforceable because not filed and approved by Commissioner), *and Olson v. Western Auto. Ins. Co.*, 222 P. 104 (Kan. 1924) (policies issued without proper regulatory approval are null and void).

Such situations can occur even where the insurer is not recalcitrant (pushing forward with a form it knows to be "illegal") or negligent (cluelessly selling insurance on a form disapproved by the commissioner). Instead, the insurer may, as a standard practice, sell on a form that has been submitted for pending approval, fully expecting that the form will be approved. If state regulators surprise the insurer by disapproving the submitted form, the insurer risks unenforceability of the problematic provision. But this may be a risk the insurer wishes to accept rather than continue to use a form it no longer wants to use.

It may seem strange to discover that private insurance policies can be subject to statutory regulation without offending traditional constitutional rights of freedom to contract. However, the courts have consistently held that insurance is affected with a strong public interest, and early constitutional objections to state regulation were rejected by the courts unless the objectives of the statute went beyond the reasonable and legitimate interests of the state. In earlier days of the insurance business, for example, a number of insurance companies dealt reprehensibly with their policyholders. The policyholders often could not read, and even if they could, they seldom understood the policies due to their extraordinary length, fine print, incomprehensible legal and trade jargon, and convoluted sentence structure. It was not until the loss actually occurred that the insureds often would discover that some hidden condition in this "Serbonian bog" of endless print had caused the forfeiture of policy coverage. As one judge sarcastically commented regarding insurance policy coverage, "the first page giveth, and the last page taketh away."

It was against this shameful behavior that state legislatures sought to protect policyholders. Among various regulatory measures, laws have been passed in practically every state relating to the content of insurance policies, and requiring that prior to the use of a policy form or provision, the insurer file with the proper state regulatory agency a copy of its proposed insurance form for approval. Indeed, some insurance policies, like fire insurance policies, are inflexible "standard policies," and any policy deviation from the required state statute will be overridden by the statutory language. *See generally* Spencer Kimball, *The Purpose of Insurance Regulation*, 45 Minn. L. Rev. 471 (1961). *But see* Daniel Schwarcz, *Reevaluating Standardized Insurance Policies*, 78 U. Chi. L. Rev. 1263 (2011) (finding considerable variation in homeowners' insurance policy language despite conventional wisdom positing strict standardization).

What happens, then, when an insurance company fails to have its insurance policy provisions, endorsements, or premium rates approved by the state insurance commissioner as mandated by state statute? The following case aptly illustrates this important issue:

## Mutual Life Ins. Co. v. Daddy$ Money, Inc.
Court of Civil Appeals of Texas
646 S.W.2d 255 (1982)

**Stephens, Justice.**

This dispute arises over the sum of death benefits due under two identically worded life insurance policies. After the death of the insured, the carrier, appellant Mutual Life Insurance Company of New York (MONY), tendered payment of $7,989.30 to the beneficiary, appellee Daddy$ Money, Inc., contending that prior to the death of the insured, premium payments had been discontinued and that, under the terms of the policies, coverage had been reduced to single-premium paid-up participating life insurance. Daddy$ Money concedes that premium payments had been discontinued prior to the death of the insured, but contends that the coverage afforded by the terms of the policies was extended term life insurance for the full face amount of the policies, in the sum of $205,000.

When the policies were originally issued, they each contained a printed provision providing that in the event of default in premium payments, the policies would continue as paid-up extended term insurance so long as the cash value remained sufficient to pay the premium for the extended term insurance. In addition, each policy contained a typed endorsement, number 72500, which provided that in the event of a default in premium payments while the policies had a cash value, such cash value would be applied to provide a reduced single-premium paid-up participating life policy.

The printed policies had been approved by the State Board of Insurance for use in Texas. The conflicting endorsement, form number 72500, had not been approved. The facts are undisputed. The insured died, after discontinuance of premium payments, within the applicable time period when the face amount of the policies would have been due the beneficiary under the terms of the printed policy if endorsement number 72500 was ineffective.

The trial court rendered a summary judgment for Daddy$ Money, holding endorsement 72500 ineffective, and awarded the beneficiary the face amount of the policies less outstanding loans against the policies, or $191,271.95, plus interest, together with reasonable attorneys' fees in the sum of $80,000 and statutory penalties. We affirm.

MONY's first point of error contends that endorsement 72500 is an enforceable provision of the policies irrespective of whether it had been approved or disapproved by the State Board of Insurance prior to its issuance. The trial court's judgment was predicated on the theory that the failure of the Board to approve a provision of a life insurance policy before its issuance renders ineffective any portion of the policy detrimental to the insured. Endorsement 72500, which provides for reduced single-premium paid-up participating life insurance for less than $8,000.00 upon a default in the payment of premiums, is clearly inconsistent with the printed provision, which provides a non-participating extended term policy for the face amount under those same circumstances. In a case involving a fire insurance policy, the Supreme Court has clearly stated that, where the provisions in a policy are inconsistent, the authorized provision must override the provision which was neither authorized nor approved....

MONY urges that life insurance policy provisions should be treated differently from fire insurance policy provisions for two reasons: (1) the Texas Insurance Code does not empower the Board to prescribe standard forms of life insurance policies or their endorsements, but only empowers the Board to disapprove life insurance policies or their endorsements for certain specific reasons, whereas the Code does empower the Board to prescribe uniform fire insurance policies and to require the insurance companies to adopt and use those forms and no others; and (2) that the intention of the legislature, by enacting statutory penalties against companies who fail to secure approval of their policies or endorsements, rather than declaring the unapproved policies or their endorsement void, was that unapproved policies or endorsements should be enforced between the company and its insured.

Although MONY advances authority for its position from other jurisdictions, we are persuaded that precedent in Texas is otherwise. In *Lyons v. Texorado Oil & Gas Co.*, 91 S.W.2d 375 (Tex. Civ. App.-Amarillo, 1935, writ ref'd), a distinction was drawn between regulatory statutes enacted for the purpose of providing revenue to the State and those which were intended to protect the public. The rule was enunciated that where a statute was enacted for purposes of providing revenue for the state, and the statute provided penalties for failure to comply with its terms, yet did not declare void contracts entered into in violation of its terms, then such fines or penalties could be assessed, but the contract should not be held void. On the other hand, where the purpose of a statute was for police protection or protection of the public in general, then contracts entered into in violation of its terms are void although the statute provided only that penalties could be assessed....

We conclude that the rationale enunciated in *Lyons v. Texorado Oil & Gas Co., supra*, is the better policy and we hold that the issuance of an unapproved endorsement to a life insurance policy, in violation of Article 3.42 of the Insurance Code, constitutes a nullity when enforcement of its terms is sought against the insured. MONY's point of error number one is overruled....

MONY next contends that endorsement number 72500 supersedes and controls the conflicting terms of the printed provisions of the policy. We agree that the law is clear that an endorsement to a policy generally supersedes and controls conflicting printed terms within the policy. However, endorsement number 72500, having never been approved by the State Board of Insurance, was a nullity insofar as its enforcement against the insured, as we held in point of error number one. Thus, the printed provisions of the policies control....

## Notes and Questions

1. The general rule in most jurisdictions is that a state insurance commission or board, authorized by statute, may approve or disapprove the format of any insurance policies and premium rates utilized within that state, but such regulatory authority cannot be used in an arbitrary manner. *See, e.g., Crown Life Ins. Co. v. Commonwealth, Dep't of Ins.*, 394 A.2d 1305 (Pa. Commw. Ct. 1978).

2. The state insurance board's decision to approve or disapprove a particular insurance policy may still be appealed to the courts in most states. But if the state board approves an insurance policy form, can this form later be held invalid by a court, or is the insurance board's decision binding on the courts? *Compare Manhattan Life Ins. Co. v. Wilson Motor Co.*, 75 S.W.2d 721 (Tex. Civ. App. 1934), *with Nixon v. Farmers Ins. Exchange*, 201 N.W.2d 543 (Wis. 1972). *See also American Diversified Mut. Life Ins. Co. v. Texas State Bd. of Ins.*, 631 S.W.2d 805 (Tex. Civ. App. 1982).

3. The *Daddy$ Money* case held that the issuance of a life insurance endorsement was a nullity since it was not approved by the Texas Insurance Board as required under the state insurance code. A number of states have followed this Texas rationale. Other states, however, have adopted the New York *Conway* rule that an insurance company's failure to have its policies approved by the state insurance commissioner would *not* render the policy invalid *per se*, but the policy would only be invalid to the extent that it conflicted with state statutory provisions or state public policy. *See, e.g., Metropolitan Life Ins. Co. v. Conway*, 169 N.E. 642 (N.Y. 1930). Which is the better reasoned view? Based upon what underlying public policy rationale?

4. When the parties to an insurance policy stipulate that the laws of a specific jurisdiction will control as to the construction and effect of that policy, it is generally held that the stipulated jurisdiction's law will control—even though that state was not the place of the contract's execution or performance. *See, e.g., Insurance Co. of N. Am. v. English*, 395 F.2d 854 (5th Cir. 1968) (applying Mississippi law as the law of insured's residence as provided in the policy even though contract arguably was as a whole performed in Alabama or Tennessee in a case arising from death due to a Tennessee Valley Authority power transmission incident).

### PROBLEM ONE

The insured, Delores Hill, contracted with a general agent of the insurer to procure what the agent told her was "all risk" insurance coverage on her two horses. She made her initial premium payment of $1,000, and the agent transmitted the policy to Hill, advising her to read her policy. On the front of the policy were the words in bold type "READ YOUR POLICY. Your coverage is subject to all the terms, conditions, exclusions and limitations in the policy." The insured did not read her policy.

In the policy was an exclusion from coverage for "death or destruction" of the horses from "combined immune deficiency, respiratory diseases and systematic infection." When one of her horses died as a result of an excluded condition, Hill brought a claim against the insurance company, which the insurer denied under its exclusion. This policy exclusion, however, had never been approved by the Oklahoma Insurance Commissioner, so Hill brought a summary judgment action against the insurer to provide coverage, for a bad faith breach of the insurance contract, and for misrepresentation of the agent, claiming compensatory and punitive damages.

Title 36 of the Oklahoma Insurance Code Section 3620 provided in relevant part: "Any insurance policy, rider, or endorsement hereafter issued and otherwise valid which contains any condition or provision not in compliance with the requirements of this Code, shall not be thereby rendered invalid, but shall be construed and applied in accordance with … the Code."

• How should the court rule in this case?

## [C] Power to Control Investments

In addition to promoting fair business practices through state administrative regulation of the insurance business, the state is also concerned with maintaining insurer solvency by regulating investments and other financial aspects of those insurance companies doing business within the state. Insurance companies are required by statute to maintain certain "reserves," or sums of money that an insurer must set aside as a fund for future unaccrued and contingent claims, as well as for those claims already accrued. *See, e.g., Arrow Trucking Co. v. Continental Ins. Co.*, 465 So. 2d 691 (La. 1985). The state insurance commissioner therefore regulates the insurers' reserves by actuarially determining a level of reserves necessary to ensure that a specific insurance plan can fulfill the commitments which it has made. *See, e.g., Blue Cross & Blue Shield v. Demlow*, 270 N.W.2d 845 (Mich. 1978); *Commonwealth, Ins. Dep't v. Safeguard Mut. Ins. Co.*, 387 A.2d 647 (Pa. 1978).

The *Safeguard Mutual* case also discusses the distinction between a "mutual" insurance company and a "stock" insurance company. A mutual insurance company is owned by its policyholders, who function as insurers as well as the insured. A stock insurance company, on the other hand, is owned by the corporate stockholders. Many mutual insurance companies pay periodic dividends to the policyholders, thereby reducing the overall cost of insurance. State insurance statutes generally regulate mutual and stock insurance companies separately, often requiring different premium reserves of each. Under what rationale?

Insurance company assets are heavily regulated as "authorized" or "unauthorized" assets under applicable state statutes, and the *Safeguard* case demonstrates when such assets may, or may not, be considered in determining insurer solvency. *See also Dearborn Nat'l Ins. Co. v. Forbes*, 44 N.W.2d 892 (Mich. 1950).

## [D] Power to Limit Classes of Insurance

State insurance regulators may also limit an insurer to selling only certain insurance products by limitations set forth in the insurer's certificate of authority. *See American Financial Sec. Life Ins. Co. v. Dep't of Ins.*, 609 So. 2d 733 (Fla. Dist. Ct. App. 1992). For example, in *Allin v. American Indem. Co.*, 55 S.W.2d 44 (Ky. 1932), the Kentucky Supreme Court held that, although no domestic Kentucky insurance company could write both fire and automobile insurance, Kentucky public policy would not be opposed to licensing a foreign insurance corporation to write only automobile insurance within the state, although its foreign charter also authorized it to write fire insurance.

Most state insurance statutes prohibit companies from writing certain types of multi-risk insurance coverage on a public policy basis. For example, life insurance companies are generally limited to providing life and health insurance policies. Non-life insurance companies may write various classes of insurance limited only by statutory provisions, and title insurance companies are usually permitted to write only title insurance policies. *See, e.g.*, VA. CODE § 38.2-135 (2002 Replacement Volume).

Recently, many insurance companies have been able to overcome these statutory prohibitions through the purchase of subsidiary insurance corporations controlled by a parent holding company. Thus, it is now possible in many states for a single "name" insurance company to write life, property, and liability insurance coverage through its various subsidiaries, although the statutory reserve requirement for each insurance category must still be maintained. *See, e.g., Conn. Gen. Life Ins. Co. v. Superintendent of Ins.*, 10 N.Y.2d 42 (1961). *But see Woodyard v. Arkansas Diversified Ins. Co.*, 594 S.W.2d 13 (Ark. 1980) (when the degree of control exercised by the parent insurer makes the subsidiary insurer a "mere tool" of the parent, court will ignore the corporate form of the subsidiary and will enforce the prohibition against multi-risk insurance).

## [E] Power to Regulate Rates

A state has the constitutional power to regulate premium rates charged for insurance. *See, e.g., John Hancock Property & Cas. Ins. Co. v. Commonwealth, Ins. Dep't*, 554 A.2d 618 (Pa. 1989); *Att'y Gen. v. Comm'r of Ins.*, 817 N.E.2d 742 (Mass. 2004) (issues around rates of return and excessive premiums for certain policyholders). "Enlightened" insurance rating is aimed at developing rates that are adequate, but not excessive or unfairly discriminatory. *See* KEETON & WIDISS, INSURANCE LAW § 8.4(a) (2d ed. 1988). *See also Blue Cross and Blue Shield, Inc. v. Elliott*, 479 A.2d 843 (Del. Super. Ct. 1984) (permissible insurance rates are those which are not unfairly discriminatory and are less than excessive and more than adequate); *Allstate Ins. Co. v. Schmidt*, 88 P.3d 196 (Haw. 2004) (state statute prohibits discrimination on basis of length of driving experience in insurance underwriting).

### Notes and Questions

1. In *State v. Ins. Servs. Office*, 434 So. 2d 908 (Fla. Dist. Ct. App. 1983), the court found that a rule promulgated by the Florida Department of Insurance which prohibited the use of sex, marital status, and scholastic achievement as automobile insurance rating factors constituted an invalid exercise of delegated legislative authority. Based on what rationale?

2. In *Hartford Acci. & Indem. Co. v. Insurance Comm'r of Commonwealth*, 505 Pa. 571, 482 A.2d 542 (1984), the Pennsylvania Supreme Court, in five separate opinions, held that different automobile insurance rates for young men and young women drivers could indeed constitute unfair discrimination under the Pennsylvania Equal Rights Amendment. If young male drivers are involved in approximately twice the automobile accidents as are young female drivers, what public policy justifies the involuntary socialization of risk and spreading of premium rates mandated by the Pennsylvania Supreme Court?

3. The European Union's European Court of Justice ruled that different insurance premiums for women and men constitute discrimination and are not compatible with the EU's Charter of Fundamental Rights. *See* C-236/09, *Association Belge des Consommateurs Test-Achats and Others* (01/03/11). Member states are thus not allowed to adopt contrary legislation that conflicts with this decision. The order includes all insurance: auto, medical, and life insurance, sold in the European Union. What do you suppose are the opposing arguments to this order? Can you explain, with reference to insurance concepts of risk, why the insurance industry is concerned? Why might certain consumers be concerned? How will costs now be spread?

## [F] Power to Prevent Withdrawal by Insurer from State

State insurance regulators regulate not only the entry of an insurer into the state but also its exit. Although a state cannot "force" an insurer to continue operating in a state indefinitely, the state may place reasonable restrictions on an insurer's exit by requiring particular filings, minimum time frames, adequate notice to policyholders, and sufficient solvency assurances so that claims "in the pipeline" will be paid even if the insurer no longer has the business incentive of continuing to attempt to sell policies in the state. *See Hartford Fire Ins. Co. v. Colorado Div. of Ins.*, 824 P.2d 76 (Colo. App. 1991).

## [G] Retaliatory Statutes

Another common feature of state regulation is the retaliatory taxation statute, which is designed to protect state-based insurers from being unduly burdened in their out-of-state operations such that non-resident insurers gain a competitive advantage over the state's own insurers. *See Guardian Life Ins. Co. v. Commonwealth*, 611 A.2d 797 (Pa. Commw. Ct. 1992):

If any other state imposes any burdens or prohibitions on insurance companies, or agents of this state doing business in such other state, which are in addition to, or in excess of, the burdens or prohibitions imposed by this Commonwealth on insurance companies and agents, like burdens and prohibitions shall be imposed on all insurance companies and agents of such other state doing business in this Commonwealth, so long as the burdens and prohibitions of such other state remain in force.

The retaliatory tax, although commonly referred to as a "tax," is not technically a tax, but is more properly a business license fee or charge, imposed to regulate insurance companies.... The purpose of the Retaliatory Statute, and of similar laws enacted in almost every state, is to encourage equal treatment of domestic and foreign insurance companies, and to break down interstate barriers. The Retaliatory Statute "is certainly not a revenue raising measure. In fact, its success might be said to depend on how little is collected under its terms rather than how much."

In order to determine if any retaliatory tax is owed, the department must calculate the economic burdens and prohibitions, primarily taxes, that Pennsylvania places on New York companies, compare that to the economic burdens and prohibitions that New York places on Pennsylvania companies, and if the New York side of the equation exceeds the Pennsylvania side, the department uses "the retaliatory tax to bring the sides into balance." Therefore, the department first must calculate the burdens and prohibitions imposed by both of the relevant states before it can compute the retaliatory tax owed, if any.

The purpose of retaliatory insurance tax statutes is to protect State X's insurance companies by discouraging sister state jurisdictions from imposing heavier burdens on State X insurance companies than State X imposes on sister state companies who do business in State X. *See, e.g., Republic Ins. Co. v. Oakley*, 637 S.W.2d 448, 451 (Tenn. 1982). Put another way, the principal purpose of retaliatory insurance tax laws is to promote the interstate business of domestic insurers by deterring other states from enacting discriminatory or excessive taxes. *See, e.g., Western & Southern Life Ins. Co. v. State Bd. of Equalization*, 451 U.S. 648, 669 (1981). Is this purpose legitimate and reasonable? Would not such retaliatory statutes restrict interstate commerce as defined by Art. 1, §8, cl. 3, of the U.S. Constitution?

## § 3.03. The State-Federal Regulatory Divide

In the following split opinion about the application of the McCarran-Ferguson Act to potentially pre-empt state regulation in the sphere of insurance, what are the tensions that exist between state and federal regulation of insurance? What subtext drives these tensions?

# United States Department of Treasury v. Fabe

Supreme Court of the United States
508 U.S. 491 (1993)

**Justice Blackmun** delivered the opinion of the Court.

The federal priority statute, 31 U.S.C. § 3713, accords first priority to the United States with respect to a bankrupt debtor's obligations. An Ohio statute confers only fifth priority upon claims of the United States in proceedings to liquidate an insolvent insurance company. Ohio Rev. Code Ann. § 3903.42 (1989). The federal priority statute pre-empts the inconsistent Ohio law unless the latter is exempt from pre-emption under the McCarran-Ferguson Act, 59 Stat. 33, as amended, 15 U.S.C. § 1011, et seq. In order to resolve this case, we must decide whether a state statute establishing the priority of creditors' claims in a proceeding to liquidate an insolvent insurance company is a law enacted "for the purpose of regulating the business of insurance," within the meaning of § 2(b) of the McCarran-Ferguson Act, 15 U.S.C. § 1012(b).

We hold that the Ohio priority statute escapes pre-emption to the extent that it protects policyholders. Accordingly, Ohio may effectively afford priority, over claims of the United States, to the insurance claims of policyholders and to the costs and expenses of administering the liquidation. But when Ohio attempts to rank other categories of claims above those pressed by the United States, it is not free from federal pre-emption under the McCarran-Ferguson Act.

The Ohio priority statute was enacted as part of a complex and specialized administrative structure for the regulation of insurance companies from inception to dissolution. The statute proclaims, as its purpose, "the protection of the interests of insureds, claimants, creditors, and the public generally." § 3903.02(D). Chapter 3903 broadly empowers the State's Superintendent of Insurance to place a financially impaired insurance company under his supervision, or into rehabilitation, or into liquidation. The last is authorized when the Superintendent finds that the insurer is insolvent, that placement in supervision or rehabilitation would be futile, and that "further transaction of business would be hazardous, financially or otherwise, to [the insurer's] policyholders, its creditors, or the public." § 3903.17(C). As liquidator, the Superintendent is entitled to take title to all assets, § 3903.18(A); to collect and invest moneys due the insurer, § 3903.21(A)(6); to continue to prosecute and commence in the name of the insurer any and all suits and other legal proceedings, § 3903.21(A)(12); to collect reinsurance and unearned premiums due the insurer, § 3903.32 and 3903.33; to evaluate all claims against the estate, § 3903.43; and to make payments to claimants to the extent possible, § 3903.44. It seems fair to say that the effect of all this is to empower the liquidator to continue to operate the insurance company in all ways but one—the issuance of new policies.

Pursuant to this statutory framework, the Court of Common Pleas for Franklin County, Ohio, on April 30, 1986, declared American Druggists' Insurance Company insolvent. The court directed that the company be liquidated, and it appointed respondent, Ohio's Superintendent of Insurance, to serve as liquidator. The United

States, as obligee on various immigration, appearance, performance, and payment bonds issued by the company as surety, filed claims in excess of $10.7 million in the state liquidation proceedings. The United States asserted that its claims were entitled to first priority under the federal statute, 31 U.S.C. § 3713(a)(1)(A)(iii), which provides: "A claim of the United States Government shall be paid first when ... a person indebted to the Government is insolvent and ... an act of bankruptcy is committed."

Respondent Superintendent brought a declaratory judgment action in the United States District Court for the Southern District of Ohio seeking to establish that the federal priority statute does not pre-empt the Ohio law designating the priority of creditors' claims in insurance-liquidation proceedings. Under the Ohio statute, as noted above, claims of federal, state, and local governments are entitled only to fifth priority, ranking behind (1) administrative expenses, (2) specified wage claims, (3) policyholders' claims, and (4) claims of general creditors. § 3903.42. Respondent argued that the Ohio priority scheme, rather than the federal priority statute, governs the priority of claims of the United States because it falls within the anti-preemption provisions of the McCarran-Ferguson Act, 15 U.S.C. § 1012.[1] ...

We granted *certiorari* to resolve the conflict among the Courts of Appeals on the question whether a state statute governing the priority of claims against an insolvent insurer is a "law enacted ... for the purpose of regulating the business of insurance," within the meaning of 2(b) of the McCarran-Ferguson Act.

The McCarran-Ferguson Act was enacted in response to this Court's decision in *United States v. South-Eastern Underwriters Ass'n*, 322 U.S. 533 (1944). Prior to that decision, it had been assumed that "[i]ssuing a policy of insurance is not a transaction of commerce," *Paul v. Virginia*, 75 U.S. (8 Wall.) 168, 183 (1869), subject to federal regulation. Accordingly, "the States enjoyed a virtually exclusive domain over the insurance industry." ...

The emergence of an interconnected and interdependent national economy, however, prompted a more expansive jurisprudential image of interstate commerce.... Thus, in *South-Eastern Underwriters*, it held that an insurance company that conducted a substantial part of its business across state lines was engaged in interstate commerce and thereby was subject to the antitrust laws. This result, naturally, was widely perceived as a threat to state power to tax and regulate the insurance industry. To allay those fears, Congress moved quickly to restore the supremacy of the States in the

---

1. [3] Section 1012 reads:

"(a) ... The business of insurance, and every person engaged therein, shall be subject to the laws of the several States which relate to the regulation or taxation of such business.

"(b) ... No Act of Congress shall be construed to invalidate, impair, or supersede any law enacted by any State for the purpose of regulating the business of insurance, or which imposes a fee or tax upon such business, unless such Act specifically relates to the business of insurance: Provided, That after June 30, 1948, the Act of July 2, 1890, as amended, known as the Sherman Act, and the Act of October 15, 1914, as amended, known as the Clayton Act, and the Act of September 26, 1914, known as the Federal Trade Commission Act, as amended, shall be applicable to the business of insurance to the extent that such business is not regulated by State Law."

realm of insurance regulation. It enacted the McCarran-Ferguson Act within a year of the decision in *South-Eastern Underwriters.*

The first section of the McCarran-Ferguson Act makes its mission very clear: "Congress hereby declares that the continued regulation and taxation by the several States of the business of insurance is in the public interest, and that silence on the part of the Congress shall not be construed to impose any barrier to the regulation or taxation of such business by the several States."

Shortly after passage of the Act, the Court observed: "Obviously Congress' purpose was broadly to give support to the existing and future state systems for regulating and taxing the business of insurance." *Prudential Ins. Co. v. Benjamin*, 328 U.S. 408, 429 (1946).

Congress achieved this purpose in two ways. The first "was by removing obstructions which might be thought to flow from [Congress'] own power, whether dormant or exercised, except as otherwise expressly provided in the Act itself or in future legislation." The second "was by declaring expressly and affirmatively that continued state regulation and taxation of this business is in the public interest and that the business and all who engage in it 'shall be subject to' the laws of the several states in these respects."

"[T]he starting point in a case involving construction of the McCarran-Ferguson Act, like the starting point in any case involving the meaning of a statute, is the language of the statute itself." *Group Life & Health Ins. Co. v. Royal Drug Co.*, 440 U.S. 205, 210, (1979). Section 2(b) of the McCarran-Ferguson Act provides: "No Act of Congress shall be construed to invalidate, impair, or supersede any law enacted by any State for the purpose of regulating the business of insurance ... unless such Act specifically relates to the business of insurance."

The parties agree that application of the federal priority statute would "invalidate, impair, or supersede" the Ohio priority scheme and that the federal priority statute does not "specifically relat[e] to the business of insurance." All that is left for us to determine, therefore, is whether the Ohio priority statute is a law enacted "for the purpose of regulating the business of insurance."

This Court has had occasion to construe this phrase only once. On that occasion, it observed: "Statutes aimed at protecting or regulating this relationship [between insurer and insured], directly or indirectly, are laws regulating the 'business of insurance,'" within the meaning of the phrase. *SEC v. National Securities, Inc.*, 393 U.S. 453, 460 (1969). The opinion emphasized that the focus of McCarran-Ferguson is upon the relationship between the insurance company and its policyholders:

> "The relationship between insurer and insured, the type of policy which could be issued, its reliability, interpretation, and enforcement—these were the core of the "business of insurance." Undoubtedly, other activities of insurance companies relate so closely to their status as reliable insurers that they too must be placed in the same class. But whatever the exact scope of the statutory term, it is clear where the focus was—it was on the relationship between the insurance company and the policyholder." *Id.*

In that case, two Arizona insurance companies merged and received approval from the Arizona Director of Insurance, as required by state law. The Securities and Exchange Commission sued to rescind the merger, alleging that the merger-solicitation papers contained material misstatements, in violation of federal law. This Court held that, insofar as the Arizona law was an attempt to protect the interests of an insurance company's shareholders, it did not fall within the scope of the McCarran-Ferguson Act. *Id.* The Arizona statute, however, also required the Director, before granting approval, to make sure that the proposed merger "would not 'substantially reduce the security of and service to be rendered to policyholders.'"

The Court observed that this section of the statute "clearly relates to the 'business of insurance.'" *Id.* But because the "paramount federal interest in protecting shareholders [was] perfectly compatible with the paramount state interest in protecting policyholders," the Arizona statute did not preclude application of the federal securities laws.

In the present case, on the other hand, there is a direct conflict between the federal priority statute and Ohio law. Under the terms of the McCarran-Ferguson Act, 15 U.S.C. § 1012(b), therefore, federal law must yield to the extent the Ohio statute furthers the interests of policyholders.

Minimizing the analysis of *National Securities*, petitioner invokes *Group Life and Health Insurance v. Royal Drug Co.*, 440 U.S. 205 (1979) and *Pireno* in support of its argument that the liquidation of an insolvent insurance company is not part of the "business of insurance" exempt from pre-emption under the McCarran-Ferguson Act. Those cases identified the three criteria, noted above, that are relevant in determining what activities constitute the "business of insurance." *See* [*Union Labor Life Ins. Co. v.*] *Pireno*, 458 U.S. 119, at 129 [(1982)].

Petitioner argues that the Ohio priority statute satisfies none of these criteria. According to petitioner, the Ohio statute merely determines the order in which creditors' claims will be paid, and has nothing to do with the transfer of risk from insured to insurer. Petitioner also contends that the Ohio statute is not an integral part of the policy relationship between insurer and insured and is not limited to entities within the insurance industry because it addresses only the relationship between policyholders and other creditors of the defunct corporation.

To be sure, the Ohio statute does not directly regulate the "business of insurance" by prescribing the terms of the insurance contract or by setting the rate charged by the insurance company. But we do not read *Pireno* to suggest that the business of insurance is confined entirely to the writing of insurance contracts, as opposed to their performance. *Pireno* and *Royal Drug* held only that "ancillary activities" that do not affect performance of the insurance contract or enforcement of contractual obligations do not enjoy the antitrust exemption for laws regulating the "business of insurance." ...

There can be no doubt that the actual performance of an insurance contract falls within the "business of insurance," as we understood that phrase in *Pireno* and *Royal Drug.* To hold otherwise would be mere formalism. The Court's statement in *Pireno* that the "transfer of risk from insured to insurer is effected by means of the contract between the parties ... and ... is complete at the time that the contract is entered," presumes that the insurance contract in fact will be enforced. Without performance of the terms of the insurance policy, there is no risk transfer at all. Moreover, performance of an insurance contract also satisfies the remaining prongs of the *Pireno* test: it is central to the policy relationship between insurer and insured and is confined entirely to entities within the insurance industry.

The Ohio priority statute is designed to carry out the enforcement of insurance contracts by ensuring the payment of policyholders' claims despite the insurance company's intervening bankruptcy. Because it is integrally related to the performance of insurance contracts after bankruptcy, Ohio's law is one "enacted by the State for the purpose of regulating the business of insurance." 15 U.S.C. § 1012(b).

The broad category of laws enacted "for the purpose of regulating the business of insurance" consists of laws that possess the "end, intention, or aim" of adjusting, managing, or controlling the business of insurance. *Black's Law Dictionary* 1236, 1286 (6th ed. 1990). This category necessarily encompasses more than just the "business of insurance." For the reasons expressed above, we believe that the actual performance of an insurance contract is an essential part of the "business of insurance." Because the Ohio statute is "aimed at protecting or regulating" the performance of an insurance contract, *National Securities*, 393 U.S. at 460, 89 S. Ct. at 568, it follows that it is a law "enacted for the purpose of regulating the business of insurance," within the meaning of the first clause of § 2(b).

Petitioner, however, also contends that the Ohio statute is not an insurance law but a bankruptcy law because it comes into play only when the insurance company has become insolvent and is in liquidation, at which point the insurance company no longer exists. We disagree. The primary purpose of a statute that distributes the insolvent insurer's assets to policyholders in preference to other creditors is identical to the primary purpose of the insurance company itself: the payment of claims made against policies....

We hold that the Ohio priority statute, to the extent that it regulates policyholders, is a law enacted for the purpose of regulating the business of insurance. To the extent that it is designed to further the interests of other creditors, however, it is not a law enacted for the purpose of regulating the business of insurance.

Of course, every preference accorded to the creditors of an insolvent insurer ultimately may redound to the benefit of policyholders by enhancing the reliability of the insurance company. This argument, however, goes too far: "But in that sense, every business decision made by an insurance company has some impact on its reliability ... and its status as a reliable insurer." *Royal Drug* rejected the notion that such indirect effects are sufficient for a state law to avoid pre-emption under the McCarran-Ferguson Act.

We also hold that the preference accorded by Ohio to the expenses of administering the insolvency proceeding is reasonably necessary to further the goal of protecting policyholders. Without payment of administrative costs, liquidation could not even commence. The preferences conferred upon employees and other general creditors, however, do not escape pre-emption because their connection to the ultimate aim of insurance is too tenuous.... By this decision, we rule only upon the clash of priorities as pronounced by the respective provisions of the federal statute and the Ohio Code. The effect of this decision upon the Ohio Code's remaining priority provisions—including any issue of severability—is a question of state law to be addressed upon remand....

**Justice Kennedy**, with whom **Justice Scalia**, **Justice Souter** and **Justice Thomas** join, dissenting.

... Relying primarily on our decision in *SEC v. National Securities, Inc.*, 393 U.S. 453 (1969), the majority concludes that portions of Ohio's priority statute are saved from pre-emption by the McCarran-Ferguson Act. I agree that *National Securities* is the right place to begin the analysis. As the Court points out, *National Securities* is the one case in which we have considered the precise statutory provision that is controlling here to determine whether a state law applicable to insurance companies was a law enacted for the purpose of regulating the business of insurance. I disagree, however, with the Court's interpretation of that precedent.

The key to our analysis in *National Securities* was the construction of the term "business of insurance." In *National Securities* we said that statutes designed to protect or regulate the relationship between an insurance company and its policyholder, whether this end is accomplished in a direct or an indirect way, are laws regulating the business of insurance. 393 U.S. at 460. While noting that the exact scope of the McCarran-Ferguson Act was unclear, we observed that in passing the Act "Congress was concerned with the type of state regulation that centers around the contract of insurance." *Id.* There is general agreement that the primary concerns of an insurance contract are the spreading and the underwriting of risk, see 1 G. Couch, Cyclopedia of Insurance Law § 1.3 (2d ed. 1984); R. Keeton, Insurance Law § 1.2(a) (1971), and we have often recognized this central principle. See *Union Labor Life Ins. Co. v. Pireno*, 458 U.S. 119, 127 n.7 (1982); *Group Life & Health Ins. Co. v. Royal Drug Co.*, 440 U.S. 205, 211–12 (1979).

When the majority applies the holding of *National Securities* to the case at bar, it concludes that the Ohio statute is not pre-empted to the extent it regulates the "performance of an insurance contract," *ante*, at 505, by ensuring that "policyholders ultimately will receive payment on their claims," *ante*, at 506. Under the majority's reasoning, see *ante*, at 493, 508, any law which redounds to the benefit of policyholders is, *ipso facto*, a law enacted to regulate the business of insurance. States attempting to discern the scope of powers reserved for them under the McCarran-Ferguson Act will find it difficult, as do I, to reconcile our precedents in this area with the decision the Court reaches today. The majority's broad holding is not a logical extension of our decision in *National Securities* and indeed is at odds with it.

The function of the Ohio statute before us is to regulate the priority of competing creditor claims in proceedings to liquidate an insolvent insurance company. On its face, the statute's exclusive concentration is not policyholder protection, but creditor priority.... The Ohio law does not regulate or implicate the "true underwriting of risks, the one earmark of insurance." *SEC v. Variable Annuity Life Ins. Co. of America*, 359 U.S. 65, 73 (1969) (footnote omitted).

To be sure, the Ohio priority statute increases the probability that an insured's claim will be paid in the event of insurer insolvency. But such laws, while they may "further the interests of policyholders," *ante*, at 502, have little to do with the relationship between an insurer and its insured, *National Securities*, 393 U.S. at 460, and as such are not laws regulating the business of insurance under the McCarran-Ferguson Act. The State's priority statute does not speak to the transfer of risk embodied in the contract of insurance between the parties. Granting policyholders priority of payment over other creditors does not involve the transfer of risk from insured to insurer, the type of risk spreading that is the essence of the contract of insurance.

Further, insurer insolvency is not an activity of insurance companies that "relate[s] so closely to their status as reliable insurers," *id.*, as to qualify liquidation as an activity constituting the "core of the 'business of insurance.'" *Id....*

In my view, one need look no further than our opinion in *National Securities* to conclude that the Ohio insolvency statute is not a law "enacted ... for the purpose of regulating the business of insurance." Even so, our decisions in *Pireno* and *Royal Drug* further undercut the Court's holding, despite the majority's attempt to distinguish them.

*Royal Drug* and *Pireno* are best viewed as refinements of this Court's analysis in *National Securities*, tailored to address activities of insurance companies that would implicate the federal antitrust laws were it not for the McCarran-Ferguson Act. Although these cases were decided in accordance with the rule that exemptions from the antitrust laws are to be construed narrowly, see *Pireno*, 458 U.S. at 126; *Royal Drug*, 440 U.S. at 231, I see no reason why general principles derived from them are not applicable to any case involving the scope of the term "business of insurance" under the McCarran-Ferguson Act.

\* \* \*

The Ohio statute here does not qualify as regulating the business of insurance under *Pireno*'s tripartite test for the same reason that it fails to do so under *National Securities:* It regulates an activity which is too removed from the contractual relationship between the policyholder and the insurance company. First, the risk of insurer insolvency addressed by the statute is distinct from the risk the policy-holder seeks to transfer in an insurance contract. The transfer of risk from insured to insurer is effected "by means of the contract between the parties — the insurance policy — and that transfer is complete at the time that the contract is entered." *Id.*, at 130. As to the second prong, the Ohio statute does not regulate the relationship between the insured and the insurer, but instead addresses the relationship among all creditors the insurer has left in the lurch. Finally, it is plain that the statute is not limited to entities within the insurance industry. The statute governs the rights of all creditors of insolvent insurance companies, including employees, general creditors, and stockholders, as well as government entities.

Even though Ohio's insurance liquidation statute is not a law enacted for the purpose of regulating the business of insurance, I underscore that no provision of federal law precludes Ohio from establishing procedures to address the liquidation of insolvent insurance companies. The State's prerogative to do so, however, does not emanate from its recognized power to enact laws regulating the business of insurance under the McCarran-Ferguson Act, but from the longstanding decision of Congress to exempt insurance companies from the federal bankruptcy code. 11 U.S.C. §§ 109(b)(2), (d). The States are not free to enact legislation inconsistent with the federal priority statute, and in my view the majority errs in applying the McCarran-Ferguson Act to displace the traditional principles of pre-emption that should apply. I would reverse the judgment of the Court of Appeals.

## Notes and Questions

1. The purpose of federal anti-trust laws, such as the Sherman Anti-Trust Act, is to prevent a business from willfully acquiring and maintaining monopoly power. The McCarran-Ferguson Act, however, exempts the insurance business from federal anti-trust laws, but only to the extent that such insurance business: (a) is regulated by the state; and (b) does not involve any boycott, coercion, or intimidation.

2. McCarran-Ferguson is generally viewed as a "reverse preemption" statute that ousts federal law from an area in favor of state law rather than a "federal override preemption" statute that ousts state law from an area in favor of federal law. But as the cases suggest, there may be a substantial zone of harmonious overlap between state and federal law applicable to insurers.

3. The McCarran-Ferguson Act has been held not to protect insurers from suit under the Racketeer Influenced and Corrupt Organizations Act ("RICO"), 18 U.S.C. § 1961 *et seq. See Humana Inc. v. Forsyth*, 525 U.S. 299 (1999). The Court found that RICO's authorization of treble damages did not invalidate, impair, or supplant any state regulation of insurers because the type of alleged misconduct (fraudulent overcharging of insureds) actionable under RICO also violated analogous state anti-fraud law.

4. Usually, it is the state insurance commissioner who takes insurers or others to task for violating state insurance regulation. However, the state Attorney General usually is empowered to enforce these same laws absent specific state law prohibitions on such activity. *See State v. American Family Mut. Ins. Co.*, 609 N.W.2d 1 (Minn. Ct. App. 2000).

## [A] Federal Oversight of Insurance

The American financial crisis of 2007–2010 prompted Congress to enact a sweeping overhaul of the federal financial regulatory framework. The changes were designed to combat the "too big to fail" problem of large financial institutions (including insurers like American International Group (AIG) which suffered a severe liquidity crisis in 2008 that was felt throughout the market) controlling large portions of the economy (many, like AIG, who required large government bailouts to avoid economic disaster). The Dodd-Frank Wall Street Reform and Consumer Protection Act, 15 U.S.C. §313, is aimed at preventing taxpayer-funded bailouts and producing greater regulation of the financial system in America. Title V of the Act addresses the insurance industry. The Act creates the Federal Insurance Office, which will:

1. Monitor all aspects of the insurance industry (with the exception of health insurance, some long-term care insurance, and crop insurance), including the identification of gaps in regulation of insurers that could contribute to financial crisis;

2. Monitor the extent to which traditionally underserved communities and consumers, minorities, and low- and moderate-income persons have access to affordable insurance (except health insurance);

3. Make recommendations to the Financial Stability Oversight Council about insurers which may pose a risk, and to help any state regulators with national issues;

4. Administer the federal Terrorism Insurance Program;

5. Coordinate international insurance matters;

6. Determine whether State insurance measures are preempted by covered agreements (states may have more stringent requirements); and

7. Consult with the States regarding insurance matters of national importance and prudential insurance matters of international importance.

The Insurance Office may also require any insurer to provide data as reasonably necessary in order to carry out the above tasks. The Act also provides direction regarding state pre-emption issues. The Act will not preempt:

1. any state insurance measure that governs any insurer's rates, premiums, underwriting, or sales practices;

2. any state coverage requirements for insurance;

3. the application of the antitrust laws of any state to the business of insurance; or

4. any state insurance measure governing the capital or solvency of an insurer, except to the extent that such state insurance measure results in less favorable treatment of a non-United States insurer than a United States insurer.

The Act also specifically holds that nothing in Title V "shall be construed to establish or provide the Office or the Department of the Treasury with general supervisory or regulatory authority over the business of insurance." Title V also permits states to agree amongst themselves on how insurance premium taxes should be paid to an insured's home state.

## *Notes and Questions*

1. How does Title V of the Dodd-Frank Act attempt to strike a tenuous balance between federal and state control of insurance? Will its measures work? Can you predict any clashes between state and federal regulation of insurance?

2. Should insurance be a federal matter entirely? If large insurer conglomerates can play such a pivotal role in bringing down the economy of the entire country, why is so much of insurance still state-regulated?

3. Do you predict litigation will be necessary to determine the meaning of the various mandates of the Federal Insurance Office? What sorts of state-controlled items do you think will require further clarification by the courts? What conflicts can you predict?

## [B] Intersection between Civil Rights Statutes and Insurance: The Americans with Disabilities Act

One of the most litigated intersections of insurance and civil rights law involves the degree to which the Americans with Disabilities Act ("ADA"), 42 U.S.C. § 12101, limits the options of insurers in issuing policies or setting the parameters of coverage. As you read the cases below, consider what, if anything, distinguishes them and the persuasiveness of the arguments for and against ADA regulation of insurance. These cases and others involving the ADA and insurance often involve questions over both the reach of the ADA and the degree to which the ADA may be in conflict with the McCarran-Ferguson Act's general bar to indirect federal regulation of the business of insurance. Recall that direct, on-point federal regulation directed at the business of insurance trumps the McCarran-Ferguson Act unless the legislation exceeds congressional power and that it may be possible for both a federal law and state insurance regulation to have "peaceful coexistence." McCarran-Ferguson is designed to preserve the general status quo of state-based insurance regulation and to prevent broad-based federal law from displacing state insurance regulation "by accident." The McCarran-Ferguson Act is not the equivalent of a constitutional provision barring all federal regulation touching upon insurance.

### John Doe and Richard Smith v. Mutual of Omaha Insurance Co.

United States Court of Appeals for the Seventh Circuit
179 F.3d 557 (1999)

**Posner, Chief Judge.**

Mutual of Omaha appeals from a judgment that the AIDS caps in two of its health insurance policies violate the public accommodations provision of the Americans with Disabilities Act. One policy limits lifetime benefits for AIDS or AIDS-related conditions (ARC) to $25,000, the other limits them to $100,000, while for other conditions the limit in both policies is $1 million. Mutual of Omaha has stipulated that it "has not shown and cannot show that its AIDS Caps are or ever have been consistent with sound actuarial principles, actual or reasonably anticipated experience, bona fide risk classification, or state law." It also concedes that AIDS is a disabling condition within the meaning of the Americans with Disabilities Act. *See Bragdon v. Abbott*, 524 U.S. 624, 118 S. Ct. 2196, 2207–09, 141 L. Ed. 2d 540 (1998). Since the Supreme Court held in *Bragdon* that infection with the AIDS virus (HIV) is a disabling condition from the onset of the infection, 118 S. Ct. at 2204, before any symptoms appear, it is apparent that both ARC and AIDS are disabilities. Mutual of Omaha does not question this, but argues only that the Americans with Disabilities Act does not regulate the content of insurance policies.

Title III of the Act, in section 302(a), provides that "no individual shall be discriminated against on the basis of disability in the full and equal enjoyment of the goods, services, facilities, privileges, advantages, or accommodations of any place of public accommodation" by the owner, lessee, or operator of such a place. 42 U.S.C. § 12182(a). The core meaning of this provision, plainly enough, is that the owner or operator of a store, hotel, restaurant, dentist's office, travel agency, theater, Web site, or other facility (whether in physical space or in electronic space, *Carparts Distribution Center, Inc. v. Automotive Wholesaler's Ass'n of New England, Inc.*, 37 F.3d 12, 19 (1st Cir. 1994)) that is open to the public cannot exclude disabled persons from entering the facility and, once in, from using the facility in the same way that the nondisabled do. The owner or operator of, say, a camera store can neither bar the door to the disabled nor let them in but then refuse to sell its cameras to them on the same terms as to other customers....

To come closer to home, a dentist cannot refuse to fill a cavity of a person with AIDS unless he demonstrates a direct threat to safety or health, *Abbott v. Bragdon, supra*, 118 S. Ct. at 2210–13; and an insurance company cannot (at least without pleading a special defense, discussed below) refuse to sell an insurance policy to a person with AIDS. *28 C.F.R. § 36.104* Place of Public Accommodation (6). Mutual of Omaha does not refuse to sell insurance policies to such persons—it was happy to sell health insurance policies to the two plaintiffs. But because of the AIDS caps, the policies have less value to persons with AIDS than they would have to persons with other, equally expensive diseases or disabilities. This does not make the offer to sell illusory, for people with AIDS have medical needs unrelated to AIDS, and the policies give such people as much coverage for those needs as the policies give people who don't have AIDS. If all the medical needs of people with AIDS were AIDS-related and thus excluded by the policies, this might support an inference that Mutual of Omaha was trying to exclude such people, and such exclusion, as we shall see, might violate the Act. But that is not argued.

Since most health-insurance policies contain caps, the position urged by the plaintiffs would discriminate among diseases. Diseases that happened to be classified as disabilities could not be capped, but equally or more serious diseases that are generally not disabling, such as heart disease, could be. Moreover, the plaintiffs acknowledge the right of an insurance company to exclude coverage for an applicant's pre-existing medical conditions. If the applicant is already HIV-positive when he applies for a health-insurance policy, the insurer can in effect cap his AIDS-related coverage at $0. This "discrimination" is not limited to AIDS or for that matter to disabilities, which is why the plaintiffs do not challenge it; but it suggests that the rule for which they contend is at once arbitrary and unlikely to do much for people with AIDS.

The insurance company asks us to compare this case to one in which a person with one leg complains of a shoestore's refusal to sell shoes other than by the pair, or in which a blind person complains of a bookstore's refusal to stock books printed in Braille. We do not understand the plaintiffs to be contending that such complaints are actionable under section 302(a), even though there is a sense in which the disabled individual would be denied the full and equal enjoyment of the services that the store offers. In fact, it is apparent that a store is not required to alter its inventory in order to stock goods such as Braille books that are especially designed for disabled people.... But it is apparent as a matter of interpretation rather than compelled by a simple reading which would place the present case on the other side of the line; and so the case cannot be resolved by reference simply to the language of section 302(a).

The common sense of the statute is that the content of the goods or services offered by a place of public accommodation is not regulated. A camera store may not refuse to sell cameras to a disabled person, but it is not required to stock cameras specially designed for such persons. Had Congress purposed to impose so enormous a burden on the retail sector of the economy and so vast a supervisory responsibility on the federal courts, we think it would have made its intention clearer and would at least have imposed some standards. It is hardly a feasible judicial function to decide whether shoestores should sell single shoes to one-legged persons and if so at what price, or how many Braille books the Borders or Barnes and Noble bookstore chains should stock in each of their stores. There are defenses to a prima facie case of public-accommodation discrimination, but they would do little to alleviate the judicial burden of making standardless decisions about the composition of retail inventories. The only defense that might apply to the Braille case or the pair of shoes case is that the modification of a seller's existing practices that is necessary to provide equal access to the disabled "would fundamentally alter the nature of ... [the seller's] services," and it probably would not apply to either case and certainly not to the Braille one.

The plaintiffs might be able to distinguish the shoestore hypothetical by pointing out that a nondisabled person might be in the market for one shoe simply because he had lost a shoe; in refusing to sell single shoes the store thus would not be refusing to adapt its service to a class of customers limited to disabled people. But the Braille case, and many others that we can imagine (such as a furniture store's decision not to stock wheelchairs, or a psychiatrist's refusal to treat schizophrenia, as distinct from his refusing to treat schizophrenics for the psychiatric disorders in which he specializes, or a movie theater's refusal to provide a running translation into sign language of the movie's soundtrack), cannot be so distinguished, although some of them might find shelter in the "fundamental alteration" defense. All are cases of refusing to configure a service to make it as valuable to a disabled as to a nondisabled customer.

That the plaintiffs are asking that a limitation be removed rather than that a physical product be added or altered cannot distinguish these cases. For the same thing is true in our example of the psychiatrist who refuses to treat schizophrenia. More important, since section 302(a) is not limited to physical products, but includes contracts and other intangibles, such as an insurance policy, a limitation upon the duty to serve cannot be confined to physical changes. An insurance policy is a product, and a policy with a $25,000 limit is a different product from one with a $1 million limit, just as a wheelchair is a different product from an armchair. A furniture store that does not stock wheelchairs knows that it is making its services less valuable to disabled than to nondisabled people, but the Americans with Disabilities Act has not been understood to require furniture stores to stock wheelchairs.

It might seem that the AIDS caps could be distinguished from the "refusal to stock" cases because the caps include complications of AIDS. If being infected by HIV leads one to contract pneumonia, the cost of treating the pneumonia is subject to the AIDS cap; if a person not infected by HIV contracts pneumonia, the costs of treating his pneumonia are fully covered. It looks, therefore, like a difference in treatment referable solely to the fact that one person is disabled and the other not.

But this is not correct. The essential point to understand is that HIV doesn't cause illness directly. What it does is weaken and eventually destroy the body's immune system. As the immune system falters, the body becomes prey to diseases that the system protects us against. These "opportunistic" diseases that HIV allows, as it were, to ravage the body are exotic cancers and rare forms of pneumonia and other infectious diseases.... To refer to them as "complications" of HIV or AIDS is not incorrect, but it is misleading, because they are the chief worry of anyone who has the misfortune to be afflicted with AIDS. An AIDS cap would be meaningless if it excluded the opportunistic diseases that are the most harmful consequences of being infected by the AIDS virus.

What the AIDS caps in the challenged insurance policies cover, therefore, is the cost of fighting the AIDS virus itself and trying to keep the immune system intact plus the cost of treating the opportunistic diseases to which the body becomes prey when the immune system has eroded to the point at which one is classified as having AIDS.... It is these *distinctive* diseases that are the target (along with the costs of directly treating infection by HIV) of the AIDS caps. This is not a case of refusing, for example, to provide the same coverage for a broken leg, or other afflictions not peculiar to people with AIDS, to such people, which would be a good example of discrimination by reason of disability.

... The end stage of many diseases is an illness different from the one that brought the patient to that stage; nowadays when a person dies of pneumonia, it is usually because his body has been gravely weakened by some other ailment. If a health insurance policy that excluded coverage for cancer was interpreted not to cover the pneumonia that killed a patient terminally ill with cancer, this would not be "discrimination" against cancer.

To summarize the discussion to this point, we cannot find anything in the Americans with Disabilities Act or its background, or the nature of AIDS and AIDS caps, to justify so radically expansive an interpretation as would be required to bring these cases under section 302(a) without making an unprincipled distinction between AIDS caps and other product alterations—unless it is section 501(c)(1) of the Act. That section provides that Title I (employment discrimination against the disabled) and Title III (public accommodations, the title involved in this case) "shall not be construed to prohibit or restrict an insurer ... from underwriting risks, classifying risks, or administering such risks that are based on or not inconsistent with State law," unless the prohibition or restriction is "a subterfuge to evade the purposes" of either title....

Remember that the right of full and equal enjoyment as we interpret it includes the right to buy on equal terms and not just the right to enter the store. For Mutual of Omaha to take the position that people with AIDS are so unhealthy that it won't sell them health insurance would be a prima facie violation of section 302(a). But the insurance company just might be able to steer into the safe harbor provided by section 501(c), provided it didn't run afoul of the "subterfuge" limitation, as it would do if, for example, it had adopted the AIDS caps to deter people who know they are HIV positive from buying the policies at all....

There is, as we have pointed out, a difference between refusing to sell a health-insurance policy at all to a person with AIDS, or charging him a higher price for such a policy, or attaching a condition obviously designed to deter people with AIDS from buying the policy (such as refusing to cover such a person for a broken leg), on the one hand, and, on the other, offering insurance policies that contain caps for various diseases some of which may also be disabilities within the meaning of the Americans with Disabilities Act....

We conclude that section 302(a) does not require a seller to alter his product to make it equally valuable to the disabled and to the nondisabled, even if the product is insurance. This conclusion is consistent with all the appellate cases to consider this or cognate issues.... And if it is wrong, the suit must fail anyway, because it is barred by the McCarran-Ferguson Act.

That Act, so far as bears on this case, forbids construing a federal statute to "impair any law enacted by any State for the purpose of regulating the business of insurance ... unless such Act specifically relates to the business of insurance." 15 U.S.C. § 1012(b). Direct conflict with state law is not required to trigger this prohibition; it is enough if the interpretation would "interfere with a State's administrative regime." *Humana Inc. v. Forsyth, 525 U.S. 299 (1999). The* interpretation of section 302(a) of the Americans with Disabilities Act for which the plaintiffs contend would do this. State regulation of insurance is comprehensive and includes rate and coverage issues, so if federal courts are now to determine whether caps on disabling conditions (by no means limited to AIDS) are actuarially sound and consistent with principles of state law they will be stepping on the toes of state insurance commissioners.

It is one thing to say that an insurance company may not refuse to deal with disabled persons; the prohibition of such refusals can probably be administered with relatively little interference with state insurance regulation, and anyway this may be a prohibition expressly imposed by federal law because encompassed within the blanket prohibition of section 302(a) of the Americans with Disabilities Act, and so outside the scope of the McCarran-Ferguson Act. It is another thing to require federal courts to determine whether limitations on coverage are actuarially sound and consistent with state law. Even if the formal criteria are the same under federal and state law, displacing their administration into federal court—requiring a *federal* court to decide whether an insurance policy is consistent with *state* law—obviously would interfere with the administration of the state law. The states are not indifferent to who enforces their laws....

It is true that we are not being asked *in this case* to decide whether the AIDS caps were actuarially sound and in accordance with state law. But if the McCarran-Ferguson Act does not apply, then we are certain to be called upon to decide such issues in the next case, when the insurer does not stipulate to them. Mutual of Omaha didn't want to get into these messy issues if it could show that the Americans with Disabilities Act did not apply. If the ADA is fully applicable, insurers will have to defend their AIDS caps by reference to section 501(c), and the federal courts will then find themselves regulating the health-insurance industry, which McCarran-Ferguson tells them not to do.

Section 501(c) itself specifically relates to insurance and thus is not within the scope of McCarran-Ferguson. But the interpretation that the McCarran-Ferguson Act bars is not an interpretation of 501(c); it is an interpretation of section 302(a) that injects the federal courts into the heart of the regulation of the insurance business by the states.

Of course, we can infer from section 501(c)—we have done so earlier in this opinion—and Mutual of Omaha does not deny, that section 302(a) has some application to insurance: it forbids an insurer to turn down an applicant merely because he is disabled. To that extent, as we have already suggested, we can accept (certainly for purposes of argument) that section 302(a) relates specifically to the business of insurance. But thus limited to a simple prohibition of discrimination, section 302(a) does not impair state regulation of insurance; no state wants insurance companies to refuse to insure disabled people. It is only when section 302(a) is interpreted as broadly as it must be for the plaintiffs in this case to prevail that McCarran-Ferguson's reverse preemption comes into play.

Both because section 302(a) of the Americans with Disabilities Act does not regulate the content of the products or services sold in places of public accommodation and because an interpretation of the section as regulating the content of insurance policies is barred by the McCarran-Ferguson Act, the judgment in favor of the plaintiffs must be reversed with directions to enter judgment for the defendant. This does not, however, leave the plaintiffs remediless. If in fact the AIDS caps in the defendant's policies are not consistent with state law and sound actuarial practices (and whether they are or not, the defendant may be bound by its stipulation, though this we needn't decide), the plaintiffs can obtain all the relief to which they are entitled from the state commissioners who regulate the insurance business. Federal law is not the only source of valuable rights. Reversed.

**Evans, Circuit Judge,** dissenting.

The Americans with Disabilities Act is a broad, sweeping, protective statute requiring the elimination of discrimination against individuals with disabilities.... Because I believe the insurance policies challenged in this case discriminate against people with AIDS in violation of the ADA, I dissent.

The majority believes we are being asked to regulate the content of insurance policies—something we should not do under the ADA. But as I see it we are not being asked to regulate content; we are being asked to decide whether an insurer can discriminate against people with AIDS, refusing to pay for them the same expenses it would pay if they did not have AIDS. The ADA assigns to courts the task of passing judgment on such conduct. And to me, the Mutual of Omaha policies at issue violate the Act.

Chief Judge Posner's opinion likens the insurance company here to a camera store forced to stock cameras specially designed for disabled persons. While I agree that the ADA would not require a store owner to alter its inventory, I think the analogy misses the mark. The better analogy would be that of a store which lets disabled customers in the door, but then refuses to sell them anything but inferior cameras. To pick up on another analogy raised at oral argument, we are not being asked to force a restaurant to alter its menu to accommodate disabled diners; we are being asked to stop a restaurant that is offering to its nondisabled diners a menu containing a variety of entrees while offering a menu with only limited selections to its disabled patrons. Section 501(c)'s "safe harbor" would allow Mutual of Omaha to treat insureds with AIDS differently than those without AIDS if the discrimination were consistent with Illinois law or could be justified by actuarial principles or claims experience. But Mutual of Omaha conceded that its AIDS and ARC caps do not fall under the ADA's safe harbor protection.

The parties stipulated that the very same affliction (e.g., pneumonia) may be both AIDS-related and not AIDS-related and that, in such cases, coverage depends solely on whether the patient has AIDS. In my view that is more than enough to trigger an ADA violation. Chief Judge Posner reasons that, although the policies appear to discriminate solely based on an insured's HIV status, they really don't, when you consider the nature of AIDS. He suggests that the phrase "AIDS related conditions" embodies a unique set of symptoms and afflictions that would make it easy for the insurance company to determine with certainty whether an expense incurred for a particular illness is "AIDS-related" and therefore subject to the cap. His analysis—charitable to Mutual of Omaha to be sure—may very well be medically sound. But it doesn't come from the insurance policies.

The policies don't even hint at what illnesses or afflictions might fall within the ARC exclusion. Nor has the medical community embraced an accepted definition for what "conditions" are "AIDS-related." The practical effect of all this, as Mutual of

Omaha concedes, is that coverage for certain expenses would be approved or denied based solely on whether the insured had AIDS. Given that the ADA is supposed to signal a "clear and comprehensive national mandate for the elimination of discrimination against individuals with disabilities," *see 42 U.S.C. § 12101*(b)(1), I would use the statute to right the wrong committed by Mutual of Omaha.

I also part company with the majority on the McCarran-Ferguson Act analysis, and I think the faultiness of its conclusion is evident in the way the issue is framed. The Chief Judge writes: "It is one thing to say that an insurance company may not refuse to deal with disabled persons; the prohibition of such refusals can probably be administered with relatively little interference with state insurance regulation.... It is another thing to require federal courts to determine whether limitations on coverage are actuarially sound and consistent with state law." Slip op. at 12. This is somewhat misleading because, as the majority acknowledges, the question of whether these caps are actuarially sound or consistent with state law has been taken out of the equation by Mutual of Omaha's concession in the parties' stipulation.

Consistent with McCarran-Ferguson we can — and we should — decide exactly what the majority seemed to think is permissible: whether an insurer may refuse to deal with disabled persons on the same terms as nondisabled persons. Because any conceivable justification for the caps (under section 501(c)) is not at issue, and because an insurer cannot legally decide to pay or not pay expenses based solely on whether an insured has AIDS and is therefore disabled under the ADA, I dissent from the opinion of the court.

## Notes and Questions

For a critical look at the *Doe v. Mutual of Omaha* opinion, *see* Lori Bloch Izzo, Note, *The ADA Does Not Regulate the Content of Insurance Policies, but What Have Cameras, Braille Books, or Wheelchairs Got to Do with It?*, 7 CONN. INS. L.J. 263 (2000–2001). In commenting on *Doe v. Mutual of Omaha* as part of a general survey of Judge Posner's insurance opinions, one of the casebook authors also raised questions about the decision:

> Posner failed to expressly note what I regard as a rather significant distinction: a refusal to cover pre-existing conditions does not preclude coverage for that condition per se — even expensive coverage — should the condition develop after the policy is in effect. Thus, Posner permits insurers to not only refuse to write coverage for persons that already have AIDS but also allows insurers to limit or exclude coverage should the originally HIV-free policyholder develop AIDS complications at some later date. As a practical matter, the distinction may mean a large difference in the number of ultimately covered persons and benefit dollars ultimately provided.

> [T]he abstract existence of the ADA "safe harbor" without concrete state regulatory pronouncements on matters of AIDS coverage does not suggest the broad-based immunity found by Posner in Mutual of Omaha. It does not follow that the ADA may not be applied to insurers simply because under

the ADA and McCarran-Ferguson, state regulation might permit insurers to discriminate because they "have to" maintain the financial integrity of their risk pools. As Judge Evans stated in dissent in *Mutual of Omaha*, the defendant insurer's stipulation that the "safe harbor" was not at issue removed this defense from the case. Without this defense, the ADA appears applicable by its terms and the state regulation is not at issue, meaning McCarran-Ferguson is not at issue.

Jeffrey W. Stempel, *An Inconsistently Sensitive Mind: Richard Posner's Celebration of Insurance Law and Continuing Blind Spots of Econominalism*, 7 Conn. Ins. L.J. 7 (2000–2001).

Does this criticism seem persuasive? Was Mutual of Omaha allowed to get the benefit of the ADA's "safe harbor" for state insurance regulation without actually having to prove the applicability of the exception to the application of the ADA? In that sense, was Mutual of Omaha allowed to stipulate away the safe harbor but use it anyway? Or was this just smart litigation strategy by the insurer? If the *Doe* case had been decided the other way, would the insurer not have had the right to make a second summary judgment motion on the basis of the safe harbor exception and state insurance regulation?

# Pallozzi v. Allstate Life Insurance Co.

United States Court of Appeals for the Second Circuit

198 F.3d 28 (1999)

**Leval, Circuit Judge.**

Plaintiffs Joseph M. Pallozzi and Lori R. Pallozzi appeal from the judgment of the United States District Court for the Northern District of New York (Scullin, J.) dismissing their complaint against Defendant Allstate Life Insurance Company ("Allstate") under Fed. R. Civ. P. 12(b)(6). The complaint alleged in main that Allstate discriminated against Plaintiffs on the basis of their mental disabilities by refusing to issue them a joint life insurance policy, thereby violating Title III of the Americans with Disabilities Act (the "Act" or "ADA"), 42 U.S.C. §§ 12181–12189. Because the complaint failed to allege that Allstate's refusal to insure Plaintiffs was without actuarial justification, the district court dismissed the action. See 998 F. Supp. at 207–08. We disagree with the court's reasoning and disposition, and therefore vacate the judgment.

A. Relevant statutory provisions.

Title III of the ADA, which generally prohibits discrimination on the basis of disability by so-called "public accommodations," provides in Section 302(a) that

> No individual shall be discriminated against on the basis of disability in the full and equal enjoyment of the goods, services, facilities, privileges, advantages, or accommodations of any place of public accommodation by any person who owns, leases (or leases to), or operates a place of public accommodation.

Title III includes a long list of private facilities that qualify as "public accommodations" so long as their operations "affect commerce," including an "insurance office, professional office of a health care provider, hospital, or other service establishment."

Section 501(c) of Title V of the ADA (the "safe harbor" provision) includes the following statement:

INSURANCE

Subchapters I through III of this chapter [i.e., Titles I through III of the ADA] and title IV of this Act shall not be construed to prohibit or restrict—

(1) an insurer, hospital or medical service company, health maintenance organization, or any agent, or entity that administers benefit plans, or similar organizations from underwriting risks, classifying risks, or administering such risks that are based on or not inconsistent with State law....

The safe harbor provision also states, in its so-called "subterfuge clause":

Paragraph (1) ... shall not be used as a subterfuge to evade the purposes of [Titles] I and III of [the Act].

The McCarran-Ferguson Act, insofar as it bears on the instant dispute, provides:

No Act of Congress shall be construed to invalidate, impair, or supersede any law enacted by any State for the purpose of regulating the business of insurance ... unless such Act specifically relates to the business of insurance.

B. Allegations of the complaint.

The Pallozzis are a married couple. Joseph Pallozzi has been diagnosed with major depression and agoraphobia, Lori Pallozzi with major depression and borderline personality disorder. Both Pallozzis have received counseling, medication, and inpatient treatment for their conditions in the past.

In October 1996, Plaintiffs applied to Allstate for a joint life insurance policy in the amount of $65,000. Allstate initially issued them a Temporary Insurance Agreement, but soon canceled the agreement based on medical information provided by Plaintiffs' psychiatrist, and refused to sell them another policy. When Plaintiffs inquired as to why they had been rejected, the carrier gave them a copy of their application and referred them to their psychiatrist for further information. Allstate refused their requests to furnish them with specific reasons for the denial.

In February 1997, Plaintiffs commenced this lawsuit against Allstate in the United States District Court for the Northern District of New York. Their complaint claimed that Allstate refused to sell them life insurance because of their mental disabilities; and that this refusal violated Title III of the ADA and failed to come within the safe harbor of Section 501(c) of the Act because the insurer's conduct violated various provisions of the New York State Insurance Law, specifically N.Y. Ins. Law §§ 2606, 2608, and 4224. It further asserted that Allstate's actions constituted a "subterfuge to evade the purposes of Title III of the ADA." The complaint sought a declaratory judgment that Allstate violated Plaintiffs' rights under Title III and New York law, and an order directing Allstate to sell Plaintiffs a life insurance policy "at a price which is based on sound actuarial principles, or actual or reasonably anticipated experience." ...

Plaintiffs advance three related arguments: (1) Title III of the ADA does regulate the underwriting practices of insurance companies; (2) its regulation of insurance underwriting is not barred by the McCarran-Ferguson Act because the ADA "specifically relates to the business of insurance"; and (3) the district court imposed unjustified pleading burdens in ruling on the motion under Fed. R. Civ. P. 12(b)(6). We agree with all three contentions.

### I. Whether the ADA regulates insurance underwriting practices.

Allstate contends that Title III of the ADA does not reach the underwriting practices of insurance companies. Plaintiffs, marshaling the text of the statute, its legislative history, and interpretive guidelines issued by the U.S. Department of Justice, argue that Title III does regulate insurance underwriting practices. We believe the text of the statute confirms Plaintiffs' position, making it unnecessary for us to examine their back-up arguments based on legislative history and administrative interpretation.

We start with the fact that Title III specifies an "insurance office" as a "public accommodation." Section 302(a) bars a "place of public accommodation" from "discriminating against [an individual] on the basis of disability in the full and equal enjoyment of [its] goods [and] services." The most conspicuous "goods" and "services" provided by an "insurance office" are insurance policies. Thus, the prohibition imposed on a place of public accommodation from discriminating against a disabled customer in the enjoyment of its goods and services appears to prohibit an insurance office from discriminatorily refusing to offer its policies to disabled persons, subject to the safe harbor provision of Section 501(c) of Title V. *See Doe v. Mutual of Omaha Ins. Co.*, 179 F.3d 557, 559 (7th Cir. 1999) (Posner, C.J.) (absent special circumstances, Title III of the ADA prohibits an insurance company from refusing to sell an insurance policy to a disabled person by reason of the person's disability).

This conclusion is reinforced by the safe harbor provision of Section 501(c) of Title V and its subterfuge clause. That provision is labeled "INSURANCE." As quoted above, it first asserts that Titles I through III "shall not be construed to prohibit or restrict — (1) an insurer ... from underwriting risks, classifying risks, or administering such risks that are based on or not inconsistent with State law." *Id.* It then provides, in its subterfuge clause, that the foregoing exemption for insurance underwriters in compliance with state law "shall not be used as a subterfuge to evade the purposes of [Titles] I and III of [the Act]." *Id.*

The exemption for insurance underwriters whose practices are "not inconsistent with State law" strongly implies that the Act is intended to reach insurance underwriting practices that are inconsistent with State law. If the ADA were not intended to reach insurance underwriting under any circumstances, there would be no need for a safe harbor provision exempting underwriting practices that are consistent with state law.... And, in any event, the subterfuge clause suggests that, notwithstanding compliance with state law, Titles I and III do apply to insurance practices where conformity with state law is used as a subterfuge to evade their purposes. Considering the net effect of these provisions, it seems clear to us that Title III was intended by Congress to apply to insurance underwriting.

Allstate argues that Title III defines the term "public accommodation" to include "insurance office[s]," not insurance companies. This choice of words, the carrier maintains, suggests that Congress intended the statute to ensure that the disabled have physical access to the facilities of insurance providers, not to prohibit discrimination against the disabled in insurance underwriting. Furthermore, Allstate contends, because insurance policies are not actually used in places of public accommodation, they do not qualify as goods and services "of [a] place of public accommodation."

We find those arguments unpersuasive. Title III's mandate that the disabled be accorded "full and equal enjoyment of the goods, [and] services ... of any place of public accommodation," *id.*, suggests to us that the statute was meant to guarantee them more than mere physical access. Cf. *Carparts Distribution Ctr., Inc. v. Automotive Wholesaler's Ass'n*, 37 F.3d 12, 20 (1st Cir. 1994) ("To ... limit the application of Title III to physical structures ... would severely frustrate Congress's intent that individuals with disabilities fully enjoy the goods, services, privileges and advantages, available indiscriminately to other members of the general public."). We believe an entity covered by Title III is not only obligated by the statute to provide disabled persons with physical access, but is also prohibited from refusing to sell them its merchandise by reason of discrimination against their disability. *Accord, Mutual of Omaha*, 179 F.3d at 559, 564. Furthermore, Allstate's insistence that the statute provides only for physical access ignores the implication of the safe harbor provision that the Act deals with the "underwriting [and] classifying [of] risks."

We find no merit in Allstate's contention that, because insurance policies are not used in places of public accommodation, they do not qualify as goods or services "of a place of public accommodation." The term "of" generally does not mean "in," and there is no indication that Congress intended to employ the term in such an unorthodox manner in Section 302(a) of Title III. Furthermore, many of the private entities that Title III defines as "public accommodations"—such as a "bakery, grocery store, clothing store, hardware store, [or] shopping center," as well as a "travel service, ... gas station, office of an accountant or lawyer, [or] pharmacy,"—sell goods and services that are ordinarily used outside the premises.

On Allstate's interpretation, a bakery's refusal to sell bread to a blind person would fall outside the scope of the statute. We see no basis for reading the statute so narrowly.... ("It is the purpose of this [Act] ... to provide a clear and comprehensive national mandate for the elimination of discrimination against individuals with disabilities ... [and] to invoke the sweep of congressional authority ... to address the major areas of discrimination faced day-to-day by people with disabilities.").We therefore hold that Title III does regulate the sale of insurance policies in insurance offices, subject to the limitations of the safe harbor provision in Section 501(c) of Title V. As we base our holding on the statutory text—which, we find, unambiguously covers insurance underwriting in at least some circumstances—we need not consider Plaintiffs' arguments that the ADA's legislative history and the interpretive guidelines issued by the Department of Justice confirm this interpretation.

## II. Whether the McCarran-Ferguson Act bars application of Title III to insurance underwriting.

Allstate contends that, even if the ADA might be read to cover insurance underwriting, the McCarran-Ferguson Act forbids such an interpretation. That Act mandates in relevant part that no federal statute "shall be construed to invalidate, impair, or supersede any law enacted by any State for the purpose of regulating the business of insurance ... unless [the statute in question] specifically relates to the business of insurance." It is understood to apply not only to federal statutes that literally "invalidate, impair, or supersede" state laws, but also to federal statutes that would "interfere with a State's administrative regimen." *Humana, Inc. v. Forsyth*, 525 U.S. 299 (1999). Allstate argues that because the ADA does not "specifically relate to the business of insurance," it falls within McCarran-Ferguson's prohibition. Plaintiffs maintain that the ADA does "specifically relate to the business of insurance," and therefore falls outside the prohibition. We agree with Plaintiffs.

In *Barnett Bank v. Nelson*, 517 U.S. 25 (1996), the Supreme Court considered whether a federal statute granting certain national banks permission to sell insurance in small towns "specifically relates to the business of insurance" within the meaning of the McCarran-Ferguson Act. *Id.* at 28. The statute conflicted with a Florida act prohibiting such sales. See *id.* at 28–29.

A unanimous Supreme Court held (per Justice Breyer) that the federal statute does "specifically relate to the business of insurance," arriving at this result by applying a four-step analysis. (1) The Court began by inquiring whether the statute "relates" to the insurance business, that is, whether it "has a connection with" insurance plans. *Id.* at 38 (internal quotation marks and citation omitted). (2) The Court next assessed whether the statute "specifically" relates to the insurance business, that is, whether it relates to the insurance business "explicitly, particularly, [or] definitely." *Id.* (internal quotation marks and citation omitted, alteration in original). (3) The Court then examined whether the statute specifically relates to the "business of insurance," that is, whether it affects "matters ... at the core of the McCarran-Ferguson Act's concern," such as "the relation of insured to insurer and the spreading of risk." *Id.* at 39. (4) Finally, the Court considered the statute in light of the McCarran-Ferguson Act's purposes, emphasizing that the Act serves "to protect state [insurance] regulation primarily against inadvertent federal intrusion." *Id.* (emphasis in original).

In applying the foregoing analysis, the Court also explained that neither the Mc-Carran-Ferguson Act's language, nor its purpose, requires the Federal Statute to relate predominantly to insurance. To the contrary, specific detailed references to the insurance industry in proposed legislation normally will achieve the McCarran-Ferguson

Act's objectives, for they will call the proposed legislation to the attention of interested parties, and thereby normally guarantee, should the proposal become law, that Congress will have focused upon its insurance-related effects.

Applying the analytic framework of *Barnett Bank* to this case leads us to conclude that the ADA does "specifically relate to the business of insurance," and therefore falls outside the scope of McCarran-Ferguson's prohibition. As for step one, the ADA clearly "relates" to the insurance business, insofar as Title III defines an "insurance office" as a "public accommodation," 42 U.S.C. § 12181(7)(F), and Section 501(c), which is labeled "INSURANCE," subjects insurance underwriting to the regulatory scope of the ADA under specified circumstances. *Id.* § 12201(c). These same provisions satisfy step two, demonstrating that the Act relates "specifically" to insurance.... They are explicit and direct in their references to insurance.

Third, we find that the ADA does regulate the "business of insurance," in that it affects "matters ... at the core of the McCarran-Ferguson Act's concern," such as "the relation of insured to insurer and the spreading of risk." Although the safe harbor provision generally exempts insurance underwriters from the reach of Titles I through III so long as they comply with state law, Congress clearly contemplated that under some circumstances—when the conditions of the safe harbor were not met—Titles I through III would apply to insurance underwriting practices, including the relation of insurers to those applying to become their insureds. As we read Sections 302(a) and 501(c), they prohibit insurance underwriters from denying life insurance policies to disabled persons by reason of their disabilities, except in the circumstances protected by the safe harbor. Such decisions to grant or deny an application for insurance are within the "business of insurance," as contemplated in step three of Barnett Bank.

Finally, turning to Barnett Bank's fourth step, consideration of the ADA in light of McCarran-Ferguson's purposes also supports our conclusion. The ADA's specific references to insurance in Title III and Section 501(c) suggest that any intrusion by the statute on state insurance regulation is not "inadvertent." These references "achieve the McCarran-Ferguson Act's objectives," because they "called ... [the ADA] to the attention of interested parties" prior to its enactment, and thereby "guaranteed ... that Congress ... focused upon its insurance-related effects." We therefore hold that the McCarran-Ferguson Act does not bar application of Title III to insurance underwriting.

Indeed, we believe the safe harbor provision of Section 501(c) was written by Congress with McCarran-Ferguson in mind, precisely to communicate that message. With the benefit of minimal decoding, we understand Congress to be saying:

> (1) Because of the general preference expressed in McCarran-Ferguson's default rule that insurance matters be regulated by State authority, rather than by us, we require a plaintiff seeking to prove a claim arising from underwriting decisions to show that the practice complained of is proscribed not only by this statute but also by State law.

(2) If, on the other hand, the insurer uses State law as a subterfuge to evade the purposes of this Act, that also will support a claim.

(3) We set forth this separate provision (under the caption "INSURANCE") to make clear that our statute "specifically relates to the business of insurance" and therefore must be interpreted, notwithstanding McCarran-Ferguson, to regulate insurance practices.

Finally we note that the Seventh Circuit in Mutual of Omaha also found McCarran-Ferguson satisfied with respect to the type of discriminatory practice at issue in this case. Although ruling on a different issue, the court expressed the view that Title III forbids an insurer's discriminatory refusal to sell its policies to a disabled person, and that this interpretation of the ADA would not be barred by McCarran-Ferguson. See *Mutual of Omaha*, 179 F.3d at 559, 564 ("Thus limited to a simple prohibition of discrimination, section 302(a) does not impair state regulation of insurance....")....

## Notes and Questions

1. Are the differences in *Pallozzi* and *Doe* explained by different facts or different courts?

2. Although most of the reported decisions tend to take a narrow view of insurance as a "public accommodation" under the ADA, tallying up the individual judges' votes reflects a considerably divided federal judiciary on this issue. *See, e.g.*, Stempel, *An Inconsistently Sensitive Mind*, *supra*, at 69. (In the course of *Doe v. Mutual of Omaha*, the Seventh Circuit was split 7–5 on the issue, and the trial court's view was in accord with the dissenters, a close vote even by the standards of a Florida election.)

## [C] State Regulation Seeking to Change Public Policy

State insurance law or insurance department action frequently is designed to accomplish a goal that, strictly speaking, is not insurance. For example, rate regulation seeks to prevent unfair or invidious discrimination in rate setting. Similarly, "redlining" by an insurer may be attacked by regulators. The entire auto insurance regulatory regime is permeated by efforts to provide some measure of assured compensation to accident victims. On occasion, insurers and regulators or state legislators may venture further afield in attempting to accomplish public policy goals through insurance regulation.

For example, in 1999, California enacted the Holocaust Victims Insurance Relief Act, CAL. INS. CODE §§ 13800–13807. The Act, abbreviated as HVIRA,

> requires insurers that do business in California and sold insurance policies, in effect between 1920 and 1945 (Holocaust-era policies), to persons in Europe to file certain information about those polices with the [California]

Commissioner [of Insurance]. The reporting requirement also applies to insurance companies that do business in California and are "related" to a company that sold Holocaust-era policies, even if the relationship arose after the policies were issued. A "related company" is any "parent, subsidiary, reinsurer, successor in interest, managing general agent, or affiliate company of the insurer." HVIRA requires the Commissioner to store the information in a public "Holocaust Era Insurance Registry." The Commissioner must "suspend the certificate of authority to conduct insurance business in the state of any insurer that fails to comply" with HVIRA's reporting requirements.

*See Gerling Global Reinsurance Corp. of Am. v. Low*, 240 F. 3d 739 (9th Cir. 2001) (footnote and citations omitted). Under HVIRA, the insurance companies must provide information about their number of Holocaust Era policies as well as the holder, beneficiary, and current status of each policy, the city of origin, domicile, or address for each named policyholder. The insurer must also certify that one of the following has occurred with regard to the policies: the proceeds of the policies have been paid; beneficiaries or heirs could not be located; a court plan exists for distributing the proceeds of the policies, or the proceeds have otherwise been appropriately distributed. *See* CAL. INS. CODE § 1384(a), (b).

In response to HVIRA, a number of insurers sued, contending that the Act violated the Commerce Clause and intruded on the federal government's exclusive power over foreign affairs. The trial court granted an injunction preventing enforcement of the Act. On appeal, the California Commissioner persuaded a panel of the Court of Appeals that HVIRA did not violate the Commerce Clause, particularly in view of the McCarran-Ferguson Act's statement in favor of state-based regulation of insurance, and that HVIRA did not impinge upon the U.S. government's power over foreign affairs. *See Gerling Global Reinsurance Corp. of Am. v. Low*, 240 F.3d 739 (9th Cir. 2001).

However, the Ninth Circuit left the trial court's injunction in place and remanded the matter to consider other insurer challenges to HVIRA, particularly the claim that HVIRA deprived the insurers of property without due process of law. On remand, the trial court found a due process violation, concluding that the penalty of suspension of an insurer's license for failure to comply with HVIRA was property deprivation without an adequate opportunity to be heard before an adjudicatory forum. In a second appellate proceeding, the Court of Appeals again disagreed with the trial court. *See Gerling Global Reinsurance Corp. of Am. v. Low*, 296 F.3d 832 (9th Cir. 2002).

Then the U.S. Supreme Court weighed in, in *American Insurance Association v. Garamendi (Insurance Commissioner, State of California)*, 539 U.S. 396 (2003). In the majority decision by Justice Souter, HVIRA was held to be pre-empted by federal law. Contrast that holding with the dissent by Justice Ginsberg, who held that HVIRA was valid and not an encroachment onto federal territory.

# [D] Insurance and Federal ERISA Pre-Emption

## [1] *The Fine Line of ERISA Pre-Emption*

The Federal Employee Retirement Income Security Act of 1974 (ERISA), 29 U.S.C. § 1001 *et seq.*, generally preempts any state laws relating to employee benefit plans covered by ERISA. However, a section of the Act, 29 U.S.C. § 1144(b)(2)(A), states that it shall not "be construed to exempt or relieve any person from any law of any state which regulates insurance, banking, or securities." Thus, ERISA "explicitly preserves state regulation of 'insurance.'" *Alessi v. Raybestos-Manhattan*, 451 U.S. 504, 523 n.19 (1981).

Although ERISA is not an insurance statute per se, it has generated a host of litigation concerning health care and insurance coverage. ERISA was enacted in response to several well-publicized defaults of major pension plans, particularly the insolvency of the Studebaker plant, which left thousands of workers without promised retirement benefits even though they had spent years or even decades with the company. As might be expected, Congress was concerned. ERISA was passed largely to shore up and police retirement plans so that the plans would be solvent and well-administered. *See generally* Jeffrey W. Stempel & Nadia von Magdenko, *Doctors, HMOs, ERISA and the Public Interest After* Pegram v. Herdrich, 36 TORT & INS. L.J. 687 (2001).

The legislative history of ERISA contains no reference to insurance law. However, Congress did not want the pension regulation it had enacted to be compromised by inconsistent state laws that might provide lower protection to workers or add to employer costs because of inconsistency and uncertainty as to compliance. Consequently, ERISA contains very broad preemption language, requiring that ERISA preempt any inconsistent state law except for what might be termed "core" insurance regulation.

This exception to the broad preemption was a clear congressional indication that Congress did not want ERISA to overrule the McCarran-Ferguson Act and the historical preference for state regulation of insurance. But when ERISA was enacted, relatively little thought had been given to how the preemption provision and its savings clause would or would not affect claims arising under insurance policies that were part of an employee benefit plan subject to ERISA. As you read the following cases, see if you can determine where to draw the line of preemption. Do employers, insurers, and lower courts have enough clear guidance to draw that line?

## Rush Prudential HMO, Inc. v. Moran

Supreme Court of the United States
536 U.S. 355, 122 S. Ct. 2151, 153 L. Ed. 2d 375 (2002)

**Justice Souter** delivered the opinion of the Court.

Section 4-10 of Illinois's Health Maintenance Organization Act, 215 Ill. Comp. Stat., ch. 125, § 4-10 (2000), provides recipients of health coverage by such organizations with a right to independent medical review of certain denials of benefits. The issue in this case is whether the statute, as applied to health benefits provided by a health maintenance organization under contract with an employee welfare benefit plan, is preempted by the [ERISA]. We hold it is not.

Petitioner, Rush Prudential HMO, Inc., is a health maintenance organization (HMO) that contracts to provide medical services for employee welfare benefit plans covered by ERISA. Respondent Debra Moran is a beneficiary under one such plan, sponsored by her husband's employer. Rush's "Certificate of Group Coverage," issued to employees who participate in employer-sponsored plans, promises that Rush will provide them with "medically necessary" services. The terms of the certificate give Rush the "broadest possible discretion" to determine whether a medical service claimed by a beneficiary is covered under the certificate. The certificate specifies that a service is covered as "medically necessary" if Rush finds:

> "(a) [The service] is furnished or authorized by a Participating Doctor for the diagnosis or the treatment of a Sickness or Injury or for the maintenance of a person's good health.

> "(b) The prevailing opinion within the appropriate specialty of the United States medical profession is that [the service] is safe and effective for its intended use, and that its omission would adversely affect the person's medical condition.

> "(c) It is furnished by a provider with appropriate training, experience, staff and facilities to furnish that particular service or supply."

As the certificate explains, Rush contracts with physicians "to arrange for or provide services and supplies for medical care and treatment" of covered persons. Each covered person selects a primary care physician from those under contract to Rush, while Rush will pay for medical services by an unaffiliated physician only if the services have been "authorized" both by the primary care physician and Rush's medical director.

In 1996, when Moran began to have pain and numbness in her right shoulder, Dr. Arthur LaMarre, her primary care physician, unsuccessfully administered "conservative" treatments such as physiotherapy. In October 1997, Dr. LaMarre recommended that Rush approve surgery by an unaffiliated specialist, Dr. Julia Terzis, who had developed an unconventional treatment for Moran's condition. Although Dr. LaMarre said that Moran would be "best served" by that procedure, Rush denied the request and, after Moran's internal appeals, affirmed the denial on the ground that the procedure was not "medically necessary." Rush instead proposed that Moran undergo standard surgery, performed by a physician affiliated with Rush.

In January 1998, Moran made a written demand for an independent medical review of her claim, as guaranteed by § 4-10 of Illinois's HMO Act, 215 Ill. Comp. Stat., ch. 125, § 4-10 *et seq.* (2000), which provides:

> "Each Health Maintenance Organization shall provide a mechanism for the timely review by a physician holding the same class of license as the primary

care physician, who is unaffiliated with the Health Maintenance Organization, jointly selected by the patient..., primary care physician and the Health Maintenance Organization in the event of a dispute between the primary care physician and the Health Maintenance Organization regarding the medical necessity of a covered service proposed by a primary care physician. In the event that the reviewing physician determines the covered service to be medically necessary, the Health Maintenance Organization shall provide the covered service."

The Act defines a "Health Maintenance Organization" as

"any organization formed under the laws of this or another state to provide or arrange for one or more health care plans under a system which causes any part of the risk of health care delivery to be borne by the organization or its providers." Ch. 125, § 1-2.

When Rush failed to provide the independent review, Moran sued in an Illinois state court to compel compliance with the state Act. Rush removed the suit to Federal District Court, arguing that the cause of action was "completely preempted" under ERISA.

While the suit was pending, Moran had surgery by Dr. Terzis at her own expense and submitted a $94,841.27 reimbursement claim to Rush. Rush treated the claim as a renewed request for benefits and began a new inquiry to determine coverage. The three doctors consulted by Rush said the surgery had been medically unnecessary.

Meanwhile, the federal court remanded the case back to state court on Moran's motion, concluding that because Moran's request for independent review under § 4-10 would not require interpretation of the terms of an ERISA plan, the claim was not "completely preempted" so as to permit removal under 28 U.S.C. § 1441. The state court enforced the state statute and ordered Rush to submit to review by an independent physician. The doctor selected was a reconstructive surgeon at Johns Hopkins Medical Center, Dr. A. Lee Dellon. Dr. Dellon decided that Dr. Terzis's treatment had been medically necessary, based on the definition of medical necessity in Rush's Certificate of Group Coverage, as well as his own medical judgment. Rush's medical director, however, refused to concede that the surgery had been medically necessary, and denied Moran's claim in January 1999.

Moran amended her complaint in state court to seek reimbursement for the surgery as "medically necessary" under Illinois's HMO Act, and Rush again removed to federal court, arguing that Moran's amended complaint stated a claim for ERISA benefits and was thus completely preempted by ERISA's civil enforcement provisions. The District Court treated Moran's claim as a suit under ERISA, and denied the claim on the ground that ERISA preempted Illinois's independent review statute.

The Court of Appeals for the Seventh Circuit reversed. Although it found Moran's state-law reimbursement claim completely preempted by ERISA so as to place the case in federal court, the Seventh Circuit did not agree that the substantive provisions of Illinois's HMO Act were so preempted....

Because the decision of the Court of Appeals conflicted with the Fifth Circuit's treatment of a similar provision of Texas law in *Corporate Health Ins., Inc. v. Texas Dept. of Ins.*, 215 F.3d 526 (2000), we granted certiorari [and] now affirm.

It is beyond serious dispute that under existing precedent § 4-10 of the Illinois HMO Act "relates to" employee benefit plans within the meaning of § 1144(a). The state law bears "indirectly but substantially on all insured benefit plans," by requiring them to submit to an extra layer of review for certain benefit denials if they purchase medical coverage from any of the common types of health care organizations covered by the state law's definition of HMO. As a law that "relates to" ERISA plans under § 1144(a), § 4-10 is saved from preemption only if it also "regulates insurance" under § 1144(b)(2)(A). Rush insists that the Act is not such a law.

In *Metropolitan Life* [*Ins. Co. v. Taylor*, 481 U.S. 58 (1987)], we said that in deciding whether a law "regulates insurance" under ERISA's saving clause, we start with a "common-sense view of the matter," under which "a law must not just have an impact on the insurance industry, but must be specifically directed toward that industry." We then test the results of the common-sense enquiry by employing the three factors used to point to insurance laws spared from federal preemption under the McCarran-Ferguson Act. Although this is not the place to plot the exact perimeter of the saving clause, it is generally fair to think of the combined "common-sense" and McCarran-Ferguson factors as parsing the "who" and the "what": when insurers are regulated with respect to their insurance practices, the state law survives ERISA. Cf. *Group Life & Health Ins. Co. v. Royal Drug Co.*, 440 U.S. 205, 211 (1979) (explaining that the "business of insurance" is not coextensive with the "business of insurers").

The common-sense enquiry focuses on "primary elements of an insurance contract [which] are the spreading and underwriting of a policyholder's risk." *Id.*, at 211. The Illinois statute addresses these elements by defining "health maintenance organization" by reference to the risk that it bears. See 215 Ill. Comp. Stat., ch. 125, § 1-2(9) (2000) (an HMO "provides or arranges for ... health care plans under a system which causes any part of the risk of health care delivery to be borne by the organization or its providers").

Rush contends that seeing an HMO as an insurer distorts the nature of an HMO, which is, after all, a health care provider, too. This, Rush argues, should determine its characterization, with the consequence that regulation of an HMO is not insurance regulation within the meaning of ERISA.

The answer to Rush is, of course, that an HMO is both: it provides health care, and it does so as an insurer. Nothing in the saving clause requires an either-or choice between health care and insurance in deciding a preemption question, and as long as providing insurance fairly accounts for the application of state law, the saving clause may apply. There is no serious question about that here, for it would ignore the whole purpose of the HMO-style of organization to conceive of HMOs (even in the traditional sense) without their insurance element."

The defining feature of an HMO is receipt of a fixed fee for each patient enrolled under the terms of a contract to provide specified health care if needed." *Pegram v. Herdrich*, 530 U.S. 211, 218 (2000). "The HMO thus assumes the financial risk of providing the benefits promised: if a participant never gets sick, the HMO keeps the money regardless, and if a participant becomes expensively ill, the HMO is responsible for the treatment...." [This type of risk spreading is] a feature distinctive to insurance....

The dominant feature [of an HMO] is the combination of insurer and provider, and "an observer may be hard pressed to uncover the differences among products that bill themselves as HMOs, [preferred provider organizations], or managed care overlays to health insurance." Thus, virtually all commentators on the American health care system describe HMOs as a combination of insurer and provider, and observe that in recent years, traditional "indemnity" insurance has fallen out of favor.... ("A common characteristic of the new managed care plans was the degree to which the roles of insurer and provider became integrated")....

On a second tack, Rush and its *amici* dispute that § 4-10 is aimed specifically at the insurance industry. They say the law sweeps too broadly with definitions capturing organizations that provide no insurance, and by regulating noninsurance activities of HMOs that do. Rush points out that Illinois law defines HMOs to include organizations that cause the risk of health care delivery to be borne by the organization itself, or by "its providers." In Rush's view, the reference to "its providers" suggests that an organization may be an HMO under state law (and subject to § 4-10) even if it does not bear risk itself, either because it has "devolved" the risk of health care delivery onto others, or because it has contracted only to provide "administrative" or other services for self-funded plans.

These arguments, however, are built on unsound assumptions. Rush's first contention assumes that an HMO is no longer an insurer when it arranges to limit its exposure, as when an HMO arranges for capitated contracts to compensate its affiliated physicians with a set fee for each HMO patient regardless of the treatment provided. Under such an arrangement, Rush claims, the risk is not borne by the HMO at all. In a similar vein, Rush points out that HMOs may contract with third-party insurers to protect themselves against large claims.

The problem with Rush's argument is simply that a reinsurance contract does not take the primary insurer out of the insurance business, cf. *Hartford Fire Ins. Co. v. California*, 509 U.S. 764 (1993) (applying McCarran-Ferguson to a dispute involving primary insurers and reinsurers); *id.*, at 772–773 ("Primary insurers ... usually purchase insurance to cover a portion of the risk they assume from the consumer"), and capitation contracts do not relieve the HMO of its obligations to the beneficiary. The HMO is still bound to provide medical care to its members, and this is so regardless of the ability of physicians or third-party insurers to honor their contracts with the HMO.

It is far from clear, though, that the terms of § 4-10 would even theoretically apply to the matchmaker, for the requirement that the HMO "provide" the covered service if the independent reviewer finds it medically necessary seems to assume that the HMO in question is a provider, not the mere arranger mentioned in the general definition of an HMO. Even on the most generous reading of Rush's argument, however, it boils down to the bare possibility (not the likelihood) of some overbreadth in the application of § 4-10 beyond orthodox HMOs, and there is no reason to think Congress would have meant such minimal application to noninsurers to remove a state law entirely from the category of insurance regulation saved from preemption.

In sum, prior to ERISA's passage, Congress demonstrated an awareness of HMOs as risk-bearing organizations subject to state insurance regulation, the state Act defines HMOs by reference to risk bearing, HMOs have taken over much business formerly performed by traditional indemnity insurers, and they are almost universally regulated as insurers under state law. That HMOs are not traditional "indemnity" insurers is no matter; "we would not undertake to freeze the concepts of 'insurance'... into the mold they fitted when these Federal Acts were passed." Thus, the Illinois HMO Act is a law "directed toward" the insurance industry, and an "insurance regulation" under a "commonsense" view.

The McCarran-Ferguson factors confirm our conclusion. A law regulating insurance for McCarran-Ferguson purposes targets practices or provisions that "have the effect of transferring or spreading a policyholder's risk; ... [that are] an integral part of the policy relationship between the insurer and the insured; and [are] limited to entities within the insurance industry." *Union Labor Life Ins. Co. v. Pireno*, 458 U.S. 119, 129 (1982). Because the factors are guideposts, a state law is not required to satisfy all three McCarran-Ferguson criteria to survive preemption, see *UNUM Life Ins. Co. v. Ward*, 526 U.S. at 373, and so we follow our precedent and leave open whether the review mandated here may be described as going to a practice that "spreads a policyholder's risk." For in any event, the second and third factors are clearly satisfied by § 4-10.

It is obvious enough that the independent review requirement regulates "an integral part of the policy relationship between the insurer and the insured." Illinois adds an extra layer of review when there is internal disagreement about an HMO's denial of coverage. The reviewer applies both a standard of medical care (medical necessity) and characteristically, as in this case, construes policy terms. Cf. *Pegram v. Herdrich*, 530 U.S., at 228–229. The review affects the "policy relationship" between HMO and covered persons by translating the relationship under the HMO agreement into concrete terms of specific obligation or freedom from duty. Hence our repeated statements that the interpretation of insurance contracts is at the "core" of the business of insurance. *E.g.*, *SEC v. National Securities, Inc.*, 393 U.S. 453, 460 (1969).

Rush says otherwise, citing *Union Labor Life Ins. Co. v. Pireno, supra*, and insisting that that case holds external review of coverage decisions to be outside the "policy relationship." But Rush misreads *Pireno*. We held there that an insurer's use of a "peer review" committee to gauge the necessity of particular treatments was not a practice integral to the policy relationship for the purposes of McCarran-Ferguson. 458 U.S. at 131–132. We emphasized, however, that the insurer's resort to peer review was simply the insurer's unilateral choice to seek advice if and when it cared to do so.

The policy said nothing on the matter. The insurer's contract for advice from a third party was no concern of the insured, who was not bound by the peer review committee's recommendation any more, for that matter, than the insurer was. Thus it was not too much of an exaggeration to conclude that the practice was "a matter of indifference to the policyholder," Section 4-10, by contrast, is different on all counts, providing as it does a legal right to the insured, enforceable against the HMO, to obtain an authoritative determination of the HMO's medical obligations.

The final factor, that the law be aimed at a "practice ... limited to entities within the insurance industry," is satisfied for many of the same reasons that the law passes the commonsense test. The law regulates application of HMO contracts and provides for review of claim denials; once it is established that HMO contracts are, in fact, contracts for insurance (and not merely contracts for medical care), it is clear that §4-10 does not apply to entities outside the insurance industry (although it does not, of course, apply to all entities within it).

Even if we accepted Rush's contention, rejected already, that the law regulates HMOs even when they act as pure administrators, we would still find the third factor satisfied. That factor requires the targets of the law to be limited to entities within the insurance industry, and even a matchmaking HMO would fall within the insurance industry. But the implausibility of Rush's hypothesis that the pure administrator would be bound by §4-10 obviates any need to say more under this third factor. Cf. *Barnett Bank of Marion Cty, N.A. v. Nelson*, 517 U.S. 25, 39, 116 S. Ct. 1103, 134 L. Ed. 2d 237 (1996) (holding that a federal statute permitting banks to act as agents of insurance companies, although not insurers themselves, was a statute regulating the "business of insurance" for McCarran-Ferguson purposes).

In sum, §4-10 imposes no new obligation or remedy like the [claim] considered in [*Pilot Life*]. Even in its formal guise, the state Act bears a closer resemblance to second-opinion requirements than to arbitration schemes. Deferential review in the HMO context is not a settled given; §4-10 operates before the stage of judicial review; the independent reviewer's *de novo* examination of the benefit claim mirrors the general or default rule we have ourselves recognized; and its effect is no greater than that of mandated-benefit regulation.

In deciding what to make of these facts and conclusions, it helps to go back to where we started and recall the ways States regulate insurance in looking out for the welfare of their citizens. Illinois has chosen to regulate insurance as one way to regulate the practice of medicine, which we have previously held to be permissible under ERISA[.] While the statute designed to do this undeniably eliminates whatever may have remained of a plan sponsor's option to minimize scrutiny of benefit denials, this effect of eliminating an insurer's autonomy to guarantee terms congenial to its own interests is the stuff of garden variety insurance regulation through the imposition of standard policy terms.... ("State laws regulating the substantive terms of insurance contracts were commonplace well before the mid-70's").

It is therefore hard to imagine a reservation of state power to regulate insurance that would not be meant to cover restrictions of the insurer's advantage in this kind of way. And any lingering doubt about the reasonableness of §4-10 in affecting the application of §1132(a) may be put to rest by recalling that regulating insurance tied to what is medically necessary is probably inseparable from enforcing the quintessentially state-law standards of reasonable medical care. See *Pegram v. Herdrich*, 530 U.S., at 236. "In the field of health care, a subject of traditional state regulation, there is no ERISA preemption without clear manifestation of congressional purpose." *Id.*, at 237. To the extent that benefits litigation in some federal courts may have to account for the effects of §4-10, it would be an exaggeration to hold that the objectives of §1132(a) are undermined. The saving clause is entitled to prevail here, and we affirm the judgment.

**Justice Thomas**, with whom **The Chief Justice, Justice Scalia**, and **Justice Kennedy** join, dissenting.

This Court has repeatedly recognized that ERISA's civil enforcement provision, §502, provides the exclusive vehicle for actions asserting a claim for benefits under health plans governed by ERISA, and therefore that state laws that create additional remedies are pre-empted.... Such exclusivity of remedies is necessary to further Congress' interest in establishing a uniform federal law of employee benefits so that employers are encouraged to provide benefits to their employees: "To require plan providers to design their programs in an environment of differing state regulations would complicate the administration of nationwide plans, producing inefficiencies that employers might offset with decreased benefits."

Of course, the "expectations that a federal common law of rights and obligations under ERISA-regulated plans would develop ... would make little sense if the remedies available to ERISA participants and beneficiaries under §502(a) could be supplemented or supplanted by varying state laws." Therefore, as the Court concedes, see *ante*, at 19, even a state law that "regulates insurance" may be pre-empted if it supplements the remedies provided by ERISA, despite ERISA's saving clause, §514(b)(2)(A), 29 U.S.C. §1144(b)(2)(A). See *Silkwood v. Kerr-McGee Corp.*, 464 U.S. 238, 248 (1984) (noting that state laws that stand as an obstacle to the accomplishment of the full purposes and objectives of Congress are pre-empted). Today, however, the Court takes the unprecedented step of allowing respondent Debra Moran to short circuit ERISA's remedial scheme by allowing her claim for benefits to be determined in the first instance through an arbitral-like procedure provided under Illinois law, and by a decisionmaker other than a court. This decision not only conflicts with our precedents, it also eviscerates the uniformity of ERISA remedies Congress deemed integral to the "careful balancing of the need for prompt and fair claims settlement procedures against the public interest in encouraging the formation of employee benefit plans." I would reverse the Court of Appeals' judgment and remand for a determination of whether Moran was entitled to reimbursement absent the independent review conducted under §4-10.

Section 4-10 constitutes an arbitral-like state remedy through which plan members may seek to resolve conclusively a disputed right to benefits. Some 40 other States have similar laws, though these vary as to applicability, procedures, standards, deadlines, and consequences of independent review.... Allowing disparate state laws that provide inconsistent external review requirements to govern a participant's or beneficiary's claim to benefits under an employee benefit plan is wholly destructive of Congress' expressly stated goal of uniformity in this area....

For the reasons noted by the Court, independent review provisions may sound very appealing. Efforts to expand the variety of remedies available to aggrieved beneficiaries beyond those set forth in ERISA are obviously designed to increase the chances that patients will be able to receive treatments they desire, and most of us are naturally sympathetic to those suffering from illness who seek further options. Nevertheless, the Court would do well to remember that no employer is required to provide any health benefit plan under ERISA and that the entire advent of managed care, and the genesis of HMOs, stemmed from spiraling health costs. To the extent that independent review provisions such as §4-10 make it more likely that HMOs will have to subsidize beneficiaries' treatments of choice, they undermine the ability of HMOs to control costs, which, in turn, undermines the ability of employers to provide health care coverage for employees.

As a consequence, independent review provisions could create a disincentive to the formation of employee health benefit plans, a problem that Congress addressed by making ERISA's remedial scheme exclusive and uniform. While it may well be the case that the advantages of allowing States to implement independent review requirements as a supplement to the remedies currently provided under ERISA outweigh this drawback, this is a judgment that, pursuant to ERISA, must be made by Congress. I respectfully dissent.

## Aetna Health Inc. v. Davila

Supreme Court of the United States
542 U.S. 200, 124 S. Ct. 2488, 159 L. Ed. 2d 312 (2004)

**Justice Thomas** delivered the opinion of the Court.

In these consolidated cases, two individuals sued their respective health maintenance organizations (HMOs) for alleged failures to exercise ordinary care in the handling of coverage decisions, in violation of a duty imposed by the Texas Health Care Liability Act (THCLA). We granted certiorari to decide whether the individuals' causes of action are completely pre-empted by the "interlocking, interrelated, and interdependent remedial scheme" We hold that the causes of action are completely pre-empted and hence removable from state to federal court. The Court of Appeals, having reached a contrary conclusion, is reversed.

Respondent Juan Davila is a participant, and respondent Ruby Calad is a beneficiary, in ERISA-regulated employee benefit plans. Their respective plan sponsors had entered into agreements with petitioners, Aetna Health Inc. and CIGNA Healthcare of Texas, Inc., to administer the plans. Under Davila's plan, for instance, Aetna reviews requests for coverage and pays providers, such as doctors, hospitals, and nursing homes, which perform covered services for members; under Calad's plan sponsor's agreement, CIGNA is responsible for plan benefits and coverage decisions.

Respondents both suffered injuries allegedly arising from Aetna's and CIGNA's decisions not to provide coverage for certain treatment and services recommended by respondents' treating physicians. Davila's treating physician prescribed Vioxx to remedy Davila's arthritis pain, but Aetna refused to pay for it. Davila did not appeal or contest this decision, nor did he purchase Vioxx with his own resources and seek reimbursement. Instead, Davila began taking Naprosyn, from which he allegedly suffered a severe reaction that required extensive treatment and hospitalization.

Calad underwent surgery, and although her treating physician recommended an extended hospital stay, a CIGNA discharge nurse determined that Calad did not meet the plan's criteria for a continued hospital stay. CIGNA consequently denied coverage for the extended hospital stay. Calad experienced postsurgery complications forcing her to return to the hospital. She alleges that these complications would not have occurred had CIGNA approved coverage for a longer hospital stay.

Respondents brought separate suits in Texas state court against petitioners. Invoking THCLA, respondents argued that petitioners' refusal to cover the requested services violated their "duty to exercise ordinary care when making health care treatment decisions," and that these refusals "proximately caused" their injuries. *Ibid.*

Petitioners removed the cases to Federal District Courts, arguing that respondents' causes of action fit within the scope of, and were therefore completely pre-empted by, ERISA § 502(a). The respective District Courts agreed, and declined to remand the cases to state court. Because respondents refused to amend their complaints to bring explicit ERISA claims, the District Courts dismissed the complaints with prejudice.

Both Davila and Calad appealed the refusals to remand to state court. The United States Court of Appeals for the Fifth Circuit consolidated their cases with several others raising similar issues. The Court of Appeals recognized that state causes of action that "duplicat[e] or fal[l] within the scope of an ERISA § 502(a) remedy" are completely pre-empted and hence removable to federal court. After examining the causes of action available under § 502(a), the Court of Appeals determined that respondents' claims could possibly fall under only two: § 502(a)(1)(B), which provides a cause of action for the recovery of wrongfully denied benefits, and § 502(a)(2), which allows suit against a plan fiduciary for breaches of fiduciary duty to the plan.

Congress enacted ERISA to "protect ... the interests of participants in employee benefit plans and their beneficiaries" by setting out substantive regulatory requirements for employee benefit plans and to "provid[e] for appropriate remedies, sanctions, and ready access to the Federal courts." The purpose of ERISA is to provide a uniform regulatory regime over employee benefit plans. To this end, ERISA includes expansive pre-emption provisions, which are intended to ensure that employee benefit plan regulation would be "exclusively a federal concern."

ERISA's "comprehensive legislative scheme" includes "an integrated system of procedures for enforcement." This integrated enforcement mechanism, ERISA § 502(a), is a distinctive feature of ERISA, and essential to accomplish Congress' purpose of creating a comprehensive statute for the regulation of employee benefit plans. As the Court said in *Pilot Life Ins. Co. v. Dedeaux*, 481 U.S. 41 (1987):

> "[T]he detailed provisions of § 502(a) set forth a comprehensive civil enforcement scheme that represents a careful balancing of the need for prompt and fair claims settlement procedures against the public interest in encouraging the formation of employee benefit plans. The policy choices reflected in the inclusion of certain remedies and the exclusion of others under the federal scheme would be completely undermined if ERISA-plan participants and beneficiaries were free to obtain remedies under state law that Congress rejected in ERISA. 'The six carefully integrated civil enforcement provisions found in § 502(a) of the statute as finally enacted ... provide strong evidence that Congress did *not* intend to authorize other remedies that it simply forgot to incorporate expressly.'"

Therefore, any state-law cause of action that duplicates, supplements, or supplants the ERISA civil enforcement remedy conflicts with the clear congressional intent to make the ERISA remedy exclusive and is therefore pre-empted.

The pre-emptive force of ERISA § 502(a) is still stronger. In *Metropolitan Life Ins. Co. v. Taylor*, 481 U.S. 58 (1987), the Court determined that the similarity of the language used in the Labor Management Relations Act, 1947 (LMRA), and ERISA, combined with the "clear intention" of Congress "to make § 502(a)(1)(B) suits brought by participants or beneficiaries federal questions for the purposes of federal court jurisdiction in like manner as § 301 of the LMRA," established that ERISA § 502(a)(1)(B)'s pre-emptive force mirrored the pre-emptive force of LMRA § 301.

Since LMRA § 301 converts state causes of action into federal ones for purposes of determining the propriety of removal, so too does ERISA § 502(a)(1)(B). Thus, the ERISA civil enforcement mechanism is one of those provisions with such "extraordinary pre-emptive power" that it "converts an ordinary state common law complaint into one stating a federal claim for purposes of the well-pleaded complaint rule." Hence, "causes of action within the scope of the civil enforcement provisions of § 502(a) [are] removable to federal court." ERISA § 502(a)(1)(B) provides:

> "A civil action may be brought—(1) by a participant or beneficiary— ... (B) to recover benefits due to him under the terms of his plan, to enforce his rights under the terms of the plan, or to clarify his rights to future benefits under the terms of the plan."

This provision is relatively straightforward. If a participant or beneficiary believes that benefits promised to him under the terms of the plan are not provided, he can bring suit seeking provision of those benefits. A participant or beneficiary can also bring suit generically to "enforce his rights" under the plan, or to clarify any of his rights to future benefits. Any dispute over the precise terms of the plan is resolved by a court under a *de novo* review standard, unless the terms of the plan "giv[e] the administrator or fiduciary discretionary authority to determine eligibility for benefits or to construe the terms of the plan."

It follows that if an individual brings suit complaining of a denial of coverage for medical care, where the individual is entitled to such coverage only because of the terms of an ERISA-regulated employee benefit plan, and where no legal duty (state or federal) independent of ERISA or the plan terms is violated, then the suit falls "within the scope of" ERISA § 502(a)(1)(B). In other words, if an individual, at some point in time, could have brought his claim under ERISA § 502(a)(1)(B), and where there is no other independent legal duty that is implicated by a defendant's actions, then the individual's cause of action is completely pre-empted by ERISA § 502(a)(1)(B).

To determine whether respondents' causes of action fall "within the scope" of ERISA § 502(a)(1)(B), we must examine respondents' complaints, the statute on which their claims are based (the THCLA), and the various plan documents. Davila alleges that Aetna provides health coverage under his employer's health benefits plan. Davila also alleges that after his primary care physician prescribed Vioxx, Aetna refused to pay for it. The only action complained of was Aetna's refusal to approve payment for Davila's Vioxx prescription. Further, the only relationship Aetna had with Davila was its partial administration of Davila's employer's benefit plan.

Similarly, Calad alleges that she receives, as her husband's beneficiary under an ERISA-regulated benefit plan, health coverage from CIGNA. She alleges that she was informed by CIGNA, upon admittance into a hospital for major surgery, that she would be authorized to stay for only one day. She also alleges that CIGNA, acting through a discharge nurse, refused to authorize more than a single day despite the advice and recommendation of her treating physician. Calad contests only CIGNA's decision to refuse coverage for her hospital stay. And, as in Davila's case, the only connection between Calad and CIGNA is CIGNA's administration of portions of Calad's ERISA-regulated benefit plan.

It is clear, then, that respondents complain only about denials of coverage promised under the terms of ERISA-regulated employee benefit plans. Upon the denial of benefits, respondents could have paid for the treatment themselves and then sought reimbursement through a § 502(a)(1)(B) action, or sought a preliminary injunction....

Respondents contend, however, that the complained-of actions violate legal duties that arise independently of ERISA or the terms of the employee benefit plans at issue in these cases. Both respondents brought suit specifically under the THCLA, alleging that petitioners "controlled, influenced, participated in and made decisions which affected the quality of the diagnosis, care, and treatment provided" in a manner that violated "the duty of ordinary care set forth in §§ 88.001 and 88.002."

Respondents contend that this duty of ordinary care is an independent legal duty. They analogize to this Court's decisions interpreting LMRA § 301. Because this duty of ordinary care arises independently of any duty imposed by ERISA or the plan terms, the argument goes, any civil action to enforce this duty is not within the scope of the ERISA civil enforcement mechanism.

The duties imposed by the THCLA in the context of these cases, however, do not arise independently of ERISA or the plan terms. The THCLA does impose a duty on managed care entities to "exercise ordinary care when making health care treatment decisions," and makes them liable for damages proximately caused by failures to abide by that duty. However, if a managed care entity correctly concluded that, under the terms of the relevant plan, a particular treatment was not covered, the managed care entity's denial of coverage would not be a proximate cause of any injuries arising from the denial. Rather, the failure of the plan itself to cover the requested treatment would be the proximate cause.

More significantly, the THCLA clearly states that "[t]he standards in Subsections (a) and (b) create no obligation on the part of the health insurance carrier, health maintenance organization, or other managed care entity to provide to an insured or enrollee treatment which is not covered by the health care plan of the entity." Hence, a managed care entity could not be subject to liability under the THCLA if it denied coverage for any treatment not covered by the health care plan that it was administering.

Thus, interpretation of the terms of respondents' benefit plans forms an essential part of their THCLA claim, and THCLA liability would exist here only because of petitioners' administration of ERISA-regulated benefit plans. Petitioners' potential liability under the THCLA in these cases, then, derives entirely from the particular rights and obligations established by the benefit plans. So, unlike the state-law claims in *Caterpillar*, [*Inc. v. Williams*, 482 U.S. 386 (1987)], respondents' THCLA causes of action are not entirely independent of the federally regulated contract itself.

Hence, respondents bring suit only to rectify a wrongful denial of benefits promised under ERISA-regulated plans, and do not attempt to remedy any violation of a legal duty independent of ERISA. We hold that respondents' state causes of action fall "within the scope of" ERISA § 502(a)(1)(B), *Metropolitan Life* [1985] and are therefore completely pre-empted by ERISA § 502 and removable to federal district court.

Ultimately, the Court of Appeals [which ruled in favor of Davila and Casad] rested its decision on one line from *Rush Prudential* [*HMO, Inc. v. Moran* 536 U.S. 355 (2002)]. There, we described our holding in *Ingersoll-Rand* [*Co. v. McClendon*, 498 U.S. 133 (1990)], as follows: "[W]hile state law duplicated the elements of a claim available under ERISA, it converted the remedy from an equitable one under § 1132(a)(3) (available exclusively in federal district courts) into a legal one for money damages (available in a state tribunal)." The point of this sentence was to describe why the state cause of action in *Ingersoll-Rand* was pre-empted by ERISA § 502(a): It was pre-empted because it attempted to convert an equitable remedy into a legal remedy. Nowhere in *Rush Prudential* did we suggest that the pre-emptive force of ERISA § 502(a) is limited to the situation in which a state cause of action precisely duplicates a cause of action under ERISA § 502(a).

Nor would it be consistent with our precedent to conclude that only strictly duplicative state causes of action are pre-empted. Frequently, in order to receive exemplary damages on a state claim, a plaintiff must prove facts beyond the bare minimum necessary to establish entitlement to an award. In order to recover for mental anguish, for instance, the plaintiffs in *Ingersoll-Rand* and *Metropolitan Life* would presumably have had to prove the existence of mental anguish; there is no such element in an ordinary suit brought under ERISA § 502(a)(1)(B). This did not save these state causes of action from pre-emption. Congress' intent to make the ERISA civil enforcement mechanism exclusive would be undermined if state causes of action that supplement the ERISA § 502(a) remedies were permitted, even if the elements of the state cause of action did not precisely duplicate the elements of an ERISA claim.

Respondents also argue—for the first time in their brief to this Court—that the THCLA is a law that regulates insurance, and hence that ERISA § 514(b)(2)(A) saves their causes of action from pre-emption (and thereby from complete pre-emption). This argument is unavailing. The existence of a comprehensive remedial scheme can demonstrate an "overpowering federal policy" that determines the interpretation of a statutory provision designed to save state law from being pre-empted.

As this Court stated in *Pilot Life*, "our understanding of [§ 514(b)(2)(A)] must be informed by the legislative intent concerning the civil enforcement provisions provided by ERISA § 502(a), 29 U.S.C. § 1132(a) [29 USCS § 1132(a)]." The Court concluded that "[t]he policy choices reflected in the inclusion of certain remedies and the exclusion of others under the federal scheme would be completely undermined if ERISA-plan participants and beneficiaries were free to obtain remedies under state law that Congress rejected in ERISA." The Court then held, based on

> "the common-sense understanding of the saving clause, the McCarran-Ferguson Act factors defining the business of insurance, and, *most importantly,* the clear expression of congressional intent that ERISA's civil enforcement scheme be exclusive, ... that [the plaintiff's] state law suit asserting improper processing of a claim for benefits under an ERISA-regulated plan is not saved by § 514(b)(2)(A)."

*Pilot Life*'s reasoning applies here with full force. Allowing respondents to proceed with their state-law suits would "pose an obstacle to the purposes and objectives of Congress." As this Court has recognized in both *Rush Prudential* and *Pilot Life*, ERISA § 514(b)(2)(A) must be interpreted in light of the congressional intent to create an exclusive federal remedy in ERISA § 502(a). Under ordinary principles of conflict pre-emption, then, even a state law that can arguably be characterized as "regulating insurance" will be pre-empted if it provides a separate vehicle to assert a claim for benefits outside of, or in addition to, ERISA's remedial scheme.

Respondents, their *amici*, and some Courts of Appeals have relied heavily upon *Pegram v. Herdrich*, [530 U.S. 211 (2000),] in arguing that ERISA does not pre-empt or completely pre-empt state suits such as respondents'. They contend that *Pegram* makes it clear that causes of action such as respondents' do not "relate to [an] employee benefit plan," ... *Pegram* cannot be read so broadly. In *Pegram*, the plaintiff sued her physician-owned-and-operated HMO (which provided medical coverage through plaintiff's employer pursuant to an ERISA-regulated benefit plan) and her treating physician, both for medical malpractice and for a breach of an ERISA fiduciary duty. The plaintiff's treating physician was also the person charged with administering plaintiff's benefits; it was she who decided whether certain treatments were covered. We reasoned that the physician's "eligibility decision and the treatment decision were inextricably mixed." We concluded that "Congress did not intend [the defendant HMO] or any other HMO to be treated as a fiduciary to the extent that it makes mixed eligibility decisions acting through its physicians."

A benefit determination under ERISA, though, is generally a fiduciary act. "At common law, fiduciary duties characteristically attach to decisions about managing assets and distributing property to beneficiaries." Hence, a benefit determination is part and parcel of the ordinary fiduciary responsibilities connected to the administration of a plan. The fact that a benefits determination is infused with medical judgments does not alter this result.... *Pegram* itself recognized this principle.

*Pegram*, in highlighting its conclusion that "mixed eligibility decisions" were not fiduciary in nature, contrasted the operation of "[t]raditional trustees administer[ing] a medical trust" and "physicians through whom HMOs act." A traditional medical trust is administered by "paying out money to buy medical care, whereas physicians making mixed eligibility decisions consume the money as well." And, significantly, the Court stated that "[p]rivate trustees do not make treatment judgments." But a trustee managing a medical trust undoubtedly must make administrative decisions that require the exercise of medical judgment. Petitioners are not the employers of respondents' treating physicians and are therefore in a somewhat analogous position to that of a trustee for a traditional medical trust.

ERISA itself and its implementing regulations confirm this interpretation. ERISA defines a fiduciary as any person "to the extent ... he has any discretionary authority or discretionary responsibility in the administration of [an employee benefit] plan." When administering employee benefit plans, HMOs must make discretionary decisions regarding eligibility for plan benefits, and, in this regard, must be treated as plan fiduciaries. Also, ERISA § 503, which specifies minimum requirements for a plan's claim procedure, requires plans to "afford a reasonable opportunity to any participant whose claim for benefits has been denied for a full and fair review by the appropriate named fiduciary of the decision denying the claim." This strongly suggests that the ultimate decisionmaker in a plan regarding an award of benefits must be a fiduciary and must be acting as a fiduciary when determining a participant's or beneficiary's claim.

The relevant regulations also establish extensive requirements to ensure full and fair review of benefit denials. These regulations, on their face, apply equally to health benefit plans and other plans, and do not draw distinctions between medical and nonmedical benefits determinations. Indeed, the regulations strongly imply that benefits determinations involving medical judgments are, just as much as any other benefits determinations, actions by plan fiduciaries. Classifying any entity with discretionary authority over benefits determinations as anything but a plan fiduciary would thus conflict with ERISA's statutory and regulatory scheme.

Since administrators making benefits determinations, even determinations based extensively on medical judgments, are ordinarily acting as plan fiduciaries, it was essential to *Pegram*'s conclusion that the decisions challenged there were truly "mixed eligibility and treatment decisions," *i.e.*, medical necessity decisions made by the plaintiff's treating physician *qua* treating physician and *qua* benefits administrator. Put another way, the reasoning of *Pegram* "only make[s] sense where the underlying negligence also plausibly constitutes medical maltreatment by a party who can be deemed to be a treating physician or such a physician's employer." Here, however, petitioners are neither respondents' treating physicians nor the employers of respondents' treating physicians. Petitioners' coverage decisions, then, are pure eligibility decisions, and *Pegram* is not implicated....

**Justice Ginsburg**, with whom **Justice Breyer** joins, concurring.

The Court today holds that the claims respondents asserted under Texas law are totally preempted by § 502(a) of the Employee Retirement Income Security Act of 1974 (ERISA or Act). That decision is consistent with our governing case law on ERISA's preemptive scope. I therefore join the Court's opinion. But, with greater enthusiasm, as indicated by my dissenting opinion in *Great-West Life & Annuity Ins. Co. v. Knudson*, [534 U.S. 204] (2002), I also join "the rising judicial chorus urging that Congress and [this] Court revisit what is an unjust and increasingly tangled ERISA regime." Because the Court has coupled an encompassing interpretation of ERISA's preemptive force with a cramped construction of the "equitable relief" allowable under § 502(a)(3), a "regulatory vacuum" exists: "[V]irtually all state law remedies are preempted but very few federal substitutes are provided." ... A series of the Court's decisions has yielded a host of situations in which persons adversely affected by ERISA-proscribed wrongdoing cannot gain make-whole relief.

"[T]here is a stark absence—in [ERISA] itself and in its legislative history—of any reference to an intention to authorize the recovery of extracontractual damages" for consequential injuries.... As the array of lower court cases and opinions documents, fresh consideration of the availability of consequential damages under § 502(a)(3) is plainly in order.

The Government notes a potential amelioration. Recognizing that "this Court has construed Section 502(a)(3) not to authorize an award of money damages against a *non-fiduciary*," the Government suggests that the Act, as currently written and interpreted, may "allo[w] at least some forms of 'make-whole' relief against a breaching *fiduciary* in light of the general availability of such relief in equity at the time of the divided bench." As the Court points out, respondents here declined the opportunity to amend their complaints to state claims for relief under § 502(a); the District Court, therefore, properly dismissed their suits with prejudice. But the Government's suggestion may indicate an effective remedy others similarly circumstanced might fruitfully pursue.

"Congress ... intended ERISA to replicate the core principles of trust remedy law, including the make-whole standard of relief." I anticipate that Congress, or this Court, will one day so confirm.

## *Notes and Questions*

1. Since the 1995 decision in *New York State Conf. of Blue Cross & Blue Shield Plans v. Travelers Ins. Co.*, 514 U.S. 645 (1995), the Court has tended to rely less on the broad preemption language in ERISA and more on traditional rules of preemption that begin with the strong presumption that state law is not displaced except when clearly necessary to effectuate a federal scheme or clearly commanded by Congress.

2. Note that the Court's generally broad view as to when a state law "relates to" an employee benefit plan has not shrunk much over time. What has arguably changed is the Court's willingness to characterize challenged state legislation as part of the state's regulation of insurance, an area of an exception to ERISA preemption.

3. Has the role of the McCarran-Ferguson Act changed as regards its use as a signpost to guide ERISA preemption? Explain.

4. *See generally* Russell Korobkin, *The Failed Jurisprudence of Managed Care, and How to Fix It: Reinterpreting ERISA Preemption*, 51 UCLA L. Rev. 457 (2003); Donald T. Bogan, *ERISA: State Regulation of Insured Plans After* Davila, 38 J. Marshall L. Rev. 693 (2005); Beverly Cohen, *Saving the Savings Clause: Advocating a Broader Reading of the Miller Test to Enable States to Protect ERISA Health Plan Members by Regulating Insurance*, 18 Geo. Mason L. Rev. 125 (2010).

5. The involvement of an ERISA plan also has significant implications regarding litigation procedure and jurisdiction. *See, e.g., Peralta v. Hispanic Bus.*, 419 F.3d 1064 (9th Cir. 2005) (finding existence of federal subject matter jurisdiction where interpretation of ERISA is "at heart" of dispute; also discussing nature and scope of fiduciary duties under ERISA); *Haw. Mgmt. Alliance Ass'n v. Ins. Comm'r*, 100 P.3d 952 (Haw. 2004) (state external review statutes directed toward health insurers impliedly preempted by ERISA); *Hardt v. Reliance Standard Life Ins. Co.*, 560 U.S. 242 (2010) (attorney fee shifting under ERISA upheld).

6. Regarding actual questions of coverage for claims made under an ERISA plan, the standard of review for denial of claims is highly deferential to the plan administrator (or its agent, an insurer). *See, e.g., Sisto v. Ameritech Sickness & Accident Disability Benefit Plan*, 429 F.3d 698 (7th Cir. 2005) (upholding plan administrator's decision that employee injured in bathroom was not eligible for work-related accident benefits on ground that worker's job did not involve bathroom and incident therefore was not "during and in direct connection with" her employment duties; Sisto did receive sickness benefits which were limited to one year in duration while accident benefits would have continued throughout the period of disability).

Cynics might ask whether company workers are supposed to go off premises when nature calls; one suspects the employer would then very much consider use of the company's bathroom to be part of the job. *But see King v. Hartford Life & Accident Ins. Co.*, 414 F.3d 994 (8th Cir. 2005) (refusing to accept plan administrator's determination that motorcycle crash injuries were insufficiently "accidental" where victim had been intoxicated at the time of the event).

## [2] ERISA Pre-Emption and State Restrictions on Insurer Subrogation

A recurring issue in bodily injury tort litigation is the degree to which a successful plaintiff must reimburse a medical insurer for benefits paid. Insurers understandably think they should be repaid if the victim recovers from the tortfeasor. As you learned in first-year torts, the collateral source rule prohibits defendant from introducing evidence of compensation the plaintiff may have received from insurers, family, go-fund-me sites and the like. Plaintiffs respond that even successful litigation seldom results in complete recovery, particularly when counsel fees and costs are subtracted from the recovery, which is typically discounted for settlement because of the risk of a defense verdict (and 90-odd percent of cases settle).

Although specifics may vary, most states follow the "made whole" principle which restricts the rights of an insurer to obtain reimbursement until the plaintiff has been fully compensated. *See generally* Johnny C. Parker, *The Made Whole Doctrine: Unraveling the Enigma Wrapped in the Mystery of Insurance Subrogation*, 70 Mo. L. Rev. 723 (2005); Matthiesen, Wickert & Lehrer, S.C., *Made Whole Doctrine in All 50 States*, available at http://www.mwl-law.com. For example, an insurer may have paid $50,000 for surgery and a hospital stay, but if the plaintiff has future medical expenses not covered by insurance, the insurer's right to reimbursement would presumably not reach this portion of a settlement, just as it would not reach portions of the settlement relating to pain and suffering. If these uninsured losses exceed the amounts received in settlement (easily possible if the claim is subject to damage caps, as is often the case for claims against the government or relating to medical malpractice), the insurer would not be able to obtain reimbursement.

ERISA has broad pre-emption language subject to a "carve-out" for state insurance regulation. Because most group medical plans are employer-provided employee benefit plans, medical insurers in these plans frequently argue that state statutes or court decisions limiting insurer reimbursement are pre-empted by ERISA.

## ILLUSTRATION

Penelope Plaintiff is hit by a negligent driver while out on her motorcycle, resulting in severe injuries that require amputation of her left leg. Penelope's employer-provided (although she contributes a significant monthly premium payment) medical insurance covers the bulk of treatment costs, paying $400,000 to medical providers. Her suit against defendant driver results in a $1.5 million settlement which provides that "payment is for general damages, including medical expenses, pain and suffering, and emotional distress but does not include special damages that duplicate any previously received medical payments, no-fault payments, wage loss, or temporary disability payments."

Medical Insurer places a lien on the settlement, seeking repayment of its $400,000. Penelope objects, citing State Law, which states:

> Where damages are recovered by judgment or settlement of a third-party claim, an insurer that has previously paid benefits to the claimant may obtain reimbursement for any amounts spent on special damages but not for general damages. Special damages are those that relate to readily quantifiable pecuniary loss, including medical and hospital expenses or loss of earnings, or out-of-pocket expenses resulting from injury.

Medical Insurer responds that the State Law limiting its right to reimbursement is pre-empted by ERISA, which "pre-empts any and all State laws as they may now or hereafter related to any employee benefit plan." *See* 29 U.S.C. §1144(a).

Penelope replies that 29 U.S.C. §1144(b)(2)(A) provides that preemption does not apply to "any law of any State which regulates insurance, banking, or securities." Consequently, state law applies, and Medical Insurer may not obtain repayment from the settlement funds (which already will be depleted by Penelope's litigation expenses and her attorney's contingency fee).

- Who has the better argument?
- Why?
- What other facts, if any, would be helpful to know in resolving the dispute?
- If Penelope prevails on the pre-emption issue, is Medical Insurer without recourse?
- How might the Insurer obtain reimbursement even if there is no ERISA pre-emption?

On very similar facts, the Ninth Circuit found no pre-emption of Hawai'i state law limiting the ERISA-plan health provider's reimbursement efforts. *See Rudel v. Hawai'i Management Alliance Ass'n,* 2019 U.S. App. LEXIS 27371 (Sept. 11, 2019) ("There are no statutory provisions of ERISA that address reimbursement limitations. Thus, no conflict exists between the Hawai'i Statutes and ERISA." "Because the Hawai'i Statutes regulate insurance and are directed at insurance practices and impact risk pooling, they are saved from express preemption ... because they do not impermissibly expand the scope of available ERISA remedies, [they] are not preempted"). *See also Singh v. Prudential Health Care Plan, Inc.*, 335 F.3d 278 (4th Cir. 2003) (making similar analysis).

# § 3.04. Specific Insurance Programs

There are some specific insurance programs that exist at both the state and federal level that do not take the form of insurance policies regulated solely by the private market (and approved in form by state regulators). For example, life insurance is very heavily regulated by state statute. Indeed, under state incontestability statutes, life insurance policies, and certain types of accident and health insurance policies, cannot be voided by the insurer after a statutory period (normally two years), even though the insured has made a material misrepresentation or concealment in the application, or has breached a warranty or condition in the policy. *See, e.g.*, KEETON & WIDISS, INSURANCE LAW § 6.6(d) (1988). Automobile liability insurance coverage is also heavily regulated by state statutes, as noted in the chapter on Automobile Insurance. Federal programs exist for flood and terrorism risks. This patchwork system of regulated insurance forms the web of compensation available for a wide variety of society's risks.

## [A] State Insurance Guaranty Acts

State insurance guaranty acts are largely patterned after a model act proposed by the National Association of Insurance Commissioners. Under such insurance guaranty acts, a state establishes a guaranty association to which all insurers doing business in the state must belong. Should any member insurer be declared insolvent or found to be potentially unable to fulfill its contractual obligations, then the state insurance guarantee association will ensure that the policyholders of the insolvent or financially disabled company receive their policy benefits. *See, e.g., Colorado Ins. Guar. Ass'n v. Harris*, 827 P.2d 1139 (Colo. 1992).

## [B] Federal Crop Insurance

Under the Federal Crop Insurance Act (7 U.S.C. § 1501 *et seq.*), Congress has authorized the Federal Crop Insurance Corporation (FCIC) to enter into contracts for crop insurance. These contracts continue in effect from year to year, but after the first year they may be cancelled by either party upon proper notice. The FCIC may also "limit or refuse [crop] insurance in any county or area on the basis of the insurance risk involved" under 7 U.S.C. § 1508(a). The purpose of the Act is to improve "the economic stability of agriculture through a sound system of crop insurance," 7 U.S.C. § 1502. *See, e.g., Rainbow Valley Citrus Corp. v. Federal Crop Ins. Corp.*, 506 F.2d 467

(9th Cir. 1974). Much litigation with crop insurance involves ascertaining the actual amount of loss. *See, e.g., A.W.G. Farms v. Federal Crop Ins. Corp.*, 757 F.2d 720 (8th Cir. 1985) (sugar beet crop damaged in freezing weather); *Citizens Bank of Jonesboro v. Federal Crop Ins. Corp.*, 547 F.2d 59 (8th Cir. 1976) (unharvested cotton crop).

## [C] Federal Flood Insurance

The National Flood Insurance Act of 1968 (42 U.S.C. § 4001 *et seq.*) was enacted by Congress to provide previously unavailable flood insurance protection to property owners in flood-prone areas. Mudslide protection was added to the National Flood Insurance Program (NFIP) in 1969. To qualify for flood insurance, a municipality or community must apply for the entire area within its jurisdiction. Individual property owners may not purchase flood insurance unless they live in a municipality or community which has entered the program. Thus, to achieve Congress' goal of preventing widespread flood damage through the implementation of broad-based flood plain management regulations, an individual who complies with the regulations still cannot obtain the benefit of the program without local government action.

Many communities apparently decided it was better to remain outside the Program and avoid paying any insurance premiums as long as they were able to collect federal disaster relief. Congress then passed the Flood Disaster Protection Act of 1973, requiring the purchase of federal flood insurance as a condition to receiving any federal construction assistance for buildings within a flood or mudslide hazard area. The Act also provided that, upon identification of a flood hazard area by the Director of the Flood Insurance Program, no federal financial assistance would be provided to a community within that area unless it was participating in the National Flood Insurance Program on or after July 1, 1975. *See generally United States v. Parish of St. Bernard*, 756 F.2d 1116 (5th Cir. 1985), *cert. denied*, 474 U.S. 1070 (1986). To deal with the threat to the viability of the program of certain geographic zones that faced repeated flood losses, Congress enacted the Flood Insurance Reform Act of 2004, Pub. L. No. 108-264. Most homes insured by the federal plan are in Texas and Florida.

Because they so directly put federal dollars at risk, flood insurance policies involve certain special protections in the law. *See, e.g., Palmieri v. Allstate Ins. Co.*, 445 F.3d 179 (2d Cir. 2006) (applying federal law) (flood insurance act precludes prejudgment interest on amounts recovered and preempts any contrary state law); *Gallup v. Omaha Prop. & Cas. Ins. Co.*, 434 F.3d 341 (5th Cir. 2005) (applying federal law) (Flood Act preempts state tort actions based on insurer's handling of claim under flood policy); *Studio Frames, Ltd. v. Standard Fire Ins. Co.*, 397 F. Supp. 2d 685 (M.D.N.C. 2005) (interest not available on judgments against flood insurers or NFIP). Similar state-supported insurance programs may have similar protection. *See, e.g., Jonathan Neil & Assoc. v. Jones*, 94 P.3d 1055 (Cal. 2004) (bad faith tort remedy not available against insurers in connection with coverage issued due to participation in California Automobile Assigned Risk Plan).

## [D] Federal Terrorism Insurance

Congress enacted the Federal Terrorism Risk Insurance Act in 2002 as a temporary measure in order to allow the insurance industry time to develop its own products and insurance management techniques for terrorism-related losses. The Act is a sort of backstop for insurers, providing federal assistance in the form of federal reinsurance to insurers in the event of a large-scale terrorist loss. The Act's program has been continually extended ever since, and is now the Terrorism Risk Insurance Program Reauthorization Act. The reinsurance program is triggered by an act of terrorism where aggregate losses must exceed $100 million for insurers. The Act requires that insurers have reserves set to cover a prescribed limit before the federal reinsurance is called upon to respond.

The private market for terrorism insurance has expanded significantly in the property and casualty realms. Losses resulting from terrorism-related activities may be covered by either stand-alone terrorism policies or enhancements to standard insurance coverage programs, with additional coverages like "active shooter insurance," "loss of attraction" insurance (for when fear of a terrorism-related event results in losses to a particular venue), "political violence" insurance or insurance for cyber-losses.

# Chapter 4

# Formation of the
# Insurer-Policyholder Relationship

## § 4.01. Crystallizing the Insurance Arrangement

The arrangement implicit in an insurance policy is a complex one. It involves the insurer agreeing to take on a future contingent risk that a policyholder wants to hopefully avoid ever happening but, in the event it does come to be, the policyholder wants to be financially protected. At heart, the deal is contractual, but the special nature of the insurance policy makes it more like a contract "on steroids." It involves real issues of equity, power imbalance, and serious financial risk for the policyholder who faces complete financial destitution if the deal goes sideways. To that end, while traditional contracts principles can be generally applicable in an insurance contract, there are always twists. This is why the raging debate between a formalist and a functionalist approach to insurance can so often affect the outcome of an insurance dispute even as the insurance bargain is forming. Watch for the tensions between these two approaches as this chapter explores how the insurance deal crystallizes and how the duties of insurer and policyholder play out at the beginning of their relationship.

## § 4.02. Validity of an Oral Insurance Contract

In the absence of a state statute to the contrary, an oral contract of insurance generally is valid if the parties expressly or impliedly agree upon the following six terms: (1) the subject matter identified; (2) the risk insured against; (3) the amount of insurance; (4) the duration of the risk; (5) the premium payment; and (6) the identities of the parties. *See, e.g., Ellingwood v. N.N. Investors Life Ins. Co.*, 805 P.2d 70 (N.M. 1991). The last element, the identification of the insurer, is especially important if the applicant orally requests insurance from a general agent who represents several different insurance companies.

State legislatures have the power to modify or prohibit oral contracts of insurance, and a minority of states have enacted such statutes. Generally speaking, however, judicial or statutory law rarely prohibits oral contracts relating to property or liability insurance, although they may more frequently regulate oral contracts related to life, health, or accident insurance. *See generally* Jerry & Richmond, Understanding Insurance Law § 31(d) (6th ed. 2018); Keeton & Widiss, Insurance Law § 2.2 (1988).

# Gulf Insurance Co. v. Grisham

## Supreme Court of Arizona
### 126 Ariz. 123, 613 P.2d 283 (1980)

**Cameron, Justice**

In May of 1974, Kenneth Martinez and Hazel A. Martinez purchased a Cessna 150 from Sawyer Aviation Company for their 17 year-old son, Gary Martinez. Title to the aircraft was taken in Hazel Martinez' name. At the time of sale, Paul Sapp, Sales Manager for Sawyer Aviation, was asked by Kenneth Martinez if insurance on the aircraft could be obtained. Mr. Sapp contacted the Simis Insurance Agency and, on 21 May 1974, Richard Simis sent a letter to Kenneth Martinez informing him of the coverage for the aircraft. The letter stated as follows:

> We have this date bound coverage on your 1970 Cessna 150, N58668G.
>
> Enclosed are Pilot Record Forms to be completed by each pilot. Please complete the form and return to us. Your policy will be issued upon receipt of the applications.
>
> The coverages bound are $100,000.00/300,000.00 bodily injury, $100,000.00 property damage (*excluding passengers*), and $6,350.00 hull coverage.
>
> Our envelope is enclosed for the return of the pilot forms.
>
> Thank you for this opportunity to be of service to you. (Emphasis added.)

Mr. and Mrs. Martinez received this letter on or about 23 May 1974. Enclosed with the letter were pilot record forms which Gary Martinez completed and returned to Simis Insurance Agency. Kenneth Martinez called Paul Sapp and told him that he expected the passengers to be covered, and in response Paul Sapp told Kenneth Martinez that the matter would be corrected.

Neither Mr. or Mrs. Martinez contacted the Simis Insurance Agency, or Gulf International Aviation Underwriters, Inc., but instead, according to Kenneth's testimony, relied upon Paul Sapp to request coverage in addition to that described in the letter of 21 May. Richard Simis testified that, on 10 July, the policy and invoice were mailed to Mr. Martinez.

The policy specifically excluded passengers while riding in the airplane piloted by a student pilot. Although Kenneth denied receiving the policy, the amount stated on the invoice as the premium was paid on 7 August 1974.On 14 August 1974, Gary Martinez, 17, a licensed student pilot, took Richard Grisham, 18, for a flight in the Cessna 150 aircraft. The airplane crashed and both men died.

The parents of Richard Grisham brought suit against the Martinezes. The plaintiff insurance company represented the Martinezes under reservation rights and brought this separate action for declaratory judgment seeking to relieve the insurance company of any responsibility to provide a defense. Depositions of the Martinezes were taken and affidavits filed by Mr. Sapp and Mr. Simis.

The court granted the plaintiff insurance company's motion for summary judgment, and the defendants appeal. It is apparent that the written contract of insurance did not cover Richard Grisham as he was a passenger specifically excluded. If there is coverage, it must be pursuant to an oral contract of insurance.

The general rule is that an oral contract of insurance is valid and enforceable.... However, there must be " ... a showing that the parties have agreed on all the essential terms of the contract, including the subject matter, the risk insured against, the time of commencement and duration of the risk, the amount of insurance and the amount of the premium." *See* 43 Am. Jur. 2d, *Insurance* § 202 at 258; *Ranger Insurance Company v. Phillips*, 544 P.2d 250, 253 (Ariz. App. 1976).

For there to have been an oral contract between Martinez and plaintiff Gulf Insurance Company, there must have been an agreement between Gulf's agent Simis Insurance Agency and Martinez. *Ranger, supra.* Defendants admit that there was no contract between the Martinezes and Simis. Defendants in their brief stated:

> It is undisputed that the MARTINEZ' never had any personal contract, either written or oral, with the SIMIS INSURANCE AGENCY or GULF INSURANCE COMPANY prior to the plane crash; all discussions or negotiations went through PAUL SAPP.

> It is also undisputed that SAPP was not on the payroll of either SIMIS AGENCY or GULF INSURANCE, but he had worked similar transactions on other occasions in the past....

It is agreed that there was no oral contract between the Simis Insurance Agency and Martinez. The Martinezes, however, claim they relied upon their dealings with Sapp, who they believed to be Simis' authorized agent. Other than the receipt of the letter and invoice from Simis to Martinez as a result of the conversation between Martinez and Sapp, the only testimony bearing on this subject was given by Kenneth Martinez:

Q Did you ever talk with anyone who you believed to be working for the Gulf Insurance Company before the accident?

A Before the accident?

Q Yes.

A Paul Sapp.

Q What made you think that he worked for the Gulf Insurance Company?

A Well, I assumed by the conversation between him and me about insurance that he must have got some kind of kick back for pointing the customers in their direction.

Q What is it that he said that led you to believe that?

A Nothing. He just asked me about the insurance, if I wanted him to get it for me.

Q You never heard of Gulf Insurance Company before that, I take it?

A No.

Q Other than your conversation with Sapp, did anybody, any adjuster or anybody else, tell you that Sapp was working for the insurance company?

A. No.

In addition, Sapp had acted for the Martinezes to acquire their initial policy from Simis. There are two main types of agency, actual (express) and ostensible (apparent). If there is evidence that the principal has delegated authority by oral or written words which authorize him to do a certain act or series of acts, then the authority of the agent is express. *Canyon State Canners v. Hooks*, (Ariz. 1952). If there is no such express authority, or if intent to create such authority cannot be implied from the actions of the principal and agent, then the next question is whether there is apparent agency. We have said:

> The ostensible agent is one where the principal has intentionally or inadvertently induced third persons to believe that such a person was its agent although no actual or express authority was conferred on him as agent. (citations omitted) *Canyon State Canners, supra*, 74 Ariz. at 73, 243 P.2d at 1025.

Keeping in mind that the party asserting the agency relationship has the burden of proving the agency, *Salt River Valley Water Users' Ass'n v. Giglio*, 549 P.2d 162 (Ariz. 1976), we note that the Martinezes have not shown Sapp to fall within either of the above-mentioned types of agency. They have not shown evidence of a written or oral agreement between Simis and Sapp or any evidence that Simis, as a principal, acted in any way so as to induce Martinez to believe Sapp was Simis' agent. All the Martinezes have shown is that Sapp's actions and representations led them to believe he was an authorized agent.

We do not believe liability should be found on the basis of such a belief. Were we to allow an unauthorized agent to bind an unknown principal to liability such as is present in this case, we would encourage fraud and injustice in the future, as anyone who represented themselves as agents could bind completely innocent principals. We therefore find no material issue of fact which would require us to set aside the granting of the motion for summary judgment.

Defendants, however, rely heavily on *Ranger Insurance Company v. Phillips, supra*, which has a fact situation close to the case at bar. In *Ranger*, the insured talked personally to a person who was an authorized agent of the insurance company:

> .... Phillips testified that student instruction was one of the services he provided and that he would not have considered insurance without such coverage. Initially he contacted his own insurance agent, Sabatelli Insurance Agency. Not being familiar with aircraft insurance, Sabatelli contacted John 'Sandy' Sanderson who was employed by American Underwriters Agencies, Inc.... Testimony at the trial revealed that Phillips spoke directly with Sanderson and told him the coverage he wanted, which included student pilots. Accordingly, Sanderson assured him he was covered by Ranger.... We find that this evidence was sufficient for the trial court to find that student pilot coverage had been sought by Phillips and contracted for by Ranger

through its agents. *Ranger Insurance Company v. Phillips, supra,* 544 P.2d at 253.

Defendant's reliance on *Ranger Insurance Company v. Phillips, supra,* is misplaced as that case involved an authorized agent and this does not. The two cases are distinguishable. We find no error.... Affirmed.

### *Notes and Questions*

1. The *Grisham* court, in addition to the oral contract question, also discussed whether Sapps was an agent of the insurer. Assuming *arguendo* that Sapps was a general agent of the insurer, would there be any recovery? Under what theory, if any?

2. Does an agent's oral contract to procure insurance fall within the Statute of Frauds because it "is not to be performed within one year of the making thereof"? *Compare* the cases of *Goldberg v. Colonial Life Ins. Co.,* 134 N.Y.S.2d 865 (App. Div. 1954), *with Monogram Products, Inc. v. Berkowitz,* 392 So. 2d 1353 (Fla. Dist. Ct. App. 1980).

3. Since an oral contract is informally made, an implied agreement on the essential terms is often as good as an express agreement. But what if an independent agent, who represents more than one insurance company, fails to specify which particular coverage would apply before loss occurs? A valid oral contract or not? *See Employers Fire Ins. Co. v. Speed,* 133 So. 2d 627 (Miss. 1961).

### **PROBLEM ONE**

A building contractor telephoned a property and liability insurance agent to obtain a builder's risk insurance policy. The agent represented a number of insurance companies. The agent orally told the contractor over the telephone that "he was covered." After this telephone conversation, the agent scribbled the words "Insure 7750 Van Buren [Street] same as 7730." An enforceable oral insurance contract? Why or why not?

# § 4.03. Insurance Binders and Conditional Receipts

Whether or not a "conditional receipt" (for life insurance) or a "binder" (for property and liability insurance) constitutes temporary insurance, and under what conditions, has been the subject of a great deal of insurance litigation. The interests of the policyholder who desires immediate protection against a risk of loss, and the needs of the insurance company in attempting to limit an undesirable risk distribution, are both legitimate concerns.

"Binding receipts" or "binders" are almost always contracts of temporary insurance, since liability and property insurance agents are normally *general agents* who can bind their insurance company to a temporary contract based on their express or implied authority, absent any limitation in the insurance contract. As a general rule, a "binder may be written or oral and founded upon words or deeds of an agent." *State Auto. Mut. Ins. Co. v. Babcock*, 220 N.W.2d 717 (Mich. 1974). For example, statements by agents, such as "You're covered," or "I'll take care of it," have been held to constitute oral binders. *See, e.g., American Universal Ins. Co. v. Kruse*, 306 F.2d 661 (9th Cir. 1962). Conduct which would lead a reasonable person to conclude that he or she is insured also has been held to establish a valid binder. *See Turner v. Worth Ins. Co.*, 472 P.2d 1 (Ariz. 1970).

For commercial property and casualty insurance, the custom and practice of the insurance industry regarding insurance binders is not consistent. Whether a binder is valid or not depends upon the particular situation, and varies with the parties' understanding, the presence or absence of a broker, and the arrangements the broker has made with the parties. In some cases, the commercial policyholder attempts to procure insurance through a broker, and the broker and the property and casualty insurance underwriter informally agree to the attachment of temporary insurance before the final policy attaches — either orally or by e-mail. Other insurers, however, insist upon a written and signed confirmation by the insurer of any proposed binder. *See, e.g.,* Stempel & Knutsen on Insurance Coverage, § 3.05[a].

As contrasted with many property agents, life insurance agents normally are only *soliciting* agents rather than *general* agents, so they do *not* generally have the power to create coverage in life insurance policies absent approval from their home office. Thus, life insurance agents can only give "conditional" receipts rather than "binding" receipts.

In the case of life insurance policies, the courts are split as to whether a "conditional receipt" issued to an applicant for life insurance constitutes temporary insurance or not. When issued by an authorized life insurance agent, this "conditional receipt," it has been argued, constitutes a temporary contract of insurance, subject to a condition-rejection by the insurance company — which would terminate this coverage if the insured is found in good faith to be uninsurable. Thus, if the insured dies during this time period, the insurance company, to avoid coverage, must prove that a valid reason for rejection of the risk existed at the time of the application. *See, e.g., Gaunt v. John Hancock Mut. Life Ins. Co.*, 160 F.2d 599 (2d Cir.), *cert. denied*, 331 U.S. 849 (1947); Edwin Patterson, Essentials of Insurance Law 99–102 (2d ed. 1957).

A small minority of courts hold that this temporary insurance, resulting from the issuance of a "conditional receipt," protects the insured until the insurer has accepted or rejected the application, and the insurer cannot terminate the risk unless the insured is notified in his *lifetime* that his application was rejected. *See, e.g., Service v. Pyramid Life Ins. Co.*, 440 P.2d 944 (Kan. 1968); *Allen v. Metropolitan Life Ins. Co.*, 208 A.2d 638 (N.J. 1965). Many other courts, however, reject this "temporary insurance" doctrine and determine the legal consequences of a "conditional receipt" on the basis of a "satisfaction" type contract, that is to say, the applicant's insurability is a condition precedent to the insurance company's affording coverage.

Thus, broadly speaking, there are three kinds of conditional receipts recognized in various jurisdictions: (1) an "approval" type conditional receipt, in which no insurance comes into effect until the insurance is approved by an authorized official of the insurer; (2) a "satisfaction" or "condition precedent" conditional receipt, in which the proposed insurance takes effect at the time of the insurance application *only* if it later appears that under objective standards of insurability, the applicant was a "standard risk" at the date of the application; and (3) unconditional "temporary" or "interim" coverage during the pendency of the application, or for a stated period of time. *See, e.g., Simpson v. Prudential Ins. Co.*, 177 A.2d 417, 422–23 (Md. 1962).

# § 4.04. Insurer's Delay in Acting upon the Insurance Application

The courts are hopelessly divided on the question of liability of an insurer for unreasonable delay in acting upon an insurance application. A majority of jurisdictions do impose liability and do so under four theories:

> (a) A tort theory, referred to as the "negligent delay" theory. The "negligent delay" theory, generally stated, is that an insurance company is under a duty to act upon an application for insurance within a reasonable period of time, and a violation of this duty, with resultant damages, subjects the company to liability for negligence. *See, e.g., Continental Life & Accident Co. v. Songer*, 603 P.2d 921, 929 (Ariz. 1979)

> (b) An estoppel theory: the insurer is estopped from denying that its delay did not imply acceptance of the application. *See, e.g., Moore v. Palmetto State Life Ins. Co.*, 73 S.E.2d 688 (S.C. 1952).

> (c) A contract theory: retention of the premium and failure to reject the application is tantamount to acceptance and inconsistent with rejection of the application offer. *See, e.g., Cartwright v. Maccabees Mutual Life Ins. Co.*, 247 N.W.2d 298 (Mich. 1976).

> (d) An implied agreement to act promptly. *See, e.g., Barrera v. State Farm Mut. Auto. Ins. Co.*, 456 P.2d 674 (Cal. 1969).

There is a strong minority view, however, which holds that mere delay does not impose either contractual or tort liability; that is, there is no presumption of acceptance nor a duty to act promptly. *See, e.g., Cameron v. First Nat'l Bank*, 607 P.2d 1113 (Mont. 1980) (no contract created); and *La Favor v. American Nat'l Ins. Co.*, 155 N.W.2d 286 (Minn. 1967) (no action *ex delicto*). *See generally* HOLMES' APPLEMAN ON INSURANCE LAW, Ch. 12, *Insurer's Liability for Delay or Failure to Act on an Insurance Application* (2d ed. 1998). Which theory was applied in the following case?

# Independent Life and Accident Insurance Co. v. McKenzie

Florida Court of Appeals
503 So. 2d 376 (1987)

**Wigginton, Judge**

This appeal is from a final judgment in favor of Gladys and Phillip McKenzie adjudging their entitlement to the proceeds of a life insurance policy.... Appellant, Independent Life and Accident Insurance Company, challenged the award by the trial court on the several bases that: the premium receipt did not create an insurance contract; the representations of appellant's agent did not estop it from denying coverage; and Independent Life was not negligent in failing to obtain the deceased's signature on the application for insurance prior to his death.

On August 8, 1983, two Independent Life agents visited Phillip and Gladys McKenzie in their Wakulla County home to discuss life insurance. At the time of the visit, the lives of Gladys and two of her adult children, Tammy Free and Randy Raker, were insured by another company, the National Standard Life Insurance Company. Phillip could not qualify for a National Standard policy due to disability. Upon discovering that Independent Life could issue Phillip a policy, the McKenzies determined to cancel the National Standard policies, including Raker's, and replace them with Independent Life policies.

The McKenzies each completed and signed applications for insurance. Free and Raker were not present at the meeting, but the agents filled out applications for them using information obtained from the National Standard policies. Phillip then paid the agents $39.23 cash for one month's coverage and was given a "Receipt for Application," which stated that the money was received "as payment on application for insurance on Phillip McKenzie and Gladys McKenzie" and also provided:

> This receipt is issued for deposit on application for insurance. The policy will be considered in force from the date of the receipt and the company will assume all liability under the terms of the policy contract....

Neither Free's nor Raker's name appears on the receipt, although the evidence at trial showed that $39.23 exceeded the monthly premium due for Gladys and Philip alone, and Independent Life admitted that the amount was "probably for all four policies." Despite the premium payment, the McKenzies concede that they were made aware at the time that Free and Raker would not be covered until their signatures were obtained on the applications. The agents repeatedly assured them, however, that they would locate the children (Free lived near her parents in Wakulla County; Raker was residing with another sister in Tallahassee) and obtain their signatures. Gladys' offer to get Raker's signature herself was rejected.

The agents contacted Tammy Free the next day and she signed her application. However, Raker was not located, and the evidence tended to show that the agents made no effort to do so. Twenty-eight days after the August meeting, on September 5, 1983, Raker was killed in an automobile accident in Leon County. Independent refused to pay on the policy since the application had never been signed. Although Raker's National Standard policy had been cancelled in favor of the Independent Life policy, Raker's death occurred within the 30-day grace period following that cancellation and National Standard paid full triple-indemnity benefits of $7,500.

On February 23, 1984, the McKenzies filed a complaint seeking a declaration of entitlement to the $10,000 proceeds of Raker's policy. Independent Life answered in April, denying the existence of a policy on Raker, and moved for summary judgment on the same ground in July; the motion was denied in April 1985. In January 1986, the McKenzies filed a trial brief, arguing entitlement to the proceeds due either to the agent's negligent delay in obtaining Raker's signature on the application or on the theory that the agent's assurances that the signature would be obtained estopped the company to deny coverage. Independent Life countered with its own brief, arguing that any policy obtained without Raker's consent was against public policy and void; that a 28-day delay in locating Raker was not unreasonable and therefore not negligent, and that estoppel was not available to create insurance coverage.

Following a November 1985 bench trial, the court entered a final judgment that Independent Life had "wrongfully withheld payment of the policy proceeds" to the McKenzies. No ground for this determination was specified. Although we do not agree that appellees should prevail on either the contract or estoppel arguments espoused by them before the lower court, the evidence and circumstances surrounding this business transaction is sufficient to support a finding of negligent delay.

Florida law requires that an individual contracting for insurance on the life of another have an "insurable interest" in that life.... An insurable interest may be predicated upon any relation such as warrants the conclusion that the person claiming the interest has an interest, arising from natural affection, in the life of the insured.... It was undisputed that the McKenzies had such an interest in Raker's life, so that they could make application for a policy covering him and be entitled to any benefits and rights provided therein.

The insurer has a duty to the "applicant" for a policy of life insurance to either accept or reject that application within a reasonable length of time after receiving the application and accepting the initial premium.... The breach of this duty can create liability in tort for negligent delay.... In our case, the "applicant" was not the potential insured but individuals with an insurable interest in the life of the insured. In such a situation, a permissible applicant, while he can pay the premium, cannot complete the application with the insured's signature so as to give rise to the duty contemplated by Huberman and Rosin. However, it must nonetheless reasonably follow that when an agent undertakes to obtain the insured's signature, a comparable duty to the actual applicant arises to do so expeditiously or to timely notify of one's inability to do so.

The evidence unmistakably shows that no effort had been made toward obtaining Raker's signature prior to his death. Under these specific circumstances, the company's agents acted negligently in failing either to obtain the signature of the insured or to inform the applicants of the impossibility of doing so. The final judgment is affirmed.

## *Notes and Questions*

1. Whether or not the courts will impose liability on insurers for a delay in acting on an insurance application is normally based on the issue of whether the delay was reasonable or unreasonable. This is normally a question of fact for the jury. *See, e.g., American Life Ins. Co. v. Hutcheson*, 109 F.2d 424 (6th Cir.) (applying Tennessee law), *cert. denied*, 310 U.S. 625 (1940).

2. Is it reasonable or unreasonable that an insurance application is delayed because the insurance agent needed additional time to obtain further information about the policyholder, or about the subject of the proposed insurance? *See, e.g., Duke v. Valley Forge Life Ins. Co.*, 341 So. 2d 1366 (La. Ct. App. 1977).

3. Those jurisdictions which impose liability on insurers for any unreasonable delay do so generally on the ground that an insurance policy, as distinguished from a purely private contract, is affected with a public interest; or that the applicant, as a matter of fair dealing, is entitled to know promptly if the application is rejected, so he or she can apply elsewhere to another insurance company. Should these grounds be sustainable to impose a contractual or tort liability against the insurance company even though the insurance application form usually states that insurance shall *not* be effective until the company has acted favorably upon the application? Why or why not? Should a premium payment always be required?

4. Should the "insurability" of the applicant matter? What if no insurance company would have issued a policy? *See, e.g., Huff v. Standard Life Ins. Co.*, 897 F.2d 1072 (11th Cir. 1990) (applying Florida law).

### PROBLEM TWO

Perry Antoine worked offshore on an oil derrick as a roustabout for an oil company. He sought to obtain insurance to protect his family in the event that he was killed or disabled, and he applied to the Hartford Insurance Company for both life and disability insurance policies. Hartford accepted his life insurance policy application at an increased premium, but it rejected Antoine's disability insurance application because of his occupation.

Mr. Antoine then applied for disability coverage with the Sentry Life Insurance Company on September 30, 1974. He heard nothing from Sentry for a number of months. Only when he was permanently disabled in an automobile accident in April of 1975 did Mr. Antoine subsequently learn that his disability insurance application had been rejected by Sentry five months earlier because of his occupation, but no one at Sentry had bothered to notify Antoine of this fact.

Mr. Antoine filed suit against Sentry based upon its unreasonable delay in acting on his disability insurance application. At no time was any premium paid to Sentry by the plaintiff.

• How should the court rule in this case?

# § 4.05. Duties of Insurance Agents Pre-Loss

The relationship of principal to agent in the insurance business generally follows the rules of agency law. A number of these concepts should be emphasized:

(a) *General agents*, normally found in liability and property insurance, possess general powers of making, modifying, or cancelling insurance contracts for the principal insurer—absent any limitation to these powers expressed in the insurance policy or elsewhere.

(b) *Special* or *Soliciting agents*, normally found in life insurance, possess limited powers confined to soliciting applications, delivering policies, and receiving initial premiums. Their powers are more ministerial than contractual, since the insurance company's home office normally possesses the sole authority to accept, reject, or cancel the insurance contract.

(c) *Brokers* solicit business from both the policyholder and the insurer. Normally a broker acts as an agent of the policyholder, but he or she may also act as an agent of the insurer—or as agent of both parties—depending on the facts of the case.

(d) An insurance agent possesses *actual or apparent authority* to act on behalf of his principal. Actual can be implied as well as express. For example, an insurer may have a historical pattern of permitting an agent to accept risks "in the field" even if this is not authorized by the formal agency agreement. Any limitations upon the agent's apparent powers cannot affect the insured unless these limitations are communicated to the insured.

(e) Any *mistake, fraud or wrongdoing* perpetrated by the agent in the course of his or her employment binds the principal insurance company, even though the conduct was not authorized. An exception to this rule exists whenever the agent and the policyholder are in collusion to defraud the insurance company. In such a situation, the principal is not bound by the agent's misconduct.

(f) Any *knowledge* possessed by the agent, material to an insurance transaction in which he is employed, will bind the insurance company, whether or not this knowledge is actually communicated by the agent to his company.

*See generally* JERRY & RICHMOND, UNDERSTANDING INSURANCE LAW § 35 (6th ed. 2018); KEETON & WIDISS, INSURANCE LAW § 2.5 (1988).

Both general and special agents are generally compensated on a commission basis, although some may have a base salary as well. The commission is typically based on a percentage of the premiums collected, with the amount varying according to the type of policy sold. For insurance products with low turnover, such as life insurance (where consumers are less likely to change insurers), the agent's commission can be quite high, perhaps more than 100 percent of the first-year premium (because once sold, the policy is likely to be kept in effect, generating premiums for years to come). For insurance products with higher turnover, such as auto insurance (where consumers are more likely to switch in search of lower rates or because of a move to another state), the percentage of commission is usually lower.

For purposes of assessing the existence of insurance and resolving coverage questions, the crucial point to remember is that the agent represents the insurer and her conduct may bind or be imputed to the insurer. The broker represents the applicant/policyholder and her conduct may bind or be imputed to the policyholder.

Frequently, there are some mixed aspects of the intermediary's role. For example, a broker may primarily be the agent of the policyholder but is the agent of the insurer for purposes of collecting premiums. The agent may primarily be an insurance company employee but still may have duties to the applicant that require the agent to respond appropriately in a given situation. For example, if an applicant wants to insure his ice rink, it would be negligent for the agent to sell a policy that expressly excludes coverage for liability claims arising out of ice-skating injuries (unless, perhaps, if this is openly discussed with the applicant and acceptance of the exclusion results in a lower premium).

Whether the agent is individually liable apart from the insurer (which may have to pay for a skating injury because of the reasonable expectations of the policyholder) depends on the facts and applicable state law of agency.

Brokers, by contrast, are expected not only to respond reasonably to specific requests by policyholders but also to act as fiduciaries toward policyholders and to act reasonably on behalf of policyholders even in the absence of specific direction. This does not, however, mean that brokers are expected to be omniscient in anticipating policyholder needs or possible claims. For example, a policyholder who purchases a reasonable amount of insurance but is later hit with an unexpectedly large claim will be unlikely to persuade the court that the broker is liable for failing to recommend higher policy limits.

In extreme cases, however, the broker may be responsible. For example, if the broker sells a drug manufacturer a $1 million package of insurance without any warning that this amount is likely to be inadequate if the product becomes the target of litigation, this could be found to be professionally negligent in view of the possibility that drug product liability lawsuits could easily far exceed this amount of coverage. *See also* Todd A. Schoenhaus & Adam M. Share, *Liability of the Insurance Broker for Breach of Duty to Advise*, Risk Mgmt. Mag. Feb. 2006, at 39. *See, e.g., AYH Holdings, Inc. v. Avreco, Inc.*, 826 N.E.2d 1111 (Ill. Ct. App. 2005) (surplus lines exchange broker had duty to inform policyholder of insurer's financial condition).

For commercial policyholders, large brokers such as Marsh & McLennan, Aon, or Willis Group do not sell individual policies so much as they help the policyholder put together an insurance program or package of policies on a variety of coverages, with both primary insurance and multiple levels of excess insurance lest the company be saddled with large liability claims. This part of the insurance world, of course, is quite distinct from that of most consumer policyholders, who simply buy auto, home, and perhaps life insurance from their friendly neighborhood agent with a storefront office in the local strip mall.

However, brokers, and even large commercial insurance brokers, are similar to agents in that the primary means of compensation is through commissions based on the amount of insurance placed, and the commissions are usually paid by insurers even though it is the policyholders who are the "clients" of the commercial brokerage firm.

Most insurance policies are contracted through insurance agents, who often emphasize the catastrophic effects of loss, and the "peace of mind" that insurance provides, when attempting to convince a prospective insured to purchase insurance coverage. *See, e.g.*, Robert Jerry, II, *Remedying an Insurer's Bad Faith Contract Performance: A Reassessment*, 18 CONN. L. REV. 271, 298–299 (1986). Yet, when loss does occur, a sales/coverage dispute regarding this promised coverage is most often resolved utilizing an insurance-as-contract analysis. *See, e.g.*, Tom Baker, *Constructing the Insurance Relationship: Sales Stories, Claims Stories, and Insurance Contract Damages*, 72 TEXAS L. REV. 1395 (1994). *Compare D'Ambrosio v. Pennsylvania Nat'l Mut. Casualty Ins. Co.*, 396 A.2d 780, 786 (Pa. Super. Ct. 1978) ("The insurer's promise to the insured to 'simplify his life', to put him in 'good hands', to back him with 'a piece of the rock', or to 'be on his side' hardly suggests that the insurer will abandon the insured in his time of need."), *aff'd*, 431 A.2d 966 (Pa. 1981), *with Rodio v. Smith*, 587 A.2d 621, 624 (N.J. 1991) ("However persuasive, 'You're in good hands with Allstate' is nothing more than mere puffery.").

––––––––

Are the following court decisions too forgiving to agents? Or, do they simply reflect practical realities in light of the agent's limited role? Would it be unfair or impossible to hold agents accountable for every communication with a potential policyholder? But, even if an agent is the employee of an insurer, does the applicant not rely on the agent's expertise? Does the applicant not have an objectively reasonable expectation that the policy purchased from the agent will be appropriate to the applicant's needs?

## Murphy v. Kuhn

Court of Appeals of New York
90 N.Y.2d 266, 660 N.Y.S.2d 371, 682 N.E.2d 972 (1997)

**Bellacosa, J.**

The question for this case is whether an insurance agent should be liable to a former customer for tortious misrepresentation and breach of implied contract. The alleged wrongdoing is a failure of the defendant insurance agent to advise plaintiff Thomas Murphy as to possible additional insurance coverage needs. The theory of the lawsuit and the asserted duty is a special relationship and special level of advisory responsibility. The Appellate Division affirmed an order of Supreme Court, which granted defendants' motion for summary judgment and dismissed the complaint. Plaintiffs appeal pursuant to leave granted by this Court. We affirm the order of the Appellate Division because no special relationship was established on this record.

Plaintiffs Thomas Murphy and Webster Golf Course, Inc. sued defendants Donald C. Kuhn, Kuhn & Pedulla Agency, Inc., and its predecessor Roman A. Kuhn Agency, alleging professional negligence and breach of implied contract. This dispute originates in a 1991 automobile accident in Florida involving Murphy's son. One person died and several others suffered serious injuries as a result of the accident. At that time, the title to the son's car was in his father's name and the personal insurance was placed under the commercial automobile policy covering Murphy's business, Webster Golf Course, Inc. After exhausting the $500,000 policy limit to settle the car accident claims, Thomas Murphy assertedly paid an additional $194,429.50 plus $7,500 in attorneys' fees. Then, he sued these defendants to recover the additional sums he had to pay personally.

Defendants began providing the property, casualty and liability insurance to plaintiffs in 1973 in connection with their golf business. Beginning in 1977, defendant Donald Kuhn also handled all of Murphy's personal insurance needs, providing him with both homeowners insurance and personal automobile coverage. In 1979, plaintiff Thomas Murphy and his partner, Edward Rieflin, completed their purchase of the Happy Acres Golf Course and formed Webster Golf Course, Inc. Happy Acres had been a client of the Roman A. Kuhn Agency since 1957.

In 1990, Kuhn placed personal automobile coverage for Murphy with The Hartford, as insurer. Later that year, Hartford notified Murphy that his coverage was in danger of cancellation due to the poor driving records of his children. Murphy then transferred the insurance covering his son's car, which was registered and titled in Murphy's name, from Murphy's personal policy to Webster Golf Course's commercial automobile insurance policy. Murphy testified at his deposition that it was his standard arrangement to place title and register his children's cars in his name. From 1984 until the time of the accident, the liability limits on the commercial policy were $250,000 per person and $500,000 total per accident. Murphy never requested higher liability coverage for his personal and family automobile insurance needs, which were subsumed within the commercial automobile liability policy.

[The trial court] concluded that, absent a request by the customer, an insurance agent "owes no continuing duty to advise, guide or direct the customer to obtain additional coverage." Therefore, acknowledging that on this record plaintiffs never specifically requested defendants to increase the liability limits on the commercial automobile policy, the court held that defendants owed no special duty of affirmative advisement to plaintiffs. The court also declined to adopt plaintiffs' "special relationship" theory.

Plaintiffs propose that insurance agents can assume or acquire legal duties not existing at common law by entering into a special relationship of trust and confidence with their customers. Specifically, plaintiffs contend that a special relationship developed from a long, continuing course of business between plaintiffs and defendant insurance agent, generating special reliance and an affirmative duty to advise with regard to appropriate or additional coverage.

Generally, the law is reasonably settled on initial principles that insurance agents have a common-law duty to obtain requested coverage for their clients within a reasonable time or inform the client of the inability to do so; however, they have no continuing duty to advise, guide or direct a client to obtain additional coverage. Notably, no New York court has applied plaintiffs' proffered "special relationship" analysis to add such continuing duties to the agent-insured relationship.

Recently, however, this Court recognized a special relationship in a commercial controversy, involving no generally recognized professional relationship. We held that the relationship between the parties "under the circumstances [there] required defendant to speak with care." [However,] "liability for negligent misrepresentation has been imposed only on those persons who possess unique or specialized expertise, or who are in a special position of confidence and trust with the injured party such that reliance on the negligent misrepresentation is justified." For example, "[p]rofessionals, such as lawyers and engineers, by virtue of their training and expertise, may have special relationships of confidence and trust with their clients, and in certain situations we have imposed liability for negligent misrepresentation when they have failed to speak with care." [See, e.g.,] *Ossining Union Free School Dist. v Anderson LaRocca Anderson*, 73 NY2d 417 [engineering consultants]; *White v Guarente*, 43 NY2d 356 [accountants]; *Ultramares Corp. v Touche*, 255 NY 170 [accountants]; *Glanzer v Shepard*, 233 NY 236 [public weighers]).

The Court concluded that given "the absence of obligations arising from the speaker's professional status" in the commercial context, "there must be some identifiable source of a special duty of care" in order to impose tort liability. "The existence of such a special relationship may give rise to an exceptional duty regarding commercial speech and justifiable reliance on such speech" (*id.*). We determined, to be sure, that "[w]hether the nature and caliber of the relationship between the parties is such that the injured party's reliance on a negligent misrepresentation is justified generally raises an issue of fact"....

Even assuming the general applicability of the "special relationship" theory in the customer-agent automobile insurance coverage setting, we conclude that the relationship between these parties was insufficiently established to warrant or justify this case surviving a defense summary judgment motion. As a matter of law, this record does not rise to the high level required to recognize the special relationship threshold that might superimpose on defendants the initiatory advisement duty, beyond the ordinary placement of requested insurance responsibilities. Rather, the record in the instant case presents only the standard consumer-agent insurance placement relationship, albeit over an extended period of time. Plaintiffs' plight does not warrant transforming his difficulty into a new, expanded tort opportunity for peripheral redress. The record does not support plaintiffs' effort in this manner to shift to defendant insurance agent the customer's personal responsibility for initiating, seeking and obtaining appropriate coverage, without something more than is presented here.

We note in this respect that Murphy never asked Kuhn to increase the liability limits on the Webster Golf Course commercial automobile policy. In fact, there is no indication that Murphy ever inquired or discussed with Kuhn any issues involving the liability limits of the automobile policy. Such lack of initiative or personal indifference cannot qualify as legally recognizable or justifiable reliance. Therefore, there was no evidence of reliance on the defendant agent's expertise.... The absence of reliance is further reflected in Murphy's deposition testimony that it was his standard procedure to simply register his children's cars in his name. Additionally, Murphy's deposition description of his relationship with Kuhn concerning the golf course's general insurance matters shows that he had not met personally with Kuhn to discuss the insurance needs of Webster Golf Course, Inc. for approximately 12 years preceding the accident in question. Rather, his partner Rieflin was the one actively and personally involved in handling the insurance needs of the golf course.

We also note that Murphy's contention that he mistakenly believed that the commercial policy had a $1,000,000 liability limit on all covered vehicles can be given no weight in resolving this dispute on this theory. The liability coverage had remained the same since 1984 and Murphy's deposition testimony failed to establish the basis for his plainly unfounded assumption. Therefore, plaintiffs are not entitled to advance beyond the summary judgment stage of this lawsuit because they failed to establish the existence of a legally cognizable special relationship with their insurance agent in this standard set of circumstances.

Plaintiffs-appellants urge this Court to avoid generally absolving insurance agents from legal principles which subject other individuals to duties beyond those rooted in the common law. They overstate the concern and effect of this decision and the principle that emanates from it. Our decision today does not break any new ground and does not immunize insurance brokers and agents from appropriately assigned duties and responsibilities. Exceptional and particularized situations may arise in which insurance agents, through their conduct or by express or implied contract with customers and clients, may assume or acquire duties in addition to those fixed at common law.

Notably, other jurisdictions have recognized such an additional duty of advisement in exceptional situations where, for example, (1) the agent receives compensation for consultation apart from payment of the premiums, (2) there was some interaction regarding a question of coverage, with the insured relying on the expertise of the agent); or (3) there is a course of dealing over an extended period of time which would have put objectively reasonable insurance agents on notice that their advice was being sought and specially relied on. In these circumstances, insureds bear the burden of proving the specific undertaking. The relationship established in the instant case does not rise to the level of these exceptional situations and we refrain from determining when the special relationship analysis may apply in the insurance context.

We do, however, take note that the uniqueness of customary and ordinary insurance relationships and transactions is manifested by "the absence of obligations arising from the speaker's professional status" with regard to the procurement of additional coverage. As stated, it is well settled that agents have no continuing duty to advise, guide, or direct a client to obtain additional coverage. No doubt, therefore, public policy considerations will have to be weighed on the question of whether to override this settled principle by recognizing additional advisement duties on insurance agents and brokers. But we do not reach that question here.

Insurance agents or brokers are not personal financial counselors and risk managers, approaching guarantor status. Insureds are in a better position to know their personal assets and abilities to protect themselves more so than general insurance agents or brokers, unless the latter are informed and asked to advise and act. Furthermore, permitting insureds to add such parties to the liability chain might well open flood gates to even more complicated and undesirable litigation. Notably, in a different context, but with resonant relevance, it has been observed that "[u]nlike a recipient of the services of a doctor, attorney or architect ... the recipient of the services of an insurance broker is not at a substantial disadvantage to question the actions of the provider of services".... Order affirmed, with costs.

### Harris v. Albrecht

Supreme Court of Utah
86 P.3d 728 (Utah 2004)

**Durham, Chief Justice:**

The instant case is one of first impression in which we determine when an insurance agent creates a contract to procure insurance or when a duty to procure insurance arises. Petitioner Rick Albrecht seeks review of the Utah Court of Appeals' reversal of the trial court's grant of summary judgment in Albrecht's favor. Albrecht is a Utah-licensed insurance agent employed by Rick Albrecht Insurance Agency, Inc. He sells policies exclusively for co-petitioner, State Farm Fire & Casualty Company (State Farm). Ken Harris earned his architecture license in 1981, formed Harris and Olsen Architects in 1987, changing the firm's name to Ken Harris Architects in 1990. Harris' business grew considerably after 1990, and he made substantial investments in equipment and office furnishings from 1995 to 1997. By the summer of 1997, the scope of the improvements prompted an interest in acquiring business insurance.

In 1989, Albrecht and Harris commenced a business relationship when Harris obtained an auto insurance policy from State Farm through Albrecht. Albrecht continued procuring various insurance policies for Harris, including an umbrella policy and coverage for his home, boat and Recreational Vehicle. They conducted most of their business over the telephone, talking every couple of months. A conversation generally consisted of requests from Harris for insurance coverage, followed by fulfillment of each request by Albrecht, without detailed discussion of different types of coverages.

In mid-summer 1997, Harris contacted Albrecht to obtain business insurance for his architectural firm. He told Albrecht "to place business and fire coverage on [his] equipment and the contents [of his office]." Harris alleged that Albrecht responded by saying that "he would take care of [it]," and "he would come out and look at [the] equipment." On December 31, 1997, a fire destroyed the building housing Harris' architectural firm. The losses totaled $1,143,855.50. Harris attributed $940,000 to the loss of architectural plans and other valuable papers. While watching the building burn, Harris called Albrecht and asked: "You placed that [business] coverage we talked about, didn't you?" Albrecht replied: "We talked about it, Ken, but we never did anything about it."

Harris brought claims against Albrecht, Rick Albrecht Insurance Agency and State Farm for breach of a contract to procure insurance and negligent failure to procure insurance. The trial court granted Albrecht's motion for summary judgment, and the Court of Appeals reversed.

Whether an insurance agent breached a contract to procure insurance or whether the agent had a duty to procure insurance are matters of first impression for this court. The Court of Appeals erred when it concluded that "whether a contract to procure insurance or a duty to procure insurance ultimately exists [are] questions of fact best left to the trier of fact." This court's precedent establishes that whether a contract or duty exists is a matter of law.

The formation of a contract requires a meeting of the minds. "Where a person seeks to enter into a contract of insurance with an insurance company or its agent it is understood that the negotiations will not ripen into a contract until the parties arrive at an agreement as to all of the elements which are essential to an insurance contract, including the subject matter to be covered, the risk insured against, the amount of the indemnity, the duration of the coverage and the premium." We conclude that no contract of insurance existed between Harris and Albrecht. They did not discuss any of the elements essential to an insurance contract except that Harris "wanted business and fire coverage on [the] equipment and the contents" of his architectural business. There was no mention, except fire, of the types of risks Harris wanted covered, the amount of indemnity, the duration of coverage, or the premium. Therefore, there was no meeting of the minds on which to base a contract of insurance.

However, the issue here is not whether an oral contract of insurance existed but rather whether an oral contract to procure insurance existed.... In entering into a contract to procure insurance, obviously the owner is seeking the same ultimate objective, that is, a contract of insurance, but the performance for which he bargains is the services of the insurance agent in obtaining the best possible terms consistent with the owner's insurance needs. Such a contract could arise even though the agent was given the authority to ascertain some of the facts essential to the creation of the ultimate contract of insurance, such as the appraised value of the property to be covered or the most advantageous premium.... "Obviously, liability for failure to procure insurance could not arise unless the agent had sufficiently definite directions from his principal to enable him to consummate the final insurance contract.... An express agreement is not necessary; the scope of the risk, the subject matter to be covered, the duration of the insurance, and other elements can be found by implication." ... Therefore, a contract to procure insurance may arise when the agent has definite directions from the insured to consummate a final contract, when the scope, subject matter, duration, and other elements can be found by implication, and when the insured gives the agent authority to ascertain some of the essential facts.

In the present case, Albrecht did not have sufficiently definite directions from Harris to consummate the final insurance contract. Harris requested fire coverage for the contents and equipment of his business and also asked for business insurance. In order for Albrecht to procure business insurance, he needed to know the type of coverage Harris desired, such as loss of income, earthquake, employee dishonesty, money and securities, and theft. Depending on the types of coverage desired, Albrecht potentially needed to know the value of all furniture and equipment, accounts receivable, and building improvements, as well as the amount of deductible Harris wanted, why Harris' business had never been insured, when Harris wanted the policy to go into effect, whether there had been any prior losses, and, crucially, the value of architectural documents and other valuable papers. Albrecht had none of this information because all of Harris' previous policies were personal. Furthermore, Harris has not cited any instance where a court has held that an insurance agent must procure part of an insurance policy while waiting for the remaining sections to be sufficiently identified.

For similar reasons, Albrecht could not identify "the scope of the risk, the subject matter to be covered, the duration of the insurance, and other elements ... by implication." Although Harris requested fire insurance for the contents and equipment in his business, too many variables remained. The auto, home, boat and RV policies offered no information from which Albrecht could determine the missing terms of the contract.

Additionally, Harris failed to give authority for Albrecht to ascertain some of the essential facts. He merely made a general request for insurance, which falls short of giving Albrecht authority. Harris was required to give explicit instructions to Albrecht rather than make a blanket request for insurance. Giving authority to the agent requires more than such a blanket request.... Albrecht lacked sufficient information from which the terms of a contract of insurance or a contract to procure insurance could be implied. The expression of a desire to procure business insurance followed by an oral affirmation of that desire is not enough to create a contract to procure insurance. Creation of a contract to procure insurance requires that the agent know or have ready access to the information needed to procure the insurance or be able to imply the terms from prior dealings. If the insured gives authority to the agent to obtain some information, he must do so explicitly.

The second issue before us is whether Albrecht assumed a duty to procure insurance when he allegedly told Harris "he would take care of that," and that he would come out and look at the equipment" after Harris called Albrecht and told him that he "wanted business and fire coverage on [the] equipment and the contents" of his architectural business.... One standard for determining whether an insurance agent has assumed a duty to procure has been stated as follows:

> [A] court must look to the conduct of the parties and the communications between them, and more specifically to the extent to which they indicate that the agent has acknowledged an obligation to secure a policy. Where an insurance agent or broker promises, or gives some affirmative assurance,

that he will procure or renew a policy of insurance under circumstances which lull the insured into the belief that such insurance has been effected, the law will impose upon the broker or agent the obligation to perform the duty which he has thus assumed. Further, if the parties have had prior dealings where the agent customarily has taken care of the customer's needs without consultation, then a legal duty to procure additional insurance may arise without express and detailed orders from the customer and acceptance by the agent.... An application from the customer is sufficient to support a duty to procure insurance. A bare acknowledgment of a contract to protect the insured against casualty of a specified kind until a formal policy can be issued is enough....

Factors that indicate a duty include (1) whether Harris gave Albrecht an application, (2) whether Albrecht made a bare acknowledgment of a contract covering a specific kind of casualty even though all the terms had not been settled, (3) whether Albrecht made promises to procure insurance that lulled Harris into believing a policy had been procured, and (4) whether there were prior dealings where Albrecht took care of Harris' needs without consultation.

The final three factors are relevant to the instant case, requiring a close look at the language used during Albrecht's and Harris' telephone call. Albrecht said "he would take care of that, he would come out and look at the equipment." This statement is not a bare acknowledgment of an obligation to procure insurance because the statement that "he would come out and look at the equipment" indicated that Albrecht needed to gather more information or do other work before procuring a policy. A bare acknowledgment occurs when an agent confirms coverage pending the issuance of a formal policy.

Albrecht's comments failed to rise to the level of a promise to procure insurance and were insufficient to lull Harris into believing a policy had been procured because they lacked the requisite specificity. An agent must affirmatively assure the insured that a policy will be procured or has been procured. Harris argues that their prior dealings lulled him into believing Albrecht would procure insurance. Rather, Harris lulled himself into believing he had an insurance policy. No reasonable and experienced businessperson would believe the conversation here gave rise to a duty to procure insurance when considered in light of its brevity and the lack of any specificity for such a complex and customized type of policy. Even if Albrecht's comments lulled Harris into believing Albrecht would procure a policy, the fact that Harris never completed an application, never received a bill or policy, and was never contacted by Albrecht in the five months after the conversation should have put Harris on notice that he did not yet have a policy. Failing to examine one's mail is not a defense.

A significant distinction exists between business insurance policies and personal insurance policies. The ease of procuring an auto or homeowner's policy contrasts sharply with the customization required for a business policy. The information available to Albrecht at the time of the telephone conversation provide the essential elements needed to create an insurance contract. A policy for an architectural business requires more customization than one for a simple retail business. Valuable papers, for which Harris now seeks to recover damages, were beyond Albrecht's authority to bind State Farm, and State Farm would likely have required Harris to take certain loss-reduction measures regarding the safe-keeping of those papers before binding them. It was impossible for Albrecht to provide Harris with a "standard business policy."

Albrecht did not acknowledge an obligation to secure an insurance policy for Harris because Albrecht did not: (1) take an application for insurance; (2) make a bare acknowledgment against casualty of a specific kind; (3) lull Harris into believing he would procure insurance or that a policy had been procured; or (4) have a pattern of prior dealings of the type sufficient to impose a duty to procure insurance. At most, Albrecht lulled Harris into believing that he would come out and look at his business.

The court of appeals cited several cases supporting its decision. We agree with Judge Davis' dissent, however, finding those cases distinguishable from the instant case because in each the agent had all the information needed to procure a policy.... Here, Harris merely requested insurance and expressed a desire to procure insurance. [In footnote 2, the Court observed that "The nature of the losses here underscores the reason summary judgment was appropriate. The most basic business policy includes $5,000 of protection for valuable papers. Albrecht only had binding authority up to $25,000 for valuable papers, and Harris could not have received such coverage without taking loss-reduction measures. It is also possible that State Farm would not have bound the policy or that Harris would not have insured his valuable papers for as much as he now claims. The latter is of particular importance because Harris offered his investment in new equipment as the reason for obtaining business insurance, as opposed to protecting valuable papers, which presumably increased in value throughout his career in contrast to the recent equipment purchases. In light of these unknowns, a jury determination of damages would be purely speculative."]

A contract to procure insurance may arise when the agent has definite directions from the insured to consummate a final contract; when the scope, subject matter, duration, and other elements can be found by implication; and when the insured gives the agent authority to ascertain some of the essential facts. A duty to procure insurance may arise when an agent accepts an application; makes a bare acknowledgment of a contract covering a specific kind of casualty; lulls the other party into believing a contract has been effected through promises; and has taken care of the insured's needs without consultation in the past.... The court of appeals erred when it failed to determine that the telephone conversation between Albrecht and Harris created neither a contract nor a duty to procure insurance. We reverse.

## Notes and Questions

1. Would it be feasible in the above cases for the applicant to at least reasonably expect that he is being sold a consumer insurance policy that at least provides the industry standard minimum of coverage? Or, that if the actual policy is not at least this comprehensive, the agent will point this out to the applicant? Or does this simply revisit the issue about the agent's obligation (or lack of obligation) to explain coverage

provisions? For the most part, agents do not have a duty to explain. But as a counterweight, an agent's lack of explanation will make it more likely that ambiguous, hidden, or unfairly surprising language is construed against the insurer.

2. *See also President v. Jenkins*, 853 A.2d 247 (N.J. 2004) (broker not liable for failing to explain gap in coverage for doctor switching medical malpractice coverage where doctor did not advise broker that former coverage that would have eliminated gap was being allowed to lapse). This holding makes sense for agents. But does it make sense for brokers? Should the broker have been required to at least inquire as to whether the doctor was planning to keep the prior coverage in force?

3. *See also Canales v. Wilson Southland Ins. Agency*, 583 S.E.2d 203 (Ga. Ct. App. 2003) (agent not liable for selling policy with U.S./Canada coverage but no coverage for Mexico when accident takes place while van driven in Mexico). The court held that even though the policyholder had been going to the agent for some time for insurance needs, this alone did not create the requisite "special relationship" that would require more of an agent. So far, the decision seems unobjectionable, if a bit harsh. But would it affect your view to know that the policyholder spoke Spanish and did not read or write English? Should the agent selling the policy have foreseen that this particular policyholder might be likely to drive from Georgia to Mexico?

4. *See also DeHayes Group v. Pretzels, Inc.*, 786 N.E.2d 779 (Ind. Ct. App. 2003) (no special relationship and no broker liability to insurer where insurer is forced to pay commercial property claim because of fire). The insurer contended that the broker should have recognized that the policyholder's sprinkler system was not adequate to protect the property. Was the insurer asking the broker to do its job?

5. The purported authority of an insurance agent to act on behalf of—and legally bind—the principal insurance company has led to continuing litigation. Consider the following fact situations:

> (a) An agent held himself out to be a general agent of a specific automobile insurance company, and provided the alleged policyholder with an application containing the company's name on the masthead. In fact, the agent had no agency connection whatsoever with this insurance company, and had in fact stolen the insurance applications from the company. Should the insurance company be legally bound by this "agent's" misrepresentation? Why or why not? *See Lumbermens Mut. Casualty Co. v. Savigliano*, 422 So. 2d 29, 30–31 (Fla. Dist. Ct. App. 1982).

> (b) The policyholder, a filling station operator, was orally promised by an agent of a worker's compensation insurance company that his insurance policy would automatically be renewed, and that his signature was not needed for the policy. Within the next two years, the filling station operator was not billed for any premiums, nor did he receive any policy in the mail. He did have other insurance policies with the same agent, however, that were automatically renewed. The insurance company argued that it should not be liable for its agent's negligence, and that the alleged policyholder could not

possibly have reasonably relied on the agent's oral promises. What result? *See Nehring v. Bast,* 103 N.W.2d 368, 376–377 (Minn. 1960).

(c) A soliciting agent orally and fraudulently misrepresented certain terms and remedies in a life insurance contract to the alleged policyholder that were different from what actually appeared in the written application. When the alleged policyholder died, the insurance company refused payment, arguing that this death was not covered by the terms of the policy. Should the insurance company be liable for its agent's representations? Why or why not? *See American Nat'l Life Ins. Co. v. Montgomery,* 640 S.W.2d 346, 349–351 (Tex. Civ. App. 1982).

6. Many legal controversies have developed regarding the issue of whether an insurance intermediary was a broker, normally representing the interests of the policyholder, or an agent, normally representing the insurance company. The Seventh U.S. Circuit Court of Appeals has identified four criteria utilized to determine whether an intermediary is an agent or a broker: (1) whether the insurer or the policyholder first called the intermediary into the transaction; (2) whether the insurer or the policyholder controls the actions of the intermediary; (3) whether the insurer or the policyholder pays the intermediary; and (4) whether the intermediary represents the interests of the insurer [an agent] or the interests of the policyholder [a broker]. *See Lazzara v. Howard A. Esser, Inc.,* 802 F.2d 260 (7th Cir. 1986).

7. An action against an insurance agent for failing to properly procure coverage for the policyholder can be maintained as a tort action for negligent failure to procure coverage, or for breach of contract to procure the insurance coverage. *See, e.g., In re Jones,* 19 B.R. 293, 295 (Bankr. E.D. Va. 1982); *Prince v. Royal Indem. Co.,* 541 F.2d 646 (7th Cir. 1976); *University Nursing Home, Inc. v. R.B. Brown & Associates, Inc.,* 506 A.2d 268 (Md. Ct. Spec. App. 1986) (a claim for failure to procure insurance coverage is a blend of tort and contract principles).

### PROBLEM THREE

The personal representative of decedent Len Bias sued the decedent's agent for failure to procure a $1 million life insurance policy in a timely manner in the decedent's life. Len Bias died from cocaine intoxication two days after he was picked by the Boston Celtics in the National Basketball Association player draft.

• How should the court rule on this case?

## § 4.06. Acceptance: Premium Payment and Policy Delivery

### [A] Delivery of the Policy

Traditionally it has been held that where the insurance application or policy requires a premium payment to effectuate the policy, failure to pay the initial premium eliminates the possibility of coverage, notwithstanding any provisions in the insurance application or conditional receipt. But there are now judicial cases recognizing a "constructive payment" and "constructive delivery" theory, as exemplified in the case excerpt of *Wanshura v. State Farm Life Ins. Co.*, 275 N.W.2d 559 (Minn. 1978):

> On the evening of November 14, 1973, Meissner [State Farm's agent] telephoned Susan [wife of the applicant] and stated that he would like to deliver the policy the following day at 4:30 p.m. He further advised Susan that the premium would be $56.10 instead of $20, [the amount quoted when the application was prepared] and she said that was fine. No mention was made of the waiver of premium disability clause. Susan then specifically inquired about the effective date of the policy—whether it was the issuance date of October 17 or the delivery date. Meissner advised her it was the issuance date. Susan asked him if he was sure and Meissner said "Yes." Susan then stated that her reason for inquiring was that John [applicant for the insurance] just got out of the hospital and had developed problems. Meissner did not ask about John's health but merely stated that he was sorry. He further stated he would come out with the policy at 4:30 p.m. the next day. The next morning Meissner canceled the appointment and the policy was never delivered or the premium collected. John Wanshura died from cancer on May 1, 1974....

> The trial court found that the premium had been tendered. The evidence as to the phone conversation between Susan Wanshura and Meissner on November 14, 1973, supports this conclusion. Likewise, the nature of the relationship of the parties supports the finding that Susan was the authorized agent of her husband. She conducted all the insurance matters with Meissner, including the homeowner and automobile coverage which led to the solicitation of the life insurance application. Meissner's dealings were with Susan, not John.

> The question of tender of insurance premiums as satisfaction of the requirement of payment of initial premium is a question of first impression with this court. Courts in other jurisdictions construing insurance clauses that require payment of the first premium have concluded that actual payment is not required and that tender of the premium is sufficient....

> We have indicated our approval of tender of payments in other contractual situations.... We now hold that under the facts of this case there was a sufficient tender of payment to satisfy the prerequisite of payment required under the contract between the parties.

The following case discusses two issues: (1) a waiver of the premium payment as a condition precedent to the policy's becoming effective and (2) when delivery of the policy to an agent can be construed as "constructive delivery" to the insured.

# Kramer v. Metropolitan Life Insurance Co.

United States District Court, District of New Jersey
494 F. Supp. 1026 (1980)

**Cohen, Senior District Judge**

In this contract action, plaintiff seeks recovery of accidental death benefits under an insurance policy issued by the defendant Metropolitan Life Insurance Company (Metropolitan) through its agent, defendant Lawrence Duffey, upon the lives of herself and her husband, Robert D. Kramer. Metropolitan has refused to pay the benefits on the grounds that the policy was never delivered nor was the first premium paid in accordance with the terms of the policy. Trial was held without a jury and this Court, having considered the testimony of all witnesses, the exhibits in evidence and the arguments of counsel, finds that the policy in question was in effect at the time of Robert Kramer's death and, therefore, plaintiff may recover under its double indemnity provision....

On March 28 or 29, 1978, defendant agent Duffey met with the Kramers at their home in Lindenwold, New Jersey for the purpose of discussing life insurance. At that time, the Kramers signed an application to Metropolitan for a family life insurance policy in the amount of $10,000.00. The parties decided that their policy would be paid for through Metropolitan's Check-O-Matic system, which provides for the payment of premiums by deductions from the insureds' checking account. To this end, the Kramers signed an "Authorization to Honor Checks," which permitted Heritage Bank to honor checks drawn on their account by, and payable to the order of, Metropolitan. The portion of that document which is pertinent to this litigation states that "[w]hen the policy is delivered, the Initial Check-O-Matic premium must be paid in cash. The Company will draw checks or issue directions, as authorized above, for all other premiums."

It is undisputed that no initial premium was paid by the Kramers at the late March meeting. However, the witnesses at trial disagree regarding why this was so. According to the plaintiff, her husband offered to pay to Duffey any amount that Metropolitan required as a first premium. However, Duffey would not accept the payment because he did not know whether Robert Kramer would be insured and how much the premium would be if he were insured due to an eye condition he suffered. Duffey, however, testified that he requested cash payment of the first premium, but that Robert Kramer refused because he preferred to wait until he was sure that the policy was issued as applied for. Duffey asserts that he then explained that coverage would not commence until the payment of the first premium was made. Consistent with plaintiff's testimony is a memorandum by Duffey, dated March 29, 1978, which states: "The reason I did not collect the first premium is because I was not sure if (Robert Kramer's) physical condition would put the company at an unfair risk."

At trial, Duffey was asked by the Court to explain the inconsistency between his direct testimony and the memorandum.... This Court is not convinced by Duffey's explanation. Upon weighing his contradictory statements against the testimony of the plaintiff, we find that Robert Kramer offered to pay the first premium, but that Duffey refused to accept it. Metropolitan eventually issued a family life insurance policy for the Kramers, and it inserted that policy into its Check-O-Matic system on June 1, 1978. The policy bore the issue date of June 5, 1978. On June 3, 1978 Metropolitan mailed to Heritage Bank the Authorization to Honor Checks which was signed by the Kramers. Duffey received the policy from Metropolitan on June 6 or 7, 1978. There was no accompanying correspondence.

On June 8 or 9, 1978, Duffey called the Kramer home to inform them that the policy had been issued. Since Robert Kramer was working late, Duffey could not deliver the policy that evening. The testimony indicates, and this Court finds, that Duffey agreed to call the Kramers the following evening, when Robert Kramer would be home, so that he could arrange to promptly deliver the policy. However, the plaintiff testified at trial that she and her husband remained at home the entire next evening, but Duffey did not call. Duffey, on the other hand, alleged that he did call, but that there was no answer.

Upon careful scrutiny of the conflicting testimony, we find that Duffey did not call the Kramers the night following his telephone conversation with the plaintiff. On June 13, 1978, Duffey finally called the Kramer home to set up an appointment to deliver the policy. However, Robert Kramer died a few hours earlier. Duffey subsequently went to the Kramer home, but refused to deliver the policy to the plaintiff's father because he claimed that it was not in effect.

The outcome of this case turns on the resolution of two issues: (1) whether Metropolitan waived the requirement that the first premium be paid in cash as a condition precedent to the policy becoming effective; and, (2) whether the policy was delivered to the insureds. Regarding the first issue, we have observed above that the Authorization to Honor Checks specifically noted that the initial premium payment had to be made in cash rather than via the Check-O-Matic system. We have made the factual determination that the Kramers did not pay the initial premium. But the plaintiff contends that the actions of Metropolitan and its agent constituted a waiver of this condition precedent....

The general rule is that in the absence of an express provision in the policy to the contrary, the actual prepayment of the premium is neither essential for a contract of insurance to be valid nor a condition precedent to the inception of the policy and the assumption of the risk by the insurer.... However, the requirement of paying the full first premium is not contrary to public policy, and it may therefore serve as a condition precedent to the liability of an insurance company.... While such a condition is valid, it is well settled that

> [a]lthough the insurer may insert conditions in the application, requiring full payment of the first premium and delivery before the policy takes effect, *such conditions are for its own benefit and may be waived*....

It is especially true that courts will look diligently for a waiver where, as here, a forfeiture of the benefits of an insurance policy will otherwise result. "A basic tenet of insurance law proclaims that forfeitures are not favored." ... The preference for waiver over a forfeiture is aptly described in 16A Appleman, *Insurance Law and Practice* § 9082, at 289–91 (1968):

> Courts are always prompt to seize upon any circumstances that indicate an election to waive the forfeiture of a contract of insurance, or any agreement to do so, on which the party has relied and acted. Forfeitures are not favored if there are any circumstances indicating a waiver thereof. Such forfeitures will be enforced only where there is the clearest evidence that such was the intention of the parties, and slight circumstances are sufficient to indicate the intention of the insurer to effect a waiver.

In the case at bar, the plaintiff urges that Metropolitan impliedly waived the required cash payment of the first premium as a result of its agent's refusal to take it when offered, and the subsequent withdrawal of four premium payments from the Kramers' checking account by the Check-O-Matic device. It is undisputed that after the Kramers' family life insurance policy was put into Metropolitan's Check-O-Matic system and the Authorization to Honor Checks was sent to Heritage Bank, and after Robert Kramer's death, ... checks were issued and charged to the Kramer account. ...

We are not convinced by Metropolitan's argument that a clerical error caused the placement of the Kramer policy into the Check-O-matic system. This is not to say that Metropolitan purposefully took the next step, *i.e.,* withdrawing premium payments from the Kramer account after Robert Kramer's death. Although we do not believe that Metropolitan intended to deny coverage and then surreptitiously continue to withdraw premiums indefinitely, it is clear that in its normal course of business it placed itself in a position whereby the payment of the *first premium* could be collected by the Check-O-Matic system. Metropolitan was aware that Duffey did not receive an initial premium from the Kramers, yet it allowed the Kramer policy to be inserted into the Check-O-Matic device. ...

We now turn to the issue of whether the policy was delivered to the Kramers. The application for insurance provides that Metropolitan

> will incur no liability by reason of this application *until a policy has been delivered* and the full first premium specified therein has actually been paid to and accepted by (Metropolitan). Upon such delivery and payment, the policy will be effective as of its date of *issue*—but only if, at the time of such delivery, the Proposed Insured and each other person to be insured [are] in the same condition of health as that represented in the application and has not consulted with or been attended or examined by a physician or other practitioner since the completion of the application. (Emphasis supplied.)

Although Metropolitan sent the policy to its agent Duffey, it is uncontroverted that it was never actually delivered to the Kramers. The question remains, however, whether the delivery to Duffey was a constructive delivery to the Kramers. It is a long recognized rule of insurance law that delivery of a policy to an agent for the purpose of delivering it to a prospective insured is tantamount to actual delivery to that prospective insured.... However, it is equally well settled that this principle of constructive delivery "does not operate where a condition was attached to the delivery to the agent which is binding upon the applicant or is such that it must be met by him."...

In the case at bar, even though we have found that the condition of paying the first premium in cash was waived by Metropolitan, the delivery of the policy to Duffey was not automatic delivery to the Kramers because of another condition in the application, emphasized in the quotation above, which requires that the insureds be in the same state of health at the time of delivery as they were in at the time of the application. Duffey had no authority to deliver the policy to the Kramers without first determining their state of health. Therefore, the mere delivery to Duffey was not constructive delivery to the Kramers. However, constructive delivery may still be found if the failure to actually deliver the policy to the insured was caused by the negligence of the agent who had possession of the policy.

We find persuasive authority for this position in the well reasoned opinion of the Washington Supreme Court in *Frye v. Prudential Insurance Company of America*, 157 Wash. 88, 288 P. 262 (1930), which states that:

> Authorities are to be found where the claim of constructive delivery has been sustained under the particular facts shown in special cases in which the local agent, through whom the application was made, having received a policy for conditional delivery, after ample time and opportunity in which to act, neglected or failed to make the delivery....

157 Wash. at 93, 288 P. at 264....

This Court finds that Metropolitan's agent, Duffey, had ample time and opportunity to deliver the family life insurance policy to the Kramers, but he did not do so. We therefore find that the policy was constructively delivered to the Kramers, and since the cash payment of the first premium was waived, that its provisions must be enforced. Plaintiff shall recover compensatory damages in the amount of $20,000, together with interest from June 13, 1978, to the date of payment. The insurance under the policy shall continue for the balance of its term on the life of the plaintiff without further premium payments....

The defendants are responsible to the plaintiff for the reasonable costs of this action. We deny plaintiff's request for the assessment of punitive damages against the defendants. Their challenge of the payment of benefits in this case did not represent such egregious conduct as to warrant their punishment.... And, while Metropolitan's taking of four premium payments subsequent to Robert Kramer's death was clearly negligent, we do not feel that it was willful, wanton or malicious.

## *Notes and Questions*

1. The "constructive delivery" theory is followed by a large number of courts, but there are still jurisdictions that apply a traditional "strict construction" approach to the delivery of the application or policy, as demonstrated in the following excerpt from *Reynolds v. Guarantee Reserve Life Ins. Co.*, 44 Ill. App. 3d 764, 3 Ill. Dec. 397, 358 N.E.2d 940 (1976):

> ... The deceased son of the plaintiffs, Mark Reynolds, executed applications for a life insurance policy and a disability insurance policy with the defendant on September 26, 1974. [The insurance company on October 18 found Mark to be an acceptable risk. Mark was killed on October 22, 1974, prior to delivery of the policy.] The defendant's authorized agent with whom Mark Reynolds dealt was John C. Drew. At this time, Mark Reynolds delivered to John Drew a check in the amount of $29.25 which represented one month's premium on both policies he applied for. Mark named the plaintiffs as policy beneficiaries in the applications. The applications which Mark signed provide, in pertinent part:

> Disability Application

> I also agree that the insurance will not take effect until (1) the application is approved and accepted by the Company at its Home Office, (2) the policy *is delivered* while the health of each proposed covered person and all other conditions remain as described in this application and (3) the first premium has been paid in full. (Emphasis added.)....

> The receipt that Mark Reynolds received in exchange for his check for premiums on the proposed policies states:

> No insurance shall take effect and no liability shall exist *unless and until* the application is approved by the Company and a policy *is issued (a) during the lifetime* and good health of all persons proposed for coverage under a life policy or (b) *while the health* and occupations of all persons proposed for a health policy *are as described in this application*, in which case the policy shall be deemed to take effect on the policy date thereof. (Emphasis added.)

> If the company declines to issue a policy, or issues a policy other than as applied for, which is not accepted upon delivery, the amount receipted above will be refunded by the company upon surrender of this receipt....

> An application for insurance is a mere offer; it creates no rights and imposes no duty on the insurer.... The parties to an application for insurance are competent to make any provision for the effective date of insurance.... Such provision may be the issuance of the policy, the date of delivery of the policy or the date of acceptance of the policy by the applicant and is binding and not contrary to public policy.... Where the application and receipt in connection with an application for insurance provide, no insurance will be

effective until a policy is issued or delivered, no contract of insurance is created where the applicant dies prior to the time such conditions are performed. . . .

Applying the principles above to the applications, receipt and facts in the instant case, it is apparent that no contract of insurance was in effect prior to the death of plaintiffs' son Mark. The applications constituted mere offers; the conditions precedent to the insurance policies taking effect had not been performed prior to Mark's death.

The plaintiffs' final contention is that it is unconscionable for the defendant to take a check from the proposed insured, cash it for its own use and refuse to provide any coverage to the proposed insured in return. There is no merit to this contention. It is not conduct that is harsh or shocking to the conscience for an insurance company to accept prepayment of premiums for proposed policies of insurance which clearly will not provide coverage until issued or delivered where the receipt for that prepayment expressly contains a provision that if the company declines to issue a policy the amount received will be refunded. . . . The language of the agreement is controlling. . . .

For the foregoing reasons, the judgment of the circuit court . . . granting defendant's motion for summary judgment is affirmed.

*Query*: Which is the better reasoned theory? Why?

### PROBLEM FOUR

Plaintiff Megee applied for a disability insurance policy with the United States Fidelity and Guaranty Insurance Company. The policy application stated that the insurance company would be liable only "when the policy is delivered and the first policy premium paid during the lifetime of and while the health of the person proposed for insurance is as here described on the policy date."

Megee's application for insurance was approved by the insurer, and the policy was sent to the agent for delivery to the applicant. On the day the agent received the policy, but prior to delivering the policy to Megee, however, Megee was disabled in an accident at work. Thereafter, Megee attempted to pay his first premium, which had not been submitted with his application since Megee wanted to see what the policy coverage was before paying for it. Megee argued that he had coverage under the insurance policy which had been constructively delivered to him, since the approved policy was already in the agent's hands.

• How should the court decide this case?

## [B] Payment of Premiums

### [1] Mode of Payment

Normally the mode of payment for an insurance premium is in cash, or as provided for in the insurance contract, or as mandated by state statute. It is also normal procedure for the insurance company or its agent to receive a check as the premium payment. But what happens if the check is not honored by the bank?

The courts have split on this issue. Some courts have held that if the insurer elects to accept a check as a premium payment, but the check is not honored by the bank, nonpayment on the check merely entitles the insurer to seek recovery from the drawer of the check, but the insurer cannot cancel the policy based on the dishonored check. *See, e.g., Statewide Ins. Corp. v. Dewar*, 694 P.2d 1167 (Ariz. 1984). Other courts, however, have held that a check is only a conditional payment, and if the check is dishonored by the bank, the premium has not been paid and the insurer can cancel the policy. *See, e.g., Snowden v. United of Omaha Life Ins. Co.*, 450 So. 2d 731 (La. Ct. App. 1984).

## [2] *Time of Payment*

The date when an insurance premium is due is normally determined by examining the insurance policy itself, since the date specified in the contract is binding on the parties, and must be enforced by the court. *See, e.g., D & P Terminal, Inc. v. Western Life Ins. Co.*, 368 F.2d 743 (8th Cir. 1966). But when an insurance policy contains inconsistent provisions as to the effective date of premium payment, or when what is stated in the policy differs from the later date of approval, acceptance, or delivery of the policy, should these ambiguities be resolved in favor of the insurer of the insured? *See, e.g., Life Ins. Co. v. Overstreet*, 603 S.W.2d 780 (Tex. 1980) (majority and dissenting opinions).

What should be the test for determining such possible "ambiguities" or "inconsistencies" in the policy regarding time of payment? What if a policyholder completed, signed, and paid an initial premium payment under an insurer's conditional receipt application on December 6, 1993, but the life insurance policy had an "effective date" of December 28, 1993. Which date should prevail? Why? *See Stauffer v. Jackson Nat'l Life Ins. Co.*, 75 F. Supp. 2d 1271 (D. Kan. 1999).

## [3] *Grace Periods*

Every individual life insurance policy, and many other types of accident, health, and disability insurance policies, have a 30- or 31-day grace period for the payment of an overdue premium. Such grace periods generally provide that an insurer cannot forfeit coverage under the policy during a given grace period for failure to pay an insurance premium prior to the end of such grace period. Grace periods were established in recognition that certain enumerated personal insurance policies are often long-term insurance contracts which require additional safeguards against policy forfeiture for nonpayment of premiums. Accordingly, such grace periods in the vast majority of states are now statutorily mandated under applicable state insurance law.

Although grace periods have general applicability to individual life insurance policies, rules applicable to group insurance policies are far more complex and conflicting, often based upon whether or not the group insurance policy is a contributory or noncontributory plan. Policies other than life insurance and its allied lines do not generally provide for a grace period, although it is a common practice with many property and liability insurance companies to set forth a short period of time during which the insured can pay an overdue premium. For additional background information on grace periods generally, *see* JERRY & RICHMOND, UNDERSTANDING INSURANCE LAW § 72 (6th ed. 2018).

### Notes and Questions

1. May an agent of a life insurance company (as opposed to the company itself) legally extend the time to pay the premium past the grace period, or accept late premium payments? *See Slocum v. New York Life Ins. Co.*, 228 U.S. 364 (1913).

2. Although policies other than life insurance do not generally provide for a grace period, may an agent for an automobile insurance company legally bind the company by orally agreeing to extend the time for a premium payment? *See Lapierre v. Maryland Casualty Co.*, 438 N.E.2d 356, 359–60 (Mass. App. Ct. 1982). If fire insurance premiums are paid in installments, and loss occurs after failure to pay an installment, but payment is *then* made and accepted by the insurance company, is the loss covered? *See Home Ins. Co. v. Caudill*, 366 S.W.2d 167 (Ky. 1963).

3. If the premium date or end of the grace period falls on a Sunday or holiday, the majority of jurisdictions hold that the premium may validly be paid on the next business day, absent a contrary provision in the insurance contract.

4. A number of states require grace period provisions in life insurance policies by state statute. Such a statutory grace period is a safeguard for the insured, and generally cannot be waived by the insured in the absence of valuable consideration. *See generally* COUCH ON INSURANCE § 76:50 (3d ed. 1998).

# § 4.07. Cancellation and Renewal of the Insurance Policy

## [A] Cancellation

The general purpose of notice provisions is to prevent the cancellation or nonrenewal of the policyholder's policy without allowing adequate time to obtain other insurance in its place. The form and content of a policy cancellation notice is determined in the policy itself, or by statutory mandate — specifically in the areas of life insurance, fire insurance, and automobile liability insurance. With many other types of insurance, however, it may be unnecessary for the insurance company to give any notice of cancellation to the policyholder.

What reasons must the insurer give to support its cancellation or failure to renew a policy? This would differ widely depending upon the specific type of insurance and varying state statutory regulation, if any. By statute, many life insurance policies, for example, after an initial two-year contestability period has tolled, may only be cancelled for non-payment of the premiums. Fire insurance and automobile liability insurance cancellation and renewal requirements also are normally controlled by statute.

Other insurance policies, however, may be cancelled or rescinded for non-payment of premiums; for a material misrepresentation or concealment in the insurance application; for a breach of warranty in the policy; or for any other good cause. Indeed, there are cases stating that, in some circumstances, the insurer may possess an unqualified right to cancel at any time, and need not give any reason whatsoever for this cancellation or failure to renew.

Cancellation of a policy can also be done by the policyholder. A common example takes place when a policyholder decides to sign up with a new insurer and then directs the old insurer to cancel his or her old policy, and refund the "unearned" premium, or the premium for future coverage through the policy period.

## Wisconsin Housing & Economic Development Authority v. Verex Assurance, Inc.

Wisconsin Supreme Court
159 Wis. 2d 57, 464 N.W.2d 10 (1990)

### Dykman, Judge

Verex Assurance, Inc. (Verex) appeals from a judgment declaring that Verex cannot rescind an insurance policy insuring the Wisconsin Housing and Economic Development Authority (WHEDA) because of alleged misrepresentations in the application process. We conclude that sec. 631.36, Stats., regulates both cancellations and rescissions and therefore affirm.

WHEDA administers the "Home Program," which enables low-income residents to secure low interest mortgage loans. WHEDA purchased the mortgage loan at issue, made by M&I Grootemaat Mortgage Corporation (M&I) to Maria Carrasco on November 28, 1984. Verex issued a primary mortgage insurance policy to M&I covering the Carrasco loan. WHEDA also obtained a mortgage pool insurance policy from Verex, insuring losses not covered by the primary policies. Both the primary and pool coverage by Verex were effective upon closing.

In May of 1985, WHEDA issued a notice of non-monetary default to Carrasco, for failing to occupy the premises. WHEDA notified Verex of the default. WHEDA later obtained a judgment of foreclosure against Carrasco. WHEDA filed a claim with Verex, requesting payment under both policies. On October 31, 1986, Verex notified M&I that it suspected Carrasco had made three misrepresentations in connection with the application for the loan, regarding the down payment, original appraisal and Carrasco's intent to occupy the premises.

In March of 1987, Verex tendered to M&I the premium paid under the primary policy on the Carrasco loan, stating that it was rescinding that policy on the ground of misrepresentation. Verex did not attempt to terminate coverage under the pool policy. However, Verex denied WHEDA's claim under the pool policy as well, contending that M&I was WHEDA's agent and therefore M&I's misrepresentations should be imputed to WHEDA for the purposes of rescinding under the pool policy.

The trial court concluded that, in order to terminate an insurance contract by any means, the insurer must comply with sec. 631.36, Stats. Because Verex did not do so, the trial court found that its attempt to terminate coverage was ineffective. Verex appeals. Section 631.36, Stats., provides, in part:

> (1) Scope of Application. (a) General. Except as otherwise provided in this section or in other statutes or by rule under par. (c), this section applies to all contracts of insurance based on forms which are subject to filing and approval under s. 631.20(1)....
>
> (2) Midterm Cancellation. (a) Permissible Grounds. Except as provided by par. (c) ... no insurance policy may be canceled by the insurer prior to the expiration of the agreed term or one year from the effective date of the policy or renewal, whichever is less, except for failure to pay a premium when due or on grounds stated in the policy, which must be comprehended within one of the following classes:
>
>> 1. Material misrepresentation [in the application];
>>
>> 2. Substantial change in the risk assumed, except to the extent that the insurer should reasonably have foreseen the change or contemplated the risk in writing the contract;
>>
>> 3. Substantial breaches of contractual duties, conditions or warranties [in the policy]; or
>>
>> 4. Attainment of the age specified as the terminal age for coverage.
>
> (b) Notice. No cancellation under par. (a) is effective until at least 10 days after the 1st class mailing or delivery of a written notice to the policyholder.

Verex contends that sec. 631.36, Stats., was intended by the legislature to regulate only cancellation. They assert that sec. 631.36 left untouched the common law remedy of rescission. The cardinal rule in all statutory interpretation is to discern the intent of the legislature.... The primary source of statutory interpretation is the language of the statute itself.... If a statute is plain and unambiguous, a court must apply its plain meaning, without resort to rules of construction.... A statute is ambiguous if reasonable persons could disagree as to its meaning....

"Cancellation" is not defined in sec. 631.36, Stats. It is thus unclear whether the legislature intended this term to include rescission. However, sec. 631.36(1)(e) provides that "[n]othing in this section prevents the *rescission* or reformation of any life or disability insurance contract not otherwise denied by the term of the contract or by any other statute." (Emphasis added.)

We conclude reasonable persons could arrive at different understandings as to whether sec. 631.36, Stats., encompasses rescission. The statute is ambiguous. We therefore turn to extrinsic aids such as the "scope, history, context, subject matter and object of the statute" to discern legislative intent....

A construction that will fulfill the purpose of the statute is favored over a construction that defeats its manifest object.... Section 631.36, Stats., is structured to allow an insurer to cancel for any reason during the first sixty days of the policy, with ten days notice. Sec. 631.36(2)(c). In addition, an insurer may cancel for the following grounds, if stated in the policy: (1) material misrepresentation; (2) substantial change in the risk assumed; (3) substantial breaches of contractual duties, conditions or warranties; or (4) attainment of a specific age. Sec. 631.36(2)(a). Finally, an insurer may cancel a policy issued for a term longer than a year or an indefinite term on its anniversary date, provided the policy contains an anniversary date cancellation clause and notice is given. Sec. 631.36(3).

Verex contends that this statute does not provide an exclusive listing of the methods by which an insurer may terminate coverage. Rather, Verex argues, it only governs when an insurer may cancel the insurance contract. Thus, Verex maintains, it may still terminate the insurance contract under the common law doctrine of rescission. Adoption of Verex's position would, in practical terms, negate the two pervasive objects of sec. 631.36, Stats.: (1) providing comprehensive regulation of the "crazy-quilt" of methods for terminating insurance contracts, and (2) providing assurances of security to purchasers of insurance.

Because the grounds for cancellation of an insurance contract listed in sec. 631.36(2)(a) essentially mirror the grounds for rescission available under the common law, both the notice and reservation of rights provisions of sec.631.36 would, under Verex's interpretation, be surplusage. When faced with the option of giving ten days' notice under sec. 631.36(2)(b) or immediately rescinding the insurance contract *ab initio*, we believe the insurer would almost always opt to rescind. Likewise, it is doubtful insurers would feel any compulsion to reserve their rights in a policy under sec. 631.36(2)(a). Thus, under Verex's interpretation, the common law of rescission rather than the statutory scheme of sec. 631.36 would most frequently be used. This result would hardly fulfill the object of regulating "the subject as broadly as possible rather than attempt to build a crazy-quilt of laws...."

Interpreting a similar statute, one court recently observed that the insurers "have it well within their power to halt the chaos which they fear."... During the first sixty days of the policy, insurers may terminate coverage for any reason with ten days notice. *See* 631.36(2)(c), Stats. If proper notice is given and rights reserved, insurers may also terminate coverage on the anniversary date of the policy, sec. 631.36(3), or for any of the grounds enumerated in sec. 631.36(2)(a), including fraud. *See* sec. 631.36(2)(a)1.

In addition, there is no requirement that an insurer accept an applicant's answers at face value and offer immediate coverage.... Rather, insurers have ample opportunity both prior to and within the initial sixty days of extending coverage to investigate the veracity of the information provided by applicants.

The effective date of coverage under both WHEDA's pool insurance policy and M&I's primary insurance policy was November 28, 1984. Verex did not cancel coverage under either policy during the first sixty days of coverage. Nor did it reserve the right, under the pool policy, to cancel for any of the grounds enumerated in sec. 631.36(2)(a), Stats., or on the policy's anniversary date, pursuant to sec. 631.36(3). In addition, Verex failed to comply with any of the notice provisions of section 631.36 necessary to terminate coverage under either the pool or primary policies. As such, Verex was precluded from terminating either policy.

## Notes and Questions

1. Compare the judicial result in *Verex, supra,* with the following case:

> A prospective insured in a homeowners insurance policy application fraudulently stated that he had suffered no property damage in the last five years. In fact, he had suffered three separate incidents of property loss amounting to tens of thousands of dollars worth of damage.

> The Supreme Court of Pennsylvania held in this case that a section of the Pennsylvania Unfair Insurance Practices Act which prohibits an insurer from cancelling or refusing to renew an insurance policy unless the policy was obtained by fraud did *not* abrogate the insurer's long-standing common law right to rescind a policy *ab initio* in the event that such fraud or misrepresentation by the insured was established, and such a common law remedy of recession *ab initio* was not inconsistent with the purposes of the Act.

*Metropolitan Property & Liability Ins. Co. v. Insurance Comm'r of Commonwealth,* 580 A.2d 300 (Pa. 1990).

*Query*: Can the holdings of these two cases be reconciled with each other regarding the similarities or distinctions between cancellation and rescission of an insurance policy?

On one hand, state public policy would tend to encourage, if not statutorily mandate, that the insurer give proper notice of cancellation to the policyholder rather than cancelling an insurance policy at will and leaving the insured unprotected. On the other hand, shouldn't an insurer have the legitimate right to limit unreasonable underwriting risks—especially when a policyholder fraudulently misrepresents a material fact in the insurance application or breaches a material condition of the policy? *See also Klopp v. Keystone Ins. Cos.,* 595 A.2d 1 (Pa. 1991) (a state statute does not preempt the insurer's common law right to rescind an automobile policy for 60 days after the policy was written); *Ferrell v. Columbia Mut. Ins. Casualty Co.,* 816 S.W.2d 593 (Ark. 1991) (state statute does not preempt the insurer's common law right to rescind coverage when a noncompulsory automobile insurance provision is involved).

2. If a state statute mandates that a notice of cancellation shall be "mailed to the insured" within a certain number of days prior to cancellation, is the actual receipt of this notice required to effectuate the cancellation? *Compare Difalco v. Industrial*

*Fire & Casualty Ins. Co.*, 400 So. 2d 1057 (Fla. Dist. Ct. App. 1981), *with Rocque v. Cooperative Fire Ins. Ass'n*, 438 A.2d 383 (Vt. 1981). How should this proof of cancellation be substantiated or rebutted? Which party has the burden of proof? *See Aultman v. Rinicker*, 416 So. 2d 641 (La. Ct. App. 1982); *Balboa Ins. Co. v. Hunter*, 299 S.E.2d 91 (Ga. Ct. App. 1983).

3. If a policy of insurance has been cancelled or has lapsed, it may still be reinstated or revived if provided for in the policy, or if both parties so agree. But is this reinstated policy a new contract of insurance, or is it merely a continuation of the old contract? Absent a specification in the policy, most courts will treat the reinstated policy as a continuation of the old policy. *See, e.g., Bruegger v. National Old Line Ins. Co.*, 387 F. Supp. 1177 (D. Wyo. 1975). *But see contra Hammond v. Missouri Property Ins. Placement Facility*, 731 S.W.2d 360 (Mo. Ct. App. 1987) (holding that the reinstatement of a lapsed policy constitutes a new contract). *See generally* Jerry & Richmond, Understanding Insurance Law § 62A[d] (6th ed. 2018).

What if the notice sent to the policyholder was ambiguous regarding the insurer's intent to cancel or renew the policy? *See Staley v. Municipal Mut. Ins. Co.*, 282 S.E.2d 56 (W. Va. 1981).

4. In the case of *Reynolds v. Infinity Gen. Ins. Co.*, 694 S.E.2d 337 (Ga. 2010), an automobile insurance company contended that its policy was not in effect on the date of the policyholder's automobile collision, due to a cancellation notice sent to the policyholder for nonpayment of premium. This cancellation notice also provided an opportunity for the policyholder to keep the policy in force by paying the past due premium within a statutory 10-day period, which the policyholder did not exercise. The court held that the cancellation notice was positive and unequivocal evidence that the policy cancellation was occurring, and the mere fact that this cancellation notice contained an option for the policyholder to avoid the imminent cancellation did not alter the clear statement that the policyholder's coverage was being terminated for nonpayment of the premium.

## [B] Policy Renewal

As discussed above, the procedural requirements for cancellation and renewal of life insurance and automobile insurance policies are very heavily regulated by state statute. Yet with many other less regulated kinds of liability and property insurance, the decision whether or not to *renew* the policy is generally left to the contractual intent of the parties themselves, and the insurer generally has an unqualified right to refuse to renew policy coverage, and does *not* need to give any reason whatsoever for its failure to renew the policy. So generally speaking, in the absence of a state statute to the contrary, an insurer is *not* obligated either to notify the insured that the insurance coverage has expired by its own terms, or to renew the coverage automatically.

For example, in the case of *Gahres v. Phico Ins. Co.*, 672 F. Supp. 249 (E.D. Va. 1987), a medical malpractice insurance company failed to win approval from the state insurance commissioner for a rate increase, so the insurer refused to renew its medical malpractice policies when the policies were ready for renewal. When the insured physicians argued that the insurer owed them a "good faith duty" to renew their policies, the court responded that "[w]hen an insurance company exercises its right under a cancellation clause, there is, then existing, a contractual relationship between the parties. By contrast, when an insurance company chooses not to renew a policy, it has already performed the contract [and] there is no obligation that remains or persists beyond the term of the contract." *Id* at 253–254. So, in the absence of such a legislative mandate in the medical malpractice area, the court was unwilling to impose any "good faith duty" on the insurer to renew its medical malpractice policies. *See also Egnatz v. Medical Protective Co.*, 581 N.E.2d 438 (Ind. Ct. App. 1991) ("absent statutory restrictions, an insured may not defeat the insurer's contractual right not to renew a policy by asserting the insurer's exercise of its option [not to renew] was arbitrary and capricious").

If the policyholder and the insurer agree to renew their insurance policy, is the renewed policy a new policy or a continuation of the old policy? Whether the renewal of an insurance policy constitutes a new and independent policy, or a continuation of the original policy, primarily depends on the intention of the parties, as ascertained from the instrument itself. *See, e.g., Reserve Life Ins. Co. v. La Follette*, 323 N.W.2d 173 (Wis. 1982). However, the courts have not been consistent on this matter. *Compare Moreau v. Sanders*, 415 So. 2d 562 (La. Ct. App. 1982) (each subsequent renewal of an insurance policy is a new and separate contract, even though a new policy is not issued), *with Meeker v. Shelter Mut. Ins. Co.*, 766 S.W.2d 733 (Mo. Ct. App. 1989) (renewal of a homeowners policy did not create a new policy, so any misrepresentation by the insured in his previous policy application, if material, would void the policy *ab initio*).

What happens if an insurance policy is renewed, but the new policy contains additional provisions not found in the original policy? The general rule with insurance policy renewal is that, in the absence of any notice or explanation by the insurer that the terms of the policy have been changed, it may be assumed by the policyholder that the same terms and conditions that applied to the old policy will also apply to the new policy. *See, e.g., Brewer v. Vanguard Ins. Co.*, 614 S.W.2d 360 (Tenn. Ct. App. 1980). But how can this general rule on policy renewal be reconciled with the prevailing rule that a policyholder is presumed to have read the terms of his or her policy and assented to its provisions? *See Parris & Son, Inc. v. Campbell*, 196 S.E.2d 334 (Ga. Ct. App. 1973).

Insurers also commonly revise or amend their policies in order to refine language, broaden coverage in response to demand, or restrict coverage due to unwanted new loss exposures. A policyholder who stays with the same insurer for decades may find the policy's scope changing in significant ways even though the policyholder thinks it has had essentially the "same" policy since the inception of the relationship. Normally, insurers cannot alter policy provisions during a given policy period. They must wait until the policy is up for renewal and then may amend the policy language in the course of charging a renewal premium for the ensuing policy period. As a matter of formal contract law, the insurer offers a slightly different insurance policy to the policyholder, who accepts by sending in a premium payment.

Both parties assume the policy is in force and rely on it, although policyholders may be at best only dimly aware of changes in coverage, which are usually outlined in a brochure-like insert to the billing sent for the renewal premium. The insert often states that it is an "Important Notice Regarding Changes To Your Policy" but the common belief is that policyholders do not bother to read it and are unlikely to seek to change insurers even if they notice that coverage has contracted to some degree. Why? Because most laypersons are busy thinking about and doing other things. In addition, they probably assume that most other insurers are making similar changes in their renewal policies, making it unlikely the policyholder could obtain broader coverage from a competing insurer.

Further, the changes may be the type of thing that is unlikely to lead to a coverage problem. For example, a major auto insurer's notice of policy revisions sent to one of the authors informs the policyholder:

> If you buy or lease a new or used car, your car policy will provide coverage for that car as a "newly acquired car" for up to 14 days after you take possession of that car. Previously, the policy provided for up to 30 days of coverage. This change applies to your new or used car whether it replaces an existing car or is an additional car in your household.

The brochure/notice also informs the policyholder that the changes are effective on the renewal date or a set future date, whichever arrives first.

Clearly, the new change gives the policyholder less protection in that it provides a shorter period of "automatic" coverage for a newly purchased vehicle. But is this change worth getting upset about? Not if the policyholder is reasonably diligent in contacting his or her insurance agent within two weeks of the purchase, which seems a reasonable course of conduct even if the car purchase itself was the result of impulse buying. The insurer undoubtedly shortened the time of automatic coverage in order to encourage swifter contact with the agent and swifter payment of the premium on a new policy, which is likely to be larger than the premium paid on the old policy covering the old car.

Regulators and courts generally permit this type of one-sided amendment of policies without much discussion. Rolling changes of this sort in standardized policies are perceived as efficient and unlikely to harm the policyholder except in rare circumstances. But rare circumstances are what make for litigation. What if, for example, the policyholder receiving the language above buys a new car, forgets to call his agent, and is involved in a multiple fatality crash 16 days later? Can the policyholder validly claim that he had an objectively reasonable expectation that his policy provided a month's worth of insurance? Or that the renewal policy was unchanged from the previous year's policy? Does it matter if the automobile purchase and accident straddle the renewal date rather than taking place after the renewal date? Who would likely win this coverage dispute, the policyholder or the insurer?

Although most insurers cannot ordinarily change policy provisions during the midst of the policy period and must wait for renewal, this is not a particularly significant impediment to the insurer. As we have seen, all that is needed by the insurer is a little planning, a printing press, and a renewal premium billing in order to accomplish even substantial changes in policy scope, all usually without any significant risk of losing customers. The conventional wisdom holds that most policyholders do not shop for insurance based on the scope of coverage but instead shop by price. If narrowing coverage keeps premiums in check, the insurer is unlikely to encounter policyholder resistance or flight because the policyholder will ordinarily not appreciate the consequences of a change restricting coverage until after a loss has taken place.

## [C] Lost Policies

How many insurance policies do you have in force? Do you have any idea where they are? Could you produce them? What if the insurer claimed never to have issued the policy you claim you have? In most personal lines of insurance, the policyholder deals somewhat regularly with an agent (or at least with an 800 number operator or online avatar in an e-chat) and presumably expects the agent or company to come up with a copy of the policy if necessary to resolve a coverage question. But what if the agent acts like she's never heard of you or produces a policy that you think is different from what was promised? What would you do?

For personal lines of insurance, where we tend to know the agent or have palpable losses that are contemporaneous with the policy period, the sort of scenario described above seems like something out of the *Twilight Zone*. But it's less farfetched for commercial insurance, where claims may arise years after the time (and policy period) during which the injury to a third party first took place.

In addition, there may have been changes in corporate form by both the commercial policyholder and the insurer. The former Ma & Pa Grocery Store Fraternal Liability Association is now part of InsuranceGiantCo, which has no record of a 1990 policy held by Jack's CornerMart, which has since become part of a national chain that cannot locate a copy of the old Jack's CornerMart policy. But Jack, who retired in 2010 and is still sharp as the metaphorical tack (he knew when to get out of the grocery business, right?) distinctly remembers purchasing general liability insurance every year he ran the store. Is this enough to prove coverage? What else is necessary?

In *City of Sharonville v. American Employers Insurance Co.*, 109 Ohio St. 3d 186, 846 N.E.2d 833 (2006), the Supreme Court of Ohio held that the City and its police officers were still covered for liability in a civil rights action despite being unable to produce the actual liability insurance policy that was allegedly covering the city for liability in 1981. The lawsuit alleged an ongoing conspiracy to cover up a murder. The City was unable to locate the policy but proved that one was in existence at the time because there was reference to it in correspondence between the insurer and City over another lawsuit at around the same time of the alleged wrongdoing in 1981. The Court thus allowed secondary evidence of the existence of insurance.

Today, a modern policyholder might well have a strong cyber-trail of e-documents that could essentially prove the existence of coverage. Bank records, too, might come into play. Does the standardization of insurance policies today make the task easier?

## [D] Transfer of Policies and Policy Rights

In today's fast-paced world of commerce, corporations can be here today and gone tomorrow. Start-ups are sold, shut down, bought out, splinter off, or grow. There are mergers, acquisitions, and a variable list of transfers in the life of a modern company. Acquiring a business has also historically meant that the business' rights under its insurance policies were also transferred — or "assigned" — at least with respect to events that occurred prior to the transfer. Part of any corporate change is the due diligence step whereby all outstanding liabilities of a company are investigated so the purchaser knows what it is getting into with the purchase. Many policies may actually state that the "policyholder" includes not only the named policyholder but its acquisitions and sometimes its successors as well.

However, a number of insurance policies contain clauses which either seek to limit or eliminate entirely the right of a policyholder to assign or transfer its rights under the policy. These "anti-assignment" or "consent-to-assignment" clauses raise issues about the policyholder's right to transfer such things as coverage and a legal defense, as owed under its insurance policy. Most courts permit the transfer of rights under an insurance policy despite these clauses, as long as the loss which is the target of coverage occurred before the transfer of the policy

This issue played out in the California courts, with the top state court eventually deciding to reject the hyper-literalist approach of upholding anti-assignment clauses in insurance. In *Henkel Corp. v. Hartford Accident & Indemn. Co.*, 29 Cal. 4th 934, 129 Cal. Rptr. 2d 828, 62 P.3d 69 (2003), the California Supreme Court upheld the anti-assignment clause so that post-loss assignment of rights under the policy vitiated coverage. This ruling creates serious insurance problems. It limits the available insurance coverage for latent claims against the company, especially those long latency claims like pollution or asbestos. It also frustrates the ability to determine consent to the assignment after the corporation goes through changes throughout the years. This remarkable state of affairs existed for some years in California, until the Court again visited the issue in *Fluor Corp. v. Superior Court*, 288 P.3d 1287, 149 Cal. Rptr. 3d 675 (2015), and effectively reversed its position in *Henkel*, disregarding the anti-assignment language of the policy.

Formalists and textualists would undoubtedly respond that if the policy has an anti-assignment clause, it should be enforced — right? The functionalist answer is that strict application of restrictions on assignment after the fact are economically inefficient and violate the widely accepted public policy that contract rights (like other property rights) should generally be freely alienable so that assets can be transferred to the entity that places most value on the asset. Are you satisfied with the functionalist response? Why or why not?

# § 4.08. Policyholder's Duties Pre-Loss

## [A] Applicant's Representations

### Edwin Patterson,
### *Essentials of Insurance Law*[1]

A representation is a statement made by the applicant for insurance or by someone acting for him and by his authority, to the prospective insurer, before the making of the contract of insurance and not embodied as a term of the contract. If the statement is made a part of the contract, it becomes a warranty and creates a condition of the insurer's promise (if the statement relates to the risk). Since a representation is no part of the contract, it is unaffected by the parol evidence rule..., and it need not be in writing, although the contract itself is in writing. However, under statutes that have been widely enacted in respect to life insurance..., only written representations, a copy of which is attached to the policy, can be used by the insurer as a defense to an action on the policy. Apart from such statutes oral representations are as effective as written ones. Yet the difficulty of proving the insured's statements by word of mouth has made the defense of misrepresentation practicable chiefly in cases where a written application is required of the insured.

A representation has legal consequences only if it is relied upon and thus induces the insurer to make a contract which it would not otherwise have made.... Practically, the representations relied upon in insurance litigation almost always relate to factors directly affecting the risk....

The law of misrepresentation is frequently identified with the law of fraud. This is erroneous. The latter is only a part of the former. A fraudulent misrepresentation is one made by a person who was aware, at the time when he made the statement, that it was false. This fact of awareness is called scienter. In most of the United States, scienter must be proved in order to recover damages for a misrepresentation. At one time in the history of English law, only a fraudulent misrepresentation would be a sufficient ground for rescission. During the nineteenth century, the English courts of equity extended the right of rescission to one who had been misled into a bargain by an innocent misrepresentation and in so doing they called it constructive fraud. Confusion has resulted. Probably in most of the United States an innocent misrepresentation is available as a defense to an action brought upon a contract thus induced. Yet in many courts the confusion persists, with uncertainty in the law....

[T]he doctrine has become established that the test is the *effect* of the misrepresentation upon the insurer, not the *culpability* (fraud or carelessness) of the insured or his agent in making it. The insured speaks at his peril. If he draws unwarranted inferences from accurate data and communicates only the former to the underwriter, his policy is voidable if the difference between data and inference is material. The safest course for the insured or his broker to pursue is to communicate the known data to the insurer and let the latter draw his own inferences. In this case, there will

---

be no misrepresentation. The insured is not responsible for the insurer's mistakes in estimating the risk....

In many branches of insurance where a written application is required, such as liability and burglary, the application is incorporated into the policy by reference..., and the statements of the insured thus become warranties. As the defense of breach of warranty is easier for the insurer to establish than the defense of material misrepresentation, the latter is seldom relied upon in such cases. If the incorporation by reference is defective, the application may still afford a defense on the basis of misrepresentation.

In applying the law of misrepresentation to life insurance, a considerable number of courts have uttered approval of the rule that *only a fraudulent misrepresentation* by the insured will avoid the policy. The law of misrepresentation has thus become unsettled and confused in many jurisdictions. The sources of this confusion are twofold. One is the failure to distinguish between fraud and innocent misrepresentation. Either the court ignores the historical development outlined at the beginning of this section or it intentionally uses "fraud" to include constructive fraud. The other distinction often overlooked is that between statements of fact and statements of opinion. Several leading cases in which the court construed the policy and application as warranting merely the good faith of the insured have been relied upon as establishing the rule that in all cases proof of bad faith is necessary to sustain the defense of misrepresentation. Where the applicant's statement is clearly one of opinion or belief, the insurer must prove fraud as well as materiality. If one eliminates the decisions based on this theory, the doctrine that innocent misrepresentation of material fact suffices to make the policy voidable is still law by the decided weight of authority.

## [B] Distinction between Warranties and Representations

Warranties are distinguished from representations in that:

(a) Warranties are parts of the insurance contract, agreed to be essential; but representations are only collateral inducements to the contract, such as an insurance application ... or a proof of loss statement after loss occurs.

(b) Warranties are always written on the face of the policy, actually or by reference. Representations may be either oral or written in a totally disconnected paper.

(c) Common law warranties are conclusively presumed to be material, but the burden is on the insurer to prove representations are material.

(d) Common law warranties must be strictly complied with, while only substantial truth is required of representations.

Vance on Insurance (3d ed. 1951).

A *warranty* is a written statement or condition appearing in the insurance policy itself or incorporated by reference, whereas a *representation* is an oral or written statement which *precedes* the policy of insurance, and which relates to the facts necessary to enable an insurance company to decide whether or not to accept the risk, and at what premium. And although the literal truth of a common law warranty is essential to the validity of the insurance policy, substantial truth and materiality is the test for a representation or statutory warranty. *See generally* Couch on Insurance §§ 82:21, 82:34 (3d ed. 2010). *See also* Jerry & Richmond, Understanding Insurance Law § 102 (6th ed. 2018); Keeton & Widiss, Insurance Law § 5.7 (1988).

## [C] Common Issues with Applicant Representations

### [1] *Innocent versus Deceitful Misrepresentations*

Almost all courts hold that a fraudulent misrepresentation will make the insurance policy voidable because "fraud vitiates all contracts." *See, e.g., Claflin v. Commonwealth Ins. Co.,* 110 U.S. 81, 3 S. Ct. 507, 28 L. Ed. 76 (1884). *See also Chism v. Protective Life Ins. Co.,* 290 Kan. 645, 234 P.3d 780 (2010) (holding that an insurer has the right to rescind an insurance policy *ab initio* for fraudulent misrepresentations in the application process). *See, e.g., Harper v. Fid. & Guar. Life Ins. Co.,* 234 P.3d 1211 (Wyo. 2010) (holding that innocent or negligent misrepresentations made in a life insurance application also would allow the insurer to rescind the policy *ab initio* during the two-year contestability period for life insurance contracts).

The elements of fraudulent misrepresentations generally include, in addition to a knowingly false representation, reliance and injury by the insurance company. Some courts in jurisdictions requiring materiality hold that materiality will be implied from the fraudulent purpose. Others hold that when a misrepresentation is fraudulently made, it is *not* necessary to determine whether that misrepresentation is material — the critical issues being whether the misrepresentation affected risk or the insurer's judgment.

The general rule in many states, however, is that even though a misrepresentation made in an insurance application is not "wilfully false or fraudulently made," if it is material to the risk of loss, it may nevertheless void the policy at the option of the insurer. So, in these jurisdictions, a material misrepresentation of fact in an insurance application, even if made in good faith, or as a result of negligence or ignorance, may *still* void the insurance policy if the insurer relies on it. Thus, in most states, actual fraud need not be established if the innocent misrepresentation was material to the risk, and was relied upon by the insurer. *See generally* Jerry & Richmond, Understanding Insurance Law § 102[a] (6th ed. 2018).

Some commentators have argued that the insurance company's traditional rescission remedy for innocent misrepresentations of fact in the insurance application overcompensates insurance companies, and that rescission allows insurers to refuse benefits to people who make innocent misrepresentations in their insurance application, even while retaining the premiums of similarly situated insureds who never file claims.

*See, e.g.*, Brian Barnes, *Against Insurance Rescission*, 120 Yale L.J. 330 (2010). Nevertheless, this common law rescission remedy based on a policyholer's misrepresentation of material facts in the insurance application is still widely recognized in the vast majority of American states.

## PROBLEM FIVE

Joseph Harper, the husband of appellant Gail Harper, purchased a life insurance policy from the Fidelity and Guaranty Life Insurance Company, and died two months after purchasing the policy. Fidelity's life insurance application required that Mr. Harper answer a number of questions about his health and health history. He represented on his application that he had never sought or received medical treatment, advice, or counseling for the use of alcohol. In light of Mr. Harper's death, within the life insurance company's two-year "contestability period," Fidelity reviewed Mr. Harper's medical records, and found that there were various medical conditions—including a history of severe alcohol abuse—that had not been disclosed on his application, and in Fidelity's estimation, were material to the issuance of the life insurance policy. Fidelity then rescinded Mr. Harper's policy coverage *ab initio*, and returned his premium payment to Mrs. Harper.

Mrs. Harper argues that Fidelity had a duty to further investigate Mr. Harper's answers on his insurance application, and that Fidelity should have obtained his medical records rather than rely on his answers in the insurance application itself. Fidelity, however, disputes the assertion that it was under any duty to investigate the answers Mr. Harper gave in his application when the application was submitted, especially because Fidelity had no reason to assume that the answers were not truthful or accurate.

• How should the court resolve this dispute?

• What about Mrs. Harper's allegations that the insurer should be estopped to deny coverage, and that the insurer was guilty of "post-claim underwriting" to defeat coverage, and that Fidelity "breached the covenant of good faith and fair dealing by denying benefits under the policy without any reasonable or fairly debatable basis, and by failing to fully and properly investigate"?

## *[2] Continuing Duty of Disclosure*

Although the application for insurance presents something of a "snapshot" of the facts affecting the risk at the time of the application, the insurer often structures the contracting process to require that the applicant notify the insurer if any material facts have changed. To take an obvious and macabre example, the representative of an applicant for life insurance should ordinarily tell the insurer that the applicant has died during the processing of the application rather than waiting for the issuance of the policy and then claiming post hoc death benefits. (Even this obvious a rule may have exceptions; if the insurer inordinately delayed issuing the policy, the applicant's estate may under some circumstances have a valid claim to benefits.) *See also Western Fire Ins. Co. v. Moss*, 11 Ill. App. 3d 802, 298 N.E.2d 304 (1973) (agent for applicant for boat owners insurance failed to disclose that boat was in tragic collision with river barge during pendency of application; insurer issued policy unaware of accident and was able to avoid payment due to lack of disclosure):

> It is now settled law in this State that a recovery may be had on a policy of insurance against a loss occurring prior to the issuance of the policy provided that neither the insured nor the insurer knew of the loss when the contract was made. *Burch v. Commonwealth County Mutual Ins. Co.*, 450 S.W.2d 838 (Tex. Sup. 1970)....
>
> We therefore conclude that Moss' insurance broker, Kamberos, was his agent, not only for the mailing of the application, but also for the ultimate procurement of a liability policy on his boat and motor; that shortly after mailing said application and days before it was received or processed Kamberos learned from his secretary that there had been an "occurrence," which he did not investigate or report to Western Fire or its agent Buschbach; that during the pendency of that application Kamberos, as Moss' agent for the procurement of the policy, was under a continuing duty to advise Western Fire or its agent Buschbach that there had been an "occurrence" (actually a fatal accident), which certainly was a change materially affecting the risk, and that his lack of knowledge of the details of said "occurrence" does not excuse the failure which constitutes, in law, a concealment or a fraud upon the insurance company, which had no hint of the fatal collision when it issued the policy; that this concealment or fraud vitiates the policy and bars any recovery as against the insurance company; and that, certainly, under Illinois law and probably generally, this is true, even though the policy was predated to be effective before the policy was actually issued.

The *Moss* case quoted above provides an excellent example of the inter-relationship of various factual and legal issues inherent in an insurance law problem, and how the court attempts to deal with them.

The major principle of required disclosure of material intervening facts during an application period is often referred to as "the *Stipcich* Rule," after *Stipcich v. Metropolitan Life Ins. Co.*, 277 U.S. 311, 48 S. Ct. 512, 72 L. Ed. 895 (1928). There, the United States Supreme Court declared that an insurance applicant has an affirmative duty to disclose any new material facts to the insurance company that occur *after* he has submitted his application, but *before* the policy is issued. If he or she fails to make this disclosure, the insurance company may, despite its prior acceptance of the application, void the policy. This rule is generally followed in life insurance cases, where the issue comes up most frequently.

The *Stipcich* Rule also covers innocent misrepresentations if they are material. It is distinguished from the doctrine of concealment in that concealment refers to undisclosed facts known to the applicant at the time of the application for insurance. The *Stipcich* Rule, on the other hand, applies to facts that become known to the policyholder after the application, but before the insurance contract becomes complete.

Another case interpreting the continuing duty of full disclosure was *Fidelity and Deposit Co. v. Hudson United Bank*, 653 F.2d 766 (3d Cir. 1981). In this case, the insured bank had procured two consecutive fidelity insurance bonds, the first from Employers Mutual (Employers), and the second from Fidelity and Deposit (F&D). In January of 1976, while covered under the Employers bond, the bank applied for a new bond from F&D to provide coverage when the Employers bond expired. Shortly after submitting this application, the bank's president found evidence of possible employee "incompetence" concerning the granting of large commercial loans. These loans had been recommended by a new loan officer-vice president. Some of the vice president's actions were "not in accord with general banking practice."

Eventually, the bank realized large losses on these loans. The president recommended that the vice president be discharged due to his incompetence. The bank sent letters, explaining the losses and denying knowledge of any intentional wrongdoing by the bank's officers, to the F&D and to Employers. The letter to Employers indicated that it felt that it had no claim for employee dishonesty under the bond, and requested confirmation. Employers replied that there was no basis for such a claim. In March, the bank informed F&D that a "possible pending fraud claim" had been brought to Employers' attention. Despite this warning, F&D issued a new fidelity bond to the bank at the expiration of the Employers bond in May 1976.

In November, the bank filed claims under the employee fidelity provisions of both of the bonds in respect to the loans made by the vice president and other losses. Employers settled out of court. F&D cancelled their bond in April 1977, but allowed the bank to purchase continuing coverage under a 12-month rider. During 1977, the bank discovered many other losses and filed claims for these with F&D. In January 1978, F&D filed suit to have the bond rescinded *ab initio*. The New Jersey District Court found for F&D and granted the recission. The insured bank appealed.

The United States Court of Appeals reversed. The opinion by Chief Judge Seitz held that the bank had not intended to defraud F&D and that it had "no actual knowledge of [the vice president's] alleged dishonesty before the effective date of the F&D bond. Therefore, F&D is entitled to rescind only if the bank can be charged as a matter of law with having had sufficient constructive knowledge of [the vice president's] alleged dishonesty before the effective date of the bond to impose upon it a duty to notify F&D." The court noted that a bank is held to have "discovered" a loss only when it has "sufficient knowledge of specific dishonest acts to justify a careful and prudent person in charging another with dishonesty or fraud.... Mere suspicion of dishonesty or wrongdoing is not enough." The fact that the bank had informed Employers of a "possible pending fraud claim" was not enough to establish the requisite knowledge of dishonesty. Furthermore, because the bank had informed F&D that there was a "possible pending fraud claim," F&D "bore the burden of requesting supplemental information from the bank."

## [3] The Test of Materiality

Under both the common law and statutory provisions, a misrepresentation generally will not void an insurance policy unless it is material. Thus, the determination whether a statement is material or not is of crucial importance. Unfortunately, the test for materiality is far from uniform. According to Professor Vance, the test of materiality is in the *effect* the representation would have on the parties in the making of the bargain. To be material, this fact need not increase the risk, nor contribute to any loss or damage suffered. It is sufficient that the true knowledge of the statement in question would have *influenced* the parties in making the bargain. VANCE ON INSURANCE 375–76 (3d ed. 1951). Professor Vance's test of materiality remains the traditional minority view today, and is *not* the better-reasoned view. *Query*: Why not? In a widely quoted leading opinion, *Penn Mut. Life Ins. Co. v. Mechanics' Sav. Bank & Trust Co.*, 72 F. 413, 430 (6th Cir. 1896), Judge Taft suggested this form of question as a test of materiality:

> Are you able to say, from your knowledge of the practice and usage among life insurance companies generally that information of this fact would have enhanced the premium to be charged, or would have led to a rejection of the risk?

The test of materiality, according to Taft was therefore the test of a "reasonably prudent insurer" in the community—whether such an insurer would have increased the premium or rejected the risk, had the true facts been known. *See also Burnham v. Bankers Life & Casualty Co.*, 24 Utah 2d 277, 470 P.2d 261 (1970). Judge Taft's test for materiality, as enunciated in the *Penn Mutual Life Insurance* case, is probably the majority and better-reasoned view of materiality today. *See, e.g.*, *Nappier v. Allstate Ins. Co.*, 961 F.2d 168, 170 (11th Cir. 1992) ("A material misrepresentation is one that would influence a prudent insurer in deciding whether to assume the risk of providing coverage.").

Professor Wigmore, however, uses a "particular-insurer standard" to test materiality by asking: Is the misrepresentation in question "one which would have influenced the [particular] insurer ... to fix a higher rate of premium or to refuse the insurance altogether"? 7 WIGMORE ON EVIDENCE § 1946. Secondarily, Wigmore would question the usage of insurers in the same community. Professor Wigmore's test of materiality, however, could tend to reward a capricious "particular insurer" who might employ some questionable or unreasonable underwriting standards not shared by other "prudent insurers" in the community.

Another leading opinion regarding the test of materiality is that of Judge Richman in the case of *New York Life Ins. Co. v. Kuhlenschmidt*, 33 N.E.2d 340, 347 (Ind. 1941), where the question to the expert witness is whether "the facts if truly stated *might* reasonably have influenced the company in deciding whether it should reject or accept the risk" or charge a substantially higher premium. (Emphasis added.) This test of materiality is also less than satisfactory, since an insurance company, attempting to avoid its policy coverage in hindsight, "might" be influenced by just about anything.

To make matters worse, according to Professor Keeton, "it has not been common for statutory draftsmen to express a clear choice among the various possible standards concerning the point of view from which materiality is determined." *See* KEETON & WIDISS, INSURANCE LAW § 5.7 (1988). *See also* JERRY & RICHMOND, UNDERSTANDING INSURANCE LAW § 102[d] (6th ed. 2018).

## *Notes and Questions*

1. Many courts define materiality in terms of whether the insurer would have rejected the risk of loss or charged a substantially higher premium. *See, e.g., Hatch v. Woodmen Accident & Life Co.*, 88 Ill. App. 3d 36, 409 N.E.2d 540 (1980). But some courts still apply Professor Vance's test and hold that materiality exists whenever the true facts would have "influenced" the parties in making the contract. VANCE ON INSURANCE 375–76 (3d ed. 1951).

2. Even though a majority of courts have characterized materiality as relating to an increased risk of loss, these courts still split as to whether a material misrepresentation *would* have influenced the insurer to reject the risk of loss or charge a substantially higher premium; or whether it *might* have influenced the insurer to reject the risk of loss or charge a substantially higher premium. *Compare Billington v. Prudential Ins. Co.*, 254 F.2d 428 (7th Cir. 1958) (applying Indiana law), *and New York Life Ins. Co. v. Kuhlenschmidt*, 218 Ind. 404, 33 N.E.2d 340, 346–47 (1941), *with Scroggs v. Northwestern Mut. Life Ins. Corp.*, 176 Cal. App. 2d 300, 1 Cal. Rptr. 189 (1959).

3. If a material misrepresentation in an insurance application may indeed void the policy coverage, what would prevent an unscrupulous insurance agent from concealing or falsifying material facts in the application to the detriment of the prospective policyholder? What would prevent an insurance agent or prospective policyholder, both acting in good faith, from making innocent but material misrepresentations in the application that may void the entire policy?

To help alleviate these problems, most states now require by statute that a copy of any life insurance application be attached to the policy. According to Professor Patterson, the reason for these "entire-contract" statutes is two-fold: (1) to abolish the technical common law doctrine of warranties vs. representations with respect to any statement made by the applicant in applying for life insurance; and (2) to require the insurer to furnish the applicant with a copy of all statements made by the applicant that might thereafter be relied upon by the insurer for voiding the policy. This attached copy at least gives the insured an *opportunity* to correct any errors in his application, and the courts have generally interpreted "entire-contract" statutes in accordance with this purpose. In addition, the courts have construed these "entire-contract" statutes as requiring the exclusion of proof by the insurer of any misrepresentations made by the insured in an application *not* attached to the policy. *See* PATTERSON, ESSENTIALS OF INSURANCE LAW 438–39 (2d ed. 1957).

4. Does the applicant have the duty to read the insurance application and policy? According to the court in the case of *Minsker v. John Hancock Mut. Life Ins. Co.*, 254 N.Y. 333, 173 N.E. 4 (1930):

> When an insured receives a policy, it is his duty to read it or have it read, and, if an application incorporated therein does not contain correct answers to the questions asked ... it is his duty to have it corrected. In such circumstances a recovery will no longer be permitted because the medical examiner incorrectly recorded the applicant's answers or because the insured was unable to read or neglected to read the policy.

5. A rather unique standard of materiality has been expressed in this way: "The fact that a specific answer is sought by the insurer ... makes that answer material." *Faulkiner v. Equitable Life Ins. Co.*, 144 W. Va. 193, 107 S.E.2d 360 (1959). But doesn't this troublesome view imply that if the insurer chooses to ask irrelevant or immaterial questions in the insurance application they then may "become" material, and an untrue answer will avoid the policy? Mercifully, this is *not* the majority approach to materiality in most jurisdictions.

*Query*: In light of these various tests for materiality, how would you, as an attorney for a national insurance company, counsel your client on how he or she should attempt to prove a material misrepresentation in court?

### PROBLEM SIX

In an application for life insurance, the policyholder identified the beneficiary as his wife. Unknown to both the policyholder and his "wife," her divorce from a prior husband was invalid, and thus her marriage to the policyholder was null and void. When the policyholder later died from a gunshot wound, the Prudential Insurance Company denied liability on the ground that the policyholder had materially misrepresented his marital status in the insurance application. He was "living together, unmarried" which was a "poor risk" according to Prudential, and it brought evidence into court showing that the company does not issue life insurance policies to applicants who cohabit or live together in an unmarried state.

The relevant state statute provided that "no statement in [an insurance] application ... shall bar a recovery ... unless ... such statement was material to the risk ... and was untrue."

- Should Prudential be liable on its policy, or was there material misrepresentation?

## [4] *Insurer's Reliance on the Applicant's Misrepresentation*

In order to constitute a ground for avoiding the insurance policy, a misrepresentation must have been *relied upon* by the insurer. *See, e.g.*, *Adams v. National Casualty Co.*, 307 P.2d 542 (Okla. 1957); *Zogg v. Bankers' Life Co.*, 62 F.2d 575 (4th Cir. 1933). Thus, a misrepresentation in an insurance application will *not* avoid the policy if the insurer had actual knowledge of the true facts or the falsity of the applicant's statements, or had enough notice to begin a reasonable inquiry to ascertain the true facts. *See, e.g., Union Ins. Exchange Inc. v. Gaul*, 393 F.2d 151 (7th Cir. 1968).

What is the effect of an independent investigation by the insurance company to test the truth of the representations made by the applicant? If the insurer makes a routine independent investigation, this may not in itself prevent the insurance company from avoiding the policy because of material misrepresentation in the application, especially when these investigations are mostly "fishing expeditions." *See New York Life Ins. Co. v. Strudel*, 243 F.2d 90 (5th Cir. 1957). But when the insurer's independent investigation either discloses the false representations, or discloses facts which place upon the insurance company the duty to investigate further, then the insurance company may *not* avoid the policy for material misrepresentations in the application. *See, e.g., John Hancock Mut. Life Ins. Co. v. Cronin*, 139 N.J. Eq. 392, 51 A.2d 2 (1947). *See also* Annot., 169 A.L.R. 361, 363 (1947).

## [5] *Incontestability Provisions*

Many statutes now require life insurance policies to contain certain provisions which are commonly called "incontestable clauses." The following passage from *Powell v. Mutual Life Ins. Co.*, 313 Ill. 161, 164–65, 144 N.E. 825, 826 (1924), explains the function of the "incontestable clause" and its relation to misrepresentations:

> Clauses in life insurance policies known as "incontestable clauses" are in general use, and in this state ( ... ) and in other states are now required by statute. In the earlier development of insurance contracts it not infrequently occurred that, after the insured had paid premiums for a large number of years, the beneficiaries under the policy found, after the maturity thereof by the death of the insured, that they were facing a lawsuit in order to recover the insurance; that in certain answers in the application it was said by the insurer that the insured had made statements which were not true, and the beneficiaries were not entitled to recover on the policy. It is needless to call attention to the fact that this situation gave rise to a widespread suspicion in the minds of the public that an insurance contract was designed largely for the benefit of the company. Recognizing this fact, and seeing the effect of it on the insurance business, numerous insurance companies inserted in their policies what is now known as an incontestable clause.... The incontestable clause now in general use is to the effect that the policy shall be incontestable after a certain period, as one or two years, except for defenses recited therein. Such a clause is generally upheld as valid, because it gives to the insurer a reasonable time in which to discover fraud, if there be such, in the securing of the insurance contract.

Incontestable clauses are favored under the law and, if ambiguous, courts tend to construe them in favor of the policyholder. *Mutual Life Ins. Co. v. Hurni Packing Co.*, 263 U.S. 167 (1923). A state statute dealing with incontestable clauses cannot be waived or contracted away by the parties. *See* Annot., 9 A.L.R.2d 1436, 1461. Further discussion of the operation and interpretation of incontestability clauses is found in

Chapter 12 concerning Life, Health, and Disability Insurance, particularly in the excerpt from *Amex Life Assurance Co. v. Superior Court*, 930 P.2d 1264 (Cal. 1997).

## [6] Concealment

## D.M. McGill, *Life Insurance*[2]

The doctrine of concealment is the final legal defense of the insurance company in its efforts to avoid liability under a contract which was obtained through the misrepresentations or concealment of material facts. Of the three basic grounds for avoidance, concealment is the narrowest in scope and the most difficult to prove....

In general law, concealment connotes an affirmative act to hide the existence of a material fact. In insurance law, however, a concealment is essentially a nondisclosure; it is the failure of the applicant for insurance to communicate to the insurer his knowledge of a material fact that the insurer does not possess.

It is general law of longstanding custom that one party to a contract is under no legal obligation during the period of negotiation to disclose to the other party information which the first party knows is not known to the second party and, if known, would be deemed material to the contract. The rationale of this rule is that prices in the market place should be set by the best-informed buyers and sellers; and as a reward for performing this economic function, such persons should be permitted to profit by their special knowledge of affairs. For some years, however, there has been a marked trend in the other direction....

In insurance, the law of concealment, [like the law of warranties and misrepresentations], developed during the eighteenth century out of cases involving marine insurance, and the law still reflects the conditions of that period. The relative inaccessibility of the property to be insured and the poor communication facilities, combined with the aleatory nature of the contract, caused Lord Mansfield, the father of English commercial and insurance law, to hold that the applicant for insurance was required by good faith to disclose to the insurer all facts known to him that would materially affect the insurer's decision as to acceptance of the risk, the amount of the premium, or other essential terms of the contract, whether or not the applicant was aware of the materiality of the facts. Even though conditions affecting marine insurance have changed, the law has not. The person seeking marine insurance today, whether he be the shipowner or shipper, must disclose all material facts in his possession to the insurer; and failure to do so, even though innocent, will permit the insurer to void the contract. Under the British Marine Insurance Act, enacted in 1906, the applicant is even "deemed to know every circumstance which, in the ordinary course of business, ought to be known by him."[3]

In English law, the doctrine of innocent concealment is strictly applied to all branches of insurance. In the United States, it is applied only to marine insurance. The American courts have felt that the circumstances surrounding fire and life in-

---

2. Copyright © 1967.
3. [1] 6 Edw. VII, Chap. 41, Sec. 18(1).

surance are so different from those obtaining marine insurance—particularly in 1766, when the marine rule originated—that a different rule is justified. Under American law, except for marine insurance, a concealment will permit the insurer to void the contract only if the applicant, in refraining from disclosure, had a fraudulent intent.[4] In other words, *except for marine insurance, a concealment must be both material and fraudulent.* In marine insurance, it need only be material.

The doctrine of concealment may be regarded as a special manifestation of the doctrine of misrepresentation. The relationship between a misrepresentation and a concealment has been compared with that existing between the heads and tails of a coin. If a misrepresentation is the heads of a coin, a concealment is the tails. One is affirmative; the other is negative. A concealment is misrepresentation by silence. It has legal consequences for the same reason that a misrepresentation does—namely, that the insurer was misled into making a contract that it would not have made had it known the facts. Hence, the general concept of materiality applied to a concealment is the same as that applicable to a misrepresentation: the effect on the underwriting decision of the insurer. "Fraudulent intent" is a subjective concept difficult to prove; many courts take the attitude that if the fact not disclosed by the applicant was *palpably material*, this is sufficient proof of fraud.[5] Experts are occasionally called upon to testify as to the materiality of a concealed fact; but in those cases settled in favor of the insurer, the judge has usually decided from his own knowledge that the fact concealed was palpably material.

The palpable materiality test is applied to the applicant's knowledge of materiality, while both the prudent-insurer and individual-insurer tests of materiality apply only to the *effect* on the insurer. In concealment cases, which are governed by statutes only in California and states that have adopted its laws, the prudent-insurer test seems to be the prevailing one.

———————

For additional information on concealment in insurance law, *see generally* Jerry & Richmond, Understanding Insurance Law § 103 (6th ed. 2018); Keeton & Widiss, Insurance Law § 5.8 (1988). *See also* Couch Cyclopedia of Insurance Law §§ 81:22–81:23, 84:1–84:25, 99:1–99:10 (3d ed. 2010).

## [7] *Concealment versus Misrepresentation*

Courts often lack precision in discussing misrepresentation and concealment defenses by an insurer. For example, in *O'Riordan v. Federal Kemper Life Assurance Co.*, 114 P.3d 753, 755 (Cal. 2005), the court speaks of whether a life insurance applicant "concealed" a history of smoking, although the case could be analyzed as a misrep-

———————

4. [2] This is not true in California. The Insurance Code (Section 330) of that state provides that "concealment, whether intentional or unintentional," entitles the insurer to rescind the contract.

5. [3] If the undisclosed fact is palpably material—that is, if its importance would be obvious to a person of ordinary understanding it can be inferred that the applicant was aware of its materiality, an essential element in fraud.

resentation problem, specifically whether the applicant answered truthfully when the insurer asked whether the applicant had "smoked cigarettes in the past 36 months."

The Court concluded that the applicant's negative answer did not bar coverage as a matter of law even though a post-death examination of medical records reflected some more recent tobacco use, arguably making the applicant's statement false (although the insurer obtained blood and urine samples that "showed no traces of nicotine"). Summary judgment was not available to the insurer and trial was required as to the decedent applicant/policyholder's state of mind (i.e., whether the applicant had intentionally misrepresented the length of time as a non-smoker).

Most policyholder lawyers, of course, regard surviving a summary judgment motion as a long step on the road to successful settlement or judgment due to the prevailing view that jurors are relatively unlikely to presume fraud by the decedent, who is represented in court by his or her widowed spouse who may desperately need the insurance policy proceeds to survive. But, at least under the formal law of misrepresentation, a misstatement of material fact need not be made with fraudulent intent. Even an innocent material misrepresentation makes the policy voidable, at least until the period of policy incontestability (usually two years), has passed.

So why was applicant's state of mind an issue in this case if the question was answered incorrectly? (Whether an applicant is a smoker is a material fact in life insurance because smokers on average die earlier than nonsmokers.) A complicating fact was that the insurer's agent had, in the course of taking the application by interview, discussed the question with the applicant. She "mentioned that she 'might have had a couple of cigarettes in the last couple of years,'" to which the agent replied: "That's not really what they're looking for. They're looking for smokers." The insurer was charged with the agent's assurances, which made the applicant's negative response to the question sufficiently true to bar a successful misrepresentation defense. In effect, the court saw the matter as converted into a concealment question, in which case an intent to mislead the insurer is required to void coverage. But this is not the typical concealment scenario, which usually has an insurer making no inquiry and the applicant intentionally withholding information the applicant subjectively knows is material to the insurer's underwriting decision.

California Insurance Code § 330 states that "[n]eglect to communicate that which a party knows, and ought to communicate, is concealment," while § 331 provides that "[c]oncealment, whether intentional or unintentional, entitles the injured party to rescind insurance." Section 332 further requires that "[e]ach party to a contract of insurance shall communicate to the other, in good faith, all facts within his knowledge which are or which he believes to be material to the contract and as to which he makes no warranty, and which the other has not the means of ascertaining." On its face, this portion of the Insurance Code can be read as a codification of the marine insurance duty of *uberimai fidei* (the "utmost good faith"), which imposes on an insurance applicant the affirmative duty of notifying the insurer of anything that the applicant reasonably thinks might be material to the risk. These statutory provisions can also be read to remove the element of knowing intent to withhold material information (as opposed to mere failure to recognize that the insurer might be interested in certain data) that is an element of common law concealment.

On closer examination, the law of California, although perhaps less forgiving to applicants than some states, does not depart from the general rule of insurance: if an insurer fails to ask a question, the applicant has no affirmative duty to volunteer information. This is reflected in court decisions long before *O'Riordan. See, e.g., Thompson v. Occidental Life Ins. Co.*, 513 P.2d 353 (Cal. 1973); *Barrera v. State Farm Mut. Auto. Ins. Co.*, 456 P.2d 674 (Cal. 1969); *Harte v. United Ben. Life Ins. Co.*, 424 P.2d 329 (Cal. 1967); *Olson v. Standard Marine Ins.* Co., 240 P.2d 379 (Cal. Ct. App. 1952). *See also Telford v. New York Life Ins. Co.*, 69 P.2d 835 (Cal. 1937) (inaccurate answer to specific question makes policy voidable even where insurer's medical examiner could observe that applicant had previously had left breast removed, but not requiring voluntary disclosure of such information in the absence of a direct question from the insurer).

Examination of the state insurance statutes as a whole suggests that the statutory provisions quoted above were not designed to dramatically alter the common law rule that an insurer must make inquiry and cannot depend on the applicant to determine when information is sufficiently relevant that it must be disclosed. Even § 332 does not require disclosure if the insurer has the "means of ascertaining" information. Insurers almost always have such means through asking questions, conducting physicals, obtaining medical records, and inspecting real property, automobiles, or business operations. Section 333 then provides that certain matters not be disclosed "except upon inquiry" by the insurer where the information (a) is known by the other; (b) can be obtained in the exercise of ordinary care; (c) is subject to waiver; (d) related to an excluded, non-material risk.

Ordinarily, rescission is permitted only where the insurer has affirmatively asked for information and received a materially inaccurate response from the applicant. If an applicant fails to appreciate the significance of undisclosed information in the absence of inquiry by the insurers, this type of nondisclosure is not tantamount to "concealment" and will not void coverage.

Although there may be some room for debate, we see *O'Riordan* as a misrepresentation case rather than a concealment case. If *O'Riordan* were a true concealment case, there would be no need for the court's discussion of precisely what was asked of Mrs. O'Riordan or what she understood was being sought by the insurer; she would be obligated to disclose material facts regarding whether she smoked irrespective of any inquiry by the insurer. Of course, *O'Riordan* could be characterized as a concealment case, and the policyholder could still prevail on the grounds that occasional backsliding by a former smoker was not in fact information that materially would affect a life insurer's underwriting decision. At the very least, the California Supreme Court seems indisputably correct in finding that the dispute was not appropriate for summary judgment because of contested questions of fact.

# § 4.09. Insurer's Limitations of Risk: Warranties

## [A] Insurer's Use of Warranties

The term "warranty" was likely first introduced into marine insurance policies during the 17th century, and later passed into the legal doctrines applicable to other types of insurance contracts as well.

An insurance warranty is a statement included in the insurance policy that the policyholder must undertake or the policy is void. *See e.g.,* Robert H. Jerry, II & Douglas R. Richmond, Understanding Insurance Law § 101 (6th ed. 2018); Keeton & Widiss, Insurance Law § 5.6 (1988). A common example in commercial liability policies for fitness gyms is to have the policyholder gym warrant as a condition of liability coverage that all participants sign a waiver or release of liability prior to using the gym equipment. Failure to have a patron sign the release voids coverage for the gym if that patron is hurt at the gym and later sues the gym in tort. *See, e.g., Colony Ins. Co. v. Dover Indoor Climbing Gym,* 974 A.2d 399 (N.H. 2009) (failure of gym to get climbing wall climber to sign waiver rendered policy inapplicable when climber sued gym after he was hurt).

Insurers seldom use the word "warranty" in their insurance policies, preferring instead to use the word "condition" or "condition precedent." When the word "warranty" is used, American courts frequently interpret the term to mean a "condition," and vice versa. A distinction between these two concepts is recognized in some jurisdictions, however, either because the distinction is mandated by statute, or because the court recognizes the theory that a failure of a condition precedent precludes the technical creation of any duty to perform a contract.

With a warranty situation, the traditional view was that any breach precludes enforcement of the contract. However, in misrepresentation situations, the party in breach may argue that a misrepresentation was not material and hence does not absolve the other party of the duty to perform. *See generally* Couch on Insurance §§ 81:10–81:18 (3d ed. 2010). For example, a policyholder may "warrant" or "state" that it has installed StrongCo locks on its doors but have in fact accepted installation of ToughCo locks because of a shortage of the former brand. If there is a burglary, traditional treatment of the statement as a warranty would vitiate coverage. But if the statement is only a representation, the policyholder would not lose coverage if ToughCo locks are equally strong and resistant to being picked or broken.

Decisions on inaccurate representation cases usually are vague about who bears the burden to prove materiality (the insurer finding a misrepresentation) or a lack of materiality (the policyholder disputing the materiality of a misstatement). Because the traditional view is that strict compliance with conditions is a prerequisite for imposing contract obligations and because an assertion of lack of materiality after a finding of misrepresentation or breach sounds in the nature of an affirmative defense, one can make a good argument that proving lack of materiality is for the party in breach. But in our view, the better approach is to place the burden of proving materiality on the insurer in cases like the StrongCo/ToughCo hypothetical above. Logically, the party seeking to avoid performing the contract (the insurer in this hypothetical) should be required to prove materiality because in the absence of material breach, it would be obligated to perform (in that there was a burglary). *See generally* E. ALLAN FARNSWORTH, CONTRACTS, Ch. 8 (4th ed. 2004). In the insurance context, an additional factor supporting our view is that the insurer is normally the more expert party on risk and will have better access to information bearing on the materiality or non-materiality of the lock substitution.

An "affirmative" warranty asserts or represents *existing* facts or conditions at the time they are made, whereas a "promissory" or "continuing" warranty stipulates that certain things shall be done or exist *in the future*, during the lifetime of the insurance policy. Although warranties may be express or implied, promissory warranties must always be contained in the policy itself, or in a paper incorporated by reference into the policy. *See* VANCE ON INSURANCE 410–12 (3d ed. 1951). The importance of distinguishing between affirmative and promissory warranties is demonstrated in the following case.

## Reid v. Hardware Mutual Insurance Co.

Supreme Court of South Carolina
252 S.C. 339, 166 S.E.2d 317 (1969)

**Moss, Chief Justice**

Hardware Mutual Insurance Company of the Carolinas, Inc., the appellant herein, on May 22, 1964, issued a fire insurance policy to Zelphia H. Reid and W.C. Reid, in the amount of $5,000.00, insuring against loss or damage by fire, for a five year period, a one story frame dwelling located in Conestee, South Carolina, owned by Zelphia H. Reid, the respondent herein [who relocated from the property].... The dwelling described in said policy was destroyed by fire on December 18, 1965, and at such time the balance of the mortgage debt owned by the respondent was $1,647.56. The appellant was notified of the loss of said dwelling by fire and demand for payment by the insureds under the aforesaid policy was made and such was refused.

[The insurer] set up as defenses: ... (5) That the aforesaid policy was void *ab initio* because the policy was written upon the basis that the dwelling was owner occupied and it was incumbent upon the respondent to notify the appellant of any change in occupancy because such was material to the risk.... The final question for determination is whether the designation, at the time the policy was issued, that the insured dwelling was "owner occupied" was a continuing warranty.

A warranty, in the law of insurance, is a statement, description, or undertaking on the part of the insured, appearing in the policy of insurance or in another instrument properly incorporated in the policy, relating contractually to the risk insured against. Generically, warranties are either affirmative or promissory. An affirmative warranty is one which asserts the existence of a fact at the time the policy is entered into, and appears on the face of said policy, or is attached thereto and made a part thereof. A promissory warranty may be defined to be an absolute undertaking by the insured, contained in a policy or in a paper properly incorporated by reference, that certain facts or conditions pertaining to the risk shall continue, or that certain things with reference thereto shall be done or omitted. . . .

While it is generally recognized that a warranty may be "promissory" or "continuing," the tendency is to construe a statement in the past or present tense as constituting an affirmative rather than a continuing warranty. Thus, a description of a house in a policy of insurance, as "occupied by" the insured, is a description merely and is not an agreement that the insured should continue in the occupation of it. . . . A statement in an insurance policy that the property is occupied by the insured as a dwelling for himself and family, is not a warranty that it shall continue to be so occupied but is only a warranty of the situation at the time the insurance is effected. . . .

There is no provision in the policy contract that the dwelling would be "owner occupied" during the term of the insurance contract nor any requirement that if the premises are otherwise occupied than by the owner, notice of such change of occupancy or use would be given to the insurer.

The insurance contract here involved contained a description of the dwelling insured as being "owner occupied." This was an affirmative warranty, not a continuing warranty, by the respondent that the dwelling was so occupied by him at the time the contract of insurance was made.

## Notes and Questions

1. Why was it important in *Reid* that the "owner occupied" warranty was interpreted as an affirmative rather than a promissory warranty?

2. The *Reid* case was distinguished in the subsequent case of *Heniser v. Frankenmuth Mut. Ins.*, 534 N.W.2d 502, 506 (Mich. 1995), where the Michigan Supreme Court held that an exclusion within a property insurance policy unambiguously excluded coverage where the plaintiff did not reside at the property. Since the plaintiff in Heniser no longer owned the property and was not residing at the property at the time of the fire, the exclusion provision took effect, and the property was not covered by insurance. "Unlike the language in *Reid* ... the phrase 'where you reside' in the policy before us is not a warranty but a statement of coverage." *Id.*

### PROBLEM SEVEN

Plaintiff Rodriguez was operating a Case Model Log Skidder—a log rolling and loading machine used in timber cutting operations—which was insured against loss by the Northwestern National Insurance Company. The Northwestern National insurance policy contained the following provisions:

It is understood and agreed by the assured that as respects the peril of Fire this insurance is NULL and VOID if any condition of this warranty is violated as respects equipment insured hereunder while operating or located in woods or forest or while land clearing.... (2) It is warranted that an Underwriters Laboratory-approved fire extinguisher with a rating of at least 1A or 10BC will be provided on each piece of equipment insured at all times such equipment is being operated.

Rodriguez did have a fire extinguisher on his log skidder when it was destroyed by fire while operating in the woods, but the fire extinguisher was not a fire extinguisher approved by Underwriters Laboratory. However, Rodriguez argued that the presence of such an approved fire extinguisher would not have reduced the risk of this particular fire because the fire was beneath the floorboards in an inaccessible transmission area, and no fire extinguisher could reach the fire, no matter what type of fire extinguisher was utilized.

• How should the court rule in this case? Explain your reasoning.

## PROBLEM EIGHT

The owner of a four-story building insured the building against fire. The insurance policy read: "Warranted that the third floor is occupied as a Janitor's residence." When the building and its contents were destroyed by fire, the insurer refused to pay on the claim, since evidence showed that a massage parlor also utilized a portion of the third floor.

• Does this constitute an affirmative or promissory warranty?

• Does it make a difference that the janitor occupied the third floor along with the massage parlor?

# [B] The Substantial Compliance Concept

Many courts now hold that a strict, literal compliance with every insurance warranty is not always necessary, and that "substantial compliance" with the warranty provision is often enough to uphold the insurance policy. Thus, an increasing number of courts have now adopted the rule of "substantial compliance" with respect to warranties, holding that promissory warranties need only be "substantially" true or "substantially" fulfilled. *See* JERRY & RICHMOND, UNDERSTANDING INSURANCE LAW § 101 (6th ed. 2018). But how "substantial" must this compliance be?

## Liverpool & London & Globe Insurance Co. v. Kearney

United States Supreme Court
180 U.S. 132 (1901)

The insured's hardware store was protected by two fire policies issued by the insurer. Each of these policies contained an "iron safe" clause, in which the insured covenanted to "keep a set of books showing a complete record of business transacted ... together with the last inventory of said business" and to "keep such books and inventory securely locked in a fireproof safe ... or in some secure place not exposed to a fire...."

The clause stated that failure to produce such books and inventory in case of a loss would void the policy.

On April 18, 1895, a fire broke out in the town and spread toward the insured's place of business. When it became apparent that the insured's store would soon be engulfed by the conflagration, the insured rushed into the store and removed the books from the safe, and carried them home for safety. In the confusion, however, the inventory was either left in the safe and destroyed by the fire, or was otherwise lost. When the insured subsequently put in a claim for the loss that resulted from the fire, the insurer refused to indemnify him, claiming that since the insured did not produce the inventory as required by the "iron safe" clauses, coverage under the policies was forfeited.

The insured brought an action for the amount of the loss in the United States District Court, which resulted in a judgment for the insured. The Court of Appeals affirmed, and the insurer appealed to the United States Supreme Court.

Although the insurer insisted that the words of the "iron safe" clause be interpreted literally, Justice Harlan affirmed the lower court's decision, ruling that insurance contracts are subject to the same rules of construction as other contracts. Thus, legal effect should be given to a reasonable intent of the parties, rather than to the rigid, literal interpretation of the language used. An exception to this general rule, noted by the Court, is that ambiguous clauses in insurance policies should be construed against the insurer.

Under these principles, Justice Harlan held that where the insured "acted in good faith and with such care as prudent men ought to exercise under like circumstances, it could not reasonably be said that the terms of the policy ... were violated." The policies would be void only if the insured failed "to produce [the books and inventory] if they are in existence when called for, or if they have been lost or destroyed by the fault, negligence, or design of the insured."

Moreover, if the insurer, as drafter of the policy, had intended to make the insured comply with strict technicalities, "it should have used words expressing that thought." Thus, the insured is not required to keep "such books as would be kept by an expert bookkeeper or accountant," and the safe is not required to be "perfect in all respects and capable of withstanding any fire however intensive and fierce"; rather, the standard to be applied is that of sufficient compliance "in the judgment of prudent men in the locality." In the opinion of the Court, this holding "does not make for the parties a contract which they did not make for themselves. It only interprets the contract so as to do no violence to the words used and yet to meet the ends of justice."

## *Notes and Questions*

1. "Iron safe" or "record warranty" clauses are very common in policies insuring stocks of goods against fire. Such a warranty requires the insured to take inventory, keep books, and preserve them in a fireproof safe or another such place protected against fire. This clause is designed to protect the insurance company against fraudulent loss-of-inventory claims.

2. It is generally held that substantial compliance with the "iron safe" clause warranty is sufficient, and it is a question of fact in each case whether or not there has been substantial compliance. However, the inventory must be sufficiently detailed to enable the insurance company to reasonably determine the amount and value of the goods. *See Dickerson v. Franklin Nat'l Ins. Co.*, 130 F.2d 35 (4th Cir. 1942) (applying West Virginia law); *Georgian House of Interiors, Inc. v. Glens Falls Ins. Co.*, 151 P.2d 598 (Wash. 1944).

3. Even with the recognition of the "substantial compliance" doctrine in many states, iron safe and inventory record warranties continue to be important areas of insurance law litigation today. *See, e.g.*, COUCH CYCLOPEDIA OF INSURANCE LAW §§ 97:5–97:7 (3d ed. 2010).

––––––––––

In *SFI, Inc. v. United States Fire Ins. Co.*, 453 F. Supp. 502 (M.D. La. 1978), the court found coverage where a burglar alarm was negligently left off overnight. The court's view was that the burglar alarm warranty was satisfied (there was, after all, a burglar alarm in place) even though the alarm was not operational at the time of the crime and property loss.

The policy in *SFI* provided that the insured must "exercise due diligence in maintaining the [burglar alarm] system." Should this mean that the burglar alarm must be turned "on," as well as be "in proper working order"? Why then did the court hold that the insured plaintiff "did use due diligence in complying with all the terms and conditions of the insurance policy"? Was this substantial compliance with the policy warranty? Why or why not?

The traditional rule requiring strict compliance with insurance warranties is that such warranties must be clearly and understandingly made. Was such a warranty clearly made in the *SFI* policy? What other insurance law concept of contract interpretation might the court have used in this case?

## [C] Common Warranties in Insurance Policies

Other standard warranties in insurance policies include:

a) "Watchkeeper" warranties, common in commercial property policies, where the policyholder warrants to keep a watchkeeper on the premises who keeps an eye on the place outside of regular business hours. *See, e.g. Hanover Fire Ins. Co. v. Gustin*, 40 Neb. 828, 59 N.W. 375 (1894) (court held substantial compliance is sufficient and coverage attached after fire loss at mill when watchkeeper left to purchase new lock); *Coffey v. Indiana Lumberman's Mutual Ins. Co.*, 372 F.2d 646 (6th Cir. 1967) (no coverage for fire loss 12 days after policyholder laid off workers at furniture plant, including watchkeepers).

b) Increase in hazard clauses are commonly found in fire insurance and other property policies so as to void coverage if the policyholder does or does not do something that substantially alters the conditions of the property to materially increase the risk of loss. For example, a business might have its sprinkler system disconnected and suffer a fire. The property policy might require the policyholder to have a functioning and monitored sprinkler system in order for coverage to attach for a fire loss. *See, e.g., Industrial Development Associates v. Commercial Union Surplus Lines Insurance Co.*, 222 N.J. Super. 281, 536 A.2d 787 (N.J. Super. App. 1988) (policyholder's negligence in disconnecting sprinkler system does not void coverage because condition of property did not change; properly still had a functioning sprinkler system, but it was just accidentally shut off).

c) How the policyholder uses the property may also feature in an insurance warranty. A business vehicle is more exposed to the risk of accidents than an occasional pleasure vehicle. A munitions factory is more hazard-prone than a warehouse for steel products. A common example is the use of a portion of the family home for commercial purposes. Many residential insurance policies exclude coverage for liability or property damage if the home is used for business, or alternatively, a higher premium may be charged. *See, e.g., Durham v. Cox*, 310 S.E.2d 371 (N.C. Ct. App. 1984) (policyholder told agent he was using garage for woodworking business, and "business purpose" exclusion in policy waived by insurer's conduct in continually underwriting policy while knowing this risk); *Badger Mut. Ins. Co. v. Hancock*, 157 S.E.2d 58 (Ga. Ct. App. 1967) (holding that the policyholder could not recover for fire loss of his garage, used for business purposes, under the policy's "business exclusion" provision).

d) Occupancy of premises also features as insurance warranties. In property insurance, the risk of loss due to vandals, vagrants, or other criminal elements entering an unoccupied building and setting it on fire or stealing, either through negligence or design, is much greater than the risk of loss in an occupied building, and therefore insurers often limit the period of time that a building may be left unoccupied or vacant. In the case of a dwelling, "occupancy" normally means a person must live or sleep in the building; a "vacant" building is one in which there is no settled intention to return and live. *See, e.g., Chiapetta v. Lumbermens Mutual Ins. Co.*, 583 A.2d 198 (Main Sup. Jud. Ct., 1990).

e) Warranties prohibiting "other insurance" coverage are commonly found in many property, medical, and automobile liability insurance policies. The purpose of an "other insurance" provision is to prevent over-insurance in the form of double or triple indemnity for a single insurable loss. If the policyholder takes out policies from two or three insurance companies to insure the same property, for example, the policyholder should not be able to collect any more recovery for loss than what they actually incurred, because otherwise they might be tempted to commit arson or another illegal act in order to obtain a windfall recovery. *See, e.g., Burgess v. North Carolina Farm Bureau Mutual Ins. Co.*, 44 N.C. App. 441, 261 S.E.2d 234 (N.C. Ct. App. 1980).

f) A warranty about where a policyholder keeps their vehicle is common in automobile insurance policies. This warranty is used not only to keep risk in check by knowing where the vehicle is used and stored, but also is used by the insurer in determining premium rates. Some urban areas may have higher probabilities of accident or theft than some rural areas. *See, e.g., Arbuckle v. (American) Lumbermens Mut. Casualty Co.*, 129 F.2d 791 (2d Cir. 1942) (applying New York law) (finding that breach of place of garaging representation or warranty is material and would defeat coverage but that insurer bears the burden to show breach of the condition).

g) Some policies may include warranties against encumbrances. An encumbrance is any right to, or interest in, property that may diminish its value. Encumbrances can include any claim, lien, encroachment, mortgage, easement, lease, inchoate right of dower or curtesy, unpaid taxes, or other such restriction. Since the value of a policyholder's interest in property generally measures the degree of care that he or she will use to preserve such property, the policyholder is required through an encumbrance warranty to truthfully state their — and others' — interest in that property. Failure to correctly define these interests may also violate the policy's "increase in hazard" warranty. There has been much litigation concerning encumbrance warranties and mortgages or deeds of trust, for example. *See, e.g., Lilledahl v. Insurance Co. of North America*, 163 A.D.2d 696, 558 N.Y.S.2d 709 (1990).

## [D] Statutory Limitations to Insurance Warranties

Numerous state legislatures have enacted statutory modifications which greatly restrict the operation of the common law warranty doctrine in insurance law, especially as it applied to insurance applications. Under these statutes, it is generally provided that a policy would not be void because of a misrepresentation or false warranty by the policyholder, unless such representation or warranty was material to the risk of loss, or — in some states — was made with a fraudulent intent.

What is material to the risk of loss? Generally speaking, the test of materiality is: Did the fact or circumstance represented or misrepresented induce the insurance company to (1) accept a risk it otherwise would have rejected; or (2) accept the risk at a lower premium. Put another way, would the insurer, governed by the usual custom and practice of insurance companies, have rejected the risk or charged a higher premium had the true facts of the applicant been properly disclosed? So, a misrepresentation or statutory warranty is material as a matter of law when the knowledge of the true facts would reasonably influence the judgment of the insurance company in making the insurance bargain, estimating the risk, or fixing the premium. But when such a misrepresentation or statutory warranty cannot be deemed material as a matter of law, the insurance company has the burden of proving this materiality as a matter of fact.

For a sample of state statutes on warranties and representations, *see* as examples FLA. STAT. §627.409; NEB. REV. STAT. §44-358; N.Y. INS. LAW §3106; VA. CODE ANN. §38.2-309. With the exception of the New York statute, the other three cited state statutes generally refer to statements or promises made in *applications* for insurance. Thus, arguably, they may not apply to warranty conditions contained in the insurance policy itself, the breach of which may still be governed by judicial interpretation, as discussed earlier in this chapter.

If an insurer attempts to rescind its policy coverage, a growing number of states, including New York, by statutory enactment now require a showing of materiality by the insurer affecting *both* the insurance application *and* insurance warranties found within the policy itself. These selected statutes state that, at least when applied to insurance applications, a breach of warranty must be *material* in order to avoid coverage. To be material, a fact need not necessarily increase the risk of loss, or contribute to any loss suffered. It is sufficient that the knowledge of this material fact would have *influenced* the parties in making the bargain. The test of materiality, in other words, as suggested by Judge Taft would be:

> Are you able to say, from your knowledge of the practice and usage among ... insurance companies *generally* that information of this fact *would have enhanced the premium to be charged* or would have led to a rejection of the risk? (Emphasis added.)

*Penn Mut. Life Ins. Co. v. Mechanics' Sav. Bank & Trust Co.*, 72 F. 413 (6th Cir. 1896). Note, however, that several state statutes will also permit avoidance of the policy upon an *immaterial*, but *willful, or fraudulent* misrepresentation.

A minority of jurisdictions have enacted a "contribute-to-loss" type statute which provides that a breach of warranty will not void the policy unless it is, in fact, a *cause* of the loss. Iowa, Kansas, Missouri, Nebraska, New Hampshire, Rhode Island, Texas, and Wisconsin have various kinds of contribute-to-loss statutes, with the Nebraska statute being one of the most comprehensive in scope. New York specifically excludes the application of its modified warranty statutes to marine insurance, as do most states by statutory or judicial case law. Why should marine insurance be an exception to the statutory rule requiring materiality in certain insurance warranties?

# § 4.10. Policyholder Defenses

The previous section considered the *insurer's* defenses to honoring an insurance bargain, including breach of warranty, misrepresentation, and concealment defenses. This section focuses on the *policyholder's* defenses, which arise whenever an insurance company or its authorized agent waives a defense, becomes estopped to assert it, or elects not to take advantage of a breach of warranty or material misrepresentation in the insurance contract. *See generally* EDWIN PATTERSON, ESSENTIALS OF INSURANCE LAW 475–477 (2d ed. 1957); COUCH ON INSURANCE §§ 238:1 *et seq.*, 239:93 (3d ed. 2010); JEFFREY W. STEMPEL & ERIK S. KNUTSEN, STEMPEL & KNUTSEN ON INSURANCE COVERAGE, §§ 5.01–5.05.

Thus, insurance law litigation dealing with breach of warranty and misrepresentation issues has been called "the happy hunting ground for waiver and estoppel" by various policyholder attorneys. As important as these concepts are, however, some courts have defined them inaccurately.

"Waiver" is the express or implied voluntary and intentional relinquishment of a known contractual right which may result from either the affirmative acts of the insurer or its authorized agent, or from the insurer's nonaction, with knowledge of the applicable facts. Because there must be a clear and requisite intent to establish such a waiver, it generally cannot be found in negligence or mistake. *See, e.g., Reserve Life Ins. Co. v. Howell*, 357 P.2d 400 (Or. 1960). Nor is it essential that a waiver be "bargained for" or supported by consideration. Even if a waiver needed a contractual foundation, a party's reliance to the waiver ordinarily would constitute a suitable substitute for contractual consideration. *See generally* JERRY & RICHMOND, UNDERSTANDING INSURANCE LAW § 25E (6th ed. 2018).

"Estoppel," on the other hand, does not require any actual surrender of a known right. Rather, it implies some misleading act, conduct, or inaction on the part of the insurer or its agent upon which the policyholder detrimentally relies. *See, e.g., Pitts v. New York Life Ins. Co.*, 148 S.E.2d 369 (S.C. 1966); *Salloum Foods & Liquor, Inc. v. Parliament Ins. Co.*, 388 N.E.2d 23, 27–28 (Ill. Ct. App. 1979); *First Am. Title Ins. Co. v. Firriolo*, 695 S.E.2d 918 (W. Va. 2010). Estoppel is an equitable principle imposed as a rule of law.

In considering waiver and estoppel problems throughout this section, it must be kept in mind that the insurance business is done almost exclusively through agents, and thus waiver and estoppel arguments applied against the insurer most often involve an act or omission by an agent or officer of the insurer who must necessarily be acting within the scope of his or her authority. And although a life insurance agent, acting as a special or soliciting agent, cannot generally bind an insurer on the acceptance of risks or the settlement of losses, a general agent in the property and liability insurance field usually does have the authority, within specified limits, to make and modify insurance bargains, and to settle certain losses on behalf of the principal insurance company, absent any contractual limitations to the general agent's powers found within the insurance policy.

## [A] Waiver and Estoppel

### Continental Insurance Co. v. Kingston

Court of Appeals of Utah
114 P.3d 1158 (2005)

**Orme, J.**

Joseph O. Kingston and D.U. Company, Inc. appeal the trial court's grant of summary judgment in favor of Continental Insurance Company premised on a theory of misrepresentation in an insurance application. We conclude the insurance company waived any right it had to rescind the policy and reverse the summary judgment.

## BACKGROUND

Except as otherwise noted, the key facts are not in dispute and may be summarized as follows. Joseph O. Kingston bought a home built in the 1800s in Bountiful, Utah, from D.U. Company, Inc. (DUC). Kingston subsequently applied for automobile and home insurance from Jackson Insurance Agency, an agent of Continental Insurance Company. Brent Christensen, an employee of Jackson Insurance Agency, helped Kingston prepare the insurance policy application. One of the questions on the application asked for the year Kingston's home was built, and Christensen entered the year "1990," rather than the actual year the home was built. Continental approved Kingston's application and issued him an insurance policy on the home.

From March 1994 through July 4, 1997, Kingston timely paid all premiums on the insurance policy. On July 4, 1997, Kingston's home caught fire, causing substantial damage to the structure and interior of the home. Two entities, Wasatch Claims Service and Fire Investigations, were retained by Continental to assess the loss to Kingston's home. Immediately after the fire occurred they inspected the home and, one week later, Fire Investigations issued a letter to Continental informing Continental that "the home is over one hundred years old." At about the same time, an agent of Continental advised Kingston that the loss was covered under the policy. As a result, Kingston hired Utah Disaster Kleenup to perform demolition work on the home. Continental paid for the demolition work done on the home and authorized restorative work to be done. In addition, Continental authorized Kingston to move into temporary housing, paid for Kingston's temporary living expenses, and told Kingston to inventory his personal property losses, for which it would also pay.

In January of 1998, pursuant to a policy provision, Continental examined Kingston under oath as part of its claims investigation. Around this time, Continental pulled Kingston's original insurance application and discovered that the application listed "1990" as the year the home was built. As a result, in March of 1998, Continental filed a complaint against Kingston and DUC in Third District Court, seeking to rescind the insurance policy on the ground that Kingston had made material misrepresentations on the application. In that same month, it sent a reservation of rights letter to Kingston and renewed Kingston's policy for an additional year. Kingston and DUC counterclaimed for breach of the insurance contract.

Subsequently, DUC filed a motion for partial summary judgment, which Kingston joined, and Continental filed a cross-motion for summary judgment. Both motions were denied by the trial court. After additional discovery, Continental renewed its motion for summary judgment alleging that, as a matter of law, Kingston made a material misrepresentation on his application. Kingston and DUC opposed Continental's motion on multiple grounds, including waiver. The trial court granted Continental's motion and dismissed Kingston and DUC's counterclaims, declaring that Continental had a right to rescind Kingston's policy based on the misrepresentation made in the application.

Kingston and DUC now appeal the denial of DUC's motion for partial summary judgment and the granting of Continental's motion for summary judgment. DUC and Kingston also appeal from the trial court's rulings on a number of other matters, including the admissibility of certain testimony of Kathleen Wentzel and Brent Christensen, as well as an award of costs to Continental. We need not reach these other matters in view of our disposition.

## ISSUES AND STANDARD OF REVIEW

On appeal, Kingston and DUC 4 (hereinafter collectively "Kingston") argue that the trial court should have granted DUC's motion for partial summary judgment because Continental waived its right to rescind the policy as demonstrated by its post-fire course of conduct. Kingston additionally argues that the trial court erred in granting Continental's motion for summary judgment because it should not have reached the issue of whether Kingston made a material misrepresentation given that Continental waived its right to rescind the policy. He argues that waiver is conclusively demonstrated by Continental's knowledge of the home's actual age, its intent to continue Kingston's policy despite knowing of the home's age, and its post-fire course of conduct.

Continental additionally argues that Kingston misrepresented that the home was a single-family dwelling, when the home was actually used as a multi-family dwelling, and that Kingston misrepresented whether the home had previously been insured. However, in its motion for summary judgment, Continental limited its material misrepresentation claim to the age of the home. Thus, we confine our discussion to the thrust of the motion for summary judgment, i.e., whether the age of the home was materially misrepresented.

In this case, the material facts are not in dispute. Thus, we must consider whether the trial court was correct in holding that Continental was entitled to rescind the policy as a matter of law because of a material misrepresentation made on the policy application. The answer, as will be seen, turns on whether Continental was barred from rescinding the policy because, as a matter of law, it waived that right. We review the trial court's legal conclusions under a correction of error standard.

## ANALYSIS

An insurer's reliance upon material misrepresentations made by an insured enables an insurer to rescind a contract at its election. *See Perkins v. Great-West Life Assurance Co.*, 814 P.2d 1125, 1130 (Utah Ct. App. 1991) (stating that contract is voidable where material misrepresentations are made by insured and insurer relies on those misrepresentations); Utah Code Ann. §31A-21-105(2) (2003) (describing when misrepresentations affect an insurer's obligations under an insurance policy). However, an insurer may forfeit the right to rescind a contract if it intentionally relinquishes that right or if its course of conduct demonstrates that it intended to relinquish that right. *See generally Soter's, Inc. v. Deseret Fed. Sav. & Loan*, 857 P.2d 935, 940–41 (Utah 1993). Once a party intentionally relinquishes the right to rescind, it is thereafter prohibited from asserting that right. *See generally id.*

In order to determine whether a party has waived its right to rescind a contract, the court must find that an "intentional relinquishment of a known right" has been made. *Phoenix Ins. Co. v. Heath*, 61 P.2d 308, 311 (Utah 1936). In *Soter's*, the Utah Supreme Court explained that "'to constitute waiver, there must be an existing right, benefit, or advantage, a knowledge of its existence, and an intention to relinquish it.'" 857 P.2d at 938 (quoting *Phoenix*, 61 P.2d at 311–12). The Court in. *Soter's* further noted "that the intent to relinquish a right must be distinct." *Id.*

On appeal, the question of waiver frequently turns upon whether a party had the requisite intent to waive the right in question. *See id.* at 940. To make this determination a court must consider all of the relevant facts before it and base its decision upon the "totality of the circumstances." *Id.* at 942. If a party did not expressly relinquish its right, then a court must examine the party's conduct to determine whether that party intended to relinquish the right in question. The intent to relinquish a right need not be express and "may be implied from action or inaction." *K&T, Inc. v. Koroulis*, 888 P.2d 623, 628 (Utah 1994).

In this case, neither party alleges that an express waiver was made. Therefore, we must determine whether waiver can be "implied from action or inaction" on Continental's part, while keeping in mind that the basis of our inquiry rests upon whether the relinquishment was distinctly made.

In a number of contexts, the Utah Supreme Court has discussed the waiver of a party's right to rescind a contract....

In the specific context of insurance, the Utah Supreme Court noted that if a party claims a right to rescission and then does any substantial act that recognizes the contract as in force, that party has usually waived its right to rescind. *See Farrington v. Granite State Fire Ins. Co.*, 120 Utah 109, 232 P.2d 754, 758 (1951). In *Farrington*, the plaintiff took insurance out on a building she described in the insurance application as "a building occupied as a skating rink," but which actually was a building with a partially collapsed roof and that was no longer used as a skating rink. *Id.* at 755. A fire destroyed the building and, within four days, the defendant insurance company had sent an agent to investigate the incident. *See id.* at 758. A month and a half later, the defendant company accepted the plaintiff's payment of the remaining balance owed on the premium. *See id.* Defendant insurer made no claim of a right to rescind the policy until approximately one year later, when the defendant denied liability, claiming a right to rescind based upon material misrepresentations made in the application. *See id.*

While waiver of the defendant's right to rescind the policy was not ultimately the controlling issue in *Farrington*, the Utah Supreme Court nonetheless thought the waiver claim merited careful analysis under the facts of the case. The Court thought it significant that "all of the facts upon which the defendant claims right of rescission were known to the defendant within a very few days of the fire," that the defendant accepted the plaintiff's premium payment, and that the defendant had allowed a great deal of time to pass without asserting a right to rescind the policy based on the facts it knew. *Id.* On such facts, our Supreme Court opined that one who claims a right to rescission must act with reasonable promptness, and if after such knowledge, he does any substantial act which recognizes the contract as in force, such as the acceptance of the more than half of the premium would be, such an act would usually constitute a waiver of his right to rescind. *Id.*

The Supreme Court's discussion of waiver in *Farrington* establishes that an insurer waives the right to rescind an insurance policy when that insurer has knowledge of facts that would give it the right to rescind the policy, and does not act promptly to assert or reserve the right to rescind the policy, or otherwise treats the policy as valid, such as by earning and collecting premiums. *See id.*

Consistent with the lessons of *Farrington*, other states have likewise precluded rescission if an insurer has acted, subsequent to a breach, in such a way as to recognize the insurance contract as in force. *See, e.g., McCollum v. Continental Cas. Co.*, 151 Ariz. 492, 728 P.2d 1242, 1245 (Ariz. Ct. App. 1986) ("When an insurer has knowledge of facts allegedly justifying a denial of coverage or the forfeiture of a policy previously issued, an unequivocal act that recognizes the continued existence of the policy or an act wholly inconsistent with a prior denial of coverage constitutes a waiver thereof."); *Johnson v. Life Ins. Co.*, 52 So. 2d 813, 815 (Fla. 1951) ("It is equally well settled in insurance law that, when an insurer has knowledge of the existence of facts justifying a forfeiture of the policy, any unequivocal act which recognizes the continued existence of the policy or which is wholly inconsistent with a forfeiture, will constitute a waiver thereof.").

Specifically, when an insurer accepts premiums after discovering facts that would justify rescission of the policy, numerous courts have precluded the insurer from later denying coverage. *See, e.g., Dairyland Ins. Co. v. Kammerer*, 213 Neb. 108, 327 N.W.2d 618, 620 (Neb. 1982) ("'Insurer is precluded from asserting a forfeiture where, after acquiring knowledge of the facts constituting a breach of condition, it has retained the unearned portion of the premium or has failed to return or tender it back with reasonable promptness[.]'") (citation omitted); *Continental Ins. Co. v. Helmsley Enters., Inc.*, 211 A.D.2d 589, 622 N.Y.S.2d 20, 21 (N.Y. App. Div. 1995) ("Where an insurer accepts premiums after learning of an event allowing for cancellation of the policy, the insurer has waived the right to cancel or rescind."); *McCollum*, 728 P.2d at 1245 (holding insurance company waived right to rescind when it had learned of fact justifying rescission but "retained and continued to accept premiums" from insured).

After careful review of the record, we conclude that the facts indicate an unequivocal intent on Continental's part to relinquish any right it had to deny coverage to Kingston, thus constituting waiver as a matter of law. Continental's course of conduct clearly demonstrated its intent to cover the losses on the home, regardless of the age of the home. At least as of July 11, 1997, if not earlier, Continental had knowledge that the home was over one hundred years old. Within days after the fire occurred, Continental sent agents to Kingston's home to assess the damage. A week after the fire, Fire Investigations, an agent of Continental, sent Continental a letter informing it that the "the home is over one hundred years old."

Notwithstanding this knowledge, and without being enough concerned about the home's age to check its records to make sure this was the risk it had underwritten, Continental or its agents paid for Kingston's living expenses, informed Kingston that his loss was covered, authorized demolition of the home's interior, undertook repairs to restore the home, obtained commitments from two contractors to do restoration work, authorized restoration work to commence on the home at Continental's expense, and required Kingston to prepare an extensive personal property inventory to establish the amount of personal property loss.

Additionally, during this time, Continental never evinced an attitude that its insurance of a home of this age would in any way be exceptional, never informed Kingston that the age of the home was a concern, and never suggested that it was going to consider rescinding the policy based on the age of the home. Under the totality of the circumstances, these acts inarguably demonstrate a distinct intent on Continental's part to continue Kingston's policy and to cover his losses without regard to the age of the home.

Continental asserts that it did not discover the discrepancy between the age of the home as listed on the application and the actual age of the home until January 1998, when it finally pulled the application and reviewed it. Therefore, Continental insists, any acts performed prior to that time should not be considered as evidence of its intent to continue the policy rather than rescind it. As indicated, we have our doubts about the materiality of the discrepancy. But even if Continental was not charged with knowledge of the discrepancy until January of 1998, it continued to bill Kingston for premiums even after it discovered the discrepancy and accepted a premium payment made by Kingston in February of 1998.

We believe these acts indicate Continental's intention to continue the policy, despite the contents of the application. See 44A Am. Jur. 2d Insurance § 1606 (2003) ("An insurer waives its right to seek rescission of a policy when it knowingly accepts premium payments following the discovery of alleged misrepresentations upon which it claims to have relied when it issued the policy[.]"); *id.* at § 1613 ("Acceptance of premiums by the insurer after learning of a breach of condition or a ground for forfeiture normally constitutes waiver or estoppel of the condition.").

Seen from another perspective, if it were extraordinary for Continental to insure homes as old as this one, it is peculiar indeed that it did not immediately review its records to see how such a decision contrary to its corporate policy had been made. The matter-of-fact way in which it greeted the information that the home was over 100 years old suggests that the age of the home was not actually of great concern, i.e., was not material.

Finally, Continental's argument that because it sent a reservation of rights letter it expressly reserved all rights to rescind the policy is not persuasive. The letter was not sent until March of 1998, subsequent to the acts mentioned above and eight months after the fire. Nevertheless, our conclusion in this case should not be taken in any way to undermine the ability of an insurance company to properly employ a reservation of rights letter in handling insurance claims.

## CONCLUSION

A contract containing material misrepresentations is voidable at the election of the injured party. Thus, any material misrepresentations made on Kingston's insurance policy application rendered the policy voidable instead of void *ab initio.*

As conclusively shown by its post-fire course of conduct, Continental intentionally relinquished its right to rescind the contract. As a result, whether a misrepresentation was made by Kingston on the policy application and whether the misrepresentation was material have no bearing on this case and, therefore, the trial court erred in granting summary judgment in favor of Continental. We reverse the decision of the trial court and remand for further proceedings consistent with this opinion.

## *Notes and Questions*

1. What theory did the *Kingston* appellate court primarily rely upon in reaching its decision—waiver or estoppel? Based on what factual evidence? Do you agree with the appellate court's reasoning? Why or why not?

*Query:* The trial court in *Kingston* concluded that Continental's denial of coverage was valid. What evidence do you think the trial court found compelling? Is misstating the age of the home material to Continental's decision to insure the home? When did Continental first learn about the age of the home?

2. The general rule is that, although doctrines of waiver and estoppel may operate to avoid conditions, warranties, or representations that would ordinarily cause the forfeiture of an insurance policy, waiver and estoppel principles do *not* operate to rewrite or enlarge those risks that were not initially covered by the policy. *See, e.g., Swiderski v. Prudential Property and Casualty Ins. Co.,* 672 S.W.2d 264 (Tex. Ct. Civ. App. 1984). Under this majority rule, may limitations or exclusions in an insurance policy ever be waived by the insurer? Likewise, it is generally held that an insurer cannot waive or be estopped to assert an insurable interest requirement. *See, e.g., Beard v. American Agency Life Ins. Co.,* 550 A.2d 677 (Md. 1988); *Hack v. Metz,* 176 S.E. 314 (S.C. 1934). *But see contra Rhead v. Hartford Ins. Co.,* 19 P.3d 760 (Idaho 2001) (minority view).

3. A contrary position was taken in *National Discount Shoes, Inc. v. Royal Globe Ins. Co.,* 424 N.E.2d 1166 (Ill. App. Ct. 1981), where the court held that an insurer may always create a new contract by an express waiver, even after loss occurs, and thus be held liable for coverage that did not actually exist at the time of loss (minority view). *Query:* Should such a contract require new consideration?

A number of courts have held that new consideration is not necessarily required under the doctrine of *promissory estoppel.* The purpose of promissory estoppel is to bridge any lack of consideration gap by using the detriment of the promisee to supply the consideration necessary to enforce the promise. Promissory estoppel does not depend on conduct which may be contractually equivocal, as do traditional waiver and equitable estoppel doctrines, but requires affirmative action which indicates a desire to be contractually bound. *See, e.g., Prudential Ins. Co. v. Clark,* 456 F.2d 932 (5th Cir. 1972) (applying Florida law).

Nevertheless, it has been repeatedly held by most courts that traditional doctrines of waiver and estoppel cannot generally be used to extend the coverage of an insurance policy, nor create new liability on the part of the insurer, but may only affect those rights that are reserved within the policy. However, even in those states that do not normally allow the creation or extension of coverage through traditional waiver and estoppel defenses, the doctrine of promissory estoppel may still be applicable in certain situations to bind the insurer. *See generally* Eric Mills Holmes, *Restatement of Promissory Estoppel*, 32 WILLAMETTE L. REV. 263 (1996) (arguing that where equitable estoppel is defensive and cannot create insurance coverage, promissory estoppel is offensive and may affirmatively create insurance coverage). *But see also* Charles L. Knapp, *Rescuing Reliance: The Perils of Promissory Estoppel*, 49 HASTINGS L.J. 1191 (1998).

4. An agent's conduct normally binds the insurer as a matter of contract, and may create estoppel against the insurer as well. *See, e.g., Guerrier v. Commerce Ins. Co.,* 847 N.E.2d 1113 (Mass. Ct. App. 2006) (holding that an agent's misstatement in an application previously signed in blank by the applicant estops the insurer from rescinding the policy on grounds of misrepresentation, since the agent's errors were imputed to the insurer rather than to the applicant). *See also Walker v. Emplrs Ins. of Wausau,* 846 N.E.2d 1098 (Ind. Ct. App. 2006) (holding that the insurer's admission that no policy exclusion applied estopped it from later asserting the applicability of a policy exclusion).

## PROBLEM NINE

Defendant insurer issued a group life insurance policy in the amount of $50,000 to a law firm in which Barwick was a partner and an insured. Under the terms of the policy, the amount of coverage was reduced by one-half when a person reached the age of 65. After Barwick attained the age of 65, the insurer's monthly billings to the law firm, which showed Barwick's correct birth date, continued to show Barwick's coverage as $50,000 and continued to charge a premium for $50,000 of life insurance coverage, which the firm paid. At the age of 66, Barwick died, and the insurer tendered payment of $25,000 to Barwick's widow. She sued for the full $50,000 amount.

• What result? Should Mrs. Barwick recover $25,000 or $50,000?

## PROBLEM TEN

Steve Clark, who enlisted in the United States Marine Corps in 1966, purchased a ten thousand dollar life insurance policy with the World Service Life Insurance Company. This policy had no war risks or aviation exclusion policies. Shortly thereafter, Robert Brummel, a soliciting agent employed by the Prudential Life Insurance Company, urged Clark to drop the World Life policy, and replace it with a Prudential life insurance policy. Brummel advised Clark that he could obtain a Prudential policy similar to the World Life policy, without any limiting war risk or aviation exclusion clause. Clark then cancelled his World Life policy, and obtained what he thought was similar coverage under the Prudential policy.

However, the Prudential policy was never delivered to Clark, and the Prudential policy did in fact contain war risk and aviation exclusion clauses.

Clark was killed in Vietnam in 1968 when his helicopter crashed and burned under enemy fire. Prudential initially agreed to pay the life insurance claim to Clark's beneficiaries, but later stated that this decision was made through "oversight and mistake," and that Clark's claim in fact was barred by the war risk and aviation exclusion clause in the Prudential policy.

- Should Clark's beneficiaries recover the life insurance proceeds in this case?

- Why or why not?

# [B] Non-Payment of Premiums: Waiver and Estoppel

The policyholder has the duty to pay premiums on or prior to the due date of the premium. Failure to do so will cause the policy to lapse (normally after a "grace period"). The insurer does not have the duty to notify the policyholder of payments due since the policy itself provides those dates. However, a course of dealing between policyholder and insurer may impose such a duty on the insurer. As with other contractual obligations, the insurer could waive the requirement of a timely premium payment, or through its conduct be estopped from relying on such obligation of the policyholder. The following case discusses waiver and estoppel defenses in the context of non-payment of life insurance premiums:

## Time Insurance Co. v. Vick

Illinois Appellate Court

250 Ill. App. 3d 465, 620 N.E.2d 1309 (1993)

On March 30, 1983, the decedent, John W. Vick, submitted an application for life insurance to plaintiff, Time Insurance Company ("Time"). Time accepted the application and issued an annually renewable term life insurance policy. The policy, dated April 1, 1983, provided for a death benefit of $100,000. Although the decedent initially elected to pay premiums on a monthly basis, as indicated by his application, he later changed the premium payment plan from a monthly to a quarterly interval. His insurance agent handled his request, which was received by Time along with the balance of the first quarterly premium on May 16, 1983. Subsequent to this mode of payment change, the decedent did not timely pay the next quarterly premium due on July 1, 1983 which caused the policy to lapse. On September 30, 1983, Time requested that the decedent complete a supplemental application in order to be considered for reinstatement.

On October 5, 1983, the decedent executed the application and submitted it along with the back premium. Time approved the application, and the decedent's policy was reinstated effective July 1, 1983. There were fourteen payments due under the policy from the date of its inception through the date of decedent's death. Thirteen of those payments were received after their respective due dates, with five of the thirteen being made after the expiration of the policy's 31-day grace period. With regard to the premium due for the quarter beginning April 1, 1986, the decedent did not mail his payment along with the April 1, 1986 quarterly premium notice until June 10, 1986, which caused the policy to again lapse. Time negotiated the check on June 16, 1986. On June 24, 1986, Time forwarded to the decedent a request to complete a supplemental application for reinstatement of the lapsed policy. The decedent executed the supplemental application on or about July 25, 1986, and it was received by Time on July 28, 1986. On July 29, Time approved reinstatement of the policy, with an effective date of April 1, 1986, based on the medical history supplied by decedent on the supplemental application.

Unbeknownst to Time, however, decedent died on that same date from a self-induced alcohol and thioridazine overdose. The decedent died intestate and was survived by his wife, Susan Vick, defendant in this cause, and their minor daughter, Melissa Vick. Decedent did not designate a beneficiary when he purchased the policy. On August 4, 1986, defendant mailed a check to Time together with the premium payment stub for the July 1, 1986 premium. Time negotiated the check on August 6, 1986. On August 30, 1986, defendant, acting through her attorney, informed Time of the decedent's death and demanded full payment of the policy amount.

In a letter dated November 10, 1986, which defendant received on November 24, Time advised defendant's attorney that the policy had been reinstated based on material misrepresentations made by the decedent in his supplemental application, and that, as a result, it was denying payment of the benefits and rescinding the policy as of the effective date of the reinstatement, April 1, 1986. Time enclosed with its letter a check in the amount of $315.60 for the premiums paid on said policy subsequent to the date of the lapse. Defendant refused to accept the check.

Time thereafter filed a complaint seeking judicial rescission of the reinstatement of the subject policy as well as its cancellation based on material misrepresentations of fact made by the decedent on his supplemental application. Time also requested the court to issue an order requiring defendant to accept the sum of $315.60 as full and final satisfaction of all demands against it under said policy and to pay the costs it incurred in bringing this action.

On Time's motion, defendant was appointed the Special Administratrix of decedent's estate for the purpose of defending the action. Defendant then petitioned the court to appoint her as Special Administratrix for the purposes of prosecuting or defending this action and filed a counterclaim at law seeking the proceeds of the policy, interest on the proceeds from the date of the decedent's death, and an additional sum of $25,000 plus reasonable attorney's fees and other costs.

On October 10, 1990, Time filed a Request to Admit Facts pursuant to Supreme Court Rule 216. Defendant did not respond. On May 15, 1991, the trial court entered an agreed order admitting the facts contained in the Request to Admit as true for purposes of this action. Defendant, therefore, admitted that decedent had been hospitalized on four separate occasions from July 12, 1983 through September 15, 1985 for the treatment of acute and chronic alcoholism, was treated on approximately a weekly basis as an outpatient by a psychiatrist from September 16, 1985 through July 25, 1986 for major depression and alcohol dependence, received and ingested the medications thioridazine and antabuse for the treatment of the respective illnesses, and died as a result of alcohol and thioridazine toxicity, leaving a note in which he indicated that he intended to end his own life.

Time then filed a motion for summary judgment, and defendant subsequently filed her own such motion. On October 23, 1991, the trial court granted Time's motion for summary judgment and ordered defendant to accept the sum of $315.60 in full and final satisfaction of all demands against Time under the policy. In addition, the reinstatement of the insurance policy was rescinded, and said policy was cancelled. It is from this order that defendant appeals.

Defendant contends that: (1) Time has waived its right to terminate the life insurance policy for non-payment of the premium due April 1, 1986 by having previously accepted late payments; (2) Time is estopped from terminating the life insurance policy for non-payment of the April 1, 1986 premium because it received and accepted the premium after the grace period expired; (3) Time did not sustain its burden of proving that it properly effectuated the termination of the policy within six months of April 1, 1986, the date of the decedent's alleged default arising from non-payment of the premium; and (4) alternatively, a genuine issue of material fact exists regarding the payment of premiums or termination of the policy.

The central issue in this case is whether the subject policy properly lapsed. Defendant concedes that if the policy did properly lapse, the decedent's estate would not be entitled to the policy proceeds because the decedent was not insurable at the time of reinstatement. Defendant, therefore, does not rely on Time's reinstatement of the policy on July 29, 1986, but rather contends that the decedent's policy did not properly lapse as a result of the non-payment of the premium due April 1, 1986 within the 31-day grace period provided by the terms of the contract. Conversely, Time avers that the subject policy was reinstated after it had properly lapsed, but that such reinstatement was based on material misrepresentations made by the decedent on his supplemental application which now requires rescission of the reinstatement.

Defendant first contends that Time, by its previous acceptance of late payments made by the decedent, has waived any right it may have had to declare a forfeiture or lapse of the decedent's life insurance policy for failure to pay the premium due April 1, 1986 before or within the 31-day grace period. Defendant points out that Time had previously accepted three payments from the decedent after expiration of the 31-day grace period without forfeiting or lapsing the policy, or requiring a reinstatement application and proof of insurability.

It is well-established that the law does not favor the forfeiture of life insurance policies, and unless the circumstances show a clear intention to claim a forfeiture for nonpayment of the premium, such forfeiture will not be enforced.... An insurer may waive a forfeiture provision in an insurance policy by an act, statement or course of conduct toward the insured which recognizes the policy as existing, although the time for payment of the premium has expired.

Furthermore, if the conduct of the insurer is such as to lead the insured to believe that a forfeiture will not be insisted upon, the insurer will be estopped from taking advantage of such forfeiture. In the present case, defendant initially alleges that five of the fourteen payments due under the policy from the date of its inception through the date of the decedent's death were received after the expiration of the policy's 31-day grace period, with Time requesting only one reinstatement application in addition to the one at issue.

A close reading of the record reveals that defendant's allegation is misleading. The policy in question includes a grace period provision which provides:

> You have 31 days to pay each premium after it falls due. Any premium unpaid at the end of the Grace Period will be in default. The policy will then terminate. . . .

It also contains a reinstatement provision which states:

> This policy may be reinstated at any time within five years after default in payment of premium. Reinstatement is subject to the conditions that follow. (1) The request must be made within five years after the policy lapsed. (2) You must show evidence satisfactory to Time that you are still insurable. (3) You must pay all overdue premiums with interest from the date due of each at the rate of 6% compounded annually.

The deposition transcript of Robert Reindl, the individual in charge of Time's life policyholder service department, reveals that Time's computer billing service generates a lapse notice after the grace period has expired when payment for a premium due has not been received. The lapse notice provides as follows:

> Your policy lapsed at the end of the grace period unless otherwise provided in the contract. However payment of the amount overdue will be accepted if received by the company during the insured's life time and on or before 60 days of the due date. After this offer expires, application for reinstatement will be required.
>
> A written offer to extend the time for payment of a premium, such as the one contained in the lapse notice above, is sanctioned by section 235 of the Illinois Insurance Code ("the Code"). . . .

A summary of the premium payments made under the subject policy, which is contained in the record, indicates that only three of the five payments made after the expiration of the 31-day grace period were made more than 60 days after the due date; those payments were for the premiums due April 1, 1983, July 1, 1983, and April 1, 1986.

The deposition testimony of Reindl indicates that the column on the payment summary entitled "Date Premium Received" reflects the date the premium was processed by Time, not necessarily the date the monies were received. According to

Reindl, although Time did not have any record as to when it actually received the monies, it could have requested a copy of the check from its bank, and he estimated that Time would have received the check within 24 hours of the date stamped on the check by the bank.

The payment summary reveals that the balance of the premium due for the quarter beginning April 1, 1983 was paid more than 60 days after the due date; however, Time's employee, Debbie Socolick, who worked in the policy service department at that time, testified at her deposition that Time received a written request from the decedent's insurance agent to change the premium payment interval on the subject policy from monthly to quarterly. The request was received by Time on May 16, 1983, and was accompanied by the balance of the premium due for the first quarter. That balance, however, does not appear on the payment summary until July 19, 1983 due to the mode of payment change.

Therefore, under the circumstances, a reinstatement was not necessary as the balance of the premium due was received by Time within 60 days of the premium due date. It should be noted that a premium based on a monthly interval was collected from the decedent at the time he submitted his application on March 30, 1983.

With regard to the premiums due July 1, 1983 and April 1, 1986, which the decedent paid more than 60 days after the due date, the record reveals that Time advised decedent his policy had lapsed and requested that he submit a supplemental application demonstrating evidence of insurability so that he could be considered for reinstatement. The decedent complied by completing and signing two supplemental applications dated October 5, 1983 and July 25, 1986. On both occasions, the policy was reinstated and made effective in 1983 and 1986, respectively.

Defendant admitted, in a signed affidavit, that the decedent received, signed and mailed the supplemental application at issue to his insurance agent on July 25, 1986. The record, therefore, reveals that Time adhered to its lapse policy without exception. Consequently, it has not waived its right to declare a forfeiture or lapse of the subject policy for non-payment of the April 1, 1986 premium within the 31-day grace period as there was no conduct on its part which would have led the decedent to believe that a forfeiture would not be enforced. It is undisputed that Time had accepted late premium payments in the past and, on one occasion, prior to the present one, reinstated the policy. However, such actions were pursuant to valid company policies referred to in the insurance policy and do not constitute waiver....

Defendant next contends that Time is estopped from terminating the policy for non-payment of the premium due April 1, 1986 because it received and accepted the premium payment from decedent after expiration of the policy's grace period. Defendant argues that Time made no attempt until November 10, 1986 to refund the premium to the decedent which it received and deposited on June 16, 1986.

According to defendant, the deposition testimony of Kathy Strozinsky, the underwriter who handled the reinstatement of decedent's policy, demonstrates that

Time did not follow company policy when it failed to refund the decedent's premium payment 30 days after sending its June 24, 1986 letter to him and not receiving the reinstatement application it requested from him. Strozinsky stated that rather than closing out the decedent's file and refunding his premium, Time reinstated his policy. Furthermore, the deposition testimony of Reindl, defendant asserts, provides similarly, and, in addition, establishes that the best evidence of Time's receipt of a premium payment is the decedent's cancelled check or money order. This last point is also noted on the back of the premium payment notices sent to decedent and provides: "Record of Payment — Your cancelled check or money order stub will be your receipt."

The doctrine of estoppel arises by operation of law and acts as a bar to the rights and privileges of an insurer where it would be inequitable to permit their assertion. . . . Unlike the doctrine of waiver, such relinquishment need not be voluntary, intended or desired by the insurer; however, the doctrine of estoppel does "necessarily require[] some prejudicial reliance of the insured upon some act, conduct or nonaction of the insurer." . . . In this case, it is undisputed that Time received and negotiated the decedent's check, representing payment for the premium due April 1, 1986 on June 16, 1986, and that it did not tender a refund until November 10, 1986.

The reason Time did not attempt to refund the premium for 147 days is twofold. First, it was waiting to receive the decedent's supplemental application to determine whether it contained evidence of insurability, an intention manifested by Time to the decedent in its June 24, 1986 letter. Time did not receive the decedent's supplemental application until July 28, 1986, and as soon as it did, it reviewed the application and reinstated the policy the following day. Secondly, Time, upon learning on August 30, 1986 that the decedent had died, began an investigation and subsequently discovered fraud in that decedent had materially misrepresented his health, inducing Time to reinstate his policy.

Furthermore, Time, having been induced to reinstate the policy, was entitled to keep the premium which it believed it had earned until such time as defendant gave notice of the decedent's death. In fact, rather than advise Time of the decedent's death on July 29, 1986 or soon thereafter, defendant paid the July 1, 1986 quarterly premium on August 4, 1986, after the decedent had already died.

Under these facts, Time is not estopped from terminating the policy since estoppel requires some prejudicial reliance by the insured. There can be none here. Defendant cannot now claim that she relied to her detriment on Time's acceptance of the check when the decedent knew that the policy had lapsed, applied for reinstatement, and failed to disclose his extensive medical history which was material to his supplemental application.

For the reasons stated herein, the judgment of the circuit court of Cook County granting summary judgment in favor of Time Insurance and denying defendant's motion for summary judgment is affirmed.

## Notes and Questions

1. In the *Vick* case, was there any action or inaction on the part of the insurer upon which the policyholder could have arguably relied to his detriment, which would thus provide the policyholder a basis to assert a defense of estoppel against the insurer? Why or why not?

2. There has been a great deal of litigation concerning whether or not an insurer had validly "accepted" a late premium payment. The following cases illustrate this continuing controversy:

(a) In *Mardirosian v. Lincoln Nat'l Life Ins. Co.*, 739 F.2d 474 (9th Cir. 1984), a life insurance policy listed husband Greg as the insured and wife Aida as the owner and beneficiary. The premium notices were mailed to Greg, but only after Aida and Greg had separated and moved into new residences, as a result of which the insurer's premium notices were returned, marked "moved—left no address." The company instituted an address search for Greg. This effort failed, and the company made no attempt to notify Aida of the prospective lapse. The policy lapsed on April 7, 1980, and Greg died on July 18, 1980. Through her attorney, Aida in December mailed a check for payment of the premium which had been due in April. An accompanying letter stated in part:

> Mrs. Mardirosian ... has furnished me with the enclosed check in the amount of $290.06 payable to the Lincoln National Life Insurance Company in payment of the premium which was due and of which she never received notice.
>
> Please accept the enclosed check in full payment of the premium due and please also pay the full amount of the proceeds to our client in care of our offices for the amount of the policy due in the year of death of Mr. Mardirosian....

The insurer cashed the check, later explaining that it deposited it in a "suspense account" until its legal department could review the matter. In a letter dated January 15, 1981, it informed Aida that her check was not a timely payment of the premium and refunded her payment. (The applicable California statutory law also provided that an insurer could not deny reinstatement unless the insurer "acts within a reasonable time.") What should be the result in this case?

(b) The policyholder, Crum, failed to pay his insurance premium within a 31-day grace period expiring on February 1st, but he did forward a premium check dated February 15th which was received by the insurer, Prudential, on February 18th, and deposited on February 22nd. Also on February 22nd, Prudential sent Crum a computer letter that any remittance could not be accepted since it would be received after the grace period, but the letter also included an application for reinstatement. Unfortunately, Crum never received this letter since he died on February 22nd. Prudential refunded Crum's net premium on March 24th. Is Prudential liable under the policy, or not? *See Crum v. Prudential Ins. Co.*, 356 F. Supp. 1054 (N.D. Miss. 1973). Can *Crum* be reconciled with the *Mardirosian* case, *supra*?

(c) In early November 1976, the policyholder Anderson was sent a letter from his automobile insurance company stating that if he didn't pay an overdue premium, his coverage would be cancelled. On November 18th, the insurer mailed Anderson a cancellation letter, but on November 19th, before receiving this second letter, Anderson tendered his late premium to the insurer's general agent, who accepted the payment and mailed it to the home office. Anderson suffered an automobile accident on November 29th, but sometime after the accident, the insurer returned the premium to its agent for return to Anderson. What result? *See Northeast Ins. Co. v. Concord General Mut. Ins. Co.*, 461 A.2d 1056 (Me. 1983).

(d) The policyholder Serenos argued that their automobile insurer should be estopped from cancelling a renewal policy because the company in the past had accepted late premium payments, and because an agent of the insurer had told the Serenos over the telephone that late payment of the renewal premium was "no problem" and could be paid when the Serenos returned to Arizona from a Florida vacation. A paragraph from the policy renewal policy entitled "Automatic Termination" read:

> If we offer to renew or continue and you or your representative do not accept, this policy will automatically terminate at the end of the current policy period. Failure to pay the required renewal or continuation premium when due shall mean that you have not accepted our offer.

What result? *See Sereno v. Lumbermens Mut. Casualty Co.*, 647 P.2d 1144 (Ariz. 1982).

3. Can an insurance company waive an initial premium payment? In *Lawrimore v. American Health & Life Ins. Co.*, 276 S.E.2d 296 (S.C. 1981), it was held that a waiver of an initial premium prepayment may be implied from an unconditional delivery of the insurance policy without requiring payment, or from extensions of time to make payment. And in *Kramer v. Metropolitan Life Ins. Co.*, 494 F. Supp. 1026 (D.N.J. 1980), an insurer was held to have waived the first premium payment to be paid in cash as a condition precedent to the policy becoming effective when the agent refused to accept the initial payment, and when the insured's Check-O-Matic banking system through which the prospective insureds had authorized premium payments had deducted and had withdrawn the premium payment from the insured's checking account.

## [C] Course of Dealing

A custom or practice on the part of the insurer to accept late or erratic premium payments from a policyholder may create a course of dealing whereby the insurer can be estopped from claiming any lapse of the policy for failure to make a timely premium payment. In *Walters Auto Body Shop, Inc. v. Farmers Ins. Co.*, 829 S.W.2d 637 (Mo. Ct. App. 1992), the court rejected application of estoppel for the policyholder and observed:

> It is a universal rule of law that in the absence of an agreement to the contrary, the delivery of a check to the creditor and his acceptance of it is not

payment of the debt or obligation until the check has itself been paid, and that when the check is not paid, it may not be said to have constituted payment of the debt or obligation for which it was given. Moreover, this rule extends as well to transactions falling within the purview of insurance law, which contemplates that insurance premiums are ordinarily to be paid in cash, and that in the absence of a different intention or agreement, the giving of a check therefor will not operate as payment.

The rule still remains that payment by check is conditional until that check is paid, in the absence of agreement or circumstances indicating the contrary.

While the record might arguably show that Farmers accepted overdue premiums as long as the amount due did not exceed 150% of the sum of the previous month's premium and service charges, it does not support a finding that, as a matter of law, Farmers waived its right to cancel when no payment at all was made and the balance fell below the required 150%.

Issues of this sort tend to be fact sensitive, making it difficult to articulate a hard-and-fast rule of when an insurer's acceptance of payment will create estoppel and when an insurer may stand on its formal contractual rights despite previous conduct that did not strictly adhere to those rights.

## *Notes and Questions*

1. Should waiver or estoppel be applied against an insurance company that had previously accepted one monthly premium after the time for its payment had passed? *See Blanton v. John Hancock Mut. Life Ins. Co.*, 345 F. Supp. 168 (N.D. Tex. 1971), *aff'd*, 463 F.2d 421 (5th Cir. 1972). What if the insurance company had a long-continuing custom of accepting late premiums notwithstanding the fact that the policy holder was delinquent under the terms of the policy? *See Rice v. Reliance Standard Life Ins. Co.*, 512 F. Supp. 1011 (D. Del. 1981).

2. What general guidelines and public policy arguments should a court utilize in determining the custom or habit of the insurer in accepting late premiums, and whether such acceptance of late premiums constitutes a waiver or estoppel defense in favor of the policyholder? *See, e.g., Guardian Life Ins. Co. v. Weiser*, 51 N.Y.S.2d 771 (Sup. Ct. 1941), *aff'd*, 268 A.D. 901, 51 N.Y.S.2d 457 (1944).

### PROBLEM ELEVEN

Policyholder paid timely premiums for several years on his life insurance policy, but then missed the premium due on January 16, 1992. The insurer, however, accepted a check on March 19, 1992, and reinstated the policy which had lapsed on February 16, 1992 (at the end of the grace period). The policyholder did not pay the premium due on March 16, 1993, and told the agent on April 16, 1993 (the last day of the grace period) that he would pay it on April 23rd. The policyholder died on April 26th without having paid the premium. Has a course of dealing been reached between the policyholder and the insurer, so that one could persuasively argue the waiver of timely premium payments? Why or why not?

## [D] Non-Waiver Agreements and Reservation of Rights Notice

If an insurance company is required under its policy to investigate certain facts related to the potential liability of its policyholder, and to defend the policyholder under its policy coverage, then the policyholder or another potential claimant might argue that the insurance company, through its continuing investigation and conduct, has waived any possible defense against coverage or is estopped to deny it. But a non-waiver agreement or a reservation of rights notice would negate any such inference.

Under a consensual non-waiver agreement, the policyholder and insurer agree that the insurer will incur the cost of investigating and defending the insurance claim, but this investigation would not preclude the insurer from later asserting a defense of non-coverage. A reservation of rights notice, on the other hand, is a unilateral notice which must be promptly delivered to the policyholder and his or her attorney, and to any other potential claimant, whenever the insurer, during the course of its investigation or its defenses of the claim, acquires information of any potential defense of non-coverage. *See generally* KEETON & WIDISS, INSURANCE LAW § 6.7(a) (1988).

## First United Bank v. First American Title Ins. Co.

Nebraska Supreme Court
496 N.W.2d 474 (1993)

First United must show that American Title assumed or continued the defense of the foreclosure action against First United without an effective reservation of rights agreement. It is uncontroverted that American Title failed to obtain a reservation of rights agreement from First United. In addressing First United's estoppel argument, the Court of Appeals stated: [W]e find that whether the Title Company was estopped to deny coverage is irrelevant because it assumed [First United's] defense without sending [First United] a reservation of rights.

Estoppel may not be used to bring the claim within the terms of the policy, where it is clear that no loss existed. Although the Court of Appeals correctly stated the general rule of estoppel, we disagree that it was "irrelevant" that American Title assumed First United's defense without notifying First United of a reservation of rights. On the contrary, this case exemplifies the precise situation in which a reservation of rights is essential to protect the interests of both the insured and the insurer. Reservation of rights is a means by which prior to a determination of the liability of the insured, the insurer seeks to suspend the operation of waiver and estoppel.

When coverage is in doubt, the insurer may offer to defend the insured, reserving all of its policy defenses in case the insured is found liable. Upon such notification the insured may either accept the reservation of rights and allow the company to defend or it may reject the reservation of rights and take over the defense itself....

The policy reasons underlying reservation of rights are two-fold: (1) to allow an insured to more ably protect its own interests by retaining control over its own defense, and (2) to avoid conflicts of interest between the insurer and its insured. The record shows, and American Title does not dispute, that First United had an opportunity to protect its own interests by accepting an offer from the Bank of Bellevue. Even though First United notified American Title of the offer, American Title did not endeavor to negotiate on behalf of its insured, nor was American Title prompted to send any reservation of rights at that point.

It is obvious that, by relying on American Title's unconditional defense, First United was denied the opportunity to control its own defense and protect its own interests. Moreover, the record indicates that, while American Title was controlling First United's defense, American Title was collecting data which would only be relevant in litigation against its insured. For example, American Title requested First United to explain how it had suffered a loss under the policy. This was not an issue in Southwest's foreclosure action against First United, but is a central issue in American Title's denial of coverage to its insured and First United's resulting breach of contract suit. Such conduct on the part of American Title at least raises the inference of divided loyalties. American Title's failure to obtain a reservation of rights agreement from First United, far from being irrelevant, was in clear violation of the policy considerations underlying such agreements. Thus, the second prong of the test is satisfied.

Finally, First United must show that it was harmed or prejudiced in some way by American Title's actions. If First United has not been prejudiced, there is no ground for the assertion of estoppel. [W]e now hold that American Title's assumption of complete control of a matter involving a possible claim for over 12 months, with the consequent need of cooperation under the terms of the policy, and without a reservation of rights agreement, constitutes a sufficient showing of prejudice as a basis for urging estoppel.

Furthermore, American Title's conduct deprived First United of the opportunity to otherwise protect its interests by entering into negotiations with Bank of Bellevue. First United has satisfied all three requirements for application of the doctrine of estoppel to American Title's defense of non-coverage under the policy. Moreover, the facts of this case … present a highly persuasive argument for the operation of the doctrine of estoppel.

We therefore adopt the exception to the general rule of estoppel and hold that when an insurance company assumes the defense of an action against its insured, without reservation of rights, and with knowledge, actual or presumed, of facts which would have permitted it to deny coverage, it may be estopped from subsequently raising the defense of non-coverage. Based on the recited uncontroverted facts, American Title is estopped from raising the defense of non-coverage to First United's suit on the policy.

## *Notes and Questions*

1. A bilateral non-waiver agreement generally reserves to each party its respective rights, provides that the insurer will defend the suit at its own expense, and ensures that nothing which is done under the agreement will be deemed to constitute a waiver

of any respective rights. A unilateral reservation of rights notice is given by the insurer that it will defend the suit, but that it still reserves all non-coverage rights it may have under the policy.

The test of the duty of a liability insurance company to defend its policyholder, under the majority rule, is found in the scope of the allegations in the complaint against the policyholder. Thus, when a legal complaint arguably brings the action within the policy coverage, the insurer is required to defend its policyholder, regardless of the ultimate outcome of the action, or its liability to the policy. *See, e.g., Socony-Vacuum Oil Co. v. Continental Casualty Co.*, 59 N.E.2d 199 (Ohio 1945).

When there is a clear duty to defend its policyholder based upon allegations in the filed complaint, an insurer cannot excuse itself from this duty to defend by seeking to require the policyholder to enter into a bilateral non-waiver agreement as a condition precedent to making such a defense. *See, e.g., Motorists Mut. Ins. Co. v. Trainor*, 294 N.E.2d 874 (Ohio 1973).

2. A reservation of rights notice must promptly be given to the policyholder "within a reasonable time" or "as soon as practical," and any unreasonable delay by the insurer will defeat its right of disclaimer. *See, e.g., Allstate Ins. Co. v. Gross*, 265 N.E.2d 736 (N.Y. 1970). ("Reasonableness" is generally determined in light of all the facts and circumstances of each particular case.)

3. What happens when the insurer unsuccessfully attempts to achieve a bilateral non-waiver agreement, and then subsequently sends a unilateral reservation of rights notice to the policyholder? Some courts have held that where an attempt to achieve a bilateral non-waiver agreement with the policyholder fails, and a unilateral reservation of rights is subsequently sent to the policyholder by the insurer, the policyholder's failure to respond makes the reservation of rights effective to preserve the insurer's rights under the policy. *Pacific Indem. Co. v. Acel Delivery Service, Inc.*, 485 F.2d 1169, 1174 (5th Cir. 1973), *cert. denied*, 415 U.S. 921 (1974). Other courts have required the policyholder's consent to the reservation of rights and will only find consent in the policyholder's silence if the reservation of rights letter informs the policyholder of their right to reject the insurer's defense of the case under the reservation and policyholder's right to have their own attorney. *Merchants Indem. Corp. v. Eggleston*, 179 A.2d 505, 512 (N.J. 1962).

Those courts require such informed consent so the policyholder can hire his or her own attorney without prejudicial delay to the defense of the underlying action, and permit the policyholder to control a case in which the policyholder may be required to pay any final judgment. *See also Diamond Service Co. v. Utica Mut. Ins. Co.*, 476 A.2d 648, 655 (D.C. 1984).

4. Many states also have codified the requirement of an insurer to issue a timely reservation of rights to all claimants. Example: "Whenever any insurer on a policy of liability insurance discovers a breach of the terms or conditions of the insurance contract by the insured, the insurer shall notify the claimant or the claimant's counsel of the breach. Notification shall be given within forty-five days after discovery by the

insurer of the breach or of the claim, whichever is later." VA. CODE ANN. § 38.2-2226. Violation of these statutory provisions can also subject an insurer to fines imposed by the State Insurance Commission.

5. Finally, when will the insurer be estopped to deny coverage based on the fact that its defense of the action on behalf of its policyholder in fact prejudiced the policyholder? Again, the courts are split on this question. Some courts apply estoppel against the insurance company only when it has conducted the action to final judgment or has settled claims. *Boulet v. Millers Mutual Insurance Ass'n*, 362 F.2d 619, 622–23 (8th Cir. 1966). Other courts, and notably the New Jersey courts, hold that prejudice to a policyholder will be presumed when the insurer undertakes the policyholder's defense even though it does not pursue the claim to settlement or final judgment. *American Legion Tri-County Memorial Hospital v. St. Paul Fire & Marine Ins. Co.*, 256 A.2d 57 (N.J. Super. 1969).

6. In the case of *World Harvest Church, Inc. v. GuideOne Mut. Ins. Co.*, 695 S.E.2d 6 (Ga. 2010), although a sister insurer had issued a written reservation of rights regarding a prior similar lawsuit, the insurer advised its policyholder that it "did not see coverage" but it did not issue a written reservation of rights prior to assuming the defense of the underlying action for almost 11 months, when it advised the policyholder that it would stop defending the policyholder because there was no coverage. *Held*: The insurer was estopped from asserting non-coverage, and prejudice was presumed, when the insurer conducted an initial defense of its policyholder without a reservation of rights notice.

### PROBLEM TWELVE

Software, Inc. is insured under a "Businessowners Policy" by Wellworth Ins. Co. In 1981, a customer sued Software alleging breach of the software contract and Wellworth defended its insured under a reservation of rights. Finally, Wellworth paid plaintiff $3,000 in settlement of the case. In 1986, another customer sued Software on similar charges.

The insurer entered into a reservation of rights and non-waiver agreement with the insured whereby the insurer would pay 50 percent of the insured's litigation fees and reserved its right to bring a declaratory judgment action to assert that the policy did not cover the claim. The suit was settled requiring the insured to pay $563,000.

Wellworth refuses to pay asserting that there is no coverage for this kind of a claim. The insured argues that because the insurer paid the $3,000 settlement in the 1981 case, it is now estopped to deny coverage or has waived its right to do so.

• What result?

## [E] Election

The "election" theory is a hybrid between waiver and estoppel. It contemplates a rule of law which restricts the actor (normally the insurer) to a choice from among a limited number of legal options. It is similar to estoppel because it is an imposed rule of law, and it is similar to waiver because a choice must still be made by the actor. Election is most commonly found in insurance law when the insurer has the option to repair or rebuild insured property or pay a monetary claim. According to Professor Keeton, although the concept of election is "more troublesome" for the courts to employ than either waiver or estoppel, it is often more useful for the policyholder to utilize since it does not require the voluntary relinquishment element for waiver, nor the detrimental reliance factor for estoppel. *See* KEETON & WIDISS, INSURANCE LAW § 6.1(b)(4) (1988); JERRY & RICHMOND UNDERSTANDING INSURANCE LAW § 25E (6th ed. 2018).

## Howard v. Reserve Insurance Co.

Illinois Appellate Court
117 Ill. App. 2d 390, 254 N.E.2d 631 (1969)

Plaintiff Howard had fire damage to his building covered by insurance policies issued by Reserve Insurance Company, Market Insurance Company and Midland National Insurance Company. These policies contained, *inter alia*, the following provisions:

> The insured shall give immediate written notice to this Company of any loss, protect the property from further damage, forthwith separate the damaged and undamaged personal property, put it in the best possible order, furnish a complete inventory of the destroyed, damaged and undamaged property....
>
> It shall be optional with this Company to take all, or any part, of the property at the agreed or appraised value, and also to repair, rebuild or replace the property destroyed or damaged with other of like kind and quality within a reasonable time, on giving notice of its intention so to do within thirty days after the receipt of the proof of loss herein required.

The fire occurred on June 14, 1963; plaintiff notified the insurance companies on June 17th and on June 25th the following reply was sent by them:

> You have notified us of a fire at the captioned address which occurred June 14, 1963, under Market Insurance Company Policy No. 5425-1167 and Reserve Insurance Company Policy No. 1025-1509.

[Adjusters representing the insurance companies and the insured could not agree on an amount for damages. Meanwhile the insured had some of the damage repaired to protect the property from further damage. When billed for this repair work, the insurance companies denied liability on the ground that the insured breached the insurance contract by depriving the insurance companies of the opportunity to exercise the option reserved to them in the policies to repair or rebuild.] It appears that efforts were made by the parties to reach some agreement as to the fire loss. There is evidence that immediately after the fire some action had to be taken by the insured in order to protect the property from further damage. In this respect, the insured complied with the provisions of the policies. Thereafter negotiations were commenced while some of the repairs to the building were being made.

The insurance companies were aware that these repairs were in progress and did not advise the insured that they should cease because the companies may exercise their option to repair or rebuild. We are mindful that the policies provided that the insurance companies had thirty days after receipt of proof of loss to exercise their option. Knowing however that the insured commenced some of the repairs which were necessary to avoid further loss and damage, the insurance companies did not say "stop further work." We agree with the trial court's statement:

> This letter (June 25, 1963) that was sent did not exercise the option, and following that letter, negotiations were going on with the adjusters for the companies with regard to amounts, and if the company had taken the position that they would exercise that option, even if that letter didn't so indicate it, it was the duty of these adjusters to say, "why do we talk about money? We don't care what you're asking or what the price is. We're going to do that ourselves."

It is difficult to draw a clear cut line between the limits to which the insured can go in its duty to "protect the property from further damage, forthwith separate the damaged and undamaged personal property, put it in the best possible order...." It is equally difficult at times to determine whether it is more reasonable to complete temporary repairs or to do only so much, and stop at some point in anticipation of the insurance company's right to exercise its option to rebuild or repair.

All of the concerned parties should approach this situation fairly and honestly. If the insurance company demands its rights under the policy it should let this be known to the insured promptly and in a "plain, simple and straightforward manner." On the other hand, the insured should not present an exaggerated and unreasonable proof of loss. Counsel for the companies, in his oral argument before this court, stated that there is no law in Illinois on the provision found in fire insurance policies on the question of the insurance company's option to repair, rebuild or replace.

It is our opinion that Illinois law recognizes all valid provisions of standard fire insurance policies including the insurance company's option to repair, rebuild or replace the property destroyed or damaged. We adopt the language of the Court of Appeals of Kentucky in *German Insurance Company v. Hazard Bank*, 104 S.W. 725 (Ky. 1907):

> In insurance contracts, as in all other contracts, it is incumbent upon the parties to deal with each other in a plain, simple, and straightforward manner, and, where an election is to be exercised under a contract, notice should be made in such manner as to leave no doubt in the mind of the opposite party of an intention to exercise it.

In the instant case, the letter of June 25, 1963, in our opinion is not clear indication of the insurance company's exercise of their option rights to repair, rebuild or replace. Said letter "insists" on compliance with the policy provisions in lines 90 to 122 relating to the duty of the insured to protect the property from further damage, but it "points out" lines 141 to 147 [quoted above] gave the insurer the options to repair, rebuild or replace. We agree with the insured that said letter did not contain a clear, unambiguous and explicit exercise of the option. Appellants ask this court to establish by its decision some guidelines to prevent future litigation. It is axiomatic that each legal controversy must be resolved within the framework of the facts and circumstances and the law therein involved. Basic guidelines may be helpful but they alone do not resolve legal controversies and possible future litigation. The above reference to the Kentucky Court of Appeals decision may be helpful.

In *Home Mutual Insurance Company of Iowa v. Stewart*, 100 P.2d 159 (Colo. 1940), the Supreme Court of Colorado suggests five criteria to make the notice of election by insurance companies effective.

(1) It must be made within a reasonable time after the damage or loss has occurred to the insured.

(2) It must be clear, positive, distinct and unambiguous.

(3) The repairs or replacements must be made within a reasonable time.

(4) It cannot be coupled with an offer of compromise or be made for the purpose of forcing a compromise, but it must be an election made with no alternative.

(5) When the election is made, the repair or replacement must be suitable and adequate.

We adopt these criteria, however, with this caution that most legal controversies present differences which must be decided individually within the legal and factual bounds therein contained.

Appellants direct our attention to the language contained in certain cases in support of their appeal. In *Aetna Insurance Co. v. Platt*, 40 Ill. App. 191 (1891), the insurance company notified the plaintiff of its intention to rebuild and repair and within eight days began such work. The question of the amount of damages was submitted to arbitrators. The Illinois Appellate Court reversed the judgment of the trial court holding that submission to arbitration to ascertain damage was not an election to pay the loss and a waiver of the right to rebuild or repair.

Both parties to this appeal direct our attention to *Eliot Five Cent Savings Bank v. Commercial Union Assurance Co.*, 7 N.E. 550 (Mass. 1886).... In the *Eliot* case immediate repairs were necessary to prevent further damage. The insurance company claimed, that the insured by entering and repairing the premises immediately after the fire, deprived the defendant of its right to elect, rebuild or repair. The Massachusetts Court said in affirming the judgment of the trial court for the insured:

The fact that the plaintiff had commenced making repairs without notice did not deprive the defendant of its right to notify the plaintiff of its intention to repair the premises. If the defendant had done so, and found that the insured was making repairs without any notice to it, both acting in good faith, it might be difficult to adjust fairly the rights of the parties. But there is nothing to show that the defendant ever entertained an intention to repair. It has never notified the insured of such intention, and it is clear that the acts of the plaintiff in making necessary repairs, in good faith, ought not, upon any principles of law or justice, to defeat the right to recover its actual loss.

For the reasons given above, the order of the trial court is affirmed.

### Notes and Questions

1. As illustrated in the *Howard* case, the election by the insurer to repair or replace the insured property as its option must be made within the time stipulated in the policy or, in the absence of any stipulation, within a reasonable time after the damage or loss has occurred. The insurer's notice to elect its option must also be clear and unequivocal. An election, once made, is irrevocable. *See also* VANCE ON INSURANCE 882–83 (3d ed. 1951).

2. When the insurer elects to repair or rebuild, the former policy of insurance is transformed into a construction contract, and the policyholder no longer has an action on the policy to recover any monetary indemnity. Likewise, the insurer cannot later claim a breach of any condition in the policy that would lead to a forfeiture. *See, e.g., Walker v. Republic Underwriters Ins. Co.*, 574 F. Supp. 686 (D. Minn. 1983) (building); *Home Indem. Co. v. Bush*, 513 P.2d 145 (Ariz. Ct. App. 1973) (vehicle).

3. If the insurer elects to repair a damaged vehicle or rebuild a damaged building, the insurer is bound by its election—even though the cost of this undertaking may be more or less than the original amount of insurance coverage under the policy. *See, e.g., Walker v. Republic Underwriters Ins. Co., supra* (building); *Venable v. Import Volkswagen, Inc.*, 519 P.2d 667 (Kan. 1974) (vehicle). The insurer must complete these repairs within a reasonable time, and put the insured property in substantially the same condition as it was prior to loss. *Id.*

4. When the insurer elects to repair or rebuild the insured property within a reasonable time, but the insurer or its agents repair, replace, or rebuild in an improper manner, then the insurer will be liable in accordance with general principles of contract law since the parties are no longer governed by any appraisal or arbitration provisions under the policy. *Home Indem. Co. v. Bush, supra.*

## [F] Reformation

Reformation is an extraordinarily equitable remedy, and the courts exercise it with great caution when, by reason of fraud or mutual mistake, the insurance policy as written does not express the real intention and actual agreement of the parties.

Since reformation is an exceptional remedy, the moving party (normally the policyholder) must prove by clear and convincing evidence, rather than by a mere preponderance of the evidence, that there was fraud or a mutual mistake of the parties, and he or she may also show by parole evidence what actually occurred in the making of the contract.

However, reformation is never a remedy for a unilateral mistake. *See generally* VANCE ON INSURANCE 257–67, 260–61 (3d ed. 1951). *See also First Am. Title Ins. Co. v. Firriolo*, 695 S.E.2d 918 (W. Va. 2010) ("The jurisdiction of equity to reform written instruments, where there is a mutual mistake, or mistake on one side and fraud or inequitable conduct on the other, if the evidence be sufficiently cogent to thoroughly satisfy the mind of the court, is fully established and undoubted.").

# Chapter 5

# The Insurable Interest Requirement

Insurable interest, like the concepts of risk shifting, risk distribution, and fortuity, is at the core of insurance theory. Just as insurance should not be obtained for intentional or certain losses, neither should insurance be purchased by someone who has no insurable interest in the subject matter that is insured. For example, it would be been pretty ridiculous for Stempel to purchase a life insurance policy on Queen Elizabeth, naming Stempel or Knutsen as beneficiary. This type of insurance transaction would be improper even if Stempel could afford the premiums. What else, in addition to macabre tastelessness, is wrong with this hypothetical insurance purchase?

The answer, of course, is that Stempel had no insurable interest in Her Majesty. As we shall see in this chapter, the beneficiary need not necessarily have an insurable interest in the proceeds of an insurance policy. For example, Stempel could get a life insurance policy on himself and make the benefits payable to a favorite charity. The "rule" of insurable interest is that the purchaser or "owner" of the policy must have an insurable interest in the thing insured, be it life, property, or a less concrete risk.

The insurable interest concept—despite being at the core of sound insurance theory—was overlooked during the early days of insurance and was actually imposed on the industry by statute. (Of course, the British Parliament got the idea of passing the insurable interest statute based on what it knew from reputable participants in the business of insurance.) Parliament was moved to act because in the absence of an insurable interest rule, insurance had become a rampant form of gambling. Ordinary Britons were buying and selling insurance over whether a coronation would be cancelled, whether war would break out, whether a well-known actor would die in a gin binge or of certain diseases. Thus, insurance was being purchased not to manage risk but to engage in wagering contracts. Wagering was not seen as healthy for society to encourage widespread, informal, uncontrolled wagering through the purchase and sale of insurance. Hence, Parliament acted and adopted the insurable interest doctrine by statute.

Today, the insurable interest doctrine is so strongly recognized as being essential to wise insurance practice that present-day insurers and American, British, and Canadian courts embrace it even without statutory guidance, although most state insurance laws have codified the insurable interest requirement. Seldom, however, do insurance policies themselves state that an insurable interest is a prerequisite to coverage under the policy. This is just something that everyone "knows" today (and may be codified in statute).

Because the insurable interest requirement is usually not expressed in the text of a policy, it can be viewed as an "implied" exclusion that courts will apply to a coverage dispute despite the lack of policy language on the issue. But in some ways, an insurer relying on a defense of lack of insurable interest is better off than an insurer relying on an exclusion. Recall that according to the basic ground rules of insurance policy construction, exclusions are strictly construed against the insurer and the insurer bears the burden of persuasion to show the applicability of an exclusion. By contrast, if the insurer interposes a defense of lack of insurable interest, it is the policyholder that bears the burden of persuasion on the issue. Further, the court will usually treat the issue of insurable interest in a neutral manner, without strict or liberal construction in favor of either policyholder or insurer.

One might argue that the insurer in this situation has its metaphorical "cake" and is eating it, too, in that the insurer sold the policy, collected premiums, and would never have challenged the validity of the policy unless a loss occurred. When faced with the loss, the insurer nonetheless has an insurable interest defense. Despite the arguable asymmetry of this situation, insurers are allowed to do this because our law and society place such importance on the insurable interest doctrine.

The insurable interest concept was initially fueled by insurance run amok as wagering or gambling. Today, that underpinning of the doctrine is less important, in part because society does not hold gambling in disrepute. Today, the strongest underpinning of the insurable interest doctrine is the idea that requiring an insurable interest makes it less likely that the policyholder will act negligently or recklessly regarding the risk or — worse yet — intentionally trigger the risk insured against or inflict a loss in order to secure insurance payments. Although there are of course no guarantees in life (that's why we have insurance, after all), as a general matter, simple self-interest works to make a policyholder with an insurable interest less likely to leave the house with the stove on, torch the house, or kill.

Today, the insurable interest doctrine exists primarily to prevent insurance from providing a financial incentive for criminal or otherwise undesirable behavior. The point is well-illustrated in movies like *Double Indemnity*, in which two lovers plot the murder of an inconvenient husband in order to collect insurance proceeds as well as to further their relationship. Of course, the unfaithful spouse does have an insurable interest in the cuckolded spouse. Thus, a cynic might ask: what good is the insurable interest doctrine? Good question. We only said the insurable interest doctrine was helpful, not foolproof.

Although spouses or children might still purchase insurance and then attempt to hasten the event that will allow them to collect, this is generally less likely than if one is allowed to purchase insurance on the life of a total stranger who might be eliminated without any compunction by the policyholder. For example, in one well-known tragic case, an aunt-in-law purchased insurance on a child and murdered the child. *See Liberty Nat'l Life Ins. Co. v. Weldon*, 100 So. 2d 696 (Ala. 1957). In another notorious case, an over-insured low-level employee was killed in a hunting "accident." *See Rubenstein v. Mutual Life Ins. Co.*, 584 F. Supp. 272, 279 (E.D. La. 1984).

When the insurable interest doctrine works, the insurer looks for insurable interest and refuses to write coverage without it. If the scheming applicant manages to get a policy anyway, the insurable interest doctrine prevents him or her from collecting, which creates some additional deterrence and disincentive for wrongful conduct. This is why, as a general matter, concepts such as incontestability (the legal ban on insurer invocation of misrepresentation defenses after the policy has been in force for a specified minimum time period), waiver, or estoppel (*see* Chapter 7) all yield to the insurable interest requirement.

What then, is an insurable interest? As the cases in this chapter show, courts tend to look for either a legal interest in the risk insured, a factual expectancy about the risk insured, or some combination of interest and expectancy that creates adequate interest in continued care toward the risk insured. For a discussion of the historical roots of the doctrine and early case law development of these concepts, see JEFFREY W. STEMPEL & ERIK S. KNUTSEN, STEMPEL & KNUTSEN ON INSURANCE COVERAGE, § 1.05. In this chapter, we review the modern status of the insurable interest doctrine according to the type of insurance at issue.

For the most part, the legitimacy of an asserted insurable interest is measured differently for different types of insurance. An insurable interest in a life is evaluated according to the time the policy is purchased, not at the time a loss occurs. For example, one can buy insurance on a spouse and continue to hold the policy after divorce. For property insurance, the timing rule is just the opposite. There must usually be an insurable interest at the time a loss occurs. A policyholder may buy homeowner's insurance but may not keep it in force and collect on it for a loss after the policyholder has sold all of her interest in the home.

As suggested by the foregoing discussion, courts usually will not treat the insurable interest requirement as subject to waiver or estoppel against the insurer, even though this has the effect of letting the insurer "have its cake and eat it, too." As revealed in "insurance for crime" cases, it is unfortunately too easy for unscrupulous applicants to obtain insurance when they lack a legitimate insurable interest. The judiciary therefore has made a tacit public policy decision that enforcing the insurable interest doctrine provides more deterrence by reducing the chance for paying off criminals than estoppel against the insurer would increase the odds that underwriters would catch a planned criminal scheme.

# § 5.01. The Insurable Interest Concept in Property Insurance

## [A] Introduction

The purpose of requiring an insurable interest in property is to prevent wagering contracts which may well result in the destruction or impairment of the property, rather than its maintenance. For example, if Smith takes out insurance on Jones' apartment building, and Smith has no interest in preserving or maintaining Jones' property, then Smith has everything to gain and nothing to lose if Jones' building burns to the ground, which may tempt Smith to commit arson, or some other illegal act. Such wagering contracts, without an insurable interest, are held to be void and unenforceable.

A person generally is said to have an insurable interest in property if he derives an economic benefit from its existence, or would suffer any loss from its destruction, whether or not he has any title to, possession of, or lien upon this property. Under the majority view only the insurer can question the lack of an insurable interest in property insurance. However, the courts are deeply divided on the question of whether an insurer may validly waive its defense of a lack of insurable interest, or be estopped from asserting it.

Some courts have taken an "intermediate position" on the question of whether the insurable interest defense should be defeated by estoppel. Courts espousing this position have held that an insurer cannot be estopped from asserting a complete lack of insurable interest, but that estoppel may be invoked to prevent a challenge by the insurer that the insurable interest is worth less than the amount due under the policy, once some kind of insurable interest has been established. Prominent scholars find this "intermediate position" the most persuasive and reconcilable approach. *See* JERRY & RICHMOND, UNDERSTANDING INSURANCE LAW, §§ 42, 44 (6th ed. 2018); ROBERT E. KEETON & ALAN I. WIDISS, INSURANCE LAW § 3.4 (1988). State statutes often define insurable interest. In cases involving these statutes, the determination of whether a person has an insurable interest in property or a life is normally a question of fact for the jury.

## [B] What Constitutes an Insurable Interest in Property?

A common judicial problem, as illustrated in *Castle Cars, infra,* concerns the question of how and when one has an insurable interest in property, whether one "derives a benefit from its existence or would suffer loss from its destruction." *See generally* JERRY & RICHMOND, UNDERSTANDING INSURANCE LAW § 46 (6th ed. 2018). More specifically, Professor Vance states that an insurable interest in property exists in the following five categories:

(a) When the insured possesses legal title to the property insured, whether vested or contingent, defeasible or indefeasible.

(b) When he has an equitable title to the property, of whatever kind and however acquired.

(c) When he possesses a qualified property or possessory right, such as that of a bailee.

(d) When he has mere possession or right of possession.

(e) When he has neither possession of the property, nor other legal interest in it, but may suffer, from its destruction, the loss of a legal right (a "legal liability" right).

WILLIAM R. VANCE, VANCE ON INSURANCE 161–179 (3d ed. 1951).

In addition to the five categories cited above which support an insurable interest in property, a sixth theory—that of a "factual expectancy"—has gained substantial acceptance in American courts. This theory is based in large part on the early English case of *Lucena v. Crauford*, 127 Eng. Rep. 630 (House of Lords 1805), and 127 Eng. Rep. 858 (House of Lords 1808), in which some questionably "insured" captured Dutch ships were lost at sea before reaching an English port. At that time, an Act of Parliament would have given the Commissioners (who insured the ships) legal title over the captured vessels if they had made it to port. The *Lucena* case contained the diverse opinions of Justice Lawrence, Lord Eldon, and a third "tribunal opinion," discussing whether a "factual expectation" to property creates a bona fide, insurable interest in the absence of a corresponding "basis of legal right" or a "present existing title."

An early American case, *National Filtering Oil Co. v. Citizens' Ins. Co.*, 13 N.E. 337 (N.Y. 1887), cited this "factual expectancy" argument to support an insurable interest in property, but the concept was not applied in the later case of *Farmers' Mut. Ins. Co. v. New Holland Turnpike Co.*, 15 A. 563 (Pa. 1888). Some American jurisdictions today do not accept the "factual expectancy" theory absent a corresponding "legal right" or "existing title" in the property itself. *See, e.g.*, CAL. INS. CODE § 283. Note the following excerpt from *Splish Splash Waterslides, Inc. v. Cherokee Ins. Co.*, 307 S.E.2d 107 (Ga. Ct. App. 1983):

> [I]t is clear that mere possession of property, although giving the possessor certain rights against a trespasser ... is in and of itself not sufficient to constitute an insurable interest.... While title may not always be the determinative factor, ... the insured must have some *lawful* interest in the property before he can have an insurable interest in the property, ... although that interest might be "slight or contingent, legal or equitable."

## Castle Cars, Inc. v. United States Fire Insurance Co.

Supreme Court of Virginia
221 Va. 773, 273 S.E.2d 793 (1981)

### Poff, Justice

This appeal poses the question whether a *bona fide* purchaser for value has an insurable interest in stolen property.

The facts are stipulated. Castle Cars, Inc. (the dealer), bought a used car for $2600 and received the seller's assignment of a title certificate issued by the Division of Motor Vehicles. That night the car was stolen from the dealer's lot. The dealer filed a claim under the theft provisions of its garagekeeper's liability insurance policy with United States Fire Insurance Company (the insurer). The insurer paid the claim, and the dealer assigned the title certificate to the insurer in accordance with the subrogation provisions of the policy.

Subsequent investigation disclosed that the car had been stolen from its rightful owner, but since it bore a Vehicle Identification Number plate which had been transferred by the thief from a wrecked vehicle of similar description, the true owner was never identified. The car was never recovered, and the insurer filed suit for reimbursement from the dealer. Finding that the dealer had no insurable interest in the stolen vehicle, the trial court entered judgment for the insurer.

The question we consider is one of first impression in this Court. Although courts in sister states are divided on the issue, they agree that a property insurance contract is void unless the insured has an "insurable interest" in the property insured.... The reasons for the rule are grounded in public policy....

Courts do not agree, however, upon what constitutes an insurable interest. The disagreement apparently stems from the disparate views expressed by Lord Lawrence and Lord Eldon in the old English case of *Lucena v. Crauford*, 2 Bos. & Pul. (H.R.) 269, 127 Eng. Rep. 630 (1806).... Lord Lawrence believed that a person has an insurable interest if he has "some relation to, or concern in the subject of the insurance" which may be prejudiced "by the happening of the perils insured against" and he "is so circumstanced with respect to" the insured subject "as to have a moral certainty of advantage or benefit" sufficient to make him "interested in the safety of the thing." ... Disagreeing, Lord Eldon felt that an interest is insurable only if it is a legal or equitable right enforceable in law or chancery. "[E]xpectation," he said, "though founded on the highest probability, [is] not interest," ... and "[i]f moral certainty be a ground of insurable interest, there are hundreds, perhaps thousands, who would be entitled to insure" the same property.... In short, Lord Lawrence held that factual expectation, if grounded in moral certainty, was sufficient, while Lord Eldon required legal or equitable entitlement.

Our Court has indicated that it considers the Eldon view too restrictive. Although the interest held insurable in *Tilley v. Connecticut Fire Ins. Co.*, 11 S.E. 120 (Va. 1890), was an enforceable equitable right, the Court expressed a view in dictum much like that of Lord Lawrence:

> Any person who has any interest in the property, legal or equitable, or who stands in such a relation thereto that its destruction would entail pecuniary loss upon him, has an insurable interest to the extent of his interest therein, or of the loss to which he is subjected by the casualty.

11 S.E. at 120.

The *Tilley* dictum influenced later decisions. In [*Liverpool & London & Globe Ins. Co. v. Bolling*, 10 S.E.2d 518 (Va. 1940)], we noted that "[e]verywhere there is a tendency to broaden the definition of an "insurable interest"; neither legal nor equitable title is necessary." ... There, in a suit on a fire insurance policy, the plaintiff alleged that her father-in-law had authorized her to use his building to conduct a business and had promised to give it to her later. On appeal from a judgment for the plaintiff, the insurance company contended that the plaintiff had no insurable interest in the building. Quoting the dictum in *Tilley*, we approved the following rule:

> Any title or interest in the property, legal or equitable, will support a contract of insurance on such property. The term "interest" as used in the phrase "in-

surable interest" is not limited to property or ownership in the subject matter of the insurance. Where the interest of the insured in, or his relation to, the property is such that he will be benefited by its continued existence or suffer a direct pecuniary injury by its loss, his contract of insurance will be upheld, although he has no legal or equitable title. 26 C.J. 20.

The rule approved by the majority was tacitly adopted by the General Assembly. By Acts 1952, c. 317, the term "insurable interest" was defined to mean "any lawful and substantial economic interest in the safety or preservation of the subject of insurance free from loss, destruction or pecuniary damage." Code § 38.1-331....

Under the facts stipulated here, the dealer had an "economic interest in the safety or preservation of the subject of insurance," Code § 38.1-331, and that interest, measured by the purchase price, was certainly "substantial." The insurer makes the point that the statute requires that an interest, "to be insurable, must also be a lawful interest" and insists that "[t]he interest held by a purchaser of stolen property cannot be lawful."

Although the dealer acquired what reasonably appeared to be proper paper title to the car, it is true that it acquired no legal title; a thief takes no title in the property he steals and can transfer none. But under the rule applied in *Bolling* and [*Insurance Company v.*] *Dalis*, [141 S.E.2d 721 (Va. 1965),] the interest need not be legal or equitable title to be insurable. And, as we construe the statute codifying that rule, a "substantial economic interest" is an insurable interest if it is "lawful" in the sense that it was not acquired in violation of the law.

As used in this context, the word "lawful" is not synonymous with the word "legal." An interest enforceable against the world is legal. An interest acquired in good faith, for value, and without notice of the invalidity of the transferor's title is lawful and enforceable against all the world except the legal owner. We share the view of those courts which have held that such an interest in a stolen motor vehicle is an insurable interest....

The parties agree that the dealer acquired its interest in the car as a *bona fide* purchaser for value without notice that the car was stolen property. Applying the principles in *Bolling* and *Dalis* and the statute as we have construed it, we hold that the interest the dealer acquired was economic, substantial, and lawful and that the trial court erred in ruling that such interest was not insurable. The judgment will be reversed and final judgment for the dealer will be entered here.

**Harrison, Justice**, dissenting

I would follow the line of cases, grounded in sound public policy, holding that no one acquires an insurable interest in stolen property. In *Bolling* and *Dalis*, relied upon by the majority, the insureds clearly had a lawful, legitimate, and substantial economic interest in the properties insured. There, neither the properties nor the insureds were in any way suspect. Here, we are dealing with stolen property acquired from a thief. The majority holds that the interest acquired by the automobile dealer was economic, substantial, and lawful. I disagree. The person from whom the dealer acquired the automobile had no title, legal or equitable, no right of possession, and could pass no "legal" or "lawful" interest in the automobile. The thief could only surrender physical possession of that which he illegally acquired and possessed.

Admittedly the dealer had a financial investment involved by virtue of his $2600 payment for the stolen vehicle. However, this investment and the benefit and enjoyment by the dealer of its purchase was assured only if the theft remained undetected and its possession of the stolen goods went unchallenged. Therefore, protection of the dealer's "interest" depended upon the success of a thief's larcenous transaction. The court that decided *Bolling*, and the General Assembly that enacted Code § 38.1-331, never envisioned that such an "interest" could become an insurable interest.

The decision in this case not only reverses public policy but comes at an inopportune time in an era of mounting crime. By broadening the definition of an insurable interest, we decrease the risk taken by the purchaser of stolen property and make easier the "fencing" of such property by robbers and thieves. It also removes the incentive for an insured purchaser to take proper precaution, to scrutinize, and to make careful inquiry of the reliability, honesty, and integrity of those who offer to sell and deliver articles of personal property. I would affirm the judgment of the lower court.

## *Notes and Questions*

1. Which of the five "interests" cited by VANCE, *supra*, did the Virginia court apply in *Castle Cars*?

2. The dissent in *Castle Cars* expresses a strong minority view, holding that one cannot acquire an insurable interest in stolen property. Under property law, title to stolen goods cannot be passed. Should a similar rule be applied to insurable interests? Should an innocent purchaser lose all? Isn't this the sort of risk that insurance companies undertake? The majority of courts in fact do recognize that a good faith purchaser does have an insurable interest in the purchased stolen goods, and a possessory right good against all the world except the true owner. *See, e.g., Butler v. Farmers Ins. Co.*, 126 Ariz. 379, 616 P.2d 46 (1980). Is the difficulty that a court has in determining whether an "innocent" purchaser is in fact innocent the primary motivation for the minority rule?

3. The majority rule, stated in the *Castle Cars* case, *supra*, that the owner of stolen property *does* have an insurable interest in that property against everyone except the true owner, is also consistent with the "factual expectancy" theory of an insurable interest: the insured has a substantial economic interest in the preservation of the stolen vehicle or other stolen property since he or she probably paid a large sum of money for the property which would be lost if the vehicle were damaged or destroyed in an automobile accident. *See, e.g.,* JERRY & RICHMOND, UNDERSTANDING INSURANCE LAW § 46 (6th ed. 2018).

## PROBLEM ONE

Howard, a licensed automobile dealer, owned and operated a used car and repossession business in Omaha, Nebraska. At the time of trial, he had purchased and sold over 150 used automobiles.

In the fall of 1988, Howard saw in the parking lot of an Omaha restaurant a 1964 red Corvette with out-of-state license plates. Howard entered the restaurant and asked two people who he believed to be the owners whether their vehicle was for sale. The two replied that it was not for sale, but Howard nonetheless handed them a business card and asked them to call him if they ever wished to sell their Corvette.

Four weeks later, Howard received a telephone call from "Jay" stating that the alleged owner "Kathern Carter" had decided to sell her Corvette at an agreed upon price of $9,500 plus food and gasoline expenses for driving the Corvette into Nebraska from another state. "Kathern Carter," however, refused to take a certified check from Howard for $9,500 and instead agreed upon a cash payment of $6,500 "for tax purposes."

"Kathern Carter" and "Jay" also told Howard that they did not have a certificate of title for the Corvette at that time since "there was a lien filed against the title" in Georgia but that certified title would be mailed to Howard in the near future. Howard subsequently admitted in court that although he normally demands a certificate of title on any out-of-state automobile, the Corvette with all its original parts was worth approximately $25,000 and therefore it was a "fantastic buy" that he didn't want to "slip through his fingers."

Howard insured his Corvette through the State Farm Mutual Automobile Insurance Company. Subsequently, Howard discovered that there was no certificate of title, that "Kathern Carter" and "Jay" were fictitious aliases, and that the Corvette was a stolen vehicle. A mysterious fire later destroyed the Corvette. After the automobile was destroyed by fire, the Nebraska State Police found alterations of the vehicle identification number, attempting to change the last three digits from "868" to "888," that Howard stated he did not discover at the time of sale.

State Farm denies coverage on the basis that Howard had no insurable interest in the stolen Corvette. Howard counters that although a car thief acquires no title in stolen property and cannot transfer any title to a stolen vehicle, nevertheless an innocent purchaser of a stolen vehicle would acquire an insurable interest in such a vehicle.

• How should the court decide this case?

## PROBLEM TWO

Atlantic Recycling leases part of an industrial park from the owner, IDA. The lease provided the following:

- The lease is renewable and includes an option to buy, with a price reduction in the amount of rent paid.

- The lease also requires Atlantic to return the property to IDA and "restore possession of the Property to IDA in good condition, reasonable wear and tear excepted." Further, the lease provides that if Atlantic returns the property to IDA in damaged condition, IDA may collect the costs of restoring the property from Atlantic.

- IDA must maintain property insurance on the industrial park at Atlantic's expense.

- If the park becomes damaged to the point Atlantic cannot occupy the premises, Atlantic will owe no rent so long as such condition persists. IDA may repair that damage but is under no obligation to repair the property. If IDA does not repair the property, the lease is terminated without penalty.

Atlantic took out an "all risk" insurance policy covering the business and the property (not the policy held by IDA in the lease) from Aspen. The property was tragically destroyed in a fire. Aspen paid the business claims but denied the property damage claims for want of an insurable interest by Atlantic in the leased property.

- How would you argue for Atlantic?

- For Aspen?

- Based on the policy concerns outlined in *Castle Cars*, how would a court decide this case?

# [C] Limits on Insurable Interest in Property

How broad or narrow can—or should—the concept of insurable interest be in order to protect the basic interests the concept is designed to protect? At what point is it stretched to become a useless insurance law tool? This next case explores the boundaries of the insurable interest concept.

## Arthur Andersen LLP v. Federal Insurance Company

Superior Court of New Jersey, Appellate Division
416 N.J. Super. 334 (2010)

**Espinosa, J.A.D.**

Plaintiff, Arthur Andersen LLP (Andersen), alleged that business losses caused as a result of property damage to the World Trade Center (WTC) and the Pentagon on September 11, 2001 were covered losses under its insurance policy. Andersen appeals from orders that granted summary judgment to the insurer, dismissing its claims. We affirm.

Andersen contends that it earned $204 million less than it expected to earn in the three and one-half months following the terrorist attacks. Andersen did not own or lease any property at the WTC or the Pentagon and cannot identify any supplier or client whose property was damaged to support this claim. Nonetheless, Andersen filed a claim under its all-risk commercial property insurance policy for business losses that it claims it suffered as a result of the property damage to the WTC and the Pentagon, based upon a comparison between expected revenue trends and actual revenue earned. This lawsuit ensued when coverage was denied by Federal Insurance Company (Federal) and Certain Underwriters at Lloyd's and Certain London Market Insurance Companies (London), (collectively, defendant insurers).

Andersen had a three layer program of commercial property insurance covering the period from September 1, 2001 through September 1, 2002....

Andersen contends that coverage for its claim is provided by the Contingent Business Interruption (CBI) provision, Clause 9.F(4)(b), and the Interdependency provision, Clause 9.F(6). Both these provisions are within the "Time Element Coverages" (Clause 9.F), which apply when a specified type of loss for a period of time of up to eighteen months is caused by damage to specified property.

The CBI provision gives the insured coverage for the loss of sales or revenue sustained when its business is interrupted as a result of damage to property that disrupts the flow of goods and services with a supplier or customer and states, in pertinent part:

> This policy ... is extended to cover *the actual loss sustained by the Insured* resulting from the necessary interruption of the business conducted by the Insured, whether partial or total, *caused by loss, damage or destruction* covered herein ... *to:* ...

> Property that directly or indirectly prevents a supplier of goods, services or information to the Insured from rendering their goods, services, or information or *property that directly or indirectly prevents a receiver of goods, services or information from the Insured from accepting or receiving the Insured's goods, services or information.* [Clause 9.F(4)(b) (Emphasis added).]

When an insured sustains losses at one insured location as a result of property damage at another insured location, the Interdependency provision provides coverage as follows:

> This policy is extended to cover *the total loss sustained by the Insured* anywhere in the world caused by loss, damage or destruction by any of the perils covered herein during the term of this policy *to any real or personal property as described in Clause 9* situated within the Territory covered by this policy. [Clause 9.F(6) (Emphasis added.)]

Andersen contends that its claim is covered under the Interdependency provision because the WTC, the Pentagon, and United Airlines Boeing 757 Aircraft (Flight 93) fall within the following definition of Real and Personal Property contained in Clause 9.A(1):

> The interest of the Insured in all real and personal property ... which is not otherwise excluded and which is owned, used, leased or intended for use by the Insured, *or in which the Insured may have an insurable interest,* or for which the Insured may be responsible for the insurance.... [(Emphasis added.)]

No evidence has been presented that Andersen insured or was responsible for insurance for either site or the airplane. As previously mentioned, Andersen did not own or lease any of this property.

In interrogatory answers, Andersen further stated that its claim of approximately $204 million in lost revenues was "based on a comparison between expected revenue trends and actual revenue earned" and could not be separated to correspond to the damage to the different properties, i.e., the WTC, the Pentagon or the United Airlines airplane. Andersen maintained that its claim was "not based on a client-by-client calculation" but rather, based upon a comparison between expected revenue trends and actual revenue earned (the generalized revenue shortfall). Some of Andersen's proposed witnesses acknowledged that various factors affected its revenues after September 11, including disruption of air traffic, governmental action to reduce the risk of future attacks, the general fear of future attacks, the economic downturn, Andersen's involvement in the Enron scandal and the choice by some potential clients to take their business to Andersen's competitors.

\* \* \*

At the heart of Andersen's arguments is the legal question whether Andersen's claim falls within the coverage provided by the CBI provision or the Interdependency provision. After carefully reviewing the record, briefs and arguments of counsel, we are satisfied that there is no merit to plaintiff's claim that its losses are covered by the CBI or Interdependency provisions of the Policy....

\* \* \*

Significantly, Andersen does not contend that it is entitled to coverage due to any ambiguity in the terms of the Policy provisions at issue here. We agree that the language of the CBI and Interdependency provisions is clear and unambiguous, and therefore, must be enforced as written.

\* \* \*

The pertinent language of the Interdependency clause provides coverage for "the total loss sustained by the Insured anywhere in the world caused by ... damage ... to any real or personal property as described in Clause 9[,]" i.e., property "in which the Insured may have an insurable interest...." Andersen argues that its claim falls within that definition because it had an insurable interest in the WTC and the Pentagon.

One must have an insurable interest in property to sustain recovery under a policy that insures risks for property damage. The purpose for this requirement is "the discouragement of illicit uses of insurance, such as wagering, and the destruction of insured property." *Miller v. New Jersey Ins. Underwriting Ass'n*, 414 A.2d 1322 (N.J. 1980). *See also Lincoln Nat'l Life Ins. Co. v. Calhoun*, 596 F.Supp.2d 882, 889 (D.N.J.2009) ("Without an insurable interest, there would be no actual loss; the contract would thus be a pure gamble.") (citation omitted).

Although it is not necessary to have legal or equitable title to have an insurable interest in real estate, it is clear that the interest in the property must have some pecuniary value and that the party who seeks to recover bears the burden of proving that value.

The test of an insurable interest in real property is "whether the insured has such a right, title or interest therein, or relation thereto, that he will be *benefited by its preservation and continued existence or suffer a direct pecuniary loss* from its destruction or injury by the peril insured against." [citation omitted; italics in original]; *See also* 33–195 *Appleman on Insurance* § 195.01 (2d ed. 2008) ("The usual rule customarily followed is that an insurable interest exists when the insured derives pecuniary benefit or advantage by the preservation or continued existence of the property or will sustain pecuniary loss from its destruction.").

Andersen did not derive any direct pecuniary benefit, such as rental income, from the existence of the WTC and Pentagon and suffered no direct loss from the damage inflicted to those buildings on September 11. Andersen argues that such proof is unnecessary; that an insurable interest means "*any* economic interest in the continued existence of the property" and exists "if the loss of the property *may* cause the insured an economic loss." (Emphasis added.)

When the trial court explored the breadth of this contention with counsel at oral argument, Andersen's counsel agreed that, based upon its interpretation, Andersen could assert a claim for lost revenue if a terrorist attack targeted and destroyed property that was completely unrelated to Andersen's ability to conduct its business, i.e., low income housing in New York. This expansive interpretation fails because it conflicts with established caselaw and subverts the policy underlying the insurable interest requirement.

The common thread in cases in which an insurable interest is found is the existence of a cognizable relationship between the insured and the property that provides the basis for the insured to derive a direct pecuniary benefit from the property or suffer a direct pecuniary loss if the property is damaged. For example, in [one prior case finding insurable interest], a nominal owner of property had a sufficient nexus to the property to create an insurable interest because of his potential liabilities—for unpaid real estate taxes or to a visitor injured on the premises. We noted that, "in the absence of insurance coverage, [the named insured] would 'suffer a direct pecuniary loss from [the property's] destruction.'" [citation omitted]. *See also Miller, supra*, (mortgagees who operated businesses from the insured property continued to have insurable interests after the city had obtained title to the property through foreclosure proceedings for nonpayment of real estate taxes); *Hyman* [*v. Sun Ins. Co.*], *supra,* 70 N.J.Super. at 100, 175 A.2d 247, and cases cited therein. In contrast to these cases, Andersen is unable to identify any relationship it had with either the WTC or the Pentagon that had an ascertainable value and provided a basis for pecuniary benefit or loss.

[The New Jersey] Supreme Court [has previously] rejected the argument that an insurable interest existed where there was a far closer relationship between the insured and a loss caused by a defect in title. The title insurance policy was issued when two brothers purchased property as partners trading as a general partnership. The policy defined "insured" as those named and those who succeeded to their interest by operation of law. The policy also provided for the continuation of insurance after title was conveyed "so long as such insured retains an estate or interest in the land ... or so long as such insured shall have liability by reason of covenants of warranty made by such insured in any transfer or conveyance of such estate or interest...." Ten years later, the general partnership conveyed the property to a limited partnership in which the brothers were the sole limited partners and a corporation owned jointly and exclusively by them was the general partner. The limited partnership did not purchase a new title insurance policy for the property.

In an unpublished opinion, this court found that the brothers were entitled to coverage under the policy because they never transferred their "beneficial interests" in the land and the general and limited partnerships were "alter egos" of the brothers.

The Supreme Court rejected this analysis and reversed, finding that the brothers had no insurable interest in the property. The Court noted that, as a matter of law, a partnership is an entity distinct from its partners and that, as principals in the limited partnership, the brothers were shielded from personal liability. The Court recognized that one of the purposes underlying the principles of insurance contract interpretation is the insurer's need for "predictable levels of risk ... in order to calculate premium rates reliably" and concluded that allowing coverage to continue under the circumstances presented "effectively extends the time of exposure and the risk to the insurer." [citation omitted]

The evidence here fails to show that Andersen derived any income, such as rent, from the existence of the WTC or that Andersen bore any potential liability to others based upon its "interest" in the WTC. In short, there are no circumstances of Andersen's association with the WTC that gave rise to the threat of a *direct* pecuniary loss to Andersen in the event the WTC was damaged.

Andersen's theory would permit an insured to allege an insurable interest in a class of property so broad as to be impossible to define and certainly not susceptible to a predictable level of risk. Just as an insurable interest cannot be viewed so narrowly as to create "a windfall for the insurer, allowing it to retain the premiums it reaped on [a] policy without providing anything in return," the interest cannot be read as broadly as Andersen argues, allowing the insured to reap a windfall recovery for a loss so clearly unanticipated in the calculation of the premium. Such an application would undermine the very purpose of an "insurable interest" requirement, reducing an insurance contract to a "pure gamble," [citations omitted] and we reject it as a matter of law.

Affirmed.

### Notes and Questions

1. How does the position of the policyholder in the *Andersen* case stretch the concept of insurable interest? Does it do so to a breaking point?

2. What is the value of a broad versus a narrow insurable interest concept?

3. How does the factual expectancy test for insurable interest dictate the result in *Andersen*?

4. Can the result in *Andersen* sit comfortably with a formalist approach to the policy text in the case? Or is the result a functionalist result? Why or why not?

### PROBLEM THREE

The policyholder had a right to use a cabin, although that right could be terminated at any time at the whim of the owner.

- Should this possession of the cabin constitute a substantial economic interest within the definition of an insurable interest?

- Why or why not?

- Would an option to buy such property constitute an insurable interest?

### PROBLEM FOUR

A son was erecting a house on land that belonged to his mother. He lived with his mother and contemplated living with her in this new house, since she had promised she would convey the land to her son when she died.

- Did the son have an insurable interest in the house?

- Could he recover for damage to the basement caused by a bulldozer that negligently back-filled the basement under an insurance policy that provided coverage against "all direct loss and damage caused by a vehicle"?

## [D] When an Insurable Interest Must Exist in Property

When does an insurable interest need to exist to be valid for property insurance purposes? At the time of application for the policy? At the time the policy is issued? Or at the time of the loss claimed? What difference does it make, and why? Should it even matter, as long as it exists at some point?

# Kingston v. Great Southwest Fire Insurance Co.

Utah Supreme Court
578 P.2d 1278 (1978)

**Ellett, Chief Justice**

The only issue involved in this case is this: Did the appellant have an insurable interest in the warehouse that was destroyed by fire?

The appellant owned a warehouse and had insurance on it with the respondent company. Just prior to the fire, Salt Lake City Corporation filed a suit in condemnation seeking to condemn the property in question. Thereafter, and prior to the fire, the city was granted an order of immediate occupancy. Despite the order, the appellant maintained possession and was using the warehouse as a place of storage for his merchandise.

The condemnation order was contested and no final judgment had been entered whereby the legal title to the property had been given to Salt Lake City. In fact, the final judgment was not entered for some eight months after the fire. The appellant began an action on the policy while the contest of the condemnation was still pending.

Our statute [U.C.A., 1953, as amended, 78-34-9] provides that the condemnor may pay seventy-five percent (75%) of the appraised value of the property into court and, if accepted, the landowner can then contest at trial only the value of the property taken and the damages resulting therefrom. In this case, the money deposited was not accepted by the landowner; therefore, all issues, including the right to condemn, were reserved for trial.

Our statutes [U.C.A., 1953, as amended, 78-34-16] further provide that the condemnor may abandon the condemnation proceedings at any time prior to the payment for the land, being liable to the landowner only for all damages sustained.

There is no claim made that Mr. Kingston, the appellant, did not have an insurable interest in the building when the policy was issued. He paid the premium and the respondent herein ought not be permitted to refuse payment simply because a lawsuit over the property is pending. If there could be a complaint about paying the money to the insured, it should only be made by the condemnor, and then only if the condemnation proceeds to judgment.

The law requires an interest in insured property to exist both at the time of issuance and at the time of loss. In the instant matter, the appellant did have an insurable interest at the time of the fire; (a) He was the legal owner thereof; (b) The condemnation proceedings could be abandoned, and he would have to take back his property as is and would have no claim against the city for damages due to the fire since the city was not responsible therefor; (c) He was in possession of the warehouse at the time of the fire.

An owner of a building who retains legal title even though he has contracted to sell it has an insurable interest therein until the purchase price is paid [citing 44 C.J.S. *Insurance* § 188a] There can be no difference in the retention of an insurable interest in a contract to sell and in a suit in condemnation. In each case, the owner has an insurable interest in the property until he is paid for it. In the case of a sale, he agrees to the deal; in the case of condemnation, the court compels him to agree.

In *American National Bank & Trust Company v. Reserve Insurance Co.* [187 N.E.2d 343 (Ill. Ct. App. 1962)] it was held that an owner had an insurable interest at the time of a destructive fire even though condemnation proceedings had not been completed. The insurer denied liability on its policy. In affirming the judgment in favor of the owner, the court said:

> It is the defendant's next contention that recovery should be denied on the grounds that the insured lacked an insurable interest in the premises at the time of the fire.... The city's petition was still pending and undisposed of at the time of the fire. A jury subsequently entered a verdict of $6775.00 in the condemnation proceedings representing the value of the property at the time the petition to condemn was filed. Defendant suggests that the jury's verdict having been affirmed ... title relates back to the date of filing the petition to condemn, upon payment of compensation by the condemning authority.
>
> We think there is no merit to this contention insofar as it is directed to the relevant question of plaintiff's insurable interest on the date of the fire. At that date, the city's petition was pending but had not been acted upon. At the date of the fire there had been no change in the legal title to the property, or even a jury verdict in the proceedings by the city. At that stage of the condemnation proceedings the city might have abandoned its petition altogether upon the payment of the property owners' expenses in the proceedings, as provided by statute.... This being so, it seems clear to us that plaintiff did have an insurable interest in the property on the day of the fire. The fact that the city continued its proceedings against the property after the fire, rather than exercising its statutory prerogative to abandon them, is certainly a fortunate circumstance for the plaintiff, but it is not an event which defendant may seize upon in an effort to avoid liability on its contract of insurance.

Accordingly, we are of the opinion that the condemnation award received by plaintiff does not limit or bar plaintiff's right to recover in this action....

## [E] Extinguishment of Insurable Interest

If the purpose of an insurable interest in property is to derive an economic benefit from its existence or suffer loss from its destruction, then the corollary would seem to apply: an insurable interest should be extinguished when the insured would *not* derive an economic benefit from the property's existence nor suffer any loss from the destruction of that property. Or should it? Compare the following two opinions and decide in each case whether the insurable interest was extinguished, or whether it still survived.

# Tublitz v. Glens Falls Insurance Co.

New Jersey Superior Court, Law Division
179 N.J. Super. 275, 431 A.2d 201 (1981)

**Baime, J.D.C.** (temporarily assigned)

This case presents a question of first impression in New Jersey. Defendant is the insurer of three buildings owned by plaintiff. On November 14, 1979, plaintiff entered into a contract for demolition of the buildings. The contract was to be performed within ten days. On November 18, 1979, one of the buildings was destroyed by fire. At issue is whether the accidental destruction of the building is a loss for which defendant must indemnify plaintiff under the fire insurance policy. The carrier has denied coverage on the ground that plaintiff has suffered no loss since it was the latter's intention to demolish the building in any event. Plaintiff maintains that defendant is liable for the actual cash value of the building. It is undisputed that the policy was in effect at the time of the fire. Plaintiff now seeks summary judgment as to liability only.

Clearly, an insured must sustain a loss before he can recover on a standard form policy.... The insurer's premiums are assumed to represent the fair equivalent of the obligation it contracted to incur without knowledge of the existence of collateral remedies....

No New Jersey court has had occasion to determine the effect of impending demolition upon the insurable interest in a building. This issue has been considered in other jurisdictions, however. It is generally held that the existence of an executory contract for demolition of a building does not deprive the owner of an insurable interest in the property....[1]

The mere fact that an executory contract exists for demolition does not render a structure worthless nor deprive it of its value as a matter of law.... The existence of such a contract does not deprive the owner of an insurable interest in his building.... A finding that an insurable interest in the building no longer exists typically involves a situation in which the demolition work has begun at the time of the fire....[2]

The reasonable expectations of the insured must be considered in determining coverage.... In this case the fire occurred before any demolition work had begun. Despite the fact that the demolition contract was scheduled to be performed within ten days, it cannot be stated with certainty that it would, in fact, be commenced

---

1. [1] An exception to this rule is recognized in cases where the executory demolition contract is subject to specific performance. *See Royal Ins. Co. v. Sisters of the Presentation*, 430 F.2d 759 (9 Cir. 1970); *Lieberman v. Hartford Ins. Co.*, 287 N.E.2d 38 (Ill. Ct. App. 1970). This exception is inapplicable to the case at bar.

2. [2] An insurable interest has been recognized even in situations where demolition has begun, however.

within that period. Performance of the contract may have been delayed by a number of factors, both within and beyond the control of the parties. So, too, plaintiff could have chosen to repudiate the contract prior to demolition. Therefore, it is reasonable to infer from all the surrounding circumstances that plaintiff expected his fire insurance coverage to be in force until demolition was actually begun.

For the reasons stated herein, I find that an insurable interest is not destroyed by the existence of an executory contract for demolition of a building. Therefore, partial summary judgment is granted in favor of plaintiff on the issue of liability. An appropriate order should be submitted.

## Chicago Title & Trust Co. v. United States Fidelity & Guaranty Co.

United States District Court, Northern District of Illinois

376 F. Supp. 767 (1973)

### Will, District Judge

… In the instant case, when the subject building was destroyed on May 1, 1972, it was an economically useless building. It was empty, secured and boarded. It had been gutted by a previous fire. It was not being used in any way.

Here, as in *Aetna State Bank v. Maryland Casualty Co.*, 345 F. Supp. 903 (N.D. Ill. 1972), it would be ludicrous to allow the plaintiff to recover a substantial amount of money representing the replacement cost less depreciation of a building that was for all practical purposes non-existent. It would be grossly inequitable for plaintiff's beneficiary to recover $43,000 for a building which less than one month prior to its destruction she had purchased for $4,000 in what appears to have been an arm's length transaction and in which building she had made absolutely no additional investment or improvements.

We hold that the *Smith v. Allemannia Fire Ins. Co.*, 219 Ill. App. 506 (1920) doctrine of rigidly defining actual cash value of a building as its reproduction costs minus depreciation is limited in application to those buildings which are being economically utilized at the time of their damage or destruction. Such a limitation may be implied from the facts of those cases which have purported to follow *Smith*. Despite the language in the various opinions, Illinois had not allowed such windfalls as plaintiff here seeks.

In the instant case, the building was economically useless at the time of the fire. While we would prefer a more flexible standard of insurable "actual cash value" than the Illinois courts have adopted so that, in cases like the instant one, an insurable interest having some relationship to the actual value, even though nominal, could be found, we conclude that under all the precedents, there was no insurable interest in the building at the time of the fire on May 1, 1972.

In cases such as the instant one, where the building is vacant, boarded up and under a court order prohibiting repair of its heating system, and, therefore, cannot be economically utilized, reproduction cost new less depreciation has little or no relationship to actual value. Other factors, such as market value or salvage value, should be considered in establishing any insurable interest of the building owner. In their present posture, however, the Illinois cases preclude consideration of such factors. They do, however, permit a finding that where, as here, a building is economically useless and was obviously purchased for its scrap or salvage value, there is no insurable interest. This is such a case.

## *Notes and Questions*

1. On the issue of extinguishing an insurable interest, is *Tublitz* consistent with *Chicago Title & Trust Co.*? Can they be distinguished?

2. *Tublitz* represents the so-called "physical loss theory" and *Chicago Title & Trust Co.* represents the "financial loss theory" for ascertaining the amount of an insured loss. For an analysis of the appropriate measure of damages in demolition cases, *see* Emeric Fischer, *The Rule of Insurable Interest and the Principle of Indemnity: Are They Measures of Damages in Property Insurance?*, 56 IND. L.J. 445, 459–62 (1981).

### PROBLEM FIVE

James falls on hard times and cannot pay the mortgage on his house. The house goes into foreclosure. While James is negotiating with the bank, the title is transferred from his name to the bank. James continues to live in the house which is destroyed by fire. As an otherwise reasonably prudent person, James held insurance to cover the house.

• Can James recover on the policy or has his interest been extinguished?

### PROBLEM SIX

The Endowment Board of Seawash University tried to recover on a fire insurance policy covering an obsolete science building that they owned. Before closing down the old building, the Board had accepted a new science center from the University, and the students used only the new building from that point of time. The Board had contractually agreed with the University to permit the demolition of the old building and to use the land for other University needs. The fire insurance policy was in effect at the time the old science building burned down.

• How should the court decide, and why?

### PROBLEM SEVEN

A man gives an expensive diamond engagement ring to his fiancée but, prior to the wedding, the ring is lost or stolen.

• Does the man have a continuing insurable interest in the ring?

• What if his fiancée had called off the wedding before the ring was lost or stolen?

• Assume that insurance coverage is taken out by the husband's parents on their daughter-in-law's diamond wedding ring since the ring is a valuable family heirloom. Should the parents have a valid insurable interest in the diamond ring? Why or why not?

# § 5.02. The Insurable Interest Concept in Life Insurance

## [A] Who Has an Insurable Interest in a Life?

Life insurance policies normally fall into two categories: (1) policies taken out by the insured themselves on their own life, for the benefit of themselves, their estate, or a designated beneficiary; and (2) policies taken out upon the life of another.

It is generally held that "every person has an insurable interest in his own life," but when a person desires to insure the life of another person for his own benefit, an insurable interest in that person's life is of paramount importance to eliminate the possibility of wagering or gaming contracts that might lead to an early and untimely death — by foul means or fair. Indeed, the English Statute of George III in 1774 made reference to this "mischievous kind of gaming" and prohibited "the making of insurances on lives ... wherein the assured shall have no interest." 14 Geo. III, c. 48 (1774). This mandatory requirement of an insurable interest in another's life was adopted into American insurance law, and is still required today because "the policy of the law requires that the assured shall have an interest to preserve the life insured in spite of the insurance, rather than to destroy it because of the insurance." VANCE ON INSURANCE 190 (3d ed. 1951).

Notwithstanding that murder-for-insurance proceeds is a genuine risk, insurers tend to be willing to write coverage largely without much scrutiny of the net worth or future prospects of a proposed applicant. The general approach to insurable interest of both insurers and the courts is to merely look for a factual or legal benefit from the continued life of the person insured. Beyond this, courts seldom worry about whether the person's life was overinsured unless there are reasonable grounds for suspecting crime or fraud. The traditional rule is that "every person has an unlimited insurable interest in his or her own life." *See generally* Peter Nash Swisher, *The Insurable Interest Requirement for Life Insurance: A Critical Reassessment*, 53 DRAKE L. REV. 477, 485, n.23, 541 (2005), *reprinted in* 55 DEFENSE L.J. 526 (2006).

When the face amounts of life insurance are large, insurers may take considerably more interest in having the policy limits be commensurate with the insured's wealth or earning power so that he or she is not "worth more dead than alive" to the beneficiaries. But it appears that insurers do not do much, if any, financial investigation as part of the underwriting process, until the policy limits approach the mid-six figures or even the million dollar mark. The notion underlying the public policy behind the insurable interest requirement in life insurance is that a well-insured person is not significantly more likely than an uninsured or underinsured person to take his own life—and there also is a suicide exclusion provision in most life insurance policies, commonly denying indemnification of the insured if death is by suicide within the first two years of the life of the policy.

Because life insurance is a common financial planning tool, insurers traditionally give middle class policyholders substantial berth in determining how much life insurance is enough. A young couple may now not have much net worth or a huge salary, but if both are junior investment bankers or Wall Street lawyers, it is not absurd for them to be considering million-dollar policies. If they buy when younger, premiums are lower or leveled. Conversely, a rural farmer may not have much income but may purchase large amounts of life insurance to assist in estate planning as well as to protect his major asset of farm acreage. In addition, of course, a higher policy limit means higher premiums, giving agents little incentive to scrutinize policy amounts in relation to policyholder wealth or prospects.

As a result of these practical factors, insurers seldom show much interest in vetting proposed life insurance policy limits until after a suspicious loss has occurred. Thereafter, insurers may seek to argue that a policyholder had an insufficient insurable interest to purchase the amount of insurance at issue. Although such arguments may have superficial appeal to lay jurors, they are inconsistent with historical practices and the legal parameters of the insurable interest doctrine. An insurer can still, of course, defend a claim on grounds of fraud, misrepresentation or concealment but should not be permitted to second guess its own decision as to policy limits. Of course, nothing is to prevent an insurer from simply refusing to write policies above certain limits for the insured in question.

But murder-for-insurance schemes unfortunately do exist, which more than justifies an insurable interest requirement for life insurance. The facts and foibles, naiveté and cunning, found in the *Rubenstein* case below, serve as a prime example of this public policy.

## Rubenstein v. Mutual Life Insurance Co. of New York

United States District Court, Eastern District of Louisiana
584 F. Supp. 272 (1984)

### Charles Schwartz, Jr., District Judge

Plaintiff, Alan M. ("Mike") Rubenstein, instituted this action to recover the proceeds of a $240,000 credit life insurance policy issued by defendant, The Mutual Life Insurance Company of New York (MONY), insuring the life of Harold J. Connor, Jr. Connor died on November 6, 1979.

Plaintiff is the beneficiary and owner of said policy; MONY claims that plaintiff is not entitled to recovery under the policy for reasons that are the subject of this suit, and refunded to plaintiff the premiums paid by plaintiff. Plaintiff is a resident of Louisiana; defendant is a corporation incorporated and domiciled in New York, authorized to do and doing business in Louisiana. Prior to, during, and after July,

1979, plaintiff was employed as a fulltime owner and operator of a taxi cab associated with the United Cab Company of New Orleans. After attending a local seminar, he purportedly became interested in starting and developing "TV Journal," a publication similar in concept to "TV Facts," to be circulated free of charge in St. Tammany Parish. Revenues were to be derived solely from paid advertisements contained in the publication.

In late July, 1979, Connor contacted plaintiff through the Louisiana Unemployment Commission in Slidell, where plaintiff had placed a notice requesting assistance in developing and operating the "TV Journal." On August 7, 1979, shortly after their initial meeting, plaintiff and Connor entered into a partnership agreement making Connor a 25% partner in the "TV Journal" business until January 1, 1980; thereafter, plaintiff would "grant" Connor a franchise for the publication of a tabloid in the St. Tammany Parish area to be entitled "TV Journal." Under the franchise aspect of the agreement, Connor was required to pay plaintiff $1000 per month for 20 years beginning on February 1, 1980, but could terminate the agreement at any time upon 60 days notice without penalty.

Also on August 7, 1979, plaintiff and Connor met with Earl Moreau, a MONY agent, regarding life insurance on Connor. Based on discussions between plaintiff, Connor and Moreau concerning plaintiff's newly established business relationship with Connor, Moreau recommended, and plaintiff applied for, a $240,000 credit life insurance policy on Connor's life, who was then 23 years old.

[As the court observed in a footnote: Credit life insurance is to be distinguished from a "key employee" business insurance policy. With the former, the insurer risks that the debtor-insured will die before he or she can repay the creditor-beneficiary an existing debt. Under the latter, the insurer risks the death of someone whose loss would be highly detrimental to the business. From his discussions with plaintiff and Connor, Moreau correctly concluded that plaintiff was ineligible for "key employee" insurance on Connor's life.]

As of the date of application, Connor had done little if any work for the "TV Journal" business; and no edition of it had been published, and no advertisements sold. No evidence was introduced to demonstrate the need for this fledgling and undercapitalized business to expend its limited resources for insurance on the life of an apparently healthy 23 year old man.

In providing information for the insurance application, plaintiff and Connor represented that Connor's annual income at the time of the application was $26,000 when in fact Connor's sole source of income was the "TV Journal" business, from which he received approximately $100 to $150 a week. Had MONY known Connor's actual income, it would not have issued the policy herein since an insured earning such limited income has no reasonable prospect of repaying a debt of $1000 per month for twenty years without the life insurance.

[Plaintiff and Connor also failed to disclose to Moreau the 60-day termination provision of the agreement, which effectively limited Connor's potential maximum debt to $2000. The court found that plaintiff and Connor knew of the falsity of their representations regarding Connor's income and termination provision and that they knew that these misrepresentations were material.]

The evidence further establishes that when plaintiff applied for the insurance policy, and when Connor died on November 6, 1979, Connor was not at all indebted to plaintiff because Connor was not obligated to begin making payments to plaintiff until February 1, 1980.

Based on the information before it, MONY agreed to issue the policy on September 28, 1979; it was thereafter delivered to plaintiff on October 6, 1979. According to plaintiff's testimony, Connor was to do all the work in preparing the "TV Journal" for publication, while plaintiff was to provide the capital. However, Connor's education was limited to high school, and prior to August 7, 1979, he had no experience in publishing and only limited experience in sales, having worked for approximately two months without success as a furniture salesman, according to Paula Andrus, Connor's girlfriend at the time. Ms. Andrus also attested to Connor's inability to balance his own checking account, further evidence of his lack of business skill.

Plaintiff, too, had no prior experience in publishing or in selling advertisements, his only sales experience of any nature having occurred "years" ago, by his own admission. Plaintiff did observe the operations of "TV Tempo" for the purpose of learning the operations of such a weekly, and prior to August 7, 1979, had taken some preliminary steps in furtherance of the "TV Journal" (e.g., contacting printers, obtaining proofs and TV listings, and figuring possible advertising rates). But, after that date, plaintiff's involvement in the operations of the "TV Journal" was nominal at best; he testified that he did not even know whether Connor had sold a single advertisement, and plaintiff himself had made only a few calls for that purpose. Plaintiff also stated that he was not aware of what bills Connor was paying, or how much he was paying Connor in salary. As further evidence of his own lack of business acumen, plaintiff explained the origin of the provision requiring Connor to pay him $1000 per month beginning February 1, 1980, by saying that they "both came up with the idea of $1000," with no further justification for the projection.

Regarding the financing of "TV Journal," plaintiff explained that he bought some furniture for the office, which was located in Connor's apartment, and that he paid Connor's salary and "whatever" else Connor needed. The evidence indicates, however, that *at most* $5000 was available as of late August, 1979, to develop the "TV Journal" until it became profitable or generated significant advertising revenues. Most of the $5000 apparently originated from a $5433 loan issued by the Bunkie Bank & Trust Company on August 22, 1979, for which Connor signed the note and plaintiff provided the collateral. Of the $5433, however, $1400 was used by plaintiff to pay off a previous personal loan from Bunkie Bank & Trust, and $1000 was given to Connor for his personal use.

Disposition of the remaining $3000 is unclear, although it appears that the money was deposited in plaintiff's personal account with the Hibernia National Bank, which account he used to pay Connor's salary. This account showed a balance of $1246 on November 7, 1979, which was immediately before Connor had planned to print the first issue. Plaintiff's only other account was one he maintained with Bunkie Bank & Trust from November, 1976 to November, 1979. It had an average balance of $1500 to $1800 before it was closed. The "TV Journal" account at the Fidelity Bank & Trust Company shows a balance that was overdrawn twice in a two month period.

[The court found that the "TV Journal" was grossly undercapitalized.]

In addition, the failure of "TV Journal" to presell any advertisements or to obtain any advertising contracts further impaired any likelihood of success; without presold advertisements, the business would have incurred substantial losses during its first six months, from which it would have had little chance of recovering. Given this slim chance of reaching the breakeven point, Connor would have had no realistic possibility of being able to cover the $1000 monthly payment to plaintiff.

The bizarre circumstances surrounding the tragic death of Harold J. Connor, Jr., even after lengthy testimony from five witnesses who were present when Connor was shot, are still largely in dispute and somewhat irreconcilable. What was established conclusively at the trial was as follows: Connor was part of a deer hunting party that included plaintiff, plaintiff's step children, David and Darryl Perry, and the Perrys' first cousin, David Kenney. They left the New Orleans area on November 5, 1979, and arrived at plaintiff's parents' home in Bunkie later that day. Thereafter, plaintiff's brother, Larry Rubenstein, and a friend of his, Michael Fournier, also arrived at the home of plaintiff's parents. Plaintiff claims that he had no prior notice of his brother's and Fournier's visit. The latter joined the hunting party early the following morning. The group traveled in plaintiff's car on a dirt road surrounded by woods to a location selected the previous evening when plaintiff visited his uncle and cousin.

When the party arrived at the location, plaintiff distributed the firearms, ammunition, and orange hunting vests to each member of the group. Thereafter, Kenney locked the car keys inside the car, and the group searched for wire with which to open the door lock. Soon after Connor was able to open the front door on the passenger side, Fournier, who was standing less than 10 feet behind Connor, discharged his gun, a single shot, 12-gauge shotgun. The pellets struck Connor in the back, slightly above the waist, and traveled generally in a lateral path through his body.

Fournier claims that the gun discharged when he tripped, and Darryl Perry, in corroborating his testimony, claims that the gun discharged about when the butt was close to the ground and while the barrel was pointed diagonally upward in the direction of Connor. This testimony, however, was flatly contradicted by the forensic scientist and pathologist, who concluded that in view of the lateral path of the pellets through Connor's body above his waist, the barrel of the gun must have been parallel (horizontal) to the ground and at waist level at the time of discharge. Further, because of its safety device, in order for the gun to have been discharged, it must have been loaded, cocked, and the trigger pulled. The firing pin could not have been activated just by the gun striking the ground. (Testimony of forensic scientist Ronald Singer and pathologist Dr. Tom D. Norman.).

The testimony of the witnesses raises more questions than it answered, in particular: why did Connor go deer hunting when according to his mother, girlfriend and cousin, he had never been hunting before and was disgusted by the idea of killing animals, and did not pack the proper clothing? And why did Fournier load his gun, cock it, have his finger on the trigger, and have it pointed at Connor?

We conclude that examined in the light most favorable to the plaintiff, his handing a shotgun and ammunition to an individual who was, according to the plaintiff, previously unknown to him, and who was, it was later learned, a convicted felon then on probation [subsequently revoked] and prohibited from carrying firearms, constitutes conduct falling well below the standard of care required of a reasonable person in possession of firearms.

Examining the evidence not in the light most favorable to plaintiff but instead with the slightest circumspection leads to the distasteful conclusion that Harold J. Connor, Jr. was killed under highly suspicious circumstances, circumstances that suggest something far more sinister than a mere "accident."

## CONCLUSIONS OF LAW

Defendant interposes three separate and independent defenses to plaintiff's claim that he is entitled to recover under the $240,000 credit insurance policy insuring the life of Harold J. Connor, Jr.: (1) that defendant was induced to execute the policy by material misrepresentations made with the intent to deceive the insurer; (2) that plaintiff as the beneficiary lacks an insurable interest in the life of the insured; and (3) that plaintiff was culpably negligent in contributing to the death of the insured, and that such negligence bars his recovery under the policy. For the purposes of this decision, we need only consider defendant's first two defenses, and make no ruling on the third.

Under Louisiana law, a life or health insurance policy is null and void if the insurer is induced to execute the policy by misrepresentations in the application that were made with the intent to deceive and if the misrepresentations materially affected the insurer's decision to accept the risk or increased the hazard assumed by the insurer.... The insurer has the burden of proving the elements of [the statute].

Consistent with the foregoing findings, wherein we found that plaintiff and Connor misrepresented Connor's salary and failed to disclose the termination provision; that they knew of the falsity and the materiality of their misrepresentations; and that each of said misrepresentations materially affected the insurer's decision to accept the risk; we find that the insurance policy in question is null and void under La. R.S. 22:619(B). We further conclude that each of the misrepresentations constitutes a separate and independent ground for invalidating the insurance policy under said statutory provision.

Louisiana law also requires that a beneficiary who procures an insurance policy upon the life of another have an insurable interest in the life of the insured. La. R.S. 22:613(A). The absence of any insurable interest on the part of the beneficiary who procures the policy invalidates the policy, and the insurer's only liability is to return the premiums paid.... The beneficiary has the burden of proving the existence of the insurable interest.

A beneficiary who is not related by blood or marriage to the insured does not have an insurable interest unless he has a reasonable expectation of pecuniary gain from the continued life of the insured, or reasonable expectation of sustaining loss from his death....

Where the beneficiary's insurable interest is a debt allegedly owed by the insured, as is herein claimed, the amount of the life insurance at the time the policy was written and at the time of the insured's death must be proportionate to the debt actually owed by the insured; if the value of the life insurance is grossly disproportionate to the amount actually owed, the beneficiary lacks an insurable interest, and the policy is null and void. Since we earlier held that Connor was not indebted to plaintiff either when the policy was written or when he died, the amount of the insurance is grossly disproportionate to the amount of the debt. Even if we consider the amount that Connor could have owed under the terms of the partnership agreement— $2000—this too is far exceeded by the face value of the policy. Accordingly, we conclude that plaintiff lacks an insurable interest in the policy herein considered.

Should we characterize the beneficiary's expectation as a pecuniary gain arising from his business partnership with the insured, rather than as a debt arising from their relationship, our findings of fact lead to only one reasonable conclusion: that an expected pecuniary advantage of $240,000 in profits over 20 years derived from "TV Journal" is grossly disproportionate to the amount Connor could have paid plaintiff on a monthly basis given the inexperience of Connor and plaintiff and the vast undercapitalization of the venture. We therefore hold that plaintiff lacks an insurable interest under this theory too....

Because an insurable interest is required by law in order to protect the safety of the public by preventing anyone from acquiring a greater interest in another person's death than in his continued life, the parties cannot, even by solemn contract, create insurance without an insurable interest; further, the insurance company cannot waive or be estopped from asserting lack of insurable interest by its conduct in issuing the policy....

### Notes and Questions

1. *Rubenstein* serves as a prime example of how wagering contracts, without a bona fide insurable interest, can lead to questionable "accidental" death, and why the rule requiring an insurable interest is designed to protect human life. What ultimately happened to Alan "Mike" Rubenstein and his avaricious quest for life insurance proceeds involving highly suspicious deaths of other people? According to Professor Robert Jerry:

> One might have hoped that Rubenstein's interest in making money through the purchase of insurance on the lives of others might have waned after his unsuccessful effort to recover on the policy on Connor's life. Tragically, that was not the case. Darrell Percy, Rubenstein's step-son, would later enter

adulthood and marry a woman named Evelyn Ann, with whom he would have a daughter, Krystal Ryan, in 1989. In 1991, Rubenstein purchased a $250,000 insurance policy on the life of Krystal, his then two-year-old step-granddaughter, and named his wife, Doris, as the beneficiary....

[In 1993] after Doris did not hear from her son, Rubenstein ... went to look for him and reported discovering three bodies, all murdered.... Darrell and Evelyn had been stabbed, and Krystal had been strangled. Later, Rubenstein would testify that he collected the insurance proceeds and "blew" the money. After a lengthy investigation, Mississippi authorities charged [Rubenstein] in September 1998 with the three murders.... Rubenstein was tried ... and he was convicted of three counts of first degree murder and sentenced to death.... In September 2000, Darrell's father brought a $15 million lawsuit against Rubenstein, his wife, and the New York Life Insurance Company, which sold the policy on Krystal's life. Among the allegations in the suit is the claim that Doris knew that her husband had murdered Connor in 1979 in an attempt to collect insurance proceeds and did nothing to thwart Rubenstein's scheme with respect to Krystal.

Robert H. Jerry, II, *May Harvey Rest in Peace:* Lakin v. Postal Life and Casualty Company, 2 Nev. L.J. 292, 296–297 (2002).

Darrell's father undoubtedly also sued the New York Life Insurance Company based on its alleged negligence in issuing life insurance to Rubenstein, who may have lacked a valid insurable interest in the life of his step-granddaughter, Krystal.

2. In *Liberty Nat'l Life Ins. Co. v. Weldon*, 267 Ala. 171, 100 So. 2d 696 (1957), an aunt-in-law who at times temporarily cared for a two-year-old girl, took out life insurance on the child from three insurance companies, and then fatally poisoned the little girl by putting arsenic in her soda. An insurable interest? If no insurable interest, are the insurance companies estopped to deny it? Could the aunt-in-law recover the insurance proceeds before her execution in the electric chair?

*Weldon* held that a life insurance company has a duty to use reasonable care not to issue a life insurance policy to one who has no insurable interest in the life insured and gave the father of the poisoned child a judgment of $75,000 against the three insurance companies.

Unfortunately, these are not rare and isolated incidents. On September 23, 2010, for example, Teresa Lewis was executed by lethal injection in Virginia for the murder-for-hire of her husband and step-son for $250,000 in life insurance proceeds. This was the first execution of a woman in Virginia since 1912, and the first execution of a woman in America since 2005. The two murder-for-hire trigger men were both sentenced to life in prison without parole.

3. It has uniformly been held that a beneficiary who murders the insured cannot recover the policy benefits, and the proceeds must be paid to the innocent contingent beneficiary or to the estate of the deceased. *See, e.g., Cockrell v. Life Ins. Co.*, 692 F.2d 1164, 1170 (8th Cir. 1982) (applying Arkansas law) (holding that a beneficiary who

intentionally and unlawfully kills the insured cannot recover the insurance proceeds, and such insurance proceeds are paid to the innocent contingent beneficiary, or the estate of the deceased); *Lunsford v. Western States Life Ins.*, 908 P.2d 79, 82 (Colo. 1995) (reaching the same conclusion by applying the Colorado "slayer statute").

However, there is an "innocent instrumentality" exception to this general rule:

> An exception to the rule that the liability of the insurer is not affected by the beneficiary's unlawfully killing the insured may arise when the beneficiary is also guilty of fraud with respect to the insurer. For example, if it is established that the beneficiary conceived of the idea of murdering the insured prior to the time the insurance was procured and with that thought in mind the beneficiary himself procured the policy, either in person or acting through the insured as an innocent instrumentality so that the insurance policy was, in actual effect, at its inception a contract between the beneficiary and the insurance company, as distinguished from a contract between the innocent insured and the company, the insurance company may defeat liability on the ground of fraud. Under this principle, recovery is barred even by the estate of the insured.

*See generally* COUCH ON INSURANCE § 58:18 (3d ed. 2010). *See also New England Mut. Life Ins. Co. v. Null*, 605 F.2d 421 (8th Cir. 1979) (applying Missouri law).

4. Most jurisdictions hold that in order to have an insurable interest in another's life, the assured must be "related by blood or law" and must have an insurable interest "engendered by love and affection." Alternatively, there must be a "lawful economic interest" in having the life of the insured continue, such as in commercial or contractual situations involving employer-employee, creditor-debtor, and partnership relations.

To best align with the policy reasons behind the insurable interest concept, what should constitute a "close relationship by blood or law"? Few courts or legislatures have formulated any general rule fixing the degree of relationships where an insurable interest in one's life is found to exist. It is, however, generally recognized that an insurable interest exists between spouses, and between a parent and minor child. A similar insurable interest has been found by some courts in grandparent-grandchild and brother-sister relationships, but a specific pecuniary benefit also must be found to support insurable interests for aunts, uncles, nieces, nephews, cousins, and various in-laws or stepchildren. *See generally* VANCE ON INSURANCE 189–97 (3d ed. 1951).

5. Assume that prospective adoptive parents signed a contract with a state welfare agency to provide a home and educational and religious advantages to a child until they decided whether or not to adopt him. Should these prospective adoptive parents have an insurable interest in that child's life prior to adoption when they obtained the life insurance policy without the child's consent, and when they subsequently assigned the policy to another trustee? Why or why not? Based on what underlying public policy arguments? *See generally* COUCH ON INSURANCE, §§ 41:1–43:18 (3d ed. 2010).

6. Should a fiancée have an insurable interest in the life of her fiancé? Why or why not?

## PROBLEM EIGHT

In 1980, Jim Lopez filed suit against Life Insurance Company of Georgia, claiming that the company's negligence had endangered his life and caused him injury. In the complaint, Lopez alleged that his total family income amounted to $9,000 per year, but nonetheless the insurance company had issued to Lopez's wife insurance coverage on his life with a face value of $260,000 at an annual premium of $7,464. Moreover, Lopez alleged that he was not aware that his wife was purchasing life insurance, and he claimed to have been tricked into signing the authorization forms, believing that his wife was purchasing a health insurance policy.

The complaint further stated that in early 1977, Lopez overheard his wife and her brother plotting to kill him. Lopez called his insurance agent immediately, informing him of this conspiracy, but the insurance company made no inquiry into the matter. In May of 1977, Lopez's wife and brother-in-law allegedly abducted him and were attempting to drown him when a deputy sheriff happened upon the scene and rescued Lopez. His complaint against Life of Georgia therefore alleges the insurance company was negligent in failing to discover the disproportion of the coverage to the family's financial circumstances, and negligence in failing to investigate the conspiracy to murder Lopez after receiving actual notice from him.

The question certified to the appellate court was: "Whether an insurer issuing an insurance policy can be liable in tort to the insured where the policy beneficiary attempts to murder the insured in order to collect the policy benefits and where the insurer had actual notice of the policy beneficiary's murderous intent."

• How should the court rule on this case?

## PROBLEM NINE

Wife took out a life insurance policy on Husband's life. Allegedly, she forged his name on the policy application with the knowledge of the insurer, and then Wife poisoned Husband with arsenic.

• Does Wife have an insurable interest in Husband's life?

• Does the insured Husband need to have knowledge of, or to consent to, the issuance of such a policy?

• Assuming Husband dies from the arsenic poisoning, may Wife recover the proceeds?

• Assuming Husband survives the arsenic poisoning, what cause of action—if any—does he have against the insurance company?

## PROBLEM TEN

Clyde Graves and James Norred established a business partnership and obtained life insurance policies on each other's lives, naming the other partner as beneficiary. This partnership was later terminated with a physical division of the partnership assets and a cessation of the business, but no formal partnership dissolution papers were filed. When James Norred died, Clyde Graves demanded full payment on Norred's life insurance policy since Graves was named as the primary beneficiary. However, Graves' claim was contested by Norred's widow Jewell Norred and the life insurance agent, who both testified that Graves told them that each partner intended that the full insurance proceeds were to go to the estate of the deceased partner (*i.e.*, James Norred's wife Jewell) in payment for his partnership interest.

   • How should the court decide this case?

## [B] When an Insurable Interest Must Exist for Life Insurance

For life insurance, there must be an insurable interest at the time the policy is procured. It does not matter if that interest has eclipsed at the time of the insured's death. This is different than the requirement in property insurance. Historically, insurable interest in the lives of others was restricted in order to stamp out any concerns for wagering on the life of someone else. In 1774 in England, by statute, the insured was required to have an insurable interest in the life insured or the policy was void. Statute 14 Geo. III, Chap. 48 § 3 (1774). In addition, that same statute also stipulated that the insured could not recover more than "the amount or value of the interest of the insured in such life or lives."

Today, life insurance is treated more as an investment vehicle and certainly not like an indemnity policy such as property insurance. To that end, requiring the purchaser of a life insurance policy to have an insurable interest in the life of the insured at the time of purchase provides some measure of restriction on the class of people who may profit from the death of the life insured. There are a number of examples of this in the life insurance world. Prime among them is the "key employee" insurance policy, where a business takes out life insurance on a key employee. The business must have an insurable interest in that employee at the time of purchase of the policy. In *Tillman v. Camelot Music, Inc.*, 408 F.3d 1300 (10th Cir. 2005), the court held that, even though employers have an insurable interest in the lives of their key employees, they do not necessarily have an insurable interest in the life of a rank-and-file employee. So, Wal-Mart would have an insurable interest in its managers but not in the greeters at the front of the store.

Yet, if the key employee who is the life insured is discharged or otherwise leaves the business, most courts will hold that the business that purchased the policy is still the owner, because it had an insurable interest in the life of that key employee at the time of purchase of the policy. This is so even if that insurable interest has effectively extinguished some time after the purchase (i.e., the death of the life insured employee or that employee's departure from the business). The insurable interest does not have to be a continuing interest. In *Liss v. Liss*, 937 So. 2d 760 (Fla. 4th DCA, 2006), the court held that, in key employee policies, it is only necessary that the insurable interest exist at the time the insurance was purchased.

## [C] Issues with Insurable Interest and Life Insurance

### [1] Who Can Challenge Insurable Interest in Life Insurance?

A clear majority of jurisdictions follow the general rule that the insurer—and *only* the insurer—may raise any question regarding the lack of an insurable interest, and this is true for property insurance as well as life insurance. *See, e.g., Ryan v. Tickle,* 210 Neb. 630, 316 N.W.2d 580 (1982) (widow of insured decedent cannot challenge validity of insurable interest of policy owner—the decedent's business partner in a situation where partners took out policies on one another to protect their mutual economic interests in mortuary business; only the insurance company has standing to dispute the insurable interest of policy purchaser).

The public policy behind this rule apparently is that the insurance company, being a party to the policy, has a legitimate interest in raising the lack of an insurable interest, whereas nonparties have no such standing to raise any lack of an insurable interest. *See generally* VANCE ON INSURANCE 199–200 (3d ed. 1951); COUCH ON INSURANCE, §§ 41:5, 41:6 (3d ed. 2010). Is this distinction persuasive to you?

A small minority of jurisdictions hold that *any* interested party may raise the question of a lack of insurable interest. What is the basis for this minority rule? *See, e.g., Smith v. Coleman,* 183 Va. 601, 32 S.E.2d 704 (1945), *set aside on rehearing on other grounds,* 184 Va. 259, 35 S.E.2d 107 (1945).

### [2] Insurable Interest and Beneficiaries to Life Insurance

It is the prevailing view in most American jurisdictions that a person may insure his or her own life, pay premiums on the policy, and name a beneficiary who has no insurable interest in him or her—if there is no state statute to the contrary, and no collusion or speculation in any attempted wagering contract. *See* COUCH ON INSURANCE § 41:19 (3d ed. 2010). *See, e.g., American Casualty Co. v. Rose,* 340 F.2d 469 (10th Cir. 1964).

A minority of states, by case decision or statute, require that the beneficiary of a life insurance policy have an insurable interest in the life of the insured, or be related to the insured by a designated degree of kinship. The rationale for this minority rule is that a beneficiary without an insurable interest might be interested in the early death of the insured, and such policies are viewed as wagers on human life and are therefore condemned as against public policy. *See, e.g., Pashuck v. Metropolitan Life Ins. Co.,* 124 Pa. Super. 406, 188 A. 614 (1936); COUCH ON INSURANCE § 41:20 (3d ed. 2010).

### [3] Assignment of Life Insurance

In a life insurance policy, there are four parties to the bargain: the insurer, the owner of the policy, the life that is being insured (*cestui que vie* or CQV for short), and the beneficiary. Usually the owner and the CQV are the same person (referred to as the insured). However, the owner and the CQV could be two separate people. A corporation buying life insurance on the life of an officer (key employee insurance) is the owner of the policy, and the officer is the CQV. The corporation may name anyone as beneficiary (usually it names itself).

The owner of a life insurance policy usually reserves in the policy powers of ownership which include the rights to change the beneficiary, to assign the policy, to "cash in" the policy for its cash surrender value, and to borrow against the policy, all without the consent of the beneficiary. The right to assign the policy gives rise to many issues. Although there is universal agreement that one may obtain insurance on his or her own life, naming anyone as beneficiary, there has been much less agreement among the jurisdictions as to whether an insured may lawfully assign a life insurance policy, before its maturity, to a person who has no insurable interest in the person whose life is insured. In addition, controversy exists as to the relative rights of a beneficiary and assignee to the proceeds of a policy. *See* VANCE ON INSURANCE 674–83 (3d ed. 1951). *See also* JERRY & RICHMOND, UNDERSTANDING INSURANCE LAW § 52[B][d] (6th ed. 2018); KEETON & WIDISS, INSURANCE LAW, §§ 3.5(d), 4.11(e) (1988).

The following case is the touchstone American jurisprudence for the concept of insurable interest as it relates to assignment of a life insurance policy.

## Grigsby v. Russell

United States Supreme Court
222 U.S. 149, 32 S. Ct. 58, 56 L. Ed. 133 (1911)

**Justice Holmes** delivered the opinion of the court

This is a bill of interpleader brought by an insurance company to determine whether a policy of insurance issued to John C. Burchard, now deceased, upon his life, shall be paid to his administrators or to an assignee, the company having turned the amount into court. The material facts are that after he had paid two premiums and a third was overdue, Burchard, being in want and needing money for a surgical operation, asked Dr. Grigsby to buy the policy and sold it to him in consideration of one hundred dollars and Grigsby's undertaking to pay the premiums due or to become due; and that Grigsby had no interest in the life of the assured. The Circuit Court of Appeals in deference to some intimations of this court held the assignment valid only to the extent of the money actually given for it and the premiums subsequently paid....

Of course the ground suggested for denying the validity of an assignment to a person having no interest in the life insured is the public policy that refuses to allow insurance to be taken out by such persons in the first place. A contract of insurance upon a life in which the insured has no interest is a pure wager that gives the insured a sinister counter interest in having the life come to an end. And although the counter interest always exists, as early was emphasized for England in the famous case of *Waine-wright (Janus Weathercock)*, the chance that in some cases it may prove a sufficient motive for crime is greatly enhanced if the whole world of the unscrupulous are free to bet on what life they choose. The very meaning of an insurable interest is an interest in having the life continue and so one that is opposed to crime. And, what perhaps is more important, the existence of such an interest makes a roughly selected class of persons who by their general relations with the person whose life is insured are less likely than criminals at large to attempt to compass his death.

But when the question arises upon an assignment it is assumed that the objection to the insurance as a wager is out of the case. In the present instance the policy was perfectly good. There was a faint suggestion in argument that it had become void by the failure of Burchard to pay the third premium *ad diem,* and that when Grigsby paid he was making a new contract. But a condition in a policy that it shall be void if premiums are not paid when due, means only that it shall be voidable at the option of the company.... The company waived the breach, if there was one, and the original contract with Burchard remained on foot. No question as to the character of that contract is before us. It has been performed and the money is in court. But this being so, not only does the objection to wagers disappear, but also the principle of public policy referred to, at least in its most convincing form. The danger that might arise from a general license to all to insure whom they like does not exist. Obviously it is a very different thing from granting such a general license, to allow the holder of a valid insurance upon his own life to transfer it to one whom he, the party most concerned, is not afraid to trust. The law has no universal cynic fear of the temptation opened by a pecuniary benefit accruing upon a death. It shows no prejudice against remainders after life estates, even by the rule in *Shelley's Case.* Indeed, the ground of the objection to life insurance without interest in the earlier English cases was not the temptation to murder but the fact that such wagers came to be regarded as a mischievous kind of gaming. St. 14 George III, c. 48.

On the other hand, life insurance has become in our days one of the best recognized forms of investment and self-compelled saving. So far as reasonable safety permits, it is desirable to give to life policies the ordinary characteristics of property. This is recognized by the Bankruptcy Law § 70, which provides that unless the cash surrender value of a policy like the one before us is secured to the trustee within thirty days after it has been stated the policy shall pass to the trustee as assets. Of course the trustee may have no interest in the bankrupt's life. To deny the right to sell except to persons having such an interest is to diminish appreciably the value of the contract in the owner's hands. The collateral difficulty that arose from regarding life insurance as a contract of indemnity only, ... long has disappeared.... And cases in which a person having an interest lends himself to one without any as a cloak to what is in its inception a wager have no similarity to those where an honest contract is sold in good faith.

Coming to the authorities in this court, it is true that there are intimations in favor of the result come to by the Circuit Court of Appeals. But the case in which the strongest of them occur was one of the type just referred to, the policy having been taken out for the purpose of allowing a stranger association to pay the premiums and receive the greater part of the benefit, and having been assigned to it at once....

On the other hand it has been decided that a valid policy is not avoided by the cessation of the insurable interest, even as against the insurer, unless so provided by the policy itself.... And expressions more or less in favor of the doctrine that we adopt are to be found also in [other cases]. It is enough to say [that] there has been no decision that precludes us from exercising our own judgment upon this much debated point. It is at least satisfactory to learn from the decision below that in Tennessee, where this assignment was made, although there has been much division of opinion, the Supreme Court of that State came to the conclusion that we adopt, in an unreported case.... The law in England and the preponderance of decisions in our state courts are on the same side.

Some reference was made to a clause in the policy that "any claim against the company arising under any assignment of the policy shall be subject to proof of interest." But it rightly was assumed below that if there was no rule of law to that effect and the company saw fit to pay, the clause did not diminish the rights of Grigsby as against the administrators of Burchard's estate.

## Note

A majority of jurisdictions uphold these sorts of assignments and follow *Grigsby*, but only if such assignments were made in good faith and *not* with the intent of encouraging wagering contracts. In the often-quoted case of *Mutual Life Ins. Co. v. Allen*, 138 Mass. 24, 30 (1884), for example, the court stated:

> We see nothing in the contract of life insurance which will prevent the assured from selling his right under the contract for his own advantage, and we are of opinion that an assignment of a policy made by the assured in good faith for the purpose of obtaining its present value, and not as a gaming risk between him and the assignee, or a cover for a contract of insurance between the insurer and the assignee, will pass the equitable interest of the assignor; and that the fact that the assignee has no insurable interest in the life insured is neither conclusive nor *prima facie* evidence that the transaction is illegal.

*See also Life Prod. Clearing LLC v. Angel*, 530 F. Supp. 2d 646 (S.D.N.Y. 2008), for a modern treatment of this topic.

There is a minority rule, referred to as the "New Jersey Rule," under which,

> the insured takes no rights in the policy during the life of the beneficiary; ... he has merely the power to divest the named beneficiary of his rights and to vest those rights in a new beneficiary; ... he has power only to revoke the appointment already made and make a new appointment, such power to be exercised only in the manner provided in the policy.

*Davis v. Modern Indus. Bank*, 18 N.E.2d 639 (N.Y. 1939), interpreting *Sullivan v. Maroney*, 78 A. 150 (N.J. Eq. 1910).

The meaning of the New Jersey rule is that a beneficiary has a vested right in the policy and can be deprived of it only by a change of beneficiary. Therefore, in a contest between a beneficiary and assignee, the beneficiary's claim is superior. In addition, the insurance company is not protected when it accepts a surrender form executed by the insured alone.

In either type of jurisdiction, a determination must be made whether the assignment of a life insurance policy to one without an insurable interest in the insured life was in fact an honest, good faith transaction, or merely a "cover-up" for an illegal wagering contract.

In a minority of jurisdictions, the view has been taken that an assignment of a life insurance policy by the insured to one with no insurable interest is void as a matter of law regardless of who pays the premiums; the parties' good faith and the absence of a preconceived intent to assign at the time of the policy issuance are considered irrelevant. The public policy behind this view is that such an assignment is a wagering contract and a temptation to commit crime.

In some states, the assignment controversy has been settled by statute, either authorizing or prohibiting assignments to persons without an insurable interest in the life of the insured. *See, e.g.,* VA. CODE ANN. § 38.2-3111:

> Assignment of life insurance policies—A policy of insurance on life, taken out by the insured himself, or by a person having an insurable interest in his life, in good faith, and not for the mere purpose of assignment, may, unless the policy provides otherwise, be lawfully assigned to any one as any other chose in action, without regard to whether the assignee has an insurable interest in the life insured or not.

In 2010, in a 5–2 decision based on its construction of the state's insurable interested statute, New York's highest court held that a person may procure an insurance policy on his or her own life and transfer it, even immediately, to anyone—even someone lacking an insurable interest and even if this was the plan from the outset. *See Kramer* v. *Phoenix Life Ins. Co.,* 940 N.E.2d 535 (N.Y. 2010).

In *Kramer,* the battle was not among family members or current and former spouses but between the widow and the assignees, commercial investors in what is known as a "stranger-owned life insurance" (often expressed as SOLI or STOLI insurance) or a "scheme" as described by the court. The case involved

> several insurance policies obtained by decedent Arthur Kramer, a prominent New York attorney, on his own life, allegedly with the intent of immediately assigning the beneficial interest to investors who lacked an insurable interest in his life. In May 2008, Arthur's widow, plaintiff Alice Kramer, as personal representative of her husband's estate [sued] seeking to have the death benefits from these insurance policies paid to her. She alleges that these policies, which collectively provide some $56,200,000 [Ed. note: not a misprint] in coverage, violate New York's insurable interest rule because her husband obtained them without the intent of providing insurance for himself or anyone with an insurable interest in his life....

> [New York Insurance Law] Section 3205(b)(1) addresses individuals obtaining life insurance on their own lives:

> Any person of lawful age may on his own initiative procure or effect a contract of insurance upon his own person for the benefit of any person, firm, association or corporation. Nothing herein shall be deemed to prohibit the immediate transfer or assignment of a contract so procured or effectuated. [940 N.E.2d at 539.] ...

There is simply no support in the statute for plaintiff and the insurers' argument that a policy obtained by the insured with the intent of immediate assignment to a stranger is invalid. The statutory text contains no intent requirement; it does not attempt to prescribe the insured' motivation. To the contrary, it explicitly allows for "immediate transfer or assignment".... This phrase evidently anticipates that an insured might obtain a policy with the intent of assigning it, since one who "immediately" assigns a policy likely intends to assign it at the time of procurement.

The statutory mandate that a policy must be obtained on an insured's "own initiative" requires that the decision to obtain life insurance be knowing, voluntary, and actually initiated by the insured.... [All that is required is that] the insured's decision must be free from nefarious influence or coercion. [940 N.E.2d at 541.]

There is a reason strangers were interested in buying the policies, but not a good one according to the *Kramer* dissent:

> Even if we ignore the possibility that the owner of the policy will be tempted to murder the insured, this kind of "insurance" has nothing to be said for it. It exists only to enable a bettor with superior knowledge of the insured's health to pick an insurance company's pocket.
>
> In a sense, of course, all insurance is a bet, but for most of us who buy life insurance it is a bet we are happy to lose.... But stranger-originated life insurance does not protect against a risk; it does not make sense for the purchaser if it is expected to be profitable for the insurance company. The only reason to buy such a policy is a belief that the insured's life expectancy is less than what the insurance company thinks it is.

*See* 940 N.E.2d at 544 (Smith, J., dissenting). Invoking *Grigsby v. Russell, supra,* the *Kramer* dissent acknowledged that *Grigsby* and the majority of cases had adopted a liberal rule permissive of assignment.

> But this rule of free assignability has always had an exception — an exception for [cases] like this case, where the insured, at the moment he acquires the policy, is in substance acting for a third party who wants to bet on the insured's death.

### Notes and Questions

1. Which view is more sound: the *Kramer* majority or the *Kramer* dissent? Or was one opinion making a ruling without regard to its wisdom? Are the opinions different in their degree of formalism and functionalism? Does it affect your assessment to

know that since Kramer's purchase of the insurance policies and sale of the policies to investors, New York's Legislature has outlawed SOLI/STOLI insurance arrangements like this?

2. The viatical settlement raises challenging legal and policy questions about insurable interest and assignment of life insurance. A viatical settlement is an arrangement where the life insured makes someone else the beneficiary of the proceeds of the insurance when the life insured dies — in exchange for the life insured being paid up-front money in the present, while still alive (of course, the life insured is paid less than the face value of the policy).

The viatical settlement industry became notorious at the start of the outbreak of HIV/AIDS. That disease was not well-known, and frequently, a diagnosis was unfortunately fatal. Investors "purchased" the right to life insurance proceeds from life insureds and then took over paying the premiums until the life insured died. The investors then collected the death benefits. The life insured enjoyed a lump sum cash payout while alive, but the beneficiary of the policy, of course, changed to the investors (instead of who was originally earmarked as the beneficiary for the life insured).

What policy and societal challenges do you see with respect to viatical settlements? How does the viatical settlement industry get around the problem of insurable interest here? For more, *see, e.g.*, "Study Paper on Viatical Settlements" (British Columbia Law Institute, 2006).

3. Groups of investors in the viatical settlement industry conglomerate to form a market in "death futures," which can ride the investment wave of varying scourges to our health. How, if at all, does this sort of mass commercial financial behavior run up against insurable interest issues?

4. An offshoot of the viatical settlement market has been the "senior settlement," where perhaps otherwise-healthy senior citizens change the beneficiary of their life insurance to an investor in exchange for up-front cash to enjoy while alive. The investor of course pays something less than the full value of the death benefit, and continues to pay the premiums. As people are living longer, this type of arrangement is growing in popularity. How — if at all — is this a different situation than the viatical settlement with the terminally ill life insured?

## PROBLEM ELEVEN

Husband's retirement life insurance policy was not cancelled when he left his employer who operated a pension retirement system. When husband died, the insurance company paid the proceeds to a pension trustee who had no insurable interest in husband's life. Wife brought an action against the insurance company and the trustee for the insurance proceeds.

• Can she recover? Why or why not?

## PROBLEM TWELVE

Lonnie Rakestraw was employed in the department of highways of the city of Cincinnati. For many years he had been a contributing member to a retirement program maintained by the city. A Cincinnati ordinance and a contract between the city and its employees mandated that any designated beneficiary in the city's retirement plan must be one who has a lawful insurable interest in the employee.

Some years prior to his death, Lonnie Rakestraw deserted his wife Lizzie and began living with Octavia Foster. Lonnie then named Octavia as the beneficiary of his retirement plan. Octavia knew of the existence of Lonnie's legal marriage to Lizzie and she did not claim that she thought Lonnie and Lizzie were divorced. Therefore, Octavia could not claim the existence of a putative marriage or a common-law marriage in Ohio. Octavia's sole claim to Lonnie's death benefits under the retirement plan was therefore predicated on the fact that Octavia, as a "de facto" spouse, had a valid insurable interest in Lonnie since Lonnie supported her economically, and since Octavia expressed love and affection for Lonnie.

- Does Octavia have a valid insurable interest in Lonnie's life?

- What party or parties can raise the lack of an insurable interest in this case?

# [D] Extinguishment of Insurable Interest in Life Insurance

The general rule that "[t]he subsequent cessation of an insurable interest does not invalidate an insurance policy which was valid when purchased" is generally accepted in respect to life insurance policies. Succinctly put, a life insurance policy valid at its inception is valid forever.

But what is the policy, and insurable interest connection, that empowers a corporation, partnership, or other business organization to purchase life insurance coverage on certain employees under a "key employee" policy? *See, e.g., Connecticut Mut. Life Ins. Co. v. Luchs*, 108 U.S. 498 (1883); COUCH ON INSURANCE § 43:13 (3d ed. 2010).

## *Notes and Questions*

In *Trent v. Parker*, 591 S.W.2d 769 (Tenn. App. 1979), Dean Trent, a former officer and shareholder of the East Lawn Memorial Park, brought a legal action to cancel two insurance policies, including a "key employee" life insurance policy on Trent's life, since he was no longer an officer of East Lawn Memorial Park and had been involved in violent arguments with his former partner, J.T. Parker. Doesn't Trent have a legitimate concern? If he is now in litigation with the business and may no longer be a "key employee" in that organization, what prevents a wagering contract type of situation where the business now has everything to gain, and nothing to lose, if Trent should suddenly die from an unfortunate "accident"? Nevertheless, the Tennessee Court of Appeals held that East Lawn Memorial Park still had an insurable interest in the life of its ex-key employee, Trent.

## PROBLEM THIRTEEN

Wartnick is an officer of Midwest Florist Supply Company, a family-run business founded by Wartnick's father. Robert Nachtsheim worked as a salesman for Midwest between 1959 and 1972. In April of 1970, Wartnick bought a $100,000 "key employee" insurance policy from the Prudential Life Insurance Company, naming Midwest as the beneficiary. In August of 1972, Robert Nachtsheim left Midwest and joined a competing florist business. On May 11, 1973, three days before the Prudential insurance policy was to lapse, Wartnick paid the annual premium to keep it in effect, even though Nachtsheim no longer worked for Midwest.

On the morning of May 24, 1973, Robert Nachtsheim was fatally shot shortly after he arrived at work. The evidence suggested the killer was someone the decedent knew: he apparently had let the killer in before opening for business; there was no evidence of robbery or a struggle; and the killer shot the decedent in the head at close range from a visible position. A large box of orchids, normally sold only to other wholesalers, had been removed from the cooler and was upside down on the floor near the decedent's body. The police and the District Attorney's office investigated the killing, but no one was charged, and it remains officially unsolved.

Prudential paid Wartnick and Midwest the life insurance proceeds over the objection of Nachtsheim's widow, Betty Nachtsheim. In October of 1976, Betty Nachtsheim sued Prudential, Midwest, and Wartnick under Minnesota's wrongful death statute for $350,000 in compensatory damages and $2 million in punitive damages.

At the time of the shooting, the Minnesota wrongful death statute required that the action be brought within three years of the wrongful act causing death, but the statute was amended in 1983 to remove any time limitations based on murder. Betty Nachtsheim alleged that her husband had been overinsured; that he had told Prudential not to renew the policy since he no longer worked for Midwest; that when the last premium was paid Midwest had no insurable interest in his life; and that Wartnick had murdered or procured to murder her husband.

- How should the court rule in this case?

- What valid cause of action—if any—would Betty Nachtsheim have against the Prudential Insurance Company?

# § 5.03. Insurable Interest and Liability Insurance

Liability insurance, like other types of insurance, must generally be supported by an insurable interest in the insured, although there are some cases holding to the contrary. The insurable interest in liability insurance does not depend on whether the insured has a legal or equitable interest in property, but upon whether the insured may be found legally liable, thus triggering some type of liability insurance policy.

Accordingly, legal or equitable title is not the test of an insurable interest in liability insurance; an individual has an insurable interest in his own personal liability if the occurrence of an insured event will cause him economic disadvantage in the form of legal liability. *See generally* Jerry & Richmond, Understanding Insurance Law § 44[c] (6th ed. 2018). Although most courts do hold as a general rule that liability insurance—like other forms of insurance—must be supported by an insurable interest, other courts have held that an insurable interest is not required for liability insurance. Under what rationale?

Normally, this is a fairly straightforward inquiry, which perhaps accounts for the relatively lower proportion of insurable interest cases involving liability insurance. If a prospective policyholder is engaging in activity that may give rise to liability claims against third parties, the prospective policyholder has an insurable interest in purchasing liability insurance to provide it with defense and indemnity protection against such possible claims. Consequently, a commercial widget maker or a service provider normally has an insurable interest in liability insurance because it may be sued by users of the product or service for bodily injury or property damage if something goes wrong (or is perceived to go wrong).

Similarly, individuals usually have an insurable interest in obtaining liability insurance if they entertain guests, drive, or publish commentary that may be perceived as defamatory (this is a standard feature in personal umbrella insurance) or simply interact with third parties who may make claims against them. Personal umbrella policies also may cover things like battery if the policyholder can surmount the intentional act defense.

# Chapter 6

# Causation and the Concept of Accident

## § 6.01. Insurance Causation

To determine the trigger for coverage in an insurance context, one needs to know the cause of the loss. A property insurance policy may provide coverage for "fire" but exclude coverage for "flood." Similarly, a liability policy may provide coverage for "legal liability" but exclude coverage for losses "expected or intended from the standpoint of the insured." When two or more causes combine together at once, or in a sequence, to produce a loss, the issue becomes all the thornier. The causation analysis therefore drives much of insurance law.

Causation in insurance differs from causation in tort—a fundamental difference to keep in mind. Causation in tort is a tool used within the fault-based context of negligence to assess fault, blame, and responsibility for falling below a certain standard. Causation is the bridge that links blameworthy conduct to responsibility to pay for a loss. The question being answered is: "Who is at fault and who pays?"

In insurance, however, the "fault" of the cause is irrelevant. The context is one of contract law, not tort. Causation in insurance is designed to answer the question, "Does a certain happening trigger coverage within the language of the insurance policy?" Insurance causation therefore bears little resemblance to the policy-laden concept of proximate cause in negligence. It only determines whether or not a certain contractual right is going to be in play. If a covered cause of loss, for example, fire, caused some damage to a house, the policy should indemnify the policyholder. The causation analysis to determine coverage in insurance is usually not concerned with "why" the fire started, or who was to blame for the fire or what circumstances led up to the fire. If fire damaged the property, the policy covers the loss unless an applicable exclusion removes coverage.

Justice Benjamin Cardozo in his landmark insurance decision of *Bird v. St. Paul Fire & Marine Ins. Co.*, 120 N.E. 86, 87–88 (N.Y. 1918), noted that an insurance relationship depends on the existence of a contract, and this distinguishes insurance law causation from tort law causation:

> In the law of torts ... there is the tendency to go farther back in the search for causes than there is in the law of contracts.... Especially in the law of in-

surance, the rule is that, "you are not to trouble yourself with distant causes".... In last analysis, therefore, it is something in the minds of men, *in the will of the contracting parties*, and *not* merely *in the physical bond of union between events*, which solves, at least for the jurist, this problem of causation [in insurance law cases].... Our guide is the *reasonable expectation and purpose* of the ordinary business man when making a business contract. It is *his intention*, expressed or fairly inferred, that counts.

*Id.*

In Cardozo's view, then, insurance causation issues are based upon a test of "proximateness" that emphasizes the *reasonable expectations of the parties* to insurance coverage, a standard that is based on contract law, rather than tort law. *See also* Peter Nash Swisher, *Insurance Causation Issues: The Legacy of* Bird v. St. Paul Fire & Marine Ins. Co., 2 Nev. L.J. 351 (2002); Erik S. Knutsen, *Confusion About Causation in Insurance: Solutions for Catastrophic Losses*, 61 Ala. L. Rev. 957 (2010); Erik S. Knutsen, *Causation in Canadian Insurance Law*, 50 Alberta L. Rev. 631 (2013).

Yet because both tort law and insurance law each use the same name to describe a crucial step in the applicable analytic framework—"causation"—courts often confuse concepts from causation in negligence and attempt to apply them in an insurance causation context. That leads to misleading and haphazard results, as tort concepts of morality and blameworthiness start to creep into judicial reasoning and warp what should be a contractual analysis.

Insurance causation becomes an issue in two scenarios: coverage disputes and loss distribution disputes. *See* Knutsen, *supra.* In coverage disputes, the policyholder and insurer are attempting to determine whether or not a certain loss is covered by a certain insurance policy. In loss distribution disputes, two or more insurers may potentially provide coverage for the same resulting loss. Whether or not one or the other insurer, or both insurers, are required to respond to the loss is typically a matter decided using insurance causation concepts. One must first determine the cause of the loss and then determine which insurer—if any—is to be responsible for indemnifying the insured. The dispute usually lies between insurers.

When trying to sort out whether or not a particular happening in the world is a trigger of insurance coverage, it can often be a challenge to sort out which among many complicated possible causes is the cause to examine. The key is to discuss the cause in relation to its sequence upon the loss.

First, start with isolating the end result loss being claimed. What is it? A burned house from a fire? Someone being accidentally shot while the policyholder was cleaning a firearm? Sewage entering a home through a sewer back-up? A pedestrian struck by a vehicle while the driver was texting?

Then, work backward from the loss to determine the relevant causes potentially at play in the analysis. Pay particular attention to those causes that are specifically triggering relevant insurance policy provisions (i.e., coverage and exclusion clauses). Assess the causal involvement and causal necessity of the particular trigger(s) of coverage.

Finally, focus on the end result of the damage, not how the damage took place. For property insurance, focus on the results of the external force which damaged the property (i.e., what part of the house did the fire damage?). Quite simply: what "touched" the property to result in the insurance claim? If it is a burned house, left as a pile of ashes, it matters little that wind pushed some fire embers to the building to get the fire going. The cause of the loss, for insurance coverage purposes, is "fire."

For liability insurance, focus on the <u>result</u> of the behavior which caused harm (i.e., what did the tortfeasor's negligent driving do that harmed the accident victim?). In this context: what category of policyholder loss-causing "behavior" resulted in the losses claimed? If, for example, a pedestrian is hit by a car driven by a distracted, texting driver, the cause of injury to the pedestrian is an automobile collision for which use of a cellphone is only tangential.

However, if the auto policy contains an exclusion of any "claims arising out of use of an electronic device" or even "out of the use of a mobile phone," the insurer may be able to bar coverage—provided that the court does not strike down the exclusion on public policy grounds as inconsistent with the protective requirement of mandatory auto insurance. In addition, a court might find literal application of this language to bring about an "absurd" result inconsistent with the purpose of auto insurance. Like it or not, legal or not, people use phones while driving. An exclusion for claims where phones are used to defeat the basic purposes of auto insurance—protecting policyholders from their own negligence and compensating victims—would appear too broad to enforce.

An exclusion for any claim "in which an electronic device is tangentially involved" or "is operating" would, by its language, have an even greater chance of being found applicable to bar coverage—but would present even greater public policy problems. This exclusionary language, if enforced literally, could deprive policyholders of coverage and victims of compensation if the car radio was on during a collision or if an unused mobile phone was in the driver's pocket or if a passenger was using a laptop while en route.

Another simple example: assume a house fire results because a policyholder left a candle burning. The policyholder ran outside to greet some friends who were passing by and forgot the candle was burning. The drapes caught fire from the candle flame and the house was damaged by fire. The policyholder's homeowners property policy is an all-risk policy which covers losses from fire. For the insurance causation analysis, one would start from the end result of the damage—the house was burned by fire. It does not matter (at the coverage stage) why the policyholder left the house or how the candle burned the drapes. The result of the external force (fire) was damage to the home. The loss is covered because fire (a covered cause) was necessarily involved in the losses to the home.

# [A] Approaches to Insurance Causation

Courts have not been uniform in how they have analyzed causation issues with respect to insurance coverage. The issue is often tricky, because parties can perceive that some causes of a loss may be covered causes, some may be excluded, and others neither covered nor excluded.

In most insurance coverage disputes revolving around causation issues, there is typically one cause of the loss that is "the" cause—the factor that drives whether or not coverage exists under the policy. Parties look to that cause and examine the text of the policy in light of the cause of the loss to determine coverage. However, in an increasingly complex world with increasingly creative lawyers, the causal tale of how a potentially insured loss came to be can become quite convoluted as parties are incentivized to either seek coverage or deny coverage. In some instances, it is not at all clear which one of a number of possible potential causes triggers insurance coverage. There may, in fact, be more than one cause acting together to produce an insured loss. Concurrently caused losses require a particular approach when assessing insurance causes. There exist three approaches (and varying permutations) among American courts as to how to resolve concurrent causation.

The most prevalent approach is the proximate cause (also called the "dominant cause") approach. The majority view today is if multiple concurrent causes contributed to the loss, and a dominant cause was a covered peril, then insurance coverage would exist for the entire loss, even though other concurrent causes were not covered under the policy. *See, e.g., W. Nat'l Mut. Ins. Co. v. Univ. of N.D.*, 643 N.W.2d 4 (N.D. 2002). While this approach is by far the most common, it is not without its problems. In a multi-causal scenario, how does one determine what is the "dominant" or "proximate" cause? The problem is even more complicated when losses arise because various causes combine to produce a loss which would otherwise never occur unless those causes acted together in that specific combination.

A minority of courts follow a more conservative approach: if a covered cause combines with an excluded cause to produce the loss, the policyholder may not recover. *See, e.g., Lydick v. Insurance Co. of North America*, 187 Neb. 97, 187 N.W.2d 602 (1971); *Vanguard Ins. Co. v. Clarke*, 475 N.W.2d 48 (Mich. 1991).

Finally, a minority of courts follow a more liberal approach to concurrent causation: if one cause in the causal chain is a covered cause, the entire loss is covered by the insurance policy. *See, e.g., State Farm Ins. Cos. v. Seefeld*, 481 N.W.2d 62 (Minn. 1992); *Salem Group v. Oliver*, 607 A.2d 138 (N.J. 1992). The Supreme Court of Canada has also adopted the liberal approach: *see Derksen v. 539938 Ont. Ltd.*, 2001 CSC 72 (Can.).

As you read the following two decisions (one about property insurance, one about liability insurance), can you tell which approach the court used? Which is more effective? Does it matter whether the issue is one of property or liability insurance?

# Leonard v. Nationwide Mutual Insurance Co.

Court of Appeals for the Fifth Circuit
499 F.3d 419 (2007)

**Edith H. Jones, Chief Judge:**

This homeowner's policy coverage dispute arose from the destruction wrought by Hurricane Katrina along the Mississippi Gulf Coast. We affirm the judgment of the district court, but to do so we must work through some erroneous reasoning that led to its conclusion.

The Leonards' home lies twelve feet above sea level on the southmost edge of Pascagoula, Mississippi, less than two hundred yards from the Mississippi Sound. Hurricane Katrina battered Pascagoula with torrential rain and sustained winds in excess of one hundred miles per hour. By midday, the storm had driven ashore a formidable tidal wave—also called a storm or tidal surge—that flooded the ground floor of the Leonards' two-story home.

*A. The Policy*

The Leonards purchased their first Nationwide homeowner's policy from Nationwide's Pascagoula-area agent, Jay Fletcher, in 1989. Although Nationwide twice revised its standard homeowner's policy language between 1989 and 2005, the Leonards' "Form HO-23-A" policy that was in force when the storm made landfall was substantially indistinguishable from the "Elite II" policy they originally purchased.

Like almost all homeowner's policies, Nationwide's Form HO-23-A is a "comprehensive," or "all-risk," policy pursuant to which all damage to dwellings and personal property not otherwise excluded is covered. Also, like almost all homeowner's policies, Nationwide's policy covers only damage caused by certain instrumentalities—or "perils"—and excludes damage caused by others. Relevant to this appeal are the policy provisions that define the scope of coverage for damage caused by (1) wind; (2) water; and (3) concurrent action of wind and water.

*1. Wind*

Wind damage both to a dwelling and to personal property is a peril insured against under Section I, clause 2 (the "wind-damages clause"), which along with pertinent prefatory language states:

Coverage A—Dwelling and Coverage B—Other Structures ( ... )

Coverage C—Personal Property

We cover accidental direct physical loss to property described in Coverage C caused by the following perils except for losses excluded under Section I— Property Exclusions: ( ... )

2. windstorm or hail.

Direct loss caused by rain ... driven through roof or wall openings made by direct action of wind, hail, or other insured peril is covered....

The policy thus covers losses caused by rain blown through a hole in a roof, wall, or window. Exclusively wind-related damage, like a blown-off roof, or a window damaged by a wind-propelled projectile, is also covered.

*2. Water*

Like most homeowner's policies, the Leonards' policy unambiguously excludes damage caused by water—including flooding—in a broadly worded exemption clause (the "water-damages exclusion"):

> Property Exclusions (Section I) ( ... )
>
> (b) Water or damage caused by water-borne material. Loss resulting from water or water-borne material damage described below is not covered even if other perils contributed, directly or indirectly, to cause the loss. Water and water-borne material damage means:
>
> 1. flood, surface water, waves, tidal waves, overflow of a body of water, spray from these, whether or not driven by wind....

When the Leonards annually renewed their policy, they received the following notice from Nationwide informing them that flood losses would not be covered, but that additional flood coverage was available upon request:

> *IMPORTANT INFORMATION*
>
> A Message From Your Nationwide Agent:
>
> Your policy does not cover flood loss. You can get protection through the National Flood Insurance Program. If you wish to find out more about this protection, please contact your Nationwide Agent.

The Leonards never purchased additional flood coverage under the federally subsidized National Flood Insurance Program ("NFIP"). *See* 42 U.S.C. §§ 4001–4027.

*3. Concurrent Action by Wind and Water*

The prefatory language introducing the water-damages exclusion addresses situations in which damage arises from the synergistic action of a covered peril, e.g., wind, and an excluded peril, e.g., water:

> 1. We do not cover loss to any property resulting directly or indirectly from any of the following. *Such a loss is excluded even if another peril or event contributed concurrently or in any sequence to cause the loss....*

Commonly referred to as an "anticoncurrent-causation clause," or "ACC clause," this prefatory language denies coverage whenever an excluded peril and a covered peril combine to damage a dwelling or personal property. The inundation of the Leonards' home was caused by a concurrently caused peril, i.e., a tidal wave, or storm surge—essentially a massive wall of water—pushed ashore by Hurricane Katrina's winds. Accordingly, argues Nationwide, losses attributable to storm surge-induced flooding are excluded under the ACC clause. The validity of the ACC clause is the key interpretive battleground of this appeal.

## B. Paul Leonard's Conversations with Fletcher

Paul Leonard testified that when he first bought his policy in 1989, he asked Nationwide's agent Jay Fletcher whether the Nationwide policy covered hurricane-related losses. According to Leonard, Fletcher responded that all hurricane damage was covered. Fletcher stated in his deposition testimony that he did not recall this conversation; the district court deemed it irrelevant to the case.

Leonard claims he spoke again with Fletcher ten years later to discuss a proposed increase in the wind/hail deductible that Nationwide was instituting on its homeowner's policies. Leonard called Fletcher after seeing advertisements for additional NFIP coverage in the wake of Hurricane Georges, which struck the Mississippi coast in 1998. Fletcher allegedly assured Leonard that he did not need additional flood coverage because Leonard did not live in an area classified Zone A for flood risk by the Federal Emergency Management Agency ("FEMA"). Fletcher purportedly added that his own property was not insured under the NFIP. Leonard does not allege that Fletcher told him the Nationwide policy covered flooding caused by a hurricane; Leonard merely inferred from Fletcher's comments that such coverage existed.

At the bench trial, the district court admitted under Federal Rule of Evidence 406 what it characterized as evidence that Fletcher "as a matter of habit and routine, expressed his opinion ... that customers [in Pascagoula] should not purchase flood insurance unless they lived in a flood prone area (Flood Zone A) where flood insurance was required in connection with mortgage loans." *Leonard v. Nationwide Mut. Ins. Co.*, 438 F.Supp.2d 684, 690 (S.D.Miss.2006). Trial evidence demonstrated that between 2001 and Katrina's landfall in late August 2005, Fletcher sold approximately one hundred eighty-seven NFIP policies to Pascagoula-area customers, twelve of whom lived in the Leonards' waterfront neighborhood.

## C. Hurricane Damage

Inspection of the Leonards' residence following the storm revealed modest wind damage. The roof suffered broken shingles and loss of ceramic granules, but its watertight integrity was not compromised. The non-load-bearing walls of the garage and the garage door were severely damaged; doors in the house and garage had been blown open. Finally, a "golf-ball sized" hole in a ground-floor window was likely caused by a wind-driven projectile.

Water damage, in contrast, was extensive. The Leonards' neighborhood had suffered a seventeen-foot storm surge, causing the entire ground floor of their residence to become inundated under five feet of water blown ashore from the Mississippi Sound. Walls, floors, fixtures, and personal property sustained extensive damage. The second floor of the house remained unscathed.

Nationwide's adjuster evaluated the storm damage and, after applying the Leonards' five hundred dollar deductible, tendered a check for $1,661.17—the amount determined attributable solely to wind. Nationwide informed the Leonards that damages caused by water and the storm surge's concurrent wind-water action were barred, respectively, by the water-damages exclusion and the ACC clause.

At trial, the Leonards offered expert testimony that the total damages actually exceeded $130,000, but this figure did not apportion damages caused by different perils. The Leonards' wind-specific assessment claimed $47,365.41, including costs for roof replacement and structural repairs to the garage.

### D. The Anti-Concurrent Causation Clause

Although the district court granted the Leonards only a meager monetary recovery for losses proven to have been caused by wind, it also summarily invalidated the ACC clause, stating that "[t]he provisions of the Nationwide policy that purport to exclude coverage entirely for damages caused by a combination of the effects of water (an excluded loss) and damage caused by the effects of wind (a covered loss) are ambiguous." *Leonard*, 438 F.Supp.2d at 693. Contrary to the district court's ruling, Nationwide's ACC clause is not ambiguous, nor does Mississippi law preempt the causation regime the clause applies to hurricane claims.

Eschewing a text-based analysis, the district court opines that the clause

does not affect the coverage for other losses (covered losses), i.e., damage caused by wind, that occur at or near the same time. Thus, [the ACC clause] does not exclude coverage for different damage, the damage caused by wind, a covered peril, *even if the wind damage occurred concurrently or in sequence with the excluded water damage.* The wind damage is covered; the water damage is not.

*Id.* at 693 (emphasis added). This conclusion is unjustifiable when read against the clause's plain language:

1. We do not cover loss to any property resulting directly or indirectly from any of the following. *Such a loss is excluded even if another peril or event contributed concurrently or in any sequence to cause the loss.* ( … )

2. Water or damage caused by water-borne material....

(1) flood, surface water, waves, tidal waves, overflow of a body of water, spray from these, *whether or not driven by wind.*

The clause unambiguously excludes coverage for water damage "even if another peril"—e.g., wind—"contributed concurrently or in any sequence to cause the loss." The plain language of the policy leaves the district court no interpretive leeway to conclude that recovery can be obtained for wind damage that "occurred concurrently or in sequence with the excluded water damage." *Leonard*, 438 F.Supp.2d at 693. Moreover, in the past we have not deemed similar policy language ambiguous. *See, e.g., Arjen Motor Hotel Corp. v. Gen. Accident Fire & Life Assurance Corp.*, 379 F.2d 265, 268 (5th Cir.1967) (affirming denial of recovery when evidence "conclusively establish [ed] that wave action, an excluded peril, at the very least contributed to the collapse of the restaurant building"). Nationwide's assertion that the district court "simply read the clause out of the contract," is not at all wide of the mark. The clause is not ambiguous.

The fatal flaw in the district court's rationale is its failure to recognize the three discrete categories of damage at issue in this litigation: (1) damage caused exclusively by wind; (2) damage caused exclusively by water; and (3) damage caused by wind "concurrently or in any sequence" with water. The classic example of such a concurrent wind-water peril is the storm-surge flooding that follows on the heels of a hurricane's landfall. The only species of damage covered under the policy is damage caused *exclusively* by wind. But if wind and water synergistically caused the *same* damage, such damage is excluded. Thus, the Leonards' money judgment was based on their roof damages solely caused by wind. Contrary to the court's damage matrix, however, had they also proved that a portion of their property damage was caused by the concurrent or sequential action of water — or any number of other enumerated waterborne perils — the policy clearly disallows recovery.

The district court seemed to fear that enforcement of the policy's concurrent causation exclusion would render *any* recovery for hurricane damage illusory. Observing that the policy denies coverage whenever a "windstorm[ ] combined with an excluded cause of loss, e.g., flooding," the court hypothesized that "an insured whose dwelling lost its roof in high winds and at the same time suffered an incursion of even an inch of water could recover nothing...." *Leonard*, 438 F.Supp.2d at 694 (discussing the weather-conditions exclusion). That fear is unfounded, with regard to the policy's wind-coverage clause, which clearly preempts the court's scenario:

> We cover accidental direct physical loss to property ... caused by the following perils....
>
> 2. windstorm or hail.
>
> *Direct loss caused by rain ... driven through roof or wall openings made by direct action of wind....*

If, for example, a policyholder's roof is blown off in a storm, and rain enters through the opening, the damage is covered. Only if storm-surge flooding — an excluded peril — then inundates the *same* area that the rain damaged is the ensuing loss excluded because the loss was caused concurrently or in sequence by the action of a covered and an excluded peril. The district court's unsupported conclusions that the ACC clause is ambiguous and that the policyholder can parse out the portion of the concurrently caused damage that is attributable to wind contradict the policy language.

Like the district court, the Leonards provide no support for their argument that the ACC clause is ambiguous. Instead, they adopt the district court's reliance on venerable Mississippi authorities regarding proximate causation of damage caused by hurricanes. *See Leonard*, 438 F.Supp.2d at 695 (citing cases reflecting "well-established Mississippi law"). Because the ACC clause is unambiguous, the Leonards can prevail only if they can demonstrate that the clause is prohibited by Mississippi caselaw, statutory law, or public policy. None of these sources of state law restricts Nationwide's use of the ACC clause to preclude recovery for concurrently caused hurricane losses.

* * *

### a. Mississippi's Default Rule: Efficient Proximate Causation

The default causation rule in Mississippi regarding damages caused concurrently by a covered and an excluded peril under an insurance policy is that the insured may recover if the covered peril was the "dominant and efficient cause" of the loss. *Evana Plantation, Inc. v. Yorkshire Ins. Co.*, 214 Miss. 321, 58 So.2d 797, 798 (1952). This rule is typically referred to as the doctrine of efficient proximate cause. To recover under the doctrine in the context of a homeowner's policy that covers wind damage but excludes damage by water, "it is sufficient to show that wind [i.e., the covered peril] was the proximate or efficient cause of the loss ... notwithstanding other factors [i.e., excluded perils like water] contributed...." [citation omitted]

The Mississippi Supreme Court frequently employed this default rule in the welter of insurance coverage cases that surfaced in the aftermath of Hurricane Camille. It is also the rule the district court and the Leonards contend must apply here. *See Leonard*, 438 F.Supp.2d at 694 (collecting cases). However, although the Mississippi Supreme Court often premised recovery for policyholders on the application of the efficient proximate cause rule, in actuality, in many of the Camille cases the court did little more than uphold jury findings that the damages suffered by policyholders were caused *exclusively by wind*, not by concurrent wind-water action.

Such cases thus do not support the Leonards' argument that the Mississippi default rule in hurricane cases is always to allow recovery for covered damages even if they are concurrent with excluded damages and irrespective of contrary policy language. In fact, the Mississippi Supreme Court intimated in one case that even if a covered peril is the efficient proximate cause of damage, a concurrently contributing cause that is excluded under a homeowner's policy may preclude recovery. *See Grain Dealers Mut. Ins. Co. v. Belk*, 269 So.2d 637, 640 (Miss.1972).

Whatever the effect of the efficient proximate cause doctrine in the Hurricane Camille cases, those decisions do not control the current case because none of the policies they involve contain ACC clauses similar to the one at issue here, nor do those cases purport to enshrine efficient proximate causation as an immutable rule of Mississippi insurance policy interpretation. The Fifth Circuit long ago explicitly recognized that efficient proximate causation does not necessarily control Mississippi contracts for hurricane damage. *See Kemp* [*v. American Universal Ins. Co.*], 391 F.2d at 534–35 ("[I]n order to recover on a windstorm insurance policy, *not otherwise limited or defined*, it is sufficient to show that wind was the proximate or efficient cause of loss or damage...." (emphasis added)). As discussed below, we reach the same conclusion here as well.[1]

---

1. [7] Insurers developed ACC clauses specifically in response to court decisions that applied the efficient proximate cause doctrine to resolve thorny issues of policy coverage for concurrently caused perils. *See* 7 COUCH ON INS. § 101:57 ("Insurers often change the terms of their policies in periodic attempts to negate the effect of the case law regarding multiple causation set forth by various jurisdictions which may have resulted from the prior terms employed by insurers in their policies."); *Preferred Mut. Ins. Co. v. Meggison*, 53 F.Supp.2d 139, 142 (D.Mass.1999) (ACC provisions have appeared in recent years in response to concurrent-causation doctrine, under which courts have found insurers "obligated to pay for damages resulting from a combination of covered and excluded perils if the efficient proximate cause is a covered peril." (citation omitted)); *Garvey v. State Farm Fire & Cas. Co.*,

*b. The Earth-Movement Cases ...*

Recent decisions involving the effect of ACC clauses and earth-movement exclusions under Mississippi law all upheld ACC clauses that abrogated the default efficient proximate causation rule and excluded damage occasioned by the synergistic action of a covered and an excluded peril. The cases reflect the general Mississippi contract principle that "where a clause in a contract does not violate any statute, or public policy, and is unambiguous and certain in its provisions, it is enforced as written." ...

*c. Other Jurisdictions*

... Only Washington and West Virginia do not allow abrogation of the default rule via an ACC clause. California and North Dakota require efficient proximate causation by statute.

*2. Public Policy*

A general background principle of Mississippi contract law holds that parties may decline to adopt common-law causation rules so long as the contract's provisions do not offend public policy.... As Mississippi has not adopted the efficient proximate cause doctrine as a matter of public policy, there is no bar to Nationwide's use of the ACC clause here. Most jurisdictions concur that ACC clauses comport with state public policy. The Alabama Supreme Court's recent decision in *State Farm Fire & Casualty Co. v. Slade*, 747 So.2d 293 (Ala.1999), is representative of this trend.

*Slade* involved an improbable set of events in which a lightning bolt caused the collapse of a retaining wall near the policyholders' swimming pool. Months later, cracks were observed in the interior and exterior walls of the adjacent dwelling. State Farm refused to cover the structural damage, asserting that lightning (a covered peril), caused subsequent earth movement (an excluded peril), resulting in the observed damage. The homeowner's policy contained an ACC clause substantively indistinguishable from the one contested here.

*Slade* held that the occasional citation of the efficient proximate cause rule in Alabama caselaw did not require the court to invalidate the disputed ACC clause because the rule is not a "principle of public policy." 747 So.2d at 314. Instead, the court adhered to Alabama's "long-standing rule against rewriting unambiguous insurance policies so long as they do not ... contravene public policy." *Id.* (citation and internal quotation marks omitted). [W]e believe that the Mississippi Supreme Court, if squarely confronted with the issue, would follow *Slade*.

For all these reasons, we conclude that use of an ACC clause to supplant the default causation regime is not forbidden by Mississippi caselaw (including the Camille cases which antedate such clauses), statutory law, or public policy. Because the ACC clause is unambiguous and not otherwise voidable under state law, it must stand.

---

48 Cal.3d 395, 257 Cal.Rptr. 292, 770 P.2d 704, 710 n. 6 (1989) (Homeowners' policy language changed because court decisions found coverage for losses not intended to be covered, threatening insurer insolvency in the event of a major catastrophe.).

## E. Water-Damages Exclusion

The Leonards' only textual argument that their policy is ambiguous focuses on the water-damage exclusion, not the ACC clause. They assert that the water damage their house sustained was caused not by flooding—an explicitly excluded peril—but by "storm surge," which they characterize as a "separate, discrete peril unique to hurricanes" and as a term commonly understood "among residents of Pascagoula" as distinct from a flood. Thus, the argument goes, because "[t]he literal wording of the 'water damage' exclusion does not contemplate the exclusion of [damage from] 'storm surge,'" recovery is available. *See* 11 Couch on Ins. § 153:48 ("Because exclusions are read narrowly, a policy excluding damage from some natural water-related perils may cover damage from other natural water phenomena."). This argument is unpersuasive.

Courts have interpreted water-damage exclusions like the one found in the Leonards' policy to encompass the peril of wind-driven inundation by water, or storm surge, for ages. Mississippi courts have upheld such exclusions before and after Hurricane Katrina.... Further, this court's most recent consideration of the term "flood" also supports Nationwide's contention that the term is unambiguous and has a concrete meaning, whether or not used in the context of an insurance policy. *See In re Katrina Canal Breaches Litigation*, 495 F.3d 191, 2007 U.S. App. LEXIS 18349 (considering the term in the context of water damage resulting from the "failure of a structure such as a dam or dike"). No decision of this court or any other of which we are aware endorses the Leonards' view that storm surge is a unique meteorological phenomenon not contemplated by water-damages exclusions like Nationwide's.

The provision explicitly exempts from coverage damage caused by "flood ... waves, tidal waves, [and] overflow of a body of water ... *whether or not driven by wind.*" (emphasis added). The phrase "storm surge" is little more than a synonym for a "tidal wave" or wind-driven flood, both of which are excluded perils. The omission of the specific term "storm surge" does not create ambiguity in the policy regarding coverage available in a hurricane and does not entitle the Leonards to recovery for their flood-induced damages. *See In re Katrina Canal Breaches Litig.*, 495 F.3d 191, 2007 U.S. App. LEXIS 18349 (stating in the context of an ACC clause that "an insured may not avoid a contractual exclusion merely by affixing an additional label or separate characterization to the act or event causing the loss." (citation omitted)); 7 Couch on Ins. § 101:39....

# GuideOne Elite Insurance Co. v.
# Old Cutler Presbyterian Church, Inc.
Court of Appeal for the Eleventh Circuit
420 F.3d 1317 (2005)

**Fay, Circuit Judge:**

The defendants, a church and the victims of a multi-crime episode that commenced on church property, appeal a district court's award of summary judgment in favor of the plaintiff insurer. The insurer initiated this diversity action seeking a declaratory judgment adjudicating the meaning, interpretation and application of a sexual misconduct exclusion contained in the church's general commercial liability policy. The district court found that the underlying crimes at the hands of a third party criminal all arose out of an act of sexual misconduct, and found the sexual misconduct exclusion applicable, thereby limiting coverage to that afforded to acts of sexual misconduct under a separate liability coverage form. We disagree, finding that the underlying crimes are not excluded by virtue of the sexual misconduct exclusion, and reverse the district court's judgment with instructions.

*Facts*

*The Incident*

The tragic facts of this case are undisputed, and though disturbing, the explicit details are, unfortunately, essential to our analysis. At around noon on October 16, 2002, J.A.W. (the "Victim"), a 31 year old mother, was picking up her three-year old daughter, E.S.W. (the "Daughter"), from the Little Disciples preschool at Old Cutler Presbyterian Church, Inc. (the "Church"). The Victim was also accompanied by her eight-month old baby boy, P.W. (the "Son"). As she was securing her children in her mini-van, a man came up behind her and tackled her while screaming, "If you want to live and you don't want to see your children die, get in the car, bitch." The perpetrator then struck her on the head, threw her into her van, and closed the door.

Once in the van, the perpetrator told the Victim that he had a knife, made her close her eyes, and stuck her with a very sharp object in the upper arm or neck before he headed into the back seat to sit next to the Daughter. The Daughter was screaming and attempted to get out of her seat and out of the van when the perpetrator pushed her back and forced her back into the seat, resulting in a bruise on her lower back. He then ordered the Victim into the passenger seat, sat himself in the driver's seat, turned-up the volume on the radio to try to mask the screams of the Victim and her children, and drove off in the van.

As they were driving, the perpetrator began engaging the Victim in conversation. He told her, "Give me your money, give me your rings, give me your pin number to your ATM card," and "I also want something else from you, there are a few other things you're going to have to do for me." [The perpetrator then engaged in repeated acts of sexual assault.]

The perpetrator next had the Victim crouch down on the passenger side of the vehicle and told her that he needed money and needed to find a bank. He told her that he was unsure how to go about getting the money because he did not want to be seen on the cameras, nor did he want to send her into the bank, for fear that she would ask someone for help. Thinking out loud, the perpetrator named the different banks in the area, dismissing them for various reasons, until he remembered that there was a Bank of America with a drive-through ATM.

He then instructed the Victim to drive and told her, "I'm going to sit in the back seat with your daughter and remember I have a knife." At that point, the perpetrator stuck the Victim with the knife and continued, "I'm not kidding around, I'm getting in the back with your children and you're going to withdraw the money, whatever you're able to withdraw and I want to see the receipt when you're done, I need to know how much money is in all your accounts."

The perpetrator drove to the Bank of America in Homestead, where he and the Victim switched places in the mini-van. The Victim was only able to withdraw $400 from the ATM and handed the receipt and money to the perpetrator. The Victim's husband's paycheck had just been deposited and, upon looking at the receipt, the perpetrator said he couldn't believe how much money the Victim had in the bank; he couldn't believe how he had gotten so lucky. He said he had to find a way to get the rest of it and that he could come back for the Victim if he needed to, because he was going to get all of the money.

The perpetrator again had the Victim switch places with him, so that he was again driving. He then told her that they were driving to a First Union bank. At First Union, he had the Victim get out of the car to withdraw money from a walk-up ATM, as this bank did not have a drive-through. After attempting to withdraw cash from her various accounts, the Victim returned to the car empty handed, explaining to the perpetrator that the ATM would not allow her to withdraw any more money. The perpetrator responded by screaming at her that "he had to have this money" but "if you know your children are in the car with me you're going to be too hysterical going into the bank, I don't know." The perpetrator then decided against sending the Victim into the bank to withdraw the money, said, "this is almost over for you," and began driving back towards the Church.

On their way back to the Church, the perpetrator [then sexually assaulted the Victim again.] He then drove into the Church parking lot but could not find a secluded area, so he drove into a wooded area opposite the Church and parked the van. The perpetrator told the Victim that he had been nice to her and that he had intended to kill her and her children but had decided against it. He told her that she should be grateful and that she did a good job pleasing him.

Before he parted, the perpetrator returned the Victim's wedding rings, stating that he did not want to arouse her husband's suspicions by having her rings missing and making her promise not to tell her husband. He then told her to go home and take a shower, left the Victim and her children in the mini-van, and walked away.

*The Policy*

On the date of the Incident, the Church was covered by a primary liability insurance policy (the "Primary Policy") issued by GuideOne Elite Insurance Company (the "Insurer"). The Primary Policy contains a Commercial General Liability coverage form (the "CGL") providing limits of $1 million per occurrence and $2 million in the aggregate, with the following exclusion:

> any "personal and advertising injury," "bodily injury" and mental or emotional pain or anguish, sustained by any person arising out of or resulting from any actual or alleged act of sexual misconduct of any kind. [The Insurer]

shall have no duty to investigate, settle, defend or pay any claim or suit asserting any act of sexual misconduct or any breach of duty contributing to such act.

(the "Sexual Misconduct Exclusion"). Neither the Primary Policy nor the CGL define "sexual misconduct." Because of the Sexual Misconduct Exclusion in the CGL, the Church also purchased Sexual Misconduct Liability coverage (the "SML"), which applies to certain delineated acts of sexual misconduct and provides for $100,000 per occurrence and $300,000 in the aggregate. Though part of the Primary Policy, the SML is a separate coverage requiring a separate premium. The SML defines "Sexual Misconduct or Sexual Molestation" as:

> any activity which is sexual in nature whether permitted or unpermitted, including but not limited to sexual assault, sexual battery, sexual relations, sexual acts, sexual activity, sexual handling, sexual massage, sexual exploitation, sexual exhibition, photographic, video or other reproduction of sexual activity, sexual stimulation, fondling, intimacy, exposure of sexual organs, lewd, or lascivious behavior or indecent exposure, fornication, undue familiarity, or unauthorized touching.

In addition to the Primary Policy, which encompasses the CGL and the SML, the Church was also covered by an umbrella policy, which covers "bodily injury" and also contains the Sexual Misconduct Exclusion found in the CGL. The limits of the umbrella policy are $5 million per occurrence and $5 million in the aggregate.

*The Lawsuit*

Upon learning of the Incident, the Church notified its Insurer, and on May 6, 2003, anticipating a lawsuit against the Church by the Victim and her family, the Insurer filed this declaratory judgment action (the "Federal Action"), seeking an adjudication of the meaning, interpretation and application of the Sexual Misconduct Exclusion. After this action was filed by the Insurer, the Church was sued for money damages in state court by the Victims (the "State Court Action"). That suit alleges that the Victim and her children were kidnapped while leaving the premises of the Church and subsequently assaulted and battered. It further alleges that the Church was negligent in failing to provide adequate security despite its knowledge of criminal activity in the area and in failing to warn patrons of that criminal activity. There is no specific mention of sexual activity or rape.

The Church then tendered the claim to the Insurer for defense and indemnity, pursuant to its CGL Policy. The Insurer made a unilateral determination that the perpetrator's subjective intent was sexual, and denied coverage under the CGL. Instead, the Insurer asserted that all the claims made by the Victims were covered only by the SML, which is subject to substantially less coverage than the CGL.

The primary issue in this case is whether allegations of the Incident in the underlying State Action against the Church constitute acts "arising out of sexual misconduct" within the meaning of the CGL, such that they trigger the Sexual Misconduct Exclusion of the Policy. Thus, we are now called upon to interpret a church's CGL Sexual

Misconduct Exclusion in a case involving multiple crimes by a third party. As the Florida Supreme Court has not yet had occasion to construe "arising out of sexual misconduct" as it is used in the standard CGL, we approach this question as one of first impression to be resolved in a manner consistent with established general precepts of policy construction in place in the State of Florida.

"Sexual misconduct," though not defined in the CGL, has a single clearly defined meaning. It is impossible to categorize the rape of the Victim as other than an act of sexual misconduct. Therefore, the rape of the Victim unambiguously falls within the Sexual Misconduct Exclusion.

As applied here, the Victim's injuries from assaults and batteries occurring during the course of the sexual acts may or may not be intertwined with the sexual misconduct, depending upon the perpetrator's purpose. However, non-sexual acts (the assaults, batteries, kidnapping, false imprisonment) occurring independent of the sexual acts, i.e., during the robbery, are not inseparably intertwined with the sexual misconduct.

Each of these non-sexual acts would constitute a crime and would have caused injuries (both physical and emotional) even without the existence of any sexual misconduct. Because the CGL does not unambiguously exclude coverage for injuries arising out of any non-sexual acts, such as kidnapping, assault, and battery, we hold that the CGL, at a minimum, covers any damages relating to the non-sexual acts of the Incident, and excludes only those injuries suffered as a result of the sexual acts.

We stress, however, and explain below, that we find that this represents coverage *at a minimum*. Under these circumstances, where the loss can be attributed to multiple causes, Florida law requires coverage of *all* of the Victim's injuries as related to the Incident.

### The Concurrent Cause Doctrine

In contending that the district court erred in granting summary judgment in favor of the Insurer, the Defendants contend the district court should have applied Florida's concurrent cause doctrine because the injuries were caused by two independent crimes, robbery as well as rape, one of which is covered. Florida's concurrent cause doctrine permits coverage under an insurance policy when the loss can be attributed to multiple causes, "as long as one of the causes is an insured risk." *American Surety & Cas. Co. v. Lake Jackson Pizza, Inc.*, 788 So.2d 1096, 1100 (Fla. 1st DCA 2001). This doctrine, however, is only applicable "when the multiple causes are not related and dependent, and involve a separate and distinct risk." *Transamerica Ins. Co. v. Snell*, 627 So.2d 1275, 1276 (Fla. 1st DCA 1993) (citations omitted). The Victims argue that the district court improperly denied coverage for their injuries because the robbery gives rise to liability covered by the Church's CGL, and the Victims' injuries were incurred, at least in part, because the perpetrator intended to commit a robbery in addition to a sexual assault.

We agree. "Causes are dependent when one peril instigates or sets in motion the other." *Paulucci v. Liberty Mut. Fire Ins. Co.*, 190 F.Supp.2d 1312, 1319 (M.D.Fla.2002). In this case, the perils were independent. Robbery and rape have separate objectives that can work in tandem to cause one loss. For example, in *Wallach v. Rosenberg*,

527 So. 2d 1386 (Fla. 3d DCA 1988), human negligence combined with weather peril to erode a sea wall, and although the policy excluded weather-related causes, it did protect the insured when loss resulted from human negligence. In affirming a verdict for the insureds, the court concluded that a "jury may find coverage when an insured risk constitutes a concurrent cause of the loss even where 'the insured risk is not the prime or efficient cause of the accident.'" *Id.* at 1387 (quoting 11 G. Couch, *Couch on Insurance 2d* § 44:268 (rev. ed.1982)).[2]

A similar approach is warranted in this case. Where two crimes combine to cause a loss, it seems "logical and reasonable to find the loss covered ... even if one of the causes is excluded from coverage." *Id.* at 1388. Robbery is not part and parcel to the crime of rape, and the same is true of kidnapping, assault, imprisonment, and battery. Perhaps the confusing element here is that the same actor committed all of the crimes. If the actions perpetrated that day, however, were only parts of one larger crime, that would obviate the rationale behind multiple criminal statutes under which an offender could be charged. In *Paulucci v. Liberty Mutual Fire Insurance Co.*, the court observed that "where loss is caused by an unrelated simultaneous earthquake and lightning strike ... the concurrent causation doctrine would apply and mandate coverage regardless of which peril was covered." 190 F.Supp.2d 1312, 1319 (S.D.Fla.2002). We can similarly analogize. Much like the broad reach of nature's action—a lightning strike and an earthquake—here, one person carried out all of the crimes. So, too, is the loss covered in this case.

The concurrent cause doctrine does not demand that we apportion the loss.... If any apportionment or allocation is appropriate under Florida law, that is a matter for the state trial court. The question before us is one of coverage and we find and hold that such exists.

In conclusion, we find that the district court erred in construing the Sexual Misconduct Exclusion in favor of the Insurer and as precluding coverage....

## Notes and Questions

1. Which approach makes more sense for concurrent causation: the proximate (or dominant) cause approach or the liberal approach? Can you see why courts disagree? *See* Peter Nash Swisher, *Insurance Causation Issues: The Legacy of* Bird v. St. Paul Fire & Marine Ins. Co., 2 Nev. L.J. 351 (2002) (arguing the proximate cause approach is an appropriate middle-ground approach to concurrent causation which respects the reasonable expectations of the parties); Erik S. Knutsen, *Confusion About Causation in Insurance: Solutions for Catastrophic Losses*, 61 Ala. L. Rev. 957 (2010) (arguing for a liberal approach to concurrent causation).

---

2. [7] In *Wallach*, the court adopted the view of the California Supreme Court, which held that "coverage under a liability insurance policy is equally available to an insured whenever an insured risk constitutes simply *a* concurrent proximate cause of the injuries. That multiple causes may have effectuated the loss does not negate any single cause; that multiple acts concurred in the infliction of injury does not nullify any single contributory act." *State Farm Mut. Auto. Ins. Co. v. Partridge*, 10 Cal.3d 94, 109 Cal.Rptr. 811, 514 P.2d 123, 130 (1973) (en banc).

2. Should insurers like the one in *Leonard*, above, be able to contract out of the concurrent cause doctrine applicable in the particular state? Anti-concurrent cause clauses have been met with only spotty success among the states. *See, e.g., Murray v. State Farm Fire & Cas. Co.*, 509 S.E.2d 1 (W. Va. 1998); *Howell v. State Farm Fire & Casualty Co.*, 267 Cal. Rptr. 708 (Cal. Ct. App. 1990).

3. California has had the most dynamic and active development of jurisprudence about concurrent causation. California enshrined the proximate cause analysis in statute, as a default rule if the insurance policy is silent on the causation issue. *See* CAL. INS. CODE § 530 (2011). However, that state also treats causation differently for property and liability insurance, in recognition of the differing nature of each type of insurance and the insurer's ability to reliably predict risks *ex ante*. *See Garvey v. State Farm Fire & Casualty Co.*, 770 P.2d 704 (Cal. 1989). For property insurance, the state upholds a conservative approach if such is demanded in the insuring agreement. *See, e.g., Julian v. Hartford Underwriters Ins. Co.*, 110 P.3d 903 (Cal. 2005). If the insuring agreement is silent as to the approach to causation, a proximate cause approach is used. For liability insurance, however, a liberal approach to concurrent causation is used. *See, e.g., State Farm Mut. Auto. Ins. Co. v. Partridge*, 10 Cal. 3d 94, 109 Cal. Rptr. 811 (1973). Do you agree that concurrent causation should be treated differently in liability insurance than in property insurance? Why or why not?

## PROBLEM ONE:
## PROPERTY INSURANCE

On May 18, 1980, Mount St. Helens in Washington State erupted in a volcanic explosion. The pyroclastic flows from that eruption, along with hot ash and debris, began melting the snow and ice flanking the mountain, and created enormous mudflows which began moving down the valley shortly after the volcanic eruption began. Approximately 10 hours after the eruption began, the policyholder's home, 25 miles away from Mount St. Helens, was destroyed by a mudflow or a combination of mudflows preceded by water damage from flooding.

The homeowner's insurance policy issued by the insurer provided the following:

"EXCLUSIONS: We do not cover loss resulting directly or indirectly from: Earth movement ... water damage ... and flood. Direct loss by fire, explosion, theft, or breakage of glass ... resulting from earth movement is covered."

The policyholders argued that their loss was caused by the volcanic "explosion." However, the insurance company rejected this claim on the basis that the damage was excluded as "earth movement" in the form of mudflows, or a combination of earth movement and water damage.

• How should the court decide this case?

• Based upon what causation rationale?

## PROBLEM TWO:
## LIABILITY INSURANCE

While on a farm, a helper assists the farmer place some boards over an opening in the side of a barn. The two men rig up a lift by which the helper on the ground could be raised up to put the boards in place. The rig consists of a wooden platform connected by cables to a length of rope. The free end of the rope was tied to the back of the farmer's pickup truck. The truck was moved slowly forward to back, so the helper could be raised or lowered to put the boards in place. The rope snapped and the helper fell to the ground and was seriously injured.

The farmer was insured by two separate liability policies, an automobile liability policy, which covered for losses "arising from the ownership, maintenance, use or operation of an automobile" and a farmowners comprehensive liability policy (which covered the farmer for "legal liability" but excluded coverage for losses "arising from the ownership, maintenance, use or operation of an automobile").

• Which policy should respond to the loss?

• One?

• Both?

• Neither?

• Why?

## [B] Direct Loss versus Remote Loss

Standard property and fire insurance policies often provide coverage to the policyholder "against all direct loss or damage by" certain physical losses (most commonly fire, but also other losses such as windstorm). But what does this provision mean? If it includes "all loss" proximately caused by fire, for example, should this necessarily be limited to the actual burning of the property or should the coverage also include loss resulting from any scorching, charring, smoke damage, or water damage used in extinguishing the fire? The following case illustrates the parameters of this particular limitation of coverage within the context of business interruption coverage in a property policy.

### Source Food Technology, Inc. v.
### U.S. Fidelity and Guar. Co.
United States Court of Appeals, Eighth Circuit
465 F.3d 834 (2006)

**Gruender, Circuit Judge**

Source Food Technology, Inc. ("Source Food") appeals the order of the district court granting summary judgment to United States Fidelity and Guaranty Company ("USF & G") on Source Food's claim for breach of contract for denial of insurance coverage based on "direct physical loss to" its property. For the reasons discussed below, we affirm the judgment of the district court.

Source Food is a Minnesota company that sells cooking oil and shortening containing beef tallow from which the cholesterol has been removed ("beef product"). The United States Department of Agriculture ("USDA") prohibited the importation of ruminants or ruminant products from Canada on May 20, 2003, after a cow in Canada tested positive for bovine spongiform encephalopathy, commonly known as "mad cow disease."

At the time the border was closed to the importation of beef, Source Food's sole supplier of beef product was Hubbert's Industries in Ontario, Canada. Hubbert's Industries manufactured and packaged the beef product in Canada using Source Food's patented manufacturing process for removing cholesterol from beef tallow. Just prior to the embargo, Source Food placed an order for beef product with Hubbert's Industries. The beef product was manufactured, packaged and loaded onto a truck for shipping to Source Food but was not shipped due to the USDA's order.

Although the parties dispute whether at this point Source Food owned the beef product, we assume, as did the district court, that the beef product inside the truck in Canada was the property of Source Food. The parties agree that there is no evidence that the beef product was contaminated by mad cow disease.

When the border was closed to the importation of beef products, Source Food was unable to fill orders and was forced to find a new supplier of beef product. Source Food's best customer, Casey's General Store, Inc., terminated its contract with Source Food seven months early because Source Food was unable to deliver the required one or two truckloads of beef product per week after May 20, 2003.

Source Food submitted a claim under its insurance policy with USF & G, which included property and business interruption coverage. Source Food claimed damages for extraordinary operating expenses, loss of profits based on the early termination of its contract with Casey's General Store, Inc., and the cost of obtaining from a new supplier in Arkansas an alternative product with cholesterol and later, when the necessary manufacturing equipment was installed, the beef product without cholesterol.

The insurance policy provides coverage for the loss of business income where there is direct physical loss to the insured's property:

> (1) "Business income." We will pay the actual loss of "business income" you sustain due to the necessary suspension of your "operations" during the "period of restoration." The suspension must be caused by *direct physical loss to Property* (other than those items listed in SECTION I.A.2.), including Property Off Premises, and result from any Covered Cause of Loss....

> (4) Action by Civil Authority. We will pay for the actual loss of "business income" you sustain and necessary "extra expense" caused by action of civil authority that prohibits access to the described premises due to *direct physical*

*loss to property*, other than at the described premises, caused by or resulting from any Covered Cause of Loss.

Section I.A.4(b)(1) and (4) (emphases added). However, the insurance policy does not define the phrase "direct physical loss to property."

The insurance claim was denied....

On appeal, Source Food argues that the closing of the border caused direct physical loss to its beef product because the beef product was treated as though it were physically contaminated by mad cow disease and lost its function. Source Food principally relies upon *Gen. Mills, Inc. v. Gold Medal Ins. Co.*, 622 N.W.2d 147 (Minn.Ct.App.2001), and *Marshall Produce Co. v. St. Paul Fire & Marine Ins. Co.*, 256 Minn. 404, 98 N.W. 2d 280 (Minn. 1959), to support its position that the impairment of function and value of a food product caused by government regulation is a direct physical loss to insured property.

Both of the Minnesota cases that Source Food relies on, as well as *Sentinel Mgmt. Co. v. New Hampshire Ins. Co.*, 563 N.W.2d 296 (Minn.Ct.App.1997), are distinguishable from this case. The insurance policy provisions in *General Mills* and *Sentinel* are comparable to the provisions at issue here. However, coverage was found to be triggered in those two cases by actual physical contamination of insured property.

The insurance policy in *General Mills* required "direct physical loss or damage to property." 622 N.W.2d at 151 (internal quotations omitted). Sixteen million bushels of General Mills's raw oats were treated with a pesticide not approved by the FDA for use on oats. *Id.* at 150. Although consumption of the contaminated oats was not hazardous to human health, the oats were in violation of FDA regulations and could not be used in General Mills's oat-based products. *Id.* at 150. Because the contamination rendered the oats unusable, General Mills was entitled to coverage for "direct physical loss or damage to property." *Id.* at 151–52.

The insurance claim in *Sentinel* was brought under a policy covering "direct physical loss to building(s)" and was based on the release of asbestos fibers and resulting contamination of apartment buildings. 563 N.W.2d at 298. The Minnesota Court of Appeals held that the asbestos contamination constituted direct physical loss to the properties because "a building's function may be seriously impaired or destroyed and the property rendered useless *by the presence of contaminants.*" *Id.* at 300 (emphasis added). As opposed to these two cases in which actual physical contamination was established, Source Food concedes that the beef product inside the truck in Canada was not physically damaged or contaminated in any manner.

The insurance policy at issue in *Marshall Produce* did not cover just "direct *physical* loss" as in Source Food's insurance policy, but rather it covered "all loss or damage by fire." 98 N.W. 2d at 285 (internal quotations omitted). The supplier in *Marshall Produce* manufactured drums of egg powder and other goods for the army. After smoke from a nearby fire penetrated the manufacturing plant, the army rejected the drums because they violated the sanitation requirements of the government contract that the "processing and storing of eggs and egg products must be done in an area free from odors, dust, and smoke-laden air." *Id.* at 296. Shortly after the fire, an inspector "examined the packaging around the cans [and] ... found smoke contamination, a very strong odor from the smoke throughout the package and around the border of the package." *Id.*

Although it was not established that the egg powder inside the drums was physically contaminated by the smoke, the Minnesota Supreme Court determined that the supplier was entitled to insurance coverage because the insurance policy covered "all loss or damage by fire" and the rejection of the goods was a loss caused by the smoke from the fire. *Id.* at 296–97. By contrast, the portions of Source Food's insurance policy at issue only provide coverage when there is direct physical loss to property, and Source Food's beef product suffered no physical contamination.

In *Pentair, Inc. v. Am. Guarantee & Liab. Ins. Co.*, 400 F.3d 613 (8th Cir. 2005), a case applying Minnesota law and discussing the same Minnesota insurance cases, we rejected an argument very similar to that made by Source Food. When an earthquake caused a loss of power to two Taiwanese factories, the factories could not supply products to a subsidiary of Pentair for two weeks. *Id.* at 614. Pentair argued that the property of the Taiwanese factories suffered "direct physical loss or damage" when the power outages prevented the factories from performing their function of manufacturing products. *Id.* at 615.

We distinguished *Sentinel* and *General Mills*, explaining that "in those cases, insured property was physically contaminated — a building by the release of asbestos fibers in *Sentinel*, and grain by application of an unapproved pesticide in *General Mills*." *Id.* at 616. Although we noted that "[o]nce physical loss or damage is established, loss of use or function is certainly relevant in determining the amount of loss, particularly a business interruption loss," we refused to adopt the position that "direct physical loss or damage is established *whenever* property cannot be used for its intended purpose" and noted that our holding was also consistent with *Marshall Produce. Id.*

Although Source Food's beef product in the truck could not be transported to the United States due to the closing of the border to Canadian beef products, the beef product on the truck was not — as Source Foods concedes — physically contaminated or damaged in any manner. To characterize Source Food's inability to transport its truckload of beef product across the border and sell the beef product in the United States as direct physical loss to property would render the word "physical" meaningless. Moreover, the policy's use of the word "to" in the policy language "direct physical loss *to* property" is significant.

Source Food's argument might be stronger if the policy's language included the word "of" rather than "to," as in "direct physical loss *of* property" or even "direct loss *of* property." But these phrases are not found in the policy. Thus, the policy's use of the words "to property" further undermines Source Food's argument that a border closing triggers insurance coverage under this policy.

Source Food did not experience direct physical loss to its property. Therefore, Source Food cannot recover the loss of business income resulting from the embargo on beef products under insurance policy provisions requiring direct physical loss to its property.

### Notes and Questions

1. The "direct loss" coverage necessarily depends on the court's causation analysis. Do you see a difference in coverage whether a particular court uses a liberal, dominant cause, or conservative approach to causation?

2. Should a short circuit electrical "flash" or an explosion of highly combustible materials that results in fire constitute "a direct loss or damage by fire"? *Compare Kreiss v. Aetna Life Ins. Co.*, 229 N.Y. 54, 127 N.E. 481 (1920), *with Scripture v. Lowell Mut. Fire Ins. Co.*, 64 Mass. 356, 57 Am. Dec. 111 (1852).

### PROBLEM THREE

A fire damaged a building to the extent that it was approximately a 50 percent loss. The city building inspector informed the policyholder that, under existing city ordinances, any property damaged to the extent of 50 percent of its value could not be repaired, and must be totally replaced. The insurer agreed to indemnify the policyholder for "all direct loss or damage by fire." Is the insurance company liable only for 50 percent of the value of the property, or 100 percent of the value since, under the city ordinance, the policyholder's loss was total?

# § 6.02. Accidental Means versus Accidental Results

The requirement that an insurable loss be "accidental" is implicit in the nature and underlying principles of insurance law. Most life, accident, property, and liability insurance policies therefore expressly require that any loss be "accidental" in a fortuitous sense, rather than an intended result, in order to be covered under the insurance policy. *See generally* KEETON & WIDISS, INSURANCE LAW § 5.4 (2d ed. 1988).

An "accident" has been defined as an event which is "unintended and unexpected," and the term "accidental" has further been interpreted to mean "happening by chance; unexpectedly taking place; not according to the usual course of things; or not as expected." *See, e.g., United States Mut. Acc. Ass'n v. Barry*, 131 U.S. 100 (1889). From what point of view should a court examine the question of whether or not a loss is accidental? The general rule is that whether or not the insured's death is accidental is normally determined from the point of view of the insured. *See, e.g., New York Life Ins. Co. v. Harrington*, 299 F.2d 803 (9th Cir. 1962); *Estate of Wade v. Continental Ins. Co.*, 514 F.2d 304 (8th Cir. 1975) (life insurance). Other courts, however, view an "accident" from the viewpoint of the injured party. *See, e.g., Haser v. Maryland Cas. Co.*, 78 N.D. 893, 53 N.W.2d 508 (1952) (liability insurance). Thus, any injury which is unintended, unexpected, or unusual is normally deemed to be "accidental." *See generally* Robert H. Jerry, II & Douglas R. Richmond, Understanding Insurance Law §64(a) (6th ed. 2018).

The corollary of this general rule is that if insurance coverage only applies to fortuitous or "accidental" occurrences, then no coverage will exist for a loss that is caused intentionally. Accordingly, many insurance policies frequently state that coverage will be provided only for an occurrence or "accident" that is "neither expected nor intended from the standpoint of the insured."

The following cases illustrate the various concepts of "accident, accidental death, or accidental means" which constitute a much-litigated area in insurance law.

## Carroll v. CUNA Mutual Insurance Society

Supreme Court of Colorado
894 P.2d 746 (1995)

Lohr, J.

... The plaintiff, Lyman Carroll, sought declaratory relief determining that benefits were payable to him as the sole beneficiary under a policy of accidental death insurance issued by the defendant, CUNA Mutual Insurance Society (CUNA), and insuring Mr. Carroll's wife, Marie Carroll. At issue was whether Mrs. Carroll's death, which resulted from a massive intracranial hemorrhage caused in turn by the rupture of a preexisting cerebral aneurysm during sexual intercourse with her husband, was a covered event under the policy.

The district court determined that Mrs. Carroll's death was not caused by an accident as required by the policy and entered judgment for CUNA. The court of appeals affirmed on a different rationale, noting that the policy language required not only that death be caused by an accident but also that it must result directly and independently of all other causes.

The court of appeals held that the circumstances of Mrs. Carroll's death did not meet this latter requirement because under the court's construction, the requirement is not satisfied "when the injury or death is due, even in part, to a preexisting bodily infirmity." Although we interpret the relevant language in the policy more narrowly than did the court of appeals, we agree that as properly construed, CUNA's policy does not provide coverage for Mrs. Carroll's death. We therefore affirm the judgment of the court of appeals.

This case arises from Lyman Carroll's claim for insurance benefits under a group accidental death and dismemberment policy issued by CUNA and covering Mr. Carroll's wife, Marie Carroll, as an "Insured Person." The insurance policy provided benefits for "bodily injury caused by an accident occurring while the Group Policy is in force as to the Insured Person and resulting directly and independently of all other causes in loss covered by the Group Policy." Upon review of the circumstances of Mrs. Carroll's death, CUNA refused payment. CUNA asserted that Mrs. Carroll's death was not caused by an "accident" and did not result "directly and independently of all other causes," as required by the terms of the insurance policy....

The circumstances of Mrs. Carroll's death are taken from the testimony of Mr. Carroll at trial. On March 22, 1990, Marie Carroll was a sixty-seven year old woman of generally good health who suffered from hypertension. At approximately 9:00 in the evening of March 22, Marie Carroll and her husband began to engage in sexual intercourse. A short time later, as Marie Carroll approached orgasm, she leaned forward and fell to the floor. When Mrs. Carroll was arising from the floor she stated that she felt as if her head had exploded and that it was burning. She told her husband she was suffering from a severe headache.

That night and the next day Mrs. Carroll had trouble verbalizing and continued to feel unwell. Mrs. Carroll, however, went about her regular activities throughout the day. At approximately 9:00 in the evening on March 23, 1990, Mr. Carroll took Mrs. Carroll to the hospital. The attending physician determined that Mrs. Carroll was suffering from a massive hemorrhage in the left side of her brain. Later that evening, Marie Carroll slipped into a coma. The next morning, after examination, Mrs. Carroll was declared brain dead.

Dr. Randall Bjork, a neurologist, testified at the trial regarding the medical causes of Mrs. Carroll's death. He stated that Marie Carroll had died from a massive intracerebral hemorrhage. According to Dr. Bjork, Mrs. Carroll suffered this hemorrhage due to the rupture of an aneurysm in her brain. The rupture occurred in part as a result of Marie Carroll's elevated blood pressure during intercourse. Dr. Bjork explained that hemorrhages occurring at the point of orgasm are a known phenomenon in the medical literature and occur at a frequency of approximately one in every 300,000 people each year.

Dr. Bjork further testified that the aneurysm probably had been present in Mrs. Carroll's brain for many years prior to the time of the rupture. He described an aneurysm as something like a "powder keg" or "time bomb." Almost anything, including ordinary events such as interviewing a baby-sitter or playing chess, can trigger its rupture. Dr. Bjork also testified that Marie Carroll's existing hypertension could have increased the likelihood that the aneurysm would rupture and the amount of hemorrhage resulting.

Mr. Carroll sought review of the court of appeals' decision by this court. We granted certiorari to determine:

> Whether the court of appeals erred in interpreting the clause in an accidental death and dismemberment insurance policy, "directly and independently of all other causes," to preclude coverage for any injury or death that is "due, even in part, to a preexisting bodily infirmity" such as Mrs. Carroll's condition.

We now hold that the court of appeals' construction of the phrase "directly and independently of all other causes" to preclude coverage when the injury or death is due even in part to a preexisting bodily infirmity was unduly narrow. Instead, we conclude that this phrase means that the accident must be the predominant cause of injury in order for the injury to be compensable. Because the trial court's findings establish that Mrs. Carroll's death was predominantly caused by her preexisting aneurysm, we hold that the insurance policy did not cover Mrs. Carroll's death. Therefore, we affirm the court of appeals' judgment but do so by adopting a different construction of the language of the policy.

The accidental death policy that CUNA issued to Mr. Carroll defines a covered "injury" as follows:

> *Injury* means bodily injury caused by an accident occurring while the Group Policy is in force as to the Insured Person and resulting directly and independently of all other causes in loss covered by the Group Policy.

For an injury to be compensable under this policy it must be caused by an accident and result directly and independently of all other causes. We first address whether Mrs. Carroll's injury was caused by an accident.

The CUNA policy does not define the term "accident." Relying on the Colorado Court of Appeals' decision in *Bobier v. Beneficial Standard Life Ins. Co.*, 40 Colo.App. 94, 96, 570 P.2d 1094, 1096 (1977), Mr. Carroll maintains that his wife's death was caused by accident because it was an "unusual or unanticipated *result* [flowing] from a commonplace cause." (Emphasis in original.) We agree.

Courts have had difficulty crafting a definition of the term "accident" that will fairly apply to all contingencies. When considering this problem some courts have attempted to distinguish between accidental means and accidental results. The basis for this distinction is the relationship between cause and effect. Under the accidental means test, the precipitating cause of the injury must be accidental or unintended. This test encompasses one common understanding of the term accident as an unexpected action or event, such as a slip or a fall, that then causes injury. Under the accidental results test, only the injury, not the precipitating cause, must be unexpected for the injury to be accidental.

Courts strictly applying the accidental means test have held that death or injury does not result from an accident or accidental means within the terms of an accident insurance policy where it is the natural result of the insured's voluntary act, unaccompanied by anything unforeseen except the death or injury. *See, e.g., Smith v. Continental Casualty Co.*, 203 A.2d 168 (D.C.1964) (insured who died from a heart attack after exerting himself in performance of his regular duties as an engineer did not die of an accident because no accident interfered with his movements)....

Commentators have criticized the distinction between accidental means and accidental results as illusory and contrary to the normal expectations of the average policy holder. The basis for the criticism is the difficulty of distinguishing between voluntary and involuntary acts....

The modern trend is to reject the distinction between accidental means and accidental results when considering whether a particular death or injury is accidental.... Under this view, the unexpected consequences of an individual's behavior provide the "accidental element" for purposes of an insurance policy....

The rejection of the distinction between accidental means and accidental results was first articulated by Justice Cardozo in his dissent in *Landress v. Phoenix Mut. Life*

*Ins. Co.*, 291 U.S. 491 (1934). In *Landress*, the insured died after suffering sunstroke. The majority stated that since the insured voluntarily exposed himself to the sun and there were no unforeseen intervening causes, the death was not caused by accidental means. Justice Cardozo stated in an oft-quoted passage that "[t]he attempted distinction between accidental results and accidental means will plunge this branch of the law into a Serbonian Bog." *Id.* at 499 (Cardozo, J., dissenting).

Justice Cardozo asserted that if the court considered the result accidental, as death from sunstroke would be, then the means must be accidental also. *Id.* at 501 (Cardozo, J., dissenting).... Thus, under this definition, as long as the resulting injury or death is unexpected, unintended, and unforeseeable then the injury or death is accidental.

In *Reed v. United States Fidelity and Guaranty Co.*, [176 Colo. 568 491 P.2d 1377 (1971),] we adopted Justice Cardozo's reasoning in *Landress* and rejected the distinction between accidental means and accidental results. In addition, we adopted the definition of accident as quoted above from the *Western* case. *See also Equitable Life Assurance Society* [*v. Hemenover*], 100 Colo. at 235, 67 P.2d at 81–82.

The insured in *Reed* was a firefighter. While fighting a fire, he was exposed to black smoke. During the course of this activity, the insured became ill and died of a heart attack on the way to the hospital. *Reed*, 491 P.2d at 1379. The administratrix of his estate brought an action against the insurer on the insured's accidental death policy. The trial court granted the insurer's motion to dismiss at the conclusion of the plaintiff's case.

We held that, viewing the evidence most favorably to the plaintiff, the "unforeseen exacerbation of his heart condition could have been an accidental injury." *Id.* at 573, 491 P.2d at 1380. Thus, although the insured undertook voluntary activity that was part of his normal employment, we held that his injury could have resulted from an accident, with the result that the motion to dismiss was improperly granted.

The Colorado Court of Appeals in *Bobier v. Beneficial Standard Life Ins. Co.*, 40 Colo.App. 94, 570 P.2d 1094 (1977), interpreted the term accident as used in an accidental death insurance policy similar to the one at issue in this case. In *Bobier*, the insured died from pneumonia as a result of aspiration. The aspiration occurred when she inhaled her own vomit during an incident in which she fell to the floor in the middle of the night. The insured's husband brought suit against the insurance company that had issued an accidental death policy covering the insured. At the conclusion of the evidence, the trial court directed a verdict for the plaintiff. The Colorado Court of Appeals reversed.

There was some dispute in the evidence as to what caused the aspiration. The insurance company presented evidence that the insured had cardiac arrhythmia, and that the cardiac arrhythmia caused an arrhythmic seizure which then caused the aspiration. *Bobier*, 570 P.2d at 1095. The plaintiff claimed that the aspiration either was the unusual or unanticipated result of the normal bodily function of regurgitating or that it was induced when the insured fell to the floor.

The court of appeals, citing *Hemenover* and *Reed*, defined accident to include an unusual or unanticipated result flowing from a commonplace cause. 570 P.2d at 1096. The court of appeals reasoned that "if a jury were to find that the inhalation of material by Mrs. Bobier [the insured] did not follow as the 'natural or probable consequence' of her vomiting, and that thus it could not have been 'reasonably anticipated,' it could conclude that an 'accident' was the cause of death."

Alternatively, if the jury were to find "that the cardiac [arrhythmia] occurred first and that the aspiration and subsequent pneumonia were merely predictable resulting mechanisms which led to death," the jury could have concluded that Mrs. Bobier's death was not accidental. 570 P.2d at 1097. Because there was evidence to support both the plaintiff's theories and those of the defendant, the court of appeals reversed the directed verdict entered for the plaintiff.

We reaffirm our adherence to the definition of accident as set forth in footnote two of Justice Cardozo's dissenting opinion in *Landress* and adopted by us in *Reed*. *See supra* at pp. 751–752. The distinction between accidental means and accidental results is too illusory to be useful. The ordinary purchaser of an insurance policy is probably unaware of the distinction between these concepts. An unanticipated or unusual result flowing from a commonplace cause may be an accident.

Although this definition is broad and could in the extreme bring about results inconsistent with common understanding, we believe that insurance companies wishing to avoid the consequences of the broadly inclusive definition of accident in *Reed* must include limiting language readily comprehensible by the ordinary purchaser.

This position is further bolstered by the fact that the definition of accident that we reaffirm today has been the law in this state for over twenty years. Insurance companies have had ample time to devise language that properly balances the actuarial risk of liability with the insurance premiums they charge consumers. Thus, we hold that a voluntary act that causes an unforeseeable, unintended, or unexpected result can be considered an accident.

Therefore, we agree with Mr. Carroll that Mrs. Carroll's death was accidental under the terms of CUNA's insurance policy. The trial court found that during intercourse Mrs. Carroll experienced elevated blood pressure on top of her preexisting hypertension. The trial court also found that the rupture of Mrs. Carroll's aneurysm occurred as part of the orgasm she experienced during sexual intercourse. The clear implication of these findings is that Mrs. Carroll's voluntary participation in sexual intercourse with her husband contributed in part to her death.

Death was certainly not an expected, intended, or foreseeable result of intercourse. We therefore find that under the definition of accident adopted in *Reed* and reaffirmed in this opinion, Mrs. Carroll's death was an accident. Thus, Mr. Carroll has satisfied the first requirement for recovery under the insurance policy.

We now consider the second requirement for recovery under the CUNA insurance policy. Under the insurance policy, to be compensable, the injury not only must be caused by accident but also must result directly and independently of all other causes in loss covered by the policy.

The court of appeals interpreted the phrase "directly and independently of all other causes" to preclude coverage when the injury or death is due even in part to a pre-existing bodily infirmity. *Carroll*, 876 P.2d at 76. Mr. Carroll argues that the phrase "directly and independently of all other causes" is ambiguous and should be construed against the insurer. Mr. Carroll further asserts that another panel of the court of appeals properly construed this phrase in *Continental Casualty Co. v. Maguire*, 28 Colo.App. 173, 4471 P.2d 636 (1970), to require only that the accident be the predominant cause of the injury. According to Mr. Carroll, the mere existence of a bodily infirmity should not automatically preclude recovery. We agree....

In *Reed v. United States Fidelity and Guaranty Co.*, 491 P.2d 1377 (1971)], we interpreted a liability clause more restrictive than the one at issue in the present case. In *Reed*, the insured died from a heart attack sustained while fighting a fire. The insured, a fifty-six year old man, also suffered from arteriosclerosis, a normal condition for his age. The insurance company argued that the insured's arteriosclerosis constituted a disease or bodily infirmity that precluded coverage for the death under the insurance policy. We held that since arteriosclerotic degeneration is a normal part of the aging process, the insured as a matter of law could not be considered diseased or infirm within the meaning of the insurance policy. *Reed*, 491 P.2d at 1380.

We recognized that precluding coverage because of infirmity caused by the normal aging process would limit the scope of recovery under these accidental injury insurance policies to an extent inconsistent with a policy holder's reasonable expectations and the insurance contract's purposes. 491 P.2d at 1380. We quoted the following statement by Chief Judge Cardozo in *Silverstein v. Metropolitan Life Ins. Co.*, 254 N.Y. 81, 171 N.E. 914, 915 (1930):

> In a strict or literal sense, any departure from an ideal or perfect norm of health is a disease or an infirmity. Something more, however, must be shown to exclude the effects of accident from the coverage of a policy. The disease or the infirmity must be so considerable or significant that it would be characterized as disease or infirmity in the common speech of men.

*Reed*, 491 P.2d at 1380.

No individual is completely free from the normal degeneration that might cause weakness or susceptibility to an accident. Requiring an individual to be highly fit in order to recover under an accidental insurance policy would effectively nullify the value of these policies for an ordinary purchaser.

Thus, the court of appeals' holding that the insurance policy in this case precludes liability any time the injury or death is due even in part to a preexisting illness or disease sweeps too broadly. The court of appeals' holding would deny recovery even if the disease is a remote cause of the injury. This is contrary to the expectations of the average policy holder and to the policies discussed in *Reed*.

We hold, therefore, that the court of appeals' decision in this case excessively limits recovery under accidental injury and death insurance policies. The proper interpretation of the clause "directly and independently of all other causes" is that contained in *Maguire*. Benefits under accidental death or injury policies of the type at issue here are recoverable as long as one can show that the accident is the predominant cause of the loss.

Other jurisdictions have interpreted the phrase "directly and independently of all other causes" in accidental injury insurance policies to mean that the accident must be the predominant cause of the injury....

Other courts have interpreted the phrase "directly and independently of all other causes" to require that the accident be the direct or proximate cause of the injury.... Courts when using the word "proximate cause," however, seem to intend no more than to distinguish between remote and predominant causes....

We, therefore, interpret the expression "directly and independently of all other causes" to require that the accident be the predominant cause of injury. The court of appeals' statement that this phrase precludes recovery whenever the injury is due, even in part, to a preexisting bodily infirmity is incorrect.

We now consider whether the trial court properly granted judgment for CUNA at the conclusion of the plaintiff's case in light of our holding that to recover under the insurance policy Mr. Carroll must prove by a preponderance of the evidence that the predominant cause of Mrs. Carroll's death was an accident....

Although the trial court based its analysis on the definition of accident in *Bobier*, the main focus of its findings is that there was little causal relationship between Mrs. Carroll's sexual activities and her death. The trial court states that "the aneurysm did not 'flow' from a commonplace cause" and that the rupture "could have occurred at any time." The main cause of Mrs. Carroll's death was her preexisting aneurysm and hypertension. Sexual intercourse was merely coincident with the rupture and not the predominant cause.

We therefore conclude that although the trial court and the court of appeals misinterpreted the law, the findings of the trial court demonstrate that it reached the correct result in entering a judgment for CUNA. The evidence even when considered in the light most favorable to Mr. Carroll supports the trial court's findings, which in turn establish that the predominant cause of Mrs. Carroll's death was her preexisting aneurysm and hypertension. Mr. Carroll has not sustained his burden of proving by a preponderance of the evidence that Mrs. Carroll's death was caused "directly and independently of all other causes." We therefore affirm the judgment of the Colorado Court of Appeals but do so based on reasoning different from that of the court of appeals.

## Notes and Questions

1. As the *Carroll* case points out, in some jurisdictions, the courts have drawn a distinction between the term "accidental means," which is interpreted as synonymous

with "cause," and "accident" or "accidental death," which is interpreted as synonymous with "result." Is it correct to reject this cause-and-effect dichotomy, holding that the terms "accidental means," "accident," and "accidental death" are legally synonymous? Under what rationale? *See, e.g., Landress v. Phoenix Mut. Life Ins. Co.*, 291 U.S. 491 (1934) (dissenting opinion by Cardozo, J., stating at 499 that attempting to distinguish accidental means and accidental results would plunge the courts into a "Serbonian Bog"); *Equitable Life Assurance Soc. of U.S. v. Hemenover*, 67 P.2d 80 (Colo. 1937) ("whatever kind of a bog that is, we concur"). *See generally* KEETON & WIDISS, INSURANCE LAW § 5.4[b][3] (1988).

*Query*: Would the insured "common man or woman in the marketplace" as a non-lawyer readily understand a distinction between "accidental means" and "accidental results"? Are these hyper-technical terms arguably ambiguous and contrary to the policyholder's reasonable expectation of coverage for accidental injuries or death? *See generally* Adam Scales, *Man, God, and the Serbonian Bog: The Evolution of Accidental Death Insurance*, 86 IOWA L. REV. 173 (2000).

2. The courts have not been uniform in determining whether an "accident" has occurred when overexertion of the insured results in death. A common—and much litigated—situation, as in the *Carroll* case, is when the insured engages in vigorous exercise which is followed by a fatal heart attack. Some courts have held that unless some mishap or fall occurred during the exercise, the heart attack was not an "accident." *See, e.g., Kolowski v. Metropolitan Life Ins. Co.*, 35 F. Supp. 2d 1059 (N.D. Ill. 1998); *Bristol v. Metropolitan Life Ins. Co.*, 122 Cal. App. 2d 631, 265 P.2d 552 (1954). Other courts would deny coverage on the ground that a preexisting health condition, such as a weak heart, caused the death rather than the "accident." *See, e.g., Duvall v. Massachusetts Indem. & Life Ins. Co.*, 295 Ark. 412, 748 S.W.2d 650 (1988). Still other courts have held that the insured's death after exertion or exercise is an "accident," since the heart attack was an unexpected or unanticipated result of the exercise. *See, e.g., Carrothers v. Knights of Columbus*, 295 N.E.2d 307 (Ill. App. Ct. 1973); *Rankin v. United Commercial Travelers*, 193 Kan. 248, 392 P.2d 894 (1964). These different judicial approaches as to what constitutes an "accidental" death from overexertion cannot be reconciled. *See generally* JERRY & RICHMOND, UNDERSTANDING INSURANCE LAW § 64[a] (6th ed. 2018).

## PROBLEM FOUR

The policyholder was playing a leisurely game of golf on a hot summer day. As he was ready to tee off toward the eighth hole, he collapsed and died. According to a medical autopsy, the insured had died of sunstroke. His life insurance policy provided double indemnity coverage only if the insured died from an accidental death "caused solely through external, violent, and accidental means."

• Should the policyholder's beneficiaries be able to recover under the life insurance policy's "accidental death" benefits?

• Why or why not?

# § 6.03. Accident or Fortuity in Tension with the Policyholder's Voluntary Actions

## Hairston v. Liberty National Life Insurance Co.

### Supreme Court of Alabama
### 584 So. 2d 807 (1991)

**Almon, Justice**

Maggie J. Hairston appeals from a summary judgment entered in favor of the defendant, Liberty National Life Insurance Company, in an action alleging breach of contract and bad faith failure to pay an insurance claim. The question presented is whether the trial court erred in holding that, as a matter of law, the death of Ms. Hairston's ex-husband, James L. Hairston, by acute ethanol poisoning, was not "accidental" within the terms of the insurance policy on Mr. Hairston's life.

The facts leading up to the death of Mr. Hairston are undisputed. On the night of his death, he and three companions went to several bars and there consumed a large amount of alcohol. The four also drank a half gallon of "Thunderbird" wine that they had purchased at a package store. After they had drunk the wine, Hairston stated that he was going home and "staggered across the street." Two days later Mr. Hairston's body was discovered in the backyard of a residence near where his drinking companions had last seen him. An autopsy was performed by the Jefferson County coroner, Dr. J.P. Garceau, who concluded that Hairston had died as a result of acute ethanol poisoning.

The trial court entered a summary judgment for Liberty National, holding that, as a matter of law, Mr. Hairston's death was not "accidental" within the meaning of that term as it was defined in the life insurance policy, and thus, that no accidental death benefits under the policy were due to be paid. It is from that judgment that Maggie Hairston appeals.

The parties do not dispute the fact that Mr. Hairston often drank excessively or that he voluntarily and intentionally drank alcohol on the night of his death. Thus, the only question for our review is whether Mr. Hairston's death could have been "accidental" within the meaning of the life insurance policy issued by Liberty National.

The accidental death provisions in the insurance policy on Mr. Hairston's life provided, in pertinent part, as follows:

> BENEFITS—Upon receipt at its Home Office of due proof that the death of the Insured resulted, directly and independently of all other causes, from bodily injury effected solely through external, violent and accidental means as evidenced by a visible wound or contusion on the exterior of the body (except in case of drowning or internal injuries revealed by autopsy) ... the Company will, subject to all provisions of the policy and to the conditions thereunder, pay to the beneficiary, in addition to the amount otherwise provided by the policy, the Additional Indemnity for Death by Accidental Means.

EXCLUSIONS FROM COVERAGE—The Additional Indemnity for Death by Accidental Means shall not be payable if the Insured's death results directly or indirectly (a) from self-destruction, or any attempt thereat, whether sane or insane, or (b) from bodily or mental infirmity or disease of any kind or medical or surgical treatment therefor, or (c) from committing or attempting to commit an assault or felony, or (d) from insurrection or war or any act attributable to war (declared or undeclared, or any conflict between the armed forces of countries) whether or not the Insured is in military service, or (e) from participating or engaging in a riot, or (f) from operating or riding in or descending from any kind of aircraft of which the Insured was a pilot, officer, or member of the crew, or in which the Insured was giving or receiving training or instruction or had any duties.

Liberty National argues that these policy provisions make this policy an "accidental means" policy as opposed to an "accidental results" policy. Thus, it contends that, although Mr. Hairston's death was accidental, the means by which the death occurred, i.e., the consumption of alcoholic beverages, was not accidental, and that, therefore, no coverage is afforded under this policy. On the other hand, Maggie Hairston contends that Alabama law does not recognize a distinction between "accidental means" and "accidental results." She contends, in the alternative, that, even if Alabama does recognize such a distinction, the circumstances surrounding Mr. Hairston's death fall within the "accidental means" provision.

In *Emergency Aid Insurance Co. v. Dobbs*, 83 So. 2d 335 (Ala. 1955), this Court recognized a distinction between "accidental results" and "accidental means." However, we also set forth a broad definition of what constitutes a death or injury by accidental means: "It is an accidental death or injury if the result is an accident whether or not due to accidental means; but it is caused by accidental means, although the means employed were voluntarily rendered, if, in the act preceding the injury, something unforeseen, unusual and unexpected occurs which produces the result." ... From this definition, it is clear that even a voluntary act that leads to an unforeseen, unusual, or unexpected result could invoke coverage under an "accidental means" policy.

In *Hearn v. Southern Life & Health Insurance Co.*, 454 So. 2d 932 (Ala. 1984), the insured's beneficiary brought an action against the insurer, alleging nonpayment of the benefits on three policies providing accidental death benefits. The insured was killed when, after a high-speed chase by a police officer, his vehicle left the road and crashed into a gully. The insured died of smoke inhalation while attempting to escape from the vehicle through a jammed door. This court, in reversing the trial court's judgment based on a directed verdict in favor of the defendant insurance company, recognized that "even where one voluntarily exposes himself to unnecessary danger, he may still die by accidental means if his death is the result of a miscalculation of speed, distance, or his driving capabilities." ...

Further, we concluded that, for insurance contract purposes, an insured is not held to intend all the probable or foreseeable consequences of his actions, and we determined that recovery is precluded only where "there is a reasonable basis for his belief that his conduct makes serious injury or death a virtual certainty." ... This Court has also held: "[O]ur point of view in fixing the meaning of this contract must not be that of the scientist. It must be that of the average man. Such a man would say that the dire result, so tragically out of proportion to its trivial cause, was something unforeseen, unexpected, extraordinary, an unlooked-for mishap, and so an accident. This test—the one that is applied in the common speech of men—is also the test to be applied by courts." ...

Our review of the insurance policy at issue and of the facts and circumstances surrounding Mr. Hairston's death leads us to the conclusion that the trial court erred in holding that, as a matter of law, this death was not an "accident" within the meaning of the policy. A jury could find that the death, while a result of the insured's voluntary actions, was something unforeseen, unexpected, and unusual, or that, as was the case in *Hearn, supra,* the insured died as the result of a miscalculation of his capabilities. Under the holdings of *Dobbs* and *Hearn,* we cannot say as a matter of law that the death was not an accident. Liberty National has not argued that any of the exclusions from coverage that Liberty National chose to insert in this policy barred Maggie Hairston's recovery under the additional indemnity provisions, that the judgment is due to be affirmed for any other reason.

The trial court erred in determining that, as a matter of law, James L. Hairston's death was not an "accident" under the terms of this life insurance policy. Maggie Hairston does not argue that the summary judgment on the bad faith claim is due to be reversed. Therefore, the judgment is affirmed as to the bad faith claim and reversed as to the breach of contract claim, and the cause is remanded for further proceedings consistent with this opinion.

## Notes and Questions

1. The *Hairston* court arguably applies the modern majority rule, that for purposes of determining coverage under an accident or life insurance policy with "accidental death" benefits, the foreseeability of death resulting from the policyholder's voluntary actions must be tested from the subjective viewpoint of the particular policyholder themself. *See also Cole v. State Farm Mut. Ins. Co.,* 753 A.2d 533 (Md. 2000); *Miller v. Continental Ins. Co.,* 40 N.Y.2d 675, 389 N.Y.S.2d 565 (1976).

In a more recent decision, *Cranfill v. Aetna Life Ins. Co.,* 49 P.3d 703 (Okla. 2002), the Oklahoma Supreme Court held that a drunken driving death was nonetheless sufficiently "accidental" for coverage. Although the decedent, Cortez Cranfill, may have been exceedingly foolish, negligent, and drunk (he also failed to buckle his seat belt), there was no evidence that he "expected or intended" to have an accident and kill or injure himself. Stated the court:

> In the context of life and accident insurance, contract terms are not analyzed under the tort principle of foreseeability. Otherwise, deaths resulting from almost any high-risk driving activity would be excluded from coverage under an accident insurance policy (e.g. driving at an excessive speed, failing to keep a proper lookout, failing to maintain brakes in good condition,

changing lanes without using a proper turn signal, floating to a stop sign). If one applied tort principles, death from such high risk activity could be said to be reasonably foreseeable. Foreseeability has a more specific meaning in the context of life and accident insurance. It is only when the consequences of the act are so natural and probable as to be expected by any reasonable person that the result can be said to be so foreseeable as not to be accidental.... The mere fact that an insured's death may have resulted from his or her own negligence, or even gross negligence, does not prevent the death from being accidental under the plain meaning of the word "accident". *Id.* 49 P.3d at 706.

*Query*: Is this a question of law for the court, or a question of fact for the jury?

2. Exclusions for death while under the influence of alcohol are found in some insurance policies. *See, e.g., Sylvester v. Liberty Life Ins. Co.*, 42 P.3d 38 (Colo. App. 2001). Can you predict some of the problems with this type of exclusion, particularly with causation? With reasonable expectations of policyholders?

3. Other courts, in analyzing whether or not an "accidental death" resulted from the policyholder's voluntary actions, however, still apply a more traditional "classic tort" approach in determining whether the policyholder's actions were the "natural and foreseeable consequence of a deliberate act" from the objective viewpoint of a "reasonable insured." *See, e.g., Patch v. Metropolitan Life Ins. Co.*, 733 F.2d 302 (4th Cir. 1984) (applying Virginia law); *Young v. J.C. Penney Life Ins. Co.*, 701 F.2d 709 (7th Cir. 1983) (applying Missouri law).

Thus, the courts are split regarding what constitutes an "accidental" death in life, health, and accident insurance policies. On one hand, some courts employ an *objective* or "classic tort" doctrine that if an injury or death was reasonably foreseeable as a natural consequence of an intentional act, then it could *not* be accidental. Courts applying this "classic tort" approach tend to look at the policyholder's voluntary acts from an objective "reasonable insured" viewpoint. *See, e.g., Floyd v. Equitable Life Assurance Soc'y*, 264 S.E.2d 648 (W. Va. 1980).

Other courts, however, have adopted a more liberal *subjective* definition of what constitutes an "accidental death," holding that when a particular policyholder commits a voluntary act, not intending to cause themself harm, this act *would* constitute an "accidental death" within the terms of the policy coverage. Courts applying this modern majority approach tend to look upon the policyholder's voluntary acts from a subjective "particular insured" viewpoint. *See, e.g., New York Life Ins. Co. v. Harrington*, 299 F.2d 803 (9th Cir. 1962) (applying California law) (finding that the death was accidental when the policyholder put a loaded gun to his temple and pulled the trigger, mistakenly thinking that the safety was engaged); *Cockrell v. Life Ins. Co.*, 692 F.2d 1164 (8th Cir. 1982) (applying Arkansas law) (pointing out that Arkansas state courts have declined to adopt the "classic tort" concept that one intends the natural and foreseeable consequence of one's deliberate acts so as to bar recovery for unintended results). Which approach is more persuasive to you? Based on what underlying rationale?

A number of courts have adopted a three-step quasi-objective "hybrid rule" or "*Wickman* test" to determine what does, and does not, constitute an "accidental" death. The First Circuit Court of Appeals in *Wickman v. Northwestern Nat'l Ins. Co.*, 908 F.2d 1077 (1st Cir. 1990) (applying federal common law), had to determine whether the decedent, who jumped or fell from a railroad bridge 50 feet above the railroad tracks, suffered an "accidental death." The policy excluded benefits "for loss directly or indirectly caused by suicide" and "intentionally self-inflicted injury" whether the insured was sane or insane. When asked "what happened" in the emergency room, before he died, Wickman replied, "I jumped off."

The *Wickman* court then had to devise a test that, following Judge Cardozo's dissent in *Landress* (the Serbonian Bog case), rejected the archaic and hyper-technical accidental means versus accidental result distinction, yet could not permit the "insured's subjective, yet unreasonably optimistic expectation of coverage." The *Wickman* court selected the "reasonable expectations of the insured" as the starting point of its analysis. The court then articulated a three-step process. First, the trier of fact is to determine *what the insured's subjective expectation was*, or whether the insured actually "expected an injury similar in type or kind to that suffered." If not, the second question was whether *the insured's expectations were reasonable*, taking into account *the particular insured's characteristics and experiences*. And third, if the trier of fact is unable to determine what the insured's subjective expectations were, then an *objective "reasonable insured" standard* is required. *Id.* at 1080–83.

"In practice," observes Professor Adam Scales, "*Wickman's* [highly influential] three step test has been collapsed into the quasi-objective inquiry contained in step three. Courts invariably bottom [their] conclusions as to coverage upon a determination of what someone like the insured would have expected to result from [his or her] assertedly accidental conduct." Scales, *Man, God, and the Serbonian Bog: The Evolution of Accidental Death Insurance*, 86 Iowa L. Rev. 173, 296 (2000).

Other courts have interpreted *Wickman* to preclude coverage only when death or serious injury is "highly likely to occur." *See, e.g., Todd v. AIG Life Ins. Co.*, 47 F.3d 1448, 1455–56 (5th Cir. 1995) (applying *Wickman* to find coverage in an autoerotic asphyxiation case, since death or serious injury was "not highly likely to occur").

*But query*: Could not a trier of fact in autoerotic asphyxiation cases, applying a quasi-objective "reasonable insured" standard under *Wickman*, also find that death *was* "highly likely to occur"?

4. It is generally held that, although suicide is not an "accidental death," if this form of self-destruction occurs while the policyholder is suffering from a mental illness, or occurs without the intent to take one's life, then it would constitute an "accidental death." Some insurance policies have therefore attempted to limit coverage for the policyholder's suicide "while sane or insane."

5. The general rule in most courts, therefore, is that a person is a victim of an "accident" when, from the victim's point of view, the occurrence causing the injury or death is not a natural or probable result of the victim's own acts. *Hoffman v. Life Ins.*

*Co.*, 669 P.2d 410 (Utah 1983). But if the policyholder is the aggressor in an assault and knew, or should have anticipated, that the other person might kill him in the encounter, then the death would not be considered "accidental." *Drew v. Life Ins. Co.*, 316 S.E.2d 512 (Ga. Ct. App. 1984). *See generally* JERRY & RICHMOND, UNDERSTANDING INSURANCE LAW §63[C] (6th ed. 2018).

*Query*: What happens if the insured husband, in a drunken state, seriously beats his wife, causing her to defend herself with deadly force? Would this constitute an "accidental death" since the husband, in his intoxicated condition, could not anticipate his wife's response to his aggressive acts? Why or why not? *See Herbst v. J.C. Penney Ins. Co.*, 679 S.W.2d 381 (Mo. Ct. App. 1984).

## PROBLEM FIVE

Which of the following factual situations should be labeled an "accidental death" for purposes of insurance coverage? Why or why not?

(a) An insured tavern keeper was shot and killed by a patron he was attempting to expel from the tavern for indecent behavior.

(b) An insured soldier is killed in battle by the enemy. (There was no "war risks" exclusion in the policy.)

(c) The policyholder shot and killed himself by placing a loaded gun to his temple and pulling the trigger, thinking, however, that the safety catch was engaged.

(d) The policyholder died after a voluntary dive from atop the Coolidge Dam in Arizona, a height of more than 139 feet. He had previously made dives from heights of 15, 25, 40, 50, and 75 feet from diving boards, ship decks, rocky ledges, and box canyons; and he stated (correctly) that the Coolidge Dam venture was to be his last dive.

(e) The policyholder burned to death in a fire which he deliberately set in order to collect fire insurance. He died when a gas furnace pilot light prematurely ignited 10 gallons of gasoline the insured had poured on the furniture and floor of the house, immolating the insured along with his house.

(f) The policyholder was found dead, hanging by his neck in the bathroom. The insurance company refused coverage based on its suicide exclusion, and based on the fact that the policyholder's death was not accidental. The policyholder's beneficiary, however, offered evidence that the policyholder's death was accidental and unintended while he was engaging in autoerotic sexual practices.

## PROBLEM SIX

The insurer issued a homeowners policy that contained an exclusion for loss arising out of an intentional fire set by "an insured." The term included the named insured and any relatives living at home. Plaintiff's 17-year-old son intentionally (not accidentally or negligently) set the house on fire.

- Should Plaintiff be able to recover for the intentional fire caused by her son?
- Why or why not?

# § 6.04. Pre-Existing Conditions, Fortuity and Accident

## Hill v. Mutual Benefit Life Insurance Co.

United States District Court, Western District of Arkansas

763 F. Supp. 1000 (1990)

### Oren Harris, District Judge

Before the court is a motion for summary judgment filed by the defendant, Mutual Benefit Life Insurance Company. The defendant seeks summary judgment dismissing plaintiff's claim for accidental death insurance benefits. The defendant also seeks to strike plaintiff's claims for bad faith and punitive damages. Plaintiff has responded to the motion....

The facts are uncontroverted. Plaintiff's husband, the decedent, purchased a life insurance policy from the defendant providing for $52,000 in accidental death benefits. The decedent made timely payment of all premiums and the policy was in full force and effect at the time of his death. Plaintiff is the sole beneficiary of the policy.

On January 9, 1989, the decedent slipped and fell while carrying a heavy mail bag on his mail route for the Post Office. Fifty-two hours later, on January 11, 1989, he died as a result of the rupturing of an abdominal aneurysm. The decedent's treating physician, Dr. John Vaughn, noted that the aneurysm had most likely been in existence for some time, and it's [sic] rupture was probably caused by the accidental fall.

Plaintiff made a claim for both term life and accidental death benefits under the life insurance policy. Defendant paid the term benefits, but denied accidental death benefits under the policy. Accidental death benefits are controlled by the following provision of the policy:

> Accidental Death Benefits: If an accidental bodily injury is sustained by an insured member, while he is insured under the Group Policy, which directly, and independently of all other causes, results in his death within ninety days from the date of such injury, the beneficiary of the insured member as designated or otherwise determined for the member's Life Insurance will be entitled to the applicable maximum amount of benefit, subject to the provisions and limitations of the Group Policy.

> Risks Not Assumed: Accidental death and dismemberment is not a risk assumed under the Group Policy if it results directly or indirectly from: ... (c) any bodily or mental infirmity, disease, or infection other than a pyogenic infection occurring through and with an accidental cut or wound.

Both parties agree that the aneurysm was a bodily infirmity. However, plaintiff contends that if not for the accidental fall, the aneurysm would not have ruptured; *i.e.* the accidental fall precipitated the death. Defendant contends that since the cause of death was due to a pre-existing bodily infirmity, it is not obligated to pay accidental death benefits.

Defendant cites *Jackson v. Southland Life Ins. Co.*, 393 S.W.2d 233 (Ark. 1965) in support of its contention. In *Jackson*, the insured had an epileptic attack, fell into a water-filled ditch, and drowned.[3] The trial judge, sitting as a jury, found that the pre-existing disease was the proximate cause of the drowning and denied coverage under the accidental insurance policy. The Arkansas Supreme Court affirmed. The court quoted the general laws regarding this topic from an American Jurisprudence volume. The court stated: "The general rule is that the mere fact that the insured is afflicted with some disease or infirmity at the time of an injury will not preclude recovery upon an accident insurance policy if an accident is the direct or proximate cause of death or disability, even though the policy excepts death or injury caused by disease or infirmity...."

"On the other hand, if the insured is afflicted with a disease or infirmity at the time an alleged accident occurs, which disease or infirmity proximately causes or substantially contributes to the death or injury resulting, such death or injury is not within the coverage of a policy which insures against death or bodily injury by accident or accidental means, independently of all other causes, or which excepts death or bodily injury produced by diseased or infirmity." Defendant contends that the second stated paragraph is the controlling law in the case at hand. The court disagrees.

First, the Supreme Court merely quoted the passages in dicta. They did not specifically adopt this as controlling Arkansas law. Second, this paragraph flies in the face of the overwhelming case law in Arkansas regarding this subject.

In *Farm Bureau Mutual Insurance Company of Arkansas, Inc. v. Fuqua*, 599 S.W.2d 427 (Ark. 1980), the facts are similar to the case at hand. The insured, age 72, fell and sustained a fracture to his right hip. He died a week later. The death certificate listed the immediate cause of death as "Renal Failure" due to "Chronic Renal Disease." The insurance company denied coverage under the accidental death provision of the policy for the same reasons in this case. The trial court, sitting as a jury, found the insured's accidental fall triggered the complications resulting in his death. Judgment was rendered in favor of the beneficiary, plus fees and penalty.

On appeal, the Arkansas Supreme Court found that the complications resulting in the death of the insured were precipitated by the accident causing the fractured hip and affirmed the trial court. The court stated: "Our exhaustive research reveals the law to be well settled in this state than [sic] an insurance company is liable on their policy of accident insurance if death resulted when it did on account of an ag-

---

3. [1] The *Jackson* case differs factually from the case in hand. There, the insured died of an accidental injury resulting from his physical infirmity. Here, the insured died from a physical infirmity triggered by an accident.

gravation of a disease by accidental injury, even though death from the disease might have resulted at a later period regardless of the injury, on the theory that if death would not have occurred when it did but for the injury, the accident was the direct, independent and exclusive cause of death at the time...."

Based upon the *Fuqua* case, the law in Arkansas seems to be contrary to what the defendant contends. That is, if the accident precipitates the death, it is the direct, independent and exclusive cause for purposes of an accidental death insurance policy. This being the case, defendant's motion for summary judgment regarding coverage under the insurance policy shall be denied.

## Notes and Questions

1. Many courts interpret a "disease or bodily infirmity" exclusion to preclude coverage whenever the pre-existing disease or infirmity is a concurrent proximate cause of the policyholder's death or disability. But if the disease or infirmity in no way causes such death or disability, or is only a remote cause, then the insurance company would be liable under its policy coverage. *See, e.g., Commercial Travelers Ins. Co. v. Walsh*, 228 F.2d 200 (9th Cir. 1955) (applying Washington law). Thus, in the case of *Brock v. Firemens Fund of America Ins. Co.*, 637 S.W.2d 824 (Mo. Ct. App. 1982), where the policyholder had a pre-existing heart condition which may have been only a remote cause of his death, the court held that the policyholder's beneficiary could recover even though the policy specifically required that death be caused by accidental injury "directly and independently of all other causes."

2. A number of courts therefore have found, as a general rule, that if there is a pre-existing disorder or illness at the time of the injury or death, recovery may still be found under "accident" or "accidental death" coverage if the injury was severe enough to have caused considerable damage, but not if the pre-existing disorder or illness was the proximate or predominant cause of such injury or death. *See, e.g., Moore v. Prudential Ins. Co.*, 278 So. 2d 481 (La. 1973).

*Query*: What was the cause of death in the *Hill* case, *supra*? Was it the policyholder's fall, or was it his pre-existing abdominal aneurysm? *See also Mooney v. Monumental Life Ins. Co.*, 123 F. Supp. 2d 1008 (E.D. La. 2000); *Bozic v. JC Penny Life Ins. Co.*, 744 N.Y.S.2d 189 (App. Div. 2002); *Reserve Life Ins. Co. v. Whittemore*, 442 S.W.2d 266 (Tenn. Ct. App. 1969) (where a fall is produced by a pre-existing bodily infirmity or disease, there is no "accident" for purposes of insurance coverage).

3. In *Gravatt v. Regence Blue Shield*, 42 P.3d 692 (Idaho 2002), the Idaho Supreme Court held that a pre-existing medical condition was *not* covered under a health insurance policy, even though it was disclosed in the insurance application, and even though a physician had misdiagnosed the ailment.

When Troy Gravatt applied for a health insurance policy, he told the insurer that he had been suffering from numbness, tingling, and reduced motor skills in his right hand and forearm, and his right leg, and that this condition had been bothering him for approximately a year.

The medical diagnosis at that time was that Gravatt had "thoracic outlet syndrome." Prior to the expiration of the policy's one-year waiting period, a subsequent medical diagnosis determined that Gravatt did not have thoracic outlet syndrome, but instead had a brain tumor that was causing his numbness. The health insurer refused to pay for surgery, noting that Gravatt's surgery was occasioned by a pre-existing condition that afflicted him prior to the effective date of the policy.

The trial court found coverage on the ground that Gravatt had not concealed his medical condition, and the cause of his surgery (the brain tumor) had not been known prior to the inception of the policy.

The Idaho Supreme Court reversed, holding that regardless of the accuracy of the medical diagnosis, Gravatt's pre-existing medical condition clearly existed prior to the inception of the insurance policy. Gravatt's numbness, whether caused by a brain tumor or some other cause, was therefore a pre-existing medical condition that was excluded under the policy.

### PROBLEM SEVEN

A lawyer who practiced law in an isolated Montana town was insured under a group accidental death and dismemberment policy. He died from a heart attack which was triggered by a wolf attack. The wolf bite was not severe enough by itself to have caused the lawyer's death. It did, however, aggravate and trigger his physical infirmity.

- Is the policyholder covered or not?
- If you were the judge, how would you rule?
- Based upon what rationale?

# § 6.05. Accidental Death by "External Means"

Due to an alleged "looseness" in defining the terms "accident" and "accidental death," many insurance companies further limit coverage in their policies to bodily injury or death caused through "violent, external, and accidental means." What constitutes such accidents by "external means"? The following case illustrates some semantic distinctions in interpreting what constitutes injury or death by "external means."

## Spaid v. Cal-Western States Life Insurance Co.

Court of Appeal of California
130 Cal. App. 3d 803, 182 Cal. Rptr. 3 (1982)

Racanelli, P.J.

On appeal from a judgment of nonsuit, we consider whether the evidence presented a question of fact under an insuring agreement providing for payment of accidental death benefits for injury sustained as a result of "external means."[4] ... We conclude that under applicable principles of law, the order of nonsuit was erroneous requiring reversal.

The record discloses the following: Decedent was found dead by the side of his bed at approximately 11 p.m. on December 29, 1972. A small pool of vomitus and an undigested piece of steak one-half inch in diameter, were found near the body. The autopsy report listed the cause of death as asphyxia due to aspiration of stomach contents. Earlier that evening, decedent appeared to choke on some meat during dinner. After he had retired about 9:30 p.m., his daughter observed him coughing very badly.

Dr. Berry, who had been summoned for assistance and pronounced Spaid dead, testified that death was caused by asphyxiation due to the lodging of a piece of meat in decedent's windpipe; he further testified that such undigested meat constituted a "foreign body" as contrasted to a natural internal substance.

Relying principally on *Spott v. Equitable Life Ins. Co.* 209 Cal. App. 2d 229 (1962), the trial court concluded that death had resulted from regurgitated *internal* matter as distinguished from external means.

Here, the sole issue is the scope of coverage; consequently the burden is on the insured to establish that death resulted from a cause and in a manner covered by the policy.... But if the ambiguity "relates to the extent or fact of coverage ... the language [of an insurance policy] will be understood in its most inclusive sense, for the benefit of the insured." ...

Applying such settled principles, we conclude that substantial evidence existed to support an inference that death was caused by external means consistent with the required construction of the insuring agreement.

In the only reported California decision, Division Three of this court concluded (in an analogous factual setting) that death by asphyxia due to bronchial aspiration of regurgitated gastric contents was the product of internal means since the regurgitated material, due to the digestive process, "had lost its identity as either solid or liquid food...." (*Spott v. Equitable Life Ins Co.*, *supra*, 209 Cal. App. 2d 229, 230–232; *accord* ... *McCallum v. Mutual Life Insurance Co. of New York*, 274 F. 2d 431 (4th Cir. 1960) [applying Virginia law]. But, contrary to respondent's assertion, *Spott* is factually distinguishable insofar as it relies on a finding of no evidence of wholly undigested pieces of food.

Initially, we question whether a logical distinction can be made on the basis of the directional trajectory of the trauma-inducing substance of external origin. Whether

---

4. [1] The relevant policy provisions provided coverage if the insured sustained bodily injuries "solely through violent, external and accidental means...." Since respondent virtually concedes that the insured's death was violent and accidental (*cf. Hargreaves v. Metropolitan Life Ins. Co.* (1980) 104 Cal. App. 3d 701, 705, the crucial [inquiry] focuses upon whether death was caused by external means.

the material was inside the body and on its way outside or in a state of descending transit is irrelevant to the foreign source of origin. Rather, the significant determination should pivot on whether the obstructing matter was undigested and thus retained its external characteristic as distinguished from digested food matter which had lost its identity and become part of the internal body substances.[5]

But, assuming the viability of the *Spott/McCallum* analysis, nevertheless a question of fact is clearly presented whether decedent's death due to asphyxia resulted from choking on undigested food (an external substance) or on his own vomitus (an internal substance).

On the evidence presented, the jury could reasonably have found that death was caused by the externally introduced and undigested piece of steak which had lodged in decedent's windpipe resulting in asphyxia. Accordingly, the failure to submit such material factual issue for jury determination constituted prejudicial error.

**Newsom, J.** [dissenting]

While the question is a close and conceptually difficult one, given the precise terms of the insurance contract, I do not think it can be said that the sole means of death here was "external," for appellant's alcoholic ingestion, and related stuporous condition, clearly contributed materially to the sad accident which led to the present claim....

I regard the reasoning of the court in *McCallum* ... as particularly persuasive, for here, as there, the substance which choked appellant "was inside the body and on its way outside during the vomiting process ... in no sense ... an external means."

## *Notes and Questions*

1. In *Spaid, supra*, which opinion is more persuasive to you? Judge Racanelli's majority opinion, or Judge Newsom's dissenting opinion?

• Why?

• Is this judicial decision just another example of Legal Functionalism versus Legal Formalism in interpreting insurance policies?

• Or is this dispute properly centered on whether the internal or external substance was the proximate or predominant cause of the policyholder's death?

• What is the possible legal rationale behind these semantic distinctions?

2. Is death as a result of failure of an artificial heart valve an excluded death because it is caused by "external means"? *See Century Cos. of America v. Krahling*, 484 N.W.2d 197 (Iowa 1992) (death by failure of valve held to be caused by internal means; valve became "functional part of the body" and coverage granted).

---

5. [2] Suppose, for example, the decedent had choked on some other indigestible substance such as a toothpick, a marble or a coin. Should the courts fashion two separate rules depending upon whether the foreign object was being swallowed for the first time or being vomited back out? We think not. (See *Peoples Life Ins. Co. v. Menard*, 117 N.E.2d 376, 380 (Ind. App. 1954)).

# Chapter 7

# Duties of Policyholder and Insurer

Life, liability, casualty, property, and other types of insurance policies generally contain provisions imposing certain duties on the insured and the insurer after loss has occurred. The insured policyholder normally is required after loss occurs to submit *notice* and *proof of loss* to the insurer, and to *cooperate* with the insurer in settling the claim. The insurer, on the other hand, owes a duty to the insured of *good faith and fair dealing* in settling the insurance claim and, with most liability insurance policies, the insurer also has a *duty to defend* the insured against third party plaintiffs.

## § 7.01. Duties of the Policyholder

### [A] Requirement of Notice of Loss: Is Prejudice to the Insurer Necessary?

The purpose of an insurance policy provision requiring a timely notice of loss is not merely to inform the insurer that an accident has in fact occurred. Rather, it also provides the insurer with an opportunity to investigate the claim and determine its rights and liabilities in the action. The policyholder must therefore give timely notice of a loss or claim by providing sufficient information to apprise the insurer of the nature of the loss or claim. But must lack of timely notice prejudice the insurer to enable avoidance of coverage?

### Molyneaux v. Molyneaux

Superior Court of New Jersey
553 A.2d 49 (1989)

[George and Dorothy Molyneaux, their children and George's mother were boating on September 9, 1984, in New York Harbor when the boat hit the wake of a ship, flew into the air, landed on its left side but did not capsize. Dorothy suffered a broken leg; the children were also injured. On August 12, 1985, Dorothy filed suit against George for personal injuries. George carried a boat and yacht policy with Mutual Insurance Co. (Mutual) that contained a personal liability provision to pay for claims arising out of the operation of the boat. But it was not until the lawsuit was filed (almost a year after the accident) that George notified United about the accident.

The insurer filed a declaratory judgment action against George and Dorothy seeking determination that it was not liable to defend or pay any claim against George on the basis that notice of the claim was given late, in violation of the insurance policy terms. George conceded that the notice was late, but contended that there was no prejudice to Mutual. The trial judge determined that Mutual was obligated to defend and indemnify in the action filed by Dorothy because there was no prejudice to Mutual as a result of the late notice. Mutual appealed.]

Mutual argues that because of the unique factual circumstances of this case, the trial judge should not have applied the appreciable prejudice standard stated in *Cooper v. Government Employees Ins. Co.*, 237 A.2d 870 (N.J. 1968) and that this standard should not apply to cases involving marine liability insurance.

In *Cooper*, the Supreme Court established a two-part test to determine forfeiture of coverage when an insured has failed to give timely notice to the insurance carrier: The insurance contract not being a truly consensual arrangement and being available only on a take-it-or-leave-it basis, and the subject being in essence a matter of forfeiture, we think it appropriate to hold that the carrier may not forfeit the bargained-for protection unless there [is] both a breach of the notice provision and a likelihood of appreciable prejudice. The burden of persuasion is the carrier's.... Since George conceded that he gave late notice, there is no dispute concerning the breach of the notice provisions of the policy. Accordingly, the hearing focused solely upon the issue of appreciable prejudice, which Mutual claims should not have been applied in this case.

Mutual relies upon two recent decisions to support its contention regarding the issue of appreciable prejudice: *Zuckerman v. National Union Fire Ins. Co.*, 476 A.2d 820 (N.J. Super. Ct. App. Div. 1984), *aff'd*, 495 A.2d 395 (N.J. 1985), and *Stables v. American Live Stock Ins. Co.*, 493 A.2d 584 (N.J. Super. Ct. App. Div. 1985). However, a review of these cases clearly shows that Mutual's reliance upon them is misplaced.

In *Zuckerman*, the Supreme Court delineated a comprehensive analysis of the distinction between a "claims made" or "discovery" policy and an "occurrence" policy. As stated by the Court, "In a discovery policy the coverage is effective if the negligent or omitted act is discovered and brought to the attention of the insurance company during the period of the policy, no matter when the act occurred. In an occurrence policy the coverage is effective if the negligent or omitted act occurred during the period of the policy, whatever the date of discovery." ...

In other words, in an "occurrence" policy, the peril insured is the occurrence itself, so that once the occurrence takes place, coverage attaches even though the claim is not made for some time thereafter. In a "claims made" policy it is the making of the claim which is the event and peril insured, regardless of when the occurrence took place....

The notice requirement in [an occurrence] policy [does] not define the coverage provided by the policy but rather [is] included to aid the insurance carrier in investigating, settling, and defending claims.... Accordingly, the requirement of notice in an occurrence policy is subsidiary to the event that invokes coverage, and the conditions related to giving notice should be liberally and practically construed....

Here, Mutual's policy is unquestionably an occurrence policy, comparable to an occurrence automobile liability insurance policy. As such, "the *Cooper* doctrine has a clear application." …

In support of Mutual's contention that it was prejudiced [by the delayed notice] and could thus decline coverage, [the insurer argued] that: (1) George Molyneaux may not have been operating the boat; (2) portions of Molyneaux's statement were unbelievable; (3) there was no police report; (4) he was suspicious because there was no collision damage or claim; (5) Molyneaux did not remember the name of the restaurant where he docked before removing his mother from the boat; (6) George could not recall whether his son had received additional medical treatment after being seen initially in the emergency room; (7) potential witnesses were lost; and (8) Molyneaux's "incredible" version of the accident precluded a product liability action against the manufacturer of the boat. Based on these "facts" [Mutual claims adjuster] Kolody concluded that Mutual was prejudiced and that there was no way to overcome the prejudice.

Items (1), (2) and (4) are merely conjecture and suspicions which may not form the basis to establish appreciable prejudice. Circumstances that are merely suspicious will not support an inference of fraud or appreciable prejudice.… Insofar as item (8) is concerned, Cobalt Boats, the manufacturer of the boat, was brought in as a defendant and held liable. Insofar as the police report is concerned, Higgins, Kolody's investigator, checked only one precinct … in New York City, because it was closest to the Holland Tunnel and he was on his way home. He was told that a search for an old police report could be made but it required an authorized signature. Kolody was so informed but he never got an authorized signature.

As to item (5), the restaurant was across the street from Bellevue Hospital where Dorothy Molyneaux had been taken. Kolody and Higgins both knew this, but never made any effort to check this out. Item (6) is totally irrelevant and as to item (7), concerning Circle Lines' witnesses, Higgins did contact Circle Lines and was informed that passenger lists are never kept. Thus, the passengers could not have been identified even if he had requested the information the day after the accident.

We are satisfied from our review of the record that Mutual failed to sustain its burden of proof that it was appreciably prejudiced by late notice of the claim. The fact that an insured's sympathy is with an injured member of the insured's family does not of itself furnish evidence that the filing of a late notice causes appreciable prejudice to the insurer.…

Under New York law [since changed — see Notes below], the insurer is not required to show appreciable prejudice in cases involving late notice of loss to a carrier. Mutual contends that the trial court committed reversible error in not applying New York law in interpreting the insurance policy in question. There is no merit to this contention.

In *State Farm, etc., Ins. Co. v. Simmons' Estate*, [1980] the Supreme Court adopted the "most significant relationship test" as it is set forth in Restatement (Second), Conflict of Laws § 6, 188 (1971). Under this test, the law of the place of the contract ordinarily governs the choice of law because this rule will generally comport with the reasonable expectations of the parties concerning the principal situs of the insured risk during the term of the policy and will furnish needed certainty and consistency in the selection of the applicable law.

In this matter, both the place of contracting and negotiation of the policy was New Jersey. George acquired the policy through Michael Rice, his local insurance agent. The insured boat was purchased, stored, docked and licensed in New Jersey. All payments to the policy were made in New Jersey. In our view the trial court did not err in applying the law of New Jersey on the issue of compliance with the notice provision the insurance policy.

## Notes and Questions

1. There are three different approaches that various jurisdictions apply regarding late notice and prejudice to the insurer.

### The Traditional "No Prejudice Required" Rule

In a minority of jurisdictions under a traditional rule (e.g., Alabama, Georgia, Idaho, and Virginia), compliance with the notice requirement is a necessary condition to coverage, where prejudice to the insurer is assumed as a matter of law. Therefore, if there is an unexcused failure to give notice, there is no coverage. *See* Randy Maniloff & Jeffrey Stempel, General Liability Insurance Coverage: Key Issues in Every State, Ch. 3 (4th ed. 2018).

Historically, New York has been the most prominent state that embraced the traditional rule most seriously. *See Security Mut. Ins. Co. v. Acker-Fitzsimons Sec. Corp.,* 293 N.E.2d 76, 78 (N.Y. 1972) (adhering to traditional rule despite arguments that requirement of prejudice to insurer was becoming the modern majority standard). New York common law also applied the "no prejudice required" rule for excess insurance as well (*see American Home Assur. Co. v. International Ins. Co.,* 684 N.E.2d 14 (N.Y. 1997)) but required a showing of prejudice before late notice could be a defense for reinsurers (*see Unigard Sec. Ins. Co. v. North River Ins. Co.,* 594 N.E.2d 571, 579–80 (N.Y. 1992)). *See* Ch. 13, *infra*; Jeffrey W. Stempel & Erik S. Knutsen, Stempel & Knutsen on Insurance Coverage § 17.05 (4th ed. 2016).

The 2009 enactment of New York Ins. Law § 3420(a) altered this traditional approach by providing that "failure to give notice within the prescribed time will not invalidate any claim made by the insured, injured person, or any other claimant, unless the failure to provide timely notice has prejudiced the insurer."

It is not clear where the statute assigns the burden of persuasion, although the most likely answer is that it is the insurer's burden since *Unigard v. North River, supra,* placed the burden of showing prejudice on the reinsurer. Regarding the statute, *see* Eric Tausend, Note, *"No Prejudice" No More: New York and the Death of the No-Prejudice Rule,* 6 Hastings L.J. 497 (2009). Although the statutory change is a break for policyholders, it is not carte blanche to permit willful tardiness. *See, e.g., Sevenson*

*Envtl. Servs., Inc. v. Sirius Am. Ins. Co.*, 64 A.D.3d 1234, 1236 (N.Y. App. Div. 2009) (15-month delay reporting job-related accident involving policyholder employee unreasonable as a matter of law).

In jurisdictions where no prejudice is required for an insurer to prevail on a late notice defense, there may be a judicial tendency to take a more liberal view of what constitutes lateness in order to avoid the harsh results of contract forfeiture. Insurance policies typically require notice as soon as practicable, a term courts construe as requiring reasonable notice. Even relatively late notice can be deemed reasonable under apt circumstances. Most obviously, a policyholder has no reason to give notice if it is unaware of a claim or if intervening events beyond the policyholder's control (e.g., disruption from war or natural disaster) impose a delay in providing notice. *See, e.g., Rekemeyer v. State Farm Mut. Auto. Ins. Co.*, 828 N.E.2d 970 (N.Y. 2005); *Great Canal Realty Corp. v. Seneca Ins. Co.*, 833 N.E.2d 1196 (N.Y. 2005) (even when applying traditional no-prejudice-required rule, New York did not consider notice required until policyholder could with reasonable diligence be aware of loss or claim).

Regardless of whether a court is being strict or lenient, notice cannot be provided until an occurrence has taken place, a claim is actually made, or circumstances arise appraising the insured of a potential claim. *But see Billings v. Commerce Ins. Co.*, 936 N.E.2d 408 (Mass. 2010) (where underlying "occurrence" is malicious prosecution, the occurrence takes place upon the filing of the allegedly malicious action, not its termination; policyholder's time to give notice begins to run upon making of purportedly malicious claim, not its resolution).

### Considering Prejudice but Placing Burden on the Policyholder

In some jurisdictions (e.g., Indiana, Iowa, Ohio) under a presumptive rule, there is a *rebuttable presumption* that failure to give notice *is* prejudicial to the insurer, and there is no coverage unless the *insured* proves that there was no prejudice to the insurer. *See* MANILOFF & STEMPEL, *supra*, Ch. 3.

### Requiring the Insurer to Prove Prejudice

Most states (e.g., Alaska, Arizona, California, Colorado, Connecticut, Delaware, Florida, Hawaii, Kansas, Kentucky, Louisiana, Maine, Maryland, Massachusetts, Michigan, Minnesota, Mississippi, Missouri, Nebraska, Nevada, New Hampshire, New Jersey, New Mexico, North Carolina, North Dakota, Oklahoma, Oregon, Pennsylvania, Rhode Island, South Carolina, South Dakota, Tennessee, Texas, Utah, Vermont, Washington, West Virginia, Wisconsin) follow the modern majority rule of requiring prejudice and requiring that the *insurer* prove actual prejudice due to any delay in notice in order to avoid coverage. *See* MANILOFF & STEMPEL, *supra*, Ch. 3 (summarizing state approaches and citing cases); *Prince George's County v. Local Gov't Ins. Trust*, 879 A.2d 81, 93–95 (Md. 2005) (same).

- Which rule did the New Jersey court apply in the *Molyneaux* case, *supra*?

- Why did the insurer in *Molyneaux* argue that New York law, rather than New Jersey law, should apply to this case?

• Which is the better reasoned rule regarding late notice and prejudice to the insurer?

The traditional rule was relatively firmly in place until the mid-20th Century and rested on the notion that the requirement of timely notice was typically styled as a "condition precedent" to coverage. Under classical contract jurisprudence, if a condition precedent had not taken place, the obligated party had no duty to perform contractual duties. *See, e.g., Fireman's Fund Ins. Co. v. Care Mgmt.*, 361 S.W.3d 800 (Ark. 2010) (following classical analysis so long as notice requirement is denominated as condition precedent to coverage).

During the last third of the 20th Century, however, courts moved decisively toward requiring prejudice from late notice before coverage could be denied. The rationale for this approach was based on the old maxim that "law abhors a forfeiture" and that policyholders should not lose otherwise available coverage simply through the oversight of untimely notice unless there is actual harm to the insurer. *Alcazar v. Hayes*, 982 S.W.2d 845 (Tenn. 1998), is a well-known case representative of this approach.

Some states continue to differentiate between primary insurers, excess insurers, and reinsurers as respects late notice. For example, Alabama follows the traditional rule for primary insurers but requires excess insurers to prove prejudice from late notice in order to deny coverage. *See, e.g., Midwest Emplrs. Cas. Co. v. East Ala. Health Care*, 695 So. 2d 1169, 1173 (Ala. 1997).

Illinois follows a bit of a hybrid rule in which unreasonably late notice absolutely permits an insurer to deny coverage. But in determining whether notice is unreasonably late, Illinois courts are instructed to use a multi-factor test which includes, among other factors, whether the insurer has been prejudiced. *See Country Mut. Ins. Co. v. Livorsi Marine, Inc.*, 856 N.E.2d 338, 346 (Ill. 2006) (lack of notice "may be a factor in determining ... whether a reasonable notice was given in a particular case yet it is not a condition which will dispense with the requirement"). The Illinois factors are (1) the specific policy language, (2) the policyholder's sophistication, (3) the policyholder's awareness of a loss or claim requiring notice, (4) the policyholder's diligence and reasonable care assessing the availability of coverage after a loss or claim, and (5) whether the insurer was prejudiced by any delay in notice.

In *Livorsi Marine*, the Illinois Supreme Court found no coverage—not even a duty to defend—due to the policyholder's late notice 20 months after it was hit with a lawsuit. Because the notice was so unreasonably late, the court found that the question of prejudice to the insurer need not be addressed.

Notwithstanding the *Livorsi Marine* outcome, the Illinois multi-factor test can in practice often look a lot like that standard notice-prejudice approach. *See, e.g., W. Am. Ins. Co. v. Yorkville Nat'l Bank*, 939 N.E.2d 288 (Ill. 2010) (finding formal notice to insurer 27 months after lawsuit filed sufficiently timely because policyholder had informed agent at time of suit and been told there was probably no coverage; no significant prejudice to insurer under the circumstances and elements of estoppels). *But see* 939 N.E.2d at 297 (Freeman, J., dissenting) (arguing at length that majority failed to faithfully apply *Livorsi Marine* methodology and "unduly expands the concept of 'actual notice'").

Wyoming has precedent embracing the traditional rule, but the precedent is old enough to raise doubts in light of the subsequently shifting legal landscape. Wyoming's leading state supreme court ruling addressing the issue is now over 40 years old. Until fairly recently, Nevada was in a similar situation in that its judicial precedent on notice had last been seriously examined in 1950 and briefly re-affirmed in 1986 but without extensive analysis of whether to reconsider the 1950 decision based on following the then-majority rule that had since become a distinct minority view. In addition, regulations promulgated by the Department of Insurance and contained in the state's Administrative Code arguably "overrule" the older case law. In *Las Vegas Metro. Police Dep't v. Coregis Ins. Co.*, 256 P.3d 958 (Nev. 2011), Nevada clearly embraced the majority rule of requiring the insurer to prove prejudice from late notice.

An alternative means by which insurers may sometimes avoid claims is the use of a contractually established limitations period for filing claims. *See, e.g., Voris v. Middlesex Mut. Assur. Co.*, 999 A.2d 741 (Conn. 2010) (in notice-prejudice jurisdiction, court finds claim for underinsured motorist benefits filed more than three years after auto accident not covered due to policy's clear three-year time limit on making such claims; limitation did not violate public policy and was not unconscionable; insurer did not mislead insured into sitting on its rights).

2. Who may give notice? Normally it is the obligation of the insured to give a timely notice of loss to the insurer, but it has also been held that a notice of loss from "any reliable source" is sufficient when an insurance policy provides that written notice of loss must be given "by or on behalf of the insured." *See, e.g., Philadelphia Electric Co. v. Aetna Casualty & Surety Co.*, 484 A.2d 768 (Pa. Super Ct. 1984). If a notice provision in an accident insurance policy is a condition precedent to coverage, and failure to furnish timely written notice may vitiate the contract as to both the insured *and* the person injured by the insured's acts, may the injured third party plaintiff also give written notice to the insurer of the accident instead of the insured?

3. *Time to give notice.* Where insurance coverage is conditioned upon the insured giving a timely notice of loss to the insurer, the insured is required to act as a reasonably prudent person in giving such notice. The facts and circumstances to be considered in determining whether the insured has met this reasonable standard normally include factors such as those used by the Illinois courts.

4. Under this timely notice test, does a bank's duty to notify its fidelity bond insurance carrier of loss arise only when it has actual knowledge of a specific fraudulent act, or as soon as it begins to suspect dishonesty and wrongdoing from its employee?

5. Note that the *Molyneaux* court makes the distinction between an "occurrence" type insurance policy, and a "claims made" (often spelled as "claims-made") insurance policy. Are the types of policies really so different as to justify dramatically different judicial approaches to the notice requirement? Keep this in mind when studying liability insurance in Ch. 9.

6. Most insured losses are not catastrophic and do not exceed the amount of primary insurance held by the policyholder, at least if the policyholder has been prudent and maintained a sufficiently large primary policy. But a significant portion of commercial property and liability claims may exceed the amount of primary insurance available, in which cases any excess insurers are also entitled to timely notice, even though many excess insurers attempt to avoid the administrative costs of monitoring or defending trial or adjusting claims, reasoning that the primary insurer will do this work in return for the generally more expensive cost of a primary policy.

When it becomes apparent that a loss or claim will exceed the primary layer and pierce the excess or umbrella layers of coverage, the primary insurer, the policyholder, or both may be responsible for giving timely notice to the excess/umbrella insurer.

## [B] Notice of Loss and Proof of Loss Distinguished

### Goodwin v. Nationwide Insurance Co.

656 P.2d 135 (Idaho Ct. App. 1982)

[Plaintiff Goodwin was injured in an automobile accident.] Nationwide argues that Goodwin failed to comply with the notice and proof of loss provisions of the insurance contract, and, therefore, cannot recover for his disability. The policy contains several notice and proof of loss provisions.

> Written *notice of injury* or of sickness upon which claim may be based must be given to the Company **within *twenty days*** after the occurrence or commencement of any loss for which benefits arising out of each such injury or sickness may be claimed, or as soon thereafter as is reasonably possible.

> Written *proof of loss of time on account of disability* or of hospital confinement for which claim is made must be furnished to the Company **within ninety days** *after the termination of the period for which claim is made.*

> Written *proof of any other loss* on which claim may be based must be furnished to the Company **not later than ninety days** *after the date of such loss.*

[Emphasis added.] The policy also contained this "escape clause."

> Failure to furnish notice or proof of claim within the time provided in the Policy shall not invalidate or reduce any claim if it shall be shown not to have been reasonably possible to furnish such notice or proof and that such notice or proof was furnished as soon as was reasonably possible.

On September 4, 1973, Nationwide first received written notice of Goodwin's injury in an auto accident. This notice consisted of a hospital insurance form, which indicated that Goodwin had been in an auto accident, that he was hospitalized from that day until the following afternoon, and that he was treated for contusions above the left eye and in the region of his right flank. Nationwide thus received, within twenty days, notice of an accident which had produced trauma. Nationwide did not, however, receive written proof of loss until October, 1975, when Goodwin filed a "statement of claim" indicating he was suffering from disabling headaches.

The trial court held that the receipt by Nationwide, eighteen days after the accident, of the hospital insurance form satisfied the twenty-day notice requirement. The trial court also held that, given the complex nature of Goodwin's claim, "it was not reasonably possible for plaintiff to furnish notice of proof within ninety days and that the notice of proof ultimately furnished was furnished as soon as was reasonably possible." Thus, the trial court determined that Goodwin had satisfied both the notice of injury and the proof of loss provisions of the policy.

Nationwide contends that Goodwin did not satisfy either requirement. The company asserts that the hospital insurance form was not a sufficient notice of injury because it failed to specify headache pain upon which Goodwin based his disability claim. We believe, however, that the notice was both timely and adequate.

The policy provision states only that the insured must give "written notice of injury or sickness upon which claim may be based." It does not require that the insured describe his injury in such detail as to specify a disability. Rather, the purpose of the notice requirement is to give the insurer a timely opportunity to investigate an injury which may give rise to a subsequent claim of disability. Upon receiving notice of an accident that has produced injury, an insurer can, if it so desires, investigate and determine the nature of the accident and the extent of any injury.

In this case, Goodwin notified the company in writing that he had been involved in an automobile accident which produced an injury serious enough to require hospitalization from that day until the afternoon of the following day, and that contusions of the head and flank were treated. This notice gave the insurer a reasonable chance to investigate the accident and the injury. It served the purposes of such a notice.... We conclude the trial court was correct in holding that the notice was sufficient under the policy.

Finally, we look at Nationwide's contention there was a failure to comply with the proof of loss requirements of the policy. As we noted the trial judge held that, under the escape clause, the proof of loss was furnished "as soon as was reasonably possible" and was timely. The threshold question, however, is whether there was even a need to apply the escape clause. We think not.

Idaho Code § 41-2111 requires a disability policy to contain a provision that "written proof of loss must be furnished to the insurer ... in case of claim for loss for which this policy provides any periodic payment contingent upon continuing loss *within ninety (90) days after the termination of the period for which the insurer is liable* and in case of claim for any other loss within ninety (90) days after the date of such loss." [Emphasis added.]

The language used in the policy, while closely conforming to the statute, says: "Written proof of loss of time on account of disability or of hospital confinement ... must be furnished within ninety days after the termination of the period for which claim is made." Reading the policy as a whole does not disclose that any different meaning should be given to this language than should be given to the statutorily required language. Absent evidence to the contrary, we will presume that Nationwide was merely restating in its own language what the statute required. The policy language cannot be construed to the derogation of an insured's rights under the statute. Therefore, we will read the policy language as though it fully conformed to the statute. Our focus will be upon the meaning of the statutory language "within ninety (90) days after the termination of the period for which the insurer is liable [ . . . for which claim is made.]"

A statute will be given its plain meaning if not ambiguous. . . . The plain meaning of the statute is that proof of claim for a disability may be submitted at any time within the duration of disability covered by the policy, and for ninety days thereafter. We note, however, as a caveat, that the statute does not displace the defense of laches where an insurance company shows substantial prejudice from "late" submission of proof of claim. No prejudice is shown in this case; the trial court expressly found there was none.

We are not asked to decide today, and we do not intimate, what the extent of an insurance company's liability might be for benefits allegedly accruing more than ninety days before the proof of claim is submitted. In this appeal Nationwide has contested only the adjudication of liability, not the amount of the judgment.

## *Notes and Questions*

1. The court in the *Goodwin* case held that the *notice of loss* or injury "within twenty days after the occurrence" was met by the hospital insurance form which, according to the court, gave sufficient notice of the insured's injuries because it gave the insurance company a reasonable chance to investigate the accident even though it failed to specify Goodwin's particular disability. Although courts generally do not insist on strict compliance with proof of loss requirements, too much informality can be fatal to the policyholder's case. *See, e.g., Parks v. Farmers Ins. Co.*, 227 P.2d 1127 (Ore. 2009) (telephone conversations describing loss were sufficient to satisfy proof of loss requirement).

2. The *proof of loss* requirement, however, had to be made "within ninety days after the termination of the period for which the claim is made." *So query*: If Goodwin's proof of loss was filed 25 months after the accident, how was this 90-day proof of loss requirement met?

3. *Goodwin* exemplifies statutory schemes enacted to protect the insured from prejudice in failing to comply with technical or minor notice and proof of loss insurance policy requirements, relating to notice and proof of loss with certain types of insurance coverage. When an insurance policy provision relating to notice and proof of loss conflicts with a statutory provision, the statutory provision prevails.

4. Normally notice and proof of loss are required to be given to the identifiable insurer. What happens, however, when *two* fire insurance companies provide coverage on the same premises as co-insurers, but notice and proof of loss is only given to one insurer?

### PROBLEM ONE

Plaintiffs Harry and Rita Reisman filed an action in Illinois against Bertaldo Delgado alleging that they suffered damages of $10,000 as a result of an automobile accident caused by Delgado's negligence. Coronet, Delgado's liability insurer, hired legal counsel to defend Delgado after Coronet received notice of this action. The action was dismissed for failure to prosecute.

When the plaintiffs filed a second action based on the same accident, Delgado had become a nonresident of Illinois, so service of process was made on the Illinois Secretary of State under applicable Illinois long-arm statutory law. Delgado failed to appear and the plaintiffs obtained a $10,000 default judgment. Coronet received notice of this second action when plaintiffs commenced proceedings to garnish the proceeds of Delgado's liability insurance policy, more than 30 days after entry of the default judgment. Delgado's policy required the insured to "notify the company of any summonses, subpoenas, or notices regarding any lawsuits as soon as possible."

• Will Delgado be Covered?

## [C] Requirement of Cooperation by the Policyholder

Liability insurance policies generally contain clauses requiring the policyholder to cooperate with the insurer in the conduct of the action by assisting settlement efforts, attending hearings and trials, and securing and giving needed evidence. The purpose of these cooperation clauses is to protect the insurer in its defense of the insured by obligating the insured not to deliberately or intentionally take any action which would adversely affect the insurer's settlement or other handling of the claim. Thus, if there is a material breach of this cooperation clause by the policyholder, then the insurer is not liable under its policy in the absence of any waiver or estoppel defenses. The duty to defend is discussed in later chapters.

But how material and substantial must the policyholder's noncooperation actually be for the insurer to avoid liability?

### American Guarantee and Liability Insurance Co. v. Chandler Manufacturing Co., Inc.

Supreme Court of Iowa
467 N.W.2d 226 (1991)

**Schultz, Justice.**

This appeal presents issues arising from a cooperation clause in a liability insurance policy issued by American Guarantee and Liability Insurance Company (American). A coverage dispute arose as an aftermath of a products liability suit involving a defective battery charger that caused a fire loss. Both the manufacturer, Chandler Manufacturing Co., Inc. (Chandler), and distributor, Maxwell City, Inc. (Maxwell), of the battery charger had a judgment entered against them. On a cross-claim, Maxwell secured a judgment against Chandler for indemnification of the entire loss. American, as Chandler's insurer, brought a declaratory judgment action seeking to void the insurance policy. American contended that it had no duty to pay Maxwell's judgment because Chandler violated the cooperation clause of the policy....

Chandler's policy with American was effective on March 13, 1982, the date of the fire loss. Chandler never notified American of the fire loss or the products liability suit which was filed against Chandler in November 1983. In October 1985 American first became aware of the suit against Chandler from a letter sent by Maxwell's attorney notifying American of Maxwell's cross-claim against Chandler. After receiving this notification, American proceeded to defend the action on behalf of Chandler. American wrote a letter to George Chandler (George), President of Chandler, notifying him of its intention to defend the action subject to a reservation of rights. The record is unclear on whether the reservation of rights letter was mailed before or after American assumed the defense of this action.

Chandler's inaction may be explained in part by the fact that Chandler went out of business in 1982 and filed for bankruptcy in 1984. Chandler's bankruptcy case was closed on December 31, 1985, without assets remaining or distributions being made to unsecured creditors.

The liability policy in this case contained terms detailing an insured's duties in the event of an occurrence, claim, or suit. One clause required an insured to notify American of any occurrences, which are defined in the policy as accidents resulting in property damage. Another clause required the insured to report any claims or suits brought against it to American. The policy also contained a cooperation clause, and a provision that "[n]o action shall lie against the Company unless, as a condition precedent thereto, there shall have been full Compliance with all of the terms of this policy...." Throughout this action American has relied upon Chandler's breach of the cooperation clause, rather than a breach of the notice provisions.

Trial of American's declaratory judgment petition was to the court. American presented evidence of George's failure to answer numerous letters sent to him at his home in Evanston, Illinois. These letters stated that Chandler should cooperate with the defense of the lawsuit and requested that George contact American's lawyer in Fort Dodge, Iowa, who was defending the action. American's lawyer also corresponded with George. George did call the lawyer once and provided oral answers to interrogatories. These interrogatories were later sent to George for his signature; he never returned them. Approximately two weeks before trial, American hand-delivered a letter notifying George of the trial and urging him to cooperate with its lawyers. However, this letter did not request that George attend the trial. George neither responded to this letter nor appeared at trial.

In its ruling, the trial court determined that the cooperation clause placed a duty on the insurer to exercise reasonable diligence in obtaining the insured's cooperation. The court concluded that "[i]t is very clear that Chandler did not cooperate with the attempts made to contact him, but this Court is not convinced that American used a sufficient degree of diligence in seeking his cooperation." The court noted that it was not addressing the issue of whether Chandler's lack of cooperation substantially prejudiced American. The trial court denied American's declaratory judgment petition based on its finding that American failed to use reasonable diligence in seeking Chandler's cooperation.

On appeal, American essentially raises two issues. First, American claims that the trial court's determination of American's lack of diligence in securing the cooperation of its insured was inappropriate. Second, American urges that the evidence shows that it did act diligently in seeking the cooperation of its insured. Both parties agree in their briefs that this matter was tried as an equitable action. Thus, our review is *de novo.*

### I. Burden of proof and the insurer's use of reasonable diligence.

American urges that the trial court's determination that Chandler breached the cooperation clause invokes a presumption that American was prejudiced by the non-cooperation of its insured. It further urges that the trial court simply ignored this presumption of prejudice by turning its attention to the issue of American's diligence in seeking the insured's cooperation. We first examine the burden of proof in this action and then turn to the issue of whether reasonable diligence is required of an insurer.

### A. Burden of proof.

Although this action seeks declaratory relief, its true nature is one of a judgment creditor seeking recovery against an insurer who insured the debtor for liability. We have recognized the rule that a judgment creditor is required to stand in the position of his debtor when seeking coverage under the debtor's liability insurance policy.... "This requirement subjects such a creditor to any defenses which would be good against the insured debtor."

We have addressed the appropriate placement of the burden of proof in disputes over breach of insurance policy terms that are a condition precedent to the insurer's liability. We have consistently required that the party claiming entitlement to coverage under the policy must prove compliance with its terms.... The party claiming coverage may meet this burden of proof by showing the following: (1) substantial compliance with the condition precedent; (2) the failure to comply was excused or waived; or (3) the failure to comply was not prejudicial to the insurer. We have also adopted and followed the rule that a substantial breach of a condition precedent which is not excused or waived must be presumed prejudicial to the insurer.... Previously, we applied these established rules governing placement of the burden of proof in a case in which breach of a cooperation clause was claimed....

We have varied these established rules regarding placement of the burden of proof when an action against an insurer is commenced by a judgment creditor of the insured, rather than by the insured itself.... We relied upon the principle that "the burden of proving a factual issue ... should rest upon the party who has possession of facts or information lacking to the other." ... We concluded that since the insurer maintained files on its transactions with the insured, it possessed firsthand knowledge of any lack of cooperation on the part of its insured. We further held that the judgment creditor did not have the burden of going forth with the evidence concerning compliance with the cooperation clause.

[W]e conclude that the insurer, American, had the burden of going forward with the evidence on the issue of Chandler's noncooperation. In our *de novo* review, we find that American met the burden of proving the noncooperation of its insured Chandler. We now turn to issues concerning the insurer's use of reasonable diligence under the cooperation clause.

B. Reasonable diligence.

The trial court concluded that the cooperation clause of the insurance policy required both the insured's cooperation and the insurer's use of reasonable diligence in obtaining that cooperation. However, neither the court nor Maxwell cited any Iowa case law in support of this reasonable diligence requirement. Instead, it relied on authority from other jurisdictions in imposing a reasonable diligence requirement on American....

In its appellate briefs, American does not seriously challenge the trial court's requirement that an insurer exercise reasonable diligence in obtaining the cooperation of its insured. Rather, American simply contends that it in fact met this requirement and such a requirement should not change the presumption of prejudice to the insurer under Iowa law. Nevertheless, we must first determine whether a reasonable diligence requirement should be imposed on insurers under Iowa law.

We first examine a cooperation clause of an insurance policy. A cooperation clause applies to conduct of the insured in the proceedings subsequent to the notice of the loss, claim or suit and prior to a determination of an insurer's liability.... The purpose of a cooperation clause is to protect insurers and prevent collusion between insureds and injured parties. The question of cooperation under a policy's cooperation clause involves not only the good faith of the insured but also the good faith of the insurer.

The majority rule appears to be that the insurer's and insured's obligations under a cooperation clause are reciprocal; the insured must cooperate with the insurer and the insurer must use reasonable diligence in obtaining the insured's cooperation.... We believe that the stated majority rule is sound and should be adopted by this court. The rule basically requires the insured and insurer to act diligently when a liability claim arises.

We find no merit in American's claim that the reasonable diligence requirement places the burden of proving prejudice on the insured. The insurer does not receive the benefit of a favorable presumption of prejudice until it is established that the insured breached the cooperation clause. The insurer's use of reasonable diligence is simply an element in the determination of whether the insured has breached the cooperation clause. The adoption of this rule adds an element of proof in determining whether the cooperation clause has been breached; it does not shift or change the burden of proof on prejudice.

Consequently, we hold that an insurer cannot avoid its obligation on a policy because of an insured's breach of a cooperation clause unless it exercises reasonable diligence in securing the insured's cooperation. The trial court correctly arrived at this same conclusion.

### II. Proof of reasonable diligence.

In our *de novo* review, we agree with the trial court's finding that American failed to use reasonable diligence in seeking Chandler's cooperation in defending the products liability lawsuit. American's claims office in Kansas City merely corresponded with George Chandler concerning the lawsuit. American suggested that George cooperate with its lawyer in Fort Dodge, Iowa, even though it knew that George was a resident of Evanston, Illinois. It did not utilize its claims office and personnel in an area near Evanston to personally contact George. After a careful review of American's correspondence and its actions and inferences therefrom, we find that American was more concerned with making a paper trail to document George's noncooperation than in securing his cooperation in defending the lawsuit. Although George Chandler was accessible, American never took his personal statement, his deposition, or attempted to secure his presence at trial. The trial court correctly concluded that American's conduct fell short of reasonable diligence.

## *Notes and Questions*

1. What proofs (as to performance of a condition precedent) does the court in *American* require of the party claiming entitlement to coverage? Why then does the court find for plaintiff, even though plaintiff did not comply with the condition precedent (the cooperation requirement)?

2. In *Home Indem. Co. v. Reed Equipment Co.*, 381 So. 2d 45 (Ala. 1980), it was held that the failure of an insured to cooperate with the insurer is inconsequential unless it is both "material and substantial." To be "material and substantial" the lack of cooperation must cause actual prejudice to the insurer.

3. The courts differ as to whether proof of prejudice by the insurer is necessary in order for an insurer to avoid liability when the insured has breached a cooperation clause in the insurance policy. A majority of courts hold that the insurer must show that it was "substantially prejudiced" or injured by the insured's noncooperation. *See, e.g., Clemmer v. Hartford Ins. Co.*, 22 Cal. 3d 865, 151 Cal. Rptr. 285, 587 P.2d 1098 (1978). Other courts, however, presume that a probability of prejudice to the insurer arises from the insured's breach of a cooperation clause and place the burden on the *insured* to show any lack of prejudice. *See, e.g., Western Mut. Ins. Co. v. Baldwin*, 258 Iowa 460, 137 N.W.2d 918 (1965). "Prejudice" resulting from the insured's noncooperation has been defined to constitute an act that affects a jury, or causes a jury to render a verdict against the insured. *See, e.g., Harleysville Ins. Co. v. Rosenbaum*, 30 Md. App. 74, 351 A.2d 197 (1976).

4. In general, a liability policyholder's typical duties of cooperation include: (1) providing relevant records surrounding a claim to the insurer; (2) attending depo-

sitions and other claim-related legal proceedings such as pre-trial conferences; (3) giving truthful testimony (falsification of facts and documents will breach the duty to cooperate); (4) making reasonable attempts to obtain cooperation of employees, family members, or friends with helpful knowledge of the case; (5) signing any papers required in connection with the claim, such as interrogatory answers, affidavits, or settlement agreements; and (6) attending trials and hearings. *See generally* STEMPEL & KNUTSEN, *supra*, § 9.02.

## PROBLEM TWO

Acme Insurance Company argues that it can escape liability on the ground that its insured, Zeno, willfully failed to appear and testify at trial, in breach of the cooperation clause in Acme's policy. Acme argues that there is a "strong possibility" that Zeno's testimony would have raised a jury question as to Zeno's alleged liability in the related personal injury accident, and that Zeno's willful failure to testify at trial thereby prejudiced Acme in its defense of Zeno.

- Has Zeno breached the duty of cooperation?
- Sufficiently to lose coverage?

## PROBLEM THREE

A liability insurer brought a declaratory judgment action in court seeking relief from its duty to pay a tort judgment against its insured, based on the insured's alleged willful failure to cooperate with the insurer in not attending a scheduled deposition on the day the insured attended the funeral of a close friend's father.

The insurer claimed that the lack of the insured's deposition was prejudicial to its case, and that the insured could have attended the deposition in the afternoon, since the funeral took place in the morning. The jury, however, held that the insured had not willfully failed to cooperate with the insurer, but the trial court judge disagreed with the jury's finding, and held in favor of the insurer.

- How should the appellate court rule in this case?

---

Why do a majority of courts require the insurer to prove actual prejudice in any breach of cooperation action? The following excerpt from *Pennsylvania Threshermen & Farmer's Mut. Casualty Ins. Co. v. Owens*, 238 F.2d 549, 550–51 (4th Cir. 1956), is instructive:

> Liability insurance is intended not only to indemnify the assured but also to protect members of the public who may be injured through negligence.... It would greatly weaken the practical usefulness of policies designed to afford public protection, if it were enough to show mere disappearance of the assured without full proof of proper efforts by the insurer to locate him.

# [D] Misstatements by the Policyholder

A deliberately false and willful misstatement of material facts made by the insured to the insurer after loss occurs is a violation of the cooperation clause and will absolve the insurer from liability under the policy. On the other hand, an unintended, accidental, or "innocent" post-loss false statement, if subsequently corrected, will not generally establish grounds for the insurer to escape liability under a breach of cooperation clause.

Some states, attempting to avoid post-loss problems of distinguishing willfully false from innocent misstatements by the insured, have passed various "anti-technicality statutes" which provide that misrepresentations made by the insured in any proof of loss will not avoid policy coverage unless they are fraudulently made, material, and the insurer was misled and caused to waive or lose some valid defense.

But such laudable consumer-oriented statutes can also be abused by the insured. *See, e.g., Aetna Casualty & Surety Co. v. Guynes*, 713 F.2d 1187, 1189 (5th Cir. 1983), involving suspected arson, where the insureds blatantly misrepresented the value of their home, their whereabouts on the night of the fire, their alleged role in another insurance fraud, and other evidence. The court, quoting from an earlier case upholding a similar insurance "anti-technicality statute" in Florida, stated: "Clearly, in the absence of a statute, the law, which is founded on truth and justice, will not regard it as unsound that a person has lost the benefit of the contract by willful, immoral, dishonest acts which the contract itself condemns." But under this "anti-technicality" statute, the insureds recovered under their policy.

# [E] Collusion between the Policyholder and the Claimant

The cooperation clause in a liability insurance policy is violated when the insured, by his or her collusive conduct, assists a third-party claimant in maintaining an action against the insured and the insurer. However, a lack of good faith on the part of the insured cannot necessarily be inferred because a close familial or other relationship exists between the insured and the injured third-party claimant that may account for a certain sympathy on the part of the insured toward the injured claimant.

## PROBLEM FOUR

The insured's nephew was injured while working on the insured's farm. The insured discussed the lawsuit with his nephew; he told his nephew that he would be at a friend's birthday party in a neighboring county where the nephew resided so service of process could be served on him; he exhibited a general animosity toward the insurer's claims adjuster; and he opposed the insurer's motion to quash this service of process based on the insured's alleged fraudulent conspiracy with his nephew.

• Did these acts constitute collusion which breached the cooperation clause and terminated the insurer's liability under the policy?

• Why or why not?

# § 7.02. Duties of the Insurer

Aside from the obligation to pay the insured when a covered loss occurs, the insurer has certain other contractual obligations to fulfill when notice of loss is given, including a duty to defend the insured in liability insurance claims, the duty to gain the insured's cooperation, and the duty of good faith and fair dealing to the insured to fairly settle claims within the policy coverage.

## [A] Duty to Defend the Policyholder

### State Farm Fire & Casualty Co. v. Eddy

California Court of Appeal
267 Cal. Rptr. 379 (1990)

[Eddy, believing he might have herpes, had a viral culture test on June 3, 1985, with negative results. He therefore believed he did not have herpes. Early in 1986, he had a continuing affair with Greenstreet who, on March 27, 1986, was diagnosed as having herpes. Thereupon, Greenstreet sued Eddy for battery and infliction of emotional distress. Eddy called upon his homeowner's insurer, State Farm, to defend him. State Farm brought a declaratory action contending that there was no coverage under the terms of its policy and also by virtue of California Insurance Code § 533. The trial court agreed and granted summary judgment to the insurer. The policy included coverage for personal liability and also had an exclusion for "bodily injury which is expected or intended by an insured." Bodily injury was defined to include "harm, sickness or disease."]

DUTY TO DEFEND

Appellants contend that although a determination on the merits might show that there was intentional conduct for which State Farm need not indemnify Eddy, the complaint alleged both negligent and intentional torts; therefore, State Farm must defend since potentially it could be required to indemnify for Eddy's negligence. We agree.

"An insurer's duty to defend is separate from its duty to indemnify. The fact that an insurer may ultimately not be liable as the indemnifier of the insured does not establish that it has no duty to defend. The duty to defend is broader than the duty to indemnify and is measured by the reasonable expectations of the insured [and the allegations found in the complaint].... Accordingly, '[a]n insurer is not absolved from its duty to defend the lawsuit merely because it is forbidden by law or contract to indemnify the liability-causing action.' [Citation.] 'An insurer, bound to defend an action against its insured, must defend against all of the claims involved in that action, even though some ... of them ultimately result in recovery for damages not covered by the policy.'" ... "An insurer ... bears a duty to defend its insured whenever it ascertains facts which give rise to the *potential* of liability under the policy." [Citing the well-known case *Gray v. Zurich Insurance Co.*, 419 P.2d 168 (Cal. 1966) (emphasis added)]....

Moreover, although State Farm argued that the policy excluded coverage for bodily injury which was "expected or intended" by an insured, Eddy's declaration in opposition to the motion for summary judgment indicated that the infliction of the disease was not expected or intended, even though the intercourse was. The tort is the transmission of disease, not the consensual sexual relations.... "[N]otice of noncoverage of the policy, in a situation in which the public may reasonably expect coverage, must be conspicuous, plain and clear."

Therefore, it was error for the court to rule there was no duty to defend.

## DUTY TO INDEMNIFY

### 1. Violation of Law

Next, appellants contend that Eddy's conduct did not amount to violation of law or fraud so as to defeat coverage.

State Farm had argued to the trial court that Eddy fraudulently induced Greenstreet to consent to intercourse, and that he committed the misdemeanor of infecting Greenstreet with a venereal disease in violation of Health and Safety Code § 3198. Because of this, the insurance contract was made unenforceable by Civil Code § 1668, which declares that all contracts which have for their object to exempt a person from responsibility for certain conduct, including fraud and violation of law, are against the policy of the law.

We shall assume for this discussion that transmission of genital herpes would constitute a misdemeanor under [California] Health and Safety Code § 3198.... The question is whether, at the time Eddy engaged in sexual intercourse with Greenstreet, he knew the act was unlawful.

Civil Code § 2773, by its language, requires actual knowledge. Even if, in retrospect, Eddy perhaps should reasonably have known that he was exposing a person to or infecting her with a venereal disease (because of his medical and dating history), the indemnity agreement would not be void....

A reading of the declarations accompanying the motion for summary judgment shows that Eddy asserted that he had a good faith belief that he did not have herpes, and that this was founded on the results of the viral culture taken in 1985....

If Eddy's asserted belief is found true, even though he committed an unlawful act, the agreement to indemnify would not be void under section 2773. If, on the other hand, it is found that at the time Eddy engaged in intercourse he knew he was committing an unlawful act, the indemnity agreement is void.

We have noted that State Farm has a duty to defend Eddy in the suit brought by Greenstreet. "Since the court in the third party suit does not adjudicate the issue of coverage, ... [t]he only question there litigated is the insured's liability.... [I]f the insurer adequately reserves its right to assert the noncoverage defense later, it will not be bound by the judgment. If the injured party prevails, that party or the insured will assert his claim against the insurer. At this time the insurer can raise the non-coverage defense previously reserved."

State Farm has reserved its right to assert its noncoverage defense. If it is found that Eddy knew at the time he had intercourse with Greenstreet that he was acting unlawfully, State Farm may at that time assert that the contract is void under section 2773.

## Notes and Questions

1. Insurers frequently agree to defend a policyholder under a "reservation of rights," in which the insurer reserves its rights to contest coverage depending on the facts elucidated during discovery or trial of the matter. The question then arises as to whether an insurer's reservation creates a conflict of interest between insurer and policyholder. If so, the policyholder is generally permitted to select its own defense counsel, with the insurer paying reasonable legal fees commensurate with what the insurer would otherwise pay counsel selected by the insurer. However, a mere reservation of rights alone normally is not viewed as creating sufficient adversity to permit policyholder choice of counsel, although there are a few jurisdictions to the contrary. *See Twin City Fire Ins. Co. v. Ben Arnold-Sunbelt Bev. Co. of S.C., LP*, 433 F.3d 365 (4th Cir. 2005) (applying Virginia law) (collecting authorities from many states).

2. Assume a long-time client of yours has been sued and wants to tender defense of the matter to its liability insurer. However, the client also wants your law firm to defend it in the action. What information will you need to determine if this is possible? What will you tell your client? Should your client still tender the matter to the insurer or should you defend the case and then send the insurer the bill? Some courts hold that reservation of rights creates conflict between insurer and policyholder that entitles the policyholder to choose its own counsel independent of the insurer.

3. ABA Formal Opinion 05-435 (Dec. 8, 2004) touches on these issues and concludes that a law firm may under certain circumstances represent a plaintiff suing a policyholder even if the firm also regularly represents the policyholder's liability insurer because the plaintiff and the defendant's liability insurer are not automatically "directly adverse."

The rationale underlying this view is the important concept that a liability insurer is generally regarded as a third party responsible for obtaining a lawyer and resolving claims but is not itself a part to the litigation. "However, a concurrent conflict may arise if there is a significant risk the representation of the individual plaintiff will be materially limited by the lawyer's responsibilities to the insurer."

The concern is that an insurer client may be so important to the law firm (because of the insurer's frequent need to hire lawyers for policyholders or its own legal work) that the law firm is compromised in its zeal for representing a plaintiff that, if it wins, will be paid at least in part by the insurer. But even then, the ABA Opinion concludes, it may be possible for the plaintiff and the insurer to waive the conflict if the attorney for the plaintiff has a reasonable belief that he or she "will be able to provide competent and diligent representation."

4. The standard answer to the question of whether to tender defense of a claim to the insurer is "always tender." Most liability insurers will not pay for any "pre-tender"

defense expenditures even if the matter is eventually tendered to them. *See* MANILOFF & STEMPEL, Ch. 4. In addition, failure to tender can create defenses to coverage such as late notice and failure to cooperate. It also is not a great way to strengthen the client-policyholder's relationship with its insurers. Sometimes common sense and practicality are as important as the precise contours of legal right.

There may be variants of any general rule. For example, Illinois has a line of cases permitting "targeted tender," in which the policyholder covered by overlapping insurers can tender the defense of a claim to a single insurer rather than providing notice and tender of defense to all insurers. *See John Burns Constr. Co. v. Indiana Ins. Co.*, 727 N.E.2d 211 (Ill. 2000).

Why would a rational policyholder do such a thing? What are the risks? What's the potential "reward" in asking only one insurer to defense when several insurance policies have arguably been "triggered" by a particular claim against the policyholder? What would you tend to advise to clients in this position? If you were practicing in a state other than Illinois that had no precedent on the issue, what would you advise the client?

5. Where there are multiple insurers implicated by a claim, the question can also arise as to the relative responsibilities of the insurers in providing a defense or paying defense costs. Sometimes insurers faced with the situation imitate "Alphonse and Gaston," two cartoon characters popular during the first half of the 20th Century (but at least dimly remembered by the authors). Alphonse and Gaston were not exactly a laugh-riot and would not threaten currently popular comedians.

Alphonse and Gaston's primary activity was continually deferring to one another about who should first go through a door. They regularly wasted countless hours with an "After you," "No, no, after you" routine similar to the famous Laurel & Hardy scene where the two say good-bye to friends for an interminable time before finally driving off. Insurers are accused of engaging in an Alphonse and Gaston routine when they delay mounting a policyholder's requested defense while hoping that another triggered insurer will rise to the occasion and defend the matter, saving the waiting insurer the time, effort, and money.

6. Unfortunately, the Alphonse and Gaston routine sometimes works. For example, a "good" liability insurer may "step up to the plate" and provide a defense of the claim and resolve the matter economically while a "bad" insurer (or insurers) continues to sit on the sideline with money that it would have otherwise spent on defense safely in the bank earning interest. Worse yet, the sitting insurer is sometimes the insurer that had primary defense responsibility while the defending insurer may have been further from the risk or even a higher level excess insurer.

For example, in *Iowa Nat'l Mut. Ins. Co. v. Universal Underwriters Ins. Co.*, 150 N.W.2d 233 (Minn. 1967), a primary insurer with a duty to defend refused but the policyholder's excess insurer stepped into the void and defended. After the matter was concluded, the defending insurer sought to be reimbursed for half of the defense costs. Incredibly, the Minnesota Supreme Court held that no good deed goes unpunished and that the defending excess insurer (which should have been able to sit on the sideline) had no right to reimbursement from the primary insurer. The formalist logic of the court was that the duty to defend is not divisible, making prorated reimbursement inappropriate. The functional effect of the decision was to reward the insurer that acted improperly toward its policyholder.

Notwithstanding that the decision is an embarrassment for even the most ardent formalist, *Iowa National* remained good law in Minnesota for more than 40 years (*see, e.g., Home Ins. Co. v. Nat'l Union Fire Ins.*, 658 N.W.2d 522, 527 (Minn. 2003)). Finally, *Iowa National* was overruled in *Cargill, Inc. v. Ace Am. Ins. Co.*, 784 N.W.2d 341 (Minn. 2010). As the *Cargill v. Ace American* court noted,

> The *Iowa National* rule does little to encourage insurers to "resolve promptly the duty to defend issue." Rather, the *Iowa National* rule encourages any insurer whose policy is arguably triggered to deny its insured a defense and, essentially, play the odds that among all insurers on the risk, it will not be selected by the insured to defend.
>
> We conclude that the *Iowa National* rule, even as we have modified it over the years, is no longer an appropriate result when multiple insurers may be obligated to defend an insured. There is little incentive for any single carrier to voluntarily assume the insured's defense. To the contrary, under *Iowa National* an insurer who voluntarily assumes the defense finds itself bearing the entire cost of the insured's defense unless the insured enters into a loan receipt agreement [which] is by no means assured.

784 N.W.2d at 352 [citations omitted].

Fortunately, most jurisdictions have adopted the reasonable view that the defending insurer in such cases is entitled to seek proportional reimbursement from other triggered insurers.

7. As should perhaps go without saying, an insurer cannot escape duty to settle responsibilities by misleading a policyholder (or any insured under the policy) into thinking that a claim is not available and that settlement is therefore not a possibility.

8. At what point in time does the duty to defend arises in CERCLA environmental pollution cases?

9. If there is an adverse judgment against the insured, and there are reasonable grounds for appeal, does the insurer also have a duty to its insured to prosecute the appeal? The courts are split on this question. *Compare Palmer v. Pacific Indem. Co.*, 254 N.W.2d 52 (Mich. Ct. App. 1977) (in a malpractice defense, the insurer, through a broad "duty to defend" clause in the policy, had to defend the insured at both the trial and appellate levels), *with Guarantee Abstract & Title Co. v. Interstate Fire & Casualty Co.*, 618 P.2d 1195 (Kan. 1980) (there is no obligation on the part of the insurer to prosecute an appeal), *and General Casualty Co. v. Whipple*, 328 F.2d 353 (7th Cir. 1964) (applying Illinois law).

10. As discussed in Ch. 13, excess insurance policies usually follow form to the underlying primary policy over which the excess policy "sits." As a result, the excess

insurer may have a duty to defend once the underlying primary policy is "exhausted" by the payment of its limits to effect settlements or pay judgments. *See, e.g., Johnson Controls, Inc. v. London Mkt.*, 784 N.W.2d 579 (Wis. 2010).

However, in many or perhaps most cases, the excess policy provides that it will pay for both defense expenditures and settlement/judgment payments and may elect to defend but has no express duty to defend. Because defense costs count against the policy limit in such instances ("defense within limits" or "burning limits" in the language of the trade as opposed to "defense outside limits," which is typical for primary policies), policyholders who have exceeded the limits of primary coverage must often be careful not to expend so much in defense costs that they effectively exhaust the excess policies that are supposed to enable them to resolve large claims.

11. As noted in *Molyneaux*, the duty to defend is separate from and broader than the duty to indemnify in that the duty to defend is based on the existence of a potential for coverage while the duty to indemnify is not imposed unless the adjudicated facts of the case bring the claim within coverage. However, if an insurer simply defends a tendered claim without saying anything, almost all courts regard the insurer to have waived any defenses it may otherwise have had regarding indemnity coverage—or to be estopped from contesting coverage (*see* Ch. 4). *See, e.g., World Harvest Church, Inc. v. GuideOne Mut. Ins. Co.*, 695 S.E.2d 6 (Ga. 2010).

The rationale for this rule is that the insurer must give the policyholder fair warning if it is contesting indemnity coverage and provide the insurer with an opportunity to retain materials and approach the defense of a claim knowing it may be adverse to its own insurer regarding its attempt to gain indemnity payments on any resulting settlement or judgment.

In order to avoid waiver or estoppel, liability insurers frequently agree to defend under a "reservation of rights," accepting tender of defense of a matter with a Reservation of Rights Letter that outlines various coverage issues on which the insurer is maintaining its right to deny coverage on the underlying claim depending on the determination of the facts in the case. Pending this determination, the insurer continues to defend, and may even seek reimbursement of some expenditures it sees as falling outside any potential for coverage even as the insurer defends the entire "suit." (*See* below regarding such recoupment actions.)

In addition to the Reservation of Rights Letter, the insurer may also file a declaratory judgment action seeking a judicial determination that it need no longer defend an action or need not cover any eventual liability that falls outside indemnity coverage.

By statute or common law, insurers are usually under some time pressure to dispatch an expeditious response to a policyholder's tender of a claim. State versions of the model Unfair Claims Practices Act promulgated by the National Association of Insurance Commissioners (NAIC) usually require some sort of insurer response (even if not a fully developed claims position) within 30 days.

12. Although court appearances and litigation activity require admission to the bar, an insurer may satisfy its duty to defend (and duty to settle, discussed below) by having adjusters respond to the claim prior to judicial proceedings. *See, e.g., Farmers Ins. Exch. v. Johnson*, 224 P.3d 613 (Mont. 2009) (insurer did not breach duty to defend by sending adjuster rather than attorney to represent policyholder defendant in mediation activity).

For the most part, this broad tolerance for the use of nonlawyer personnel by insurers is sensible as a means of lowering disputing costs (adjusters are generally less expensive than attorneys), so long as the adjuster is conscientious and sufficiently qualified by training and experience. But it comes closer to being the unauthorized practice of law than most people (including the legal profession) realize.

The practice of law is generally defined as the rendering of legal services, including but not limited to court appearances or representation in negotiations, as well as the providing of legal advice. *See Linder v. Ins. Claims Consultants, Inc.*, 560 S.E.2d 612 (S.C. 2002) (public adjusters permitted to evaluate amount of loss but not to interpret insurance policies, negotiate coverage disputes, or advise claimant as to whether to accept offer of settlement).

Under this standard, some states have found "public" adjusters (those used by policyholders to help present claims to the insurance company) as engaging in unauthorized law practice. *See, e.g., Utah State Bar v. Summerhayes & Hayden*, 905 P.2d 867 (Utah 1995); *Professional Adjusters, Inc. v. Tandon*, 433 N.E.2d 779 (Ind. 1982). Although "in-house" adjusters on the insurance company payroll have not been as targeted, it is hard to distinguish their work from that of the public adjuster or an attorney at a negotiation, arbitration, or mediation. The major substantive difference is that a liability insurance company adjuster, as a representative of the insurer controlling defense and settlement of a claim, is not advising the policyholder or claimant — but the in-house adjuster is surely representing the insurer in an adversary proceeding against the claimant. In the course of this activity, the adjuster is of course making legal as well as factual assessments.

If courts were being formalist, the widespread use of nonlawyer personnel might create grave problems for insurers (unauthorized practice of law is a felony in some states). However, the long-standing use of nonlawyer adjusters and the perceived efficiencies of the status quo have led courts to take a functionalist view.

As a practical matter, an able and experienced adjuster is often more adept at resolving claims than most lawyers, although some of this effectiveness is not only the insurance skills of the adjuster but also his or her informal legal knowledge. As law professors, we have seen more than a few adjusters attend law school, often coming to their first year with substantially more practical knowledge about tort law and litigation than their peers.

13. Liability insurance is often referred to as "litigation insurance" because of the view that its primary value is as much to fend off claims and free policyholders to concentrate on business or enjoy peace of mind as it is to pay any claims reaching

judgment. Consequently, insurers cannot "walk away" from duty to defend obligations merely by depositing the policy limits with the court. *See Am. Serv. Ins. Co. v. China Ocean Shipping Co. (Am.)*, 932 N.E.2d 8 (Ill. App. 2010).

If an insurer interpleads the policy limits, it must still continue to provide a defense to its insureds, at least until policy limits are exhausted. In conducting itself, the insurer must act in good faith as if there were no policy limits to exhaust. For example, the insurer cannot reflexively pay the entire policy limits to the first injured party, particularly if the injuries are relatively minor, as a means of terminating the duty to defend. Rather, the insurer must continue to defend vigorously until such time as policy limits are exhausted by good faith defense and settlement efforts. *See also City of Hartsville v. S.C. Mun. Ins. & Risk Fin. Fund*, 677 S.E.2d 574 (S.C. 2009) (insurer retained continuing duty to defend after dismissal of negligent misrepresentation claim because remaining civil conspiracy claim continued to expose policyholder to liability).

Alternatively, insurers are not necessarily required to fight claims until the last ounce of blood is spilled. *See, e.g., Mortensen v. Stewart Title Guar. Co.*, 235 P.3d 387 (Idaho 2010) (title insurer permitted to pay amount of judgment against policyholder rather pursuing appeal, as desired by policyholder).

Nor are insurers required to act as timeless custodians of everything related to a claim. Further, even in unusual cases, the insurer's first duty remains to the policyholder. *See, e.g., Am. Family Mut. Ins. Co. v. Golke*, 768 N.W.2d 729 (Wis. 2009) (insurer bringing subrogation action against roofers whose alleged negligence led to fire damaging policyholder home had not engaged in spoliation when it destroyed the damaged roof of the home in order to permit rebuilding of home; insurer had given roofers adequate notice and opportunity to retrieve the material in question).

## [1] *The Standard for Determining the Existence of a Duty to Defend: The Four Corners/Eight Corners Rule and the Role of Extrinsic Evidence*

The *Eddy* case illustrates the general rule of liability insurance policies that *the duty to defend is broader than the duty to pay*, based on the rationale that: "An insurer ... bears a duty to defend its insured whenever it ascertains facts which give rise to the potential of liability under the policy. In the instant case the complaint itself, as well as the facts known to the insurer, sufficiently apprised the insurer of [this potential liability]." *Gray v. Zurich Ins. Co.*, 419 P.2d 168 (Cal. 1966). Thus, in the vast majority of jurisdictions, if the allegations of a complaint set forth a *possibility* of coverage, the duty to defend will exist, even though the lawsuit may be groundless, false, or frivolous.

This focus on the face of the complaint made against a policyholder/defendant is commonly known as the "four corners rule" because it directs the court to examine the four corners of the complaint. If any of the allegations of the complaint, if true, would fall within a coverage provision of the policy, there is the requisite "potential for coverage" and the liability insurer's duty to defend is triggered. Because this analysis implicitly requires not only an examination of the face of the complaint but also the face of the applicable liability policy, it is often called the "eight corners" rule (four corners of the complaint plus four corners of the policy). *See* Maniloff & Stempel, Ch. 5.

The four corners/eight corners analysis has historically dominated duty to defend decisions and remains the universal starting point for analysis. However, there is also a substantial, once clearly minority, view that the allegations in a complaint are not necessarily determinative of an insurer's duty to defend. As a result, insurers may be required in many states and circumstances to consider whether extra-complaint information brings a case potentially within coverage. Similarly, an insurer's declaratory judgment action seeking a determination that it need not defend may include presentation of additional evidence rather than merely an argument that the face of the complaint creates no potential for coverage.

Empirically, it appears that what the once-clear minority rule is gaining in popularity and that most jurisdictions do not permit consideration of evidence outside the complaint in addressing duty to defend questions. *See* Maniloff & Stempel, *supra*, Ch. 5. Most states find the duty to defend triggered not only by the face of the complaint but by the potential for coverage reflected in the complaint, including the court's use of judicial notice and a common sense reading of the situation as well as the introduction of extrinsic evidence by the policyholder. In that way, the policyholder is not deprived of coverage merely because the third party (or its counsel) pleaded poorly.

Conversely, the insurer can be said to be vulnerable to the clever pleading of the third-party claimant, who will almost always want to trigger the insurer's duty to defend and possible coverage, thereby increasing the pool of funds potentially available to pay a settlement. Insurers in this position may in most states use extrinsic information to defeat the potential for coverage. But to be safe, in most states the insurer must seek to do this by filing a declaratory judgment action seeking the court's determination that there is no duty to defend. In the meantime, the prudent liability insurer will also defend the action against the policyholder during the pendency of the declaratory judgment action. In the absence of a defense, the insurer that loses a declaratory judgment may face considerable damages exposure for whatever harms may befall the undefended policyholder.

As has been observed, the four corners rule is a universal inclusionary standard but is not usually employed as an exclusionary standard by courts.

- How far, however, must an insurer or court go beyond the four corners to provide coverage?

- For example, is it sufficient that the insurer be responsible for considering extra-complaint facts of which it is aware?

- What about facts told to the insurer by the policyholder-defendant (who obviously wants coverage and will know what to say to try and get it after talking with counsel)?

• Must the insurer do more and investigate the facts and circumstances of the claim in order to determine if coverage is possible under the terms of the liability policy?

Almost two-thirds of the states (Alabama, Alaska, Arizona, Arkansas, California, Colorado, Connecticut, Georgia, Hawaii, Illinois, Indiana, Iowa, Kansas, Maryland, Massachusetts, Michigan, Minnesota, Missouri, Montana, Nebraska, Nevada, New Hampshire, New Mexico, North Carolina, North Dakota, Ohio, Oklahoma, Oregon, South Dakota, Utah, Virginia, and Washington) permit consideration of extrinsic evidence to a substantial degree, with some states unclear on the point.

More than a third of the states (Delaware, Florida, Idaho, Kentucky, Louisiana, Maine, Mississippi, Pennsylvania, Rhode Island, South Carolina, Tennessee, Texas, Vermont, West Virginia, Wisconsin, and Wyoming) continue to impose the traditional four corners/eight corners approach without significant exception.

The case for consideration of extrinsic information is strongest where the information already lies within the possession of the insurer or is made available to the insurer by the policyholder. Fewer states are willing to impose on the insurer an affirmative duty of investigation to determine if facts outside the complaint bring an otherwise non-defense action within the potential for coverage to require a defense. *But see Waste Management of Carolinas, Inc. v. Peerless Ins. Co.*, 340 S.E.2d 374, 377–78 (N.C. 1986) ("Where the insurer knows or could reasonably ascertain facts that, if proven, would be covered by its policy, the duty to defend is not dismissed because the facts alleged in a third-party complaint appears to be outside coverage or within a policy exception to coverage.").

## Fitzpatrick v. American Honda Motor Co., Inc.

Court of Appeals of New York
78 N.Y.2d 61, 571 N.Y.S.2d 672, 575 N.E.2d 90 (1991)

**Titone, J.**

It is well established that a liability insurer has a duty to defend its insured in a pending lawsuit if the pleadings allege a covered occurrence, even though facts outside the four corners of those pleadings indicate that the claim may be meritless or not covered. The issue in this appeal is whether the insurer has a duty to defend in the opposite circumstance, i.e., where the pleadings do not allege a covered occurrence but the insurer has actual knowledge of facts demonstrating that the lawsuit does involve such an occurrence. Under these facts, we hold that the insurer cannot use a third party's pleadings as a shield to avoid its contractual duty to defend its insured.

The plaintiff in the main action, Linda Fitzpatrick, sought recovery for the wrongful death of her husband, John Fitzpatrick, who died on October 31, 1985 while operating a three-wheel all-terrain vehicle. The complaint alleged that the vehicle in question was owned by defendant Frank Moramarco and that Moramarco had given Fitzpatrick permission to use it in connection with the performance of certain yardwork and household chores. According to the complaint, codefendant Cherrywood Property

Owners Association (CPOA, the owner of the property on which the accident occurred, had retained Moramarco, and Moramarco, acting as CPOA's agent, had in turn hired Fitzpatrick as an "independent contractor."

In fact, Moramarco was an officer, shareholder and director of an independent concern called Cherrywood Landscaping, Inc. (CLI), which had been retained by CPOA to do landscaping work on CPOA's property. The vehicle involved in Fitzpatrick's accident had been purchased by Moramarco on behalf of CLI for use in its landscaping and gardening business. CLI had also purchased a liability insurance policy from National Casualty Co. (National), which indemnified the corporation against having to pay damages for bodily injury and property damage arising out of its business. While the policy was not an "owner's policy" and Moramarco was not a specifically named insured, the terms of the policy included as "insured persons" "any executive officer, director or stockholder [of the named insured (i.e., CLIs)] while acting within the scope of his duties as such."

Shortly after Moramarco was served with papers in the main action, he notified National and requested that the insurer provide him with a defense. National, however, refused, stating that the policy it had issued to CLI did not appear to cover the claim against Moramarco.

In subsequent correspondence, Moramarco advised the insurer that the vehicle involved in the Fitzpatrick accident was "owned for and used exclusively for landscaping operations" and that the claims asserted against him in the main action all arose out of activities he undertook for CLI the named insured. The same circumstances were brought to the insurer's attention in a letter from its own agent in which the company was urged to reconsider its prior decision. Nonetheless, National maintained that it was not required to provide a defense because the complaint did not name CLI and Moramarco, the named defendant, was not insured as an individual.

Moramarco thereafter commenced a third-party action against National seeking payment of his legal fees in the main action, as well as "judgment over" for any judgment entered against him in the main action. National promptly moved, pursuant to [New York] CPLR [Civil Practice Laws and Rules] 3211(a)(1) and (7), to dismiss the third-party complaint. Relying wholly on the absence of allegations in the Fitzpatrick complaint suggesting that the claim against Moramarco arose in connection with his activities as an officer, shareholder or director of the insured CLI National argued that it had no duty to defend or indemnify Moramarco under the terms of the policy. In response, Moramarco submitted proof to show that, despite the complaint's inaccuracies, the Fitzpatrick claim actually did involve a covered event.

The [trial court] denied National's dismissal motion, holding that the question of whether its policy covered the Fitzpatrick accident "must await a plenary trial." The Appellate Division, however, reversed and dismissed the third-party complaint. The court held that the allegations in the complaint are the determinative factor in resolving whether the provisions of an insurance policy have been "activated" in a particular action. Since the Fitzpatrick complaint named Moramarco only in his individual capacity and the insured, CLI, was never even mentioned, the Appellate Division concluded that the existing documentary evidence, i.e., the Fitzpatrick complaint and the National policy, was sufficient to warrant dismissal of Moramarco's third-party claim. This Court granted Moramarco leave to appeal from the Appellate Division order. We now reverse.

This Court has repeatedly held that an insurer's duty to defend its insured arises whenever the allegations in a complaint state a cause of action that gives rise to the reasonable possibility of recovery under the policy. In the present appeal, National asks this Court to hold that the converse is also true. According to National, the complaint allegations are, in all cases, the *sole* determining consideration and, consequently, an insurer is relieved of the duty to defend whenever the complaint allegations do not on their face set forth a covered cause of action. However, the position National advocates is neither compelled by our prior case law nor consistent with sound legal principles and policies. Accordingly, we reject it.

The rationale underlying the cases in which the "four corners of the complaint" rule was delineated and applied, is based on the oft-stated principle that the duty to defend is broader than the duty to indemnify. In other words, as the rule has developed, an insurer may be contractually bound to defend even though it may not ultimately be bound to pay, either because its insured is not factually or legally liable or because the occurrence is later proven to be outside the policy's coverage.

It follows logically from this principle that an insurer's duty to defend is called into play whenever the pleadings allege an act or omission within the policy's coverage. Even where there exist extrinsic facts suggesting that the claim may ultimately prove meritless or outside the policy's coverage, the insurer cannot avoid its commitment to provide a defense, since "[a] complaint subject to defeat because of debatable theories must [nevertheless] be defended by the insured." ... Accordingly, the courts of this State have refused to permit insurers to look beyond the complaint's allegations to avoid their obligation to defend and have held that the duty to defend exists "[i]f the complaint contains any facts or allegations which bring the claim even potentially within the protection purchased".... The holdings thus clearly establish that an insurer's duty to defend is at least broad enough to apply when the "four corners of the complaint" suggest the reasonable possibility of coverage.

However, to say that the duty to defend is *at least* broad enough to apply to actions in which the complaint alleges a covered occurrence is a far cry from saying that the complaint allegations are the *sole* criteria for measuring the scope of that duty. Indeed, in these circumstances, where the insurer is attempting to shield itself from the responsibility to defend despite its actual knowledge that the lawsuit involves a covered event, wooden application of the "four corners of the complaint" rule would render the duty to defend narrower than the duty to indemnify—clearly an unacceptable result. For that reason, courts and commentators have indicated that the insurer must provide a defense if it has knowledge of facts which potentially bring the claim within the policy's indemnity coverage.

We agree with these authorities and hold that, rather than mechanically applying only the "four corners of the complaint" rule in these circumstances, the sounder approach is to require the insurer to provide a defense when it has actual knowledge of facts establishing a reasonable possibility of coverage. This holding fits easily and appropriately within the existing rules governing coverage disputes, which certainly do not require us to extend the "four corners of the complaint" rule to a situation such as this one, where it has not been applied before and, in fact, has no apparent value.

Although it has been argued that the "four corners of the complaint" rule has the advantage of certainty (see, dissenting opn., at 73), there is no reason to believe that the rule we adopt here will engender any more litigation. Contrary to the dissenters' assertion the above cited authorities do not uniformly impose on the insurer an obligation to investigate; rather, their holdings on this point are mixed. In any event, the duty we recognize here, i.e., the duty to defend when the facts *known* to the insurer indicate coverage, does not depend upon, or even imply, a corollary duty to investigate. Indeed, there is nothing in this case, where the insurer was actually notified of the salient facts by both its insured and its own agent, that requires us to create a duty to investigate where none previously existed.

The conclusion we reach here flows naturally from the fact that the duty to defend derives, in the first instance, not from the complaint drafted by a third party, but rather from the insurer's own contract with the insured. While the allegations in the complaint may provide the significant and usual touchstone for determining whether the insurer is contractually bound to provide a defense, the contract itself must always remain a primary point of reference. Indeed, a contrary rule making the terms of the complaint controlling "would allow the insurer to construct a formal fortress of the third party's pleadings thereby successfully ignoring true but unpleaded facts within its knowledge that require it to conduct the insured's defense."

Further, an insured's right to a defense should not depend solely on the allegations a third party chooses to put in the complaint. This is particularly so because the drafter of the pleading may be unaware of the true underlying facts or the nuances that may affect the defendant's coverage and it might not be in the insured's (or the insurer's) interest to reveal them.

The principle that an *insurer* may not rely on the pleadings to narrow the scope of its duty to defend also finds support in the practical realities that prevail under modern pleading rules. As one commentator has observed, "considering the plasticity of modern pleadings, in many cases no one can determine whether the third party suit does or does not fall within the indemnification coverage of the policy until the suit itself is resolved" (7C Appleman [on Insurance] § 4684, at 83). This observation is particularly apt in the context of New York's liberal pleading rules, which permit the pleadings to be amended to conform to the proof *at any time*, provided that no prejudice is shown.

The facts in this case—where the complaint on its face did not state a covered claim but the underlying facts made known to the insurer by its insured unquestionably involved a covered event—present a clear example.

The insurer here refused to defend Frank Moramarco because he was sued, albeit mistakenly, as an employee of CPOA and the owner of the injury-causing vehicle. Had the complaint correctly identified Moramarco as an officer and/or shareholder of the insured CLI he would have unquestionably been covered for this lawsuit, since the policy provided that "any executive officer, director or stockholder [of CLI] while acting within the scope of his duties as such" was an additional "insured person" under the policy.

Further, the insurer promised to "defend any suit against the insured seeking damages on account of bodily injury or property damage" arising out of CLI's landscaping and gardening business—a condition plainly satisfied here. To deny Moramarco an insurance-company sponsored defense under these circumstances merely because the attorney for the plaintiff in the main action accidentally mischaracterized Moramarco's role would be to afford the insurer an undeserved windfall at the expense of its insured.

Indeed, relieving the insurer of its duty to defend is particularly imprudent and counterproductive where, as here, the inaccuracies in the plaintiff's pleadings are likely to become apparent when the true facts are developed on the record and the role of the insured in the incident is fully exposed. At that point, the trial court could well grant a request by the plaintiff to conform the pleadings to the proof, in which event the insurer's core policy obligation to defend Frank Moramarco as an additional insured would unquestionably be triggered. Moramarco should not be required to wait until that point is reached before obtaining an insurance-company sponsored defense, since a "provision for defense of suits is useless and meaningless unless it is offered when the suit arises" (7C Appleman, *op. cit.* §4684, at 83).

In sum, application of the "four corners of the complaint" rule in these circumstances is not required by our prior cases and is not even supported by the rationale usually offered in support of the rule. Further, invocation of the rule here and in analogous cases leads to an unjust result, since it exalts form over substance and denies an insured party the benefit of the "litigation insurance" for which it has paid. These factors militate in favor of a rule requiring the insurer to provide a defense where, notwithstanding the complaint allegations, underlying facts made known to the insurer create a "reasonable possibility that the insured may be held liable for some act or omission covered by the policy"....

We therefore hold that National cannot ignore the facts made known to it by its insured and rely instead on the *Fitzpatrick* complaint alone to assess its duty to defend Moramarco.

## Notes

Consistent with the *Fitzpatrick* approach is *Pekin Ins. Co. v. Wilson*, 930 N.E.2d 1011 (Ill. 2010), which found that the policyholder was entitled to a defense notwithstanding that the plaintiff's complaint had framed the action as an assault-and-battery that seemingly would make the policy's intentional injury exclusion applicable (*see* Chapter 1 regarding the fortuity requirement in insurance and the intentional act exclusion). The policyholder had counterclaimed, asserting self-defense. The court did not limit its examination to the complaint alone but also considered this affirmative defense, finding that the pleadings as a whole showed a potential for coverage and thus activated the insurer's duty to defend.

If an insurer wrongfully refuses to defend an action against the insured, the insurer can be held liable for reasonable attorney's fees and expenses incurred by the insured in defending himself. However, in a case where there was no contractual duty on the part of an excess liability insurer to defend the insured against claims falling within the "umbrella" coverage of its policy, the insured could not recover counsel fees in defending against the claim. A wrongful failure to defend the insured can result in a bad faith action against the liability insurer as well.

A liability insurer that refuses to defend its insured does so at its peril; for if the insured loses his or her case, then the insurance company probably will have to pay the legal judgment anyway, even though the plaintiff's allegations may initially have appeared to be false, fraudulent, or groundless. On the other hand, if the insurance company does defend its insured, then the insured may claim that the insurer has waived any of its policy defenses, or is estopped to deny them, and the insurer again may be liable for the judgment.

What, then, should legal counsel for a liability insurer do if it is determined that there is no coverage under its policy, yet, because the plaintiff's pleadings allege facts which would potentially come under policy coverage, it must still defend its insured? To protect its rights, the insurer should obtain a non-waiver agreement or issue a reservation of rights notice to its insured and to the plaintiff, and then attempt to obtain a declaratory judgment from the court as to whether or not it must defend its insured.

## [2] Fee-Shifting in Insurance Disputes

Because insurance is an aleatory contract in which premium payment precedes the need for insurance protection, an asymmetry exists that may disadvantage policyholders or allow opportunistic behavior by less scrupulous insurers.

Consider the problem of a policyholder suffering a house fire or being sued for alleged negligent infliction of injury. At this point, the policyholder is vulnerable. It has already paid premiums to the insurer rather than saving and self-insuring against these risks. Because the fire has already occurred or the lawsuit has been filed, it is now largely too late to purchase insurance, at least at any reasonable price (although there still may be enough fortuity regarding the eventual amount of the loss to permit some market for such policies).

The policyholder needs protection—either rebuilding or defense now. But if the insurer disagrees about coverage (or potential for coverage regarding the liability insurer's duty to defend) and refuses to pay or files a declaratory judgment action, the policyholder is forced to expend litigation costs if it hopes to collect the insurance to which it thinks it is entitled. Even if the policyholder eventually prevails, it has suffered additional financial loss when it was supposed to have the protection of insurance.

Although this often is the case for other contracts (the party injured by breach is not made completely whole because of transaction costs pursuing remedies), it seems particularly unfair that this should befall a policyholder that was correct regarding coverage because insurance is purchased to provide protection and "peace of mind."

As a result, most states, by statute or common law, provide for the recovery of counsel fees and related expenses incurred vindicating rights under an insurance policy. States divide over whether the policyholder's right to counsel fees (an exception to the "American Rule" in which litigants generally pay their own legal fees) is automatic upon prevailing or is established only where the insurer's coverage position was unreasonable or it otherwise acted in bad faith. *See* MANILOFF & STEMPEL, *supra*, Ch. 8.

Many states (e.g., California, Connecticut, Illinois, Iowa, Mississippi, North Carolina, North Dakota, Pennsylvania, Rhode Island, South Dakota, Tennessee, Virginia, Wisconsin, and Wyoming) require something more than mere success by the policyholder.

However, an equal or greater number of states (Arkansas, Delaware, Florida, Georgia, Hawaii, Idaho, Kansas, Maine, Maryland, Massachusetts, Montana, Nebraska, New Hampshire, New Jersey, New York, Oregon, South Carolina, Utah, Washington, and West Virginia) make fee-shifting to the successful insurer something close to automatic, while others (e.g., Missouri) give the court wide discretion in coverage cases.

Some states (e.g., Michigan, Minnesota) have fee-shifting for successful policyholders when there has been a breach of the duty to defend but not for coverage actions generally.

A significant number of states (Alabama, Kentucky, Louisiana, New Mexico, Ohio, and Vermont) do not provide for fee-shifting in insurance matters, although there still may be an opportunity for fee-shifting if an established exception to the American Rule (e.g., creation of a common fund or benefit, a contract provision, litigation misconduct) applies. *See* MANILOFF & STEMPEL, *supra*, Ch. 8.

Insurers may, in theory, obtain fees where the policyholder has acted in bad faith or violated civil litigation requirements (e.g., FED. R. CIV. P. 11, 28 U.S.C. § 1927; COLO. REV. STAT. ANN. § 13-17-101; NEV. REV. STAT. ANN. § 18.010 (which applies only to awards of less than $20,000)) that positions be reasonable under the law and supported by at least some evidence and that the claim or prosecution of the case not be vexatious or in bad faith. But this is relatively rare.

Alaska Civil Rule 82 provides for fee-shifting from loser to winner along the lines of the "English Rule." *See State v. Native Village of Nunapitchuk*, 156 P.3d 389, 394 (Alaska 2007). Arizona gives courts discretion to make counsel fee awards in any contractual action. *See Lennar Corp. v. Auto-Owners Ins. Co.*, 151 P.3d 538, 553 (Ariz. Ct. App. 2007) (applying ARIZ. STAT. ANN. § 120341.01(A)). Texas is similar. *See* TEX. CIV. PRAC. & REM. CODE § 37.009. But fee awards for contracts other than insurance policies are relatively rare. In addition, there may be offer-of-judgment fee-shifting opportunities particular to insurance actions. *See, e.g.,* OKLA. STAT. ANN. tit. 36 § 3629(B).

In awarding fees, trial courts have substantial but not limitless discretion. Fee awards can be challenged as either excessively generous or unduly miserly. *See, e.g.,* *Snider v. Am. Family Mut. Ins. Co.*, 244 P.3d 1281 (Kan. Ct. App. 2011) (trial court's award of $5,000 counsel fees in connection with successful prosecution of policyholder's $5,000 claim was abuse of discretion in view of reasonable legal work required to prevail against nonpaying insurer; case remanded with instruction that $19,500 was amount of reasonable fee award; prevailing insured had requested $44,000 in fees). Lest we gasp too much at the size of the fees requested and awarded in relation to the amount obtained, consider this.

> Snider contends that the small amount of attorney fees awarded by the trial court in this case would be punitive against Snider and his attorney and would grant insurance companies full discretionary power to deny modest insurance claims without the fear of being held accountable for the attorney fees incurred by the insured.

244 P.3d at 1286. Work property of Snider's was stolen from storage and the insurer contended, erroneously we now know, that the property was not covered "contractor's equipment" under Snider's commercial property insurance.

## [3] *Reimbursement of Counsel Fees and the Policyholder's Costs of Defense*

One of the central maxims of duty to defend jurisprudence is that the insurer is required to defend the entire case so long as there is at least one covered claim set forth in the complaint. Thus, if a plaintiff sues the policyholder and alleges five separate counts or causes of action, there will be a duty to defend if even one of the five counts of the complaint comes within coverage. This is a rule supported by text of the insurance policy (and by formalist principles) because the typical primary liability insurance policy states that it has a duty to defend any "suit" against the policyholder. A "suit" is typically defined as any civil pleading seeking relief in the courts of law. Some policies, such as Directors and Officers liability policies, may even provide coverage for criminal claims against an individual officer or director, but usually only after the return of a grand jury indictment or prosecution by information.

But what if an insurer defends a matter on the basis of one covered claim among many uncovered claims? Can the insurer then attempt to recoup some of the expenditures by seeking reimbursement from the policyholder? *Compare Buss v. Superior Court*, 939 P.2d 766 (Cal. 1997) (liability insurer may seek reimbursement of defense costs expended on uncovered third-party claims in multi-claim litigation provided insurer shoulders the burden of demonstrating uncovered claims sufficiently separate factually from covered claims and where insurer has properly reserved such rights prior to assuming defense of litigation), *with Shoshone First Bank v. Pacific Emplrs. Ins. Co.*, 2 P.3d 510 (Wyo. 2000) (no insurer right to seek reimbursement).

# General Agents Insurance Company of America, Inc. v. Midwest Sporting Goods Company

Supreme Court of Illinois
828 N.E.2d 1092 (2005)

**Justice Thomas** delivered the opinion of the court.

At issue in this case is whether, following a declaration that an insurer has no duty to defend its insured, the insurer is entitled to reimbursement of the amounts paid for the defense of its insured in the underlying lawsuit. The circuit and appellate courts held that the insurer was entitled to reimbursement. For the following reasons, we reverse the judgments of the circuit and appellate courts.

The City of Chicago and Cook County sued Midwest Sporting Goods Company (Midwest) and other defendants for creating a public nuisance by selling guns to inappropriate purchasers. Midwest tendered defense of the suit to General Agents Insurance Company of America (hereinafter Gainsco), its liability carrier. Gainsco denied coverage. The City of Chicago and Cook County then filed their first amended complaint against Midwest and other defendants. Midwest again tendered defense of the suit to Gainsco. On July 23, 1999, Gainsco responded to Midwest's independent counsel as follows:

> We wish to acknowledge and confirm our receipt and review of the First Amended Complaint that you forwarded to our office on behalf of your client and our Insured, Midwest Sporting Goods, Inc. by letter dated April 28, 1999. This letter will supplement Gainsco's letter of December 3, 1998 denying coverage with respect to the plaintiff's original complaint in this matter. We have had an opportunity to review the allegations of the First Amended Complaint, as well as the policy documentation, and without waiving the Company's rights or defenses under the Policy, would like to call the following points to your attention.
>
> * * * [The letter then quotes certain policy language.]
>
> The policy only applies to damages because of property damage or bodily injury caused by an occurrence. The First Amended Complaint does not seek damages because of property damages or bodily injury. As such, the claim is not covered under the Policy.
>
> The First Amended Complaint alleges that the Insured is liable to the plaintiffs for various acts of intentional and/or willful conduct. As a consequence, and based upon the above-noted policy provisions, the claim may not be covered under the Policy.
>
> Additionally, to the extent that the claim involves periods of time that fall outside of the periods of time to which the coverage afforded by the Company covers, the claim is not covered by the Policy.
>
> Please note that to the extent that the claim seeks injunctive relief, the claim is not a claim for damages and, thus, is not afforded coverage under

the Policy. Further, to the extent that the claim is for punitive or exemplary damages, the claim is not afforded coverage under the Policy.

Subject to the foregoing, and without waiving any of its rights and defenses, *including the right to recoup any defense costs paid in the event that it is determined that the Company does not owe the Insured a defense in this matter*, the Company agrees to provide the Insured a defense in the captioned suit. In light of the competing interests between the Company and the Insured in respect of the coverage for this matter, the Company agrees to the Insured's selection and use of your firm as its counsel in this matter. However, the Company notes its right to associate with the Insured and its counsel in the defense of the underlying litigation.

\* \* \*

Please note that any acts taken by or on behalf of the Company are taken under and pursuant to a full reservation of its rights and defenses under the Policy. Likewise, we will understand that any acts taken by or on behalf of the Insured are taken pursuant to a reservation of rights as well. (Emphasis added.)

Based upon the record in this case, it does not appear that Midwest ever responded to Gainsco's reservation of rights letter. Midwest thereafter accepted Gainsco's payment of defense costs.

Gainsco filed a declaratory judgment action seeking, *inter alia*, a declaration that it did not owe Midwest a defense in the underlying litigation. The declaratory judgment action also asserted a claim for recovery of all defense costs paid to Midwest's independent counsel on behalf of Midwest in the underlying litigation. [The trial court held] that Gainsco had no duty to defend Midwest in the underlying litigation. [T]he trial court noted that the issue before it was whether the plaintiffs in the underlying complaint were seeking damages in the nature of economic loss or bodily injury. The trial court held that based upon case law, the damages sought by the plaintiffs in the underlying case amounted only to economic loss, and therefore held that Gainsco was entitled to summary judgment on its declaratory judgment action.

[Editors' Note: This ruling is typical of cases considering whether a general liability policy covers third party claims seeking purely injunctive relief, including municipal attempts to attempt to regulate the availability of firearms. However, where a claim of this sort also may seek monetary damages against the source of the alleged public nuisance, the prevailing view is that there exists a potential for coverage triggering the duty to defend at least until this contingency is resolved against the policyholder.]

Gainsco then filed a motion for entry of judgment for recovery of defense costs, seeking to recover the defense costs that it had paid to Midwest's independent counsel for Midwest's defense of the underlying litigation. The trial court ordered Midwest to pay Gainsco $40,517.34....

Midwest argues that Gainsco failed to establish any legal basis that would entitle it to an award of reimbursement of defense costs. Midwest notes that the insurance policy between Midwest and Gainsco contains no provisions allowing Gainsco to recover defense costs. Further, because there was an express written insurance contract between the parties, Gainsco cannot claim that it is entitled to recover defense costs under a theory of unjust enrichment. In addition, Gainsco's reservation of rights letter could only reserve the rights contained within the insurance policy and could not create new rights. In any event, the language in the reservation of rights letter clearly establishes that Gainsco paid the defense costs pursuant to the insurance policy.

Gainsco responds that each of the preceding arguments must fail because there is no contract governing the parties' relationship. Gainsco argues that its duty to defend extended only to claims for damages that were payable or potentially covered under a Gainsco policy. Here, as the circuit and appellate courts found, the Gainsco policies did not apply to the underlying litigation. In addition, Gainsco notes that numerous decisions, including *Buss*, ... support the trial court's decision.

An insurer's duty to defend its insured is much broader than its duty to indemnify its insured. An insurer may not justifiably refuse to defend an action against its insured unless it is clear from the face of the underlying complaint that the allegations set forth in that complaint fail to state facts that bring the case within or potentially within the insured's policy coverage.

A court must compare the allegations in the underlying complaint to the policy language in order to determine whether the insurer's duty to defend has arisen. If the underlying complaint alleges facts within or potentially within policy coverage, an insurer is obligated to defend its insured even if the allegations are groundless, false or fraudulent. The allegations in the underlying complaint must be liberally construed in favor of the insured.

In addition, if several theories of recovery are alleged in the underlying complaint against the insured, the insurer's duty to defend arises even if only one of several theories is within the potential coverage of the policy. When the underlying complaint against the insured alleged facts within or potentially within the scope of policy coverage, the insurer taking the position that the complaint is not covered by its policy must defend the suit under a reservation of rights or seek a declaratory judgment that there is no coverage.

In the instant case, as noted, Gainsco chose both to defend under a reservation of rights and to seek a declaratory judgment that there was no coverage. Gainsco's reservation of rights letter provided that it reserved the right to recoup any defense costs paid in the event it was determined that Gainsco did not owe Midwest a defense.

The gravamen of Midwest's argument on appeal is that Gainsco could not reserve the right to recoup defense costs because the insurance contract between the parties does not contain a provision allowing Gainsco the right to recoup defense costs. In turn, the gravamen of Gainsco's response is that there is no contract governing the relationship between the parties because both the circuit and appellate courts have held that the policies issued by Gainsco to Midwest did not apply to the underlying litigation. Accordingly, Gainsco maintains that it had no duty to defend Midwest and thus is entitled to recoup the amounts paid for Midwest's defense.

In support of its argument, Gainsco points to decisions from other jurisdictions where courts have held that an insurer may recover its defense costs if it specifically reserves the right to recoup those costs in the event it is determined that the insurer does not owe the insured a defense.

In *Buss v. Superior Court*, the court also addressed whether an insurer could recover reimbursement of defense costs from its insured. The underlying action in that case asserted 27 causes of action, of which only one claim potentially fell within policy coverage. The insurer accepted defense of the underlying action, but reserved all of its rights, including the right to deny that any cause of action was actually covered and the right to be reimbursed for defense costs in the event it was later determined that there was no coverage.

In addressing the issue, the court first noted that in a "mixed" action, involving claims that are at least potentially covered and claims that are not, an insurer nonetheless has a duty to defend the claim in its entirety. The court then stated that with regard to "mixed" claims, an insurer may not seek reimbursement for claims that are at least potentially covered, but may seek reimbursement for defense costs as to the claims that are not even potentially covered. The court explained that with regard to defense costs for claims that are potentially covered, the insured had paid premiums and the insurer had bargained to bear those costs, so that there was no right of reimbursement implied in the policy or implied in law.

The [*Buss*] court noted exceptions would exist if the policy itself provided for reimbursement or if there was a separate contract supported by separate consideration. However, with regard to claims that are not even potentially covered, the insured had not paid premiums to the insurer and the insurer did not bargain to bear those costs. Consequently, the court reasoned that the insurer has a right to reimbursement implied in law as quasi-contractual. Under the law of restitution, the insured has been "enriched" through the insurer's bearing of unbargained-for defense costs, an enrichment that must be deemed unjust.

Finally, Gainsco notes that other jurisdictions also have found that an insurer may recover defense costs from its insured where the insurer agrees to provide the insured a defense pursuant to an express reservation of rights, including the right to recoup defense costs, the insured accepts the defense, and a court subsequently finds that the insurer did not owe the insured a defense. [Citations omitted.] In general then, the decisions finding that an insurer is entitled to reimbursement of defense costs are based upon a finding that there was a contract implied in fact or law, or a finding that the insured was unjustly enriched when its insurer paid defense costs for claims that were not covered by the insured's policy. Although such reasoning was not the basis for the appellate court's decision in this case, Gainsco notes that this court may affirm the appellate court on any basis, and urges this court to adopt the reasoning of the courts in the preceding cases.

Upon review, we find the analysis of those decisions refusing to allow reimbursement to be more persuasive and more on point with Illinois case law than the cases cited by Gainsco. For example, in *Shoshone First Bank v. Pacific Employers Insurance Co.* (Wy. 2000) ... [the] court rejected the insurer's claim that it had the right to allocate defense costs for uncovered claims because its reservation of rights letter had specifically reserved the right to allocate the fees, expenses and indemnity payments when the case was resolved. The court stated:

> The insurer is not permitted to unilaterally modify and change policy coverage. We agree with the Supreme Court of Hawaii that a reservation of rights letter "does not relieve the insurer of the costs incurred in defending its insured where the insurer was obligated, in the first instance, to provide such a defense." *First Insurance Co. of Hawaii, Inc. v. State, by Minami* (Haw. 1983). [The insurer] could have included allocation language in the Policy, but it failed to do so. We look only to the four corners of the policy to determine coverage, and where the policy is unambiguous, extrinsic evidence is not considered. [Citation.] The Policy issued to Shoshone by [the insurer] states a duty to defend, and allocation is not mentioned. In light of the failure of the policy language to provide for allocation, we will not permit the contract to be amended or altered by a reservation of rights letter."

> A reservation of rights letter does not create a contract allowing an insurer to recoup defense costs from its insureds.

> [T]o allow the insurer to force the insured into choosing between seeking a defense under the policy, and run the potential risk of having to pay for this defense if it is subsequently determined that no duty to defend existed, or giving up all meritorious claims that a duty to defend exists, places the insured in the position of making a Hobson's choice. Furthermore, endorsing such conduct is tantamount to allowing the insurer to extract a unilateral amendment to the insurance contract. If this became common practice, the insurance industry might extract coercive arrangements from their insureds, destroying the concept of liability and litigation insurance.

We agree with the analysis of the court in *Shoshone First Bank.* As a matter of public policy, we cannot condone an arrangement where an insurer can unilaterally modify its contract, through a reservation of rights, to allow for reimbursement of defense costs in the event a court later finds that the insurer owes no duty to defend. We recognize that courts have found an implied agreement where the insured accepts the insurer's payment of defense costs despite the insurer's reservation of a right to reimbursement of defense costs. However, recognizing such an implied agreement effectively places the insured in the position of making a Hobson's choice between accepting the insurer's additional conditions on its defense or losing its right to a defense from the insurer.

The United States Court of Appeals for the Third Circuit, applying Pennsylvania law, also has ruled that an insurer cannot recover defense costs even when it defends under a reservation of rights to recover defense costs if it is later determined there is no coverage. *Terra Nova Insurance Co. v. 900 Bar, Inc.*, 887 F.2d 1213 (3d Cir. 1989). The court reasoned that:

A rule permitting such recovery would be inconsistent with the legal principles that induce an insurer's offer to defend under reservation of rights. Faced with uncertainty as to its duty to indemnify, an insurer offers a defense under reservation of rights to avoid the risks that an inept or lackadaisical defense of the underlying action may expose it to if it turns out there is a duty to indemnify [footnote omitted]. At the same time, the insurer wishes to preserve its right to contest the duty to indemnify if the defense is unsuccessful. Thus, such an offer is made at least as much for the insurer's own benefit as for the insured's. If the insurer could recover defense costs, the insured would be required to pay for the insurer's action in protecting itself against the estoppel to deny coverage that would be implied if it undertook the defense without reservation.

Again, we find the reasoning of the *Terra Nova* court to be more persuasive than the authorities cited by Gainsco. We agree that when an insurer tenders a defense or pays defense costs pursuant to a reservation of rights, the insurer is protecting itself at least as much as it is protecting its insured. Thus, we cannot say that an insured is unjustly enriched when its insurer tenders a defense in order to protect its own interests, even if it is later determined that the insurer did not owe a defense.

Certainly, if an insurer wishes to retain its right to seek reimbursement of defense costs in the event it later is determined that the underlying claim is not covered by the policy, the insurer is free to include such a term in its insurance contract. Absent such a provision in the policy, however, an insurer cannot later attempt to amend the policy by including the right to reimbursement in its reservation of rights letter.

Moreover, as the Supreme Court of Hawaii recognized, "affording an insured a defense under a reservation of rights agreement merely retains any defenses the insurer has under its policy; it does not relieve the insurer of the costs incurred in defending its insured where the insurer was obligated, in the first instance, to provide such a defense." *First Insurance Co. of Hawaii, Inc. v. State of Hawaii*, 66 Haw. 413, 422, 665 P.2d 648, 654 (1983), Gainsco's reservation of rights letter could retain only those defenses that Gainsco had under its policy. Gainsco concedes that the insurance policies at issue did not provide for reimbursement of defense costs. Consequently, Gainsco's attempt to expand its reservation of rights to include the right to reimbursement must fail.

[W]e note that Gainsco's reservation of rights letter reveals some uncertainty concerning coverage. With regard to allegations in the underlying claim that Midwest was liable to the plaintiffs for various acts of intentional and/or willful conduct, Gainsco's reservation of rights letter stated that "the claim *may not be* covered under the Policy." (Emphasis added.) Given this uncertainty, Gainsco correctly agreed to pay Midwest's defense costs in the underlying action and sought a declaratory judgment that it did not owe Midwest a defense. Gainsco thus remained obligated to defend Midwest as long as any questions remained concerning whether the underlying claims were covered by the policies.

Because Gainsco's obligation to defend continued until the trial court found that Gainsco did not owe Midwest a defense, Gainsco is not entitled to reimbursement of defense costs paid pending the trial court's order in the declaratory judgment action. The fact that the trial court ultimately found that the underlying claims against Midwest were not covered by the Gainsco policies does not entitle Gainsco to reimbursement of its defense costs.

In sum, we acknowledge that a majority of jurisdictions have held that an insurer is entitled to reimbursement of defense costs when (1) the insurer did not have a duty to defend, (2) the insurer timely and expressly reserved its right to recoup defense costs, and (3) the insured either remains silent in the face of the reservation of rights or accepts the insurer's payment of defense costs. We choose, however, to follow the minority rule and refuse to permit an insurer to recover defense costs pursuant to a reservation of rights absent an express provision to that effect in the insurance contract between the parties.

## *Notes and Questions*

1. It is not all that clear which approach to recoupment enjoys majority rule status. If one looks at all cases, the pro-recoupment *Buss* approach holds sway but if one looks only at state supreme courts, the anti-*Buss* approach of *Shoshone First Bank* (Wyo. 2000), *General Agents Ins. v. Midwest Sporting Goods* (Ill. 2005), and *Am. & Foreign Ins. Co. v. Jerry's Sport Ctr., Inc.*, 2 A.3d 526, 546 (Pa. 2010), is the majority.

California has reiterated its support of the *Buss* approach. *See Scottsdale Ins. Co. v. MV Transportation*, 115 P.3d 460, 471 (Cal. 2005). Notwithstanding that California is often a trend-setter as well as the largest state, the *Buss* decision has received a mixed response in other states. At the state supreme court level, only Montana has expressly embraced California's approach in permitting recoupment of fees for defense of claims ultimately deemed beyond any potential for coverage. *See Travelers Cas. & Sur. Co. v. Ribi Immunochem Research*, 108 P.3d 469, 480 (Mont. 2005). Rejecting *Buss* and its theory underlying recoupment are nearly a fifth of state supreme courts (Alabama, Alaska, Arkansas, Hawaii, Idaho, Illinois, Pennsylvania, Texas, and Wyoming). *See, e.g., Am. & Foreign Ins. Co. v. Jerry's Sport Ctr., Inc.*, 2 A.3d 526, 546 (Pa. 2010); *Excess Underwriters at Lloyd's v. Frank's Casing Crew & Rental Tools, Inc.*, 246 S.W.3d 42, 43 (Tex. 2008).

Colorado and a few other states (e.g., Massachusetts) could be viewed as modified *Buss* or *Buss*-light states while some have no instructive authority. A number of other states appear receptive to *Buss* at lower court or federal court levels but lack definitive state supreme court decisions as yet (e.g., Connecticut, Florida, Kentucky, Michigan, Nevada, New Jersey, New Mexico, New York, Ohio, Oklahoma, Tennessee, and Virginia) while some appear to be trending anti-*Buss* (e.g., Iowa, Maryland, Minnesota, Mississippi, Missouri, and Utah). For a sustained look at recoupment and the issue of insurer rights to obtain reimbursement of defense costs, *see* MANILOFF & STEMPEL, *supra*, Ch. 7 (2011).

2. Regardless of the scorecard concerning cases in insurer recoupment of fees, the question remains: Is it a good idea? Professor Robert Jerry, co-author of a well-respected insurance law textbook for students (ROBERT H. JERRY, II & DOUGLAS R. RICHMOND, UNDERSTANDING INSURANCE LAW (6th ed. 2018)), has endorsed the concept. *See* Robert H. Jerry, II, *The Insurer's Right to Reimbursement of Defense Costs*, 42 ARIZ. L. REV. 13 (2000). Although Dean Jerry's analysis on any insurance topic is always worthy of consideration, many other law professors (us included) are not nearly as enthusiastic about insurer recoupment actions. Particularly troubling is that the standard liability insurance policy promises to defend "suits" against the policyholder (not merely potentially covered "claims") and contains no specific language authorizing reimbursement of defense costs for uncovered claims.

Although insurers have taken the position that they can create contracts to this effect by specifying so in a reservation of rights letter sent to the policyholder after tender of the defense of the lawsuit, our view is that this does not create a separate contract allowing recoupment. After the claim has been made and the policyholder seeks a defense from the insurer pursuant to the policy for which premiums were previously paid, the policyholder is metaphorically over a barrel and likely to accept a defense even if it ostensibly comes with strings attached in the form of the insurer's purported right to recoupment. This can hardly be called freedom of contract.

Where recoupment has been permitted, this has been either on equitable grounds or because the insurer expressed a reserved right to recoupment when it agreed to defend the claim. This is a bit like a surgeon bargaining with a patient who is already anesthetized and is on the operating table. After a policy is sold, premiums collected, and a claim arises, the policyholder as a practical matter needs a defense. The policyholder should not be expected to refuse a defense in which the insurer is adding a recoupment reservation that was not expressly in the policy. Arguably, as the Illinois Supreme Court observed, this is changing the rules in the middle of the game. Where the focus is, as it should be, on the policy as issued and on the relative purpose and function of liability insurance (a/k/a "litigation insurance"), the better view appears to be one that restricts the insurer's ability to seek reimbursement for defense costs expended on a matter under the language and operation of the typical standard general liability policy.

Dean Jerry and others disagree on this point and by now can also argue that sophisticated policyholders purchasing liability insurance now have constructive notice that their liability carriers may seek recoupment of defense expenditures that can be isolated to claims in a suit that are clearly beyond the scope of policy coverage. It's a better argument in 2011 than it was in 1997 when *Buss* was decided (although there was *Buss*-like precedent prior to *Buss* in the lower courts). But recoupment does give insurers leverage over policyholders by virtue of judicial activism and concepts of equity rather than by express terms of a contract agreement. Ordinarily, insurers are seen as the litigants arguing for strict enforcement of contract terms and dismissing appeals to equity (often made by policyholders) as improper.

3. The American Law Institute's *Restatement of the Law, Liability Insurance* ("RLLI") provides

> Unless otherwise stated in the insurance policy or otherwise agreed to by the insured, an insurer may not seek recoupment of defense costs from the insured, even when it is subsequently determined that the insurer did not have a duty to defend or pay defense costs.

*See* RLLI § 21. The Comments and Reporters Notes to the RLLI defend this position not only because is seen as the emerging view but upon a substantive rationale akin to that expressed in *General Agents* and Note (2) above. To that we add that it just seems unfair for an insurer to promise to defend potentially covered "suits" in the policy and then pull the proverbial "switcheroo" on policyholders via a reservation of rights letter by attempting to coerce the policyholder into accepting possible recoupment of claims-linked defense costs as a condition of receiving a defense.

As might be expected during debate over the RLLI, many insurers opposed § 21 and would have preferred that the ALI embrace *Buss v. Superior Court.* Critics of § 21 and the RLLI generally received a bit of a boost in *Catlin Specialty Insurance Co. v. CBL & Associates Properties*, 2018 Del Super. LEXIS 342 (Del. Superior Ct., Aug. 9, 2018) (applying Tennessee law).

The *Catlin* court declined to follow the RLLI approach and permitted a liability insurer to seek refund of defense costs. CBL, an operator of shopping centers, was sued by a tenant salon for a decade of electricity overcharges and, in what was either ignorant stupidity or stealthy brilliance by the salon's counsel, appears to have alleged that the overcharges resulted only from a fraudulent scheme by CBL with no alternative allegations of negligence. *See Catlin Specialty Insurance Co. v. CGL & Associates Properties*, 2017 Del Super. LEXIS 471 (Del. Superior Court June 20, 2017) (also choosing Tennessee law advocated by Catlin rather than Florida law (the situs of the shopping center at issue) as advocated by CBL out of a Delaware choice of law preference for the home state of the policyholder in such conflicts).

The insurer defended under a reservation of rights that included—you guessed it—language giving the insurer the right to seek recoupment if it should prevail in a declaratory judgment action seeking a finding of no potential for coverage. Quoting an earlier decision in the litigation,

> The Court found in Catlin's favor on the duty to defend—"Because the only reasonable interpretation of the allegations in the Underlying Action sound in intentional conduct and the Policy does not cover such acts," [therefore,] Catlin had no duty to defend CGL Defendants.

2018 Del Super. LEXIS 342 at *3.

Having won the declaratory judgment action, Catlin sought repayment of its defense expenditures. The court agreed and, in doing so, considered RLLI § 21 but declined to follow it. The court, having chosen Tennessee as the state of applicable law, was also influenced by a 2007 federal court case in Tennessee, even though federal trial court opinions are not binding precedent in state courts. Like the Tennessee federal court, the Delaware state trial court was persuaded that the majority rule was one permitting recoupment and also noted that this would be consistent with Tennessee law on unjust enrichment. According to the *Catlin* court: "Restatements are mere persuasive authority—until adopted by a court; they never, by mere issuance, override controlling case law." 2018 Del. Super. LEXIS 342 at *8.

The *Catlin* court is of course correct that Restatements are only "soft law" that distills the "hard" law of judicial precedent and is not controlling. But we disagree with the implicit view in *Catlin* that a federal trial court opinion can count as "controlling" case law. This view does not follow the rules of the division of federal and state judicial authority. We also are supporters of RLLI § 21 and thus have concerns that it is substantively wrong to permit recoupment where there is a potentially covered claim. But *Catlin* was the type of case that is particularly favorable to the insurer in that it involved what appears to be a completely uncovered fraud claim.

*Catlin* involves a form of recoupment far different than cases like *Buss* and *General Agents*. In the type of recoupment case that has driven the debate, the complaint against the policyholder alleges one or more potentially covered claims as well as one or more that is not. Consequently, in cases like *Buss* and *General Agents*, the insurer was obligated to defend the "suit" against the policyholder. The question then became whether the insurer could get back some of the money it spent on parts of the suit that did not involve potentially covered claims.

By contrast, *Catlin* was a case in which there was never a potential for coverage for the "suit" against CBL because the complaint alleged only intentional fraud that was not possibly subject to coverage as determined by the four corners/eight corners face-of-the-complaint test. *Catlin* is therefore a quite different case than the others that have animated the interstate division over recoupment. In *Catlin*, the insurer could—if it were willing to take the risk of being held in breach of the duty to defend—have refused to defend and been vindicated. That is quite a different case than one where there is a clear potential for coverage for at least part of the lawsuit against the policyholder. Consequently, *Catlin* is not really a rejection of the rationale of RLLI § 21 so much as it is a declination to apply § 21 to a particularly extreme case.

### [4] *The Role of Insurer-Appointed Defense Counsel and the Relative Rights of Insurer and Policyholder*

In the triangular or tripartite relationship between the policyholder facing a claim, the counsel selected by the defending insurer, and the liability insurer, the question has arisen as to the exact nature of counsel's relationship to the other parties. Without doubt, the defending attorney and the policyholder/defendant have an attorney-client relationship and the attorney is subject to the full range of requirements provided by the law of lawyer professional responsibility. There is debate, however, over whether the insurer controlling the relationship is also a "client."

Analytically, we favor the "one-client" model that treats the lawyer's only client as the insured defendant facing a claim and characterizes the insurer as a third-party payor, albeit one with significant contract rights. Under this model, the attorney-client relationship is only between the lawyer and the policyholder, not between the lawyer and the insurer. This is true even though the liability insurer, under the terms of most standard policies, selects counsel for the policyholder and pays counsel for the policyholder. *See State Farm Mut. Auto. Ins. Co. v. Traver*, 980 S.W.2d 625 (Tex. 1998).

Under this approach, if the insurer-selected attorney commits malpractice, the policyholder's recourse is a malpractice suit against the lawyer and not a malpractice suit against the insurer. *See also Lifestar Response of Ala., Inc. v. Admiral Ins. Co.*, 17 So. 3d 200 (Ala. 2009) (insurer not vicariously liable for attorney's alleged negligence and wrongdoing as insurer, although controlling defense and settlement of the claim, did not control the attorney's exercise of professional judgment). However, the insurer may in some cases be legally liable due to negligence or recklessness in selecting counsel. For example, Acme Insurance knows that Larry Lawyer is incompetent or unethical but hires him anyway for the defense of Peggy Policyholder, Acme can be charged with breaching its contract duties to Policyholder and bad faith as well.

A majority of states appear, however, to have adopted a "two-client" model in which the insurer is also a client of the attorney defending the claim against the policyholder. *See* Johnny Parker, *The Expansion of Defense Counsel Liability to Include Malpractice Claims by Insurance Companies: How the West Was Won*, 46 TORT TRIAL & INS. PRAC. L.J. 33, 38 n. 27 (2010) (listing Alabama, Alaska, California, Hawaii, Illinois, Indiana, Massachusetts, Minnesota, Mississippi, Nevada, New Jersey, North Carolina, Pennsylvania, Utah, Vermont, and Washington as two-client model states). *See also* Douglas R. Richmond, *A Professional Responsibility Perspective on Independent Counsel in Insurance*, INS. LITIG. RPTR., Vol. 33, No. 1 (Feb. 2, 2011); James M. Fischer, *The Professional Obligations of* Cumis *Counsel Retained for the Policyholder but Not Subject to Insurer Control*, 43 TORT TRIAL & INS. PRAC. L.J. 173 (2008).

However, Professor Parker's scorecard, although helpful, must like many attempts to categorize the states, be viewed with caution. Of the 16 states he lists with precedent embracing the two-client model, only seven of these jurisdictions have state supreme court precedent on this issue. Frequently, lower state court and federal court attempts to predict the rulings of the state supreme court regarding insurance matters prove inaccurate. Consequently, care is required before a state can be said to have adopted a given model or rule. *See generally* MANILOFF & STEMPEL (conducting 50-state surveys on 20 important issues on which states have divided, but tending to avoid rigid categorization, particularly where the state supreme court has not spoken).

Nonetheless, despite the perils of categorizing our misgivings about it, the two-client model appears to have more support in the case law. Under this arrangement, if the defending attorney errs in some significant way in conducting the defense producing a detrimental result for the insurer, the insurer may have a claim against the policyholder's appointed attorney. *See Paradigm Ins. Co. v. Langerman Law Offices, P.A.*, 200 Ariz. 146, 24 P.3d 593 (2001) (insurer may make claim against counsel for failing to realize that other insurance was available to pay prior to the appointing insurer's policy). However, it is not at all clear that the insurer would not be able to make such claims under a theory of breach of contract (the agreement that the lawyer as a vendor would provide adequate services defending the case) rather than as a matter of attorney-client privilege.

The distinction between the one-client and two-client models may be (dare we say it) largely academic in that all two-client model states also make it clear that in the event of a conflict, the attorney's primary duty is to the insured defendant rather than to the insurer. *See* Parker, *How the West Was Won*, *supra*. *See, e.g., Paradigm v. Langerman*, *supra* (referring to policyholder as primary client and insurer as secondary client); *Nev. Yellow Cab Corp. v. Eighth Judicial Dist. Court of Nev.*, 152 P.3d 737, 739 (Nev. 2007) (in case of conflict, attorney's loyalty must be to policyholder defendant as main client); *Spratley v. State Farm Mut. Auto. Ins. Co.*, 78 P.3d 603, 607 (Utah 2003) (same); *Pine Island Farmers Coop v. Erstad & Riemer, P.A.*, 649 N.W.2d 444, 451 (Minn. 2002) (same). These cases and other two-client model state cases also permit the insurer to pursue claims of professional negligence against the insurer-appointed defense counsel. Summarizing the case law, Professor Parker observed:

> In the insurance context, the dual representation doctrine provides that where the interests of the insurer and insured coincide, both may be considered clients of the defense counsel retained to represent the insured. The doctrine provides for a conditional or qualified extension of the attorney-client relationship to include both parties except where a conflict between the interest of the insurer and that of the insured exists. If a conflict exists, the insured is the sole client of defense counsel.

*See* Parker, *How the West Was Won*, *supra*, at 39.

So, does it matter which approach a state may take when it appears that all states get to the same place in the end? Perhaps. In addition to the issue of potential insurer claims for attorney professional negligence (on either a lawyer malpractice or breach of contract theory), there is the issue of counsel's conduct when faced with a potential conflict situation.

### PROBLEM FIVE

Plaintiff StartCo sues defendant Acme Corporation, alleging that Acme engaged in unfair trade practices impeding StartCo's ability to enter the relevant market, resulting in StartCo's bankruptcy. The complaint is open-ended about whether these alleged unfair practices were intentionally designed to thwart StartCo or were merely the consequence of Acme's ordinary (but allegedly improper) business practices. Acme tenders the claims to its insurer, Stoneheart, which in turn, retains Stewart Stainless (of the blue chip firm Stainless, Sterling & Gold).

Stainless is diligently preparing to answer the complaint and defend the litigation when an officer from Acme states:

> This was no accident. We knew StartCo could be a threat to our bottom line and made sure that they would have trouble getting apartment permits

from our friends in county government or merchandise from necessary vendors, since we could put the squeeze on those vendors as well. In addition, we arranged for StartCo facilities to receive some annoyingly frequent visits from local "vandals." And we sure spread the word about how crappy their merchandise was supposed to be.

Pursuant to ordinary case monitoring protocol, Stainless is to write a regular report to Stoneheart regarding what he has learned and the status of the case.

- What should Stainless do?

- What should the Report say?

- What, if any questions, can Stainless answer if posed questions by the Stoneheart adjuster on the case?

- What are the insurance coverage implications of Stainless's conduct?

- Should Stainless report the conversation to anyone at Acme? Who? In what manner?

- Do the answers to any of these questions change depending on whether Stainless is operating in a state where:

- Only the policyholder is his client?

- Both the insurer and the policyholder are clients, but the attorney's primary loyalty is to the policyholder in case of conflict of interest between policyholder and insurer?

- Is the likely result different regarding attorney participation and insurance coverage depending on whether the relevant jurisdiction follows the one-client or two-client model of the policyholder-counsel-insurer relationship?

## [5] *Policyholder Rights to Select Counsel*

In the typical liability insurance situation, a plaintiff sues the policyholder alleging negligent infliction of injury. The policyholder then tenders the claim to the insurer, which examines the allegations of the complaint and agrees to provide a defense if the complaint creates a potential for coverage. Pursuant to the terms of the standard general liability policy, the insurer selects counsel to defend the policyholder from the insurer's list of approved lawyers and law firms (typically termed "panel counsel"). This permits the insurer to quickly select defense counsel in which it has confidence based on the insurer's prior approval of these firms based on investigation and experience.

In addition, insurers are famous (or infamous depending on who you ask) for driving a hard bargain with panel counsel, keeping lawyer hourly rates and overall legal fees relatively low in relation to litigation costs generally. In return for agreeing to lower legal fees, panel counsel are relatively assured of a steady stream of work from solvent clients (collecting billed fees can become an issue with clients, even commercial clients, facing cash flow problems or bankruptcy).

The linkage of insurers as institutional "clients" of the law firm or at least purchasers of legal services in bulk (depending on whether the state in question follows a one-client or two-client model of the tripartite relationship) creates some occasional friction as insurers, in addition to negotiating low hourly rates, may also be aggressive in reviewing counsel's bills or may impose upon selected counsel guidelines or rules for defending claims (an area explored at greater length below). Despite this recurrent tension, many policyholders and their regular counsel have concerns that insurer panel counsel will be unduly loyal to insurers and insufficiently devoted to policyholder defendants.

Against this backdrop, the issue arises as to whether the policyholder defendant must accept the panel counsel selected by the insurer to defend a claim. The short but perhaps unsatisfying answer is the classic law school response of "it depends." In general, if there are no questions as to panel competence and the interests of insurer and policyholder align, the policyholder lacks any legal right to refuse the insurer's choice of counsel and/or to interfere with the insurer's prerogative to defend or settle the case as it sees fit.

There are, of course, exceptions. Regarding competence, for example, a policyholder can rightfully insist on new counsel to defend a complex professional liability or intellectual property claim if the insurer has chosen inexperienced counsel better equipped for slip-and-fall claims or fender-bender automobile lawsuits.

Regarding settlement and control of the case, the policyholder may be able to insist that the insurer fulfill its "duty to settle" (discussed at greater length below and in Chapter 9) where there is a significant risk of a judgment against the policyholder in excess of the policy limits. In addition, particular insurance policies may give policyholders a role in the resolution of cases. For example, some liability policies sold to professionals require the insured's consent to settlement so that a doctor or lawyer can object to settlement of a malpractice claim viewed as weak. The doctor's or lawyer's concern is that payment for a weak claim or overpayment on a legitimate claim will harm the professional's reputation or encourage further lawsuits.

In addition, even in the absence of a legal right to countermand the insurer's choice of counsel, a policyholder may be able to reach a voluntary agreement with the insurer to use counsel of the policyholder's choice, particularly where the policyholder's preferred attorney has special expertise, familiarity with the situation, and is willing to work for the rates agreed to by panel counsel (or the policyholder is willing to make up the difference for preferred counsel's higher rate).

The major exception to the general rule of insurer selection of counsel takes place if there is a conflict of interest between policyholder and insurer. In the typical case, as discussed above, the interests of insurer and policyholder are aligned. For example, in a slip-and-fall premise liability case, both the insurer and the policyholder share the same interest in vetting the plaintiff's claim (e.g., screening for fraudulent claims) and paying as little as possible to resolve legitimate claims so long as refusal to make a reasonable settlement does not foment needless litigation expense or the risk of an excess verdict.

Regarding litigation, the insurer is essentially a litigation factory, defending claims throughout a wide area. It is relatively indifferent to the tension and cost of litigation, a business expense it amortizes. By contrast, policyholders, particularly individuals, may dislike the inconvenience and anxiety produced by litigation. For the most part, however, the law is indifferent to this concern, so long as the insurer adequately defends claims and protects the policyholder from the risk of an excess judgment. For insurers, litigation is potentially a necessary part of its business model in order to avoid paying settlements it regards as too generous to claimants.

But where there is a misalignment of insurer and policyholder interests, particularly where counsel's defense may have an impact on coverage, the policyholder is ordinarily permitted to select its own defense counsel, with state law varying on the responsibility for compensation at any level higher than comparable panel counsel rates. *See* Maniloff & Stempel, Ch. 6.

What separates the various states from one another, however, is the degree of conflict required. In some states (e.g., Arkansas, Louisiana, Maryland, Massachusetts, Mississippi, Missouri, Montana, New Jersey, and New York) a mere reservation of rights by the insurer appears to be sufficient to create the requisite conflict requiring independent counsel while in other states (e.g., Alaska, California, Delaware, Georgia, Kansas, Oklahoma, Pennsylvania, Rhode Island, and Texas), there must be an actual conflict in which counsel's actions may help the insurer in a coverage dispute at the expense of the policyholder defendant (and client) the lawyer is professionally required to protect. In other states (e.g., Alabama and Washington), insurer-selected defense counsel is under a "heightened" duty of good faith to the policyholder but is not required to withdraw or cede to policyholder-selected counsel unless a concrete conflict develops. *See generally* Maniloff & Stempel, *supra*, Ch. 6.

What type of conflicts are sufficient in the states that do not treat a reservation of rights alone as triging policyholder's prerogative to select counsel? As illustrated in one treatise:

> The classic example of an asserted conflict of interest, giving rise to a demand by an insured for independent counsel, is a suit alleging that the insured's liability is based on intentional or negligent conduct (or some other alternative causes of action where one is covered and one is not):
>
> > Under a typical liability insurance policy coverage is available for negligent acts but not for intentional acts. The insurer therefore would benefit from either a defense verdict or a finding of intentional wrongdoing. The insured, on the other hand, would benefit from either a defense verdict or a finding of negligence. Absent informed consent of both the insurer and the insured, an attorney trying to represent both the insured and the insurer would face an insurmountable conflict of interest. [Quoting *Arm-*

*strong Cleaners, Inc. v. Erie Ins. Exch.*, 364 F. Supp. 2d 797, 806 (S.D. Ind. 2005).]

In this situation, an insured may fear that its counsel, wanting to please the insurer, in hopes of continuing to benefit from its status as panel counsel, will handle the case in such a way that any damage award is based on intentional rather than negligent, conduct.

Another possible conflict of interest arises if "the insurer knows it can later assert non-coverage, it … may offer only a token defense of its insured. If the insurer does not think that the loss on which it is defending will be covered under the policy, it may not be motivated to achieve the lowest possible settlement or in other ways treat the interests of the insured as its own." [Quoting *Continental Ins. Co. v. Bayless & Roberts*, 608 P.2d 281, 289–90 (Alaska 1980); *see also CHI of Alaska v. Employers Reinsurance Corp.*, 844 P.2d 1113, 1118 (Alaska 1993).]

*See* Maniloff & Stempel, *supra*, at 219–20.

California law in this regard is particularly well-developed, largely formed in the well-known case *San Diego Fed. Credit Union v. Cumis Ins. Society, Inc.*, 208 Cal. Rptr. 494 (Cal. Ct. App. 1984), which continues to have enough importance that policyholder-selected independent counsel are to this day commonly referred to as "*Cumis* counsel." However, a subsequently enacted statute, Cal. Civ. Code Ann. § 2860, which largely codifying the *Cumis* case holding, differs in some degree from the case and sets forth currently applicable state law.

In general, the California approach (and that of the seeming majority of jurisdictions) provides for independent counsel when there is both a conflict of interest and the potential that the outcome of a looming coverage dispute (e.g., the question of whether injury to the claimant was intentional or accidental) could be controlled by counsel's conduct of the defense.

In addition, the statute helpfully provides minimum competence/experience requirements for defense counsel and that the rates to be paid to independent counsel are limited to what would otherwise have been paid to panel counsel. This provision makes it less attractive for insurers to fight a policyholder's request for independent counsel and it appears from conversations with policyholders and insurer representatives that carriers are quite accommodating to these requests from California policyholders. *See also* Douglas R. Richmond, *A Professional Responsibility Perspective on Independent Counsel in Insurance*, Ins. Litg. Rptr., Vol. 33, No. 1, at 5, 11 (Feb. 2, 2011) (suggesting that insurers include a *Cumis* endorsement to policies specifying payment of insurers' regular rates for such work, criteria for selection, and that counsel must provide insurer with information).

But is paying independent counsel only up to the rates the insurer would otherwise pay panel counsel—and having the policyholder responsible for any additional charges—fair to the policyholder? Massachusetts implicitly answers in the negative and has refused to adopt a per se rule of limiting payment of independent counsel to panel counsel rates. *See, e.g., Northern Sec. Ins. Co. v. R.H. Realty Trust*, 941 N.E.2d 688 (Mass. App. Ct. 2011) (approving reimbursement rate of $225 to policyholder who funded independent counsel rather than $150 panel counsel rate sought by insurer). The Massachusetts rule is that when an insurer seeks to defend under a reservation of rights, the policyholder may refuse and the insurer is then required to "pay the reasonable charges of the insured's retained counsel." *Id.* at 691, citing *Herbert A. Sullivan, Inc. v. Utica Mut. Ins. Co.*, 788 N.E.2d 522 (Mass. 2003), and *Magoun v. Liberty Mut. Ins. Co.*, 195 N.E.2d 514 (Mass. 1964). The rationale for avoiding strict linkage with panel counsel rates is that:

> The insured was entitled to have a reasonable fee paid, based on market rather than panel rates. Panel rates, the judge correctly observed, often reflect, first, what Northern Security was able to bargain for as a large insurance company handling various cases involving many attorneys, who presumably wish to continue receiving referrals; and second, the justifiable interest of a company such as Northern Security to keep its legal costs down, especially in routine cases, which may be at odds with an insured's desire to pay more for legal representation in the hope of minimizing legal exposures.

941 N.E.2d at 692 (also expressly noting that independent counsel worked for substantially less than his usual $375/hour rate as a favor to the insured).

The *R.H. Realty Trust* case can also be read as implicitly suggesting that complexity of the case appeared beyond that of routine cases for which panel counsel are paid lower rates. Although the issue is seldom expressly addressed in the cases, policyholders could buttress this argument by noting that while insurers typically pay comparatively low rates to panel counsel defending policyholders in routine tort litigation, these same insurers commonly pay dramatically higher rates to lawyers the insurers retain in coverage litigation in which the insurer is attempting to avoid paying a claim. A layperson might argue that what is sauce for the good should be sauce for the gander.

Further, although insurers in Massachusetts and similar states may not have the protection of a ceiling on rates at panel counsel level, the insurer often has the option of withdrawing its reservation of rights (which deprives the policyholder of the right to independent counsel absent an actual conflict of interest) and using panel counsel. Although this precludes a later defense to paying any resulting judgment or settlement, it may be a prudent option in cases where the legal fees will be substantial (whatever the hourly rate) in absolute terms or relative to the stakes of the case and the insurer's indemnity coverage defense has a low probability of success.

## [6] Issues of Insurer Control over Counsel

The previous section might give the reader the impression that insurer-selected defense counsel are something like the keystone cops and that their work is frequently subject to suits claiming malpractice or its contract breach equivalent. That would be the wrong impression. Insurance defense lawyers, like most attorneys, are highly competent. To be sure, some cases go better than others. But malpractice or its equivalent is comparatively rare. Similarly, most lawyers by training and orientation seek to represent the policyholder using the attorney's best judgment.

In recent years, as new forms of legal services delivery and new efforts at insurer cost control have emerged, concern has arisen as to whether these market-driven initiatives intrude too greatly on the professional responsibility of the insurance defense attorney. Among these are in-house counsel or "staff counsel." Another vehicle for the delivery of legal services is the "captive" law firm, a group of lawyers holding themselves out as a law firm but in fact working exclusively for one insurer, either as exclusive independent contractors or employees. Both forms of legal services delivery have met with some criticism questioning whether attorneys in this position can give policyholder's the full loyalty to which they are entitled. The concern is that lawyers in these organizations are not sufficiently independent of the insurer and therefore can not fully serve the policyholder client. *See* ABA MODEL RULE OF PROFESSIONAL RESPONSIBILITY 1.7 (attorney should not accept employment where his performance for the client may be "materially limited" by his responsibilities owed to others).

The argument is that there is an inevitable trade-off between defending claims well and saving the insurer money. For the most part, courts have permitted staff counsel and captive law firms, so long as there is sufficient disclosure to the policyholder of the nature of the appointed attorney's business arrangement. *See Cincinnati Ins. Co. v. Wills*, 717 N.E.2d 151 (Ind. 1999). However, Kentucky and North Carolina have forbidden use of staff counsel to defend claims against policyholders.

A related issue is whether aggressive insurer efforts to manage and control the performance of appointed counsel creates impermissible conflicts and inadequate service for the policyholder. The Montana Supreme Court, in *In re Ugrin, Alexander, Zadick & Higgins, P.C.*, 299 Mont. 321, 2 P.3d 806 (2000), strongly criticized excessive insurer management of counsel, invalidating rules of one carrier that required the adjuster's permission to conduct legal research, make motions, or take more than minimal discovery. As a result of this case and substantial customer criticism, many insurers have backed away from micro-management and sometimes eschew case management guidelines and fee auditing altogether. However, there is some evidence to indicate that many courts would accept reasonably broad and flexible insurer guidelines that do not unduly interfere with the lawyer's professional judgment.

## [7] Consequences of Breach of the Duty to Defend

### Century Surety Co. v. Andrew

Nevada Supreme Court
432 P.3d 180 (Nev. 2018) (en banc)

**Douglas, C.J.:**

An insurance policy generally contains an insurer's contractual duty to defend its insured in any lawsuits that involve claims covered under the umbrella of the insurance policy. In response to a certified question submitted by the United States District Court for the District of Nevada, we consider "[w]hether, under Nevada law, the liability of an insurer that has breached its duty to defend, but has not acted in bad faith, is capped at the policy limit plus any costs incurred by the insured in mounting a defense, or [whether] the insurer [is] liable for all losses consequential to the insurer's breach." We conclude that an insurer's liability where it breaches its contractual duty to defend is not capped at the policy limits plus the insured's defense costs, and instead, an insurer may be liable for any consequential damages caused by its breach. We further conclude that good-faith determinations are irrelevant for determining damages upon a breach of this duty.

## FACTS AND PROCEDURAL HISTORY

Respondents Ryan T. Pretner and Dana Andrew (as legal guardian of Pretner) initiated a personal injury action in state court after a truck owned and driven by Michael Vasquez struck Pretner, causing significant brain injuries. Vasquez used the truck for personal use, as well as for his mobile auto detailing business, Blue Streak Auto Detailing, LLC (Blue Streak). At the time of the accident, Vasquez was covered under a personal auto liability insurance policy issued by Progressive Casualty Insurance Company (Progressive), and Blue Streak was insured under a commercial liability policy issued by appellant Century Surety Company. The Progressive policy had a $100,000 policy limit, whereas appellant's policy had a policy limit of $1 million.

Upon receiving the accident report, appellant conducted an investigation and concluded that Vasquez was not driving in the course and scope of his employment with Blue Streak at the time of the accident, and that the accident was not covered under its insurance policy. Appellant rejected respondents' demand to settle the claim within the policy limit.

Subsequently, respondents sued Vasquez and Blue Streak in state district court, alleging that Vasquez was driving in the course and scope of his employment with Blue Streak at the time of the accident. Respondents notified appellant of the suit, but appellant refused to defend Blue Streak. Vasquez and Blue Streak defaulted in the state court action and the notice of the default was forwarded to appellant. Appellant maintained that the claim was not covered under its insurance policy.

Respondents, Vasquez and Blue Streak, entered into a settlement agreement whereby respondents agreed not to execute on any judgment against Vasquez and Blue Streak, and Blue Streak assigned its rights against appellant to respondents. In addition, Progressive agreed to tender Vasquez's $100,000 policy limit. Respondents then filed an unchallenged application for entry of default judgment in state district court. Following a hearing, the district court entered a default judgment against Vasquez and Blue Streak for $18,050,183.

The default judgment's factual findings, deemed admitted by default, stated that "Vasquez negligently injured Pretner, that Vasquez was working in the course and scope of his employment with Blue Streak at the time, and that consequently Blue Streak was also liable." As an assignee of Blue Streak, respondents filed suit in state district court against appellant for breach of contract, breach of the implied covenant of good faith and fair dealing, and unfair claims practices, and appellant removed the case to the federal district court.

The federal court found that appellant did not act in bad faith, but it did breach its duty to defend Blue Streak. Initially, the federal court concluded that appellant's liability for a breach of the duty to defend was capped at the policy limit plus any cost incurred by Blue Streak in mounting a defense because appellant did not act in bad faith. The federal court stated that it was undisputed that Blue Streak did not incur any defense cost because it defaulted in the underlying negligence suit.

However, after respondents filed a motion for reconsideration, the federal court concluded that Blue Streak was entitled to recover consequential damages that exceeded the policy limit for appellant's breach of the duty to defend, and that the default judgment was a reasonably foreseeable result of the breach of the duty to defend. Additionally, the federal court concluded that bad faith was not required to impose liability on the insurer in excess of the policy limit. Nevertheless, the federal court entered an order staying the proceedings until resolution of the aforementioned certified question by this court.

## DISCUSSION

Appellant argues that the liability of an insurer that breaches its contractual duty to defend, but has not acted in bad faith, is generally capped at the policy limits and any cost incurred in mounting a defense.[1] Conversely, respondents argue that an insurer that breaches its duty to defend should be liable for all consequential damages, which may include a judgment against the insured that is in excess of the policy limits.[2]

In Nevada, insurance policies are treated like other contracts, and thus, legal principles applicable to contracts generally are applicable to insurance policies. The general rule in a breach of contract case is that the injured party may be awarded expectancy damages, which are determined by the method set forth in the *Restatement (Second) of Contracts § 347* (Am. Law Inst. 1981). The *Restatement (Second) of Contracts § 347* provides, in pertinent part, as follows:

> [T]he injured party has a right to damages based on his expectation interest as measured by
>
> (a) the loss in the value to him of the other party's performance caused by its failure or deficiency, plus
>
> (b) *any other loss, including incidental or consequential loss, caused by the breach, less*
> (c) any cost or other loss that he has avoided by not having to perform. (Emphasis added.)

---

1. [2] The Federation of Defense & Corporate Counsel, Complex Insurance Claims Litigation Association, American Insurance Association, and Property Casualty Insurers Association of America were allowed to file amicus briefs in support of appellant.

2. [3] The Nevada Justice Association was allowed to file an amicus brief in support of respondents.

An insurance policy creates two contractual duties between the insurer and the insured: the duty to indemnify and the duty to defend. "The duty to indemnify arises when an insured becomes legally obligated to pay damages in the underlying action that gives rise to a claim under the policy." On the other hand, "An insurer bears a duty to defend its insured whenever it ascertains facts which give rise to the potential of liability under the policy."

In a case where the duty to defend does in fact arise, and the insurer breaches that duty, the insurer is at least liable for the insured's reasonable costs in mounting a defense in the underlying action. Several other states have considered an insurer's liability for a breach of its duty to defend, and while no court would disagree that the insurer is liable for the insured's defense cost, courts have taken two different views when considering whether the insurer may be liable for an entire judgment that exceeds the policy limits in the underlying action.

The majority view is that "[w]here there is no opportunity to compromise the claim and the only wrongful act of the insurer is the refusal to defend, the liability of the insurer is ordinarily limited to the amount of the policy plus attorneys' fees and costs." [The rationale of these courts is that a] "refusal to defend, in itself, can be compensated for by paying the costs incurred in the insured's defense." In sum, "[a]n [insurer] is liable to the limits of its policy plus attorney fees, expenses and other damages where it refuses to defend an insured who is in fact covered," and "[t]his is true even though the [insurer] acts in good faith and has reasonable ground[s] to believe there is no coverage under the policy."

The minority view is that damages for a breach of the duty to defend are not automatically limited to the amount of the policy; instead, the damages awarded depend on the facts of each case. The objective is to have the insurer "pay damages necessary to put the insured in the same position he would have been in had the insurance company fulfilled the insurance contract." Thus, "[a] party aggrieved by an insurer's breach of its duty to defend is entitled to recover all damages naturally flowing from the breach." Damages that may naturally flow from an insurer's breach include:

> (1) the amount of the judgment or settlement against the insured plus interest [even in excess of the policy limits]; (2) costs and attorney fees incurred by the insured in defending the suit; and (3) any additional costs that the insured can show naturally resulted from the breach.

We conclude that the minority view is the better approach. Unlike the minority view, the majority view places an artificial limit to the insurer's liability within the policy limits for a breach of its duty to defend. That limit is based on the insurer's duty to indemnify but "[a] duty to defend limited to and coextensive with the duty to indemnify would be essentially meaningless; insureds pay a premium for what is partly litigation insurance designed to protect ... the insured from the expense of defending suits brought against him." Even the *Comunale* court recognized that "[t]here is an important difference between the liability of an insurer who performs its obligations and that of an insurer who breaches its contract." [*Comunale v. Traders*

& *Gen. Ins. Co.*, 50 Cal. 2d 654, 328 P.2d 198, 201 (Cal. 1958)]. Indeed, the insurance policy limits "only the amount the insurer may have to pay in the performance of the contract as compensation to a third person for personal injuries caused by the insured; they do not restrict the damages recoverable by the insured for a breach of contract by the insurer." *Id.*

The obligation of the insurer to defend its insured is purely contractual and a refusal to defend is considered a breach of contract. Consistent with general contract principles, the minority view provides that the insured may be entitled to consequential damages resulting from the insurer's breach of its contractual duty to defend. *See* Restatement of Liability Insurance § 48 (Am. Law Inst., Proposed Final Draft No. 2, 2018). Consequential damages "should be such as may fairly and reasonably be considered as arising naturally, or were reasonably contemplated by both parties at the time they made the contract." The determination of the insurer's liability depends on the unique facts of each case and is one that is left to the jury's determination.

The right to recover consequential damages sustained as a result of an insurer's breach of the duty to defend does not require proof of bad faith. Thus, even in the absence of bad faith, the insurer may be liable for a judgment that exceeds the policy limits if the judgment is consequential to the insurer's breach. An insurer that refuses to tender a defense for "its insured takes the risk not only that it may eventually be forced to pay the insured's legal expenses but also that it may end up having to pay for a loss that it did not insure against." Accordingly, the insurer refuses to defend at its own peril.

However, we are not saying that an entire judgment is automatically a consequence of an insurer's breach of its duty to defend; rather, the insured is tasked with showing that the breach caused the excess judgment and "is obligated to take all reasonable means to protect himself and mitigate his damages." ... *Conner v. S. Nev. Paving, Inc.*, 103 Nev. 353, 355, 741 P.2d 800, 801 (1987) ("As a general rule, a party cannot recover damages for loss that he could have avoided by reasonable efforts.").

### *CONCLUSION*

In answering the certified question, we conclude that an insured may recover any damages consequential to the insurer's breach of its duty to defend. As a result, an insurer's liability for the breach of the duty to defend is not capped at the policy limits, even in the absence of bad faith.

### *Note*

A look at the trial record reveals the Nevada Supreme Court's description of the victim's brain injuries as "significant" to be an understatement. They were, in the words of the trial court, "catastrophic," and placed the victim in a diminished state requiring constant care. *See Andrew v. Century Surety Co.*, 134 F.3d 1249 (D. Nev. 2015).

The federal district court hearing the case (originally filed in state court but removed to federal court by the insurer—which routed appeal to the Ninth Circuit resulting in the certified question to the Nevada Supreme Court that was answered in excerpted opinion) calculated damages at approximately $18 million in a default judgment proceeding. The default occurred because neither the driver nor the small family business trucking company had funds sufficient to hire defense counsel. Insurer attorneys might wonder, of course, if this amount would have been reduced—or even if liability could have been avoided—had the case be vigorously defended.

This prompts the question: What on earth was the insurer thinking when it declined to defend the claim? In the federal district court proceedings, the duty to defend dispute centered on whether the insurer was bound by the pleadings (which alleged that the driver was on duty for the trucking company at the time of the collision) or whether the insurer could consider extrinsic evidence to defeat the duty to defend rather than to create it, as was the situation in *Fitzpatrick v. American Honda, supra,* the ATV case of the New York Court of Appeals.

The federal district court, applying Nevada law per *Erie R.R. v. Tompkins,* ruled that state law took a pure "four corners/eight corners" approach and that, if a duty to defend was triggered on that basis, it could not be undone by additional information, at least not by additional information negating coverage. In particular, the insurer had taken a statement of the driver in which he stated he was off work and heading home at the time of the collision.

The range of considerations permitted in determining the duty to defend can be a matter of reasonable debate. It certainly can be worth an insurer or policyholder pursuing a declaratory judgment on the question. But if this was what the insurer wanted, it should have simultaneously defended the action while pursuing declaratory relief on both the question of duty to defend (which it would have lost if the trial court was correct about application of the four corners test, which we think it was) and the duty to indemnify, which it might well have won if the driver really was off duty and not within the scope of his employment. The insurer would still likely need to provide a defense for a significant amount of time, but it could perhaps have saved not only the $20 million judgment but perhaps also its $1 million policy limits.

Or, perhaps more practically, the insurer should have simply settled the case for policy limits. Liability was clear. The victim was minding his own business riding a bicycle properly on the shoulder of the road when the truck negligently moved enough to the right so that the cyclist was clipped in the head at fairly high speed by outstretched side-view mirrors on the truck. Sure, a good defense attorney might be able to prove some negligence on the part of the victim—but more than the 50 percent comparative negligence necessary to result in a defense judgment under the law of Nevada and most other states? Sure, $1 million is a lot of money—but it is a lot less than $18 million. And this is without considering the costs of defense. Century Surety may have though it was saving this by not defending—but then it spent substantial legal fees litigating the duty to defend question and the ensuing damages-for-breach-of-duty-to-defend question.

See if you agree or disagree with our analysis after studying the "duty to settle" material below. We realize that hindsight is 20-20 but still are at a loss to understand the insurer's decisionmaking. It could have saved itself a lot of money if it had been a bit more humble about the strength of its duty to defend position. The ironic upside is that the insurer's error effectively expanded policy limits from $1 million to $20 million, providing more resources for a tragically injured victim.

## More on the Consequences of Breach of the Duty to Defend

As noted in the Nevada Supreme Court's opinion, there is a split in the courts as to whether an insurer's damages for breach of the defense duty is limited to policy limits. We are not as sure as was the court about which is the current "majority" rule. More recent cases appear to agree with the *Century Surety v. Andrew* court that policy limits no longer protect a liability insurer that has breached its duty to defend, even in the absence of bad faith accompanying the breach. Also, the American Law Institute's *Restatement of the Law, Liability Insurance* ("RLLI"), adopts a similar view, making a black-letter pronouncement that "[a]n insurer that breaches the duty to defend a legal action forfeits the right to assert any control over the defense or settlement of the action." *See* RLLI § 19.

The Comments and Reporters' Note accompanying the Section make it even clearer that a defense-breaching insurer may be held responsible for consequential damages without regard to policy limits. Lest insurers get too worried, however, it should be remembered that policyholders or their assignees must still prove damages with reasonable certainty, and consequential damages must be within the contemplation of the parties at the time of contracting. Consequently (we could not resist the pun), the core consequential damage liability for a breaching insurer will usually be the amount of a judgment in excess of policy limits. But as reflected in *Century Surety*, this can be an enormous amount if an insurer fails to defend a suit presenting a large damages exposure for the policyholder.

Another possible consequence of breach of the duty to defend is that the insurer may lose the right to contest coverage. In an earlier draft of the RLLI, the ALI endorsed this view but then later retreated, much to the chagrin of an observer who prematurely praised the ALI for moving in this direction. *See* Jeffrey W. Stempel, *Enhancing the Socially Instrumental Role of Insurance: The Opportunity and Challenge Presented by the ALI Restatement Position on Breach of the Duty to Defend*, 5 UC IRVINE L. REV. 587 (2015). As noted above, the final RLLI § 19 simply stripped non-defending insurers of settlement control and implicitly bound breaching insurers to reasonable, non-collusive settlements made by undefended policyholders, who are entitled to protect themselves from claims when their insurers do not.[3]

Although a majority of states permit the non-defending, breaching insurer to contest coverage, the scorecard is not as lopsided as commonly presumed. *See id.* at 586,

---

3. The earlier version of this RLLI Section (then § 21 in RLLI Tentative Draft No. 2, March 28, 2014) stated that the breaching insurer "loses … the right to contest coverage for the claim" and also provided that "[d]amages for breach … include the amount of any judgment entered into against the insured or the reasonable portion of a settlement entered into by or on behalf of the insured after

n. 30. Of the roughly 30 states that have relatively clear precedent on the issue, roughly 60 percent follow the traditional rule of allowing breaching insurers to nonetheless contest coverage. Among the minority rule states are Alaska, Illinois, Montana, New Jersey, New Mexico, North Carolina, Ohio, Rhode Island and Washington, a group that encompasses a good deal of the U.S. population. New York briefly adopted this approach, as well, but reconsidered and reversed itself because of the state's strong rules of stare decisis. *See K2 Investment Group, LLC v. American Guarantee & Liability Ins. Co.*, 993 N.E.2d 1249 (N.Y. 2013); *K2 Investment Group, LLC v. American Guarantee & Liability Ins. Co.*, 6 N.E.3d 1117 (N.Y. 2014). California, Texas and Wisconsin all have arguably inconsistent precedent. Had the "forfeiture of coverage for breach" advocates enjoyed slightly better luck, a clear majority of the U.S. population could be subject to the "minority" rule.

Looking at precedent in this way also raises an interesting question (at least to us; most lawyers seem not to care): what exactly do we mean by "minority" and "majority" rules? The traditional view is that the number of states is what counts. But one might be better served both in determining the strength of a legal position studying its impact by looking at the population percentage subject to a particular legal regime.

For example, one might have an approach (let's take something very nontraditional like ending absolute immunity for prosecutors) that is the law in only five states, with 45 states rejecting the non-immunity rule. But if the five states abrogating immunity are California, Texas, Illinois, Florida and New York, this would place nearly 40 percent of the American population under the non-immunity rule. If this non-traditional rule was in place in these jurisdictions for a decade without adverse consequences, it would be strong evidence that fears of adverse impact on public servants in the absence of immunity (the rationale for the traditional rule) were overstated.

Alternatively, one might determine majority and minority rules by focusing primarily on cases less than 20 years old, or some other, older temporal metric for issues that are not extensively litigated. This would capture more of the modern trend, which is generally perceived as the emerging "better" view of the law.

Perhaps the leading case on the minority view side of the ledger is *Employer's Insurance of Wausau v. Ehlco Liquidating Trust*, 708 N.E.2d 1122 (Ill. 1999). Unfortunately, the court labeled this an "estoppel" upon the insurer, which can be misleading and result in higher burdens on policyholders seeking coverage in the aftermath of a defense breach. *See* Stempel, 5 UC IRVINE L. REV. at 604–10. Other prominent minority rule cases are *Burd v. Sussex Mutual Ins. Co.*, 267 A.2d 7 (N.J. 1970), and *Farmers Union Mutual Ins. Co. v. Staples*, 90 P.3d 381 (Mont. 2004). Influential cases backing the majority rule are *Gedeon v. State Farm Mutual Auto. Ins. Co.*, 188 A.2d 320, 322 (Pa. 1963), *Timberline Equipment v. St. Paul Fire & Marine Ins. Co.*, 576 P.2d 1244 (Or. 1978), and *Capstone Building Corp. v. American Motorist Ins. Co.*, 67 A.3d 961, 999 (Conn. 2013).

---

breach, subject to the policy limits, and the reasonable defense costs incurred by or on behalf of the insured" in addition to the amount of any excess judgment or other provable consequential damages. We remain disappointed that the ALI did not stay with this formulation of the section.

### [8] The "Duty to Settle" and Policyholder Prerogatives Regarding Settlement

The duty to defend potentially covered claims also carries with it the duty to settle the claim if the policyholder's liability has become reasonably clear and the matter can be settled for a reasonable amount within the available policy limits. This at a minimum includes a duty to accept reasonable settlement demands from claimants, particularly if there is a significant risk of a judgment against the policyholder exceeding policy limits. Most courts also recognize that the insurer also has an affirmative duty to attempt to achieve a reasonable settlement and protect the policyholder/defendant.

In some situations, there may in essence be a duty not to settle—at least when the policyholder objects, settlement is costly to the policyholder, and the amount paid is unreasonable. In such cases, the policyholder would have preferred that the liability insurer keep fighting on its behalf. *See, e.g., Roehl Transp., Inc. v. Liberty Mut. Ins. Co.*, 784 N.W.2d 542 (Wis. 2010) (insurer's settlement of case where policy had high deductible may constitute bad faith where insurer settled too quickly and easily and was essentially using the policyholder's money rather than its own to resolve the claim).

But what happens if the insurer refuses to defend or otherwise get involved in effectuating settlement? A considerable body of law has emerged finding that where an insurer wrongfully refuses to defend, the policyholder may not only settle the claim but that the insurer's failure bars it from contesting the reasonableness of the settlement. *See Evanston Ins. Co. v. ATOFINA Petrochemicals, Inc.*, 256 S.W.3d 660 (Tex. 2008); *Benjamin v. Amica Mut. Ins. Co.*, 140 P.3d 1210, 1216 (Utah 2006); *Red Giant Oil Co. v. Lawlor*, 528 N.W.2d 524, 531–32 (Iowa 1995).

Situations where an insurer does not deny a duty to defend but nonetheless fails to effect settlement present another variant of the problem, as addressed in the following case.

## Miller v. Shugart

Supreme Court of Minnesota
316 N.W.2d 729 (1982)

**Simmonett, J.**

While Milbank Mutual Insurance Company was litigating whether it had coverage for both the insured car owner and the driver, the insured owner and the driver settled with the injured plaintiff and confessed judgment for a stipulated sum. After the coverage question was decided adversely to Milbank, plaintiff commenced a garnishment action against Milbank to collect on the judgment. Milbank appeals from an order in the garnishment proceeding granting plaintiff summary judgment to collect from Milbank on defendants' confessed judgment to the extent of the policy limits plus interest. Finding that Milbank must indemnify, we affirm plaintiff's recovery of the policy limits but reverse the ruling on interest.

Plaintiff Lynette Miller was injured in an automobile accident on June 19, 1976, when a car owned by defendant Barbara Locoshonas and driven by defendant Mark Shugart, in which Lynette was a passenger, struck a tree. Locoshonas had an auto liability policy with Milbank. Milbank, however, contended Shugart, the driver of the car, was not an agent of the owner and thus not covered under the policy. To determine this coverage question, Milbank, shortly after the accident, commenced a declaratory judgment action. Milbank provided separate counsel at its expense to represent the insured and the driver.

On January 8, 1979, judgment was entered in the declaratory judgment action adjudging that Milbank's policy afforded coverage to both Locoshonas and Shugart. On January 31, 1979, plaintiff Lynette Miller commenced her personal injury action against Locoshonas and Shugart. In April 1979 Milbank appealed the declaratory judgment decision to this court, and in April 1980 we summarily affirmed.

Twice while the appeal was pending, counsel for Locoshonas and Shugart advised Milbank they were negotiating a settlement with plaintiff's attorney and invited Milbank to participate in the negotiations. Milbank refused, pointing out it could not do so while the coverage question was unresolved.

In September 1979, plaintiff and the two defendants signed a stipulation for settlement of plaintiff's claims in which defendants confessed judgment in the amount of $100,000, which was twice the limit of Milbank's policy. The stipulated judgment further provided that it could be collected only from proceeds of any applicable insurance with no personal liability to defendants. Milbank was advised of the stipulation. Judgment on the stipulation was entered on November 15, 1979.

In May 1980, following this court's summary affirmance on the coverage issue, plaintiff Miller served a garnishment summons on Milbank. Milbank interposed an answer to the supplemental complaint setting out the history of the litigation and alleging that the confession of judgment was in violation of its policy and that Milbank was thus not bound by the judgment. Plaintiff then moved for summary judgment in her favor for $50,000, the policy limits, plus interest and costs. Milbank countered with its own motion for summary judgment, claiming defendants had breached the cooperation clause of the policy, that garnishment did not lie, and that the confessed judgment was invalid. The trial court granted plaintiff's motion, adjudging plaintiff was entitled to recover the $50,000 limits plus interest on $100,000.

Three main issues present themselves: (1) Does garnishment lie, (2) may Milbank avoid responsibility for the confessed judgment, and (3) if Milbank is bound by the judgment, must it also pay interest on the entire $100,000?

Milbank says there has never been a trial on the merits, that the purported judgment, insofar as it is concerned, is still an "unliquidated tort claim," and that, consequently, the sum due plaintiff is not "due absolutely," and so garnishment does not lie. Milbank overlooks, however, that as between plaintiff and the defendants the tort claim has been liquidated and reduced to a judgment. So long as this has occurred, the basis for garnishment exists....

What Milbank is really saying is that the judgment does not liquidate the claim because it obligates the defendants to pay nothing. While it is true that defendants need not pay anything, it is also true that the judgment effectively liquidates defendants' personal liability. We hold, therefore, that plaintiff may seek to collect on that judgment in a garnishment proceeding against the insurer.

The next question is whether the judgment stipulated to by the plaintiff and the defendant insureds is the kind of liability the insurer has agreed under its policy to pay. This involves an inquiry into whether the judgment is the product of fraud or collusion perpetrated on the insurer and whether the judgment reflects a reasonable and prudent settlement.

We first must deal with a threshold issue. Milbank argues the indemnity agreement of its policy has been voided because the insureds breached their duty under the policy to cooperate. We disagree.

Under the auto liability policy, Milbank has a duty to defend and indemnify its insureds, and the insureds have a reciprocal duty to cooperate with their insurer in the management of the claim. Plaintiff contends that defendants were relieved from their duty to cooperate because Milbank breached its duty to defend. We would put the issue differently. Milbank has never abandoned its insureds nor, by seeking a determination of its coverage, has it repudiated its policy obligations. Milbank had a right to determine if its policy afforded coverage for the accident claim, and here Milbank did exactly as we suggested in *Prahm v. Rupp Construction Co.*, 277 N.W.2d 389, 391 (1979), where we said a conflict of interest might be avoided by bringing a declaratory judgment action on the coverage issue prior to trial. This is the route Milbank followed, appropriately providing another set of attorneys to defend the insureds in the declaratory judgment action.

On the other hand, while Milbank did not abandon its insureds neither did it accept responsibility for the insureds' liability exposure. What we have, then, is a question of how should the respective rights and duties of the parties to an insurance contract be enforced during the time period that application of the insurance contract itself is being questioned. Viewed in this context, Milbank's position, really, is that it has a superior right to have the coverage question resolved *before* the plaintiff's personal injury action is disposed of either by trial or settlement. It is unlikely plaintiff could have forced defendants to trial before the coverage issue was decided. Put this way, the question becomes: Did the insureds breach their duty to cooperate by not waiting to settle until after the policy coverage had been decided? In our view, the insureds did not have to wait and, therefore, did not breach their duty to cooperate.

While the defendant insureds have a duty to cooperate with the insurer, they also have a right to protect themselves against plaintiff's claim. The attorneys hired by Milbank to represent them owe their allegiance to their clients, the insureds, to best represent their interests. If, as here, the insureds are offered a settlement that effectively relieves them of any personal liability, at a time when their insurance coverage is in doubt, surely it cannot be said that it is not in their best interest to accept the offer. Nor, do we think, can the insurer who is disputing coverage compel the insureds to forego a settlement which is in their best interests.

On the facts of this case we hold, therefore, that the insureds did not breach their duty to cooperate with the insurer, which was then contesting coverage, by settling directly with the plaintiff.

The next issue is whether Milbank may avoid the stipulated judgment on the grounds of fraud or collusion. We hold as a matter of law that the judgment was not obtained by fraud or collusion.

We start with the general proposition that a money judgment confessed to by an insured is not binding on the insurer if obtained through fraud or collusion.... In this case, however, Milbank has not made any showing of fraud or collusion. In its answer to the supplemental complaint, Milbank has neither pleaded fraud or collusion nor pleaded facts for such a defense. *See* Rules of Civil Procedure, Rule 9.02 ("In all averments of fraud or mistake, the circumstances constituting fraud or mistake shall be stated with particularity.") Neither, in opposing plaintiff's motion for summary judgment, has Milbank submitted affidavits or other evidence to make out any fact issue of fraud or collusion. Rules of Civil Procedure, Rule 56.05.

As we understand Milbank's argument, it is that the fraud and collusion consist of the defendant insureds settling the claims over Milbank's objections and contrary to the insurer's best interests, and in confessing judgment for a sum twice the amount of the policy limits. This conduct, however, need be neither fraudulent nor collusive. As we have just held, the defendant insureds had a right to make a settlement relieving them of liability. They also advised Milbank of what they were doing. Moreover, they waited to settle until after the district court had found coverage to exist. We see nothing improper in defendants' conduct. Nor is there anything wrong with the insureds' confessing judgment in an amount double the policy limits, since plaintiff, in her motion for summary judgment, has recognized Milbank's coverage is only $50,000 and seeks to recover no more than that sum from Milbank. The interest question will be addressed separately.

This is not to say that Milbank's position is enviable. As the trial court observed, it had "serious doubts about the propriety of the procedure whereby the insurer is placed in a 'no-win' situation as was done here." If the insurer ignores the "invitation" to participate in the settlement negotiations, it may run the risk of being required to pay, even within its policy limits, an inflated judgment. On the other hand, if the insurer decides to participate in the settlement discussions, ordinarily it can hardly do so meaningfully without abandoning its policy defense. Nevertheless, it seems to us, if a risk is to be borne, it is better to have the insurer who makes the decision to contest coverage bear the risk. Of course, the insurer escapes the risk if it should be successful on the coverage issue, and, in that event, it is plaintiff who loses.

We hold, as a matter of law, on the showing made on plaintiff's motion for summary judgment, that the stipulated judgment against the defendant insureds was not obtained by fraud or collusion.

Although having found that the stipulated judgment is untainted by fraud or collusion, our inquiry is not at an end. It seems to us there must also be a showing that the settlement on which the stipulated judgment is based was reasonable and prudent.

The settlement stipulation recites that defendants confess judgment in favor of plaintiff in the amount of $100,000 "upon the condition that plaintiff agree that her judgment may be satisfied only from liability insurance policies in force at the time ...and that this judgment is not satisfiable nor may it be a lien upon any other assets of defendants...." Defendants agreed judgment could be entered *ex parte* adjudging the driver Shugart negligent although the parties further agreed, somewhat inconsistently, that the stipulation "does not constitute an admission by either defendant of his or her negligence," and it was also agreed the stipulation and judgment could not be used as an admission by the defendants in any other lawsuit.

Plainly, the "judgment" does not purport to be an adjudication on the merits; it only reflects the settlement agreement. It is also evident that, in arriving at the settlement terms, the defendants would have been quite willing to agree to anything as long as plaintiff promised them full immunity. The effect of the settlement was to substitute the claimant for the insureds in a claim against the insurer. Thus on this appeal we see only the plaintiff claimant and the defendants' insurer in dispute, with the insureds taking a passive, disinterested role. Moreover, it is a misnomer for the parties to call plaintiff's judgment a "confessed" judgment. If this were truly a confessed judgment or even a default judgment, it is doubtful that it could stand. It seems more accurate to refer to the judgment as a judgment on a stipulation.

In these circumstances, while the judgment is binding and valid as between the stipulating parties, it is not conclusive on the insurer. The burden of proof is on the claimant, the plaintiff judgment creditor, to show that the settlement is reasonable and prudent. The test as to whether the settlement is reasonable and prudent is what a reasonably prudent person in the position of the defendant would have settled for on the merits of plaintiff's claim. This involves a consideration of the facts bearing on the liability and damage aspects of plaintiff's claim, as well as the risks of going to trial. This can be compared with the somewhat analogous situation in which a joint tortfeasor seeking contribution from a co-tortfeasor must prove the settlement made was reasonable.

The trial court granted plaintiff summary judgment against Milbank for its policy limits of $50,000. The question is whether the record shows, as a matter of law, that the stipulated judgment, to the extent of $50,000, was reasonable and prudent. Not much proof was submitted to the trial court on this issue at the hearing on the motions for summary judgment. Nonetheless, it does appear, without dispute, that this was a one-car accident, with the plaintiff as passenger, in which the car left the road and hit a tree. As to damages, the settlement stipulation recites, and it is undisputed by Milbank, that plaintiff suffered "severe and disfiguring personal injuries," that no-fault benefits in excess of $20,000 were paid and that the no-fault benefits were likely to total $35,000 or more. The trial court states in its memo that Mr. Forsythe, retained by Milbank to represent the insureds, had reviewed the liability and damage aspects of the claim and had concluded "there was a substantial likelihood that ultimately judgment would be entered against his clients * * * for more than any possible insurance coverage...." On this showing, not disputed, we conclude the trial court did not err in granting summary judgment in favor of plaintiff and against Milbank to the extent of $50,000.

## Notes and Questions

1. Is the *Miller-Shugart* approach too favorable to policyholders? Does *Miller-Shugart* make it unduly likely that the third-party claimant and the policyholder-defendant will enter into "sweetheart" settlements and leave the insurer stuck with the tab? Why or why not?

2. Before you empty your tear ducts for the poor liability insurer, consider the means by which insurers can protect themselves from being "stuck" with an inflated judgment or settlement in states like Pennsylvania or Minnesota. What are they? Is that enough to make a case like *Miller v. Shugart* "fair"?

3. In contrast to the *Miller v. Shugart* approaches, many — perhaps even most — courts appear to require the policyholder who is denied a defense to "prove up" its losses in a claim against the insurer for failure to defend. Instead of simply using the amount of an adverse judgment as the basic component of damages, the policyholder must show how the insurer's failure to defend led to a larger damages award than would be the case had the insurer provided a competent defense when asked. Is this approach too good a deal for the insurer? Can't an insurer simply sit back, willfully breach a duty to defend, and then be no worse off than it would have been had it shouldered its duty, so long as the policyholder was able to retain adequate counsel and resolve the case within acceptable parameters?

4. *See also Century Indem. Co. v. Aero-Motive Co.*, 336 F. Supp. 2d 739 (W.D. Mich. 2004) (finding $5 million settlement and consent judgment unreasonable where it was twice the amount of plaintiff's highest prior demand and several times counsel's valuation; concluding that settlement resulted from bad faith conduct by policyholder; *Miller-Shugart* treatment also unavailable because insurer was in fact defending claim when improper settlement made); *Safeway Ins. Co. v. Guerrero*, 106 P.3d 1020 (Ariz. 2005) (rejecting insurer's claim of intentional interference with contractual relations against claimant's attorney negotiating a settlement and assignment of policy rights with policyholder-defendant).

5. Arizona has perhaps an even more well-developed *Miller-Shugart* jurisprudence than Minnesota, with such agreements known as "*Morris, Damron*, or *Morris-Damron*" settlements in Arizona. *See Guerrero*, 106 P.3d at 1022; *United Servs. Auto. Ass'n v. Morris*, 154 Ariz. 113, 741 P.2d 246 (1987); *Damron v. Sledge*, 105 Ariz. 151, 460

P.2d 997 (1969). The distinction is that a *Morris* settlement occurs even where the insurer is defending the claim but where the policyholder can credibly assert an anticipatory breach of the insurer's duty to indemnify. A *Damron* agreement results in situations where the insurer fails to defend at all.

## [B] The Insurers' Duty of Good Faith and Fair Dealing

Insurers also have a duty of good faith and fair dealing toward the policyholder. Although policyholders also have similar duties of fair conduct toward the insurer, greater burden rests on the insurer. Also, the legal "teeth" put into the doctrine are differential. For example, an aggrieved policyholder may sue the insurer in a "bad faith" cause of action. In more than half the states, this is styled as a tort action or statutory claim permitting exemplary damages. For the most part, courts do not permit an insurer to sue the policyholder for "reverse bad faith," but the insurer may obtain monetary relief for the consequential damages ensuing from policyholder breach of duties that insures the insurer. In addition, insurers may become great tipsters for local law enforcement authorities, who are usually interested in devoting prosecutorial resources to egregious insurance fraud (e.g., fake car accident rings) even if they are not interested in prosecuting the isolated policyholder who inflates a claim. Chapter 12 discusses bad faith in detail.

## [C] The Effect of Failure to Settle

### Mid-America Bank & Trust Co. v. Commercial Union Insurance Co.

Appellate Court of Illinois
587 N.E.2d 81 (1992)

**Justice Howerton** delivered the opinion of the court.

This is an appeal of a verdict against an insurance company in a case brought for negligence and for bad faith in refusing to settle a claim within the policy limits.

A truck hit a 13-year-old boy; he suffered brain damage. The truck was insured by Commercial Union under a policy that had limits of $50,000 per person and $100,000 per occurrence. Plaintiff's attorney sent a letter offering to settle for the policy limits. The offer remained open but was never accepted.

Commercial Union hired third-party defendant as its lawyer. On the advice of Commercial Union, and because of the possibility of damages exceeding the policy limits, the owner of the truck hired his own attorney.

Plaintiff, almost three years later on May 3, 1980, again offered to settle for $50,000. The third-party defendant instead offered $30,000, "take it or leave it," but did not tell the truck owner that he was going to offer this amount. Plaintiff was offended and withdrew all offers.

Six days later, third-party defendant offered to pay $50,000, stating that he always had had authority to settle for that amount. Plaintiff refused to accept the offer and the case was tried. A jury awarded plaintiff $911,536.50, an amount in excess of the coverage.

Thereafter, the owner of the truck settled with plaintiff. As part of that settlement, he assigned to plaintiff all claims he had against Commercial Union in exchange for plaintiff's covenant not to execute the $911,536.50 judgment against him.

Plaintiff, then, sued Commercial Union for negligence and for the tort of bad faith in settling the original claim.

Commercial Union filed a third-party complaint against its lawyer, third-party defendant, whose estate has since been substituted, seeking indemnity and contribution. A jury awarded plaintiff $686,536.00, being the unpaid balance of the previous judgment, and also found Commercial Union to be 75% at fault and third-party defendant 25% at fault. The circuit court entered judgment and also awarded attorney fees and costs and ordered interest assessed against Commercial Union and third-party defendant at 9%, to be computed from December 3, 1983, for a total judgment of $1,099,791.95.

Both Commercial Union and third-party defendant make several arguments on appeal. We need only consider four: (1) that the circuit court erred by denying Commercial Union's motion for directed verdict; (2) that the circuit court erred by dismissing Commercial Union's indemnity claim; (3) that the circuit court erred by allowing certain expert testimony; and (4) that the circuit court erred in awarding post-judgment interest. We affirm in part, vacate in part and remand with directions.

Commercial Union first argues that the circuit court erred in denying its motion for directed verdict. We disagree and affirm....

There is evidence in the record from which a jury could infer that Commercial Union acted negligently or in bad faith. Plaintiff's letter to the owner of the truck in July 1977 stated, "[w]e want to indicate to you that we would settle this case now for the amount of the insurance policy limits, even though the injuries in this case may justify a jury verdict in excess of the average policy." Eight days later, Commercial Union's claims adjuster reported to the company that, "this case, ... has a value of upward to $1,000,000...." The adjuster also indicated that the chance of losing exceeded 10%, and he recommended that Commercial Union increase their reserve to $50,000.

A memo dated October 19, 1977, from the branch claims manager to the claims supervisor, stated in part: "The next thing I want done and I want it done immediately, is to acknowledge receipt of the lawyer's lien letter wherein he makes policy limits demand and advise him that we cannot give consideration to his policy limits demand at this time because we have no information in our file in regards to any specials or any medical reports in our file to indicate what the boy's injuries are. I think we pretty well know what the injuries are but I think we can put the lawyer off on his policy limits demand so that we are not in bad faith by telling him that we have nothing to support his policy limits demand." This memo also recognized the possibility of a million-dollar verdict, that there was at least a 30 to 40% chance of losing, and gave authority to settle for $50,000.

Commercial Union argues that it offered to pay the policy limits, and six days later plaintiff refused that offer, there being no change of circumstances during that six-day period that would justify refusal, and therefore, plaintiff failed to prove a cause of action. We disagree. Commercial Union's argument asks us to focus only on that six-day period but to ignore the three-year period wherein plaintiff had an offer to settle outstanding. This we cannot do, because this three-year period is relevant, since it, together with the above memoranda and the statement, "30,000, take it or leave it," is the very essence of plaintiff's claim.

In negotiating settlements in which recovery may exceed policy limits, the insurer must give the interest of the insured consideration at least equal to its own.... A cause of action against an insurer exists if the insurer's refusal to settle a claim within the policy limits amounts to negligence, or bad faith ... and when it does, the insurer may be held liable for the entire judgment entered against the insured and cannot complain of its amount.... In the case at bar, Commercial Union was aware of the offer, the extent of the injury, the possibility of bad faith, the possible personal liability of the owner of the truck, and the risk of excess liability if the case were tried. For almost three years there was a clear opportunity to settle within the policy limits, but Commercial Union refused. We conclude that the circuit court properly denied the motion for directed verdict.

## Notes and Questions

1. As demonstrated in *Commercial Union Insurance Company*, courts hold a liability insurance company liable *in excess* of its policy limits if that insurer fails to exercise "good faith and fair dealing" in considering offers to settle a claim for an amount within the policy limits. Put another way, the insurer must act in good faith and deal fairly with any offers to settle in order to protect the insured from excess liability should the case be tried in court. *See generally* 14 Couch on Insurance 2d §§ 51:3–51:31 (1982). The problem, however, is to determine what constitutes, or does not constitute, an insurer's "good faith."

2. No single test of an insurer's "good faith" effort to settle has been uniformly adopted by the courts. Some courts have held that, in the absence of willful "bad faith," actual fraud, or misrepresentation, the insurer is entitled to protect its own interests in refusing to settle. Other courts have held the insured's interest in any settlement offer must be given equal weight with the insurer's interest; and some courts give the insured's interest priority. *See generally* Maniloff & Stempel, Ch. 20.

3. Under the traditional view, an error or mistake in judgment by the insurer in failing to settle a claim within policy limits after an honest and fair investigation would not constitute "bad faith" on the part of the insurer. Although the error might have amounted to negligence against the insurer, it is not sufficient to show "a dishonest purpose or moral obliquity" to demonstrate bad faith.

4. A number of courts have rejected the traditional rule that an insurer's duty to settle is limited to the exercise of good faith and fair dealing toward the insured. Instead, these courts hold that the insurer may indeed be liable for negligence in rejecting a reasonable offer to settle within policy limits under the insurer's duty to exercise reasonable care. But the mere fact that a claimant was successful in a court action when the insurer refused to settle the claim within policy limits prior to trial does not, in itself, establish that the insurer was negligent in refusing to settle.

### PROBLEM SIX

Manchester Insurance Company sued attorney William Knight, Jr., for malpractice, alleging that Knight had been negligent in defending Manchester in a suit concerning the company's liability for damages in excess of the policy limits. The negligence complained of was Knight's failure to settle the company's case with the plaintiff's attorney, Bernard Reese. Reese had offered to settle the case for $20,000, and this offer to settle was open through the trial. Manchester had authorized Knight to settle for $17,000, but when Reese asked Knight prior to the jury selection if there was any offer of settlement, Knight replied, "I have no comment on that." Reese then offered to settle for $20,000, but again Knight replied, "I have no comment on that."

Reese later stated that, although he would not have settled for less than $10,000 each for both claims, he might have changed his position if Knight had not said "no comment" when asked about his authority to settle. The jury gave a verdict to the plaintiffs for $75,000.

- Did Knight's action in stating "no comment" to Reese's settlement offers constitute a breach of the duty to exercise good faith on behalf of the insurer?

- Would it constitute a breach of the duty to exercise reasonable care?

- Can Knight's actions in this failure to settle be imputed to the insurance company?

## [D] Direct Actions by the Injured Party against the Insurer

It has also been held that the rights of an injured third party with respect to an automobile liability insurance policy irrevocably attach at the time of the accident and cannot be destroyed either by a subsequent cancellation of the policy or by a mutual rescission made by the insurer and the insured. Are the statutory rights of an injured third party in an automobile liability insurance context absolute, or are they subject to any defenses? Without enabling legislation, the right to direct action by the injured third party against the liability insurer generally does not exist.

# Chapter 8

# Property Insurance

## § 8.01. An Overview of Property Insurance

Property insurance is first party insurance. It is designed to indemnify the policyholder for injury to, or loss of, covered property. The fire insurance issued in colonial times and the marine insurance underwritten at Lloyd's Coffee House covering the cargo of merchant ships are among the earliest forms of property insurance. At its most basic, the property insurance concept is quite simple. The policyholders pool their funds in the form of premium payments. If one of the policyholders suffers a covered property loss, the insurance fund (administered by the insurance company) pays the policyholder a sum of money designed to compensate the policyholder for the loss. The insurer is able to do this by spreading and pooling the risk as well as investing the premium payments. As long as not too many of its policyholders suffer property loss within a compressed time, the insurer will be able to pay claims and still make money.

There can be significant disputes between insurer and policyholder about what is the appropriate measure of value for the damaged or destroyed property. But everyone agrees on the concept—the policyholder should be indemnified for the loss according to the terms of the insurance policy. Over-indemnification is to be avoided because it may create moral hazard or adverse selection. Under-indemnification is also to be avoided because then the property insurance would fail to make the policyholder "whole"—remembering that the concept of being "made whole" is controlled by the contract, not the general standards of fairness or morality.

Because property insurance is first party insurance, there will perhaps be heightened concern over possible adverse selection and moral hazard. For that reason, the typical property insurance policy and the governing law impose upon the policyholder certain requirements of making a timely and adequate "proof of loss" if there is damage to the property. The policy also typically provides a significant deductible so that the insurer is not required to provide coverage (and the attendant costs of administration) for small claims. To illustrate: if the neighborhood juvenile delinquent dents or knocks down a mailbox, the homeowner generally shoulders this sort of loss. But if the pipes burst due to a sudden cold snap, flooding the house, the homeowner submits this larger claim to the insurer, paying the amount of the deductible before coverage attaches.

Over the years, the basic fire policy has evolved into a "homeowners" policy. It is still primarily first party property coverage but also usually provides a component of liability coverage for the homeowner if a third party should sue the homeowner for negligence (which can include failure to maintain the property in a safe condition, among many other negligent acts insured against). The property insurance portion of the homeowners policy is triggered primarily by losses that could arise from the property itself and from losses to contents within the property. The liability insurance coverage provided by the homeowners policy is not typically restricted to only those acts of negligence arising on one's property. The liability insurance coverage is usually triggered by the insured being sued as a result of an "occurrence." The "occurrence" could happen anywhere in the world. For example, if a passerby slips on the unshovelled sidewalk and sues the homeowner, the liability coverage in the homeowners policy generally is triggered. The liability portion of a homeowners or other "property plus" policy is addressed in the Liability Insurance segment of this book. Questions of coverage under a homeowners or business owners policy involving intentional conduct, trigger, and other coverage issues will for the most part be determined according to liability insurance principles rather than property insurance principles.

The typical homeowners policy delineates insurance coverage on the "Dwelling" itself and "Other Structures" as well as "Personal Property." Special limits are provided on coverage for certain hard-to-insure, subject-to-fraud items such as money, securities, and jewelry. These types of items are thought to be problematic because an unscrupulous policyholder can contend that these were in the house but the contention is hard to verify. For example, after all but the most devastating fires, there is usually pretty tangible evidence of the damage to furniture, clothing, and the like. But what if the policyholder claims to have had $1 million of bearer bonds or cash in the closet? How does the insurer disprove that one? There are ways, of course, but they are expensive ways, prompting insurers to simply lower the limit of coverage on these types of items. As with most insurance, the policyholder who really does have a lot of expensive jewelry or priceless art can usually purchase some increased coverage for an additional premium. But such endorsements are usually not limitless. At some point, the insurance company will say "no" and suggest that the policyholder simply use a safe deposit box.

Most property policies also list the property that is "not covered." This of course makes perfect sense for the insurer to both limit his or her risks and to avoid litigating dubious claims from policyholders who might otherwise argue that the family car or airplane or hovercraft is part of the household property. Business data is often specifically excluded, because the homeowners insurer does not desire to become a business insurer. If the policyholder needs insurance protection for items because he or she runs a small business from the home, the obvious solution is for the policyholder to purchase a modest commercial policy.

The homeowners policy, like most property policies, also covers "Loss of Use" and provides coverage for ancillary things like "debris removal" after a loss. Usually, the homeowner will be reimbursed for the reasonable cost of protecting the property from future covered loss. The typical property policy of this type generally excludes "earth movement" or "earthquake" coverage, which tends to exclude coverage for loss caused by a mudslide as well, unless other covered causes were responsible for the loss. Wind damage may be covered, but in many places vulnerable to hurricanes, homeowners usually are required to purchase separate windstorm coverage through an add-on endorsement or through a stand-alone windstorm policy.

There is also a limitation on coverage for loses incurred because of "Ordinance or Law," which means expenses incurred because a change in the law requires them. For example, a city may determine that it needs to toughen up the building code to make homes more wind-resistant and make the changes retroactive, requiring the homeowner to incur home remodeling costs. Many property policies (and liability policies for that matter) exclude ordinance or law coverages altogether.

The homeowners policy or "specified perils" property policy, after stating what property is covered, then has a separate section for "Perils Insured Against"—in essence stating what injurious forces are covered, for both the dwelling/other structures and personal property. To obtain property insurance coverage, the policyholder must generally show both that covered property has been damaged and that it has been damaged by a covered peril listed in the policy.

Modern homeowners property insurance policies are typically written on an "all-risk" basis in which the insuring agreement broadly states that it covers injury to the property. Of course, explicit exclusions following an all-risk insuring clause can still defeat coverage. But the all-risk format puts a greater risk of non-persuasion upon the insurer in the event of dispute. By contrast, under the typical named-perils policy, the policyholder has the burden to first establish coverage before there is even any talk of exclusions. Consequently, the policyholder bears more of a burden of persuasion as to these types of policies.

Common exclusions in a property policy include: Ordinance or Law (subject to the lower limit set out earlier in the policy), Earth Movement, Water Damage (which is why homeowners in a flood plain should buy flood insurance), Power Failure, Neglect by the policyholder, War, Nuclear Hazard, Intentional Destruction, Terrorism and Governmental Action. As discussed in Chapter 1, all of these exclusions attempt to eliminate providing a coverage that would undermine prudent insurance operations because the excluded perils are either not fortuitous or would undermine the risk pooling and underwriting of the insurer. For example, if House A is contaminated by a nuclear meltdown, Houses B through Z are probably being subjected to the same nuclear force, a correlated risk. As discussed in Chapter 1, an insurer taking on correlated risks of any significance will have a rough time remaining solvent.

The standard property policy also includes conditions of coverage. These are contractual requirements that must be satisfied if the policyholder is to enjoy his or her rights on the contract and are akin to the contract law concept of "conditions precedent" to the operation of a contract right. For example, the policy imposes upon the policyholder a duty to give notice of the loss and a duty to provide the insurer with sufficient information to evaluate the loss.

The "Conditions" section of the policy also typically contains a "co-insurance" clause. In the area of property insurance, "co-insurance" means something different than in health insurance, the area in which most consumers are probably familiar with the term. For health insurance, co-insurance refers to the portion of a medical claim that must be shouldered by the policyholder. Usually, it is an 80/20 ratio, with the policyholder paying 20 percent of medical bills (after satisfaction of the deductible). This serves the insurer's goal of discouraging adverse selection and moral hazard because the medical coverage is not totally "free" even if the insured's employer is paying all the premiums. In health insurance, the term co-insurance refers to a cost-sharing arrangement between insurer and policyholder.

In property insurance, the term co-insurance refers to a ratio of insurance coverage in force that must be maintained by the policyholder if the policyholder is to be entitled to full indemnity on a covered loss. To the extent that the policyholder has fallen below this co-insurance ratio, coverage is not lost completely, but instead is reduced pro rata. The purpose of the property co-insurance clause is to encourage the policyholder to keep sufficient insurance in force. This means that the premiums will be higher and in theory provide the insurer with enough premium revenue to justify the risks insured.

A reason for property co-insurance is that most property losses are not total losses. For example, there may be a kitchen fire in the home that is extinguished relatively quickly. It may cost a fair amount to replace the kitchen but probably less than the full policy limits, even if those limits are low. The insurer's fear is that, without a co-insurance provision, policyholders might be tempted to underinsure the home, reducing premium payments but still leaving insurers on the hook for less-than-total losses such as our hypothetical kitchen fire. Without the co-insurance clause (sometimes called a co-insurance penalty), the policyholder loses this gamble only if there is a total loss, or something close to it. With the co-insurance clause, the underinsuring policyholder gets a reduced payment for the small losses commensurate with the reduced premiums it paid because it underinsured the property. For a more complete discussion of property co-insurance, see ROBERT H. JERRY, II & DOUGLAS R. RICHMOND, UNDERSTANDING INSURANCE LAW §93[b] (6th ed. 2018).

Remember, per the discussion in Chapter 2 regarding policy interpretation, that "Conditions" or "Definitions" in a policy may be treated either as part of the insuring agreement (on which the policyholder bears the burden of persuasion to show compliance and hence coverage) or as an exclusion on which the insurer bears the burden of persuasion. It depends on whether the condition/definition is simply a straightforward condition/definition or operates in the nature of a restriction on coverage. Even where the language is clear, if the restriction on coverage is unfair or hidden, a court may apply the reasonable expectations approach for the benefit of the policyholder.

On the whole, property insurance is designed to cover significant episodes of damage brought about by some external or independent force rather than from the deficiencies of the property or the mere passage of time. For example, "wear and tear" is not a covered property insurance event. Everything gets old and worn eventually. The paint on the exterior of a home may have faded enough over the years to require repainting, but this is not an insured event. The policyholder must pay for this out of general home maintenance dollars—not insurance. However, if there is a lightning strike on the southeast corner of the house, the costs of repainting the entire house to match the paint on the new wood replacing the lightning-damaged wood is probably covered. *See Hampton Foods, Inc. v. Aetna Casualty & Surety Co.*, 787 F.2d 349 (8th Cir. 1986) (applying Missouri law).

Similarly, if there is a garden variety rainstorm and the living room window leaks, insurers generally consider this not to be covered. They reason that this results from a deficiency in the integrity of the home structure and not from a covered peril. However, if there is wind-driven rain that forces damaging moisture through a perfectly good window, this is a covered property loss under most policies.

The unifying concept here is that property insurance covers the fortuitous loss that ordinarily does not take place but is visited on the property by other forces. It does not provide a long-term guarantee of the property's functional utility and performance.

# § 8.02. Scope of Property Insurance Coverage

## [A] Coverage for Direct Physical Loss

Property insurance generally covers "direct physical loss or damage to tangible property." So, some external force must somehow damage the property. And the property needs to be "tangible." But what if that property is ephemeral, existing only in digital form on a computer? How is something damaged physically if it cannot even be touched?

### Ashland Hospital Corp. v. Affiliated FM Insurance Co.

United States District Court, E.D. Kentucky,
2013 WL 4400516

**David L. Bunning, District Judge.**

#### I. FACTUAL BACKGROUND

A. The Hospital purchases a data storage network

In 2007, Plaintiff Ashland Hospital Corporation, d/b/a King's Daughter's Medical Center, contracted with technology company and manufacturer, EMC Corporation, to sell, install and support a computer data storage network known as the DMX4. The DMX4 is the Plaintiff's "primary computer data repository, which runs a number of essential hospital functions and is critical to patient health and safety." (Doc. # 70-1, at 6). Plaintiff used the DMX4 to store all of its electronic records, including medical records, schedules, and lab reports. EMC "markets the unit as having the highest degree of availability—99.999%," (Doc. # 69-1, at 5), and thus the unit's guarantee of information availability is its key feature. EMC installed the DMX4 within one of Plaintiff's data centers and monitored it in real-time from a remote location.

B. The Hospital's data center overheats

On March 24, 2010, the air conditioning equipment in the data center failed, causing elevated temperatures (hereinafter "the overheat event"). Alarms within the DMX4 alerted EMC that various component parts of the unit had been exposed to increased temperatures. The DMX4 ultimately went into a failed state, rendering the system unavailable for a period of several hours. During this period, Hospital personnel could not access important information including physician orders, patient schedules, and historical medical records. Certain data was "completely corrupted and had to be restored from a backup." (Doc. # 70-2, at 25). [The hospital's insurer denied the claim.]

* * *

B. The phrase "direct physical loss or damage" includes a loss of reliability

The Policy "insures against all risks of *direct physical loss or damage* to insured property except as excluded under this policy." (Doc. # 70-4, at 18) (emphasis added). The central question for the Court is whether the phrase "direct physical loss or damage" includes a loss of reliability suffered by a data storage network due to heat exposure.

As a federal court sitting in diversity, the Court's task is to predict how the Kentucky Supreme Court would rule if it were deciding this question of state law....

As an initial matter, the parties dispute whether the term "physical" modifies the term "damage." Neither of these terms are defined in the Policy (nor is the term "loss" defined, for that matter). Naturally, Defendant argues that "physical" does modify "damage," while Plaintiff argues it does not. However, even if the Court were to adopt Defendant's interpretation, the Court would still find that coverage exists. Therefore, since it need not resolve this issue, the Court assumes without holding that the term "physical" modifies the term "damage."

The Court presses on to the heart of the matter. Plaintiff contends that the DMX4's loss of reliability constitutes "direct physical loss or damage" for three reasons. First, it asserts that the DMX4's components were physically altered by the overheat event. Second, it contends that this physical alteration compromised the system's reliability, even though it could still function after the overheat event. And third, because the system's reliability is the "entire function or purpose of the unit" (Doc. # 70-1, at 17), and the purpose of insuring the unit was to protect that reliability, Plaintiff posits that the loss of reliability is a covered event. Plaintiff emphasizes that this reliability is essential because "[a] device that could provide 80% availability would be a completely different device due to the importance of the data it stores and the severity of the consequence if the data is unavailable." (Doc. # 70-1, at 17). It contends that the if the Court ignores the reliability of the DMX4, its insurance coverage becomes illusory.

Defendant takes the opposite view. It contends that "direct physical loss or damage" does not include a loss of reliability for two reasons. First, it asserts that a loss of reliability is an "intangible" or "non-physical" concept, and that to prove "direct physical loss or damage" Plaintiff must present "*distinct, demonstrable,* physical alteration of the property" that is "tangible" or "perceptible" to the senses. (*Id.* at 17) (emphasis added). Second, it posits that coverage does not exist unless this demonstrable physical alteration rendered the DMX4 unable to function.

The Court agrees with Plaintiff that the phrase "direct physical loss or damage," as applied to Plaintiff's data storage network, encompasses a loss of reliability caused by excessive temperature. There are two reasons the Court makes this finding. First, the component damage at issue here is undeniably "direct" and "physical": it is "direct" because the harm flows immediately or proximately from the heat exposure, and it is "physical" because the harm results from physical alteration to the components themselves.

It is undisputed, for instance, that disk drive damage occurs on a microscopic level through a process called "ionic migration," in which "lubricants are thinned or ... move around because they're more fluid [as a result of heat exposure]." (Doc. # 69-8, at 48). It is also undisputed that heat exposure can degrade the disk drives "Annualized Failure Rate," meaning their annual risk of failure—or in other words, their reliability. There is no question, therefore, that degradation of a disk drive's Annualized Failure Rate due to heat exposure is a *physical* process. The Court therefore rejects Defendant's contention that a loss of reliability is "clearly [an] intangible/non-physical concept" and that to "equate [it] to direct physical loss or damage would render the word 'physical'... meaningless." (Doc. # 71-1. at 24).

The Court also rejects Defendant's contention that the Policy requires Plaintiff to produce visible proof of disk drive damage by conducting physical testing such as a "tear down analysis." EMC's Frederick Sproule explained that a tear down analysis is not only extremely time-consuming, expensive, and labor intensive, but also quite frequently yields inconclusive results. (Doc. # 69-3, at 21). Perhaps this is why Defendant itself never conducted this test or any other physical testing, despite receiving an extension of time from this Court to do so. Given the inherent difficulty at play, the Court holds that visibly witnessing microscopic disk drive damage is not required to prove a loss of reliability.

Second, the Court declines Defendant's invitation to interpret the phrase "direct physical loss or damage" as requiring proof that the DMX4 permanently lost its ability to function. Adopting this view would ignore both the core function and value of the DMX4, and the purpose of insuring it. As stated above, the core function and value of the DMX4 is to provide Plaintiff 99.999% guaranteed reliability of critical data. According to Chad Phipps, Plaintiff's head of Information Technology, the Hospital chose to spend top dollar on the DMX4, rather than settling for a less expensive storage network, because the DMX4 offered the highest guarantee of reliability. (Doc. # 69-4, at 49). In short, its value—its insurable risk—is its reliability.

Were the Court to hold that in order to obtain coverage, Plaintiff must await the DMX4's total failure and the concomitant loss of critical patient data, it would defeat the objective of insurance. This principle was aptly explained by the Seventh Circuit in *Eljer Manufacturing, Incorporated v. Liberty Mutual Insurance Company,* 972 F.2d 805 (7th Cir.1992). The question in that case was as follows:

> If a manufacturer sells a defective product or component for installation in
> the real or personal property of the buyer, but the defect does not cause any

tangible change in the buyer's property until years later, can the installation itself nonetheless be considered a 'physical injury' to that property?

*Id.* at 808. At issue were a large number of claims against the manufacturer of defective plumbing systems. *Id.* at 807. Some of the claims involved systems that had leaked, and some involved systems which had not yet leaked, but which the property owners replaced in anticipation of a leak. *Id.* The appellate court was asked to determine whether, for insurance purposes, the "physical injury" to property occurs when the defective plumbing system is installed, when it leaks, or at some point in between. *Id.* at 808–809.

The court held that the injury occurred when the systems were installed because the defective plumbing system was "like a time bomb placed in an airplane luggage compartment: harmless until it explodes. Or like a silicone breast implant that is harmless until it leaks. Or like a defective pacemaker which is working fine now but will stop working in an hour." *Id.* at 807, 814. The Court went on to explain that the purpose of having insurance is to protect against the risk of a large loss, not just to provide reimbursement after the loss has occurred:

> The central issue in this case—when if ever the incorporation of one product into another can be said to cause physical injury—pivots on a conflict between the connotations of the term "physical injury" and the objective of insurance. The central meaning of the term as it is used in everyday English ... is of a harmful change in appearance, shape, composition, or some other physical dimension of the "injured" person or thing. If water leaks from a pipe and discolors a carpet or rots a beam, that is physical injury, perhaps beginning with the very earliest signs of rot.... The ticking time bomb, in contrast, does not injure the structure in which it is placed, in the sense of altering the structure in a harmful, of for that matter in any, way—until it explodes. But these nice, physicalist, "realistic" (in the philosophical sense) distinctions have little to do with the objectives of parties to insurance contracts. The purpose of insurance is to spread risks and by spreading cancel them. Most people (including most corporate executives) are risk averse, and will therefore pay a premium to avoid a small probability of a large loss. Once a risk becomes a certainty—once the large loss occurs—insurance has no function.

*Id.* at 808–09.

The heat-exposed data storage components in this case are like the hyperbolic ticking time bomb referenced by the Seventh Circuit: harmless until they fail. For insurance purposes, the "loss" or "damage" occurs when the components were exposed to excessive heat, not when the components fail. A contrary holding would frustrate the risk-spreading objectives of insurance. Moreover, the argument for coverage is even stronger in this case than it was in *Eljer* because in that case there was no allegation of physical alteration to the residences at issue, whereas in this case Plaintiff has alleged physical alteration to the DMX4's components.

Defendant cites several cases for the proposition that "direct physical loss or damage" does not encompass a loss of use, access, function, or reliability. However, these cases are inapposite because, unlike the instant case, they do not involve damage to the insured property itself. For instance, in *America Online, Inc. v. St. Paul Mercury Insurance Company*, 207 F.Supp.2d 459, 461, 470 (E.D.Va.2002), customers sued AOL claiming that its internet access software caused damage to their computers, computer data, software, and systems by causing their computers to freeze and to crash. AOL's general liability policy provided that its insurer would pay the amounts AOL was legally required to pay for property damage, which the policy defined as "physical damage to tangible property of others." *Id.* at 462.

The district court held that St. Paul had no duty to defend AOL against the customers' claims for damage to their computer data, software and systems because those items are not "tangible" property. *Id.* at 462. It further found that although the customers' computers *were* tangible property, the customers had not alleged physical injury to the "body or substance" of the computers. *Id.* at 469. *See also, North River Ins. Co. v. Clark*, 80 F.2d 202, 203 (9th Cir.1935) (locomotive not "damaged" when bridge burned, leaving it stranded and useless to its owner); *Source Food Technology v. USF & G Co.*, 465 F.3d 834, 835 (8th Cir.2006) (Canadian company's truckload of beef that was not permitted to enter the United States due to a legal regulation did not sustain "direct physical loss" because the beef itself was not contaminated); *Pentair, Inc. v. American Guar. and Liability. Ins. Co.*, 400 F.3d 613, 614 (8th Cir.2005) (corporation did not sustain "direct physical loss or damage" when two of its Taiwanese factories suffered a power outage because the factories themselves were undamaged).

Each of Defendant's cited cases are therefore inapposite because unlike the computers in *America Online,* the locomotive in *Clark,* the beef in *Source Food,* and the Taiwanese factories in *Pentair,* the DMX4's components were physically compromised, as described below. Therefore, the Court holds that the phrase "direct physical loss or damage" is unambiguous and includes a loss of reliability caused by excessive temperature.

In the alternative, to the extent that there is any ambiguity in the phrase, the Court resolves the ambiguity in favor of Plaintiff in order to protect its reasonable expectations of coverage. The doctrine of reasonable expectations provides that "the insured is entitled to all the coverage he may reasonably expect to be provided under the policy. Only an unequivocally conspicuous, plain and clear manifestation of the company's intent to exclude coverage will defeat that expectation." *Simon v. Continental Insurance Company*, 724 S.W.2d 210, 212 (Ky.1987). The Kentucky Supreme Court has explicated the doctrine as follows:

> An insurance company should not be allowed to collect premiums by stimulating a reasonable expectation of risk protection in the mind of the consumer, and then hide behind a technical definition to snatch away the protection which induced the premium payment.

*Aetna Cas. & Sur. Co. v. Kentucky*, 179 S.W.3d 830, 837 (Ky.2005). Here, Plaintiff's expectation was that Defendant would provide coverage if the DMX4's components lost reliability due to heat exposure. Defendant should not be allowed to collect premiums from Plaintiff and then assert that it was only insuring microscopic disk drive damage visible to the human eye that causes total system failure. This is especially true given that Defendant *itself* struggled with how to interpret the phrase "direct physical loss or damage." Defendant's adjustor, Terry MacKenzie, wrote to Plaintiff that Defendant needed to determine whether the DMX4 "has been compromised, i.e. damaged." (Doc. # 70-11, at 3).

The Court therefore holds that even if there is ambiguity in the Policy's language, coverage exists for a loss of reliability. Having determined the meaning of the phrase "direct physical loss or damage" as a matter of law, the Court must consider whether a genuine dispute of material fact exists regarding whether such loss or damage occurred in this case.

\* \* \*

… Based upon all of the aforementioned uncontradicted facts, no rational fact finder could find that the DMX4 did not suffer a loss of reliability due to heat exposure. *See Ercegovich v. Goodyear Tire & Rubber Co.,* 154 F.3d 344, 349 (6th Cir.1998) ("If, after reviewing the record in its entirety, a rational fact finder could not find for the nonmoving party, summary judgment should be granted."). Coverage therefore exists.…

## Notes and Questions

1. Insurance for so-called cyber-losses is complex. While most property insurers may argue that coverage for cyber-losses is excluded via a "direct physical loss" coverage clause, is such a practice defensible in today's modern society, where electronic data is so vital to so much? Does it not seem strange that if the Ashland Hospital kept its records in paper form in a steel filing cabinet, and lost those records through some event, that that loss would be covered? Should it really matter whether the property is in digital format? *See* Erik S. Knutsen & Jeffrey W. Stempel, *The Techno-Neutrality Solution to Navigating Insurance Coverage for Cyber Losses,* 122 PENN ST. L. REV. 645 (2018).

2. Note the Court's extensive discussion of *Eljer Manufacturing, Inc. v. Liberty Mutual Insurance Company,* 972 F.2d 805 (7th Cir.1992), an opinion by Judge Richard Posner that we like so well it was excerpted in the Fourth Edition of this casebook in Chapter 9 on Liability Insurance. (For the Fifth Edition, we moved the case to the Teacher's Manual should your instructor wish to assign it or provide more detail.)

In that case, part of the Seventh Circuit's concern about a "ticking time bomb" was that the manufacturer/policyholder would have trouble obtaining liability coverage if recognition of a triggering event was postponed until there was an actual visible leak in the defective plumbing systems. Because the problem was known prior to such actual leaks, future liability insurers would likely have specific exclusions in their policies, leaving the policyholder "high and dry" (no pun intended) if the insurer on the risk at the time of installation (when there was arguable damage through incorporation of the defective product into the plumbing system) was not required to provide coverage.

Notwithstanding the erudition of the *Eljer Manufacturing v. Liberty Mutual* opinion and the prestige of its author, the Illinois Supreme Court eventually sided with liability insurers on this issue and required an actual leak to trigger coverage, although it agreed that under New York law, which was applicable to some of the homes and lawsuits, defective component incorporation was sufficient physical injury. *See Travelers Insurance Co. v. Eljer Manufacturing, Inc.*, 757 N.E.2d 481 (Ill. 2001).

We agree with the Seventh Circuit and New York and disagree with Illinois on this issue—but the two *Eljer Manufacturing* cases nicely illustrate different "mainstream" or "legitimate" approaches to the matter. *Ashland Hospital* follows the Seventh Circuit but fails to note the differences in types of coverage. Should an insurer's or court's approach to what constitutes sufficiently "physical" property damage vary by type of policy?

One argument for insurers is that a property insurance policyholder should always be able to have high enough limits based on the estimated costs of rebuilding, while a liability insurance policyholder cannot estimate that risk as accurately because the final tally of the financial obligation depends upon less predictable jury verdicts. Does that argument apply to *Ashland Hospital*? Would it apply to the homeowners who had the defective Eljer plumbing fixtures in their homes and then sought to collect property insurance for repair after leaks develop? Or are they in danger of cancellation as well? Realistically? Why or why not?

## [B] Coverage under "All Risk" Policies

An "all risk" insurance policy is very broad in scope of coverage, but is not an "all loss" policy. It contains certain express or implied exclusions that have developed over the years, and "all risk" insurance policies generally cover: (1) losses caused by a fortuitous or accidental event; and (2) losses from an external, extraneous cause rather than an internal or inherent defect in the subject matter. For a discussion comparing all-risk insurance policies with specific-risk policies, see generally KEETON & WIDISS, INSURANCE LAW § 5.1(b)–(d) (2d ed. 1988). For purposes of an "all risk" policy coverage, then, an event which is "inevitable" or certain to take place is not a "fortuitous event"; and a court must gauge this inevitable or fortuitous event by standing in the shoes of the parties at the time the policy was made. *See, e.g., Standard Structural Steel Co. v. Bethlehem Steel Corp.*, 597 F. Supp. 164 (D. Conn. 1984).

### Great Northern Insurance Co. v. Dayco Corp.

United States District Court, Southern District of New York
637 F. Supp. 765 (1986)

#### Milton Pollack, Senior District Judge

[Dayco, a manufacturer of V belts appointed Edith Reich, dba FTC, as its sales agent for the Soviet Union. She was paid a commission on each sale, before payment by the purchaser. Reich defrauded Dayco through a scheme of "double contracting":

presenting fictitious purchase orders to Dayco (with much higher prices) and different contracts (invoices with lower prices than she quoted at the time of the order) to Russian customers. When the Russians became "delinquent" in their payments in an amount in excess of $6,000,000, Dayco demanded payment from them. The Russians maintained they had paid for all the shipments. Dayco then employed an attorney, Mr. Huhs, fluent in Russian, to investigate the matter. When the fraud was discovered, Dayco filed a claim for loss under its all risk policy with Great Northern Insurance Co. Great Northern then filed this declaratory judgment action seeking a decree that it was not liable.]

## I. Burden of Proof

Under an all risks policy, the insured has the burden to establish a prima facie case for recovery. The insured need only prove the existence of the all risks policy, and the loss of the covered property. *See Pan American World Airways, Inc. v. Aetna Casualty and Surety Co.*, 505 F.2d 989, 999 (2d Cir. 1974) [reproduced in Chapter 1, *supra*]. The very purpose of an all risks policy is to protect the insured in cases where it is difficult to explain the disappearance of the property; thus, the insured need not establish the cause of the loss as part of its case. *See Atlantic Lines Limited v. American Motorists Insurance Co.*, 547 F.2d 11, 13 (2d Cir. 1976); *Holiday Inns Inc. v. Aetna Insurance Co.*, 571 F. Supp. 1460, 1463 (S.D.N.Y. 1983).

Dayco has demonstrated, by competent and admissible evidence, that its sales agent, Edith Reich, made representations that she had secured the contracts with the Russians as reported to Dayco; that Dayco genuinely believed Reich's representations and released the goods to the Russians in reasonable reliance on the alleged contracts; that Reich's representations were false in that the contracts which Reich presented to Dayco were not made; that as a result of its reliance on Reich's fraudulent representations, Dayco was deprived of its goods; and that Dayco had been unable to recover those goods. This evidence is sufficient to establish a *prima facie* case for recovery.

Once the insured has established a *prima facie* case, the insurer must prove that the claimed loss is excluded from coverage under the policy; the insurer must show that the loss was proximately caused by the excluded peril. The burden on the insurer is especially difficult because the exclusions will be given the interpretation which is most beneficial to the insured. It is not sufficient for the insurer to offer a reasonable interpretation under which the loss is excluded; it must demonstrate that an interpretation favorable to it is the only reasonable reading. *See Pan American*, 505 F.2d at 999–1000. Great Northern based its case at trial on two exclusions contained in the insurance policy: an employee infidelity exclusion and a provision requiring the insured to protect the property from further damage....

## II. Exclusion for Employee Infidelity

Great Northern argued at trial that two of Dayco's employees who were the most intimately associated with Edith Reich and the FTC transaction—Edwin Gordon, Senior Vice-President, and Jeanette Curry, Manager of the International Division—received over $100,000 each from Reich and that these two individuals aided Reich in her fraudulent scheme. Great Northern thus contends that Dayco's losses are excluded by the employee infidelity exclusion in the policy.

The policy provides that it "does not insure against physical damage caused by or resulting from: "... i) Theft, mysterious disappearance, conversion or infidelity by an employee of the insured. Actual physical damage to the Insured's property as a result of a willful act of malicious intent shall be deemed not to be an act of infidelity"....

The phrase "caused by or resulting from" in reference to an excluded peril requires the insurer to prove that the excluded peril is the proximate cause of the loss. *See Pan American*, 505 F.2d at 1006. The concept of proximate cause when applied to insurance policies is a limited one; New York courts give an especially narrow scope to the inquiry.... "[T]he horrendous niceties of the doctrine of so-called 'proximate cause' employed in negligence suits applies in a limited manner only to insurance policies." *New York, New Haven & Hartford Railroad Co. v. Gray*, 240 F.2d 460, 465 (2d Cir. 1957).

In the context of insurance policies, "the causation inquiry stops at the efficient physical cause of the loss; it does not trace events back to their metaphysical beginnings." *Pan American*, 505 F.2d at 1006. The concept of proximate cause is what the average person would ordinarily think of as the cause of the loss.

[T]he common understanding is that in construing [insurance] policies we are not to take broad views but generally are to stop our inquiries with the cause nearest to the loss. This is a settled rule of construction, and if it is understood, does not deserve much criticism, since theoretically at least the parties can shape their contract as they like....

In this case, the evidence clearly demonstrates that Edith Reich was the cause of Dayco's loss. It was Reich who presented the fictitious contracts to Dayco and induced Dayco to produce and ship goods pursuant to the contracts. Reich's actions were the direct and precipitating cause of Dayco's loss; no loss would have occurred without Reich's fraud.

Although it was shown that Gordon and Curry accepted money from Reich, this fact is not sufficient to establish that the employee infidelity exclusion applies to Dayco's loss. Great Northern had the burden of proving that the dishonest acts of Curry and Gordon were the proximate cause of the loss. Great Northern failed to satisfy this burden since there was no proof that either Curry or Gordon were co-conspirators with Reich or that either of them were involved, in any way, in Reich's fraudulent scheme....

There was no evidence that either Gordon or Curry knew that the contracts presented by Reich were fictitious, or that either of them participated, in any manner, in Reich's fraud. Both Gordon and Curry testified credibly to the effect that they always believed that the contracts with the Russians were valid and would be fulfilled; and that they did not know that the contracts were fictitious or that the orders as submitted to Dayco did not represent actual orders. No evidence was presented which in any way contradicted this testimony."

Where a policy expressly insures against direct loss and damage by one element but excludes loss or damage caused by another element, the coverage extends to the loss even though the excluded element is a contributory cause." *Essex House v. St. Paul Fire & Marine Insurance Co.*, 404 F. Supp. 978, 985 (S.D. Ohio 1975)....

The rationale underlying this rule of construction is that an insurance company can draft its policy as it desires; "if the insurer desires to have more remote causes determine the scope of the exclusion, he may draft language to effectuate that desire." *Pan American*, 505 F.2d at 1007. The rule is particularly applicable to all risks policies where the insured specifically purchases comprehensive coverage.

### III. Employment of Reasonable Means to Protect Property from Further Damage

Paragraph 12(a) of the insurance policy, entitled Protection of Property, states that "The insured's primary duty is to act in every respect as if no insurance existed. The Insured shall employ every reasonable means to protect the property from further damage, including the prompt execution of temporary repairs where necessary for such protection and separate damaged from undamaged personal property."

Great Northern contends that in accordance with this clause, once Dayco discovered the fraud, it had a duty to attempt to get back the goods and that Dayco failed to satisfy this duty. Thus, Great Northern argues that the loss is excluded by this clause.

Great Northern's argument that the Protection of Property clause excludes Dayco's loss is unpersuasive. To prove that the claimed loss is excluded, Great Northern must demonstrate that its interpretation of the clause is the only reasonable reading of it. *See Pan American*, 505 F.2d at 999–1000. Pursuant to this rule of construction, it is questionable whether the clause can be interpreted to impose an affirmative duty on the insured to secure the return of property which is no longer in its control.

Nevertheless, even if the clause can be interpreted to place such a duty on the insured, Dayco has clearly satisfied its burden under the clause. Dayco retained John Huhs to investigate the existence or nonexistence of the contracts purportedly procured by Reich and to ascertain what had happened to Dayco's goods after shipment. Mr. Huhs met with representatives of Tractoroexport in Moscow on two occasions and made inquiries to determine what had happened to Dayco's goods after they were shipped to Russia. The Tractoroexport representatives stated that they no longer had Dayco's merchandise and that they had no knowledge as to the whereabouts of the goods. Dayco's inquiries were sufficient to satisfy any duty which it may have had to attempt to secure the return of its property.

Great Northern has failed to carry its burden of proof to establish that it is relieved from liability under the insurance policy by any exclusion contained therein. Accordingly, as to the declaratory judgment phase of this action, Dayco is entitled to a decree from this Court that Great Northern is obligated to indemnify Dayco for the loss of its goods, under the insurance policy. In addition, Dayco is entitled to an award of attorneys' fees for its defense of this declaratory judgment action....

[The balance of this case, dealing with the subject of damages, is omitted.]

## *Notes and Questions*

As the *Dayco* decision succinctly summarized, a policyholder in an "all risk" policy has the initial burden to establish a *prima facie* case by showing the existence of the "all risk" policy, and the loss of the covered property. Once the policyholder has established this *prima facie* case, the insurer must then prove that the claimed loss is excluded from coverage under the policy and that the loss was caused by the excluded peril. So, although the fact situation in the *Dayco* case is rather unique, the burden of proof requirements on both the policyholder and the insurer were still fairly standard and straightforward in the analysis made by Judge Pollack.

*Query*: If sales agent Edith Reich fraudulently forged a number of fictitious policies, what then was "fortuitous" about Dayco's losses under the "all risk" policy, since there was a theft, mysterious disappearance, and employee infidelity exclusion in the Great Northern policy?

### PROBLEM ONE

A "bridge strand" or lifting cable used in the dismantling of an old bridge and the erection of a new replacement bridge was found to be defective due to exposure to the weather, ordinary wear and tear, or internal deficiencies within the cable itself.

- Was this damage caused by a "fortuitous event" that would trigger coverage under an "all risk" insurance policy?

- What if the damage to the cable was actually caused by an engineering miscalculation in the design of the cable guides?

- Would this be a "fortuitous event" under "all risk" policy coverage?

## [C] Specified Risk versus All-Risk Policies

Sometimes, it can be difficult to discern just what particular risks a specified risk property policy does cover, as the next case demonstrates.

## Northwest Airlines, Inc. v. Globe Indemnity Co.

Supreme Court of Minnesota
303 Minn. 16, 225 N.W.2d 831 (1975)

Yetka, Justice

[Plaintiff Northwest Airlines, Inc. (Northwest) had a "Blanket Crime Policy" issued by defendant Globe Indemnity Co. (Globe). On November 24, 1971, an individual who identified himself as "D.B. Cooper" hijacked plaintiff's Flight 305. He threatened to blow up the plane unless $200,000 cash and four parachutes were delivered to the plane at Seattle. Plaintiff made arrangements with a Seattle bank to deliver that much cash to plaintiff's terminal at the Seattle airport, a "premises" of plaintiff within the meaning of the subject insurance policy. The $200,000 was delivered and one of plaintiff's officials gave a receipt for the money while it was *inside the terminal* (emphasis in the original), then delivered it to the hijacked plane, which had landed at the airport. The official handed the money to a stewardess who, in turn, surrendered it to Cooper, along with four parachutes.

Cooper then ordered the plane to take off for Mexico. Approximately halfway between Seattle and Portland, Cooper parachuted from the plane. Neither he nor the money have ever been located.]

The "Blanket Crime Policy" underlying this appeal provides coverage as set forth in five insuring agreements, which may be described in general terms as follows:

(1) Employee dishonesty coverage.

(2) Loss inside the premises coverage.

(3) Loss outside the premises coverage.

(4) Money orders and counterfeit paper currency coverage.

(5) Depositor's forgery coverage.

Plaintiff seeks recovery under the following insuring agreements, which state in relevant part:

LOSS INSIDE THE PREMISES COVERAGE

II. Loss of Money and Securities by the actual destruction, disappearance or *wrongful abstraction* thereof *within the Premises* or within any Banking Premises or similar recognized places of safe deposit.

LOSS OUTSIDE THE PREMISES COVERAGE

III. Loss of Money and Securities by the actual destruction, disappearance or *wrongful abstraction* thereof outside the Premises while being conveyed by a *Messenger* or any armored motor vehicle company, or while within the living quarters in the home of any Messenger.

Loss of other property by Robbery or attempt thereat outside the Premises while being conveyed by a *Messenger* or any armored motor vehicle company, or by theft while within the living quarters in the home of any Messenger. (Italics supplied.)

Section 3 of the conditions and limitations of the policy provides the following definitions of terms relevant to the issues presented in this appeal:

"Money" means currency, coins, bank notes, Federal Reserve notes, precious metals of all kinds and bullion; and travelers checks, register checks and money orders held for sale to the public.

"Employee" means any natural person (except a director or trustee of the Insured, if a corporation, who is not also an officer or employee thereof in some other capacity) while in the regular service of the Insured in the ordinary course of the Insured's business during the Policy Period and whom the Insured compensates by salary, wages or commissions and has the right to govern and direct in the performance of such service, but does not mean any broker, factor, commission merchant, consignee, contractor or other agent or representative of the same general character....

"Premises" means the interior of that portion of any building which is occupied by the Insured in conducting its business.

"Messenger" means the Insured or a partner of the Insured or any Employee who is duly authorized by the Insured to have the care and custody of the insured property outside the Premises.

The trial court determined that there was a wrongful abstraction of money from within plaintiff's premises or from within plaintiff's bank premises, and also outside the premises while the money was being conveyed by a messenger as defined in the policy. From judgment for plaintiff in the amount of $180,000 plus interest and costs and disbursements, defendant appeals.

To recover, defendant correctly states that plaintiff must establish:

(1) That it suffered a loss of money.

(2) That the loss resulted from the actual wrongful abstraction thereof.

(3) That the wrongful abstraction is a risk covered in the policy.

Defendant attacks the first element on grounds that the trial court's finding that plaintiff "suffered a loss of $200,000 in money by means of wrongful abstraction thereof within the meaning of the contract of insurance" is too general. This assertion must fail because:

(a) The court found that plaintiff obtained $200,000 in cash and delivered it to a stewardess who, in turn, delivered said money to the hijacker.

(b) A fair reading of the findings establishes that the hijacker jumped from the airplane with the money.

(c) The court found that none of the $200,000 has been recovered.

In the light of the foregoing, we cannot agree that the taking of the $200,000 is not a "loss of money" as defined in the policy.

Defendant maintains that the insuring agreement was intended to cover only specific money that plaintiff might have on its premises at any particular time from ticket sales and other receipts, and could not include borrowed money and that, therefore, the money taken really did not belong to Northwest Airlines. However, we see little reason for a distinction between money which plaintiff has on hand itself, which it borrowed, or which it could readily borrow.

The second requisite element, wrongful abstraction, is not defined in the policy and the parties agree that said term is unambiguous. The applicable rule of interpretation is found in *Orren v. Phoenix Ins. Co.*, 288 Minn. 225, 228, 179 N.W.2d 166, 169 (1970), which states:

... Where the language used in a insurance contract is unambiguous, it must be given its ordinary and usual meaning the same as the language of any other contract, and this court cannot under the guise of construction redraft the contract.

Defendant characterizes the hijacking as extortion, which is "wrongful" according to the definition of extortion provided by defendant. Thus, the hijacking was wrongful. The term "abstract" is defined in *Webster's New International Dictionary* (2d ed. 1947) p. 10, as "to take secretly or dishonestly." In light of the above-quoted rule from the *Orren* case it would appear clear that airline hijacking for ransom is indeed wrongful abstraction.

Defendant argues also that extortion is not a peril insured against by the policy. Defendant proposes that the rule of "*expressio unius est exclusio alteris*" is applicable because the inclusion of coverage for wrongful abstraction thereby excludes coverage for extortion and hijacking losses. We do not agree with these contentions.

Defendant contends that wrongful abstraction cannot occur when the taking is consented to by the owner.... We reject this argument also. To say that, in the circumstances of this case, plaintiff in any way consented to its $200,000 loss is contra to logic as well as to law.

In summary, it is fair to state that the term "wrongful abstraction" is as broad in scope as it is possible to envision. Had defendant desired to couch coverage in more restrictive terms, it was its duty to do so since it is obvious that plaintiff would not voluntarily suggest more restrictive language which would naturally work to its detriment.

Defendant contends the third requisite element for coverage under Insuring Agreement II, wrongful abstraction within the premises, has not been fulfilled. It argues that the wrongful abstraction took place when Cooper assumed control of the airplane. Thus, it concludes that, since the $200,000 was not at the covered premises at that moment, there was no loss of money due to wrongful abstraction. This argument, too, must fail in the cold light of the fact that the hijacking consisted of a continuing course of related events beginning with the takeover of the airplane and culminating with the hijacker's successful escape with the money which was, when taken, owned by plaintiff.

During cross-examination both of plaintiff's officers in charge of insurance testified that they believed Insuring Agreement II provided coverage because they considered the airplane was a "premises" under this provision. When confronted with the definition of "premises" set forth in the policy, both witnesses admitted they were mistaken (as "premises" clearly does not include airplanes). Defendant thus argues that the "misconstruction and misinterpretation" by plaintiff's executives should not be the basis of finding that coverage existed under the policy. However, the decision of the trial court was not reached on the erroneous interpretation that the airplane was the "premises."

In continuation of the above argument, defendant concludes that since the wrongful taking did not occur until the hijacker first exercised dominion over the money (*i.e.,* when the money was delivered to him aboard the airplane) the wrongful taking did not occur within "premises" as defined in the policy.

When that policy is read as a whole, we find it to be in the nature of a blanket or all-risk policy, as opposed to one which covers only specified risks. As defendant's counsel admitted in oral argument, mere unforeseeability of the manner in which the loss was sustained will not *per se* constitute grounds for the insurer to deny coverage. In the present case, where there is blanket coverage and the risk at issue was not excluded, the insurer must fulfill its contractual obligation to indemnify the insured.

Moreover, as noted above, both parties have strongly argued that there is no ambiguity present in the policy at issue. However, the very fact that their respective positions as to what this policy says are so contrary compels one to conclude that the agreement is indeed ambiguous. The rule is well settled that ambiguous language will be strictly construed in favor of the insured. [In footnote two of the opinion, the Court observed: "Defendant contends that the rule of strict construction should not be applied against it because the policy at issue was the result of arm's-length negotiations between defendant and a sophisticated insured which was represented by its own insurance experts. However, the record shows that the basis for the policy at issue was a printed form supplied by defendant. The specific provisions at issue were taken verbatim therefrom."]

## *Notes and Questions*

1. How did the court here convert a specified perils policy into one of all-risks? Was it justified in doing so? Why?

2. Why do you think the insurance market supports the existence of both specified perils coverage and all-risks coverage?

3. Coverage for loss or theft of property may be limited by the insurance company only to loss or theft occurring "on" or "within" the "premises." But what is the scope of the term "premises"? With homeowner's insurance, it has been held that the loss of personal property in a separate building on the rear of a home lot was covered under a fire insurance policy as occurring on the "premises," rather than falling under a clause excluding coverage for property away from the "premises." *See Stout v. Washington Fire & Marine Ins. Co.*, 385 P.2d 608 (Utah 1963). But other courts have held to the contrary.

How "premises" is defined for purposes of insurance coverage presents a multitude of examples and illustrations. How was the term "premises" explained and utilized in the *Globe* case? Can the "premises" of an airline really equate to rocketing through the air at 30,000 feet on a plane?

4. There is a liability insurance coverage known as a "premises-operations" policy which covers injury or loss on the policyholder's premises while a manufacturing or other activity is in progress, and prior to the activity's completion, resulting from an act of negligence or omission. This "premises-operations" insurance coverage is distinguished from product liability insurance, which covers loss or injury once a product has been completed and distributed in the marketplace. *See, e.g., Lindley Chemical, Inc. v. Hartford Acci. & Indem. Co.*, 322 S.E. 2d 185 (N.C. Ct. App. 1984).

## PROBLEM TWO

John Sheehan, a farmer assisted by three employees, was harvesting feed corn and storing it in five storage bins which he rented from a government agency. The bins were located on government property several miles from Sheehan's farm. Sheehan's employees negligently dumped feed corn into a nearby bin leased to Robert Davis. Davis' bin was partially filled with certified seed corn which was rendered worthless when the feed corn was commingled with it. Sheehan's insurance policy coverage for farming operations excluded the unloading of vehicles "while away from the premises." "Premises" was defined in the policy as "all premises which the Named Insured or his spouse owns, rents or operates as a farm or maintains as a residence and includes private approaches thereto and other premises and private approaches thereto for use in connection with said farm or residence, except business property."

- Should Sheehan's storage bin liability be covered or excluded under the policy?

# § 8.03. Triggering Coverage in Property Insurance

Insurance is not applicable until an insured event occurs. In most cases, the time of injury or destruction is obvious, particularly with perils such as fire or windstorm. But what about more subtle or less apparent injury with delayed manifestation? What juncture is the point of trigger for these? The issue becomes more important if Insurer A is on the risk at the time the problem started, and Insurer B is on the risk at the time the problem became obvious. Insurer A will predictably argue that the apt trigger is the date on which the damage became apparent. Insurer B will argue that insurance coverage is triggered by the early stages of the process resulting in the now-obvious damage. Which insurer should win the argument, A or B? What contextual factors should be important to a court in deciding such a dispute over trigger?

## Prudential-LMI Commercial Insurance v. Superior Court

Supreme Court of California
51 Cal. 3d 674, 274 Cal. Rptr. 387, 798 P.2d 1230 (1990)

Lucas, J.

Petitioner Prudential-LMI Commercial Insurance (Prudential) and real parties in interest (plaintiffs) each seek review of a Court of Appeal decision issuing a writ of mandate directing summary judgment in favor of Prudential. The action involves progressive property damage to an apartment house owned by plaintiffs and insured over the years by successive insurers, including Prudential.

We granted review to address three issues: (i) when does the standard one-year limitation period (hereafter one-year suit provision) contained in all fire policies (pursuant to Ins. Code § 2071) [all further statutory references are to the Insurance Code unless otherwise noted] begin to run in a progressive property damage case; (ii) should a rule of equitable tolling be imposed to postpone the running of the one-year suit provision from the date notice of loss is given to the insurer until formal denial of the claim; and (iii) when there are successive insurers, who is responsible for indemnifying the insured for a covered loss when the loss is not discovered until several years after it commences?

The last issue can be resolved by placing responsibility on (a) the insurer insuring the risk at the time the damage began, (b) the insurer insuring the risk at the time the damage manifested itself, or (c) all insurers on the risk, under an allocation (or exposure) theory of recovery.

As explained below, we hold that the one-year suit provision begins to run on the date of inception of the loss, defined as that point in time when appreciable damage occurs and is or should be known to the insured, such that a reasonable insured would be aware that his notification duty under the policy has been triggered.

We also hold that this limitation period should be equitably tolled from the time the insured files a timely notice, pursuant to policy notice provisions, to the time the insurer formally denies the claim in writing.

In addition, we conclude that in a first party property damage case (i.e., one involving no third party liability claims), the carrier insuring the property at the time of manifestation of property damage is solely responsible for indemnification once coverage is found to exist.

As we explain further below, we emphasize that our holding is limited in application to the first party progressive property loss cases in the context of a homeowners insurance policy. As we recognized in *Garvey v. State Farm Fire & Casualty Co.*, (1989) 48 Cal.3d 395, 405–408 [257 Cal.Rptr. 292, 770 P.2d 704], there are substantial analytical differences between first party property policies and third party liability policies. Accordingly, we intimate no view as to the application of our decision in either the third party liability or commercial liability (including toxic tort) context.

### 1. The Policy

Plaintiffs, as trustees of a family trust, built an apartment house in 1970–1971 and insured it with four successive fire and extended coverage property insurers between 1971 and 1986. Prudential insured the risk between October 27, 1977, and October 27, 1980. It issued an all-risk homeowners policy which insured against "All Risks of Direct Physical Loss except as hereinafter excluded." The policy insured for both property loss and liability.

As noted above, we are concerned here only with the first party property loss portion of plaintiffs' policy. It insured against all risks of direct physical loss subject to the terms and conditions set forth in the policy, which provided definitions and general policy provisions explaining to the insured the coverages and exclusions of the policy. The specified exclusions included loss "caused by, resulting from, contributed to or aggravated by any earth movement, including but not limited to earthquake, mudflow, earth sinking, rising or shifting; unless loss by fire or explosion ensues, and this Company shall then be liable only for such ensuing loss."

The policy contained several standard provisions adopted from the "California Standard Form Fire Insurance Policy" and section 2071, entitled "Requirements in case loss occurs." The provisions in relevant part required the insured to: "give written notice ... without unnecessary delay, protect the property from further damage ... and within 60 days after the loss, unless such time is extended in writing by this company, the insured shall render to this company a proof of loss, signed and sworn to by the insured, stating the knowledge and belief of the insured as to the following: the time and origin of the loss, [and] the interest of the insured and all others in the property...."

In the same section of the policy, the provision entitled "When loss payable" required the insurer to pay the amount of loss for which the company may be liable "60 days after proof of loss ... is received by this company and ascertainment of the loss is made whether by agreement between the insured and this company expressed in writing or by the filing with this company of an award as [otherwise provided in the policy—i.e., pursuant to the policy arbitration and appraisal provisions]."

Plaintiffs' policy also contained the standard one-year suit provision first adopted by the Legislature in 1909 as part of the "California Standard Form Fire Insurance Policy." (*See* §§ 2070, 2071.) It provided: "No suit or action on this policy for the recovery of any claim shall be sustainable in any court of law or equity unless all the requirements of this policy shall have been complied with, and unless commenced within 12 months next after inception of the loss." With this background in mind, we turn to the facts underlying this claim.

## 2. The Facts

While replacing the floor covering in an apartment unit in November 1985, plaintiffs discovered an extensive crack in the foundation and floor slab of the building. In December 1985, they filed a claim with their brokers, who immediately notified Prudential and the other companies that had issued insurance policies on the property during plaintiffs' period of ownership. Prudential conducted an investigation of the claim, which included an examination under oath of plaintiffs in February 1987. Prudential concluded the crack was caused by expansive soil that caused stress, rupturing the foundation of the building.

In August 1987, shortly before receiving formal written notice that their claim had been denied under the policy's earth movement exclusion, plaintiffs sued Prudential, the three other insurers that had insured the property between 1971 and 1986, and their insurance brokers or agents, alleging theories of breach of contract, bad faith, breach of fiduciary duties and negligence.

\* \* \*

## 5. Progressive Loss Rule

We next examine allocation of indemnity between successive first party property insurers when the loss is continuous and progressive throughout successive policy periods, but is not discovered until it becomes appreciable, for a reasonable insured to be aware that his notification duty under the policy has been triggered. Although the Court of Appeal here held that plaintiffs' claim was time-barred under section 2071, it observed in dictum that apportionment of damages between all insurers who insured the risk during the time of the development of the injury would be the "equitable result." The court based its reasoning on a line of cases applying the "continuous exposure theory" of loss allocation, which apportions payment between those insurers whose policies insured the risk during the period from the date when damage first occurred to the date of its discovery by the insured.

The foregoing theory was first announced in the context of a third party construction defect case [citation omitted], and more recently found application in cases involving asbestos-related bodily injury. [citations omitted] In 1983, the Court of Appeal relied on these cases to conclude that apportionment of liability among successive insurers was the only equitable method for determining which carrier should pay in a third party property damage case, when the loss (leakage from a swimming pool) continued over two separate policy periods. (*California Union Ins. Co.* [*v. Landmark Ins. Co.*, 145 Cal. App.3d 462,193 Cal. Rptr. 461 (1983)].)

Prudential argues that even assuming the applicable one-year suit provision does not bar the suit, it should not be responsible for any covered loss because plaintiffs presented no evidence that a loss was suffered during the period of its policy term (Oct. 27, 1977, to Oct. 27, 1980). It also asserts that because its policy period ended in 1980—five years before the damage was allegedly discovered by plaintiffs—it should not be responsible for indemnification of *any* covered loss.

Prudential asks the court to adopt a "manifestation rule" of property coverage that fixes liability for first party property losses solely on the insurer whose policy was in force at the time the progressive damage became appreciable or "manifest." In discussing both the manifestation and continuous exposure theories, we keep in mind the important distinction that must be made in a causation analysis between first party property damage cases and third party liability cases.

### The Manifestation and Exposure Theories

The first case to discuss a manifestation theory in the first party property context was *Snapp v. State Farm Fire & Cas. Co.*, (1962) 206 Cal.App.2d 827, 831–832 [24 Cal.Rptr. 44] (*Snapp*). The *Snapp* court was called on to resolve the insurer's contention that its homeowners policy did not cover a loss to the insured residence resulting from the movement of unstable fill. The homeowners policy was written by State Farm for a three-year term commencing in 1956 and consisted of the "California Standard Form Fire Insurance Policy" and an endorsement extending the coverage to insure against property loss.

The loss "materialized" and thus became "ascertainable" during State Farm's policy period and continued to progress after the policy term expired. State Farm first argued that because the instability of the fill made the resulting earth movement "inevitable," the loss was not a "fortuitous" event, and hence not covered under the policy. State Farm relied, in part, on sections 22 and 250, which codify the "loss-in-progress rule" and provide that an insurance contract indemnifies only against contingent or unknown events (§ 22), and any such contingent or unknown event may be insured against subject to the limitations of the Insurance Code (§ 250).

The court rejected this argument, however, and held that although the loss may have been "inevitable," such inevitability did not alter the fact that "at the time the contract of insurance was entered into, the event was only a *contingency* or *risk* that might or might not occur within the term of the policy." (*Snapp*).

State Farm next asserted that even assuming it was responsible for the loss, its liability became "terminable" on the date its policy expired and therefore it was not liable for the "continuing damage or loss" after expiration. In rejecting State Farm's argument, the *Snapp* court noted that the question of whether the insurer was liable for the loss was a legal rather than factual issue. The court held, "[t]o permit the insurer to terminate its liability while the fortuitous peril which materialized during the term of the policy was still active would not be in accord either with applicable precedents or with the common understanding of the nature and purpose of insurance; it would allow an injustice to be worked upon the insured by defeating the very substance of the protection for which his premiums were paid." [*Snapp*]

Thus the court determined, "[o]nce the contingent event insured against has occurred during the period covered, the liability of the carrier becomes *contractual* rather than *potential* only, and the sole issue remaining is the extent of its obligation, and it is immaterial that this may not be fully ascertained at the end of the policy period." (*Id.* at p. 832.) The court concluded the date of "materialization" of a loss determines which carrier must provide indemnity for a loss suffered by the insured, and the carrier insuring the risk at the time the damage is first discovered is liable for the entire loss.

Next, in *Sabella v. Wisler*, (1963) 59 Cal.2d 21, 25 [27 Cal.Rptr. 689, 377 P.2d 889] (*Sabella*), the insurer claimed that damage to the insured's residence was not fortuitous and thus not covered because "the damage occurred as a result of the operation of forces inherent" in the underlying soil conditions (including uncompacted fill and defective workmanship in the installation of a sewer outflow that ultimately broke). *Sabella* rejected the insurer's contention that the loss was "not fortuitous and hence not a 'risk' properly the subject of insurance." (*Id.*) Relying on *Snapp, Sabella* held that even if it were inevitable that the damage would have occurred at some time during ownership of the house, the loss was covered because such loss was a contingency or risk at the time the parties entered into the policy....

The next California case to address the problems arising in progressive property damage cases presented the issue of which carrier should indemnify insureds for a loss that occurred over two separate policy periods. In *California Union Ins. Co.*, 145 Cal.App.3d 462, a third party liability insurance case, the insureds installed a swimming pool during Landmark Insurance Company's policy period. The pipes to the pool (and possibly the pool itself) began to leak during Landmark's policy period and continued to leak during the term of the subsequent insurer, California Union.

Repairs which the parties believed corrected the leakage were made during Landmark's policy term. Nonetheless, because the underlying cause of the damage had not been discovered, the repairs were ineffective and additional damage occurred after California Union insured the risk.

Because the case involved liability policies, the Court of Appeal relied on three out-of-state liability cases that had apportioned payment between successive insurers when the damage or injury had continued during the separate policy periods. One case involved construction damage (*Gruol Construction Co. v. Insurance Co. of North America, supra,* 11 Wn.App. 632 [524 P.2d 427]), and the others involved asbestos-related bodily injury ...

The *California Union Ins. Co.* court determined that it was faced with a "one occurrence" case, involving continuous, progressive and deteriorating damage, notwithstanding the fact that new damage occurred to the pool after certain repairs had been made (*California Union Ins. Co., supra,* 145 Cal.App.3d 462, 468–474), and held both insurers jointly and severally liable for the damages (*id.* at p. 476). It reasoned that in a third party liability case "involving continuous, progressive and deteriorating damage," the carrier insuring the risk when the damage first becomes apparent remains responsible for indemnifying the loss until the damage is complete, notwithstanding a policy provision which purports to limit coverage to losses occurring within the parameters of the policy term....

In *Home Ins. Co.* [*v. Landmark Ins. Co.* (1988)], 205 Cal.App.3d 1388, the sole issue was "which of two first party insurers is liable for the loss from continuing property damage manifested during successive policy periods." (*Id.* at p. 1390.) Home insured the Hotel del Coronado against property damage for the period September 1, 1980, through October 1, 1986. The concrete facade of portions of the structure "first began to visibly manifest deterioration in the form of ...'spalling' (cracking and chipping)" in or about December of 1980. (*Id.* at p. 1391.) The spalling continued after it was first discovered by the insured and became progressively worse over time, extending through the expiration of Home's coverage and the inception of the Landmark policy.

Although the damage was initially discovered in the first of the two policy periods, and continued through both policy periods, apparently it was impossible to determine the extent of damage occurring during each period, and thus the amount of coverage owed by each insurer could not be determined. In a subsequent declaratory relief action, the trial court determined that under the manifestation and loss-in-progress rules, Home was solely at risk. (*Id.* at p. 1392.)

The Court of Appeal affirmed, holding that the "date of manifestation determines which carrier must provide indemnity for a loss suffered by its insured." The court rejected Home's reliance on *California Union Ins. Co.,* for the proposition that the loss-in-progress rule is inapplicable to claims for continuing and progressive property damage. As the *Home Ins. Co.* court observed, *California Union Ins. Co., supra,* had been "based on the exposure theory ... commonly used in asbestos bodily injury cases.... Common sense tells us that property damage cases, even those involving continuous damage such as the one before us, differ from asbestos bodily injury cases where injury is immediate, cumulative and exacerbated by repeated exposure. We believe the rationale for apportioning liability in the asbestos cases is not a basis to deviate from settled principles of law."

Thus, the *Home Ins. Co.* court reasoned, *California Union Ins. Co.* should not be applied to the property damage case before the court. Accordingly, the court held that "as between two first-party insurers, one of which is on the risk on the date of first manifestation of property damage, and the other on the risk after the date of the first manifestation of damage, the first insurer must pay the entire claim."

Because *California Union Ins. Co.*, addressed a third party liability question, its analysis necessarily differed in many respects from the one we undertake here. As one court observed, in first party cases applying the rule finding coverage only on actual occurrence of injury, no damage or injury of any kind has taken place until manifestation; the cause instead lies dormant until it later causes appreciable injury. By contrast, when damages slowly accumulate, the exposure theory should apply. (*Ibid.*) As [one commentator] observes, "The issue of continuous and progressive losses has not arisen frequently in the context of first party cases (perhaps because homeowner's policies were [originally drafted] to cover only sudden damage such as fire and windstorm, and not gradual damage such as settlement)." ...

Other commentators have warned against confusing first and third party issues. "Applying the terminology that has grown up around bodily injury [liability] insurance coverage cases in the context of coverage for property damage implies that the considerations are identical and obscures the real differences between the two types of problems." (Arness & Eliason, *Insurance Coverage for "Property Damage" in Asbestos and Other Toxic Tort Cases* (1986) 72 Va.L.Rev. 943, 973, fn. 108.) Accordingly, and because the issue of whether an allocation or exposure theory should apply in the third party property damage liability context is not before the court, we leave its resolution to another date.

As stated by the *Home Ins. Co.* court, the manifestation rule in the first party context "promotes certainty in the insurance industry and allows insurers to gauge premiums with greater accuracy. Presumably this should reduce costs for consumers because insurers will be able to set aside proper reserves for well-defined coverages and avoid increasing such reserves to cover potential financial losses caused by uncertainty in the definition of coverage."

Based on the reasoning set forth in *Snapp, Sabella* and *Home Ins. Co.*, we conclude that in first party progressive property loss cases, when, as in the present case, the loss occurs over several policy periods and is not discovered until several years after it commences, the manifestation rule applies. As stated above, prior to the manifestation of damage, the loss is still a contingency under the policy and the insured has not suffered a compensable loss. Once the loss is manifested, however, the risk is no longer contingent; rather, an event has occurred that triggers indemnity unless such event is specifically excluded under the policy terms.

Correspondingly, in conformity with the loss-in-progress rule, insurers whose policy terms commence after initial manifestation of the loss are not responsible for any potential claim relating to the previously discovered and manifested loss. Under this rule, the reasonable expectations of the insureds are met because they look to their present carrier for coverage. At the same time, the underwriting practices of the insurer can be made predictable because the insurer is not liable for a loss once its contract with the insured ends unless the manifestation of loss occurred during its contract term.

One final question must be addressed regarding the application of a manifestation rule of coverage in progressive loss cases: how does the rule relate to our rules of delayed discovery and equitable tolling announced above? We have previously defined the term "inception of the loss" as that point in time when appreciable damage occurs and is or should be known to the insured, such that a reasonable insured would be aware that his notification duty under the policy has been triggered. We conclude that the definition of "manifestation of the loss" must be the same.

Under this standard, the date of manifestation and hence the date of inception of the loss will, in many cases, be an issue of fact for the jury to decide. When, however, the evidence supports only one conclusion, summary judgment may be appropriate. For example, when the undisputed evidence establishes that no damage had been discovered before a given date (i.e., no manifestation occurred), then insurers whose policies expired prior to that date could not be liable for the loss and would be entitled to summary judgment. The litigation can then be narrowed to include only the insurers whose policies were in effect when the damage became manifest.

### Conclusion

Based on the principles discussed above, we conclude plaintiffs should be allowed to amend their complaint to allege that their delayed discovery of the loss at issue was reasonable, and that they timely notified Prudential of the loss without unnecessary delay following its manifestation. If it is found that plaintiffs' delayed discovery of the loss was reasonable, then the rule of equitable tolling would operate to toll the one-year suit provision from the date the insured filed a timely notice of loss to Prudential's formal denial of coverage.

Whether Prudential must then indemnify plaintiffs for any covered claim under the policy necessarily depends on whether that insurer was the carrier of record on the date of manifestation of the loss. Although it appears from the present record that manifestation of loss occurred in November 1985, after Prudential's policy had expired, we note that plaintiffs have joined other insurers in the litigation. Therefore, in the absence of conclusive evidence, we decline to speculate concerning the date manifestation of loss occurred. The decision of the Court of Appeal is reversed and the cause remanded for proceedings consistent with our opinion.

*Notes and Questions*

Should the analysis focus on trigger or on causation? *Contra State Farm Fire & Casualty Co. v. Von Der Lieth*, 2 Cal. Rptr. 2d 183, 820 P.2d 285 (1991). There is some obvious overlap. Are the two cases consistent? Does *Von Der Lieth* suggest any movement toward a more expansive or more restrictive trigger of property insurance coverage? As discussed in *Prudential-LMI*, above, courts have largely taken a different approach to the trigger of liability insurance coverage, one in which the bodily injury or property damage to the third party making a claim against the policyholder need not be visibly manifest. *See* Randy Maniloff & Jeffrey Stempel, General Liability Insurance: Key Issues in Every State, Ch. 15 (2011).

### PROBLEM THREE

Your lovely chalet in the Pacific Northwest looked like a million (and cost nearly that) when you bought it 10 years ago. Unbeknownst to you, it was afflicted with a condition known as "dry rot" in which the wood was decomposing underneath the exterior. You did not notice the problem until the dry rot broke through six years ago. Now, it appears the condition permeates the whole house, requiring extremely expensive repairs, maybe even making the structure a total loss.

- Which insurer should pay: the property insurer you used when you bought the house 10 years ago?
- The one you switched to six years ago?
- The one you were with four years ago?
- The insurer you are with today?
- None of them?
- All of them? Why?
- Exactly when does property damage occur under this scenario?

# § 8.04. The Innocent Co-Insured Problem

When a policyholder acts alone in perpetrating a fraud or causing a loss in a manner that otherwise falls outside of coverage (e.g., causing intentional injury), the matter is relatively straight-forward: there is no coverage. Similarly, where two policyholders individually or in concert cause uncovered injury, there is no coverage. But what if one policyholder intentionally destroys property while the other policyholder is genuinely innocent? This is not an uncommon scenario in arson or drug forfeiture cases.

One spouse (usually the husband) may be chest-deep in crime and fraud while the other spouse has no knowledge of the other's nefarious conduct. Although it is perhaps sweet that love can be so occasionally blind, should this permit the "innocent" co-insured to collect insurance despite the misconduct of the "guilty" insured?

# Borman v. State Farm Fire & Casualty Co.

Supreme Court of Michigan
446 Mich. 482, 521 N.W.2d 266 (1994)

**Levin, J.**

This Court granted leave to appeal, limited to the issue whether § 2832 of the Insurance Code, providing the form of the standard fire insurance policy, "prohibits an insurer from denying coverage to an insured who is innocent of wrongdoing based upon the wrongdoing of any other coinsured."

We hold that the provisions of the insurance policy issued by defendant State Farm Fire & Casualty Co., insofar as they deny coverage to an insured who is innocent of wrongdoing by another insured, are inconsistent with the provisions of the standard policy, and, thus, contrary to the provisions of the standard policy, and are therefore void insofar as fire insurance coverage is involved.

We further hold that State Farm is subject to liability under the policy to the plaintiff's decedent, who was an innocent insured, in the same manner and to the same extent as if the inconsistent provisions were not contained in the policy.

Dennis Borman commenced this action against State Farm as personal representative of the estate of Lillian Roach to recover for the loss of personal property belonging to Roach that was destroyed in December, 1988, by a fire at an adult foster care home that her grandson, Gary Borman, was purchasing on land contract. The fire was set or arranged to be set by Gary Borman or persons in privity with him. Roach was not complicit in the wrongdoing.

The circuit court granted summary disposition for State Farm relying on the basis of language in the policy excluding coverage for intentional wrongful acts by "any insured," citing this Court's decision in *Allstate Ins. Co. v. Freeman*, 443 N.W.2d 734 (Mich. 1989). The Court of Appeals reversed, relying on this Court's decision in *Morgan v. Cincinnati Ins. Co.*, 307 N.W.2d 53 (Mich. 1981).[1]

In *Morgan*, Helen and Robert Morgan owned a home as tenants by the entireties. The home was extensively damaged by a fire started by Robert Morgan. Divorce proceedings were then pending. The insurer claimed that the policy was voided when Robert Morgan intentionally started the fire. The insurer relied on the first sentence of the standard insurance policy prescribed by § 2832 of the Insurance Code.

Concealment fraud.

This entire policy shall be void if, whether before or after a loss, the insured has wilfully concealed or misrepresented any material fact or circumstance concerning this insurance or the subject thereof, or the interest of the insured therein, or in case of any fraud or false swearing by the insured relating thereto.[2]

\* \* \*

---

1. [5] 198 Mich.App. 675, 499 N.W.2d 419 (1993).
2. [6] M.C.L. § 500.2832; M.S.A. § 24.12832, repealed by 1990 P.A. 305.

This Court rejected the insurer's contention that "*the* insured" should be read as "*any* insured," with the result that the entire policy would be void if any insured committed fraud. The Court in *Morgan* said "[w]e believe such a reading is unwarranted," and read "the insured" as voiding the policy only in the event of fraud by the insured who committed the fraud. This Court said:

> We ... hold that the provision voiding the policy in the event of fraud by "the insured" is to be read as having application only to the insured who committed the fraud and makes claim under the policy. The provision has no application to any other person described in the policy as an insured.

> Henceforth whenever the statutory clause limiting the insurer's liability in case of fraud by the insured is used it will be read to bar only the claim of an insured who has committed the fraud and will not be read to bar the claim of any insured under the policy who is innocent of fraud.[3]

State Farm contends that *Morgan* does not govern disposition of this case because the homeowner's policy provides that the policy is void "as to you or any other insured" if any person insured under the policy causes or procures a loss to property covered under the policy for the purpose of obtaining insurance benefits, or intentionally conceals or misrepresents any material fact or circumstance and provides that in such event the insurer "will not pay you or any other insured for this loss."

In *Morgan*, the insurer claimed that the first sentence of the standard policy bars recovery by an insured who seeks to defraud the insurer and by any other person insured under the policy, including an insured who is innocent of wrongdoing. This Court responded that the language of the standard policy applies only to the insured who committed the fraud and has no application to any other person insured under the policy. This Court thus read the standard policy as providing in effect for recovery by an innocent insured under that statutorily mandated fire policy.

The provisions in the homeowner's policy relied on by State Farm cover the same subject matter, fraud on the insurer, as the first sentence of the standard policy. While the standard policy contemplates "[a]dded provisions" — "any other provision or agreement *not inconsistent* with the provisions" of the standard policy — because the provisions of the homeowner's policy relied on by State Farm cover the same subject matter as the first sentence of the standard policy, and provide for less coverage to innocent insureds than is mandated under the first sentence as construed by this Court in *Morgan*, the provisions of the homeowner's policy relied on by State Farm are "inconsistent with the provisions" of the standard policy and hence "absolutely void." Thus, State Farm is liable to Lillian Roach's estate, insofar as fire insurance coverage is involved, in the same manner and to the same extent as if the inconsistent provisions were not contained in the policy.

---

3. [9] *Id.*, at pp. 276–277, 307 N.W.2d 53.

State Farm and amicus curiae Auto Club Group Insurance Company contend that barring recovery by innocent insureds is necessary to address the problems of affordability and cost control for the insurer and the consumer. State Farm asserts that when a home is destroyed by fire, State Farm usually incurs a net loss after the mortgage holder or loss payee is paid and any litigation is successfully defended. It contends that homeowner's insurance will become more affordable if the equity of innocent coinsureds is forfeited to fire insurers.

Amici curiae on behalf of innocent coinsureds contend that many cases of homeowners' arson are related to domestic violence, and an inability of the innocent spouse to recover insurance proceeds may increase the guilty party's incentive to commit arson.[4]

We do not rest decision on any resolution of the merits of that policy debate. We have reviewed the case law in other jurisdictions and find support for the view set forth in *Morgan* in cases construing "the insured" where a standard policy is prescribed by the legislature....

We recognize that courts in other jurisdictions have enforced against innocent insureds contractual provisions voiding policies for fraud, concealment, or intentional acts by "an" or "any" insured, but in none of these cases did the court advert to any conflict with a standard policy prescribing a provision voiding the policy because of the wrongful conduct of "the insured."

**Robert P. Griffin, J.** (dissenting).

I respectfully dissent.

Defendant State Farm's fire insurance policy precludes recovery by "*any* insured" if a coinsured has "intentionally concealed or misrepresented any material fact"; the Michigan standard policy precluded recovery by "*the* insured." (Emphasis added.) Plaintiff Borman argues on appeal that use of the term "any insured" in defendant's policy violates the legislative intent underlying the standardized statutory policy. The majority has adopted plaintiff's reasoning and holds that the policy must not be construed to deny coverage to an innocent coinsured for the intentional wrongs of another insured.

However, I view this case from a different perspective. The real question is whether the statute ... permitted modification of the statutorily mandated fire insurance policy so as to change the ambiguous term "the insured" to "any insured," as well as to create a new policy exclusion for intentional acts of "any person insured under the policy." Because the modifications reflected in the policy at issue are unambiguous and consistent with the statutory scheme, I would hold that the term "any insured," as it is used in this policy, precludes recovery by an innocent coinsured.

---

4. [10] It is contended that domestic violence is largely motivated by a desire of one spouse to control and dominate the other. That the abuser's desire to control is threatened when the abused partner attempts to leave the relationship, and the abuser may resort to threatening and actual conduct designed to constrain the abused partner to rejoin the abuser, and depriving the abused partner of a home for herself and her children may and has been part of the abuser's plans.

This fraud provision in the Michigan standard policy has been interpreted by this Court to allow recovery by an innocent coinsured despite the wrongdoing of another coinsured. *Morgan v. Cincinnati Ins. Co.*, 411 Mich. 267, 307 N.W.2d 53 (1981). In *Morgan*, the plaintiff and her husband owned a home, as tenants by the entireties, that was insured by the defendant. The husband purposely set fire to the home, causing extensive damage. The insurer refused to pay the plaintiff, claiming that because she and her husband owned inseparable interests in the property as tenants by the entireties, the husband's fraud was imputed to the plaintiff. The insurer further argued that the standard policy at issue, which incorporated "the insured" language of § 2832, precluded coverage of the plaintiff. Applying § 2832 to the fire insurance policy, the *Morgan* Court resolved the ambiguity of the statutory term "the insured" in favor of the plaintiff and stated:

> The insurer in this case would have us read this provision as if it stated "[t]his entire policy shall be void if ... *any* person *insured*" has committed fraud. We believe such a reading is unwarranted, and hold that the provision voiding the policy in the event of fraud by "*the insured*" is to be read as having application only to the insured who committed the fraud and makes claim under the policy. The provision has no application to any other person described in the policy as an insured.
>
> Henceforth whenever the statutory clause limiting the insurer's liability in case of fraud by *the insured* is used it will be read to bar only the claim of an insured who has committed the fraud and will not be read to bar the claim of any insured under the policy who is innocent of fraud. [*Morgan, supra*, at pp. 276–277, 307 N.W.2d 53 (emphasis added).]

Obviously, *Morgan* did not address the effect of § 2832 or other provisions of the Insurance Code in the present context where more explicit and unambiguous policy language has been used. Rather, it dealt only with the limited situation in which the statutory language of § 2832 was set forth verbatim in an insurance contract.

We do not read this Court's decision in *Morgan* as mandating coverage for all innocent coinsureds under all circumstances. Indeed, *Morgan* took pains to provide instruction concerning the use of unambiguous language in policy provisions governing innocent coinsureds:

> We no longer consider the application of the theory of implied suretyship appropriate in insurance law. *In Michigan limitations on recovery under an insurance policy must be clearly stated in the contract.* The implication of a mutual obligation of suretyship among several insured persons is in effect a limitation on recovery by implication and not to be permitted under Michigan law.
>
> Furthermore, since the provision quoted above does not expressly create a joint obligation of suretyship, to read the fraud provision as creating one would be contrary to the reasonable expectations of an insured. *An ordinary person seeing his or her name included in an insurance contract without limiting language would suppose his or her interest to be covered.* It appears that the

instant policy names "Robert Morgan and Helen Morgan," without more, as the insured under the policy. [*Id.*, at p. 277, 307 N.W.2d 53 (emphasis added).]

In response to *Morgan*, defendant, as well as many other insurers, have revised their fire policies to make the language unambiguous. As a result, defendant's policy includes an intentional act provision, and language in the fraud provision has been modified to make clear that it applies to "any insured," rather than to "the insured," thereby rectifying the *Morgan* concern that the "the insured" language was not sufficiently explicit.

When the language of an insurance policy is clear and unambiguous, the contract should be enforced. Here, the policy's language excluding coverage for the concealment or fraud by "you or any other insured" unambiguously excludes an insured, even an innocent one. This Court has already interpreted the term "any insured" to include an innocent insured.

Moreover, while the insurance commissioner can reject insurance contracts that conflict with the statute, the commissioner explicitly approved the instant policy. Evidence of approval by the commissioner "should be somewhat persuasive of its compliance with the statute." [citations omitted]

I conclude that the policy language at issue in this case is not inconsistent with the statute or the standard policy. While the Legislature used the term "the insured," instead of "any insured," nothing in the legislative history indicates that it intended to preclude the coverage exclusion at issue here.

## Sager v. Farm Bureau Mutual Insurance Co.

Supreme Court of Iowa
680 N.W.2d 8 (2004)

**Streit, J.**

A battalion of Beanie Babies has marched a legal question before us. While on a quest to torch his wife Ramona's Beanie Baby collection, Robert Sager nearly burnt down the family house. Ramona now seeks to collect under the couple's homeowners policy with Farm Bureau for Robert's pyromaniacal actions. The policy, however, contains an exclusion for "intentional loss" at the hand of "an insured." In a matter of first impression, we hold Iowa's standard fire insurance policy, as set forth in Iowa Code section 515.138 (1999), renders the exclusion unenforceable. We reverse and remand for further proceedings.

The facts are stipulated. Robert Sager intentionally set a fire in the basement of a house he shared with his wife Ramona in DeWitt. Angry after Ramona told him she was ending their relationship, Robert torched Ramona's Christmas decorations in the basement of their house.[5] The fire quickly spread, and portions of the house were

---

5. [1] At a deposition conducted months later, Robert described the scene and his subsequent actions as follows:

She had Beanie Babies everywhere and I was sick of them sons of bitches and I decided

soon engulfed in flames. Robert's pyromaniacal act caused approximately $100,000 damage to the house and its contents. Not surprisingly, Robert and Ramona later divorced.

At the time of the fire, Robert and Ramona were named insureds under a homeowners policy with Farm Bureau Mutual Insurance Company. When Ramona sought payment, Farm Bureau denied her claim. To justify its nonpayment, Farm Bureau cited exclusions in the policy for "intentional loss"....

The "intentional loss" exclusion barred recovery for "any loss arising out of any act committed ... (1) [b]y or at the direction of an 'insured'... and (2) [w]ith the intent or expectation of causing a loss." Farm Bureau contended this exclusion precluded payment to Ramona because Robert, *an insured*, had purposefully started the fire.

In *Vance v. Pekin Insurance Company*, we held that where one spouse had intentionally set fire to the family home, an innocent coinsured spouse could not recover under a homeowners policy which clearly and unequivocally excluded coverage from losses resulting from the intentional acts of "*an insured*." 457 N.W. 2d at 593 (emphasis added). In *Vance*, we adopted the so-called "best reasoned rule," according to which "recovery depends ... on a contract analysis of the insurance policy provisions." *Id.* (citing Leane E. Cerven, Note, *The Problem of the Innocent Co-Insured Spouse: Three Theories of Recovery*, 17 Val. U.L.Rev. 849, 867–68 (1983)). We explicitly noted this contract analysis followed the recent trend in other courts away from analyses centering upon property rationales or the marital status of the parties. *See id.*

We have consistently applied this contract analysis ever since.... Other courts have followed suit. *See, e.g., Watson v. United Serv. Auto. Ass'n*, 566 N.W.2d 683, 688 (Minn.1997) ("The majority of courts use a contract-based theory which focuses on a contractual analysis of the insurance policy provisions ..."; policies which contain "an insured" bar recovery to an innocent coinsured spouse).... *See generally* 10 Lee R. Russ & Thomas F. Segalla, *Couch on Insurance 3d* § 149:49 (2003) ("whether arson by one coinsured spouse bars innocent coinsured spouse from recovering under policy depends not on property rationales or marital rights and obligations, but on contract analysis of insurance policy provisions ...").

*Vance* contained an intentional loss exclusion similar to the case at bar. In *Vance*, we interpreted the phrase "an insured" in the policy to mean "an unspecified insured" who intentionally sets fire to the house. 457 N.W. 2d at 593. That is, under the express

---

I was going to barbecue them. I had a big brush pile that I was going to burn outside and I had decided I was going to get all her Beanie Babies and take them out and barbecue the sons of bitches and went to get the charcoal lighter. Christmas has always been another big issue between us just because, you know, she sees it differently than I do, and I went in the basement to get the charcoal lighter and take it upstairs and fry her Beanie Babies and all her Christmas stuff was sitting there and I sprayed some charcoal lighter on her Christmas stuff and threw a couple of matches at it and it flared up a lot faster than I thought it was going to ...

According to Ramona, 150 Beanie Babies and Buddies perished in the fire. She claimed $1100 in damages for these collectible dolls.

terms of such a policy, if any insured sets fire to the house, all insureds are barred from recovering. *Id.* As a threshold matter, then, we find the provisions of the insurance contract at issue in this case bar Ramona's claim. As in *Vance*, the policy explicitly excludes coverage for "any loss arising out of any act committed ... (1) [b]y or at the direction of *an 'insured*'... and (2) [w]ith the intent or expectation of causing a loss." (Emphasis added.) Applying a contract analysis, Robert's malfeasance plainly bars Ramona's right to recover.

After *Vance* was decided, however, a new question arose in other jurisdictions: If an innocent coinsured spouse is denied coverage under the express terms of the policy, do those policy provisions then violate the mandatory coverage provisions in state statutes? Citing a relatively recent Minnesota decision, *Watson v. United Services Automobile Association*, 566 N.W.2d 683 (Minn.1997), Ramona claims her policy, if interpreted to bar an innocent coinsured spouse from recovery, violates the mandatory minimum coverage set by Iowa statute.

Found in Iowa Code section 515.138, our state's standard fire insurance policy "lists various permissible standard provisions for fire policies...." *Thomas v. United Fire & Cas. Co.*, 426 N.W.2d 396, 397 (Iowa 1988). That is,

> It shall be unlawful for any insurance company to issue any policy of fire insurance upon any property in this state ... different from the standard form of fire insurance policy herein set forth.... An insurer may issue a [different] policy ... if such policy includes provisions with respect to the peril of fire which are the substantial equivalent of the minimum provisions of such standard policy....

Iowa Code § 515.138. Insurance companies which offer or issue policies "other or different from the standard form" are guilty of a simple misdemeanor. *Id.* § 515.140. Such policies, however, nonetheless remain binding upon the insurance company. *Id.; cf. A.A. Cooper Wagon & Buggy Co. v. Nat'l. Ben Franklin Ins. Co.*, 188 Iowa 425, 430, 176 N.W. 309, 311 (1920) (recognizing, under earlier version of our standard fire insurance policy, that where policy does not conform to standard fire insurance policy, it is still binding upon the insurer). As we recently stated in another context,

> Notwithstanding the principle that the meaning of an insurance contract is generally determined from the language of the policy, statutory law may also affect our interpretation of policy provisions.... [W]hen a policy provision conflicts with a statutory requirement, the policy provision is ineffective and the statute controls.

*Lee v. Grinnell Mut. Reins. Co.*, 646 N.W.2d 403, 406 (Iowa 2002) (citations omitted).

The standard fire insurance policy itself is too lengthy to set forth here. As we have previously pointed out, however, "[t]he standard type of insurance policy is what is generally known as the New York type. It was first adopted in the state of New York and has been followed in Iowa and many other states since its original adoption." ... Like other jurisdictions employing the New York policy, Iowa's standard fire insurance policy does not contain an exclusion for intentional loss; the policy does, however, consistently refer to "the insured" in policy exclusions.

For example, the standard policy excludes coverage for losses due to "neglect of *the insured* to use all reasonable means to save and preserve the property at and after a loss...," as well as losses occurring "[w]hile the hazard is increased by any means within the control or knowledge of *the insured*." Iowa Code § 515.138 (emphases added).

Ramona argues the consistent use of the phrase "the insured" in the policy evinces a legislative intent to apply the exclusions only to the malfeasant insured, and not also to the innocent insured; when a homeowners policy denies coverage whenever "an insured" intentionally causes the loss, it conflicts with statute.

When interpreting our standard fire insurance policy, we look to the decisions of other jurisdictions with a similar policy.... Doing so, we discover Ramona's argument is supported by the great weight of authority. As the court of appeals noted, courts presented with this same question—and a growing number at that—have almost unanimously ruled in favor of the innocent coinsured spouse.... The Nebraska Supreme Court, for example, reasoned as follows:

> [W]hile there is no specifically designated intentional acts exclusion in the [standard policy], it includes other provisions dealing generally with the insurer's right to void coverage based upon conduct of "the insured." In each instance, the standard policy uses language indicative of a several obligation whereby the insured bears the responsibility for his or her own conduct. We find no provision ... creating a joint obligation whereby the wrongful actions of one insured could prejudice the rights of an innocent co-insured.

*Volquardson*, 647 N.W.2d at 610; *see also Watson*, 566 N.W.2d at 691 (because the Minnesota standard fire insurance policy consistently used "the insured" and not "an insured," the policy's intentional loss provision incorporated an additional contract term; the policy thus was "at odds with the rights and benefits of the Minnesota standard fire insurance policy" because it failed to provide coverage for innocent coinsured spouses); *Lane*, 747 N.E.2d at 1272 (same).

Farm Bureau contends the foregoing cases are distinguishable because of a difference in the Iowa statute. As indicated, Iowa's statute only prohibits those policies which are not the "substantial equivalent" of the statutory policy. Iowa Code § 515.138. Although this "substantial equivalent" provision is, so far as we can tell, somewhat peculiar to Iowa, it is not unique. *See* 1959 Iowa Acts ch. 329 (adding "substantial equivalent" proviso to standard fire policy). In *Volquardson*, for example, the Nebraska Supreme Court rejected an identical claim. 647 N.W.2d at 609. The relevant Nebraska statute stated a director of insurance may approve a non-standard policy "if such policy with respect to peril of fire includes provisions which are the substantial equivalent of the minimum provisions of the standard policy." Nebraska Rev. Stat. § 44-501(6) (1998). The Nebraska Supreme Court, however, ruled

> [t]here is an obvious substantive difference between joint and several obligations of multiple insureds with respect to a coverage exclusion based upon

conduct. Where the obligation is joint, commission of a proscribed act by one insured voids coverage as to all. However, where the obligation is several, the proscribed conduct defeats the policy rights of the insured who committed the act but not those of an innocent coinsured.

*Volquardson*, 647 N.W.2d at 609. We agree with this assessment, and hold the policy, insofar as it bars recovery to an innocent coinsured spouse, is not the substantial equivalent of Iowa Code section 515.138.

Lastly, we reject Farm Bureau's contention that accepting Ramona's argument "overrules" *Vance*. Farm Bureau maintains we must assume that we considered and rejected Ramona's statutory argument in *Vance*, because in that case we denied recovery to an innocent coinsured spouse — notwithstanding the fact Iowa Code section 515.138 was "on the books" at that time. Farm Bureau points out that *Vance* was written in response to a certified question from the federal district court; certified questions, it alleges, are different than cases taken on direct appeal, because our review in certified questions is not limited to issues raised, briefed, and argued by the parties.

We reject this argument. We were not presented with the standard fire insurance policy in *Vance*, and our answers to certified questions are no different than our decisions on direct appeal, insofar as both proceedings are *adversarial*. In either sort of case, we generally consider only questions argued by the parties; answers to certified questions should not be understood as all-encompassing court-approved treatises on a given body of law.

Farm Bureau's argument also ignores the organic nature of law: the law develops over time, in no small part due to the ability of lawyers to develop new arguments. Unfortunately, the best arguments are not marshaled before us in every case. We do not, then, "overrule" *Vance*, because in that case we were not presented with the statutory argument. Instead, our decision today simply "adds a second step to the contractual analysis." *Watson*, 566 N.W.2d at 689 (citations omitted).

Because we find the intentional loss provision is unenforceable against Ramona, we need not decide whether it is also rendered unenforceable due to ambiguity.

## Notes and Questions

1. Today, many courts and policymakers appear to recognize that sometimes the co-insured spouse is innocent even if informed. A wife or girlfriend may be the victim of domestic abuse and have been in no realistic position to keep a violent husband or boyfriend from committing arson. There is an NAIC model law on the topic and several states have enacted legislation to protect the co-insured who is the victim of domestic abuse. *See, e.g.,* NEB. REV. STAT. §44-7406; MD. CODE ANN. INS. §27-504 (1999). Washington has such a law (WASH. REV. CODE §48.18.550 (2000)) that states that an exclusion of co-insureds shall not apply to deny coverage to a domestic abuse victim for property loss, provided the victim has filed a police report, cooperates with the domestic abuse investigation, and was not an active party in creating the

property loss. Washington appears to have no similar provision for liability insurance and there is case law denying liability coverage to a wife whose husband has committed coverage-disqualifying intentional torts—a result that seems at odds with the state's apparent recognition of the problem for property insurance. *See Mutual of Enumclaw Ins. Co. v. Cross*, 10 P.3d 440 (Wash. 2000).

*Kulubis v. Texas Farm Bureau Underwriters Ins. Co.*, 706 S.W.2d 953 (Tex. 1986), represents something of a modern evolution and compromise for its time in that it permits the innocent co-insured to have prorated recovery. *See also Texas Farmers Ins. Co. v. Murphy*, 996 S.W.2d 873 (Tex. 1999) (following same approach to community property). The traditional rule barred any recovery by the innocent co-insured, primarily on the theory that the property interest between them was blended and indivisible or that misconduct was imputed between policyholders since they are in a joint enterprise of sorts. In addition, there was probably silent support for the traditional rule because of a judicial view that the allegedly innocent co-insured perhaps really did know what was going on.

2. Where a property insurance policy speaks of excluding coverage because of misconduct of "the insured," some courts have found coverage for the innocent co-insured by viewing the term as sufficiently uncertain as to preclude operation against an insured who was not "the insured" perpetrating the misconduct. *See Steigler v. Insurance Co. of North America*, 384 A.2d 398 (Del. 1978). Other courts have found coverage for the innocent co-insured on the basis of state statutes requiring coverage, interpreting such statutes to preclude depriving the innocent co-insured of that coverage merely because of the sins of another policyholder. *See, e.g., Morgan v. Cincinnati Ins. Co.*, 307 N.W.2d 53 (Mich. 1981).

3. Where insurers have revised language to preclude coverage because of the coverage-defeating acts of "an" insured or "any" insured, this has usually been successful in preventing recovery by the innocent co-insured. *See, e.g., Utah Farm Bureau Ins. Co. v. Crook*, 980 P.2d 685 (Utah 1999); *Noland v. Farmers Ins. Co.*, 892 S.W.2d 271 (Ark. 1995). Unless, of course, there is an applicable statute requiring coverage in a manner that overrides even this more pro-insurer policy language. *See, e.g., Watson v. United Servs. Auto. Ass'n*, 566 N.W.2d 683 (Minn. 1997); *Osbon v. National Union Fire Ins. Co.*, 632 So. 2d 1158 (La. 1994).

4. Notwithstanding the cases excerpted above and other cases in which innocent property insureds have obtained coverage, the insurer's use of an exclusion based on the conduct of "any" insured rather than "the" insured is often effective so long as it is not inconsistent with other provisions of a policy such as a severability clause or provision stating that the policy limits are fully available to each insured. Liability insurers have been particularly successful in avoiding coverage based on the misconduct of a single insured by using the broader "any" insured language. *See* RANDY MANILOFF & JEFFREY STEMPEL, GENERAL LIABILITY INSURANCE: KEY ISSUES IN EVERY STATE, Ch. 9 (4th ed. 2018) (finding that majority of courts enforce the literal "any" insured language notwithstanding severability clause). For a scholarly review of the issue, *see* John F. Dobbyn, *Subrogation and the Innocent Spouse Dilemma*, 78 ST. JOHN'S L. REV. 1095 (2004).

# § 8.05. Place of Loss Limitations

Coverage limitations are not restricted only to those concerning the causes and results of the peril of loss insured against. An insurer may also limit its coverage territorially, applying only to those losses occurring within the United States, or within some other designated country. But these territorial "place of loss" limitations have had their problems of interpretation, as illustrated below.

## Vargas v. Insurance Co. of North America

United States Court of Appeals, Second Circuit
651 F.2d 838 (1981)

**Sofaer, District Judge.**

This is an appeal from a grant of summary judgment to defendant-appellee Insurance Company of North America ("INA") in a declaratory judgment action brought to determine whether INA is liable under an aviation insurance policy issued to Joseph Khurey for his single-engine Piper Arrow. The policy, issued on December 13, 1977, provided in part that it would apply "only to occurrences, accidents or losses which happen ... within the United States of America, its territories or possessions, Canada or Mexico." An endorsement, added to the policy on December 14, 1977, extended the territorial limits to include the Bahama Islands.

On December 23, 1977, Khurey, his wife, and his daughter were killed when the plane crashed into the sea approximately twenty-five miles west of Puerto Rico. The family had been traveling from New York to Puerto Rico, and they had stopped in Miami and Haiti to rest and refuel. The crash occurred on the last leg of the trip, while the Khureys were en route from Haiti to Puerto Rico. Puerto Rico is a "territory" of the United States....

INA denied insurance coverage on the ground that the loss did not occur "within" the United States, its territories, or its possessions. INA claims that the policy covers losses that occur only in the enumerated areas or in territorial waters within three miles adjacent to the coasts of such areas. Appellants read the language more broadly, to include coverage for losses that occur while the plane is traveling between two points that are both within areas expressly covered.

Under New York law, which governs this case, an ambiguous provision in an insurance policy is construed "most favorably to the insured and most strictly against the insurer." ... The insurer bears a heavy burden of proof, for it must "'establish that the words and expressions used [in the insurance policy] not only are susceptible of the construction sought by [the insurer] but that it is the only construction which may fairly be placed on them.'" ... The insurer is "obliged to show (1) that it would be unreasonable for the average man reading the policy to [construe it as the insured does] and (2) that its own construction was the only one that fairly could be placed on the policy." *Sincoff v. Liberty Mutual Fire Insurance Co.* 11 N.Y.2d 386, 390, 230 N.Y.S.2d 13, 16, 183 N.E.2d 899, 901 (1962).

Thus, the question in this case is narrow: is the insurer's interpretation of the contract the only reasonable and fair construction as a matter of law? The District Court granted summary judgment for appellee, concluding that the policy could not reasonably be construed to cover any loss that occurs beyond the territorial limits of the United States or its possessions, Canada, or Mexico. We disagree.

The policy is readily susceptible of a reasonable and fair interpretation that would cover the flight at issue in this case. The policy was for an airplane, which is not merely an object but also a mode of transportation, capable of long-distance travel over water as well as land. The parties knew that the plane would fly substantial distances as it transported the insured and various passengers to their contemplated destinations. The policy, moreover, provided coverage for losses both within the continental United States and within territories more than three miles beyond the continental United States. It is reasonable to construe this coverage of United States territories (some of which are ocean islands), not as restricted to the airspace immediately above them, but rather as including destinations to and from which the plane could travel without forfeiting coverage.

Appellants' construction is more consistent with the realities of airplane travel. So long as the plane is on a reasonably direct course from and to geographic areas covered by the policy, the plane could reasonably be said to be within the contemplated territorial limits. Coverage of "ordinary and customary" routes has frequently been implied in analogous marine insurance contracts.... If the plane were flown on an unreasonable course between two covered points, coverage could be lost.

Appellants' construction is supported by the language of the policy. The territory clause limits coverage to occurrences "within the United States of America, its territories or possessions, Canada or Mexico." The word "within" can reasonably be construed to mean "inside the borders" of the places specified. On the other hand, the term can also reasonably be construed to mean "inside an area that includes the places specified as well as such area as must be crossed in passing to and from the places specified." The policy's "Extension of Territorial Limits Endorsement" is consistent with the latter construction. The endorsement is phrased, not in terms of specific places, but rather in terms of "geographical limits"; and the controlling clause provides that the "limits set forth in the [c]onditions of this policy ... are extended to include" the places covered by the endorsement. Thus, the "limits" may be read as describing the outside boundaries of an area within which flights, on reasonable routes, are covered.

Appellee concedes that this construction is appropriate with respect to specific places covered by an Extension of Territorial Endorsement. It acknowledges that the insured "requested an endorsement to cover flights *to* the Bahamas." Appellee's Brief at 13 (emphasis added).

The extension was not explicitly drafted to include the Bahama Island and the route over which a plane would have to fly to get to and return from the Bahamas. Yet, the addition of "The Bahama Islands" to the covered territory reasonably implied that trips to and from those islands, on reasonable routes, would also be covered.

Otherwise, an insured would be forced to ship his plane to and from places covered by the policy, although those places are well within the aircraft's known range and capacity.

If inclusion of "The Bahama Islands" carries with it inclusion of any reasonable route to and from those islands, then the policy itself should be construed to include reasonable routes to and from any location covered by the policy's territory clause, and within the aircraft's known capacity.

Appellee argues that the terms of the insurance contract are so clear that the court need not resort to rules of construction. The coverage provision of the contract is in fact ambiguous, and the insurer could have avoided that ambiguity by defining the territorial limits with more precision. Had appellee wished to preclude coverage for trips to and from places included in the territory provision, language to accomplish that objective was readily available....

In *Peerless Insurance Co. v. Sun Line Helicopters, Inc.*, 180 So. 2d 364, 365–66 (Fla. App. 1965), the policy applied "only to occurrences ... while the aircraft is within the United States of America (excluding Alaska), its territories or possessions, Canada or Mexico, or its being transported between ports thereof...." An emergency during a flight between the United States and Puerto Rico caused the pilot to crash-land on an island in the Bahamas. The trial court found the word "being transported between ports" to be ambiguous, and it therefore construed them to include situations in which the plane was transporting a pilot between places covered by the territory condition.

In affirming, the appellate court deemed it significant that the insurance company had amended its policy on another aircraft owned by the insured to limit coverage for transportation between ports to situations in which the aircraft was "dismantled," thus making clear that actual flights were not covered. The policy in this case is even more ambiguous than that originally issued in *Peerless*, and the insurer bears the responsibility for not adopting a clear exclusion....

[I]t is appellee's construction that appears unreasonable in terms of aviation practice. If the policy excluded coverage for all flights over waters beyond the territorial limits, then flights between certain points within the continental United States would have to stay within the territorial limits in order to remain covered. Yet the most direct routes between many points within the continental United States pass over waters beyond the territorial limits; for example, the most direct route form New York City to Miami takes aircraft more than three miles beyond the coast.

The same is true of many other routes, including routes between points within the territorial United States and points in Mexico, Canada, or Alaska, all of which are areas covered by the policy. Were INA's construction accepted, a pilot would be required to follow a less-direct route to avoid losing coverage, and the economic and air-safety consequences of utilizing indirect routes are likely to be far more significant than the costs of covering routes between areas expressly covered, as suggested by INA's price quotation for coverage for the Caribbean....

Another factor that undermines appellee's case for summary judgment is the intent of the parties.... In this case, Khurey revealed in his original insurance application his intention to fly the insured aircraft outside the United States. He responded affirmatively to a question on the application, "Will aircraft be used outside Continental United States?" and to the request for details, he replied, "for vacations." It was in fact on a flight outside the continental United States, during a Christmas vacation, that Khurey and his family were killed.

In addition, appellants allege that Khurey's wife came from Puerto Rico and that the family expected to vacation there occasionally. Appellants have not had an opportunity to prove this allegation or to establish that INA agents knew of Khurey's intentions. But the purported intention is entirely consistent with a belief on Khurey's part that the insurance policy covered flights between the United States and Puerto Rico.

Because appellee failed to prove that its construction of the insurance policy was the only fair and reasonable one, the decision granting it summary judgment is reversed. On the present record, the appellants, rather than the appellee, are entitled to summary judgment in the coverage issue. INA may, however, raise factual questions that would render summary judgment in appellants' favor inappropriate. This and other issues will be for the trial court to determine on remand.

The order of the District Court is reversed, and the case is remanded for proceedings consistent with this opinion.

## Notes and Questions

1. If the *Vargas* aviation insurance policy limited coverage on any losses to those occurring "within the United States of America [and] its territories and possessions," how did the court justify coverage when the airplane crashed 25 miles west of Puerto Rico, in international waters? What connection, if any, does a flight to Puerto Rico have on the policy's territorial extension endorsement to fly to the Bahamas? What if the pilot had crashed in international waters during a flight to Hawaii?

2. In the case of *Foremost Insurance Co. v. Eanes*, 134 Cal. App. 3d 566, 184 Cal. Rptr. 635 (1982), the policyholder's motor home was involved in an accident while the vehicle was loaned to friends who were driving it in Mexico. Their automobile insurance stated that it applied only "to accidents which occur ... while the automobile is within the United States of America, its territories or possessions, or Canada." The policyholder's attorney argued that this limitation was ambiguous, because "it was reasonable for the insured to expect that 'accident' referred not just to the injury-causing event ... but also included the negligent or wrongful act of the insured [in loaning the vehicle for the Mexican trip] which constituted the legal cause of the injury." To argue that the loan of the vehicle constitutes the "accident" in this case, responded the court, "strains credulity."

3. An extensive analysis of "all risk" policies covering airliners that have been hijacked and destroyed by terrorists can be found in *Pan American World Airways, Inc. v. Aetna Casualty & Surety Co.*, 368 F. Supp. 1098 (S.D.N.Y. 1973), *aff'd*, 505 F.2d 989 (2d Cir. 1974), excerpted in Chapter 1, *supra*.

## PROBLEM FOUR

St. Elmo Raymond Montayne, a qualified pilot, leased an aircraft for the purpose of transporting a passenger on a charter flight from Fort Lauderdale to Orlando, Florida. After becoming airborne, the passenger forced the pilot at gun point to depart from the flight plan and to proceed to a directed location in the interior of Cuba. A landing was made there in a pasture.

The passenger alighted and joined certain persons who were there to meet him. The pilot then took off to return to the United States. After gaining an altitude of approximately 4,000 feet, he was overtaken by a Cuban military aircraft which attacked him and damaged the plane by gunfire. He escaped and made a forced landing. Rebel forces hid him and the plane for several days, after which he took off and returned to his point of departure in Broward County, Florida.

The policyholder owner of the aircraft brought action against the insurance company for the damages to its aircraft under the following policy provisions:

### Coverage

To pay for all physical loss of or to the aircraft ... in flight caused by fire, explosion, lightning, theft, robbery or vandalism, excluding fire or explosion resulting from crash or collision of the aircraft with the ground, water or any object....

This policy applies only to occurrences, and losses to the insured aircraft which are sustained, during the policy period, while the aircraft is within the United States of America, Canada or the Republic of Mexico, or is being transported between ports thereof, and is owned, maintained and used for the purposes stated as applicable thereto in the Declarations.

This Policy does not apply: ... to loss due to war, whether or not declared, invasion, civil war, insurrection, rebellion or revolution or to confiscation by duly constituted governmental or civil authority.

The insurer refused to cover this loss based on the fact that: (1) there was no theft, since there was no permanent deprivation of the aircraft; (2) the loss occurred outside the policy's territorial limitations; and (3) the loss was caused under the policy's "war, civil war, insurrection, rebellion, or revolution" exclusion.

• What result?

# § 8.06. Theft and Mysterious Disappearance

In many property insurance policies which cover theft, there may also be an additional endorsement that covers — or an exclusionary clause that does *not* cover — any loss resulting from a "mysterious disappearance" of the insured property. Such a sample coverage provision under "Perils Insured Against" might read: "Theft, meaning any act of stealing or attempt to steal, or mysterious disappearance (except mysterious disappearance of a precious stone or semi-precious stone from its setting in any watch or piece of jewelry)."

How is this term "mysterious disappearance" to be interpreted as it relates to theft? The following case gives one illustration.

## Benson v. Bradford Mutual Fire Insurance Corp.

Court of Appeals of Illinois
121 Ill. App. 3d 500, 76 Ill. Dec. 774, 459 N.E.2d 689 (1984)

**Seidenfeld, Presiding Justice.**

Plaintiff's appeal from a directed verdict in favor of the defendant raises the issue of the quantum of proof required to submit a theft claim to the jury in a suit on an insurance policy providing coverage for "[t]heft or attempt thereat, excluding ... mysterious disappearance...."

Elmer Benson, as a debtor in possession under bankruptcy proceedings (Benson), sued Bradford Mutual Fire Insurance Corporation (Bradford) claiming that 2400 to 2500 hogs had been stolen from him sometime between September 1975 and August 1977. This amounted to approximately 60% of his herd. Suit was brought after Bradford had refused to pay the claim, alleging failure to comply with reporting terms under the policy and denying that the loss was from theft.

Benson was a farmer who operated a feed store business in Sandwich, Illinois. Benson operated his feeder pig business on his own farm and on 7 other nearby farms from March 19, 1977 to March of 1980. His home farm and some of the others were converted cattle farms but several were built for or substantially modified for raising hogs.

Benson introduced bills of sale, purchase agreements with Swift, and weight tickets to show that he purchased 20,023 feeder pigs during the two-year time period and to show that he sold 15,156 of these to Swift. Accounting for the difference, he testified that Swift replevied 1763 hogs; he sold 60 hogs to third parties; he used 2 hogs himself; 12 hogs were accidentally electrocuted; and 4 hogs died in a road accident. He introduced his farm record books which showed that 375 hogs died in 1976 and 195 died in 1977. Deducting all the hogs accounted for, the records indicate that 2474 hogs were missing.

Benson testified that he generally counted his hogs when they were purchased and again when they died, were sold, or were otherwise disposed [of]. A neighboring experienced hog farmer testified that he accounted for his hogs the same way. Other experienced hog farmers, acquainted with Benson's operation, testified that he maintained good, typical, or reasonable conditions on his farm. Benson testified that there was no evidence of the hogs escaping, but that if they had it was unlikely that large numbers of hogs simply wandered off, because if a hog gets loose it usually stays close to the pen near the other pigs and near food. He did not notice any drop in feed consumption....

The farms used by Benson were spread out over 75 miles in two counties, although, Benson testified, the major loss was at his own farm. There were caretakers at the other farms whose responsibility was apparently limited to providing the pens and helping with their feeding and medication. Benson introduced testimony of Patricia Smith who lived on a farm, from which Benson reported 40 pigs missing, in a house 200 yards from the pens which were 40 feet from the road. She testified that on two occasions she had heard trucks going into the farm and had heard pigs squealing late at night, but she did not look, and saw nothing. Bradford introduced testimony that Patricia Smith had stated to an investigator, however, that she knew nothing about an alleged theft of pigs, or anything about trucks on the farm....

Bradford introduced testimony tending to show that a higher death rate, not accurately reflected in what it characterized as poor bookkeeping methods, accounted for the loss and that Benson's bookkeeping methods were contrary to good farm management practices. An expert pig farmer stated that if he kept as many pigs as Benson did, he would take periodic inventory.... Bradford introduced evidence of other probable causes for Benson's loss. Benson's hired man testified for the defense that many pigs died from overcrowding or exposure....

Bradford's expert swine consultant testified that a typical death rate in an operation like Benson's could vary from 8% to 30%; and that the winter of 1976 to 1977 was especially hard on pigs raised in open lots such as Benson's.

At the close of Benson's evidence, Bradford moved for a directed verdict, asserting that insufficient evidence of theft had been introduced. The court denied defendant's motion for a directed verdict. At the close of all evidence, however, the trial court ruled (1) that there was enough conflicting evidence to go to the jury on the issue of plaintiff's technical compliance with the policy, but (2) that there was insufficient evidence of theft to withstand defendant's motion for a directed verdict....

Evidence of theft of livestock is, by the nature of the activity, difficult to prove. However, cases where livestock thefts were proven presented stronger evidence than plaintiff presented here. Accurate records and close observation permitted relatively swift discovery of the thefts in cases where it was proven. Plaintiff's witness Alabastro who lived in the area and had reported stolen pigs, testified he had noticed a drastic feed consumption drop during the month in which the loss occurred. Plaintiff's witness Leppert testified to tire tracks near the time of his loss.

In contrast, defendant took no monthly counts, reported no feed consumption drop, reported no approximate dates when he discovered losses, nor reported any temporal relationship between the unlocked gates or unusual truck noises and any specific losses. Here the sole piece of direct evidence plaintiff presents is that 1400 pigs disappeared over a two year period....

No case has been found in Illinois considering what quantity of evidence a plaintiff must present to go to the jury in order to prove theft of livestock within the coverage of an insurance policy which excludes mysterious disappearance. There are, however, various cases in other jurisdictions which have been referred to by the parties. A plaintiff must prove more than mere disappearance to prove theft...."Theft" as used in an insurance policy, where it is not defined, is given its popular meaning as covering any wrongful appropriation of another's property to the use of the taker...."Theft" must be construed to mean something other than escape, mysterious disappearance, inventory shortage, wrongful conversion or embezzlement, because these are specific exclusions in the insurance policy....

It is, of course, true that the circumstances in each of the cases dictate whether the insured has offered sufficient proof to go to the jury....

In the case before us, the evidence does not establish a reasonable inference of theft. It was shown that the caretakers were in a position to see the pens and to hear anything unusual, yet, with the exception of Mrs. Smith, who lived on the Moyer farm and who reported hearing a truck in the night once, none of the caretakers testified.... Benson at no time noticed any reduced feed consumption by his herd. This appears to be contrary to his claim that practically 60% of his herd had been stolen. The nature and quality of Benson's farm records taken as a whole did not amount to positive evidence of the loss by theft....

Moreover, Bradford presented a credible explanation which would account for substantially greater losses from disease. Under the circumstances we cannot conclude that theft was a logical explanation for the loss.

### Notes and Questions

1. The insured in *Benson* had to prove a sufficient probability of theft, since the "mysterious disappearance" of his hogs was excluded from coverage. Do you agree with the court that Benson did not present enough evidence to take the issue of theft to the jury?

2. The court in *Corcoran v. Hartford Fire Ins. Co.*, 333 A.2d 293 (N.J. Super. Ct. 1975), interpreted a homeowners insurance policy that included "mysterious disappearance" of property under its coverage. Admitting that the courts are split as to how "mysterious disappearance" is defined, the *Corcoran* court concluded that:

> the better-reasoned rule is that in order for a plaintiff to recover under a "mysterious disappearance" clause as is contained in the instant homeowner's policy, it is not necessary to first prove the probability of theft. Mere proof of mysterious disappearance will establish plaintiff's right to recovery.

A substantially narrower view of the scope of coverage under a "mysterious disappearance" clause was taken by the courts in *Brier v. Mutual Ins. Co.*, 213 A.2d 736,

737–38 (Conn. 1965), and *Austin v. American Casualty Co.*, 193 A.2d 741 (D.C. 1963). In the *Austin* case, 193 A.2d 741 at 742, the court stated:

> [T]he mysterious disappearance addition to the theft policy reduces the quantum of proof necessary to establish a theft by permitting a finding of theft from proof of a mysterious disappearance under circumstances which suggest the probability of theft. Thus recovery is generally allowed where the article disappears from some place where the insured has left it, either intentionally or unintentionally. Disappearance under these circumstances suggests a probability that the article was taken by a thief. On the other hand, recovery is generally disallowed where the owner has no recollection of when he last had possession of the article and cannot say when or from what place the article disappeared. Such circumstances suggest the probability that the article was lost or mislaid rather than stolen.

Which theory is preferable? Based upon what underlying legal and public policy rationale?

3. It is common in burglary or theft insurance policies for the insurance company to limit its liability to cases where there exist "visible marks" or "visible evidence" of a forcible entry. Although courts generally have recognized the validity of this "visible marks" requirement, some courts have held it to be unconscionable. *See, e.g., C & J Fertilizer, Inc. v. Allied Mut. Ins. Co.*, 227 N.W.2d 169, 181 (Iowa 1975) ("Defendant never offered any evidence ... which might support a conclusion [that] the [visible marks] provision in issue, considered in its commercial setting, was either a reasonable limitation on the protection it offered or should have been reasonably anticipated by plaintiff.... [T]he above provision is unconscionable...."). Alternatively, some courts have found the literal language of the visible marks requirement to impermissibly defeat the objectively reasonable expectations of the policyholder, as in *Atwater Creamery Co. v. Western National Mut. Ins. Co.*, 366 N.W.2d 271 (1985), set forth in Chapter 2, *supra*.

What constitutes "visible marks" or "visible evidence" of a forcible entry? *Rosenthal v. American Bonding Co.*, 100 N.E. 716 (N.Y. 1912) (entering a storeroom through an unlocked door or with a spare key); *Norman v. Banasik*, 283 S.E.2d 489 (N.C. 1981) (removal of a door bolt by unscrewing it, but leaving no marks on the bolt); *Weldcraft Equipment Co. v. Crum & Forster Ins. Co.*, 312 A.2d 68 (Pa. Super. Ct. 1973) (picking a lock); *Thomas Jefferson Ins. Co. v. Stuttgart Home Center, Inc.*, 627 S.W.2d 571 (Ark. Ct. App. 1982) (removing screen, unfastening a window, and knocking over a flower pot).

4. In property, casualty, or fire insurance policies, a provision might also require an inventory method of proving loss. Under this provision, the insured is required to make and keep books and inventories of the insured merchandise, and these documents cannot be supplemented by parol evidence. To establish the amount of loss, the insured may introduce into evidence the last invoice prior to loss, as well as the average sales profit and amounts receivable.

5. The most common form of property insurance provides indemnity protection when tangible physical property is damaged "by the elements" so to speak, e.g., fire, wind, water, hail (frozen water), or other externally imposed physical injury such as vandalism. As discussed in this subsection, general property policies sometimes cover theft and sometimes exclude it.

In addition to general property insurance, policyholders may purchase insurance against loss from crime or employee dishonesty. These policies typically cover only physical taking of property or money but may also cover losses caused by more subtle crimes such as fraud, forgery, or securities law violations. Directors and Officers Insurance acts to protect companies from the liability consequences of wrongdoing that may lie at the boundary between misfeasance and outright intentional wrongdoing or crime.

Even a fairly broad crime policy is relatively limited in its scope of coverage and should not be confused with an all-risk property policy insuring against damage from the elements or other external forces. Nor should it be confused with a general liability policy.

# § 8.07. Occupancy and Vacancy

A typical restriction on property coverage is that the insurance is not in force if the covered property is vacant or unoccupied for any significant length of time. The restrictions on coverage, the definition of the terms, and the time periods involved tend to vary among property policies. The purpose of these restrictions, however, is uniformly the same. Insurers fear that property is more vulnerable to loss if someone is not on the property. For example, a home is more likely to be burglarized when the owners are away. Similarly, a small fire might be caught and extinguished quickly by the home residents. However, in their absence, it may become a large fire and destroy the entire home. Of course, those sorts of things can happen even if the policyholder has left the house only to go to work or to run to the grocery store. Insurers cannot reasonably require that homeowners post round-the-clock sentries but they can limit coverage if the property is empty for too long a time. The following case addresses these tensions.

## Langill v. Vermont Mutual Insurance Co.

United States Court of Appeals for the First Circuit
268 F.3d 46 (2001)

**Coffin, Senior Circuit Judge.**

In this Massachusetts diversity case plaintiff-appellant, Grace Langill, the insured owner of a residential property, challenges the invocation by defendant-appellee insurance company, Vermont Mutual Insurance Co., of a statutorily required "vacancy" exclusion in plaintiff's policy, to deny coverage for fire damage to the property. Appellant appeals from a partial summary judgment granted to defendant prior to trial. We affirm.

## Factual Background

The insured premises are a rental dwelling at 158 Mansfield Avenue (158) in Norton, Massachusetts, some thirty-five to forty feet away from appellant's own residence at 156 Mansfield Avenue. In February 1999, two tenants who had lived at 158 for twelve years moved out, leaving the property in a condition showing considerable wear and tear. Soon after their departure, appellant's husband undertook to refurbish the house by cleaning, removing debris, filling nail holes, painting walls, repairing several windows, and installing Venetian blinds. During this period, doors were kept locked, utilities were maintained, and heating oil was supplied. In the premises were Mr. Langill's tools, a step ladder, two chairs, a mattress, frame and box spring, a radio and an ash tray.

It was Mr. Langill's practice to spend one to two hours a day working at 158 starting at 11:00 a.m. or noon. A longer time would place undue strain on his arm. He would sometimes visit the premises at night to smoke or meet with friends; he had coffee there with a friend six or seven times. On one night, after an argument with appellant, he had stayed all night.

On May 4, 1999, Mr. Langill was at 158 from 10:30 a.m. until approximately noon. He spent the rest of the day at his house, save a visit to a store to buy a newspaper. At 2:00 a.m. on May 5, he was awakened by appellant and saw "a big orange ball" of fire at 158. By this time the fire was well advanced on one wall. The Norton Fire Investigator concluded that the fire was an arson.

Appellant's "Dwelling Fire Policy" included, as required by Massachusetts General Laws ch. 175 § 99, the following exclusionary clause:

> 27. Vacancy. Unless otherwise provided in writing, we will not be liable for loss caused by fire or lightning occurring while a described building is vacant, whether intended for occupancy by owner or tenant, beyond a period of sixty consecutive days for residential purposes of three units or less, and thirty consecutive days for all other residential purposes.

## Discussion

The question presented to us and to the district court is whether under Massachusetts law, the undisputed facts depict a dwelling that had been, at the time of the fire, "vacant" for more than sixty consecutive days. This is a matter of law and our review is de novo. We also are bound by the Massachusetts rule that "[b]ecause the language of the standard policy is prescribed by statute..., the rule of construction resolving ambiguities in a policy against the insurer is inapplicable.... Instead, we must ascertain the fair meaning of the language used, as applied to the subject matter." *Bilodeau v. Lumbermens Mut. Cas. Co.*, 467 N.E.2d 137, 140 (Mass. 1984) (internal citations and quotations omitted).

Two Massachusetts cases have been called to our attention. The earlier is *Will Realty Corp. v. Transportation Ins. Co.*, 22 Mass.App.Ct. 918, 492 N.E.2d 372 (1986). After a tenant was evicted and left a rundown house, the windows were boarded and the only activity occurred on two days when workmen removed from the house doors, windows and sinks. A fire destroyed the building several months later. In reversing a ruling that the property had not been "vacant," the court said, "the policy provision reflects the commonplace observation that the risk of casualty is higher when premises remain unattended.... [P]remises may be vacant despite sporadic entry." 22 Mass.App.Ct. at 919, 492 N.E.2d at 373.

A more recent case is helpful, not so much in its precise holding, as in its discussion of policy underlying the "vacancy" exclusion. *See Aguiar v. Generali Assicurazioni Ins. Co.*, 47 Mass.App.Ct. 687, 715 N.E.2d 1046 (1999). A restaurant, which had closed for the season on Labor Day, was destroyed by fire approximately two months later. (At the time, Mass. Gen. Laws ch. 175 §99 provided for a vacancy period of only thirty days before the vacancy exclusion could be invoked.) Before the fire, the restaurant had been unoccupied and utilities had been shut off.

In affirming the trial court's ruling that the property had been vacant for the required period, the appeals court "illuminated why an insurer would be concerned about an unoccupied building" by explaining that arsonists had attempted to destroy the building several times in the months before they ultimately succeeded. 47 Mass.App.Ct. at 689, 715 N.E.2d at 1047.

Moreover, in discussing the insured's argument that he reasonably expected to be covered under the insurance policy, the court commented:

> [w]hen reasonable expectations analysis comes into play, it is more likely to do so when the task is to interpret an ambiguous provision rather than an unambiguous one whose meaning, as in this case, no one disputes.... They could not reasonably have expected that leaving the building vacant did not alter the underwriting condition.

47 Mass.App.Ct. at 691, 715 N.E.2d at 1048.

Neither case neatly covers the facts in the case at bar. In both cases no activity was going on in the premises. In *Aguiar*, at least, the premises were not devoid of contents. It is clear, however, that the court was not equating "vacant" with "abandonment," as do some jurisdictions. *See, e.g., Jerry v. Kentucky Cent. Ins. Co.*, 836 S.W.2d 812, 815 (Tex.App.1992) ("entire abandonment"). It is also clear that having the building "attended" and "occupied" is the central theme.

The question remains whether this requirement can be satisfied by regular visits and activities, although of relatively brief nature, by someone other than a resident of the building. We are helped by reflecting on the reasons underlying vacancy exclusions. In considering the vacancy exclusion of a policy insuring a warehouse, the Fourth Circuit explained:

> When a building is not in use, it is more likely that potential fire hazards will remain undiscovered or unremedied. Chances are also greater that a fire in a vacant building will burn for a longer period and cause greater damage before being detected.

*Catalina Enter. v. Hartford Fire Ins. Co.*, 67 F.3d 63, 66 (4th Cir.1995). Surely, these considerations are even more applicable to one insuring a dwelling.

When we review the undisputed facts of this case, in light of these policy concerns, we can readily see their lack of fit. That is, the approximation to an inhabited abode is not measurably advanced by the motley and sparse inventory of chairs, mattress, and step ladder. Nor does the midday hour or so of work activity convey the appearance of residential living. And random evening visits hardly provide the appearance of somebody being at home or effective anti-vandal protection. The fact is that none of the activities of Mr. Langill or others changed the fact that at the critical and likely times for vandalism and arson, there was no one in the house to discourage, see, or hear marauders, or to hear the activation of smoke detectors.

A recent New York case seems both apposite and persuasive. In *Lamoureux v. New York Cent. Mut. Fire Ins. Co.*, 244 A.D.2d 645, 663 N.Y.S.2d 914 (N.Y.App.Div.1997), the insured building was a one-family residence located adjacent to and behind plaintiff's residence. The premises were destroyed by fire three months after the plaintiff's tenant had moved out. The policy excluded coverage for loss if the building were vacant over 60 consecutive days. Plaintiff's principal challenge to a finding of vacancy was that he was personally renovating the house and was inside the building every day for a couple of hours.

The court reversed the trial court's denial of the insurer's motion for summary judgment, "[g]iving the word vacant its plain and ordinary meaning...." 244 A.D.2d at 646, 663 N.Y.S.2d at 915. It also ruled that because "plaintiff himself was never an inhabitant of the premises, the fact that he frequented the premises for the purpose of renovation is not germane to the issue of vacancy." *Id.*

We think the Massachusetts courts would similarly rule on the record before us. When we consider the nature of the hazard sought to be guarded against, the sustained presence of a resident, particularly in the hours of darkness, appears logically as the critical factor where the premises are a dwelling. Of course, this also assumes the presence of furnishings and amenities "minimally necessary for human habitation." *American Mut. Fire Ins. Co. v. Durrence*, 872 F.2d 378, 379 (11th Cir.1989).

We recognize, as this case illustrates, that there is a wide continuum between residency and absolute absence of human presence from the premises. And we do not intend to foreclose the possibility of a set of facts not involving a resident but so paralleling the conditions of residency as to avoid application of the exclusion clause. But we think that in general the multi-factor approach urged by appellant is inconsistent with Massachusetts law.

What seems preeminent in this insurance context, for both insurer and insured, is predictability. To the extent that a multi-factor approach is suggested, such as including the presence or absence of tenants, the habitability or absence thereof, the number, nature, duration, and regularity of activities and visits by non-residents, and the proximity of the insured site to the residence, any predictability is fatally compromised.

Appellant has vigorously invoked dictionary definitions and case law to serve his purpose. As might be suspected, where a host of things can be spoken of as "vacant," from rooms and houses to stores, positions, and expressions, definitions are legion. Appellant has relied on those that stress a space being "devoid of contents." *Webster's New World Dictionary*, 1968 ed., p. 1606. This is a perfectly good definition but it has been impliedly rejected by *Aguiar*.

Moreover, reference to absence of contents would be more relevant if one were considering whether a warehouse were vacant. The absence of that for which the premises were intended to be used would seem to be the proper object of inquiry. Appellee's choice of another of Webster's definitions seems more of a fit: "untenanted; not in use, as a room or a house." *Id.*

We note as well that the language of the provision, "whether intended for occupancy by owner or tenant," directs us to give no special consideration to purpose of the building as one to rented rather than one to be used by appellant.

Appellant's reliance on cases illustrates the hazard of focusing on text to the exclusion of context. For example, cases are cited for the proposition that efforts to rehabilitate property preclude a finding of vacancy.... *Knight* involved installing new equipment, painting, and making ready a service station and restaurant for reopening and *Limbaugh* similar activities to ready a recreation hall and package liquor store for opening.

In both cases there were policy exclusions if the premises were "unoccupied" for sixty days. *Knight* relied on the reasoning of *Limbaugh*, in which the court said:

> The word "occupancy" itself, as used in insurance policies, refers to the presence of persons within the building. This is particularly true as it relates to dwelling houses. They are expected to be places of human habitation where people live and dine and sleep. This cannot be said of a recreation hall and package liquor store, for the nature of the occupancy does not warrant the conclusion.

*Limbaugh*, 368 S.W.2d at 924. The court accordingly held that cleaning and repainting the interior of the liquor store "would be an activity consistent with its occupation as such." *Id.* at 925.

Not only does the meaning of "vacancy" depend on the type of premises involved, but also the type of insurance policy. Appellant seeks comfort from *Ellmex Constr. Co., Inc. v. Republic Ins. Co.*, 202 N.J.Super. 195, 494 A.2d 339 (N.J.Super.Ct.App.Div.1985), which held that the presence in a model home of realtors for four days every week constituted sufficient presence to defeat a thirty day vacancy exclusion clause.

But the court noted that the policy involved was a "builder's risk" policy, which should not be interpreted as are policies insuring ordinary homeowners. 202 N.J.Super. at 204, 494 A.2d at 344. The latter policies, observed the court, "may, and usually do, require the insured dwelling to be occupied as a place of abode." 202 N.J.Super. at 203–04, 494 A.2d at 343. It consequently felt free to depart from this standard and, resolving ambiguity against the insurer, held that defendant had not required that the premises be "occupied" twenty-four hours per day.

Finally, it is important to distinguish cases according wide elasticity to the word "occupancy," after finding the word ambiguous and construing the term in favor of the insured. *See Smith v. Lumbermen's Mut. Ins. Co.*, 101 Mich. App. 78, 300 N.W.2d 457 (1981); *Drummond v. Hartford Fire Ins. Co.*, 343 S.W.2d 84 (Mo.Ct.App.1960). In *Smith*, the court held that where the insurer knew that a dwelling was under a contract of sale, a temporary vacancy pending arrival of the new resident-owner was "not within the vacancy clause, absent a clear expression of intent in the insurance policy." 101 Mich. App. at 86, 300 N.W.2d at 460. Likewise, in *Drummond* the court, relying on early precedent, held that the presence of a caretaker one day and night each week during the specified vacancy period constituted "possessio pedis" and was sufficient. 343 S.W.2d at 87. Suffice it to say that neither case would be considered relevant in interpreting the mandatory vacancy provision under Massachusetts law.

# § 8.08. Business Interruption Insurance

Businesspersons frequently speak of having "business interruption coverage" as though it is a separate form of stand-alone insurance. Technically, business interruption coverage is a type of property loss coverage that is added to the basic property coverage for loss to the property itself. Sometimes it is part of a blended multi-risk policy sold to commercial policyholders and sometimes it is sold more as a standard endorsement to a property insurance policy.

The standard Business Income Property Insurance Coverage Form defines "Business Income" as net income and the continuing normal operating expenses of the business. It is designed to compensate the policyholder not only for revenue lost but also for the continuing economic obligations a policyholder may owe to employees and vendors if it is to remain a viable business entity pending repair or replacement of property damage so that the business may resume full operation.

Business interruption coverage can be complex both in terms of determining what is covered and the amount of the business income lost. There may also be issues regarding whether the business must be completely shut down to collect this type of coverage as opposed to partially closed or suffering reduced output.

Many business interruption policies do not attach until a designated time after a property loss, usually 60–90 days. This type of coverage is in the nature of "catastrophic" business income coverage in that it is designed to be activated only when the business interruption is prolonged and serious, with the policyholder essentially self-insuring for smaller versions of this risk.

Many policies also provide business income coverage in the event the source of the reduction in income is not damage to the policyholder's property but instead a loss of supplies due to a supplier's inability to provide the promised goods. For example, after the September 11, 2001 terrorist attacks on the World Trade Center Towers, all public commercial airline travel was halted for several days, making it difficult or impossible for some supplies to reach businesses. Under appropriate circumstances, this would be covered under these forms of business interruption policies. Similarly, government regulations and delays imposed due to the salvage efforts at the World Trade Center site could create covered business loss claims. *See* Jeffrey W. Stempel, *The Insurance Aftermath of September 11*, 37 Tort & Ins. L.J. 817, 824–27 (2002).

The devastation of widespread hurricanes, wildfires and floods in America have not only led to tight property insurance markets but also launched a rash of business interruption claims. These claims were often more problematic than usual because of both the magnitude and length of the "BI" claims (which made insurers less willing to pay in close cases and which presented expanded problems of valuation and concern that businesses were not doing all they could to resume operations) and because of uncertainty as to whether physical loss that interrupted commerce resulted from covered or uncovered causes.

## Broad Street, LLC v. Gulf Insurance Co.

Supreme Court, Appellate Division, First Department, New York
37 A.D.3d 126, 832 N.Y.S.2d 1 (2006)

**Nardelli, J.**

In this appeal, we are asked to determine the scope of the business interruption coverage afforded in a commercial property insurance policy issued by defendant Gulf Insurance Company to plaintiff Broad Street, LLC, the owner of a lower Manhattan building which was temporarily closed in the aftermath of the September 11, 2001 destruction and mass murder at the World Trade Center.

At the core of this dispute is the meaning of the policy term "necessary suspension"; plaintiff asserts the term should be interpreted to mean the suspension of "normal business activities," whereas defendant submits the term is clear and unambiguous and is triggered only by a total interruption of business operations.

Plaintiff Broad Street, LLC (Broad Street) owns and operates the building designated as 25 Broad Street, New York, New York. The building, which is located approximately three blocks from the World Trade Center site, consists of 345 residential units and three commercial spaces.

There is no dispute that following the events of September 11, 2001, the building was completely shut down from that day to September 18, 2001, at which time tenants were permitted back into their units. Plaintiff's staff, during the week the building was closed, cleaned the common areas, as well as the apartments, especially those with windows that had been left open, and replaced all of the air filters in the building.

There is also no dispute that a commercial property insurance policy was issued to plaintiff by defendant Gulf Insurance Company and covered the building at the time in question. The policy provides, in pertinent part:

> "We will pay for the actual loss of Business Income you sustain due to the necessary suspension of your 'operations' during the 'period of restoration.'

The suspension must be caused by direct physical loss of or damage to property at the premises described in the Declarations ... caused by or resulting from any Covered Cause of Loss."

"Operations" is defined in the policy as "your business activities occurring at the described premises"; "period of restoration" is defined as the period that "begins on the date of direct physical loss or damage caused by or resulting from the Covered Cause of Loss at the described premises" and "[e]nds on the date when the property at the described premises should be repaired, rebuilt or replaced with reasonable speed and similar quality."

Plaintiff, by letter dated September 24, 2001, informed defendant that the building had sustained damage "in the form of smoke and soot in all common areas, building systems and apartments in addition to lost gas and steam service," and that the building had been evacuated from September 11 through September 17 [Mr. Brendan Harte, the superintendent of the building, testified at an examination before trial conducted on February 12, 2004, that all of the building's utilities, including gas and hot water, were restored by September 17 or 18]. Plaintiff further stated that its business interruptions losses:

"are on-going as we have not resumed normal business operations. While some tenants have returned to the building, other [sic] have not. Normal business-life in the vicinity of our residential building has not resumed due to on going [sic] transportation limitations, street closures and limited deliveries.

"Moreover, utilities, including phone and cable, to the building continue to be interrupted. There are public health warnings related to air quality that continue during the clean up effort.

"All of this is not only disruptive to our existing tenancy, it is also seriously affecting our ability to rent vacant apartments and retail space."

The tenants of the building, through counsel, informed plaintiff, by letter dated December 28, 2001, that:

"The problems encountered by financial district Residents are legion, and have been well documented by the media and in various legal actions: temporary ouster from their homes only to return to dust-filled apartments; the lingering, and potentially harmful, stench from Ground Zero that has caused many residents to experience respiratory or other complications with long-term effects yet to be determined; the morbid reality of a mass graveyard just a few blocks away."

Tenants' counsel further noted that due to security measures, streets in the area were closed to vehicles, and tenants had to walk a block or more to hail a taxi. Counsel concluded that the building and the area were no longer what the tenants had bargained for when they executed their leases and, as a result, sought, inter alia, a full rent credit from September 11 through September 30; a rent reduction from October 1, 2001 through September 30, 2002; an option to surrender the lease upon 30 days' notice; and monthly air-and water-quality testing. Plaintiff eventually provided a number of concessions to its tenants, including rent abatements or reduced rents to those who remained in the building.

Plaintiff subsequently commenced the within action by the service of a summons and complaint in August 2002, seeking coverage for the business losses it sustained up to the commencement of the action, which were purportedly in excess of $17 million, plus a declaratory judgment declaring that defendant is obligated to pay plaintiff's loss of business claims for the entire period of restoration.

Defendant answered the complaint and, after the completion of discovery, moved for partial summary judgment seeking an order: that under the terms of the policy, the period of restoration during which plaintiff is entitled to recover its actual loss of business income is from September 11, 2001 through and including September 17, 2001; that any loss of income sustained after September 17, 2001 is not within the policy coverage; and that any consequential damages are dismissed with prejudice.

Defendant did not, and does not now, contest that its policy covered plaintiff's losses from September 11 through September 17, but asserts that under the unambiguous terms of the policy, in order to be covered, the business losses must occur during a "necessary suspension," which means a total cessation of plaintiff's business. Defendant argues that once tenants were permitted to return to the building after September 17, plaintiff's claims no longer fell within the parameters of the policy.

The motion court denied defendant's motion, finding issues of fact as to whether plaintiff was prevented, after September 17, "from providing functionally equivalent services to the residential tenants occupying apartments at the time of the attack." Defendant appeals and we now reverse.

Initially, we reject plaintiff's contention that defendant has waived its argument that the policy requires a complete cessation of operations for the full period of its business income loss in order to trigger coverage because it never raised this argument before the motion court. A review of the record reveals that defendant clearly and repeatedly argued that coverage for plaintiff's income loss was limited to the week-long period when plaintiff's operations were suspended; that when the building was opened, utilities were restored, and tenants were returning, plaintiff's operations could no longer be considered suspended; that coverage was only for the "necessary suspension of operations," in other words, once the insured has resumed operations, the required element of a "suspension of operation" is no longer present; and that this did not mean "normal operations," but only "necessary suspensions," which in this case lasted only until September 18....

Turning to the merits of defendant's argument, our analysis begins with the well-established principles governing the interpretation of insurance contracts, which provide that the unambiguous provisions of an insurance policy, as with any written contract, must be afforded their plain and ordinary meaning, and that the interpretation of such provisions is a question of law for the court.... If, however, there is ambiguity in the terms of the policy, any doubt as to the existence of coverage must be resolved in favor of the insured and against the insurer, as drafter of the agreement....

A contract of insurance is ambiguous if the language therein is susceptible of two or more reasonable interpretations..., whereas, in contrast, a contract is unambiguous if the language has "a definite and precise meaning, unattended by danger of misconception in the purport of the [agreement] itself, and concerning which there is no reasonable basis for a difference of opinion"....

In this matter, contrary to the finding of the motion court, we perceive of no ambiguity in the governing language of the subject insurance policy. Indeed ... this Court addressed the very issue pivotal on this appeal and determined that in order for business interruption insurance to be triggered, there must be a "'necessary suspension,' i.e., a total interruption or cessation" of operations (*54th St. Ltd. Partners*, 306 A.D.2d at 67, 763 N.Y.S.2d 243; *see also Royal Indemn. Co. v. Retail Brand Alliance, Inc.*, 822 N.Y.S.2d at 269).

Numerous other jurisdictions have considered the foregoing policy language and arrived at the same conclusion (*see e.g. Apartment Movers of Am., Inc. v. One Beacon Lloyds of Texas*, 170 Fed. Appx. 901, 901 [5th Cir.2006] [a slow down in business experienced by the insured was not a "'necessary suspension of your operations' so as to trigger coverage for loss of business income"]; *Madison Maidens, Inc. v. American Mfrs. Mut. Ins. Co.*, 2006 U.S. Dist. LEXIS 39633 [S.D.N.Y.2006] [although plaintiff's offices sustained serious flood damage, uncontroverted evidence that at least two of plaintiff's employees were able to perform their normal duties indicated that there was no cessation of business to trigger the insured's business interruption coverage]; *Keetch v. Mutual of Enumclaw Ins. Co.*, 66 Wash.App. 208, 831 P.2d 784 [1992] [although plaintiff's motel was buried in six inches of ash following a volcanic eruption, and, as a result, suffered a dramatic decrease in occupancy, it remained open and, therefore, could not recover under its business interruption policy]; *Buxbaum v. Aetna Life & Cas. Co.*, 103 Cal.App.4th 434, 126 Cal.Rptr.2d 682 [Cal. Ct. App.], *review denied* 2003 Cal. LEXIS 2251 [2002] [since the plaintiff law firm suffered water damage to its offices, but since attorneys working in the office continued to bill hours on the day the flood damage was discovered there was no suspension of operations to trigger the business interruption loss provisions of the policy]). The *Buxbaum* court succinctly stated that:

> "[i]n order for business income coverage to apply, the Policy requires that there be a 'necessary suspension' of operations. This term is not defined in the policy.... [¶] Webster's Third New International Dictionary defines 'suspension' as 'the act of suspending or the state or period of being suspended, interrupted, or abrogated.' 'Suspended' is defined as 'temporarily debarred, inactive, inoperative.' These definitions comport with what appears to be the common understanding of the term 'suspension,' that is, that it connotes a temporary, but *complete, cessation* of activity. Thus, if one were to apply the plain, ordinary meaning to the use of the phrase 'NECESSARY SUSPENSION' within the policy, in order for a claim to fall within the coverage provision

it would require that any direct physical loss of or damage to property result in the cessation of [the insured's] operations."

quoting *Home Indemnity Company v. Hyplains Beef, L.C.*, 893 F.Supp. 987, 991–992 [D.Kan.1995], *affd.* 89 F.3d 850 [10th Cir.1996] (internal quotation marks omitted) (emphasis in original); *American States Ins. Co. v. Creative Walking, Inc.*, 16 F.Supp.2d 1062 [E.D.Miss.1998], *affd.* 175 F.3d 1023 [8th Cir.1999] [a claim for lost income was limited to the 13-day period in which the insured's business was suspended after a water main break, despite the longer lasting slow-down in business].

Accordingly, we find that plaintiff's business interruption loss is restricted to the period between the September 11 attack on the World Trade Center and September 18, when tenants were again allowed to reside in their apartments.

We find unavailing plaintiff's reliance on section G.1. of the policy, under "Loss Conditions," entitled "Resumption of Operations," which states:

"a. Business income loss, other than Extra Expense, to the extent you can resume your 'operations,' *in whole or in part*, by using damaged or undamaged property (including merchandise or stock) at the described premises or elsewhere.

"b. Extra expense loss to the extent you can return 'operations' to normal and discontinue such Extra Expenses."

While plaintiff maintains that this mitigation provision, which reduces payments to the extent operations can be resumed "in whole or in part" conflicts with any interpretation of "necessary suspension," which requires total cessation of operations, the plain meaning of the word "resume" indicates that in order for the provision to apply, there must necessarily have been a stoppage of operations " 'from which it was necessary to begin anew' " (*see Buxbaum* ...).

We reject plaintiff's argument that because it was unable to provide a habitable environment for its residents by September 18, it cannot be considered to have resumed operations. In the first instance, plaintiff submits no evidence to support the conclusion that *any* tenant, let alone *every* tenant, was prevented from returning to their units due to a breach of the warranty of habitability. The majority of the tenants' letters submitted by plaintiff, which are unsworn and inadmissible in any event, seek rent reductions, not release from their leases. Further, plaintiff's own superintendent testified that air filters were changed as often as tenants requested, that the building's HVAC system was undamaged, and that air quality testing, commenced the September in question, was continued on an "ongoing basis," with results within acceptable limits.

Plaintiff also contends that it should be covered under defendant's policy for the "period of restoration," which extended well beyond the one-week period its tenants were barred from their apartments. This argument, however, is also unavailing as the restoration period is only as long as necessary for plaintiff to resume operations, as it is tied in to the requirement that there be a "necessary suspension of your operations" (*see Admiral Indem. Co. v. Bouley Intl. Holding, LLC*, 2003 U.S. Dist. LEXIS

20324 [S.D.N.Y.2003] [where the court held that defendant restaurant's restoration period following the September 11 attack ended when it began serving Red Cross volunteers, even though it had not opened, because the period of restoration ended when the business could resume operations]; *Streamline Capital, L.L.C. v. Hartford Cas. Ins. Co.*, 2003 WL 22004888 [S.D.N.Y.2003] [business income coverage only applies to the suspension of plaintiff's operations, indicating that the period of restoration is dependent only on replacing what is necessary to resume those operations]; *accord Duane Reade, Inc. v. St. Paul Fire & Marine Ins. Co.*, 411 F.3d 384, 395–396 [2nd Cir.2005]).

Finally, the complaints and dissatisfaction voiced by plaintiff, and its tenants, revolve around the dust, smell and inconvenience of lower Manhattan. The policy, however, expressly states that the "period of restoration" does not include any increased period required due to enforcement of any ordinance or law which "[r]equires any insured or others to test for, monitor, clean up, remove, contain, treat, detoxify or neutralize, or in any way respond to, or address the effects of pollutants."

In sum, the record establishes that plaintiff had resumed operations as of September 18, 2001, in that it had cleaned most of the debris from the September 11 attacks, changed the building's air filters, re-established all utilities and allowed tenants to return. Moreover, the air filters continued to be changed regularly, as the tenants forwarded requests, and ongoing air testing was performed indicating the air quality was within acceptable Environmental Protection Agency levels. Thus, plaintiff was no longer suffering a "necessary suspension" of its business operations.

Accordingly, the order of the Supreme Court, New York County (Edward H. Lehner, J.), entered September 19, 2005, which denied defendant's motion for partial summary judgment seeking an order: that under the terms of the policy, the period of restoration during which plaintiff is entitled to recover its actual loss of business income is from September 11, 2001 through and including September 17, 2001; that any loss of income sustained after September 17, 2001 is not within the policy coverage; and that any consequential damages are dismissed with prejudice, should be reversed, on the law, without costs, the motion granted and the matter remanded for further proceedings.

## Notes and Questions

A subset of business interruption coverage is contingent business interruption coverage. This type of insurance coverage provides indemnity for losses when a business related to the policyholder's business suffers an interruption such that it affects the policyholder's business. These types of claims are most common in the supply chain industry. For example, if there is a fire at a tire manufacturing plant that supplies the tires for an auto manufacturer, the tire plant may not be able to produce tires for some time. The auto manufacturer may suffer a resulting business interruption because its key supplier suffered a business interruption. In today's world of interdependent commerce, contingent business interruption insurance provides a business with the opportunity to insure against these supply chain risks. The trigger of coverage for contingent business interruption insurance is typically the same type of trigger one would expect for property damage to the policyholder's property: direct loss to tangible physical property. So, if the tire manufacturer suffered a direct loss to tangible physical property at its plant, the auto manufacturer's contingent business interruption coverage may be triggered if the auto manufacturer had its operations interrupted.

# § 8.09. Property Coverage and Large-Scale Disasters

Large-scale disasters, both human made and natural, pose special challenges to property insurance. The many property claims left in the wake of a hurricane, tsunami, flood, wildfire, volcano, storm, terrorist event, electrical failure, large-scale structural defect like a building or highway can all be a nightmarish tangled web for insurers and insureds alike. The holdings in some cases can often be conflicting, making it difficult for parties to find consistency. On the other hand, the results of often a single case can have a rippling effect to prompt either mass claims settlement or mass claims denial.

There also frequently may be complex coverage and exclusionary issues about concurrently caused losses. Property damage due to large-scale disasters is often the result of multi-causal environmental or human-made factors. Finally, there may also be troubling issues of governmental liability — did the responsible government properly plan for this foreseeable event or did it properly respond after the loss?

There are often also jurisdictional issues when a disaster cuts across state lines. Courts tend to focus on the propriety of removal of state cases to federal court. *See, e.g., Wallace v. La. Citizens Prop. Ins. Corp.*, 444 F.3d 697 (5th Cir. 2006) (applying federal procedural law) (reversing trial court's remanding of removed case and returning to trial court for further proceedings; Appeals Court suggests that removal and consolidation of Hurricane Katrina-related claims may be appropriate under Multiparty, Multiforum Trial Jurisdiction Act, 28 U.S.C. § 1441(e)(1)(B), in class action based on 28 U.S.C. § 1369, which seeks class action commonality on theory that claims arise from the "same accident"); *Koppel v. Eustis Ins., Inc.*, 2006 U.S. Dist. LEXIS 31378 (E.D. La. May 19, 2006) (remanding removed Katrina-related claim of agent negligence in failing to procure contents of flood coverage; federal establishment and regulation of flood insurance program did not establish complete federal preemption of state law-based tort claims against agent selling flood insurance); *Landry v. State Farm Fire & Cas. Co.*, 2006 U.S. Dist. LEXIS 38703 (E.D. La. June 8, 2006) (rejecting insurer's Rule 59(a) motion to amend court's prior order of remand after removal). Strategically, policyholders in mass disaster cases tend to favor state court and particular venues within the affected states while insurers tend to prefer to remove coverage claims to federal court, which is thought to have a bench and jury venire more sympathetic to insurers and more willing to find that contested policy language defeats coverage.

# In re Katrina Canal Breaches Litigation

United States Court of Appeals for the Fifth Circuit
495 F.3d 191 (2007)

**King, Circuit Judge:**

On the morning of August 29, 2005, Hurricane Katrina struck along the coast of the Gulf of Mexico, devastating portions of Louisiana and Mississippi. In the City of New Orleans, some of the most significant damage occurred when levees along three major canals—the 17th Street Canal, the Industrial Canal, and the London Avenue Canal—ruptured, permitting water from the flooded canals to inundate the city. At one point in Katrina's aftermath, approximately eighty percent of the city was submerged in water.

Each plaintiff in this case is a policyholder with homeowners, renters, or commercial-property insurance whose property was damaged during the New Orleans flooding. Despite exclusions in their policies providing that damage caused by "flood" is not covered, the plaintiffs seek recovery of their losses from their insurers.

Their primary contention is that the massive inundation of water into the city was the result of the negligent design, construction, and maintenance of the levees and that the policies' flood exclusions in this context are ambiguous because they do not clearly exclude coverage for an inundation of water induced by negligence. The plaintiffs maintain that because their policies are ambiguous, we must construe them in their favor to effect coverage for their losses.

We conclude, however, that even if the plaintiffs can prove that the levees were negligently designed, constructed, or maintained and that the breaches were due to this negligence, the flood exclusions in the plaintiffs' policies unambiguously preclude their recovery.

Regardless of what caused the failure of the flood-control structures that were put in place to prevent such a catastrophe, their failure resulted in a widespread flood that damaged the plaintiffs' property. This event was excluded from coverage under the plaintiffs' insurance policies, and under Louisiana law, we are bound to enforce the unambiguous terms of their insurance contracts as written. Accordingly, we conclude that the plaintiffs are not entitled to recover under their policies.

## I. FACTUAL BACKGROUND AND PROCEDURAL HISTORY

The cases in this appeal are a handful of the more than forty currently pending cases related to Hurricane Katrina that have been consolidated for pretrial purposes in the Eastern District of Louisiana. In several of the consolidated cases, property owners are suing their insurers to obtain recovery under homeowners, renters, and commercial-property policies for the damage their property sustained during the inundation of water into the city that accompanied the hurricane. This appeal involves four such cases … "the *Vanderbrook* action," … "the *Xavier* action," … "the *Chehardy* action," and … "the *Humphreys* action." …

A. *The Vanderbrook Action*

In the *Vanderbrook* action, eight individuals ("the *Vanderbrook* plaintiffs") filed a petition for damages in Louisiana state court against their insurers. The *Vanderbrook* plaintiffs allege that "[s]ometime between 10:00 and 11:00 a.m. on August 29, 2005, before the full force of [Hurricane Katrina] reached the City of New Orleans, a small section of the concrete outfall canal wall known as the 17th Street Canal, suddenly broke, causing water to enter the streets of the [c]ity," resulting in damage to their insured property. They assert that the water damage "was not the result of flood, surface water, waves, [tidal] water, tsunami, seiche, overflow of a body of water, seepage under or over the outfall canal wall or spray from any of the above but was water intrusion, caused simply from a broken levee wall."

The *Vanderbrook* plaintiffs allege that their insurers have refused to adjust or pay for their losses, despite "a sudden break in the concrete wall of the levee outfall canal" not being described in any of their policies as an excluded loss. They assert that their insurance policies are contracts of adhesion and are "unduly and unreasonably complex," resulting in their lack of understanding of the policies' provisions. And they allege that the policies' exclusions are so "oppressive" to them and "unreasonably favorable" to the insurers that the exclusions are unconscionable and void....

.... The Hanover, Standard Fire, and Unitrin policies provide coverage for risk of direct physical loss to structures on the property as well as for certain risks of loss to personal property, as long as the loss is not an excluded peril. The policies contain the following flood exclusion:

> We do not insure for loss caused directly or indirectly by any of the following. Such loss is excluded regardless of any other cause or event contributing concurrently or in any sequence to the loss....

> ... Water Damage, meaning:

> ... Flood, surface water, waves, tidal water, overflow of a body of water, or spray from any of these, whether or not driven by wind....

\* \* \*

### III. DISCUSSION

The policies in this case—which are homeowners, renters, and commercial-property policies—are all-risk policies. All-risk policies "create[ ] a special type of coverage that extends to risks not usually covered under other insurance; recovery under an all-risk policy will be allowed for all fortuitous losses not resulting from misconduct or fraud, unless the policy contains a specific provision expressly excluding the loss from coverage." ... Insurers may, however, limit their liability under all-risk policies: "[A]bsent a conflict with statutory provisions or public policy, insurers, like other individuals, are entitled to limit their liability and to impose and to enforce reasonable conditions upon the policy obligations they contractually assume." ... But "[e]xclusionary provisions in insurance contracts are strictly construed against the insurer, and any ambiguity is construed in favor of the insured." ...

## B. *Flood Exclusions*

The plaintiffs contend that their policies' flood exclusions do not unambiguously exclude coverage for losses caused by an inundation of water resulting from a breached levee where the breach occurred in part because the levee was negligently designed, constructed, or maintained. The plaintiffs urge us to conclude that the term "flood" is ambiguous in this context and that the policies must be construed in favor of coverage. By contrast, the insurers maintain that the policies unambiguously exclude coverage for the inundation of water resulting from the breached levees.

The Louisiana Supreme Court has not interpreted a flood exclusion in the context of breached levees. We must therefore make an *Erie* guess and determine, in our best judgment, how that court would resolve the issue if presented with this case.

The plaintiffs first contend that because the term "flood" is not defined in the policies, it is ambiguous — indeed, the *Chehardy* plaintiffs say that the term's undefined status makes it per se ambiguous — requiring us to construe the term in favor of coverage. But the fact that a term used in an exclusion "is not defined in the policy itself . . . alone does not make the exclusion ambiguous; instead, [the court] will give the term its generally prevailing meaning." . . .

The plaintiffs also maintain that because the insurers could have more explicitly excluded floods that are caused in part by negligence, their failure to do so in these policies makes the flood exclusions ambiguous. Specifically, the *Chehardy* plaintiffs point to evidence that before Hurricane Katrina struck, the insurer defendants knew about the availability of policy forms that more explicitly excluded floods caused in part by man but that they elected not to amend their policies' language accordingly.

Xavier, which was insured through Travelers, also points to its policy's "earth movement" exclusion, which excludes earth movements "whether natural or man made"; Xavier asserts that Travelers thus knew how to clearly exclude man-made floods but did not do so. Similarly, the district court compared the flood exclusions in most of the policies with those in the policies of State Farm and Hartford Insurance Company of the Midwest, remarking that those insurers succeeded with little effort in clearly excluding water damage resulting from negligent acts and that the other insurers could have done so as well.

But the fact that an exclusion could have been worded more explicitly does not necessarily make it ambiguous. . . . Nor does the fact that other policies have more explicitly defined the scope of similar exclusions. . . .

We therefore reject the plaintiffs' arguments that the flood exclusions in the policies before us are ambiguous in light of more specific language used in other policies.

Furthermore, even where the scope of an exclusion is not readily apparent, we do not immediately construe that exclusion in favor of coverage. Instead, we first apply the general rules of contract construction set forth in the Civil Code. *La. Ins. Guar. Ass'n*, 630 So. 2d at 764. Under those rules, we give the words of a contract their "generally prevailing meaning." La. Civ. Code Ann. art. 2047. Dictionaries, treatises, and jurisprudence are helpful resources in ascertaining a term's generally prevailing meaning.... When the words of a policy provision are clear and unambiguous in the context of the facts of the case and do not lead to an absurd result, we apply the provision as written without any further interpretation....

To ascertain the generally prevailing meaning of the term "flood," we begin by considering dictionary definitions of the term. Each of the dictionaries we have accessed lists more than one definition of "flood," but the existence of more than one definition of a term does not itself make the term ambiguous.... Likewise, when "a word has two meanings, one broad and one more restrictive included within the broader meaning, it does not follow that the narrower meaning was intended." ...

The Oxford English Dictionary has two pertinent definitions of "flood": (1) "[a]n overflowing or irruption of a great body of water over land not usually submerged; an inundation, a deluge" and (2) "[a] profuse and violent outpouring of water; a swollen stream, a torrent; a violent downpour of rain, threatening an inundation." 5 OXFORD ENGLISH DICTIONARY 1075–76 (2d ed.1989). [The Court continued to examine definitions in three other dictionaries plus an encyclopedia]....

We also consider the definitions of "flood" in treatises. Appleman's Insurance Law and Practice defines "flood waters" as "those waters above the highest line of the ordinary flow of a stream, and generally speaking they have overflowed a river, stream, or natural water course and have formed a continuous body with the water flowing in the ordinary channel." 5 JOHN ALAN APPLEMAN & JEAN APPLEMAN, INSURANCE LAW AND PRACTICE § 3145 (1970). And *Couch on Insurance* defines "flood" as "the overflow of some body of water that inundates land not usually covered with water." STEVEN PLITT ET AL., COUCH ON INSURANCE § 153:54 (3d ed.2006) [hereinafter COUCH]. Couch also states that the term "flood" is generally unambiguous. *Id.* § 153:49.

Additionally, we look to jurisprudence, both from Louisiana courts and from courts outside Louisiana.... [The court found no helpful Louisiana jurisprudence.]

Where courts outside Louisiana have considered whether a flood exclusion similar to the ones here unambiguously precludes coverage for water damage resulting from the failure of a structure such as a dam or dike, they have uniformly declared that the inundation of water falls within the language of the exclusion....

The most prominent such case is *Kane*, which arose in the context of the failure of the Lawn Lake Dam in Colorado. *See* [*Kane v. Royal Ins. Co. of Am.*, 768 P.2d 678 (Colo. 1989),] at 679. As a result of the dam failure, water swept into the Fall River and inundated the plaintiffs' insured property, causing extensive damage. *Id.* The plaintiffs argued that their all-risk policies provided coverage for the damage, even though the policies contained flood exclusions. *Id.* at 680.

The Colorado Supreme Court rejected this argument and construed the term "flood" as extending to the water damage resulting from the dam failure. The court relied in part on dictionary definitions and the definition of "flood" in Appleman's treatise and observed that "[t]he inundation of insureds' normally dry land falls squarely within these generally accepted definitions of the term 'flood.'" *Id.* at 681. Concluding that the term was unambiguous in light of its generally accepted meaning and in the context of the facts of the case, the court declared that "there is no doubt that this large-scale inundation of water was a 'flood.'" *Id.*

In *Wallis v. Country Mutual Insurance Co.*, an Illinois intermediate court stated that the "plain and ordinary meaning" of "flood" is "water that escapes from a watercourse in large volumes and flows over adjoining property in no regular channel ending up in an area where it would not normally be expected." 309 Ill.App.3d 566, 243 Ill.Dec. 344, 723 N.E.2d 376, 383 (2000). The court held that it was immaterial that a particular watercourse was originally man-made as long as it had a defined bed, visible banks, and a recurrent water flow. *See id.* Indeed, the court observed that a permanent watercourse with these characteristics is considered a natural watercourse. *See id.* at 382; *see also* BLACK'S LAW DICTIONARY 1623 (8th ed. 2004) ("If [a man-made] watercourse is of a permanent character and has been maintained for a sufficient length of time, it may be considered a natural watercourse....").

Accordingly, the *Wallis* court held that water that had overflowed a man-made creek's banks and damaged the plaintiff's house was a flood within the plain and ordinary meaning of the term, *id.* at 383, and that the plaintiff's loss was excluded by his insurance policy's flood exclusion, *id.* at 384.

In light of these definitions, we conclude that the flood exclusions are unambiguous in the context of this case and that what occurred here fits squarely within the generally prevailing meaning of the term "flood." When a body of water overflows its normal boundaries and inundates an area of land that is normally dry, the event is a flood. This is precisely what occurred in New Orleans in the aftermath of Hurricane Katrina. Three watercourses—the 17th Street, Industrial, and London Avenue Canals—overflowed their normal channels, and the levees built alongside the canals to hold back their floodwaters failed to do so. As a result, an enormous volume of water inundated the city. In common parlance, this event is known as a flood.

Additionally, a levee is a *flood*-control structure; its very purpose is to prevent the floodwaters of a watercourse from overflowing onto certain land areas, i.e., to prevent floods from becoming more widespread.... By definition, whenever a levee ruptures and fails to hold back floodwaters, the result is a more widespread flood. That a levee's failure is due to its negligent design, construction, or maintenance does not change the character of the water escaping through the levee's breach; the waters are still floodwaters, and the result is a flood.

The plaintiffs, however, attempt to inject ambiguity into the term "flood" by asserting that a reasonable interpretation of the term is that it refers only to inundations of water with "natural" causes, not those with a "non-natural" cause. The plaintiffs rely primarily on cases interpreting flood exclusions in the context of broken water mains. They also assert, applying two canons of construction, *noscitur a sociis* and *ejusdem generis*, that a flood includes only natural events because the other terms in the water-damage exclusions are natural phenomena. Additionally, they contend that a reasonable policyholder would expect that only naturally occurring floods would be excluded.

Before we address these contentions, we first question the notion that the flood in this case was non-natural. The plaintiffs focus on the alleged negligent design, construction, or maintenance of the levees as being the cause of the flood, and we accept as true (for the purpose of assessing the motions to dismiss) their allegation that the canals' floodwaters would not have reached their property had the negligence not occurred. This focus, however, ignores the sizeable natural component to the disaster: a catastrophic hurricane and the excess water associated with it.

The non-natural component is simply that in certain areas, man's efforts to mitigate the effect of the natural disaster failed, with devastating consequences. But if man's failure to adequately prepare for a natural disaster could alone transform the disaster into a non-natural event outside the scope of a policy's exclusion, it is difficult to conceive how an insurer could ever exclude the resulting loss; any natural event could be recharacterized as non-natural either because man's preventative measures were inadequate or because man failed to take preventative measures at all.

Even if we accept the plaintiffs' characterization of the flood in this case as non-natural, we disagree that the term "flood" in this context is limited to natural events. The plaintiffs first maintain that dictionary definitions support their interpretation, but the dictionaries we have reviewed make no distinction between floods with natural causes and those with non-natural causes. Indeed, the Columbia Encyclopedia specifically states that a flood may result from the bursting of a levee. *See* Columbia Encyclopedia 1002. Similarly, Appleman's treatise states: "A 'flood,' contemplated by the exclusion, can result from either natural or artificial causes." 5 John Alan Appleman & Jean Appleman, *supra*, at § 3145 (Supp.2007) (citing *Kane*, 768 P.2d 678).

\* \* \*

The plaintiffs finally contend that the reasonable expectations of homeowners insurance policyholders would be that damage resulting from man-made floods would be covered. "[A]scertaining how a reasonable insurance policy purchaser would construe the clause at the time the insurance contract was entered" is one way that ambiguity in an exclusion clause may be resolved. *La. Ins. Guar. Ass'n*, 630 So.2d at 764. But "Louisiana law ... precludes use of the reasonable expectations doctrine to recast policy language when such language is clear and unambiguous." *Coleman v. Sch. Bd. of Richland Parish*, 418 F.3d 511, 522 (5th Cir.2005). As we have explained, the flood exclusions in the policies are unambiguous in the context of the specific facts of this case; thus, we need not resort to ascertaining a reasonable policyholder's expectations. For the sake of thoroughness, however, we will briefly address a few of the parties' arguments.

First, the plaintiffs assert that because their policies are all-risk policies, they have a heightened expectation of coverage and that a reasonable policyholder thus would not expect water damage resulting from third-party negligence to be excluded. Although a few courts have stated that insureds with all-risk policies have "heightened expectations" of coverage, *see, e.g., Murray v. State Farm Fire & Cas. Co.,* 203 W.Va. 477, 509 S.E.2d 1, 14 (1998), we are not aware of any Louisiana court that has so held. And although all-risk policies do generally extend to all fortuitous losses, this is true only to the extent that the policy does not expressly exclude the loss from coverage. *See Alton Ochsner Med. Found.,* 219 F.3d at 504.

Each policy in this case contains a specific provision expressly excluding damage caused by flood, and none of the exclusions indicates that whether a particular flood is excluded depends on whether its cause is purely natural. Given the generally prevailing use of the term "flood," we believe a reasonable policyholder would expect a massive inundation of water from a breached levee to be excluded, notwithstanding the all-risk nature of the policies.

Second, the plaintiffs assert that because many of the policies contained a "Hurricane Deductible Endorsement," reasonable policyholders would expect those policies to cover damage resulting from a hurricane. Many of the policies contained an endorsement materially similar to the following, from Humphreys's policy with Encompass Indemnity:

> We will pay only that part of the total of the loss for all Property Coverages that exceeds the hurricane deductible stated on the Coverage Summary. The hurricane deductible shown on the Coverage Summary applies to all covered property for direct physical loss or damage caused directly or indirectly by a hurricane as defined below. Such deductible applies regardless of any other cause or event contributing concurrently or in any sequence to the loss. No other deductible provision in the policy applies to direct physical loss caused by a hurricane. In no event will the deductible applied for a hurricane loss be less than the property deductible shown on the Coverage Summary.
>
> Hurricane means wind, wind gust, hail, rain, tornado, cyclone or hurricane which results in direct physical loss or damage to property by a storm system that has been declared to be a hurricane by the National Weather Service....
>
>    ....
>
> All other provisions of this policy apply.

The plaintiffs assert that in light of this language, a reasonable policyholder would have expected the water damage in this case to be covered. Humphreys goes a step further and argues that the hurricane-deductible endorsement in her policy actually expands coverage to extend to any property damage caused by a hurricane.

But the plain language of the hurricane-deductible endorsements indicates that they do nothing more than alter the deductible for damage caused by a hurricane. Nothing in the language of the endorsements purports to extend coverage for floods or to restrict flood exclusions; indeed they do not even include flood or water (other than rain) in the definition of "hurricane." Further, the endorsements state that all other provisions of the policies apply, indicating that the flood exclusions remain in effect. The hurricane-deductible endorsements therefore would not give a reasonable policyholder the impression that flood resulting from a breached levee would be covered.

Finally, several defendants argue that in light of flood insurance available though the National Flood Insurance Program ("NFIP"), a reasonable policyholder would not expect homeowners policies to cover the flooding in this case. The defendants assert that we may consider the NFIP in interpreting "flood" because custom and industry usage is relevant under article 2053 of the Civil Code. They contend that the NFIP's existence over many years has made it clear to property owners that standard all-risk policies do not cover flood damage, regardless of whether the cause of the flood is natural or non-natural, and that property owners who want flood coverage must purchase it through the NFIP; a reasonable policyholder thus would not expect the inundation of water in this case to be covered under a standard homeowners, renters, or commercial-property insurance policy.

The plaintiffs, in contrast, urge us not to consider the NFIP, contending that it has no bearing on this appeal. And to the extent the NFIP may be relevant, the plaintiffs argue that a reasonable policyholder would expect the NFIP to provide coverage for naturally occurring floods but that floods induced by negligence would be covered under standard all-risk policies.

We do not rely upon the NFIP to decide this appeal. Our decision is based instead upon our determination that the flood exclusions in the policies before us unambiguously preclude the plaintiffs' recovery. But to the extent that the NFIP's definition of "flood" is further evidence of the term's generally prevailing meaning, we note that it is consistent with our interpretation. Standard insurance policies issued under the NFIP define "flood" as follows:

> [a] general and temporary condition of partial or complete inundation of two or more acres of normally dry land area or of two or more properties (one of which is [the policyholder's] property) from:
>
> a. Overflow of inland or tidal waters,
>
> b. Unusual and rapid accumulation or runoff of surface waters from any source,
>
> c. Mudflow.

44 C.F.R. Pt. 61, App. A(1), App. A(2), App. A(3) (2006); *see also* Federal Emergency Management Agency, FloodSmart.gov: What is a Flood?, http://www.floodsmart.gov/floodsmart/pages/whatflood.jsp (last visited July 25, 2007).

The NFIP makes no distinction between inundations of water caused by natural levee ruptures and those caused by man-made ruptures (even if such a distinction were workable). The canals' overflowing into the City of New Orleans due to the levee ruptures was certainly an overflow of inland waters as used in the NFIP's definition, and it may also have been an unusual and rapid runoff of surface waters.

In sum, we conclude that the flood exclusions in the plaintiffs' policies are unambiguous in the context of the facts of this case. In the midst of a hurricane, three canals running through the City of New Orleans overflowed their normal boundaries. The flood-control measures, i.e., levees, that man had put in place to prevent the canals' floodwaters from reaching the city failed. The result was an enormous and devastating inundation of water into the city, damaging the plaintiffs' property.

This event was a "flood" within that term's generally prevailing meaning as used in common parlance, and our interpretation of the exclusions ends there. The flood is unambiguously excluded from coverage under the plaintiffs' all-risk policies, and the district court's conclusion to the contrary was erroneous.

## C. Efficient Proximate Cause and Anti-Concurrent-Causation Clauses

Lastly we turn to the doctrine of efficient proximate cause. Under this doctrine, as it is applied in many jurisdictions, where a loss is caused by a combination of a covered risk and an excluded risk, the loss is covered if the covered risk was the efficient proximate cause of the loss.... The efficient proximate cause of the loss is the dominant, fundamental cause or the cause that set the chain of events in motion. *See* COUCH, *supra*, at § 101:45.

Many of the insurance policies at issue in this appeal excluded "loss caused directly or indirectly by" flood "regardless of any other cause or event contributing concurrently or in any sequence to the loss." This language, which the district court referred to as an anti-concurrent-causation clause, has been recognized as demonstrating an insurer's intent to contract around the operation of the efficient-proximate-cause rule. *See, e.g., TNT Speed & Sport Ctr., Inc. v. Am. States Ins. Co.*, 114 F.3d 731, 732–33 (8th Cir.1997).

The district court considered the anti-concurrent-causation clauses in this case and concluded that they are inapplicable here because there were not two separate causes of the plaintiffs' damage. The court remarked that this case does not present a combination of forces that caused damage and that it therefore is not analogous to cases where Hurricane Katrina may have damaged property through both wind and water. *Cf. Tuepker v. State Farm Fire & Cas. Co.*, No. 1:05-CV-599, 2006 U.S. Dist. LEXIS 34710 (S.D.Miss. May 24, 2006) (unpublished opinion) (Hurricane Katrina case involving alleged damage from wind, rain, and storm surge), *appeal docketed*, Nos. 06-61075 & 06-61076 (5th Cir.).

Instead, the court stated that "in this case the 'cause' conflates to the flood," meaning that the alleged negligent design, construction, or maintenance of the levees and the resulting flood were not separate causes of the plaintiffs' losses. Consequently, the court concluded that the anti-concurrent-causation clauses needed not be addressed at that time but stated that they may need to be addressed at later stages in the litigation.

On appeal, several insurers rely in part on the language in their anti-concurrent-causation clauses to demonstrate that floods are excluded regardless of the cause. The *Chehardy* plaintiffs respond that "the District Court correctly determined that the anti-concurrent causation clauses were inapplicable," contending that the cause of their damage ("man-made inundation of water or inundation resulting from third-party negligent acts") was a covered peril. Xavier responds that the district court "correctly noted that [the anti-concurrent-causation clause] is inapplicable because there is no separate or other cause of damage."

We agree with the district court's determination that we need not address whether insurers may contract around the efficient-proximate-cause rule under Louisiana law, nor need we address the operation of the efficient-proximate-cause rule itself in this case. The efficient-proximate-cause doctrine applies only where two or more distinct actions, events, or forces combined to create the loss.... But here, on these pleadings, there are not two independent causes of the plaintiffs' damages at play; the only force that damaged the plaintiffs' properties was flood.

To the extent that negligent design, construction, or maintenance of the levees contributed to the plaintiffs' losses, it was only one factor in bringing about the flood; the peril of negligence did not act, apart from flood, to bring about damage to the insureds' properties. Consequently, as the plaintiffs argue and as the district court held, the efficient-proximate-cause doctrine is inapplicable....

Moreover, to the extent that the plaintiffs do attempt to recharacterize the cause of their losses by focusing on negligence as the cause rather than water damage, their argument fails. "An insured may not avoid a contractual exclusion merely by affixing an additional label or separate characterization to the act or event causing the loss." *Kish*, 883 P.2d at 311; *Chadwick* [*v. Fire Ins. Exch.*], 21 Cal.Rptr.2d at 874 [(Cal. Ct. App. 1993)]. "If every possible characterization of an action or event were counted an additional peril, the exclusions in all-risk insurance contracts would be largely meaningless." *Chadwick*, 21 Cal.Rptr.2d at 874.

Thus, in *Pieper v. Commercial Underwriters Insurance Co.*, where a policy covered loss caused by arson but excluded loss caused by brush fire, a brush fire caused by arson was excluded. 69 Cal.Rptr.2d at 557–58. The *Pieper* court determined that the cause of the brush fire was irrelevant; the plaintiffs' property was damaged by one cause alone, brush fire, and thus, the efficient-proximate-cause rule was inapplicable. *Id.*

And in *Kish v. Insurance Co. of North America*, where a policy covered loss caused by rain but excluded loss caused by flood, the court held that the insured could not avoid the operation of the flood exclusion by merely recharacterizing the flood as rain. 883 P.2d at 311–13. The court held that there was one cause of the plaintiffs' loss— rain-induced flood—which was excluded, and concluded that the efficient-proximate-cause rule was inapplicable. *Id.* We similarly reject any attempt on the plaintiffs' part to avoid the operation of the flood exclusion by recharacterizing the flood as negligence; the sole cause of the losses for which they seek coverage in this litigation, flood, was excluded from coverage regardless of what factors contributed to its development.

In sum, we need not address the applicability of anti-concurrent-causation clauses or the efficient-proximate-cause rule because, as pleaded, there was not more than one separate cause of the plaintiffs' losses. As the district court recognized, there are other cases arising in the context of Hurricane Katrina where these issues may come into play, but this is not the case for their resolution.

## *Notes and Questions*

1. Is the court's decision a formalist or functionalist one?

2. Why the heavy reliance on dictionaries and encyclopedias to define the terms? Does that tend to lead to a more formalist or functionalist decision?

3. Can you predict how courts dealing with insurance cases about large-scale disasters often boil the issues down to the turns of meanings of a specific word in a policy, despite the alleged failings of government intervenors to respond or prepare for the loss with proper public infrastructure? What sorts of insurance coverage litigation might arise from earthquakes, tsunamis, nuclear events, floods or wildfires?

4. How is insurance to respond when the causality of many losses resulting from large-scale disasters is so complex? For example, in the devastating earthquake-driven tsunami in northern Japan in 2011, there was not only loss resulting from earthquake and tsunami but also the leakage of radiation from damaged nuclear plants. How is property and liability insurance supposed to respond when the causes of losses impinge on both human-made and natural causes?

# § 8.10. Valuation and the Property Insurance Claim

When an insured loss occurs, the amount of loss is often determined by various "terms of art" appearing within the policy. This section identifies and discusses terms of art in the insurance field, such as "occurrence," "cash value," "valued versus unvalued policies," "cost to repair or replace," "appraisal of damage," and also examines general concepts and statutory limitations related to loss.

## [A] Actual Cash Value, Replacement Cost and Depreciation

Property insurance policies often contain a provision which limits loss to the "actual cash value" of the property at the time of loss, less depreciation. Such a provision might read:

> This company shall not be liable beyond the actual cash value of property at the time any loss or damage occurs, and the loss or damage shall be ascertained or estimated according to such actual cash value with proper deduction for depreciation, however caused, and shall in no event exceed what it would then cost to repair or replace the same with material of like kind and quality.

But how should "actual cash value" be determined? In addition to fair market value, replacement cost, and depreciation, should other factors such as location and obsolescence also be considered? Should the insured be able to submit further proof of loss and additional value under a "broad evidence standard"? The courts are far from uniform in answering these questions. *See, e.g., Ohio Casualty Ins. Co. v. Ramsey*, 439 N.E.2d 1162 (Ind. Ct. App. 1982):

> Because a fire insurance policy is a contract of indemnity, the intent of the parties to the policy is to place the insured in the same financial position he would have been in had no loss occurred....
>
> It has been said that in order to indemnify the insured, the term "actual cash value" will be given a meaning which takes into account the character of the insured property and the extent of the loss. Thus, real property is treated differently than personal property, and total losses are treated differently than partial losses....
>
> Fair market value is the price at which property would change hands between a willing buyer and seller, neither being under any compulsion to consummate the sale.... In certain areas of the law in which fair market value is the measure of damages, the prevailing rules permit proof of all possible elements of value in establishing market value. In eminent domain proceedings, for instance, Indiana courts allow evidence of "anything affecting the sale value" of the condemned property.... Specific consideration has been given to three factors or "approaches" in estimating the fair market value of property taken by eminent domain:
>
>> (1) the current *cost of reproducing* the property less depreciation from all sources; (2) the "*market data*" approach or value indicated by recent sales of comparable properties in the market, and (3) the "*income-approach*," or the value which the property's net earning power will support based upon the capitalization of net income. This three-approach means of reaching market value is usually combined.... All three methods have been judicially approved....
>
> [citation omitted] Courts in the area of fire insurance law have apparently considered evidence of comparable sales ("market data" approach) as the *sole* criterion of fair market value, rejecting evidence of income ("income" approach) and reproduction costs ("cost of reproducing" approach).... Probably because market value in this limited sense is not the true test of indemnity, most courts have rejected fair market value as the exclusive measure of "actual cash value" under a fire insurance policy such as Ramsey's....
>
> A number of courts have defined "actual cash value" as the cost of replacing the property at the time of loss — less an appropriate depreciation deduction.... Although the provision at issue specifies that the insurer's liability shall not exceed "the amount which it would cost to repair or replace the property with material of like kind and quality within a reasonable time after such loss," courts adopting the replacement-cost-less-depreciation test have, in effect, made the quoted phrase the substantive measure of "actual cash value."

One author offers the following analysis of the relative strengths and weaknesses of the test:

Property owners in jurisdictions which have adopted the replacement-cost-less depreciation test are able to estimate accurately the value of property when insuring it.

*But the inflexibility of this rule is also its most objectionable feature. While it may be appropriate where, as in the majority of cases, the insured property is being used for its intended purposes, the test will result in excessive recovery where the property is obsolete.* Many structures today have a high replacement value because of the inflated cost of building materials even though their true commercial value—represented by rentals, prospective profits, usefulness to the present owner, location and age—is considerably less. The "moral hazard" [promoting arson by allowing recovery in excess of actual loss] against which the principle of indemnity is directed may, therefore, be increased through the use of the replacement cost-less depreciation test. [citation omitted]

As the italicized language indicates, courts adopting replacement cost less depreciation as the test of "actual cash value" fail to recognize that under the "cost of reproducing" approach to determining the fair market value of property taken by eminent domain ... depreciation is not restricted to physical wear and tear, but has been extended to embrace the effect of obsolescence (loss of adaptability)....

Possibly because the law in this area has traditionally assigned restrictive meanings to the terms "fair market value" and "replacement cost less depreciation," a number of courts in recent years have rejected market value and replacement cost as the exclusive tests of "actual cash value."

They have adopted the broad evidence rule, under which the fact finder may consider all available evidence logically tending to establish "actual cash value." *E.g., McAnarney v. Newark Fire Insurance Co.*, (1928) 247 N.Y. 176, 159 N.E. 902.... In *McAnarney*, a leading case on point, the New York Court of Appeals expressed the broad evidence rule as follows:

Where insured buildings have been destroyed, the trier of fact may, and should, call to its aid, in order to effectuate complete indemnity, every fact and circumstance which would logically tend to the formation of a correct estimate of the loss. It may consider original cost and cost of reproduction; the opinions upon value given by qualified witnesses; the declarations against interest which may have been made by the assured; the gainful uses to which the buildings might have been put; as well as any other fact reasonably tending to throw light upon the subject....

247 N.Y. at 184–85, 159 N.E. at 905.

Thus, in applying the rule, a court may take into account market value, replacement cost, and depreciation. In addition, such factors as location and obsolescence may be considered. [The court also noted in a footnote that: "A structure is obsolete when a reasonable owner would not rebuild it in case of destruction. Obsolescence is caused by changes and improvements in building design or construction or by the presence of other factors which make the use to which the building has heretofore been put impracticable."] ...

The disadvantage of the broad evidence standard is its lack of predictability. But its overriding allure is its ability to aid the fact finder in ascertaining the true economic value of insured property—the objective of indemnity.... We therefore adopt the broad evidence rule as the measure of recovery for a total loss to real property insured under a policy containing a liability-limiting clause such as the one in this case.

In so doing, we suggest that every factor considered by appraisers in assessing the fair market value of condemned property merits consideration by the fact finder under the broad evidence rule: Evidence of the cost of reproduction less depreciation and obsolescence, prices comparable properties have brought, and income from the property may be admitted to show the "actual cash value" of insured property.... Furthermore, the trier of fact may properly consider declarations against interest; matters affecting the credibility of witnesses, including valuation experts; and any other evidence which will aid in determining "actual cash value."

In *Travelers Indem. Co. v. Armstrong*, 442 N.E.2d 349, 354–57 (Ind. 1982), the Indiana Supreme Court summarized the four methods for determining "actual cash value" for losses sustained:

Historically, four methods have been judicially sanctioned for determining the actual cash value of losses under policy provisions....

(1) *Replacement cost, without deduction for depreciation.* The method ... has been criticized as follows:

"The most striking development in the partial loss cases has been the emergence of a minority view that recovery may be had for the cost of reconstruction without any depreciation allowance. The rationale of these cases is that if a depreciation deduction is taken, the insured will realize a sum that is insufficient to pay for repairing the property at the time of the loss. Where the damage is to a substantial portion of the structure, the repair of which would appreciably extend the normal life of the building, recovery of full repair cost would permit the insured to profit by his loss since he is thereby receiving the cost of a new building for an old building. Where, on the other hand, the damaged portion is structurally insignificant, the failure to consider depreciation is justifiable." 49 Colum. L. Rev. 818, 826.

Even when that article was written in 1949, the hazard of windfall profit was recognized. Footnote 60 states:

"Since depreciation is always deducted in computing total loss, an insured may recover more for a partial loss under this minority rule than for a total loss. Thus, if the insured has a building valued at $100,000 which has depreciated $20,000, he would recover $80,000 in a case of total loss. If his loss was $90,000 under this minority view, he would collect the full $90,000." *Id.*

(2) The *market value test* has been adopted in relatively few jurisdictions, the most prominent being California. *Jefferson Ins. Co. of New York v. Superior Court of Alameda County*, (1970) 3 Cal.3d 398, 90 Cal. Rptr. 608, 475 P.2d. 880. In the case of partial damage or destruction of a building by fire, it is speculative, since there may be no established market. The rule has been criticized in this way.

"It is commonly said that a building has no recognized market value in the ordinary sense since each structure is in theory unique. Further, the market value of its structure is bound up with the value of the land on which it stands and if the land is not marketable the building will have a decreased value. The majority of the courts, therefore, have rejected market value as the sole definition or standard of 'actual cash value,' but have allowed juries to consider it as a factor in computing the actual cash value of a building." 49 Colum. L. Rev. 818, 820.

(3) The *replacement cost with deduction for depreciation* used to be the majority rule.

"At least fourteen jurisdictions have adopted the reproduction or replacement cost less depreciation standard of measuring the actual cash value. The New York Standard Fire Insurance Policy says recovery shall not exceed 'the amount which it would cost to repair or replace the property with material of like kind and quality....'

"This provision is acknowledged to have been intended as an upper limit of the insured's recovery, but courts have generally adopted it as the rule of measurement of actual cash value in those states using replacement cost method. Its primary advantage is that of certainty but the inflexibility of the rule is also its most objectionable feature. It results in over-compensation in those cases where substantial obsolescence has taken place apart from corresponding depreciation." Insur. L.J., July, 1973, p. 368.

The replacement cost with deduction for depreciation has been described by its adherents as follows:

"Of the three rules generally applicable to partial losses, the one that squares with the basic principle of indemnity and affords a reasonable guide to insureds in determining insurable value and to insurers in determining the amount of loss is replacement cost less depreciation, with depreciation given its broad meaning as exemplified in the *McAnarney* case in situations where obsolescence is a material factor." Ins. L.J., 1953, 685, 688.

It, nevertheless, cannot always be said that the insured has been "indemnified" if he is required to expend a substantial sum from his own pocket to restore his building, albeit to an improved condition, when it suited his purpose in its pre-loss condition.

(4) The fourth method that has been employed is the so-called *Broad Evidence Rule* which originated with the case of *McAnarney v. New York Fire Insurance Company*, (1928) 247 N.Y. 176, 159 N.E. 902.

> The Broad Evidence Rule has now become the majority rule, having been adopted in at least twenty-three states.

> > "More than twenty-three states have adopted some form of the broad evidence rule. It is clear that obsolescence cases like the early *McAnarney* case and demolition and abandonment of building cases have been responsible for most breaking of traditional valuation rules. These appear to be the primary areas where existing doctrines simply could not be stretched enough to meet indemnity and equity principles." Insur. L.J., 1973 at p. 369.

> The fourth approach, the *Broad Evidence Rule*, instead of being a fixed rule, is a flexible rule. It permits an appraiser or a court or a jury to consider any relevant factor.

In *Strauss Bros. Packing Co. v. American Ins. Co.*, 98 Wis. 2d 706, 298 N.W.2d 108 (1980), the Wisconsin Supreme Court held that, although market value was the proper test for determining the actual cash value of farm products, the "broad evidence rule" gave the court the right to consider all facts "reasonably tending to throw light upon the subject." Under established case law, the measure of damages for injury or destruction of a growing crop is the difference between the crop value at maturity, less the expense of cultivation, harvesting, and marketing of the probable crop which was prevented from maturing; and, by analogy, the same calculations should be used when determining the actual cash value of growing livestock, such as calves and minks.

*Query*: Which of the four methods of determining "actual cash value" is most persuasive? Does what is being valued make a difference?

## [B] Valued Policies

In marine insurance, and occasionally property insurance, the policy stipulates a certain value for the insured cargo or property, rather than leaving the value to be determined at the time of loss. Such a policy is termed a "valued policy." If no such stipulation appears, the policy is referred to as "open" or "unvalued."

Non-marine property insurance policies are seldom valued, but many states have adopted valued policy statutes (particularly those states in flood and hurricane-prone areas). The theory behind these valued policy statutes is that the denial of any opportunity to contest the valuation of the property when the claim is filed by the policyholder will cause the insurer to investigate more carefully before underwriting the risk of loss, and policies for excessive amounts will therefore not be written. However, valued policies may also tempt the policyholder to obtain excessive coverage, and then destroy the property.

A variant on the valuation problem is the presence of "valued" policies. A "valued" policy is one that provides that in the event of a "total" loss, the amount paid to the policyholder will be the face value of the policy. This relieves the policyholder of the burden of proving up the amount of the loss through documentary or expert evidence and also prevents the insurer from delaying resolution or the claim or chiseling the policyholder by quibbling about the value of the property destroyed.

As one might expect in light of their operation, valued policies did not come into existence due to the altruism of the insurance industry. State legislators, beginning in the late 19th and early 20th centuries, enacted legislation requiring valued policies in order to combat perceived abuses and to protect policyholders from financial devastation from the total loss of a home or similarly important property.

Today, approximately 20 states have valued policy statutes of some form. Most are in the South or West, reflecting the populist origins of the legislation. Normally, valued policy laws apply only to personal insurance sold to individuals and not to commercial policies or corporate policyholders. However, even without the coercion of such legislation, insurers may often write valued policies—commercial as well as personal—because these are perceived to be an attractive product by prospective policyholders. The premiums charged also logically will reflect the greater exposure to the insurer in a valued policy.

Of course, the valued policy provision does not eliminate all debate over interpretation and application. For example, there can be questions over whether there has really been a "total" loss, which is generally defined as property that is more than 50 percent damaged, is damaged beyond repair, or where the costs of repair will approach or exceed the cost of complete replacement. *See Kelly v. Commercial Union Ins. Co.*, 709 F.2d 973 (5th Cir. 1983) (applying Louisiana law). Put another way, if the property has "lost its essential character," there has been a total loss. *See Stahlberg v. Travelers Indem. Co.*, 568 S.W.2d 79 (Mo. Ct. App. 1978). If government regulations require rebuilding, this is also usually construed to constitute a total loss. *See Liverpool & London & Globe Ins. Co. v. Nebraska Storage Warehouses, Inc.*, 96 F.2d 30 (8th Cir. 1938) (applying Nebraska law).

- Are valued policies a good idea?

- Or, even if a good idea for some purposes, do they violate the indemnity principle? Do they encourage moral hazard for fraud?

"On balance," concludes Professor Keeton, "the principle of indemnity would be better served by repeal of valued policy statutes." *See generally* Keeton & Widiss, Insurance Law (2d ed. 1988). The casebook authors disagree, concluding that valued policy laws are an appropriate legislative response to problems of loss valuation and policyholder protection that do not impose undue burdens on insurers. *See* Jeffrey W. Stempel & Erik S. Knutsen, Stempel & Knutsen on Insurance Coverage, §15.04.

# Chauvin v. State Farm Fire & Casualty Co.

United States Court of Appeals for the Fifth Circuit
495 F.3d 232 (2007)

### W. Eugene Davis, Circuit Judge

Plaintiffs are homeowners who sued their insurers, alleging that their homes were totally destroyed in Hurricanes Katrina and/or Rita. They appeal the district court's order granting the defendant-insurers' motions to dismiss and/or motions for judgment on the pleadings, concluding that Louisiana's Value Policy Law does not apply when a total loss does not result from a covered peril. For the following reasons, we AFFIRM the order of the district court dismissing the homeowners' claims.

## I. BACKGROUND

Plaintiffs (the "homeowners"), both individuals and putative class representatives, are homeowners who allege that Hurricanes Katrina and/or Rita rendered their homes total losses. When their homeowner's insurers (the "insurers") refused to reimburse them for the full value of their homes as stated in their policies (the "agreed face value"), the homeowners filed suit against the insurers, alleging that they were entitled to the agreed face value pursuant to La.Rev.Stat. Ann. § 22:695, Louisiana's Valued Policy Law ("VPL"). All of the insurance policies cover damage caused by wind and rain, but contain a clause excluding coverage for damage caused by flood.[6]

The insurers filed Fed. R. Civ. Proc. 12(b)(6) motions to dismiss and Fed. R. Civ. Proc. 12(c) motions for judgment on the pleadings, arguing, *inter alia*, that (1) the VPL applies only to a total loss resulting from fire; and (2) even if the VPL extends to perils other than fire, the VPL does not allow full recovery when the total loss is not caused by a covered peril. In response, the homeowners argued that the VPL does apply to non-fire perils and that the VPL requires an insurer to pay the agreed face value when (1) the property is rendered a "total loss," even if the "total loss" is due to an excluded peril; so long as (2) a covered peril causes some damage, no matter how small, to the property.

In a well-reasoned opinion, the district court granted the insurers' motions. Assuming without deciding that the VPL applied to non-fire perils, the district court first held that, regardless of whether the statutory language of the VPL is considered ambiguous, the homeowners' interpretation would lead to absurd consequences. The court concluded that the focus of the VPL was on establishing the value of the property in the event of a total loss, and was not intended to expand coverage to excluded perils. Thus, the court determined that the VPL does not apply when a total loss does not result from a covered peril.

---

6. [3] The exclusion found in Allstate's policy is typical. It reads:
> We do not cover loss to the property described in *Coverage A—Dwelling Protection or Coverage B—Other Structures Protection* consisting of or caused by:
>     1. Flood, including but not limited to surface water, waves, tidal water or overflow of any body of water, or spray from any of these, whether or not driven by wind.

The homeowners then filed the instant appeal. While this appeal was pending, the homeowners filed a motion asking us to certify the questions regarding the construction of the VPL to the Louisiana Supreme Court, which we denied. The homeowners also filed a motion requesting that we stay our decision in this case pending the appeal of two Louisiana state court decisions, which we also denied.

Because we conclude that the VPL does not apply to a total loss not caused by a covered peril, we assume for purposes of this opinion that the VPL applies to non-fire perils.

## A. THE LANGUAGE OF LOUISIANA'S VALUED POLICY LAW

The homeowners maintain that they are entitled to the agreed face value of their policy under the VPL because their homes sustained some damage from wind, a covered peril, even though the total loss resulted from flooding, a non-covered peril. On the other hand, the insurers contend that the VPL does not require them to pay the agreed face value of the policy because the total loss was not caused by a covered peril.

In determining which interpretation of the VPL the Louisiana Supreme Court would likely adopt, we begin with the language of the statute and the rules of construction provided in the Louisiana Civil Code. Louisiana's VPL provides, in relevant part:

> A. Under any fire insurance policy insuring inanimate, immovable property in this state, if the insurer places a valuation upon the covered property and uses such valuation for purposes of determining the premium charge to be made under the policy, *in the case of total loss the insurer shall compute and indemnify or compensate any covered loss of, or damage to, such property* which occurs during the term of the policy at such valuation without deduction or offset, unless a different method is to be used in the computation of loss, in which latter case, the policy, and any application therefor, shall set forth in type of equal size, the actual method of such loss computation by the insurer....[7]

The statutory interpretation articles in the Louisiana Civil Code provide that "[w]hen a law is clear and unambiguous and its application does not lead to absurd consequences, the law shall be applied as written and no further interpretation may be made in search of the intent of the legislature."[8] However, "[w]hen the language of the law is susceptible of different meanings, it must be interpreted as having the meaning that best conforms to the purpose of the law." When interpreting a statute, "[t]he words of a law must be given their generally prevailing meaning," and "[w]hen the words of a law are ambiguous, their meaning must be sought by examining the context in which they occur and the text of the law as a whole."

---

7. [12] La.Rev.Stat. Ann. § 22:695(A) (emphasis added). The parties do not dispute that the homeowner's policies involved in this suit are "valued policies" within the meaning of the VPL.

8. [13] La. Civ. Code art. 9.

We agree with the district court that the language of the VPL is not clear and unambiguous. In particular, the critical language in the statute providing that "in the case of a total loss the insurer shall compute and indemnify or compensate any covered loss of, or damage to, such property" is susceptible of two possible meanings: (1) in the event of a total loss, an insurer is required to pay the homeowner the agreed full value of a policy as long as a covered loss causes some damage to the property, even if a non-covered peril renders the property a total loss; or (2) an insurer is only required to pay the homeowner the agreed face value of a policy when the property is rendered a total loss by a covered loss. We therefore must interpret the statute in a manner that best conforms to the purpose of the law.

The VPL was enacted to fix the value of the insured property in the event of a total loss and thus, operates as a form of liquidated damages.[9] As stated by the Louisiana Fourth Circuit Court of Appeal:

> Valued policy laws or so-called total losses statutes dealing with Fire Ins. policies were enacted by many states in the late 1800's and early 1900's principally as a protective measure for insureds. In general, these valued policy laws require that in case of total loss to an insured's property from certain specified perils, the amount stated in the policy declarations is considered the value of the structure at the time of loss and is payable in full. In other words, if the value of property is less than the amount of insurance on a policy covering a building in a state having such a law, the insurer is precluded in most states from arguing that a lesser sum be paid, i.e., actual cash value....

The legislative intent of these laws was to prevent over-insurance and other abuses, that is, to keep insurers and their representatives from writing insurance on property for more than it is actually worth.

A second reason for valued policy laws is to encourage insurers and producers to inspect risks and assist prospective insureds in determining insurable value of properties.... It follows that failure of an insurer to inspect a risk for valuation purposes can lead to over-insurance and can produce a moral hazard as well. In other words, if a building is insured for more than its actual worth, an insured might be indifferent about loss prevention. This situation might even give an insured an incentive to intentionally cause damage to his structure.

In other words, according to the Louisiana courts, the VPL was adopted for two main purposes: (1) to keep insurers from writing insurance on property for more than it was actually worth, collecting premiums based on that overvaluation, and later arguing that the property was worth less than the face value when the property was destroyed; and (2) to discourage intentional destruction of property by insureds when they are permitted to over insure their property.

---

9. [20] *See Hart v. N. British & Mercantile Ins. Co.*, 182 La. 551, 162 So. 177, 181 (1935); *The Forge, Inc. v. Peerless Cas. Co.*, 131 So.2d 838, 840 (La.App.2d Cir.1961).

## B. APPLYING THE VPL TO CLAIM OF TOTAL LOSS CAUSED BY A NON-COVERED PERIL

After considering the purposes of the VPL, we are convinced that the insurers' construction of the VPL best conforms with its legislative purpose and thus, the VPL only requires an insurer to pay the agreed face value of the insured property if the property is rendered a total loss from a covered peril.[10]

As the district court observed, the homeowners' interpretation does nothing to further the purpose of the VPL. In particular, a finding that the statute requires insurers to pay the agreed face value of the property, even if an excluded peril (flooding) causes the total loss, runs counter to the VPL's effort to link insurance recoveries to premiums paid. Such an interpretation of the statute would force the insurer to pay for damage resulting from a non-covered peril for which it did not charge a premium. Also, because the focus of the VPL is on valuation (to set the *amount* payable when there is a total loss), not on coverage, the statute signals no intent to expand coverage to excluded perils.

Contrary to the homeowners' assertion, the insurers' construction of the VPL does not render the statute meaningless. In the case of a total loss resulting from a covered peril, the VPL continues to function as a liquidated damages clause by preventing insurers from challenging the value of the insured property and guaranteeing that the homeowners receive payment corresponding to the valuation of the property that was used to calculate their premiums. In addition, the homeowners' interpretation would lead to absurd results. As the district court stated:

> If the VPL has the meaning plaintiffs ascribe to it, an insured holding a valued homeowner's policy that covered wind damage but specifically excluded flood losses could recover the full value of his policy if he lost 20 shingles in a windstorm and was simultaneously flooded under 10 feet of water. The insurer would thus have to compensate the covered loss of a few shingles at the value of the entire house. In effect, the insurer would be required to pay for damage not covered by the policy and for which it did not charge a premium. Such a result would be well outside the boundaries of any party's reasonable expectation of the operation of an insurance contract.

Moreover, we find the cases cited by the homeowners in support of their interpretation of the VPL unpersuasive....

Similarly, the out-of-state cases cited by the homeowners are distinguishable and we decline to follow them. In particular, the wording of the Florida VPL is different from the Louisiana VPL and, thus, we find the Florida cases[11] relied on by the home-

---

10. [23] None of the homeowners assert claims for wind damage outside of their total loss claims under the VPL. As such, we only hold that a total loss resulting from a non-covered peril does not trigger the VPL. Our decision has no bearing on the insurers' potential liability for incidental damage to the homeowners' property by wind or any other peril covered by the relevant insurance policies.

11. [29] *See Fla. Farm Bureau Cas. Ins. Co. v. Cox*, 943 So.2d 823 (Fla.Dist.Ct.App.2006) (holding that insurer owed homeowners full amount of policy when they suffered a total loss, "in not insignifi-

owners inapposite to the issue currently before us, which involves the interpretation of the language of the Louisiana VPL.[12]

Accordingly, the district court correctly concluded that Louisiana's VPL does not apply when a total loss does not result from a covered peril.[13]

## II. CONCLUSION

For the aforementioned reasons, we AFFIRM the judgment of the district court dismissing the homeowners' claims.

### Notes and Questions

Do you agree or disagree with Professor Keeton's comment that "On balance, the principle of indemnity would be better served by repeal of valued policy statutes." What are the public policy arguments pro and con for valued versus unvalued policies? Did the result in the case serve the purposes and goals of a valued policy statute? Does it encourage fraud on the part of insured property owners?

## [C] Cost to "Repair or Replace"

If the measure of damages was limited to replacement value less depreciation or to fair market value, many insured property owners would be put to hardship in attempting to replace the lost residence. Take a residence that is 30 years old that has a replacement cost of $100,000 and depreciation of $60,000 (or fair market value of $40,000). If there is a total loss and the proceeds of insurance were only $40,000, how could the insured build a $100,000 residence? To protect homeowners from this predicament, most homeowners policies sold today include what is called "replacement cost coverage." Under these clauses, if at the time of loss the limit of liability for a dwelling is at least 80 percent or more of the replacement cost of the dwelling, the

---

cant part as the result of windstorm damage," although an excluded peril, water, contributed to the damage); *Mierzwa v. Fla. Windstorm Underwriting Ass'n*, 877 So. 2d 774, 775–76 (Fla.Dist.Ct.App. 2004) (holding that if the insurer "has *any* liability at all to the owner for a building damaged by a covered peril and deemed a total loss, that liability is for the face amount of the policy." (citation omitted) (emphasis in original)).

12. [30] Compare Fla. Stat. §627.702(1) (2003) with La.Rev.Stat. Ann. §22.695(A). At the time *Mierzwa* was decided, the Florida VPL stated, in relevant part:

In the event of the total loss of any building, structure, mobile home ... located in this state and insured by any insurer as to a covered peril, ... the insurer's liability, *if any*, under the policy for such total loss, shall be in the amount of money for which such property was so insured as specified in the policy and for which a premium has been charged and paid.

Fla. Stat. §627.702(1) (emphasis added). The Florida legislature has since amended this statute to provide that an insurer is not responsible for damage caused by excluded perils. *See* Fla. Stat. §627.702(1)(a) (2005) (inserting the phrase "if caused by a covered peril" into Florida's VPL).

13. [31] In light of our recent decision in *In re Katrina Canal Breaches Litigation*, No. 07-30119, 2007 WL 2200004 (5th Cir. Aug.2, 2007), in which we vacated a judgment of the district court which held that language in some insurance policies excluding flooding was ambiguous and, thus, water damage from levee breaches was covered by insurance policies, the homeowners' request that we remand this case based on that district court decision is now moot.

insurer will cover the full cost of repairing or replacing the dwelling without deduction for depreciation. Under replacement cost coverage, no proceeds will be paid unless the policyholder actually repairs or replaces the damaged property. Read the following case to see how the provision operates. *See, e.g., Whitmer v. Graphic Arts Mut. Ins. Co.*, 410 S.E.2d 642 (Va. 1991).

In *Edmund v. Fireman's Fund Ins. Co.*, 42 N.C. App. 237, 256 S.E.2d 268 (1979), the policyholder's home, which was destroyed by fire, was insured by a policy with a face amount of $30,000. The policyholder received almost $23,000 from the insurer, representing the actual cash value of the dwelling, but the policyholder sued to recover an additional $6,000 which, together with the $23,000 received, would equal the replacement cost. Although the policy included a replacement cost provision, the provision was not relevant in determining the amount of the policyholder's claim after his residence was destroyed by fire because the duty to pay replacement cost was contingent upon actual replacement, and the policyholder bought another house and lot rather than rebuilding. Thus, the policyholder failed to satisfy the burden of proving that the replacement value of the house was greater than the amount paid by the insurer and was denied recovery.

In *United States Fire Ins. Co. v. Welch*, 163 Ga. App. 480, 294 S.E.2d 713 (1982), a collision caused the insured to drive his car into a lake. His insurance policy provided collision coverage for the actual cash value of the damaged vehicle or the amount necessary to repair or replace it less the deductible amount, whichever was less. The term "repair" meant to restore the vehicle to "substantially the same condition and value as existed before the damage occurred." At the insurer's election, repairs were made at a cost of $2,171, but the repairer would not guarantee the condition of the vehicle, only the parts replaced and the repairs actually made. Even after the repairs, the value of the car was $3,600 less than before the accident. The insurer paid the insured the repair cost less the deductible, but the insured nevertheless sued for the post-repair loss in value. Finding for the plaintiff, the court held that the correct measure of loss was the difference between the market value of the automobile immediately before the collision and its market value immediately after being repaired, less the deductible.

## [D] Appraisal of Damage

Standard fire insurance policies and other property insurance policies often provide that if the insurer and the policyholder fail to agree on the value of the property or the amount of loss, either party may demand an appraisal. The appraisal is normally conducted by two appraisers, one appointed by each party, with a disinterested umpire resolving any differences between them. As a general rule, such appraisal clauses apply only to valuation of property and not to other disputed issues. Appraisers may also be selected under state insurance statutes.

Arbitration clauses, on the other hand, purportedly serve as an alternative to court action, as applied, for example, to uninsured motorist insurance. But according to

Professor Keeton, arbitration clauses have been less favorably treated by the courts, and their enforcement, when allowed, "has created many more problems because of their wider scope [than appraisal clauses] and the wider range of problems for which clear-cut answers are not provided in the policy provisions themselves." *See generally* KEETON, INSURANCE LAW BASIC TEXT §§ 452–455 (1971). *See also Smithson v. United States Fidelity & Guar. Co.*, 411 S.E.2d 850 (W. Va. 1991) (failure to follow policy's appraisal procedure ordinarily bars policyholder claim; appraisal term of policy not unconscionable; but insurer's delay in asserting appraisal provision may excuse policyholder's noncompliance; claims considered in appraisal procedure are final determinations as to those elements of loss and may not be recovered again in subsequent litigation).

## [E] The Nature of Loss: Physical Loss— Financial Loss Dichotomy

Assume that certain real property destroyed by fire is insured by both the mortgagor and mortgagee, the lessor and lessee, or the vendor and purchaser—all of whom have an insurable interest in the property. Can both parties recover the full amount of the insured loss? Or under insurance indemnity principles, can there only be one recovery for the loss? If the damaged or destroyed property is restored or repaired by the mortgagor or lessee, can the mortgagee or lessor also recover from the insurer? The courts are deeply divided on these questions, depending on which theory they follow—the "physical loss" theory (or "New York rule") of *Foley v. Manufacturers' & Builders Fire Ins. Co.*, 152 N.Y. 131, 46 N.E. 318 (1897), or the "financial loss" theory (or "Wisconsin rule") of *Ramsdell v. Insurance Co. of North America*, 197 Wis. 136, 221 N.W. 654 (1928).

Under the New York rule enunciated in *Foley*, the rights of an insurer and a policyholder under a fire insurance policy are established at the time of the fire and loss. Assuming that the policyholder had an insurable interest in the insured property, the fact that the policyholder may have ultimately recouped her loss from another source does not relieve the insurer of its liability. In other words, the rights of the parties under this "physical loss" theory become fixed at the moment of loss, and no evidence is admissible as to subsequent events. *See, e.g., Citizens Ins. Co. v. Foxbilt, Inc.*, 226 F.2d 641 (8th Cir. 1955); *Alexandra Restaurant, Inc. v. New Hampshire Ins. Co.*, 272 A.D. 346, 71 N.Y.S.2d 515 (1947), *aff'd*, 297 N.Y. 858, 79 N.E.2d 268 (1948).

Under the Wisconsin rule, however, no loss would be recoverable by the lessor of a building under a fire insurance policy if the building was restored by the insured lessee who recovered the loss from his insurer. In other words, under this "financial loss" theory, insurance is a contract of indemnity where the insured's actual pecuniary loss may be recovered, but nothing more. *See, e.g., Glens Falls Ins. Co. v. Sterling*, 219 Md. 217, 148 A.2d 453 (1959). This "physical loss" versus "financial loss" dichotomy is further discussed in the following case.

# Mission National Insurance Co. v. Schulman

United States District Court, District of Connecticut
659 F. Supp. 270 (1986)

### Thomas P. Smith, United States Magistrate

This action sounding in tort and contract relates to a property insurance policy issued by the plaintiff to the defendants Schulman and Schulman Investment Company ("Schulman") for a building leased by Schulman to the defendant United Organics Corporation ("UOC"). Pending before the court is Schulman's motion for summary judgment, Rule 56, F.R. Civ. P. For the reasons set out below, that motion should be denied.

The recitation of pertinent facts begins with the execution of the insurance policy ("policy") for a building owned by Schulman located at 387 Ludlow Street, Stamford, Connecticut ("Building 13") and occupied by lessee UOC. Paragraph 19 of the policy detailed a subrogation agreement. A subrogation receipt signed by Schulman contained the warranty that "no settlement has been made by the undersigned with any person or corporation against whom a claim may lie, and [that] no release has been given to anyone responsible for the loss...."

The lease agreement between Schulman and UOC, a manufacturer of chemicals, provided, *inter alia*, that (1) "the tenant shall keep the demised premises in good condition ... and free from trash, inflammable material, explosive materials and noxious odors, that (2) the tenant agrees to indemnify and save the landlord harmless from all claims and liability for losses of or damage to property, and that (3) the tenant agrees to comply with all laws, ordinances, rules and regulations ... applicable to the business to be conducted by the tenant in the demised premises...."

Fire substantially destroyed Building 13 on January 4, 1983. The plaintiff then paid Schulman a settlement in April 1983 of $191,921.00, following Schulman's execution of a sworn statement in proof of loss and subrogation receipt described above.... After learning from the Stamford Fire Marshall's Office that the fire was caused by a chemical reaction among the chemicals used by UOC and that the absence of fire detection and extinguishing devices, among other things, contributed to the spreading of the fire, the plaintiff placed UOC on notice of its subrogation claim, only to be informed by UOC on November 20, 1984, that it had repaired all fire damage to the property.

The plaintiff filed suit after learning that UOC had repaired the damaged building. Count One alleges breach of contract against Schulman relating to the subrogation agreement. Count two alleges fraud and misrepresentation against Schulman relating to the subrogation agreement and the proof of loss statement submitted by it.... As part of its answer, Schulman admitted that "the defendants ... were aware of the repairs made by United Organics Corporation," while UOC pled accord and satisfaction with Schulman as a special defense.

It is of course well settled that to prevail on a motion for summary judgment the moving party must demonstrate the absence of any genuine issue of material fact and that it is entitled to judgment as a matter of law. . . . In judging the merits of such a motion the court resolves all ambiguities and draws all reasonable inferences in favor of the party against whom summary judgment is sought. Accordingly, on a defendant's motion for summary judgment, the court considers all pleadings and other evidence in a light most favorable to the plaintiff.

Schulman's argument supporting its motion for summary judgment is direct and focuses on whether it incurred the loss reported to the plaintiff despite the fact that Building 13 was repaired by UOC at no cost to Schulman. This issue, it contends, is determined by the application of New York law, given that the insurance contract was executed in New York and because "generally Connecticut applies the law of the place of a contract to determine the validity and construction of the contract."

No genuine issue of material fact exists, Schulman argues because, under the so-called New York rule governing insurance contracts and the role of third parties in making repairs at no cost to the insured, UOC's action in repairing Building 13 is irrelevant to the analysis and has no effect on *the loss incurred by it because its loss occurred at the time of Building 13's destruction.* [Emphasis added by authors.] All subsequent events simply do not matter under the analysis set out in *Alexandra Restaurant, Inc. v. New Hampshire Insurance Co. of Manchester*, 272 App. Div. 346, 71 N.Y.S.2d 515 (1947), *affirmed*, 297 N.Y. 858, 79 N.E.2d 268, which noted in part, citing the landmark New York case on the issue, that "the fact that improvements on land may have cost the owner nothing or that if destroyed by fire, he may compel another person to replace them without expense to him, or that liability of a third person in no way affects the liability of an insurer, in the absence of any exemption in the policy. *Foley v. Manufacturers' Fire Insurance Company*, 156 N.Y. 131, 133, 76 N.E. 318, 319 (1897)."

While Schulman's statement of the law relating to Connecticut's governing choice of law principles is accurate as far as it goes, it nonetheless is not the applicable statement of the law here because it fails to consider that in cases such as the one at bar the place of performance essentially controls the choice of law analysis. . . . Since the insurance policy at issue here covered property in Connecticut, there is but little question that Connecticut law controls.

Though Connecticut has as its capital the insurance capital of the world, it has yet to address squarely the issue of whether the so-called New York rule or the so-called Wisconsin rule relied upon by the plaintiff should apply in circumstances such as [those] now before the court. As a result, this court, sitting in diversity, must make an estimate of what the Connecticut Supreme Court would do if faced with this issue. . . .

In contrast to the New York rule, the Wisconsin rule, principally set out in *Ramsdell v. Insurance Company of North America*, 197 Wis. 136, 221 N.W. 654 (1928), looks not only to the relationship between insurer and insured but to the actions of the third party to determine whether a cognizable loss has occurred. The *Ramsdell* court noted that it looks to the substance of the whole transaction rather than to seek a metaphysical hypothesis upon which to justify a loss that is no loss.

The clash between the New York and Wisconsin rules has split the jurisdictions that have considered the issue. *See, e.g., Citizens Insurance Company v. Foxbilt, Inc.,* 226 F.2d 641, 644 (8th Cir. 1955) (cases cited therein). Courts that have followed — wisely, in this court's opinion — the Wisconsin rule have focused on the nature of the insurance contract itself. The Maryland Appellate Court in *Glens Falls Insurance Company v. Sterling,* 219 Md. 217, 148 A.2d 453, 454 (1959), for example, explicitly contrasted the two theories, writing that "we think that logic, reason, and justice as well as the previous decisions of the court, commit us to the doctrine enunciated in the *Ramsdell* case, *supra.* It is an elementary principle of insurance law that fire insurance ... is a contract of personal indemnity, not one from which a profit is to be realized.

As early as 1847, this court stated that a fire insurance policy was a contract of indemnity and the right to recover 'must be commensurate with the loss actually sustained by the insured.' This position is echoed, first, in 44 C.J.S. Insurance § 224, where we find that" fire insurance is a personal contract with the insured and not a contract *in rem,* its purpose being not to *insure property against fire* [the "physical loss" theory; emphasis added by authors], but to insure the owner of the property against loss by fire" [the "financial loss" theory; emphasis added by authors]. And, second, in 45 C.J.S. Insurance § 915, it is stated that "since a contract for insurance against fire ordinarily is a contract of indemnity ... [the] insured is entitled to receive the sum necessary to indemnify him, or to be put, as far as practicable, in the same condition pecuniarily in which he would have been had there been no fire; that is, he may recover to the extent of his loss occasioned by the fire, but no more, and he cannot recover if he has sustained no loss." To follow the contrary principle, it has been suggested, "would convert insurance into a wagering device." 66 A.L.R. 1344.

This court's determination that Connecticut would follow the Wisconsin rule does not rest merely on the wisdom of that rule, as an intermediate Connecticut appellate court has made clear that Connecticut also considers the type of contract at issue here to be a contract of indemnity.

In *Hartford Accident and Indemnity Co. v. Chung,* 37 Conn. Sup. 587, 429 A.2d 158, 160–169 (Conn. Super. Ct. 1981), the Appellate Session of the Connecticut Superior Court, on facts similar to the ones involved here, said that "it is from the very nature of a contract of insurance as a contract of indemnity that the insurer, upon paying to the insured the amount of a loss, total or partial, becomes ... subrogated in a corresponding amount to the insured's right of action against the person responsible for the loss."

That Connecticut considers a fire insurance policy to be a contract of indemnity is, as a result, persuasive on the issue of whether the Connecticut Supreme Court would follow the Wisconsin rule, given that that rule has as its central principles the characterization of a fire insurance policy as one of indemnity and the principle that there can be no loss if a third party has made repairs at no cost to the insured, which, of course, is precisely what occurred here.

Having disposed of Schulman's argument that it is entitled to summary judgment as a matter of law, the issue narrows to whether there exists a genuine issue of material fact. This issue is easily disposed of in light of UOC's affirmative defense of full accord and satisfaction and Schulman's submission of a proof of loss statement. Schulman's argument that UOC did not understand what it was saying when pleading this defense is not well taken, making it clear that a genuine issue of material fact exists as to whether Schulman violated the plaintiff's subrogation rights and entitled the plaintiff to recover the insurance proceeds paid to Schulman.... Without addressing other factual issues, it is clear that on this issue alone, Schulman's motion for summary judgment should be denied.

## Notes and Questions

1. Which rule did the *Schulman* court adopt — the New York "physical loss" theory, or the Wisconsin "financial loss" theory? Under what rationale?

2. Although the New York "physical loss" rule has been adopted in various states including Massachusetts, Pennsylvania, and Michigan, other courts and commentators have criticized this theory since it violates the indemnity principle of insurance law by providing double or multiple recovery for a single loss:

> Such a rule, it seems, is of questionable soundness both in point of principle and precedent, in view of the fact that the essential nature of an insurance contract is one of indemnity, and not of profit. Adherence thereto would convert insurance into a wagering device.

68 A.L.R. 1344.

What general principles of insurance law would support the New York "physical loss" rule?

3. Assume that a vendor of certain real property has an insurance policy on the property. A purchaser buys the property without his own insurance coverage, and insurance is never mentioned in the contract of sale. Then, before legal title is actually conveyed from the vendor to the purchaser, the property is destroyed by fire. Who should receive the insurance proceeds from this loss? The vendor or the purchaser? Should the insurance coverage run with the property or is it a personal contract solely between the named insured and the insurer?

It might be argued that the expectation of "the common person in the marketplace" would be that the insurance should run with the property, and the purchaser should recover the insurance proceeds. This theory was developed by early English precedent in *Rayner v. Preston*, 18 Ch. D. 1 (1881), and *Castellain v. Preston*, 11 Q.B.D. 380 (1883), but this rule was later changed by British statutory law in 1922.

Under *Brownell v. Board of Education*, 239 N.Y. 369, 146 N.E. 630 (1925), the New York Court of Appeals held that such insurance coverage did *not* run with the property, but was based upon a personal contract between the vendor and the insurer, so the purchaser could recover nothing. Some courts have held that even if insurance coverage is based on the theory of a personal contract between the vendor and his insurer, the vendor must hold these proceeds in "constructive trust" for the purchaser. *See, e.g., Vogel v. Northern Assurance Co.*, 219 F.2d 409 (3d Cir. 1955); *Insurance Co. of North America v. Alberstadt*, 383 Pa. 556, 119 A.2d 83 (1956).

*Query*: In drafting a contract of sale for real property, how can an astute attorney easily avoid these horrible complexities and pitfalls?

# § 8.11. Coinsurance

Generally, fires do not result in total destruction, especially where there are sprinkler systems. Therefore, property owners (both inventory and building owners), realizing this, would only insure up to 40 percent or 50 percent of the value of the property and *feel* that they are fully insured (*i.e.*, they would recoup 100 percent of the actual loss). This would be a great detriment to insurers, since the premium charged is the same percentage of each thousand dollars of coverage, and if partial losses (with only partial premiums) are in fact "full losses," the insurer would make very little profit (if any) on the lessened premiums. Therefore, insurers require that policyholders buy coverage close to the full value (usually 80 percent) of the insured property. If the policyholder does not carry at least this amount of coverage, the policyholder becomes a coinsurer on any loss. Assume inventory worth $100,000 is insured in the amount of $60,000, the policy having an 80 percent coinsurance clause. There is a loss of $40,000. The policyholder purchased insurance coverage for only sixty percent of the insured property's value. The policyholder was supposed to insure for eighty percent of the property's value. Therefore, the insurer will not indemnify the full value of the policyholder's loss.

The liability of the insurer is:

$$[\$60,000 \text{ (amount of insurance)} \div (.80 \times \$100,000)] \times \\ \$40,000 \text{ (amount of loss)} = \$30,000$$

and the policyholder bears $10,000 of the loss. If the loss were a total loss (*i.e.*, $100,000), the policyholder would recover $60,000, the face of the policy. If the amount of insurance had been $80,000 (or more), then the insurer would have had to pay the full $40,000 loss in the partial loss above (and the face of the policy in case of a total loss). *See, e.g., Schnitzer v. South Carolina Insurance Co.*, 62 Or. App. 300, 661 P.2d 550, *review dismissed*, 295 Or. 259, 705 P.2d 1157 (1983) (illustrating the application of this formula in situations where more than one property is insured (*blanket policy*) and the hazards faced if the insured "does not know what he/she is doing").

# § 8.12. Subrogation

## [A] How Subrogation Operates

Subrogation in insurance law is the right of the insurance company to "step in the shoes" of its insured in order to recover from a legally responsible third party, in tort or contract, for the loss paid by the insurer to its insured. *See, e.g., Mann v. Glens*

*Falls Ins. Co.*, 541 F.2d 819 (9th Cir. 1976). Such a subrogation action may exist by operation of law, or it may exist through a conventional contractual agreement between the parties.

Subrogation clauses are generally found in property and liability insurance policies, and in some classes of casualty insurance. The subrogation doctrine, however, has no application to life or accident insurance. In medical and hospitalization insurance policies, the inclusion or omission of subrogation clauses has varied from policy to policy, and from state to state.

For a general overview of the subrogation doctrine in insurance law, see VANCE ON INSURANCE 786–99 (3d ed. 1951); JERRY & RICHMOND, UNDERSTANDING INSURANCE LAW § 96 (6th ed. 2018); and KEETON & WIDISS, INSURANCE LAW § 3.10 (2d ed. 1988). *See also Shelter Ins. Cos. v. Frohlich*, 498 N.W.2d 74 (1993) (providing general explanation of concept and process and noting that policyholder's full compensation for a loss generally is a prerequisite to subrogation unless the insurance policy specifically provides otherwise).

> Although courts have expressed various rationales for the conclusion that an insured must be fully compensated for a loss before the insurer is entitled to subrogation, the underlying premise seems to be that, under principles of equity, an insurer is entitled to subrogation only when the insured has received, or would receive, a double payment by virtue of an insured's recovering payment of all or part of those same damages from the tort-feasor. As observed in *Rimes v. State Farm Mut. Auto. Ins. Co.*, 106 Wis. 2d at 276–77, 316 N.W.2d at 355: "[W]here either the insurer or the insured must to some extent go unpaid, the loss should be borne by the insurer for that is a risk the insured has paid it to assume." ... Allowing an insurer to subrogate against an insured's settlement when an insured has not been fully compensated would mean that all the insured's settlement could be applied to a medical payment subrogation claim with nothing left to compensate the insured for excess medical bills or personal injuries. Insurance companies accept premiums in exchange for medical payment coverage and may be obligated to pay medical expenses regardless of their insured's negligence or whether a third-party tortfeasor is liable and, therefore, must pay damages. In addition, there is little empirical substantiation that possible reimbursement through successful subrogation is considered in determining insurance premiums for medical payment coverage.

*National Union Fire Ins. Co. v. Ranger Ins. Co.*, 190 A.D.2d 395, 599 N.Y.S.2d 347 (1993), engaged in more extensive discussion of the principle that a volunteer's payment does not give rise to a subrogation claim. The facts in that case are as follows: a customer was injured on the premises of a shopping center which had liability insurance policies with both insurers. The customer filed suit against the shopping center which turned the pleadings and summons over to National. National proceeded to defend the insured.

On the eve of trial, it discovered that its policy contained an endorsement stating, "this policy excludes shopping centers." Ranger's policy had no such exclusion. National settled with the plaintiff in the amount of $100,000 and then made claim against Ranger in subrogation. Here is how the court held:

> At the time the payment was made, National was not acting under any mistake of fact or law and makes no such claim in this action. Because National was not obligated under its policy of insurance, it became a volunteer with no right to recover the monies it paid on behalf of its insured. It is well settled that "[a] mere volunteer or intermeddler will not be substituted in the place of a person whose rights he seeks to acquire, simply because he has paid a debt, or discharged an obligation, for which that person was responsible."

In *Hartford Accident & Indem. Co. v. CNA Ins. Cos.*, 99 A.D.2d 310, 472 N.Y.S.2d 342 (1984), it was held that an equitable subrogee is vested with no greater or different rights and remedies than those possessed by the subrogor; and where an insurer seeks to assert an equitable right of subrogation for *pro rata* contribution from a coinsurer, the insurer is subject to any defense or claim which may be raised against the insured.

Another axiom of subrogation is that the insurer may not make a subrogation claim against a policyholder — or any "insured" (named or unnamed) under the policy. *See Reich v. Tharp*, 167 Ill. App. 3d 496, 521 N.E.2d 530 (1987). The rationale for this rule: (1) subrogation rights only exist against a third party to whom the insurer owes no duty; and (2) to allow subrogation under this situation would permit the insurer, in effect, to pass the loss from itself to its own insured and to thus avoid the coverage which the insured purchased.

In some cases, in the absence of an express lease provision which establishes a tenant's liability for any negligently started fire, the tenant "stands in the shoes" of the insured landlord for the purpose of defeating a subrogation action. *See, e.g., Rizzuto v. Morris*, 22 Wash. App. 951, 592 P.2d 688 (1979); *Monterey Corp. v. Hart*, 216 Va. 843, 224 S.E.2d 142 (1976). *But see Zurich-American Ins. Co. v. Eckert*, 770 F. Supp. 269 (E.D. Pa. 1991), *contra*. How was the landlord-tenant rule applied to the life tenant situation in *Reich*?

In *Miller v. Russell*, 674 S.W.2d 290 (Tenn. Ct. App. 1983), the court held that when an insurance policy was taken out by the mortgagors for the mutual benefit of both themselves and the mortgagees, the mortgagors and mortgagees were coinsured under the policy, and the insurer had no right of subrogation against the negligent mortgagees.

## [B] Subrogation and Settlement

What happens if the insured makes settlement with a third-party tortfeasor or another party liable for the loss? Does this release destroy the insurer's right to subrogation? Does it matter whether or not the release was made before or after the insurer has settled with its insured? *See Group Health, Inc. v. Heuer*, 499 N.W.2d 526 (Minn. Ct. App. 1993).

On February 6, 1989, Sara Parsons entered into a settlement agreement with all the tortfeasors, and provided them with a general release. Under the terms of the settlement, she received $2.4 million from the involved insurance carriers. $700,000 was paid from a $1 million liability policy covering Lindholm. All of the other carriers paid their policy limits.

Group Health brought this action in April 1990, seeking to enforce its subrogation rights. All of the respondents moved for summary judgment, claiming they had not received adequate notice of Group Health's subrogation interest prior to their settlement with Sara Parsons. Group Health responded with a motion for partial summary judgment, seeking a determination that respondents had received adequate notice.

The district court [held] ... that the tortfeasors did not receive appropriate or adequate notice of Group Health's subrogation interest?

A subrogor is generally entitled to no greater rights than those possessed by the subrogee.... Thus, an insured may defeat an insurer's right of subrogation by settling with and releasing all potential claims against the alleged tortfeasors. However, a settlement entered into in willful disregard of a known subrogation claim will not defeat that claim.... Such willful disregard is similar to committing a fraud upon the insurer.

Actual notice may be proved by direct or circumstantial evidence.... Formal, written express notice was not given in this case.... Nor is there any other direct evidence that respondents had actual notice: Group Health did not attend pretrial conferences, attempt to intervene, or otherwise attempt to contact respondents.... Group Health contends that respondents were placed on notice of its subrogation interests by means of unilateral references to Group Health by Parsons' attorney. However, these references were insufficient to put respondents on notice of any subrogation interests.

Subrogation is an equitable concept arising out of payment of another's obligation, and its purpose is to prevent unjust enrichment.... To this extent, equity will not permit a tortfeasor to benefit by receiving a windfall.... However, one asserting the right to subrogation cannot thereby profit from his own inaction.

Group Health should not be allowed to sleep on its rights when it had adequate opportunity to protect itself.

## Notes and Questions

1. It is generally held that an insurer is barred from asserting its right of subrogation against a third-party tortfeasor when the insured settles with the tortfeasor and executes a valid release prior to the insurer making payment on the claim. *See, e.g.,*

*Prudential Lines, Inc. v. Firemen's Ins. Co.*, 91 A.D.2d 1, 457 N.Y.S.2d 272 (1982). The consequence to the insured of such an act was explained in *Tate v. Secura Ins.*, 587 N.E.2d 665 (1992), as follows:

> The applicable principles supporting Secura's contention are succinctly stated in *Allstate Ins. Co. v. Meeks* (1986), Ind. App., 489 N.E.2d 530, 533: In summary, an insured who destroys the insurer'scontractual subrogation rights breaches the insurance contract and, as a result, extinguishes his right of action on the policy. An insured destroys the insurer's contractual subrogation right by releasing the tortfeasor prior to settling with the insurer because it is that very settlement which enables the insurer to protect its subrogation right by giving notice thereof to the tortfeasor. However, where the insurer has given notice to the tortfeasor of its payment and thereafter makes settlement and obtains a release, it will not be a defense as against the insurer in enforcing its rights as subrogee.... Similarly, the rule does not apply where the doctrines of waiver and estoppel are available....

2. If a release between the insured and the tortfeasor contained a reservation of the insured's right to be indemnified by his insurer, would the insurer have a right of subrogation against the tortfeasor? *See, e.g., Connecticut Fire Ins. Co. v. Erie R. Co.*, 73 N.Y. 399 (1878); *Holbert v. Safe Ins. Co.*, 114 W. Va. 221, 171 S.E. 422 (1933). What if the release is ambiguous or releases the tortfeasor only from certain claims? *See Record v. Royal Globe Ins. Co.*, 83 A.D.2d 154, 443 N.Y.S.2d 755 (1981), where the release was found to be limited only to the insured wife's pain and suffering and loss of services, and thus the release had not impaired the subrogation rights of the insurer so as to preclude the insureds from recovering under their automobile liability insurance policy.

3. Where a tortfeasor or other liable third party makes a settlement with the insured after the insurer has paid the claim, with actual or constructive knowledge of this payment, then this settlement will not affect the insurer's right to subrogation since such settlement would constitute fraud of the insurer's rights and would be a void agreement.

4. When a release is obtained by a tortfeasor from the insured after the insured has received payment from its insurer, and the tortfeasor did not have knowledge of the insurance coverage, is the release a defense to the insurer's subrogation claim? Should the loss fall on the insurer who fails to notify the third-party tortfeasor of its settlement and resulting subrogation claim, or the third-party tortfeasor who fails to inquire as to the existence of any insurance? *See, e.g., Aetna Casualty & Surety Co. v. Norwalk Foods, Inc.*, 125 Misc. 2d 986, 480 N.Y.S.2d 851 (Civ. Ct. 1984), declining to follow *Camden Fire Ins. Ass'n v. Bleem*, 132 Misc. 22, 227 N.Y.S. 746 (City Ct. 1928).

## [C] Subrogation and Defenses

Because the insurer in any subrogation action "stands in the shoes" of its insured, and because the insurer has no greater rights than those possessed by the insured, it follows that any defenses that are valid against the insured are also applicable against the insurer. *See Great West Casualty Co. v. MSI Ins. Co.*, 482 N.W.2d 527 (Minn. Ct. App. 1992); *Southland Corp. v. Self*, 36 Conn. Supp. 317, 419 A.2d 907 (1980).

The rule that a subrogee has no greater rights than a subrogor was applied in *Blume v. Evans Fur Co.*, 126 Ill. App. 3d 52, 81 Ill. Dec. 564, 466 N.E.2d 1366 (1984). The insured in *Blume* left her mink coat with Evans Fur Company after signing a receipt which stated the value of the coat to be $300 and which limited Evans' liability to that amount, even though both the insured and Evans knew that the coat was worth in excess of $4,000. Evans lost the coat, and after paying its insured the value of the coat, the insurer filed a subrogation claim. The court held that the insurer was bound by the limitation of liability provision in the bailment agreement.

In *Holyoke Mut. Ins. Co. v. Concrete Equipment, Inc.*, 394 So. 2d 193 (Fla. Dist. Ct. App. 1981), an insurance company which had paid an insured corporation's loss became a subrogee of that corporation, and was permitted—but not required—to maintain an action against a third-party tortfeasor in the name of the insured corporation, even though the corporation had been dissolved.

In *Allstate Ins. Co. v. Ville Platte*, 269 So. 2d 298 (1972), the insured was contributorily negligent in causing the fire that burned his home to the ground. The insurer paid him the loss and then sued the other negligent party in subrogation. The court held that contributory negligence was a complete defense to the action.

Other defenses which may be brought against the insurer-subrogee in addition to contributory negligence and contractual limitations include: the equitable doctrine of unclean hands; illegality; immunity from suit; limitation of liability; laches; the statute of limitations; and an absence of authority to bring suit. *See generally* Couch on Insurance 3d § 224. In a subrogation action brought by the insurer, should the tortfeasor be able to counterclaim on any matter he could assert against the insured? *Compare Ohio Farmers Ins. Co. v. McNeil*, 103 Ohio App. 279, 3 Ohio Op. 2d 193, 143 N.E.2d 727 (1956), *with First Farmers & Merchants Nat'l Bank v. Columbia Casualty Co.*, 226 F.2d 474 (5th Cir. 1955) (applying Alabama law).

## [D] Common Subrogation Issues

### [1] Waiver or Estoppel of Subrogation Rights

"Parties to an agreement may waive their insurer's right of subrogation," *Continental Ins. Co. v. Faron Engraving Co.*, 577 N.Y.S.2d 835, 836 (N.Y. 1992). *Accord Sexton v. Continental Casualty Co.*, 816 P.2d 1135 (Okla. 1991).

The running of the statute of limitations on a claim against the tortfeasor would not bar the insured from claiming under the policy even though the insurer now has no subrogation rights: "the initial responsibility to act to protect subrogated rights rests upon the insurer.... [W]hen an insurer sits on these rights, it cannot be heard to complain when the statute of limitations has run." *Selected Risks Ins. Co. v. Dierolf*, 350 A.2d 526, 529 (N.J. 1975).

If an insurer enters into a settlement agreement with the injured party upon a claim the insurer disputes, it can preserve the issues only if it specifically reserves, in the settlement agreement, the right to raise the issues later. By having settled a claim with the claimant and another insurance company arguably liable on the claim, the insurer waived its right to seek contribution from the other insurer (where the settlement did not reserve its right to do so). *See Jefferson Ins. Co. v. Travelers Ins. Co.*, 614 A.2d 385 (Vt. 1992).

### [2] *Mortgages, Leases and Subrogation*

Property insurance policies contain a provision variously called a mortgage clause, or a "union" or "standard" mortgage clause. In this provision, the insurance company agrees to protect the mortgagee's interests in the property regardless of any violation of the policy terms by the mortgagor.

Under this clause, the insurer will have a right of subrogation against the insured mortgagor upon payment of loss to the mortgagee and upon the claim that no liability exists to the mortgagor. *See, e.g., Quincy Mut. Fire Ins. Co. v. Jones*, 486 S.W.2d 126 (Tex. Civ. App. 1972).

*Query*: What constitutes a *bona fide* claim of insurer nonliability to the mortgagor? *See McAlpine v. State Mut. Fire Ins. Co.*, 295 N.W. 224 (Mich. 1940).

Where the insurer is under an obligation to both the mortgagor and mortgagee, however, it is not entitled to subrogation, since its payment to the mortgagee is regarded as being in discharge of its obligation to the mortgagor. *See, e.g., United Stores of America, Inc. v. Fireman's Fund Ins. Co.*, 420 F.2d 337 (8th Cir. 1970).

When the mortgagee obtains a separate insurance policy covering only his interest, however, the insurer may be entitled to be subrogated to the rights of the mortgagee as against the mortgagor. *See, e.g., United Stores of America, Inc. v. Fireman's Fund Ins. Co., supra; Twin City Fire Ins. Co. v. Walter B. Hannah, Inc.*, 444 S.W.2d 131 (Ky. Ct. App. 1969).

In the absence of a "union" or "standard" mortgage clause, if there is a simple loss-payable clause to the mortgagee in the mortgagor's policy, the insurance company, upon payment of the loss to the mortgagee, will not be subrogated to the mortgagee's rights under the mortgage. Why not? *See Capital Fire Ins. Co. v. Langhorne*, 146 F.2d 237 (8th Cir. 1945).

Lease situations also challenge the subrogation concept. A lease agreement may stipulate how a tenant is liable to a landlord for losses to the property. But does the lease or the landlord's insurance policy control? How do leases mesh with subrogation rights in a lessor-lessee situation? *See, e.g., Dix Mutual Ins. Co. v. Laframboise*, 597 N.E.2d 622 (Ill. 1992).

### [3] *Loan Receipt Method*

A loan receipt agreement is an arrangement between the insured and his insurer whereby the insurer advances a "loan" to the insured for the amount of loss, and this loan must be repaid only in the event of a recovery by the insured against the third-party tortfeasor. The purposes of a loan receipt agreement are to make prompt payment to the insured and to keep the insurer out of litigation by avoiding a subrogation action in which the insurer must, in its own name, prosecute the claim against the tortfeasor. *See, e.g., C & C Tile Co. v. Independent School Dist.*, 503 P.2d 554 (Okla. 1972) (the primary purpose of a loan receipt agreement is to prevent disclosure of the insured's insurance to the jury in an action against the tortfeasors).

Although they are "legal fictions," loan receipt agreements have been held to be valid in many jurisdictions. Other courts have held such agreements to be legal shams and, based on the insurer's "payment" to its insured, have allowed the tortfeasor to raise the point that the insurer, rather than the insured, is the real party in interest. *See, e.g., Kopperud v. Chick*, 27 Wis. 2d 591, 135 N.W.2d 335 (1965).

# § 8.13. Title Insurance

Title Insurance involves real property but it does not insure the real property or other physical property against loss. Rather, title insurance protects the purchaser of real estate if the title obtained by the buyer is impaired in some way. "Defects in titles may stem from sources such as forgery of public record, forgery of titles, invalid or undiscovered wills, defective probate procedures, and faulty real estate transfers." *See* James S. Trieschmann, Robert E. Hoyt & David W. Sommer, Risk Management and Insurance 187–88 (12th ed. 2004). The title insurer agrees to indemnify the property owner against loss suffered by reason of unmarketability of the title or from "loss or damage by reason of liens, encumbrances, defects, objections, estates, and interests" except those listed in a schedule of defects found during a title search of the property. The goal is that the title search should be done well and reveal all defects, with buyer and seller then negotiating impact of those defect on the terms of the sales transaction. Title insurance provides compensation for defects that are missed by the title search, but does not insure the property against physical injury or the owner against commercial loss.

Title insurance also normally includes a duty to defend the owner in legal proceedings concerning title to the property. The premium is paid once and the policy remains in force from the time of issuance forward. However, if the property is sold or otherwise transferred, the title insurer's commitment ends and the new owner must purchase a new policy of title insurance. "Title insurance is thus narrower than general property or liability insurance and backward-looking in that it assumes the risk of a deficient examination of title. By contrast, general property insurance and liability insurance is forward-looking in that it assumes the risk that adverse events will take place in the future." *See* Stempel & Knutsen on Insurance Coverage, § 22.13[D].

Because of its more limited scope and significant premiums in relation to risk assumed, title insurance has been regarded by some as overpriced relative to the value of the product. Even if the criticisms are well-founded, it is still hard to imagine the modern American home market without title insurance. In addition, title insurance may serve a related useful role by encouraging better recordkeeping regarding chain of title and by making real property markets more transparent and efficient. In that respect, title insurance may make for better real estate transactions and documentation just as the inspection component of boiler and machinery insurance has made for safer industrial equipment. Useful treatises on title insurance include JOYCE PALOMAR, TITLE INSURANCE LAW (2017), and JAMES L. GOSDIN, TITLE INSURANCE: A COMPRE-HENSIVE OVERVIEW (4th ed. 2015).

A risk management cousin of sorts to title insurance is private mortgage insurance, which insures against the risk of defaults on mortgages. Premium payment is commonly included as part of a buyer's regular mortgage payments. *See generally Quintin Johnstone, Private Mortgage Insurance*, 39 WAKE FOREST L. REV. 783 (2004).

# Chapter 9

# Liability Insurance

## § 9.01. The Purpose and Design of Liability Insurance

Liability insurance is the "casualty" insurance that is typically lumped with "property" insurance to form the "property and casualty" arena of insurance products. This is distinguished from "life and health" insurance, which is the other major area into which insurance is typed and divided. Property insurance (the topic of the previous chapter) is first-party insurance and liability insurance is third-party insurance. Property insurance exists to compensate the policyholder for the loss of her possessions. Liability insurance exists to protect the policyholder from claims by third parties and to prevent adverse judgments from bringing financial ruin to the policyholder.

Liability insurance, like health insurance, is something of a latecomer to the indemnity field. As noted in Chapter 1, the oldest forms of insurance were essentially property insurance — efforts to transfer and spread the risk of loss of merchant goods in transit or personal or real property due to fire or other destructive forces. Modern life insurance developed in the 18th century and there was at least some market for life insurance in continental Europe as early as the 1400s. Industrial accident insurance developed in the late 19th century and Workers' Compensation Insurance at the turn into the 20th century, which also was the approximate time of the automobile and the first liability policies. Medical expense insurance began in earnest during the mid-20th century.

Why was liability insurance relatively late in coming? The conventional wisdom is that it was not thought necessary until the sharp increase in injuries to persons and property that were inflicted not by natural forces but by other human beings acting carelessly. Consequently, the rise of the automobile brought both a revolution in tort law and insurance. So, too, did the industrial revolution, although its legal effect was to some degree delayed as industrialists fended off tort liability quite effectively until the 20th century through doctrines such as assumption of the risk, contributory negligence, and the fellow-servant rule as well as the concept of privity that largely prevented consumers from suing product manufacturers directly.

As we now know, the citadel of privity eventually fell and product liability litigation became a staple of tort law, often with manufacturers facing "strict" liability if the product when used as intended was unreasonably dangerous to the user. The negligence rules evolved so that plaintiffs were not barred from recovery unless they were more at fault than the defendant. Concepts of assumption of risk and injury by a fellow servant also evolved to be more receptive to plaintiff claims that injury resulted from defendant policy or activity and that plaintiffs were not assuming risk merely by coming to work, walking along a road, or being on certain property.

The net effect of these changes in society and law was to create a vastly expanded market for liability insurance. Even when suits by workers against employers were carved off into a separate category of workers compensation by statute, this merely moved the insurance need from a general liability need to a need for workers compensation insurance. As the 20th century progressed, liability suits became more common. In addition, various statutory causes of action were created that went beyond traditional common law torts for physical injury: e.g., antitrust; securities violations; discrimination.

Enterprising insurers seized upon this growing need to offer liability insurance for sale and profit. As noted above, it appears that automobile liability insurance and employers liability insurance were the first such products, followed later by general liability insurance and still later by professional liability insurance such as legal malpractice, medical malpractice, errors and omissions, and directors and officers insurance.

All liability insurance has this common feature: it agrees to pay judgments against the policyholder or reasonable settlements made by or on behalf of the policyholder as a result of liability claims against the insured. As we will see later in this chapter, the liability need not result from a claim for relief classified as a "tort" but that is the most common type of claim covered under a general liability policy.

Most liability policies also provide the policyholder with a defense to liability claims asserted against the policyholder by third parties. For that reason, liability insurance is often referred to as "litigation insurance" in that it protects the policyholder from the financial burdens and distractions of civil litigation at least as much as it protects the policyholder against adverse judgments or settlements. For many liability claims, the litigation costs rival or exceed any resulting judgments. A relatively high percentage of liability claims are not successful. Some are even utterly meritless. But nearly all have the potential to involve the policyholder in significant litigation at substantial expense.

Liability insurance that includes a defense obligation of the insurer thus protects the policyholder by transferring (to the insurer) and spreading (among a pool of similarly situated but not closely correlated policyholders) the risk of expensive, time-consuming, distracting litigation as well as the risk that the third-party claims will be successful in litigation and result in a judgment or settlement that must be paid.

Liability insurance appears to have begun to routinely include a duty to defend component during the 1930s and 1940s. Insurers marketed the insurance product as containing both indemnity and defense components for the reasons set forth above because this provided a more attractive, saleable product. The policyholder got both liability judgment insurance and litigation insurance for a single premium. Although the price of the premium was higher than it would have been without the defense component, it was still an attractive and convenient package for the policyholder. The policyholder paid one premium and in return received the "peace of mind" that came from knowing that if it was sued for negligence or similar alleged wrongdoing, the liability insurer would step in and defend the claim and either eliminate it (through motions or a successful result at trial) or settle it or pay it if the claimant prevailed at trial.

As we will see in this chapter, the actual operation of liability insurance is considerably more complicated than this simple schematic. In particular, there can be difficult questions of when liability coverage attaches or is "triggered" as well as whether the third-party claim against the policyholder is "covered" or is excluded. In addition, there are a considerable number of technical concerns facing policyholder and insurer regarding the processing of claims and the insurer's administration of the defense and resolution of cases (although many of these are also present with other types of insurance). The policyholder must give timely notice of a loss and make an adequate proof of loss. The insurer must adjust the first-party property loss in competent good faith. However, the responsibilities of policyholder and insurer are more involved in the context of liability insurance. Because of a policyholder defendant's dependency on the insurer to defend and resolve claims, liability insurance has proven a more fertile ground for the rise of "bad faith" claims against insurers. Consequently, we shall discuss the concepts of bad faith and the relative rights and responsibilities of insurer and policyholder at some length in this chapter as well as in Chapter 12.

# § 9.02. The Organization of the General Liability Policy

The most common form of pure general liability policy is the CGL — commercial general liability — policy drafted by the Insurance Services Office for use by insurers. CGL used to stand for "comprehensive general liability" but the title was changed in 1986 in order to prevent policyholders from arguing that the title of the policy implied that policy language should be more broadly construed because of the "comprehensive" nametag.

The CGL has a basic insuring agreement that provides that the insurer will provide coverage for third-party claims against the policyholder that make the policyholder "legally obligated to pay damages" for either "bodily injury" or "property damage" to which the insurance applies, which means that judgments resulting from claims not covered under the policy remain the policyholder's problem.

The bodily injury or property damage must be caused by an "occurrence," which is defined as "continuous or repeated exposure to substantially the same general conditions." The term "occurrence" replaced the word "accident" with the 1966 revision of the CGL and was designed to eliminate questions of whether the activity giving rise to injury and liability must be episodic and isolated (e.g., an automobile accident) or could be lengthier in its damage-creating timeline (e.g., a defective component that gradually destroyed a building or tainted food that gradually poisoned a consumer). With the change to "occurrence" language, insurers opted for the latter approach. However, as discussed in Chapter 1 concerning fortuity, an injury that the policyholder subjectively expects or intends is not an "occurrence" within the meaning of the CGL policy.

Bodily injury is defined as "bodily injury, sickness or disease," including resulting death. Property damage is defined as "physical injury to tangible property." If the third party's claim for bodily injury or property damage is successful, the insurer will pay the resulting settlement or judgment. It is the policyholder's burden to demonstrate that the claim comes within the insuring agreement. Once this is done, it is the insurer's burden to demonstrate the applicability of an exclusion if the insurer argues that an exclusion applies to bar coverage. The modern view is that liability insurance provides liability coverage and that the insurer will pay the settlement or judgment rather than requiring that the policyholder advance the money and then seek repayment from the insurer.

Older cases and policies may present the problem of whether the policy is a liability policy or an "indemnity" policy, the latter requiring that the insurer reimburse the policyholder rather than pay the judgment directly. Today, most liability policies are, at the risk of sounding tautological, read as being liability policies and not indemnity policies unless there is clear language to the contrary

The standard CGL policy provides that the insurer has the "right and duty to defend" the policyholder against any "suit" seeking "damages" and that the insurer has control over the litigation and settlement — including retention of counsel who will defend the policyholder. However, as we shall see, the duty of good faith imposed upon the insurer requires that the insurer conduct itself reasonably in the defense and that the insurer give equal consideration to the interests of the policyholder.

In addition, the attorney retained to defend the policyholder has a lawyer-client relationship with the policyholder and may not act adversely to the policyholder. In some states, the policyholder is regarded as the only "client" of the attorney while in other states the primary client is the policyholder and the secondary client is the insurer. Either way, the attorney's duties to the policyholder outweigh any duties to the insurer. Insureds can be individuals, family members, businesses, trusts, or other organizations. An employee acting within the scope of employment is usually an "insured," which makes sense in that many if not most claims against commercial entities stem from isolated acts by employees rather than conduct of the organization per se.

Structurally, the CGL is organized into a "Coverage A" (the bodily injury and property damage component) and a "Coverage B" (the "personal and advertising injury") component. The declarations page or "dec sheet" at the front of the policy lists the basics: the name of the policyholder or "named insured," and any named "additional insureds" as well as the policy period, the policy limits, and the premium charged.

The typical policy has a "per occurrence" or "per claim" limit which is the most the insurer will pay in settlement or for a judgment. The modern CGL form also has an "aggregate" limit, which is the most the insurer will pay for all covered settlements or judgments subject to a particular policy and policy period.

The declarations page also lists the particular version of the CGL issued as well as endorsements sold with the CGL. The standard form CGL is periodically revised (ISO copyrights the forms even though only the most extreme insurance nerd would deem the forms page turners), and there are variant versions of the basic form.

The most significant distinction is that a CGL may be written on a "claims-made" basis (where the making of a claim is the triggering event for coverage) rather than an "occurrence" basis (where the date of injury to the third-party claimant is the triggering event for coverage). Or, more precisely, these policies are usually "claims made and reported" policies that require not only a claim against the policyholder but that the claim be reported to the insurer before the end of the policy period or an "extended reporting period" (usually ranging from 30 to 90 days after the policy period) provided as part of the insurance product.

In addition, policyholders often purchase "tail" coverage which is in essence the purchase of a significantly longer extended reporting period. For example, a builder with a claims-made CGL form may decide to cease operations. But it knows that it remains at risk of construction defects that may not yet have been discovered and suits that have not yet been filed. It may therefore purchase several years of tail coverage to deal with a possible "pipeline" of claims.

The CGL form begins with an insuring agreement that typically states that the insurer "will pay those sums that the insured becomes legally obligated to pay as damages because of 'bodily injury' or 'property damage' to which this insurance applies." In addition to specified exclusions, limits on coverage include the requirement that the injury to a claimant take place in the "coverage territory" and during the policy period. Coverage territory is usually defined as the U.S. and its possessions and Canada as well as international travel between places within the coverage territory.

General liability—as opposed to more delineated types of liability (e.g., professional liability, directors' or officers' liability)—largely includes the liability incurred by the policyholder's regular activity and includes staples of litigation such as premises liability (e.g., slip-and-fall).

The CGL policy also covers personal and advertising injury in Part B. Personal injury claims are things like trespass and defamation. Advertising injury is complex enough to merit its own course but generally refers to one business inflicting injury upon another through misleading and disparaging advertising. Coverage C of the standard policy covers medical expenses for which the policyholder may be liable.

CGL coverage extends to some types of contractual liability, but reaches this result a bit circuitously. The policy first provided that there is no coverage for an obligation "to pay damages by reason of the assumption of liability in a contract or agreement." But immediately thereafter, the CGL form states that this exclusion does not apply to liability "[t]hat the insured would have in the absence of the contract or agreement" or liability assumed in an "insured contract" provided that the injury took place after the insured contract was executed. The policy then states that the following are insured contracts subject to coverage.

- A contract for a lease of premises
- A sidetrack agreement
- Any easement or license agreement
- An obligation, as required by ordinance, to indemnify a municipality
- An elevator maintenance agreement
- "That part of any other contract or agreement pertaining to your business ... under which you assume the tort liability of another party to pay for [injury] to a third person or organization. Tort liability means a liability that would be imposed by law in the absence of any contract or agreement." However, this exception to the exclusion for contract-based liability "does not include that part of any contract or agreement."

Right after the insuring agreement, the typical CGL form states that the insurer has the "right and duty to defend" the policyholder against any "suit" seeking damages, subject to limitations in the policy such as an exclusion. As illustrated later in this Chapter, there may be controversy over whether a demand placed upon the policyholder or an action against the policyholder qualifies as a "suit." Coverage will hinge on the answer. The duty to defend ends when the applicable policy limits are exhausted through the payment of judgments or settlements by the insurer.

As noted in Ch. 1, insurance is normally not available for intentionally inflicted injury. But as we saw in Ch. 1, application of this principle and its codification in the "expected or intended injury" exclusion can become complicated.

The typical CGL policy also includes "products/completed operations" coverage, but this is not certain and can become a trap for the unwary purchaser. In addition, a CGL may have lower limits of coverage for product liability or completed operations claims.

Following the insuring agreement is a list of exclusions applicable to Coverage Part A, barring coverage for a variety of risks. Among the more important and frequently litigated exclusions are for claims related to: workers compensation; employers' liability; pollution; vehicle operation (planes, cars, boats and even drones); mobile equipment; damages to the policyholder's own property or own work; recall of defective products; electronic data breaches; and copyright violations.

Also excluded are claims involving "impaired" property, which can be roughly defined as property that can be restored to good condition through the simple correction of any of the policyholder's defective work. This can be a complex and fact-dependent area of coverage dispute. For now, consider this relatively simple

## ILLUSTRATION

Eddy Electrician does the wiring at 123 Elm Street and installs a defective circuit breaker box. As a result, the home has no working electricity. Hatti

Homeowner sues Eddy, seeking repair of the electric system and damages for loss of use of her home. Because the electrical wiring is Eddy's "own work," that exclusion—which is designed to prevent vendors obtaining insurance for simply doing their work incorrectly—is applicable. *See Weedo v. Stone-E-Brick*, 81 N.J. 233, 405 A.2d 788 (1979), infra.

But as we will also see, where poor quality work causes damage to other property (including loss of use), the "your work" exclusion is not applicable. However, in this case, all that is necessary to make things right is replacing the defective circuit breaker box (which was Eddy's work) with a working circuit breaker box. There was loss of use to other parts of the house that were not Eddy's work, but the problem can be easily fixed by just subbing out the bad circuit breaker box. The property was impaired, but the impairment was rectified by a simple repair of poor work by the vendor that did not involve tearing into or modifying other parts of the home.

If the lack of electricity had gone on too long, however, so that there was damage to the home from the lack of electricity—e.g., from frozen pipes (assume an electric heat home, even if that's not currently fashionable) or extreme heat (no air conditioning could lead to warping or desiccation that causes damage)—there would then be injury to property other than the vendor's work that would require repair rather than just the replacement of the defective circuit breakers.

That type of claim should be covered, even if it does seem like rewarding Eddy for the initial bad work and failure to correct the problem promptly. But general liability insurance is sold to protect policyholders from negligence, so the result is not odd once one understands that insurance is a form of risk management and not a morality play. However, if Homeowner sought replacement of the circuit breakers in April and Eddy intentionally refused because of a billing dispute and pipes subsequently burst in December, the vendor's fault might transform from negligence to expected or intended injury.

---

A core exclusion in a CGL policy is the liquor liability exclusion that blocks coverage from a policyholder "contributing to the intoxication of any person," violating any liquor statute or regulation, or serving underage drinkers. The exclusion is so broadly written that it states that the exclusion applies even if claims against the policyholder are pleaded as negligence actions or inadequate supervision actions. However, there is an exception to the exclusion where booze is brought on company property even if the company is not a bar, restaurant, or other entity dealing with alcohol as part of its regular business operations. The exclusion in the standard form CGL policy is targeted at those businesses rather than liquor related liability stemming from informal social events. However, CGL policies may be sold with an endorsement (CG 21 50) that expressly makes the liquor liability exclusion applicable to consumption of alcohol on the policyholder's premises or, conversely, with an endorsement (CG 21 06) that provides coverage for BYOB (bring your own bottle) events.

For each of these common exclusions, there is usually available another type of insurance policy that will cover the risk. The policyholder can (and usually is usually required to by state law) buy workers compensation insurance or environmental impairment insurance or product recall insurance. Liquor liability insurance has long been a separate product. Although considered essential for bars and restaurants, it is viewed by most policyholders as a poor market characterized by low policy limits, high premiums and what might be termed "B" list carriers that may have solvency or service problems.[1] Vehicular insurance is commonplace, with auto insurance being effectively required in all states and constituting the most prevalent type of insurance. America loves cars and has more of them then homes. The CGL policy itself fills some of this role in that some of the intellectual property exclusion of Part A may be replaced by Part B's personal and advertising injury coverage.

## PROBLEM ONE

- Why do CGL insurers want so badly to avoid coverage for liquor liability?
- Why not include liquor liability coverage in the standard CGL form and just have insurers charge higher premiums?

## PROBLEM TWO

For many years, the standard CGL policy has not contained an aggregate limit for general liability claims but did have an aggregate limit for products/completed operations claims. Guess what happened? Things like this.

JuiceCo is a builder of electric power plants insured by UtilityProtection Insurance Company. Power plants require a lot of insulation, which during JuiceCo's heyday meant lots of use of asbestos-containing products which remained in the power plant after construction was done. In the two or three decades after having worked on the power plants, hundreds of workers sue JuiceCo, which cannot assert Workers Compensation immunity because the workers were independent contractors working with subcontractors hired by JuiceCo.

---

1. *See* Jeffrey W. Stempel, *Making Liquor Immunity Worse: Nevada's Undue Protection of Commercial Hosts Evicting Vulnerable and Dangerous Patrons*, 14 Nev. L.J. 866 (2014). Perhaps unsurprisingly, Nevada is a bit different in that it is one of a handful of states that do not impose "dram shop" liquor liability on commercial purveyors of alcohol—but then goes one "better" by imposing social host liability that is akin to dram shop liability. Bob Booze can serve obviously drunk patrons at his bar and faces no liability when one of those patrons knocks off a pedestrian on the way home. And, as discussed in the article, the law has been interpreted so broadly that what would otherwise be vendor misconduct for negligent security or the like has been immunized because alcohol was involved. But if Bob lets his daughter's boyfriend have one too many egg nogs at the family's holiday celebration, liability ensues. What happens in.... Oh, never mind. It's enough to make you want to be a Canadian.

JuiceCo tenders defense of the claim to its CGL insurer. The policy provides $1 million of per occurrence policy limits with no aggregate limit on general operations liability as well as $1 million per occurrence limit on completed operations liability, with a $5 million aggregate limit on completed operations liability. The insurer defends the claims and begins settling them seriatim for reasonable amounts. The amount of settlement payments quickly exceeds $5 million.

- May UtilityProtection stop defending or paying claims?

- On what basis?

- What will be JuiceCo's response?

- Who has the better of the argument?

- What more would you like to know?

- What if the suits are by workers operating the Power Plant rather than the workers who built the plant?

- How does this change you analysis?

## PROBLEM THREE

Policyholder leases computers from Vendor and signs a lease that includes a "hold harmless" agreement that not only waives any potential claims against the computer maker for injuries arising out of the use or operation of the computers but also promises to indemnify Vendor for any liability arising out of Policyholder's use of the computers.

Sure enough, the computers overheat, causing a fire on Policyholder's premises that spreads to other tenants in the building. The tenants and the building's landlords sue Policyholder and Computer Vendor. Policyholder tenders its defense to its CGL insurer, which defends under a reservation of rights. Trial results in a judgment holding both liable for $1 million in losses, assigning 50 percent of fault to Computer Vendor and 50 percent to policyholder. Insurer refuses to pay any portion of the judgment, arguing that Policyholder's potential liability arose out of a voluntarily assumed contract.

- Is Insurer's argument persuasive?

- What should Insurer's responsibility—if any—be?

- Could Insurer successfully have refused to defend?

---

Related to the duty to defend found in standard CGL policies, the standard CGL form contains a "Supplementary Payments" provision that applies both to Coverage A (bodily injury and property damage) and to Coverage B (personal and advertising injury). It provides that the insurer will pay "with respect to any claim" it investigates or settles or any "suit" against the policyholder:

All expenses incurred

Up to $250 for bail bonds

(More munificently) the cost of bonds to release attachments, but only for bond amounts within the applicable limit of insurance

"[a]ll reasonable expenses incurred" by the policyholder at the insurer's request "to assist [the insurer] in the investigation or defense" of the claim or suit but not including counsel fees or expenses "taxed against the insured."

Prejudgment interest awarded against the policyholder. However, if the insurer should "make an offer to pay the applicable limit of insurance," it "will not pay any prejudgment interest based on that period of time after the offer."

"[a]ll interest" on the full amount of any judgment that accrues after entry of the judgment" and before the insurer has paid, offered to pay, or deposited in court the part of the judgment that is within the applicable limit of insurance.

These supplementary payments do not "reduce the limits of insurance" and are, therefore, like defense costs in the typical CGL policy, "outside limits" and do not erode policy limits by amounts spent on the supplementary payments. *See* ISO CGL Form CG 00 01 04 13 pp. 8–9 (2012).[2] Summarizing parameters of these provisions, one commentator stated:

First, a supplementary payments provision does not create coverage. Coverage under the policy is created by the insuring agreements. Second, a supplementary payments provision does not increase the policy's liability limits; the policy's liability limits are always those stated in the declarations.... Third, a supplementary payments provision does not create or expand and insurer's duty to defend. [I]t simply enables the insurer's payment of defense expenses in addition to its policy limits. Furthermore, the obligation to pay defense expenses is limited to cases the insurer actually defends. A supplementary payments provision neither requires the insurer to reimburse the insured's expense in a case the insured defends without the insurer's participation, nor requires the insurer to pay the insured's pre-tender defense expenses.[3] Fourth, a supplementary payments provision does not grant third parties rights under the policy. A supplementary payments provision is intended to benefit the insured, not strangers to the contract. Third parties are at best incidental beneficiaries of supplementary payments provisions and cannot enforce them.

---

2. There is similar supplementary payments language in the liability portion of homeowners and automobile insurance. *See, e.g.,* ISO Homeowners-3 Form HO 00 03 05 11), pp. 20–21 (2010).

3. Insurers have generally been successful at avoiding payment of pre-tender defense costs, with courts reasoning that notification and tender to the insurer is a condition precedent to receiving the benefits of the duty to defend promised in the standard liability policy. *See* Randy Maniloff & Jeffrey Stempel, Commercial General Liability Insurance Coverage: Key Issues in Every State Ch. 4 (4th ed. 2018).

Douglas R. Richmond, *The Subtly Important Supplementary Payments Provision in Liability Insurance Policies*, 66 DePaul L. Rev. 763, 766–67 (2017) (citations omitted) (also addressing issues arising pursuant to supplementary payments provisions such as whether insurer must pay for supersedeas bonds). *See also* Timothy H. Wright, *Key Coverage Issues Presented by the Supplementary Payments Provision*, New Appleman on Insurance, Current Critical Issues in Insurance Law (Spring 2016); James P. Bobotek & Ruth Kochenderfer, *Trap or Treasure: Often Overlooked Provisions in General Liability Policies*, New Appleman on Insurance Current Critical Issues in Insurance Law (Winter 2012); Michael Sean Quinn & Olga Seelig, *Liability Insurance and Supplementary Payments*, 25 Ins. Litig. Rep. 133 (2003).

## § 9.03. What Constitutes "Bodily Injury"?

### Voorhees v. Preferred Mutual Insurance Co.

Supreme Court of New Jersey
128 N.J. 165, 607 A.2d 1255 (1992)

**Garibaldi, J.**

The primary issue in this appeal is whether a homeowner's insurance policy providing coverage for bodily injuries caused by the insured will cover liability for emotional distress accompanied by physical manifestations. We hold that it will. Further, we hold that the event causing the distress will be deemed an accidental occurrence entitling the insured to coverage when the insured's actions, although intentional, were not intentionally injurious.

I

In the underlying suit, filed in 1985, Eileen Voorhees was sued by her child's teacher for her comments questioning the teacher's competency and fitness. The complaint against Voorhees indicates that Voorhees and other parents had expressed their concern about the teacher at an open school–board meeting and had requested that their children be removed from her class. The school board decided to relieve the teacher of her teaching duties pending the results of a psychiatric examination. Local newspapers published stories regarding the controversy. The teacher alleged that [t]he January 17, 1985 issue of *The Cranford Chronicle*, one of the defendant newspapers in this case, quotes the defendant, Eileen Voorhees, as speaking for the parents of some of the school children of the plaintiff and as saying that she, Eileen Voorhees, was glad the Board of Education had finally "done something." The article goes on to quote the defendant, Eileen Voorhees, as having stated, "We have been warning them since September that there were serious problems which should be investigated. I'm just sorry it took an incident like the one on December 10 to convince them."

After the psychiatric examination, the schoolteacher was considered fit to resume teaching, and did so at a special assignment. The teacher sued Voorhees, the local Board of Education, the Superintendent of Schools, the school principal, the local newspapers, and one other parent seeking compensation for the injuries she had suffered due to their behavior. Count four of the complaint, concerning Voorhees and the other parent, alleged that [a]t various times and on various dates * * * defendants [other parent] and Eileen Voorhees made false and erroneous statements about the competency and fitness of the plaintiff....

As a direct and proximate result of the foregoing, plaintiff was damaged in her reputation as a professional teacher and has been unable and remains unable to function in her customary teaching assignment.

The teacher alleged that the parents' accusations and the school system's response caused her extreme emotional distress. Medical evidence generated in response to interrogatories revealed that the emotional distress associated with the events had resulted in "an undue amount of physical complaints," including "headaches, stomach pains, nausea, [and] body pains."

Voorhees was insured under a homeowners policy issued by Preferred Mutual Insurance Company. That policy obligated the insurer to

> pay * * * all sums for which any *insured* is legally liable because of *bodily injury* * * * caused by an *occurrence* to which this coverage applies[, and to] defend any suit seeking damages, provided the suit results from *bodily injury* * * * not excluded under this coverage.

In its definitions section, the policy stated that

*Bodily injury* means bodily harm, sickness or disease to a person including required care, loss of services and death resulting therefrom.

*Occurrence* means an accident.

The policy excluded coverage for "liability caused intentionally."

Voorhees requested Preferred Mutual to defend her against the schoolteacher's suit. The carrier refused on two grounds: one, that the policy expressly excluded coverage for liability created by intentional acts; and two, that the teacher's claim sounded in libel and/or slander, causes of action that result in "personal" rather than "bodily" injury claims, and are therefore not covered under the policy. [Ed. note: *see* §9.15 regarding Personal Injury and Advertising Injury Coverage in Part B of the CGL policy.]

The underlying case settled for $750 in August 1987. Voorhees alleges she spent more than $14,000 defending the suit. In September 1988, Voorhees filed this suit against Preferred Mutual for damages for breach of the insurance contract. Both parties moved for summary judgment.

The dispute centers on whether the complaint alleges a covered claim. Preferred Mutual argues that the complaint sets forth only one cause of action, for defamation. Because such a claim is not based on a plaintiff's personal distress and humiliation, but is based instead on the harm to the plaintiff's relations with others—the harm to the plaintiff's "relational" interest—it is not covered by a bodily-injury policy. Voorhees, on the other hand, alleges that the complaint sets forth various alternative causes of action, among them outrage and the negligent infliction of emotional distress, both of which fall within the policy's coverage.

As written, the complaint alleges outrage and negligent infliction of emotional distress just as convincingly or unconvincingly as it does defamation [using words like "reckless" and "negligent" as well as "intentional"]. The complaint notified Preferred Mutual that plaintiff would argue multiple, alternative causes of action, potentially including, but not limited to, defamation.

Voorhees' homeowner's-insurance policy requires Preferred Mutual to defend her against any suits alleging "bodily injury," defined as "bodily harm, sickness or disease." Authorities dispute whether emotional-distress injuries are covered under bodily-injury insurance policies.

The terms of that dispute focus on two primary considerations: (1) whether the term "bodily injury" is ambiguous and should thus be construed against the insurer; and (2) whether finding coverage for emotional distress under a bodily-injury policy would conflate the coverage provided by bodily-injury policies with the broader coverage traditionally provided by personal-injury policies ...

Many of the courts addressing the ambiguity of the phrase "bodily injury" in light of claims for emotional distress have done so in all-or-nothing terms, ignoring the specific nature of the injuries alleged and the context in which they occurred. We believe that one cannot evaluate the "ambiguity" of a phrase like "bodily injury" in a vacuum. Whether the term is ambiguous depends on the context in which it is being used.

In the present case, the schoolteacher's alleged emotional injuries resulted in certain physical consequences, including nausea, headaches, and the like. This case thus requires us to address the "ambiguity" of the phrase "bodily injury" in the context of emotional injuries that have led to physical consequences. We thus reserve the discussion of its ambiguity when emotional distress does not result in physical consequence for our companion case ...

A significant number of courts have held that when emotional distress results in physical manifestations, it is covered under a bodily-injury policy. For example, in *Holcomb v. Kincaid*, 406 So.2d 646 (La. Ct. App.1981), the plaintiff in the underlying action alleged that the insured's fraudulent marriage to her had caused emotional distress resulting in a "rash, falling hair, weight loss, and symptoms of a stroke." *Id.* at 648. The court held that the term bodily injury was ambiguous and should thus be construed against the insurer, and that those physical manifestations "appear to fit within the policy definition of bodily injury ...."

Even a number of jurisdictions denying coverage for emotional distress unaccompanied by physical symptoms have noted that if plaintiff had alleged physical symptoms, the duty to defend would have been triggered.

We conclude that the term "bodily injury" is ambiguous as it relates to emotional distress accompanied by physical manifestations. That ambiguity should be resolved in favor of the insured. Moreover, we find such an interpretation to be in accord with the insured's objectively-reasonable expectations. That "emotional distress can and often does have a direct effect on other bodily functions" is well recognized.... An insured who is sued on account of an injury involving physical symptoms could reasonably expect an insurance policy for liability for bodily injuries to provide coverage.

We conclude, therefore, that "bodily injury" encompasses emotional injuries accompanied by physical manifestations. Here the injured party's emotional distress resulted in physical manifestations. Attached to the schoolteacher's answers to interrogatories was a medical report by a psychiatrist who had examined the teacher. In his report the doctor states that the teacher had informed him that she suffered from "headaches, stomach pains, nausea, depression, and body pains." The doctor found such physical complaints "real" and consistent with the teacher's emotional distress allegations. We note that the physical manifestations necessary to trigger coverage under a "bodily injury" policy do not, *per se*, demonstrate the severe emotional distress necessary to sustain a claim for the infliction of emotional distress. We are defining the term "bodily injury" under insurance law, not tort law.

C. Interpreting "Occurrence"

The insurance policy defines an occurrence as an "accident." In essence, the insurance company limits its coverage to accidental occurrences to preclude coverage for insureds whose conduct is intentionally-wrongful.

The key interpretive question is what should be deemed "accidental": the *act* or the *injuries* resulting from the act? ... New Jersey's lower courts generally focus on the accidental nature of the resulting *injury*.... "The general rule is that coverage exists * * * for the unintended results of an intentional act, but not for damages assessed because of an injury which was intended to be inflicted."...

We adhere to the prevalent New Jersey rule and hold that the accidental nature of an occurrence is determined by analyzing whether the alleged wrongdoer intended or expected to cause an injury. If not, then the resulting injury is "accidental," even if the act that caused the injury was intentional. That interpretation prevents those who intentionally cause harm from unjustly benefitting from insurance coverage while providing injured victims with the greatest chance of compensation consistent with the need to deter wrong-doing. It also accords with an insured's objectively-reasonable expectation of coverage for unintentionally-caused harm.

The general trend appears to require an inquiry into the actor's subjective intent to cause injury. Even when the actions in question seem foolhardy and reckless, the courts have mandated an inquiry into the actor's subjective intent to cause injury....

When the actions are particularly reprehensible, the intent to injure can be presumed from the act without an inquiry into the actor's subjective intent to injure. That objective approach focuses on the likelihood that an injury will result from an actor's behavior rather than on the wrongdoer's subjective state of mind....

Absent exceptional circumstances that objectively establish the insured's intent to injure, we will look to the insured's subjective intent to determine intent to injure. Voorhees' actions were a far cry from the type of egregious behavior that justified an objective approach in [other cases] and thus do not justify a departure from the general rule requiring an inquiry into the insured's subjective intent to injure.

Although Voorhees' statements were unquestionably intentional, there is little evidence that she intended or expected to injure the schoolteacher. Our impression is that she was motivated by concern for her child rather than by a desire to injure the teacher. Regardless of our impressions, the complaint itself included an allegation of negligent infliction of emotional distress. An allegation of negligence presumes the absence of an intent to injure. Preferred Mutual thus had the duty to defend until the negligence claim had been dismissed.

[Dissenting opinion of **Clifford, J.**, omitted.]

## Notes and Questions

1. Although the cases are divided, the majority of modern decisions appear to align with the *Voorhees* approach holding that primarily mental or emotional injuries constitute covered "bodily injury" so long as there are sufficiently discernible physical symptoms or manifestations of the mental or emotional injury. *See* RANDY MANILOFF & JEFFREY STEMPEL, GENERAL LIABILITY INSURANCE COVERAGE: KEY ISSUES IN EVERY STATE, Ch. 11 (4th ed. 2018).

However, most courts, including the New Jersey Supreme Court, also hold that where such sufficiently detectable physical consequences of emotional distress are absent, there is no bodily injury within the meaning of the standard CGL policy. *See, e.g., SL Industries, Inc. v. American Motorists Ins. Co.*, 128 N.J. 188, 607 A.2d 1266 (1992) (decision announced in tandem with *Voorhees*). Other courts take a broader view and have held that coverage exists for purely mental or emotional injury on the ground that this nonetheless constitutes illness and disease as well as injury to a portion of the body (the brain). *See, e.g., Lavanant v. General Acci. Ins. Co.*, 79 N.Y.2d 623, 584 N.Y.S.2d 744, 595 N.E.2d 819 (1992).

Counting roughly (i.e., placing the states into broad categories as the possible expense of losing some nuance in these fact-specific cases), almost 10 states (e.g., Hawaii, Indiana, Iowa, Maine, Vermont, Wisconsin, Wyoming—and of course New York) treat "pure" emotional injury unaccompanied by tangible physical symptoms as covered bodily injury (e.g., *Lavanant*) while almost 20 states (e.g., California, Colorado, Connecticut, Idaho, Kentucky, Maryland, Massachusetts, Michigan, Minnesota, Montana, Nebraska, New Hampshire, North Dakota, South Carolina, Texas, Washington, West Virginia—and of course New Jersey) follow the *Voorhees* approach.

Some states could be viewed as unwilling to find bodily injury even where there emotional distress is accompanied by physical symptoms (e.g., perhaps Louisiana and Rhode Island). A surprisingly large number of states (e.g., Alabama, Alaska, Arizona, Florida, Georgia, Illinois, Kansas, Mississippi, Nevada, New Mexico, North Carolina, Ohio, Oregon Pennsylvania, South Dakota, Tennessee, Virginia) have lower state court or federal court precedent on the issue but no definitive state high court precedent (and hence are not in our rough count) or seem to lack any instructive authority (e.g., Arkansas, Delaware, Utah). *See also Littlefield v. State Farm Fire & Casualty Co.*, 857 P.2d 65, 70–71 (Okla. 1993) (loss of consortium claim not bodily injury to husband because it was based on physical injury to wife; although husband suffered loss of society, he was not physically injured).

The Missouri Supreme Court has held that emotional distress suffered from witnessing a grisly car accident can qualify as covered sickness or disease under an auto insurance policy in view of the state's uninsured motorist law. *See Derousse v. State Farm Mut. Auto. Ins. Co.*, 298 S.W.3d 891 (Mo. 2009). Although the *Derousee* court chose not to reach the issue of whether there was also bodily injury, its decision goes at least as far as *Voorhees* and may be consistent with *Lavanant*. The facts in *Derousse* were particularly compelling, as the injuries witnessed were particularly gruesome.

2. Which of these alternative views is more persuasive?

(a) Only damage to the physical body itself is covered?

(b) Mental/Emotional injury is covered if accompanied by tangible physical symptoms?

(c) Mental/Emotional injury is covered if accompanied by detectable physical characteristics?

(d) Mental/Emotion injury is covered (so long as proven with sufficient certainty)?

3. In evaluating these alternative holdings, which rule is most supported by:

(a) the language of the CGL policy?

(b) the purpose of the CGL?

(c) the likely intent of insurers?

(d) the objectively reasonable expectations of the policyholder?

# § 9.04. What Constitutes "Property Damage"?

The standard form Commercial General Liability (CGL) policy defines property damage as "physical injury to tangible property" (the pre-1966 version of the CGL policy simply spoke of property damage and was more susceptible to being held to cover intangible injury to property, which prompted insurers to change the form).

A question of tangible property damage can arise in any number of situations where the policyholder suffers genuine economic harm that may or may not be the result of physical injury to property. Even if physical injury to tangible property is slight, this usually suffices to qualify as property damage under the CGL form. But the policyholder may do injurious things that nonetheless fail to constitute bodily injury or property damage. *See, e.g., Concord Gen. Mut. Ins. Co. v. Green & Co. Bldg. & Dev. Corp.*, 160 N.H. 690 (2010) (leaking carbon monoxide from policyholder vendor's defective work on chimney not property damage when no other portion of home was physically impaired).

In one most unusual example of a property damage claim (which almost sounds like a bad skit on "Saturday Night Live"), a group of elementary students was inadvertently exposed to hard-core pornography when shown what was supposed to be a Christmas pageant (the provider of recycled videotapes had failed to properly erase the pre-existing porno pageant and replace it with the Christmas pageant). As a result, Scholastic, the well-known provider of children's media, sued the provider of the tapes. The provider in turn sought coverage from its liability insurer. The court ruled that the type of injury in question was not one involving physical injury to tangible property. *See Schaefer/Karpf Productions v. CNA Ins. Companies*, 64 Cal. App. 4th 1306, 76 Cal. Rptr. 2d 42 (1998).

The court reached a similar conclusion of no property damage when the policyholder supplier was liable for losses incurred by the retailer due to mislabeling that resulted in underpricing of the product sold. *See Wis. Label Corp. v. Northbrook Prop. & Cas. Ins. Co.*, 233 Wis. 2d 314, 607 N.W.2d 276 (2000). As you read the next case, consider whether it carries the concepts of intangibility too far, particularly in view of the subject matter involved. In *Wisconsin Label, supra*, the court was dealing with price tags. In *Kazi v. State Farm, infra*, the court deals with a claim that at least touches upon real property, one of the most tangible things about which law concerns itself. Or is *Kazi* nonetheless correct because of the nature of the claim involving the real property at issue?

## Kazi v. State Farm Fire and Casualty Company

Supreme Court of California
24 Cal. 4th 871, 103 Cal. Rptr. 2d 1, 15 P.3d 223 (2001)

**Chin, J.**

We granted review to determine whether comprehensive liability insurers who insure only for tangible property losses owe a duty to defend in a dispute involving the right to use an implied easement. Case law and treatises have always acknowledged that actions over easement ownership, interference, or the right to use an easement concern "pure rights in property" or intangible rights only.... [W]e conclude, in contrast to the Court of Appeal, that an insurer providing a liability policy that covers damage to tangible property on the insured's premises has no duty to defend an easement dispute. For reasons explained below, we therefore reverse the Court of Appeal judgment and remand the matter for proceedings consistent with this conclusion.

### I. FACTS AND PROCEDURAL HISTORY

Plaintiffs Zubair M. Kazi and Khatija Kazi (the Kazis) purchased land (Parcel A) from the State of California's Santa Monica Mountains Conservancy (Conservancy). C. David Tollakson and Lynn L. Tollakson (the Tollaksons) also purchased Conservancy land (Parcel B). In an informational booklet, the Conservancy informed prospective buyers that Parcels A and B shared a common driveway 20 feet in width that straddled the boundary line between the two parcels. The deeds made no reference to any express easement for a common driveway. When the Tollaksons bought Parcel B, however, they relied on the representations made in the informational booklet to assume an implied easement existed on Parcel A for a "common driveway, for ingress, egress, and a right of way over and across Parcel A, parallel to the Boundary Line and for a width of not less than ten feet, all of which is appurtenant to Parcel B...."

In order to facilitate building on their property, the Kazis graded an access road on Parcel A, at or near the boundary line of Parcel B. Although the access road did not involve Parcel B, the Tollaksons complained to the Kazis that the grading interfered with their claimed implied easement and right-of-way over the Kazis' parcel, effectively ousting them from use and possession of their own Parcel B. When the Kazis denied the existence of an implied easement over Parcel A, the Tollaksons sued them in May 1990.

The Tollaksons' complaint against the Kazis asserted causes of action for (1) declaratory and injunctive relief, (2) quiet title, (3) trespass to the common driveway easement, and (4) ejectment from the common driveway easement. Each cause of action essentially alleged that the Kazis' access road obstructed the Tollaksons' alleged implied easement over Parcel A. The complaint specifically noted that the entire dispute concerned the "right of way over and across Parcel A, parallel to the Boundary Line and for a width of not less than ten feet, all of which is appurtenant to Parcel B...."

The complaint alleged no physical damage to either parcel, but essentially asserted that the Tollaksons would not have purchased Parcel B without the easement over Parcel A for the common driveway because without it, Parcel B was not buildable. * * *

In August 1990, the Kazis tendered defense of the Tollaksons' complaint to their liability insurance carriers, defendants Farmers Insurance Exchange (Farmers), the primary insurance carrier, State Farm Fire and Casualty Company (State Farm), and Truck Insurance Exchange (Truck). These policies covered property damage and personal injury, which included a duty to defend and indemnify the Kazis in an underlying lawsuit involving third party property damage or personal injury.

Farmers insured the Kazis under a Farmers E-Z-Reader Car Policy that included a "Comprehensive Personal Liability Insurance Endorsement" providing liability coverage for "damages which an insured becomes legally obligated to pay because of ... property damage resulting from an occurrence to which this coverage applies." The policy defined property damage as "physical injury to or destruction of tangible property, including loss of its use." The insurers did not intend these policies to cover disputes involving claims over intangible property rights.

Before the insurers responded to the demand for a defense, the Kazis settled the Tollakson action on the eve of trial in November 1990. As part of the settlement, the parties agreed that the mutual common driveway alleged in the complaint did not exist. Instead the Kazis agreed to record a deeded easement in a portion of Parcel A to enable the Tollaksons to construct and maintain a separate driveway on Parcel B.

The settlement agreement also gave the Kazis an option, at the Tollaksons' expense, to "process a lot line adjustment" so that the easement the Kazis granted to the Tollaksons would become part of Parcel B. Following the settlement, State Farm reimbursed the Kazis for the fees and costs it found reasonably attributable to the six-month defense and settlement.

Not satisfied with the reimbursement, the Kazis filed the present bad faith action against their insurers, suing them for breach of contract, breach of the duty of good faith and fair dealing, and negligent handling of their claim. The insurers' answer to the complaint asserted that they had no duty to defend or indemnify the Kazis in the underlying Tollakson lawsuit because it involved an easement dispute and their policies did not cover intangible property actions. Truck and Farmers also cross-complained against the Kazis in declaratory relief, seeking a declaration that they had no duty to defend the Kazis, that their policies provided no coverage for the Tollaksons' claims, and that they had no duty to indemnify the Kazis for their costs.

First, we look to the policies' definition of the term "tangible property." "Tangible property" is not ambiguous, and coverage therefore does not turn on alternative meanings. Consistent with an insured's reasonable expectations, "tangible property" refers to things that can be touched, seen, and smelled. To construe tangible property as including a legal interest in an easement or in property "requires a strained and farfetched interpretation." Instead, an easement is a nonpossessory " 'interest in the land of another that gives its owner the right to use the land of another or to prevent the property owner from using his land.' " An easement right is akin to goodwill, an anticipated benefit of a bargain, or an investment, none of which is considered tangible property.

It is especially important to distinguish an easement right from fee simple property ownership. Fee simple title provides an owner "the right to the surface and to everything permanently situated beneath or above it." By contrast, an appurtenant easement is a burden on land that creates a right-of-way or the right to use the land only. It represents a limited privilege to use the land of another for the benefit of the easement holder's land, but does not create an interest in the land itself.

An easement is therefore an incorporeal or intangible property right that does not relate to physical objects but is instead imposed on the servient land to benefit the dominant tenement land. Being incorporeal, the right to an easement is limited to the intangible benefit of access to the easement holder's property. In other words, it is an intangible legal right. The owner of the dominant tenement may maintain an action for the enforcement of this intangible right and may recover damages from a party for obstructing the easement. Awardable damages compensate the plaintiff for loss of use of the easement and the diminished value of the lot it benefitted. The ability to recover damages for obstruction of an easement, however, does not change the intangible nature of the property right for purposes of interpreting insurance liability coverage.

## Note

The CGL policy also covers claims that the policyholder's negligence causes "loss of use" to a third party's property. The drafters of the modern CGL policy form used as an example a situation in which a policyholder's defective construction crane collapsed in front of a restaurant, thereby making the restaurant inaccessible to patrons and reducing the restaurant's income. If the restaurant owner sued the crane maker, there would be loss of use general liability coverage. *See* George H. Tinker, *Comprehensive General Liability Insurance—Perspective and Overview*, 25 Fed'N Ins. Counsel Q. 217, 232 (1975). *See, e.g., Sola Basic Industries, Inc. v. United States Fidelity & Guaranty Co.*, 280 N.W.2d 211 (Wis. 1979). The claimant's property need not be injured—just unavailable. But the property for which use is lost must itself be physical. *See Lucker Mfg. v. Home Ins. Co.*, 23 F.3d 808, 818–20 (3d Cir. 1994) (applying Pennsylvania and Wisconsin law).

# § 9.05. Defining and Counting the Liability Insurance "Occurrence"

## Michigan Chemical Corporation v. American Home Assurance Company

United States Court of Appeals for the Sixth Circuit
728 F.2d 374 (1984)

**Contie, Circuit Judge.**

The defendants, American Home Assurance Company (American Home), Aetna Casualty and Surety Company (Aetna) and Insurance Company of North America (INA) have filed an interlocutory appeal in response to a partial summary judgment granted by the district court in favor of the plaintiffs, Michigan Chemical Corporation (MCC) and American Mutual Reinsurance Company (Amreco). Since the district court's order involves a controlling question of law upon which there is substantial ground for difference of opinion, and since an immediate appeal will materially advance the ultimate termination of this litigation, this court has jurisdiction pursuant to 28 U.S.C. § 1292(b). We reverse and remand for further proceedings consistent with this opinion.

MCC filed a declaratory judgment action in the district court in order to determine how much insurance coverage was available to pay farmers who had sustained property damage resulting from the distribution of contaminated livestock feed throughout Michigan. The record reflects that in early 1973, MCC produced and distributed both a magnesium oxide livestock feed supplement and a flame retardant which contained the toxin polybrominated biphenyl (PBB). These substances were packaged in nearly identical brown fifty-pound bags. The sole difference between the magnesium oxide and PBB bags was the stenciled trade names of the respective products, "Nutrimaster" and "Firemaster."

The district court found that MCC accidentally shipped PBB rather than magnesium oxide to Farm Bureau Services on May 2, 1973. The court did not determine whether any other accidental shipments occurred. Farm Bureau Services then mixed the PBB with regular feed and sold the resulting product to dairy farmers. In October of 1973, the farmers began complaining that some animals were rejecting the feed and that ingestion caused decreased milk production. After Farm Bureau Services and state authorities discovered that the feed was contaminated, 28,679 cattle, 4,612 swine, 1,399 sheep and over 6,000 chickens and other farm animals were destroyed. Their owners filed hundreds of claims against MCC and Farm Bureau Services.

MCC and Amreco have contended throughout this litigation that each claim filed against MCC constitutes an "occurrence" within the meaning of the insurance policies. They argue that there can be no occurrence until injury takes place because an indemnifiable event stems not from an insured's abstract act of negligence, but arises only when damage is suffered. The plaintiffs therefore assert that the five insurers are liable for $28 million per filed claim, subject to the $28 million aggregate annual limit of all the policies combined. Since all of the property damage took place in 1973 and 1974, the plaintiffs argue that MCC's total liability coverage is $56 million.

Conversely, [the insurers] contend that the only "occurrence" was the May 2, 1973 accidental shipment of PBB. Although injury must be suffered before the insured becomes liable, the timing of the injury only determines the policy year to which that injury is assigned. The *number of occurrences* is said to be governed by the cause of the accident rather than its effects. Since the cause of the property damage in this case allegedly was a single mis-shipment of PBB, the defendants conclude that MCC's maximum coverage is $28 million.

To date, MCC and Farm Bureau Services have paid over $45 million in claims. The five insurers have acknowledged that one occurrence took place and have contributed $28 million to the settlement of these claims.

The district court found the definitions of "occurrence" in the insurance policies to be ambiguous and therefore construed the policies against the defendants. Hence, MCC's argument that the number of occurrences equals the number of claims was held to be reasonable.

This interlocutory appeal presents the question of what constitutes a separate "occurrence" under each of the five insurance policies. The Lloyd's policy contains the following definition:

> The term "Occurrence" wherever used herein shall mean *an accident or a happening or event* or a continuous or repeated exposure to conditions *which unexpectedly and unintentionally results in* personal injury, *property damage* or advertising liability *during the policy period.* All such exposure to substantially the same general conditions existing at or emanating from one premises location shall be deemed one occurrence. [Emphasis supplied.]

The Travelers' policy, contains a similar definition:

> "Occurrence" means *as respects property damage 1) an accident* or 2) continuous or repeated exposure to conditions *which results in injury to or destruction of tangible property,* including consequential loss resulting therefrom, *while this agreement is in effect.* All damages arising out of such exposure to sub-

stantially the same general conditions shall be considered as arising out of one occurrence. [Emphasis supplied.]

The parties agree that the minor differences in the wording of these provisions are immaterial. Although the terms "event" and "happening" in the Lloyd's policy may potentially be broader in scope than the term "accident," the district court found, and the parties do not dispute, that the term "accident" encompasses the incidents which transpired here. Accordingly, we need not discuss whether the Lloyd's policy provides wider liability coverage for property damage than does the Travelers' policy.

Second, the defendants have argued that the distribution of contaminated feed throughout Michigan was a continuous or repeated exposure to a general condition and that all such exposure constitutes one occurrence under the second sentence of both definitions.

The vast majority of courts (including two courts which have interpreted the precise language of the definition of occurrence in the Lloyd's policy) have concluded that although injury must be suffered before an insured can be held liable, the number of occurrences for purposes of applying coverage limitations is determined by referring to the cause or causes of the damage and not to the number of injuries or claims. The number and timing of injuries is relevant in addressing the distinct question of the policy period to which each injury will be assigned.

The definitions of "occurrence" in the present insurance policies reflect this approach. First, these provisions in essence refer to an "accident" which results in injury during the policy period. The language makes the accident constituting the occurrence logically distinct from the injuries which later take place. Second, the insurance policies under review afford coverage on an "occurrence" rather than on a "claim" basis. The use of the former term "indicates that the policies were not intended to gauge coverage on the basis of individual accidents giving rise to claims, but rather on the underlying circumstances which resulted in the claims for damages." ... We hold that where the courts over such an extended period of time have reached virtually a uniform result in interpreting the term "occurrence" (including two courts which have interpreted the exact language of the Lloyd's policy), and where the policy language reflects this approach, the policy terms admit of only one reasonable interpretation. The terms therefore are unambiguous and require no further construction.

We are aware of only one case which calculated the number of occurrences by referring to the number of injuries rather than to the cause or causes of those injuries. See *Elston-Richards Storage Co. v. Indemnity Insurance Co. of North America*, 194 F. Supp. 673, 678–82 (W.D. Mich. 1960), *aff'd*, 291 F.2d 627 (6th Cir. 1961). Although this court decided *Elston-Richards*, the holding is not binding because the current litigation involves Illinois law. We are persuaded that if the Illinois courts were presented with the current case, they would follow the overwhelming majority of decisions which have held that the number of occurrences is determined by examining the cause or causes of the damage.

The plaintiffs attempt to distinguish the cases upon which the defendants rely by arguing that in most of the cited cases, injuries or damages were suffered immediately after the causal event took place. This scenario contrasts with the present situation in which several months elapsed between the mis-shipment or mis-shipments of PBB and the resulting property damage. One commentator has suggested that if a single cause and numerous injuries are closely linked in time and space, then there has been one occurrence, but if a cause and its effects are temporally removed, then each injury constitutes an occurrence. This argument, however, was considered and rejected by the Third Circuit:

> The fact that there were multiple injuries and that they were of different magnitudes *and that injuries extended over a period of time* does not alter our conclusion that there was a single occurrence.... Indeed, the definition of the term "occurrence" in the Appalachian policy contemplates that one occurrence may have multiple and disparate impacts on individuals *and that injuries may extend over a period of time.* [Emphasis supplied.]

## *Notes and Questions*

Along with the problem of occurrence counting is that of defining an occurrence. *Voorhees v. Preferred Mutual, supra,* contains a good summary of the approach of most courts regarding the issue of whether an event is sufficiently "accidental" to be an "occurrence." Section 9.12, *infra,* contains additional discussion of the issue in the context of claims against commercial builders. Some of the debate is largely a revisiting of the issues addressed in Chapter 1 regarding whether events are sufficiently accidental or fortuitous.

A variant of the problem takes place if the policyholder is sued for misrepresentation. If the misrepresentation is fraudulent, coverage is unavailable because the injury is expected and intended and does not result from an accident. But savvy claimant's counsel will almost always plead negligent misrepresentation in hopes that the misspeaking defendant has insurance coverage. Many and perhaps even most courts resist coverage in these cases, reasoning that the statements that led to the alleged harm and the lawsuit were intentional rather than accident.

But in true cases of negligent misstatements (rather than fraud for which the victim is hoping to find insurance coverage), the error and the harm both were unintentional, suggesting that the better view is that coverage exists. At the very least, there would seem a potential for coverage triggering the duty to defend (*see* the chapter on Duty to Defend). *See, e.g., Sheets v. Brethren Mut. Ins. Co.,* 679 A.2d 540 (Md. 1996) (misstatements as to integrity of home's sewage system leading to purchase and then problems with home were covered). *But see Am. Family Ins. Group v. Robnik,* 787 N.W.2d 768 (S.D. 2010) (negligent misrepresentation leading to expected injury not a covered accident or occurrence; misspeaking policyholder was aware of plumbing problems in home he was selling and capped drains to obscure the problem); *Rock v. State Farm Fire & Cas. Co.,* 917 N.E.2d 610 (Ill. Ct. App. 2009) (no coverage where misrepresentation did not lead to property damage; misrepresentation of absence of water damage to home not covered). *See generally* H. Brent Brennenstuhl, Annot., *Negligent Misrepresentation as "Accident" or "Occurrence" Warranting Insurance Coverage*, 58 A.L.R.5 th 483 (1998).

But back to counting occurrences once you find them.

1. As you have gleaned it from the *Michigan Chemical* case above, summarize the law of occurrence counting. What tests have been used or could be used? What test is primarily used? In contrast to the *Michigan Chemical* approach, *see Owners Ins. Co. v. Salmonsen*, 366 S.C. 336, 622 S.E.2d 525 (2005) (finding distribution of defective stucco to be one occurrence rather than multiple occurrences based on number of sales).

2. As a general matter, almost every state now employs "cause" analysis rather than "effects" analysis, but the differences in application among the states can vary greatly. *See* RANDY MANILOFF & JEFFREY STEMPEL, GENERAL LIABILITY INSURANCE COVERAGE: KEY ISSUES IN EVERY STATE, Ch. 9 (4th ed. 2018).

3. As examples of courts tending to find fewer occurrences, *see Stonewall Ins. Co. v. E.I. du Pont de Nemours & Co.*, 996 A.2d 1254 (Del. 2010) (manufacturer policyholder's production of unsuitable product triggered only one occurrence); *Donegal Mut. Ins. Co. v. Baumhammers*, 938 A.2d 286 (Pa. 2007) (one occurrence where insured's son shot neighbor, drove to other locations, and shot others, all over two-hour period); *Ramirez v. Allstate Ins. Co.*, 811 N.Y.S.2d 19 (N.Y. App. Div. 2006) (two infants ingestion of lead paint chips in apartment is one occurrence); *Bomba v. State Farm Fire and Cas. Co.*, 379 N.J. Super. 589, 879 A.2d 1252 (2005) (shooting of two police officers a single occurrence).

*But see Addison Ins. Co. v. Fay*, 905 N.E.2d 747 (Ill. 2009) (death of two juveniles when caught in quicksand while crossing gravel pit constituted two occurrences); *Koikos v. Travelers Ins. Co.*, 849 So. 2d 263 (Fla. 2003) (injuries to two patrons shot at restaurant by same perpetrator within seconds constituted two occurrences). In a similar vein regarding insurance coverage for asbestos claims, *see Plastics Eng'g Co. v. Liberty Mut. Ins. Co.*, 759 N.W.2d 613 (Wis. 2009) (each asbestos plaintiff's repeated exposure was one occurrence, resulting in many occurrences and policyholder's ability to obtain full benefits of older liability policies without aggregate limits but no need for policyholder to satisfy the per-occurrence deductible for each triggered policy).

Occurrence-counting cases are particularly fact-sensitive and arguably result oriented in that policyholders and insurers are not always consistent, tending to argue for more occurrences when it is in their interest and for fewer occurrences when that helps their respective causes. For example, a policyholder may generally obtain more potential coverage when there are several occurrences — although the policy's aggregate limit puts a strict ceiling on coverage, with many liability policies having an aggregate limit that is the same as the per occurrence limit. But if the policy provides for high deductibles or retentions, the policyholder may have most coverage from a finding of fewer occurrences, depending on the size of the respective claims.

The cases discussed above regarding shooting claims are obviously in tension if not completely inconsistent. The *Koikos* each-victim-is-an-occurrence approach seems sounder for cases involving shootings or similar acts of serial destruction by a single tortfeasor, particularly under the facts of the two cases. In both *Baumhammers* and *Koikos*, the assailants did not spray a single burst of fire but separately fixated on separate targets and shot separately, albeit within a very short time frame. And, as the *Koikos* court emphasized, an occurrence requires injury; until a bullet hits someone (or at least comes close enough to inflict mental anguish), there is no injury.

*See also Owners Ins. Co. v. Salmonsen*, 622 S.E.2d 525, 526 (S.C. 2005) (finding one occurrence in product liability coverage case based on policyholder defendant placing product in stream of commerce; differing from *Michigan Chemical* approach were major distributional events were occurrences). For product distribution cases, either the *Salmonsen* approach or a *Michigan Chemical* approach finding of more occurrences linked to significant multiple junctures of sale or distribution may be more apt depending on the facts of the respective cases.

4. Is the *Michigan Chemical* court being too "cute" and too pro-policyholder by considering each shipment as an occurrence when the root cause of the problem appears to have been one mix-up at the warehouse? Why or why not? Think in terms of the purpose of liability insurance and reasonable policyholder expectations as well as the insurer's underwriting criteria and approach to risk distribution. Does this make the *Michigan Chemical* result seem more correct or less correct?

Another aspect of this issue that could affect older cases is the possibility that a cause-centered-on-injury approach has the potential to greatly multiply the financial responsibility of primary insurers issuing policies without an aggregate limit. Although today nearly every policy sold has an aggregate limit, this was not the case for older policies sold before the 1980s and certainly not for those sold prior to the 1960s. Some of these policies are still being disputed in long-tail liability cases such as those involving asbestos and pollution. As a result, a finding of multiple occurrences effectively requires the primary insurer to cover all of the liability unless an individual claim exceeds the per-occurrence limit and reaches the first layer of excess liability insurance coverage (*see* the chapter regarding excess, umbrella, and reinsurance).

By contrast, a highly batched approach to occurrence counting in these cases makes it much more likely that excess coverage will be implicated. This, along with the size of the deductibles or retentions in the policies, makes for yet another strategic consideration when policyholders and insurers argue and courts seek a result that is fair as well as consistent with legal doctrine. It also explains why differently situated insurers may argue for a different approach to occurrence counting or explain why the same insurer or policyholder may argue for one approach in Court A and another approach in Court B.

5. As in other areas of law, advocates debating the number of occurrences will attempt to define the term with varying degrees of generality depending on the interests of their clients. A party seeking one occurrence will want the most generality, e.g.,

"it all stems from one mislabeling problem." A party seeking multiple occurrences, even under a cause theory, will argue for a narrower concept of cause, e.g., "there can be no injury without a separate and distinct sale ... or shipment ... or feeding." Consider this as permissible advocacy if you litigate this issue in practice but remember, the position you take in Court A could come back to haunt you (and the next client) in Court B.

6. The potential to make conceptually inconsistent arguments as to what constitutes an occurrence is an example of what attorneys term a "positional conflict," a situation in which lawyers or law firms may find themselves arguing "X" in Court A and "Non-X" in Court B. Although this is not a conflict as palpable as representing a plaintiff and a defendant in the same case, it nonetheless presents a conflict in that the lawyer's success in convincing Court A of X may have an adverse affect on the second client, who would like Court B to conclude that "Non-X" is the proper result. For that reason, positional conflicts are treated quite seriously when they take place in the same jurisdiction (e.g., if Court A and Court B are different panels of the same state Supreme Court or Court of Appeals) although less seriously when Court A and Court B are not related.

7. Insurance coverage litigation can present significant problems of positional conflict. For example, it is hard to ethically claim in Court A that a pollution exclusion applies to even smoke from a hostile fire and then dispute this assertion in Court B when, due to standardization, the language of the exclusion is exactly the same.

# § 9.06. What Is a "Claim" or "Suit" for Purposes of Duty to Defend?

## Hazen Paper Company v. United States Fidelity & Guaranty Company

Supreme Judicial Court of Massachusetts
407 Mass. 689, 555 N.E.2d 576 (1990)

**Wilkins, J.**

Hazen Paper Company (Hazen) brought this action in October, 1986, seeking, among other things, a declaration that its insurer (USF&G) was obliged to defend and indemnify it with respect to claims against Hazen arising out of alleged environmental pollution by a facility to which Hazen had sent solvents for recycling from 1976 to 1979.

In 1983, the United States Environmental Protection Agency (EPA) notified Hazen by letter that Hazen was a potentially responsible party (PRP) under the Comprehensive Environmental Response, Compensation, and Liability Act of 1980 [CERLCA or "Superfund"] because of the release of hazardous substances at the Re-Solve, Inc., hazardous waste facility in North Dartmouth; that the EPA and the Massachusetts

Department of Environmental Quality Engineering (DEQE) (now the Department of Environmental Protection) had incurred and would incur expenses for remedial action taken in response to releases of hazardous substances at that site; and that they intended to seek from Hazen, and others, reimbursement for costs incurred and commitments toward the cost of future response measures. In 1986, the DEQE by letter notified the Re-Solve Generators Committee (and Hazen) that, pursuant to G.L. c. 21E (1988 ed.), it was seeking reimbursement for the cost of removing 115 drums of hazardous material from the Re-Solve site.

USF&G denies any obligation to defend Hazen against the governmental claims, argues that the claims do not fall within the basic recitation of the scope of policy coverage, and asserts that, in any event, the pollution exclusion clause relieves it of any duty to indemnify Hazen with respect to those claims. The applicable USF&G policies, which include standard comprehensive general liability insurance coverage, provide that USF&G will pay all sums Hazen "shall become legally obligated to pay as *damages* because of ... *property damage* to which this insurance applies, caused by an occurrence, and [USF&G] shall have the right and duty to defend any *suit* against the insured seeking *damages* on account of such ... property damage" (emphasis supplied).

USF&G disclaims any duty to afford Hazen a defense with respect to the claims asserted in the letters of the EPA and DEQE because neither letter involves a "suit" against Hazen within the meaning of the word "suit" in the policy. USF&G denies any duty to indemnify Hazen with respect to claims for reimbursement for cleanup costs, arguing that such costs are not "damages" within the policy terms and that, in any event, any amounts payable by Hazen are not amounts Hazen is obliged to pay because of "property damage." ...

Hazen [argues] that the letters of notification from those agencies had the same practical effect as the filing of a complaint in a legal action because Hazen's rights and obligations could be substantially affected by actions and determinations occurring before any lawsuit would be commenced. The policy provides that USF&G has the "duty to defend any suit against [Hazen] seeking damages on account of ... property damage" to which the insurance applies.... Literally, there is no suit. That fact alone has been sufficient to provide the answer for some courts.... It is, however, not sufficient to provide an answer for us.

A superficial view of the EPA letter might lead one to conclude that it is not analogous to a complaint.... ]It states], however, declaring that "the only form of voluntary involvement" that EPA would consider is "commitment to a complete implementation of all the measures needed on the site proper and reimbursement of the expenses already incurred by EPA and DEQE." It then describes those measures. EPA asked for a written response within thirty days, announced a planned meeting for all potentially responsible parties, and requested information and records regarding hazardous substances that Hazen sent to the Re-Solve facility. The letter advised Hazen of criminal penalties for any failure to furnish the requested information.

The question is a close one. The authorities are divided on the point. We conclude that the litigation defense protection that Hazen purchased from USF&G would be substantially compromised if USF&G had no obligation to defend Hazen's interests in response to the EPA letter. * * *

The consequences of the receipt of the EPA letter were so substantially equivalent to the commencement of a lawsuit that a duty to defend arose immediately. The EPA letter was not the equivalent of a conventional demand letter based on a personal injury claim [which is only informal action falling short of a suit].

Hazen's obligation to respond positively to the EPA letter was strong. The prospects of avoiding financial responsibility were minimal because liability is not based on fault and the available defenses are very limited [under the law]. Moreover, the risk to which Hazen was exposed was substantial because, as a practical matter, its liability is joint and several. Early involvement in the settlement discussions is thus often crucial to protect one's interests. Any court action by EPA is limited to the administrative record and judicial review considers only whether the EPA "decision was arbitrary and capricious or otherwise not in accordance with law". Thus participation in the development of that record can be crucial. Settlement of EPA claims against potentially responsible parties with protection against claims for contribution is a desired goal. The situation was such that the opportunity to protect Hazen's interests could well have been lost, long before any lawsuit would be brought. It would be naive to characterize the EPA letter as a request for voluntary action. Hazen had no practical choice other than to respond actively to the letter.

The early involvement of an insurer in such a process is obviously important to the insured (and very possibly to the insurer), assuming, of course, that the claim is one that falls within the coverage of the policy. We turn now to the question of the extent to which cleanup costs are within the coverage of the policy. [The court concluded they were.] ... We explicitly reject the reasoning of some courts that incorporates "[p]revious judicial interpretations" into the insurance contract to narrow the scope of the word "damages" and thus purport to eliminate any ambiguity. Lay people should not reasonably be expected to know such limitations. * * * The important point is that, if Hazen is legally liable to pay certain amounts because of property damage for which the law holds it responsible, and USF&G is legally obliged to pay "damages on account of ... property damage."

## Foster-Gardner, Inc. v.
## National Union Fire Insurance Company of Pittsburgh, PA

Supreme Court of California
18 Cal. 4th 857, 77 Cal. Rptr. 2d 107, 959 P.2d 265 (1998)

**Brown, J.**

In this case we determine whether environmental agency activity prior to the filing of a complaint, in this case an order notifying the insured that it is a responsible party for pollution and requiring remediation, is a "suit" triggering the insurer's duty to defend under a comprehensive general liability insurance (CGL) policy. Two Courts of Appeal have ruled on the issue reaching opposite conclusions. We granted review in both cases....

## I. FACTS AND PROCEDURAL BACKGROUND

Since 1959, plaintiff Foster-Gardner, Inc. (Foster-Gardner) has operated a wholesale pesticide and fertilizer business in Coachella, California (Site). In August 1992, Foster-Gardner received an "Imminent and Substantial Endangerment Order and Remedial Action Order" (Order) from the Department of Toxic Substances Control (DTSC) of the California Environmental Protection Agency. DTSC issued the Order pursuant to the Carpenter-Presley-Tanner Hazardous Substance Account Act (HSAA), California's "Superfund" law.

The Order stated the following: As a finding of fact Foster-Gardner was "the owner and operator of the Site, [was] a responsible party, and has incurred liability for cleaning up the Site." As a conclusion of law, Foster-Gardner was a "responsible party" or "liable person" within the meaning of [the law]....

Foster-Gardner tendered defense of the DTSC Order to four of its insurers, National Union Fire Insurance Company of Pittsburgh, PA, and Pacific Indemnity Company (Pacific), Fremont Indemnity Company (Fremont), and Ranger Insurance Company (Ranger) (insurers). Pacific's policies were in effect from May 1984 to May 1986, Fremont's policies from June 1983 to July 1984, and Ranger's policies from December 1970 to December 1980.

All insurers had issued CGL polices containing the following language with minor nonmaterial differences: "The company will pay on behalf of the insured all sums which the insured shall become legally obligated to pay as damages because of ... bodily injury or ... property damage to which [this] insurance applies, caused by an occurrence, ... and the company shall have the right and duty to defend any suit against the insured seeking damages on account of such bodily injury or property damage, ... and may make such investigation and settlement of any claim or suit as it deems expedient, but the company shall not be obligated to pay any claim or judgment or to defend any suit after the applicable limit of the company's liability has been exhausted by payment of judgments or settlements."

While the policies consistently treated the terms "suit" and "claim" as separate and noninterchangeable, these terms were not defined in the policies.... The insurers either refused to defend, or agreed to defend subject to a reservation of rights and have not, in Foster-Gardner's view, adequately funded that defense.

## II. DISCUSSION

### 3. Out-of-state Authority

While the issue of whether environmental agency activity prior to the filing of a complaint is a "suit" within the meaning of a CGL policy is one of first impression in California, numerous other state and federal courts have considered this question. These cases have arisen as a consequence either of underlying CERCLA proceedings, underlying state proceedings pursuant to statutes modeled after CERCLA (similar to the HSAA), or both. Essentially three approaches have evolved, generally referred to as the literal, functional, and hybrid approaches.

a. The "literal meaning" approach

Under the "literal meaning" approach, the term "suit" is deemed unambiguous, referring to actual court proceedings initiated by the filing of a complaint. When no complaint has been filed, there is no "suit" the insurer has a duty to defend.... In addition to the plain meaning of the term "suit," some courts find support for their conclusion in the connection between the filing of a complaint and the duty to defend. Generally the issue of whether an insurer's duty to defend has arisen is determined by looking to the allegations in the underlying complaint and comparing these allegations to the policy provisions.... Because they conclude the term "suit" does not encompass administrative agency orders and other activity, courts have noted that the insurer would be put in the position of providing coverage for which it did not contract or receive payment.

b. The "functional" and "hybrid" approaches

Under the "functional" approach, any receipt of a PRP letter or other precomplaint environmental agency activity constitutes a "suit." In a refinement of the "functional" approach, other courts have determined that a PRP letter or other precomplaint environmental agency action is a "suit" only if it is sufficiently coercive and threatening. This is the "hybrid" approach. These courts essentially do not consider a mere preliminary notification to be a "suit," but conclude a proceeding becomes a "suit" if it progresses beyond the mere notification or request for voluntary action stage. Because the Order received by Foster-Gardner in this case is considerably past the mere notification stage, we need not differentiate between the two approaches here.

Under both the functional and hybrid approach, the term "suit" is deemed ambiguous, and interpreted to refer to proceedings other than those in a court of law initiated by the filing of a complaint. Some courts are persuaded that "the fact that another reasonable interpretation of the term 'suit' exists simply creates an ambiguity." Having found ambiguity, courts then determine that an insured would reasonably expect a defense of the administrative agency's order or other activity.

[C]ourts have [also] relied on certain policy considerations, such as the need to encourage prompt and efficient hazardous waste cleanup. "[I]f the receipt of a PRP notice is held not to trigger the duty to defend under CGL policies, then insureds might be inhibited from cooperation with the EPA in order to invite the filing of a formal complaint.... A fundamental goal of CERCLA is to encourage and facilitate voluntary settlements.... It is in the nation's best interests to have hazardous waste cleaned up effectively and efficiently."

B. Analysis

While a claim may ultimately ripen into a suit, 'claim' and 'suit' are not synonymous." Foster-Gardner's construction of the term "suit" is not reasonable. There is nothing in the policy language to support the interpretation that some precomplaint notices are "suits" and some are not. Rather, the unambiguous language of the policies obligated the insurers to defend a "suit," not, as Foster-Gardner asserts, the "substantive equivalent" of a "suit." ... Moreover, the policies do not treat the terms "suit" and "claim" as interchangeable, but consistently treat them separately. This careful separation indicates that the insurers' differing rights and obligations with respect to "suits" and "claims" were deliberately and intentionally articulated in the policies. The effect of such policy language is that "an insurer owes a duty to defend 'suits' but no duty to defend 'claims' which have not yet become 'suits.' Instead, the insurer has the discretionary right to investigate and settle 'as it deems expedient.'"

Rather, by specifying that only a "suit," and not a "claim" triggers the duty to defend, insurers have drawn an unambiguous line to define and limit their contractual obligation. This delineation encourages stability and efficiency in the insurance system. In exchange for a higher premium, the policies might have obligated the insurer to defend any "demand" against the insurer, or to provide a defense whenever the insured is subject to government compulsion or investigation. They did not....

The fact that damaging, perhaps even irrefutable, findings will be made [in the administrative proceeding] does not mean that a duty to defend arises in the criminal proceeding.... [B]ecause we conclude the insurers here did not contract and receive premiums to defend anything but a civil lawsuit, requiring them to defend the Order would result in an unintended windfall for Foster-Gardner.

Moreover, it is indeed arguable that an insured's early intervention in a dispute outside the civil action context may reduce any indemnity for which the insurer is ultimately held liable. That does not alter the scope of the insurer's duty to defend....

Our conclusion that a "suit" is a court proceeding initiated by the filing of a complaint creates a "bright-line rule that, by clearly delineating the scope of risk, *reduces the need for future litigation*....

This is a contract issue, and imposition of a duty to defend CERCLA proceedings that have not ripened into suits would impose on the insurer an obligation for which it may not be prepared.... Whatever merit there may be to these conflicting social and economic considerations, they have nothing whatsoever to do with our determination whether the policy's disjunctive use of 'suit' and 'claim' creates an ambiguity."

[Dissenting opinion of Kennard, J. omitted.]

### Notes and Questions

1. Which case is more persuasive: *Hazen Paper* or *Foster-Gardner*? Why?

2. Is there arguably another approach construing the term "suit" than the alternatives set forth in these cases?

3. Which view of "suit" is more consistent with the purposes of liability insurance?

4. In *Ameron Internat. Corp. v. Insurance Co. of State of Pennsylvania*, 242 P.3d 1020 (Cal. 2010), the California Supreme Court found that an administrative adjudicative proceeding seeking payment from a government contractor for defective performance

qualified as a suit under the contractor's liability policies because it had a greater "quasi-judicial" nature such that "*Foster-Gardner*'s rule does not apply here." *Id.* at 1022. Further, the U.S. Dept. of the Interior Board of Contract Appeals (IBCA) "pleading requirements meet the standards for a complaint under our Code of Civil Procedure." Therefore, "[i]t would exalt form over substance to find such a complaint before the IBCA insufficient simply because the IBCA is not a court of law, particularly when the basis of the insurer's' position is that they rely on the substantive contents of a complaint in order to make their coverage decisions." *Id.* at 1029. In addition, "a reasonable policyholder would believe that a policy providing coverage for a 'suit' would provide coverage for the IBCA proceedings. As the legislative purpose indicates, the IBCA proceedings provides contractors with their 'day in court.'" *Id.* at 1030.

Justice Kennard, the lone dissenter in *Foster-Gardner*, concurred separately in the unanimous *Ameron* decision, reiterating her criticism of the *Foster-Gardner* decision, arguing that the *Ameron* majority's distinctions were strained.

> When it was decided in 1998, *Foster-Gardner* represented a distinctly minority view.... Since *Foster-Gardner* was decided, no sister state court has adopted its "literal meaning approach," or its resulting "bright-line rule," in construing the term "suit" in a CGL insurance policy, while courts in nine sister states and federal courts apply the law of two other sister states have rejected that approach, instead adopting either the "functional equivalent" approach or the "hybrid" approach that the *Foster-Gardner* majority rejected [and the *Hazen*, excerpted above, employed; Justice Kennard then cited a dozen cases, including four state supreme court cases following *Hazen*'s approach and reaching a similar outcome.] Thus, over the past 12 years, it has become increasingly apparent that *Foster-Gardner* lies far outside the mainstream of American insurance law.

> Here, the court * * * implicitly rejects *Foster-Gardner*'s reasoning.... Although I would prefer that *Foster-Gardner* be overruled, the decision here is at least a step in the right direction.

*See also Governmental Interinsurance Exch. v. City of Angola*, 8 F. Supp. 2d 1120, 1130 (N.D. Ind. 1998) ("'vast majority of courts ... have found that all kinds of coercive administrative actions are ... "suits" covered by general liability insurance policies.'").

5. Does *Ameron* change your views on the issue? Does it matter that despite losing many if not most of these disagreements, insurers have continued to stick with largely the same policy language? Is the absence of change tacit acceptance of the non-California decisions? Does that mean liability insurers in California have an economic advantage over those in other states? Does the discrepancy present any strategic opportunities for policyholders dealing in government contracts, chemical manufacture, or other activities that may be more subject to government administrative proceedings than the norm?

6. As discussed above concerning occurrence-counting, there may be a distributional divide separating primary and excess insurers on this issue. As reflected above, the typical primary policy speaks of defending "suits." By contrast, many excess or

umbrella policies (*see* the chapter regarding excess, umbrella, and reinsurance) talk about covering "claims" against the policyholder but differ regarding whether they have any defense obligation, although many such policies provide that the excess insurer will defend if the primary policy is exhausted or inapplicable. In a case like *Foster-Gardner*, then, the California Supreme Court decision absolves the primary insurer of defense obligations but an excess insurer that has a contingent duty to defend claims may be required to step into the role normally assumed by the primary insurer. For the most part, this potential discrepancy is on its way to becoming moot, at least in Superfund cases, because the typical general liability policy has excluded superfund coverage since the 1986 revision to the standard form CGL policy.

# § 9.07. The Concept of an Uninsurable "Known Loss"

## General Housewares Corp. v. National Surety Corporation

Court of Appeals of Indiana, Fourth District
741 N.E.2d 408 (2000)

**Sullivan, Judge.**

Appellants, General Housewares Corporation and its wholly owned subsidiary, Chicago Cutlery, Inc., (collectively "Housewares"), challenge the trial court's entry of summary judgment in favor of National Surety Corporation (National). We reverse and remand [finding the known loss doctrine inapplicable].

The Known Loss Doctrine

Housewares claims that the trial court erred by applying the "known loss" doctrine to its third-party liability insurance policies. Both parties claim, and our research reveals, that no Indiana court has recognized this doctrine. Therefore, this is a matter of first impression in Indiana.

The "known loss" doctrine is a common law concept deriving from the fundamental requirement in insurance law that the loss be fortuitous. Simply put, the known loss doctrine states that one may not obtain insurance for a loss that has already taken place. Id. Describing the known loss doctrine, commentators have noted that "losses which exist at the time of the insuring agreement, or which are so probable or imminent that there is insufficient 'risk' being transferred between the insured and insurer, are not proper subjects of insurance." 7 Lee R. Russ and Thomas F. Segalla, Couch on Insurance § 102:8 at 20 (3d ed. 1997).

This principle has been referred to by various names, including "loss in progress," "known risk," and "known loss." ... "Loss in progress" refers to the notion that an insurer should not be liable for a loss which was in progress before the insurance took effect. Id. Although the term "known loss" has been limited to those situations where a loss has actually occurred, ... most courts have defined the doctrine to also include losses which are "substantially certain" to occur or which were a "substantial probability." ... Despite some differences between the various labels used, we agree with the Illinois Supreme Court, which noted that the term " 'known loss' most adequately describes the doctrine." ... Therefore, we will use the term "known loss" to encompass the fortuity principle.

### General Application of the Known Loss Doctrine

Although the known loss doctrine is recognized by many jurisdictions, there is some disagreement as to how the doctrine should be applied. Some courts have required actual knowledge on the part of the insured.... Other courts have been less stringent and have required only a "reason to know," or "evidence of probable loss," or determined whether a "reasonably prudent" insured would know that the loss is highly likely to occur....

In the present case, both parties suggest that the known loss doctrine should depend upon a party's actual knowledge. We agree. The very term "known loss" indicates that actual knowledge upon behalf of the insured is required before the doctrine will apply. This is ordinarily a question of fact.

Exactly what the insurer is required to know before the known loss doctrine will apply must also be determined. As noted above, there has been no unanimity among courts which have considered this issue. Some courts merely require knowledge of a "substantial probability" of loss. The First Circuit ... adopted a "substantially certain" test. Although these standards may seem similar, we prefer the language in Selman to that of Outboard Marine.

The term "probability" indicates the presence of contingency and fortuity, the lack of which is the very essence of the known loss doctrine. Even if there is a probability of loss, there is some insurable risk, and the known loss doctrine should not apply...."Certainty," on the other hand, refers not to the likelihood of an occurrence, but rather to the inevitability of an occurrence. Therefore, a "substantially certain" loss is one that is not only likely to occur, but is virtually inevitable. The inquiry should be more of temporality than probability—when an event will occur, not whether an event will occur. We also note that, because the effect of the known loss doctrine is to avoid coverage, the burden of proving that the loss was known is on the party seeking to avoid coverage....

Therefore, we hold that if an insured has actual knowledge that a loss has occurred, is occurring, or is substantially certain to occur on or before the effective date of the policy, the known loss doctrine will bar coverage. This is not to say, however, that parties may not explicitly agree to cover existing losses. Indeed, the known loss doctrine is inapplicable "if the insurer also knew of the circumstances on which it bases the defense." ...

* * *

The "expected or intended occurrence" exclusions and the known loss doctrine serve different functions. The expected or intended exclusions focus upon the time of the act for which insurance is sought, while the known loss doctrine looks to the time the insurance contract is entered into. The Second Circuit summarized the distinction:

"The 'expected or intended' claim requires consideration of whether, *at the time of the acts causing the injury,* the insured expected or intended the injury, an inquiry that generally asks merely whether the injury was accidental. The 'known loss' defense requires consideration of whether, *at the time the insured bought the policy (or the policy incepted),* the loss was known. The contentions may overlap, but they are distinct...."

*Stonewall Ins. Co. v. Asbestos Claims Mgmt. Corp.* (1995) 2d Cir., 73 F.3d 1178, 1215 (citations omitted) (emphasis supplied) *modified on other grounds by 85 F.3d 49.* Because Housewares insured against liability to a third party and not property damage, we look to see if the insured knew of a liability, rather than whether property damage was known.

Housewares claims that the known loss doctrine should not apply in the present case because, although it may have known of conditions which could lead to liability, its liability was "unknown" until it was fixed in amount. Housewares argues that, because it was not aware (and in some cases is still not aware) of the full extent of its liability, the known loss doctrine is inapplicable to it policies. We disagree [and] hold that there is a distinct difference between knowledge of the existence of liability and knowledge of the full extent of liability.

The existence of liability can be known without the full extent of liability being fixed. For example, if one negligently injures a pedestrian with one's automobile, one's liability is substantially certain. However, it may be months before the dollar amount of liability is certain, and the known loss doctrine bars purchasing insurance after the accident. An insured's liability need not be fixed to a monetary certainty; if the known liability has occurred or is substantially certain to occur, the known loss doctrine bars coverage.

## Notes and Questions

1. What distinction, if any, is there between the "known loss" doctrine and the "intentional act" or "expected and intended" exclusion (discussed in Chapter 1, *supra*)?

2. What is the difference, if any, between the known loss doctrine and the fortuity requirement for insurability?

3. Does the court in the above case not only articulate the doctrine correctly but apply it correctly so as not to undercut the objectively reasonable expectations of the policyholder? Why or why not?

4. Is there a danger that too expansive a view of the known loss concept could result in depriving a policyholder of coverage simply because of the realities of its business? For example, a prescription drug manufacturer is almost certain to be sued by at least a few customers who suffer adverse reactions to the drug. Should the pharmaceutical company have CGL coverage? Why or why not?

5. What about a home builder that is sued over alleged defects in the construction of the house? Under what circumstances would the known loss doctrine properly apply?

# § 9.08. Is Liability Insurance Coverage Limited to Only "Tort" Claims?

## Vandenberg v. The Superior Court of Sacramento County

Supreme Court of California
21 Cal. 4th 815, 88 Cal. Rptr. 2d 366, 982 P.2d 229 (1999)

Baxter, J.

[W]e must determine whether a commercial general liability (CGL) insurance policy that provides coverage for sums the insured is "legally obligated to pay as damages" may cover losses arising from a breach of contract. We [conclude that] the coverage phrase "legally obligated to pay as damages," as used in a CGL insurance policy, may provide an insured defendant with coverage for losses pleaded as contractual damages.

The underlying litigation involves damage to a parcel of land that Vandenberg used as an automobile sales and service facility. Before 1958, owners Eugene and Kathryn Boyd operated an automobile dealership on the property. From 1958 to 1988, Vandenberg leased the property from Boyd under a series of leases. In 1988 Vandenberg discontinued the business and possession of the land reverted to Boyd.

To prepare the property for sale, Boyd removed three underground waste oil storage tanks. Testing revealed contamination of soils and groundwater underlying the property. Boyd filed an action against Vandenberg, alleging causes of action for breach of contract, breach of the covenant of good faith and fair dealing, public and private nuisance, negligence, waste, trespass, strict liability, equitable indemnity, declaratory relief, and injunctive relief. The Boyd complaint alleged Vandenberg had installed and operated the waste oil storage tanks and the tanks were the source of the petroleum contamination.

Vandenberg had obtained CGL insurance from several companies over the years, including Phoenix Assurance Company of New York (Phoenix), the Glens Falls Insurance Company (Glens Falls), Continental Insurance Company (Continental), TIG Insurance Corporation, Centennial Insurance Company (Centennial), and United States Fidelity and Guaranty Company (USF&G) (collectively insurers). The policies provided coverage to Vandenberg for sums he was "legally obligated to pay as damages" because of property damage. However, certain of the policies, including policies issued by US F&G and Centennial, also contained a so-called pollution exclusion, under which property damage caused by a pollutant or contaminant was not covered except for a "sudden and accidental" discharge.

Vandenberg tendered defense of the Boyd action to his insurers, but only USF&G agreed to provide a defense. During judicially supervised settlement proceedings, Vandenberg, Boyd, and USF&G reached an agreement among themselves to resolve the Boyd litigation. The agreement provided that its parties would contribute jointly to the investigation and remediation of the contamination, with USF&G bearing the largest share of the cost. Boyd agreed to release USF&G from any claims. Vandenberg agreed to release USF&G from claims for bad faith, breach of the contract, and extracontractual damages. Boyd released all claims against Vandenberg except those based on the theory that the contamination constituted a breach of the lease agreements.

*Boyd and Vandenberg* agreed to resolve the reserved *breach of lease* issues through arbitration or by trial, depending upon their agreement on an arbitrator and arbitration schedule. Vandenberg conditioned his agreement to the settlement upon the arbitration being "binding." USF&G agreed to defend Vandenberg, but the ultimate issues of USF&G's coverage and indemnity obligations, as well as any claim by Vandenberg for counsel fees [paid to independent counsel].

Among other things, the arbitrator found that the contamination stemmed primarily from the underground waste oil tanks and was caused in part by Vandenberg's improper installation, maintenance and use of the tanks. The arbitrator indicated the discharge of contaminants was not sudden and accidental. The arbitrator's award of over $4 million to Boyd was confirmed by a superior court judgment.

The insurers rejected Vandenberg's request for indemnification. He then filed the underlying action against his insurers, alleging various causes of action arising out of the failure to defend, settle, or indemnify in the Boyd action. The trial court ... found Vandenberg had no coverage under the policies for the arbitration award because the claims submitted to the arbitrator were contractual. The Court of Appeal ... ruled that coverage under the insurance policies in question could not be determined by reference to the "general rule" that damages for an insured's nonperformance of a contract are not covered under CGL insurance policies.... Rather, the court reasoned, when there is damage to property, the focus of the inquiry should be the nature of the risk or peril that caused the injury and the specific policy language, not the form of action brought by the injured party.

We granted the insurers' petitions for review to consider the circumstances, if any, in which private contractual arbitration decisions may have collateral estoppel effect in favor of nonparties, and whether CGL policy language indicating coverage for sums the insured becomes "legally obligated to pay as damages" can include losses pled as breach of contract.

[Part I of the Court's discussion concerning the preclusive impact of arbitration omitted.]

The CGL insurance policies issued by all the insurers in this case provided coverage for sums Vandenberg was legally obligated to pay as damages because of property damage. We next consider whether this coverage language in a CGL insurance policy necessarily precludes coverage for losses pleaded as contractual damages.

In holding that coverage for property damage losses is not necessarily precluded because they are pled as contractual damages, the Court of Appeal properly focused on the property itself and the nature of the risk causing the injury. Acknowledging the line of decisions espousing a general rule of noncoverage for contractual damages, the Court of Appeal nevertheless concluded "the general rule is not a universal bar to insurance coverage whenever a contract is involved. Rather, the focus of coverage for property damage is the property itself." Coverage under a CGL insurance policy is not based upon the fortuity of the form of action chosen by the injured party. Thus, as the Court of Appeal stated, determination of coverage must be made individually by considering "the nature of [the] property, the injury, and the risk that caused the injury, in light of the particular provisions of each applicable insurance policy."

The insurers contend CGL insurance policies limiting coverage to amounts the insured is "legally obligated to pay as damages," or using similar language, refer to tort liability and not contractual liability. A long line of decisions supports their position, holding that any liability arising ex contractu, as opposed to ex delicto, is not covered under such policies. The underlying reasoning of these cases is that the phrase "legally obligated to pay as damages" describes liability based upon a breach of a duty imposed by law, i.e., tort, rather than by contract. We disagree. The nature of the damage and the risk involved, in light of particular policy provisions, control coverage....

Insurance policies are contracts construed in accordance with the parties' mutual intent at the time of contract formation, as inferred from the written provisions. The "clear and explicit" meaning of the provisions, interpreted in their "ordinary and popular sense," controls judicial interpretation unless "used by the parties in a technical sense or a special meaning is given to them by usage." If the meaning a layperson would ascribe to insurance contract language is not ambiguous, courts will apply that meaning.

Even if a provision raises doubts as to coverage in the minds of legally trained observers due to a sophisticated legal distinction, courts will not assume the distinction was incorporated into the policy. Whatever ambiguity a phrase possesses due to a party's legal knowledge is resolved in favor of coverage....

Nothing in the respective policies between Vandenberg and any of the insurers suggests any special or legalistic meaning to the phrase "legally obligated to pay as damages." A reasonable layperson would certainly understand "legally obligated to pay" to refer to any obligation which is binding and enforceable under the law, whether pursuant to contract or tort liability. Further, a reasonable layperson, cognizant that he or she is purchasing a "general liability" insurance policy, would not conclude such coverage term only refers to liability pled in tort, and thus entirely excludes liability pled on a theory of breach of contract. Under general insurance principles, we must interpret the phrase "legally obligated to pay as damages" in accordance with the ordinary and popular sense, not the legalistic, and erroneously premised, interpretation of the language urged by insurers.

Moreover, the arbitrariness of the distinction between contract and tort ... is evident when we consider the same act may constitute both a breach of contract and a tort. Predicating coverage upon an injured party's choice of remedy or the form of action sought is not the law of this state. [C]ourts must focus on the nature of the risk and the injury, in light of the policy provisions, to make that determination.

Insurance treatises concur with this approach. "[W]hether a particular claim falls within the coverage afforded by a liability policy is not affected by the form of the legal proceeding. Accordingly, the legal theory asserted by the claimant is immaterial to the determination of whether the risk is covered." (9 Couch, Insurance (3d ed. 1997) § 126:3, p. 126–8.) Insurance commentators explain: "The expression 'legally obligated' connotes legal responsibility that is *broad* in scope. It is directed at civil liability ... [which] can arise from either unintentional (negligent) or intentional tort, under common law, statute, or contract." (Malecki & Flitner, Commercial General Liability (6th ed. 1997) p. 6, italics added.) "The coverage agreement [which] embraces 'all sums which the insured shall become legally obligated to pay as damages ...' is intentionally broad enough to include the insured's obligation to pay damages for breach of contract as well as for tort, within limitations imposed by other terms of the coverage agreement (e.g. bodily injury and property damage as defined, caused by an occurrence) and by the exclusions...." (Tinker, *Comprehensive General Liability Insurance — Perspective and Overview* (1975) 25 Fed. Ins. Coun. Q. 217, 265.)

Accordingly, we uphold the Court of Appeal's determination that Vandenberg's insurers cannot avoid coverage for damages awarded against Vandenberg in the Boyd action solely on grounds the damages were assessed on a contractual theory.

[Dissenting opinion of BROWN, J. omitted.]

## Notes and Questions

In *Shade Foods, Inc. v. Innovative Products Sales & Marketing, Inc.*, 78 Cal. App. 4th 847, 870, 93 Cal. Rptr. 2d 364, 380 (2000), the court had this reaction to *Vandenberg*:

> In the present case, the jury found that IPS was negligent and that it breached implied and express warranties to Shade. The latter finding was based on jury instructions presenting alternative theories of breach of warranty, including breach of express warranty, implied warranty of merchantability, and implied warranty of fitness for particular purpose.
>
> In light of the *Vandenberg* decision, the insuring agreement clearly now covers IPS's liability for negligence. The *Vandenberg* court decisively rejected the interpretation of the "legally obligated to pay" language as precluding coverage for actions involving both contractual and tort liability for the same loss....

*See also Lee v. USAA Cas. Ins. Co.*, 86 P.3d 562, 564–65 (Mont. 2004) (policy "contains no exclusion for liability arising out of a contract, which is an exclusion often included in these types of liability insurance policies").

# § 9.09. When Is Coverage Triggered?

## Singsaas v. Deiderich

Supreme Court of Minnesota
307 Minn. 153, 238 N.W.2d 878 (1976)

Amdahl, J.

The parties stipulated, for purposes of this declaratory judgment action only and so far as material here, that prior to December 1971, Jerome A. and Daniel Diederich organized a business partnership doing business as Diederich Bros. Construction Company (Diederich). They subsequently purchased a policy of insurance from respondent, Western Casualty & Surety Company. The policy contained both a products hazard endorsement and a completed operations hazard endorsement, and its stated term was from November 24, 1971, to November 24, 1974.

On or about December 6, 1971, Diederich negligently performed some work in connection with repairs and modification on a manlift located in a grain elevator structure owned and operated by the Burr Farmers Elevator & Supply Company in the village of Burr, Minnesota. The negligent work consisted of using a cast iron socket clamp into which a soft metal, called babbitt, was placed for the purpose of holding the end of the manlift hoisting cable. Diederich decided to go out of business and requested cancellation of the policy. The policy was canceled on July 21, 1972, and some amount of premium was refunded to Diederich. On August 8, 1972, plaintiff Bruce Singsaas, an employee of the Burr Farmers Elevator & Supply Company, used the manlift and the cable came loose from the cast iron socket, causing the manlift to fall, rendering him a permanent paraplegic.

The policy by its terms applied to bodily injuries caused by an "occurrence" and "occurrence" was defined in the policy as:

> "'[O]ccurrence' means an accident, including injurious exposure to conditions which results, *during the policy period*, in bodily injury or property damage neither expected nor intended from the standpoint of the insured." (Italics supplied.)

The policy further provided that it applied "only to bodily injury... which occurs during the policy period...."

The issue is: Does a liability insurance policy containing a completed operations hazard endorsement provide coverage where the policyholder's negligent acts during a time the policy is in effect result in injury after a policy has been canceled and the policy specifically provides that its coverage is limited to accidents which result, during the policy period, in bodily injury and to bodily injury which occurs during the policy period? We agree with the trial court and answer the question in the negative.

The definition of "occurrence" in the policy is derived from a 1966 revision of a nationally standardized liability policy form. The underwriting intent of the language is to make coverage depend upon whether bodily injury results during the policy period. This intent is emphasized by the further explicit provision, noted *supra*, that "[t]his insurance applies only to bodily injury... which occurs during the policy period...."

The trial court decision is consistent with the generally accepted rule that the time of the occurrence is not the time the wrongful act was committed but the time the complaining party was actually damaged.

The majority rule, which follows the underwriting intent, has been criticized as contrary to the intent of the insured party when purchasing completed operations and products liability coverage to protect himself from liability resulting at any time from a negligent act performed during the policy period. However, such intent is no less frustrated when the policy limit selected by the insured is less than the economic consequences of an injury and no one would argue that the insurance carrier should pay an amount larger than its policy limits. The rule does not preclude an insured from purchasing the insurance coverage he desires....

It is also argued that the policy language would permit the insurer to avoid liability by canceling the policy before an injury occurred if it learned of any negligent work. However, the possibility of cancellation by the insurer is not an appropriate reason to reject the majority rule here and we do not reach nor answer issues arising by reason of insurer cancellation, as it was the insured who canceled the policy.

# § 9.10. Insurer's Liability for Progressive Injuries — When Does the Injury Occur?

Liability insurance covers the policyholder for liability claims arising from the policyholder's operations as well as for claims arising after completion of operations or due to products manufactured by the policyholder. Although there can be some considerable separation between the time of a liability-creating act and the liability-creating damage due to policyholder operations, this type of "long-tail" or latent injury claim is more common for product liability claims.

What happens, however, when Insurance Company A initially provides products liability coverage, but the product-related injury or disease does not manifest itself until some years later, when Insurance Company B or C is providing similar coverage to the same manufacturer for its defective products? Which insurance company is ultimately liable for these injuries?

Three distinct major legal theories have evolved to answer this question: the "exposure" theory; the "manifestation" theory; and the "injury in fact" theory, which in many cases become a "continuous" trigger. In addition, there is case law supporting combinations of these theories. *See* Randy Maniloff & Jeffrey Stempel, General Liability Insurance Coverage: Key Issues in Every State, Ch. 16 (5th ed. 2018) (characterizing situation as involving five different approaches to trigger).

Under the exposure trigger, bodily injury or property damage takes place when the claimant is exposed to the injurious situation allegedly created by the policyholder. Under a manifestation theory, injury or damage takes place when the loss is reasonably capable of detection. Under an injury-in-fact or actual injury approach, something more than mere exposure is required but the damage need not be manifest in order to trigger a liability policy. Under the continuous trigger, all insurance on the risk is triggered from the time of first injurious exposure to the date of discovery of the insurer. *See* Maniloff & Stempel, *supra*, Ch. 16; Jeffrey W. Stempel & Erik S. Knutsen, Stempel & Knutsen on Insurance Coverage § 14.09[b] (4th ed. 2016).

Much of the case law in this area arises out of injurious product claims where the injury or damage has not been recognized for years. Disputes over liability coverage for asbestos injury and environmental contamination claims made much of the law in this area. When these and kindred cases are examined in more detail, they are more consistent than commonly supposed. For example, most of the "exposure" trigger asbestos coverage cases are really taking about "injurious exposure," which is quite consistent with most applications of the "actual injury" trigger in that even a non-obvious, unnoticed, hard-to-detect injury triggers coverage if the actual injury can be shown retrospectively.

Once again, asbestos cases provide a good example of the concept. When persons were initially exposed to asbestos fibers, they did not immediately gasp and collapse. Rather, they inhaled the asbestos, which began subtly causing harm over a period of years. After sufficient time, symptoms became "manifest" and these persons sued, prompting the asbestos-manufacturing defendants to seek liability insurance coverage. Although a few courts embraced the manifestation trigger, most courts correctly concluded that actual injury could take place well before the third-party claimants knew they had lung problems from years of asbestos particles in their lungs. Just as important, the claimants were alleging that the asbestos was doing damage for years prior to manifestation, triggering the liability insurers' duty to defend.

In addition, because of the nature of asbestos particle interaction with lung tissue and damage to the human body, many courts concluded that there was "continuous" trigger continuing after the claimant's original injurious exposure to the asbestos. As a result, many policies and policy periods were considered to be triggered even if there was no new exposure to additional asbestos sources after the initial exposure. As a result, many insurance policies were triggered, much to the consternation of insurers. Although different insurers argued for different triggers (undoubtedly based on the manner in which different triggers would reduce the insurer's respective responsibility), the insurance industry as a whole preferred that fewer policies be triggered.

The popularity of the continuous trigger increased the liability of many insurers. To some extent, insurers were able to recoup some of this legal and economic loss in jurisdictions where they persuaded courts to pro-rate the respective responsibility of insurers according to time on the risk, policy limits, or some combination of both as this prevented some insurers from being required to pay their entire policy limits when triggered, even if the policyholder faced claims exceeding policy limits. *See gen-*

*erally* STEMPEL & KNUTSEN §§ 14.09, 14.10; Jeffrey W. Stempel, *Assessing the Coverage Carnage: Asbestos Liability and Insurance After Three Decades of Dispute*, 12 CONN. INS. L.J. 349 (2005). Regarding trigger for long-tail claims, key cases of note are:

- *Insurance Co. of N. Am. v. Forty-Eight Insulations*, 633 F.2d 1212 (6th Cir. 1980), *cert. denied*, 454 U.S. 1109 (1981) (applying Illinois and New Jersey law) (leading exposure trigger case);

- *Eagle-Picher Industries, Inc. v. Liberty Mut. Ins. Co.*, 682 F.2d 12 (1st Cir. 1982), *cert. denied*, 460 U.S. 1028 (1983) (leading manifestation trigger case);

- *American Home Products Corp. v. Liberty Mut. Ins. Co.*, 565 F. Supp. 1485 (S.D.N.Y. 1983), *aff'd as modified*, 748 F.2d 760 (2d Cir. 1984) (important actual injury case—but note, Second Circuit modified portion of trial court opinion requiring that damage from prescription drug DES, the subject of the third-party claims, be diagnosable; if allowed to stand, diagnosability requirement would have converted injury-in-fact trigger in some cases to something much more like manifestation trigger);

- *Keene Corp. v. Insurance Co. of N. Am.*, 667 F.2d 1034 (D.C. Cir. 1981), *cert. denied*, 455 U.S. 1007 (1982) (applying general principles of law) (leading continuous trigger case).

## *Notes and Questions*

1. In determining the insurer's liability for latent product-caused injuries, what are the strengths and weaknesses of the following three theories: (a) the exposure theory; (b) the manifestation theory; (c) the injury-in-fact or "triple trigger" theory? Which theory is most persuasive to you? Why?

2. The courts initially had to grapple with these latent mass tort injuries involving asbestos products. *See, e.g., Insurance Co. of N. Am. v. Forty-Eight Insulations*, 633 F.2d 1212 (6th Cir. 1980), *reh'g granted in part*, 657 F.2d 814 (6th Cir.), *cert. denied*, 454 U.S. 1109 (1981). But products liability mass tort litigation is by no means limited to asbestos-related injuries. Diethylstilbestrol (DES), a synthetic drug that for a quarter of a century was manufactured by numerous American pharmaceutical companies, was taken on prescription by millions of pregnant women to avoid spontaneous abortions and other disorders stemming from low levels of the estrogen hormone. It was discovered in 1971 that there was a linkage between DES and a number of maladies, including cancer. Thousands of lawsuits by daughters of DES mothers have been brought against various drug manufacturers and their insurers. In DES cases, the courts must often grapple with the "exposure," "manifestation," and "injury in fact" theories of insurer liability, as well as the meaning of the term "occurrence." *See, e.g., Kremers-Urban Co. v. American Employers Ins. Co.*, 119 Wis. 2d 722, 351 N.W.2d 156 (1984).

Outside of the realm of long-tail latent injuries such as asbestos and pollution, trigger analysis is less uncertain and generally more straight-forward, as in *Singsaas v. Diederich, supra*. However, construction defect claims can present an additional set of considerations. *See* Maniloff & Stempel, *supra*, Ch. 16. Emerging mass torts (or perhaps only large torts in relation to asbestos, the juggernaut all mass torts), may present similar trigger issues as well as a range of coverage questions because of the newness of the underlying claims. Examples are:

- *Climate Change Litigation. See, e.g.*, Travis S. Hunter, Comment, *Ambiguity in the Air: Why Judicial Interpretation of Insurance Policy Terms Should Force Insurance Companies to Pay for Global Warming Litigation*, 113 Penn St. L. Rev. 267 (2008); Jeffrey W. Stempel, *Insurance and Climate Change Litigation*, *in* Adjudicating Climate Change: Sub-National, National, and Supra-National Approaches (William C.G. Burns & Hari M. Osofsky eds., Cambridge 2009).

- *Chinese Drywall Home Damage Litigation. See, e.g.*, *Amerisure Ins. Co. v. Albanese Popkin the Oaks Dev. Group, L.P.*, 2010 U.S. Dist. LEXIS 125918 (S.D. Fla. Nov. 30, 2010) (adopting manifestation trigger rather than continuous trigger urged by policyholder); Jeff Casale, *Drywall cases hinge on exclusions*, Bus. Ins., Feb. 7, 2011, at 1 (discussing emergence of construction defect litigation related to installation of Chinese-manufactured drywall which emitted noxious fumes causing injury to homes and disturbing occupants); Lynne McCristian, *We Are Not the Maytag Man*, Fla. Underwriter, Nov. 2009, at 10 (insurance industry representative takes position that most Chinese drywall claims are merely sub-standard performance of policyholder work without requisite injury to property other than the policyholder's own work); [To the extent that the defective drywall injures parts of the home other than the drywall, we think she is wrong; although liability policies are not warranty or service agreements, they do respond if there is property damage to things other than the policyholder's own work.]; Thomas McKay II et al., *Chinese Drywall: Background, Scope and Insurance Coverage Implications—Part 2* (Nov. 2009), *available at* http://mondaq.com (outlining issues and likely insurer defenses to coverage). Regarding triggered property damage taking place prior to visibility, *see D.R. Sherry Constr., Ltd. v. Am. Family Mut. Ins. Co.*, 316 S.W.3d 899 (Mo. 2010) (CGL policy trigger by cracks in drywall prior to problems with home becoming apparent).

- *Claims of Sexual Abuse by Clergy. See, e.g.*, Peter Nash Swisher & Richard C. Mason, *Liability for Clergy Sexual Abuse Claims*, 17 Conn. Ins. L.J. 355 (2011).

### Illustrative Mass Torts

(a) *Dalkon Shield.* The Aetna Insurance Company agreed to a settlement with the A.H. Robins Company of approximately $70 million in addition to over $244 million that Aetna and Robins have already paid out in over 6,000 claims related to Robins' Dalkon Shield intrauterine device. Although sale of the Dalkon Shield was stopped in 1974 in the U.S., and worldwide in 1975, there are still thousands of pending cases against the Robins Company based on its allegedly defective product. Aetna, as Robins' primary products liability insurer, had been determining its liability coverage based on the "manifestation" theory. *See* Richmond Times-Dispatch, Nov. 2, 1984, at 1.

On August 21, 1985, after resolving 9,230 Dalkon Shield cases for over $378 million with another $107 million in legal fees and related expenses, but with over 5,000 cases still pending and another 8,000 cases estimated would be filed in the coming years, A. H. Robins Company filed a Chapter 11 bankruptcy petition in federal court, following a precedent set by the Manville Corporation in 1982 with asbestos-related litigation. *See Dalkon Shield Claimants' Comm. v. Aetna Cas. & Sur. Co. (In re A. H. Robins Co.)*, 88 B.R. 755 (E.D. Va. 1988).

In fact, there were more than 200,000 claims made against A.H. Robins, which ultimately set up two court-approved Dalkon Shield trust funds to partially compensate the injured plaintiffs. The larger trust would pay claimants $2.25 billion from A.H. Robins and American Home Products its successor corporation; $50 million from the Aetna Insurance Company in settlement of a class action lawsuit against Aetna; and $5 million from two Robins family members.

The smaller trust fund was supplemented by Aetna insurance policy coverages totaling $350 million for late-filed claims, future claims, or other claims not otherwise compensated by the trusts. This final reorganization plan was approved by 94.4 percent of the claimants, by 99.5 percent of Robins' stockholders, and by the unanimous consent of the major creditors. *In re A.H. Robins Co.*, 880 F.2d 779 (4th Cir. 1989). *See generally* Ronald Bacigal, Limits of Litigation: The Dalkon Shield Controversy (1990).

(b) *Agent Orange.* There also was a settlement of $180 million in the Agent Orange case, brought by about 15,000 Vietnam veterans and their families against seven chemical companies that manufactured Agent Orange, a dioxin-contaminated defoliant used in the Vietnam War. Insurance coverage litigation continued for years thereafter.

### The "Non-Cumulation" Clause

When multiple policies in consecutive policy years are triggered, the "noncumulation of liability" clause commonly found in general liability policies may act to limit the amount of policy proceeds available. *See, e.g., Liberty Mut. Ins. Co. v. Treesdale, Inc.*, 418 F.3d 330 (3d Cir. 2005) (applying Pennsylvania law) (limiting benefits under policy to limits of a single policy although asbestos-related claims spanned several policy years); *Hiraldo v. Allstate Ins. Co.*, 5 N.Y.3d 508, 840 N.E.2d 563 (2005) (limiting insurer's responsibility for lead poisoning claim under landlord's liability policy to one annual aggregate policy limit of $300,000 even though the injuries spanned three years). *But see Spaulding Composites Co. v. Aetna Cas. & Sur. Co.*, 176 N.J. 25, 819 A.2d 410 (2003) (refusing to give effect to noncumulation clause as respects multiyear asbestos and instead determining liability insurer's coverage responsibility according to pro-ration formula generally applied in all cases involving coverage under consecutive liability policies). *See* § 9.11 regarding coordination of coverage and allocation of responsibilities among insurers.

A typical noncumulation clause states

It is agreed that if any loss covered hereunder is also covered in whole or in party under any other excess policy issues to the Assured prior to the inception date hereof the limits of liability hereon ... shall be reduced by any amounts due to the Assured on account of such loss under such prior insurance.[4]

The non-cumulation clause at issue in *Hiraldo v. Allstate*, provides that "[r]egardless of the number of ... policies involved" the insurer's maximum responsibility "resulting from one loss will not exceed the limit of liability" stated on the policy's declarations sheet.

Noncumulation provisions typically also include a "batching" clause that provides that all injuries resulting from one accident or "continuous or repeated exposure to the same general conditions" shall be considered to be a single loss. In *Hiraldo*, only one policy out of three issued by Allstate to a landlord was obligated to provide coverage for an underlying claim for bodily injury caused by residential exposure to lead paint. Each policy was subject to a $300,000 limit of liability and the underlying plaintiffs obtained judgments totaling approximately $700,000. Said the Court:

> If each of the successive policies had been written by a different insurance company, presumably each insurer would be liable up to the limits of its policy. Why should plaintiffs recover less money because the same insurer wrote them all? Some courts have held that successive policy limits may be cumulatively applied to a single loss, where the policies do not clearly provide otherwise. But here, the policies do clearly provide otherwise. The non-cumulation clause says that "regardless of the number of ... policies involved, [Allstate's] total liability under Business Liability Protection coverage for damages resulting from one loss will not exceed the limit of liability ... shown on the declarations page." That limit is $300,000, and thus Allstate is liable for no more.

840 N.E.2d at 564 (citations omitted).

If the policy limits vary during consecutive years on which a single triggered liability insurer is on the risk, the policy year with the highest policy limits would presumably be the one invoked by a court. One commentator has described the non-cumulation cause as another form of "other insurance" clause that may require co-ordination of benefits but does not necessarily cap the insurer's liability, particularly when consecutive policy periods are triggered and implicated. *See* Christopher C. French, *The "Non-Cumulation Clause"; An "Other Insurance" Clause by Another Name*, 60 U. KAN. L. REV. 375 (2011–12) (courts should treat non-cumulation clauses as they do other insurance clauses with sufficient regard for doctrines such as contra proferentem and policyholder reasonable expectations). *See, e.g., First United Methodist Church of Stillwater, Inc. v. Philadelphia Indemnity Insurance Co.*, 423 P.3d 29 (Okla Ct. Civ. App. 2016) (non-cumulation clause ambiguous in context of dispute and would be construed against insurer).

One emerging important aspect of a non-cumulation clause is that some courts have viewed the clause as inconsistent with pro-rating insurer responsibility for

---

4. *See, e.g., Stonewall Ins. Co. v. E.I. du Pon de Nemours & Co.*, 996 A.2d 1254, 1259 (Del. 2010).

long-tail torts across multiple policy years. *See, e.g., In re Viking Pump, Inc. & Warren Pumps LLC*, 52 N.E.3d 1144 (N.Y. 2016). Thus, what otherwise might be a case where a court would impose pro-ration by time on the risk and perhaps policy limits as well, the presence of a non-cum clause may be viewed as a contractual agreement altering whatever default rule of pro-ration would otherwise prevail in the jurisdiction.

### Multi-Year and "Stub" Policies

A related issue concerning trigger and available coverage is the problem of whether policy limits in a multi-year policy (liability policies are often sold on a three-year basis to commercial policyholders) are annual limits or limits applicable to the entire time period of the policy. For example, if a policy covering 2007–2009 has a stated aggregate limit of $6 million, what happens if the policyholder is hit with judgments of $4 million in 2007, $3 million in 2008, and $4 million in 2009? Does the policy provide coverage for all of this liability or only $6 million of the liability? Although the case law is mixed and depends to some degree of course on the wording of the policy's Declarations Page and its clarity, the industry norm is one of annualized limits unless the policy language and understanding of the parties is clearly to the contrary. *See Union Carbide Corp. v. Affiliated FM Ins. Co.*, 947 N.E.2d 111 (N.Y. 2011).

And related to this is the issue of so-called "stub" policies where insurance is in effect for a year or period of years but also contains an extension, often the result of a planned change in coverage. In the example above, there might be a policy covering 2007–2009 and covering January and February of 2010. If the policyholder is hit with a claim applicable to February 2010, does the policyholder have $6 million of coverage carrying over from 2009 (assuming that the limits are annualized), meaning $2 million with what's left of the 2009 limits — or does the policyholder have an additional $5 million of coverage for occurrences taking place and causing injury during January–February of 2010? Or is the correct figure $1 million (one-sixth of the annual $6 million limits). *See Union Carbide v. Affiliated FM, supra* (remanding case to trial court for fact-finding on the issue).

As a general rule, absent clear policy language and party understanding to the contrary, stub policy limits should be the same as a new set of annualized limits. This probably seems counter-intuitive at first glance. It may even seem like a windfall for the policyholder to receive a full year's policy limit while paying only a two-month premium. But by the same token, the liability insurer is on the risk for only two months, not the full year it would be with an annual policy — so there is proportionality between premium and protection. In addition, the purpose of the liability policy is to protect the policyholder to the level anticipated when a policy is purchased. If the intended risk management decision is to have $6 million of coverage in place in case of serious injury to a third party, this level of protection should be in place throughout the year. The nature of fortuity and risk is that one never knows whether a tort-spawning incident will take place in January, February, July, or December. Pro-rating policy limits thus defeats the insuring intent and purpose and makes for ineffective risk management.

# § 9.11. Coordination of Coverage and Allocation of Insurance Proceeds

Under the basic principles of insurance law previously discussed, it would violate public policy to permit a policyholder to profit from an insured loss. Over-indemnification is to be avoided, even if there is enough insurance in force to pay for the over-indemnification. When two or more insurance policies are triggered by a claim and apply to the claim or loss, there policies must be coordinated and the respective policy proceeds allocated as between the insurers.

Where the claim or loss involves only a single policy period, there are several accepted means of allocation, all largely driven by "other insurance" clauses found in most insurance policies. Other insurance clauses tend to come in three flavors:

(1) an "escape" clause that provides that if other insurance applies, the instant insurance is not applicable and the insurer "escapes" from its insuring agreement.

(2) an "excess" clause that provides that if other insurance applies, the instant insurance operates as excess insurance and is only payable after the other "primary" insurance is exhausted.

(3) a "pro-rata" clause that apportions applicable insurance coverage according to their relative policy limits.

*See* STEMPEL & KNUTSEN § 13.02 (also noting presence of "excess pro rata" and "excess-escape" hybrid clauses).

When two applicable policy periods each have pro-rata coordination clauses, a court can apply and give complete effect to both policy provisions. Problems arise, however, when the coordination clauses of different policies are in conflict. In such situations, courts tend to take one of three quite different approaches:

(1) "Clause-matching," in which the court juxtaposes the different policy terms and determines which term takes precedence. Most courts engaging in this textualist sport for avoiding coverage (typically the goal of both insurers with the different coordination clauses) find that an "escape" clause trumps an "excess" clause which trumps a "pro-rata" clause. Clause-matching has more than a few problems. First, the different insurers are hardly contracting with one another, which undermines the premise that great deference should be given to policy language against another insurer that did not purchase the policy language at issue (although the insurer with the clause providing reduced coverage does have a decent argument that the text defines the scope of the insurance product, e.g., a policy with an escape clause is designed to provide less coverage than a policy with an excess clause and so on). Second, this method tends to reward the insurer with the most stingy policy language, even if this disappoints the reasonable expectations of the policyholder and is inconsistent with the context of the contract generally. For example, each insurer may have charged similar premiums for similar risk, which makes it arguably unfair to allow one insurer a windfall of providing no coverage (and pocketing the premium) simply because the policyholder had other insurance.

(2) Pro-ration when faced with conflict. Under this approach, if the "other insurance" clauses of different applicable policies are in conflict, the court simply imposes pro-ration by operation of law and pro-rates coverage according to the applicable policy limits of the different policies. This methodology, generally associated with the Oregon Supreme Court case *Lamb-Weston, Inc. v. Oregon Auto. Ins. Co.*, 219 Or. 110, 341 P.2d 110 (1959), has been both praised and criticized. Supporters of the approach like its functional approach and tendency to spread the insurance coverage burdens, which is seen as consistent with the risk-spreading aspect of insurance generally. *See* Stempel on Insurance Contracts § 13.03, at 13-8 & 13-9. Critics view the approach as insufficiently faithful to contract text and the judicial equivalent of "splitting the baby" or compromising without regard to the relative strength of competing legal arguments, a "lazy way" of insurance coordination. *See* Appleman (Second) On Insurance § 4906, at 344.

(3) Imposing primary insurance responsibility on the insurance policy that is "closest to the risk," with other policies operating as excess insurance in accordance with their respective closeness to the risk in question. *See, e.g., Auto Owners Ins. Co. v. Northstar Mut. Ins. Co.*, 281 N.W.2d 700 (Minn. 1979); *Integrity Mut. Ins. Co. v. State Auto. & Casualty Underwriters Ins. Co.*, 239 N.W.2d 445, 447 (Minn. 1976). Although strong textualists tend to criticize this approach, it has been praised by many, particularly law professors, for reflecting economic reality better than either clause-matching or pro-ration by fiat. *See, e.g.,* STEMPEL & KNUTSEN § 13.03; Susan Randall, *Coordinating Liability Insurance*, 1995 Wis. L. Rev. 1339. *See also Illinois Nat'l Ins. Co. v. Farm Bureau Mut. Ins. Co.*, 578 N.W.2d 670 (Iowa 1998) (rejecting closest to the risk approach not on substantive grounds but because pro-ration is simpler and easier to apply and conserves judicial resources). In addition, courts may determine the policy closest to the risk not so much through a functional analysis of the relative primacy of the multiple insurance policies but according to particular criteria such as the age of a policy or whether the claimant is a "named insured" under one policy but merely an "insured" under other policies. *See* ROBERT H. JERRY, II & DOUGLAS R. RICHMOND, UNDERSTANDING INSURANCE LAW § 97[d] (6th ed. 2018).

(4) There is also the issue of how to pro-rate applicable coverage. Should each insurer bear an equal share? Should the percentage of coverage responsibility be based on the policy limits? On the premiums received by the respective insurers? Courts have used all three methods, with "equal shares" pro-ration and "pro-ration by limits" being most popular. *See* Robert H. Jerry, II & Douglas R. Richmond, Understanding Insurance Law § 97[e] (4th ed. 2007); STEMPEL & KNUTSEN § 13.03. *See, e.g., Allstate Ins. Co. v. Chicago Ins. Co.*, 676 So. 2d 271 (Miss. 1996); *Lamb-Weston, supra.* Pro-ration by premiums is a minority view that appears to have lost judicial support during the latter 20th century for reasons that are not altogether clear. *See, e.g., Insurance Co. of Texas v. Employers Liability Assurance Corp.*, 163 F. Supp. 143 (S.D. Cal. 1958) (one of the more "recent" cases using this approach). Pro-ration by premiums seems to make at least as much sense as pro-ration by one of the other methods, arguably more sense in that the insurers are required to pay in proportion to their profits.

## Interstate Fire & Casualty Company v. Auto-Owners Insurance Company

Supreme Court of Minnesota

433 N.W.2d 82 (1988)

Yetka, J.

The dispute in this case is between two insurance companies as to which one is the primary insurer responsible to pay damages to Kenneth DeCent. DeCent, a student at a public high school, was injured during a physical education class taught by David Trefethen and assisted by Jim Leitch, a high school senior. The school district had general liability insurance with Continental Insurance Company and umbrella liability insurance with respondent, Interstate Fire & Casualty Company.

The injured plaintiff, Kenneth DeCent, settled for the Continental policy limits of $500,000 and an additional $310,863 paid by Interstate. Leitch was covered also by his father's homeowners liability policy written by appellant, Auto-Owners Insurance Company. Interstate claims reimbursement from Auto-Owners for the $310,863 it paid towards the settlement.

The trial court found for Auto-Owners, holding that Interstate should pay as it was "closest to the risk." The court of appeals reversed and found that Auto-Owners had the primary liability and should thus reimburse Interstate. We reverse the court of appeals and reinstate the grant of summary judgment for Auto-Owners awarded by the trial court.

The facts of this case are basically undisputed. On March 28, 1977, Kenneth DeCent, a junior high school student, was injured in an accident occurring on school property during a physical education class. The accident occurred while DeCent was awaiting his turn to wrestle. DeCent picked up a basketball and began bouncing it against the wall. The ball got loose and both Leitch—the student supervisor—and DeCent went to recover it. In order to prevent DeCent from reaching the ball, Leitch grabbed him around the waist and lifted him off the ground. Leitch then either fell or dropped De-Cent on his head, breaking DeCent's neck. DeCent is now a quadriplegic.

DeCent's parents brought suit against the school, various administrators and teachers at the school, and Jim Leitch. The DeCents settled all claims against named defendants for $810,863. The school's primary insurance carrier, Continental Insurance Company, paid $500,000, and Interstate, the school's secondary insurer, paid the remaining $310,863.

Interstate brought this suit seeking reimbursement from Auto-Owners for the $310,863 settlement paid to Kenneth DeCent. Auto-Owners insured Jim Leitch, the student supervisor, under his father's homeowners insurance. The policy provides [liability coverage and that if there is other applicable insurance, the policy will pay a pro-rata share of liability up to policy limits.]

The Interstate policy was an umbrella policy with a limit of $1,000,000. It contained the following "excess" insurance provision:

OTHER INSURANCE: If other valid and collectible insurance with any other insurer is available to the insured covering a loss also covered by this policy, (other than insurance that is specifically in excess of the insurance afforded by this policy) the insurance afforded by this policy shall be in excess of and shall not contribute with such other insurance. Nothing herein shall be construed to make this policy subject to the terms, conditions and limitations of other insurance.

Auto-Owners moved for summary judgment on the grounds that either Interstate's policy came before Auto-Owners' policy in the order of priority of payment or Auto-Owners did not cover Leitch in this situation because he was engaged in a "business pursuit." Interstate filed a cross-motion for summary judgment, arguing that it was entitled to reimbursement from Auto-Owners because its policy was secondary to Auto-Owners'.

The trial court granted appellant's motion for summary judgment, finding that Interstate's policy was "closest to the risk" and that Leitch was engaged in a business pursuit so that he was not covered under the Auto-Owners policy. Interstate appealed. The court of appeals reversed, finding that Leitch was not engaged in a business pursuit at the time of the accident so the Auto-Owners policy did cover him. It also found that the two insurance policies operated on different levels. Auto-Owners' policy was primary and Interstate's was an umbrella policy designed only to cover any excess loss after the primary insurer had paid....

The heart of this dispute is the interpretation of the respective other insurance clauses. Auto-Owners' policy contains a "pro rata" clause to govern other insurance. It provides that if there is other valid and collectible insurance, Auto-Owners will pay only its pro rata share of the loss in the proportion that the limit of its policy bears to the aggregate limits of all valid and collectible insurance or in equal shares if the other policies so provide. Interstate's policy contains an "excess" clause to govern other insurance. It provides that its liability is limited to the amount by which the loss exceeds the coverage provided by other valid and collectible insurance.

The threshold question in this appeal is whether a pro rata and an excess clause conflict. Appellant argues that they do; consequently, the court must determine which policy is "closest to the risk." Respondent argues that the two clauses can be reconciled so that the "closest-to-the-risk" analysis is unnecessary.

Minnesota has taken a different approach than the majority of jurisdictions in deciding whether excess and pro rata clauses conflict. The majority position reconciles the two clauses by interpreting the policy containing the excess clause as secondary coverage where there is another policy covering the same risk. The courts reason that, where an excess clause is inserted in a liability insurance policy, the usual intent of the insurer is to provide only secondary coverage. On the other hand, a pro rata clause "is intended to become effective only when other valid and effective *primary* insurance is available."

In this case, the trial court found that the two clauses did conflict and Interstate's policy was "closest to the risk." In reversing the granting of summary judgment, the court of appeals did not apply the "closest-to-the-risk" test because it did not find a conflict between the two clauses. The court adopted the reasoning of ... that, in the pro rata clause, other valid and collectible insurance refers only to *primary* insurance. Since Interstate's coverage was only secondary, Auto-Owners' pro rata provision did not apply to it; consequently, Auto-Owners was not entitled to summary judgment....

In Minnesota, this court does not simply look at the type of "other insurance" clauses involved. In *Integrity Mutual Insurance v. State Automobile & Casualty Underwriters Insurance Co.*, 307 Minn. 173, 175, 239 N.W.2d 445, 446 (1976), this court explained that the better approach was to "allocate respective policy coverages in light of the total policy insuring intent, as determined by the primary risks upon which each policy's premiums were based and as determined by the primary function of each policy." In *Integrity*, this court found that an excess clause and a pro rata clause do conflict.

Appellant argues that, because this court found that an excess and a pro rata clause conflict in *Integrity*, the court must employ the "closest-to-the-risk" analysis in this case. Auto-Owners lists three factors that the court set out in considering which policy is "closest to the risk:"

(1) Which policy specifically described the accident-causing instrumentality?

(2) Which premium is reflective of the greater contemplated exposure?

(3) Does one policy contemplate the risk and use of the accident-causing instrumentality with greater specificity than the other policy—that is, is the coverage of the risk primary in one policy and incidental to the other?

While the underlying carrier is said to be primary and the umbrella carrier is said to be excess, this is not the same relationship as between two carriers in the usual primary-excess situation, where one insurer is primary because "closest to the risk," thereby leaving the other insurer as excess.

Here, Interstate designed its coverage to be secondary to Continental's, the underlying carrier. The policy specifically so provides. Continental, however, is not contesting its coverage; it has already paid up to its limits. The relationship between Interstate's and Auto-Owners' coverage is not as specifically defined. Interstate's policy does not name Auto-Owners as an underlying insurer. Because Interstate and Auto-Owners do not stand in relationship to each other as umbrella carrier and underlying carrier as in *Jostens*, [*Inc. v. Mission Insurance Co.*, 387 N.W.2d 161 (Minn. 1986),] further analysis is necessary.

It appears to us that, in this case, rather than applying the three-part "closest-to-the-risk" test, it is more helpful to use the broader approach set out in *Integrity* of allocating respective policy coverages in light of the total policy insuring intent, as determined by the primary policy risks and the primary function of each policy....

[T]he umbrella carrier, contracted with the school district to provide coverage in excess of the underlying insurance provided by Continental, the primary carrier.

While it is true that Interstate relied on Continental's primary coverage in setting its premium, Interstate was not further relying on each student having a family homeowners policy when it calculated its risk in insuring the school district. The umbrella policy contemplated coverage for accidents and injuries sustained on school property during school events. This injury caused by a student supervisor during a physical education class is precisely the type of risk Interstate intended to cover in providing catastrophic insurance to the school district. To hold that Auto-Owners is the primary insurer for this accident would be to ignore the intent of the respective policies.

## *Notes and Questions*

Sometimes, the other insurance clauses of a policy will arguably come into conflict with policy terms different than another policy's other insurance clause. *See, e.g., State Auto Prop. & Cas. Ins. Co. v. Springfield Fire & Cas. Co.*, 916 N.E.2d 157 (Ill. Ct. App. 2009). In that case, an insurer selected to defend a claim pursuant to the Illinois rule that a policyholder may engage in "targeted tender" and submit a claim to only one of several triggered insurers. The target insurer attempted to require another triggered insurer to pay first pursuant to the target insurer's "excess" style other insurance clause but the court refused, holding that a policy's other insurance clause does not supersede a policyholder's right to "deselect" coverage and direct the claim at a single insurer. Regarding the target tender option in Illinois, see *John Burns Constr. Co. v. Indiana Ins. Co.*, 727 N.E.2d 211 (Ill. 2000).

As noted above, the problem of "other insurance" clauses generally applies to a single policy period. The advent of long-tail, multi-year claims against policyholders from the 1970s forward created a new type of coordination problem of "consecutive" allocation of triggered policies. *See* MANILOFF & STEMPEL, Ch. 18 (Chapter authored by Shane R. Heskin).

In essence, as addressed in the *Con Ed. v. Allstate* and *Goodyear v. Aetna* cases below, courts have tended either to require pro-ration of coverage among trigger insurance policies (the pro-rata or apportionment approach) or have permitted policyholders to access all triggered policies to the full policy limits (the "all sums" or "joint & several" approach). Calling the all sums approach a joint & several liability approach is a misnomer because those coverage cases do not provide insurer liability without regard to "fault" or contractual obligation but in fact insist only on requiring a trigger insurer's policy limits to be fully available rather than potentially reduce availability to the policyholder through pro-ration.

The jurisdictions are quite divided, with roughly nine states (e.g., California, Illinois, Montana, Ohio, Oregon (by statute), Pennsylvania, Washington, West Virginia, Wisconsin) adopting the "all sums" or vertical method in which the policyholder may completely draw trigger insurance up to the policy limits available for a given policy or "tower" of insurance coverage that includes excess and umbrella liability insurance sitting atop its primary insurance (*see* the chapter regarding excess and umbrella insurance). Another 16 states (e.g., Colorado, Connecticut, Georgia, Kansas, Kentucky, Louisiana, Maryland, Massachusetts, Minnesota, probably Missouri, Nebraska, New

Hampshire, New Jersey, New York, Utah, Vermont) apply some form of pro-ration to allocate insurer responsibility in cases of consecutively triggered policy years.

In addition to *Con Ed. v. Allstate* and *Goodyear v. Aetna*, reproduced below, important illustrative cases in this area *Boston Gas Co. 1 v. Century Indem. Co.*, 910 N.E.2d 290 (Mass. 2009) (pro-rating consecutively triggered insurer liability by time on the risk; policyholder responsible for any period of no insurance after temporal apportionment applied); *Plastics Eng'g Co. v. Liberty Mut. Ins. Co.*, 759 N.W.2d 613 (Wis. 2009) (each triggered liability insurer responsible for paying full policy limits if covered claims equal or exceed that amount).

Despite the decades of asbestos and pollution coverage litigation, almost 20 states (e.g., Alabama, Alaska, Arizona, Arkansas, Florida, Idaho, Iowa, Maine, Michigan, Nevada, New Mexico, North Carolina, North Dakota, Oklahoma, South Carolina, South Dakota, Tennessee, Virginia, Wyoming) continue to have little or no instructive authority on the question while the approach of some states (e.g., Delaware, Hawaii, Indiana) is a matter of disagreement among observers. *See* Maniloff & Stempel, Ch. 18. *See also CPC Int'l v. Northbrook Excess & Surplus Ins. Co.*, 668 A.2d 647, 649 (R.I. 1995) (adopting manifestation trigger for latent injury claims, which largely obviates the need for any apportionment, creating an all sums approach but one confined to a single policy period).

Among pro-rata jurisdictions, there are several methods of allocating insurer responsibility, including the "apportioned share setoff," the "pro tanto method," "horizontal exhaustion," and various hybrids. *See* Maniloff & Stempel, Ch. 18.

A key early decision in the insurance coverage wars over asbestos liability was *Keene Corp. v. Insurance Co. of N. Am.*, 667 F.2d 1034 (D.C. Cir. 1981), *cert. denied*, 455 U.S. 1007 (1982). *Keene* adopted a multiple or continuous trigger and permitted the policyholder to determine how to assign claims to several triggered policies, permitting the policyholder to maximize coverage. However, the policyholder was restricted to one policy per assigned claim and could not "spill over" to another triggered policy. The *Keene* court seemed not to see anything different about consecutive policy periods and concurrent policy coordination, at least that is the seeming presumption in the opinion that use of the respective policies "other insurance" clauses could readily resolve allocation issues. How was *Keene* able to accomplish this? Or is the *Keene* approach not apt for the multi-year liability claims situation?

*Keene* has been referred to as a "joint-and-several-liability" approach and is also known as a "pick-and-choose" approach or a "pick-and-spike" approach because it allows the policyholder to engage in "vertical" allocation by assigning particular claims and coverage responsibilities to a particular policy year (as opposed to requiring a "horizontal" allocation of insurer responsibilities across a number of policy years). This of course was a rather favorable allocation system for policyholders, one that caused complaint among insurers, who referred to this as "joint-and-several" liability that was unfair to the insurers. The *Keene* approach has been successfully challenged by insurers during the intervening two decades. Is the *Keene* approach to allocation too favorable to policyholders? Why or why not?

It has been suggested that methods of allocation follow the court's chosen method of trigger. *Keene* adopted a multiple or continuous approach to trigger. Does it necessarily follow that once having adopted this type of trigger methodology, the *Keene* court was logically required to allow the policyholder to avoid allocation and select a given policy to respond to a given claim?

The policyholder's victory in the *Keene* case elevated its lawyer, the late Eugene R. Anderson, to national prominence. Ironically, *Keene* was the first major insurance case for Anderson, whose practice had previously centered on commercial and tax litigation. *Keene* literally changed Anderson's career and practice and he then specialized in insurance coverage litigation on behalf of policyholders, becoming one of the "deans" of the insurance bar. *See* Eugene R. Anderson, *A "Keene" Story*, 2 Nev. L.J. 489 (2002) (appearing in the *Law Journal* Symposium on "Favorite Insurance Cases") (relating Anderson's account of the *Keene* litigation and noting that prior to *Keene*, Anderson "had wanted to be a tax lawyer" and obtained an LL.M in taxation from NYU).

Among key cases rejecting the *Keene* approach and requiring pro-ration of insurer responsibility in multi-year tort claims were *Northern States Power Co. v. Fidelity & Cas. Co.*, 523 N.W.2d 657 (Minn. 1994); *Owens-Illinois v. United Ins. Co.*, 138 N.J. 437, 650 A.2d 974 (1994); and *Stonewall Ins. Co. v. Asbestos Claims Mgmt. Corp.*, 73 F.3d 1178 (2d Cir. 1995). These mid-1990s decisions appeared to give momentum to the view that pro-ration by time on the risk was preferable to policyholder-directed allocation. But the states remain roughly evenly divided on this issue, as illustrated by the two cases excerpted below. Although temporal pro-ration has been in something of a period of ascendency, there are significant decisions to the contrary from important jurisdictions and the courts continue to diverge on the issue.

## Consolidated Edison Company of New York, Inc. v. Allstate Insurance Company

Court of Appeals of New York
98 N.Y.2d 208, 746 N.Y.S.2d 622, 774 N.E.2d 687 (2002)

**Kaye, Chief Judge.**

Central to this appeal by an insured against its insurers [is] how any liability should be allocated. This case presents something of a time capsule in that nineteenth century technology polluting twentieth century properties will have significant twenty-first century financial ramifications.

For approximately 60 years—from 1873 to 1933—Consolidated Edison's corporate predecessors owned and operated a manufactured gas plant in Tarrytown, New York. The site was later sold to Anchor Motor Freight, Inc. In 1995, Anchor notified Con Edison that, during an investigation it was conducting pursuant to Department of Environmental Conservation (DEC) requirements, it discovered contamination at the site. Anchor alleged that the manufactured gas plant caused the contamination and demanded that Con Edison participate in the investigation and remediation.

After its own investigation, Con Edison entered into an agreement with the DEC to clean up the site, and commenced this declaratory judgment action against 24 insurers that had issued it general liability policies between 1936 and 1986, demanding defense and indemnification for environmental damages arising from the contamination caused by the Tarrytown plant. The policies that were the subject of the complaint were issued in layers, and provided for a self-insured retention in the amount of $100,000 per year from 1936 to 1961, and $500,000 per year from 1961 to 1986. Con Edison's total coverage in excess of the retention ranged between $2 million and $49.5 million during each of the relevant years.

Defendant Travelers Indemnity Company, which provided coverage for liability in excess of $20 million from 1964 to 1970, moved for dismissal on the ground that, as to it, the claim was nonjusticiable. Travelers argued that where there is both continuous, progressive property damage and successive insurance, liability should be allocated pro rata among the insurers. Applying a pro rata allocation to damage estimates most favorable to Con Edison, Travelers contended that its excess insurance policies would not be reached in any given policy year. Nineteen other defendants cross-moved to dismiss the complaint against them on the same ground. In response, Con Edison argued against pro rata allocation, asserting that it should be permitted to allocate all liability to any defendant for any one year it elects within the coverage period.

The [trial] court ruled that only for the purposes of determining the motion to dismiss, it would prorate the damages and dismiss all policies that would not be reached by that method. The court took the highest projection of damages by Con Edison's expert ($51 million), divided by the number of years named in the complaint (50), and thus determined that policies that attach at levels above $1.1 million were nonjusticiable because they would not be reached even if Con Edison prevailed at trial. As the court stated:

> Here, we have policies from 24 insurers that can be called upon to answer for the claim, all of which are overlapping. The damages cannot be attributed to any specific year or years because there is no documentation nor are there any witnesses that address specific discharges. What is known is that the damages for later years is less than earlier years, because the amount of pollution has diminished over time. Under the circumstances... it would be inequitable to put the parties to the expense of trying claims under excess policies issued in later years, when those policies would not be reached if pro rata allocation is applied.

The court added, "this necessarily is not the formula I will use at trial since both the plaintiff and defendants should have an opportunity to explore the issue of allocation to the plaintiff based upon a complete record and then the formula can be modified to conform to the proof." Con Edison appealed from that order.

The jury found that there was property damage at the site during the years that the three defendants' policies were in effect, but that the property damage was not the result of an "accident" or "occurrence," and thus there was no coverage. Con Edison appealed, arguing that the court erred in assigning it the burden of establishing that the property damage was the result of an "accident" or "occurrence." We now affirm

Generally, it is for the insured to establish coverage and for the insurer to prove that an exclusion in the policy applies to defeat coverage

We next consider whether the Trial Court properly prorated the estimated prospective damages for purposes of the motion to dismiss.

Where, as here, an alleged continuous harm spans many years and thus implicates several successive insurance policies, courts have split as to whether each policy is liable for the entire loss, or whether each policy is responsible only for a portion of the loss. This is a matter of first impression for this Court, though Federal courts have predicted New York's answer. In determining a dispute over insurance coverage, we first look to the language of the policy. We construe the policy in a way that "affords a fair meaning to all of the language employed by the parties in the contract and leaves no provision without force or effect".

Here, the dispute centers on two policy terms: "all sums" and "during the policy period." In the words of a representative Travelers policy:

"1. Coverage

"To indemnify the insured for all sums which the insured shall be obligated to pay by reason of the liability

"(a) imposed upon the insured by law, or

"(b) assumed by the insured ...,

"for damages, direct or consequential, and expenses, all as more fully defined by the term ultimate net loss, on account of * * * property damage, caused by or arising out of each occurrence.

"3. Policy Period:

"This policy applies only to 'occurrences' as defined herein, happening during the policy period.

"Definitions

"4. Occurrence

"The term 'Occurrence' wherever used herein, shall mean an event, or continuous or repeated exposure to conditions, which causes injury, damage or destruction during the policy period. All such exposure to or events resulting from substantially the same general conditions *during the policy period* shall be deemed one occurrence" [emphasis supplied].

Con Edison urges that it should be permitted to collect its total liability—"all sums"—under any policy in effect during the 50 years that the property damage occurred, up to that policy's limit. In a subsequent action, the indemnifying insurer could then seek contribution from the other insurers who also provided coverage during the relevant period. This is referred to as "joint and several allocation," by analogy to joint and several tort liability.

The insurers, by contrast, argue that a straightforward reading of the phrase "during the policy period" limits an insurer's liability to "all sums" incurred by the insured "during the policy period." Under this reading, referred to as "pro-rata allocation," the liability is spread among the policies....

While Con Edison points to precedents of this Court in support of its position, the cases do not in fact support joint and several allocation. In *York-Buffalo Motor Express, Inc. v National Fire & Marine Ins. Co.* (294 NY 467, 63 N.E.2d 61 [1945]), where two insurers provided concurrent coverage for a car accident, we allowed the insured to recover the whole amount from either insurer. The present case, however, involves multiple successive insurers and a continuous harm. In *Continental Cas. Co. v Rapid-American Corp.* (80 N.Y.2d 640, 593 N.Y.S.2d 966, 609 N.E.2d 506 [1993]), we addressed whether defense costs should be allocated among several policy periods, as well as periods of self-insurance. After noting that the duty to defend is broader than the duty to indemnify, we held that "pro rata sharing of defense costs may be ordered, but we perceive no error or unfairness in declining to order such sharing, with the understanding that the insurer may later obtain contribution from other applicable policies". We left open the issue whether indemnification should be prorated among the applicable policies.

Con Ed maintains that pro rata allocation among the insurers would only be appropriate if the policies contained "other insurance" clauses providing for such allocation. This argument mistakes the function of "other insurance" clauses. Such clauses apply when two or more policies provide coverage during the same period, and they serve to prevent multiple recoveries from such policies. Here, by contrast, the issue was whether any coverage potentially existed at all among certain high-level policies that were in force during successive years. "Other insurance" clauses have nothing to do with this determination.

Joint and several allocation in the present factual setting is inconsistent with the unambiguous language of the policies before us. Con Edison concedes that it is impossible to determine the extent of the property damage that is the result of an occurrence in a particular policy period. Indeed, its theory of the case was that while the plant was in operation—long before any of the policies were issued—there were leaks, spills and drips that eventually migrated to the groundwater. Con Edison planned to establish that the dispersion of the pollutants was a gradual, continuous process, thus creating an inference that there was an accident or occurrence during each and every policy period, though there is no evidence of an accident during any particular policy period.

Con Edison wants to combine this uncertainty-based approach, which implicates many successive policies, with an entitlement to choose a particular policy for indemnity. Yet collecting all the indemnity from a particular policy pre-supposes ability to pin an accident to a particular policy period.... Although more than one policy may be implicated by a gradual harm..., joint and several allocation is not consistent with the language of the policies providing indemnification for "all sums" of liability that resulted from an accident or occurrence "during the policy period".

Pro rata allocation under these facts, while not explicitly mandated by the policies, is consistent with the language of the policies. Most fundamentally, the policies provide indemnification for liability incurred as a result of an accident or occurrence during the policy period, not outside that period.... Con Edison's singular focus on "all sums" would read this important qualification out of the policies. Proration of liability among the insurers acknowledges the fact that there is uncertainty as to what actually transpired during any particular policy period....

We recognize ... that there are different ways to prorate liability among successive policies. Here, the court prorated liability based on the amount of time the policy was in effect in comparison to the overall duration of the damage. [T]he New Jersey Supreme Court contemplated proration by multiplying the number of years the insurer provided coverage by the limits of the policies, and held that each insurer would be liable for that portion of the liability corresponding to the ratio of the total coverage provided by that insurer to the total coverage provided by all the policies in effect. Other courts have prorated coverage based on the proportion of injuries suffered during relevant policy periods. Courts also differ on how to treat self-insured retentions, periods of no insurance, periods where no insurance is available and settled policies under various allocation methods.

Here, [the trial court applied] "time on the risk" and thus dismissed claims against policies that would not be reached under Con Edison's highest estimate of damages. That was not error. We note, however, that this conclusion does not foreclose pro rata allocation among insurers by other methods either in determining justiciability or at the damages stage of a trial. Clearly this is not the last word on proration.

Finally, Con Edison asserts that the Trial Court's proration of damages deprived it of the benefits of valuable premium payments over many years. However, the proration ruling dismissed only certain high-level insurers—Con Edison did get to try its claims to a jury, albeit unsuccessfully, against three of the insurers who provided coverage for 34 years. And even applying pro rata allocation, had Con Edison succeeded in persuading the jury of the merits of its position, it might well have been entitled to recover under policies issued from 1936 to 1961, when the self-insured retention was $100,000. In the end, the result is dictated not by the pro rata allocation, but by Con Edison's inability to convince the jury that the property damage was the result of an "accident" or "occurrence" as required by its insurance policies.

# Goodyear Tire & Rubber Company v.
# Aetna Casualty & Surety Company

Supreme Court of Ohio
95 Ohio St. 3d 512, 2002 Ohio 2842 (2002)

**Francis E. Sweeney, Sr., J.**

In 1993, appellants, Goodyear Tire & Rubber Company and others (collectively "Goodyear"), filed this action against appellees Aetna Casualty & Surety Company and several other insurance companies (collectively the "insurers") seeking declaratory judgments concerning insurance claims for pollution cleanup costs at twenty-two sites. Numerous claims, defendants, and specific insurance policies were disposed of through pretrial motions. The remaining parties agreed to limit the evidence in this case to claims relating to two waste disposal sites. Those sites are the Motor Wheel Site in Lansing, Michigan, and the Army Creek Landfill in New Castle, Delaware.

After Goodyear had presented its case at trial, the insurers moved for directed verdicts on various grounds. The trial court granted the directed verdicts to all defendants without providing a specific basis for its decision. The court of appeals reversed the trial court on a number of the motions for directed verdicts. No appeal has been taken from these reversals. The appellate court affirmed the trial court on the remaining motions for directed verdict. Goodyear asserts that this was error. The consolidated cases are now before this court pursuant to the allowance of discretionary appeals....

## II. *Allocation*

In determining whether the directed verdicts were properly granted, we must first decide whether the lower courts erred in the method used to allocate insurance coverage among the multiple insurers. Allocation deals with the apportionment of a covered loss across multiple triggered insurance policies.... The issue of allocation arises in situations involving long-term injury or damage, such as environmental cleanup claims where it is difficult to determine which insurer must bear the loss.

The parties are in agreement as to which primary insurance policies have been called into play, and there is no dispute that there was continuous pollution across multiple policy periods that gave rise to occurrences and claims to which these policies apply. However, they disagree as to the appropriate method for distributing losses across the triggered policies.

There are two accepted methods for allocating coverage. One approach, favored by Goodyear, permits the policyholder to seek coverage from any policy in effect during the time period of injury or damage. This "all sums" approach allows Goodyear to seek full coverage for its claims from any single policy, up to that policy's coverage limits, out of the group of policies that has been triggered. In contrast, the insurers urge us to apply the pro rata allocation scheme implicitly adopted by the court of appeals.

Under the pro rata approach, each insurer pays only a portion of a claim based on the duration of the occurrence during its policy period in relation to the entire duration of the occurrence. It divides "a loss 'horizontally' among all triggered policy periods, with each insurance company paying only a share of the policyholder's total damages." For the reasons that follow, we agree with Goodyear's position and adopt the "all sums" method of allocation.

The starting point for determining the scope of coverage is the language of the insurance policies. The policies at issue require the insurer to "pay on behalf of the insured *all sums* which the insured shall become legally obligated to pay as damages because of... property damage to which this policy applies caused by an occurrence." (Emphasis added.) The policies define "property damage" as "injury to or destruction of tangible property *which occurs during the policy period....*" (Emphasis added.) The italicized portions of this language provide the point of contention.

It is well settled that "insurance policies should be enforced in accordance with their terms as are other written contracts. Where the provisions of the policy are clear and unambiguous, courts cannot enlarge the contract by implication so as to embrace an object distinct from that originally contemplated by the parties."...

There is no language in the triggered policies that would serve to reduce an insurer's liability if an injury occurs only in part during a given policy period. The policies covered Goodyear for "all sums" incurred as damages for an injury to property occurring during the policy period. The plain language of this provision is inclusive of all damages resulting from a qualifying occurrence. Therefore, we find that the "all sums" allocation approach is the correct method to apply here.

Interpreting the policy language in this manner is a practice that has been frequently implemented in other jurisdictions.... In particular, support for this approach can be found in the frequently cited case of *Keene Corp. v. Ins. Co. of N. Am.* (C.A.D.C.1981). In *Keene*, an action for declaratory relief was brought to discern the rights and obligations of parties under comprehensive general liability policies issued to an insured that was liable for bodily injuries arising from asbestos-related diseases. The asbestos was deemed to cause bodily injury in more than one policy period, and it was determined that multiple policies had been triggered.

The court went on to rule that each insurer whose insurance policy had been triggered would be liable in full for the indemnification and defense costs of the insured relating to the asbestos claims. In reaching this conclusion, the *Keene* court noted that there was nothing in the triggered policies that "provides for a reduction of the insurer's liability if an injury occurs only in part during a policy period." This being so, the court reasoned that the insured would have reasonably expected "complete security from each policy it purchased."

Like the insured in *Keene*, we are persuaded that Goodyear expected complete security from each policy that it purchased. This approach promotes economy for the insured while still permitting insurers to seek contribution from other responsible parties when possible. Therefore, we find that when a continuous occurrence of environmental pollution triggers claims under multiple primary insurance policies, the insured is entitled to secure coverage from a single policy of its choice that covers "all sums" incurred as damages "during the policy period," subject to that policy's limit of coverage. In such an instance, the insurers bear the burden of obtaining contribution from other applicable primary insurance policies as they deem necessary.

For each site, Goodyear should be permitted to choose, from the pool of triggered primary policies, a single primary policy against which it desires to make a claim. In the event that this policy does not cover Goodyear's entire claim, then Goodyear may pursue coverage under other primary or excess insurance policies. The answer to the question of what insurance may be tapped next is dependent upon the terms of the particular policy that is put into effect by Goodyear.

At this juncture, we are unable to determine which policy Goodyear will invoke, and thus we are also unable to determine whether the primary policy limits will be exhausted. Since Goodyear may find it necessary to seek excess insurance coverage, we find that the lower court erred in granting directed verdicts in favor of the excess insurers. The excess insurers should be included in the proceedings so that their rights and obligations can be considered in the event that their policies become a factor. We reverse the judgment of the court of appeals on this question.

[Dissenting opinion of **Frederick N. Young, J.,** omitted.]

## *Notes and Questions*

1. Which approach is more satisfying, that of *Consolidated Edison* or *Goodyear*? What are the respective advantages and disadvantages of each approach? Exactly who benefits when each approach is used? Is that the "right" result? — on contract grounds? — on equity grounds? — on public policy grounds? In Ohio and other "all sums" jurisdiction, a triggered insurer that provides coverage is entitled to seek contribution from other triggered insurers. *See, e.g., Pa. Gen. Ins. Co. v. Park-Ohio Indus.,* 930 N.E.2d 800 (Ohio 2010).

2. One author has been extremely critical of the *Consolidated Edison* approach, especially of the Minnesota Supreme Court's extension of the approach in *Domtar, Inc. v. Niagara Fire Ins. Co.,* 563 N.W.2d 724 (Minn. 1997). In *Domtar,* the court allocated coverage responsibility of long-term contamination of an industrial site across more than 40 years, many of them years in which the policyholder had no insurance in force. *See* Jeffrey W. Stempel, Domtar *Baby: Misplaced Notions of Equitable Apportionment Create a Thicket of Potential Unfairness for Insurance Policyholders,* 25 Wm. Mitchell L. Rev. 769 (1999). *See also* James F. Hogg, *The Tale of a Tail,* 24 Wm. Mitchell L. Rev. 515 (1998) (addressing problems of allocation across policy years when some years were insured on an occurrence basis while others insured on a claims-made basis).

3. *See also Federated Rural Elec. Ins. Exch. v. Nat'l Farmers Union Prop. & Cas. Co.,* 805 N.E.2d 456 (Ind. Ct. App. 2004) (where two policies triggered, coverage for the matter must be pro-rated between triggered concurrent insurers; policyholder can only recover proportional amount from each insurer).

# § 9.12. Common Exclusions

Regarding standardized contracts, a classic saying is that the "large print giveth and the small print taketh away." Insurers would respond that, regarding standard form insurance policies, the print is the same size (for the most part) and that exclusionary language is an essential aspect of crafting the insurance product to fulfill its purpose and to preserve the integrity of the insurer's risk pools. So long as exclusions are read reasonably, with regard to the principles of strict construction against the insurer, there should be no unfairness. In addition, policyholders have the protection of the contra proferentem canon and the reasonable expectations principle. See how these competing views of exclusions bear out on the cases below, which address some of the most commonly litigated exclusions.

In addition to the exclusions discussed in the case that follows, the standard form CGL policy lists a number of exclusions, many of which were noted in § 9.01, *supra*. In addition, other portions of the policy form, although not denominated exclusions, may reduce coverage and be construed as exclusions by courts. Further, insurance policies may contain specifically targeted exclusions that "laser out" from coverage a particular type of risk or even a specifically denominated risk (e.g., "any and all liability arising out of operations at the PollutCo Plant in Mudville").

For examples of invocation of exclusions, see, e.g., *ACE American Ins. Co. v. RC2 Corp.*, 600 F.3d 763 (7th Cir. 2010) (enforcing exclusion in commercial liability policy for claims arising out of exposure to defective products in the U.S., which was outside the coverage area of the policy); *Flomerfelt v. Cardiello*, 997 A.2d 991 (N.J. 2010) (homeowners' insurer refuses defense to claim against policyholder, asserting exclusion for claims arising out of use, transfer, or possession of controlled dangerous substances; court finds potential for coverage and duty to defend because some theories of liability in plaintiff's complaint, if proven at trial, would avoid exclusion); *W. Nat'l Mut. Ins. Co. v. Decker*, 791 N.W.2d 799 (S.D. 2010) (business pursuits exclusion in homeowner's policy precludes coverage for claim against policyholder arising out of babysitting activity); *Liberty Mut. Ins. Co. v. Lone Star Indus.*, 290 Conn. 767 (2009) (enforcing silica exclusion); *Gilbert Tex. Constr., L.P. v. Underwriters at Lloyd's London*, 327 S.W.3d 118 (Tex. 2010) (enforcing contractual liability exclusion in policy, which bars coverage for claims against the policyholder based solely on indemnity agreements or similar contracts); *Giacomelli v. Scottsdale Ins. Co.*, 354 Mont. 15 (2009) (enforcing special event participant exclusion to preclude coverage of racetrack for claims brought by injured jockeys); *N. Sec. Ins. Co. v. Rosenthal*, 980 A.2d 805 (Vt. 2009) (business pursuits exclusion applicable to claim against homeowners who also hosted relationship counseling retreats for paying clients when client/guest fell through open trapdoor at home); *Thornburg v. Schweitzer*, 240 P.3d 969 (Kan. Ct. App. 2010) (exclusion for claims brought against policyholder by household residents applies to bar coverage for wrongful death claim when couple's 7-year-old child was killed by dog that was part of family Mastiff-raising business). *See also Blankenship v. City of Charleston*, 679 S.E.2d 654 (W. Va. 2009) (no coverage for sale of beer at concession stand at concert open to the public as it was activity beyond the ordinary concept of a private swim club, the subject of the insuring agreement).

# [A] Exclusions for the Ordinary Economic Risks of Commercial Activity

## Weedo v. Stone-E-Brick, Inc.

Supreme Court of New Jersey
81 N.J. 233, 405 A.2d 788 (1979)

**Clifford, J.**

[T]he question is whether [a general liability] policy indemnifies the insured against damages in an action for breach of contract and faulty workmanship on a project, where the damages claimed are the cost of correcting the work itself. The Appellate Division held that certain exclusions of the policy, when read together, were ambiguous and hence had to be resolved against the insurer. We reverse.

Pennsylvania National Mutual Insurance Company (hereinafter Pennsylvania National) issued a general automobile liability policy to Stone-E-Brick, Inc., a corporation engaged in masonry contracting. As part of the policy there was included Comprehensive General Liability Coverage (hereinafter CGL). During the term of the policy Calvin and Janice Weedo contracted with Stone-E-Brick to pour a concrete flooring on a veranda and to apply stucco masonry to the exterior of their home. The completed job revealed cracks in the stucco and other signs of faulty workmanship, such that the Weedos had to remove the stucco and replace it with a proper material.

Thereupon the Weedos instituted suit against Stone-E-Brick and its principal, defendant Romano, alleging in pertinent part that

> [a]s a result of the defective and unworkmanlike manner in which the defendants applied the said stucco, plaintiffs were compelled to and did cause the defects existing therein to be remedied, where possible, and the omissions to be supplied, and, in general, *were compelled to and did furnish all the work, labor, services and materials necessary to complete the application of the said stucco in accordance with the contract and were compelled to and did expend large sums of money for that purpose in excess of the price which plaintiffs agreed to pay defendants for the application of said stucco, all of which was to plaintiffs' damage.* [Emphasis supplied.]

While the same CGL policy was in effect, Stone-E-Brick performed roofing and gutter work on a house being constructed for plaintiffs Gellas, under a sub-contract agreement with the general contractor, defendant Vivino. After completion of the home the Gellases brought suit against Vivino based on breach of contract due to defects in workmanship and seeking recovery of costs "in connection with the repair and/or replacement of material necessary to correct the defects in construction."

Vivino in turn sought indemnification from Stone-E-Brick by way of third-party complaint, contending that plaintiffs' damages were the result of Stone-E-Brick's "faulty workmanship, materials or construction."

Thereafter Stone-E-Brick requested that Pennsylvania National take over the defense and indemnify it in regard to both complaints. The carrier refused, asserting that the policy of insurance did not furnish coverage for the claims made or, in the alternative, that exclusionary clauses specifically precluded coverage. * * *

Under the CGL provisions of the policy in question Pennsylvania National agreed to pay "on behalf of the insured all sums which the insured shall become legally obligated to pay as damages because of bodily injury or *property damage to which this insurance applies*, caused by an occurrence." (Emphasis supplied.) This is the standard language found in the great majority of CGLs written in this country. These provisions, developed by casualty rating bureaus over a period of nearly fifty years, have become an established norm of underwriting policy. [Citing, *inter alia*, to Roger Henderson, *Insurance Protection for Products Liability and Completed Operations— What Every Lawyer Should Know*, 50 Neb. L. Rev. 415, 418 (1971), a leading article on the issue.]

In the present instance Pennsylvania National's policy undertook to furnish certain coverage to Stone-E-Brick as a concern engaged in masonry contracting. In order to determine whether the claims of plaintiffs fall within the coverage provided, we start with an examination of the insured's business relationships with its customers.

In the usual course of its business Stone-E-Brick negotiates with homeowners to provide masonry work. As part of the bargaining process the insured may extend an express warranty that its stone, concrete and stucco products and services will be provided in a reasonably workmanlike fashion.... Regardless of the existence of express warranties, the insured's provision of stucco and stone "generally carries with it an implied warranty of merchantability and often an implied warranty of fitness for a particular purpose." ... These warranties arise by operation of law and recognize that, under common circumstances, the insured-contractor holds himself out as having the capacity to apply the stonework in a workmanlike manner, and further, that the homeowner relies upon the representation and anticipates suitable goods and services....

Where the work performed by the insured-contractor is faulty, either express or implied warranties, or both, are breached. As a matter of contract law the customer did not obtain that for which he bargained. The dissatisfied customer can, upon repair or replacement of the faulty work, recover the cost thereof from the insured-contractor as the standard measure of damages for breach of warranties....

[A] principal justification for imposing warranties by operation of law on contractors is that these parties are often "in a better position to prevent the occurrence of major problems" in the course of constructing a home than is the homeowner. The insured-contractor can take pains to control the quality of the goods and services supplied. At the same time he undertakes the risk that he may fail in this endeavor and thereby incur contractual liability whether express or implied. The consequence of not performing well is part of every business venture; the replacement or repair of faulty goods and works is a business expense, to be borne by the insured-contractor in order to satisfy customers....

There exists another form of risk in the insured-contractor's line of work, that is, injury to people and damage to property caused by faulty workmanship. Unlike business risks of the sort described above, where the tradesman commonly absorbs the cost attendant upon the repair of his faulty work, the accidental injury to property or persons substantially caused by his unworkmanlike performance exposes the contractor to almost limitless liabilities. While it may be true that the same neglectful craftsmanship can be the cause of both a business expense of repair and a loss represented by damage to persons and property, the two consequences are vastly different in relation to sharing the cost of such risks as a matter of insurance underwriting.

In this regard Dean Henderson has remarked:

> The risk intended to be insured is the possibility that the goods, products or work of the insured, once relinquished or completed, will cause bodily injury or damage to property other than to the product or completed work itself, and for which the insured may be found liable. The insured, as a source of goods or services, may be liable as a matter of contract law to make good on products or work which is defective or otherwise unsuitable because it is lacking in some capacity. This may even extend to an obligation to completely replace or rebuild the deficient product or work. This liability, however, is not what the coverages in question are designed to protect against. The coverage is for tort liability for physical damages to others and not for contractual liability of the insured for economic loss because the product or completed work is not that for which the damaged person bargained. [Henderson, *supra*, 50 *Neb.L.Rev.* at 441.]

An illustration of this fundamental point may serve to mark the boundaries between "business risks" and occurrences giving rise to insurable liability. When a craftsman applies stucco to an exterior wall of a home in a faulty manner and discoloration, peeling and chipping result, the poorly-performed work will perforce have to be replaced or repaired by the tradesman or by a surety. On the other hand, should the stucco peel and fall from the wall, and thereby cause injury to the homeowner or his neighbor standing below or to a passing automobile, an occurrence of harm arises which is the proper subject of risk-sharing as provided by the type of policy before us in this case. The happenstance and extent of the latter liability is entirely unpredictable—the neighbor could suffer a scratched arm or a fatal blow to the skull from the peeling stonework. Whether the liability of the businessman is predicated upon warranty theory or, preferably and more accurately, upon tort concepts, injury to persons and damage to other property constitute the risks intended to be covered under the CGL.

We agree with Pennsylvania National that, given the precise and limited form of damages which form the basis of the claims against the insured, either exclusion is, or both are, applicable to exclude coverage. In short, the indemnity sought is not for "property damage to which this insurance applies."

Our review of twenty years' worth of judicial treatment of the "business risk" exclusion demonstrates that, if nothing else, the underwriting policy sought to be articulated by [the exclusionary clauses at issue have been] widely recognized as a valid limitation upon standard, readily-available liability insurance coverage. Indeed, several courts have remarked in ruling upon the impact of these clauses that the terms used to convey the "business risk" exclusions are straightforward and without ambiguity....

In this case Stone-E-Brick's interpretation of the policy would result in coverage for repair and replacement of its own faulty workmanship. * * * As we have endeavored to make clear, the policy in question does not cover an accident of faulty workmanship but rather faulty workmanship which causes an accident....

[Dissenting opinion of Pashman, J., omitted.]

## American Family Mutual Insurance Company v. American Girl, Inc.

Supreme Court of Wisconsin
268 Wis. 2d 16, 673 N.W.2d 65 (2004)

**Diane S. Sykes, J.**

This insurance coverage dispute presents an array of legal issues pertaining to the proper interpretation of coverage and exclusion language in several post-1986 commercial general liability ("CGL") and excess insurance policies. The dispute initially focuses on the meaning of "property damage" and "occurrence" in the standard CGL insuring agreement's grant of coverage. The parties also dispute the applicability of several exclusions: for "expected or intended" losses; "contractually-assumed liability"; and certain "business risks" (a/k/a "your work" or "your product" exclusions). There is a question about the applicability of the "professional services liability" exclusion in certain excess policies. Finally, the parties dispute the effect of the economic loss doctrine on the availability of insurance coverage, as well as the application of the common law "known loss" doctrine to certain of the policies.

The factual context is a construction project gone awry: a soil engineering subcontractor gave faulty site-preparation advice to a general contractor in connection with the construction of a warehouse. As a result, there was excessive settlement of the soil after the building was completed, causing the building's foundation to sink. This caused the rest of the structure to buckle and crack. Ultimately, the building was declared unsafe and had to be torn down. The general contractor, potentially liable to the building owner under certain contractual warranties, notified its insurance carriers of the loss.

Contractually-required arbitration between the owner and the contractor was initiated and stayed pending resolution of coverage questions involving several of the contractor's insurers. The circuit court, on summary judgment, found coverage under some but not all of the policies. The court of appeals reversed, concluding that the "contractual liability" exclusion in each of the policies excluded coverage. We reverse.

The threshold question is whether the claim at issue here is for "property damage" caused by an "occurrence" within the meaning of the CGL policies' general grant of coverage. We hold that it is. The CGL policies define "property damage" as "physical injury to tangible property." The sinking, buckling, and cracking of the warehouse was plainly "physical injury to tangible property." An "occurrence" is defined as "an accident, including continuous or repeated exposure to substantially the same general harmful condition." The damage to the warehouse was caused by substantial soil settlement underneath the completed building, which occurred because of the faulty site-preparation advice of the soil engineering subcontractor. It was accidental, not intentional or anticipated, and it involved the "continuous or repeated exposure" to the "same general harmful condition." Accordingly, there was "property damage" caused by an "occurrence" within the meaning of the CGL policies.

We also conclude that the economic loss doctrine does not preclude coverage. The economic loss doctrine generally operates to confine contracting parties to contract rather than tort remedies for recovery of purely economic losses associated with the contract relationship. The doctrine does not determine insurance coverage, which turns on the policy language. That the property damage at issue here is actionable in contract but not in tort does not make it "non-accidental" or otherwise remove it from the CGL's definition of "occurrence." ... We further hold that because the property damage at issue here was neither expected nor intended, the "expected or intended" exclusion does not apply.

The "contractually-assumed liability" exclusion (upon which the court of appeals rested its no-coverage conclusion) eliminates coverage for damages the insured is obligated to pay "by reason of the assumption of liability in a contract or agreement." We conclude that this language does not exclude coverage for all breach of contract liability. Rather, it excludes coverage for liability that arises because the insured has contractually assumed the liability of another, as in an indemnification or hold harmless agreement. There is no indemnification or hold harmless agreement at issue here, so this exclusion does not apply.

We also conclude that while the "business risk" or "your work" exclusions ordinarily would operate to exclude coverage under the circumstances of this case, the "subcontractor" exception applies here. The subcontractor exception to the business risk exclusion restores coverage if "the work out of which the damage arises" was performed by a subcontractor.

In addition, we conclude that the "professional services liability" exclusion in the excess policies applies under the circumstances of this case. And finally, coverage under the policies issued after the property damage loss was substantially known to the parties is barred by the "known loss" doctrine.

## I. FACTS AND PROCEDURAL HISTORY

In 1994 The Pleasant Company ("Pleasant") entered into a contract with The Renschler Company for the design and construction of a large distribution center warehouse, dubbed the "94DC," on Pleasant's Middleton, Wisconsin, campus. Under the terms of the contract, Renschler warranted to Pleasant that the design and structural components of the 94DC would be free from defects, and that Renschler would be liable for any consequential damages caused by any such defects. (Pleasant changed its name to American Girl, Inc., several days before the issuance of this opinion; we will refer to the company as it was known throughout these proceedings.)

Renschler hired Clifton E.R. Lawson (Lawson), a soils engineer, to conduct an analysis of soil conditions at the site. Lawson concluded that the soil conditions were poor and recommended "rolling surcharging" to prepare the site for construction. Surcharging is a process by which soils are compressed to achieve the density required to support the weight of a building or other structure. The process usually involves placing large quantities of earth above the soil and allowing the earth to bear down on the soils. Typically this requires bringing in enough earth to cover the entire site, which can be very costly, and so for large projects like the 94DC, small areas of the site are compressed individually, and the earth is rolled from one area to the next.

The surcharging was done according to Lawson's professional advice, and the building was substantially completed in August 1994. Pleasant took occupancy, and soon thereafter the 94DC began to sink. By the spring of 1995 the settlement at one end of the structure had reached eight inches.

Renschler became aware of the problem in March 1995, and Lawson was subsequently advised. In the fall of 1995 Renschler re-hung approximately 30 exterior panels and windows that were leaking as a result of the settlement. The building continued to sink throughout 1996. By early 1997, the settlement approached one foot, the building was buckling, steel supports were deformed, the floor was cracking, and sewer lines had shifted. In January or February 1997, the parties met to discuss the settlement damage and the options for remediation. [The Court found that this meeting "triggered application of the know loss doctrine," making later injury uninsurable.]

In August 1997 Renschler notified its liability insurance carrier, American Family Mutual Insurance Company. American Family conducted an investigation of the claim and at first concluded that coverage existed for the claim. In January 1998 the insurer reserved $750,000 for the claim, and in May 1998 paid Renschler $27,501 for services performed relating to remediation of the damage that had occurred up to that point. In early 1999 remediation alternatives were estimated to cost between $4.1 and $5.9 million. Renschler hired engineers to conduct evaluations of the floor from March through September 1999. The engineers advised Renschler that the structural steel was so over-stressed that the building was no longer safe for occupancy. In late 1999 or early 2000 the building was dismantled. By that time, the settlement was approximately 18 inches. Renschler's geotechnical expert concluded that Lawson was negligent in the performance of his engineering/geotechnical work. It is undisputed that Lawson's faulty soil engineering advice was a substantial factor in causing the settlement of the 94DC.... Arbitration was stayed pending resolution of the coverage issues....

The court of appeals [holding] that the exclusion for property damage "for which the insured is obligated to pay damages by reason of the assumption of liability in a contract or agreement" precluded coverage, because Renschler's liability to Pleasant derived entirely from its obligations under the construction contract. The court of appeals also held that there was no coverage under American Family's excess policies, as well as the policies of the other insurers, on the basis of identical "contractual liability" exclusions in those policies. The court did not address the other coverage issues. We accepted review.

Exclusions are narrowly or strictly construed against the insurer if their effect is uncertain. We analyze each exclusion separately; the inapplicability of one exclusion will not reinstate coverage where another exclusion has precluded it. Exclusions sometimes have exceptions; if a particular exclusion applies, we then look to see whether any exception to that exclusion reinstates coverage. An exception pertains only to the exclusion clause within which it appears; the applicability of an exception will not create coverage if the insuring agreement precludes it or if a separate exclusion applies.

### III. DISCUSSION

#### A. The CGL policies

The precursor of today's standard commercial liability insurance contract was promulgated in 1940 and has since undergone five principal revisions, the most recent of which came into use in 1986. Today, most CGL insurance in the United States is written on standardized forms developed by the Insurances Services Office, Inc. (ISO).... Jeffrey W. Stempel, Law of Insurance Contract Disputes §§ 14.01, 14.02 (2d ed. 1999).... Until 1966, standard CGL policies provided coverage for liabilities arising out of injury or damage "caused by an accident." ... In response to uncertainty over whether the term "accident" included harm caused by gradual processes, the insurance industry removed the "accident" language from the insuring agreement and replaced it with the broader term "occurrence," defined as an accident, but also including gradual accidental harm; this coverage language is used to this day.... Standard CGL policies, including those at issue in this case, now cover "sums that the insured becomes legally obligated to pay as damages because of 'bodily injury' or 'property damage' ... caused by an 'occurrence' that takes place in the 'coverage territory.' "

The CGL insuring agreement is a broad statement of coverage, and insurers limit their exposure to risk through a series of specific exclusions. There are exclusions for intended or expected losses; for contractually-assumed liabilities; for obligations under worker's compensation and related laws; for injury and damage arising out of aircraft and automobiles; and for several so-called "business risks." ... The "business risk" exclusions, also known as "your work," "your product," and "your property" exclusions, have generated substantial litigation. 2 Stempel, *supra* § 14.13, 14-127. "Insurers draft liability policies with an eye toward preventing policyholders from … converting their liability insurance into protection from nonfortuitous losses such as claims based on poor business operations. The 'own work' and 'owned property' exclusions are two important and frequently litigated policy provisions designed to accomplish this purpose." The 1986 version of the CGL contains a modified "business risk" exclusion that provides an exception for the work of subcontractors, id., and will be discussed in greater detail below.

The CGL policies at issue here contain 15 separate exclusions lettered "a" through "n" of subsection I.A.2. This case requires an examination of several of these: exclusion (a), for expected or intended losses; exclusion (b), for contractually-assumed liabilities; and exclusions (j) and (l), the business risk exclusions for property damage to the insured's work. As we have noted, however, our first task is to determine whether the claimed loss is covered by the language of the insuring agreement's initial grant of coverage.

B. The CGL's insuring agreement

i. "Property damage" and the economic loss doctrine

The policy defines "property damage" as "physical injury to tangible property, including all resulting loss of use of that property." The sinking, buckling, and cracking of the 94DC as a result of the soil settlement qualifies as "physical injury to tangible property." …

American Family characterizes Pleasant's claim against Renschler as one for economic loss rather than property damage, and argues that the economic loss doctrine bars coverage. The economic loss doctrine generally precludes recovery in tort for economic losses resulting from the failure of a product to live up to contractual expectations. The economic loss doctrine is "based on an understanding that contract law and the law of warranty, in particular, is better suited than tort law for dealing with purely economic loss in the commercial arena." … The economic loss doctrine operates to restrict contracting parties to contract rather than tort remedies for recovery of economic losses associated with the contract relationship. The economic loss doctrine is a remedies principle. It determines how a loss can be recovered—in tort or in contract/warranty law. It does not determine whether an insurance policy covers a claim, which depends instead upon the policy language.

The economic loss doctrine may indeed preclude tort recovery here (the underlying claim is in arbitration and not before us); regardless, everyone agrees that the loss remains actionable in contract, pursuant to specific warranties in the construction agreement between Pleasant and Renschler.

To the extent that American Family is arguing categorically that a loss giving rise to a breach of contract or warranty claim can *never* constitute "property damage" within the meaning of the CGL's coverage grant, we disagree. "The language of the CGL policy and the purpose of the CGL insuring agreement will provide coverage for claims sounding in part in breach-of-contract/breach-of-warranty under some circumstances." 2 Stempel, supra § 14A.02[d], 14A-10. This is such a circumstance. Pleasant's claim against Renschler for the damage to the 94DC is a claim for "property damage" within the meaning of the CGL's coverage grant.

ii. "Occurrence"

Liability for "property damage" is covered by the CGL policy if it resulted from an "occurrence." "Occurrence" is defined as "an accident, including continuous or repeated exposure to substantially the same general harmful conditions." The term "accident" is not defined in the policy. The dictionary definition of "accident" is: "an event or condition occurring by chance or arising from unknown or remote causes." Webster's Third New International Dictionary of the English Language 11 (2002). Black's Law Dictionary defines "accident" as follows: "The word 'accident,' in accident policies, means an event which takes place without one's foresight or expectation. A result, though unexpected, is not an accident; the means or cause must be accidental."

No one seriously contends that the property damage to the 94DC was anything but accidental (it was clearly not intentional), nor does anyone argue that it was anticipated by the parties. The damage to the 94DC occurred as a result of the continuous, substantial, and harmful settlement of the soil underneath the building. Lawson's inadequate site-preparation advice was a cause of this exposure to harm. Neither the cause nor the harm was intended, anticipated, or expected. We conclude that the circumstances of this claim fall within the policy's definition of "occurrence."

[In footnote 5, the majority noted that "Justice Roggensack's dissent asserts that the soil settlement and resultant property damage were expected by the parties because the construction contract contained a warranty against defects. While the warranty in question was specifically inserted in the construction contract under the subheading 'Additional Warranties,' it is nevertheless stated in broad and general terms. The provision of a general warranty against defects does not support a conclusion that the contract parties expected a particular loss to occur."]

American Family argues that because Pleasant's claim is for breach of contract/breach of warranty it cannot be an "occurrence," because the CGL is not intended to cover contract claims arising out of the insured's defective work or product. We agree that CGL policies generally do not cover contract claims arising out of the insured's defective work or product, but this is by operation of the CGL's business risk exclusions, not because a loss actionable only in contract can never be the result of an "occurrence" within the meaning of the CGL's initial grant of coverage. This distinction is sometimes overlooked, and has resulted in some regrettably overbroad generalizations about CGL policies in our case law. Despite this broad generalization, however, there is nothing in the basic coverage language of the current CGL policy to support any definitive tort/contract line of demarcation for purposes of determining whether a loss is covered by the CGL's initial grant of coverage. "Occurrence" is not defined by reference to the legal category of the claim. The term "tort" does not appear in the CGL policy.

[Prior precedent] interpreting pre-1986 CGL policies, never discussed the insuring agreement's initial grant of coverage; rather, the cases were decided on the basis of the business risk exclusions. * * * Hence we need not address the validity of one of the carrier's initially-offered grounds of non-coverage, namely, that the policy did not extend coverage for the claims made even absent the exclusions." *Weedo* [*v. Stone-E-Brick*] does not hold that losses actionable as breaches of contract cannot be CGL "occurrences,"...

If, as American Family contends, losses actionable in contract are never CGL "occurrences" for purposes of the initial coverage grant, then the business risk exclusions are entirely unnecessary. The business risk exclusions eliminate coverage for liability for property damage to the insured's own work or product—liability that is typically actionable between the parties pursuant to the terms of their contract, not in tort. If the insuring agreement never confers coverage for this type of liability as an original definitional matter, then there is no need to specifically exclude it. Why would the insurance industry exclude damage to the insured's own work or product if the damage could never be considered to have arisen from a covered "occurrence" in the first place?

The court of appeals has previously recognized that the faulty workmanship of a subcontractor can give rise to property damage caused by an "occurrence" within the meaning of a CGL policy. In *Kalchthaler v. Keller Construction Co.*, 224 Wis. 2d 387, 395, 591 N.W.2d 169 (Ct. App. 1999), a general contractor subcontracted out all the work on a construction project; the completed building subsequently leaked, causing over $500,000 in water damage. The court of appeals noted that the CGL defined "occurrence" as "an accident," and further noted that "an accident is an 'event or change occurring without intention or volition through carelessness, unawareness, ignorance, or a combination of causes and producing an unfortunate result.'" The court of appeals concluded that the leakage was an accident and therefore an occurrence for purposes of the CGL's coverage grant.... The same is true here.... This brings us to the policy exclusions. American Family invokes several.

C. The "expected or intended" exclusion

Exclusion (a) eliminates coverage for "'property damage' expected or intended from the standpoint of the insured.'" American Family argues that given the poor soil conditions at the site, and Renschler's recognition that special measures were required to prepare the soil to carry the weight of the 94DC, Renschler expected that some settlement would occur, and therefore this exclusion applies. We disagree.

American Family does not argue that "property damage" was expected or intended by the insured (which is what the exclusion requires), only that some degree of settlement must have been expected under the circumstances. This is insufficient to trigger the exclusion....

D. The "contractually-assumed liability" exclusion

The court of appeals held that exclusion (b), for contractually-assumed liabilities, applied to preclude coverage under all the policies at issue in this case. Exclusion (b) states:

This insurance does not apply to:

. . . .

b. "Bodily injury" or "property damage" for which the insured is obligated to pay damages by reason of the assumption of liability in a contract or agreement. This exclusion does not apply to liability for damages:

(1) Assumed in a contract or agreement that is an "insured contract," provided the "bodily injury" or "property damage" occurs subsequent to the execution of the contract or agreement; or

(2) That the insured would have in the absence of the contract or agreement.

"The key to understanding this exclusion ... is the concept of liability assumed." As one important commentator has noted,

Although, arguably, a person or entity assumes liability (that is, a duty of performance, the breach of which will give rise to liability) whenever one enters into a binding contract, in the CGL policy and other liability policies an "assumed" liability is generally understood and interpreted by the courts to mean the liability of a third party, which liability one "assumes" in the sense that one agrees to indemnify or hold the other person harmless.

The term "assumption" must be interpreted to add something to the phrase "assumption of liability in a contract or agreement." Reading the phrase to apply to all liabilities sounding in contract renders the term "assumption" superfluous. We conclude that the contractually-assumed liability exclusion applies where the insured has contractually assumed the liability of a third party, as in an indemnification or hold harmless agreement; it does not operate to exclude coverage for any and all liabilities to which the insured is exposed under the terms of the contracts it makes generally.

This reading is consistent with the general purposes of liability insurance because it enables insurers to enforce the fortuity concept by excluding from coverage any policyholder agreements to become liable after the insurance is in force and the liability is a certainty. Limiting the exclusion to indemnification and hold-harmless agreements furthers the goal of protecting the insurer from exposure to risks whose scope and nature it cannot control or even reasonably foresee. The relevant distinction "is between incurring liability as a result of a breach of contract and specifically contracting to assume liability for another's negligence."

Courts in other jurisdictions have held that the contractually-assumed liability exclusion "refers to a specific contractual assumption of liability by the insured as exemplified by an indemnity agreement." ... This interpretation of exclusion (b) is consistent with the evolution of the CGL policy over time.

Prior to the 1986 revision, the exclusion for contractually-assumed liabilities was achieved through language in the insuring agreement that granted coverage for "contractual liabilities." Coverage was extended to certain types of contractual obligations but not others. With the 1986 revision, however, this language was moved into the exclusions section, and the basic coverage for certain contractual obligations was retained by inserting an exception to the exclusion for "insured contracts." ... This case does not involve a claim for "contractually-assumed liability," properly understood. The breach of contract/warranty liability at issue here is Renschler's direct liability to its contract partner, Pleasant, pursuant to warranties in the construction contract. Renschler is not claiming coverage for a claim made against it pursuant to a third-party indemnification or hold harmless agreement.

E. The "business risk" exclusions

The business risk exclusions (j) through (n) preclude coverage generally for property damage to the work of the insured. Several of these are implicated here. The first, exclusion (j), contains the following language:

> This insurance does not apply to:
>
> j. "Property damage" to:....
>
> (6) That particular part of any property that must be restored, repaired or replaced because "your work" was incorrectly performed on it....
>
> Paragraph (6) of this exclusion does not apply to "property damage" included in the "products-completed operations hazard.

The policy defines "your work" as:

> a. Work or operations performed by you or on your behalf;....

"Your work" includes:

> a. Warranties or representations made at any time with respect to the fitness, quality, durability, performance or use of "your work;"

Renschler's work on the 94DC, as well as Lawson's engineering work under subcontract to Renschler, both fall within the definition of "your work." Exclusion (j) comes into play because Pleasant's claim against Renschler involves the repair and replacement of the 94DC.

However, if the property damage that occurred falls within the "products-completed operations hazard," exclusion (j) does not apply. The "products-completed operations hazard" includes:

> All "bodily injury" and "property damage" occurring away from premises you own or rent and arising out of "your product" or "your work" except:
>
> (1) Products that are still in your physical possession; or
>
> (2) Work that has not yet been completed or abandoned.

The damage to the 94DC occurred away from premises that Renschler owns or rents, and it arose out of Renschler's "own work" because, as we have indicated, Renschler's work on the 94DC falls within the policy definition of "your work." Work on the 94DC was substantially completed in August 1994, and Pleasant occupied the premises at that time. The settlement was noticed in March 1995. Damage to the property therefore occurred after the work had been completed, so exception (2) does not apply. Thus the property damage at issue in this case falls within the "products-completed operations hazard" and exclusion (j) does not apply.

This brings into play exclusion (l), for "property damage to your work" inside the "products-completed operations hazard":

This insurance does not apply to:

l. "Property damage" to "your work" arising out of it or any part of it and included in the "products-completed operations hazard."

This exclusion does not apply if the damaged work or the work out of which the damage arises was performed on your behalf by a subcontractor.

By its terms, exclusion (l) would operate to exclude coverage under the circumstances of this case but for the exception that specifically restores coverage when the property damage arises out of work performed by a subcontractor. It is undisputed that Lawson's negligent soils engineering work was a cause of the soil settlement and resultant property damage to the 94DC.

This subcontractor exception dates to the 1986 revision of the standard CGL policy form. Prior to 1986 the CGL business risk exclusions operated collectively to preclude coverage for damage to construction projects caused by subcontractors. Many contractors were unhappy with this state of affairs, since more and more projects were being completed with the help of subcontractors.

In response to this changing reality, insurers began to offer coverage for damage caused by subcontractors through an endorsement to the CGL known as the Broad Form Property Damage Endorsement, or BFPD. Introduced in 1976, the BFPD deleted several portions from the business risk exclusions and replaced them with more specific exclusions that effectively broadened coverage. Among other changes, the BFPD extended coverage to property damage caused by the work of subcontractors. In 1986 the insurance industry incorporated this aspect of the BFPD directly into the CGL itself by inserting the subcontractor exception to the "your work" exclusion....

[Courts have] recognized that the effect of the 1986 revision of the CGL could not be defeated by reliance upon broad judicial holdings interpreting pre-1986 policies that did not contain the subcontractor exception. "For whatever reason, the industry chose to add the new exception to the business risk exclusion in 1986. We may not ignore that language when interpreting case law decided before and after the addition. To do so would render the new language superfluous."

Courts in other jurisdictions have reached the same conclusion when interpreting the post-1986 subcontractor exception or policy endorsements containing identical language. American Family cites conflicting authorities which appear to hold that damage to an insured's work caused by a subcontractor is not covered because of the "your work" exclusion, but these authorities are no longer controlling because they construed policies that did not include the subcontractor exception. Noting the apparent conflict between *Kalchthaler*, and similar cases on the one hand, and contrary cases on the other, one commentator has pointed out that "those cases [finding no coverage] involved the older policy language while the current policy specifically provides that the 'own work' exclusion does not apply 'if the damaged work or the work out of which the damage arises was performed on your behalf by a subcontractor.'" 2 Stempel, *supra* § 14.13[a], 14-132.

This interpretation of the subcontractor exception to the business risk exclusion does not "create coverage" where none existed before, as American Family contends. There is coverage under the insuring agreement's initial coverage grant. Coverage would be excluded by the business risk exclusionary language, except that the subcontractor exception to the business risk exclusion applies, which operates to restore the otherwise excluded coverage.... Accordingly, Renschler's CGL base policies with American Family cover Pleasant's claim.

We also agree with the circuit court's application of the "continuous trigger.... The continuous trigger theory interprets the term "occurrence" in CGL policies to include continual, recurring damage as well as damage that occurs at one moment in time.... The property damage to the 94DC occurred continuously over a period extending from the later part of the 1994–95 policy term, throughout the 1995–96 policy term, and well into the 1996–97 policy term. Settlement had reached eight inches by the spring of 1995, when the first policy was still in force, and continued throughout 1996 and into 1997, by which time it was approaching one foot. Accordingly, under the continuous trigger holdings of Society Insurance and Wisconsin Electric, the policies for the years 1994–95, 1995–96, and 1996–97 cover this loss.

### N. Patrick Crooks, J. *(dissenting)*.

I disagree with the majority's conclusion that there is coverage under the CGL policies issued by American Family. Although I agree with Justice Roggensack's dissent, I write separately to address an issue the majority concedes is relevant, yet touches on only briefly. In this case, there are contract claims for breach of warranty resulting in economic loss. Breach of contract/breach of warranty resulting in economic loss is not a covered "occurrence" under the plain language of the CGL policies' general grant of coverage. American Family and the other CGL insurers have no duty to defend or indemnify Renschler against Pleasant's damage claims, since the CGL policies at issue do not cover the contract claims, and the economic loss doctrine prevents any tort claim as well. Thus, I conclude there can be no coverage in this case, as the requirements for both liability and recovery of damages are not satisfied.

### Patience D. Roggensack, J. *(dissenting)*.

Before considering exceptions to coverage in the American Family insurance policy, we must first conclude that there has been an "occurrence" because the policy does not provide coverage under any circumstances unless the "'property damage' is caused by an 'occurrence.'" Renschler Company asserts that the act that caused damage to the Pleasant Company's building was Clifton Lawson's allegedly inaccurate advice concerning compaction of the subsoil prior to the building's construction, which permitted the building to sink. However, it was known that if subsoil compaction was not properly done, the completed building would sink and the damage to the building that has occurred would very likely occur. Therefore, the cause of the damage was simply the continuation of prior existing unstable subsoil conditions. Accordingly, I conclude the property damage at issue here was not caused by an accident, which is how "occurrence" is defined in the policy. Without an "occurrence," there is no potential coverage under Renschler's CGL policy. Because the majority concludes otherwise, I respectfully dissent....

The majority's equation of "accidental" with "unintentional" begs the question presented here: whether the sinking of the building was an unforeseen event or one that resulted from an unknown cause. "Accident" is the operative word in the policy definition of "occurrence." An "accident" has been variously defined as: "an event that takes place without one's foresight or expectation — an event that proceeds from an unknown cause, or is an unusual effect of a known cause, and therefore not expected." or "an event or condition occurring by chance or arising from unknown or remote causes." ... "The word 'accident,' in accident policies, means an event which takes place without one's foresight or expectation. A result, though unexpected, is not an accident; the means or cause must be accidental. Here, the settling was not an unexpected outcome of construction. It was a known possibility. Furthermore, the settling did not take place due to an unknown cause. It was well recognized that the soil conditions were unfavorable to construction and if they continued there would be problems.

In sum, all the definitions of "accident" require, at a minimum, an unexpected event or an unexpected cause. Here, it does not matter whether we focus on the sinking building or the continuation of unstable subsoil conditions, neither was unexpected. The unstable subsoil conditions were known and their correction required to prevent the building from sinking. In fact, the risk that the building would sink after construction was assumed by Renschler in its contract with Pleasant, showing a continuation of the unstable subsoil conditions was a potential and known risk of constructing the building on the site Pleasant chose. * * * Furthermore, we have equated "accident" with negligence. However, negligence is a tort, and as we have earlier explained, Pleasant cannot sue Renschler for a tort. Therefore, if we use the definition in Doyle, there will be no coverage under the policy because Renschler will never be "legally obligated to pay" Pleasant based on negligence.

Additionally, this analysis fits squarely within the purpose of a CGL policy. It is written to cover the risks of injury to third parties and damage to the property of third parties caused by the insured's completed work. It is not written to cover the business risk of failing to provide goods or services in a workmanlike manner to the second party to the contract. * * * And finally, the happening of an accident is entirely unpredictable; by its very definition, it is not something one can plan to occur. Therefore, a contractor would have difficulty budgeting to meet that risk; hence the need for insurance. However, here, the risk that the unstable subsoil conditions would continue was a known risk. If Renschler did not want to shoulder that risk, it could have required a performance bond or a warranty from Lawson similar to the one Pleasant obtained from it.

The majority also asserts that if contract claims are never "occurrences" then there is no need to have the business risk exclusion. That argument ignores the fact that the policy at issue is a standard CGL policy. It is issued to many contractors to cover myriad circumstances that may be very dissimilar from the facts that form the basis for Pleasant's claim. Therefore, in a claim based on different facts, there may be an occurrence and yet the business risk exclusion may preclude coverage. For example, if a contractor builds a building and a wall spontaneously collapses on a passer-by because of poor workmanship in constructing the wall, there would be an occurrence in regard to the unforeseen falling of the wall, and the damage to the injured person would be covered. However, the repair of the defective wall would be excluded from coverage under the business risk exclusion.

## Notes and Questions

1. Which is more persuasive in *American Family v. American Girl*: the majority or the dissents?

2. Perhaps the leading, if immodestly titled, article on this coverage question is Roger C. Henderson, *Protection for Products Liability and Completed Operations—What Every Lawyer Should Know*, 50 Neb. L. Rev. 415 (1971). But not every claim by a customer is an uncovered claim of defective workmanship. Sometimes the claim does sound as much in tort as contract and does meet the CGL policy insuring agreement standard for alleging covered bodily injury or property damage.

3. It is also important to remember that changes in policy language take place with some frequency, even in the relatively stable world of standardized insurance policies. For example, a lawyer today will ordinarily err if she relies upon pre-1966 precedent concerning what constitutes property damage because the 1966 CGL revision changed the definition of property damage to require that the damage to the property be "physical injury" and that the property injured be "tangible." (But remember, there may still be coverage for a claim that the policyholder's wrongdoing caused loss of use of third-party property even though the claimant's property was not itself physically injured.) So, for example, a frequently cited "classic" case such as *Hauenstein v. St. Paul-Mercury Indem. Co.*, 65 N.W.2d 122 (Minn. 1954) or *Geddes & Smith, Inc. v. St. Paul Mercury Indem. Co.*, 334 P.2d 881 (Cal. 1959) is usually not aptly invoked for guidance in a modern property damage coverage dispute.

When reading insurance cases, especially older ones, attorneys must be alert to the possibility that the standard insurance policy at issue has been revised or that there are case-specific differences in the policy language due to particular endorsements or some individual modifications of the policy by agreement between the parties.

4. In 1986, the standard CGL form was amended to provide coverage where any claims of injury relating to policyholder's "own work" was due to operations "per-

formed by a subcontractor." What was the effect of the change? Was it a wise change in light of the basic insurance concepts examined in Chapter 1? *See also O'Shaughnessy v. Smuckler Corp.*, 543 N.W.2d 99 (Minn. Ct. App. 1996):

> The Business Risk Doctrine is the expression of a public policy applied to the insurance coverage provided under CGL policies. The policy behind the doctrine provided the rationale for a broad interpretation of a limitation on coverage under the "work performed" exclusion prior to the 1986 change in CGL policies.... The "risk" refers to a contractor's risk that he or she "may be liable to the owner resulting from failure to properly complete the building project itself in a manner so as to not cause damage to it."
>
> > this risk is one the general contractor effectively controls and one which the insurer does not assume because it has no effective control over those risks and cannot establish predictable and affordable insurance rates.... [*Knutson Constr. Co. v. St. Paul Fire & Marine Ins. Co.*, 396 N.W.2d 229, 234 (Minn. 1986).]

The rationale behind the Business Risk Doctrine has been articulated as follows:

> If insurance proceeds could be used to pay for the repairing and/or replacing of poorly constructed products, a contractor or subcontractor could receive initial payment for its work and then receive subsequent payment from the insurance company to repair and replace it.... Equally repugnant on policy grounds is the notion that the presence of insurance obviates the obligation to perform the job initially in a workmanlike manner.

*Knutson*, 396 N.W.2d at 235.... We note that this rationale is less applicable to a claim by a general contractor for the defective work of its subcontractor. A general contractor has minimal control over the work of its subcontractors by definition, and the fact that the general contractor receives coverage will not relieve the subcontractor of ultimate liability for unworkmanlike or defective work. In such a case, an insurer will have subrogation rights against the subcontractor who performed the defective work. Presumably, the Business Risk. Doctrine will preclude the subcontractor from recovering from its own insurer. Thus, the goal of the Business Risk Doctrine would still be achieved because ultimate responsibility for poor workmanship would lie with the one who performed it.

## The Continuing Battle over Coverage in Construction Defect Litigation

As cases such as *Weedo* and *American Girl* illustrate, the business risk limitations in general liability policies are most commonly litigated in actions concerning coverage for defective construction claims. There is a substantial portion of the CGL form devoted to the business risk exclusions, including the "your property" or "own property" exclusion, the "your work" exclusion, and the "impaired property" exclusion.

From an insurer's perspective, exclusions pose a problem, of course, in that because they are exclusions they are strictly and narrowly construed against the insurer, with the insurer bearing the burden of persuasion to demonstrate the applicability of the exclusion. As a result, insurers have taken to fighting coverage for construction defect claims by arguing that defective work is not an "accident" or "occurrence," issues on which the policyholder generally bears the burden of proof or where the court's review is neutral.

As a result, there are many cases concerning whether faulty workmanship can be an occurrence, with substantial variation among the states, at least analytically. *See* MANILOFF & STEMPEL, Ch. 12 (2011). Where defective construction damages portions of a home other than the policyholder/builder's own work or where the defective work was done by a subcontractor, coverage usually exists. *Id.* at 221–25.

However, a surprising number of courts take the position that faulty workmanship is not an accident or occurrence unless it causes physical injury to tangible property or loss or use for something other than the policyholder's work product. *See* MANILOFF & STEMPEL, Ch. 12 (listing Arkansas, Colorado, Connecticut, Delaware, Georgia, Iowa, Maine, Maryland, New Hampshire, New Jersey (but only in the lower courts; *Weedo, supra*, remains well-reasoned good law), Oregon, Pennsylvania, South Carolina, Utah, West Virginia, Wyoming as states with precedent to this effect). *See also Hathaway Dev. Co. v. Am. Empire Surplus Lines Ins. Co.*, 686 S.E.2d 855, 860 (Ga. Ct. App. 2009) ("construction defects constituting a breach of contract" not an occurrence).

Analytically, this view is incorrect. Regardless of whether harm is done to other property, faulty work can of course be accidental if it takes place unintentionally. But even if accidental, these errors are not covered under the standard CGL policy unless there is injury to property other than that of the policyholder and no other policy exclusions apply. Although there are some builders who intentionally cut corners, the more common construction defect problems happen because of negligence, which is an accident, which is exactly what the CGL policy was designed to cover absent an applicable exclusion. *See* STEMPEL & KNUTSEN, Chs. 14, 25.

By adopting the view that any work done wrong by a commercial vendor must not have been accidental unless it damages other property, some courts have committed a logical error and also provided insurers with an undue tactical advantage by permitting them to avoid fighting these coverage disputes on the basis of the business risk exclusions, which should be the battleground. In practice, however, the distinction may be modest because a policyholder would in any event have to prove injury to something other than the policyholder's own work to obtain CGL coverage. *See, e.g., Concord Gen. Mut. Ins. Co. v. Green & Co. Bldg. & Dev. Corp.*, 8 A.3d 24 (N.H. 2010) (taking view that faulty work alone is not occurrence but that if faulty work damages other property, there is coverage). *But see Tri-Etch, Inc. v. Cincinnati Ins. Co.*, 909 N.E.2d 997 (Ind. 2009) (security company's negligent delay in responding to problems with scheduled setting of night alarm not an "occurrence."). Although the *Tri-Etch* decision, like many of the construction defect cases, seems analytically incorrect (i.e., the company's failure was negligent and accidental rather than intentional), the result is arguably correct in that the policy also contained an alarm services exclusion. The court clearly saw the policyholder/defendant's failing as more apt for Errors and Omissions coverage (described in § 9.16, *infra*) than CGL coverage.

The view that a contract breach cannot be an occurrence is also wrong, of course, for the reasons set forth in *Vandenberg, supra*. A breach of contract claim against a policyholder can be covered so long as it was sufficiently fortuitous and caused bodily injury or property damage. Although many contract breaches are intentional (e.g., the breacher finds a better or less expensive supplier and spurns the original deal), many are largely or completely unintentional (e.g., war prevents obtaining supplies needed to fulfill the contract from arriving; a fire destroys the premises on which the contract was to be performed). For a better reasoned approach, *see Bituminous Cas. Corp. v. Kenway Contr., Inc.*, 240 S.W.3d 633, 640 (Ky. 2007) (contractor's demolition of residential structure when it was supposed to take down only the carport an occurrence under the CGL policy).

This is not to say that decisions making this error of analysis (i.e., that bad work cannot be accidental or that breach of contract or warranty cannot be accidental) are not often right concerning the bottom line of coverage due to the application of business risk or other exclusions. But when courts find contractors errors not to be occurrences (as opposed to uncovered occurrences due to the applicability of an exclusion), they may undermine the purpose of the general liability policy, which is to protect the policyholder from claims arising out of its negligent activity (or bad luck; sometimes vendors are sued simply because a customer or third party is disgruntled, is searching for a compensatory deep pocket, etc.).

Put another way, it must be possible for faulty work to be accidental and subject to CGL coverage — otherwise there would be no need for the business risk exclusions. Similarly, the CGL policy form and the insurance industry must have contemplated providing coverage for defective work to a substantial degree — or otherwise there would not be the subcontractor exception to the "your work" exclusion.

Where a policyholder's defective work or nonperformance was substantially certain to create injury, courts may be justified in finding that the contract breach was insufficiently accidental. *See, e.g., Keneke Roofing, Inc. v. Island Ins. Co.*, 98 P.3d 246 (Haw. 2004) (contractor's abandonment of roofing contract which exposed building to elements made wager damage so foreseeably inevitable as to negate coverage). However, if the contractor in a case like this was forced to abandon the project due to factors beyond its control or failed to follow through because of negligence, a case like *Keneke Roofing* would appear to be incorrectly reasoned.

Despite the widespread standardization of liability policies, there can be variance that is crucial to the question of coverage in construction defect matters. *See, e.g., Westfield Ins. Co. v. Sheehan Constr. Co.*, 564 F.3d 817 (7th Cir. 2009) (applying Indiana law) (where policyholder purchased CGL policy that lacked subcontractor exception to the "your work" exclusion, no coverage available under circumstances of case).

The issue of CGL coverage for construction defect claims remains one of the more active areas of coverage litigation. *See, e.g., Am. Empire Surplus Lines Ins. Co. v. Hath-*

*away Dev. Co.*, 707 S.E.2d 369 (Ga. 2011) (claim against policyholder due to alleged injuries to claimant property caused by policyholder's defective plumbing work covered; faulty work can constitute an occurrence); *Crossmann Cmtys. of N.C., Inc. v. Harleysville Mut. Ins. Co.*, 2011 S.C. LEXIS 2, at *24–*25 (Jan. 7, 2011) ("We hold that where the damage to the insured's property is no more than the natural and probable consequences of faulty workmanship such that the two cannot be distinguished, this does not constitute an occurrence."); *Sheehan Constr. Co. v. Cont'l Cas. Co.*, 935 N.E.2d 160 (Ind. 2010) (finding coverage via the subcontractor exception to the "your work" exclusion). *But see Sheehan Constr. Co. v. Cont'l Cas. Co.*, 938 N.E.2d 685 (Ind. 2010) (on rehearing, court finds late notice to insurer, raising presumption of prejudice under Indiana law that policyholder did not rebut; no coverage); *Lamar Homes, Inc. v. Mid-Continent Cas. Co.*, 242 S.W.3d 1 (Tex. 2007) (finding coverage under builder's CGL policy for construction defect claims; taking approach similar to Wisconsin Supreme Court in *American Girl v. American Family*, *supra*); *Travelers Indem. Co. of Am. v. Moore & Assocs.*, 216 S.W.3d 302 (Tenn. 2007) (coverage for construction defect claims); *U.S. Fire Ins. Co. v. J.S.U.B. Inc.*, 979 So. 2d 871 (Fla. 2007) (coverage available under CGL for construction defect claims); *Auto-Owners Ins. Co. v. Pozzi Window Co.*, 984 So. 2d 1241 (Fla. 2008) (no coverage for contractor's defective window installation absent water intrusion damaging additional property other than windows themselves); *Auto-Owners Ins. Co. v. Home Pride Cos.*, 684 N.W.2d 571 (Neb. 2004) (claims against policyholder for faulty work are an occurrence if there is injury or property damage to something other than policyholder's own work).

### Additional Insureds

An additional insurance coverage issue that frequently crops up in construction defect or other liability claims related to commercial operations involves the status of "additional insureds" under a potentially applicable policy. *See, e.g., Kassis v. Ohio Cas. Ins. Co.*, 913 N.E.2d 933 (N.Y. 2009) (landlord an additional insured under tenant's CGL policy).

Recall that the primary or "named" insured generally purchases the policy and that some individuals or entities are "insureds" under the policy by operation of the policy language. Commercial liability policies also frequently designate entities other than the main policyholder as "additional insureds" by name. For example, a general contractor may insist as part of its arrangements with subcontractors that the general contractor be named as an additional insured on all subcontractor policies. This gives the general contractor more protection generally and specifically helps the general contractor if it should be sued because of mistakes made by a subcontractor.

Controversies can arise as to the scope of liability coverage offered to an additional insured. For example, a common controversy is whether the insurance provides coverage only where the additional insured is accused of "active" negligence or is sued merely for vicarious liability. You can see how this would matter in many construction defect claims in which a general contractor did not actually do the allegedly defective work but the plaintiff seeks to hold the contractor responsible for mistakes made by subcontractors.

Although there is division among the courts, the majority approach has traditionally been to cover additional insureds for both active negligence and vicarious exposure. *See* MANILOFF & STEMPEL, Ch. 13; STEMPEL & KNUTSEN § 25.06; Douglas R. Richmond, *The Additional Problems of Additional Insureds*, 33 TORT & INS. L.J. 945, 958 (1998). *See, e.g., Fed. Ins. Co. v. Am. Hardware Mut. Ins. Co.*, 184 P.3d 390 (Nev. 2008); *Acceptance Ins. Co. v. Syufy Enters.*, 69 Cal. App. 4th 321 (1999).

Relatively recent versions of additional insured endorsements or policy language tend to restrict the coverage available to additional insureds. However, broader endorsements remain in common use as well. *See generally* Randy J. Maniloff, *Coverage for Additional Insured-Venders: Recent Markdowns by ISO and New York's High Court*, 19–36 MEALEY'S LITIG. REP. INS. 1 (July 26, 2005); Randy J. Maniloff, *Additional Insured Coverage and Legislative Changes on the Horizon — Taking ISO's 07 04 Additional Insured Revisions a Step Further*, 19–22 MEALEY'S LITIG. REP. INS. 11 (2005) (also found at Fc&S CASUALTY & SURETY VOLUME (Apr. 2005), at M.24-1); Fc&S Casualty & Surety Volume, *Additional Insured Endorsements: ISO's Revisions* (May 2004), at M.23-1; Laurence A. Steckman & Bruce M. Strikowsky, *Recurring Problems in Additional Insured Litigation*, 18–23 MEALEY'S LITIG. REP. INS. 14 (Apr. 20, 2004).

## [B] The "Qualified" Pollution Exclusion

A major font of litigation during the past 40 years has been pollution-related environmental liability. Like mass tort and mass property damage cases, these environmental pollution cases inevitably generate enormous legal disputes, often involving hundreds of millions of dollars, between the insured and the insurer, and between primary insurers, excess insurers, and reinsurers.

During the early years of the CGL policy form (1943–1966), there was some debate over whether gradual or ongoing pollution qualified as an "accident" under the then-prevailing language of the policies. The traditional position of many in the industry was that an accident was confined in time and space. But this position was never particularly sound intellectually. Courts increasingly rejected insurer arguments that ongoing negligence or other liability-creating behavior could not be an accident.

Eventually, insurers ran up a figurative white flag of sorts and switched from an accident form to the modern "occurrence" form, which retained the fortuity concept but specifically provided that continued exposure to substantially the same conditions was a covered occurrence subject to liability insurance coverage if it caused injury to third parties and led to a claim. The drafting history of the 1966 CGL form makes use of environmental examples to illustrate the difference between the 1955 accident form and the 1966 occurrence form.

But with the move to an occurrence form, there also came increase risk that insurers would provide pollution liability coverage under the CGL policy. Combined with increasing national and legal consciousness about the dangers of pollution and contaminant-related injury, this raised considerable industry fear. Liability insurance companies, in order to avoid such pollution liability claims, have drafted and incorporated various pollution exclusion clauses into their CGL policies. Insurers reacted by putting in wide use by 1970 a "qualified" pollution exclusion added to the standard CGL form as an endorsement. The exclusion was added to the basic CGL form in the 1973 revision.

This version of the pollution exclusion was qualified rather than absolute in that it excluded coverage for claims or injuries arising out of pollution-related liability and contained a broad definition of pollutants—but it also contained an exception to the exclusion that restored coverage if the discharge in question had been "sudden and accidental." During the 1970s and the early 1980s, insurers and policyholders disputed whether pollution need only be unintentional to be covered or instead had to be both accidental and abrupt. Policyholders argued that sudden was essentially a synonym for accidental and could point to supportive dictionary definitions. Insurers argued that the common understanding of "sudden" includes a time element and that the policyholder's proffered construction was redundant and therefore not an accurate interpretation of the 1970 Pollution Exclusion Endorsement or the 1973 CGL Form. Policyholder's countered by pointing out drafting history materials in which industry representatives had minimized the reach of the exclusion.

Courts split on the issue, eventually leading to the use of an "absolute" pollution exclusion in the 1986 revision of the CGL form (*see* § 9.12[C], *infra*). *See* MANILOFF & STEMPEL, Ch. 14 (2011). Although batting .500 would put a baseball player in Cooperstown, it was too low and unpredictable a winning percentage for insurers wishing to cover as little pollution liability as possible (although, as discussed below, with the accumulation of cases on the issue post-dating the change, it now appears insurers batted about .600 using the qualified exclusion). Despite the change in the basic CGL form, coverage disputes involving older policies with the qualified exclusion continue to crop up, with courts continuing roughly to divide in half. Some courts find unintended pollution (or even unintended injury, which is a clear misreading of the qualified pollution exclusion language) covered while an equal or slightly greater number find pollution coverage only if the discharge in question was abrupt as well as unexpected.

Approximately 20 states (probably California,[5] Connecticut, Delaware, Florida, Idaho, Iowa, Kansas, Maine, Maryland, Massachusetts, Michigan, Minnesota, Montana, Nebraska, New York, North Carolina, Ohio, Oklahoma, Tennessee, Utah, Wyoming) take the pro-insurer temporal view barring coverage for gradual pollution claims while another 13 states (Alabama, Colorado, Georgia, Illinois, Indiana, New Hampshire, New Jersey, Oregon, Pennsylvania, Rhode Island, South Carolina, West Virginia, Wisconsin) have adopted the pro-policyholder view that only claims resulting

---

5. *See State of California v. Allstate Ins. Co.*, 201 P.3d 1147, 1156 (Cal. 2009) (focusing on characteristics of discharge rather than damage done but unclear about degree of speed required in discharge). The highly involved facts of *State v. Allstate*, which arises out of pollution at the notorious Stringfellow Acid Pits, perhaps rates a novel, or at least a law review article.

from non-accidental pollution are excluded, often finding the qualified exclusion ambiguous and resolving the coverage decision against the insurer on that basis. Amazingly in view of the hotly contested nature of the issue, some states (e.g., Alaska, Arkansas, Hawaii, Nevada, North Dakota, Vermont) still have little or no instructive authority on this version of the exclusion, and perhaps never will while many states (e.g., Arizona, Kentucky, Louisiana, Mississippi, New Mexico, South Dakota, Texas, Virginia) have no definitive state supreme court precedent on the issue. *See* MANILOFF & STEMPEL, *supra*, Ch. 14.

As we have been suggesting (perhaps ad nauseum) throughout this casebook, different judicial approaches to contract interpretation (and to "the law" generally) tend to lead to different outcomes in contested cases. This can make not only for dramatic state-to-state variance for insurance law but also can make for great variance among lower courts in the absence of clear guidance from the relevant state supreme court. This problem can be particularly pronounced for federal courts, which in diversity cases look to the relevant state law (and most insurance law disputes are governed by state law, requiring federal courts to find and apply applicable state law using the choice of law rules of the forum state).

Georgia provides a good example of federal courts failing to correctly predict state supreme court sentiment about the meaning of the qualified exclusion. *Compare Claussen v. Aetna Casualty & Surety Co.*, 676 F. Supp. 1571 (S.D. Ga. 1987) (federal court applying Georgia law predicts that Georgia Supreme Court will construe qualified pollution exclusion to bar claims for gradual but unintended pollution), *with Claussen v. Aetna Casualty & Surety Co.*, 259 Ga. 333, 380 S.E.2d 686 (1989) (Georgia Supreme Court in fact construes qualified pollution in manner opposite to that predicted by federal court and finds that gradual but unintended pollution damage is covered despite qualified pollution exclusion).

The Georgia Supreme Court's decision in *Claussen* came as a result of a certified question sent to the Georgia High Court by the United States Court of Appeals for the Eleventh Circuit, which was reviewing the federal trial court decision in *Claussen*. As a result of the Georgia Supreme Court decision, the Eleventh Circuit reversed the federal District Court, providing an interesting illustration of the benefits of certification. The problem of divergence may even exist within the same state supreme court. *See, e.g., Dimmitt Chevrolet v. Southeastern Fid. Ins. Corp.*, 636 So. 2d 700 (Fla. 1993) (reversing itself and giving broader, more coverage-reducing construction of qualified pollution exclusion). *See also Alabama Plating* Co. *v. United States Fid. & Guar. Co.*, 690 So. 2d 331, 336 (Ala. 1996) (finding that qualified pollution exclusion did not bar coverage for gradual but unintentional pollution; decision based in part on drafting history of the exclusion and insurer representations made to state insurance regulators).

*Alabama Plating* is also notable because it is one of the few cases to hold that the meaning of the pollution exclusion is established by representations made to state insurance regulators by agents of insurers. This perspective, referred to perhaps misleadingly as "regulatory estoppel" argues that individual insurers are bound by insurance industry representations to the effect that the qualified pollution exclusion barred only intentional pollution. For the most part, state courts have spurned the regulatory estoppel argument. *But see* (in addition to *Alabama Plating*) *Morton Int'l v. General Accident Ins. Co.*, 629 A.2d 831 (N.J. 1993). However, if the issue of prior insurer statements to regulators as to the meaning of a policy provision is characterized not as estoppel (either equitable or promissory) but as merely part of the background surrounding the insurance policy, its invocation by courts seems considerably less controversial. *See* STEMPEL & KNUTSEN, § 14.11[b][2].

## [C] The "Absolute" Pollution Exclusion

### Kent Farms, Inc. v. Zurich Insurance Company

Supreme Court of Washington
140 Wn.2d 396, 998 P.2d 292 (2000)

**Johnson, J.**

This case involves the applicability of an insurance pollution exclusion clause to a claim based on a negligence tort. The Court of Appeals ruled the clause did not apply. We affirm.

In August 1994, Steve Gugenberger delivered diesel fuel to Kent Farms, Inc. (Kent Farms). After filling the farm's fuel storage tank, he closed the tank's intake valve and started to remove the delivery hose. Because of a faulty intake valve, fuel back-flowed over him. He struggled to replace the hose, to stop the potential spill of thousands of gallons of diesel fuel. Fuel was driven into his eyes, his lungs, and his stomach, causing him significant injury.

Gugenberger filed suit against Kent Farms in Adams County Superior Court. Kent Farms had a commercial farm liability insurance policy underwritten by Zurich Insurance Company (Zurich Insurance) in force at the time. Among other things, the policy provided it would pay "those sums that the 'insured' becomes legally obligated to pay as damages because of 'bodily injury' or 'property damage' to which the insurance applies. We will have the right and duty to defend any 'suit' seeking those damages."

Kent Farms turned to Zurich Insurance for help. Zurich Insurance refused to pay the claim or defend Kent Farms against the suit on the grounds the coverage was precluded by a pollution exclusion clause in the policy. At summary judgment, the trial court found the exception did not apply to exclude coverage. The Court of Appeals upheld the trial court on the grounds that diesel fuel "is not a pollutant when used as intended" and, thus, was not covered by the clause.

The court also found the clause ambiguous under these facts because it could be read as excluding any injury involving diesel fuel, or only traditional environmental injuries. Zurich Insurance petitioned this court for review of the Court of Appeals decisions, which we granted.

For the purpose of this appeal, Zurich Insurance agrees the claim is a "bodily injury" as defined by the insurance policy. Therefore, the issue is whether the pollution exclusion clause applies to a claim not based on environmental damage but on personal injury arising from alleged negligence on the part of the insured. Zurich Insurance's pollution exclusion clause reads as follows:

2. Exclusions

This insurance does not apply to:

....

c. (1) "Bodily injury" and "property damage" arising out of the actual, alleged or threatened discharge, dispersal, seepage, migration, release or escape of pollutants:

....

Pollutants means any solid, liquid, gaseous or thermal irritant or contaminant, including smoke, vapor, soot, fumes, acids, alkalis, chemicals and waste. Waste includes materials to be recycled, reconditioned or reclaimed.

Here, the underlying injury and cause of action are rooted in negligence, not in environmental harm caused by pollution. The plaintiff alleges negligence in the maintenance and design of a fuel storage facility that resulted in immediate bodily injury when a high-pressure jet of liquid struck him. We must decide whether the fact a pollutant appears in the causal chain triggers application of the exclusion clause. * * *

Put another way, we are required to view the exclusion in light of the whole policy to determine whether, in that context, the exclusion applies. We begin by examining what the exclusion and similar exclusions are intended to accomplish.

The qualified pollution exclusion clause, a precursor to the clause at issue here, came into existence so insurers could avoid the "yawning extent of potential liability arising from the gradual or repeated discharge of hazardous substances into the environment." Later, various forms of absolute pollution exclusion clauses, including the clause here, were incorporated into insurance policies in the wake of expanded environmental liability under the Comprehensive Environmental Response, Compensation, and Liability Act of 1980, 42 U.S.C. §§ 9601–9675 (1995) (CERCLA). These clauses were clearly intended to exculpate insurance companies from liability for massive environmental cleanups required by CERCLA and similar legislation. *See generally* Jeffrey W. Stempel, *Reason and Pollution: Correctly Construing the "Absolute" Exclusion in Context and in Accord with its Purpose and Party Expectations*, 34 Tort & Ins. L.J. 1, 5 (1998). The insurance companies' objective in creating both clauses was to avoid liability for environmental pollution. To read the absolute exclusion clause more broadly ignores the general coverage provisions.

This exclusion clause does not deal with the discharge of substances that may also be pollutants directly onto (and into) an individual; rather, this clause specifically addresses those situations in which injury was caused by environmental damage. We, therefore, hold the absolute pollution exclusion clause relates to environmental damage, and not to the facts of this case.

Zurich Insurance argues the pollution exclusion clause applies because diesel fuel is a pollutant. However, this reasoning misunderstands the nature of the claim. Gugenberger was not polluted by diesel fuel. It struck him; it engulfed him; it choked him. It did not pollute him. Most importantly, the fuel was not acting as a "pollutant" when it struck him any more than it would have been acting as a "pollutant" if it had been in a barrel that rolled over him, or if it had been lying quietly on the steps waiting to trip him. To adopt Zurich Insurance's interpretation would unjustly broaden the application of the exclusion far beyond its intended purpose.

To apply the pollution exclusion clause to the injury in this case would be contrary to this court's previous stance on interpreting exclusion clauses. We have previously held the average purchaser of a comprehensive liability policy reasonably expects broad coverage for liability arising from business operations and "exclusions should be construed strictly against the insurer." ...

This approach is consistent with that of other courts that have found such pollution exclusion clauses do not apply much beyond traditional environmental torts.... The New York Court of Appeals held that a similar clause did not apply to injuries arising from the inhalation of asbestos fibers, on the grounds it was ambiguous whether the clause applied to the release of asbestos fibers indoors. *Continental Cas. Co. v. Rapid-American Corp.* 80 N.Y.2d 640, 653, 593 N.Y.S.2d 966, 609 N.E.2d 506 (1993).

The results and theories of these cases are consistent with the analytical approach we follow in deciding the scope of the pollution exclusion. The exclusion, when viewed in the context of its purpose, does not apply merely because a potential pollutant was involved in the causal chain. Instead, the exclusion applies to "occurrences" involving the pollutant as a pollutant. Our approach is consonant with the understanding of the average purchaser of insurance and consistent with the provisions of the insurance policy as a whole; that is, the pollution exclusion clause was designed to exclude coverage for traditional environmental harms. We will not expand the scope of the exclusion clause beyond its intended purpose.

## The Quadrant Corporation v. American States Insurance Company

Supreme Court of Washington
154 Wn.2d 165, 110 P.3d 733 (2005)

**En Banc, Bridge, J.**

A tenant in an apartment building was overcome by fumes and became ill after a restoration company applied sealant to a nearby deck. The tenant sued the restoration company and the owners of the apartment building. Both the restoration company and the building owners settled and the owners now claim that their business liability insurance should cover the loss.

The business liability policies at issue here both contain absolute pollution exclusion clauses, which the insurers now argue apply to exclude coverage for the tenant's claim. The building owners contend that after this court's decision in *Kent Farms, Inc. v. Zurich Insurance Co.*, 998 P.2d 292 (2000), the pollution exclusion cannot be applied to exclude occurrences that are not "traditional environmental harms." The owners also assert that if it is applied as the insurers suggest, the pollution exclusion would render the policy illusory with regard to the restoration company.

We hold that the plain language of the absolute pollution exclusion clause encompasses the injuries at issue here and therefore the tenant's claim is excluded from coverage. We find that the *Kent Farms* case is distinguishable on its facts and instead we adopt the reasoning of *Cook v. Evanson*, 920 P.2d 1223 (1996), a case similar to this one in that it involved injuries that resulted from toxic fumes. Furthermore, we conclude that the pollution exclusion clause does not render the policies illusory with respect to the building owners because the insurance policy will still cover a variety of claims, including slip and fall accidents, despite the pollution exclusion. We note that the restoration company is not a party to this case and, thus, the question of whether the insurance contract is illusory with respect to the restoration company is not properly before us. The insureds' request for attorney fees is denied....

The facts of this case are not in dispute. Roy Street Associates owns an apartment building located at 200 Roy Street in Seattle. In 1996, the building owners hired Pacific Restoration to make repairs and improvements on the building. In the course of completing the repair work, Pacific Restoration applied waterproofing sealants to the surface of a deck. The parties agree that Pacific Restoration used PC-220 and Polyglaze AL, manufactured by Polycoat Products. Both contain various chemicals, including a toxic substance called toluene diisocyanate (TDI), whose fumes can irritate the respiratory tract and, in high concentrations, can cause central nervous system depression....

Delores Kaczor was a tenant in the apartment adjacent to the deck. Pacific failed to warn Kaczor that it would be applying the sealant and then failed to properly ventilate the area. Fumes entered her apartment as the deck dried, making her ill enough to require hospitalization. Specifically, Kaczor's estate claimed that exposure to the fumes caused "exacerbation of her preexisting chronic obstructive pulmonary disease" and led to her "debilitating and declining health." Kaczor filed a lawsuit against Pacific Restoration and the building owners claiming personal injury and property damage. Kaczor died in 1998 and her lawsuit was dismissed without prejudice. In 1999, her estate filed a second lawsuit based on Kaczor's injuries. That suit was settled for $30,000 and dismissed in July 2000.

\* \* \*

*Application of the Absolute Pollution Exclusion in this Case:* Unlike the diesel fuel in *Kent Farms*, *Cook* involved a substance whose toxicity could cause injury even when used as intended. Thus, the *Cook* reasoning and not the *Kent Farms* rule would control when fumes caused injury and where the pollutant was being used as it was intended. Because the tenant in this case was injured by fumes emanating from water proofing material that was being used as intended, the air in her apartment was "polluted." Thus, the pollution exclusion applied and the court affirmed the summary judgment dismissal of the insureds' suit. We agree.

In this case, the policy language clearly states that the liability coverage does not apply to *bodily injury* or *property damage* arising out of the dispersal, *seepage, migration,* release, or escape of a *gaseous irritant,* including vapors, *fumes* and chemicals, at any *premises owned by the insured* or *any premises onto which a contractor* or subcontractor hired by the insured *has brought a pollutant.* The language clearly applies to bodily injury and property damage; it is not limited to actions for cleanup costs....

When considering the facts of this case, it is difficult to see how a reasonable person could interpret the policy language such that it would not encompass the claim at issue here. The Kaczor estate claims that she suffered *bodily injury and property damage* when the deck sealant *fumes* drifted or *migrated* into her apartment. The sealant was applied at property owned by the insureds.

The insureds argue that this court's decision in *Kent Farms requires* us to conclude that the absolute pollution exclusion can be applied only to exclude liability for "traditional environmental pollution." The *Kent Farms* court examined the history of the absolute pollution exclusion, but to do so, the court must have concluded that the exclusion was ambiguous with regard to the facts of that case. An absolute pollution exclusion clause can be ambiguous with regard to the facts of one case but not another. The *Kent Farms* facts are not present here. Where, as here, the exclusion unambiguously applies to the facts of the case at hand, the plain language must be applied without reference to extrinsic evidence regarding the intent of the parties....

While the *Kent Farms* case included language regarding the purpose behind the pollution exclusion, the court was careful to explain that the exclusion applies to "'occurrences' involving the pollutant *as a pollutant.*" In other words, the *Kent Farms* court distinguished between cases in which the substance at issue was polluting at the time of the injury and cases in which the offending substance's toxic character was not central to the injury.

Given Washington's clear rules for insurance contract interpretation, we reject the reasoning of other states that have declined to apply the pollution exclusion in fumes cases. The pollution exclusion at issue here unambiguously precludes coverage for the Kaczor claim and we decline to find ambiguity where none exists. Therefore, we affirm the Court of Appeals holding that the absolute pollution exclusion applies to these facts, distinguishing *Kent Farms* and adopting the reasoning in *Cook.*

Illusory Contract

The insureds contend that if the pollution exclusion is interpreted broadly, the exclusion will swallow all covered occurrences, making the policy illusory.... We conclude that because the pollution exclusion does not preclude coverage for many accidents that could occur on the building owners' property, the exclusion does not render the insurance contracts illusory. For example, slip and fall injuries would clearly fall outside of the pollution exclusion. Therefore the covered "occurrences" and excluded incidents are not mutually exclusive, and the exclusion does not render the insurance contracts illusory.

**Chambers, J.** (dissenting).

The majority embarks upon the noble quest of clarifying the law. Unfortunately, the majority confuses the "occurrence," or coverage triggering event, with the consequent damages. Specifically, the majority confuses a non polluting *event* covered by the policy with the resulting *damages*, which were caused by pollutants. Because we look at the occurrence to determine coverage, not the resulting damage, I respectfully dissent.

Our jurisprudence has been consistent in analyzing pollution exclusions. "The relevant inquiry is whether there has been a polluting event." In my view, the pollution exclusion operates only on polluting events. But if the "occurrence" triggering coverage was not a polluting event, then there is coverage. As we said, "'[i]f the initial event, the "efficient proximate cause," is a covered peril, then there is coverage under the policy regardless whether subsequent events within the chain, which may be causes-in-fact of the loss, are excluded by the policy.'" This initial event, the efficient proximate cause, should not be confused with the resulting damage. This is not new. This court has long adopted the "efficient proximate cause" rule for determining whether an event is covered or not.

> "Where *a peril specifically insured against sets other causes in motion* which, in an unbroken sequence and connection between the act and final loss, produce the result for which recovery is sought, *the insured peril is regarded as the 'proximate cause' of the entire loss.*
>
> "It is the efficient or predominant cause which sets into motion the chain of events producing the loss which is regarded as the proximate cause, not necessarily the last act in a chain of events."

Consider an auto accident in which a driver was saturated in fuel, and suffered specific injuries from the irritating nature of the chemical compound and its noxious fumes. There would be coverage for this "occurrence" and the resulting damages. In this example, the occurrence is the alleged negligent act which caused the motor vehicle collision. The mere fact that a pollutant was involved in the causal chain of events does not trigger the pollution exclusion. There is coverage so long as "a covered peril sets in motion a causal chain" even when "the last link of which is an uncovered peril." The covered peril here was the alleged negligence of the contractor and apartment owner in performing routine work necessary to maintain the apartment building.

[T]he policies at issue are commercial comprehensive general liability policies. For our purposes, the apartment owners are insured under both policies. Because these are broad and comprehensive policies we must not only interpret them as would an average person purchasing insurance but we must also strictly construe any exclusions against the insurers....

Here, coverage is broad. The Americans States' policy says, "We will pay those sums that the insured becomes legally obligated to pay as damages because of 'bodily injury' or 'property damage' to which this insurance applies." As any exclusion must be read within the context of the coverage provided, we must first examine the definitions of "occurrence" within the policies. Both policies have the identical definition of occurrence: "'Occurrence' means an accident, including continuous or repeated exposure to substantially the same general harmful conditions." Thus, the insured is led to understand that his insurance coverage extends to the continuous or repeated exposure to harmful conditions....

[T]he specific contentions against the apartment owner was the failure to assure proper ventilation or to warn of the fumes.

The question before this court is whether the average purchaser of a comprehensive liability policy understand that the act or applying waterproofing to the exterior wall of an apartment building would be an act of "discharge, dispersal, seepage, migration, (or) release" of a pollutant.... This court has never held that mere injury by a pollutant triggers a pollution exclusion. This court has always examined the pollution exclusion by determining whether the "occurrence" was a polluting event. A polluting event is the discharge, dispersal, seepage, migration, release or escape of pollutants. This court, when addressing this question within the plain, ordinary, and popular meaning in accord with the understanding of the average purchaser of insurance has adopted the traditional meaning of pollution. This court has also always viewed pollution exclusions from their traditional purpose of avoiding massive exposure for environmental damage. This history is an integral part of a proper understanding of the clauses. * * * *see also generally* Jeffrey W. Stempel, *Reason and Pollution: Correctly Construing the "Absolute" Exclusion in Context and in Accord with its Purpose and Party Expectations*, 34 Tort & Ins. L.J. 1, 5 (1998).

The majority distinguishes *Kent Farms* on the grounds that *Kent Farms* did not explicitly recite that it found the clause ambiguous. Therefore, it concludes, *Kent Farms* discussion of the history of the clause was, apparently, not binding on future courts. But read as a whole, it is clear the court believed that the clause was ambiguous, at least as applied to the facts of *Kent Farms*, as it referred approvingly to the Court of Appeals holding that the clause was ambiguous and proceeded to review the drafting history of the clause.

Against that backdrop, it is clear that applying the clause to exclude this type of harm is appropriate only if the "occurrence" that triggers coverage is a polluting event. In my view, the average consumer of a general liability policy would not understand that applying wood preservative to the exterior of an apartment building was a polluting event. As this court has already noted, expanding the exclusion to cover any type of occurrence that involves pollution would be an "opportunistic afterthought," outside the intent of the drafters. I conclude this does violence to the meaning of the exclusion and our recent unanimous *Kent Farms* opinion. Accordingly, I respectfully dissent.

## Notes and Questions

1. What's going on regarding the opinions of the Washington Supreme Court in *Kent Farms* and *Quadrant Corp.*? Can the cases be reconciled on their different facts or is something else at work such as changes in the court's membership or the court's views of contract and insurance law? Which case do you expect to become the dominant law of Washington?

2. Which case's analysis is most persuasive? Which perspective do you expect to win out over time? Or will the states simply remain divided over the scope and applicability of the absolute pollution exclusion. Remember, the exclusion has been around in substantially this form for more than 20 years.

3. Currently, approximately seven states (e.g., Florida, Georgia, Iowa, Nebraska, Oklahoma, Pennsylvania, South Dakota) appear to take a fairly literal interpretation of the absolute exclusion and invoke it to deny even claims traditionally covered under the CGL that are not normally viewed as environmental contamination or toxic tort claims. Another 13 states (Alabama, Arkansas, California, Illinois, Indiana, Louisiana, Maryland, New Hampshire, New Jersey, New York, Ohio, Wisconsin, Wyoming) are reluctant to read the exclusion literally or broadly or to use it to preclude coverage for traditional general liability matters.

As the above juxtaposition of *Kent Farms* and *Quadrant* shows, some states like Washington are arguably inconsistent, hard to classify, or have been affected by changes in state supreme court membership. A number of states (e.g., Delaware, New Mexico, North Dakota, Rhode Island, Vermont) lack any real instructive authority or lack definitive state supreme court authority (e.g., Arizona, Colorado, Hawaii, Kansas, Kentucky, Maine, Michigan, Minnesota, Mississippi, Missouri, Nevada, North Carolina, Oregon, South Carolina, Tennessee, Utah), even though some of these states can be seen as trending in one direction or the other regarding zeal for applying the exclusion.

There is also some confusion in that some states (e.g., Alaska, Connecticut, Montana, Texas, Virginia, West Virginia) have applied the exclusion only to genuine contamination claims but have done so in language (e.g., describing the exclusion as "clear and unambiguous") that suggests these states might apply the exclusionary language literally and broadly to preclude traditional general liability coverage. *See* Maniloff & Stempel, Ch. 15.

4. For a relatively spirited debate on the issue, *compare* William P. Shelley & Richard C. Mason, *Application of the Absolute Pollution Exclusion to Toxic Tort Claims: Will Courts Choose Policy Construction or Deconstruction?*, 33 Tort & Ins. L.J. 749 (1998), with Jeffrey W. Stempel, *Reason and Pollution: Correctly Construing the "Absolute" Exclusion in Context and in Accord with Its Purpose and Party Expectations*, 34 Tort & Ins. L.J. 1 (1998).

# § 9.13. The Problem of Government-Mandated Expenditures

Since the 1986 revision of the standard CGL policy, it has been pretty clear that standard liability insurance does not provide coverage when the policyholder is asked to pay or expend money as a result of a government-administered program designed to rectify problems such as pollution or land condition generally. Prior to this change in language, there was significant debate — and litigation — concerning whether government claims for remediation or reimbursement! for remediation constituted a claims for "damages" within the meaning of the CGL policy. As the following two cases illustrate, courts divided nearly in half on the issue, even when allegedly applying the same governing law. Although current ISO policy language appears to moot this issue, there remain some pending claims or potential claims involving older CGL policies where the issue can occasionally crop up.

The differing approaches and results in these "Superfund coverage" cases provides a dramatic illustration of the differing insurance coverage jurisprudence. This is well-illustrated by the insurance coverage battles surrounding contamination near Times Beach, Missouri. Waste water containing dioxin and other contaminants had been sprayed on dirt roads as a dust suppressant, resulting in substantial soil contamination. Pursuant to the federal Superfund law, government regulators required clean-up and remediation of affected property. Not surprisingly, those required to effect this expensive cleanup turned to their insurers.

The first appellate court to take on the issue was the federal U.S. Court of Appeals for the Eighth Circuit, a jurisdiction that encompasses several Midwestern states, including Missouri, the site of the problem and the state that provided the applicable law. The Eight Circuit held that CERCLA response costs were not "damages" within the meaning of the CGL policy. *See Continental Ins. Cos. v. Northeastern Pharmaceutical & Chemical Co.*, 842 F.2d 977 (8th Cir. 1988) (en banc). Then another policyholder and insurer pressed the issue before the District of Columbia Circuit. Applying Missouri law, the D.C. Circuit found coverage. *See Independent Petrochemical Corp. v. Aetna Casualty & Sur. Co.*, 944 F.2d 940 (D.C. Cir. 1991). When the issue finally came before the final authority—the Missouri Supreme Court—it determined that environmental cleanup costs constituted damages under the language of the pre-1986 CGL. *See Farmland Indus. v. Republic Ins. Co.*, 941 S.W.2d 505 (Mo. 1997). The 1986 ISO revisions to the standard CGL clearly exclude Superfund response expenses from coverage.

Not only do courts applying the same law differ on this issue, at least one state supreme court has reversed itself within a relatively short time. *See Johnson Controls, Inc. v. Emplrs. Ins.*, 264 Wis. 2d 60, 665 N.W.2d 257 (2003) (holding that CERCLA response costs are covered under standard CGL policy, *rev'g City of Edgerton v. General Cas. Co.*, 184 Wis. 2d 750, 517 N.W.2d 463 (1994), *cert. denied*, 514 U.S. 1017 (1995), on the basis of additional information regarding the background and drafting history of CGL provision providing coverage regarding actions "for damage").

# § 9.14. "Claims Made" versus "Occurrence" Liability Coverage

Insurance companies have developed a number of different approaches to define the period of time for which specific insurance coverage is to be provided. One common technique is to define the duration of coverage based upon the "occurrence" of an insured event within a particular time period specified in the policy. Automobile liability insurance policies and homeowner's insurance policies are two common examples of such "occurrence" coverage. Other liability insurance policies, including some types of professional liability insurance and newer comprehensive general liability insurance policies, provide coverage for claims that are made during the coverage period, rather than for occurrences during the coverage period. Basically, "occurrence" policies provide coverage if the insured event giving rise to liability occurred during the policy period, regardless of when the act or neglect was discovered or when the claim was filed with the insurer. "Claims made" policies, on the other hand, provide coverage if the act or neglect is discovered and brought to the insurer's attention during the policy's term, regardless of when the act occurred. *See generally* KEETON & WIDISS, INSURANCE LAW §5.10(d)(1)–(3) (1988).

One disadvantage of an "occurrence" policy is the problem of the long "tail," or the lapse of time between the date of the insured event and the time the claim is made. For example, a medical or legal professional may commit an act of malpractice in one year, but the consequences of this malpractice may not be apparent until several years later. Also, in progressive disease and progressive injury cases — such as asbestosis litigation — it is very difficult to determine exactly when the insured "occurrence" actually happened. Thus, "claims made" coverage helps the insurer to accurately calculate the premiums, since under an "occurrence" policy the premiums collected in one year may be inadequate to pay out on future claims, and the insurer may have trouble under an "occurrence" policy in accurately matching the premiums against the payable proceeds.

A "claims made" policy, however, is not without its own disadvantages — but these are generally viewed as falling on the policyholder rather than the insurer. One disadvantage is that it provides no prospective coverage for the professional who wants to go out of business or change jobs and yet have coverage in the future for events occurring during the last years of practice. This problem, however, can be overcome through the purchase of "tail" coverage. Another disadvantage is that the claims-made policy provides unlimited retroactive coverage. To control this potential problem, insurers typically insert a requirement that the act or neglect resulting from the claim must have occurred after a specified date — the "Retroactive Date" of the policy. This limits retroactivity of a policy, but it creates the possibility of a gap in coverage for some insureds. *See generally* JERRY & RICHMOND, Understanding Insurance Law §62A[e].

Even though many consumers still do not properly understand the underlying rationale — and the pitfalls — of claims-made policies, such policies have generally been upheld by the courts on public policy grounds, in the absence of ambiguous policy language. *See, e.g., Scarborough v. Travelers Ins. Co.*, 718 F.2d 702 (5th Cir. 1983); *Gulf Ins. Co. v. Dolan, Fertig & Curtis*, 433 So. 2d 512 (Fla. 1983). *But see contra Jones v. Continental Casualty Co.*, 303 A.2d 91 (N.J. Super. 1973), where the claims-made policy contained ambiguous language, and where the reasonable expectations of the insured would be disappointed. *See also* Note, *The "Claims Made" Dilemma in Professional Liability Insurance*, 22 UCLA L. Rev. 925 (1975).

Perhaps the greatest distinction between claims-made and occurrence policies—
and the most litigated aspect of the difference—involves the mechanics of notice
and the consequences of late notice. As discussed in §9.01, the prevailing rule for
notice regarding an occurrence policy is that late notice defeats coverage only if
the insurer is prejudiced. By contrast, most courts accept the insurer position that
the nature of the claims-made policy makes late notice a fatal problem of policyholders, at least if the policy requires that claims be both made against the policyholder and reported to the insurer during the policy period. *See, e.g., Catholic Med.
Ctr. v. Exec. Risk Indem., Inc.*, 867 A.2d 453 (N.H. 2005); *Hasbrouck v. St. Paul Fire
& Marine Ins. Co.*, 511 N.W.2d 364 (Iowa 1993); *Gulf Ins. Co. v. Dolan, Fertig &
Curtis*, 433 So. 2d 512 (Fla. 1983). *See also Prodigy Communs. Corp. v. Agric. Excess
& Surplus Ins. Co.*, 288 S.W.3d 374 (Tex. 2009) (even where notice not prompt, in-
surer must show prejudice if notice nonetheless given within policy period, at least
where notice provision provides for notice "as soon as practicable" rather than "im-
mediately," "promptly," or within a given date); *Fin. Indus. Corp. v. XL Specialty Ins.
Co.*, 285 S.W.3d 877 (Tex. 2009) (same).

The argument of insurers is that receipt of the claim within the specified time defines the scope of the policy's coverage and that timely notice is an essential definition
of the coverage rather than merely a requirement placed on the policyholder after
loss or the filing of a lawsuit. Prompt notice is thus a condition precedent to coverage
for which there must be strict compliance if there is to be coverage.

In addition to making this traditional, quite formalist contract interpretation argument, claims-made insurers make a functional or public policy argument as well
by contending that the very nature of the claims-made policy is designed so that the
insurer is able to know exactly what claims it will face arising out of a particular
policy period as soon as the policy period is over. Armed with this knowledge, the
insurer can then promptly set apt reserves and determine whether to renew coverage,
continue to write certain lines of coverage, set premiums and the like. *See Root v.
American Equity Specialty Ins. Co.*, 130 Cal. App. 4th 926, 945 (2005) (although in
this case, the court found the policyholder was excused from its late notice by the
circumstances of the case).

*Query:* This argument appears persuasive as a general matter. Certainly, insurers
were surprised and upset when they found out about asbestos and pollution claims
years or even decades after the end of an occurrence policy period but were nonetheless
required to defend and pay, a factor that led to greater use of the claims-made form
for general liability insurance as well as in its traditional markets of Professional Liability, Errors & Omissions, and Directors & Officers Liability. But should these
factors require a complete forfeiture of coverage if the policyholder has missed the
reporting deadline by only days, weeks, or perhaps a month or two? This is still considerably different than the leeway accorded policyholders under the traditional notice-prejudice rule for occurrence policies. *See* Bob Works, *Excusing Nonoccurrence
of Insurance Policy Conditions in Order to Avoid Disproportionate Forfeiture: Claims-
Made Formats as a Test Cas* e, 5 Conn. Ins. L.J. 505, 515 (1998).

What if the policyholder has knowledge of a claim (or facts likely to give rise to a claim) at the time of renewal of coverage and intentionally holds off telling the insurer until after a new policy is in place? Does that make you more sympathetic to the insurer's position? *See United States v. Strip*, 868 F.2d 181, 188–89 (6th Cir. 1989) (policyholder with knowledge of claim at early stage of policy period should not wait months to near-end of policy before reporting claim). But what if the policyholder is in good faith attempting to resolve the claim for an amount less than its deductible or self-insured retention? Would the timing of any renewal negotiations or purchase of subsequent insurance again affect your thinking about what rule should apply?

At the margin, courts may be distinguishing between cases based on slight differences in the claims-made policy language (at least we think they are slight; insurer or policyholder counsel may disagree). Where the policy clearly requires that claims be both made against the policyholder and reported to the insurer prior to the expiration of the policy period, courts appear to be giving this requirement very strict construction and barring coverage for missing the deadline even slightly. *See, e.g., Maynard v. Westport Ins. Corp.*, 208 F. Supp. 2d 568, 574 (D. Md. 2002); *Catholic Med. Ctr. v. Exec. Risk Indem., Inc.*, 867 A.2d 453, 455 (N.H. 2005).

But where the policy simply states that it covers only claims made against the policyholder during the policy period, some courts appear willing to apply at least a modest version of the notice-prejudice rule and bar coverage only where the claim is reported sufficiently after the policy period's expiration to cause prejudice to the insurer. *See, e.g., Pension Trust Fund v. Fed. Ins. Co.*, 307 F.3d 944 (9th Cir. 2002); *Hardwick Recycling & Salvage, Inc. v. Acadia Ins. Co.*, 869 A.2d 82, 84, 96 (Vt. 2004); *Zuckerman v. National Union Fire Ins. Co.*, 495 A.2d 395 (N.J. 1985); *Gazis v. Miller*, 892 A.2d 1277 (N.J. 2006). *But see Lexington Ins. Co. v. Rugg & Knopp, Inc.*, 165 F.3d 1087 (7th Cir. 1999) (applying Wisconsin law) (finding state statute, which codifies notice-prejudice rule by its terms applies to claims-made-and-reported policy as well as to occurrence policies).

## PROBLEM THREE

Efficient Builder used Vest Plastic Plumbing (VPP) technology throughout McMansion Acres, a 500-home development in Posh Suburb outside Millenial City that was built during Years 1, 2 and 3. The homes sell like proverbial hotcakes at high prices. Builder's ordinarily very good profits on such subdivisions is increased roughly twenty (20) percent because VPP plumbing is so much cheaper than traditional metal pipe plumbing.

Builder is sufficiently encouraged that it used VPP plumbing in Woke Towers, its new urban high-rise development in the former Warehouse District of Millenial City. Although the condominium units of Woke Towers are a different type of structure for a completely different demographic, Builder reasons that "plumbing is plumbing" and expects to score equal or greater profit from the high-rise development, which is being built during the Years 4 and 5.

Trouble arises in McMansion Acres. In Year 4, several of the homes start to have leaky plumbing, which consulted construction experts attribute to the VPP plumbing, which is showing signs of problems throughout the country in developments were it has been used. Soon more of the McMansions are sprouting leaks.

Based on data from Ranger Ridge, the oldest suburban development to use VPP piping that was completed roughly five years before the McMansion Acres construction began, construction experts predict that half of all VPP units will develop sufficiently significant leak problems to require replacement. Another 10–15 percent will require minor repairs of a problematic linkage or two, while roughly a third of the VPP homes will remain problem free for the estimated 75-year useful life of the plumbing.

Builder has in place each year a $215 million tower of liability insurance covering all of its operations that includes $15 primary general liability insurance with a $5 million deductible and two $100 million layers of excess general liability insurance (see the chapter regarding excess and umbrella insurance). Replacement of the entire plumbing system in a single McMansion costs roughly $150,000 because of the size of the homes and the need to tear out and replace walls to get to the plumbing.

At the beginning of Year 5, the 40 McMansion owners who have experienced leaky plumbing sue Builder, seeking class action status on behalf of the entire subdivision. Their theory of the case is that all of the 40 homes with leaks need completely new plumbing systems and that Builder should pay for this as well as establishing a compensation fund sufficiently large that it can pay for the remaining homes that may develop minor leaks or require total plumbing replacement.

Builder tenders defense of the claims to the Primary Insurer. Insurer accepts defense of the action involving 40 homes but states that it will not defend any class action portion of the case and will not pay for any plumbing repairs in homes that have yet to spring a leak before the end of the policy period.

Primary Insurer refuses to renew coverage for the next policy year unless the policy has a specific VPP plumbing claims exclusion. Builder begins shopping for a new primary insurer but has no luck. Word has gotten around the insurance community about VPP plumbing, and all insurers are excluding such claims from otherwise available coverage.

Primary Insurer also commences a Declaratory Judgment action against Builder seeking a court decision stating that Insurer need not cover any claims related to VPP plumbing in Woke Towers unless there has been an actual physical leak of the plumbing. Insurer is hoping to make it to the end of the year (which is also the end of the policy period) without any such leaks, as the high rise was only recently completed.

You are outside counsel to Builder. The CEO wants your opinion on the following questions if coverage matters are litigated to conclusion:

- Do the Year 1 CGL policies apply to the McMansion claims?

- Do the Year 2 CGL policies apply to the McMansion claims?

- Do the Year 3 CGL policies apply to the McMansion claims?

- Do the Year 4 CGL policies apply to the McMansion claims?

- Do the Year 5 CGL policies apply to the McMansion claims?

- On what factor(s) does the answer to these questions turn?

- What will be Insurer's position when it is forced to explain in more detail?

- Who is likely to prevail?

- Do the Year 4 CGL policies apply to potential Woke Towers Claims?

- Do the Year 5 CGL policies apply to potential Woke Towers Claims?

- Why or why not?

- More precisely, when is coverage triggered in these matters?

- What particular evidence may be crucial to determining trigger?

- Should insurer responsibility be pro-rated by years on the risk?

- Why or why not?

- What are the conditions that may make pro-ration important or unimportant in these situations?

- Where do the excess policies in each Year's tower fit in?

- Should the excess insurers be notified of the McMansion Claims?[6]

- By whom—Builder? Primary Insurer? Both?

- Should the excess insurers be notified about potential Woke Towers claims?

- By whom—Builder? Primary Insurer? Both?

- What are the public policy and practical commercial consequences of the different choices to be made regarding trigger, allocation, and other coverage issues presented in this claim and similar claims?

# § 9.15. Coverage "B" of the Commercial General Liability Policy: "Personal Injury" and "Advertising Injury"

Most commonly, liability policies are called upon to provide defense and payment for claims alleging bodily injury or property damage. However, the standard CGL policy also contains a second portion or "Part B" (Part A being the coverage for bodily

---

6. *See* the chapter on excess and umbrella insurance.

injury/property damage) that provides coverage for the policyholder confronted with third-party claims alleging "advertising injury" or "personal injury."

"Advertising injury" claims are those claiming that the third party has been damaged by the advertising activities of the policyholder. Examples would be policyholder advertising that successfully but wrongfully disparages the third party's products or services. Other covered advertising injuries are violation of privacy, infringement of "copyright, title, or slogan," or misappropriation of another's advertising ideas or style of doing business. The policyholder's advertising must be the source of the claimed injury. It is usually not enough that the policyholder has advertised some facet of an operation claimed to have wrongfully caused injury to a third party. *See* Donald S. Malecki & Arthur L. Flitner, Commercial General Liability (7th ed. 2001); Stempel & Knutsen, § 14.06; *Bank of the West v. Superior Court*, 2 Cal. 4th 1254, 10 Cal. Rptr. 2d 538, 833 P.2d 545 (1992). *But see J.A. Brundage Plumbing & Roto-Rooter v. Massachusetts Bay Ins. Co.*, 818 F. Supp. 553 (W.D.N.Y. 1993) (taking broad view of advertising injury coverage). *See also* David Gauntlett, Insurance Coverage of Intellectual Property Assets (2d. ed. 2019); David Gauntlett, IP Attorney's Handbook for Insurance Coverage in Intellectual Property Disputes (2d ed. 2014).

As examples of advertising injury cases, *see Dogloo, Inc. v. Northern Ins. Co.*, 907 F. Supp. 1383 (C.D. Cal. 1995) (addressing questions of misappropriation of trade dress as advertising injury); *Advance Watch Co. v. Kemper Nat'l Ins. Co.*, 99 F.3d 795 (6th Cir. 1996) (holding trade dress action not to come within advertising injury coverage). *See also Mylan Labs. v. Am. Motorists Ins. Co.*, 700 S.E.2d 518 (W. Va. 2010) (no advertising injury coverage for policyholder allegedly conducting "scheme to fraudulently manipulate the average wholesale price of its drugs" due to some advertising of price spreads among pharmaceutical products); *Super Duper v. Pa. Nat'l Mut. Cas. Ins. Co.*, 683 S.E.2d 792 (S.C. 2009) (claim against policyholder for trademark infringement may come within advertising injury coverage); *Santa's Best Craft, L.L.C. v. Zurich Am. Ins. Co.*, 941 N.E.2d 291, 302–04 (Ill. Ct. App. 2010) (policyholder's selective invitation to vendors to see product allegedly infringing claimant's product was not sufficiently wide dissemination of marketing communication to meet definition of advertising injury).

"Personal injury" coverage in the CGL policy covered third-party claims against the policyholder alleging false arrest, malicious prosecution, wrongful eviction or entry onto property, defamation, or violation of privacy. Note that under this portion of Part B CGL coverage, the defamation or invasion of privacy need not be advertised, although it must be "published," an element of these claims that is normally satisfied so long as a person other than claimant or defendant becomes aware of the defamatory or privacy-invading material.

Because of the nature of personal injury coverage, the ground rules for determining fortuity and the expected/intended injury exclusion are different than for Part A coverage under the CGL. *See generally* Stempel & Knutsen § 14.05. For an example of a case rejecting an insurer's invocation of an exclusion to its personal injury coverage in a defamation claim against the policyholder, see *Pharmacists Mut. Ins. Co. v. Myer, Cooper and MMG Ins. Co.*, 993 A.2d 413 (Vt. 2010). *But see Chrysler Ins. Co. v. Greenspoint Dodge of Houston, Inc.*, 297 S.W.3d 248 (Tex. 2009) (upholding and applying "known-falsity" exception to otherwise available defamation coverage).

Because advertising involves media, technological changes can produce new varieties of claims. For example, the invention of the fax machine enabled mass advertising by "junk faxes" akin to junk mail, which in turn spawned litigation by recipients of the unwanted faxes against the senders of junk faxes. In response, Congress enacted the Telephone Consumer Protection Act (TCPA), 47 U.S.C. § 227, which prohibits the use of fax machines, computers, or other devices to send unsolicited advertisements to a fax machine, permitting injured persons to seek recovery of $500 per violation. Most courts have found that such claims are covered under the advertising injury provisions of the CGL policy absent a specific junk fax exclusion. *See* Maniloff & Stempel, Ch. 19. *See, e.g., Park Univ. Enters. v. Am. Cas. Co.*, 442 F.3d 1239 (10th Cir. 2006) (applying Kansas law) (transmission of fax is publication of advertisement and its receipt can constitute invasion of recipient's privacy; CGL insurer must defend junk fax claim against policyholder); *Terra Nova Ins. Co. v. Fray-Witzer*, 869 N.E.2d 565, 574–76 (Mass. 2007) (TCPA is remedial rather than penal statute; no public policy bar to insurance coverage); *Valley Forge Ins. Co. v. Swiderski Elecs., Inc.*, 860 N.E.2d 307, 315 (Ill. 2006) (same; volitional sending of faxes does not in itself make policy's "expected or intended injury" exclusion applicable; insurer bears burden to demonstrate that policyholder sent fax with subjective intent of inflicting injury). For a contrary approach and rationale, *see Am. States Ins. Co. v. Capital Assocs. of Jackson County, Inc.*, 392 F.3d 939 (7th Cir. 2004) (applying Illinois law, incorrectly we now know, to bar CGL coverage for junk fax claim).

# § 9.16. Additional Types of Liability Coverage

This Chapter has focused on general liability insurance because it is by far the most common and commonly litigated type of liability insurance. In a basic casebook of finite length (although the book may seem interminable to you at this point in the semester), it would be hard to justify any different approach. But be aware that there are other types of liability insurance that are also pervasive, important, and the source of many coverage disputes.

## [A] Errors and Omissions Insurance

Errors and Omissions ("E & O") insurance is, as the name implies, insurance that covers professionals or quasi-professionals for mistakes of professional judgment (or lack of judgment) that injure their clients/customers. Like CGL insurance, E & O coverage generally includes a duty to defend claims and attempt to defeat or settle them without trial.

Unlike CGL insurance, E & O coverage is more commonly written on a claims-made basis (*see* § 9.14) and the costs expended on defense are more commonly subtracted from the policy limits available to settle claims or pay judgments against the policyholder. This is "defense within limits" or "burning limits" coverage as contrasted with the "defense outside of limits" coverage typically available in general liability policies. Many of the other types of more specialized liability policies, particularly professional liability policies, are likely to share the claims-made and burning limits policies found in E & O policies.

What rationales might support such differences? Does the presence of burning limits create additional opportunities for insurer bad faith or misjudgment? How? *See generally* Gregory S. Munro, *Defense Within Limits: The Conflicts of "Wasting" or "Cannibalizing" Insurance Policies*, 62 Mont. L. Rev. 131 (2001).

## [B] Professional Liability

Professional liability or malpractice insurance is sold to doctors, lawyers, and other professionals. Like E & O insurance, it is commonly sold on a claims-made basis and may or may not have burning limits regarding defense costs. The primary coverage battlegrounds in reported cases involves intentional infliction of harm to a patient or client or the question of whether a professional's misconduct was part of the misrendering of professional services or was instead simply tortious conduct that took place outside the professional role and was merely committed by a tortfeasor who happened to be a lawyer or doctor. An example of the former category is assault and battery or fraud by the professional. An example of the latter is the professional defaming a client or having an affair that leads to charges of alienation of affections by the wronged spouse.

## [C] Directors and Officers Liability Insurance

Directors and Officers Liability ("D & O") insurance is again a product that does what its name suggests: defend and insure directors and officers of corporations or similar business entities. For reasons related to corporate law, securities law, and business torts, directors and officers are often named as defendants in suits stemming from alleged corporate wrongdoing. The phenomenon stems from the nature of the business entity, which is its own legal "person" but which is actually run by its constituents: officers, directors, middle managers, lawyers, accountants, and other workers. When a rank-and-file worker makes a mistake, this most likely leads to a general liability claim as when the company driver is in an accident or a factor produces adulterated food or beverages. But where corporate misfeasance is found, this usually involves upper management and directors. Contemporary news accounts of the great corporate collapses of the early 21st century suggest that much of the directors' contribution or fault may stem from being inattentive or too compliant with management while officers are more likely to be the active perpetrators of corporate wrongdoing.

A significant number of claims against businesses involve something far milder than the raptors of Enron. For example, a company may be sued over an allegedly misleading proxy statement or press release, particularly if the company proves not to have been as close to FDA approval of a wonder drug, obtaining of oil leases in Mineralistan, etc. Plaintiff and defense lawyers and their respective allies continue to argue over the merits and worth of such suits. Plaintiffs argue that corporate mis-statement works fraud on the market and injures investors while defendants charac-terize many of these suits as raids by voracious lawyers seeking compensation that will go in large part to the lawyers simply because a company has not performed as well as indicated. Regarding the politics of business liability and the frequency of corporate wrongdoing, both sides can claim victory. Plaintiffs have the Sarbanes-Oxley Act of 2002 while defendants have the Private Securities Litigation Reform Act of 1995, the Securities Law Uniform Standards Act of 1998, and (at least to a degree) the Class Action Reform Act of 2005. *See generally* Jeffrey W. Stempel, *Class Actions and Limited Vision: Opportunities for Improvement Through a More Functional Approach to Class Treatment of Disputes*, 83 Wash. U. L.Q. 1127, 1139–54 (2005) (reviewing legislation and public policy debate over utility of class actions against businesses).

Whatever the merits of the respective positions in this ongoing debate, the fact remains that there remains much litigation directed at both allegedly errant companies and their directors and officers. Consequently, there is a brisk market for D & O in-surance (which got even better after Sarbanes-Oxley). Premiums per amount of cov-erage are comparatively high and policyholders may have substantial retentions but few companies of any size go without it. Modern D & O policies typically provide coverage in one section for the individual directors and officers while in another section providing coverage for the corporate entity itself, although many policies in force still follow the traditional approach of insuring the individual directors and of-ficers only. The distinction is important because a typical securities class action or business wrongdoing claim will have multiple counts, some against only individuals, some against the entity, some against all, and some against others such as outside accountants, lawyers, or bankers. Because most litigation settles, there can be sig-nificant battles over how much of a settlement is subject to applicable D & O insurance. *See* Stempel & Knutsen, § 19.06.

In addition to battles over allocation and apportionment regarding settlement, there are of course straight out coverage battles. For example, D & O insurance, like general liability insurance, typically excludes coverage for intentionally inflicted injury or criminal wrongdoing, which presents definitional problems akin to general liability battles over the intentional act exclusion. In addition, a single claim may present elements of both negligence and worse. D & O policies can have either a duty to defend or a duty to reimburse the policyholder for defense costs. In the latter situation, there can be issues regarding the reasonableness of defense costs and the timing of reimbursement. Like E & O coverage, D & O coverage is normally written on a claims-made basis and a "defense within limits" basis. *See generally* Stempel & Knutsen, § 19.01.

# [D] Environmental Claims Liability Insurance

As discussed in §§ 9.12 and 9.13, the issue of general liability coverage for pollution and environmental cleanup claims has been a major battleground during the past 25 years even though the standard CGL policy has since 1986 contained an "absolute" pollution exclusion. Litigation continues both because some claims involve older policies without the exclusion (remember, groundwater contamination can take place for decades before it is noticed) and because some cases present divisive issues of whether the exclusion properly applies (e.g., carbon monoxide poisoning from a leaky furnace, toxic fumes from construction work, chemical burns from handling equipment).

For the most part, however, the absolute pollution exclusion has been effective in doing what the insurance industry intended to do: bar general liability coverage for waste disposal, contamination, and cleanup claims. As a result, a policyholder that has exposures in these areas cannot expect coverage from its CGL policy. To have coverage, the policyholder will need to either "buy" its way out of the exclusion by paying a higher premium in return for an endorsement excising the exclusion or will need to procure a separate policy covering environmental pollution and related claims. These types of policies are available as separate purchases, typically with relatively high premiums and low policy limits in relation to general liability policies. This is perhaps expected. A reasonable insurer approached by BelchCo, a smelting company, undoubtedly knows that the prospective policyholder is seeking this separate coverage because it knows it presents a larger than normal risk in this area. A local bookstore is unlikely to present such claims, no matter how bad the coffee produced by its attached café.

Like other liability products thought to involve higher than normal risks, environmental claims policies tend to be written on a claims basis and defense within limits. They may also have a high policyholder retention and specific exclusions. For example, InsureCo may be willing to insure most of BelchCo's operations but not the infamous Kill City facility that has old technology and is already under investigation by the EPA. In writing coverage, InsureCo would use a specific exclusion to "laser-out" coverage for any liabilities arising out of the operations of the Kill City plant.

# [E] Employer's Liability, Workers Compensation, and Employment Practices Insurance

General liability insurance is structured to protect the policyholder from claims by third parties. Employees of an insured company may or may not be third parties, depending on the claim and one's point of view. Certainly, insurers do not view the CGL policy as providing coverage for employment-related claims and it contains exclusions designed to avoid coverage for employee claims. The notion is that employee claims should be under a different insurance product. Historically, Employers' Liability ("EL") or Workers' Compensation ("WC") policies have been those products, although there are occasionally worker claims held to fall within CGL coverage. Over time, insurers have revised the CGL to make this less likely. *See* STEMPEL & KNUTSEN § 21.02.

Consequently, the EL and WC coverages of a company are important to protecting it from employee claims. In addition, because claims of race and gender discrimination are not usually covered under these policies, a relatively recent product, employment practices liability ("EPL") has come into the market with some force.

## [1] *Workers' Compensation*

Workers' compensation insurance generally tracks the workers' compensation statutes in effect in the employer's state and sets forth the benefits the employer must pay. Employer liability for on-the-job injuries is strict and without regard to fault but the WC insurer has a right to investigate and defend claims. Certain defenses such as "serious and willful misconduct" are available. For example, if a factory worker is horsing around and injures himself trying to do a triple somersault into a cleaning vat, this probably is not covered (but remember, each case is different as are state laws and court decisions). Similarly, if the worker throws out his shoulder attempting to hit a co-worker, this is probably not covered. However, the same worker who burns his hand on a soldering iron is typically covered under WC insurance. Injury from clear violation of health and safety laws may also be excluded. *See generally* Arthur Larson & Lex K. Larson, Larson's Workers' Compensation Law (2002); Peter J. Kalis, Thomas M. Reiter & James R. Segerdahl, Policyholder's Guide to the Law of Insurance Coverage § 12.02 (1997). *See also Swenson v. Nickaboine*, 793 N.W.2d 738 (Minn. 2011) (state workers' compensation law applicable to Indian lands notwithstanding tribal sovereignty).

A major source of much workers' compensation litigation is the question of whether the employee was acting within the scope of his or her employment when injured. If the answer is "yes," then the employee is covered by WC insurance, which also means under the statutes of nearly every state that recovery against the employer is limited to WC benefits, although other entities contributing to the injury might also be sued in tort. One explanation for the popularity of product liability actions against manufacturers is that injured workers may receive relatively modest WC benefits when injured at work while using a manufacturer's equipment.

As a means of seeking additional compensation, the rational worker might be more inclined to also blame the product maker for the injury. Like much in litigation, this is a two-edged sword. A jury might have no trouble finding the worker seriously injured but find the product liability claim farfetched if the injury appears to result clearly from an unsafe workplace rather than a defectively designed or manufactured product. What most lay jurors do not know, of course, is that the employer cannot be sued in tort and that the employer's liability is cabined by the WC statute and benefits.

If the answer about on-the-job injury is "no," of course, then WC insurance is not applicable and the injured worker must pursue other avenues of relief. In some cases, an injury may not be job related for purposes of WC coverage but may result in a court action implicating CGL coverage or other insurance held by the employer or another entity arguably responsible for the worker's injury. In such cases, the respective insurers may have adverse interests and argue for different characterizations of whether the injury was sufficiently work-related to be subject to WC treatment. For example, if a worker is injured while attending a business "team building" exercise involving white water rafting during a conference/meeting at a hotel/resort, the WC insurer may argue that this is not a work-related injury while the CGL carrier will argue that it was. Depending on the answer, a different insurer may pay and the amount recoverable may vary. In addition, the nature of employer immunities frequently found in WC statutes can create some arguable gaps in coverage. *See, e.g., Bias v. Eastern Associated Coal Corp.*, 640 S.E.2d 540 (W. Va. 2006). *See also Everett Cash Mut. Ins. Co. v. Taylor*, 926 N.E.2d 1008, 1012–14 (Ind. 2010) (workers compensation exclusion in CGL policy not applicable where policyholder not required to obtain workers compensation coverage and vendor injured on property had failed to maintain worker's compensation coverage; injury to vendor's employee while working on policyholder property an occurrence for purposes of CGL coverage).

## Notes and Questions

1. Remember that workers' compensation was enacted in the late 19th and early 20th Centuries in order to provide workers with a remedy because the tort law of the time, which had strong employer defenses based on assumption of risk and the fellow servant rule, made recovery in tort very difficult for workers at a time when workplaces were far more dangerous than today. Has a century of business evolution made workers' compensation an unwitting enemy of the worker? Are revisions to the system in order?

2. Alternatively, employers and insurers frequently argue that WC insurance has become excessively costly because its no-fault premise and broad coverage make it easy for malingering workers to claim injury, prevail on dubious claims, and extend their absences through over-extended recuperation and rehabilitation periods (with expensive physical therapy or other treatment). Without doubt, WC insurance premium are relatively high compared to other forms of liability insurance even though WC benefits are set by a schedule rather than ad hoc by courts or juries. Does this mean workplace injury is still too frequent in society? That workers are taking unfair advantage? That insurers are overpricing the product or failing to control and monitor claims? During the 2002 California gubernatorial campaign, then-candidate Arnold Schwarzenegger actually used WC insurance rates as a campaign issue, making reform to lower rates part of his platform. What is the current state of political debate, if any, regarding workers' compensation in your state?

## [2] Employers' Liability Insurance

EL insurance is designed to protect the employer against liability from traditional physical injury torts that may be brought by an employee and wall outside of WC coverage. EL insurance is designed to fill gaps between the basic WC policy and CGL coverage. Consequently, it is not unusual to see these policies sold as a package or at least assembled as a package by the policyholder's broker in order to attempt to avoid gaps in coverage. *See* STEMPEL & KNUTSEN § 21.03.

## *[3] Employment Practices Liability Insurance*

EPL insurance is designed to provide defense against and indemnity for the non-traditional liability for worker claims alleging discrimination. Recall that prior to the 1964 Civil Rights Act, race, gender, and religious discrimination by private employers was perfectly legal. *See* JAMES B. DOLAN, JR., THE GROWING SIGNIFICANCE OF EMPLOYMENT PRACTICES LIABILITY INSURANCE, The Brief (Winter 2005), at 30. EPL insurance products became significantly available in the mid-1990s and initially could be had only for relatively low limits at high premiums. Since then, the product has become more affordable and protective. Regarding EPL coverage generally, *see* CLARANCE E. HAGGLUND, BRITTON D. WEIMER, T. MICHAEL SPEIDEL & ANDREW F. WHITMAN, EMPLOYMENT PRACTICES LIABILITY: GUIDE TO RISK EXPOSURES & COVERAGE (1998); ANDREW KAPLAN, RACHEL MCKINNEY, BETH A. SCHROEDER & LEONARD SURDYK, THE EPL BOOK: A PRACTICAL GUIDE TO EMPLOYMENT PRACTICES LIABILITY AND INSURANCE (1997); BARBARA A. O'DONNELL, THE FIRST WAVE OF DECISIONS INTERPRETING EMPLOYMENT PRACTICES LIABILITY POLICIES, The Brief (Fall 2005), at 39.

In addition, EPL insurance, like Boiler & Machinery insurance (*see* STEMPEL & KNUTSEN § 22.04), can have a preventive effect in reducing the number of claims against the employer by spotting potential problems before they turn into actual losses or claims. Before a B & M insurer will provide coverage, it has its expert engineers inspect the machinery to be insured. If the machinery is suffering from material defects, the insurer will not write B & M coverage. However, the prospective policyholder now knows that Boiler No. 3 needs to be repaired or replaced before it can get insurance. Fixing Boiler No. 3 now is ordinarily much less expensive than having it explode in the middle of manufacturing operations. Many policyholders purchase B & M coverage in order to obtain the inspection as much as for the coverage. Similarly, a wise EPL insurer will not write discrimination coverage until it is assured that the policyholder has in place adequate anti-discrimination protocols and procedures by which an employee may seek help if harassed on the job.

Like other policies, EPL insurance may be written with a specified exclusion for claims arising out of a certain facility or from the actions of a particular person. For example, the insurer's investigation may reveal that the Bugtussle office of AcmeCo is a little Peyton Place awash in inter-office affairs. Even if the liaisons started as consensual, these things have a way of leading to sexual harassment claims. Similarly, former regional manager Bill Bigot may have just been forced out of the company after his membership in the Aryan Nations came to light. Even if Bigot no longer works for Acme, he may have engaged in acts of discrimination that will lead to claims during the policy period. In such cases, a prudent EPL insurer would either demand a higher premium or by endorsement exclude claims related to Bigot or the Bugtussle office.

# [F] Suretyship

Suretyship is an agreement in which one contracting party agrees to act in the event of a contingency. As a result, it is often considered to be the equivalent of insurance and at other times considered distinct from insurance. Although "either too much or too little can be made of the technical differences between suretyship and insurance," traditional orthodoxy of insurance has posited that the two differ primarily in that

(a) the surety bond involves three parties (surety, principal, and obligee) while the insurance policy involves two parties (insurer and insured), although with liability insurance third-party claimants are always waiting in the wings. This may be important for purposes of "its effect on misrepresentation, concealment, or other fraud." The fraud of a contractor, unlike the fraud of a co-insured, cannot extinguish the surety's liability. "Only when principal and obligee conspire to defraud the surety will fraud void the surety arrangement."

(b) the surety arrangement generally permits the surety to seek indemnity from a contractor whose negligence caused the default requiring the surety to pay. By contrast, the insurer usually has no claim for indemnity or other relief (e.g., subrogation) as a result of negligence on the part of the policyholder. "The ability to seek reimbursement for losses from its own insured is an important distinction between suretyship and insurance."

*See* MARK S. DORFMAN, INTRODUCTION TO RISK MANAGEMENT AND INSURANCE, 410–11 (7th ed. 2002). *See also Surety Underwriters v. E & C Trucking*, 10 P.3d 338 (Utah 2000) (contract under which surety agreed to issue $50,000 bond if obligor gave surety consideration was "insurance contract" under Utah law and required license for engaging in such business; absent license, contract was unenforceable.

Neither of these traditional distinctions, however important, bears on the question of whether sureties should be liable for bad faith conduct toward the policyholder, an issues that has divided courts. The distinctions, or lack thereof, between suretyship and insurance may become important to questions of regulation and liability. It has become particularly important in recent years because of differing precedent over the issue of whether a bad faith claim can be made against a surety as it can be made against a conventional insurer.

In general, the rules and norms of contract construction applicable to insurance policies are also applicable to surety agreements. At the margin, however, the surety agreement may be more strictly construed by some courts in order to protect the interests of the surety. Historically, a surety has been described as a "favorite of the law." However, that maxim arose at a time when sureties were usually individual guarantors rather than the large insurance companies that act as sureties today.

The modern insurer-surety accepts risk transfer and spreads contingent risk much in the manner of a conventional insurer. As a result, judicial treatment of insurance and suretyship appears to be converging, including attendant bad faith exposure for sureties. Sureties and their counsel, however, usually argue with considerable success that sureties are different than insurers and should be immunized from bad faith and punitive damages exposure. The principal or obligor of a surety payment or performance bond will argue to the contrary where it believes it has been treated with bad faith by a surety. The recent judicial trend generally favors permitting insurance-like bad faith claims against sureties but the jurisdictions remain divided.

As you read the case below, ask yourself which view of surety bad faith liability is more persuasive. *See generally* Troy L. Harris, *Good Faith, Suretyship, and the Ius Commune*, 53 Mercer L. Rev. 581 (2002); Aron J. Frakes, Note, *Surety Bad Faith: Tort Recovery for Breach of a Construction Performance Bond*, 2002 U. Ill. L. Rev. 497 (2002). *See also* Stempel & Knutsen, § 22.13.

## Transamerica Premier Insurance Company v. Brighton School District 27J

### Supreme Court of Colorado
### 940 P.2d 348 (Colo. 1997)

**Chief Justice Vollack** delivered the Opinion of the Court.

We granted certiorari to review the court of appeals decision to determine whether Colorado recognizes the existence of a common law tort claim against a commercial surety who fails to reasonably proceed with the payment of a claim under a performance bond.... We conclude that allowing this cause of action to proceed in the commercial surety context is justified by the special nature of the suretyship agreement and by the reasoning set forth in our prior decisions authorizing bad faith actions against insurers.

[The Court's presentation of the facts is omitted—assume that the surety engaged in unreasonable conduct in response to a claim, including undue delay that would be sufficient to support a bad faith claim if done by a liability insurer.]

In Colorado, every contract contains an implied duty of good faith and fair dealing. Actions based upon a breach of this duty were traditionally limited to contract damages because the duty of good faith and fair dealing concerned the faithful performance of a contract's terms.... "The motivation of the insured when entering into an insurance contract differs from that of parties entering into an ordinary commercial contract. By obtaining insurance, an insured seeks to obtain some measure of financial security and protection against calamity, rather than to secure commercial advantage. The refusal of the insurer to pay valid claims without justification, however, defeats the expectations of the insured and the purpose of the insurance contract. It is therefore necessary to impose a legal duty upon the insurer to deal with its insured in good faith."... In *Travelers Insurance Co. v. Savio*, 706 P.2d 1258 (Colo. 1985), we extended the "basic rationale" of Trimble to authorize actions in tort where an insurer was alleged to have handled a first-party workers' compensation claim in bad faith. We noted that, "since workers compensation serves the same purpose as insurance in general, the Trimble rationale demands that the provider of such compensation deal fairly and in good faith with an employee asserting a compensable injury." We also elaborated on the proper standard for evaluating such claims as follows:

In the first-party context an insurer acts in bad faith in delaying the processing of or denying a valid claim when the insurer's conduct is unreasonable and the insurer knows that the conduct is unreasonable or recklessly disregards the fact that the conduct is unreasonable.... [Colorado statutory law] provides that every contractor that is awarded a public works contract for more than $50,000 must submit a performance bond executed by a qualified commercial surety to the public entity in charge of the project. Under the terms of the performance bond, in the event the contractor (the principal) fails to fulfill its obligations to the public entity (the obligee) under the public works contract, the commercial surety must guarantee performance and/or satisfy debts resulting from unpaid labor and materials.

The issue in this case concerns whether we should extend our [insuer bad faith] holdings to include situations in which a commercial surety company fails to act in good faith when processing claims made by an obligee pursuant to the terms of a performance bond. We conclude that the rationale for providing insureds with a cause of action in tort for an insurer's bad faith in processing a claim applies with equal force in the commercial surety context....

We have previously explained that commercial sureties receiving consideration for the issuance of surety bonds serve a purpose similar to that of insurers: "Generally speaking, a contract of suretyship by a surety company is governed by the same rules as the contracts of other sureties, but some distinctions are made by the courts in construing such contracts. The doctrine that a surety is a favorite of the law, and that a claim against him is strictissimi juris, does not apply where the bond or undertaking is executed upon a consideration by a corporation organized to make such bonds or undertakings for profit. While such corporations may call themselves 'surety companies,' their business is in all essential particulars that of insurers."

The insurance statutes reflect a legislative intent to include sureties as part of the regulatory scheme governing insurance. Section 10-1-102(8), 4A C.R.S. (1994), defines the term "insurer" as "every person engaged as principal, indemnitor, surety, or contractor in the business of making contracts of insurance." Similarly, section 10-3-1102(2), 4A C.R.S. (1994), of the Deceptive Practices Statute §§ 10-3-1101 to -1114, 4A C.R.S. (1994 & 1996 Supp.), defines the terms "insurance policy" and "insurance contract" to include suretyship agreements. The Deceptive Practices Statute expressly prohibits unfair claim settlement practices and lists a variety of penal measures available in the event a commercial surety engages in unfair settlement practices. See § 10-3-1104(h), 4A C.R.S. (1994); § 10-3-1108, 4A C.R.S. (1994).

Furthermore, section 10-3-1113(1), 4A C.R.S. (1994), provides: "In any civil action for damages founded upon contract, or tort, or both against an insurance company, the trier of fact may be instructed that the insurer owes its insured the duty of good faith and fair dealing, which duty is breached if the insurer delays or denies payment without a reasonable basis for its delay or denial." These statutes indicate persuasive legislative support for treating a commercial surety contract as a form of insurance agreement and for treating a commercial surety which fails to settle its obligations in good faith in the same way that our tort law treats insurers who process a claim in bad faith.

More specifically, most other jurisdictions that have considered this issue have recognized a separate cause of action in tort for a commercial surety's bad faith in processing claims made under a surety bond. * * * We agree with the reasoning of those cases which authorize a bad faith cause of action in the commercial surety context and conclude that a similar result in the present case represents a logical extension of our [insurer bad faith precedents].

A special relationship exists between a commercial surety and an obligee that is nearly identical to that involving an insurer and an insured. When an obligee requests that a principal obtain a commercial surety bond to guarantee the principal's performance, the obligee is essentially insuring itself from the potentially catastrophic losses that would result in the event the principal defaults on its original obligation. When the principal actually defaults, the commercial surety must assume or correct any flaws in performance pursuant to the terms of the original contract, thereby eliminating the obligee's risk of loss in the venture.

Although the parties to a suretyship agreement are on equal footing in terms of bargaining power when they enter into the agreement, it is the commercial surety who controls the ultimate decision of whether to pay claims made by the obligee under the terms of the surety bond. For this reason, the commercial surety has a distinct advantage over the obligee in its ability to control performance under the secondary agreement. As with insurers, commercial sureties must proceed with the payment of claims made pursuant to a surety bond in good faith. Otherwise, the core purpose of the suretyship agreement, which is to insulate the obligee from the risk of a default, is defeated.

Recognizing a cause of action in tort for a commercial surety's breach of its duty to act in good faith compels commercial sureties to handle claims responsibly. When the commercial surety withholds payment of an obligee's claim in bad faith, contract damages do not compensate the obligee for the commercial surety's misconduct and have no deterrent effect to prevent such misconduct in the future. As the Arizona Supreme Court explained ... contract damages "offer no motivation whatsoever for the insurer not to breach. If the only damages an insurer will have to pay upon a judgment of breach are the amounts that it would have owed under the policy plus interest, it has every interest in retaining the money, earning the higher rates of interest on the outside market, and hoping eventually to force the insured into a settlement for less than the policy amount."

Transamerica argues that the unique features of suretyship distinguish it from insurance and that the suretyship agreement is, in essence, a financial service. We disagree. As explained above, the suretyship agreement provides the obligee with financial security by eliminating the risk of default in the original agreement between the principal and the obligee. While there may be differences in the form of the suretyship agreement and the obligations of the parties, its substance is essentially the same as insurance.

[In footnote 4, the Court noted that "We recognize that the commercial surety is put in an awkward position in handling simultaneous claims made by the principal and the obligee. The Supreme Court of Hawaii has explained the surety's dilemma as follows:

> Clearly, the surety owes a duty of good faith and fair dealing to both the principal and the obligee on the bond. If the surety pays too quickly to the obligee, it may invite liability claims from the principal. Conversely, if it refuses to pay anything pending an arbitration or judicial proceeding to determine its liability on the bond, the surety may incur liability to the obligee for failing to act promptly on a valid claim. Although the commercial surety's obligations may be more complex than those of an insurer, this complexity does not authorize a commercial surety to disregard its obligation to act in good faith.]

[In footnote 5, the Court stated: "In *Suver v. Personal Serv. Ins. Co.*, 11 Ohio St. 3d 6, 462 N.E.2d 415 (Ohio 1984), the Supreme Court of Ohio elaborated on the differences and similarities between insurers and sureties as follows: 'It is true that a financial responsibility bond is not the same as an insurance policy and that a surety is not an insurer and may therefore act in its own interest. But the nature of the differences between the two is neither complete nor absolute. Rather, the financial responsibility bond and the insurance policy differ primarily in whom they protect and to whom the duty runs.... These differences are not so pronounced as to require the creation of a cause of action in one case and its denial in the other. Precisely the same policy arguments and rationale hold true in both settings.... Moreover, to insulate the issuer of a financial responsibility bond from liability for the deliberate refusal to pay its obligations arising from the bond is to encourage the routine denial of payment of claims for as long as possible. This court should not provide an incentive to act in bad faith.'"]

Accordingly, we hold that Colorado common law recognizes a cause of action in tort for a commercial surety's failure to act in good faith when processing claims made by an obligee pursuant to the terms of a performance bond. In evaluating these causes of action, we adopt the rule ... that a commercial surety acts in bad faith when the surety's conduct is unreasonable and the surety knows that the conduct is unreasonable or recklessly disregards the fact that its conduct is unreasonable. By imposing this legal duty on the commercial surety, our holding ensures that the expectations of the obligee and the purposes of the suretyship agreement are given effect while recognizing the surety's right to refuse invalid claims.

**Justice Kourlis** dissenting:

The majority recognizes a common law cause of action in tort for a commercial surety's failure to act in good faith when processing claims made by an obligee pursuant to the terms of a performance bond. In support of that result, the majority concludes that "the rationale for providing insureds with a cause of action in tort for an insurer's bad faith in processing a claim applies with equal force in the commercial surety context." Because I believe that there are essential differences between the surety/obligee

The fact that the General Assembly treats sureties similarly to insurers in some contexts should not thereby subject sureties to bad faith liability. * * * These statutes group insurers and sureties together because both enter into contracts to pay a benefit upon a determinable risk contingency, and, hence, both can be similarly regulated. However, it is not the fact that an insurer contracts to pay a benefit upon the occurrence of a particular event that justifies the creation of a tort action for bad faith breach. Rather, in the context of a third-party claim, it is the quasi-fiduciary relationship, and in the context of a first-party claim it is the injured party's vulnerability following an unforeseen calamity and the unequal bargaining power between insurer and insured. Those circumstances are not present in this case.

# § 9.17. The ALI Restatement of Liability Insurance

August 2019 marked formal publication of the American Law Institutes' *Restatement of the Law, Liability Insurance* ("RLLI"), a project begun in 2011 and approved at the May 2018 ALI Annual Meeting. Restatements, of course, are well known to law students and lawyers. A Restatement is designed to collect and synthesize the law of a given area. In addition to those concerning Torts and Contracts, the ALI has published Restatements regarding Judgments, Conflict of Laws, Foreign Relations, and other areas of law.

The Restatement format has "black letter" sections setting forth a Rule, followed by Comments and Illustrations concerning the Rule, followed by a Reporter's Note, which is something of a mini-treatise collecting caselaw regarding the black letter and commentary such as treatises and law review articles. Restatements were among the first projects undertaken by the ALI, which was formed in 1923 by prominent lawyers, judges, and academics seeking improvement of American law.

Summarizing, the Institute notes that "Restatements are primarily addressed to courts. They aim at clear formulations of common law and its statutory elements or variations and reflect the law as it presently stands or might appropriately be stated by a court." *See* RLLI at x (boldface removed). A Restatement rule should have at least some support in caselaw but need not be the majority rule. Rather, in examining the legal landscape, the ALI may embrace the judicial approach viewed as superior if it is the minority rule, even a distinct minority. *See Nature of a Restatement, reprinted in* RLLI at x–xi.

This section briefly reviews the RLLI and its primary provisions. For more examination, see MANILOFF & STEMPEL, *supra*, Ch. 23; STEMPEL & KNUTSEN ON INSURANCE COVERAGE § 14; Jay M. Feinman, *The Restatement of the Law of Liability Insurance as a Restatement: An Introduction to the Symposium*, 68 RUTGERS U. L. REV. 1 (2015), and accompanying Symposium articles.

Astute readers will see that the RLLI, in attempting to deal with the broad aspects of liability insurance, is not limited to the matters discussed in this Chapter but extensively examines the contract construction issues faced in Ch. 2 and the respective duties of policyholder and insurer addressed in Ch. 7.

# [A] The Structure and Content of the RLLI

## Definitions and Interpretation

After addressing some general concepts, the RLLI covers liability insurance topics in roughly the order they arise in litigation. Section 1 provides some fourteen (14) definitions. RLLI § 2 addresses "insurance-policy interpretation," noting that unless otherwise provided in the RLLI or by other law, "the ordinary rules of contract interpretation apply to the interpretation of liability insurance policies."

RLLI § 3 adopts a view that the "plain meaning" of policy text is "the single meaning, if any, to which the language of the term is reasonably susceptible when applied to the claim at issue in the context of the insurance policy as a whole, without reference to extrinsic evidence reading the meaning of the term" and further provides that terms are to be interpreted according to such a plain meaning "unless extrinsic evidence shows that a reasonable person in the policyholder's position would give the term a different meaning," a position that has proved controversial. "That different meaning must be more reasonable than the plain [textual] meaning in light of the extrinsic evidence, and it must be a meaning to which the language of the term is reasonably susceptible." RLLI § 3(2) of the RLLI permits policyholder expectations to determine the meaning of a disputed term only if the policy language is reasonably susceptible to such a construction. Pursuant to RLLI § 4, ambiguous policy language is automatically construed against the insurer. However, the insurer has the opportunity to persuade the court that "a reasonable person in the policyholder's position would not give the term that interpretation."

## Known Liabilities

RLLI § 46 addresses a "known liability" (and contrasts it with a known risk), providing that "[u]nless otherwise stated in the policy, a liability insurance policy provides coverage for a known liability only if that liability is disclosed to the insurer during the application or renewal process for the policy" (§ 46(1)). A "liability is known only when, prior to the inception of the policy period, the policyholder knows that, absent a settlement, an adverse judgment establishing the liability in an amount that would reach the level of coverage provided under the policy is substantially certain" (§ 46(2)).

## Notice

RLLI § 35 provides that for occurrence basis policies, late or defective notice by a policyholder "excuses an insurer from performance of its obligations ... only if the insurer demonstrates that it was prejudiced as a result." However, for claims-made policies, a stricter view applies, and the insurer can avoid coverage when notice is late without regard to prejudice, unless: the policy does not contain an extended reporting period; the claim at issue is made too close to the end of the policy period to allow the insured a reasonable time to satisfy the condition; and the insured reports the claim to the insurer within a reasonable time.

### The Duty to Cooperate

RLLI § 29 and § 30 address the duty to cooperate and adopt the prevailing view that the policyholder must cooperate with the insurer in defending a suit, providing specifics, but also stating that the breach of the cooperation duty will not bar coverage unless "the insurer demonstrates that the failure caused or will cause prejudice to the insurer" (§ 30(1)).

### Insuring Agreements and Exclusions

After addressing the duties of defense and cooperation, the RLLI provides an explanation of concepts and terms. For example, RLLI § 31(1) notes that an "insuring clause" is "a term in a liability insurance policy that grants insurance coverage," while § 31(3) adopts the universal judicial position that such clauses are to be "interpreted broadly." The RLLI also notes that a provision of a policy may be a coverage-granting insuring clause even when it is not so denominated in the policy. The RLLI takes a similar view of exclusions, in that "[w]hether a term in an insurance policy is an exclusion does not depend on where the term is in the policy or the label associated with the term in the policy." Exclusions are to be "interpreted narrowly," while "[a]n exception to an exclusion narrows the application of the exclusion" and "does not grant coverage beyond that provided in the insuring clauses in the insurance policy." The RLLI also provides that "[u]nless otherwise stated in the insurance policy, words in an exclusion regarding the expectation or intent of the insured refer to the subjective state of mind of the insured."

### Trigger

RLLI § 33 deals with trigger of coverage and, although not using that language, reflects prevailing law regarding trigger. For example, if an occurrence policy is triggered by injury to the claimant, the time of initial injury constitutes trigger. But an insurer can specify that all potentially covered injury is deemed to have arisen at a particular time. In effect, claims-made policies do this by making the claim against the policyholder the trigger of coverage rather than focusing on the date of injury to the claimant as in occurrence policies.

### Conditions

RLLI § 34 deals with conditions in the insurance policy, defining a condition as "an event under the control of an insured, policyholder, or insurer that, unless excused, must occur, or must not occur, before performance under the policy becomes due under the policy" (§ 34(1)). As with insuring clauses and exclusions, RLLI § 34(2) provides that "[w]hether a term in a liability insurance policy is a condition does not depend on where the term is located in the policy or the label associated with the term in the policy." Consistent with the view that failure to adhere to certain policy provisions should not result in disproportionate forfeiture, RLLI § 34(3) provides that "failure of an insured to satisfy cooperation conditions ... does not relieve the insurer of its obligations under the policy unless the failure caused prejudice to the insurer."

### Waiver and Estoppel

RLLI §§ 5 and 6 address waiver and estoppel, respectively, restating traditional doctrine. They have been essentially uncontroversial.

### Misrepresentation

Regarding misrepresentation, RLLI § 7(1) makes any statement of fact in an application for insurance into a representation. RLLI § 7(2) permits the insurer to deny a claim or rescind the entire policy on the basis of an "incorrect" representation if the representation is "material" and was "reasonably relied" upon by the insurer in issuing or renewing the policy. The insurer must show that it would have not issued the policy but for the incorrect representation or would have issued the policy "only with substantially different terms." A material representation is one that would have prompted a "reasonable insurer" to "not have issued the policy" or to only "have issued the policy under substantially different circumstances."

The RLLI adoption of an objective approach to determining materiality may place some pressure on jurisdictions using the subjective standard (most prominently California) to reconsider their approach—although where a state has a long-established subjective approach, RLLI-spurred change is unlikely but may take place in states with unclear or inconsistent precedent on the point.

### The Duty to Defend

Sections 10 through 23 of the RLLI address the duty to defend. RLLI § 10 provides that, "unless otherwise stated in the policy," the insurer issuing a policy with a duty to defend has control over the defense and settlement of the action, "including the selection and oversight of defense counsel" as well as the "right to receive from defense counsel all information relevant to the defense or settlement of the action" unless the information is confidential as provided in RLLI § 11. RLLI § 11(2) provides that "an insurer does not have the right to receive any information of the insured that is protected by attorney-client privilege, work-product immunity, or a defense lawyer's duty of confidentiality under the rules of professional conduct if that information could be used to benefit the insurer at the expense of the insured." While issues of client identity and disclosure of information can create difficulties for defense counsel, it is an accepted occupational hazard and has not made §§ 10 and 11 controversial.

### Determining Whether a Defense Is Owed

RLLI § 13 sets forth the prevailing rule on when the duty to defend is triggered and states that the duty is triggered if the allegations of the claim create a potential for coverage "without regard for the merits of those allegations." More controversial is § 13(2)(b) that provides that the insurer must also defend when it is aware of "[a]ny additional allegation known to the insurer, not contained in the complaint, or comparable document stating the legal action, that a reasonable insurer would regard as a basis for adding an allegation to the action." *See W. Hills Dev. Co. v. Chartis Claims, Inc.*, 385 P.3d 1053, 1055 (Ore. 2016) (noting RLLI adoption of four corners/eight-corners approach generally). The RLLI does not adopt the more pronounced pro-policyholder position of requiring a liability insurer to investigate and seek facts that create a potential for coverage.

### Terminating the Duty to Defend

RLLI § 13(3) states that once the duty to defend is triggered, it remains in effect unless the insurer prevails in a declaratory judgment action terminating the duty or the case is resolved or "unless facts as to which there is no genuine dispute establish as a matter of law" that one of the following situations exists: the defendant is "not an insured" under the applicable policy (§ 13(3)(a)); the "vehicle involved in the accident is not a covered vehicle" under the applicable policy (§ 13(3)(b)); the claim "was reported late under a claims-made-and-reported policy" and the late notice is not excused (§ 13(3)(c)); the action is subject to a prior litigation or related claim exclusion in a claims-made policy (§ 13(3)(d)); or the policy has been "properly cancelled" (§ 13(3)(3)).

RLLI § 18, states that the duty "terminates only upon the occurrence of one or more of the following events" and then lists these events, including: explicit waiver by the insured of its right to a defense of the action; final adjudication of the action; final adjudication or dismissal of part of the action that eliminates any basis for coverage of any remaining components of the action; settlement of the action that fully and finally resolves the entire action; partial settlement of the action (consented to by the insured) that eliminates any basis for coverage of remaining components of the action; exhaustion of the applicable policy limit; a correct insurer determination that there is no duty to defend; or final adjudication that there is no duty to defend.

### Defense Requirements

When the duty to defend is operative, RLLI § 14 sets forth the "basic obligations" of the duty, while § 15 addresses reservation of rights. The defending insurer must make "reasonable efforts to defend the insured from all of the causes of action and remedies sought in the action, including those not covered by the liability insurance policy." RLLI § 14(3) also sets forth the common understanding that "[u]nless otherwise stated in the policy," defense costs are "in addition to policy limits" and are borne by the insurer rather than merely reimbursed after payment by the policyholder.

### Reservations of Rights

Regarding reservation of rights, RLLI § 15 largely codifies existing precedent and practice by providing counsel an extensive template or even what one might call a roadmap for properly defending (which is based on the potential for coverage standard) pursuant to a reservation of the insurer's right to contest ultimate coverage of the claim (which is based on an actual facts standard). Section 15 provides that an insurer defending a legal action "may later contest coverage for that action *only* if it provides *timely notice* to the insured, *before* undertaking the defense, of any ground for contesting coverage of which it knows or should know" (RLLI § 15(1) (emphasis added)). Once defense of an action has begun, the insurer that has been defending without reservation may later reserve rights if the insurer "learns of information that provides a ground for contesting coverage" so long as it gives notice to the policyholder within a reasonable time.

RLLI § 15(3) provides that to be effective, notice of a reservation of rights "must include a written explanation of the ground, including the specific insurance-policy terms and facts upon which the potential ground for contesting coverage is based, in language that is understandable by a reasonable person in the position of the insured."[7] Where the insurer lacks sufficient information to make a decision, it may initially reserve rights but must then conduct a reasonably diligent investigation of the matter and provide a "final answer" (to borrow a game-show phrase) as to its position within a reasonable time.

### When Independent Counsel Is Required

RLLI § 16 addresses the issue of when an insurer must provide "independent" (meaning not insurer-selected) defense counsel to the policyholder. That duty is triggered when "there are facts at issue that are common to the legal action for which the defense is due and to the coverage dispute such that the action could be defended in a manner that would benefit the insurer at the expense of the insured." When a conflict requiring independent counsel arises under § 16, RLLI § 17 provides that the insurer "does not have the right to defend the action," and the policyholder "may select defense counsel and related service providers, although the insurer "has the right to associate in the defense of the legal action."

In funding independent counsel, the insurer "is obligated to pay the reasonable fees of the defense counsel and related service providers on an ongoing basis in a timely manner," and the provision of information regarding the defense to the insurer by the policyholder "does not waive the confidentiality of the information with respect to third persons." Although the current "reasonable fees" language of § 16(3) does not expressly set the fees of independent counsel at panel counsel rates as do many courts and California by legislation (CALIF. CIV. CODE § 2860), this is the presumptively logical starting place for determining reasonable rates.

### When Multiple Insurers Have Defense Obligations

RLLI § 20 sets forth a regime for governing situations in which "multiple" insurers have a duty to defend. In essence, § 20 adopts a modified version of the "targeted tender" approach of several jurisdictions, perhaps most notably Illinois, which allows the policyholder to designate the insurer it wishes to respond and then offloads to multiply-triggered insurers the task of working out their respective responsibilities so that the policyholder is not harmed by multiple insurers each waiting for another to make the first move.

---

7. *See* Randy Maniloff, *The Definitive Reservation of Rights Checklist: 50 Things That Every ROR Needs* (described in COVERAGE OPINIONS, Vol. 4, Issue 10 (Oct. 28, 2016)). *See also* Randy Maniloff, *When a Reservation of Rights Letter is Not Effective*, LAW360 (Jan. 25, 2017). *See, e.g., Hoover v. Maxum Indem. Co.*, 730 S.E.2d 413, 417 (Ga. 2012) (unclear ROR letter construed against insurer; letter "not valid if it does not fairly inform the insured of the insurer's position."); *Advantage Buildings & Exteriors, Inc. v. Mid-Continent Casualty Co.*, 449 S.W.3d 16, 22–24 (Mo. Ct. App. 2014) (failure to clearly explain basis for reservation of rights makes ROR letter ineffective and insurer is estopped to provide coverage).

### Coverage of Defense Costs Without a Duty to Defend

RLLI § 22 discusses liability policies that do not provide for an ongoing duty to defend but instead reimburse the policyholder for defense costs incurred in connection with a potentially covered claim. *See Morden v. XL Specialty Ins.*, 177 F. Supp. 3d 1320, 1340–41 (D. Utah 2016)(noting RLLI distinction between duty to defend and duty to pay policies). For such policies, the "scope of the insurer's defense-cost obligation is determined using the rules governing the duty to defend stated" in RLLI §§ 13, 18–20 and 23. The insurer is subject to the reservation of rights protocols set forth in § 15. Regarding the time period for reimbursing the policyholder's defense expenditures, the RLLI punts a bit by saying that in the absence of a specific policy provision, "the insurer's obligation to pay defense costs is determined based on all the facts and circumstances, unless otherwise provided in the policy."

### Consequences of Breach of the Duty to Defend

Particularly controversial was an earlier draft of RLLI § 19 that provided that an insurer in breach of the duty to defend lost the right to contest coverage, even if the breach was not in bad faith. Current RLLI § 19 simply states that "[a]n insurer that breaches the duty to defend a legal action loses the right to assert any control over the defense or settlement of the action." *See Nationwide Mut. Fire Ins. Co. v. D.R. Horton, Inc.*, 2016 U.S. Dist. LEXIS 160148 at *20, n. 6 (S.D. Ala. Nov. 18, 2016) (citing earlier draft of RLLI on this point). The more controversial former § 19(2) provided that "[a]n insurer that breaches the duty to defend without a reasonable basis for its conduct must provide coverage for the legal action for which the defense was sought, notwithstanding any ground for contesting coverage that the insurer could have preserved by providing a proper defense under a reservation of rights...."

Insurers prefer a rule that limits the penalty for a non-bad faith breach of the duty to defend to the simple remedy of reimbursing defense costs incurred by the policyholder that should have been defended by the insurer. A majority of states have adopted this approach. With the removal of former § 19(2), insurers gained some ground regarding the final version of the RLLI. However, § 50(2) and commentary notes that forfeiture of coverage defenses may be an apt remedy where an insurer's breach of the duty to defend was in bad faith.

An earlier RLLI draft embraced the minority rule of automatic loss of coverage defenses for breach of the duty to defend. A substantial minority of states uses this approach that strips the breaching insurer of coverage defenses. The more recent former § 19(2) used what many deemed a hybrid standard of "bad faith lite" as the prerequisite to losing coverage defenses. By contrast, the RLLI now appears to have acceded to the majority rule that a mere breach of the duty to defend, unless particularly unreasonable or unusually blameworthy, will not strip the insurer of coverage defenses.

### Insurer Recoupment of Defense Expenditures

RLLI § 21 deals with the issue of recoupment of defense costs expended by the insurer in connection with uncovered claims. It provides that "[u]nless otherwise stated in the insurance policy or otherwise agreed to by the insured, an insurer may not seek recoupment of defense costs from the insured, even when it is subsequently determined that the insurer did not have a duty to defend or pay defenses costs."

### Potential Insurer Liability for Defense Counsel Conduct

Insurers have objected to RLLI § 12. Section 12 provides that insurers may in some instances be held responsible for the professional negligence of defense counsel if "[d]efense counsel is an employee of the insurer acting within the scope of employment" or the insurer "negligently selects or supervises defense counsel, including retaining counsel with inadequate liability insurance." Pursuant to RLLI § 12, if the defense is conducted in a substandard manner, the insurer could be held responsible. This implicates the situation in which the attorney is not an insurer employee but is selected by the insurer to defend a case but may receive problematic supervision from the insurer.

Insurers have opposed § 12(2) on the ground that the non-employee attorney is an independent professional who should alone be responsible for any legal malpractice that adversely affects a defendant-policyholder. And several states have precedent adopting this view. But there is authority to the contrary, as well, that the RLLI has found persuasive. It is important to remember that § 12 does not provide for strict liability of defense attorneys or insurers—or even any change in the standard of care, the elements of a professional negligence action, or the range of damages recoverable. RLLI § 12 does, however, allow the policyholder alleging attorney malpractice to name the insurer as a co-defendant who may also be held responsible if the requirements of § 12(2) can be proven by the disgruntled policyholder.

### The "Duty to Settle"

RLLI §§ 24–28 deal with settlement and what has traditionally been termed an insurer's "duty" to settle. Helpfully, the RLLI does not use this potentially misleading term and instead speaks of an insurer's "Duty to Make Reasonable Settlement Decisions," which is discussed in detail in RLLI § 24, which provides that an insurer controlling defense of a case "has a duty to the insured to make reasonable settlement decisions to protect the insured from a judgment in excess of the applicable policy limit." A reasonable settlement is defined as "one that would be made by a reasonable insurer who bears the sole financial responsibility for the full amount of the potential judgment." Further, the "insurer's duty to make reasonable settlement decisions includes the duty to make its policy limits available to the insured for the settlement of a covered legal action that exceeds those policy limits if a reasonable insurer would do so in the circumstances." This provision has attracted some criticism from insurers. RLLI § 25 notes that "[a] reservation of the right to contest coverage does not relieve an insurer of the duty to make reasonable settlement decisions."

### Policyholder Settlement Options

Where the insurer is defending but is unwilling to settle or has failed to settle, the policyholder is permitted to take affirmative action without violating the standard policy language giving insurers control of case resolution requiring cooperation of the policyholder, provided that several requirements are satisfied, including that: the insurer is given the opportunity to participate in the settlement process; the insurer declines to withdraw its reservation of rights after receiving prior notice of the proposed settlement; it would be reasonable for a person who bears the sole financial responsibility for the full amount of the potential covered judgment to accept the settlement; and a settlement of covered and uncovered claims is allocated reasonably.

Where there are multiple actions against the policyholder, the insurer's duty to settle of course remains but becomes more complicated in situations where it appears the cumulative value of the claims will exceed policy limits. In such cases, RLLI § 26(1) states that "the insurer has a duty to the insured to make a good-faith effort to settle the actions in a manner that minimizes the insured's overall exposure." The insurer "may satisfy this duty by interpleading the policy limits to the court."

### Remedies when Insurers Unreasonably Fail to Settle

RLLI § 27 adopts the widely used "excess judgment" measure of damages for breach of the duty to make reasonable settlements. RLLI § 28 provides that where an underlying insurer has breached the duty to make reasonable settlement decisions, "an excess insurer has an equitable right of subrogation for loss incurred as a result."

### Assignment

RLLI § 36 deals with assignment of rights under a policy and adopts standard contract law, which generally supports liberal assignment as a means of maximizing the utility of property and contract rights. It further provides, "[r]ights of an insured under an insurance policy relating to a specific claim that has been made against the insured may be assigned without regard to an anti-assignment condition or other term in the policy restricting such assignments." This portion of the RLLI adopts the longstanding view that, after a claim has been made, assignment of the policy does not increase the insurer's risk because when the events giving rise to the claim took place, the insured on the risk was the original insured. *See Ocean Accident & Guaranty Corp. v. Southwestern Bell Telephone Co.*, 100 F.2d 441 (8th Cir. 1932). Somewhat less clear in case law is a situation that takes place when the original policyholder's conduct has given rise to a number of claims that may be the first wave of claims yet to come (perhaps even the metaphorical tip of the iceberg), as is the case involving product liability or other mass torts or mini-mass torts. RLLI § 37(3)(a)–(c) addresses such situations.

### Policy Limits and Number of Occurrences

RLLI § 37 addresses policy limits, defining the term, including the distinction between per-occurrence limits and aggregate limits, while § 38 takes a brief, generalist stab at the vexing issue of determining the number of occurrences that does little more than state the prevailing common law rule of "cause" analysis (rather than "effects" analysis) in broad terms.

### Attachment of Excess Insurance Policies

Regarding attachment, the RLLI takes as a presumptive rule the approach of *Zeig v. Massachusetts Bonding Co.*, 23 F.2d 665 (2d Cir. 1928) (applying New York law), and provides that an excess insurer must attach when the underlying limits are satisfied by payment from any source — RLLI § 39 then backs away from the *Zeig* approach if it is "otherwise stated in the excess insurance policy." For example, if the excess policy has language stating that the underlying limit can be satisfied only by payment by the underlying insurer(s) (and nobody else), this language presumptively controls. Policyholder counsel oppose this provision, while insurer counsel support it.

### Allocation of Insurer Responsibility and Contribution

The RLLI addresses coordination of coverage in several sections. RLLI § 40 states the prevailing view that "[w]hen more than one insurance policy provides coverage to an insured for a legal action, the insurers are independently and concurrently liable to the insured under their policies, subject to the limits of each policy," except as provided in § 41(2), regarding apportionment of coverage responsibility in long-tail tort claims. The RLLI adopts the prevailing view that the duty to defend is indivisible and not subject to allocation.

RLLI § 41 states that when multiple insurers are consecutively triggered by claims of injury taking place in a number of policy periods over several years (or, in the case of asbestos or pollution claims, potentially several decades), each insurer's coverage responsibility can be pro-rated by time on the risk and policy limits rather than requiring each triggered insurer to be responsible for "all sums" (or "those sums" in more recent policy language) covered up to the policy limits. Case law in the area has been split. *See* andy Maniloff & Jeffrey Stempel, General Liability Insurance Coverage: Key Issues in Every State, Ch. 18. *See also Nooter Corp. v. Allianz Underwriters Ins. Co.*, 2017 Mo. App. LEXIS 977, *33 (Mo. Ct. App. Oct. 17, 2017) (citing RLLI in the course of defining terms and surveying jurisdictional split on the allocation issue).

RLLI § 41 sets forth a template for allocating coverage responsibilities in cases of a multi-year, multi-insurer claim. Regarding contribution, RLLI § 42(1) states that "[a]n insurer that indemnifies an insured for a legal action has a right of contribution against any other insurer with an indemnification obligation to that insured for that action" if certain conditions are met. Where multiple insurers are involved, with some settling coverage matters with the policyholder, RLLI § 43 provides that, "[i]n determining the declarations of rights and amount of any judgment to be entered against a liability insurer with respect to the insurer's obligation to provide coverage for a legal action brought against an insured, the amount of the insured's losses that are subject to the declaration or judgment are reduced by the amount paid for those losses by any insurers that settled with and were released by the insured with respect to that legal action."

### Public Policy and Punitive Damages

RLLI § 44 deals with terms that are imposed by operation of law, stating that a "term that is required by law to be included in a liability insurance policy is so included by operation of law notwithstanding its absence in the written policy" (§ 44(1)). A liability insurance policy term is "unenforceable on public-policy grounds if legislation provides that it is unenforceable or the interests in its enforcement is clearly outweighed in the circumstances by a public policy against the enforcement of such term" (§ 44(2)).

Regarding claims against the policyholder that may allege more than mere negligence (e.g., recklessness, willful, wanton conduct), RLLI § 45(1) provides that unless "barred by legislation or judicially declared public policy," insurance policies provide at least potential coverage for such claims—the types of claims that may create punitive damages liability—and that allegations of bad conduct do not relieve an insurer of the duty to defend unless otherwise provided in the policy or a clear legislative or judicial ruling that such claims are not insurable under the applicable law.

Regarding payment of settlements or judgments, the RLLI § 45(2) provides that "[e]xcept as barred by legislation or judicially declared public policy, a term in a liability insurance policy providing coverage for civil liability arising out of aggravated fault is enforceable," including civil liability for: criminal acts, expected or intentionally caused harm, fraud, or other conduct involving aggravated fault. RLLI § 45(3) states that issues of coverage in such situations are "a question of interpretation governed by the ordinary rules of insurance-policy interpretation."

### Remedies

RLLI §§ 47 and 48 address the remedies that may be available to insurer and policyholder in disputes over the policy. Such remedies include an award of compensatory damages, a declaration of rights, court costs and counsel fees for the prevailing party, and "[i]f so provided in the liability insurance policy or otherwise agreed to by the parties," recoupment of defense costs (§ 47(5)). This last provision takes the sting out of RLLI § 21 that generally bars recoupment because liability insurers usually promise in the policy to defend "suits" rather than only "covered claims." An insurer that wants to establish a right to recoupment can do this through the policy—and need not have such a right judicially created.

RLLI § 47(4) provides that when "[t]he insured substantially prevails in a declaratory-judgment action brought by an insurer seeking to terminate the insurer's duty to defend under the policy," the insured may recover reasonable attorneys' fees and other costs incurred in that action. This provision has proved controversial among insurers and was the subject of several complaints prior to the 2017 ALI Annual Meeting. Insurers argue that the issue of counsel fees recovery should be left to the state, particularly state legislation. The RLLI adopts the view that if an insurer subjects the policyholder to fighting a "two-front war" (the initial liability claim against the policyholder and the declaratory judgment action "brought by an insurer"), the insurer that fails should compensate the policyholder for the legal expenses involved in defending and prevailing in the declaratory action.

RLLI § 48 sets forth an extensive list of damages that "an insured may recover for breach of a liability policy," including all reasonable costs of the defense of a potentially covered legal action that have not already been paid by the insurer, all amounts required to indemnify the insured for a covered legal action that have not already been paid by the insurer, reasonable attorneys' fees and other costs incurred in the legal action establishing the insurer's breach of the duty to defend, other foreseeable losses caused by breach of the policy, and, in the case of a breach of the duty to make reasonable settlement decisions, the damages stated in RLLI § 27, which are largely the amount of the judgment in excess of the policy limits. This is an extensive array of damages. But in order to recover even a single item of these damages, a policyholder will need to prevail in its action against the insured, at least in part.

### Bad Faith

The RLLI § 49 test for holding an insurer in bad faith requires that the insurer fail "to perform under a liability insurance policy" and that this be "[w]ithout a reasonable basis for [the insurer's] conduct" and "[w]ith knowledge of its obligation to perform or in reckless disregard of whether it had an obligation to perform." RLLI § 50 provides as damages for bad faith breach: reasonable attorneys' fees and other costs incurred by the insured; "[a]ny other loss to the insured proximately caused by the insurer's bad-faith conduct"; and, if available pursuant to applicable state law, punitive damages.

# Chapter 10

# Life, Health and Disability Insurance

## § 10.01. Introduction

Life, disability, and health insurance are all first-party coverages involving a bilateral policy and potential claims between insurer and policyholder. In a sense, these are the ultimate first-party coverages in that they involve the policyholder's own physical condition or that of his or her immediate family. By contrast, property insurance, although of course important, more often involves protecting the value of material that is of less concern to the policyholder. All three of these lines of insurance are also notable in that the problems of information asymmetry and adverse selection that insurers fear are presented in more pronounced form as compared to other coverages. The policyholder may know something the insurer does not about property or liability exposures, but the insurer is more able to investigate these things. By contrast, the insurer can probably never develop as much information as the policyholder about the policyholder's health and disability or life issues. The applicant for life insurance could be considering suicide two years and a day after issue of the policy and this would be most difficult for the insurer to discover.

These problems are accentuated to a degree because all three of these lines of insurance are typically (usually in the case of health insurance) sold as group policies. A given insured person becomes insured simply by belonging to the group, making it even more difficult for the insurer to investigate problems of adverse selection or moral hazard. Provisions such as requiring an employee to be a "full-time" employee are written into group policies in order to discourage adverse selection in which persons likely to face inordinate life, health, or disability risk take a job in order to get on to the group life, disability, or health plan.

Of course, it remains difficult to become too sorry for insurers even when they face the potential of life insurance scams, malingering workers avoiding a return to work, or hypochondriacs running up medical bills over hangnails. The insurer, after all, sets the terms for the transaction, controls the contracting process, and drafts the policy language. The "full-time" requirement discussed above is an example of the type of provision limiting coverage that the insurer can place in a group policy (although it has obviously worked better for insurers in Illinois than in New York— *see Krauss v. Manhattan Life Insurance Co. of New York* in Ch. 2).

Group insurance can present something of an underwriting challenge to the insurer. By selling the coverage on a group basis, the insurer is by definition unable to make individual underwriting decisions. However, the insurer is not forced to sell a group policy and may simply refrain from taking on risks it does not like. Even if the initial sale of a group policy proves a bad deal for the insurer, the insurer can cut its losses by refusing to renew or cancelling if its sale of the policy was induced by misrepresentation.

But in the main, the group insurer is "betting" on the law of large numbers and low underwriting costs to work in its favor. The underwriting costs are low in relation to the premiums received, usually from the very solvent employer (hence few collection problems) or from payroll deductions for the worker's share (hence few collection problems). But the primary insurer's line of defense is careful setting of the coverage parameters. The insurer structures the policy to limit its exposure to unwanted risks.

At a minimum, insurers limit their risk with policy limits and aggregate limits as well as sub-limits on particular types of health problems. Most group health policies have a cap on lifetime medical coverage. The cap is pretty high (frequently a million dollars or more) but this at least protects the insurer from paying really high claims for really catastrophic and long-term medical problems.

Group policies usually have a waiting period as well, before full coverage attaches and may also refuse to cover pre-existing conditions until a minimum waiting period (longer than the initial waiting period for eligibility) has passed. For disability insurance, there is usually a minimum waiting period from the time of the injury until benefits are payable (usually 180 days). This prevents the insurer from covering short-term disability that resolves itself within six months (at least resolves itself enough in order to permit the injured worker to return to the job).

In addition, it is also typical for these types of insurance products to have a co-pay or cost-sharing provision (although not for life insurance). For example, for most health insurance, there is a co-payment for each doctor visit or other service. After this initial amount for which the insured is responsible, the insurer covers a high percentage of the costs, but not all. Typical of health insurance is an 80 percent/20 percent arrangement. HMOs (Health Maintenance Organizations) may cover a higher percentage or even all the costs but in return give the insured reduced choice of service provider or require the insured to pass through more gatekeeping mechanisms in order to receive services (or receive payment for the services). It is this type of provision that has created some of the political backlash against HMOs. For example, an HMO may require approval of the insured's primary physician before paying for an emergency room visit. But the reason the insured went to the ER is because the problem arose on a Saturday night when the primary physician was unavailable.

In addition, there is usually a deductible for which the policyholder is responsible before the group health coverage attaches. Typical is something like $500 for a family, which means that the insured pays all of the first $500 of a year's medical bills. Thereafter, coverage attaches but is subject to the up-front co-pay (which cynics might describe as a rolling second deductible) and percentage co-pay arrangement. In short, insurers are not in this for their health but to make money and they attempt to design the insurance product to facilitate that goal.

# § 10.02. Life Insurance

Life insurance is both a form of risk transfer and financial planning, as acknowledged by the Supreme Court nearly a century ago in the *Grigsby v. Russell*, 222 U.S. 149 (1911), case (*see* Ch. 5) holding that life insurance policies may be assigned despite the general restrictions on assignment of an insurance policy. Although frequently offered in group form, life insurance is still primarily sold on an individual basis—at least in terms of the amount of coverage if not the frequency. Most group life policies limit the benefits to the employee's salary or a relatively small multiple of annual salary (two or three times). By contrast, life insurers are willing to underwrite extremely large life insurance policies for wealthy individuals or businesses purchasing coverage on key employees.

Group life underwriting is minimal or non-existent, individual life underwriting can be rigorous, particularly for policies with a large face value. Even for small policies (excluding so-called "industrial life" policies that are designed primarily just to cover funeral expenses), most insurers now require a medical examination that includes a blood pressure reading and a blood test.

In addition, life insurance underwriting typically involves submission by the applicant of a lengthy application asking an array of questions regarding past medical treatment, family history, and other personal and economic information. If any of the applicant's answers are inaccurate, this can provide a basis for a misrepresentation defense and rescission of the policy if the applicant becomes a policyholder. In addition to issues of misrepresentation in underwriting, frequent sources of litigation particular to life insurance include beneficiary change, incontestability, and suicide or foul play.

Traditionally, once a life insurance carrier has determined that a valid claim has been presented, the carrier is obligated to settle the claim by making a full payment in the amount of the policy to the beneficiary or beneficiaries. All insurance regulations mandate that insurers pay valid claims promptly. Some life insurers, however, have used alternative methods of settlement which do not involve a full payment of the policy proceeds, but instead periodic payments drawn on by the beneficiary. This allows the life insurer to hang on to the proceeds for a longer period of time.

# [A] Incontestability Clauses in Life Insurance

## Amex Life Assurance Co. v.
## Superior Court of Los Angeles County

Supreme Court of California
14 Cal. 4th 1231, 930 P.2d 1264, 60 Cal. Rptr. 2d 898 (1997)

Chin, J.

In 1991, the Amex Life Assurance Company (Amex) issued a life insurance policy to Jose Morales. The policy contained what is called an "incontestability" CLAUSE: "We will not contest coverage under the Certificate [of insurance] after it has been in force during the life of the Covered Person for two years from the Certificate Effective Date, if all premiums have been paid." As early as 1915, this court described this type of incontestability clause—now required by statute in all group and individual life insurance policies—as "'in the nature of ... statutes of limitations and repose....'"

After the premiums have been paid and the insured has survived for two years, the insurance company may not contest coverage even if the insured committed fraud in applying for the policy. The incontestability clause, we have explained, "'is not a stipulation absolutely to waive all defenses and to condone fraud. On the contrary, it recognizes fraud and all other defenses but it provides ample time and opportunity within which they may be, but beyond which they may not be, established.'" ... In this case, Morales knew he was HIV (human immunodeficiency virus) positive when he applied for life insurance. He lied on the application form and sent an impostor to take the mandatory medical examination. With minimal effort, Amex could have discovered the fraud even before it issued the policy, but instead it collected the premiums for more than two years until Morales died.

After the beneficiary filed a claim, Amex discovered from information long available that an impostor had taken the examination, and it denied the claim. Today, while recognizing that it is too late to contest coverage due to fraud, Amex urges us to adopt the so-called "impostor defense" that some states recognize. As generally applied, the defense provides that when a person applies for a life insurance policy and takes the medical examination but names another person as the insured, the policy does not insure the named person but, if anyone, the person who completed the application and took the examination.

We need not decide whether to adopt the impostor defense because the facts of this case do not come within it. Here, the named insured, Morales, himself applied for the policy and did everything except take the medical examination. The policy insured him, not someone else. The fraud, though abhorrent and clearly justifying rescission of the policy during the two-year contestability period, is not qualitatively different from other types of fraud California courts have held may not be used to contest coverage once the contestability period has expired if the premiums have been paid. Therefore, Amex, which did nothing to protect its interests but collect premiums until Morales died after the contestability period, may no longer challenge coverage on the basis that an impostor took the medical examination. For these reasons, we affirm the judgment of the Court of Appeal, which reached a similar conclusion.

Jose Morales applied for a life insurance policy from Amex in January 1991. Although he apparently knew he was HIV positive, he lied on the application form and denied having the AIDS (acquired immune deficiency syndrome) virus. As part of the application process, Amex required him to have a medical examination. In March 1991, a paramedic working for Amex met a man claiming to be Morales and took blood and urine samples. It is not disputed in this proceeding that this man was an impostor. On his application, Morales listed his height as five feet six inches, and his weight as one hundred forty-two pounds. The examiner stated the man claiming to be Morales was five feet ten inches tall and weighed one hundred seventy-two pounds. The examiner also noted that the man produced no identification and appeared to be "unhealthy or older than stated age." The blood sample tested HIV negative.

Amex issued Morales a life insurance policy containing the incontestability clause effective May 1, 1991. All premiums have been paid. Morales died of AIDS-related causes on June 11, 1993. Shortly before his death, he sold his policy to Slome Capital Corp. (Slome), a viatical company engaged in the business of buying life insurance policies at a discount before the insured's death. In the interim, another insurance company assumed Amex's policies. (For convenience, we will refer to both companies collectively as Amex.) Amex states that after Morales died, an "informant" advised it that an impostor, and not Morales, appeared for the medical examination.

Amex conducted an investigation and then denied Slome's claim for the policy proceeds. The letter denying the claim noted the discrepancies between the stated height and weight of the applicant and the person who appeared for the medical examination. It stated that a handwriting expert determined that the person who signed the insurance application was not the person who signed the medical test form and medical questionnaire. The expert's report stated that the signatures contained "gross differences." The letter concluded "that the person who was examined and gave blood is different from the person who applied for coverage. The only possible explanation for this is that the applicant, who we have reason to believe was previously diagnosed as HIV positive, intended to deceive Amex in order to get insurance coverage." Amex denied payment on the basis that "[w]hen Mr. Morales applied for life insurance on his own life but substituted another individual for himself in the examination so that the policy would be issued based on the other person's medical condition, he caused Amex to issue a policy on the life of someone other than himself."

Slome sued Amex for breach of contract, insurance bad faith, and equitable estoppel. The superior court denied Amex's motion for summary judgment, ruling that "California does not recognize the impostor defense to the incontestability clause." Amex filed the instant proceeding in the Court of Appeal seeking a writ of mandate directing the superior court to grant its summary judgment motion. The court granted the petition as to the bad faith cause of action but, finding that the impostor defense, even if it exists, does not apply here, denied it in all other respects.

The [appellate court] concluded that its "refusal to adopt the impostor defense on these facts will place a minimal burden on insurance companies: before providing a medical exam and issuing a policy, they must at least take reasonable steps to ensure the person being examined is the person he claims to be. A contrary ruling will undermine the public policy of requiring diligence by the insurer and instead place a potentially heavy burden on policyholders and the courts as a result of litigation arising from the additional policy contests which are sure to ensue." (Fn. omitted.) [A concurring judge urged] "the Legislature to consider narrow changes in the law relating to incontestability clauses" and to provide an exception "when a person other than the insured takes" the mandatory physical examination. We granted Amex's petition for review.

## II. DISCUSSION

### A. Incontestability Clauses

"Incontestability clauses have been used by the insurance industry for over one hundred years to encourage persons to purchase life insurance." ..."Insurance companies initially offered the incontestability clause as a policy provision because of public distrust of insurers and their promises to pay benefits in the future." Today, these clauses are "required by statute in most states because without them, insurers were apt to deny benefits on the grounds of a pre-existing condition years after a policy had been issued. This left beneficiaries, particularly those in life insurance settings, in the untenable position of having to do battle with powerful insurance carriers. *See* 7 *Williston on Contracts* § 912.394 (3d ed. 1963) (noting that these clauses came from the 'early greed and ruthlessness of the insurers' who 'too often ... resisted liability stubbornly on the basis of some misstatement made by the insured at the time of applying for the policy')." ...

The "clauses are designed 'to require the insurer to investigate and act with reasonable promptness if it wishes to deny liability on the ground of false representation or warranty by the insured.' ...'It prevents an insurer from lulling the insured, by inaction, into fancied security during the time when the facts could best be ascertained and proved, only to litigate them belatedly, possibly after the death of the insured.'... Justice Holmes stated succinctly the purpose behind the incontestability clause: "The object of the clause is plain and laudable — to create an absolute assurance of the benefit, as free as may be from any dispute of fact except the fact of death, and as soon as it reasonably can be done."....

The California experience followed the usual historical pattern: Incontestability clauses came first, then statutes requiring them. We first confronted an incontestability clause [and] concluded "that a provision in a life insurance policy to the effect that after being in force the specified time, it shall be incontestable, precludes any defense after the stipulated period on account of false statements warranted to be true, even though such statements were fraudulently made."

This conclusion does not condone fraud but merely establishes a time limit within which it must be raised. "'It is not a stipulation absolutely to waive all defenses and to condone fraud. On the contrary, it recognizes fraud and all other defenses but it provides ample time and opportunity within which they may be, but beyond which they may not be, established. It is in the nature of and serves a similar purpose as statutes of limitations and repose, the wisdom of which is apparent to all reasonable minds. It is exemplified in the statute giving a certain period after the discovery of a fraud in which to apply for redress on account of it and in the law requiring prompt application after its discovery if one would be relieved from a contract infected with fraud.'" ...

Years after [the Court's initial decision regarding incontestability], the Legislature enacted statutes requiring every life insurance policy to contain an incontestability clause: in 1935 for group policies (Ins. Code,§ 10206 ["[t]he policy shall provide that the validity of the policy shall not be contested, except for nonpayment of premiums, after it has been in force for two years from its date of issue"]), and, effective in 1974, for individual policies (Ins. Code § 10113.5 ["[a]n individual life insurance policy delivered or issued for delivery in this state shall contain a provision that it is incontestable after it has been in force, during the lifetime of the insured, for a period of not more than two years after its date of issue, except for nonpayment of premiums"]). (The parties question which of these two statutes applies to the policy of this case. As the Court of Appeal recognized, it does not matter; for our purposes, the two statutes are substantially identical.)

The Court of Appeal opinion summarized the case law ...: "Numerous decisions ... have held that even gross fraud by an insured who lied about his health in applying for life insurance falls within the terms of an incontestability provision.... The Court of Appeal discussed the "[s]ound public policy considerations" behind this rule.... It has often been held that a provision of that kind is valid because it is in the nature of a limitation of the time within which the defendant [insurer] may avoid the policy for this cause.

Such a provision is reasonable and proper, as it gives the insured a guaranty against possible expensive litigation to defeat his claim after the lapse of many years, and at the same time gives the company time and opportunity for investigation, to ascertain whether the contract should remain in force. It is not against public policy, as tending to put fraud on a par with honesty.'" 'The incontestable clauses are enforced with particularity by the courts because of the desirable purpose which they have. It is their purpose to put a checkmate upon litigation; to prevent, after the lapse of a certain period of time, an expensive resort to the courts—expensive both from the point of view of the litigants and that of the citizens of the state.

In that way, it is a statute of limitations upon the right to maintain certain actions or certain defenses.... The need for such protection becomes especially clear for life insurance policies, where the contest is usually made after the named insured has died, robbing the beneficiaries of their most potent witness."

A recent decision has reaffirmed the continuing application of incontestability clauses to fraud claims. In *United Fidelity Life Ins. Co. v. Emert* (1996) 49 Cal. App. 4th 941 [57 Cal. Rptr. 2d 14], the insurance company issued Emert a life insurance policy with a disability rider. Although knowing he was HIV positive, Emert stated on the application he did not have an "immune deficiency disorder," and, when asked to list all physicians he had seen in the last five years, listed only a general practitioner and not an HIV specialist who had been treating him regularly. After the two-year contestability period, Emert submitted a disability claim. Relying on many of the cases cited above, the Court of Appeal held that the incontestability clause prevented the insurance company from contesting the claim on the basis of the fraudulent conduct. With this backdrop, we now consider the "impostor defense" that Amex seeks to assert.

B. The "Impostor Defense"

A few decisions outside California have allowed an insurer to contest a claim despite the incontestability clause when an impostor claimed to be the named insured. The first was *Maslin v. Columbian Nat. Life Ins. Co.* (S.D.N.Y. 1932) 3 F. Supp. 368 (*Maslin*). In *Maslin*, the insurance company issued policies insuring "Samuel Maslin." After the period of contestability expired, the company asserted the defense "that an impostor posing as Samuel Maslin made the application and took the physical examination for the policies...." (*Id.* at p. 369.) The court recognized the general rule "that after the passage of the stipulated time [of contestability] the insurance company is precluded from contesting the policy on the ground of false representations by the insured, even those made fraudulently." (*Ibid.*) "The view is that even though dishonest people are given advantages under incontestability clauses which any right-minded man is loath to see them get, still the sense of security given to the great majority of honest policyholders by the presence of the clause in their policies makes it worth the cost. The time allowed to the insurance company after issuance of the policy to investigate the case and uncover any fraud is deemed a fair check against trickery or deception by the insured." (*Ibid.*)

Nevertheless, the *Maslin* court found the defense of "the alleged impersonation of Samuel Maslin by another who is said to have made the application and, more important still, to have taken the physical examination, is not barred by the incontestability clause. In substance, the defendant's position is that it never insured the life of the plaintiff's son at all and never had any contract or contractual dealings with him; that the man it insured was another person altogether, a healthy man whom the defendant's medical examiner saw and accepted as a risk and who chose to call himself Samuel Maslin.... If the facts pleaded are borne out by the proof, the defendant is under no liability to the plaintiff. There cannot be the slightest doubt that the person whom an insurance company intends to make a contract with and intends to insure is the person who presents himself for physical examination." [T]wo decisions applying New Jersey law recognized a defense under facts similar to those here, but the law regarding incontestability clauses in New Jersey is very different than in California.

C. Application to This Case

The basic rationale of the cases recognizing the impostor defense is that when a person applies for the insurance and takes the medical examination, but uses the name of someone else who then dies, no contract ever existed insuring the life of the person who has died and whose name is stated in the insurance policy. No California decision has considered this question.... Amex argues it insured, if anyone, the person who appeared for the medical examination, not Morales, and that to the extent the policy purported to insure Morales, it was void from the beginning or, to use the term in the cases, *ab initio*. The incontestability clause, it further argues, does not prevent a claim the policy never insured Morales.

In this case, however, there *was* a meeting of the minds on the identity of the person with whom Amex was dealing. Morales, the named insured, personally applied for the insurance. Amex insured his life, not someone else's. Amex did not know that an impostor appeared for the medical examination and, we may assume, would not have insured Morales's life had it known the true facts. But the fraud is similar to other frauds that the incontestability clause clearly covers. If, for example, an applicant falsely claims on the application to be healthy and then appears for the medical examination but somehow substitutes a healthy blood sample for the tainted one, the fraud would be similar in effect to that here, but there could be no question whose life was being insured.

Rejecting the impostor defense under these facts furthers the policy behind incontestability clauses. When the named insured applies for the policy, and the premiums are faithfully paid for over two years, the beneficiaries should be assured they will receive the expected benefits, and not a lawsuit, upon the insured's death. The incontestability clause requires the insurer to investigate fraud before it issues the policy or within two years afterwards. The insurer may not accept the premiums for two years and investigate a possible defense only *after* the beneficiaries file a claim. Here, with minimal effort, Amex could have discovered the fraud at the outset, as it did finally from information available before it issued the policy. The person who appeared for the examination did not produce identification although Amex could easily have demanded it. The impostor's height and weight differed considerably from Morales's. The signatures of the applicant and the impostor were transparently different.

Amex ignored this information and merely accepted the premiums for the entire period of contestability. Then it became too late to claim for the first time that an impostor took the medical examination. Beneficiaries have the right to expect that after the premiums are paid for the specified time, the insurer will promptly pay the policy proceeds upon the insured's death. The incontestability clause protects that right. In some cases, to be sure, the fraud will be harder to discover than here. But presumably, it would be no easier to discover fraud two years after the events than at the outset. More importantly, if the fraud is harder to discover, *defending* against a claim of fraud would also be more difficult after years have passed and the named insured—no doubt the key witness—has died.

Again, we agree with the Court of Appeal: "[T]he deception could well have been discovered at the start had Amex simply required all applicants to produce photographic identification before conducting a medical exam and issuing a policy. Given the relatively light burden of such a requirement, combined with the burden of diligence which *[Insurance Code] section 10113.5* places on the insurer, application of the incontestability clause to bar Amex's challenge is proper. [¶] To hold otherwise might lead to no end of mischief as insurance companies who have taken no steps to verify the identity of their applicants or medical examinees then comb their files after the incontestability period expires, looking for some basis to contend that someone other than the named insured took part in the application or examination process. Both the courts and the Legislature have recognized the occasional inequity which the incontestability clause may allow. The inequity here was no different. While Morales's fraud was abhorrent, he did nothing more than adopt another means of supplying false information to further his own application. Amex was deceived by this, but always intended to contract with Morales."

We conclude that, after the contestability period has expired, an insurer may not assert the defense that an impostor took the medical examination if, as here, the named insured personally applied for insurance.

## Notes and Questions

1. In the aftermath of the *Amex Life* decision, the California Legislature amended the Insurance Code to effectively overturn the result of the case. The relevant statutory section now provides that an insurance policy is void *ab initio* if the applicant presents photographic identification during the application process and "if an imposter is substituted for a named insured in any part of the application process, with or without the knowledge of the named insured." *See* Cal. Ins. Code § 10113.5.

2. Does the Legislature's reaction suggest that the California Supreme Court erred? Or, is this an example of the system working the way it should, with a court showing its insulation from popular sentiment (after all, who can side with a scammer even if we have empathy because of his tragic medical condition)? The court applies legal doctrine in a technical and relatively value-free manner. The elected legislature then may interject social values into the system by making judgments about the relative blameworthiness of conduct. Alternatively, is *Amex Life* a case of a court losing sight of the ethical forest because of doctrinal trees?

## [B] Change of Beneficiaries

Unless the life insured has designated an irrevocable beneficiary in a life insurance policy, the insured may change the beneficiary at any time because, under the majority rule, a designated beneficiary has no vested interest in the policy. *See, e.g., Davis v. Metropolitan Life Ins. Co.*, 285 Ill. App. 398, 2 N.E.2d 141 (1936).

A minority of courts, however, follow the "New Jersey Rule" under which a beneficiary of a life insurance policy takes a vested interest in the proceeds payable on the death of the insured, and this interest is defeasible only to the extent provided in the policy. *See, e.g., Metropolitan Life Ins. Co. v. Woolf*, 138 N.J. Eq. 450, 47 A.2d 340 (1946). Yet it is also true under the "New Jersey Rule" that the insured may reserve in the policy the right to affect the interest of the beneficiary. *See Phoenix Mut. Life Ins. Co. v. Connelly*, 188 F.2d 462 (3d Cir. 1951). But what must the insured do to validly effect this change of beneficiary in a life insurance policy? The following case discusses the applicable requirements.

# Rendleman v. Metropolitan Life Insurance Company

United States Court of Appeals, Seventh Circuit
937 F.2d 1292 (1991)

**Cummings, Circuit Judge.**

[Larry Rendleman, an employee of the State of Illinois, was insured under his employer's Group Life Insurance Program as well as the Group Health Insurance Program. Larry married Tammy on May 3, 1986, and on May 12, 1986, when Fort Dearborn Life Ins. Co. was the carrier of the group insurance, he made a written designation (on the proper form) of Tammy as beneficiary and his father Elbert as contingent beneficiary. In 1987 the employer changed its carrier to Metropolitan Life. In 1988 Larry and Tammy were divorced and Larry completed a form which dropped Tammy from the Group Health Program only. Larry was killed in an auto accident in 1989. Both Tammy and Elbert and Dorothy (the parents) filed claims for the insurance proceeds.]

A. Beneficiary Designation

Initially, the parents argue that the form designating Tammy Rendleman as the beneficiary under the life insurance policy was invalid, because it was executed when another policy with a different insurance carrier was in effect. They maintain that because the successor policy did not incorporate the prior designation form and because it contained language that it represented the entire agreement between the parties, there was no valid designation of beneficiary during the effective dates of the policy and therefore, the proceeds are payable to them under the default provision of the policy. The ex-wife counters that the beneficiary designation form completed in 1986 retained its validity despite the fact that the company that supplied the life insurance coverage had changed. As such, she argues that the district court properly entered summary judgment in her favor.

None of the parties cite any authority for their conflicting arguments with respect to the continuing validity of a beneficiary designation under a group life insurance policy where the provider is changed. Our own research has found only a few cases that have addressed the question. In *Davis v. Travelers Ins. Co.*, 196 N.W.2d 526 (Iowa 1972), the Iowa Supreme Court did face the issue now before us on appeal. In *Davis*, the decedent became an employee of the Pepsi-Cola General Bottlers in 1963 and as such, was covered under a group life insurance policy issued by the Travelers. In 1963, the decedent had executed a designation of beneficiary form naming his then wife as his beneficiary. Thereafter, the insured and his wife (the named beneficiary) were divorced and the insured remarried.

At some point prior to the insured's death, Pepsi and the Travelers renegotiated the insurance and a successor policy with substantially the same provisions was issued. The successor policy was in effect at the time of the insured's death. Both the ex-wife and the widow, as the executor of her late husband's estate, filed claims for the insurance proceeds. The executor argued that the two different policies of insurance required independent beneficiary designations in order to be effective. The *Davis* court affirmed an entry of summary judgment which rejected that argument. The court noted that the designation of beneficiary card did not make reference to effective dates of the policy.

In addition, the court emphasized that the successor policy was merely a replacement policy under which the coverage was to remain constant. "Where the renewal agreement so recites, or unless it provides otherwise, the terms and conditions of the existing policy are not changed, enlarged, or restricted by a renewal but are merely continued in force as binding on the parties; and an agreement to renew, in the absence of expression to the contrary, is presumed to contemplate the same terms and conditions as the existing insurance, the only change being the time of its expiration." *Davis*, 196 N.W.2d at 530 (quoting 44 C.J.S. Insurance § 285).

As such, the court concluded that the beneficiary designation completed prior to the effective date of the policy in force at the time of death operated to direct payment to the decedent's ex-wife. *Contra; Taylor v. Harrison*, 445 S.W.2d 270 (Tx. Ct. App. 1969) and *Leath v. Tillery*, 424 S.W.2d 505 (Tx. Ct. App. 1968) (designation of a beneficiary under one policy was not effective for a subsequent and different policy).

The rationale of ... *Davis* is controlling in this instance, even though the insurance companies that provided the insurance in this case were not related entities. The policy provisions in this instance establish that the required documents for naming, changing, or adding a beneficiary were located with the employer. In addition, the employer maintained the record-keeping function under ... [the] policy. The beneficiary designation became effective when it was delivered to the employer, and the insurance company had no requirement that it even be advised of the beneficiary until a claim was made. As the appellee ex-wife argues, there is nothing in the policy to suggest that a prior designation became ineffective when the group life insurance carrier was changed. In fact, the policy language refers to the "designated beneficiary." The use of that language lends support to the proposition that the policy presupposes that a beneficiary designation be made before the effective date of the policy. Thus, the ex-wife remained the designated beneficiary.

The conclusion that the beneficiary designation is continuing in nature and is not canceled as a result of the change in carriers is strengthened by the fact that here the original enrollment form is handled in the same manner as the beneficiary designation form, in that the employer retains possession of the form and uses it to obtain from the insurance company the type of coverage an employee has selected.

The logical conclusion to draw from the State's handling of the enrollment and beneficiary designation forms is that the employee makes a determination as to his choice of coverage and his beneficiary, and thereafter the State contracts with an insurance company to provide the desired coverage at the best price. If prior beneficiary designations were revoked each time the State switched insurance carriers, the group life insurance program would be thrown into a state of unnecessary upheaval.…

The procedures used for enrolling and designating beneficiaries in Rendleman's case show that the employees, the employer, and the insurance companies contemplated a situation where the beneficiary designation would be ongoing unless the insured changed the named beneficiary form. As intended by this set-up, a court should give effect to the last beneficiary designation form. There was no error in the magistrate judge's determination that Tammy Rendleman was the only designated beneficiary under the policy at issue and as such was entitled to the proceeds.

B. Change of Beneficiary

The parents argue in the alternative that the decedent effectively revoked his beneficiary designation prior to his death and thus, they argue that the proceeds pass to them pursuant to the default provision of the policy. To change a beneficiary, the policy provided the following instructions to the insured: If you desire to change a named beneficiary, add a beneficiary, or change the address of a beneficiary, you must inform your Group Insurance Representative at your enrolling agency or retirement system, and request that the change be made. You will be given a new Beneficiary Designation Form which you should complete. It is your responsibility to ensure that the beneficiary designation is current. The Beneficiary Designation Form is not effective unless signed by you and is on file with the agency or retirement system at the time of your death.

The parents argue that the action taken by the decedent prior to his death in telling Jeff Hutchinson that he did not want his ex-wife to collect his life insurance and in obtaining the necessary change of beneficiary form was sufficient to remove her as a beneficiary under the policy. The parents argue that the decedent clearly expressed his intent to change his beneficiary and took sufficient steps to effectuate the change even though he never completed the requisite change of beneficiary form. In *Travelers Ins. Co. v. Smith*, 106 Ill. App. 3d 318, 62 Ill. Dec. 216, 435 N.E.2d 1188 (1st Dist. 1982), the Appellate Court of Illinois noted that in cases such as the one at bar where an interpleader action is filed, the insurance company waives strict compliance with the terms of the policy dictating the procedure for changing a beneficiary. Nevertheless, the court also noted that "[o]bviously before the designation can be changed, the insured must intend to change the beneficiary. But *mere intent is not enough; there must be at least some overt act evidencing this intent.*" [Emphasis added.]

Similarly, in *Dooley v. James A. Dooley Associates Employees Retirement Plan*, 92 Ill. 2d 476, 65 Ill. Dec. 911, 442 N.E.2d 222 (1982), the Illinois Supreme Court stated "While certainty of intent is essential, it will not suffice without more. There must be a combination of intent to make the change and positive action towards effecting that end. Substantial compliance requires (a) a clear expression of the insured's intention to change beneficiaries, plus (b) his concrete attempt to carry out his intention as far as was reasonably in his power. Intent alone is not sufficient. In addition, the insured must have done all he reasonably could do under the circumstances to carry his intention into execution." ... Here the decedent plainly did not do "all he reasonably could do under the circumstances to carry his intention into execution."

In *Connecticut General Life Ins. Co. v. Gulley*, 668 F.2d 325 (7th Cir. 1982), this Court placed the Illinois cases concerning substantial compliance with the policy provisions for changing an insurance beneficiary in two categories: those where the insured took a number of positive steps to change the beneficiary but was not in strict compliance with the policy requirements, and those cases where the insured took virtually no steps to implement the change. The *Gulley* court noted that in the second category of cases "[t]ypically, the only evidence of an attempted change was an oral statement by the insured that he intended to change the beneficiary of his insurance policy. Although recognizing that strict compliance with the terms of the policy is not essential, the courts have required more concrete evidence of intent in order to effect a change of beneficiary." 668 F.2d at 327.

The case before us resembles more nearly the second category of cases recognized by this Court in *Gulley*. The only evidence in the record reflects that the decedent came upon a co-worker, Jeff Hutchinson, at the prison and [told him that] ... he did not want his ex-wife to collect the proceeds of the policy upon his death.... There is no evidence that the beneficiary designation form was ever completed.... Even though the decedent expressed his intent to remove his ex-wife as the life insurance beneficiary, he did not carry out his intention. As such, we hold that the district court properly entered summary judgment in favor of the decedent's ex-wife, since there was no revocation of the prior beneficiary designation.... Therefore, the decision of the district court granting summary judgment in favor of Tammy Rendleman and awarding her the policy proceeds is AFFIRMED.

### Notes and Questions

1. As stated in *Smith*, quoted in the main case, in addition to the insured having an intent to change the beneficiary, there must also be some overt act evidencing that intent; and when the insurer has specified the method of changing a beneficiary in the policy, there must be compliance with this method. Was strict compliance with the policy terms required or only substantial compliance? Did the insured "comply" with the policy requirements? What was the purpose of the insurer's filing an interpleader action in this case?

2. Many jurisdictions hold that substantial compliance with the policy requirements for changing a beneficiary will suffice, but the question as to what constitutes substantial compliance will depend on the particular policy provisions and facts of each case. *See, e.g., Allen v. Abrahamson*, 12 Wash. App. 103, 529 P.2d 469 (1974); *Provident Mut. Life Ins. Co. v. Ehrlich*, 508 F.2d 129 (3d Cir. 1975) (applying Pennsylvania law).

3. May an insured validly change the beneficiary of an annuity or a group life insurance policy through a provision in the insured's last will and testament? Will this constitute substantial compliance? *See, e.g., Kane v. Union Mut. Life Ins. Co.*, 84 A.D.2d 148, 445 N.Y.S.2d 549 (1981) (change through will permitted if sufficiently clear but clarity lacking in this instance).

4. Absent a controlling statute does the insured have a right to change the beneficiary when the policy is silent on the issue? *Compare Bingham v. United States*, 296

U.S. 211 (1935) (apparently applying federal common law) (unless power reserved in policy, beneficiary change not permitted, at least for purposes of assessing tax), *with Boehmer v. Kalk*, 144 N.W. 182 (Wis. 1913) (implied policyholder right to assign policy or change beneficiary even if not expressly reserved in policy). (Note as well: under most state laws, the proceeds of a life insurance policy go directly to the beneficiary without being considered part of the decedent policyholder's estate).

5. In instances of marital breakdown, life insurance is an asset that is dealt with as part of property settlement. A life insurance policy is a financial instrument of value that often may form part of a settlement. A spouse may, for example, be left on a life insurance policy as a beneficiary even though the marriage has broken down. To change the beneficiary, courts often hold that there must be clear evidence of such a change (like the insured submitting the insurer's change form) in order to alter the beneficiary after death when the beneficiary is an ex-spouse. *See, e.g., Eschler v. Eschler*, 849 P.2d 196 (Mo. 1993).

6. In *Gillespie v. Moore*, 635 S.W.2d 927 (Tex. Civ. App. 1982), a separation agreement incorporated into a divorce decree provided that the wife surrendered her ownership rights and her beneficiary rights to a life insurance policy on the husband's life. Even though she continued to be the beneficiary named in the policy, the court held she could not recover the insurance proceeds when her ex-husband died. How can this case be distinguished from *Eschler*? *See also Costello v. Costello*, 379 F. Supp. 630 (D. Wyo. 1974).

7. The corollary of this general rule is that whenever a divorce decree or separation agreement requires the insured to name certain persons as beneficiaries of a life insurance policy, those beneficiaries will prevail over any subsequent change of beneficiary made after the divorce or agreement. *See, e.g., In re Estate of Lemer*, 306 N.W.2d 244 (S.D. 1981) (husband required to name his three minor children as beneficiaries of a life insurance policy); *Posey v. Prudential Ins. Co.*, 383 So. 2d 849 (Ala. App.), *cert. denied*, 383 So. 2d 851 (Ala. 1980) (husband ordered to name his son as irrevocable beneficiary of all his life insurance policies).

8. Some states have statutes addressing the effect of divorce on the beneficiary of life insurance benefits (*see, e.g.,* VA. CODE § 20-111.1). What policy reasons can you articulate for the various approaches to the issue?

## PROBLEM ONE

The insured properly executed a change of beneficiary form in favor of his daughter and left it with her. After the insured's death, his daughter mailed this form to the insured's employer (a condition precedent to its effectiveness under the policy), although her father had never instructed her to mail the form nor evidenced an intent that she should do so.

• Was there substantial compliance?

# [C] Assignment of Life Insurance

The general rule is that, in the absence of fraud, an absolute assignment of a life insurance policy, other than as collateral, divests the beneficiary of any interest in the policy proceeds and vests the assignee with this interest. *See, e.g., Bourne v. Haynes*, 235 N.Y.S.2d 332 (1962).

An assignment of a life insurance policy to a creditor as collateral security for a debt is valid only to the extent of that debt plus reasonable expenses, and the creditor must account to the beneficiaries or the estate of the insured for any proceeds in excess of the debt. *See, e.g., Employers Modern Life Co. v. Lindley*, 404 N.E.2d 1036 (Ill. App. 1980), *Warnock v. Davis*, 104 U.S. 775 (1882).

Who should recover the insurance proceeds when a debt is barred by the statute of limitations—the beneficiary or the creditor assignee? *Compare Hawkins v. Southern Pipe & Supply Co.*, 259 So. 2d 696 (Miss. 1972), *with Gallaher v. American-Amicable Life Ins. Co.*, 462 S.W.2d 626 (Tex. Civ. App. 1971). Does the beneficiary have any recourse? *See In re Estate of Winstead*, 144 Ill. App. 3d 502, 493 N.E.2d 1183(1986).

# [D] Insurance Gothic: Beneficiary and Life Insurer Misconduct

## *[1] Beneficiary Misconduct*

It is generally held that a beneficiary who willfully and unlawfully kills the insured is barred from any recovery of the life insurance proceeds. Under what rationale? *See, e.g., Chute v. Old American Ins. Co.*, 6 Kan. App. 2d 412, 629 P.2d 734 (1981) (disapproved in *Harper v. Prudential Ins. Co.*, 233 Kan. 358, 662 P.2d 1264 (1983)).

### Diep v. Rivas

Court of Appeals of Maryland
357 Md. 668, 745 A.2d 1098 (2000)

Opinion by **Rodowsky, J.**

This interpleader action involves $150,000 in life insurance benefits payable as a result of the murder of a wife by her husband who then committed suicide. At issue is the ultimate recipient of the proceeds. After interpreting the insurance contract to provide for payment to relatives of the husband as contingent beneficiaries, the Court of Special Appeals ... then applied the slayer's rule to disqualify the contingent beneficiaries from receiving payment and awarded the proceeds to the wife's father. For the reasons set forth below, we reverse.

The murder and suicide took place during an argument at the marital home in Howard County on April 2, 1996. There were no children of the marriage. The murder victim, Maria Rivas, is survived by her father, the respondent, Dr. Hector Rivas, and the murderer/suicide, Xuang Ky Tran (Tran), is survived by his brother and sister, the petitioners, An Diep and Vanessa Diep. Tran was employed by IIT

Research Institute (IIT) which was the holder of a group accidental death and dismemberment benefit policy (the Policy) issued by Continental Casualty Company (CNA) and effective January 1, 1990. Insofar as relevant to the instant matter, the Policy is comprised of the application for the master policy and the master policy. The record also contains the form certificate issued to IIT employees who were covered by the Policy. By its terms the certificate is not the Policy but "is merely evidence of insurance provided under the Policy."

Following the death of Maria Rivas, CNA was confronted with conflicting claims for the benefits payable upon her death. The petitioners and the respondent sought payment based on their respective interpretations of the "Payment of Claim" provision applicable, where, as here, no beneficiaries had been specially designated. That policy provision reads in relevant part:

> "Benefits for loss of life of the Insured will be payable in accordance with the beneficiary designation in effect at the time of payment. If no such designation is in effect at that time, the benefits shall be paid to the surviving person or persons in the first of the following classes of successive preference beneficiaries of which a member survives the Insured:
>
> > "The Insured's (a) spouse; (b) children, including legally adopted children; (c) parents; (d) brothers and sisters; or (e) estate.... If two or more persons become entitled to benefits as preference beneficiaries, they shall share equally.
>
> "Benefits for loss of life of any insured family member will [be] payable to the Insured, if living, otherwise in the same manner as above."

The respondent contends that the applicable classes of successive preference beneficiaries are the relatives of Maria Rivas, while the petitioners contend that the applicable classes of successive preference beneficiaries are the relatives of Tran. The respondent further contends that, if the applicable classes of successive preference beneficiaries are the relatives of Tran, then they are disqualified by the slayer's rule from taking the insurance benefits. CNA responded to the conflicting claims by interpleading the claimants in the Circuit Court for Montgomery County.

There were cross-motions for summary judgment. The circuit court agreed with the respondent's construction of the Policy and, in *dicta*, commented that the slayer's rule did not apply. The Court of Special Appeals agreed with the petitioners' construction of the Policy, but held that the slayer's rule did apply. This Court issued the writ of certiorari.

In Maryland, the slayer's rule exists as a matter of public policy embodied in the common law. This Court first applied the doctrine in *Price v. Hitaffer*, 164 Md. 505, 165 A. 470 (1933), a case in which a husband murdered his wife and almost immediately thereafter committed suicide. The wife died intestate, and an orphans' court excluded the heirs and personal representatives of the murderer from the distribution of the victim's estate. The Court stated the issue to be: "Can a murderer, or his heirs and representatives through him, be enriched by taking any portion of the estate of the one murdered?" ... *Price* held that the statutes of descent and distribution must be construed in light of the strong public policy represented by

> "one line of decisions [that] apply the common-law principle of equity that no one shall be permitted to profit by his own fraud, to take advantage of his own wrong, to found any claim upon his own iniquity, or to acquire property by his own crime, and hold that provisions of a will and the statutes of descent and distribution should be interpreted in the light of those universally recognized principles of justice and morality; that such interpretation is justified and compelled by the public policy embraced in those principles or maxims, which must control the interpretation of law, statutes, and contracts."

The slayer's rule was applied in *Chase v. Jenifer*, 219 Md. 564, 150 A.2d 251 (1959), to disqualify a wife who was the named beneficiary of insurance on her husband's life from receiving the death benefits where the wife had killed the husband under circumstances constituting voluntary manslaughter, because "the killing [was] both felonious and intentional." ... There appears not to have been any contingent beneficiary named in the policy involved in *Chase*.

The contest was between the victim's personal representative and the slayer, and the proceeds were paid to the victim's estate. Whether the slayer's rule applies to homicides under circumstances constituting involuntary manslaughter was answered in the negative in *Schifanelli v. Wallace*, 271 Md. 177, 315 A.2d 513 (1974). We explained that

> "the rule which prevents a beneficiary who has intentionally killed the insured from recovering on an insurance policy is grounded on the public policy against permitting a wilful and felonious killer to profit by his felony. Thus, it has no application where even though the acts of the beneficiary cause death, they are without the intent to do so; where the death is the result of accident, or even when caused by such gross negligence on the part of the beneficiary that he is guilty of involuntary manslaughter, the beneficiary may still recover...."

More recently, ... we held that the slayer's rule does not apply to a person who was not criminally responsible within the meaning of [the] Maryland Code.... [A] daughter had murdered her mother who left a will under which the daughter was the sole beneficiary. The contest was between the slayer and her brother who was a contingent beneficiary under the will. Inasmuch as the holding ... permitted the daughter to inherit under the will, the alternate disposition to the brother did not come into effect. In the instant matter the Court of Special Appeals extended the slayer's rule to the petitioners for two reasons, the first of which is as follows:

> "The Dieps also state, and we agree, that they are not guilty of any wrongdoing. That fact, however, has no bearing on eligibility. If the law provided that innocent secondary beneficiaries were not excluded by the Slayer's Rule, the public policy reason for the rule would be eroded significantly and, arguably, the murder/suicide statistics would increase dramatically."

This rationale conflicts with the principle underlying the slayer's rule. The rule is designed to prevent one from taking "advantage of his own wrong" or acquiring "property by his own crime." ... Inasmuch as the not criminally responsible murderer, and the person who kills another unintentionally, but through gross negligence, may acquire property as a result of homicides committed by them, the petitioners, who are completely blameless in the murder of Maria Rivas, are not precluded from taking the Policy proceeds resulting from her death. Indeed, to visit the consequences of Tran's crime on his brother and sister conjures up the ghosts of corruption of the blood which is prohibited by Article 27 of the Maryland Declaration of Rights.

The Court of Special Appeals also based its extension of the slayer's rule to the petitioners on an erroneous interpretation and application of a statement by this Court ... that "these principles [of the slayer's rule] apply not only to the killer but to those claiming through or under him." From the preceding sentence the Court of Special Appeals concluded:

> "... a beneficiary under a policy of insurance on the decedent's life when the homicide is unintentional even though it is the result of such gross negligence as would render the killer criminally guilty of involuntary manslaughter."

> "Tran never having acquired any right to the proceeds, the secondary beneficiaries have no interest to assert because their claim is through Tran as surviving brother and sister.

> "[Precedent] states expressly that the Slayer's Rule is applicable to those claiming 'through or under' the slayer. Tran's brother and sister are without question claiming through and under Tran, who was the insured as defined in the policy."

The sentence ... on which the Court of Special Appeals relies reiterates one aspect of the holding in *Price*. *Price* involved the slayer's claim to a husband's fifty percent share, under the facts of that case, in the victim's intestate estate. There, although the husband committed suicide almost immediately after the murder, there was a brief interval during which he survived his murdered wife so that the claim to the fifty percent share was asserted by the heirs and personal representatives of the deceased slayer.

The claim of the heirs and personal representatives was by and through the slayer because they claimed in the right of the slayer as surviving spouse. The Court rejected the claim by and through the briefly surviving spouse, not because the heirs and personal representatives were disqualified themselves by the slayer's rule, but because the slayer, at the instant of the murder, lost his interest in the victim's estate. *Id.* at 508, 165 A. at 471.

The foregoing is made plain by the passage in the *Price* opinion in which the Court rejects an argument that application of the slayer's rule violated Article 27 of the Maryland Declaration of Rights. The opinion in *Price* in relevant part reads:

> "In the view that we take of the case, the constitutional and statutory prohibition against corruption of blood and forfeiture of estate by conviction has no application, because by reason of his murderous act the husband never acquired a beneficial interest in any part of his wife's estate. These provisions apply to the forfeiture of an estate held by the criminal at the time

of the commission of the crime, or which he might thereafter become legally or equitably entitled to. In other words, it is a constitutional declaration against forfeiture for a general conviction of crime. There can be no forfeiture without first having beneficial use or possession. One cannot forfeit what he never had. The surviving husband in the case before us, never having acquired any interest in his wife's estate, there is nothing upon which the constitutional or statutory prohibition can operate. By virtue of his act he is prevented from acquiring property which he would otherwise have acquired, but does not forfeit an estate which he possessed."

In the instant matter the petitioners do not claim through or under or in the right of Tran. Because Tran murdered Maria Rivas, he never acquired the right to collect the death benefits, just as the murderer in *Price* never acquired the right to take as surviving husband under the inheritance statutes. Further, if the insurance policy in the instant matter named Tran as the sole beneficiary, and his personal representative sought to collect from CNA on Tran's purported contract right, the "through or under" language from *Ford* [*v. Ford*, 307 Md. 105, 512 A.2d 389 (1986)], would be applicable. Similarly, the "through or under" language could ordinarily be applicable if Tran were the sole beneficiary, had murdered his wife but did not commit suicide, and then assigned his purported claim to the Policy proceeds to an innocent third party. Tran could not assign that which he did not possess.

Here, the facts do not fall within the "through or under" statement from *Ford*. The petitioners do not claim in the right of Tran. They claim based on the promise made by CNA to pay "the surviving person or persons in the first of the following classes of successive preference beneficiaries of which a member survives the Insured." Their claim is in their own right as contingent beneficiaries under the contract of insurance.

In cases involving life insurance, where the policy provides both for a primary beneficiary and a contingent beneficiary and where the primary beneficiary is disqualified under the slayer's rule, the majority rule awards the policy proceeds to an innocent contingent beneficiary. In these cases typically the contest is between the estate of the insured and the contingent beneficiary. In these cases the courts reason, expressly or impliedly, that looking to the terms of the contract best effectuates the intent of the insured.

The minority position is that if the primary beneficiary survives the insured, but is disqualified under the slayer's rule, then the insured's estate recovers, rather than the contingent beneficiary, because the contingency that the primary beneficiary predecease the insured has not been satisfied.

In the instant case the condition for payment to any contingent beneficiary has not been met because Tran, the "Insured," briefly survived his spouse. As a matter of substance, however, Tran, because of his suicide, cannot benefit in any way from an award of the proceeds to the petitioners.... Most of the cases that follow the majority rule differ from the instant matter in that the insured-victim was also the owner of the policy and selected the contingent beneficiaries. Here Tran, by not specially designating beneficiaries, left in effect as contingent beneficiaries the classes of persons predetermined in the Policy. This is not a difference of substance under the facts of this case.

Tran's default selection of contingent beneficiaries seems to have been made more than five years before the murder. What is more important, there is not a suggestion that the petitioners were accomplices in that crime. Further, even if one assumes that a motive on the part of the murderer to benefit innocent contingent beneficiaries were relevant, there is no evidence of such a motive presented here.

## Notes and Questions

1. Should a conviction of involuntary manslaughter bar a beneficiary from recovering the life insurance proceeds? *See Quick v. United Ben. Life Ins. Co.*, 23 N.C. App. 504, 209 S.E.2d 323 (1974), *rev'd*, 287 N.C. 47, 213 S.E.2d 563 (1975). What if the intentional killing of the insured by the beneficiary was done in self-defense? *See Franklin Life Ins. Co. v. Strickland*, 376 F. Supp. 280 (N.D. Miss. 1974). Is an actual criminal intent necessary to bar the beneficiary from any recovery? *See Harper v. Prudential Ins. Co.*, 233 Kan. 358, 662 P.2d 1264 (1983).

2. If a beneficiary who feloniously kills the insured is barred from any recovery, what happens to the insurance proceeds? *See Cockrell v. Life Ins. Co.*, 692 F.2d 1164 (8th Cir. 1982); *Estate of Jeffers*, 134 Cal. App. 3d 729, 182 Cal. Rptr. 300 (1982).

### [2] Life Insurer Misconduct

It may also be that insurer misconduct by inappropriately selling the policy in the first place can result in enough incentive for a beneficiary to act with ill intent toward a life insured.

## Bacon v. Federal Kemper Life Assurance Company

Supreme Judicial Court of Massachusetts
400 Mass. 850, 512 N.E.2d 941 (1987)

**Nolan, J.**

This appeal arises out of a wrongful death action in which a jury found the defendant, Federal Kemper Life Assurance Company (Kemper), liable for causing the death of Edwin C. Bacon. Adelaide R. Bacon was the wife of Edwin C. Bacon. Kemper is an insurance company which carried a life insurance policy on the life of Bacon. Bacon was found dead in his Boston office on July 30, 1974. In July, 1977, the plaintiff filed a complaint against Kemper alleging both that Kemper's breach of contract and its negligence in accepting and recording a change of beneficiary caused Bacon's murder by his business associate, James Blaikie, Jr. The complaint alleged that Blaikie had forged Bacon's signature on the change of beneficiary form and murdered him in an attempt to collect the proceeds of the life insurance policy.

The life insurance policy, which is central to this case, was issued by Kemper to Edwin C. Bacon on July 1, 1971. The policy carried a face amount of $50,000 and a term of five years. The beneficiary was a trust established by Bacon for his wife and children. In September, 1973, Bacon submitted an application to change the beneficiary of the policy to another but similar trust, known as the Edwin C. Bacon Trust of August 28, 1973. Kemper acknowledged the change of beneficiary by sending Bacon a printed and unsigned form.

Bacon was disturbed by Kemper's response. In October, 1973, Bacon's concerns were communicated in a letter to Kemper. Bacon expressed his understanding that Massachusetts law required that the change of beneficiary form be accepted and signed by a company officer. As Bacon put it, this assurance was essential so that both parties knew they were operating from the same facts and because fifty thousand dollars was a considerable sum of money for his family. An officer of Kemper replied (correctly) to Bacon that its legal department's research had not uncovered any such Massachusetts law.

On July 19, 1974, Kemper's home office received another request to change the beneficiary on Bacon's policy. The form, bearing the purported signature of Bacon, requested that the principal beneficiary be designated as James F. Blaikie, Jr., and the Edwin C. Bacon Trust listed as the contingent beneficiary. Bacon's "signature" was witnessed by Blaikie. The application was quickly processed and approved. A letter, dated July 24, 1974, acknowledging the change was sent to Bacon's business address.

Bacon habitually went to his office late in the morning and remained there until very late at night. His wife, in contrast, preferred to arise early in the morning and went to bed before he came home. When she awoke on the morning of July 30, 1974, she realized that her husband had not come home the previous night. She went to his office, arriving there around 7:30 A.M. Mrs. Bacon had to locate the building superintendent because her husband's office door was locked. Upon opening the door, they discovered Bacon's body lying face down on the floor next to a water cooler.

Shortly afterwards, the police and coroner arrived. When Bacon's body was removed from the office, a note was discovered under his chest. The note, printed in block letters, stated: "I can't stand it anymore." An autopsy was performed later that day. The medical examiner determined that the cause of death was sodium cyanide poisoning.

In August, 1974, Kemper received proof of Bacon's death from Blaikie and a request for the proceeds of the policy. A similar claim was made by Bacon's wife in September. Faced with these conflicting claims, Kemper submitted the last change of beneficiary form to a handwriting expert. The expert concluded that Bacon had not signed that form. Consequently, in December, 1974, Kemper instituted an action of interpleader for an adjudication of the rival policy claims.

On June 12, 1975, a judge of the Superior Court entered a judgment, pursuant to Mass. R. Civ. P. 58(a), as amended, 371 Mass. 908 (1977), discharging Kemper "from any and all liability whatsoever on its policy" and enjoining the claimants from making "any further claim or commencing or prosecuting this action or any further action or actions ... on account of said policy of insurance or anything growing out of the same." Thereafter the judge determined that the proceeds be distributed to the Edwin C. Bacon Trust. Three years later, the plaintiff commenced the present action.

In order to impose liability on Kemper for the death of Edwin Bacon, the plaintiff had the burden of proving by a preponderance of the evidence that (a) Blaikie murdered Bacon; (b) Kemper owed a duty to Bacon; (c) Kemper breached that duty, and (d) Kemper's breach of duty was the proximate cause of Bacon's murder. Kemper contends that it was entitled to the entry of judgment in its favor because the plaintiff's proof was insufficient as a matter of law with respect to each of these issues.

There was sufficient evidence to warrant a finding that Blaikie murdered Bacon and that Kemper owed a duty of care to Bacon in effectuating a change of beneficiary. However, we conclude that there was no evidence to warrant a finding of a breach of duty by Kemper after reviewing the evidence in the light most favorable to the plaintiff and after giving the plaintiff the benefit of every inference favorable to her....

Kemper correctly argues that the evidence was insufficient to justify the jury's finding that its conduct fell below the standard of a reasonably prudent insurance company. Kemper claims that there was no evidence which proved that it knew or should have known that its acceptance and approval of the change of beneficiary request exposed Bacon to an unreasonable risk of harm from criminal conduct by a third party. We agree.

The plaintiff contends that Kemper acted unreasonably in approving the beneficiary change because it was not signed by a disinterested witness and because Kemper did not attempt to verify whether Blaikie was actually Bacon's business partner. In addition, the plaintiff claims that the October, 1973, letter Bacon sent to Kemper was further evidence that Kemper should have known that the beneficiary change request was suspicious.

The facts relied on by the plaintiff are simply too innocuous to have aroused Kemper's suspicion that Bacon had not consented to the change of beneficiary. William Jones, a former head of Kemper's policyholder service department, whose deposition was read in evidence by the plaintiff, conceded that it was not unusual for a business partner to be listed as a beneficiary on a policy. Moreover, even though Kemper required a beneficiary to have an insurable interest in an insured's life, and Blaikie would qualify in that respect, there is no such requirement under our law.... Thus, it is immaterial who was listed as the beneficiary.

Nor can we say that Blaikie's signature as witness was enough to put Kemper on notice that the request was doubtful. Although Jones testified that he thought the requirement of a disinterested witness had been added as a precaution against fraud or foul play, he did not explain how it could obviate such a possibility. It is conceivable that it could prevent a potential beneficiary from exercising undue influence over an insured, but that obstacle could easily be overcome by a beneficiary forging the witness' signature. An insurance company would have no way of knowing if the witness' signature was forged. At the time the application in this case was received, the disinterested witness requirement was no longer in effect. The woman who assumed Jones' position in April, 1974, testified that she made the decision to eliminate that requirement because the company was receiving too many complaints from agents that it was a hindrance to insureds.

Finally, the plaintiff produced no expert testimony that such a requirement was considered good practice in the insurance industry or has any support in law. The only duty that the law imposes on an insurance company to protect its insured is that the company take reasonable steps to determine whether the insured has consented to the policy or the change of beneficiary.

In the cases in which an insurance company has been found liable for harm to its insureds, the company either had actual knowledge that the insured had not consented to the policy, ... or should have known that the person who procured the policy did not have an insurable interest in the life of the insured.... Here, the Kemper clerk charged with processing change of beneficiary requests compared Bacon's signature on that request with his signature on the original policy application request. Those signatures were identical to the naked eye. Only an expert, after careful examination, was able to conclude that one was a forgery.

Kemper acted reasonably as a matter of law in approving the request. Therefore, there was no breach of duty. The judgment for the plaintiff is reversed, and judgment is to be entered in favor of Kemper. [Concurring opinion of O'CONNER, J. omitted.]

**Abrams, J.** (dissenting, with whom **Liacos, J.**, joins).

The court today departs from its test "whether 'anywhere in the evidence, from whatever source derived, any combination of circumstances could be found from which a reasonable inference could be drawn in favor of the plaintiff.'" ... Because the court departs from its test, I dissent.

I agree with the court that the clerk's comparison of signatures is some evidence that Kemper was not negligent in processing the change of beneficiary form. There was, however, other evidence which indicates negligence on the part of the company. William Jones, the former head of the policyholder service department, said that Kemper required a disinterested third party to witness the signature of the insured. Jones also stated that the beneficiary of a policy would not qualify as a disinterested witness. Jones's successor said that she eliminated Kemper's requirement of a disinterested witness, although there was no evidence she had authority to do so.

The jury could have believed the testimony of Jones that a signature of a disinterested witness was required on a change of beneficiary application and that, because there was no signature of a disinterested witness on the forged application, Kemper had failed to follow its own internal procedures developed to protect against fraud and foul play. The failure of Kemper to follow its company procedures is some evidence of negligence....

Moreover, the evidence indicates that Bacon had submitted an application to change the beneficiary of his life insurance policy in September, 1973. After this change was processed, Bacon wrote a letter expressing concern to the company regarding the change of beneficiary procedure because the amount of the policy was a significant amount of money to his family. Nine months later, Kemper received a second change of beneficiary application bearing the forged signature of Bacon shifting the proceeds of the policy away from his family.

Jones stated that, on the basis of this information alone, he might have been suspicious of the requested change of beneficiary and would have inquired further into the matter before processing the request for a change. Although the Kemper clerk had Bacon's entire file before her in processing the change of beneficiary and could see the prior correspondence regarding the change of beneficiary procedures, she did not investigate this change of beneficiary request.

If the jury credited Jones's testimony and rejected the clerk's actions in only comparing the signatures, that was evidence that Kemper violated its duty to act with reasonable care with respect to Bacon. The credibility of the witnesses is for the jury and it is inappropriate for this court to substitute its judgment on questions of fact....

Although I believe a per se rule which imposes a duty on insurance companies to verify all change of beneficiary applications is inappropriate, on the basis of the facts of this case, the jury could reasonably have inferred that Kemper had a duty to investigate more fully this change of beneficiary. The insured took extraordinary steps to inform Kemper of his concerns for his family and, only nine months later, the insured seemed to have had a dramatic change of heart, switching the beneficiary away from his family, and this change was witnessed by the new beneficiary. These facts support the jury's determination that Kemper was negligent in handling this particular change of beneficiary application.

In addition, although not required by law, Kemper required a beneficiary to have an insurable interest in an insured's life. While a partner has an insurable interest in the life of another partner, the evidence showed that Kemper made no attempt to ascertain whether Blaikie was, in fact, a partner of Bacon. The clerk simply accepted the application for change of beneficiary without any further investigation. The jury could have found that this failure of the clerk to verify that the company policy concerning insurable interest was adhered to in this application was evidence of negligence.

Finally, there was evidence that the Kemper's clerks responsible for change of beneficiary applications handled ten to twelve requests a day. The jury could reasonably have inferred that the benefit from scrutinizing those few applications which were witnessed by the new beneficiary outweighed the cost of doing so. Kemper's failure to scrutinize those few applications would permit a reasonable inference that Kemper failed to exercise due care in the circumstances.

There was evidence which, if believed, provided a factual basis for an inference that Kemper did not take reasonable steps to determine whether Bacon consented to the change of beneficiary. Instead of adhering to well-established principles of review, the court makes the factual determination that Kemper acted with reasonable care. On the evidence admitted, the jury could have found that Kemper acted reasonably or the jury could have found that Kemper failed to follow its own procedures and exercise a reasonable amount of care in processing the change of beneficiary form. The jury could properly have concluded that Kemper was negligent. "[W]e have no authority to take upon ourselves the duties of a tribunal of fact, and to determine what verdicts should have been rendered by the jury."

## *Notes and Questions*

1. For a more tangled but equally suspicious case akin to *Bacon*, see *Lakin v. Postal Life & Casualty Ins. Co.*, 316 S.W.2d 542 (Mo. 1958). For an in depth analysis of the *Lakin* case, see Robert H. Jerry, II, *May Harvey Rest in Peace:* Lakin v. Postal Life and Casualty Company, 2 Nev. L.J. 292 (2002).

2. Sometimes, the dark side can be the insurer's side. For example, a famous evidence case that involved a $25,000 (worth $641,000 in 2019 dollars) life insurance claim, *Mutual Life Ins. Co. v. Hillmon*, 145 U.S. 285 (1892), featured a battle over the use at trial that could be made of a letter supposedly written by someone who knew the decedent had expressed plans to travel. The Court resolved the issue by holding that the letter could come in as evidence even though it was hearsay because it reflected the speaker's intent to travel to a certain area (a rule of evidence now codified as Fed. R. Evid. 803(3)).

Part of the insurer's defense in offering the letter was to suggest that the person insured was not the dead body later found (because the insured had intended to travel away from the area where the corpse was found). In effect, the insurer was suggesting that the decedent had not died but merely left his wife (the claimant in the case, who eventually prevailed in state court even though the insurer was able to use the letter in question in support of its case but had the result reversed by the a subsequent U.S. Supreme Court opinion). Thickening the plot: the decedent died of a gunshot wound, but one eventually ruled an accident.

Recent scholarship led an evidence professor to conclude that the letter was likely fabricated by the insurer as part of its defense. *See* Marianne Wesson, A Death at Crooked Creek: The Case of the Cowboy, the Cigarmaker, and the Love Letter (2014). In 2006, the corpse in question in the case (which Mrs. Hillmon contended was her husband and which the insurer contended was another man) was exhumed from its Kansas grave for DNA testing, which proved inconclusive due to decomposition of the body. However, comparison of skeletal remains with photos of Mr. Hillmon and the other man suggests that the body was that of Hillmon. In effect, the insurer's deception had been rewarded by the Supreme Court.

# [E] Life Insurance and Intentional Injury

## Todd v. AIG Life Insurance Company

United States Court of Appeals for the Fifth Circuit
47 F.3d 1448 (1995)

**Byron R. White, Associate Justice (Ret.).**

This case, a suit for recovery of benefits under the Employee Retirement Income Security Act of 1974 ("ERISA"), 29 U.S.C.§ 1001 et seq., involves the construction of an accidental death insurance policy and arises from the unfortunate death by asphyxiation of appellee's husband. The insurer refused to pay the policy's benefits after concluding that the death was not accidental.

The district court granted summary judgment in appellee's favor, finding that the loss resulted from an accident within the terms of the policy, holding that liability extended beyond the insurer to the employee welfare benefit plan and its administrator, and awarding attorneys' fees. The defendants appealed. We affirm the district court's judgment regarding policy coverage but reverse on the extended liability issue and remand for a proper determination of attorneys' fees.

Richard A. Todd was found dead at his home in Rockwall, Texas, on April 25, 1991. The cause of death was determined to be autoerotic asphyxiation, the practice of limiting the flow of oxygen to the brain during masturbation in an attempt to heighten sexual pleasure. When found, Todd was lying on his bed with a studded dog collar around his neck; the collar, in turn, was attached to two leather leashes of differing lengths, one of which passed over Todd's back and attached to an ankle.

Apparently, Todd gradually tightened the collar around his neck by pulling on the leashes, thereby reducing the supply of oxygen reaching his brain. Instead of simply restricting the flow of oxygen enough to increase his sexual gratification, however, Todd tightened the collar to the point at which he passed out.

Todd apparently designed the system of leashes to loosen the ligature in the event he became unconscious; unfortunately, the collar failed to release and ultimately terminated the flow of oxygen permanently. The autopsy report listed the cause of death as "asphyxia due to ligature strangulation," ruling the manner of death "accidental."

At the time of his death, Todd was covered by an "Accidental Death and Dismemberment Insurance" policy provided by his employer, E-Systems, Inc., as part of an employee welfare benefit plan falling within the ambit of ERISA. AIG Life Insurance Company issued the E-Systems policy, which was administered by the Group Accident Insurance Plan ("GAI"), with David V. Roberts serving as the plan administrator.

Appellee, Nancy J. Todd, was the decedent's wife and his beneficiary under the policy. Shortly after her husband's death, appellee presented her claim for benefits to the E-Systems employee welfare benefit plan and AIG through a claims processing organization, the American International Adjustment Company ("AIAC"). In an October 1991 letter written on behalf of AIG, an AIAC claims examiner denied appellee's claim, finding that "the circumstances of [Todd's] death point to the fact that he was risking his life by his actions" and explaining that "[a] death [cannot] be considered accidental … if from the viewpoint of the Insured, his conduct was such that he should have anticipated that in all reasonable probability he would be killed." …

Appellants present three issues on appeal: whether Todd's death was covered by the AIG accidental death insurance policy, whether the ERISA employee welfare benefit plan and its administrator can be held liable for the benefits owed by the insurer, and whether the district court's calculation of attorneys' fees was proper. We consider each in turn.

The first issue in this case is whether, on the facts before it, the district court erred in ruling the death to be accidental within the meaning of the policy insuring the plan.…

… First, the policy defines "injury" as "bodily injury caused by an accident occurring while this policy is in force as to the Insured Person and resulting directly and independently of all other causes in loss covered by this policy." Second is a schedule of benefits payable:

> Accidental Death and Dismemberment Indemnity: When injury results in any of the following losses to an Insured Person within 365 days of the date of the accident, the Company will pay in one sum the indicated percentage of the Principal Sum.

This provision is followed by a list of possible losses and corresponding benefits; death of the insured entitles the beneficiary to payment of the entire value of the policy. The policy contains various exclusions from coverage, including loss due to "suicide or any attempt thereat," but there is no general exclusion for self-inflicted injury.

We deal first with AIG's submission, presented to the district court and renewed here, that as a matter of federal law governing ERISA employee benefit plans the court should announce a *per se* rule that death or other bodily injury caused by autoerotic activity is never the result of an accident within the meaning of an accidental death or injury policy insuring such a plan. The essence of the argument is that common to all such activities is the intentional strangulation for the purpose of inducing asphyxia, which in this case led to death. "The 'injury,'" it is said, "was the strangulation and the resulting asphyxia," and it could not have been "caused by an accident" because the injury was plainly intentionally inflicted. So viewed, there is no ambiguity in the policy language and hence no room for the *contra proferentem* rule in cases such as this.

The district court, having noted the variety and ambiguity of dictionary and case-law definitions of the words "accident" and "accidental," and having reviewed the sparse history and current knowledge of autoeroticism, did not believe that the cases dealing with such activities warranted such a *per se* rule. We also are not impressed with AIG's submission. It is true that Todd intended to strangle himself to reduce the flow of blood and oxygen to the brain thereby creating the condition of asphyxia, a word denoting a shortage of oxygen reaching the brain or other bodily tissue. That condition need not result in the loss of consciousness, which it will, of course, if prolonged for more than a few moments. The longer the asphyxia lasts, the greater the injury, and it need last only a few minutes for death to ensue.

In this case, even if we assume that Todd intended the degree of injury from asphyxia that would cause him to lose consciousness, it is plain enough that this condition is not an injury that necessarily leads to death. It is commonplace for those who suffer from such a condition to regain consciousness and survive without any permanent damage. What killed Todd was not the mere loss of consciousness from the temporary lack of oxygen in his brain; it was the further injury to the brain and other bodily functions caused by the prolonged lack of oxygen-laden blood.

To claim that such additional injury was intended is to aver that Todd intended to die, which AIG expressly agrees he did not. *See* Brief of Appellants 15. Perhaps bodily injuries "intentionally" inflicted by the insured are not caused by accident, even without a policy exclusion of intentional injuries; but in our view the injuries that caused death in this case, and very likely in other similar cases, were not intentionally inflicted. The claimed basis for announcing a *per se* rule of federal law — that death by autoeroticism of the kind involved in this case cannot be accidental — is thus untenable.

It is true that the federal courts of appeals to have dealt with cases of this kind have denied recovery under the applicable insurance policy. But none of those cases, which AIG cites in support of its *per se* rule proposition, purports to lay down any federal law governing ERISA insurance cases. None of them involved an ERISA plan; each of them was a diversity action controlled by state law which dictated either that the death was not accidental or that a self-inflicted injury exclusion barred recovery under the policy.

Of course, the central question in this case remains to be decided: whether, even though Todd did not intend or expect to die, the injury that killed him was or was not an "accident" within the meaning of the policy. That word, without more, the district court observed, has no single, generally accepted meaning either in the dictionaries, the cases construing it, or in common parlance. Hence, after considering the published writings about autoerotic practices, the court turned to the cases dealing with such activities for help.

One of the few cases dealing specifically with deaths from autoeroticism, *Sims v. Monumental General Insurance Company*, 960 F.2d 478 (1992), came from this Circuit. It was not an ERISA case and was governed by Louisiana law. Recovery was denied under an accidental death policy, not because the death was not accidental, an issue the court carefully avoided, but because the policy expressly did not cover losses, including death, "resulting directly or indirectly, wholly or partly from ... [an] intentionally self inflicted injury." We noted that recovery had also been denied by the Fourth Circuit in two similar cases, ... on the ground that, under Virginia law, the deaths were not accidental; we also explained that, in another similar case, ... the Wisconsin Court of Appeals had ruled that a death from autoeroticism was accidental and covered by the insurance policy at issue. The *Sims* court neither agreed nor disagreed with these three cases.

The essence of the two Fourth Circuit cases rejecting coverage was explained as follows:

> Death was the natural result of a voluntary act unaccompanied by anything unforeseen except death or injury.... [The decedent] is bound to have foreseen that death or serious bodily injury *could* have resulted when he voluntarily induced unconsciousness with a noose around his neck. We are thus of opinion that his death was not an accident under Virginia law....

*International Underwriters*, [*Inc. v. Home Ins. Co.*], 662 F.2d at 1087 (emphasis added). *Sims* also noted *Sigler v. Mutual Benefit Life Ins. Co.*, 663 F.2d 49 (8th Cir.1981). That decision rejected coverage for an autoerotic death based both on a self-inflicted injury exclusion in the policy and on its view, relying on *Runge* [*v. Metropolitan Life Ins. Co.*, 537 F.2d 1157 (1976)], that the death was not accidental "since a reasonable person would have recognized that his action *could* result in his death." *Id.* at 49 (emphasis added).

In ... the Wisconsin case, the sole issue was whether the term "accidental death" in the insurance policy included death by autoerotic asphyxiation. The intermediate appellate court held that the death was accidental. In doing so, based on decisions of the Wisconsin Supreme Court, it rejected the notion that death could not be accidental if it was a foreseeable or the natural result of a force or event voluntarily set in motion by the insured.

In the court's view, it was not enough that the act *might* or *could* have caused the injury or death; only "when an insured participates in some act where serious injury or death is highly probable or an inevitable result"—only when it can be concluded that the insured, in effect, intended that result—can the result of his conduct be held not to be accidental. As the court saw it, autoerotic activity may be risky but death is not a normal, expected result of this behavior; it was not of such a nature that Kennedy knew or should have known that it probably would have resulted in death.

The district court in the instant case also discussed the decision by the Texas Court of Civil Appeals in *Connecticut General Life Insurance Company v. Tommie*, 619 S.W.2d 199 (1981), another case that involved a claim that a death from autoerotic activity was accidental and covered by the applicable insurance policy. The plaintiff relied on two experts, both of whom testified that death is not the normal or expected result of the kind of autoerotic activity in the case and that death would not be reasonably expected. The court affirmed the jury verdict that the death was accidental, ruling that it could be otherwise only" "when the consequences of the act are so natural and probable as to be expected by any reasonable person'" and were, in effect, intended by the insured.

This ruling was based on the Texas Supreme Court decision in *Republic Nat'l Life Ins. Co. v. Heyward*, 536 S.W.2d 549, 557 (Tex.1976), which held: "Injuries are 'accidental' and within the coverage of an insurance policy ... if, from the viewpoint of the insured, the injuries are not the natural and probable consequence of the action or occurrence which produced the injury; or in other words, if the injury could not reasonably be anticipated by [the] insured, or would not ordinarily flow from the action or occurrence which caused the injury."

After the review of these autoerotic death cases, which were governed by state law and which produced inconsistent results, the district court sought help from two ERISA cases that did not involve autoerotic activity. In *Brown v. American International Life Assurance Co.*, 778 F. Supp. 912 (S.D.Miss.1991), an arsonist, a participant in an ERISA plan, died in the fire she had lit. The court ruled her death accidental because she plainly had the subjective expectation that she would survive and because, on the facts presented, this expectation was not unreasonable. *Id.* at 918.

The second ERISA case that impressed the district court was *Wickman v. Northwestern Nat'l Ins. Co.*, 908 F.2d 1077 (1st Cir.), *cert. denied*, 498 U.S. 1013, 111 S. Ct. 581, 112 L. Ed. 2d 586 (1990). There the deceased had climbed over a bridge guardrail and was holding on with one hand when he fell and later died from his injuries. The court of appeals affirmed the judgment below that the death was not caused by an accident. The magistrate had found that serious bodily injury was substantially certain to happen and that "Wickman knew or should have known that serious bodily injury was a probable consequence substantially likely to occur as the result" of his conduct. *Id.* at 1081. This finding, the court of appeals said, "equates with a determination either that Wickman expected the result, or that a reasonable person in his shoes would have expected the result, and that any other expectation would be unreasonable." *Id.* at 1089.

The district court in the case before us quoted the above passages from *Wickman* and ruled that as a matter of law Todd's death from autoerotic conduct was not substantially certain to happen and that he reasonably expected to survive.

Having surveyed the authorities upon which the decision was based, we affirm the judgment of the district court that Todd's death was accidental and within the coverage of the policy insuring the employee benefit plan. That Todd neither intended nor expected to die as the result of his autoerotic conduct AIG does not dispute. Indeed, it did not invoke the policy's provision excluding coverage for suicide. Nor does it question the averments in Mrs. Todd's affidavit filed with her motion for summary judgment that Todd was gainfully employed at the time of his death and that the Todds had been married for many years, had two children, were planning a family vacation soon, and were building a new house. The district court's finding that Todd did not expect to die is well founded.

The district court held, however, and the parties agree, that the deceased's expectation of survival, without more, is not enough. In this respect, the court adopted the essentials of the *Wickman* approach. That expectation must be reasonable; and, as we see it and as we think the district court saw it, the expectation would be unreasonable if the conduct from which the insured died posed such a high risk of death that his expectation of survival was objectively unrealistic. The district court concluded that the risk of death involved in the conduct at issue must reach the level of "substantial certainty" before the resulting death could be deemed nonaccidental....

We think the district court description of what is and is not an accident fell within the rules for construing insurance contracts, including the principle of *contra proferentem*. That is, what the district court did is consistent with, if not necessarily compelled by, the rule that we interpret such policies in favor of the insured. [F]or death under an accidental death policy to be deemed an accident, it must be determined (1) that the deceased had a subjective expectation of survival, and (2) that such expectation was objectively reasonable, which it is if death is not substantially certain to result from the insured's conduct. This holding was appropriate.

This leaves us with the question whether the district court erred in holding that, as a matter of law, the autoerotic conduct in this case did not risk death to a "substantial certainty" (or its equivalents). In our opinion, there was no error. The record is silent on whether and how often Todd had previously practiced this conduct without dying. But the materials before the court clearly indicated that the likelihood of death from autoerotic activity falls far short of what would be required to negate coverage under the policy we have before us.

In a treatise on autoerotic deaths, the authors observe that "autoerotic or sexual asphyxia refers to the use of asphyxia to heighten sexual arousal, more often than not with a nonfatal outcome." Hazelwood, Dietz & Burgess, Autoerotic Fatalities 49 (1983).... In addition, an article by Jane Brody in the New York Times of March 27, 1984, observes that, according to researchers, "in a small but significant number of cases" of autoeroticism, "the person dies before he can restore his oxygen supply."

We cannot say the trial judge erred in his final ruling on this phase of the case. AIG complains that it was error to grant summary judgment to Mrs. Todd but does not allege that there was a factual dispute that required a trial; it asks only that we reverse and order judgment for AIG on its claim that no death from autoeroticism can be deemed an accident. This left to the judge to decide as a matter of law whether the risk of death from autoerotic activity in general is sufficient to deny coverage as nonaccidental. As we see it, the trial court ruled correctly.

We add this postscript to this part of the case. It may be that all this writing is necessary to affirm this part of the judgment for appellee, but it is doubtful that it should have any longlasting significance for deciding cases like this. The life insurance companies have ample ways to avoid judgments like this one.

## Notes and Questions

1. Similarly addressing autoerotic asphyxiation is *Estate of Thompson v. Sun Life Assur. Co.*, 603 F. Supp. 2d 898 (N.D. Tex. 2008), in which the Estate argued a "parade of horribles" should the court find autoerotic asphyxiation non-accidental. The court responded:

> Finally, Ruiz provides various examples of accidental deaths that also would
> not be covered should the Court hold that Thompson's death by autoerotic

asphyxiation is not covered. But all of the examples provided by Ruiz are distinguishable. She points to the example of a deep-sea diver who drowns due to equipment malfunction or the hunter who shoots himself while cleaning his gun. However, the diver does not intend to partially drown himself nor the hunter to partially shoot himself. A person engaged in autoerotic asphyxiation indisputably intends to partially strangle himself. Ruiz also gives the example of a practitioner of martial arts. This example is inapposite to this case because martial artists train themselves to employ their techniques safely, in a controlled environment, under the supervision of a teacher with advanced skills. Thus, their intent to suffer injury and survive could be seen as objectively reasonable.

How would you measure the reasonableness of the "intent to survive" other high-risk activities?

2. Other courts are split regarding whether death from autoerotic asphyxiation is "accidental" or not. *Compare Runge v. Metropolitan Life Ins. Co.*, 537 F.2d 1157 (4th Cir. 1976) (applying Virginia law) (holding that autoerotic asphyxiation was a "foreseeable consequence of a deliberate act" and therefore was *not* "accidental"), and *Sigler v. Mut. Ben. Life Ins. Co.*, 663 F.2d 49 (8th Cir. 1981) (applying Iowa law) (similar holding to *Runge*), with *Kennedy v. Washington Nat'l Ins. Co.*, 401 N.W.2d 842 (Wis. Ct. App. 1987) (finding that autoerotic asphyxiation was an "accidental" death), and *Connecticut General Life Ins. Co. v. Tommie*, 619 S.W.2d 199 (Tex. Civ. App. 1981) (similar holding to *Kennedy*).

*Query*: Which is the better reasoned approach?

# § 10.03. Health Insurance

## [A] Pre-Existing Conditions

A standard provision in many health, life, and accident insurance policies is the "pre-existing condition" exclusion to coverage. This exclusion generally precludes coverage whenever a preexisting illness, disease, or bodily infirmity is a concurrent proximate cause of the insured's illness, disability, or death.

A "pre-existing condition" generally means a condition for which an insured person "was treated or received medical advice or which was manifested" during a specified period immediately preceding the effective date of the policy. Thus, if a person is changing employment, or is in another situation where he or she would be covered by a different health care insurer, and that person has a pre-existing illness or infirmity, it may be extremely difficult to obtain health insurance coverage under a new policy. The following case, however, demonstrates that the insurer cannot use a pre-existing condition exclusion in an unjustified manner.

# Harrell v. Old American Insurance Company

Court of Appeals of Oklahoma
829 P.2d 75 (1991)

**Brightmire, Judge.**

The holder of a hospital confinement policy brought this action to recover damages for the insurer's breach of the insurance contract and failure to deal in good faith with its insured. Judgment was entered for the plaintiff on a jury verdict for both compensatory and punitive damages. The insurer appeals. We affirm.

In 1984, Jessie Harrell, the thirty-seven-year-old plaintiff, bought a hospitalization insurance policy from the defendant, Old American Insurance Company. The contract provided in part that should Harrell suffer a covered loss (hospital confinement), Old American would pay her $30 per day while she was in the hospital. In December 1984, the policy lapsed for non-payment of the monthly premium, but was soon reinstated effective January 31, 1985.

On April 29, 1985, Harrell walked into the hospital and was admitted for the following elective surgical procedures: Revision of a 1979 gastric stapling operation, a right hernia repair, and a bunionectomy on both of her feet. A presurgical physical examination disclosed that Harrell's temperature, pulse, blood pressure, and respiration were normal. She was expected to be in the hospital for only five to seven days.

The next day Harrell was taken to surgery where the contemplated procedures were carried out. The operative reports state that the "patient tolerated this procedure well … ; and [she was] removed to the Recovery Room in a good condition."

At first, Harrell's convalescence was satisfactory. On the second postoperative day, however, she began "spiking" a temperature accompanied by a rapid pulse and respiration rate. Her condition did not immediately improve.

Testing eliminated a suspected pulmonary embolus (arterial obstruction) as the cause, but did disclose that she had an abnormal accumulation of fluid in the left chest cavity and a possible infection below her diaphragm. On May 4, 1985, exploratory surgery was carried out and a subphrenic (below the diaphragm) abscess was found and drained. Additional surgeries were necessary on May 21 and June 19, 1985, following which Harrell's condition began to slowly improve.

The acute postoperative onset of the infection-related sickness required Harrell to be confined in the hospital for some sixty days beyond the five or so days originally anticipated. So, Harrell, while still in the hospital, submitted a claim to Old American for benefits under her hospitalization policy. Old American's claims examiner ordered a copy of Harrell's hospital records.

Then without talking to either the treating physicians or Harrell, the claims examiner sent this inquiry to Old American's medical consultant: "This insured was hospitalized 042985 to 070285. The policy lapsed 120384 and was reinstated 01-31-85. According to the medical records we have received what do you consider pre-existing and do you believe this entire confinement was medically necessary?" The response by Dr. Alberg was crisp and laconic: "decline entire confinement as pre-existing."

Consequently, on July 23, 1985, the claims examiner wrote Harrell and informed her that the claim was denied because her "hospitalization was due to a pre-existing condition manifested, (prior to December 3, 1984)."On August 20, 1985, Harrell again wrote the claims examiner saying that she was "just sick" about the denial of her claim and added that she could not "understand how your 'medical consultant' could come to such a conclusion." Harrell asked Old American to reconsider the claim and explained that she was "in desperate need of this money."

The response was a second rejection letter sent a week later repeating in substance what the examiner had said earlier. It is significant on the issue of bad faith that prior to mailing the letter the record does not disclose that the examiner asked either the company doctor about the medical significance of the sudden sickness that set in on the third postoperative day, or the company counsel about the relevant law, or Harrell about additional facts pertaining to her postoperative complications. Finally, Harrell wrote Old American yet a third time pleading for a reconsideration of her claim by its "medical staff."

But it never happened. For after Dr. Alberg gave his initial opinion recommending the denial of the claim, Old American never submitted the claim for reconsideration by Alberg, by any other medical or legal expert, nor, as we said, did it ever attempt to communicate with any of Harrell's doctors.

Eventually Harrell sued Old American for: (1) Breach of contract, and (2) willful bad faith failure to deal with her. The case was tried to a jury, which returned a verdict in favor of Harrell and awarded compensatory damages of $1,800 on her breach of contract claim, $40,000 on her bad faith claim, and $250,000 punitive damages.

From this judgment Old American appeals and advances the following assignments of error: (1) The trial court improperly denied its motion for summary judgment; (2) the bad faith claim and punitive damages request should not have been submitted to the jury; (3) the evidence was insufficient to support actual damages for bad faith; (4) the punitive damages award was excessive; (5) the instructions given were contrary to law; and (6) the punitive damages award violates due process and constitutes an excessive fine.

Old American's first complaint—that the trial court erred in denying its pretrial motion for summary judgment—is summarily rejected for the obvious reason that the propriety of the ruling became moot by virtue of the trial proceedings....

Old American's remaining assignments of error relate to Harrell's bad faith theory of recovery and the adjunctive punitive damages award. They may be summarized and reframed this way: There is no evidence to support a finding that Old American rejected Harrell's claim in bad faith, or if there is, then both the compensatory and punitive damages awards are excessive, and the punitive damages award is unconstitutional.

In the main the argument is that, although Harrell's hospital confinement should have lasted no more than seven days for the surgeries she had been admitted for, the postoperative problems she encountered were complications resulting from the operative procedures and therefore Old American could in good faith construe the policy provisions as excluding coverage for the extended hospitalization. To begin with it is fundamental that when there is doubt about the meaning or interpretation of an insurance policy provision it will be construed in a light most favorable to the insured.... Whatever doubts there might have been about the meaning of the material provisions of Old American's policy were correctly resolved by the trial court as a matter of law in instructions numbered 11 and 12. Instruction No. 11, to which Old American did not object to, informed the jury that:

> "[T]he insurance contract provides in pertinent part as follows: We will pay benefits for hospital confinement resulting from sickness or injury as described and defined herein. 'Sickness' means sickness or disease of a covered person *which first manifests itself after the effective date* and while *the policy is in force* except as provided in the reinstatement provision. *"Pre-existing condition" means a condition* for which a covered person was treated or received medical advice *or which was manifested during the 12-month period immediately preceding* the *Effective Date*. A condition is manifested when it is active and where distinct symptoms are evident to a Covered Person and are of sufficient severity, in the opinion of a physician, to cause a person to seek medical diagnosis or treatment. Reinstatement. *The reinstated policy* will cover only loss (confinement) that results from an injury sustained after the reinstatement date or *sickness that starts more than 10 days after such date.* In all other respects your rights and ours will remain the same, subject to any provisions noted or attached to the reinstated policy." (Emphasis added.)

Instruction No. 12 reads: "You are instructed that the Court has ruled that complications of surgery are not set forth in the policy as specific limitations or exclusions to coverage in the insurance contract; and the Court has ruled that the first 5 days of hospital confinement by the plaintiff are not to be considered by the jury, as they come within the conditions of the policy of Pre-existing conditions."

It is also a fact that the company physician—who is said to have advised Old American to deny Harrell's claim on the ground her extended stay was due to a "pre-existing condition"—admitted he did not mean that "the [spiked] temperature or the infection [was] pre-existing" but only the abnormalities which she entered the hospital to have surgically corrected. One can assume he communicated this important distinction to the claims examiner.

Beyond this the jury could reasonably find that the doctor was not particularly interested in a deeper probe into the operative facts. He did not, for instance, bother to inquire—after reading the record and discovering that the cause of Harrell's extended stay was not a consequence of the "pre-existing" gastric stapling, the right hernia, or the bunions—about the etiology of the postoperative infectious condition that overtook Harrell.

Indeed, the jury could find that the veteran claims examiner ... deliberately ignored the relevant provisions of the policy requiring the company to pay benefits for hospital confinement resulting from "sickness or disease ... which first manifests itself after the Effective Date and while the policy is in force." The claims examiner also ignored the policy definition of the phrase "Pre-existing Condition" as set out above as well as the reinstatement clause. In this respect her letters to Harrell were misleading and therefore self-serving and unfair.

Finally, there is no evidence that the claims examiner sought legal advice regarding the coverage question. It is reasonable to infer that the reason she did not was either because she knew there was coverage or she did not want confirmation of what the court set out in Instruction No. 12. Tort liability may be imposed upon a clear showing that the insurer unreasonably and in bad faith, withheld payment of the claim of its insured....

It can be seen, therefore, that the evidence justified the trial court's conclusion that it clearly and convincingly demonstrated a course of conduct on the part of Old American employees and agents which manifested "a wanton or reckless disregard for the rights of [Harrell]." ... Thus the trial court did not err in submitting the issue of punitive damages to the jury without any restriction on the amount it could award.

Nor was the award of punitive damages excessive in view of stipulated evidence that Old American at the time of trial had "Assets of $132,590,742; Liabilities of $100,170,560; Capital and Surplus of $32,420,182." Likewise, the compensatory damages award of $40,000 for Old American's bad faith treatment of Harrell was founded on sufficient evidence that Harrell was subjected to mental anguish, distress, embarrassment, and harassment by creditors; and that she experienced anxiety and worry as a consequence of Old American's willful failure to deal with her fairly. Determining fair and adequate compensation for these detrimental elements was a duty imposed upon the jury by law as explained by the court's instructions. From the evidence we find no basis to conclude that the award is excessive.

## Notes and Questions

Most courts have interpreted a pre-existing "disease or bodily infirmity" exclusion to preclude coverage whenever the pre-existing disease or bodily infirmity is a concurrent proximate cause of the illness, disease, or death. *See, e.g., Sekel v. Aetna Life Ins. Co.*, 704 F.2d 1335 (5th Cir. 1983). But if the disease or infirmity in no way causes the illness or disability, or is only a remote cause, then the insurance company would still be liable under its policy coverage. *See, e.g.,* 43 Am. Jur. 2d *Insurance* §§ 608–616.

### PROBLEM TWO

Mrs. Bird became gravely ill and was hospitalized for cirrhosis of the liver. While in the hospital, she racked up enormous medical bills. Mrs. Bird had been a life-long alcoholic but had quit drinking 10 years earlier. She had actually not had a drop to drink for the past 10 years of her life. She was insured by her health insurer for the past 7 years, so she was "dry" at the time she started the policy.

• Does Mrs. Bird's health insurance policy pay for her medical bills?

## [B] "Experimental" Medical Treatment

### Adams v. Blue Cross/Blue Shield of Maryland

United States District Court, District of Maryland
757 F. Supp. 661 (1991)

In 1990, Plaintiffs Alexandra Adams and Kelly Whittington were diagnosed as having advanced breast cancer, a potentially fatal disease. Both women were advised by their treating physicians that High Dose Chemotherapy with Autologous Bone Marrow Transplant (hereinafter "HDCT-ABMT") would be the best available care for them. Because the treatment is very expensive, costing approximately $100,000.00, Plaintiffs requested their insurance carrier Blue Cross-Blue Shield of Maryland (hereinafter "Blue Cross") to confirm in advance that it would pay for the treatment.

However, Blue Cross denied coverage for both, relying upon a policy provision which excluded coverage for "experimental and investigative" treatments. While acknowledging that the policy would cover the use of HDCT-ABMT for several other diseases, Blue Cross took the position that the treatment was "experimental" when used to treat breast cancer, and that Plaintiffs were not eligible for coverage. This Court is asked to decide whether under the benefit plan Blue Cross must pay for Plaintiffs' treatment....

Essentially, Blue Cross contends that it can deny coverage for the Plaintiffs' HDCT-ABMT treatment because a policy provision in the Blue Cross benefit plan states that "the plan will not pay for services ... that are experimental or investigative in nature." The plan provision specifically defines the term "experimental or investigative" to mean "any treatment ... not generally acknowledged as accepted medical practice by the suitable medical specialty practicing in Maryland, as decided by us." Blue Cross argues that HDCT-ABMT is experimental under that definition and, accordingly, is not covered by the plan.

As discussed at length below, this Court has concluded that High Dose Chemotherapy with Autologous Bone Marrow Transplant is not an "experimental" treatment for Plaintiffs' breast cancer under the definition of "experimental" prescribed in the Blue Cross plan. This Court finds that at the time Blue Cross decided to deny coverage to Plaintiffs, the suitable medical specialty practicing in Maryland, *i.e.* Maryland oncologists, generally acknowledged HDCT-ABMT as accepted medical practice.

The Court heard convincing trial testimony that in April and July of 1990, the dates on which the Blue Cross decisions were made for Alexandra Adams and Kelly Whittington, respectively, Maryland oncologists considered HDCT-ABMT to be accepted medical practice. The Court also heard testimony that Maryland oncologists regularly refer breast cancer patients to institutions which administer the treatment, such as Duke University Medical Center, Johns Hopkins Medical Center, and Georgetown University Medical Center. Experts testified that the treatment was at the relevant time being offered at many major medical centers across the country, and the Court finds this, too, to be persuasive evidence that the treatment was generally acknowledged as accepted medical practice.

Disregarding the specific plan language, Blue Cross decided to deny Plaintiffs coverage based on its own independent evaluation of published scientific research results, completely ignoring the consensus of opinion of members of the Maryland oncological community. As is discussed at length below, Blue Cross's decision was both incorrect and unreasonable. The benefit plan does not allow Blue Cross to form its own independent evaluation of the treatment from scientific data, selectively dismissing the opinion of the very decision makers to which the plan requires Blue Cross to defer, *i.e.*, medical oncologists practicing in Maryland.

Blue Cross also argued that the treatments were experimental based on the fact that the treatments at issue were to be given on research protocol at teaching hospitals. But the fact that treatment is provided at teaching centers "on protocol" does not alter the fact that at the relevant times Maryland oncologists generally acknowledged the treatment to be accepted medical practice. Of course, researchers maintain an interest in collecting further information about HDCT-ABMT. However, physicians refer their patients for HDCT-ABMT for the primary purpose of medical treatment, and under the plan definition it is of little consequence that the treatment also provides information to research investigators.

Indeed, physicians deliver many of today's accepted medical treatments at major teaching hospitals, whose practice it is to collect data on the patients they treat. The author Rose Kushner, a breast cancer victim who was for many years a source of comfort, information and inspiration to women with breast cancer, observed prior to her own death from the disease in 1990 that it is of no great moment that treatment given at teaching hospitals also provides the opportunity for data collection.

> It is a personal decision whether or not to go to a research hospital. [Such institutions] do make certain demands on patients that non-research hospitals do not make. Physicians, nurses, psychologists, and social workers often interview and question patients. Members of the medical staff may want to examine their wounds ... As for being part of a "random sample," I may have been, for all I know. My operation may have been done using a new type of scalpel, while a sample of other women were cut by an older instrument. I honestly don't know. But what difference does it make?

As discussed below, whether HDCT-ABMT treatment is experimental as defined by the Blue Cross plan does not turn on a determination by Blue Cross based upon its own evaluation of the scientific data. Nor does the question turn on whether the treatment is provided on an experimental protocol. Rather, it turns only upon whether at the relevant times medical oncologists practicing in Maryland generally acknowledge the treatment as accepted medical practice. This Court finds that they did at the pertinent time and that Blue Cross improperly denied insurance coverage to Mrs. Adams and Mrs. Whittington.

Breast cancer is frequently treated with chemotherapy drugs which are designed to kill cancer cells. Administered in low doses, chemotherapy can be given to patients on an outpatient basis and is usually administered in several cycles of continuing treatment. However, the effectiveness of low-dose chemotherapy for more advanced forms of breast cancer is limited because the dosage frequently is not toxic enough to kill the more aggressive cancer cells.

Currently, doctors use a variety of dosages and drug mixtures, or "cocktails," in administering low-dose therapy (sometimes called "conventional chemotherapy"). To date, no standard dosages or preparative regimens exist for low-dose chemotherapy. Indeed, ongoing research continues to evaluate the effectiveness of different dosages and preparative regimens.

High Dose Chemotherapy with Autologous Bone Marrow Transplant is a procedure in which physicians administer relatively high doses of chemotherapy drugs in conjunction with a bone marrow "transplant." In addition to destroying cancer cells, high doses of chemotherapy also destroy the patient's bone marrow and blood cells, both of which play an essential role in immunity to disease and infection. Stripped of her bone marrow and certain blood cells, the patient is open to opportunistic infection and disease following treatment with high-dose chemotherapy. To counteract this potentially lethal side effect, a portion of the patient's bone marrow is harvested from the patient prior to her treatment with toxic chemotherapy drugs. After chemotherapy treatment is completed, the healthy marrow is then reinfused to "rescue" the patient. The marrow quickly multiplies to replace the marrow destroyed during high-dose chemotherapy.

The relevant plan language in the Blue Cross contract excludes as "experimental" those procedures or treatments which are "not generally acknowledged as accepted medical practice by the suitable practicing specialty in Maryland, *as decided by us*" (emphasis added). The Court finds this language vague and ambiguous and, in any event, certainly not clear and unequivocal. The Court cannot find from such language that those who drafted the Blue Cross plan intended to secure for Blue Cross the power to determine eligibility benefits or to construe ambiguous or disputed terms, much less the power to change definitions set forth specifically in the plan.

Thus, this Court finds that the contractual language does not entitle Blue Cross to judicial deference with respect to either resolving disputes over eligibility determinations or the interpretation or definition of ambiguous terms.

The pertinent contract plainly sets forth the definition for "experimental and investigative"—an experimental procedure is a procedure "not generally acknowledged as accepted medical practice by the suitable practicing medical specialty in Maryland."

The Court finds that the term "generally acknowledged" is not ambiguous. The term refers to a consensus of acknowledgement by practicing Maryland oncologists. The parties debate the meaning of the term "accepted medical practice." Blue Cross argues that "accepted medical practice" is a "standard practice" which has (1) proven itself through a rigorous process of clinical testing and amassing of scientific evidence,

(2) has known risks and benefits, and (3) is a practice not in the process of being tested to gather generalizable knowledge.

This Court interprets the term "accepted medical practice" consistently with the focus of the contractual language on the Maryland medical community standards. Plaintiffs' experts, as well as relevant Maryland case law, have defined "standard care" or "accepted medical practice" to be a practice utilizing the degree of skill and diligence employed by the ordinary prudent practitioner in his or her field and community.... In determining what is "accepted medical practice," a practice which conforms to "accepted medical standards," courts usually look to expert testimony regarding what practice is accepted in the community of practitioners....

### COVERAGE WAS INCORRECTLY DENIED.

In contrast to the Blue Cross experts, Plaintiffs' expert witnesses utilized a practical definition of what constitutes "accepted medical treatment," one which is both consistent with the standard legal definition discussed earlier and, most importantly, consistent with the contract language. Appropriately, Plaintiffs' experts focused on whether a majority of Maryland oncologists viewed the treatment as accepted medical practice, or were in fact referring their patients for the procedure. Based on Plaintiffs' experts' testimony, this Court finds that a consensus existed as of April and July of 1990 among Maryland oncologists that HDCT-ABMT for breast cancer was an "accepted medical practice."

Moreover, as Plaintiffs' experts point out, and as the district court noted in *Pirozzi v. Blue Cross-Blue Shield of Virginia*, 741 F. Supp. 586, 591 (E.D. Va. 1990), HDCT-ABMT treatment is in use at many major medical centers, including the most highly respected medical centers around the country. "This is convincing evidence that the treatment has 'scientifically proven value' and is 'in accordance with generally accepted standards of medical practice.'" *Id.*

Although it is not necessary to support the preceding conclusion, the Court determines that even if it were to accept the Blue Cross definition of the term "accepted medical practice," which turns on scientific criteria, HDCT-ABMT would satisfy Blue Cross' purely scientific criteria.

First, the Court finds from expert testimony that at the relevant time, HDCT-ABMT satisfied the five scientific criteria developed by Blue Cross' own Technology Evaluation Committee. In July of 1990, the procedure was evaluated according to the five TEC criteria by a panel of highly qualified physicians, ... [who] issued a report entitled "High Dose Chemotherapy and Autologous Bone Marrow Support for Breast Cancer: A Technology Assessment," in which they concluded that HDCT-ABMT as treatment for breast cancer satisfied all five of the TEC criteria.... Thus, even if one accepts the Blue Cross definition of "accepted medical practice" as dependent upon scientific criteria, the Court finds that Blue Cross' determination that HDCT-ABMT was experimental and investigative runs counter to the evidence presented at trial in this case.

Questions with regard to the net health benefits of the procedure, in particular, response rates and disease-free survival, have been sufficiently answered so as to allow

Maryland oncologists to choose HDCT-ABMT as an appropriate treatment alternative, and to justify the conclusion that the treatment is an accepted medical practice. The Court finds it necessary to defer, as Blue Cross should have done under the terms of its own plan, to the opinion of the consensus of Maryland oncologists.

A decision to deny benefits can be held arbitrary and capricious if the plan administrator's interpretation is unreasonable, *see* [*Firestone Tire and Rubber Co. v.*] *Bruch*, 109 S. Ct. at 954 [1989)], or if the administrator "entirely failed to consider an important aspect of the problem [or] offered an explanation for its decision that runs counter to the evidence."... The plan administrator must "examine the relevant data and articulate a satisfactory explanation for [his] action."...

The Court finds the Blue Cross decision to be arbitrary and capricious for two reasons. First, as discussed above, the Court finds the Blue Cross interpretation of "accepted medical practice" to be unreasonable because it is inconsistent with the language in the exclusion provision. Thus, the Blue Cross decision deriving from an unreasonable definition of terms is itself unreasonable. Alternatively, accepting arguendo Blue Cross' focus on scientific criteria, Blue Cross' decision was unreasonable because it ran counter to the evidence before Dr. Keefe. [Dr. Keefe was Medical Director of Blue Cross and it was he who denied plaintiff's claim.]For the foregoing reasons, this Court finds in favor of the Plaintiffs, and rules that Blue Cross-Blue Shield of Maryland must pay for High Dose Chemotherapy with Autologous Bone Marrow Transplant treatments for Mrs. Alexandra Adams and Mrs. Kelly Whittington.

## Holder v. Prudential Insurance Co. of America

United States Court of Appeals, Fifth Circuit
951 F.2d 89 (1992)

**Edith H. Jones, Circuit Judge.**

Plaintiff-appellant Joe Frank Holder sued defendants-appellees Prudential Insurance Company of America and its agent, Andy Mathis for coverage of a medical procedure performed on his now-deceased wife. The district judge found that the treatment was "experimental in nature" and had not yet been "commonly and customarily" recognized throughout the medical profession, as a result of which it was excluded from coverage under the terms of the policy. Plaintiff appeals. We affirm.

In 1987, Wanda Maurine Holder was diagnosed with breast cancer. The tumor and surrounding tissue were removed from her breast and she underwent standard chemotherapy. In October 1987, a recurrence of the cancer was discovered and diagnosed, and Mrs. Holder was referred by her treating physician to M.D. Anderson Hospital in Houston, Texas for further treatment. There she underwent additional chemotherapy. Mrs. Holder was approached by her doctors at M.D. Anderson Hospital to accept a treatment of high-dose chemotherapy coupled with an autologous bone marrow transplantation ("HDC-ABMT"). Mrs. Holder signed a consent form for the treatment which noted that the procedure was an "experimental study"; she participated in the treatment and died of complications.[1] Mrs. Holder was a beneficiary under a health insurance plan provided by her husband's employer and purchased from Prudential Health Insurance Company of America ("Prudential"). Mr. Holder submitted a claim to Prudential for hospital and physician expenses associated with the HDC-ABMT treatment. Prudential partially denied coverage based on the policy exclusion for experimental treatment.

Plaintiff's contention on appeal is that the district court erred in finding the HDC-ABMT treatment experimental and therefore excluded from policy coverage. The parties do not here dispute that this court reviews a district court's factual findings under the clearly erroneous standard of review.... The policy provided that it did not cover treatment not reasonably necessary for medical care. To be "reasonably necessary," a treatment must be ordered by a doctor and customarily recognized as appropriate, and it could not be experimental in nature.[2]

The trial court was presented with two live expert witnesses and the deposition testimony of two others. The court found the testimony of Dr. Fehir, a M.D. and a Ph.D. in immunology and transplantation biology offered by Prudential, to be "most compelling."

The opinions of the experts were conflicting on the experimental nature of the treatment extended to Mrs. Holder. Although HDC-ABMT was not considered "experimental" in the treatment of other cancers (leukemia, Hodgkin's disease, and lymphoma), the issue was whether it was experimental in the treatment of Stage IV metastatic breast cancer. Clinical studies were referred to which showed that this procedure for the treatment of this disease was still being investigated at the time of Mrs. Holder's treatment. Further, the protocol used on her was only given to twenty or thirty women nationwide and was regulated by the FDA.

---

1. [1] The consent form, signed by Mrs. Holder, provided:

2. PURPOSE OF STUDY: This is an *experimental study* which uses high doses of mitoxantrone, etoposide (VP-16) and thiotepa (MVT) in the treatment, combined with bone marrow transplantation. The use of higher-than-normal doses of chemotherapy carries with it a greater risk of complications to both the blood-forming cells of the body (the marrow) and other organs. Therefore, the purposes of this study are: 1) to find if such a combination is associated with acceptable toxicity to organs other than the bone marrow when used with the infusion of autologous marrow; and 2) to determine if, at these high doses, there is a significant response rate [shrinkage of the tumor].

Emphasis added.

2. [3] The policy provides that it does NOT cover:

Non-essentials, check-ups — Anything not ordered by a doctor or not reasonably necessary for medical care of sickness or injury. To be "reasonably necessary," a service or supply must be ordered by a doctor and be commonly and customarily recognized throughout the doctor's profession as appropriate in the treatment of the diagnosed sickness or injury. It must neither be *educational or experimental in nature*, nor provided.

Emphasis added.

The trial court was in the best position to view the evidence and weigh the testimony of the expert witnesses, among whom Dr. Fehir's testimony was found to be most credible. The court also relied on the signed consent form describing the treatment as an "experimental study." Upon reviewing the record and evidence presented, we cannot say that the trial court was clearly erroneous in its findings.

Plaintiff alternatively appears to argue that as a matter of law HDC-ABMT treatment for Stage IV metastatic breast cancer is not experimental. This contention must also fail. The various district court decisions that found coverage despite such exclusionary provisions are readily distinguishable from the case at hand.[3] Of course, it is the nature of medical research that what may one day be experimental may the next be state of the art treatment. Had Mrs. Holder undergone a similar treatment more recently under an accepted protocol, this case may have turned out differently.[4]

Prudential and Mathis, through a separate appeal, assert that the district court erred in not awarding attorney fees in this ERISA action. Under ERISA the court has discretion to award attorney fees to either party. 29 U.S.C. § 1132(g)(1). This court uses a five factor test to determine whether a party is entitled to attorney fees. *See Ironworkers Local No. 272 v. Bowen*, 624 F.2d 1255, 1266 (5th Cir. 1980). Prudential argues that this five factor test is suspect when the defendant is the prevailing party because the test appears to be geared toward the plaintiff.... The decision to award attorneys' fees is committed to the discretion of the district court.

We need not decide whether to embrace the Seventh Circuit's test because even if that test were to be applied, we cannot say that the district court abused its discretion

---

3. [4] *See Pirozzi v. Blue-Cross Blue-Shield of Va.*, 741 F. Supp. 586 (E.D. Va. 1990) (The court found coverage under the policy but was based on different policy language. The court noted the limited nature of the decision and that "Of course, a different experimental exclusion, or different expert testimony, or a plan that conferred broad discretion on the administrator might well require a different result.").... *But compare Thomas v. Gulf Health Plan, Inc.*, 688 F. Supp. 590 (S.D. Ala. 1988) (it is undisputed that autologous bone marrow transplantation for the treatment of breast cancer is still considered experimental or investigative, even though such treatment is no longer considered experimental by Blue Cross for certain other types of cancer); *Sweeney v. Gerber Products Co. Medical Benefits Plan*, 728 F. Supp. 594 (D. Neb. 1989) (A High dose chemotherapy accompanied by ABMT as a treatment for breast cancer is in an early stage of development ... the treatment is investigational and experimental (as those terms are ordinarily defined) and has not yet been commonly and customarily (as those terms are ordinarily defined) recognized throughout the medical profession as appropriate treatment of metastic breast cancer. The consensus in the literature is that the treatment is investigational ... the doctor's own forms ..."experiment" [sic] ... several different protocols are being experimented with. Different doctors are experimenting with different drugs in different dosages.").

4. [5] Several recent studies and the cases in which they have been applied to compel coverage of HDC-ABMT treatment for Stage IV metastatic breast cancer lead to the conclusion that the treatment, under a different protocol than that administered to Mrs. Holder, may no longer be considered experimental. *See White v. Caterpillar, Inc.*, 765 F. Supp. 1418 (W.D. Mo. 1991); *Bucci v. Blue Cross-Blue Shield of Connecticut, Inc.*, 764 F. Supp. 728 (D. Conn. 1991); *Adams v. Blue Cross/Blue Shield of Maryland Inc.*, 757 F. Supp. 661 (D.C. Md. 1991).

here. The experimental nature of Mrs. Holder's treatment raised an undecided issue of fact. Holder's experts stated that the treatment was not experimental in nature, while the case law has split. To impose attorneys' fees upon Holder under these circumstances would have added insult to injury.

For the foregoing reasons, the judgment of the district court is AFFIRMED.

### *Notes and Questions*

1. In the *Adams* case, *supra*, the Maryland District Court found that High Dose Chemotherapy with Autologous Bone Marrow Transplant (HDC-ABMT) was not "experimental" treatment on advanced breast cancer, and therefore Blue Cross/Blue Shield of Maryland could not deny coverage based on its policy provision that excluded coverage for "experimental and investigative" treatments. How did the court justify its finding that HDC-ABMT was not "experimental" treatment in *Adams*?

2. In the *Holder* case, *supra*, however, the Fifth Circuit Court upheld a District Court decision that HDC-ABMT treatment for advanced breast cancer was in fact "experimental in nature" and therefore excluded from coverage under a Prudential Health Insurance policy. Based upon what underlying rationale?

3. *Query*: Can the *Adams* and *Holder* decisions be reconciled? If so, how? And which party should determine whether medical treatment is in fact "experimental" or not?

## [C] Coordinating Health Insurance Coverage

### Blue Cross and Blue Shield of Kansas, Inc. v. Riverside Hospital

Supreme Court of Kansas
237 Kan. 829, 703 P.2d 1384 (1985)

McFarland, J.

This is a dispute between two employee health care group plans as to which plan has primary coverage and which plan has secondary coverage relative to certain medical expense claims. The facts are not in dispute and may be summarized as follows. Leslie Stadalman is an employee of defendant Riverside Hospital and, as such, is a "covered person" under that institution's employee health care plan. Leslie Stadalman is the wife of Gregory Stadalman. Mr. Stadalman is employed by the City of Wichita and is covered under his employer's Blue Cross-Blue Shield group health plan. The Blue Cross-Blue Shield plan provides coverage for Mr. Stadalman's dependents.

In the Fall of 1982, Leslie Stadalman incurred medical expenses in the amount of $1,963.19. The Riverside plan refused to pay the claims on the basis it provided only secondary coverage. Blue Cross-Blue Shield (plaintiff) initially refused to pay the claims for the same reason—that its plan provided only secondary coverage. Ultimately, Blue Cross-Blue Shield paid the claims, expressly reserving the right to seek contribution and indemnity from Riverside. This action resulted.

BLUE CROSS-BLUE SHIELD PLAN

The Blue Cross-Blue Shield plan contains the following provisions:

"NON-DUPLICATION OF BENEFITS.

"M.1 *The Plans will not duplicate benefits for covered health care services for which You are eligible under any of the following Programs:*

"*Group, blanket, or franchise insurance.*

"Group practice, individual practice, and other prepayment coverage on a group basis. (This includes group and franchise contracts issued by Blue Cross and Blue Shield Plans.)

"Labor-management trusteed plans.

"Union welfare plans.

"Employee benefit organization programs.

"Self-insurance programs providing benefits to employees or members of the self-insurer.

"Coverage under government programs (except Medicare; see Part 4, Section A.3) for which the employer must contribute or deduct from his employees' pay, or both.

"Individual health insurance contracts are not included as Programs.

"M.2 To avoid duplicate benefit payments, one Program will be 'Primary' and others will be 'Secondary'.

"a. *When the Plans are Primary, benefits will be paid without regard to other coverage.*

"b. *When the Plans are Secondary, the benefits under this Certificate may be reduced. The benefits for Covered Services will be no more than the balance of charges remaining after the benefits of other Programs are applied to Covered Services.*

"A 'Covered Service' is a health care service for which benefits are available to You under this Certificate or at least one Program. When benefits are provided in the form of services, the cash value of these services will be used to determine the amount of benefits You may receive.

"M.3 Under this Certificate, the *Plans are Secondary when:*

"a. *You are covered as a dependent under this Certificate but are covered as an employee, union, or association member under another Program;* or

"b. You are covered as a dependent of a female under this Certificate but as the dependent of a male under another Program; or

"c. The other Program does not have a non-duplication of benefits provision; or "d. The first three rules do not apply and the other Program has been in force for You longer than this Certificate.

"In all other instances, the Plans are Primary under this Certificate." (Emphasis supplied.)

## RIVERSIDE PLAN

The Riverside Plan contains the following provisions:

"1. ELIGIBILITY FOR COVERED PERSONS: The following persons will be eligible for coverage under the Plan;

"(a) All permanent full-time employees in Active Service at their customary place of employment who work a minimum of 30 hours per week for the Employer.

"(b) All other persons are excluded."

The term "covered person," only applies to Riverside employees. Coverage to a "covered person" is supplied without cost under the single plan. If family coverage is desired by the "covered person," he or she must contribute thereto. Other family members so covered are referred to as "covered dependents." The plan provides coverage for covered services on a self-insurance basis up to $20,000.00 per incident. Any amount required for covered services in excess of $20,000.00 is covered by a reinsurance contract issued to the health benefit plan.

The Riverside plan contains the further provision:

## NON-DUPLICATION OF BENEFITS

"This Plan has been *designed* by specific action of the Board of Directors of Osteopathic Hospital *to coordinate payment of benefits with other plans so as to avoid overpayments. This Plan requires that if any person covered hereunder is also covered under any other plan* (as defined below), *the other plan shall be primary and this Plan shall pay the balance of expenses up to the total eligible charges.* In no event shall the combined payments exceed 100%.

"However, it is the intent of the Plan to be primary as regard to any participant who is not covered under any other Plan as defined below.

"*Plan means any plan providing benefits or services for any health or dental care under any group, franchise, blanket insurance,* health maintenance plan, union welfare, governmental plan, or any coverage required by statute." (Emphasis supplied.)

## JUDGMENT OF THE DISTRICT COURT

The district court held the non-duplication of benefits provisions of the two plans to be conflicting and mutually repugnant and directed that the Stadalman claim be paid 50% by each plan. Both Blue Cross-Blue Shield and Riverside were aggrieved by this determination and duly appealed therefrom.

\* \* \*

## ISSUE NO. 2. UNDER THE TWO EMPLOYEE HEALTH CARE GROUP PLANS HEREIN, WHICH PLAN IS PRIMARY AND WHICH PLAN IS SECONDARY RELATIVE TO THE STADALMAN CLAIMS?

As applicable to the narrow issue raised herein, both plans have quite similar purposes. They are group health care plans provided by employers to their employees without cost to the employees where only the employee is covered (single coverage). If the employee desires family coverage, he or she must contribute to the cost of the coverage. These plans seek to provide adequate financially responsible coverage at the lowest cost.

In keeping with this goal, benefits should not be duplicated where an individual has coverage under more than one such plan—hence the need for non-duplication of benefits clauses, or as sometimes referred to, "coordination of benefits" clauses. In modern American society, husbands and wives frequently both work outside the home with each being covered by his or her own employee health care group plan. Family coverage, in such circumstances, sets up the potential for duplication of benefits where one or both has family coverage under a plan.

Duplication of benefits accomplishes none of the goals of such plans, serving only to run up the cost of the plans. Hassles, such as the one before us, increase the costs of administration of the plans and can delay payment of the medical bills (or reimbursement to the employees who have previously paid the bills). Obviously, litigation of the dispute between plans as to coverage should be avoided wherever possible.

For this reason, the Insurance Commissioner of Kansas requires non-duplication of benefits provisions such as included in the Blue Cross-Blue Shield plan. The provisions spell out when the plan is primary and when it is secondary in a variety of foreseeable circumstances. Specifically, K.A.R. 40-4-34 (1982 Supp.) provides:

> "National association of insurance commissioners' coordination of benefit guidelines, June 1980 edition, are hereby adopted by reference subject to the following exceptions: [exceptions not applicable herein]."

The Riverside plan is not in accord with said regulation and guidelines and is not required to be. If both plans are studied side by side, as equals, it would appear Leslie Stadalman has two secondary coverages and no primary coverage. This is an untenable position to maintain, and this led the district court to hold the plans to be mutually repugnant. This approach was followed (relative to automobile liability policies) in *Western Cas. & Surety Co. v. Universal Underwriters Ins. Co.*, 232 Kan. 606, wherein we held:

> "The 'other insurance' clauses before us are nearly identical excess coverage provisions. In discussing the general rules relative to this situation, Am. Jur. 2d states:
>
> "'[W]here two or more policies provide coverage for the particular event and all the policies in question contain "excess insurance" clauses—it is generally held that such clauses are mutually repugnant and must be disregarded, rendering each company liable for a pro rata share of the judgment or settlement, since, if literal effect were given to both "excess

insurance" clauses of the applicable policies, neither policy would cover the loss and such a result would produce an unintended absurdity.'

7A Am. Jur. 2d, Automobile Insurance § 434, pp. 87–88. Authorities in the field of insurance have similarly commented:

> "'The fact that each insurer has attempted to make his coverage "excess" would not change the result of protecting the insured up to the total of all applicable policies. The courts, which found the insured with two policies, will not leave him with none, but will require the insurers, in the ordinary instance, to prorate the loss.

> "'One of the popular approaches to prorating is to say that where one has conflicting excess clauses, they are mutually "repugnant" — in other words, they cannot be excess to each other, since they are identical. It is a sort of "After you Alphonse; no you, Gaston" act which the courts refuse to countenance.'

8A Appleman, Insurance Law and Practice § 4909 pp. 395–403 (rev. 1981).

> "Conflicting 'other insurance' excess coverage provisions are generally held to be mutually repugnant.

> "We conclude the conflicting 'other insurance' excess coverage provisions herein are mutually repugnant and must be disregarded." 232 Kan. at 611.

In *Western Cas.*, we concluded:

> "[T]he most appropriate method of proration here is to prorate the loss equally up to the limits of the lower policy. Inasmuch as the loss herein was less than the limits of the lower policy, the loss herein should be prorated equally between Western and Universal." 232 Kan. at 613.

The difficulties of such a proration procedure when applied to employee health care group plans has been pointed out by Blue Cross-Blue Shield — the two plans have different deductibles, covered services, and coinsurance provisions.

Leslie Stadalman is an employee of Riverside and coverage was provided to her as a "covered person" as defined by the plan. Mrs. Stadalman, as a "covered person" (as opposed to a covered dependent), received the coverage as a part of her employment, and, as required by ERISA, was fully advised of the plan in writing. The Riverside plan was intended to provide her coverage but would not pay duplicate benefits with those she would have under another group employee plan. We believe the logical approach is to look to her own plan first in determining the effect of non-duplication of benefits provisions. The Riverside plan (repeated for convenience) provides:

> "This Plan has been designed by specific action of the Board of Directors of Osteopathic Hospital to *coordinate payment of benefits with other plans so as to avoid overpayments.* This Plan requires that if any person covered hereunder is also covered under any other plan (as defined below), the other plan shall

be primary and this Plan shall pay the balance of expenses up to the total eligible charges. In no event shall the combined payments exceed 100%." (Emphasis supplied.)

If Mrs. Stadalman had held two jobs with primary coverage provided by the two respective employers, the Riverside plan would intend to avoid duplication of benefits by becoming secondary. As a dependent of Gregory Stadalman under his Blue Cross-Blue Shield family plan, Leslie Stadalman has Blue Cross-Blue Shield coverage that is only excess (secondary) in nature. Her own group plan is primary unless another group plan provides primary coverage. The Blue Cross-Blue Shield plan does not provide primary coverage to Mrs. Stadalman by virtue of the fact she is a covered employee in her own group plan. Therefore, there is no potentiality for duplication of benefits or overpayment. In such circumstances, generally, the primary coverage of Riverside should pay all benefits due thereunder on the claims, and the excess claims should be submitted to Blue Cross-Blue Shield for determination of benefits due under its secondary coverage.

On the specific claims involved herein, the parties do not directly address the matter of whether the Riverside plan, as the provider with primary coverage, would provide full coverage therefor. There are inferences that such is the case, but we are not satisfied that the parties have agreed such is true. Therefore, we decline to reverse and enter judgment against Riverside for the entire amount of the claims paid by Blue Cross-Blue Shield. This aspect of the case must be determined by the district court.

The judgment of the district court is reversed and the case is remanded with directions to enter judgment against defendant consistent with this opinion.

## [D] ERISA Pre-Emption

The majority of people with health insurance are insured as part of their employee benefits with their employers. Employers typically pay all or a large portion of the employee's health benefits. However, as discussed in the chapter on Insurance Regulation, benefits under most employer-provided benefit plans are governed by federal law, not state law, via the Employment Retirement Income Security Act (ERISA). This has resulted in health benefit plan legal issues becoming a sub-area of practice that touches on state-federal regulation issues and employment law (and yes, insurance).

For this reason, a primary question when dealing with health insurance issues in America is to determine how, if at all, state laws apply to a federally regulated health plan. The complexities of ERISA pre-emption are beyond this casebook (and could well be an entirely separate course in itself). Many issues arise in this area of law that do not arise in other areas of insurance, squarely because of the ERISA pre-emption issue. For example, if a health insured suffers injury as a result of some medical mishap due to an issue with decisions by a health insurer, that insured is better off with a medical malpractice action than an action against the insurer about coverage issues.

Pre-emption of state law for such issues as health insurance benefits denials makes this area of law doubly complex. States can mandate benefits that employers must provide but are powerless to mandate the remedies for breach of those obligations. Also, denial of benefits issues in ERISA cases are determined under a different standard of review than the run of the mill contract case: a de novo standard to questions of interpretation.

## [E] Affordable Care Act

The 2010 Patient Protection and Affordable Care Act (PPACA, sometimes also called ACA or "Obamacare") plus the Health Care and Education Reconciliation Act of 2010 (HCERA) moved health insurance in the United States toward the direction of becoming closer to a form of social insurance by 2014. The U.S. already has Medicare, which provides health insurance for the elderly and injured workers, and Medicaid, which provides health insurance for some poor, including children from low income families.

The Affordable Care Act has several main objectives. First, the legislation is intended to reduce the number of Americans who have no health insurance. Second, the legislation seeks to reduce health care costs including the costs of health insurance. Third, the legislation expands coverage to include pre-existing conditions. These reforms take effect gradually.

ACA created the obligation on large employers to offer health insurance for the life of their employees, through a tax credit encouragement system. It allowed children to remain insured under their parents' policies until 26 years of age. The law also expanded Medicare availability to seniors. The Act requires all Americans who can afford it to either purchase health insurance or pay a fee to offset the coverage of uninsured Americans.

Most notably for insurance purposes, this new legal regime mandated that, in the individual and small-group health insurance markets, insurers make available minimum essential coverage to all potential insureds at a reasonable price, even those with pre-existing conditions who otherwise would typically not be able to be insured in the traditional insurance marketplace. This includes guaranteed renewal. Through insurance exchanges, private health insurers can offer health care plans, the effect of which is to almost treat the individual and small-group market as one large risk pool. Potential insureds have experience-rated pricing for only four risk factors: individual versus family, geographic region, age, and tobacco use.

Constitutional challenges continue to be had with the ACA on all fronts: from the employer-mandated insurance front to the individual and small-group market solutions under ACA.

*Query*: Should universal health care insurance coverage be mandated in the United States as well, based on underlying public policy rationales? Why or why not?

# § 10.04. Disability Insurance

## [A] The Meaning of Disability and the Scope of Disability Insurance

### Phillippe v.
### Commercial Insurance Co. of Newark, New Jersey

Court of Appeals of Louisiana
574 So. 2d 374 (1990)

After a thorough review and evaluation of the record, we are convinced the evidence supports the facts found and the reasons assigned by the trial court.... Accordingly, we affirm the judgment of the trial court, adopting its reasons as our own.... All costs are to be paid by the defendant.

### I. BACKGROUND

This is an action on a policy of disability insurance issued to Doyle F. Phillippe by Commercial Insurance Company of Newark, New Jersey (Commercial). Mr. Phillippe's petition alleged that in about 1974 he purchased a policy of disability insurance from Commercial which provided for lifetime payments to him in the event he was wholly and continuously disabled from performing the duties of any gainful occupation for which he was reasonably qualified. Mr. Phillippe asserted that his sole qualification for employment was as a dentist, and that an accident involving his right hand had rendered his practice of dentistry impossible. For some ten years prior to March 16, 1986, Commercial paid weekly benefits to him. It ceased payments on that date. Mr. Phillippe alleged that Commercial terminated his benefits arbitrarily and capriciously, without conducting any investigation into his ability to perform any gainful occupation. He prayed for judgment ordering Commercial to pay weekly benefits to him of $500.00 per week from March 16, 1986 to date of trial, declaring him to be disabled within the meaning of Commercial's policy, and for statutory penalties and attorney's fees against Commercial.

Commercial admitted in its answer that it issued a policy of disability insurance to Mr. Phillippe, but asserted that the relevant provisions, terms and exclusions of the policy limited its liability to the 520 weeks of benefits which it paid to Mr. Phillippe prior to March 16, 1986. The parties stipulated that Commercial paid Mr. Phillippe disability benefits of $500.00 per week for a period of ten years commencing in February of 1976 and terminating in March of 1986. They also stipulated that Dr. Phillippe can no longer practice dentistry in the same manner as he had prior to losing his right thumb in an accident in February of 1976.

### II. APPLICABLE POLICY PROVISIONS

The policy of insurance issued to Dr. Phillippe by Commercial was introduced into the record as Plaintiff's Exhibit 1. The pertinent disability provision is set forth therein as follows:

## ACCIDENT INDEMNITY FOR TOTAL LOSS OF TIME

PART II. If such injury shall within one year from date of accident wholly and continuously disable and prevent the Insured from performing every duty pertaining to his occupation and if the Insured be regularly attended by a legally qualified physician or surgeon, other than himself, the Company will pay the weekly indemnity for the number of days commencing with the first day of disability following the Waiting Period Accident stated in the application, but for a period not exceeding Maximum Accident Indemnity Period, as stated in the application. If the Maximum Accident Indemnity Period stated in the application exceeds five hundred and twenty weeks after the payment of the weekly indemnity for five hundred and twenty weeks as aforesaid, the Company will continue the payment of weekly indemnity so long as the Insured shall live and be wholly and continuously disabled by reason of such injury from performing the duties of any gainful occupation for which he is reasonably fitted.

These accident indemnity provisions were superseded by an Extended Accident and Sickness Rider attached to the policy, which made the following language controlling:

## ACCIDENT INDEMNITY FOR TOTAL LOSS OF TIME

PART II. If such injury shall within one year from date of accident wholly and continuously disable and prevent the Insured from performing every duty pertaining to his occupation and if the Insured be regularly attended by a legally qualified physician or surgeon, other than himself, the Company will pay the weekly indemnity for the number of days commencing with the first day of disability following the Waiting Period Accident stated in the application, but for a period not exceeding Maximum Accident Indemnity Period, as stated in the application. If the Maximum Accident Indemnity Period stated in the application exceeds five hundred and twenty weeks after the payments of the weekly indemnity for five hundred and twenty weeks as aforesaid, the Company will continue the payment of weekly indemnity so long as the Insured shall live and be wholly and continuously disabled by reason of such injury from performing the duties of any gainful occupation for which he is reasonably fitted.

The language of the policy thus provided that in the event an insured were disabled from performing his customary occupation at the time of his injury, Commercial obligated itself to pay weekly benefits for a maximum of five hundred and twenty (520) weeks, at which time Commercial's obligation would continue only so long as the insured was unable to perform the duties of *any* gainful obligation [sic] for which he is reasonably fitted" (emphasis added).

## II. RELEVANCE OF DR. PHILLIPPE'S ABILITY TO ENGAGE IN OTHER GAINFUL ACTIVITY

Dr. Phillippe asserted that evidence of occupations for which he may be suited other than the practice of general dentistry is irrelevant to the determination of this matter, in light of Louisiana jurisprudence regarding policy provisions such as the one contained in the Commercial policy. It is his position that the specific language of the Commercial policy is superseded by a succinct line of Louisiana jurisprudence which holds that in interpreting disability policies, the insured may be denied benefits only if it is found that he can perform substantially the duties of his usual and customary occupation at the time of his injury. Dr. Phillippe thus contends that ability to engage in a new occupation is of no moment, regardless of the language which may be contained in his policy. The plaintiff cited a number of cases in support of this position.

In *Foret v. Aetna Life and Casualty Company*, 337 So. 2d 676 (App. 3rd Cir., 1976), Mr. Foret contended that he was unable to perform the duties of his prior occupation as a roustabout or any gainful occupation due to constant abdominal pain. Aetna, the group disability insurer of Mr. Foret's employer, asserted that he was capable of returning to his former occupation. The medical testimony presented clearly favored the plaintiff's contention that he could not work as a roustabout. The Aetna policy provision regarding total disability read as follows:

Article II — Section 1(f):

"Reasonable occupation" means any gainful activity for which the employee is, or may reasonably become, fitted by education, training or experience, but shall not mean any such activity if it is in connection with an approved rehabilitation program.

Article II — Section 1(g):

"Total disability" or "totally disabled" means, during the first twenty-four months of any one period of disability, that the employee is unable, solely because of disease or accidental bodily injury, to work at his own occupation; and, thereafter during the continuance of such period of disability, that the employee is unable, solely because of disease or accidental bodily injury, *to work at any reasonable occupation.* (Emphasis added.)

Aetna's policy thus provided that for two years, the plaintiff's ability to perform his own occupation governed his entitlement to benefits; and that thereafter only his inability to work at any reasonable occupation would entitle him to continued benefits. The Third Circuit found that although the trial court did not expressly address the separate tests for disability within these distinct time periods in finding Mr. Foret to be totally disabled, its failure to do so was not erroneous when considered in light of Louisiana jurisprudence on the issue.

The Court stated, at p. 682: "Our courts have adopted a policy of liberal interpretation respecting accident insurance policies which provide benefits for total permanent disability, or the inability to engage in any occupation for compensation or profit.... Policy provisions similar to those above referred to have consistently been construed to mean the insured will be denied benefits only when he can perform substantial and material duties of his occupation in the usual and customary manner. That the insured may engage in some other occupation does not disqualify him insofar as concerns policies of this character."

However, this court finds the following language to indicate a significant distinguishing factor between Foret and the instant matter: The plaintiff, who has only an 11th grade education with no special training or skills, is not fitted by training or experience for any type work except manual labor. As aforestated we find no manifest error in the trial court's conclusion that by reason of plaintiff's physical condition he has been, since October 16, 1971, unable to perform heavy manual labor such as that required by a roughneck or roustabout.

Under these circumstances, when the policy provisions in question are construed in light of the jurisprudence we have no hesitancy in concluding that plaintiff has established his "total disability" within the meaning of the policy for an indeterminate period beyond the initial twenty-four month period." (*Foret*, page 682).The court's appreciation of this finding is that under the facts peculiar to *Foret*, where the insured was clearly fit only for manual labor and could not perform his usual occupation, *i.e.*, manual labor, he was of course unable to perform any other. Thus, no error could be found in the trial court's failure to specifically direct its attention to a two-tiered level of examination of Mr. Foret's capacity to engage in gainful activity.

The court finds itself to be compelled to agree with Commercial's contention that it is entitled to a two-tiered examination of the disability provisions of its policy. The cited jurisprudence basically relates to the initial determination of whether Dr. Phillippe was rendered incapable of performing his usual duties as a practicing dentist by the loss of his thumb. The parties have stipulated that he was. As a result, he was paid weekly benefits for ten years in accordance with the policy provisions. The terms of the policy clearly and unambiguously stated that after this initial 520 week period, benefits would continue only if he remained unable to pursue any gainful occupation for which he is reasonably fitted.

A contract of insurance is the law between the parties.... Each provision which is clear and unambiguous must be given its full effect. In the court's opinion, the definition to be given to the term "total disability" for purposes of making an initial determination of entitlement to benefits is not the issue in this matter. The cited jurisprudence does not address the question of whether, after paying benefits for a period of ten years, an insurer may rely upon policy provisions which in effect redefine "total disability" at that point to cease paying benefits. The primary public policies and concerns which presented themselves in the cited jurisprudence are simply not present under such circumstances. Considering all of these factors, the court finds that Commercial was entitled to present evidence of Dr. Phillippe's ability to engage in any gainful occupation for which his education and training rendered him fit at the trial of this matter, which must be given due consideration.

## IV. EVIDENCE PRESENTED

### A) Dr. Phillippe

Dr. Doyle Phillippe testified that he was 55 years of age at the time of the trial of this matter, and that his education and training consisted solely of completion of the requirements for the practice of dentistry. Dr. Phillippe also stated that he has not actively practiced dentistry for over ten years as a result of the loss of his thumb. He practiced for approximately 15 years prior to his injury. Dr. Phillippe acknowledged that he has engaged in real estate investments in the past, even prior to his accident. Those activities related to the development of a mobile home park, a rental property, and a small office building. Between 1978 and 1983 Dr. Phillippe acquired, developed and sold a small shopping center in Gonzales, Louisiana. In addition to the above activities, Dr. Phillippe also testified that he has invested in computer and construction equipment. Finally, he acknowledged that for a brief time after his injury, he was employed as a contract dental consultant for the State of Louisiana....

### B) Robert Porche

Mr. Porche testified on behalf of Commercial as an expert in vocational rehabilitation. Mr. Porche expressed the opinion that Dr. Phillippe's education and experience qualified him for a number of occupations, which are ... work in pharmaceutical sales, dental supply sales, and insurance sales. It was also Mr. Porche's opinion that Dr. Phillippe's investment experience qualified him to work as a real estate investor or developer, building consultant or resident leasing agent. He also felt that Dr.Phillippe could retrain himself in the field of oral pathology.

Under cross examination, Mr. Porche detailed the means by which he arrived at his conclusions regarding occupations for which he found Dr. Phillippe to be qualified. Mr. Porche testified that after gathering factual information about Dr. Phillippe's past education and experience, the pertinent information was compared with the requirements of a number of potential occupations and a list of occupations comparable with his education and experience was thus produced.

### C) Dr. Paul Ware

Dr. Ware testified by deposition on behalf of Dr. Phillippe, as an expert in the field of psychiatry. Dr. Ware's particular area of expertise is forensic psychiatry and neurology as they apply to the law. Dr. Ware met with Dr. Phillippe on January 4, 1978. At that time he diagnosed Dr. Phillippe as a man suffering from chronic depression and compulsive personality disorders, which he attributed to the loss of Dr. Phillippe's ability to practice dentistry.

Dr. Ware again examined Dr. Phillippe on August 30, 1988, for the purpose of performing a psychiatric evaluation. Dr. Ware's opinion was that Dr. Phillippe was not a candidate for retraining for another occupation, due to his age, work background, and personality. It was Dr. Ware's opinion that his personality is not compatible with the type of personality normally associated with a salesman of any type.

Under cross examination, Dr. Ware testified that at the time of his second examination, Dr. Phillippe did not exhibit symptoms of depression, and was psychologically sound, in his opinion. He found Dr. Phillippe to be intelligent and capable of sound assessment and evaluation of situations.

D) Exhibits Introduced by Commercial

The first ten exhibits offered by the defendant were Dr. Phillippe's income tax returns for the years 1977 through 1986. They indicate that in 1977, Dr. Phillippe's income was earned through interest earnings, dental office rental, rental of a commercial building, and trailer park rental income. In 1978, he received income as a dental consultant for the State of Louisiana, of $7,750.00, and engaged in the development of Oak Terrace Plaza Shopping Center in Gonzales. He also apparently operated a jewelry and gift shop for some time during this ten year period. Dr. Phillippe also invested in several other areas during this time, notably in equipment and rental activities. Dr. Phillippe's L.S.U. and Loyola School of Dentistry transcripts were also placed into evidence by the defendants.

## V. FINDINGS OF FACT

The court makes the following findings of fact based upon the evidence presented: Dr. Doyle F. Phillippe, at the time of his accident in 1976, had practiced general dentistry for some 15 years. His educational background and training was as a dentist. Subsequent to the loss of his right thumb in a hunting accident, he was rendered incapable of practicing general dentistry. Dr. Phillippe's income related activities between 1976 and the date of trial consisted of a brief stint as a dental consultant for the State of Louisiana, real estate investment and rental, and equipment rental.

The court accepts as fact Dr. Ware's testimony regarding Dr. Phillippe's inability to work in the area of sales due to his personality type. Mr. Porche's assertion that Dr. Phillippe's past purchase and development of land evidences ability to "sell" is at best tenuous. With regard to his opinion that Dr. Phillippe could with additional training, become an oral pathologist, the court cannot and will not find that Dr. Phillippe has a duty to undertake such a labor. No provision of the Commercial policy was ever shown to require such action on the part of Dr. Phillippe. In fact, the conduct of Commercial with regard to the entire issue of total disability forces the court to realize the inherent inequity of considering the two tiered analysis of disability set forth in the policy. It is difficult to conceive of any activity in which an individual could engage which could not be contrived to translate into a gainful occupation which disqualifies him from receipt of disability benefits.

The manner in which Mr. Porche arrived at his conclusions bears ample proof of that fact. He essentially fed into a computer the facts of Dr. Phillippe's past which he chose to rely upon, and received an impressive list of occupations for which Dr. Phillippe was qualified in return. The alternative, for Dr. Phillippe, was to remain absolutely motionless for the remainder of his life, lest he engage in some activity which "qualified" him for an occupation.

The court must find that Commercial has failed to establish by a preponderance of the evidence any occupation for which Dr. Phillippe's training and experience reasonably qualify him. The evidentiary basis for each and every occupation set forth by Mr. Porche is some fact of Dr. Phillippe's past work and investment history, which was applied to a chart of possible occupations without regard to whether Dr. Phillippe was in fact capable of carrying out the duties entailed in such occupations, or the current economic feasibility of these occupations in the area in which Dr. Phillippe lives. In the court's opinion, such testimony is of very little evidentiary value.

The court finds Dr. Phillippe to be totally disabled as that term is defined within the Commercial policy. Accordingly, he is entitled past due benefits and judicial interest thereon from date of demand in the case of those benefits accruing prior to his filing of suit, and thereafter on each payment from the date each payment was due until they are paid. He is further entitled to the declaratory relief prayed for.

## VI. PLAINTIFF'S ENTITLEMENT TO PENALTIES AND ATTORNEY'S FEES

The court must deny the plaintiff's request for punitive damages and attorney's fees, in spite of the fact that it finds the conduct of Commercial to have been less than admirable in this matter. Having bound itself to continue to pay benefits to Dr. Phillippe for life in the event he remained totally disabled, Commercial certainly owed him a duty to undertake a reasonable investigation of his ability to engage in other gainful activity prior to ceasing payment of benefits. The evidence presented indicated that Commercial fell short in discharging that duty.

Finally, the amount which Commercial may have paid Dr. Phillippe in the past is totally irrelevant to the determination of what they may owe him in the future. Having contracted for disability indemnity and accepted premiums for the same, Commercial bound itself to pay whatever sum Dr. Phillippe's disability entitled him to.

Nevertheless, the defendant was entitled to a judicial determination of what were in fact substantial legal and factual questions regarding the applicable provisions of its policy of insurance. The court cannot find Commercial's factual and legal defenses to be correct; however, their reasonableness under the circumstances of this matter are not seriously subject to question. The plaintiff's demands for penalties and attorney's fees is therefore dismissed....

## VII. CONCLUSION

For these reasons, the Court grants judgment in favor of the plaintiff, Dr. Doyle F. Phillippe, and against the defendant, Commercial Insurance Company of Newark, New Jersey, as follows: a) Dr. Doyle F. Phillippe is granted a declaratory judgment finding him to be totally disabled within the intent and meaning of the policy of disability insurance issued to him by Commercial and Commercial is ordered to pay such benefits as may hereafter accrue thereunder; b) Dr. Phillippe is granted judgment for past benefits due of $500.00 per week for the period of time commencing on March 15, 1986, and continuing until the date of signing of a formal judgment; together with legal interest from August 28, 1987 until paid on those weekly benefits due for the period of time commencing on March 15, 1986 and terminating on August 28, 1987; and legal interest on weekly benefits coming due between August

28, 1987 and the date of formal judgment from the date each weekly benefit payment became due until paid; and c) Commercial is cast for all costs of this matter.

## Dowdle v. National Life Insurance Company
United States Court of Appeals for the Eighth Circuit
407 F.3d 967 (2005)

**Riley, Circuit Judge.**

John A. Dowdle, Jr., M.D. (Dr. Dowdle), an orthopedic surgeon, brought this diversity action against National Life Insurance Company (National Life), seeking a declaratory judgment determining Dr. Dowdle is entitled to total disability benefits under the terms of his disability policies with National Life. After National Life removed the action to federal court, the parties cross-moved for summary judgment.

The district court granted summary judgment to Dr. Dowdle, concluding he is entitled to total disability benefits, because he cannot perform the material and substantial duties of his occupation. National Life appeals, maintaining Dr. Dowdle is not entitled to total disability benefits. Because we agree with the district court's determination that Dr. Dowdle is totally disabled under the policies as interpreted by Minnesota law, we affirm the district court's grant of summary judgment in favor of Dr. Dowdle.

On December 31, 1987, National Life issued a disability income policy (disability policy) to Dr. Dowdle. In the event Dr. Dowdle became totally disabled, the disability policy would provide a maximum monthly benefit of $13,050. The disability policy defines "total disability" as the inability "to perform the material and substantial duties of an occupation." Dr. Dowdle paid an additional premium to obtain an "own occupation rider" to the disability policy, which expands Dr. Dowdle's protection by defining "occupation" as "the occupation of the Insured at the time a disability, as defined in the Total Disability provision of the policy, begins."

Dr. Dowdle also purchased a "residual disability income rider," which defines "partial disability" as the inability "1. to perform one or more of the important daily duties of an occupation as defined in this policy; or 2. to engage in an occupation as defined in this policy for as much time as was usual prior to the start of disability."

On June 30, 1988, National Life issued a professional overhead expense disability policy (overhead expense policy) to Dr. Dowdle. This overhead expense policy would reimburse Dr. Dowdle's overhead expenses in the event he became disabled. The overhead expense policy uses the same definition for "total disability" as the disability policy. The overhead expense policy defines "total disability" as the inability "to perform the material and substantial duties of the Insured's occupation." The overhead expense policy defines "occupation" as "the occupation of the Insured at the time such disability begins." The overhead expense policy defines "partial disability" as the inability "1. to perform one or more of the important daily duties of the Insured's occupation as defined in this policy; or 2. to engage in the Insured's occupation as defined in this policy for as much time as was usual prior to the start of disability."

On the applications for both the disability income and the overhead expense policies (collectively, policies), Dowdle identified his occupation as an orthopedic surgeon. The applications also required Dowdle to list his specific duties. Dowdle identified his duties as seeing patients, performing surgery, reading xrays, interpreting data, and promoting referrals.... Before becoming disabled, Dr. Dowdle was a shareholder of Summit Orthopedics. Dr. Dowdle worked 50 to 60 hours per week, plus call duties. In an average week, Dr. Dowdle devoted 5 half-days to surgery and 5 half-days to office consultations, seeing 15 to 20 patients in each half-day session. Dr. Dowdle earned an average of $85,915 per month from Summit Orthopedics.

Surgery and surgery-related care comprised 85% of Dr. Dowdle's practice.... Outside his orthopedic surgery practice, Dr. Dowdle also performed independent medical evaluations (IMEs) for EvaluMed, Inc., a company Dr. Dowdle co-founded. Dr. Dowdle devoted an average of 1 hours to an IME: hour for discussion and examination, and 1 hour for review of medical records and preparation of the report. Dr. Dowdle often completed IMEs in the evening at his home. Dr. Dowdle performed an average of 7 IMEs per week. Performing IMEs was not part of Dr. Dowdle's normal duties as an orthopedic surgeon.

On September 9, 2000, Dr. Dowdle suffered injuries, including a closed head injury and a right calcaneal (heel bone) fracture, when the private aircraft he was piloting crashed shortly after takeoff. As a result of Dr. Dowdle's injuries, he is unable to stand at an operating table for an extended period of time. Consequently, he can no longer perform orthopedic surgery.... On November 16, 2000, Dr. Dowdle filed a claim with National Life for total disability benefits. National Life started paying Dr. Dowdle $28,050 per month, the maximum total disability benefits.

On February 7, 2001, Dr. Dowdle resumed performing office visits. Initially, Dr. Dowdle worked 1 half-day per week. He now works 6 half-days per week at Summit Orthopedics, seeing 15 to 20 patients during each half-day session. Since Dr. Dowdle resumed working after the accident, Summit Orthopedics considers Dr. Dowdle an independent contractor and pays Dr. Dowdle based upon a percentage of fees he generates. Dr. Dowdle earns an average of about $11,700 per month from Summit Orthopedics.... Dr. Dowdle describes his post-accident duties as follows:

> It's taking care of patients who have spinal injury and illnesses and doing the office portion of it and handling them and directing their care. And when they get to a place, if they need surgery, I hand it off to two of my partners who do the surgical treatment. Otherwise I manage their medicines. I manage their work injury and rehab and injections and all the rest, the same thing as I've done previously.

Dr. Dowdle also resumed performing IMEs for EvaluMed.

In light of his ability to resume office consultations, National Life determined that, as of February 7, 2001, Dr. Dowdle was residually disabled rather than totally disabled. National Life reasoned that, because Dr. Dowdle resumed his office practice and performed IMEs, duties he performed before his disability, Dr. Dowdle is only partially disabled. National Life continues to provide monthly residual disability benefits under the policies.... National Life argues Dr. Dowdle is not totally disabled under the terms of the policies, because Dr. Dowdle is able to conduct office consultations and other nonsurgical tasks. Conversely, Dr. Dowdle argues that, under Minnesota law, he is entitled to total disability benefits, even though he can perform some non-surgical duties.

Agreeing with Dr. Dowdle, the district court concluded, "since Dr. Dowdle is unable to perform any orthopedic surgery, he is unable to perform the substantial and material parts of his occupation in the customary and usual manner and with substantial continuity. Accordingly, Dr. Dowdle is entitled to 'total disability' benefits" under both policies. National Life appeals, arguing the district court erred in: (1) construing the policies in favor of Dr. Dowdle; and (2) concluding Dr. Dowdle is totally disabled, because he still is able to conduct an office practice and perform IMEs.

As an initial matter, we note the procedural posture of this appeal is different from the cases cited by the parties. In each of these cases, the appellate court reviewed a verdict to determine if the facts supported a finding of total disability. In the instant case, National Life appeals from an order granting summary judgment. We find it appropriate to decide this case on summary judgment, because the parties do not dispute the facts, the parties agree the issues are purely legal, and neither party desires to take this case to trial....

We review de novo the district court's grant of summary judgment, viewing the record in the light most favorable to the nonmoving party. Summary judgment is proper if the evidence shows there are no genuine issues of material fact and the moving party is entitled to judgment as a matter of law. We review de novo a district court's interpretation of a contractual provision in an insurance policy as a question of law. We apply Minnesota law in this diversity action.

National Life argues the district court erroneously construed the policies in favor of Dr. Dowdle, because the district court failed to make a threshold finding that the policy provisions at issue are ambiguous.... Under Minnesota law, if the "insurance policy language is clear and unambiguous, the language used must be given its usual and accepted meaning." However, if the "policy language is ambiguous, it must be interpreted in favor of coverage."

The parties agree orthopedic surgery was a material and substantial duty of Dr. Dowdle's occupation. However, the parties dispute whether Dr. Dowdle is totally disabled, because he still can conduct an office practice and perform IMEs. National Life contends the policies require that Dr. Dowdle be unable to perform "all" of the material and substantial duties of his occupation in order to qualify as totally disabled. Conversely, Dr. Dowdle contends the district court correctly held "total disability" means the inability to perform "the most important part" of his occupation.

Our review of the disputed policy language leads us to conclude ambiguity exists. The policies' definitions of "total disability" are susceptible to differing interpretations, because the policies do not speak in terms of "any," "all," "some," or "the most important part" of Dr. Dowdle's duties. Because the policies' definitions of "total disability" are susceptible to multiple interpretations, we conclude the district court properly construed the policies in favor of Dr. Dowdle.

In interpreting total disability policies with similar language, courts have taken one of two approaches. National Life urges us to apply the line of cases in which courts have interpreted similar language in total disability policies to mean an insured must be unable to perform "all" of his material and substantial duties to be considered totally disabled. These courts have held an insured's ability to perform just one material and substantial duty precludes a determination of total disability.

The other approach, adopted by the Minnesota Supreme Court *Weum v. Mutual Benefit Health & Accident Ass'n*, 54 N.W.2d 20, 31–2 (Minn. 1952), assesses a total disability if the insured's inability to perform certain duties precludes continuation in his or her regular occupation. In Weum, the insured, an obstetrician and gynecologist, sustained an injury which impaired his ability to deliver babies. For some time, the insurance company paid total disability benefits. When the insurance company ceased making total disability benefit payments, Dr. Weum sued. Id. Dr. Weum claimed he was totally disabled because, after his accident, he was unable to perform the work required of an obstetrician.

The policy at issue in *Weum* provided for total disability "if such injuries ... *shall wholly and continuously disable the Insured.*" The *Weum* court upheld an instruction to the jury that Dr. Weum should be considered "wholly and continuously disabled" if he was "unable to perform the substantial and material acts necessary to the successful prosecution of his occupation or employment in the customary and usual way." The court also upheld the jury verdict finding Dr. Weum totally disabled, even though he resumed an office practice. The court noted Dr. Weum "was so physically handicapped as a result of his injury that he would have been unable to perform the most important part of his specialty." The *Weum* court specifically rejected the argument that the fact an insured earns a substantial post-accident income bars a finding of total disability.

In the years since its 1952 decision in *Weum*, the Minnesota Supreme Court consistently has held, when applying an occupational disability clause like the provision present in the instant case, a determination of total disability does not require "a state of absolute helplessness or inability to perform any task relating to one's employment." Under Minnesota law, an insured may be entitled to total disability benefits, regardless of the number of important duties an insured still can perform in isolation.

Under the Minnesota law set forth in *Weum* and its progeny, the district court correctly concluded Dr. Dowdle is totally disabled. At the time he incurred his disability, Dr. Dowdle was engaged predominantly in the occupation of an orthopedic surgeon. The parties agree Dr. Dowdle's IME practice was separate and distinct from his surgery practice. Therefore, the fact that Dr. Dowdle performed IMEs both before and after the accident has no bearing on whether Dr. Dowdle can perform the "material and substantial duties" of being an orthopedic surgeon. National Life concedes Dr. Dowdle can no longer perform orthopedic surgery, which is clearly the most important substantial and material duty of Dr. Dowdle's occupation as an orthopedic surgeon. Because Dr. Dowdle's disability prevents him from performing the most important part of his occupation, he is entitled to total disability benefits under Minnesota law. We affirm the judgment of the district court.

## Notes and Questions

1. Do you agree with the Louisiana Court of Appeals that Dr. Phillippe was "totally disabled" as that term was defined in the Commercial Insurance Company policy? Why or why not? Might the court also have believed the testimony of Robert Porche, an expert in vocational rehabilitation, that Dr. Phillippe's education and experience qualified him for a number of other occupations? Why or why not? What does this tell you about litigation regarding the scope and meaning of the term "disability" in health and accident insurance policies?

2. The case of *Moore v. American United Life Ins. Co.*, 150 Cal. App. 3d 610, 197 Cal. Rptr. 878 (1984), restates the following rules regarding the scope and meaning of the term "disability":

> (a) When insurance coverage provisions in a general disability policy require "total inability to perform any occupation," total disability will result whenever an insured employee is prevented from working in a "real world" environment with reasonable continuity in his or her customary occupation, or any other occupation in which he or she might reasonably be expected to engage, in view of that employee's station and physical and mental capacity. The employee's age, education, training, and experience are specific ingredients of those physical and mental capacities; and

> (b) Recovery under a general disability policy would not be precluded because the insured employee is able to perform sporadic tasks, or give attention to simple or inconsequential matters incident to the conduct of business.

3. The basic test of "disability" is whether the policyholder may obtain employment in the open labor market either in his previous occupation, or such occupation which by education, training, and experience he might reasonably be expected to pursue. *See, e.g., Anair v. Mutual Life Ins. Co.*, 114 Vt. 217, 42 A.2d 423 (1945).

4. In litigation over disability insurance, a major question is whether the employee is "totally" or "partially" disabled:

> Such language does not impose a requirement that an insured must be absolutely helpless in order to qualify as totally disabled. A person may be able to do some work for compensation in an endeavor for which he is trained or qualified and yet be totally disabled within the fair and reasonable intendment of the policy.... It is generally said that to justify a recovery the disability must be such as renders an insured *unable to perform all the substantial and material acts necessary to the prosecution of his business or occupation in a customary and usual manner.*

> To be distinguished is the partial disability clause ... which provides that
> the insured is partially disabled when he is prevented from performing "one
> or more of the important duties of his occupation."

*Erreca v. Western States Life Ins. Co.*, 19 Cal. 2d 388, 396, 121 P.2d 689 (1942) (emphasis supplied). Moreover, self-employed insureds have been held competent to testify as to the extent of their disability. *See, e.g., Dittmar v. Continental Casualty Co.*, 29 N.J. 532, 150 A.2d 666 (1959).

5. One of the authors (Stempel) finds the outcome in *Dowdle v. National Life* both correctly decided and personally pleasing. Dr. Dowdle performed successful knee reconstruction on Stempel decades ago at the University of Minnesota Hospital when Dowdle was still a resident physician. As the case illustrates, Dr. Dowdle subsequently more than recouped his medical school tuition.

*Dowdle v. National Life* also illustrates that for many workers, their vocational talents and opportunities for compensation may vary considerably according to various aspects of their jobs. For example, Dr. Dowdle as a surgeon may have had few peers in his community but there may be many more doctors who are comparably skilled at office consultation (this as well as the economics of modern medicine probably helps explain the dramatic difference in his compensation after he could no longer do surgery). As doctors often put it, you either "have good hands or you don't" just as many basketball players can set screens but relatively few can consistently knock down three point shots under pressure.

Similarly, a lawyer may have exceptional talents in court but be only a good to average brief writer. After a serious injury (e.g., lost voice, facial disfigurement, chronic fatigue syndrome), the lawyer may no longer be able to try cases but can still research and write. However, unless this attorney is also a masterful writer or legal theorist, the lawyer's value to the firm and clients may be dramatically lowered even though the lawyer is still "working" after the injury.

For that reason, *Dowdle v. National Life* represents a correct approach to construction of "high-end" disability policies that define disability with reference to the policyholder's particular skills at the time the policy is placed rather than by mere ability to be gainfully employed in the field. Of particular importance, of course, is whether the policy is a high-end policy that pays when the policyholder cannot return to specific employment as opposed to a "Brand X" policy that pays only if the policyholder is completely unable to work.

## PROBLEM THREE

Dr. Jones, a dentist, has an Accidental Death and Dismemberment policy which pays $250,000 on total disability and $250,000 on death. Dr. Jones was involved in a terrible car crash. His left arm was crushed. As a result, his arm was fused at the elbow. Dr. Jones cannot move his arm from the elbow down to his fingers (including his wrist).

Disability benefits are payable 12 months from the date of the disability, providing that "total disability" is still ongoing. The policy states that "total disability" coverage is triggered by "loss of use of one arm." Death benefits are payable on "accidental death" of the insured.

Dr. Jones cannot perform any dental tasks that require two hands. He can still dress himself in the morning, but it takes an hour. His wife needs to help him with his belt. He can still drive by using his right hand and bending the arm to the wheel.

Dr. Jones dies in a plane crash 11 months and 29 days after his auto accident. He was in a private, two-person plane at the time, taking flying lessons. In fact, he was the student piloting the plane at the time of the crash. Dr. Jones had retired from dentistry practice (thanks to long term disability insurance) and led a typical family and home life, married with two children. He was, however, often depressed that he had to give up his dentistry profession after the accident. He had always wanted to learn how to fly a plane.

- Does Dr. Jones' widow (the beneficiary under the policy and under his will) get the disability benefit payment?

- Does Dr. Jones' widow get the death benefit payment?

- Assess the arguments among the beneficiaries and insurers' positions. Which arguments are strongest? Which will prevail?

## [B] The Limits of Conditions for Receipt of Disability Payments

Although one can agree to most anything by contract (it is a free country and all that), there are limits on what the judiciary will enforce. *See, e.g., Heller v. Equitable Life Assurance Soc.*, 833 F.2d 1253 (7th Cir. 1987) (doctor claiming disability due to carpal tunnel syndrome need not undergo surgery as condition of receiving disability policy benefits). Or are there? In *Heller*, the disability policy at issue did not clearly state that the policyholder was required to undergo surgery if necessary to attempt to return to work. What if it had? Would a court enforce coercive but sufficiently clear language of this sort? Would it depend on the degree of danger posed by the surgery? The likelihood of success from the surgery?

## [C] Disability Insurance and Illusory Coverage

In *Cody v. Connecticut General Life Ins. Co.*, 387 Mass. 142, 439 N.E.2d 234 (1982), the court implied that a disability policy with no substantial value in application may be deemed sufficiently illusory to be regulated or perhaps even construed to provide acceptable coverage (in accordance with policyholder reasonable expectations, presumably). The issue in *Cody* was whether the coordination of benefits provisions made the disability policy essentially worthless after consideration of social security and other benefits that were required to pay prior to any payments under the policy.

Application of the coordination formula in the instant case left the policyholder with essentially nothing in return for his premium payments. However, because the court foresaw other situations in which the policy would have sufficient value to justify the premium, the court refused to find the coverage illusory. Although the policyholder was unsuccessful in *Cody*, the case can be read as holding the door at least ajar for this type of argument in other cases.

# Chapter 11

# Automobile Insurance

## § 11.01. Introduction

Automobile insurance is certainly the most widely sold insurance. Due to state financial responsibility laws, drivers effectively must have auto insurance in order to license a car. Unfortunately, the state-mandated minimum levels of coverage are almost ridiculously too low (as little as $10,000 per person injured in one state, with $25,000 per person a common limit—when the loss suffered by a seriously injured victim can easily be in the millions of dollars considering the cost of future care and medical expenses alone). As a result, a surprisingly large number of auto accidents and lawsuits involve underinsured drivers as well as those illegally driving without any insurance. The financial responsibility laws are not rigorously enforced. For example, after obtaining the minimum insurance necessary to license a vehicle, irresponsible drivers often let the insurance lapse but continue to drive, resulting in a surprisingly large number of accidents and cases involving uninsured motorists.

Because auto insurance is ubiquitous and produces a high volume of disputes, it was a substantial factor in bringing about the duty to defend that now is a common feature of liability insurance. Auto insurers discovered that they could offer this additional feature at an additional premium and make money despite the frequent unpredictability of litigation costs by concentrating the defense work with experienced panel counsel who would agree to relatively low rates of pay in return for the steady high volume business produced by the large number of auto mishaps in America. The same economic logic led to use of captive law firms and in-house counsel to defend automobile tort actions in the late 20th century. Although general liability insurers were coming to the same views at about the same time, the situation and experience of the auto insurers was the driving force (bad pun intended) in showing that insurance with a duty to defend component could be profitably sold and administered on a widespread basis.

The mandatory nature of automobile insurance has tended to make it far more regulated than is typical for many other lines of insurance. Legislatures and insurance regulators have tended to mandate certain levels of coverage and certain policy provisions. Courts have frequently given somewhat different construction to auto policies in order to vindicate the positive law set forth by other branches. As a result, the law of auto insurance coverage frequently is not pure neo-classical contract law and the interpretation of particular policy provisions is less likely to be literal and textualist.

In addition, the comprehensive "no-fault" insurance arrangements in many states may give rise to distinguishable precedents regarding auto coverage. Just the same, as reflected in the cases excerpted in this chapter, insurers retain substantial latitude in policy drafting and in authoring policy terms that limit coverage.

## § 11.02. History of Automobile Insurance

First, of course, came the automobile — with auto insurance in some form not far behind. It appears that liability insurance for automobile owners, at least for commercial automobile operators, was sold as early as the 1890s. *See Phillipsburg Horse Car Co. v. Fidelity & Casualty Co.*, 160 Pa. 350, 28 A. 823 (1894). This expanded into liability insurance and collision insurance for consumer policies as well. The duty to defend, with attendant insurer control of the defense, came later. All this appears to have been in place by the 1930s. Comprehensive auto property coverage (discussed below) was not as widespread until the 1950s or 1960s, perhaps reflecting higher rates of automobile theft or vandalism as the 20th century rolled on.

The basic automobile policy as it presently exists has been in roughly the same form since the 1970s, with some occasional modification of exclusions or tweaking of policy language. Perhaps the largest modification in recent memory is the addition of "anti-stacking" language designed to prevent a policyholder owning multiple automobiles with a policy on each car from combining the various policy limits into one "super-sized" policy limit should one of the vehicles be involved in a catastrophic action.

## § 11.03. Structure of the Modern Automobile Policy

Auto insurance is actually a combination of several different types of insurance. The standard ISO-drafted auto policy contains a number of permutations to coverage that are unique in structure to auto insurance. The policy itself is a combination of liability and property insurance for automobiles. The typical auto policy always provides liability insurance for the owner and authorized drivers. The liability insurance typically covers losses "arising out of the ownership, maintenance, use or operation" of a motor vehicle. Accidents resulting from driving motorcycles and many all-terrain vehicles are thus, by extension, not covered.

In addition to the overall policy limits, there are usually territorial limits of coverage. If one plans to drive the vehicle outside the United States or Canada, a separate insurance policy will be required. Ordinarily, the liability portion of a driver's own auto insurance policy provides protection when the policyholder is driving a rental vehicle within the coverage territory (and typically many credit cards offer some type of property coverage for auto rentals). Health care coverage to the policyholder or other injured persons up to a set limit is also included.

The standard auto policy also provides uninsured motorist coverage, which stands in for liability insurance coverage if the policyholder or other insured person is hit by a third-party tortfeasor who lacks insurance. If the at-fault motorist has no applicable auto insurance, the victim's uninsured motorist coverage is called upon to indemnify the policyholder. As an additional option, the policyholder may also purchase underinsured motorist coverage. This type of insurance coverage makes up the difference between the underinsured at-fault motorist's liability insurance limits and the limits of the injured policyholder. Many states require that the policyholder be offered this option because the problems of being hit by an underinsured third party are nearly as pronounced as if the third party had no insurance. For example, the policyholder may be hospitalized for a year and permanently disabled after being hit broadside by a tortfeasor running a red light at an intersection. If the tortfeasor has only $10,000 of auto liability insurance in circumstances such as this, it is tantamount to being uninsured.

The property insurance component of the standard automobile policy provides coverage for damage to the insured vehicle so the owner can repair or replace a vehicle damaged in an accident. The property component is divided into two subcomponents: collision damage coverage and comprehensive coverage. Collision coverage is for typical vehicular accidents occurring when the auto is in motion and strikes an object (or another vehicle strikes the insured vehicle). Comprehensive coverage provides indemnity to the policyholder for a variety of perils such as if the vehicle is vandalized, stolen, or injured by other external forces such as a hailstorm or fire.

Some states also require that insurers offer some form of no-fault accident benefits payable to the insured driver upon injury resulting from a motor vehicle accident. These first party no-fault benefits are often called Personal Injury Protection (or "PIP") and pay for some limited benefits (such as medical expenses and wage loss). The benefits are triggered without regard to the fault of the driver who caused the accident.

# § 11.04. Common Issues in Automobile Insurance

## [A] Who Is an "Insured"?

Automobile insurance policies designate who is insured by the policy in one of two ways: (1) by specifically designating certain people (i.e., the owner of the car or frequent drivers in a household) as "insureds" under the policy or (2) by use of an "omnibus" clause which states that persons who drive the insured vehicle with the permission of the named insured are also additional insureds. However, if the driver using the named insured's automobile does not in fact have permission, there usually is no coverage. *See State Farm Mut. Auto. Ins. Co. v. Eastman*, 158 Cal. App.3d 562 (1984) (but coverage may be found where facts support claim of implied permission). Likewise, in many homeowners insurance policies, other members of the named insured's household also are insured under the policy. *See also Cole v. State Farm Ins. Co.*, 128 P.3d 171 (Alaska 2006) (former wife living with ex-husband after reconciliation is not "spouse" under husband's auto insurance policy).

Medical payment coverage in automobile insurance policies also designate additional insureds by their relationship to the named insured, and typically include members of the named insured's household, and sometimes guests in the insured's household.

## State Farm Automobile Insurance Co. v. Bottger

Supreme Court of South Dakota
793 N.W.2d 389 (2011)

**Meierhenry, J.**

While attempting to drive Alisia Ludwig's car out of a ditch, Andrew Bottger pinned Sarah Kosinski under the car. Kosinski sued Bottger for her injuries. Both Ludwig (the owner of the car) and Bottger (the driver of the car) were insured. Ludwig's car was insured by State Farm Automobile Insurance Company. Bottger was an insured driver on his mother's insurance policy with AMCO Insurance Company. The State Farm policy provided coverage to "any other person while using such a car if its use is within the scope of consent of you and your spouse[.]" The AMCO policy excluded coverage when an "insurer" was "[u]sing a vehicle without a reasonable belief that 'insurer' [wa]s entitled to do so."

The insurance companies sought declaratory judgment on whether coverage existed under the omnibus clause of the State Farm policy or under the exclusion clause of the AMCO policy. The trial court determined that Kosinski's injuries were not covered under either policy because Bottger did not have express or implied permission to drive at the time Kosinski was injured. We affirm as to Ludwig's State Farm policy because Ludwig had expressly withdrawn permission for Bottger to drive her car. We reverse and remand as to Bottger's AMCO policy for the trial court to determine whether Bottger had a reasonable belief that he was entitled to drive the car at the time the accident occurred.

Most of the facts are not in dispute and are not challenged as clearly erroneous on appeal. The events leading up to Kosinski's injury started in a corn field in Union County, South Dakota, where Ludwig, Kosinski, and Darci Irwin attended a high school drinking party. Ludwig drove her car to the party but needed a sober driver to drive the car back to her residence in Elk Point, South Dakota. The three young women asked Bottger if he was sober and capable of driving them to Elk Point in Ludwig's car. Bottger assured them he was sober enough to drive. Relying on his claim of sobriety, Ludwig allowed Bottger to drive her car.

The young women soon realized that Bottger was intoxicated and that his fast and erratic driving on the gravel road was placing them in danger. Ludwig directed Bottger to "pull the car over and stop." Kosinski and Irwin also "yell[ed] at [him] from the back seat to slow down or pull over." Bottger disregarded their requests. He continued speeding, missed a turn at a T-intersection, and crashed into a steep ditch.

No one was injured from the crash, but the car was wedged and stuck. All the passengers, except Bottger, got out of the car. Ludwig angrily demanded Bottger get of the car. Kosinski, who was standing in front of the vehicle, also told Bottger to get out of the vehicle. Even so, Bottger remained behind the wheel in an attempt to dislodge the vehicle by rocking it back and forth. Ludwig and Irwin climbed out of the ditch onto the road where Ludwig used her cell phone to contact someone to help remove the car from the ditch. A few minutes later, Bottger got the car to move forward, but in doing so, pinned Kosinski under the car.

*State Farm coverage depends on Bottger's status as an omnibus insured with express or implied permission to drive.*

South Dakota law mandates that automobile liability policies insure the person named in the policy and "any other person as insured, using any insured vehicle or vehicles with the express or implied permission of the named insured." SDCL 32-35-70. "The general rule is that the omnibus clause creates liability coverage in favor of the omnibus insured 'to the same degree as the [named] insured.'" ...

The specific language of the State Farm omnibus clause provides coverage if Bottger's use of the car was "within [Ludwig's] scope of consent." Undisputedly, Bottger initially had permission to drive Ludwig's car. The trial court, however, determined that "Ludwig expressly withdrew her permission and consent almost immediately after Bottger started driving when it became apparent to her that he was intoxicated." For the most part, the trial court's finding that Ludwig expressly withdrew her permission disposes of the coverage issue under the State Farm policy. [Because we affirm based on Ludwig's express revocation of permission, we need not address the trial court's determination that Bottger's intoxication was outside the scope of permission or a material deviation from Ludwig's initial express permission.]

At the hearing, Ludwig testified that she allowed Bottger to drive because he assured her he was sober. Ludwig also indicated that as soon as Bottger started driving, she realized he was not sober and specifically asked him to stop so she could find someone else to drive. As Bottger sped along the gravel road, Ludwig claimed that she repeatedly told him to stop and pull over, and then told him — more than once — to get out of the car after it crashed in the ditch. Bottger's memory of the events was unclear. He did not remember if Ludwig told him to stop driving or get out of the car.

Kosinski argues that Ludwig "expressly consented to Bottger's operation of her car for the venture from the [party] to their homes in Elk Point." Further, Kosinski contends that Bottger's attempt to get the car out of the ditch was a continuation of the "original permitted objective," regardless of Ludwig's request to "pull the car over and stop."

Kosinski points out that allowing one to avoid insurance coverage merely by claiming that consent was withdrawn seconds before an accident would contravene the purpose of the omnibus legislation. We are mindful of that concern. We have said that to prove express permission, "the evidence must be of an affirmative character, directly, and distinctly stated, clear and outspoken, and not merely implied or left to inference." [*Estate of*] *Trobaugh*, 2001 S.D. 37, 623 N.W.2d at 502 (internal citation omitted). Proof of revocation of permission requires the same level of proof.

Thus, effective revocation of permission must be clearly expressed by words or actions. One court explained that acts such as retrieving the keys, locking the vehicle, or removing the permitted driver are relevant factors "in determining whether permission has been revoked." [citation omitted]. But "the law [does not] impose[] an affirmative obligation to take such additional steps when the insured has expressly prohibited the use of the vehicle." *Id.*

The trial court found that Ludwig expressly revoked Bottger's permission to drive. The evidence supports the trial court's findings. Ludwig's revocation was affirmatively, directly, and distinctly stated. It was "clear and outspoken, and not merely implied or left to inference." *Trobaugh*, 2001 S.D. 37, ¶ 22, 623 N.W.2d at 502. Therefore we affirm the trial court's determination that there was no coverage under the State Farm policy's omnibus clause.

> *AMCO covers Bottger as an insured unless Bottger did not have a reasonable belief that he was entitled to drive Ludwig's vehicle.*

The language of Bottger's insurance contract, on the other hand, requires a different analysis. Bottger had liability coverage as a named insured under his mother's AMCO policy. The policy covered Bottger when driving his own vehicle as well as other vehicles. The policy contained an exclusionary provision that read as follows: "We do not provide Liability Coverage for any 'insured'... [u]sing a vehicle without a reasonable belief that that 'insured' is entitled to do so." AMCO claims the exclusion clause applies because Bottger did not have a reasonable belief that he was entitled to drive Ludwig's vehicle at the time of the accident. Although Bottger's permission, or lack thereof, determines coverage under Ludwig's State Farm liability policy, it does not necessarily determine coverage under Bottger's own liability policy.

The legal inquiry and focus are different between the two policies. With an exclusion clause, the legal inquiry changes from the automobile owner's perspective to the driver's perspective.... The Supreme Court of Georgia described the inquiry as "a mixed objective/subjective determination of the user's state of mind—the reasonableness of the user's subjective belief of entitlement." *Hurst v. Grange Mut. Cas. Co.*, 266 Ga. 712, 713, 470 S.E.2d 659, 661 (1996). The Court explained:

> The exclusion clause at issue differs from the traditional "omnibus" clause which authorizes coverage for a non-owner's permissive use of a vehicle. The new clause is couched in terms of entitlement rather than permission, causing a shift in the inquiry from an objective determination—whether the owner or one in legal possession of the car gave the user permission—to a mixed

objective/subjective determination of the user's state of mind—the reasonableness of the user's subjective belief of entitlement.

*Id.* (citations omitted). The Eleventh Circuit Court of Appeals also differentiated the focus of an exclusion clause as follows: "permissive use clauses focus[ ] on the owner's perspective. Specifically, the inquiry center [s] on whether the owner ha[s] expressly or impliedly given permission to the user. [An] entitlement clause reverses the inquiry. It focuses on how the situation appear[s] to the user of the automobile." ...

This approach is consistent with the risk assumed by the insurer. The insurer assumes the risk that if its insured "reasonably believes that he or she has the permission of the owner, the insured will be operating the other automobile with the same degree of care as was initially anticipated by the insurer when it issued the automobile policy." 8A Lee R. Russ, et al., *Couch on Insurance* 3d § 118:33 (2010).

As applied here, the focus of the AMCO policy exclusion is whether Bottger reasonably believed that he was entitled to drive rather than whether he had Ludwig's permission. The subjective/objective test "for determining whether the insured's (Bottger's) belief was reasonable is not necessarily what a reasonable person would believe, but is instead measured by the reaction of a reasonable person of the same age, personality and social environment, subject to such accompanying influences on the person's judgment and mind as may be credibly discerned from the subject evidence." *Id.* Consequently, "[o]ne might have a reasonable belief in his entitlement to use a vehicle, even though he has no permission to do so, and one might have the owner's permission to use a vehicle but still have no reasonable belief that he is entitled to do so." 46 C.J.S. *Insurance* § 1505 (2010).

Whether an insured has a reasonable belief that he is entitled to drive another's vehicle is a question of fact. When an insurance company seeks to avoid liability under a policy because of an excluded risk, it has the burden of proving the facts that constitute the exclusion. *State Auto. and Cas. Underwriters v. Ishmael*, 87 S.D. 49, 202 N.W.2d 384, 386 (1972).

The trial court's determination that the AMCO policy did not offer coverage focused on whether Bottger had "implied or express permission." This was a mistake because the trial court should have focused on whether Bottger reasonably believed that he was entitled to drive the vehicle out of the ditch. The trial court entered two findings concerning Bottger's subjective belief. The trial court found that (1) "Bottger subjectively believed that he was being helpful by trying to remove the car from the ditch," and (2) "Bottger subjectively believed he had permission to operate the Ludwig vehicle." The trial court, however, concluded that "[c]overage for Bottger under the AMCO policy is excluded because he did not have Ludwig's express or implied consent." Nowhere in the trial court's memorandum decision or in the findings of facts or conclusions of law does the trial court address the exclusion clause inquiry—whether Bottger had a reasonable belief that he was entitled to drive the vehicle.

We reverse and remand for the trial court to apply the language of the exclusion clause under the subjective/objective test discussed above. The trial court must determine whether Bottger believed he was entitled to drive the vehicle at the time of the accident; and if so, whether that belief was reasonable "as measured by the reaction of a reasonable person of the same age, personality and social environment, subject to such accompanying influences on the person's judgment and mind as may be credibly discerned from the [ ] evidence."

## Notes and Questions

1. Disputes over whether a driver has "permission, express or implied," to use the named insured's vehicle as required under the omnibus clause, and thereby becoming an additional insured under the named insured's insurance policy, continue to be a great source of litigation. Three judicial interpretations of the omnibus clause provision have emerged.

The first interpretation, which Professor Keeton calls the "strict construction" view, is that the use of the vehicle by the borrower must be clearly within the scope of the named insured's permission. So, under this rule, the implied consent to use a vehicle to and from work would not extend to a son's pleasure trip to the seashore since consent is limited "to the purpose for which it is given." *See Eagle Fire Co. v. Mullins*, 120 S.E.2d 1 (S.C. 1961).

The second, or "liberal," interpretation of the omnibus "permission" clause finds almost any use of the vehicle to be within the policy coverage, as long as the borrower received the named insured's initial permission to drive the vehicle. Under this interpretation, for example, the subsequent "bar hopping" of the borrower driver, although not anticipated or intended by the named insured, would be covered. *See, e.g., Matits v. Nationwide Mut. Ins. Co.*, 166 A.2d 345 (N.J. 1960). *See also Spears v. Preble*, 661 P.2d 1337 (Okla. 1983).

The third, and majority, interpretation is the "minor deviation" rule, under which coverage would be defeated by a material — but not minor — deviation in the scope of permission intended by the named insured. So, for example, if the date of a named insured's daughter was given permission to drive the father's car to a movie and directly back home, coverage would *not* be excluded when an accident occurred while the young couple were "driving around" after they decided not to go to the movie, since this was only a "minor deviation" from the permitted use. *See, e.g., Ryan v. Western Pacific Ins. Co.*, 408 P.2d 84 (Ore. 1965); *Grange Ins. Assn. v. Ochoa*, 691 P.2d 248 (Wash. Ct. App. 1984).

Any one of these theories, however, will still rest on the initial threshold question: did the first borrower give actual or implied permission to the second borrower to drive the vehicle? If not, then no question of delegation ever arises, and the secondary borrower will not be insured under the omnibus clause. May the second borrower then be liable under his or her own automobile insurance policy?

2. Permissive user motor vehicle omnibus statutes have been adopted in almost all states with the public policy purpose of entitling the permissive user to the same quantity and quality of coverage as afforded to the named insured. *See, e.g., American*

*Motorists Ins. Co. v. Kaplan*, 161 S.E.2d 675 (Va. 1968). Why was this legislation enacted, and who does it ultimately benefit?

### PROBLEM ONE

John Figenshow operated a wholesale lumber and trucking business in Tonasket, Washington. His vehicles were insured by Grange Insurance Association. Among those vehicles was a 1977 Chevrolet pickup which his employee, Alan Clifford, was permitted to drive in connection with the business and for his personal use.

On June 29, 1981, Mr. Clifford permitted his son Darin, who was age 15 and not licensed, to drive the pickup from a restaurant to their home to obtain his swimming trunks, a distance of about three and one-half miles.

Although he was told to go "right down and right back," Darin deviated 9–12 miles from his route to pick up some friends.

While returning to the restaurant, Darin lost control of the truck and crashed into a tree. Each of the four friends he had picked up sustained injuries in the accident.

- Should Darin be covered as a borrower's borrower?
- Under what theory?

## [B] "Owned" versus "Non-Owned" Vehicles

Automobile insurance companies often provide or limit coverage depending on whether the automobile is "owned" or "non-owned." The following case explores some of the ramifications of these "owned" and "non-owned" concepts in automobile liability insurance policies.

### Simon v. Lumbermens Mutual Casualty Co.

Supreme Court, Nassau County
107 Misc. 2d 816, 436 N.Y.S.2d 139 (1981)

#### James F. Niehoff, Justice.

[Karen Vascellaro, living in Rhode Island, owned a 1968 Mercury, which was insured by Aetna Casualty. Susan Vascellaro, Karen's sister, living with her father Vincent in Nassau County, N.Y., was driving the Mercury with Karen's permission when she struck Brenda Simon, plaintiff herein. Vincent had an auto liability policy with defendant Lumbermens Mutual Casualty Co.]

Brenda J. Simon, the injured pedestrian, and her father, Robert K. Simon, have instituted a negligence action against the defendants, Susan J. Vascellaro and Karen L. Vascellaro, in this Court. In the present action they seek a declaration to the effect that the father's insurance with Lumbermens constitutes excess insurance coverage.

The Lumbermens policy obligates that carrier to pay on behalf of the "insured" damages to person or property "arising out of the ownership, maintenance or use of the owned vehicle or any non-owned automobile." (Part I—Liability). The policy goes on to state that the following are "insureds" under Part I:

(b) With respect to a non-owned automobile,

(1) the named insured,

(2) any relative, but only with respect to a private passenger automobile or trailer

provided his actual operation or (if he is not operating) the other actual use thereof is with the permission, of the owner and is within the scope of such permission....

In the case at bar, Susan, as the daughter of Vincent J. Vascellaro residing in the same household as her father, is a relative of Vincent and, so, qualifies as an "insured" under the Lumbermens policy. The car in question, the 1968 Mercury owned by her sister Karen, was a private passenger car and, at the time of the accident, was being used by Susan with the permission of Karen, the owner, and within the scope of the permission granted. Thus, all of the elements necessary to bring the Lumbermens policy into play as excess coverage exist in this case provided Karen's car was a "non-owned automobile."

Manifestly, the car was not owned by either Susan or her father Vincent. But, the matter cannot end there. The policy defines a "non-owned automobile" as meaning "an automobile ... not owned by or furnished for the regular use, of either the named insured or any relative, other than a temporary substitute automobile."

Thus, for Lumbermens to become an excess insurer of the non-owned Mercury automobile it must be shown that the vehicle was not "furnished for the regular use" of Susan.

Susan and her mother both testified that Karen brought the car from Rhode Island to the Vascellaros' home in Nassau County in late August or early September of 1978. Susan was not licensed to drive at that time. Karen went with her in the car a number of times in order to let Susan practice her driving. Susan became licensed on September 14, 1978. From that time on no one drove the car but Susan..., both to school and to work and whenever she needed a car....

The question, then, boils down to whether or not Karen's automobile was furnished for Susan's regular use within the definition of non-owned automobile in the Lumbermens policy. For the reasons set forth hereinafter the Court is of the opinion that Karen's car was furnished for Susan's regular use and, therefore, is not entitled to coverage as a non-owned automobile....

In the instant case, Susan had what amounted to exclusive use of the subject vehicle for a six week period before the accident. According to her testimony, she used it at least twice daily and without any restrictions having been placed upon her use of the car. In that same period her father drove the car twice and only when it required repairs. Indeed, it is clear that Karen gave Susan the use of the car so that Susan could use it "regularly."

Under such circumstances the Court is led to but one conclusion, namely, that the 1968 Mercury is not a "non-owned vehicle" and that Lumbermens is not liable for any portion of any judgment which may be entered in the negligence action against Susan and Karen.

Without question, the insurer, Lumbermens, agreed for a single premium to afford coverage to a relative of the named insured when using a non-owned private passenger vehicle which was "not furnished for the regular use" of such relative.

As the Appellate Division, Third Department, wrote in *McMahon v. Boston Old Colony Insurance Company*, [67 A.D.2d 757, 412 N.Y.S.2d 465] "The purpose of such a provision [coverage on a non-owned vehicle] is to provide protection for the occasional or infrequent use of a vehicle not owned by the insured; it is not a substitute for insurance on automobiles which are furnished for his regular use."

On the basis of the facts in this case Lumbermens is entitled to a judgment declaring that it is not liable for any portion of any judgment which may be entered in the underlying negligence action against Susan J. Vascellaro and Karen L. Vascellaro.

## *Notes and Questions*

1. As discussed in the *Simon* case, the usual definition of a "non-owned" automobile in the policy requires that the automobile: (1) is not owned by, or furnished for regular use, of either the insured or any relative, other than as a temporary substitute automobile; and (2) is used with the implied or express permission of the owner. Did the driver in the *Simon* case comply with this coverage? What is the rationale underlying these "owned" and "non-owned" coverage provisions? Contrast with *New York Cent. Mut. Fire Ins. Co. v. Jennings*, 195 A.D.2d 541, 600 N.Y.S.2d 486 (1993).

2. Automobile liability insurance coverage has also been held to be contingent upon acquisition of ownership, rather than acquisition of operability. Thus, a truck which was inoperable at the time of acquisition but was later made operable was an "owned automobile" within the meaning of the automobile liability policy at the time of its acquisition. *See, e.g., Lacoste v. Price*, 453 So. 2d 986 (La. Ct. App. 1984).

## PROBLEM TWO

David Garroutte purchased a 1956 Chevrolet automobile before he left for military service. David did not purchase any insurance on his car, but when he returned to active duty, he left the automobile in the custody and control of his father, Wayne. The father then bought an automobile policy on the car with coverage similar to the "owned" and "non-owned" provisions in the *Simon* case. David and Wayne both stated that the automobile was for the "use and benefit of the members of Wayne Garroutte's household."

Michael Garroutte, the brother of David and son of Wayne, who was also in the armed services, was home on a 72-hour leave, and was given permission by his father Wayne to drive the car. Michael was involved in a one-car accident which injured plaintiff Coombs.

- Should Michael be covered as an insured under the policy's "non-owned" automobile coverage provisions?

## [C] What Is an "Automobile"?

Automobile insurance is mandated by statute precisely because the state has determined that there is some social good in having compensation at the ready in the event of an automobile accident. Yet what is an "automobile" or "motor vehicle"? What did the insurer and policyholder agree to cover? Today, there are many kinds of motorized vehicles, from motorcycles and all-terrain vehicles (ATVs) to scooters, parade floats, and golf carts.

- Does one's automobile insurance respond when the policyholder is in an accident with a riding lawn mower?

The larger question must then be:

- what types of accidents are meant to be covered by this mandatory, legislated insurance?

- is the answer different under a formalist approach as opposed to a functionalist approach?

- what is an "automobile" or "motor vehicle"?

### Lake v. State Farm Mutual Automobile Insurance Co.

Court of Appeals of Washington (Div. 2)
110 P.3d 806 (2005)

**Morgan, J.**

The question in this case is whether a four-wheel all terrain vehicle (ATV) is a "motor driven cycle." The trial court answered yes, and so do we. Thus, we affirm.

On August 10, 2001, Adina Lake was a passenger on an ATV that its owner, Shane Bergstrom, was driving on some sand dunes. She was thrown off and injured.

The ATV was a 1989 Yamaha Banshee. It had four wheels and was steered by using handlebars. It was ridden by straddling the engine on a long, narrow, saddle-type seat. It was powered by a two-stroke twin cylinder ATV engine which, according to Yamaha, "is a direct descendant of our legendary RZ350 sport bike." Yamaha advised in the owner's manual that it was "designed for off-road use only"; that it was "illegal to operate … on any public street, road or highway"; and that it should "never" be used to carry passengers. A picture follows.

The Banshee was not insured, but Lake had underinsured motorist coverage (UIM) through State Farm. Her policy obligated State Farm to "pay damages for bodily injury sustained by an insured that an insured is legally entitled to collect from the owner or driver of an underinsured motor vehicle," provided that "there is no coverage for bodily injury to an insured or property damage while an insured is operating or occupying … a motorcycle or a motor driven cycle."

After filing a claim that State Farm denied, Lake sued for a judgment declaring that her injuries were covered. The trial court granted State Farm's motion for summary judgment, denied Lake's cross-motion for summary judgment, and entered final judgment for State Farm.

On appeal, the parties debate two questions. First, can a motor vehicle designed only for off-road use be a "motor vehicle" within the meaning of State Farm's policy? Second, is the ATV in issue here a "motor driven cycle" within the meaning of State Farm's policy? The second question is dispositive, so we need not address the first.

In *State Farm Mutual Auto Insurance Co. v. Gates*, 83 Wash.App. 471, 921 P.2d 1096 (1996), *review denied*, 131 Wash.2d 1004, 932 P.2d 643 (1997). Jessica Boyd, age 16, was injured while a passenger on an ATV driven by a friend. She sought coverage under Gates' (her parents') State Farm policy. The Gates' policy was identical to Lake's insofar as pertinent here. After examining several definitions of the word "motorcycle," we summarized as follows:

Several common threads run through all of these definitions. First, *a motorcycle* has two or three wheels; second, *a motorcycle* has handlebars, not a steering wheel; third, *a motorcycle* has a saddle seat. The ATV on which Boyd was a passenger had all of these characteristics. We hold, therefore, that the language of State Farm's exclusion is not ambiguous and that the average insurance buyer would understand that ATVs are included within the terms "motorcycle" or "motor driven cycle." Thus, Boyd is not covered under the UIM provisions of State Farm's policy.

*Gates*, 83 Wash.App. at 476–77, 921 P.2d 1096 (emphasis added).

*Gates* differs from this case in only one respect — the ATV there had three wheels, while the ATV here had four. Emphasizing this difference, Lake invites us to distinguish *Gates* and hold that the ATV in issue here, the Banshee, was *neither* a "motorcycle" *nor* a "motor driven cycle." We decline for several reasons.

First, *Gates* focused on the definition of motorcycle, not on the definition of "motor driven cycle." It held that a three-wheeled ATV *is* a motorcycle. It did not hold, for it had no need to address, that a four-wheeled ATV is *not* a motorcycle.

Second, even if we assume that a "motorcycle" has two or three wheels, a "motor driven cycle" necessarily has more.

Third, although several standard dictionaries define a "motorcycle" as having two or three wheels, they also define "cycle" and "quadricycle" so as to indicate that the Banshee in issue here is a "motor driven cycle."

Finally, we think that an average purchaser of insurance viewing the Banshee would readily believe, without doubt or ambiguity, that it is a "motor driven cycle." *See Gates*, 83 Wash.App. at 476–77, 921 P.2d 1096 ("average insurance buyer would understand that ATVs are included within the terms 'motorcycle' or 'motor driven cycle'").... Like the trial court, we conclude that the Banshee was a "motor driven cycle" that was excluded from State Farm's UIM coverage.

## [D] Loss "Arising Out of Ownership, Maintenance, or Use" of a Vehicle

The phrase "arising out of the ownership, maintenance, or use of an insured vehicle" which appears as the key coverage clause in most automobile liability insurance policies illustrates the way in which a primary definition of coverage can likewise restrictively defeat coverage if it is interpreted in an exclusionary manner. For example, should "arising out of" refer narrowly to the actual "use" or "maintenance" of a vehicle, or should it have a much broader meaning in order to validate the "reasonable expectation" of the insured to coverage?

# North Star Mutual Insurance Co. v. Peterson

Supreme Court of South Dakota
749 N.W.2d 528 (2008)

**Meierhenry, J.**

This case involves a question of automobile insurance coverage for injuries sustained when a gun discharged while deer hunters were waiting to be transported to the fields. The circuit court found that the automobile liability policy covered the gunshot injuries.

Milbank Insurance Co. (Milbank) issued the automobile liability policy in question to Peterson Farms. Brad, Lenny and Danny Peterson were general partners in Peterson Farms. In addition to the Milbank automobile liability policy, Peterson Farms had an umbrella liability policy from North Star Mutual Ins. Co. (North Star). The circuit court found coverage under Milbank's personal automobile liability policy. Milbank appeals. The court found no coverage under North Star's umbrella policy because of exclusions specified in the policy. The ruling as to North Star's coverage has not been appealed.

In a trial to the court, the parties stipulated to most of the relevant facts. The day before the accident, Brad Peterson had been deer hunting with his sons Jeb and Shane. Eleven-year-old Jeb was using his father's Winchester Model 94, .30-.30 lever action rifle to hunt varmints such as coyote or fox.

While the hunting party was loading the rifles into the pickup at the conclusion of the hunt, a friend drove up and assisted young Jeb with loading the rifle into the vehicle. The friend ejected the round out of the chamber and opened the lever. The open lever made the rifle safe from discharge; however, its magazine still held ammunition.

The friend placed the rifle into the back seat of the Peterson's vehicle. He propped it near the middle of the backseat of the pickup with the barrel end on the floor and the butt leaning against the back of the seat. The hunting party then returned to Brad's home driving through fields and over country roads. The rifle remained in the vehicle.

The next morning, Brad, Shane and Lenny's fourteen-year-old son, Mitch again went deer hunting. While hunting, they walked through a slough and got their clothing wet. They removed and threw the wet hunting clothes in the pickup's backseat on top of the rifle. The hunting party then returned to Brad's home. Later that afternoon, Brad, Shane, Mitch and Jeb prepared to go hunting again. They got into the pickup: Brad and Shane in the front seat, Mitch and Jeb in the backseat.

The rifle was still in the backseat situated between Jeb and Mitch. Jeb noticed that the wet hunting clothes were lying on the rifle and that the barrel had moved sideways and was unsafely pointed at Mitch's leg. Jeb grasped the rifle in an attempt to reposition it away from Mitch's leg. As he moved the rifle, it discharged and struck Mitch's left ankle and grazed his right ankle.

The pickup engine was on and idling but the pickup was not moving at the time of the accident. The hunting party assumed that the vehicle's movement over the two days had jostled the rifle causing the lever to close and that their wet hunting clothing on top of the gun had caught and pulled the trigger. There was no evidence that anyone had handled the gun since its placement in the pickup the day before.

Milbank brought a declaratory judgment action asking the circuit court to determine whether its automobile liability policy with Peterson Farms covered Mitch's bodily injuries arising from this hunting accident. The dispute centers on the language in Milbank's insurance policy defining coverage. The terms of the policy provide that "[Milbank] will pay damages for 'bodily injuries' or 'property damage' for which any insured becomes legally responsible because of an auto accident...." The policy further defines an "insured" as "you or any family member for the ownership, maintenance or use of any automobile or trailer." ... Milbank raises the following issue on appeal:

Whether the circuit court erred in holding that the shooting incident of November 24, 2001, was the result of an "auto accident" as that term is used in the Milbank insurance policy.

.... Milbank argues that the accidental discharge of the firearm in the backseat of the vehicle cannot be considered an "auto accident" as that term is defined under any common sense analysis. Milbank views the situation as one where an accident took place in an automobile and did not constitute an automobile accident. Milbank claims that the auto was merely the site of the occurrence and that there was no causal connection between the vehicle's use and the injury-producing event.

Nevertheless, Milbank does not dispute that the policy covers accidents arising out of the "ownership, maintenance and use" of the vehicle. Milbank conceded during oral arguments that the statutory language covering "damages arising out of the ownership, maintenance, or use of the vehicle," must be considered when interpreting the insurance policy and that the language was, in effect, part of the policy. SDCL 32-35-70.

Additionally, the policy uses these terms in its definition of insured. The Milbank policy defines "insured" as "you or any family member for the ownership, maintenance or use" of a vehicle. The policy also provides that "[w]hen this policy is certified as future proof of financial responsibility, this policy shall comply with the law to the extent required." South Dakota law of financial responsibility requires insurance "against loss from the liability imposed by law for damages arising out of the ownership, maintenance, or use of the vehicle or vehicles...." SDCL 32-35-70. Thus, a fair interpretation of the term "auto accident" would be an accident arising out of the "ownership, maintenance and use" of the automobile.

In *Lyndoe v. American Standard Ins. Co.*, we analyzed insurance coverage of an accidental shooting in an automobile. 245 N.W.2d 273 (S.D. 1976). In that case, Loren Lyndoe was riding through downtown Custer in a truck driven by his brother, James. Lyndoes pulled their vehicle over to the side of the road to talk to an acquaintance in another vehicle. 245 N.W.2d at 273–74. While the vehicles were parked side by side, the acquaintance attempted to hand a .38 caliber pistol through his driver's side window to Loren. Loren reached for the gun through his window. Before Loren touched the gun, it discharged and struck Loren in the mouth.

The policy language in *Lyndoe* provided as follows:

> The company shall pay on behalf of the insured all sums which the insured shall become legally obligated to pay as damages because of:
>
> Coverage A-bodily injury caused by accident and arising out of the ownership, maintenance or use of the automobile.
>
> "[U]se" of the automobile includes loading and unloading.

245 N.W.2d at 275.

Although much of the analysis in *Lyndoe* centered on whether passing the gun into the window constituted "loading or unloading" the vehicle, the basic question was whether the accident arose out of the "use" of the vehicle. *Id.* We said, "[s]ome causal connection between the 'use' of the vehicle ... and the accident must exist." *Id.* (citations omitted). We also adopted a broad view of the 'use' clause in automobile coverage policies. *Id.* at 650, 245 N.W.2d at 276. We noted as follows:

> Some of the cases [from other jurisdictions] involved efforts by a plaintiff to include his injuries within an automobile policy providing coverage under a "use" clause, while others involved an effort by an insurer to exclude injuries from a homeowner's policy because of a clause excluding automobile "use." In the latter policy the "use" clause is given a narrow interpretation, while in the former, courts have adopted a broader interpretation. *Therefore the broader view of the "use" clause must be adopted in this case.*

*Id.* at 649–50, 245 N.W.2d at 276 (emphasis added).

Even under the broader view, we determined that the vehicle in *Lyndoe* was the mere situs of the accident and the injury did not arise from the 'use' of the vehicle. *Id.* We analyzed it as follows:

> Here the parties were within the City of Custer and not on a hunting expedition. They were merely discussing past and possible future hunting. The pistol was not to be delivered for the purpose of hunting nor for any use other than an examination by plaintiff followed by a return to Stender. It has been held that under a "loading and unloading" clause, the efficient and predominating cause of the accident must arise from the "use" of the vehicle. (citations omitted).
>
> Stender's actions were a continuation of the conversation between the parties and could well have taken place elsewhere except for the temporary storage of the pistol in the vehicle. His independent act of reaching out the window of the vehicle was the event which discharged the pistol. Only his hand and arm extended outside the vehicle. Plaintiff admitted that he could have reached the pistol from his vehicle which was approximately two feet away. The vehicle was merely the [s]itus from which Stender reached in attempting to deliver the pistol to plaintiff.

> We find this case more analogous to those cases where a gun was passed or moved within a vehicle than to those cases where a person stepped from his vehicle and attempted to remove a gun. We conclude that the policy's provisions cannot be interpreted so broadly as to allow coverage here.

*Id.*

Milbank argues that *Lyndoe* supports its analysis and the absence of coverage because *Lyndoe* distinguishes between cases where firearms discharge while loading and unloading them from vehicles and cases where firearms discharge while being handled inside the automobile. Generally, cases from other jurisdictions that concern coverage of hunting accidents fall into categories. The Supreme Court of New Mexico lists the categories as follows:

> 1) accidents in which the actual movement of the vehicle caused the firing of the gun, as in transport; 2) accidents in which the discharged gun was being removed from or placed in a gun rack in the vehicle; 3) accidents in which the gun was being loaded into or unloaded from the vehicle; 4) accidents arising from use of the vehicle as a gun rest; and 5) accidents in which the vehicle is described as a "mere situs" for the accident, such as when children play with guns in a standing vehicle.

*Sanchez v. Herrera*, 783 P.2d 465, 467 (N.M. 1989) (citation omitted). *See also Cameron Mut. Ins. Co. v. Ward*, 599 S.W.2d 13, 15–16 (Mo.Ct.App.1980) (the court analyzed and categorized cases from several jurisdictions).

Milbank urges us to adopt the nexus test set forth by the South Carolina Supreme Court in *Peagler v. USAA Ins. Co.*, 628 S.E.2d 475 (S.C. 2006). The *Peagler* court used a three-part test ... to determine whether an injury arose from the "ownership, maintenance, or use" of a vehicle.... The court explained the test as follows: "The party seeking coverage must show (1) a causal connection exists between the vehicle and the injury, (2) no act of independent significance breaks the causal link between the vehicle and the injury, and (3) the vehicle was being used for transportation purposes at the time of the injury." The *Peagler* court specifically rejected precedent of other courts that find coverage when accidents occur during the loading and unloading of a vehicle. The court narrowly limited coverage to instances where the plaintiff could demonstrate that the vehicle "was an active accessory to the injury."

The three-part test followed in *Peagler* is unique to South Carolina law dating back to 1975. Most jurisdictions do not use such a restrictive test. We find this restrictive and narrow approach not in sync with *Lyndoe*, where we clearly adopted a broad view when applying a "use" clause in an automobile liability policy. Nevertheless, even with a broad interpretation, a plaintiff still has to show some causal connection between the injury and the vehicle.

Other courts have recognized a causal connection and found coverage when a gun discharges in a vehicle in conjunction with a hunting expedition. We referred to this causal connection by implication in *Lyndoe*. Our language in *Lyndoe* implied that if the parties had been on a hunting expedition, our analysis would have been different. We said:

> Here the parties were within the City of Custer and *not on a hunting expedition*. They were merely discussing past and possible future hunting. The pistol was not to be delivered *for the purpose of hunting* nor for any use other than an examination by plaintiff followed by a return to Stender.

*Lyndoe*, 90 S.D. at 650, 245 N.W.2d at 276 (emphasis added).

Mitch Peterson's injury undisputedly occurred during the "use" of the vehicle on a hunting trip. Whether the vehicle was more than "mere situs," however, requires additional analysis. For purposes of coverage under the policy, there must be a causal connection between the accident that injured Mitch Peterson and the use of the pickup truck.

Other jurisdictions have required "for coverage to apply, '[t]he injury must also have a causal connection to the inherent use of the vehicle.'" *Kemp v. Feltz*, 174 Wis.2d 406, 497 N.W.2d 751, 755 (Ct.App.1993) (holding that use of a truck as a "mobile hunting vehicle is consistent with the truck's inherent use" for transportation of hunters); *see, e.g., Sanchez*, 783 P.2d at 467 (concluding "that emptying a gun within the cab of a pickup truck is foreseeably incident to use of that vehicle for hunting")…. We find this causal connection analysis more persuasive than the narrow three-part test used in *Peagler*….

The Kansas Supreme Court, in a strikingly similar hunting accident case, applied a causal connection analysis to find coverage. *Garrison v. State Farm Mut. Auto. Ins. Co.*, 258 Kan. 547, 907 P.2d 891 (1995). In *Garrison*, two men were hunting doves. They stopped the car for one of the hunters to get out. A gun stowed between the front seats of the vehicle discharged while one of the men was getting out of the car. No one knew why the gun discharged. The discharge struck the other passenger in the leg causing serious injury. *Id.* at 893.

The terms of the liability policy were similar to Milbank's policy. The policy covered damages "which an *insured* becomes legally liable to pay because of … *bodily injury* to others … caused by accident resulting from the ownership, maintenance or use of *your car*." *Id.* The policy also "promise[d] to pay damages for bodily injury … for which the law holds *you* responsible because of a *car accident*…." *Id.* at 894. The court explained the causal connection as follows:

> [F]or insurance coverage to exist for accidental bodily injury, there is no requirement that the vehicle be either the proximate cause of the injury or physically contribute to the discharge of the gun. Coverage exists where the minimal causal connection between the use of the vehicle and injury is provided by the foreseeable and reasonable use of the vehicle for hunting.

*Id.* at 895.

The court found that the car was more than the mere situs of the injury, and endorsed the statement that "Kansas follows the majority rule that there must be some causal connection between the use of the insured vehicle and the injury." *Id.* at 895 (citation omitted). The court held that "under the facts of this case, the injury sustained by Garrison, the driver, when a shotgun inside the car accidentally discharged as it was removed from the car, was a natural and reasonable incident arising out of the use of the car for hunting." *Id.* at 896.

Other courts have used a similar inquiry.... The Wisconsin Supreme Court found automobile liability insurance coverage for a hunting accident because using a truck "for a hunting trip is reasonably consistent with the inherent use of the truck." In *Allstate Ins. Co. v. Truck Ins. Exchange*, the Wisconsin Supreme Court considered whether an accidental shooting on a hunting trip in a van was covered by the "use" provision in the insured's automobile liability policy. 63 Wis. 2d 148, 216 NW2d 205 (Wis 1974). In that case, the passenger accidentally shot the driver while unloading the rifle from the vehicle for the purposes of shooting an elk.

The Wisconsin Supreme Court held that the use of a van for carrying hunters and guns when the van was outfitted for hunting "was reasonable and could be expected." The court found coverage "[i]f it can reasonably be expected that this van would be used to go on such a hunting outing, the necessary incidentals for such a hunting trip will be transported in the van, i.e., rifles, ammunition, equipment and supplies." *Id.* The court used the following test to determine whether the "use" of the vehicle was the cause of the bodily injuries:

> In determining whether the negligent act that caused bodily injury arose out of the 'use' of a motor vehicle within the coverage of a motor vehicle liability policy, the court must consider whether it was a natural and reasonable incident or consequence of the use of the vehicle for the purposes shown by the declarations, though not foreseen or expected. Thus, it has been held that one who entered an automobile in order to move it a short distance so as to enable him to park his own automobile was 'using' such when, because of defective brakes, the car rolled into a third car and caused injuries thereto. However, it has been held that an injury need not be the direct and proximate result, in a strict legal sense, of the use of an automobile to come within coverage of a policy indemnifying against liability for damages caused by accident and arising out of the ownership, maintenance or use of the automobile. This principle has been applied in cases where the injuries for which recovery was sought did not result from the movement of the vehicle.

*Id.* at 211 (citation omitted). The court concluded that this accidental shooting fell within the "use" provision of the automobile liability policy. *Id.* The gun's accidental discharge was a natural and reasonable consequence of transporting guns on a hunting trip. *Id.* The New Mexico Supreme Court posed the inquiry as follows: "the proper inquiry in hunting accidents involving automobiles is whether the use made of the vehicle at the time of the accident logically flows from and is consistent with the foreseeable uses of that vehicle." *Sanchez*, 783 P.2d at 467.

In the circuit court's memorandum decision it stated: "Having reviewed [the pertinent cases] it is my conclusion that there is coverage for this type of accident under the Milbank policy because it clearly happened on a hunting expedition." Furthermore, the circuit court concluded: "that the vehicle was not the mere situs of the accident, but that the loading of the rifle into the vehicle, its location in the vehicle and its movement were part of the use of the vehicle in the hunting expedition." We agree with the circuit court's logical conclusion that the vehicle was being used in a hunting expedition....

Clearly, an inherent use of a pickup truck is for transportation, which may involve driving through fields and over country roads. Here, the vehicle was being used to transport deer hunters to the field along with their equipment, clothing and guns. Transporting hunters and guns is a foreseeable and inherent use of a pickup truck in this State. Thus, it logically follows that when a pickup is being used in a hunting expedition where guns are being transported, the accidental discharge of the firearm can be said to be causally connected to the vehicle's use. The vehicle need not be the cause of the discharge only that its use is causally connected.

The circuit court found that the Milbank policy covered the hunting accident because the accident occurred in connection with the use of a vehicle in conjunction with a hunting expedition, and because the vehicle was more than the mere situs of the accident. Based on the undisputed facts and the language of the policy, we affirm.

ZINTER, J. (with KONENKAMP J.) (dissenting).

Was this shooting an "auto accident"? I agree that the "use" of a pickup for hunting is foreseeable, and that the transportation of firearms may be incident to use of a vehicle if the vehicle is actually being used on a hunting expedition. Under the undisputed and stipulated facts, however, this case involved the accidental discharge of a firearm that was merely being repositioned in a pickup that was still parked in the insured's driveway *before* the pickup even left for the hunting expedition. Therefore, under all analogous cases, the shooting was not an "auto accident." [Remainder of dissent omitted.]

## Wilson v. Progressive Northern Insurance Co.

Supreme Court of New Hampshire
151 N.H. 782, 868 A.2d 268 (2005)

**Duggan, J.**

The plaintiff, Stephany Wilson, appeals an order of the Superior Court (Smukler, J.) granting summary judgment to the defendant, Progressive Northern Insurance Company (Progressive). Progressive cross-appeals. We reverse in part and affirm in part.

For summary judgment purposes, the parties do not dispute the following facts. On May 7, 2000, in Falmouth, Massachusetts, the plaintiff and a friend hailed a black, four-door Lincoln taxicab. The plaintiff's dog accompanied them. As the plaintiff and her dog were entering the taxicab, the taxi driver shut the car door on the dog's tail. The dog lunged toward the plaintiff and bit her face.

The taxi driver transported the plaintiff to the Falmouth Hospital, where she received treatment for her injuries. The driver, however, left without providing the plaintiff any identifying information about himself or the taxi company. At the time of the accident, the plaintiff was a named insured under an automobile liability insurance policy issued by Progressive.

Finally, Progressive argues that the plaintiff's injuries did not arise out of the use of the taxicab. We disagree.

As noted above, interpretation of the terms of an insurance policy is a question of law for this court to determine. Under the policy, Progressive is obligated to pay for damages which "aris[e] out of the ownership, maintenance, or use of an uninsured motor vehicle."

In *Walsh v. Amica Mutual Insurance Co.*, we interpreted the phrase "[a]rising out of" an automobile's use to mean "originating from, or growing out of, or flowing from the use." *Walsh v. Amica Mut. Ins. Co.*, 141 N.H. 374, 375, 685 A.2d 472 (1996) (brackets and quotation omitted). We explained that "[t]he term 'use' refers to use of the automobile in its inherent nature as a vehicle." *Id.* Thus, to warrant coverage, "the operator must have been using his vehicle or behaving as a motorist at the time the plaintiff was injured." *Id.* (quotation omitted).

A causal connection must exist between the use of the vehicle and the resulting harm in order to invoke coverage. *Akerley v. Hartford Ins. Group*, 136 N.H. 433, 436, 616 A.2d 511 (1992). Although proximate causation is not required, a tenuous connection with an automobile is not sufficient for coverage. "The fact that the vehicle may have served as the situs of [the] injury does not make such use of the vehicle one which would be sufficient to warrant coverage."

Thus, in *Walsh*, we concluded that where the operator of the vehicle got out of the car and used the windshield to steady his weapon as he shot at the plaintiff, that use was "not a normal use for which a vehicle is intended; consequently, any connection to the plaintiff's injuries is too tenuous to warrant coverage."

Progressive relies on [other precedent] in which the intervenor was bitten by the plaintiff's dog as she loaded brochures into the plaintiff's automobile. We held that the automobile policy at issue did not provide coverage for the plaintiff because the injury did not arise from an "auto accident," which requires, "at the very least, the involvement of an automobile." Although the injury occurred while the intervenor was loading items into the automobile, there was no causal connection between the automobile and the injury. Because the automobile was merely the situs of the injury, we concluded that the dog bite could not be considered an "auto accident."

Here, by contrast, the injury was the result of the taxi driver closing the car door, an act that is part of using the automobile. The fact that the dog, not the door, was the immediate cause of the injury does not negate the allegation that the driver's negligence in closing the door was sufficient to establish more than a tenuous connection between the use of the vehicle and the injury to the plaintiff. Thus, we conclude that the plaintiff's injuries arose out of the use of an uninsured motor vehicle.

Accordingly, we conclude that ... the plaintiff's injuries arose from the use of the taxicab.

# McKenzie v. Auto Club Insurance Association

Supreme Court of Michigan
458 Mich. 214; 580 N.W.2d 424 (1998)

**Clifford W. Taylor, J.**

This case presents the issue whether plaintiff is entitled to personal injury protection (PIP) benefits under the no-fault act, MCL 500.3101 et seq.; MSA 24.13101 *et seq.*, for injuries sustained when he was nonfatally asphyxiated while sleeping in a camper/trailer attached to his pickup truck. We conclude that plaintiff's injury is not covered by the no-fault act because it did not arise out of the use of a motor vehicle "as a motor vehicle" as required by MCL 500.3105(1); MSA 24.13105(1).

Whether an injury arises out of the use of a motor vehicle "as a motor vehicle" turns on whether the injury is closely related to the transportational function of automobiles. We accordingly reverse the judgment of the Court of Appeals and remand for entry of summary disposition in favor of defendant.

The basic facts are undisputed. While on a hunting trip, plaintiff and Hughie McKenzie slept in a camper/trailer attached to the back of plaintiff's pickup truck. The camper/trailer was equipped with a propane-fueled, forced-air heater. Ostensibly, because of either poor ventilation or improper exhaust in the unit itself, carbon monoxide fumes from the heater leaked into the camper/trailer and overcame the two men. Fortunately, they were found the following day and recovered after being hospitalized.

Plaintiff filed the present suit for PIP benefits under his no-fault insurance contract with defendant. Defendant moved for summary disposition, contending that there was no coverage because the camper/trailer was not being used "as a motor vehicle" at the time the injury occurred as required by § 3105. The trial court granted summary disposition for plaintiff, finding *Koole v. Michigan Mut. Ins. Co,* 337 N.W.2d 369 (Mich. Ct. App. 1983), controlling. The Court of Appeals affirmed.

This case turns on whether plaintiff's injury, incurred while sleeping in a parked camper/trailer, arose out of the use of a motor vehicle "as a motor vehicle" as contemplated by § 3105. We are able to arrive at this ultimate question because all agree that this injury was occasioned while a person was occupying the vehicle as required by MCL 500.3106(1)(c); MSA 24.13106(1)(c).

As a matter of English syntax, the phrase "use of a motor vehicle 'as a motor vehicle'" would appear to invite contrasts with situations in which a motor vehicle is not used "as a motor vehicle." This is simply to say that the modifier "as a motor vehicle" assumes the existence of other possible uses and requires distinguishing use "as a motor vehicle" from any other uses.

While it is easily understood from all our experiences that most often a vehicle is used "as a motor vehicle," i.e., to get from one place to another, it is also clear from the phrase used that the Legislature wanted to except those other occasions, rare as they may be, when a motor vehicle is used for other purposes, e.g., as a housing facility of sorts, as an advertising display (such as at a car dealership), as a foundation for construction equipment, as a mobile public library, or perhaps even when a car is on display in a museum.

On those occasions, the use of the motor vehicle would not be "as a motor vehicle," but as a housing facility, advertising display, construction equipment base, public library, or museum display, as it were. It seems then that when we are applying the statute, the phrase "as a motor vehicle" invites us to determine if the vehicle is being used for transportational purposes.

Accordingly, we are convinced that the clear meaning of this part of the no-fault act is that the Legislature intended coverage of injuries resulting from the use of motor vehicles when closely related to their transportational function and only when engaged in that function.

Moreover, requiring that an injury be closely associated with the transportational function of a vehicle before coverage is triggered has support in much of our prior case law....

In *Turner v. Auto Club Ins. Ass'n*, 528 N.W.2d 681 (Mich. 1995), a truck involved in a multiple vehicle accident smashed into a building and started a fire when the truck's gas tank exploded. This Court held that the damage to the building arose out of the use of the truck "as a motor vehicle." This holding was not surprising in that it indicated that no-fault insurance generally covers damage directly resulting from an accident involving moving motor vehicles. This, of course, is consistent with the approach that focuses on transportational function because moving motor vehicles are quite obviously engaged in a transportational function.

In *Putkamer v. Transamerica Ins. Corp. of America*, 563 N.W.2d 683 (Mich. 1997), this Court held that injuries incurred while entering a vehicle with the intent to travel arose out of the use of a motor vehicle as a motor vehicle. Because entering a vehicle in order to travel in it is closely related to the transportational function, *Putkamer* also comports with this approach.

In *Winter v. Automobile Club of Michigan*, 446 N.W.2d 132 (Mich. 1989), this Court denied no-fault insurance coverage when it held that an injury resulting when a cement slab fell from a crane attached to a parked tow truck did not arise out of the use of a motor vehicle "as a motor vehicle." The *Winter* Court's holding turned on the fact that the truck was parked....

In [prior precedent], this Court held that injuries arising from assaults in motor vehicles lacked a sufficient causal connection to the use of a motor vehicle as a motor vehicle to be compensable under the no-fault act. These holdings also support the approach articulated here because assaults occurring in a motor vehicle are not closely related to the transportational function of a motor vehicle.

Additionally, the analysis in *Thornton* [*v. Allstate Ins. Co.*, 425 Mich. 643, 391 N.W.2d 320 (1986),] supports this approach. In *Thornton*, the Court held that injuries sustained by a taxi driver in the course of an armed robbery did not arise out of the use of a motor vehicle as a motor vehicle. It clearly concluded that only injuries arising out of the "functional use of a motor vehicle as a motor vehicle" triggered no-fault coverage. 425 Mich. at 661. It found that the taxi was merely the situs of the robbery. *Thornton*, 425 Mich. at 660.

It held that, while robbery-related injuries were arguably " 'foreseeably identifiable' with the occupational or commercial use of a motor vehicle *as a taxicab*, the relation of the gunshot wound to the functional use of a motor vehicle as a motor vehicle was at most, merely 'but for,' incidental, and fortuitous." *Thornton*, 425 Mich. at 661. It focused on whether the alleged injury was causally related to the "vehicular use," "functional character," or "functional use" of a motor vehicle. *Thornton*, 425 Mich. at 660–661. These terms were intended to distinguish use "as a motor vehicle" from other possible uses of a vehicle. Our approach here, focusing on transportational function, makes the same distinction and provides a more specific definition for these terms.

The dissent relies heavily on *Bialochowski v. Cross Concrete Pumping Co.*, 428 Mich. 219; 407 N.W.2d 355 (1987), which is also inconsistent with the approach posited here. In *Bialochowski*, this Court concluded that an injury incurred while a cement truck was unloading its product arose out of the use of a motor vehicle as a motor vehicle. The Court stated at 228:

> Motor vehicles are designed and used for many different purposes. The truck involved in this case is a cement truck capable of pouring cement at elevated levels. Certainly one of the intended uses of this motor vehicle (a motor vehicle under the no-fault act) is to pump cement. The accident occurred while this vehicle was being used for its intended purpose. We hold that the phrase "use of a motor vehicle as a motor vehicle" includes this use.

We find this holding utterly antithetical to the language of § 3105. As discussed above § 3105's requirement that injuries arise out of the use of a motor vehicle "as a motor vehicle" clearly distinguishes use "as a motor vehicle" from other possible uses. *Bialochowski* eviscerates this distinction by holding that the use of the vehicle at issue to pump cement constitutes use "as a motor vehicle." Obviously, motor vehicles are designed and used for various purposes as the *Bialochowski* Court noted. In fact, only in the context of various possible uses would a limitation to use "as a motor vehicle" be necessary. Where the Legislature explicitly limited coverage under § 3105 to injuries arising out of a particular use of motor vehicles—use "as a motor vehicle"—a decision finding coverage for injuries arising out of any other use, e.g., to pump cement, is contrary to the language of the statute. Accordingly, we are convinced that *Bialochowski* was wrongly decided.

Accordingly, we hold that whether an injury arises out of the use of a motor vehicle "as a motor vehicle" under § 3105 turns on whether the injury is closely related to the transportational function of motor vehicles.

If we apply this test here, it is clear that the requisite nexus between the injury and the transportational function of the motor vehicle is lacking. At the time the injury occurred, the parked camper/trailer was being used as sleeping accommodations. This use is too far removed from the transportational function to constitute use of the camper/trailer "as a motor vehicle" at the time of the injury. Thus, we conclude that no coverage is triggered under the no-fault act in this instance.

[Dissenting opinion omitted.]

# Blish v. Atlanta Casualty Co.

Supreme Court of Florida
736 So. 2d 1151 (1999)

**Shaw, J.**

We have for review *Atlanta Casualty Co. v. Blish*, 707 So. 2d 1178 (Fla. 5th DCA 1998), based on conflict with *Hernandez v. Protective Casualty Insurance Co.*, 473 So. 2d 1241 (Fla. 1985), and *Government Employees Insurance Co. v. Novak*, 453 So. 2d 1116 (Fla. 1984). We have jurisdiction. Art. V § 3(b)(3), Fla. Const. We quash *Blish*.

Karl Blish left work on January 6, 1995, drove a coworker home, spent a few minutes at the coworker's house, and then headed home himself. Blish's pickup truck had a blowout on U.S. 1 in Brevard County and he pulled over to change the tire. He jacked up the truck and was loosening the lug nuts when he was attacked from behind by several assailants. The men choked and beat him (he testified that he "might have went unconscious") and stole between eighty and a hundred dollars from his pocket.

After the attack, Blish recovered his glasses, did his best to finish changing the tire, and drove home ("I just barely got the tire on and I drove home."). He did not go to the hospital or call police because he did not think that he had been hurt badly enough ("I was just going to write it off as a loss, I guess."). A week later, he experienced severe abdominal pain, was rushed to the hospital in an ambulance, and was diagnosed as suffering from a ruptured spleen, which doctors removed.

Blish filed a claim for benefits under the PIP portion of his auto insurance policy with Atlanta Casualty Company ("Atlanta"). Atlanta denied the claim, and Blish filed suit. The county court granted summary judgment in favor of Atlanta, and the circuit court sitting in its appellate capacity reversed, ruling that Blish had established a sufficient nexus between his use of the truck and his injuries. The district court reversed, concluding that the attackers had made no effort to possess or use Blish's truck:

> In our case, there is nothing in the record to suggest that the assailant wanted anything other than the victim's money. No effort was made to possess or use the automobile. The fact that the victim was changing his tire when he was robbed does not make the robbery "arise from the maintenance or use" of his vehicle.

*Blish*, 707 So. 2d at 1179. This Court granted review based on conflict with *Hernandez v. Protective Casualty Insurance Co.*, 473 So. 2d 1241 (Fla. 1985) (finding PIP coverage where the insured was stopped by police for a traffic infraction and was injured during the ensuing arrest), and *Government Employees Insurance Co. v. Novak,* 453 So. 2d 1116 (Fla. 1984) (finding PIP coverage where the insured was shot in the face by a stranger and pulled from her car, which the stranger then stole).

Blish claims that the district court erred in reasoning that recovery must be denied because the assailants made no attempt to "possess or use" the vehicle. He contends that under the facts of this case there was a sufficient connection between the maintenance and use of the vehicle and the resulting injury to justify PIP coverage. We agree.

The controlling statute, section 627.736, Florida Statutes (1995), requires that motor vehicle insurance policies issued in Florida provide personal injury protection (PIP) benefits for bodily injury "arising out of the ownership, maintenance, or use of a motor vehicle":

> 627.736 Required personal injury protection benefits....
>
> (1) REQUIRED BENEFITS.—Every insurance policy complying with the security requirements of s. 627.733 shall provide personal injury protection to the named insured ... to a limit of $10,000 for loss sustained by any such person as a result of bodily injury, sickness, disease, or death *arising out of the ownership, maintenance, or use of a motor vehicle.*...

§ 627.736, Fla. Stat. (1995) (emphasis added).

This Court in *Government Employees Insurance Co. v. Novak*, 453 So. 2d 1116 (Fla. 1984), explained that the phrase "arising out of" in the above statute means that there must be "some nexus" between the motor vehicle and the injury:

> Construction of the clause "arising out of the use of a motor vehicle" is an [easy] matter. It is well settled that "arising out of" does not mean "proximately caused by," but has a much broader meaning. *All that is required is some nexus between the motor vehicle and the injury.*

*Novak*, 453 So. 2d at 1119 (emphasis added). The Court went on to explain that the phrase "some nexus" should be given a liberal construction in order to effectuate legislative intent to extend coverage broadly:

> The clause, "arising out of the use of a motor vehicle," is framed in such general, comprehensive terms in order to express the [legislative] intent to effect broad coverage. Such terms should be construed liberally because their function is to extend coverage broadly.

The Court subsequently circumscribed the parameters of the "some nexus" standard in *Hernandez v. Protective Casualty Insurance Co.*, 473 So. 2d 1241 (Fla. 1985), by pointing out that PIP coverage is not applicable where the motor vehicle, through pure happenstance, is the situs of an unrelated injury-causing event:

> It is not enough that an automobile be the physical situs of an injury or that the injury occur incidentally to the use of an automobile, but that there must be a causal connection or relation between the two for liability to exist.

Both this Court and the district courts have applied the above rules to deny coverage where the motor vehicle was the mere situs of an unrelated injury-causing event, and to find coverage where there was "some nexus," i.e., some "causal connection or relation," between the vehicle and the injury. The results under these standards, however, have not been consistent. In an effort to resolve these inconsistencies, we now set forth the following guidelines.

First, legislative intent—as always—is the polestar that guides an inquiry under section 627.736(1). Thus, as noted above, the language of the statute must be liberally construed in order to effect the legislative purpose of providing broad PIP coverage for Florida motorists. Novak. Second, a key issue in deciding coverage is whether the type of injury sustained by the insured was reasonably in the minds of the contracting parties. Accordingly, when construing the phrase "arising out of" noted above, courts should ask: Is the injury a reasonably foreseeable consequence of the use (or the ownership, or the maintenance) of the vehicle?

In the present case, Blish's injuries were an unfortunate but eminently foreseeable consequence of the use and maintenance of the pickup truck: Blish was using the truck for routine transportation purposes after dark when the truck sustained a mechanical failure, i.e., a blowout; he responded in a normal and foreseeable fashion, i.e., he attempted to change the tire on site with the tools and spare tire he carried in the vehicle for that purpose; he was in the act of repairing the vehicle, i.e., he was turning the lug nuts on the faulty tire, when he was injured.

Under these circumstances, the actual source of the injury-causing blow is not dispositive—whether it came from a negligent driver in a passing vehicle or a violent group of passing thugs is not decisive. It was the use and maintenance of the truck that left Blish stranded and exposed to random acts of negligence and violence, and he was in the very act of performing emergency maintenance on the vehicle when he was injured.

Acts of violence are an ageless and foreseeable hazard associated with the use of a vehicle—for once a person sets out in a vehicle, he or she is vulnerable. The highwaymen and desperados of bygone times preyed on the wayfarer, and these villains are with us still. Each Floridian today, when he or she gets behind the wheel, faces a variety of dangers: a car-jacking at a stoplight, or a strong-arm robbery at a deliberately staged rear-end collision, or a road rage assault in rush hour traffic, or even a random shooting by an anonymous sniper from an overpass. The danger is particularly acute when the motorist is stranded as the result of a disabled vehicle.

The scenario in the present case is every motorist's nightmare. Losses resulting from a violent encounter with this ageless road hazard—i.e., the highwayman or opportunistic thug—might reasonably be said to be very much in the contemplation of Florida consumers when they are contracting to purchase auto insurance. The motivation of the assailant—whether it be to "possess or use" the vehicle, or to steal the victim's wallet or purse, or simply to harm the victim—is a nonissue to the consumer. We note that insurance companies were placed on notice at the time of enactment of section 627.736(1)—and certainly by the time that Novak and Hernandez were decided—that the statute contemplates broad coverage.

Based on the foregoing, we hold that Blish's injuries were a reasonably foreseeable consequence of his use and maintenance of the pickup truck. The injuries thus "arise out of the ownership, maintenance, or use of a motor vehicle" and are covered under the PIP portion of his auto insurance policy. We quash *Blish*.

## Notes and Questions

1. Are the excerpted cases reconcilable? Or do some courts just have a different conceptual approach to answering this question? Identify the different orientations, if you think that is the source of the difference in these cases rather than factual distinctions. Does the formalist-functionalist distinction outlined in Chapter 2 explain these differences? Or is there something else at work that divides courts on these questions?

2. Does it matter whether the insurance in question is third-party liability insurance or first party uninsured, underinsured, or no-fault benefits? Should it matter? Should it matter if provisions in the coverage granting instrument are legislatively mandated, down to the language in the instrument? *See* Erik S. Knutsen, *Auto Insurance as Social Contract: Solving Automobile Insurance Coverage Disputes Through a Public Regulatory Framework*, 48 ALBERTA L. REV. 715 (2011).

3. For still more cases on this issue, see, e.g., *Lancer Ins. Co. v. Garcia Holiday Tours*, 345 S.W.3d 50 (Tex. 2011) (tour bus driver gave tuberculosis to high school band who rode the bus; no commercial automobile liability coverage because disease did not result from vehicle's use but instead from use of unhealthy driver, so bus not a substantial factor in producing passengers' injuries); *Sunshine State Ins. Co. v. Jones*, 77 So. 3d 254 (Fla. Dist. Ct. App. 4th Dist. 2012) (no coverage for "use" of vehicle when boy grabbed steering wheel to annoy girlfriend); *Keppler v. American Family Mut. Ins. Co.*, 588 N.W.2d 105 (Iowa 1999) (liability from dog biting child does not "arise from use" of automobile merely because dog was in van at time it bit child; as in many other auto coverage cases, the court paid some attention not only to the overall context of the incident but also to specific facts as to whether the car engine was running or the keys were in the ignition); *State Farm Mut. Auto. Ins. Co. v. DeHaan*, 900 A.2d 208 (Md. 2006) (injury to policyholder when shot by intruder stealing car not injury arising from "use" of motor vehicle; instrumentality of injury was handgun and not automobile used in normal or intended manner); *Peagler v. USAA Ins. Co.*, 368 S.C. 153, 628 S.E.2d 475 (2006) (no auto insurance coverage where, while putting on seatbelt, wife killed by discharge of firearm being removed from pickup truck cab by husband; insufficient causal connection between truck and accidental shooting); *Estate of Nord v. Motorists Mut. Ins. Co.*, 105 Ohio St. 3d 366, 826 N.E.2d 826 (2005) (injury incurring when paramedic dropped syringe did not arise out of use of ambulance as a vehicle) (but has the Court ever tried to use a syringe at 70 m.p.h.? Curiously, the *Nord* opinion does not describe the incident in any detail; the reader is not even told if the ambulance was in motion at the time); *Tex. Farm Bureau Mut. Ins. Co. v. Sturrock*, 146 S.W.3d 123 (Tex. 2004) (when foot became entangled with truck door while exiting vehicle, injury was covered under auto policy personal injury protection benefits).

What would the Florida Supreme Court that decided *Blish* think of the *DeHaan* and *Peagler* analyses and results? If nothing else, case reports continue to teem with "ownership, maintenance or use of an automobile" cases. Why is that? Are courts too zealous in guarding the boundary between auto incidents and efforts to obtain auto insurance for non-auto losses? Or are courts not fully considering the impact on claimants who may not have other forms of compensation? Extensive life insurance and disability insurance is a middle class or upper middle class type of asset—and many injured persons are lower on the economic rung and lack such coverage.

4. Automobile liability insurance policies generally cover accidents or injuries "arising out of ownership, maintenance, or use" of the insured vehicle. But what does the term "use" of the insured vehicle actually mean? The courts do not have a uniform answer to this question, as the above cases demonstrate.

All courts appear to agree that a causal connection or causal nexus must exist between the injury or loss on the one hand, and the ownership, maintenance, or use of the automobile on the other hand, in order to comply with the insurance policy coverage provision for loss "arising out of the ownership, maintenance or use" of the automobile.

Where the courts differ—and differ widely—is the degree of the causal connection that is required between the loss and the "use" of the automobile. Put another way, the courts have differed regarding whether a substantial causal nexus is required to find coverage under the insurance policy, or if only a minimal or "sufficient" causal nexus is necessary.

5. An example of a thornier variant on the use of an automobile coverage disputes is *Pemco Ins. Co. v. Schlea*, 63 Wis. App. 107, 817 P.2d 878 (1991), where the court held that a claim arising out of policyholder's abduction and sexual abuse of a woman did not arise from an automobile "accident" so as to trigger no-fault benefits. According to the majority:

> The policy defines "accident" as "an unexpected and unintended occurrence" resulting from ownership, maintenance, or use of a motor vehicle or trailer.

> The fact that the vehicle is the "mere 'situs'" of an accident does not bring the occurrence within the coverage of the policy.... The injury must result from the type of motoring risk that the parties intended to cover by the automobile policy....

> Here, Evans used the vehicle to transport Schlea. However, there is not a sufficient causal connection between this use and Schlea's injuries to invoke coverage because her injuries did not result from the natural and reasonable use of the vehicle. Kidnapping, assault, and rape are not motoring risks against which the parties intended to insure. Further, the vehicle did not contribute toward her assault and rape; it was the mere "situs" of Evans' violent acts.

The dissenting judge took a different view:

> While using a vehicle as a means of transporting a victim and as a place to commit a rape is not either a "reasonable" or "traditional" use of an automobile, it is, in my judgment, a use nonetheless.
>
> In order for an accident to result from the use of a vehicle, this court need only find that there is a causal connection between the use of a vehicle and the resulting accident. Such a connection exists if the vehicle contributed in any way to produce the injury. *Transamerica Ins. Group v. United Pac. Ins. Co.*, 92 Wn.2d 21, 593 P.2d 156 (1979).
>
> If Evans had been in an accident in the same car while he was transporting Schlea to the scene of the rape, would the majority say that this was not an occurrence resulting from the use of a motor vehicle? I think not. To me, there is little difference between that scenario and the present where the vehicle was used to perpetrate these crimes which resulted in injury to Schlea. The simple fact is that Schlea was injured as a result of Evans' use of the automobile to kidnap and rape her.

Which was the better reasoned approach in the *Schlea* case? The majority opinion or the dissenting opinion? Based upon what underlying legal justification and public policy rationale? *See, e.g., Concord Gen. Mut. Ins. Co. v. Doe*, 8 A.3d 154 (N.H. 2010), a case which upheld the *Wilson* case excerpted above (about the dog in the taxicab), in determining whether or not uninsured motorist coverage was available in the context of a sexual assault in a vehicle.

6. Courts applying a more formalistic approach to automobile insurance policy disputes tend to require a substantial causal connection between the injury and the "use" of the automobile, largely based upon traditional principles of insurance law contract interpretation. *See, e.g., State Farm Mut. Auto. Ins. Co. v. Smith*, 691 P.2d 1289 (Idaho 1984) (an automobile insurance policy provision requiring an injury to "arise out of the use" of the automobile connotes a substantial causal nexus between the injury and use, and this causal nexus must be more than incidental and fortuitous).

However, those courts applying a more functional approach to automobile insurance policies in order to validate the reasonable expectations of the policyholder generally state that a direct causal connection is not required in the legal sense, and only a minimal or "sufficient" causal nexus is necessary. *See, e.g., Allstate Ins. Co. v. Gillespie*, 455 So. 2d 617 (Fla. Dist. Ct. App. 1984) (the causal nexus between the loss and the "use" of the automobile does not need to be direct or substantial, since only a minimal causal connection is required). *See generally* Peter Nash Swisher, *Judicial Rationales in Insurance Law: Dusting Off the Formal for the Function*, 52 Ohio St. L.J. 1037, 1066–70 (1991).

7. *Loading and Unloading a Vehicle.* Automobile insurance policies often contain a clause dealing with bodily injury or property damage "arising out of the loading or unloading" of the vehicle. Other courts have interpreted "loading and unloading" a vehicle as a "use" of the vehicle within the policy. But the courts split on whether the materials "loaded or unloaded" should be interpreted under a "*coming to rest*" or a "*completed operations*" doctrine.

For example, assume that cement is unloaded from a policyholder's cement truck on a construction site into a crane bucket. This crane bucket of cement is then moved to a second floor office building construction site, but before it is off-loaded, the crane operator comes in contact with a high tension electrical wire, and is electrocuted. Coverage under the policyholder's auto policy or not? *Compare Estes Co. of Bettendorf v. Employers Mut. Casualty Co.*, 402 N.E.2d 613 (Ill. 1980), *with Drewelow v. Iowa Nat'l Mut. Ins. Co.*, 596 F.2d 334 (8th Cir. 1979) (applying Minnesota law).

8. *Entering or Alighting from a Vehicle.* A person has not ceased "using" or "occupying" a vehicle "until they have severed their connection with it—*i.e.*, when they are on their own without any reference to it." *See, e.g., Miller v. Loman*, 518 N.E.2d 486 (Ind. Ct. App. 1987).

But what does this mean? Some courts, applying a liberal interpretation regarding this scope of coverage, hold that a person is still "alighting" from a vehicle until that person has reached a "zone of safety." *See, e.g., State Farm Mut. Auto. Ins. Co. v. Holmes*, 333 S.E.2d 917 (Ga. Ct. App. 1985); *Joins v. Bonner*, 504 N.E.2d 61 (Ohio 1986). Other courts, however, adopt a more restrictive definition of "getting out of" or "alighting" from a vehicle including: (1) the distance between the accident and the automobile; (2) the time separating the accident and the exit from the vehicle; (3) the individual's opportunity to reach a "zone of safety"; and (4) the individual's intentions regarding the automobile. *Miller v. Loman, supra.*

9. *Query*: In determining whether or not injuries "arise out of the ownership, maintenance, or use" of an insured vehicle, should the courts look only for a "minimal" or "sufficient" causal nexus between the loss and the "use" of the vehicle? Or must a "substantial" causal nexus be required in order for such insurance coverage to exist? Based upon what underlying legal principles or public policy rationales? *See generally* Swisher, *Dusting Off the Formal for the Functional, supra* note 6, at 1066–70 (1991); Peter Nash Swisher, *Insurance Causation Issues: The Legacy of Bird v. St. Paul Fire & Marine Ins. Co.*, 2 Nev. L.J. 351, 371–376 (2002); Erik S. Knutsen, *Confusion About Causation in Insurance: Solutions for Catastrophic Losses*, 61 Ala. L. Rev. 957 (2010); Erik S. Knutsen, *Auto Insurance as Social Contract: Solving Automobile Insurance Coverage Disputes Through a Public Regulatory Framework*, 48 Alberta L. Rev. 715 (2011).

## PROBLEM THREE

How would you, as a judge, resolve the following cases? Would you find coverage based upon loss "arising out of the ownership, maintenance, or use" of the automobile, or not? Explain your reasoning.

(a) On the way to his car, an insured was injured when he slipped and fell in an icy automobile parking lot.

(b) While leaving her house, the insured was shot by an assailant in her driveway after she refused his request to give him a ride.

(c) The insured automobile driver collided with another car. The driver of the other car became enraged, and came after the insured with a knife. The insured rolled up his window to avoid the other driver's attack, but the other driver attempted to stab the insured through the car's open sunroof. The insured thereupon obtained a handgun from his glove compartment and shot the other driver.

• Would it have made any difference if the insured was the initial aggressor?

• Why or why not?

(d) The injured plaintiff claimed that he was in the process of towing the insured's car when he was hit by an uninsured motorist, and plaintiff argues that his injuries therefore arose out of the "use" of the insured's car.

• Is he entitled to coverage under the policy?

(e) Three people were sitting in the backseat of a station wagon parked at a bonfire party. One of the people, aided by the other two, threw an M-80 explosive firework device out of the rear of the station wagon. The firework landed in a glass of beer held by a woman. The ensuing explosion caused her substantial injuries.

• Did her injuries "arise out of the use" of the insured automobile or not?

(f) Assume that some store employees negligently loaded wood paneling in plaintiff's station wagon, and during the plaintiff's drive home from the store, the paneling shifted, fell upon the plaintiff, and caused her serious injuries.

• Is it relevant, or irrelevant, that the harm was sustained at a different place and time than the initial loading?

# [E] Loss Distribution Disputes Implicating Auto Insurance

While loss "arising out of the ownership, maintenance, or use" of a vehicle generally defines the terms of coverage in automobile insurance policies, it generally is *excluded* from coverage in most homeowners and other non-vehicular insurance policies. Tom

Baker calls these phrases "market segmentation clauses"—phrases which act as a coverage clause in one policy and an exclusion clause in another. TOM BAKER, INSURANCE LAW AND POLICY 455 (2d ed. 2008).

This can create a real contest among two or more insurers who may be called upon to respond to the same loss. For example, a loss distribution dispute may occur if an accident involving a car plus some other tortious behavior potentially triggers both an automobile policy (which covers for losses "arising from ownership, maintenance or use" of a vehicle) and a homeowners policy (which covers for all legal liability but excludes losses "arising from ownership, maintenance or use" of a vehicle). *See* Knutsen, *Confusion About Causation in Insurance: Solutions for Catastrophic Losses*, 61 ALA. L. REV. 957 (2010).

## Penn National Insurance Co. v. Costa

Supreme Court of New Jersey
198 N.J. 229, 966 A.2d 1028 (2009)

**Rivera-Soto, J.**

This appeal presents a conflict in coverage between dueling insurance carriers. A person was injured when he slipped and fell on an icy driveway; his head struck an automobile jack then being used to change a flat tire on a pickup truck. The injured person was not involved with the tire repair, and no claim was made that the repairs were being carried out negligently. He sued for his injuries and the homeowners insurance carrier settled that claim. The homeowners insurance carrier then asserted that the accident should have been covered by the automobile insurance carrier that covered the pickup truck.

The trial court held that the accident was not covered by the automobile insurance policy, and, therefore, the homeowners insurance policy was required to respond. The Appellate Division, however, reversed. It concluded that the claim was within the coverage afforded by the automobile insurance policy.

We do not agree. Coverage under an automobile insurance policy is afforded to protect "against loss resulting from liability imposed by law for bodily injury, death and property damage sustained by any person arising out of the ownership, maintenance, operation or use of a motor vehicle [.]" N.J.S.A. 39:6B-1(a). Whether any such liability is compensable under an automobile insurance policy—that is, whether the injury arises out of one of the qualifying criteria of "the ownership, maintenance, operation or use of a motor vehicle"—depends on whether there was a substantial nexus between one or more of the qualifying criteria and the injuries sustained.

Because there was no substantial nexus between the injuries suffered and "the ownership, maintenance, operation or use of a motor vehicle[,]" we reverse the judgment of the Appellate Division holding the automobile insurance carrier liable for the injured person's losses, and we reinstate the judgment of the trial court assessing such liability on the homeowners insurance carrier.

As developed in the context of cross-motions for summary judgment, the relevant facts are as follows. Frank Costa owned and operated a business that repaired large trucks, and his home was located adjacent to his business. Ernest Arians was employed by Costa as a mechanic.

On January 20, 2004, as Arians was leaving Costa's business for his lunch break, he walked past Costa's home and saw Costa changing a tire on a pickup truck parked in his home's driveway. Arians walked up the driveway, approached Costa and offered to help replace the flat tire. Costa waved off that offer, telling Arians, "No, I'll do it. I'll take care of it, go to lunch." As Arians headed off to lunch, he slipped on some ice or snow remaining on the driveway, fell, and struck his head on the bumper jack Costa was using to lift the pickup truck and replace the flat tire. Arians suffered severe injuries as a result of the blow.

Arians sued Costa to recover for the injuries Arians suffered. Penn National Insurance Company (Penn National), Arians's personal automobile insurance carrier, also filed an action in subrogation against Costa, his business and his homeowners insurance carrier, Farmers Insurance Company of Flemington (Farmers).

In its suit, Penn National sought to recover what it had paid in personal injury protection benefits to Arians. [*See N.J.S.A. 39:6A-4* (statutorily requiring coverage for "personal injury protection benefits for the payment of benefits ... to the named insured and members of his family residing in his household who sustain bodily injury as a result of an accident while occupying, entering into, alighting from or using an automobile, or as a pedestrian, caused by an automobile or by an object propelled by or from an automobile").]

Both actions were consolidated. Farmers then answered and filed a third-party complaint, naming Arians and Gulf Insurance Company (Gulf), Costa's automobile insurance carrier, as third-party defendants. Farmers asserted that Arians's injuries arose out of the maintenance of Costa's car and, for that reason, Gulf was liable for Arians's injuries. Farmers claimed that, according to the explicit terms of its homeowners insurance policy covering Costa's home and driveway, it specifically "do[es] not cover bodily injury or property damage arising out of ... [t]he maintenance, operation, ownership or use (including loading or unloading) of any ... motor vehicles ... owned or operated by, or rented or loaned to any insured."

Not surprisingly, Gulf, Costa's automobile insurance carrier, took the opposite view. It claimed that its coverage was limited to what is required by law—insurance coverage to protect "against loss resulting from ... bodily injury ... sustained by any person *arising out of* the ... maintenance, operation or use of a motor vehicle[,]" N.J.S.A. 39:6B-1(a) (emphasis supplied)—and that Arians's injuries did not arise out of the maintenance being performed on Costa's pickup truck.

Farmers and Gulf filed cross-motions for summary judgment, each claiming that the other was liable for Arians's injuries. [In the interim, Farmers had settled and paid Arians's claim against Costa in exchange for $400,000. As a result, the practical issue joined in this appeal is which insurance carrier is to bear the cost of that settlement: either Farmers or Gulf. The injured party—Arians—already has been made whole by insurance and no longer retains a stake in the outcome.] Ruling that Arians's injuries properly were subject to coverage under Costa's homeowners insurance policy and not under Costa's automobile insurance policy, the trial court relied on *Wakefern Food Corp. v. General Accident Group*, quoting that:

> When an accident, such as the one here presented, is occasioned by negligent maintenance of the premises and the only connection to that event is the fact that the motor vehicle and its operator are present because a delivery or pick-up is to be made, no realistic social or public policy is served by straining to shift coverage. [188 N.J. Super. 77, 87, 455 A.2d 1160 (App.Div.1983).]

The trial court explained that "that's exactly the principle that should be applied here." It noted that "[w]e should not be shifting the coverage to the automobile, the motor vehicle coverage, but rather it is the negligen[t] accumulation, purportedly, of the ice and snow on the property that is the nexus of the case." Concluding that Arians's injuries "should be covered by the homeowner's policy[,]" the trial court denied Farmers' motion for summary judgment, and granted Gulf's cross-motion for summary judgment.

Farmers appealed, and the Appellate Division reversed.... The panel referenced the substantial nexus test applied in *American Home Assurance Co. v. Hartford Insurance Co.*, 190 N.J. Super. 477, 464 *A.* 2d 1128 (App.Div.1983), in respect of coverage for injuries caused in the "maintenance ... of a motor vehicle[,]" and determined that "Arians'[s] injuries were directly connected with the maintenance of Costa's pickup[,]" ... It therefore concluded that "Arians' [s] injuries were not solely related to the existence of ice and snow but directly connected with the maintenance of the Ford pickup, thus coming within the exclusion in the homeowner's policy, and meeting the required substantial nexus" with the automobile insurance policy. *Ibid.*

We granted Gulf's petition for certification to determine the scope of automobile liability insurance coverage in respect of "loss[es] resulting from ... bodily injury, death and property damage ... arising out of the ... maintenance, operation or use of a motor vehicle[.]" N.J.S.A. 39:6B-1(a). For the reasons that follow, we reverse the judgment of the Appellate Division and reinstate the judgment of the Law Division.

Gulf, the automobile insurance carrier, asserts that "the mere fact that the plaintiff in a premises liability lawsuit struck his head on a car jack as he fell forward [does not] implicate the automobile liability coverage instead of the homeowners coverage[.]" It further claims that it is unfair, in a premises liability case, to shift responsibility to an automobile insurance carrier "simply because the victim struck something related to the repair of an automobile while he was falling due to the dangerous conditions on the ground[.]"

In response, Farmers, the homeowners insurance carrier, asserts that Arians's accident arose from the maintenance of a motor vehicle and, therefore, it is proper to require that the automobile insurance carrier respond in damages. Farmers urges that the reasoning and conclusions of the Appellate Division were correct and should be affirmed.

The coverage portions of the homeowners insurance policy and the automobile insurance policy at issue are mutually exclusive. By the terms of Section IID.1.A of the Farmers homeowners insurance policy, coverage for "bodily injury ... arising out of ... [t]he maintenance ... of any ... motor vehicles ... owned or operated by, or rented or loaned to any insured" is specifically excluded.

On the other hand, by statute and in almost identical terms, Gulf's automobile insurance policy specifically covers that which is specifically excluded under the homeowners insurance policy, that is, any "loss resulting from ... bodily injury ... sustained by any person arising out of the ... maintenance ... of a motor vehicle[.]" N.J.S.A. 39:6B-1(a).

Thus, this appeal presents a straightforward question: did Arians's injuries "arise out of" the maintenance of Costa's pickup truck? If the answer to that inquiry is "yes," then Costa's automobile insurance policy as issued by Gulf is obliged to respond; if the answer to that inquiry is "no," then it falls to Farmers, as Costa's homeowners insurance carrier, to assume liability. Our task, then, is to define when and in what circumstances an injury "arises out of" the maintenance of an automobile, a task to which we now turn.

As the Appellate Division correctly noted, several cases have been decided in the parallel context of injuries that "arise out of" the *use* of an automobile. *See Penn Nat'l Ins. Co., supra,* 400 N.J. Super. at 151, 946 A.2d 592 (collecting cases). Those cases reject the proposition that "the words 'arising out of the use' require or justify the interpretation that before coverage exists it must appear that the injury is a direct and proximate result, in a strict legal sense, of the use of the automobile." *Westchester Fire Ins. Co. v. Continental Ins. Cos.,* 126 N.J. Super. 29, 37, 312 A.2d 664 (App.Div.1973), *aff'd o.b.,* 65 N.J. 152, 319 A.2d 732 (1974). Instead, the cases generally hold that

> the phrase "arising out of" must be interpreted in a broad and comprehensive sense to mean "originating from" or "growing out of" the use of the automobile. So interpreted, there need be shown only a substantial nexus between the injury and the use of the vehicle in order for the obligation to provide coverage to arise. The inquiry should be whether the negligent act which caused the injury, although not foreseen or expected, was in the contemplation of the parties to the insurance contract a natural and reasonable incident or consequence of the use of the automobile, and thus a risk against which they might reasonably expect those insured under the policy would be protected. Whether the requisite connection or degree of relationship exists depends upon the circumstances of the particular case. [*Id.* at 38, 312 A.2d 664 (citation omitted).]

The almost universal utility of the substantial nexus test in the area of insurance coverage questions is evident from the breadth of contexts to which it has been applied....

That said, precious few cases have dealt with what the Appellate Division defined as "the more limited criteria of maintenance of a motor vehicle [.]" *Penn Nat'l Ins. Co., supra*, 400 N.J. Super. at 152, 946 A.2d 592. The Appellate Division identified but one case that squarely addressed whether certain injuries arose out of the maintenance of a motor vehicle. In that case, *American Home Assurance Co. v. Hartford Insurance Co.*, 190 N.J. Super. 477, 464 A.2d 1128 (App.Div.1983), the driver of a car took it to a service station to replace a tire. The service station operator placed the car on a hydraulic lift in order to replace the tire.

As he was doing so, the driver went to the rear of the car, opened the trunk, and was observed "'reaching in, sort of bending over' the trunk." *Id.* at 480, 464 A.2d 1128. The service station operator then raised the lift, unaware that, in the interim, the driver had climbed into the trunk of the car. After the car was raised to a height of some "six or seven feet above the floor of the service bay[,]" and as the service station operator was completing the tire replacement, he "heard a 'sort of thud' and then a 'groan.'" *Id.* at 481, 464 A.2d 1128. The car driver, apparently unaware that the car had been raised on the lift, stepped out of the trunk thinking it was still on the ground and was injured in the fall.

As that case unfolded, the question became which insurance carrier was required to respond to the driver's claim for damages: the service station's liability policy or the automobile policy covering the car. The court defined the core issue as "whether [the car driver]'s injury arose out of the maintenance or use of the automobile." As a threshold matter, it found that the activity involving the car at the time of the driver's injuries "more precisely constitutes 'maintenance' of the automobile." *Ibid.* It then reasoned that "the accident arose out of the maintenance of the automobile [and that] the maintenance of the automobile did not have to be the direct and effective cause of the accident." It explained that "[c]overage is afforded if there is a substantial nexus between the injury and the maintenance of the automobile." *Ibid.* It therefore concluded that "it is manifest that there was a substantial nexus between [the service station operator's negligent] maintenance of the automobile and [the driver]'s injury, thereby affording [the service station operator] coverage for [the driver]'s injury under the comprehensive automobile liability … policies."

The Appellate Division endorsed that rationale. We do so also. In the aggregate, *Westchester Fire Insurance Co.*, *Wakefern*, and *American Home Assurance Co.* demonstrate that, in order to trigger coverage under the liability portion of an automobile insurance policy, the injuries claimed must arise out of the performance of one of the qualifying criteria—either the "ownership, maintenance, operation or use of a motor vehicle [,]" N.J.S.A. 39:6B-1(a).

Those cases also explain that, at least in respect of the latter three criteria of "maintenance, operation or use of a motor vehicle[,]" automobile insurance coverage only comes into play if the injuries were caused by a negligent act and that negligent act, "although not foreseen or expected, was in the contemplation of the parties to the insurance contract a natural and reasonable incident or consequence of the use of the automobile, and thus a risk against which they might reasonably expect those insured under the policy would be protected." *Westchester Fire Ins. Co., supra*, 126 N.J. Super. at 38, 312 A.2d 664.

Synthesized into a more streamlined proposition, we explicitly hold that, in order to determine whether an injury arises out of the maintenance, operation or use of a motor vehicle thereby triggering automobile insurance coverage, there must be a substantial nexus between the injury suffered and the asserted negligent maintenance, operation or use of the motor vehicle. We address, then, the application of that test to the circumstances presented in this case.

Distinguishing *Wakefern, supra*, the Appellate Division concluded that "Arians'[s] injuries were directly connected with the maintenance of Costa's pickup." *Id.* at 153, 946 A.2d 592. It asserted that "[i]t is undisputed that Farmers insured Costa, Costa was maintaining the vehicle at the time of the accident, and Arians approached with the intention to help Costa." *Ibid.* It also noted that "Arians'[s] injuries were the direct consequence of his head hitting the protruding post of the bumper jack, which was being used for the vehicle's maintenance." *Ibid.* For that reason, the panel concluded that "Arians'[s] injuries were not solely related to the existence of ice and snow but directly connected with the maintenance of the Ford pickup, thus coming within the exclusion in the homeowner[ ]s policy, and meeting the required substantial nexus." *Ibid.*

We cannot agree. Arians's injuries must bear a substantial, and not an incidental, nexus to the negligent maintenance of Costa's pickup truck. In that respect, there has been no allegation whatsoever that Costa in any way was negligent in the manner in which he repaired the flat tire—that is, how he performed the maintenance activities—on his pickup truck. That the negligence that caused Arians's injuries was Costa's failure to keep his driveway clear of snow and ice is beyond dispute; the fact that, in the act of falling, Arians's head struck a jack being used to repair a flat tire is an unfortunate but entirely incidental happenstance to the maintenance activity Costa was performing on his truck.

Thus, unlike the car driver in *American Home Assurance Co., supra*, whose injuries bore a substantial nexus to the negligently performed maintenance activity of lifting the car while the driver was in the area of the car trunk, there is no rational linkage between the negligent failure to clear the driveway of snow and ice and the entirely non-negligent maintenance activity in which Costa was engaged. Again, this must be so because a substantial nexus exists only when "the negligent act which caused the injury, although not foreseen or expected, was in the contemplation of the parties to the insurance contract a natural and reasonable incident or consequence of the [maintenance] of the automobile[.]" *Westchester Fire Ins. Co., supra*, 126 N.J. Super. at 38, 312 A.2d 664. In a nutshell, that simply was not the case here.

In our view, *Wakefern* presents the clearest analysis and conclusions most consistent with our statement of the substantial nexus test. Echoing circumstances and considerations similar to the ones presented here, it explains that "[w]hen an accident ... is occasioned by negligent maintenance of the premises and the only connection to that event is the fact that the motor vehicle [is] present..., no realistic social or public policy is served by straining to shift coverage." *Wakefern, supra*, 188 N.J. Super. at 87, 455 A.2d 1160. Driving the point home, it further notes that, in this setting, "no reasonable contractual expectations are disappointed or denied and the reasonable expectation of the parties ... is hardly placed at hazard." *Ibid.* (citation and internal quotation marks omitted).

That reasoning applies with equal force here. It compels the serially logical conclusions that Arians's injuries did not arise from the maintenance of Costa's pickup truck; that Gulf's automobile insurance coverage was not triggered; and that the homeowners insurance policy issued by Farmers must respond to Arians's claim.

## Cawthon v. State Farm Fire & Casualty Co.

United States District Court for the
Western District of Missouri, Western Division
965 F. Supp. 1262 (1997)

### Nanette K. Laughrey, J.

On March 26, 1993, Jeffrey Cawthon ("Jeffrey") was fatally injured in the backyard of his grandfather, Thomas Michael Langton ("Langton"). Langton was trying to remove a tree limb which became embedded in the ground two days earlier when he cut down a big tree. Langton had devised a plan for the limb removal and asked his son, Robert Cawthon, to help. Langton tied a nylon rope to the trailer hitch of his pickup truck and instructed Robert to put the rope around a large, nearby tree. At Langton's direction, the rope was placed at a 90-degree angle to the tree and then attached to the embedded tree limbs. As Langton drove his pickup slowly forward, the first tree limb was dislodged and catapulted forward, striking Jeffrey in the stomach. Jeffrey died three to four hours later as a result of his injuries.

Jeffrey's mother, Sandra Cawthon, filed suit in state court against Langton to recover for the wrongful death of her son. In that action, she asserted that Langton was negligent in devising the plan to remove the tree, failing to warn Plaintiff and Jeffrey, failing to clear the area before pulling the tree branches from the ground, and failing to inspect the manner in which the tree branches were tied. Plaintiff specifically alleged that Langton was not negligent in the operation of the truck. Judgment was entered against Langton in the amount of $500,000 and Langton was given credit for $25,000, the amount previously paid to Plaintiff by State Farm Mutual Insurance Company pursuant to Langton's automobile insurance policy.

At the time of the accident, Langton also had a homeowner's insurance policy with State Farm Fire & Casualty Company. That policy covers personal liability "because of bodily injury or property damage, to which this coverage applies, caused by an occurrence." An occurrence is defined as an accident which occurs during the policy period. In addition, that policy contains a provision excluding coverage for "bodily injury or property damage arising out of the ownership, maintenance, [or] use of a motor vehicle owned or operated by the insured." It is my task to determine if this exclusion precludes Plaintiff from recovering her state court judgment from State Farm Fire & Casualty Company.

The question in this case is whether the death of Jeffrey Cawthon arose out of the use of the motor vehicle operated by the insured. In *Schmidt* [*v. Utilities Ins. Co.*, 182 S.W.2d 181 (Mo. 1944)], a case involving an automobile insurance policy, the Missouri Supreme Court held that the "words 'arising out of ... use' are very broad, general, and comprehensive [and] ... are ordinarily understood to mean 'originating from' or 'having its origin in', 'growing out of' or 'flowing from.'" ... While one Missouri court has found the term "use" and "arising out of" to be facially unambiguous, ... the proper application of this term to the myriad of legal and factual constructs in insurance disputes is anything but clear....

At one end of the factual spectrum is the automobile being operated on a public highway causing damage as a result of a collision with an object or a person. At the other end of the spectrum are injuries occurring adjacent to the vehicle or connected to it by the thinnest of evidentiary threads, *i.e.*, the vehicle was merely used to bring the participants to the place where liability occurred. The matter is further complicated because the term "use" is found in automobile insurance policies where vehicle use is a prerequisite for coverage, as well as in homeowner's insurance policies where vehicle use will preclude coverage. Missouri has not addressed this particular fact pattern in the context of a homeowner's policy, so my job is to predict how a Missouri court would resolve the dispute.

Plaintiff has two main arguments for why the vehicle exclusion clause of the homeowner's policy should not apply in this case. First, Plaintiff argues that the exclusion clause is not triggered unless the vehicle is being operated negligently. Because Plaintiff carefully plead her case to avoid alleging the negligent operation of the truck and because there is no evidence that Langton was negligent in the operation of his truck, Plaintiff states that the use of the truck cannot be the proximate cause of Jeffrey's death. Second, even if the Court finds that the use of the truck contributed to Jeffrey's death, the Court should also find that this use was concurrent with Langton's negligence in devising the plan to remove the tree and failing to clear the area. When concurrent acts cause injury, there will be insurance coverage if either act independently would have been covered.

Defendant's main argument is that the use of the truck did cause Jeffrey's death because it was a necessary component of Langton's plan for the removal of the tree. "The accident occurred because of the force exerted upon the tree branch by the pickup truck."

Both parties agree that Missouri law requires a causal connection between the injury and the vehicle before there is "use" under either a homeowner's or auto insurance policy.... Both parties agree that an incidental, fortuitous or casual connection is insufficient.... Plaintiff strongly argues that the causal connection required by Missouri law must be proximate.

Missouri cases give little consistent guidance on this question. In *Martin v. Cameron Mut. Ins. Co.*, 763 S.W.2d 710 (Mo. App. 1989), the court, interpreting an auto insurance policy, held that the connection between the injury and the use of the vehicle need not be proximate cause "in the strict legal sense of causation permeating general tort law." *Id.* at 711. There must simply be some causal connection. In *Bituminous Cas. Corp.* [*v. Aetna Life and Cas.*], 599 S.W.2d at 519 [(Mo. App. 1980)], the court held that the standard was whether the insured's control of a vehicle was the proximate cause of the accident, but then also cited the above language in Martin. Proximate cause was the implied standard in *Beauty Supplies, Inc. v. Hanover Ins. Co.*, 526 S.W.2d 75 (Mo. App. 1975). Why the court chose that standard was not discussed. Several other jurisdictions have referred to proximate cause as the correct standard for determining whether there is a sufficiently close connection between the vehicle and injury.

The relevant Missouri cases fall roughly into two categories. First, there are the auto insurance cases where vehicle use is a prerequisite to coverage. In these cases, the Missouri courts seem to deny coverage only when the auto is merely the site of the injury, *Cameron*, 599 S.W.2d at 18; or when the injury is separated from the use of the truck by time or distance, ... [*State Farm v.*] *Flanary*, 879 S.W.2d at 722 [(Mo. App. 1994)]. When there is any plausible connection between the use of the vehicle and the injury, the courts have found insurance coverage. *State Farm Mut. Auto. Ins. Co. v. Whitehead*, 711 S.W.2d 198 (Mo. App. 1986). In that case, a shootout occurred in a moving vehicle because the driver of the vehicle was attempting to transport a suspected burglar to jail. The court found coverage because the "shooting resulted because the car was being used to take [the burglar] where he preferred not to go." *Id.* at 201. In *Bituminous Cas. Co.*, 599 S.W.2d at 519, a bulldozer operator attempted to dislodge a pickup truck mired down in a landfill. In the pushing process, the driver of the pickup was struck by the bulldozer blade. The court found insurance coverage under the pickup truck's insurance because the bulldozer operator was "using" the pickup with the permission of its owner.

A second category of cases involves homeowner's insurance with a vehicle exclusion clause. Only one Missouri case has been cited by counsel which clearly fits into this category. In *Steelman v. Holford*, 765 S.W.2d 372 (Mo. App. 1989), the court refused to find vehicular use so as to trigger an exclusion clause in a homeowner's policy. The claimant was the victim of a random shooting while operating his vehicle on a public highway. The court held that there was no causal connection between the operation of the truck and the victim's injury, because the vehicle was merely the situs of the injury.

The problem with all of these cases is that they are not factually analogous. Plaintiff, trying to show that there is coverage, cites *Flanary* where the court denies auto insurance coverage. Defendant, trying to show there is no coverage, emphasizes *Steelman*, where the court finds that there is homeowner's coverage. This odd pattern of advocacy illustrates the quandary. Will the Missouri courts, having interpreted the term "use" broadly in the context of an automobile insurance policy, necessarily interpret it in the same way in a homeowner's policy?

The majority rule in other jurisdictions seems to be that the term will be broadly interpreted in an auto policy to provide coverage but narrowly interpreted in a home-owner's policy, likewise to provide coverage.... Appleman argues that the term should not be interpreted uniformly. He says: "The policyholder should be entitled to coverage under an automobile policy whenever liability settles upon him while he was using an insured automobile without regard to the manner or purpose of use." *Id.* at 76. A homeowner's liability policy, however, insures against an occurrence. "The court has a legitimate interest in determining whether the use of the automobile was the 'occurrence' which produced the liability." *Id.* at 77.

Even if the phrase were unambiguous, I would still find that the use of the truck was not the proximate cause of Jeffrey's injuries....

Plaintiff argues that many different means could have been used to pull the limb, and the truck was not a necessary part of the plan. Defendant responds that this fact is irrelevant and does not "negate the truth that the truck was used." Plaintiff's argument, however, shows how the truck is remote in the chain of causation. It was the rope being placed at the 90-degree angle and leveraged against the tree that produced the thrust that catapulted the limb forward. That result would not have occurred without the negligently placed ropes regardless of whether a truck, a horse, or a tractor had been used. The fact that the result would have been the same regardless of the source of the power shows remoteness in terms of proximate cause and independence for purposes of concurrent causation.

Courts in foreign jurisdictions are split on cases similar to this one. There are two closely analogous cases outside Missouri which apply similar exclusions to deny coverage, and three that do not apply the exclusion. In *Hagen v. Aetna Cas. & Sur. Co.,* 675 So. 2d 963 (Fla. App. 1996), the court held that an auto use exclusion in a commercial general liability policy precluded coverage. In that case, a rug delivery was being made to a retailer. The retailer did not have a forklift to unload the carpet, so a rope was tied to a carpet roll. The rope was then attached to the bumper of the retailer's pickup truck. When the pickup drove forward, the carpet was pulled out and fell on the man delivering the carpet.

The court held that the term "use" was unambiguous and the vehicle use exclusion did apply because the driver of the truck was negligent in failing to clear the area before driving the truck forward. The negligence was related to the movement of the truck, and neither the rope nor the carpet was defective. The only defective part of the plan was failing to warn the victim to get out of the way. That negligence was inextricably tied to the movement of the vehicle and the auto use exclusion clause applied.

Likewise, in *State Farm Fire and Cas. Co. v. Huyghe,* 144 Mich. App. 341, 375 N.W.2d 442 (Mich. App. 1985), the court applied the vehicle use exclusion clause to deny coverage. The insured drove his car under a clothesline, pulling it free and causing the attached cleat to strike his mother-in-law in the head. The court held that the clothesline was negligently placed because of its proximity to the garage and moving vehicles and the consequence of that negligence could not arise without a motor vehicle. In other words, all aspects of the insured's negligence were related to the use of a vehicle.

In both of these cases, the courts relied heavily on the fact that all allegations concerning the negligence of the insured and, hence, the basis for the insured's liability, were intertwined with the way in which the vehicle was operated. In *Hagen*, the negligence was the failure to warn people out of the way before moving the vehicle forward. In *Huyghe*, the negligence was in driving under the clothesline and causing it to break, and also in the location of the clothesline in the path of vehicles. The injuries were directly connected to vehicle-related negligence by the insured.

There are three closely analogous cases outside Missouri in which courts refused to find as a matter of law that the vehicle use exclusion applied. In *Lawver v. Boling*, 71 Wis. 2d 408, 238 N.W.2d 514 (Wis. 1976), a son helped his father attach some boards to the side of the family barn. The son was put on a lift chair and hoisted up by a rope attached to his father's vehicle. After some time, the rope frayed as it rubbed against the barn and the son fell. The court held that insurance coverage could be available under a farmer's general liability policy, even though it contained a vehicle use exclusion clause. The court emphasized that the insured had paid a premium for liability not caused by the vehicle and, therefore, coverage would be available if the jury found that the accident was caused in part by the negligent rigging of the ropes and the negligent choice of materials.

In *Johns v. State Farm Fire & Cas. Co.*, 349 So. 2d 481 (La. App. 1977), the insured attached a rope to the pickup truck and tied the other end to a helper's waist. The helper then climbed up the tree using the rope as a safety device. The vehicle was moved forward to make the rope taut. The rope broke and the helper fell causing serious injuries. The court of appeals held that summary judgment could not be granted for the insurance company because the vehicle use exclusion clause did not necessarily apply. If the driver of the vehicle caused the injury in part by the operation of the vehicle and in part by the plan for climbing the tree, there would be coverage under the homeowner's policy.

Finally, in *Kalell v. Mut. Fire & Auto Ins. Co.*, 471 N.W.2d 865 (Ia. 1991), the insured was pulling a dead limb on a rope attached to a pickup truck when the limb caused injury. The court in that case also held that a summary judgment for the insurance company was in error because there was a possibility that the jury would find that the injury was caused by both the negligent operation of the vehicle and the plan for the removal of the limb.

In *Kalell*, *Johns* and *Lawvers*, the courts relied on the doctrine of concurrent causation to avoid a judgment against the insured. That doctrine provides that if one event is covered by insurance and another is excluded, there will be insurance coverage unless the excluded event is the sole proximate cause of the injury. Another requirement of the doctrine is that the two events must be independent and separate. Comment, *Insurance Law-Concurrent Causation: Examination of Alternative Approaches*, 527 S. Ill. U.L.J. (1985).

The doctrine of concurrent causation has been recognized in Missouri. All these cases, however, involved allegations of negligent supervision or entrustment. The Missouri courts uniformly held that to recover for negligent supervision or negligent entrustment, a plaintiff had to show that a vehicle had been negligently operated. Hence, the injury was not caused by two separate and independent events and the doctrine of concurrent causation did not apply. In the case before me, the insured's liability was triggered by his negligent plan for the removal of the tree. The negligent operation of the truck was not a necessary element in the state court action. Liability did not flow from the negligent operation of a vehicle.

Based on Missouri precedent, the court finds that the operation of the vehicle and the negligent plan for tying the ropes were, at most, concurrent causes of Jeffrey's death. The use of the truck was an antecedent, independent factor which contributed to Jeffrey's injuries. The vehicle exclusion clause, therefore, does not preclude coverage for the negligent plan.

Finally, Mr. Langton paid for two policies to cover damages for which he became legally liable. His liability in state court arose out of the manner in which he arranged the ropes around the tree, not the operation of the truck. He was in his backyard performing a household task and the vehicle only provided the horsepower to apply leverage on the rope. Under these circumstances, it is reasonable for him to expect that his homeowner's policy would provide protection.

### *Notes and Questions*

1. The phrase "arising out of the ownership, maintenance, or use of a vehicle" frequently is utilized to *define* coverage in automobile insurance policies, but this same term also is utilized to *exclude* coverage in homeowners insurance policies and in other non-vehicular insurance policies. Thus, very often, this legal question of coverage interpretation hinges on whether the automobile insurer or the homeowners insurer ultimately will be liable to the insured. *See, e.g., Waseca Mut. Ins. Co. v. Noska,* 331 N.W.2d 917 (Minn. 1983); *Farmers Fire Ins. Co. v. Kingsbury,* 118 Misc. 2d 735, 461 N.Y.S.2d 226 (1983).

2. Because there is a contest between two policies (both with perhaps differing limits of insurance), the way in which a case's causal story is framed is key. This often comes into play at the pleading stage, where cases are pleaded to "catch coverage." *See* Ellen S. Pryor, *The Stories We Tell: Intentional Harm and the Quest for Insurance Funding,* 75 TEX. L. REV. 1721 (1997).

3. In *Lawrence v. State Farm Fire & Cas. Co.,* 133 P.3d 976 (Wyo. 2006), the court enforced the automobile exclusion in a homeowners policy regarding a third party claim of negligence in giving "gas money" to an unlicensed teenage driver for a road trip to Billings that resulting in an accident causing a passenger's death. The court held that knowingly funding an unlicensed, underage driver's use of a car may have been grossly negligent but the tragic death nonetheless arose out of use of an automobile, which is excluded from general liability coverage under both homeowners and business policies.

4. In *Foremost Ins. Co. v. Levesque*, 868 A.2d 244 (Me. 2005), an automobile loading exclusion did not defeat coverage under a homeowners policy where injury took place in a home during the delivery of a washing machine that had come by truck. The injury was sufficiently land-based and separated from vehicle use to be outside the scope of auto coverage.

### PROBLEM FOUR

Coverage or no coverage in the following loss distribution disputes:

(a) A homeowner's insurance policy excluded, and an automobile policy included, coverage for bodily injury or property damage "arising out of the ownership, maintenance, operation or use" of a motor vehicle. The insured threw an egg from a moving vehicle while traveling at approximately 40 miles per hour. The egg struck and seriously injured a pedestrian.

• Which policy should provide the primary insurance coverage: the homeowners policy or the automobile policy?

(b) Defendant, who was driving an automobile owned by Elodie Bailey, struck and killed a nine-year-old boy. However, insurance coverage is claimed under a homeowner's policy instead of under an automobile policy based upon a tort theory of negligent entrustment of an automobile.

• Should coverage exist under the homeowner's policy?

# § 11.05. Uninsured and Underinsured Motorist Coverage

## [A] Scope of Uninsured Motorist Coverage

Uninsured Motorist (UM) coverage in automobile insurance policies is designed to protect the policyholder, members of their family, and other permissive users under the policy from any injury caused by uninsured motorists. First offered in New York in the mid-1950s, UM coverage has been written into automobile insurance policies in almost all states by statutory enactment. UM coverage is not actually an additional liability coverage, but has been interpreted to be direct compensation to the insured or any permissive user who is injured by an uninsured motorist who is at fault. *See, e.g., Motorists Mut. Ins. Co. v. Speck*, 393 N.E.2d 500 (Ohio Ct. App. 1977).

The minimum UM coverage required by statute differs from state to state and, in most states, UM coverage may be rejected or lower policy limits may be selected by the insured. The UM statute normally contains a definition of the term "uninsured vehicle" and, in most states, the UM statute requires that the insured be legally entitled to recover from the uninsured tortfeasor. *See* Keeton & Widiss, Insurance Law § 4.9(e) (1988); Jerry & Richmond, Understanding Insurance Law § 135 (6th ed. 2018). *See also* Thomas & Widiss, Widiss' Uninsured and Underinsured Motorist Insurance (3d ed. 2005).

# Zarder v. Humana Insurance Co.

Supreme Court of Wisconsin
324 Wis.2d 325, 782 N.W.2d 682 (2010)

**Ann Walsh Bradley, J.**

Acuity, A Mutual Insurance Company, seeks review of a published court of appeals decision affirming the circuit court's denial of Acuity's motion for declaratory judgment. Acuity sought a declaration that the accident here was not a hit-and-run accident under the terms of the uninsured motorist (UM) policy issued to James and Glory Zarder. The circuit court and court of appeals determined that Acuity was not entitled to a declaratory judgment even though the occupants of the vehicle that allegedly struck thirteen-year-old Zachary Zarder stopped to check on his wellbeing before departing.

Acuity asserts that both the circuit court and the court of appeals erred. It contends that, under the facts of this case, the vehicle involved in the accident was not a "hit-and-run" vehicle because the unidentified driver stopped to check on Zarder's wellbeing before leaving the scene of the accident. Further, Acuity argues that this court's discussion of the term "hit-and-run" in *Hayne v. Progressive Northern Insurance Co.*, 115 Wis.2d 68, 73–74, 339 N.W.2d 588 (1983) controls the outcome of this case.

We conclude that Acuity's focus on the unidentified driver's intention when leaving the accident scene is not relevant to our determination of whether there is coverage under the terms of the insurance policy. Further, we conclude that *Hayne* does not control the outcome of this case. We, therefore, apply the standard rules of construction to the Zarders' UM policy.

Given that the phrase "hit-and-run" in the Zarders' UM policy is susceptible to more than one reasonable construction, we determine that it is ambiguous. We therefore construe the phrase "hit-and-run" in favor of coverage. Having concluded that there is coverage for this type of accident under the policy, we need not examine the requirements of Wis. Stat. §632.32(4) (2007–08). Accordingly, we affirm the court of appeals, but we modify the rationale and remand to the circuit court for further proceedings.

For the purposes of this interlocutory appeal, the facts are undisputed. Thirteen-year-old Zachary Zarder was riding his bicycle on a New Berlin municipal street on a snowy evening in December 2005 when his bicycle was struck by an unidentified motorist. The car stopped approximately 100 feet from Zarder. Three occupants got out of the car and approached Zarder, who remained at the accident scene.

Sandra and Edward Miller were walking in the neighborhood when the accident occurred. Sandra Miller said that she heard a young male voice say, "A car is coming." Sandra saw a car and heard a crash of metal.

Within seconds, the Millers arrived at the accident scene. They saw Zarder sitting in the snowbank beside his bicycle. They saw three young men exit a car, approach Zarder, and ask if he was okay. Sandra overheard Zarder assure the occupants that he was okay. [According to a New Berlin police report, Zarder "advised that after [the occupants] had checked on his wellbeing, he had assured them that he was all right and they were released from the scene. Zachary advises that he did not feel that the vehicle was driving recklessly or speeding at the time of the accident, however, he did advise that the vehicle appeared to have taken the corner too short thereby crossing into his lane and striking him."] The occupants then returned to their car and drove away. Sandra later signed an affidavit stating: "It did not appear that the subject car was fleeing the accident scene."

The Millers also asked Zarder if he was injured, and he said that he was not. Later, however, it became apparent that he was in fact injured. The Zarders contacted the New Berlin Police Department and reported the accident the same evening.

Officer Jeffrey Kuehl investigated the accident. He located car parts in the roadway of the accident scene and interviewed witnesses, but he was unable to identify the vehicle or its driver. Kuehl later stated in an affidavit: "[T]he December 9, 2005 accident was not investigated as a hit-and-run accident because the unidentified vehicle stopped at the scene and inquired as to Zachary Zarder's health and well-being[.]"

As a result of the accident, Zarder's leg and arm were fractured, requiring two surgeries. His health insurance policy, issued by Humana, was insufficient to cover his medical bills. The Zarders therefore sought coverage under their automobile insurance policy.

As required by Wis. Stat. § 632.32(4), the Zarders' policy included uninsured motorist (UM) coverage. The policy provided:

> We will pay damages for bodily injury which an insured person is legally entitled to recover from the owner or operator of an uninsured motor vehicle. Bodily injury must be sustained by an insured person and must be caused by accident and result from the ownership, maintenance or use of the uninsured motor vehicle.

The policy defined "uninsured motor vehicle" in part as "a land motor vehicle or trailer which is ... [a] hit-and-run vehicle whose operator or owner is unknown and which strikes [an insured]."

After Acuity rejected the Zarders' claim, they filed suit, claiming UM coverage. Zarder's medical insurer, Humana Insurance Company, was also listed as a defendant because it may have subrogation rights against Acuity. Acuity answered, denying coverage. It asserted "that under the circumstances of this case the policy in question [does not] provide [ ] uninsured motorist insurance coverage benefits since the vehicle that allegedly struck the Plaintiff, Zachary Zarder, did not constitute a 'hit and run' vehicle under the law[.]" It also asserted contributory negligence as an affirmative defense.

Acuity filed a motion for declaratory judgment in circuit court, seeking a no coverage declaration in connection with the Zarders' claims. It did not specifically interpret the terms of the UM policy. Rather, it argued that the policy "does not expressly define what qualifies as a 'hit-and-run' vehicle. Consequently, Wisconsin courts' [statutory] construction of the phrase 'hit-and-run' in an insurance coverage context is instructive, given the absence of a definition of the same in either the policy or [Wis. Stat. § 632.32,] the omnibus statute."

Acuity cited *Hayne v. Progressive Northern Insurance Co.*, a decision by this court, which held that the statutory term "hit-and-run" unambiguously requires physical striking. 115 Wis.2d 68, 339 N.W.2d 588 (1983). *Hayne* concluded: "[T]he plain meaning of 'hit-and-run' consists of two elements: a 'hit' or striking, and a 'run,' or fleeing from the scene of an accident." *Id.* at 73–74, 339 N.W.2d 588. Acuity argued that under *Hayne*, the unidentified vehicle was not a 'hit-and-run' vehicle because the driver stopped to check on Zarder rather than "fleeing from the scene of [the] accident."

After briefs and oral arguments, the circuit court denied Acuity's motion for declaratory judgment. Although the court did not specifically interpret the terms of the policy, it determined that Zarder was "hit" within the meaning of the term "hit-and-run." [The court commented that the Millers heard the impact and that the hit resulted in property damage to the bike.]

Wisconsin Stat. § 632.32 is Wisconsin's omnibus motor vehicle coverage statute. It provides that every motor vehicle insurance policy issued in Wisconsin must contain certain mandatory provisions. One of these requirements is set forth in Wis. Stat. § 632.32(4), which mandates uninsured motorist (UM) coverage. It includes "unidentified motor vehicle[s] involved in [] hit-and-run accident[s]" within the definition of "uninsured motor vehicle." Wis. Stat. § 632.32(4)(a)2.b.

The Zarders' policy defines "uninsured motor vehicle" in part as "a land motor vehicle or trailer which is ... [a] hit-and-run vehicle whose operator or owner is unknown and which strikes [an insured]." Although the term "hit-and-run" is not defined in the policy, Acuity asserts that the meaning of "run" is not "lacking in clarity." It asserts that the term means to "flee without stopping."

Acuity advances two arguments in support of this conclusion. The first is tied to the particular facts of this case and focuses on the intent of the unidentified driver. The second is based on our prior decision in *Hayne*, 115 Wis.2d 68, 339 N.W.2d 588. We address each argument in turn.

At oral argument, Acuity's counsel explained: "When you look at the facts of this case, we clearly do not have a 'flee' from a common sense standpoint because the facts show that the occupants of the vehicle checked on the wellbeing of Zachary Zarder. There was no attempt by them to shield their identity. There was no attempt by them to run from the scene of the accident." Under these facts, Acuity asserts, there is no coverage.

From this explanation, it appears that Acuity's definition hinges upon the intent of the unidentified driver and whether that driver attempted to evade responsibility by leaving the scene of the accident. However, we note that a definition that focuses on the unidentified driver's intentions in leaving the scene of an accident is antithetical to the purpose of UM coverage. As applied here, the purpose is to compensate an injured person who is the victim of an unidentified motorist's negligence, subject to the terms of the policy. *See Theis* [*v. Midwest Security Ins. Co.*], 232 Wis.2d 749, ¶¶ 28–29, 606 N.W.2d 162.

The intention of the unidentified driver—while central in the context of a criminal hit-and-run charge under Wis. Stat. § 346.67—is not relevant here. In construing an insurance policy, our focus is not on what the unidentified driver intended. Rather, our focus is on what the parties to the contract intended. One of the circumstances that may arise under the policy is when the victim sustains injury or damages, but the tortfeasor is unknown.

Although the court of appeals looked to Wis. Stat. § 346.67 in defining the term hit-and-run, we do not find the scope and application of that statute to be helpful to the interpretation of this insurance policy. Insurance coverage for a hit-and-run accident involving an unidentified vehicle is not coextensive with the criminal culpability of the driver of that vehicle under Wis. Stat. § 346.67.

Whatever the unidentified driver's motivation for leaving the accident scene—good, bad, or indifferent—it has no effect on the insured's inability to recover from that unidentified driver's liability policy. The question here is whether the parties contracted for coverage for this accident under the terms of the insurance policy....

Acuity acknowledges that with respect to what constitutes a run, dictionary definitions of "hit-and-run" are "less than identical" and that they "do not mirror one another." Nevertheless, it points to the conclusion in *Hayne* that the statutory term "hit-and-run" is "unambiguous" and "clear on its face." 115 Wis.2d at 76, 339 N.W.2d 588. "Because this Court has ruled the term 'hit-and-run' is unambiguous," Acuity contends that finding controls "irrespective of whether the discussion concerns the Acuity policy or, alternatively, the Omnibus statute."

In *Hayne*, the insured swerved to avoid an oncoming car, lost control of his vehicle, and was injured. 115 Wis.2d at 69, 339 N.W.2d 588. There was no contact between Hayne's vehicle and the oncoming car, which was never identified. *Id.* Hayne filed suit against his insurer, asserting a claim under his UM policy. *Id.* at 69–70, 339 N.W.2d 588. This court interpreted Wis. Stat. § 632.32(4) and determined that it did not mandate UM coverage for an accident involving an unidentified motor vehicle when there was no physical contact between the insured and the unidentified vehicle. *Id.* at 69, 339 N.W.2d 588.

In reaching this determination, the court consulted several dictionaries, reasoning that "[t]hese definitions clearly indicate that the plain meaning of 'hit-and-run' consists of two elements: a 'hit' or striking, and a 'run', or fleeing from the scene of an accident." *Id.* at 73–74, 339 N.W.2d 588. The court concluded: "The clear statutory language of sec. 632.32(4)(a)2.b. reflects a legislative intent that the statute apply only to accidents in which there has been physical contact."[1] *Id.* at 74, 339 N.W.2d 588.

We find Acuity's argument that *Hayne* controls the outcome here unpersuasive for the following three reasons. First, although *Hayne* determined that the term "run" in the statutory phrase "hit-and-run" means "fleeing from the scene of an accident," this definition leaves unanswered the question presented in this case. The court of appeals correctly recognized that the *Hayne* definition of hit-and-run "begged the question" because "while the court seemingly equated 'run' with 'flee,' it did not define or discuss the circumstances that determine when a 'flee' has occurred." *Zarder*, 316 Wis.2d 573, ¶¶ 12, 14, 765 N.W.2d 839. Although Acuity asserts that "run" means "fleeing the scene without stopping," the phrase "without stopping" does not appear in *Hayne's* definition of "hit-and-run."

Second, even though *Hayne* pronounced the physical contact requirement unambiguous, other aspects of the definition of "hit-and-run" may not be unambiguous. A word or phrase may be unambiguous in one situation, and yet be ambiguous in another. *Seider v. O'Connell*, 2000 WI 76, ¶ 43, 236 Wis.2d 211, 612 N.W.2d 659. "Permitting the facts of a case to gauge ambiguity simply acknowledges that reasonable minds can differ about a statute's application when the text is a constant but the circumstances to which the text may apply are kaleidoscopic." *Id.*

In *DeHart v. Wisconsin Mutual Insurance Co.*, we discussed the applicability of the *Hayne* decision to new factual situations. 2007 WI 91, ¶ 15, 302 Wis.2d 564, 734 N.W.2d 394 (citing *Smith v. Gen. Cas. Ins. Co.*, 2000 WI 127, ¶ 13, 239 Wis.2d 646, 619 N.W.2d 882 (discussing *Hayne*)). We cited the Legislative Council Note to Wis. Stat. § 632.32(4)(a)2.b., which provides: "A precise definition of hit-and-run is not necessary for in the rare case where a question arises the court can draw the line." *Id.* (citing Legislative Council Note, ch. 102, Laws of 1979). "Although we have established that the term 'hit-and-run' unambiguously includes an element of physical contact, we recognize that [the statute] does not specifically define 'hit-and-run.'" *Id.* "Accordingly," we concluded, "the term 'hit-and-run' has been construed on a case-by-case basis," and "[p]rior decisions explaining and interpreting the physical contact requirement are instructive to our determination in this case." *Id.*

Third, the court in *Hayne* was interpreting the language of a statute. Here, however, we interpret the language in an insurance policy. This distinction is relevant because the court applies different rules when construing a statute than it does when construing an insurance contract.

---

1. [16] We later explained the public policy rationale behind the holding in *Hayne:* "One public policy concern is of primary relevance to our analysis, that of preventing fraud. The physical contact element unambiguously included in the term 'hit-and-run' in Wis. Stat. § 632.32(4)(a)2.b. prevents fraudulent claims from being brought by an insured driver who is involved in an accident of his or her own making." *Smith v. Gen. Cas. Ins. Co.*, 2000 WI 127, ¶ 25, 239 Wis.2d 646, 619 N.W.2d 882.

Most importantly, when there is ambiguity in an insurance policy, it is construed in favor of coverage. By contrast, when there is ambiguity in a statute, the court looks to the legislature's intent in enacting it. "[T]he reasonable expectation of the insured regarding the language of the policy is not relevant to [an] analysis of Wis. Stat. § 632.32(4)(a)2.b." *Smith*, 239 Wis.2d 646, ¶ 27, 619 N.W.2d 882. We conclude that *Hayne* does not control the outcome of this case.

Accordingly, we turn to the language of the Zarders' policy and apply the standard rules of construction. The policy provides UM coverage for bodily injury which an insured person is legally entitled to recover from the owner or operator of "[a] hit-and-run vehicle whose operator or owner is unknown and which strikes [an insured]." The policy term "hit-and-run" is undefined.

A reasonable insured could conclude that a hit-and-run vehicle is a vehicle which strikes an insured and then flees the scene of the accident without stopping. However, a reasonable insured might also conclude that a hit-and-run vehicle is one that strikes an insured and then leaves the scene of the accident without the driver providing identifying information.[2]

Given that the phrase "hit-and-run" in the Zarders' policy is susceptible to more than one reasonable construction, we conclude that it is ambiguous. We therefore construe the phrase hit-and-run in favor of coverage. Ambiguous terms in an insurance contract are construed in favor of coverage for the insured.

## Notes and Questions

1. *Query*: What is the legislative purpose and underlying public policy rationale for uninsured and underinsured motorist statutes?

2. Many state UM statutes define two classes of insureds. For example, Va. Code § 38.2-2206(B) provides that an insured of the first class is "the named insured and, while resident of the same household, the spouse of the named insured, and relatives, wards or foster children of either, while in a motor vehicle or otherwise." Insureds of the second class include "any person who uses the motor vehicle to which the policy applies, with the expressed or implied consent of the named insured, and a guest in the motor vehicle to which the policy applies or the personal representative of any of the above."

3. "Stacking" is a term that refers to obtaining insurance proceeds from multiple coverages for a single loss, as long as the insured does not recover for more than his or her loss. And if the policy language—and statutory language—are ambiguous about permissive "stacking" of coverages, such ambiguity is generally interpreted against the insurer. *See* Jerry & Richmond, Understanding Insurance Law § 137

---

2. [18] This definition is consistent with the term's common and ordinary meaning, as found in some dictionary definitions. For instance, the *American Heritage Dictionary* defines "hit-and-run" as "[b]eing or involving the driver of a motor vehicle who leaves the scene of an accident, especially one in which a pedestrian or another vehicle has been struck." *American Heritage Dictionary of the English Language* 858 (3d ed. 1992).

(6th ed. 2018); Keeton & Widiss, Insurance Law § 5.9(b) (1988). Some UM statutes allow the insurer to limit intra-policy stacking, but not inter-policy stacking. Under what rationale? *See, e.g., Goodville Mut. Casualty Co. v. Borror*, 221 Va. 967, 275 S.E. 2d 625 (1981).

4. A subset of uninsured motorist cases involve one-car accidents and so-called "phantom vehicles" or "miss-and-run" drivers (as contrasted with hit-and-run drivers). In the typical case, an insured vehicle goes off the road and hits a tree or rolls over. The policyholder claims that the accident occurred because the driver took evasive action to avoid collision with a negligent driver who continued on (obviously not stopping to help the victim who left the road). These things happen all the time. But so do vehicles leaving the road without the help of any miss-and-run third parties (think of drivers taking a tight corner too fast in an SUV or dozing off or using a mobile device while driving). In these cases, a skeptical insurer may suspect that the story of a phantom driver is a convenient way for a policyholder to attempt to access the UM coverage.

The result of this climate of suspicion and ambiguous accident scenes has produced a genre of phantom vehicle claims. Courts divide on whether physical contact is required in the absence of clear language in the policy. Responding to this, insurers frequently have added policy language requiring physical contact or corroborating evidence of another (uninsured because unindentified) vehicle. But many courts have found such provisions to violate public policy or legislation designed to protect the rights of policyholders alleging injury due to a phantom vehicle. *See* Jeffrey W. Stempel & Erik S. Knutsen, Stempel & Knutsen on Insurance Coverage § 27.09. *See, e.g., Allstate Ins. Co. v. Killakey*, 580 N.E.2d 399 (N.Y. 1991) (physical contact requirement satisfied by circumstantial evidence); *Mayfield v. Allied Mut. Ins. Co.*, 436 N.W.2d 164 (Neb. 1989) (policy provision requiring physical contact enforceable and not against public policy). As noted by the court in *Vanderhoff v. Harleysville Ins. Co.*, 997 A.2d 328 at 332 (Pa. 2010), "a phantom vehicle uninsured motorist claim is fertile ground for fraud." Why?

## [B] Nature of Underinsured Motorist Coverage

In the majority of states, uninsured motorist or UM coverage is now supplemented with underinsured motorist or UIM coverage. Under such coverage, if the injured person possesses liability insurance in excess of the liability coverage carried by the third party tortfeasor, and if the injured person's loss exceeds the limits of the tortfeasor's coverage, then the injured person's own underinsured motorist coverage normally picks up the difference. Thus, the insured who is injured by another driver is provided with coverage as though they were injured by a driver with policy limits equal to their own. In some states, underinsured motorist coverage is mandatory. In other states, underinsured motorist coverage is optional, and in a number of states, underinsured motorist coverage is included unless the insured specifically rejects such coverage in writing. *See generally* Jerry & Richmond, Understanding Insurance Law § 135[c] (6th ed. 2018).

UM and UIM disputes continue to provide a steady stream of cases, many of them state specific. Regarding UM coverage, see, e.g., *Gabriel v. Premier Ins. Co.*, 840 N.E.2d 548 (Mass. 2006) (hit-and-run driver is uninsured, entitling victim to UM benefits under his own auto policy); and *GEICO Gen. Ins. Co. v. Northwestern Pac. Indem. Co.*, 115 P.3d 856 (Okla. 2005) (UM coverage primary to any available excess liability policies).

Regarding UIM coverage, see, e.g., *Welin v. Am. Family Mut. Ins. Co.*, 717 N.W.2d 690 (Wis. 2006) (state statute requires payment of additional UIM benefits to injured policyholder notwithstanding policy language); *Cole v. State Farm Ins. Co.*, 128 P.3d 171 (Alaska 2006) (UIM benefits that would be available to "spouse" not available where victim and claimant merely lived together even though they had once been married); and *Eaquinta v. Allstate Ins. Co.*, 125 P.3d 901 (Utah 2005) (UIM benefits not available to motorist for death of adult child who was not part of claimant's household).

### PROBLEM FIVE

Assume that plaintiff Insured has $100,000 in UIM coverage with the Nationwide Insurance Company. Plaintiff is seriously injured by multiple tortfeasors in a three-car collision. Defendant A has $25,000 liability coverage and Defendant B has $50,000 liability coverage. Plaintiff Insured obtains a jury verdict for $1,000,000 and collects the liability limits from Defendants A and B respectively.

- How much does Nationwide have to pay the Insured under its UIM coverage?

# § 11.06. No-Fault Automobile Insurance

Many states have enacted legislation for no-fault automobile insurance with either mandatory or optional coverage. No-fault automobile insurance (now often called "personal injury protection" or "PIP") was recommended in 1932 as a means to alleviate some of the inequities resulting from automobile injuries and to reduce the number of cumbersome and time-consuming legal battles that ensued in order to determine which driver was "at fault" under traditional tort principles. *See* Noel Dowling, *Compensation for Automobile Accidents: A Symposium*, 32 COLUM. L. REV. 785 (1932). It was not until 1971 in Massachusetts, however, that the first mandatory no-fault automobile insurance statutes were enacted — over stiff opposition — with two major objectives: (1) to provide first-party coverage for personal injuries to an insured from his or her own insurance company, regardless of which driver was at fault; and (2) to eliminate in whole or part the tort liability concept of fault for those personal injuries resulting in damages below a monetary threshold established by statute. *See* NO-FAULT AND UNINSURED MOTORIST AUTOMOBILE INSURANCE (2005).

In most instances, no-fault laws apply only to personal injuries, and cover such costs as medical and hospital expenses, lost wages, and substituted services up to a statutory limit. A victim generally cannot sue the wrongdoer for "fault" damages unless the injured party has incurred costs in excess of the statutory threshold or, in the alternative, the injured party has sustained certain statutorily prescribed injuries such as death, dismemberment, disfigurement, or the permanent loss of a bodily function. Damages for pain and suffering, however, are severely curtailed or eliminated.

Although tort liability for personal injury is abolished under most no-fault automobile accident statutes, recovery for property damage may still be instituted under the conventional tort system.

## McIntosh v. State Farm Mutual Automobile Insurance Co.

Minnesota Supreme Court
488 N.W.2d 476 (1992)

**Simonett, Justice.**

May an intentional assault qualify as an "accident" for purposes of either no-fault or uninsured motorist coverage or both? On October 1, 1987, Robert Taylor parked his uninsured car near the home of his former girlfriend, Twaya McIntosh. When McIntosh came out of the house, she got into her own car, a Dodge automobile, accompanied by a male companion and her 6-month-old son (whose father is Taylor). Taylor walked over to the Dodge and confronted McIntosh about a bedroom set purchased when the two were still living together. Taylor asked McIntosh to go back into the house with him, and opened his coat to reveal a. 38 caliber revolver.

Rather than returning to the house with Taylor, McIntosh drove away and a car chase ensued. Taylor tried (unsuccessfully) to ram the Dodge from the rear and the side, and, as the two cars proceeded on the city streets, he fired four shots at the McIntosh automobile. The chase continued onto the freeway, where Taylor fired yet another shot at the rear of McIntosh's car. He then pulled alongside the passenger side of the Dodge and fired a shot that shattered the window glass, missing the male passenger (who ducked), but striking McIntosh in the head. Taylor was convicted of first degree attempted murder and first degree assault of McIntosh.

McIntosh carried insurance for her car with defendant State Farm Mutual Automobile Insurance Company. When State Farm refused to pay no-fault and uninsured motorist benefits, McIntosh brought this declaratory judgment action in district court. The trial court granted State Farm's motion for summary judgment, concluding that McIntosh was not injured in an accident. The court of appeals affirmed. We granted McIntosh's petition for further review.

Plaintiff McIntosh does not deny, nor could she, that she was injured because of an intentional assault by her former boyfriend. She contends, however, that the shooting, from her perspective, was an "accident." State Farm does not claim, on the facts here stipulated, that the incident, from McIntosh's perspective, was not an accident.

The dispositive issue in this appeal, then, might be put: For the purposes of uninsured motorist and no-fault coverages, is an intentional assault to be viewed from the perspective of the person assaulted or of the assailant?

Under its uninsured motorist coverage, State Farm agrees to pay damages an insured is legally entitled to collect from the driver of the uninsured vehicle. The policy states, though, that: "The bodily injury must be caused by accident arising out of the operation, maintenance or use of an uninsured motor vehicle...."

This brings us to [this case], where the trial court and the court of appeals again followed *Petersen v. Croft*, 447 N.W.2d 903 (Minn. App. 1989). We granted further review to resolve the question of whose perspective defines "accident." Our court of appeals has taken a minority position, as most jurisdictions have chosen to view an incident involving a motor vehicle from the victim's perspective.

While the victim's injury must be caused by an "accident," neither our No-Fault Act nor the insurer's policy defines the term. The word, however, has a generally understood meaning. As any dictionary says, an accident is simply a happening that is unexpected and intended.... The problem is not with what the term means, but to whom the meaning applies.

Those jurisdictions that find coverage for intentional assaults take the view that the injured insured has, indeed, experienced an unexpected happening and that the character of the assailant's conduct is irrelevant. Under this reasoning, though, as *Petersen* points out, it is difficult to conceive of any incident (aside from when the victim is the assailant) that is not an accident. The term "accident" must have been inserted in the coverage clause for a reason, and the fact no allowance is made under uninsured motorist or no-fault coverage for an intentional act exclusion arguably suggests that the word "accident" is intended to create such an exclusion. The fact remains, however, that the statutes governing these coverages do not distinguish between negligent and intentional acts, and plaintiff contends that courts should not impose this distinction.

The major premise for the argument in favor of viewing an assault from the victim's perspective is that uninsured motorist and no-fault coverages are "first party coverages." The insured buys this coverage, much like health or disability insurance, to protect herself against motor vehicle injuries. In this context, it should not matter whether the injuries were inflicted intentionally or negligently, because the economic consequences for the victim are identical in either case. The insured has paid the same premium in either instance, and, so it is argued, it would be incongruous to deny benefits simply because the injuries were intentionally inflicted. Plaintiff also argues that one of the No-Fault Act's primary goals is to "relieve the severe economic distress of uncompensated victims of automobile accidents." The question remains, however, whether the coverages involved are, in fact, first party coverages.

Arguably, uninsured motorist coverage is not first party coverage, in which case the arguments based on the first party nature of the coverage apply only to basic economic loss benefits. Appleman points out that it is not accurate to suggest that uninsured motorist coverage resembles an accident rather than a liability policy; that the coverage "more closely resembles what most courts have stated it to be, namely, a substitute liability policy which stands as proxy for that which the uninsured motorist chose not to carry."

Interestingly, the Uniform Motor Vehicle Accident Reparations Act (UMVARA) does not define the word "accident." In the committee comment to section 2 of the Act it is said the word is used as "a generic term applied to the incident which immediately gives rise to liability." In other words, the term "accident" takes its meaning from the context in which it is used. Thus, for payment of "basic reparation benefits" (*i.e.*, for no-fault benefits), the committee comment says the term "accident" should be considered "[f]rom the point of view of the victim who did not intentionally injure himself," but when used in the context of security for tort liability an "accident" should be considered "from the point of view of the person causing the harm." It is significant, we think, that uninsured motorist coverage more closely corresponds to security for tort liability than it does to basic reparation benefits....

We must take a closer look, therefore, at the nature of the coverages involved here. This requires us to consider separately uninsured motorist coverage and no-fault benefits coverage under our statutes.

Uninsured motorist coverage is purchased to protect against the risk that the motorist who injures the purchaser is uninsured (or underinsured) and unable to pay the damages the purchaser is entitled to recover under tort law. The victim, in other words, collects under her own policy the compensation that the liability carrier would have paid if the uninsured motorist had been insured. Thus, the focus under uninsured motorist coverage is on the conduct of the uninsured motorist. Indeed, we do not think those who pay premiums into a pool for uninsured motorist coverage reasonably expect those funds to be available to pay compensation for injuries for which, if the uninsured motorist were insured, his insurance company would not have to pay.

Under true first party coverage, the insured would not be denied recovery if contributorily negligent, and yet under uninsured motorist coverage, the victim's recovery is reduced or even completely denied for the victim's contributory negligence. Uninsured motorist coverage is not no-fault coverage; fault on the part of the uninsured motorist must be proven under tort law. In other words, under uninsured motorist coverage, the distinction between coverage and liability under that coverage is radically different than it is under first party coverage.

In our view, uninsured motorist coverage is not true first party coverage. We agree, therefore, with the court of appeals in *Petersen* and *Wilson v. State Farm Mut. Auto. Ins. Co.*, 451 N.W.2d 216 (Minn. App. 1990), and hold that "accident," under uninsured motorist coverage, is to be viewed from the perspective of the tortfeasor. This approach best fits the nature of the coverage. We affirm the court of appeals decision denying uninsured motorist benefits to plaintiff McIntosh.

This brings us to no-fault benefits coverage. No-fault benefits are paid "for bodily injury to an insured, caused by accident resulting from the maintenance or use of a motor vehicle as a vehicle...." Coverage is not limited to damage caused by an uninsured or underinsured motor vehicle, nor is it limited to a tortfeasor's vehicle. Coverage applies, too, if the insured is injured while operating her own automobile in a single car incident. The insured's contributory negligence is irrelevant, recovery being disallowed only for the victim's intentional self-inflicted injuries.

Insurance for economic loss benefits is purchased to protect the insured against risk of injury arising from the maintenance or use of a motor vehicle regardless of whether the tortfeasor was negligent or acted intentionally, or even if there were no tortfeasor. It is enough if the victim accidentally injures herself. In other words, the focus is not on the tortfeasor; rather, no-fault benefit eligibility is dependent exclusively on the injured victim and whether she has been hurt under circumstances arising from the use of a motor vehicle. This is true first party coverage.

Consequently, we conclude that for the purpose of no-fault benefits coverage the term "accident" is to be understood from the perspective of the injured victim. We reverse the contrary ruling of the court of appeals with respect to no-fault benefits coverage, and hold that McIntosh's no-fault coverage does extend to her injuries. To be eligible for no-fault benefits McIntosh must also, of course, meet the use requirement established in *Continental Western Ins. Co. v. Klug*, 415 N.W.2d 876 (Minn. 1987), by proving that her injury resulted from an accident arising out of the use of a motor vehicle.

To summarize, an "accident" is viewed from the perspective of the tortfeasor for uninsured-underinsured motorist coverage, but from the victim's perspective for the purpose of economic loss benefits coverage. This simply reflects the truism that while words have a life of their own, they take on the coloration of their habitat. The approach we adopt here is consistent with the use of the term "accident" in the Uniform Act, and it is consistent with the principles underlying first party coverage.

### *Notes and Questions*

1. The Hawaii Supreme Court made the following observation in *Barcena v. Hawaiian Ins. & Guar. Co.*, 678 P.2d 1082 (1984):

> 1. The purpose of the No-Fault Insurance Law is to create a system of reparations for accidental harm and loss arising from motor vehicle accidents, to compensate those damages without regard to fault, and to limit tort liability for these accidents. If the accident causing accidental harm occurs in the State, every person, insured under the law, and his survivors, suffering loss from accidental harm arising out of the operation, maintenance, or use of a motor vehicle has a right to no-fault benefits.
>
> 2. The statutory system of reparations embodied in the No-Fault Insurance Law is bottomed on the compulsory coverage of all motor vehicles and operators under the no-fault insurance policies and on the partial abolition of tort liability.
>
> 3. One to whom harm befalls from an auto accident, except in those specific situations where tort liability has not been abolished, cannot seek recompense

from a negligent perpetrator of harm; he must look instead to sources designated in the No-Fault Insurance Law.

4. [To make] "no-fault benefits" [unavailable] to an insured motorist who suffered accidental harm and incurred *rehabilitation expenses* cannot be reconciled with the No-Fault Insurance Law's declared purpose to create a no-fault system of reparations, its partial abolition of tort liability, and its establishment of a right to "no-fault benefits" for loss from accidental harm arising out of the operation of a motor vehicle. [Emphasis by editors.]

2. Can the insured receive double recovery for the same injury? Some states provide by statute that the insurer may be reimbursed for its payments under first party coverage through three statutory remedies: (a) the insurer's payments may be reduced by the amount received from collateral sources, such as workers compensation benefits, social security, and Medicare; (b) the insurer paying first-party benefits may be subrogated to the rights of the insured against the party at fault and his insurer; and (c) if the injured party meets the statutory threshold requirement and sues the wrongdoer in a conventional tort action, he may be required to reimburse his own insurer out of any recovery he receives from the other party. May an injured plaintiff "stack" both no-fault and uninsured motorist insurance coverages to recover twice for the same loss? *See, e.g., Tucci v. State Farm Ins. Co.*, 469 A.2d 1025 (Pa. 1983).

3. Some no-fault statutes provide provisions for arbitration, normally between the insured and the insurer over the amount of benefits, but also between insurers regarding any contested subrogation or reimbursement rights. *See, e.g., Griffith v. Home Indem. Co.*, 84 A.D.2d 332, 446 N.Y.S.2d 55 (1982); *Paxton Nat'l Ins. Co. v. Merchants Mut. Ins. Co.*, 74 A.D.2d 715, 425 N.Y.S.2d 673 (1980), *aff'd*, 421 N.E.2d 118 (N.Y. 1981).

4. Some commentators, such as Professor Jeffrey O'Connell at the University of Virginia Law School, have argued that a no-fault program should not be limited only to automobile insurance and to workers compensation insurance, but should be expanded to include no-fault coverage for all other injuries as well—including medical malpractice, products liability, and most other traditional tort actions and claims. *See, e.g.,* O'Connell, *A "Neo No-Fault" Contract in Lieu of Tort: Preaccident Guarantees of Postaccident Settlement Offers.*, 73 Cal. L. Rev. 898 (1985); O'Connell, *Balanced Proposals for Products Liability Reform*, 48 Ohio St. L.J. 317 (1987); O'Connell, *Alternatives to the Tort System for Personal Injury*, 23 San Diego L. Rev. 17 (1986).

Such a comprehensive no-fault system covering most accidents has already been instituted in New Zealand but with limited success and with some serious operational challenges since its inception. *See, e.g.,* Harris, *Accident Compensation in New Zealand: A Comprehensive Insurance System*, 37 Mod. L. Rev. 361 (1974); O'Connell, Brown & Vennell, *Reforming New Zealand's Reform: Accident Compensation Revisited*, New Zealand L.J. 399–402 (Nov. 1988). *But see also* Miller, *An Analysis and Critique of the 1992 Changes to New Zealand's Accident Compensation Scheme*, 52 Md. L. Rev. 1070 (1993); Sir G. Palmer, *New Zealand's Accident Compensation Scheme: Twenty Years On*, 44 U. Toronto L.J. 223 (1994).

*Query*: What public policy arguments would support Professor O'Connell's proposal to extend no-fault coverage to other areas of tort and insurance law as well? What public policy arguments would not support such an extension of these no-fault programs?

# § 11.07. Automobile Property Damage

## Gonzales v. Farmers Insurance Co. of Oregon

Supreme Court of Oregon
345 Or. 382, 196 P.3d 1 (2008)

**Durham, J.**

This is an action on an automobile insurance policy. Plaintiff's insured vehicle suffered property damage in an accident. Defendants paid for repairs to the vehicle, but the repairs did not restore the vehicle to its pre-accident condition. Defendants contended that they were responsible for only the cost of the repairs. Plaintiff claimed that the policy made defendants liable for plaintiff's entire "loss" and that, if the attempted repair could not restore the vehicle to its pre-accident condition, then defendants were responsible for the diminution of the value of the vehicle due to the accident.

The trial court granted defendants' motion for summary judgment. The Court of Appeals reversed. Citing two decisions from this court, the Court of Appeals determined that an insurer in these circumstances must restore the vehicle to its pre-loss condition or, if it could not do so, pay the insured the difference in the repaired vehicle's fair market value before and after the collision.... For the reasons expressed below, we affirm the decision of the Court of Appeals.

The Court of Appeals opinion sets forth the pertinent facts:

> "In January 1998, plaintiff's 1993 Ford pickup truck, which was insured under the terms of a 'car policy Oregon' issued by defendant[s], was damaged in a collision. As a result, plaintiff incurred $6,993.40 in repair costs, which defendant paid, minus the deductible. However, notwithstanding those repairs, the pickup could not be completely restored to its 'pre-accident condition.' Consequently, even after being repaired, the vehicle's market value was diminished."

*Gonzales*, 210 Or.App. at 57, 150 P.3d 20. Defendants did not compensate plaintiff for the alleged diminished value of his truck.

Plaintiff, along with another individual, brought a class action against defendants. Plaintiff alleged that his automobile insurance policy required defendants, when they elected to repair a vehicle that had suffered property damage, to restore the vehicle to its pre-loss condition. Additionally, plaintiff alleged that that obligation required defendants to pay for the amount of loss of value to the vehicle if the vehicle could not be restored to its pre-loss condition, called "diminished value." Based on those allegations, plaintiff asserted claims for breach of contract, breach of the implied duty of good faith and fair dealing, and unjust enrichment.

Defendants moved for summary judgment, arguing that the policy did not cover diminished value. Instead, defendants argued, the policy obligated defendants to repair plaintiff's vehicle. Defendants contended that the plain and ordinary meaning of the word "repair" in the policy did not incorporate a duty to pay diminished value. Plaintiff responded that the plain meaning of "repair" encompassed restoration of the vehicle's pre-loss physical condition and, if that were not possible, payment for diminished value....

Before we turn to our analysis, we set forth the relevant wording from the insurance policy in some detail. The policy provides that defendants "will pay for loss to [the] insured car caused by collision less any applicable deductibles." The policy defines "loss" as "direct and accidental loss of or damage to [the] insured car, including its equipment." Defendants' liability for that loss is limited by the following provision:

"**Limits of Liability**

"Our limits of liability for loss shall not exceed:

"1. The amount which it would cost to repair or replace damaged or stolen property with other of like kind and quality; or with new property less an adjustment for physical deterioration and/or depreciation."

The policy also describes how loss will be paid by defendants: "We will pay the loss in money or repair or replace damaged or stolen property." Finally, the policy outlines the rights and responsibilities of the insurer and the insured, and provides, in part:

"**RIGHTS AND RESPONSIBILITIES**

"* * * *

"The insured has *the right to payment for the loss in money or repair or replacement* of the damaged or stolen property, *at the option of the* [*insurer*]."

(Boldface and capitalization in original; emphasis added.) The policy includes no definition of "repair." Neither does it expressly include or exclude coverage for diminished value in those terms.

We begin our analysis by noting that this case calls for the interpretation of the terms of the automobile insurance policy that defendants issued. This case does not call on the court to decide the principles applicable generally to diminished value claims in property damage disputes of all kinds.

The policy contains an unambiguous promise by defendants to pay plaintiff "for loss to your insured car caused by collision ..." and defines "loss" to mean "direct and accidental loss of or damage to your insured car, including its equipment." (Boldface omitted.) The policy also entitles plaintiff "to payment for the loss in money or repair or replacement of the damaged or stolen property," at defendants' option.

The parties' central dispute turns on the meaning of the word "repair" in the policy. Specifically, plaintiff argues that "repair" includes restoration of the pre-loss condition and value of the insured property, while defendants argue that "repair" refers to only the restoration of the function and appearance of the insured property. Not surprisingly, the parties offer different definitions of "repair." Defendants offer the following definition from *Webster's Third New Int'l Dictionary:* "**1 a**: to restore by replacing a part or putting together what is torn or broken * * *. **b**: to restore to a sound or healthy state." *Webster's Third New Int'l Dictionary* 1923 (unabridged ed. 2002).

Plaintiff, on the other hand, contends that defendants' definition is incomplete and cites other definitions from *Webster's:* "**2**: to make good: REMEDY * * *. **3**: to make up for: compensate for." *Id.* at 1923. Plaintiff also faults defendants for failing to include a definition of "restore," because it is part of the definition of "repair." "Restore" means "to bring back to or put back into a former or original state" *Id.* at 1936. Based on those definitions, plaintiff asserts that "repair" includes the duty to restore the vehicle's value.

Despite their differences, the definitions of "repair" cited by both plaintiff and defendants focus on the restoration of property, either to its former state or to a healthy state. Another source, *Black's Law Dictionary*, defines "repair" as "[t]o mend, remedy, restore, renovate[;][t]o restore to a sound or good state after decay, injury, dilapidation or partial destruction." *Black's Law Dictionary* 1298 (6th ed. 1990). Like the definition from *Webster's*, that definition focuses on the restoration of property to a former state.

An interpretation of the same or similar policy terms in this court's prior case law can supply helpful contextual evidence of the intent that underlies the use of those terms in the policy in question here. The parties acknowledge that two prior decisions by this court are pertinent to that inquiry, although, as noted, they disagree about the legal effect of those cases. We turn next to a consideration of that contextual evidence.

This court's two previous decisions addressed whether similar automobile insurance policies required payment for diminished value when the insurer had not restored or could not restore the vehicle to its pre-loss condition. The first case, *Rossier* [*v. Union Automobile Ins. Co.*], 134 Or. 211, 291 P. 498, addressed the issue of the proper measure of property damages under an automobile insurance policy. The policy contained a general provision indemnifying the insured against loss or damage by reason of accidental collision. The policy also provided that the insurer's liability was limited to "'the actual cost of replacement of the property damaged or destroyed, and in no event, to exceed the true cash value of the automobile current at time loss or damage occurs.'" *Id.* at 213, 291 P. 498 (quoting the policy at issue).

The court determined that that provision contemplated "that the insurer had the right to replace or repair broken or damaged parts in an effort to put the automobile in substantially the same condition as it was prior to the collision." *Id.* at 214, 291 P. 498.

The court addressed the question of the proper measure of the insurer's monetary liability as a matter of contract interpretation:

"Unquestionably the primary object or purpose of the plaintiff was to be indemnified against loss or damage to his automobile resulting from accidental collision. It is common knowledge that the nature and extent of damage to a car may be such that replacement or repair of broken parts will not compensate the insured for his loss. In the instant case plaintiff had a new car. It had been driven only 140 miles. A mechanic called as an expert witness, speaking of the damage to the automobile, said, 'It was a wrecked car, you absolutely can't put a wrecked car back in the condition it was before the wreck.' The frame was sprung; rear axles bent; upholstery seared with acid; doors battered; rear wheel broken; windows shattered and otherwise injured. To award him damages for the actual cost of replacement of broken or damaged parts would, indeed, be inadequate relief. That there would be diminution of value as the result of collision as here shown seems obvious. In many instances the injury to the automobile may be of such nature and extent that, after repairs have been made, there will be no diminution of value. Under such circumstances cost of repairs would be equivalent to the difference between the value of the automobile before and after collision."
*Id.* at 215, 291 P. 498.

The court also determined that the policy term "replacement" embraced the *repair or replacement* of damaged property:

"'Replacement' as thus used means, in our opinion, the restoration of the property to its condition prior to the injury. Such restoration may or may not be accomplished by repair or replacement of broken or damaged parts. It cannot be said that there has been a complete restoration of the property unless it can be said that there has been no diminution of value after repair of the car." *Id.* at 215–16, 291 P. 498.

.... On the basis of the foregoing reasoning, the court in *Rossier* concluded that the trial court had applied the correct measure of damages:

"The conclusion reached in the instant case that the proper measure of damages is the difference between the fair cash value of the car before and after the injury is supported by the weight of authority[.]" *Id.* (citations omitted).

*Rossier* is helpful in resolving the present dispute, even though the court in that case did not separately define the term "repair." The court rejected the contention that an insurer can satisfy its obligation to restore a vehicle to its pre-accident condition without diminished value solely by paying for the cost of repairs. According to *Rossier*, if repairs to a vehicle do not restore the vehicle to its pre-accident condition, then the correct measure of damages is "the difference between the fair cash value of the automobile before and after the collision." *Id.* at 212, 291 P. 498.

In *Dunmire* [*Co. v. Ore. Mut. Fire Ins. Co.*], 166 Or. 690, 114 P.2d 1005, the second case relied upon by plaintiff and the Court of Appeals, this court addressed a slightly different provision than that at issue in *Rossier*. In *Dunmire*, the policy limited the insurer's liability to "'what it would then cost to repair or replace the automobile, or parts thereof, with other of like kind and quality.'" *Id.* at 699, 114 P.2d 1005 (quoting policy). The trial court had awarded to the plaintiff in that case the difference between the value of the car before the accident and after the accident, minus the deductible. *Id.* ...

Defendants contend that *Rossier* and *Dunmire* are distinguishable and, if they are not distinguishable, that those cases should be overruled. ...

We disagree with defendants' reading of *Dunmire*. The policy in that case phrased the insurer's obligation in the disjunctive: "repair or replace." Thus, the policy did afford the insurer the opportunity to satisfy its liability by choosing either to repair or replace the damaged vehicle. The policy under consideration here afforded defendants the same substantive choice. Defendants' contention provides no basis for distinguishing *Dunmire*.

We conclude that *Dunmire's* interpretation of "repair" applies to the provision at issue here. Under *Dunmire*, "repair" encompasses the restoration of the vehicle to its condition prior to the collision. ... We see no reason to overrule that well-established legal interpretation. Therefore, under the policy at issue, if an attempted "repair" does not or cannot result in a complete restoration of the vehicle's pre-loss condition, the vehicle is not "repair[ed]," and the resulting diminution of value of the vehicle remains a "loss to [the] insured car caused by collision" for which defendants are liable under their policy. [We note that *Dunmire* was decided in 1941. Thus, the definition of repair adopted in *Dunmire* has been part of the legal landscape for well over 60 years. Nothing in *Dunmire* or this case, however, prevents insurers from including a definition of repair in automobile policies that excludes diminished value from coverage. According to plaintiffs, many insurance policies do exclude such coverage.]

The particular context of the word "repair" in the instant policy also demonstrates that defendants' obligation includes payment for diminished value where repair cannot restore a vehicle to its pre-loss condition.

The policy requires defendants to pay for "loss to [the] insured car caused by collision less any applicable deductibles." The policy defines loss broadly: "direct and accidental loss of or damage to [the] insured car." Defendants do not dispute that the policy definition of loss is broad enough to include diminished value. "Repair," therefore, when viewed in the context of this policy, which contains a broad definition of loss, incorporates the concept of restoration of a vehicle's preloss condition or, if the insurer cannot or will not restore the vehicle to that condition, payment for diminished value.

In the "limits of liability" provision, the word "repair" appears in the same sentence as the phrase "of like kind and quality." Plaintiff contends that that phrase modifies both the word "repair" and the word "replace." Because the word "quality" in that phrase signifies value, plaintiff argues, "repair" must restore the automobile to the same quality or condition that existed before the accident. Significantly, the provision at issue in *Dunmire* contained the same phrase. On the basis of *Dunmire*, we agree that the phrase "of like kind and quality" is another factor supporting our conclusion that defendants are obligated to restore the damaged vehicle or, if the vehicle cannot be restored, to compensate plaintiff accordingly.

We hold that "repair," as used in the policy at issue in this case, requires defendants to restore plaintiff's vehicle to its pre-loss physical condition. If defendants do not or cannot so restore plaintiff's vehicle, defendants must compensate plaintiff for the diminished value of the vehicle.

Defendants assert that plaintiff's claim, when reduced to its essence, would lead to an absurd result: if an insurer has restored a vehicle to its pre-loss condition, an insurer nevertheless is obligated to pay for diminished value that results from only stigma attached to that vehicle because the vehicle has been involved in a collision. Defendants argue that the supposed negative perception of prospective buyers regarding a repaired car's worth following a collision is not included in the policy's definition of "repair."

In this case, plaintiff does not claim damages for stigma, as defendants describe that concept above. Plaintiff submitted an affidavit in opposition to defendants' summary judgment motion that stated that he was "not satisfied that [his] vehicle had been repaired with like kind and quality parts, and was not restored to its pre-loss condition. The vehicle had a number of problems that did not exist before." Plaintiff also submitted two expert affidavits describing the inability of body shops to restore pre-loss physical condition in certain circumstances. Because this case involved a genuine dispute about whether defendants had restored the vehicle to its pre-loss condition, we need not decide whether the policy requires payment for a claim based solely on "stigma." ...

## American Manufacturers Mutual Insurance Co. v. Schaefer

Supreme Court of Texas
124 S.W.3d 154, 47 Tex. Sup. Ct. J. 40 (2003)

O'Neill J. delivered the opinion of the Court.

In this case, we must decide whether the Texas Standard Personal Auto Policy obligates an insurer to compensate a policyholder for a vehicle's diminished market value when the car has been damaged but adequately repaired. We hold that it does not, and accordingly reverse the court of appeals' judgment.

Gary Schaefer purchased a standard automobile insurance policy from American Manufacturers Mutual Insurance Company (AMM). Part D of the policy, entitled "Coverage for Damage to Your Auto," provides that AMM will pay for "direct and accidental loss to your covered auto...." The payment obligation is subject to a contractual limitation of liability that reads, in pertinent part, as follows:

LIMIT OF LIABILITY
Our limit of liability for loss will be the lesser of the:
1. Actual cash value of the stolen or damaged property; or

2. Amount necessary to repair or replace the property with other of like kind and quality; or

3. Amount stated in the Declarations of this policy.

The policy also provides for the method of paying the loss:

**PAYMENT OF LOSS**

We may pay for loss in money or repair or replace the damaged or stolen property.

In October 1995, Schaefer's vehicle was involved in an accident. It was inspected by an AMM adjuster, and the insurance company elected to repair the vehicle. Schaefer does not dispute the quality or adequacy of the repairs. Instead, he maintains that its value decreased $2,600 due to market perceptions that a damaged and subsequently repaired vehicle is worth less than one that has never been damaged. Schaefer claims that the policy obligates AMM to compensate him for that diminished value.

Schaefer filed this class action against AMM and several other insurance companies that issue policies containing the same standard language. He claims that AMM's refusal to compensate him for his vehicle's diminished market value violated the Texas Insurance Code and breached the insurance contract.

The parties dispute whether the policy language obligates AMM to pay Schaefer for the diminished value of his fully repaired vehicle. Schaefer argues that a vehicle's diminished market value is a "direct or accidental loss" that AMM is required to compensate under the policy's insuring provision. Schaefer contends that construing the policy otherwise frustrates its underlying purpose to fully indemnify the insured. Citing as authority a number of cases from Texas and other jurisdictions, Schaefer contends that the policy language requiring AMM to pay the amount necessary "to repair or replace" with "other of like kind and quality" contemplates the payment of diminished value. AMM's payment obligation is further evidenced, Schaefer claims, by the policy's failure to expressly exclude diminished value from coverage under the policy's "Exclusions" section.

While Schaefer focuses on the "loss" language of the policy's insuring provision, AMM emphasizes the limitation of liability and payment provisions. AMM does not dispute that the term "loss" could encompass diminished value, but contends that the insuring language must be construed in light of the "Limit of Liability" section, which limits the insurer's liability to the lesser of the vehicle's actual cash value or the amount necessary to repair or replace it. According to AMM, the term "repair or replace" does not encompass any concept of "value." Like Schaefer, AMM cites cases from Texas and other jurisdictions that support its position.

AMM also urges our consideration of the Texas Department of Insurance's interpretation of the policy language as not obligating an insurer to pay for a fully repaired vehicle's diminished value. *See Tex. Dep't of Ins. Commissioner's Bulletin*, No. B-0027-00 (Apr. 6, 2002) ("[A]n insurer is not obligated to pay a first party claimant for diminished value when an automobile is completely repaired to its pre-damage condition. The language of the insurance policy does not require payment for, or refer to, diminished value.").

We agree with AMM that the policy's plain language, when read in context, giving effect to all contractual provisions, is unambiguous and does not require payment for diminished value when a vehicle has been fully and adequately repaired. While a vehicle's diminished value may be a "direct loss" under the policy's insuring provision, AMM's obligation to compensate the insured for that loss is circumscribed by the policy's "Limit of Liability" section. That section states, in pertinent part, that AMM's liability for loss is limited to the damaged vehicle's "actual cash value" or the amount needed "to repair or replace" the vehicle, whichever is less. We must give the policy language its ordinary and generally accepted meaning unless the policy shows that the words used are intended to impart a technical or different meaning.

The concept of "repair" with regard to a vehicle connotes something tangible, like removing dents or fixing parts. *See* BLACK'S LAW DICTIONARY 1298 (6th ed. 1990) (defining "repair" as "to mend, remedy, restore, renovate; to restore to a sound or good state after decay, injury, dilapidation or partial destruction"); *see also Siegle v. Progressive Consumers Ins. Co.*, 819 So. 2d 732, 736 (Fla. 2002) (stating "'repair' means to restore by replacing a part or putting together what is torn or broken"); *Carlton* [*v. Trinity Universal Ins. Co.*], 32 S.W.3d at 464 [(Tex. App.—Houston [14th Dist.] 2000, pet. denied)] (defining "repair" as "bring[ing] back to good or useable condition").

We do not believe that the ordinary or generally accepted meaning of the word "repair" connotes compensating for the market's perception that a damaged but fully and adequately repaired vehicle has an intrinsic value less than that of a never-damaged car.... To expand the ordinary meaning of "repair" to include an intangible, diminished-value element would be "ignoring the policy['s] language or giving the contract['s] text a meaning never intended." *Siegle*, 819 So. 2d at 738 (interpreting identical policy language).

A number of other state courts interpreting similar or identical policy language have expressly relied on the definition of "repair" articulated in *Carlton*.... The plain meaning of AMM's obligation under the policy's "Limit of Liability" section, paragraph 2, is to restore the vehicle, either through repair or replacement, to the same physical and operating condition it was in before the damage occurred.

In addition to applying the plain meaning of the policy's language, we must also read the policy as a whole, giving effect to each provision.... Interpreting the policy's "repair or replace" language to include diminished value, as Schaefer urges, would render other provisions of the policy meaningless. The policy provides that the insured is entitled to "the lesser of" actual cash value or the amount necessary to repair or replace the vehicle. To incorporate diminished value into the "repair or replace" provision would render the "lesser of" language meaningless.

The insurer's obligation to compensate the loss would be cumulative—repair or replace *and* pay diminished value—in effect insuring the vehicle's "actual cash value" in every instance and undermining the insurer's right under the policy to choose a course of action. *See Pritchett* [*v. State Farm Mut. Ins. Co.*], 834 So.2d at 791–92 [(Ala. Civ. App. 2002)] (holding that insurer's option to pay the vehicle's full value or make repairs would be meaningless if the policy were read to cover diminished value)....

It may be true, as Schaefer contends, that in some instances—say, when a very expensive car is damaged—an insurer will spend less money if it elects to repair and pay diminished value damages rather than declare the car a total loss and pay its actual cash value. But requiring an insurer, who elects repair, to additionally pay cash for the market's diminished perception incorporates an intangible value element into the repair provision that simply does not appear in the policy's language.

Inserting the concept of diminished value into the repair provision would similarly render the policy's "Payment of Loss" section meaningless. Under this section of the policy, the insurer has an option to pay the insured in "money *or* repair *or* replace[ment]" (emphasis added). Including diminished value in the concept of repair would force an insurer that chooses to compensate a loss by exercising the repair option to also pay money, ignoring the clause's disjunctive language.

Schaefer also points to modifying language in paragraph two of the policy's Limitation of Liability provision, which refers to the [a]mount necessary to repair or replace the property with other *of like kind and quality* (emphasis added). He contends that the phrase "of like kind and quality" modifies both "repair" and "replace," and obligates the insurer to compensate for a damaged vehicle's pre-accident value because the word "quality" encompasses the concept of value. But whether or not intrinsic value generally inheres in the word "quality," and assuming without deciding that the phrase "of like kind and quality" modifies both "repair" and "replace," we must look to the ordinary meaning of the words that are modified.

We have said that the words "repair" and "replace," with regard to a vehicle, connote something tangible, like removing dents, fixing parts, or replacing the vehicle with a comparable substitute. Thus, if an insurer elects to repair a vehicle and must replace parts in doing so, it must use parts "of like kind and quality." Likewise, if an insurer elects to replace the vehicle, it must do so with a vehicle "of like kind and quality." ... Schaefer's interpretation strains the policy's plain terms.

Schaefer also contends that the policy covers diminished-value damages because they are not expressly excluded in the policy's "Exclusions" section. But an exclusion's purpose is to remove from coverage an item that would otherwise have been included. Absence of an exclusion cannot confer coverage. Because the policy's language does not obligate AMM to pay for the diminished value of a car that has been fully and adequately repaired, the failure to include diminished-value damages in the policy's Exclusion section is immaterial.

We note that diminished value claims have taken different forms.... They have arisen when repairs are incomplete or faulty, or when the insurer elects to repair when declaring a total loss is the better option. Id. Neither is the case here. AMM elected to repair the damaged vehicle, and Schaefer does not contend that the repairs were faulty, incomplete or inadequate. If he did, then the insurer might be liable for breaching its obligations under the policy's terms. But Schaefer would still only be entitled to the remedies outlined in the policy, which do not include compensation for a fully repaired vehicle's diminished market value.

We acknowledge that Schaefer's repaired vehicle may command a smaller sum in the market than a like vehicle that has never been damaged, and that awarding Schaefer diminished value in addition to repair would go further to make him whole. But we may neither rewrite the parties' contract nor add to its language.

Schaefer's standard automobile insurance policy does not obligate AMM to compensate Schaefer for his fully repaired vehicle's diminished market value. Accordingly, we reverse the judgment of the court of appeals and render judgment in favor of AMM.

## Notes and Questions

1. The above cases illustrate the two divergent "lines" of cases concerning policyholder attempts to recover because of the "inherent diminished value" of a car that has been in an accident, irrespective of the quality of the repair to the automobile. Beginning in the first half of the 20th century, courts began to address the issue. *See, e.g., Haussler v. Indemnity Co. of America*, 227 Ill. App. 504 (1923) (essentially rejecting inherent diminished value theory). A smattering of decisions have been rendered since but the issue took on renewed vigor in the 1990s, as policyholder counsel not only "rediscovered" the issue but also sought class action status, raising the stakes considerably. *See* Jeffrey W. Stempel & Erik S. Knutsen, Stempel & Knutsen on Insurance Coverage § 27.08 for a more complete discussion of the issue and commentary.

2. Which approach to the diminished value question is more persuasive: *Gonzales* or *Shaefer*?

3. How important is differing policy language? Or is the issue one that should be resolved on the basis of insurance concepts? What is the purpose of the property insurance component of a typical automobile policy? What are the objectively reasonable expectations of a policyholder whose car is in a fender bender? Does one expect repair of the car or compensation based on any difference in resale value?

4. What, if any, weight should be accorded the views of insurance regulators on an issue such as the diminished value controversy?

5. In the continuing battle over diminished value coverage, insurers appear to have some momentum. *See, e.g., Allgood v. Meridian Sec. Ins. Co.*, 836 N.E.2d 243 (Ind. 2005) (standard auto policy does not obligate insurer to pay for diminished value of car after repairs); *Culhane v. Western Nat'l Mut. Ins. Co.*, 704 N.W.2d 287 (S.D. 2005) (no coverage for diminished value unless policyholder can demonstrate that car cannot be repaired to its former physical, mechanical, and operating condition). Culhane went so far as to describe rejection of diminished value coverage as not only the majority view but an "almost unanimous" view. That is probably a little overboard, at least historically (*see* Jeffrey W. Stempel & Erik S. Knutsen, Stempel & Knutsen on Insurance Coverage § 27.08) but close to correct regarding modern case law.

6. More important, the argument for diminished value coverage is just not particularly persuasive in that it tends to convert insurance for physical damage into insurance for economic injury that normally is not covered under standard property

policies. Stempel feels more strongly about this than Knutsen, and readers should know that Stempel has been a retained expert for a large insurer in one of these cases. To test the logic of diminished value for auto damage, try a thought experiment substituting home damage.

For example, if a family is slaughtered by a serial killer (assume a messy serial killer as in all the *Halloween* and *Texas Chain Saw* movies), there will be the physical damage to the property, which can be cleaned up by ServiceMaster or similar vendors. The home will then be "good as new" but will likely have a diminished market value because of its spooky and tragic past, which not even the best realtor will be able to suppress. The Amityville Horror is logically worth less than the same house down the block absent a niche market buyer. But should physical injury insurance compensate the policyholder for this type of loss? Most courts have answered "no" regarding auto insurance.

We could use the same macabre "situs of atrocity" hypothetical for cars and presumably have the same result. The car might be worth less because it was the scene of a crime but if the repairs are adequate, there is no remaining physical damage to the car. The tricky part may be the determination of the quality of repairs. Laypersons may have difficulty knowing when the vendor selected by an auto insurer has truly repaired a damaged vehicle to the extent it is good as new. Anecdotally, drivers who have been in accidents have long complained that even after repair, the vehicle "just doesn't drive right, like it used to." They may be right, and this may well be because their insurers cut corners on repairs. There may even be a small subset of cases where even with thorough repair, the car seems to perform as if it is still at least slightly damaged. Most of you have probably seen the Carfax advertisements suggesting that buyers want to avoid vehicles that have been previously damaged; the implicit message is that, even if repaired, these cars are bad news. But notwithstanding popular perception, it appears that repair can restore automobiles to their former condition if the repairs are adequate in scope and done correctly. Where the insurer does this, should it be obligated to also compensate the policyholder due to a market-based discount imposed on auto resales simply because the car was once in an accident?

7. There may also be disputes as to the type and quality of repairs and parts used in fixing an automobile after a collision. Some insurers have a practice of paying for repair of damaged policyholder vehicles with parts made by manufacturers other than the original automaker (i.e., aftermarket parts). *See, e.g., Avery v. State Farm Mut. Auto. Ins. Co.*, 835 N.E.2d 801 (Ill. 2005) (reverse of a $1 billion class action certification).

## § 11.08. Rights of an Injured Third Party against Another Insurer

Some states, through legislation, allow injured third party accident victims the right to take direct legal action against the insurer of a tortfeasor who has been denied coverage for a loss by that insurer. *See, e.g.*, Wis. Rev. Stat. §§ 632.24, 632.34;

LA. REV. STAT. ANN. §§ 22:655, 22:983. Georgia, for example, has a direct action statute limited to motor vehicle accidents. GA. CODE ANN. § 46-7-12. Without enabling legislation, the right to direct action by the injured third party against the liability insurer does not generally exist. *See, e.g., Logan v. Hollier*, 424 So. 2d 1279 (La. Ct. App. 1982). *But see Strutz v. State Farm Mut. Ins. Co.*, 609 A.2d 569 (Pa. Super. Ct. 1992), where the court said: "To be considered a third-party beneficiary in this state it is necessary to show both parties to the contract had an intent to benefit the third party through the contract and did, in fact, explicitly indicate this intent in the contract."

# § 11.09. State Automobile Liability Insurance Regulation

## [A] Financial Responsibility Laws

The primary purpose of automobile financial responsibility statutes in the various states is to protect the public by requiring certain drivers to prove their ability to compensate innocent third parties who may be injured through the negligence of such drivers. The statutes are not designed to protect the named insured. *See, e.g., Hutcheson v. Alabama Farm Bureau Mut. Cas. Ins. Co.*, 435 So. 2d 734 (Ala. 1983). These state financial responsibility statutes may provide: (1) the negligent driver involved in a motor vehicle accident must furnish proof of financial responsibility as a condition of not having his or her license suspended or revoked; (2) that this proof of financial responsibility be demonstrated as a condition for reinstatement of the negligent driver's suspended license; or (3) it may provide for the revocation or suspension of a driver's license if that driver fails to satisfy any judgment against him or her.

Thus, financial responsibility statutes are "first bite" laws that are designed to require motor vehicle liability insurance coverage as a precondition to the continued use of a state's highways, but only after a driver has been involved in an accident, convicted of various traffic offenses, had a driver's license suspended, or been held liable on an unpaid judgment for damages. *See, e.g., Larson v. Occidental Fire & Casualty Co.*, 79 N.M. 562, 446 P.2d 210 (1968). *See also* 7 AM. JUR. 2D *Automobile Insurance* § 20 (1980). For an example of the consequences of violation of state financial responsibility laws, *see Tomai-Minogue v. State Farm Mut. Auto. Ins. Co.*, 770 F.2d 1228 (4th Cir. 1985) (applying Virginia law) (failure to pay premiums results in suspension of driver's license at request of insurer). In the *Tomai-Minogue* decision, the court discussed the public policy rationale behind financial responsibility statutes:

> The governmental interest at stake is hardly inconsequential. The statute aims to ensure that motorists are financially responsible and will satisfy promptly any judgments against them. While that interest may seem slight where a parked car was bumped, it is anything but trivial when accidents involve loss of human life, injury to other motorists, and extensive property damage. Financial responsibility statutes are not simply designed to safeguard

insurance companies, but serve the more general societal purpose of ensuring that those responsible for highway accidents pay the resulting losses without the necessity for cumbersome enforcement proceedings. Where an adverse judgment has not been satisfied by the motorist, Virginia has opted to suspend the license now and discuss the matter later. We decline to undercut that legitimate choice by requiring the taking to be later and the talking to be first.

## [B] Compulsory Insurance Programs

States also may require policyholder participation in specific insurance programs, such as workers compensation, or may require insurer participation in specific programs designed to increase insurance availability or consumer protection (such as a guarantee fund to provide compensation for policyholders of insolvent insurers). *See also Nationwide Mut. Ins. Co. v. Roberts*, 134 S.E.2d 654 (N.C. 1964) (insurer participation in automobile assigned risk pool required as a condition of doing business in state). The *Roberts* court held that because the primary purpose of compulsory motor vehicle liability insurance is to compensate the innocent victim rather than to protect the tortfeasor, "there is no reason why the victim's right to recover from the insurance carrier should depend upon whether the conduct of its insured was intentional or negligent." Is this argument persuasive to you? Why or why not? What are the insurer's rights, if any, regarding compulsory coverage?

## [C] Assigned Risk Policies

An "assigned risk" plan in state compulsory automobile financial responsibility statutes generally provides that automobile liability insurance carriers in the state are required to insure certain high risk drivers who qualify under the plan, but who are unable to secure liability insurance coverage on a voluntary basis. The right of the insurers to cancel such "assigned risk" policies is also narrowly restricted by statute. "Assigned risk" plans differ from state to state, however. *See, e.g., Virginia Farm Bureau Mut. Ins. Co. v. Saccio*, 133 S.E.2d 268 (Va. 1963) (describing Virginia's plan); *Allstate Ins. Co. v. Dorr*, 411 F.2d 198 (9th Cir. 1969) (discussing California plan).

## [D] Mandatory Minimum Limits of Automobile Liability Insurance

Underinsurance in America is a huge problem in the auto accident world. Many drivers do not have sufficient financial limits of their insurance to adequately compensate someone who may be injured in an accident as a result of the driver's negligence. Most states have enacted mandatory minimum levels of automobile liability insurance that each driver must carry. However, these minimum levels are, in the views of the casebook authors, shockingly low. Most drivers also choose to purchase merely the minimum required limits. The most common financial limits of automobile liability policies in the United States are $25,000 per person, or $50,000 per accident. *See, e.g.,* Nev. Rev. Stat. Ann. §§ 690B.020(2), § 485.3091 ($25,000/$50,000); Ala. Code §§ 32-7-23(a), 32-7-6(c) ($25,000/50,000); Mo. Rev. Stat. Ann. § 303.030 ($25,000/$50,000).

*Query:* How do these minimum limits make sense when the injury cost to an auto accident victim for a very serious injury is often in the multiple millions of dollars? Can you rationalize why most states have not changed the limits for decades? Why would the present limits in Florida at $10,000 per person/$30,000 per accident differ from Maine and Alaska where the minimum limit is $50,000 per person/$100,000 per accident?

# Chapter 12

# "Bad Faith" Litigation and Claims Administration

## § 12.01. The Concepts of Good Faith, Bad Faith and Fair Claims Handling

### [A] Defining Bad Faith

Chapter 9 concerned the respective duties of policyholder and insurer and discussed the insurer's duty of good faith and fair dealing as well as the duty to make reasonable attempts to settle claims. This chapter takes a more sustained look at the good faith obligation and related topics such as bad faith claims and the relationship between insurer, policyholder, and counsel.

It is of course hornbook law that there is in every contract an implied obligation of good faith and fair dealing. *See* E. Allan Farnsworth, Contracts § 7.17 (4th ed. 2004); American Law Institute, Restatement (Second) of The Law of Contracts § 205 (1981). This duty applies even when the contracting parties are sophisticated business persons, and to insurance policies.

But in ordinary contracts, the duty of good faith often seems to be more rhetorical than real. And the standard of good faith is not all that elevated. For example, the Uniform Commercial Code, which governs transactions among merchants, defines "good faith" as "honesty in fact" and "observance of reasonable commercial standards of fair dealing." *See* U.C.C. § 1-201(20). Although the latter phrase could be interpreted to impose more significant duties upon contracting parties, in many cases, the judicial focus is upon the mere honest-in-fact prong without much emphasis on reasonable and fair behavior. If this occurs, a merchant can be mean-spirited, unreasonable, and obstreperous—but excused from bad behavior if not dishonest, a dispiriting result.

Many courts also find bad faith where a party has acted in such a way as to deprive the other contract party of the benefit of the bargain—a rule of thumb we find useful. One might also define bad faith as something akin to the Golden Rule: the insurer should treat its policyholders as it would itself want to be treated regarding responsiveness, investigation, communication, and decision-making regarding claims. The American Law Institute *Restatement of the Law, Liability Insurance* § 49 (2019) ("RLLI") defines bad faith as an insurer's failure to perform pursuant to a liability insurance policy "(1) [w]ithout a reasonable basis for its conduct" and ("(2) [w]ith knowledge of its obligation to perform or in reckless disregard of whether it had an obligation to perform."

The duty of good faith is significantly more pronounced in the context of insurance as compared to non-insurance contract law. Although most courts have stopped short of labeling the insurer-policyholder relationship a fiduciary relationship, it is widely accepted that the arrangement is "fiduciary in nature." Some courts have in fact deemed the relationship to be a true fiduciary one akin to that of doctor-patient or attorney-client where the policyholder is placing trust in an insurer and relying on the insurer, as is the case when a liability insurer has control over defense of a claim. *See* the Chapters on Liability and Automobile Insurance, *supra*.

The insurer's duty of good faith to its policyholder requires that insurers comport themselves to an acceptable minimal level of conduct. The insurer cannot deal with its policyholders in an amoral or arm's-length manner but instead is in a relationship with its policyholder that is fiduciary in nature. Further, an insurer's good faith duties require it not only to stand by its contracts with policyholders but to adequately perform their contractual obligations.

The law and concept of insurance bad faith is closely related to the respective duties owed by insurer and policyholder, particularly the insurer's duty to defend claims under standard liability policies. Because the policyholder's fate is "in the hands" of the insurer, it has long been accepted that a liability insurer owes the policyholder greater, semi-fiduciary duties to the policyholder beyond the duties owed between parties in conventional, arm's-length contract relationships.

There is, of course, a similar dependency of first-party policyholders when faced with catastrophic loss such as destruction of one's home. Consequently, most jurisdictions now also recognize heightened obligations of good faith—and liability for bad faith—in the context of first-party insurance or for liability insurance that is "indemnity only" without a duty to defend. However, in application, the bad faith standard appears to be more vigorously applied against liability insurers who have failed to defend or settle claims as opposed to first-party insurers who have undervalued claims or otherwise mistreated the policyholder.

In a majority of states there is a separate tort claim available to the policyholder where the insurer acts in bad faith. This is not the situation for noninsurance contracts. In addition, in states were bad faith is a tort, a policyholder that satisfactorily demonstrates bad faith by the insurer may recover punitive damages, which are usually only available for ordinary breaches of contract where the contract breach is accompanied by an independent tort such as fraud.

The Arizona Supreme Court has summarized state law regarding the insurer's obligation of good faith in the context of an insurer's obligation to provide a good faith defense to liability claims against the policyholder. According to the court, "[h]ere are the basic rules."

The tort of bad faith arises when the insurer "intentionally denies, fails to process or pay a claim without a reasonable basis." *Noble v. National Am. Life Ins. Co.*, 128 Ariz. 188, 190, 624 P.2d 866, 868 (1981). While an insurer may challenge claims which are fairly debatable, *id.*, its belief in fair debatability "is a question of fact to be determined by the jury." *Sparks v. Republic Nat'l Life Ins. Co.*, 132 Ariz. 529, 539, 647 P.2d 1127, 1137 (1982). An insurance contract is not an ordinary commercial bargain; "implicit in the contract and the relationship is the insurer's obligation to play fairly with its insured." *Rawlings v. Apodaca*, 151 Ariz. 149, 154, 726 P.2d 565, 570 (1986). The insurer has "some duties of a fiduciary nature," including "equal consideration, fairness and honesty." *Id.* at 155, 726 P.2d at 571. Thus, an insurer may be held liable in a first-party case when it seeks to gain unfair financial advantage of its insured through conduct that invades the insured's right to honest and fair treatment," and because of that, "the insurer's eventual performance of the express covenant — by paying the claim — does not release it from liability for 'bad faith.'" *Id.* at 156, 726 P.2d at 572. And in *Deese* [*v. State Farm Mut. Auto. Ins. Co.*], 172 Ariz. at 508, 838 P.2d at 1269, we noted than an insurance contract provides more than just security from financial loss to the insured. We said, "the insured also is entitled to receive the additional security of knowing that she will be dealt with fairly and in good faith." *Id.* Thus, if an insurer acts unreasonably in the manner in which it processes a claim, it will be held liable for bad faith "without regard to its ultimate merits. *Id.* at 509, 838 P.2d at 1270.

*Zilisch v. State Farm Mut. Auto. Ins. Co.*, 196 Ariz. 234, 237–38, 995 P.2d 276, 279–80 (2000).

Pretty good rhetoric for policyholders, huh? But before you get too carried away planning how to spend your contingency portion of a bad faith punitive damages award, check out the governing precedent applicable to your case — and remember, in the wake of the U.S. Supreme Court's opinion in *State Farm Mut. Auto. Ins. Co. v. Campbell*, 538 U.S. 408 (2003) (discussed later in this Chapter), really large punitive damages awards will be much harder to sustain. *Campbell* rhetorically suggests that punitive damages awards more than nine times greater than the accompanying compensatory damages award will be viewed as suspect, at least where compensatory damages are substantial, and also contains other language critical of punitive damages generally.[1] However, despite any limits on punitive damages, successful bad faith claimants may be entitled to considerable compensation for injuries proximately inflicted by insurer misconduct such as loss of business, remediation costs, and the like. This is largely true even in states that view an insurance bad faith action as sounding in contract rather than tort.

---

1. However, where compensatory damages are relatively small and defendant conduct sufficiently reprehensible, post-*Campbell* courts have permitted much higher ratios of punitive damages in order to vindicate the punishment and deterrence rationales of punitive damages.

*Zilisch* arose in the context of the insurer's handling of an underinsured motorist (UIM) claim,[2] but its reasoning is equally applicable to insurer conduct regarding sales, underwriting, and cancellation. Continued the court:

> The carrier has an obligation *to immediately conduct an adequate investigation, act reasonably* in evaluating the claim, and *act promptly in paying* a legitimate claim. *It should do nothing that jeopardizes the insured's security under the policy. It should not force an insured to go through needless adversarial hoops to achieve its rights under the policy.* It cannot lowball claims or delay claims hoping that the insured will settle for less. Equal consideration of the insured requires more than that.

> [W]hile fair debatability [regarding interpretation of the policy, the law, or coverage] is a necessary condition to avoid a claim of bad faith, it is not always a sufficient conduction. The appropriate inquiry [in making a finding of bad faith conduct by the insurer] is whether there is sufficient evidence from which reasonable jurors could conclude that *in the investigation, evaluation, and processing of the claim, the insurer acted unreasonably and either knew or was conscious of the fact that its conduct was unreasonable.*

*Zilisch, supra,* 196 Ariz. at 238, 995 P.2d at 280 (emphasis added). The *Zilisch* analysis is consistent with the position of RLLI § 49 and with the other definitions of bad faith noted above.

But what constitutes an unreasonable position? Or a situation in which there is not even a potential for coverage that in turn triggers a liability insurer's duty to defend? For those mapping the legal landscape for pro-insurer and pro-policyholder doctrine, one might view the these disparate situations as creating something of an equilibrium: insurers will often be "stuck" defending a claim that seems at the edge of coverage but they also, because of the volume of insurance coverage cases and disparate state law (as reflected throughout this casebook), have some significant ability to exercise discretion or challenge coverage with relative freedom from bad faith liability. *See* Randy J. Maniloff & Jeffrey W. Stempel, General Liability Insurance Coverage: Key Issues in Every State Ch. 21 (4th ed. 2018) (highlighting state-to-state difference is 19 crucial areas bearing on coverage and bad faith).

New York precedent suggests that "gross disregard" of the policyholder's interests or a "reckless failure to place on equal footing the interest of its insured with its

---

2. Astute readers may have already noted that uninsured motorist (UM) and underinsured motorist (UIM) insurance is technically first-party insurance that is purchased by the policyholder as part of its own automobile insurance. But as discussed in the Chapter on umbrella, excess and overlapping coverage, UIM insurance is actually a hybrid in that it is purchased by the policyholder and its role is to act as liability insurance for the uninsured/underinsured tortfeasor. Consequently, our view (which we realize is contested) is that the UM/UIM insurer should respond to claims as if it were a liability insurer. UM/UIM carriers implicitly acknowledge this by requiring proof of the uninsured/ underinsured tortfeasor's liability before paying claims.

own interests" (at least for liability insurers considering a settlement offer) is sufficient to constitute bad faith by the insurer. *See Greennidge v. Allstate Ins. Co.*, 446 F.3d 356, 362 (2d Cir. 2006) (applying New York law) (collecting cases). Although unreasonable insurer behavior is often enough to demonstrate bad faith, many states require both the absence of a reasonable basis for the insurer's conduct or claim denial and that the insurer know it had no reasonable basis or acted with "reckless disregard" of the policyholder's interests, a position the RLLI viewed as the "majority" rule.

Constructive knowledge by the insurer is sufficient to meet the RLLI standard, and there are also precedents stating that sufficiently unreasonable behavior may be considered bad faith irrespective of insurer intent or state of mind. We are partial to the latter view, both because it reduces the amount of judicial inquiry and also because a policyholder is just as injured by unreasonable conduct whether the conduct is intentional or merely "innocently" unreasonable.

For purposes of compensatory damages available to the policyholder, insurer state of mind should be largely irrelevant. By analogy, consider a driver who negligently takes a turn at twice the speed limit, veering into oncoming traffic and seriously injuring an oncoming driver minding her own driving business in her own lane of the road. In the ensuing tort claim for negligent driving, no court would excuse the tortfeasor for sincerely thinking that he could maintain control because he had seen it work out fine for The Rock, Jason Statham, and Vin Diesel.[3] We see no reason that lack of evil intent should be any more of a defense (regarding compensatory damages) in a bad faith action. Punitive damages, of course, are another matter, and (as noted below) some degree of conscious disregard for policyholder rights is required before such damages can be imposed.

Although simple negligence in claims-handling or coverage evaluation is not sufficient to constitute bad faith, the duty of good faith requires that insurers respond reasonably to a reasonable claim or requests by the policyholder or third parties. The insurer must act as though it were responsible for the entire claim. *See* RLLI § 24 ("[a] reasonable settlement decision is one that would be made by a reasonable insurer that bears the sole financial responsibility for the full amount of the potential judgment.").

In addition to bad faith exposure, insurers may become defendants for other alleged breaches of tort or contract duty. *See, e.g., Pehle v. Farm Bureau Life Ins. Co.*, 397 F.3d 897 (10th Cir. 2005) (applying Wyoming law) (insurance applicants stated cognizable claim against life insurer that denied applications but failed to reveal to them that blood tests obtained by insurer showed applicants to be HIV-positive; insurer has duty to make sufficient disclosure of adverse health information in screening tests so that reasonable applicant may inquire further).

---

3. Less so for co-star Paul Walker. *See* Joel Landau, *Paul Walker dead at 40: 'Fast and Furious' star killed in fiery car crash*, New York Daily News (Nov. 30, 2013).

## [B] Unfair Claims Handling: The NAIC Model Act and State Analogs

Statutes may by their textual terms or the statutory design also act to preclude certain actions against insurers or insurance entities. *See, e.g., Maes v. Audubon Indem. Ins. Group*, 127 P.3d 1126 (N.M. Ct. App. 2006) (auto insurers providing coverage pursuant to state FAIR plan immune from bad faith tort liability). In addition, state consumer protection statutes, although not expressly aimed at insurance claims, may apply to claims handling.

The dominant claims-handling legislation is the Unfair Claims Settlement Model Act promulgated by the National Association of Insurance Commissioners (NAIC) that has been adopted in some form in nearly every state. The core of the Act is Section 3 prohibiting unfair claims settlement practices and Section 4 listing various unfair practices. The Model Act deems an insurer's engagement in any of the listed practices as "improper claims practice" if (A) "It is committed flagrantly and in conscious disregard" of the Act and rules promulgated pursuant to the Act or (B) the practice "has been committed with such frequency to indicate a general business practice to engage in that type of conduct."

The Model Act is "soft law" that has no force unless adopted by a state. Although adopting states generally follow the Model Act, there are often slight differences. For example, Nevada's version of the Act has a few wording changes favorable to policyholders (e.g., removing the requirement that insurer misrepresentations be "knowing") and also provides a private right of action, while many state versions of the act provide only regulatory remedies. Nevada Revised Statute 686A.310 defines "any of the following acts by an insurer" as an unfair claims practice.

(a) Misrepresenting to insureds or claimants pertinent facts or insurance policy provisions relating to any coverage at issue.

(b) Failing to acknowledge and act reasonably promptly upon communications with respect to claims arising under insurance policies.

(c) Failing to adopt and implement reasonable standards for the prompt investigation and processing of claims arising under insurance policies.

(d) Failing to affirm or deny coverage of claims within a reasonable time after proof of loss requirements have been completed and submitted by the insured.

(e) Failing to effectuate prompt, fair and equitable settlements of claims in which liability of the insurer has become reasonably clear.

(f) Compelling insureds to institute litigation to recover amounts due under an insurance policy by offering substantially less than the amounts ultimately recovered in actions brought by such insureds, when the insureds have made claims for amounts reasonably similar to the amounts ultimately recovered.

(g) Attempting to settle a claim by an insured for less than the amount to which a reasonable person would have believed he or she was entitled by reference to written or printed advertising material accompanying or made part of an application.

(h) Attempting to settle claims on the basis of an application which was altered without notice to, or knowledge or consent of, the insured, or the representative, agent or broker of the insured.

(i) Failing, upon payment of a claim, to inform insureds or beneficiaries of the coverage under which payment is made.

(j) Making known to insureds or claimants a practice of the insurer of appealing from arbitration awards in favor of insureds or claimants for the purpose of compelling them to accept settlements or compromises less than the amount awarded in arbitration.

(k) Delaying the investigation or payment of claims by requiring an insured or a claimant, or the physician of either, to submit a preliminary claim report, and then requiring the subsequent submission of formal proof of loss forms, both of which submissions contain substantially the same information.

(l) Failing to settle claims promptly, where liability has become reasonably clear, under one portion of the insurance policy coverage in order to influence settlements under other portions of the insurance policy coverage.

(m) Failing to comply with the provisions of NRS 687B.310 to 687B.390, [relating to cancellation and renewal of policies] inclusive, or 687B.410 [relating to insurer withdrawal from the market].

(n) Failing to provide promptly to an insured a reasonable explanation of the basis in the insurance policy, with respect to the facts of the insured's claim and the applicable law, for the denial of the claim or for an offer to settle or compromise the claim.

(o) Advising an insured or claimant not to seek legal counsel.

(p) Misleading an insured or claimant concerning any applicable statute of limitations.

Where a state unfair claims practices statute permits a private right of action, an aggrieved policyholder can pursue both statutory relief and common law claims for bad faith and breach of contract. The are not mutually exclusive. *See American Family Mutual Ins. Co. v. Barriga*, 418 P.3d 1181 (Colo. 2018) (general rule against double recovery for single harm not applicable where policyholder obtains damages for breach of contract as well as statutory award for unreasonable delay and denial of insurance benefits).

In addition, multiple statutory remedies are not necessarily mutually exclusive so long as the total amount recovered by the policyholder is not larger than the amount of actual injury to the policyholder. *See Zhang v. Superior Court*, 304 P.3d 163 (Cal. 2013) (policyholder may bring claims pursuant to state Unfair Competition Law that is based on violations of state Unfair Insurance Practices Act even though the Insurance Act does not itself provide a private right of action).

## [C] Insurance Intermediary Liability

Individuals working as adjusters for insurers (either as employees or independent contractors) generally cannot be sued for bad faith in that they are agents of a disclosed principal (the insurer). *See, e.g., Sherner v. Nat'l Loss Control Servs. Corp.*, 329 Mont. 247, 124 P.3d 150 (2005) (independent contractor adjuster and its employee); *Hamill v. Pawtucket Mut. Ins. Co.*, 179 Vt. 250 (2005) (independent contractor adjuster). If the individual has affirmatively committed a tort in connection with the claim (e.g., the assault and battery of shoving the claimant during an argument), the individual may become a defendant, but not an insurance bad faith defendant.

Similarly, independent adjusters retained by insurers to handle claims, as agents for a disclosed principal (the insurer) generally may not be separately sued for bad faith absent extenuating circumstances. *See* Jeffrey W. Stempel, *The "Other" Intermediaries: The Increasingly Anachronistic Immunity of Managing General Agents and Independent Claims Adjusters*, 15 Conn. Ins. L.J. 599 (2008); Chad G. Marzen, *The Personal Liability of Insurance Claims Adjusters for Insurance Bad Faith*, 118 W. Va. L. Rev. 411 (2015).

But support for imposing liability on intermediaries may be on the rise. *See, e.g., Keodalah v. Allstate Ins. Co.*, 413 P.3d 1059 (Wash. Ct. App. 2018) (state Supreme Court review pending) (duty of good faith imposed on "all persons" involved with insurance claims applies to insurance adjusters as well as insurers even where individual adjuster or service is independent contractor), followed in *Cherkin v. GEICO Gen. Ins. Co.*, 2018 U.S. Dist. LEXIS 216896 (W.D. Wash. Dec. 27, 2018) (applying *Keodalah* and refusing to dismiss individual defendants involved in claim handling); *Mort v. Allstate Indem. Co.*, 2018 U.S. Dist. LEXIS 153999 (W.D. Wash. Sept. 10, 2018) ("in the months since *Keodalah*, the Court has allowed plaintiffs to add claims against individual insurance adjusters—including when doing so destroys complete diversity for jurisdictional purposes."). *See also Halliday v. Great Lakes Ins. SE*, 2019 U.S. Dist. LEXIS 128364 (D.V.I. Aug. 1, 2019) (applying traditional rule to bar claim against adjuster for ordinary negligence but permitting direct action against adjuster alleging gross negligence); *De Dios v. Indemnity Ins. Co. of North America*, 2019 Iowa Sup. LEXIS 56 (May 10, 2019) (Appel J.; Wiggins, J., dissenting) (arguing that majority erred by refusing to permit claim against third party administrator of workers compensation claim).

## Questions Regarding Some Conceptual Issues of Bad Faith and Unfair Claims Handling

Some courts take the position that there cannot be bad faith by an insurer if the matter at issue was not in fact covered by the insurance policy at issue. In other words, other jurisdictions may take an approach requiring breach of contract as a prerequisite to a successful bad faith action. Other courts takes the opposite view and hold that insurer misconduct alone may support bad faith liability even if the insurer could have denied the claim successfully had it acted in good faith.

• Which approach creates the right balance of incentives for insurers?

Insurers are frequently heard to complain that bad faith liability concerns frequently prompt them to err in favor of paying doubtful claims or defending suits under marginal circumstances because of the risk of bad faith liability.

- How persuasive is this argument?

- Why or why not?

- If you are persuaded that insurers have been chilled in their ability to fight suspect claims, what alternative would you propose?

- Should bad faith liability be replaced with another enforcement mechanism?

- What alternative mechanism?

- Or should bad faith (at least as a tort) be eliminated?

Professor Roger Henderson has proposed that bad faith law be codified, with caps on damages, at least for first-party insurance matters. *See* Roger C. Henderson, *The Tort of Bad Faith in First-Party Insurance Transactions: Refining the Standard of Culpability and Reformulating the Remedies by Statute*, 26 U. Mich. J.L. Reform 1 (1992).

- Good idea?

- Why doesn't Professor Henderson suggest a similar statutorily confined remedy for third-party insurance bad faith? If you do not see his implicit basis for distinction now, think about it again after you have read some of the additional material in this chapter.

## PROBLEM ONE

In January, Defendant Driver negligently causes a collision resulting in serious injury to Plaintiff and her infant daughter, who has traumatic brain injury from the crash.

Driver is as bad at risk management as he is at driving, carrying automobile liability insurance with policy limits of only $25,000 per person and $50,000 per accident.

In March, Plaintiffs' counsel writes Driver and his Insurer, demanding payment of the policy limits. No specific response time is stated in the demand letter.

Insurer fails to respond. In September, Plaintiff sues. In October, Insurer offers the policy limits. Plaintiffs refuse saying the offer is too late.

Plaintiffs eventually obtain a $5 million judgment against Driver. Insurer writes a check for $50,000 but refuses to pay the amount in excess of policy limits.

Driver assigns his rights pursuant to the policy to Plaintiff, who then sues Insurer, who moves for summary judgment.

- What arguments would Insurer proffer?

- Should the court grant summary judgment?

- Explain.

# § 12.02. History of Bad Faith Actions

Although the concept of a covenant of good faith inherent in contractual relations has been part of the legal fabric for some time, separate causes of action for bad faith are a product of 20th Century, primarily the latter third of the 20th Century. *See* Stephen S. Ashley, Bad Faith Actions: Liability and Damages § 2:03 (2d ed. 1997) (early 20th Century cases tended to completely reject concept that insurer had any duty beyond contract compliance); *see, e.g., Market Street Assocs. Ltd. Partnership v. Frey*, 941 F.2d 588 (7th Cir. 1991) (applying Illinois law) (Posner, J.) (covenant of good faith is not some "newfangled leftist" concept when applied to traditional contract litigation). Beginning in mid-century, courts began to recognize that a third-party liability insurer has certain duties toward the policyholder because of the policyholder's reliance on the insurer for defense and indemnity. *See* Ashley, *supra* § 2:05; *See, e.g., Hilker v. Western Auto. Ins. Co.*, 204 Wis. 1, 231 N.W. 257 (1930), *aff'd on rehearing*, 204 Wis. 1, 235 N.W. 413 (1931).

The legal basis for these early decisions was not completely clear as to whether obligations owed to a policyholder sounded in contract, tort, equity, or public policy. *But see* Ashley §§ 2:06–2:08 (viewing early bad faith actions as grounded in tort concepts). Similarly, it was not clear whether an insurer's liability for failure to settle or mishandling defense of a matter constituted a separate cause of action or simply provided additional insight on a policyholder's breach of contract claim.

According to the common view of bad faith history, the law of insurer bad faith took a significant turn with the case of *Comunale v. Traders & General Ins. Co.*, 50 Cal. 2d 654, 328 P.2d 198 (1958), in which the California Supremes Court found a bad faith action to sound both in contract and tort. The *Comunale* Court implied a covenant of good faith and fair dealing that arises out of the contractual relationship but creates a duty of care toward the policyholder, with breach of the duty constituting a tortious action. At least, that is the rationale in California as well as in most other jurisdictions that treat bad faith as a separate tort cause of action.

These relatively early bad faith cases were almost exclusively claims of bad faith handling of defense and settlement by a third-party liability insurer. First-party bad faith actions appear not to have been recognized until 1970 and not to have been endorsed by a state Supreme Court until 1973. *See Gruenberg v. Aetna Ins. Co.*, 9 Cal. 3d 566, 108 Cal. Rptr. 480, 510 P.2d 1032 (1973). In *Gruenberg*, the California Supreme Court defined first-party insurer bad faith as acting unreasonably in withholding of indemnity payments due under a policy. According to the *Gruenberg* Court, the insurer commits bad faith and is subject to being sued in tort if it "fails to deal fairly and in good faith with its insured by refusing, without proper cause, to compensate its insured for a loss covered by the policy." 510 P.2d at 1036–37.[4]

---

4. Astute readers will note that this definition does not require the insurer to be knowingly acting without proper cause. *See also* Ashley, Bad Faith Actions § 5A:07, at 5A-18 ("An egregious misinterpretation of a policy may support a first-party bad faith claim. Resolution of such cases often turns

After *Gruenberg*, many states did recognize a separate cause of action in tort for insurer bad faith. However, differences in state bad faith law are as not as simple or limited as dividing the states into "tort" or "contract" jurisdictions or into "broad" and "narrow" camps on the issue. State approaches to bad faith, even within the sub-sample of states that treat bad faith claims as a separate tort action, are more of a continuum in which there are a variety of differences in state bad faith adjudication based not only on the articulated definition of bad faith but also by the courts' actual decisions in contested cases.

## § 12.03. Different Concepts of Bad Faith and Differences among the States

As noted above, there are state law differences concerning the law of insurer bad faith appear to be even more pronounced. *See* STEPHEN S. ASHLEY, BAD FAITH ACTIONS: LIABILITY AND DAMAGES § 2.01, at 2-2 (insurer bad faith "field of law suffers from more than its share of inconsistency and irrationality"); ROBERT H. JERRY, II, UNDERSTANDING INSURANCE LAW § 25G (6th ed. 2018) (" 'good faith' and 'bad faith' remain elusive concepts with no universally accepted definitions"); JEFFREY W. STEMPEL & ERIK S. KNUTSEN, STEMPEL AND KNUTSEN ON INSURANCE COVERAGE § 10.02 (4th ed. 2016) (noting differing state law as to definition of bad faith irrespective of whether bad faith is viewed as matter of tort or contract); ROBERT E. KEETON & ALAN I. WIDISS, INSURANCE LAW: A GUIDE TO FUNDAMENTAL PRINCIPLES, LEGAL DOCTRINES, AND COMMERCIAL PRACTICES § 6.2, at 625 (2d ed. 1988) (The " 'good faith' doctrine has not been developed in the same way or to the same extent throughout the nation."). *See, e.g.,* RANDY MANILOFF & JEFFREY STEMPEL, GENERAL LIABILITY INSURANCE COVERAGE: KEY ISSUES IN EVERY STATE Ch. 21 (50-state survey of first-party and third-party bad faith standards).

These areas of law remain distinct from state-to-state irrespective of whether a policyholder plaintiff is claiming mere breach of contract, bad faith breach of contract, or an independent tort action for insurer bad faith. The law of bad faith also differs in practice depending on whether the claim of bad faith arises in connection with a first-party insurance claim (e.g., for repair of damaged property, collection of medical benefits) or a third-party claim (for defense of a lawsuit and payment of any resulting judgment or settlement). Liability insurance has been a particularly fertile field for bad faith law because the duty to defend creates additional opportunities for error, oversight, or self-dealing.

Breach of the insurance contract itself does not necessarily indicate bad faith. People breach contracts for a variety of reasons: inability to perform; incompetence; a genuine

---

upon the application of the controlling principles of policy interpretation."). But as noted in § 12.01, some degree of actual or constructive knowledge of unreasonableness is required in the bad faith doctrine of most states. This suggests to us that although insurers lost the "war" as the bad faith cause of action became part of American law, they often won "battles" regarding the shape of the doctrine.

difference of opinion as to their contract obligations (that is ultimately rejected by the court, making it a breach rather than simply insisting on one's rights). The insurer's position must be unreasonable. An "unreasonableness" standard is something peculiar to insurance law in most states. Under general contract the degree of a party's error in interpreting its contract rights is essentially irrelevant to breach of contract litigation. Either the party is in breach or it is not. Subject to possible Rule 11 problems if asserting a frivolous contention, breach is breach whether a breaching party's contention is well-taken (but unsuccessful) or ridiculous to the point of absurdity.

In noninsurance litigation, the state of mind of the breaching party is also essentially irrelevant. The breaching party may know that its position refusing to pay under a contract is borderline absurd. The breacher may even know it is obligated to pay but may choose to use the money for other priorities, forcing the other party to the contract to pursue relief in the courts. This may lead to litigation sanctions (if the victimized party can clear the practical hurdle of "proving" that the breacher "knew" its position was untenable or was objectively unreasonable) but it ordinarily does not lead to enhanced contract damages for the victim.

By contrast, insurance is different than "regular" contract law in this regard. If the insurer's coverage position or refusal to pay is unreasonable, the insurer may be found in bad faith and this may provide the policyholder with (depending on the state) either (a) a separate cause of action in tort or (b) enhanced contract damages. Courts have been historically slower to recognize the bad faith cause of action for first-party claims out of a view that first-party insurance was more like "regular" contract law than third-party insurance, in which the policyholder may face potentially bankrupting liability exposure and is dependent on the insurer to defend the claim and provide "litigation insurance."

Most courts recognize that first-party policyholders are also extremely vulnerable after a loss and in a less advantageous position than most contract disputants. Most homeowners simply do not have the resources to fund their own recovery from a major disaster and then engage in years of litigation with their own insurer. The same is true regarding life, health, or disability insurance. Imagine the average family if the major income earner dies in his or her forties, is permanently disabled at age 35, or needs a bone marrow transplant in order to survive. As a result, the modern view is that there is something special about the first-party insurance policy that supports a bad faith right of action even though bad faith breach is not normally recognized in other contract contexts.

### ILLUSTRATION ONE

Policyholder's house has just been destroyed by fire. Insurer refuses to pay on the ground that the fire was not fortuitous because it grew out of a fire set down the street by the 13-year-old pyromaniac home on a weekend furlough from youth prison — the fire was expected and intended by the juvenile delinquent.

The insurer's defense is frivolous (assuming that the pyromaniac is not the child of Policyholder or otherwise qualifies as an "insured" under the policy). Policyholder did nothing to intentionally harm his home. But the home is gone and the policyholder needs the money immediately to restore the structure and put his family's life back together.

---

In addition, the handling of a matter may form the basis for a bad faith claim if insurer's coverage position is reasonable or even if the coverage position prevails at trial. In addition, the majority of states to consider the question have ruled that an insurer's conduct during the litigation itself may form the basis for a bad faith claim.

### ILLUSTRATION TWO

Policyholder's home is flooded by storm runoff that overwhelmed the city's antiquated drainage system. Policyholder immediately notifies Insurer, which urges retention of a vendor to clean up and dry out the damage, recommending the most expensive such vendor in the area. Policyholder pays and submits the bill to Insurer, making a claim for reimbursement and damage to the home as well.

Insurer states that it is "adjusting" the claim and requests multiple proofs of loss from Policyholder as well as urging Policyholder to provide a professional appraisal of the loss valuation (which Policyholder does at her own expense), even though there is an appraisal clause in the policy that provides for appraisal to be paid for by the home insurer. Insurer also criticizes Policyholder for failing to take pictures of the damage before it was cleaned up and questions the amount of damage to home and personal property.

After a year, Insurer states its final coverage position—that the policy's water damage/flood exclusion applies because the water that damaged the home was the product of a flood rather a burst or leaking pipe, bathtub overrun, etc. By this time, the short one-year statute of limitations for suing the city (on a theory of negligence because of the city's inadequate drainage system) has run, so Policyholder may not sue the city for relief.

Most courts would find Insurer's coverage position absolutely correct if the policy has a standard form water damage/flood exclusion. Flood damage is normally excluded from homeowner insurance, and Policyholder's home was damaged by a flood.

However, Insurer's conduct in failing to inform, misinforming, delaying, and implicitly deceiving Policyholder may give rise to a claim for common law bad faith or a statutory unfair claims handling action.

Some courts might deem Insurer's conduct enough for equitable estoppel in favor of Policyholder, but this is probably not a winning argument in most courts, because the Insurer's conduct, bad as it is, may not be seen as a sufficient representation of coverage. There is also substantial precedent for the proposition that equitable estoppel should not create coverage if the policy itself does not promise coverage. However, this would not preclude an argument for coverage pursuant to promissory estoppel if Insurer's conduct could be characterized as a representation inducing reasonable detrimental reliance.

Because estoppel arguments are unlikely to be successful, the availability of the bad faith remedy may be useful in filling doctrinal gaps to protect Policyholder from blameworthy insurer behavior.

- Assuming the court in the above situation finds Insurer's conduct to constitute bad faith, what should be Policyholder's remedies?

There can also be considerable variation in the respective state law of contract interpretation, including contract construction methodology, the contra proferentem canon, use of extrinsic evidence, the relative role of party intent and policy purpose and the application of considerations of reasonable expectations of policyholder or insurer. These state-to-state differences impact bad faith claims regardless of whether they are denominated as tort or contract claims.

A significant divide among the states is the contract-tort fault line. Most states treat insurer bad faith as an independent tort, while others treat insurer bad faith as a matter of contract, at least for first-party claims. And in some states, bad faith, like prohibitions about unfair claims handling, are statutory rather than based on common law. Even among the states that treat insurer bad faith as a matter of contract rather than tort, there are pronounced differences among these states regarding not only the definition of bad faith but also differences concerning the available remedies for bad faith breach by an insurer.

A recent survey provides a state-by-state survey concerning both first-party and third-party bad faith standards. *See* RANDY MANILOFF & JEFFREY STEMPEL, GENERAL LIABILITY INSURANCE COVERAGE: KEY ISSUES IN EVERY STATE, Ch. 21 (4th ed. 2018). Despite the differences between states, one can restate the essence of the bad faith standard as something like the following: An insurer commits bad faith when it acts with intentional or reckless disregard of the rights of the policyholder in either adopting a coverage position or its treatment of the policyholder, particularly regarding its handling of a claim. Despite all the nuanced differences discussed above, experienced policyholder and insurer counsel have a rough operating definition of bad faith that guides them in assessing claims across the country.

States also vary to a degree concerning their characterization of the degree to which the insurer-policyholder relationship is fiduciary. Insurer counsel tend to strongly argue against the fiduciary characterization. Conversely, policyholder counsel commonly insist the relationship is indeed fully fiduciary. Regarding first-party insurance, insurer counsel appear to have the better of the argument. Courts generally stop short of deeming those relationships fiduciary, characterizing the first-party insurance relationship as arm's-length and adversarial despite the aleatory nature of the insurance policy and the insureds' reliance upon the insurer in a time of need (at least for consumer policyholders who may have little independent financial ability to overcome a serious loss).

But courts also commonly describe the insurer-policyholder relationship as semifiduciary, fiduciary in nature, or analogous to established fiduciary relationships such as doctor-patient or attorney-client.

Regarding liability insurance, particularly where the liability insurer controls defense and settlement of a third-party claim against the policyholder, placing the insured in a position of dependency, many courts treat the relationship as fiduciary. *See, e.g., Short v. Dairyland Ins. Co.*, 334 N.W.2d 384 (Minn. 1983); *Ammerman v. Farmers Ins. Exch.*, 430 P.2d 576, 579 (Utah 1967). But rather than stating that the insurer must act as a trustee and give primacy to policyholder interests before its own, courts tend to state that the insurer must give at least equal consideration to the interests of the policyholder. *See, e.g., Egan v. Mutual of Omaha Ins. Co.*, 620 P.2d 141 (Cal. 1979).

Although this standard might not strictly meet the expectations imposed on classic fiduciaries such as lawyers, doctors, and bankers, the distinction is not great and any difference is of little practical moment. Lawyers, although fiduciaries, expect to get paid and may sue their own clients to collect past due bills (although they dislike doing so because these types of deadbeat clients have an annoying tendency to counterclaim for legal malpractice; the trait is so common that lawyer malpractice insurers commonly give a premium reduction if the law firm agrees to forgo such collection attempts). When they do pursue collection, the lawyers may reveal information that would otherwise be confidential pursuant to Model Rules of Professional Conduct R. 1.6.

Similarly, lawyers may give testimony adverse to clients if necessary to defend themselves in a disciplinary proceeding. Lawyers under some circumstances are permitted and required to act adversely to clients to warn potential victims and to protect the integrity of the justice system (e.g., correcting perjured testimony).

Thus, being even a classic fiduciary does not in practice require placing client interests first in all cases. By comparison to fiduciary activity in the real world, the "equal consideration to the interests of the insured" standard, particularly when the insurer is controlling defense of a lawsuit against the policyholder, tends to look a lot like the work of a fiduciary. Regardless of the label, significant duties attach to the insurer.

Labeling may be important, however, to the extent that a given jurisdiction permits a cause of action for breach of fiduciary duty. To the extent that this is a permissible action in a given state, policyholders would presumably be able to make such claims against insurer. More commonly, however, courts tend to find that the availability of a bad faith claim is sufficient to preclude claims alleging breach of fiduciary duty. But in states permitting only contract damages rather than tort damages, the distinctions surrounding fiduciary characterization could be important. Breach of fiduciary duty is commonly considered a tort for which punitive damages may be available in apt cases.

# § 12.04. Insurance Bad Faith Litigation in Operation

In light of the above discussion, the discerning reader might ask whether the law of bad faith can even be studied as part of a law school overview course of insurance law. We of course answer in the affirmative, perhaps guided by our desire to sell a few casebooks. It is true, however, that practicing lawyers must be sensitive to the nuances of bad faith law in the state that provides the governing law for any dispute in question. General principles alone will suffice to start but cannot be relied upon. State variances must be checked. For further discussion of insurance bad faith, see STEMPEL & KNUSTEN, Ch. 10, and ROBERT H. JERRY, II & DOUGLAS R. RICHMOND, UNDERSTANDING INSURANCE LAW § 25G (6th ed. 2018).

As to case law, rather than continue to attempt to characterize it, we now follow the advice of T. S. Eliot: "do not go and ask 'what is it?' Let us go and make our visit."[5]

## [A] The Tort Law Approach to Bad Faith

### [1] Liability Insurance

## Crisci v. The Security Insurance Company of New Haven, Connecticut

Supreme Court of California
66 Cal. 2d 425, 58 Cal. Rptr. 13, 426 P.2d 173 (1967)

**Peters, J.**

In an action against The Security Insurance Company of New Haven, Connecticut, the trial court awarded Rosina Crisci $91,000 (plus interest) because she suffered a judgment in a personal injury action after Security, her insurer, refused to settle the claim. Mrs. Crisci was also awarded $25,000 for mental suffering. Security has appealed.

June DiMare and her husband were tenants in an apartment building owned by Rosina Crisci. Mrs. DiMare was descending the apartment's outside wooden staircase when a tread gave way. She fell through the resulting opening up to her waist and was left hanging 15 feet above the ground. Mrs. DiMare suffered physical injuries and developed a very severe psychosis. In a suit brought against Mrs. Crisci the DiMares alleged that the step broke because Mrs. Crisci was negligent in inspecting and

---

5. T. S. Eliot, *The Love Song of J. Alfred Prufrock* (1917).

maintaining the stairs. They contended that Mrs. DiMare's mental condition was caused by the accident, and they asked for $400,000 as compensation for physical and mental injuries and medical expenses.

Mrs. Crisci had $10,000 of insurance coverage under a general liability policy issued by Security. The policy obligated Security to defend the suit against Mrs. Crisci and authorized the company to make any settlement it deemed expedient. Security hired an experienced lawyer, Mr. Healy, to handle the case. Both he and defendant's claims manager believed that unless evidence was discovered showing that Mrs. DiMare had a prior mental illness, a jury would probably find that the accident precipitated Mrs. DiMare's psychosis. And both men believed that if the jury felt that the fall triggered the psychosis, a verdict of not less than $100,000 would be returned.

An extensive search turned up no evidence that Mrs. DiMare had any prior mental abnormality. As a teenager Mrs. DiMare had been in a Washington mental hospital, but only to have an abortion. Both Mrs. DiMare and Mrs. Crisci found psychiatrists who would testify that the accident caused Mrs. DiMare's illness, and the insurance company knew of this testimony. Among those who felt the psychosis was not related to the accident were the doctors at the state mental hospital where Mrs. DiMare had been committed following the accident. All the psychiatrists agreed, however, that a psychosis could be triggered by a sudden fear of falling to one's death.

The exact chronology of settlement offers is not established by the record. However, by the time the DiMares' attorney reduced his settlement demands to $10,000, Security had doctors prepared to support its position and was only willing to pay $3,000 for Mrs. DiMare's physical injuries. Security was unwilling to pay one cent for the possibility of a plaintiff's verdict on the mental illness issue. This conclusion was based on the assumption that the jury would believe all of the defendant's psychiatric evidence and none of the plaintiff's. Security also rejected a $9,000 settlement demand at a time when Mrs. Crisci offered to pay $2,500 of the settlement.

A jury awarded Mrs. DiMare $100,000 and her husband $1,000. After an appeal (*DiMare v. Cresci*, 58 Cal. 2d 292 [23 Cal.Rptr. 772, 373 P.2d 860]) the insurance company paid $10,000 of this amount, the amount of its policy. The DiMares then sought to collect the balance from Mrs. Crisci. A settlement was arranged by which the DiMares received $22,000, a 40 percent interest in Mrs. Crisci's claim to a particular piece of property, and an assignment of Mrs. Crisci's cause of action against Security. Mrs. Crisci, an immigrant widow of 70, became indigent. She worked as a babysitter, and her grandchildren paid her rent. The change in her financial condition was accompanied by a decline in physical health, hysteria, and suicide attempts. Mrs. Crisci then brought this action.

The liability of an insurer in excess of its policy limits for failure to accept a settlement offer within those limits was considered by this court in *Comunale v. Traders & General Ins. Co.*, [328 P.2d 198]. It was there reasoned that in every contract, including policies of insurance, there is an implied covenant of good faith and fair dealing that neither party will do anything which will injure the right of the other to receive the benefits of the agreement; that it is common knowledge that one of the usual methods by which an insured receives protection under a liability insurance policy is by settlement of claims without litigation; that the implied obligation of good faith and fair dealing requires the insurer to settle in an appropriate case although the express terms of the policy do not impose the duty; that in determining whether to settle the insurer must give the interests of the insured at least as much consideration as it gives to its own interests; and that when "there is great risk of a recovery beyond the policy limits so that the most reasonable manner of disposing of the claim is a settlement which can be made within those limits, a consideration in good faith of the insured's interest requires the insurer to settle the claim."

In determining whether an insurer has given consideration to the interests of the insured, the test is whether a prudent insurer without policy limits would have accepted the settlement offer.

Several cases, in considering the liability of the insurer, contain language to the effect that bad faith is the equivalent of dishonesty, fraud, and concealment. Obviously a showing that the insurer has been guilty of actual dishonesty, fraud, or concealment is relevant to the determination whether it has given consideration to the insured's interest in considering a settlement offer within the policy limits. The language used in the cases, however, should not be understood as meaning that in the absence of evidence establishing actual dishonesty, fraud, or concealment no recovery may be had for a judgment in excess of the policy limits.

*Comunale v. Traders & General Ins. Co.*, makes it clear that liability based on an implied covenant exists whenever the insurer refuses to settle in an appropriate case and that liability may exist when the insurer unwarrantedly refuses an offered settlement where the most reasonable manner of disposing of the claim is by accepting the settlement. Liability is imposed not for a bad faith breach of the contract but for failure to meet the duty to accept reasonable settlements, a duty included within the implied covenant of good faith and fair dealing. [R]ecovery may be based on unwarranted rejection of a reasonable settlement offer and that the absence of evidence, circumstantial or direct, showing actual dishonesty, fraud, or concealment is not fatal to the cause of action.

Amicus curiae argues that, whenever an insurer receives an offer to settle within the policy limits and rejects it, the insurer should be liable in every case for the amount of any final judgment whether or not within the policy limits. As we have seen, the duty of the insurer to consider the insured's interest in settlement offers within the policy limits arises from an implied covenant in the contract, and ordinarily contract duties are strictly enforced and not subject to a standard of reasonableness.

Obviously, it will always be in the insured's interest to settle within the policy limits when there is any danger, however slight, of a judgment in excess of those limits. Accordingly the rejection of a settlement within the limits where there is any danger of a judgment in excess of the limits can be justified, if at all, only on the basis of interests of the insurer, and, in light of the common knowledge that settlement is one of the usual methods by which an insured receives protection under a liability policy, it may not be unreasonable for an insured who purchases a policy with limits to believe that a sum of money equal to the limits is available and will be used so as to avoid liability on his part with regard to any covered accident.

In view of such expectation an insurer should not be permitted to further its own interests by rejecting opportunities to settle within the policy limits unless it is also willing to absorb losses which may result from its failure to settle.

The proposed rule is a simple one to apply and avoids the burdens of a determination whether a settlement offer within the policy limits was reasonable. The proposed rule would also eliminate the danger than an insurer, faced with a settlement offer at or near the policy limits, will reject it and gamble with the insured's money to further its own interests. Moreover, it is not entirely clear that the proposed rule would place a burden on insurers substantially greater than that which is present under existing law.

The size of the judgment recovered in the personal injury action when it exceeds the policy limits, although not conclusive, furnishes an inference that the value of the claim is the equivalent of the amount of the judgment and that acceptance of an offer within those limits was the most reasonable method of dealing with the claim.

Finally, and most importantly, there is more than a small amount of elementary justice in a rule that would require that, in this situation where the insurer's and insured's interests necessarily conflict, the insurer, which may reap the benefits of its determination not to settle, should also suffer the detriments of its decision. On the basis of these and other considerations, a number of commentators have urged that the insurer should be liable for any resulting judgment where it refuses to settle within the policy limits.

We need not, however, here determine whether there might be some countervailing considerations precluding adoption of the proposed rule because, under *Comunale v. Traders & General Ins. Co.*, and the cases following it, the evidence is clearly sufficient to support the determination that Security breached its duty to consider the interests of Mrs. Crisci in proposed settlements.

Both Security's attorney and its claims manager agreed that if Mrs. DiMare won an award for her psychosis, that award would be at least $100,000. Security attempts to justify its rejection of a settlement by contending that it believed Mrs. DiMare had no chance of winning on the mental suffering issue. That belief in the circumstances present could be found to be unreasonable. Security was putting blind faith in the power of its psychiatrists to convince the jury when it knew that the accident could have caused the psychosis, that its agents had told it that without evidence of prior mental defects a jury was likely to believe the fall precipitated the psychosis, and that Mrs. DiMare had reputable psychiatrists on her side. Further, the company had been told by a psychiatrist that in a group of 24 psychiatrists, 12 could be found to support each side.

The trial court found that defendant "knew that there was a considerable risk of substantial recovery beyond said policy limits" and that "the defendant did not give as much consideration to the financial interests of its said insured as it gave to its own interests." That is all that was required. The award of $91,000 must therefore be affirmed.

We must next determine the propriety of the award to Mrs. Crisci of $25,000 for her mental suffering. In *Comunale v. Traders & General Ins. Co.*, it was held that an action of the type involved here sounds in both contract and tort and that "where a case sounds both in contract and tort the plaintiff will ordinarily have freedom of election between an action of tort and one of contract." ... An exception to this rule is made in suits for personal injury caused by negligence, where the tort character of the action is considered to prevail [citations], but no such exception is applied in cases, like the present one, which relate to financial damage [citations]." Although this rule was applied in *Comunale* with regard to a statute of limitations, the rule is also applicable in determining liability....

Fundamental in our jurisprudence is the principle that for every wrong there is a remedy and that an injured party should be compensated for all damage proximately caused by the wrongdoer. Although we recognize exceptions from these fundamental principles, no departure should be sanctioned unless there is a strong necessity therefor.

The general rule of damages in tort is that the injured party may recover for all detriment caused whether it could have been anticipated or not.... In accordance with the general rule, it is settled in this state that mental suffering constitutes an aggravation of damages when it naturally ensues from the act complained of, and in this connection mental suffering includes nervousness, grief, anxiety, worry, shock, humiliation and indignity as well as physical pain.

The commonest example of the award of damages for mental suffering in addition to other damages is probably where the plaintiff suffers personal injuries in addition to mental distress as a result of either negligent or intentional misconduct by the defendant.... Such awards are not confined to cases where the mental suffering award was in addition to an award for personal injuries; damages for mental distress have also been awarded in cases where the tortious conduct was an interference with property rights without any personal injuries apart from the mental distress....

We are satisfied that a plaintiff who as a result of a defendant's tortious conduct loses his property and suffers mental distress may recover not only for the pecuniary loss but also for his mental distress. No substantial reason exists to distinguish the cases which have permitted recovery for mental distress in actions for invasion of property rights. The principal reason for limiting recovery of damages for mental distress is that to permit recovery of such damages would open the door to fictitious claims, to recovery for mere bad manners, and to litigation in the field of trivialities.... Obviously, where, as here, the claim is actionable and has resulted in substantial damages apart from those due to mental distress, the danger of fictitious claims is reduced, and we are not here concerned with mere bad manners or trivialities but tortous conduct resulting in substantial invasions of clearly protected interests.

Recovery of damages for mental suffering in the instant case does not mean that in every case of breach of contract the injured party may recover such damages. Here the breach also constitutes a tort. Moreover, plaintiff did not seek by the contract involved here to obtain a commercial advantage but to protect herself against the risks of accidental losses, including the mental distress which might follow from the losses. Among the considerations in purchasing liability insurance, as insurers are well aware, is the peace of mind and security it will provide in the event of an accidental loss, and recovery of damages for mental suffering has been permitted for breach of contracts which directly concern the comfort, happiness or personal esteem of one of the parties....

It is not claimed that plaintiff's mental distress was not caused by defendant's refusal to settle or that the damages awarded were excessive in the light of plaintiff's substantial suffering.

## Notes and Questions

1. If we had used this case as a Problem, we would have probably been criticized as being unrealistic. No insurer could be that bad, right? Although cases like *Crisci* are particularly egregious, one need not search too long before finding similar examples of insurer misconduct.

2. But playing devil's advocate, would the insurer's conduct not have been arguably proper outside the insurance setting? For example, assume Stempel lends purchase money to Knutsen and takes a security interest in Knutsen's Hudson Bay Mansion (big assumption on all counts). Knutsen defaults and implores Stempel not to foreclose until the following month, because Knutsen is about to receive a large bequest that will enable him to pay off the loan. Is there any legal restriction on Stempel's right to foreclose, no matter how unwise and mean-spirited it may be?

   • Why is insurance different?

   • According to the *Crisci* court?

   • According to your view of the insurer-policyholder relationship?

   • Are there greater or reduced business and social incentives toward decent behavior in the typical insurance arrangement as compared to the typical lending transaction or sale of merchandise?

3. *Crisci* is a more than 50-year-old precedent. Have evolving attitudes toward insurer responsibilities, particularly regarding defense and settlement of claims by a liability insurer, eliminated the need for a bad faith remedy for policyholders in Ms. Crisci's position? Compare *Crisci* to the RLLI.

   (1) When an insurer has the authority to settle a legal action brought against the insured, or the insurer's prior consent is required for any settlement by the insured to be payable by the insurer, and there is a potential for a judgment in excess of the applicable policy limit, the insurer has a duty to the insured to make reasonable settlement decisions.

(2) A reasonable settlement decision is one that would be made by a reasonable insurer that bears the sole financial responsibility for the full amount of the potential judgment.

(3) An insurer's duty to make reasonable settlement decisions includes the duty to make its policy limits available to the insured for the settlement of a covered legal action that exceeds those policy limits if a reasonable insurer would do so in the circumstance.

RLLI § 24.

[A liability] insurer that breaches the duty to make reasonable settlement decisions is subject to liability for any foreseeable harm caused by the breach, including the full amount of damages assessed against the insured in the underlying legal action, without regard to the policy limits.

RLLI § 27.

- How does the RLLI black letter rule differ from *Crisci*?

- If the California Supreme Court had applied the RLLI to *Crisci*, how would the result differ, if at all?

- Which approach (if they actually are different) would be preferred by (i) Policyholders? (ii) Insurers? (iii) Attorneys? (iv) Policymakers, including insurance regulators?

## [2] Additional Bad Faith Problems Stemming from the Duty to Defend

A common source of insurer bad faith is mishandling of the defense obligation in a liability insurance situation. The attorney retained by the liability insurer to defend a claim against the policyholder may be paid by the insurer but the insurer's primary client (in many states the "only" client) is the policyholder. Consequently, defense efforts where counsel's activity reflect more concern for the insurer's money than the successful and expeditious protection of the policyholder (through settlement, summary judgment motions, etc.) may lead to bad faith liability.

The general rules of bad faith of course apply to the insurer direction of defense efforts through insurer-retained counsel. The important thing to remember (something that many attorneys unfamiliar with insurance practice do not immediately understand) is this: the standard liability insurance policy is a contract that gives the liability insurer the right and duty to control the defense, including settlement, as well as to select counsel. But the lawyer selected by the insurer works for the policyholder or at least primarily for the policyholder (in states that treat both policyholder and insurer as "clients" absent a conflict, at which time the attorney must protect the policyholder's interests).

Both the defense lawyer (because of professional responsibility rules) and the insurer (because of the duty of good faith) must act properly in conducting the defense. As outlined in the *Deese* decision and the materials at the beginning of this

Chapter, that generally means: giving at least equal concern to the rights of the policyholder; not "gambling" with the policyholder's fate by rolling the dice on a claim that should be settled if possible; and acting with loyalty toward the policyholder rather than self-dealing (by the insurer) or with misplaced loyalty toward the insurer by counsel.

At the same time, the insurer is not required to throw money at frivolous third-party claims and may defend them appropriately, even vigorously so long as it pays adequate attention to the rights of the policyholder. Similarly, an insurer may commit bad faith where it settles a claim too easily, thereby forcing the perhaps faultless policyholder to pay substantial amounts within the deductible or self-insured retention applicable to a policy.

Recall that the duty to defend is based on a potential for coverage, as determined by the face of the complaint (and the policy), often as supplemented by extrinsic evidence and is broader than the duty to indemnify. As a result, a policyholder need not prove that the insurer is required to pay a resulting damage award in order to demonstrate that that insurer is obligated to defend.

Intertwined with the liability insurer's duty to defend is the "duty to settle," more accurately described by the RLLI as a duty to make reasonable settlement decisions. Where the insurer refuses to accept a reasonable settlement offer or exhibits insufficient effort at settling, the insurer's failings may be considered not only a breach of the duty to settle but also bad faith that may entitle the policyholder not only to insurer coverage of any excess judgment (which should follow even in the absence of bad faith) but also to compensatory and perhaps punitive damages.

As part of the litigation process, policyholder or claimant counsel dismayed by an insurer's failure to settle frequently attempt to "set up" a possible bad faith claim by writing to the insurer urging settlement and outlining why under the facts of this particular case the insurer's duties of good faith and fair dealing require acceptance of a settlement offer or offering of the full policy limits in settlement. (Claimants' counsel may write these letters anticipating that if a settlement payment from the insurer does not ensue, claimant may settle with the policyholder in return for an assignment of the policyholder's right to coverage and any bad faith claims the insured may have against the insurer.)

These letters often have a local nomenclature, usually derived from a prominent failure-to-settle bad faith case in a given jurisdiction. In New Jersey, this communication "is commonly called a '*Rova Farms* Letter,' named after the leading case to address the issue [in the state; see *Rova Farms Resort, Inc., v. Investors Ins. Co.*, 323 A.2d 495 (N.J. 1974)]. In West Virginia the same demand comes by way of a *Shamblin* Letter [after *Shamblin v. Nationwide Mut. Ins. Co.*, 396 S.E.2d 766 (W.Va. 1990)]. And in Texas it's a *Stowers* Demand [after *American Indem. Co. v. G.A. Stowers Furniture Co.*, 39 S.W.2d 956 (Tex. 1931). And so forth." *See* Randy J. Maniloff, *Betting the* Rova Farm: *Rejecting a Demand to Settle Within Limits*, Binding Authority, Aug. 9, 2010.

The insurer must at least attempt to settle a claim against the policyholder when the insured's liability is "reasonably clear," which is that case when a reasonable person would conclude that the defendant policyholder is liable to the plaintiff claimant. *See Peterson v. St. Paul Fire & Marine Ins. Co.*, 239 P.3d 904, 913–14 (Mont. 2010).

But, of course, even when it is pretty clear that the policyholder is likely to be held liable, the amount of reasonable compensation is not clear. Insurers must endeavor to eliminate the claim through settlement by offering an amount (or accepting an amount) within the range of reasonable compensation, as determined by the likely range of jury verdicts on this issue.

Because this is an inexact science, insurers are allowed significant leeway in making or refusing settlement offers. However, an unduly frugal approach in rejecting offers or in "low-balling" plaintiffs may be so unreasonable as to constitute bad faith. In assessing the reasonableness of insurer behavior, a court may consider the following factors:

- The probability of the policyholder defendant's liability;
- The amount of the policy limits;
- The extent of the claimant's damages;
- The adequacy of the insurer's investigation;
- Whether the insurer followed its own defense attorney's advice regarding settlement;
- Whether any misrepresentations were made by the policyholder which may have misled the insurer in settlement negotiations; and
- The openness of the communications between insurer and policyholder.

*See Truck Ins. Exch. v. Bishara*, 916 P.2d 1275, 1279–80 (Idaho 1996).

In addition, an insurer defending a claim may commit bad faith through the manner in which it handles the claim. As an example, consider the following:

> Because a primary insurer's duty to defend includes settlement duties and an insurer must give equal consideration to the insured's interest, we hold that a covenant of good faith and fair dealing includes a duty to adequately inform the insured of settlement offers. This includes reasonable offers in excess of the policy limits. Failure to adequately inform an insured is a factor to consider in a bad-faith claim and, if established, can be a proximate cause of any resulting damages.
>
> [However,] the insurer does not [absent express policy language] have an independent duty to file an interpleader action on behalf of an insured. Nor is an insurer required to agree to a proposed stipulated judgment between the insured and the claimant if that stipulated judgment is beyond the policy limits.

*Allstate Ins. Co. v. Miller*, 212 P.3d 318, 319 (Nev. 2009).

The duty of good faith and fair dealing—and with it the potential for a bad faith action—also applies as between primary insurers and excess insurers. It also can apply even when there is in theory a sufficient "tower" of liability coverage to protect the policyholder against an excess judgment. *See, e.g., R.G. Wegman Constr. Co. v. Admiral Ins. Co.*, 629 F.3d 724 (7th Cir. 2011).

During the heat of litigation, things can become complex. Policyholders may be tempted to shade the truth or resist disclosing information. Insurers may be tempted to cut corners, shade the truth, or take unfair advantage of a policyholder through their superior economic might and litigation sophistication and experience. The following cases provide examples of insurers who strayed from the path of good faith.

## Ellwein v. Hartford Accident and Indemnity Company

### Supreme Court of Washington
### 142 Wn. 2d 766, 15 P.3d 640 (2001)

Petitioners Nancy and Tom Ellwein seek review of the summary judgment dismissal of their claims of bad faith against Respondent Hartford Accident and Indemnity Company. At issue is whether Hartford acted in bad faith when handling the Ellweins' underinsured motorist claim. We hold that, with respect to Hartford's misappropriation of the Ellweins' accident reconstruction expert, Hartford did act in bad faith.

### I. Facts

On November 28, 1989, Nancy Ellwein was driving to a work meeting when she was severely injured in an automobile accident. Mrs. Ellwein was turning left in an intersection controlled by traffic lights when her car was hit by an oncoming vehicle driven by Jason Gleason. In addition to Mrs. Ellwein and Gleason, there were two other eyewitnesses, Larry Schultz and Kenneth MacDougall, who were driving vehicles near the intersection. MacDougall's vehicle suffered minor damage as a result of the accident.

Following the accident, three insurance companies became involved-Respondent Hartford on behalf of Mrs. Ellwein; Allstate Insurance on behalf of Gleason; and Safeco Insurance on behalf of MacDougall. Shortly after the accident, both Allstate and Safeco brought subrogation claims against Hartford. In response to these claims, Gordon Woodley, an attorney Mrs. Ellwein and her husband hired to assert liability claims against Gleason, wrote to Hartford requesting that it not jeopardize the Ellweins' potential claims against Gleason by conceding comparative fault in resolving the property damage subrogation claims. In December 1989, as part of its investigation of the accident, Hartford hired accident reconstruction expert William Cooper.

Hartford provided Cooper with statements it had taken from eyewitnesses Schultz and MacDougall near the time of the accident. In these statements, both Schultz and MacDougall asserted that Mrs. Ellwein began her turn while the traffic light remained yellow and that Gleason struck Mrs. Ellwein's vehicle in the intersection when the traffic light was red. MacDougall further asserted that when Ellwein started into the intersection, Gleason was far enough away from the light that he assumed Gleason would stop. Neither MacDougall nor Schultz, however, asserted that Gleason appeared to be speeding.

In August 1990, Cooper submitted his report. Based on the statements of Schultz and MacDougall, and his own independent calculations, Cooper determined that: (1) Gleason's estimated speed was approximately 63 miles per hour (m.p.h.), above the 45 m.p.h. speed limit for that area; and (2) while Gleason was "there to be seen" by Mrs. Ellwein, Gleason likely ran the red light when he hit Mrs. Ellwein's car. On January 7, 1991, stating its opinion was based on Cooper's report, and noting Woodley's request to refrain from admitting liability, Hartford wrote Safeco asserting that Mrs. Ellwein was not at fault regarding the accident. Internally, however, Hartford was preparing to defend itself from a "potentially large" uninsured motorist claim by the Ellweins.

In an interoffice memorandum dated April 4, 1991, without notice to the Ellweins, Hartford outlined a plan to help fully understand its potential "exposures." Part of this plan involved Hartford conducting an independent investigation of the accident scene. The memorandum also noted that, although Cooper had "not proved entirely beneficial" as a court witness on other claims, his report could still be used to support Hartford's claim of comparative negligence by Mrs. Ellwein. In this memorandum, Mrs. Ellwein's comparative negligence was estimated to be 50 percent. *See* CP at 139–42.

In August 1991, Woodley wrote to Hartford notifying it of a settlement between the Ellweins and Allstate for Gleason's policy limits of $100,000, and made an Underinsured Motorist (UIM) policy limit demand. Woodley asserts that Hartford misled him by stating that the UIM policy limits were only $100,000. The context of this miscommunication, however, is unclear because Woodley failed to provide any further details. Nevertheless, on September 12, 1991, Hartford wrote a letter to the Ellweins clarifying that their policy limit was $1,000,000.

By November 1991, however, public signs of Hartford's comparative fault defense to the uninsured motorist claim began to emerge. In response to the Ellweins' UIM arbitration demand, Hartford's attorneys wrote a letter to Woodley in which they implied that Cooper was Hartford's witness and that Cooper's conclusions might change as additional evidence was developed. Hartford proceeded by providing Cooper with the following information: (1) the investigating police officer's supplemental accident report; (2) McDougall's statement dated January 12, 1990; (3) Schultz's statement dated December 11, 1989; (4) Gleason's statement dated January 8, 1989; (5) MacDougall's transcribed statement dated November 29, 1989; (6) Gleason's transcribed statement dated November 29, 1989; (7) Schultz's declaration dated August 5, 1992; and (8) McDougall's declaration dated September 22, 1992.

Much of this "new" information implicated Mrs. Ellwein as the cause of the accident. For example, both McDougall's and Schultz's versions of events changed. MacDougall opined that Mrs. Ellwein took no evasive action, and that Gleason may have entered the intersection when the light was yellow. Furthermore, Schultz now accused Mrs. Ellwein of "attempting to beat the light."

On October 7, 1992, as predicted, Cooper gave a sworn declaration in which he revised his initial findings and conclusions. Specifically, Cooper stated that: (1) Gleason entered the intersection on a yellow light, not a red light as previously reported; (2) Gleason's speed was irrelevant because he was there to be seen; (3) Gleason had no reason to believe Mrs. Ellwein would turn in front of him due to the road design; and, thus, (4) the accident was solely caused by Mrs. Ellwein's failure to yield. On October 8, Hartford brought a motion to dismiss before the arbitrators in which it asserted that Mrs. Ellwein was solely to blame.

The Ellweins responded by hiring accident reconstruction expert John Hunter. After reviewing the evidence, Hunter provided a declaration consistent with Cooper's original report. Based on Hunter's report, the arbitrators denied the motion. In a memorandum dated October 15, a Hartford employee in the Seattle office stated:

> [Having] been able to get their reconstruction expert to reevaluate his position[,] we now feel there is a comparative negligence issue involved in this case in which it appears that the insured may be at fault. We have confirmed that both parties had a yellow light at the time of the accident. Our insured would then be at fault for failing to yield the right of way by making a left hand turn in front of the claimant.
>
> The injuries are still quite substantial as verified by our independent medical examination. Our defense counsel has evaluated the case in the area of $600,000–$700,000. We feel that this has been cut down by at least 50% based upon comparative negligence which would put the loss below our reserve.

On November 13, Hartford offered the Ellweins $300,000 to settle their UIM claim. Hartford's offer was based on its assessment that the Ellweins' gross damages equaled $800,000, discounted by 50 percent for Mrs. Ellwein's contributory negligence and $100,000 for the amount received from the Gleason settlement. The Ellweins did not accept, and prior to the arbitrator's decision, Hartford raised its offer to $400,000. Again, the Ellweins did not accept.

On November 17, the arbitrator ruled that Gleason was solely at fault, and awarded the Ellweins gross damages of $929,803.39. Following the arbitration award, the Ellweins brought suit against Hartford in federal court for bad faith and Consumer Protection Act violations for the handling of their UIM claim. The Ellweins voluntarily dismissed their federal suit and refiled in state court over a year later.

In the interim, Hartford's home office senior supervisor, William Solito, destroyed the home office file on the Ellweins' claim. Solito explained that it was company policy to destroy the home office file when a claim is closed, and the only items not still available in the field office file were his notes regarding discussions he had with his superiors regarding the Ellweins' claim. Solito, however, admitted that he understood there "was a chance, not a likelihood" the case would be re-filed.

In total, two trials were scheduled for the Ellweins' bad faith action. In the first trial, held in August 1995, the Ellweins asserted that Hartford acted in bad faith by: (1) forcing the Ellweins into arbitration to recover insurance benefits; (2) failing to make a reasonable settlement offer; and (3) bringing a summary judgment motion before the arbitrators without reasonable justification.

During this trial, attorney Dwayne Richards testified as an expert witness on the Ellweins' behalf. Richards stated that, in his opinion, Hartford treated the Ellweins unfairly in handling their claim—putting its financial interests before those of its insured. Richards further testified that Hartford unfairly forced the Ellweins into arbitration when it had all the information necessary to resolve the claim by November 1992. Richards also opined that, while Hartford correctly evaluated the value of the case, it "did everything [it] could to avoid paying that amount and basically wanted to gamble on a verdict that hopefully [it] would get a windfall to the detriment of their own insured." Finally, Richards testified that Hartford acted improperly regarding Cooper by attempting "to do everything they [could]" to change Cooper's opinion.

At the close of trial, the Ellweins requested a spoliation instruction based on Solito's file destruction. The Ellweins' request was denied, and the first trial resulted in a hung jury. On retrial, the Ellweins made substantial changes to their liability theories. In addition to their previous allegations regarding Hartford's low settlement offers, and the propriety of bringing a summary judgment motion before the arbitrators, the Ellweins asserted that Hartford acted in bad faith by: (1) "misappropriating" Cooper as its accident reconstruction expert; (2) misleading the Ellweins' attorney regarding the UIM policy limits; and (3) refusing to provide the Ellweins with recorded witness statements taken by Hartford after the accident. On Hartford's subsequent summary judgment motions, the trial court dismissed all of the Ellweins' bad faith claims against Hartford.

## II. Summary of Issues

A. Did Hartford act in bad faith by basing its settlement offers on 50 percent comparative fault?

B. Did Hartford act in bad faith by using accident reconstruction expert Cooper to its advantage after originally hiring Cooper to defend the Ellweins?

C. Did Hartford commit bad faith by misrepresenting to the Ellweins' attorney that the policy limits were $100,000, instead of $1,000,000?

D. Was the jury entitled to infer that the notes Solito destroyed contained unfavorable evidence toward Hartford?

## III. Analysis

### A. Bad Faith Settlement Offers

[W]e completely concur with the Court of Appeals' finding that dismissal of the bad faith claim regarding Hartford's settlement practices was warranted. As the court noted, it is undisputed that Hartford, as a UIM insurer, had a general right to assert a comparative fault defense. Furthermore, the ambiguous and somewhat conflicting eyewitness reports alone created an issue as to whether Gleason entered the light on the yellow. Had Gleason entered the light on the yellow, Mrs. Ellwein would have been at least partially responsible for the accident by breaching in her statutory duty to yield. *See RCW 46.61.185* (duty to yield imposed upon driver turning left at intersection).

Consequently, even absent Cooper's revised report, this claim of bad faith was properly dismissed because of Hartford's legitimate basis for asserting comparative fault.

### B. "Misappropriation" of an Expert Witness

The Ellweins assert that, by continuing to use accident reconstruction expert Cooper as its own witness after the UIM claim was made, Hartford violated its duty of good faith. Hartford refutes this claim, arguing that Cooper was *its* witness because it retained him on its own behalf. Under Hartford's theory, as a UIM insurer, it "stood in the shoes" of the underinsured motorist and, thus, was under no obligation that would have prevented it from utilizing Cooper's services in defending against the UIM claim. While we agree that insurers' duties differ in the UIM context, we nevertheless find that Hartford acted in bad faith with respect to Cooper.

The real issue in this case is: what is the nature of a UIM insurer's duty of good faith toward its insured? Or, more specifically, does a UIM insurer violate its duty of good faith by hiring an expert for its insured to aid in the insured's liability representation, and then retaining that expert to aid in *its* defense of an insured's UIM claim? In addressing this issue, we (1) compare the nature of the reservation of rights context and the UIM context to determine the applicable duty of good faith and (2) apply that duty to the facts of this case. When an insurer defends its insured under a "reservation of rights," an insurer is nearly a fiduciary of the insured....

While the insurer does not have to place the insured's interests above its own, it is required: to give "equal consideration" to the insured's interests. Thus, an insurance company's duty of good faith rises to an even higher level than that of honesty and lawfulness of purpose toward its policyholders: an insurer must deal fairly with an insured, giving equal consideration *in all matters* to the insured's interests.

[Washington precedent has listed] four specific criteria to meet this "enhanced obligation": First, the company must thoroughly investigate the cause of the insured's accident and the nature and severity of the plaintiff's injuries. Second, it must retain competent defense counsel for the insured. Both retained defense counsel and the insurer must understand that only the *insured* is the client. Third, the company has the responsibility for fully informing the insured not only of the reservation of rights defense itself, but of *all* developments relevant to his policy coverage and the progress of his lawsuit. Information regarding progress of the lawsuit includes disclosure of all settlement offers made by the company. Finally, an insurance company must refrain from engaging in any action which would demonstrate a greater concern for the insurer's monetary interest than for the insured's financial risk.

On the other hand, the relationship between a UIM insurer and its insured "is by nature adversarial and at arm's length." ... UIM insurance provides an excess layer of coverage that is designed to provide full compensation for all amounts that a claimant is legally entitled to where the tortfeasor is underinsured.... "Legally entitled to" is the operative phrase, as a UIM insurer "stands in the shoes" of the tortfeasor, and its liability to the insured is identical to the underinsured tortfeasor's, up to the UIM policy limits.... Stated otherwise, UIM insurers are allowed to assert liability defenses available to the tortfeasor because UIM insurance is designed to place the insured in the same position as if the tortfeasor carried liability insurance.... The injured party is not entitled to be put in a better position by having been struck by an uninsured motorist as opposed to an insured motorist.

As is evident from the above, [the] "enhanced obligation" rule is simply unworkable in the UIM context. How could a UIM insurer "stand in the shoes" of the tortfeasor, with the ability to assert liability defenses, while at the same time give "equal consideration" to the insured's interest? UIM coverage requires that a UIM insurer be free to be adversarial within the confines of the normal rules of procedure and ethics. To require otherwise would contradict the very nature of UIM coverage.

Having found that an "enhanced" duty does not exist does not mean, however, that the duty of good faith simply disappears after a UIM claim is made. Many other courts have held, as we do today, that the duty of good faith and fair dealing survives within the UIM relationship. This is because, although the relationship becomes adversarial, the insured still has "the 'reasonable expectation' that he will be dealt with fairly and in good faith by his insurer...."....

The rule we adopt does not mean that the insurer is precluded from defending the uninsured motorist or from evaluating the claim any differently than it would have had it provided third party coverage. What it does mean, however, ... is that the insurer must deal in good faith and fairly as to the terms of the policy and not overreach the insured, despite its adversary interest.

Applying this basic standard of good faith, we find that Hartford committed bad faith as a matter of law. First, we find Hartford's claim that it believed Cooper was its expert disingenuous. Hartford clearly understood Cooper to be the Ellweins' expert, and intended to manipulate his conclusions, as is evidenced by its apparent satisfaction in having been able "to get *their* reconstruction expert to *reevaluate* his position." Second, although no previous Washington case is precisely on point regarding experts, a rule prohibiting the use and manipulation of the insured's expert by the insurer can be easily extrapolated from the analogous rule dealing with attorneys.

[I]t is presumed that insurers understand that an attorney hired by the insurer to defend the insured has only the *insured* for a client. We see no reason to treat an expert hired under similar circumstances differently. Both are hired to support the *insured's* defense. Both are hired at a time when the insurer clearly owes the insured a duty to not self-deal. Consequently, Hartford can not avoid the claim of bad faith based on "the presence of a res nova question of law...." *Guitreau v. State Farm Mut. Auto. Ins. Co.*, 540 So. 2d 1097, 1102 (La. Ct. App. 1989) ("[W]here sufficient jurisprudence exists to give guidance to insurance companies in determining whether a claim should be denied, the risk of erroneous interpretation falls on the insurer.")....

Finally, we find it particularly troubling that the insurer may "commingle" the liability representation file with the UIM file in such a way. If the insurer truly "stands in the shoes" of the tortfeasor, the benefits of the adversarial relationship should be accompanied by its costs. UIM insurers should be prohibited from using or manipulating an expert where it would be unable to do so if it were, in fact, the tortfeasor.

Having found that Hartford committed bad faith as a matter of law by misappropriating the Ellweins' expert, we reverse the Court of Appeals' dismissal of this claim. Furthermore, in the name of judicial economy, we remand for the entry of summary judgment for the Ellweins on this claim and for a determination of damages.

## C. Alleged Bad Faith Misrepresentation of Policy Limits

The Ellweins further claim that Hartford committed bad faith by misleading their attorney regarding the UIM policy limits. However, the sum total of the Ellweins' evidence of the misrepresentation is their attorney's bare assertion that Hartford misled him. The Ellweins fail to provide any context for this alleged misrepresentation, nor any evidence that the Ellweins were denied access to the policy, which clearly stated the UIM policy limits. Consequently, this unsupported allegation of misrepresentation was properly dismissed....

## D. Spoliation Instruction

The final issue raised in the Ellweins' petition for review is whether the jury should have been allowed to infer that Solito's destruction of the home office file "concealed unreasonable and bad faith activity" by Hartford. More specifically, the Ellweins argue that the trial court erred in failing to give a spoliation of evidence instruction similar to the following:

> "If defendant failed to produce evidence which is under its control and reasonably available to it and not reasonably available to plaintiff, then you may infer that the evidence is unfavorable to the defendant who could not have produced it and did not."

However, because liability is no longer a question, and the only issue that remains is damages, such an instruction is not necessary.... Consequently, we decline to address this issue. *See, e.g.*, *Hayden v. Mut. of Enumclaw Ins. Co.*, 141 Wn. 2d 55, 68, 1 P.3d 1167 (2000) (principles of judicial restraint dictate that courts should avoid resolving issues unnecessary to the resolution of the case).

### IV. Conclusion

In sum, we affirm the trial court's dismissal of the misrepresentation and low settlement offer bad faith claims. However, having found that Hartford committed bad faith by "misappropriating" the Ellweins' accident reconstruction expert, we reverse the trial court's dismissal of that count and remand for a determination of damages.

# Lockwood International, B.V. v. Volm Bag Company, Inc.

United States Court of Appeals for the Seventh Circuit
273 F.3d 741 (2001)

**Posner, Circuit Judge.**

This diversity suit, based on Wisconsin law, presents a novel but potentially quite important issue of insurance law: whether a liability insurer, asked to defend (or pay the defense costs in) a suit against its insured that contains some claims that are covered by the insurance policy and others that are not, can limit its responsibility to defend by paying the plaintiff in the liability suit to replead the covered claims as uncovered claims.

For simplicity we treat the case as a three-cornered dispute among a single plaintiff, Lockwood; a single intervenor, North River, the insurance company; and a single defendant, Volm.

It began with Lockwood, a foreign manufacturer of machines for weighing and bagging produce, suing Volm, which Lockwood had appointed to be its exclusive North American distributor. Lockwood's complaint charged that Volm had secretly formed and funded a new company, Munter, staffed by former employees of Lockwood that Volm had lured to work for Munter. Having done so, the complaint continued, Volm stole Lockwood's intellectual property and manufactured machines that copied Lockwood's.

To complete its infamy, Volm then—by disparaging Lockwood and its products (even spreading false rumors about Lockwood's financial solidity), by soliciting purchases of Lockwood products and then substituting knock-offs of them manufactured by Munter, and by warning customers that Lockwood machines infringed a Volm patent (acquired by fraud, the complaint alleged)—had induced customers for weighing and bagging machines to switch their orders from Lockwood's machines to Munter's. The complaint charged that these acts constituted breach of fiduciary duty, tortious interference with contract, unfair competition, and conspiracy. The suit is still pending.

North River had issued a commercial general liability (CGL) policy to Volm. Under the heading "personal injury," the policy covers product and producer disparagement. Under the heading of "advertising injury," it covers (so far as bears on this case and does not duplicate "personal injury") misappropriation of "advertising ideas or style of doing business" or "infringement of copyright," provided the misappropriation or infringement occurs "in the course of advertising" the insured's products.

Since the complaint expressly charged disparagement of Lockwood and its products, and strongly implied (especially in the bait and switch allegation) that Volm had appropriated Lockwood's "advertising ideas or style of doing business," North River agreed to handle Volm's defense. Had the case gone through to judgment or settlement in the usual way, North River would probably have borne the entire expense of conducting Volm's defense ... although its duty of indemnifying Volm for any damages that it was determined through judgment or settlement to owe Lockwood would have been limited to so much of the judgment or settlement as was fairly allocable to the claims in Lockwood's suit that were covered by the policy.... The difference reflects the greater difficulty of apportioning defense costs than damages. E.g., *Grube v. Daun*, 173 Wis. 2d 30, 496 N.W.2d 106, 122 (Wis. App. 1992); cf. Jeffrey W. Stempel, Law of Insurance Contract Disputes § 9.03[c], pp. 9-67 to 9-68 (2d ed. 2000).

Four years into Lockwood's suit, North River paid Lockwood $1.5 million to file an amended complaint that would delete the covered claims. Lockwood agreed to credit that amount against any judgment it might obtain against Volm. Since the policy limit was only $1 million, the agreement (to which Volm was not a party) protected Volm up to the policy limit against having to pay any covered claims.

With the agreement in hand, North River, which had already intervened in the litigation to obtain a declaration of its duties to the insured, asked the district court to rule that it had no further duty to defend or indemnify Volm, since the effect of the amended complaint was to eliminate any possible liability of Volm to pay the covered claims in Lockwood's original complaint. The district judge agreed and entered a partial final judgment against Volm, which was immediately appealable because it resolved the claim of one of the parties, namely North River. Fed. R. Civ. P. 54(b).

Volm then appealed. It asks us to rule that North River must continue to pay its defense costs notwithstanding the settlement between North River and Lockwood.

North River's lawyer acknowledged at argument — what is anyway obvious — that either he or other counsel for North River had gone over the amended complaint with Lockwood's counsel line by line to make sure that all insured claims had been deleted. In other words, the insurance company sat down with its insured's adversary to contrive a complaint that would eliminate any remaining contractual obligation of the insurance company to defend the insured. (We limit our attention to defense costs, ignoring indemnity, in view of the fact that North River's settlement agreement with Lockwood gave Volm more than the policy limit; thus only defense costs are at issue in this appeal.)

It did this without consulting the insured or obtaining the latter's agreement. We have difficulty imagining a more conspicuous betrayal of the insurer's fiduciary duty to its insured than for its lawyers to plot with the insured's adversary a repleading that will enable the adversary to maximize his recovery of uninsured damages from the insured while stripping the insured of its right to a defense by the insurance company. The limits of coverage, whether limits on the amount to be indemnified under the policy or, as in the present case, on the type of claims covered by the policy, create a conflict of interest between insurer and insured.... The insurer yielded to the conflict, in effect paying its insured's adversary to eliminate the insured's remaining insurance coverage.

It is true as North River points out that if in the course of litigation the covered claims fall out of the case through settlement or otherwise, the insurer's duty to defend his insured ceases. E.g., *Meadowbrook, Inc. v. Tower Ins. Co.*, 559 N.W.2d 411,

416 (Minn. 1997); *Conway Chevrolet-Buick, Inc. v. Travelers Indemnity Co.*, 136 F.3d 210, 214–15 (1st Cir. 1998); *North Bank v. Cincinnati Ins. Cos.*, 125 F.3d 983, 986 (6th Cir. 1997). That is the easiest case for readily apportioning defense costs between covered and uncovered claims.

Nor can the insured prevent the insurer from settling covered claims for an amount that protects the assured from having to pay anything on those claims out of his own pocket, merely because the settlement, by giving the insured all that he contracted for, will terminate the insurer's duty to defend the entire suit.... But North River did not merely settle covered claims; as part of the settlement it paid Lockwood to convert some of the covered claims to uncovered claims. That was not dealing in good faith with its insured.

An example may help make this clear. Suppose that a suit against the insured makes two claims, both covered by the defendant's liability insurance policy. The insurer could settle one claim for $1 million and both for $2 million, but $2 million is too high. Instead it says to the plaintiff, "I'll give you $1.5 million to settle the first claim if you'll agree to redraft the second so that it's an uncovered claim, which you can of course continue to press against my insured." The only purpose of such a deal would be to spare the insurance company the expense of defending against the second claim, even though it was a covered claim when filed and would have continued to be a covered claim had it not been for the insurer's bribe of the plaintiff.

The duty of good faith is read into every insurance contract, ... as it is into contracts generally ... in order to prevent opportunistic behavior by the contracting party that has the whip hand.... That was North River, which neither needed nor sought its insured's permission to settle with Lockwood and by doing so exposed the insured to having to bear its own defense costs for the remainder of the litigation.

North River's maneuver is also defeated by the principle that the duty to defend depends on the facts alleged rather than on the pleader's legal theory...."The insured is covered against particular conduct alleged against it regardless of the label placed on that conduct by the pleader." ... If Lockwood was alleging what was in fact personal injury or advertising injury within the meaning of the policy, the fact that, whether at North River's urging or otherwise, it redrafted its complaint to change the name of the tort it was charging Volm with, but retained the same factual allegations that had triggered North River's initial duty to defend, would be ineffective to terminate that duty....

To recapitulate: North River had every right to settle the claims that gave rise to its duty to defend in the first place—the covered claims and the potentially covered claims in Lockwood's suit—in order to avoid having to defend the claims in the same suit that were not actually or potentially covered. But that is not what North River did. The duty to defend turns on the facts alleged rather than on the theories pleaded; and even after its deal with North River, Lockwood was alleging facts that could well, depending on the course of trial, describe a covered claim. Thus North River did not leave behind only clearly uncovered claims when it tried to shuck off its contractual responsibility to pay for its insured's defense.

It is irrelevant that the trial may show that Lockwood's only meritorious claims against Volm are ones that are not within the scope of the policy. The duty to defend (and hence to reimburse for defense costs when the insurance company doesn't provide the lawyer for the insured) is broader than the duty to indemnify. The reason goes beyond the practical difficulties, noted earlier, involved in apportioning defense costs between covered and uncovered claims. The duty is broader because it "is triggered by arguable, as opposed to actual, coverage." ... The insured needs a defense before he knows whether the claim that has been made against him is covered by the policy, assuming there is doubt on the question.

If the duty to defend were no broader than the duty to indemnify, there would be the paradox that an insured exonerated after trial would have no claim against the insurance company for his defense costs, since the company would have no duty to indemnify him for a loss resulting from a judgment or settlement in the suit against the insured. The duty to defend must therefore be broader than the duty to indemnify, and so the fact that North River paid the policy's limit on indemnification does not exonerate it.

### Notes and Questions

1. After reading *Ellwein* and *Lockwood*, is it fair to conclude that insurers (or their counsel) sometimes act as their own worst enemies? In each of these cases, was the insurer not "too clever by half" (a/k/a too smart for its own good) by attempting to push its information advantage as an insurer to the limit?

2. Recall that in *Crisci*, the bad faith was an unreasonable refusal to settle and protect a vulnerable policyholder. What was the bad faith in *Ellwein*? In *Lockwood*?

3. In each of these cases, could the insurer have achieved its goal without acting in bad faith? How?

4. Revisiting the public policy questions asked at the close of the *Crisci* excerpt, we again ask: do instances of bad insurer behavior justify imposing a heightened standard of good faith on insurers as compared to other contracting parties? Why or why not?

## [B] The Measure of Damages from Bad Faith Conduct

To perhaps state the obvious, a policyholder must actually suffer some injury from an insurer's bad faith conduct in order to recover damages. Some courts address the matter by stating that harm is an essential element of a bad faith claim. *See Werlinger v. Clarendon Nat'l Ins. Co.*, 120 P.3d 593 (Wash. Ct. App. 2005). In our view, it is more accurate to say that a policyholder may prove bad faith without showing injury but can recover no compensation absent a showing of harm.

As noted above, several of the contract bad faith jurisdictions permit only traditional contract remedies. Ordinarily, this means that the damages claimed by the policyholder must be within the contemplation of the parties and fall within the rule of *Hadley v. Baxendale*, 9 Ex. 341, 156 Eng. Rep. 145 (1854). Some courts see lost policyholder profits as recoverable as a consequential damage in a bad faith action, but appear to require that the *Hadley v. Baxendale* rule be met and that the losses be reasonably foreseeable to the insurer. Other contract bad faith states have been willing to provide a broader scope of contract-based damages on the theory that the insurer committing bad faith has breached an obligation on which the policyholder was depending. Courts in these jurisdictions may permit policyholders to recover emotional distress damages. But these states appear to differ regarding whether physical injury is a prerequisite to emotional distress recovery and the degree of manifestation required to constitute the requisite physical injury. A few decisions in contract bad faith states support full-fledged punitive damages if the insurer's conduct is sufficiently wrongful.

The tort bad faith states exhibit similar variation in the amount recoverable. This may involve differences over the punitive damages recovery, where the states have differing punitive damage standards and limits, as discussed below. *See* Richard L. Blatt et al., Punitive Damages: A State by State Guide to Law and Practice § 3.2 (2003) (dividing state tests for award of punitive damages into four rough categories of "proof of malice," "more egregious than gross negligence but not requiring proof of malice," "gross negligence," and a very broad catchall category of "proof of various conduct requirements"); Maniloff & Stempel, Key Issues, *supra*, Ch. 20.

One study suggests that states permitting bad-faith claims in first-party insurance matters generally have higher claims settlement offers to policyholders. *See* Mark J. Browne, Ellen S. Pryor & Bob Puelz, *The Effect of Bad-Faith Laws on First-Party Insurance Claims Decisions*, 33 J. Legal Stud. 355 (2004). The question remains, of course, whether these higher offers reflect the possibility of a bad faith claim prompting fairer treatment by the insurer or instead reflect the insurer offering more due to the mere fear that a groundless bad faith claim is always a possibility if the policyholder is unsatisfied and refuses to accept the insurer's offer.

The ALI's RLLI § 48 provides the following list of "damages that an insured may recover for breach of a liability insurance policy" as including:

(1) In a case of a policy that provides defense coverage, all reasonable costs of the defense of a potentially covered legal action that have not already been paid by the insurer, subject to any applicable limit, deductible, or self-insured retention of the policy;

(2) All amounts required to indemnify the insured for a covered legal action that have not already been paid by the insurer, subject to any applicable limit, deductible, or self-insured retention of the policy;

(3) In the case of a breach of the duty to make reasonable settlement decisions, the damages stated in § 27 [the amount of a judgment against the policyholder in excess of policy limits that could have been avoided had the insurer made reasonable settlement decisions];

(4) Any other loss, including incidental or consequential loss, caused by the breach, provided that the loss was foreseeable by the insurer at the time of contracting as a probably result of a breach, which sums are not subject to any limit of the policy.

RLLI § 47 further provides "remedies that may be available in an action determining the rights of parties under a liability insurance policy" as including:

(1) An award of damages under § 48;

(2) A declaration of the rights of the parties;

(3) Court costs or attorneys' fees to a prevailing party when provided by state law or the [insurance] policy;

(4) If so provided in the liability insurance policy or otherwise agreed by the parties, an award of a sum of money due to the insurer as recoupment of the costs of defense or settlement;

(5) Collection and disbursement of interpleaded policy proceeds;

(6) Payment or return of premiums;

(7) Indemnification of the insure by the insured when state law permits recovery from highly culpable insureds; and

(8) Prejudgment interest.

## The RLLI as a Damages/Remedies Checklist

- Which of the forms of relief listed in RLLI §§ 47 & 48 are necessarily limited to liability insurance?

- Why or why not?

- Should other forms of relief have been added to §§ 47 & 48?

- Which forms?

- Why?

- Assuming the role of a state legislator, would you codify RLLI §§ 47 & 48?

- With what additions, subtractions, or deletions?

Regarding illustrative cases concerning damages available for bad faith conduct or breach of the duty to defend or settle, see, e.g., *Nunn v. Mid-Century Ins. Co.*, 244 P.3d 116 (Colo. 2010) (amount in excess of policy limits constitutes damage proximately caused by insurer's failure to settle and raises presumption of bad faith; also approving assignment of claim from policyholder to claimant); *Weinstein v. Prudential Prop. & Cas. Ins. Co.*, 233 P.3d 1221 (Idaho 2010) (insurer's intentional delay in paying claim is bad faith entitling policyholder to punitive damages); *Perera v. United States Fid. & Guar. Co.*, 35 So. 3d 893 (Fla. 2010) (injuries incurred by policyholder must have sufficient causal link to insurer's bad faith to be recovered in bad faith action by policyholder).

## [C] Punitive Damages

The tort-contract divide among the states in bad faith jurisprudence has substantial implications for the available remedies. As students remember from first year torts and contracts: generally, punitive damages are not available in connection with a breach of contract action (although they may be if the contract breacher also committed an independent tort such as fraud), but punitive damages are generally available to a tort claimant if it can be demonstrated that the defendant acted with the requisite standard of reprehensibility toward the plaintiff. In most states, this is defined as "conscious disregard" for the rights of the plaintiff, or a similar verbal standard. Some courts will accept a seemingly lower threshold such as "reckless indifference" to policyholder rights.

As with bad faith law generally, there is considerable variance among the states regarding punitive damages standards and judicial willingness to police punitive awards. States may also differ as to limitations on punitive awards. Students should be very clear on one thing: even if bad faith is proven, this does not automatically entitle the policyholder to punitive damages from the insurer. Punitive damages are not automatically available against the insurer. The policyholder must further demonstrate, usually (but not always) by clear and convincing evidence, that the insurer's misconduct went beyond mere bad faith but was more blameworthy.

In addition, states with the same or close to the same verbiage setting the punitive damages standard may, as a practical matter, impose these standards differently. Beyond this, state law varies as to the amount of punitive damages that may be recoverable by similarly situated policyholders. Even within a given state, there may be considerable variance in the manner in which courts seek to articulate the standard for punitive damages. *See, e.g., Linthicum v. Nationwide Life Ins. Co.*, 150 Ariz. 326, 330–31, 723 P.2d 675, 679–80 (1986) (listing 13 "various characterizations of conduct allowing recovery of punitive damages" under Arizona law including: malice; spite or ill will; evil intent or bad motive; gross negligence; wanton, reckless or willful acts; intentional misconduct; fraud; oppression; extreme, aggravated, or outrageous conduct; conduct involving an unreasonable risk of causing distress; reckless disregard for or indifference to the rights, interests, or safety of others; criminal acts or conduct; and the perhaps tautological "acts done in bad faith").

In addition to state common law regarding punitive damages, many states have statutes governing the imposition and amount of punitive damages. There are also federal constitutional restrictions on punitive damages. Most relevant for insurance purposes (but applicable to punitive damages generally) is *State Farm Mutual Automobile Insurance Company*, 538 U.S. 408 (2003) in which the Court overturned a $145 million punitive damages award, remanding the case to the Utah Supreme Court.

The case grew out of a tragic accident that stemmed largely from Curtis Campbell attempting to pass six vehicles in a row. Utah State student Todd Ospital, driving an oncoming car, attempted to avoid collision with Campbell but went out of control, hitting a van driven by Robert Slusher- one of the vans Campbell was passing.

Slusher was badly injured and Ospital was killed. Campbell, a State Farm policy-holder, was sued.

During the course of Campbell's defense, the insurer and insurer-provided counsel engaged in unreasonable conduct that favored its own interest at the expense of the policyholder. Most egregious was repeated rejection of opportunities to settle for Campbell's low ($25,000 per person/$50,000 per accident) limits. The jury returned a quarter-million verdict against Campbell. Adding insult to injury, State Farm took the position that the damages exceeding the policy limits were Campbell's problem. Curtis and his wife Inez sued the insurer for bad faith. See also *Campbell v. State Farm Mutual Automobile Ins. Co.*, 65 P.3d 1134 (Utah 2001) (approving jury's $ I 45 million punitive damages award in spite of trial court's remittitur to $25 million).

The U.S. Supreme Court, building on earlier precedent suggesting constitutional limits on punitive damages, held that the Due Process Clause places an outer limit on punitive damage awards based on three factors or guideposts: (1) the reprehensibility of defendant's conduct; (2) the size of the punitive award relative to the compensatory damages; and (3) the size of the award relative to government penalties imposed for similar conduct. The Court also ruled that the conduct forming the basis of a punitive award must be conduct sufficiently connected to the state in question and to harm caused in that state. Regarding ratio, the Court stated that in cases of significant compensatory damages, punitive damages should generally not be more than nine times the amount of the compensatory award.

Applied to the Campbell claim, this meant that a significant portion of insurer misconduct proffered at trial to show reprehensibility had to be discounted. In addition, because the harm to the Campbells was deemed largely economic (although their compensatory damage claim contained a strong emotional distress component), the Court found the insurer behavior less reprehensible than did the lower courts. The generally low regulatory or statutory fines levied for insurer misconduct also augured in favor of a lower punitive award. Most important, the Court found that a $145 million punitive damages judgment was just too much in that it was 145 times the $1 million emotional distress award in the case.

Justices Scalia and Thomas dissented on doctrinal grounds, arguing that the Constitution did not place limits on state common law awards of punitive damages. Justice Ginsburg also dissented, viewing the insurer's conduct as dramatically more egregious than the Court majority and sufficient to justify a large award in order to punish past misconduct and deter future similar misconduct. She also took issue with the majority's evidentiary limits. On remand, the Utah Supreme Court reiterated its distain for State Farm's behavior and entered a punitive damages judgment of $9 million, effectively the outer limit what the U.S. Supreme Court would permit. *See Campbell v. State Farm Mut. Auto. Ins. Co.*, 98 P.3d 2004), cert denied, 543 U.S. 874 (2004)

Justice Robert Jackson famously observed regarding the U.S. Supreme Court (with what appears to be humility rather than grandiosity) that "[w]e are not final because we are infallible but we are infallible only because we are final." *Brown v. Allen*, 344 U.S. 443, 540 (1953) (Jackson, J., concurring). It is worth remembering that the hierarchy of the judiciary required in order to have adequate finality and guidance for lower courts is something of a rule of necessity rather than a vote of confidence that the U.S. Supreme Court will consistently contain the nine best (however one defines best) attorneys in America.

In *Campbell v. State Farm*, six Justices saw the punishment of the insurer as too harsh or legally impermissible (because bad conduct took place outside Utah). But it should be remembered that more judges or justices viewing the case approved a jury's $145 million punitive damages award. The trial judge, six Utah Supreme Court Justices, and Justices Ginsburg—as well as the jurors—were all much more upset about State Farm's conduct[6] than were Justices Kennedy, O'Connor, Stevens, Souter, Breyer, and Chief Justice Rehnquist.

For a post-script on the Campbell case, see *Christensen & Jensen, P.C. v. Barrett & Daines*, 194 P.3d 931 (Utah 2008). Scott Barrett, the attorney representing Robert Slusher in the original action against Todd Ospital and Curtis Campbell and who was part of the Ospital-Slusher-Campbell peace pact (aided by Ospital's original counsel, L. Rich Humpherys of Christensen & Jensen, who had been retained by Allstate, the Ospital family's auto insurer), sought greater compensation from the subsequent bad faith litigation. The court rejected Barrett's argument that he was entitled to an equal share of the counsel fees since Humpherys and his firm had done the great bulk of the work prosecuting the bad faith claim against state farm during the more than 20 years between the time of the *Slusher v. Ospital & Campbell* trial in 1983 and the eventual payment of the bad faith punitive damages award in 2004.

In what is perhaps a window into the lack of information laypersons have in seeking counsel, Barrett was selected as Slusher's lawyer in 1981 because in the aftermath of the accident, Slusher was rushed to the hospital in nearby Logan, Utah, where his parents joined him for the recovery vigil. Seeking a lawyer, they consulted the yellow pages, by which Barrett benefitted by having a name at the front of the alphabet. *See* JEFFREY W. STEMPEL, LITIGATION ROAD: THE STORY OF *CAMPBELL V. STATE FARM* 65 (2008), which also provides an extensive history of the tragic accident, the underlying tort litigation, and the tortuous path of the bad faith litigation.

Recall that in the original trial against Mr. Campbell as the driver who attempted to pass six vans on an uphill road, the injured Mr. Slusher and the estate of the deceased Todd Ospital (an honors student with more than 60 years of life expectancy when killed) were awarded $135,000 and $50,000, amounts we find shockingly low ($349,000 and $129,000 in 2019 dollars) (which begins to look a little less shocking), and that provides a window on the vagaries of American litigation.

---

6. Because Justices Scalia and Thomas focused more on their view that the Constitution did not place limits on state punitive damages, it is harder to determine whether they viewed the punitive damages award as too high in relation to the insurer's misconduct.

Trial of the original case was in Logan, Utah, in Cache (pronounced "cash") County, roughly 83 miles and three counties north of Salt Lake City, where the bad faith trial was held years later. Utah lawyers refer with both humor and pathos to a "Cache County Discount" because the area is so well-known for low-cum-stingy verdicts. If the accident had taken place only a little further south, trial would have been held in Box Elder, Weber or Davis Counties, which are not known for high verdicts and would likely have resulted in far more compensation for the victims. As suggested by the large punitive damages award, trial in more urbane Salt Lake would likely have resulted in a much larger judgment in the underlying auto collision claim. *See generally* Marianne Funk, *Utah Jury Awards Trail U.S. Average*, Deseret News (Oct. 24, 1991) (state ranks 43rd in verdict size, with average award of $150,000 in wrongful death cases, with "most of Utah's rural counties ... 13.4 percent below the national average").

## [D] Institutional Bad Faith

In many if not most bad faith cases, the bad faith results from the errors of a few persons or even a single person (e.g., an adjuster, an attorney, an agent) for which the insurer is responsible because of vicarious liability. However, in some cases, the bad faith may result from an intentionally adopted, company-wide policy that is adhered to by the insurer even when the insurer knew or should have known that it violated its duty of good faith to its policyholders. In commenting on some auto insurers' practices of offering in settlement only the amounts set forth by their computerized models, one of us (Stempel) has referred to this as "institutionalized bad faith." *See also* Jay M. Feinman, Delay Deny Defend: Why Insurance Companies Don't Pay Claims and What you can Do About it (2010) (arguing that such company-wide policies placing insurer interests above those of policyholders are common and perhaps the rule rather than the exception).

More officially, a prominent insurance broker's counsel has deemed bad faith resulting from company policy as "institutional" bad faith, which will probably not become the preferred description. *See* Douglas R. Richmond, *Defining and Confining Institutional Bad Faith in Insurance*, 46 Tort Trial & Ins. Prac. L.J. 1 (2010). *Accord* James A. Varner et al., *Institutional Bad Faith: The Darth Vader of Extra-Contractual Litigation*, 57 Fed'n Def. & Corp. Couns. Q. 163 (2007).

Although the term and the concept have yet to find their way into the case law to any significant degree, there are cases essentially arguing a theory of institutional bad faith rather than merely that the insurer is responsible for the bad faith conduct of its agents on the ground. *See, e.g., Niver v. Travelers Indem. Co.*, 433 F. Supp. 2d 968 (N.D. Iowa 2006) (arguing that company incentive programs were in bad faith by encouraging adjusters to short-change policyholders); *Lopez v. Allstate Ins. Co.*, 282 F. Supp. 2d 1095 (D. Ariz. 2003) (arguing that insurer's "Claim Core Process Redesign" or CCPR and treatment of "Minor Impact Soft Tissue" or MIST injuries was unfairly designed to underpay and failed to take into account individual circumstances of claims); *White v. Continental Gen. Ins. Co.*, 831 F. Supp. 1545 (D.

Wyo. 1993) (arguing unsuccessfully that health insurer had standard practice of "post-claim underwriting" in which it sought to refuse coverage by refraining from issuing a policy after becoming aware of a claim and that insurer uses an incentive plan in which adjusters were rewarded for denying claims or chiseling on claims); *Zilisch v. State Farm Mut. Auto. Ins. Co.*, 995 P.2d 276 (Ariz. 2000) (quoted at the beginning of this chapter) (insurer allegedly adopted national practice of seeking to systematically underpay underinsured motorist claims in order to enhance profits) (an argument reminiscent of that of the Campbell plaintiffs in *Campbell v. State Farm, supra); Crackel v. Allstate Ins. Co.*, 92 P.3d 882 (Ariz. Ct. App. 2004) (claim similar to *Lopez v. Allstate, supra*).

Institutional bad faith claims may be difficult to prove in part because courts (and most everyone else) agree that insurers should be given significant discretion in attempting to manage their businesses in a manner that discourages the inefficiency of overpayment of claims, which provides some support for carefully tailored employee compensation programs or computer models for assessing claims.

However, some observers, such as Professors Feinman and Stempel, have significant problems with insurers ever using claims as a profit center and also object to ironclad use of a computer model for valuing claims in the absence of individual (human) agent discretion and supervision. But insurance industry veterans like attorney Richmond defend some of the challenged practices as essential to maintain the efficiency necessary for successful operations of insurers. *See* Richmond, *Defining and Confining Institutional Bad Faith, supra*, at 29 ("nothing wrong" with cost control initiatives that reward employees for reduced claims costs if implemented properly but noting that "some policies require careful thought before they are implemented") (*id.* at 27). *See also id.* at 26–32 (providing extensive list of recommendations for insurers seeking to avoiding institutional bad faith liability).

But it appears that one insurer has managed to adopt a company policy sufficiently drenched in unfairness to the policyholder that even these often disparate analysts agree that a case of institutional bad faith was established. In *Merrick v. Paul Revere Life Ins. Co.*, 594 F. Supp. 2d 1168 (D. Nev. 2008), the court found that UnumProvident Corporation, the parent of Paul Revere, engaged in a pattern and practice of bad faith. *See* Richmond, *Defining and Confining Institutional Bad Faith, supra*, at 21–26. *See also id.* at 24 ("Long story short, UnumProvident and Paul Revere abused Merrick just as they did many other insureds.") and at 25 ("description of the facts in *Merrick* makes UnumProvident look more like the diabolical insurer caricatured in John Grisham's novel *The Rainmaker*"). *See, e.g., Hangarter v. Provident Life & Accident Ins. Co.*, 373 F.3d 998, 1011–14 (9th Cir. 2004) (applying California law) (a case similar to *Merrick* involving the UnumProvident "family"). *See also* John H. Langbein, *Trust Law as Regulatory Law: The Unum/Provident Scandal and Judicial Review of Benefits Denials Under ERISA*, 101 Nw. U.L. Rev. 1315, 1317–20 (2007).

In many ways, *Campbell v. State Farm, supra*, was based on a theory of institutional bad faith as well as the alleged misconduct of employees or agents on the ground, particularly the defense attorney selected by State Farm to defend the original auto accident case. But after the U.S. Supreme Court's ruling limiting the use of evidence from other states, affecting other policyholders, or involving other insurance operations, there may be additional practical limits on the ability to prove up allegations of institutional bad faith. Much of the material that the Court deemed inadmissible because it involved different states and different insurance products arguably is relevant under a theory of institutional bad faith. To date, however, these evidentiary questions have not been discussed at length in reported opinions. Where there is institutional bad faith intentionally disregarding the rights of policyholders, punitive damages would seem in order. Although the Supreme Court has now restricted their availability, substantial punitive awards remain a possibility, as reflected in *Campbell* on remand.

## [E] Additional Litigation Issues

### [1] *Expert Witnesses*

Regarding litigation and proof of bad faith, states vary as to whether expert testimony is required to prove up a bad faith claim, with the majority of states rejecting any such requirement. *See, e.g., Am. Family Mut. Ins. Co. v. Allen*, 102 P.3d 333 (Colo. 2004) (expert testimony not required; affirming bad faith judgment for policyholder).

The right answer, as in so many areas of law, will vary with the type of claim. Policyholders (and their assignees) should not be required to procure potentially costly experts unless the theory of the case involves something highly specialized or even esoteric. For example, if an American policyholder contends that payment of a claim in British Pounds is unreasonable (because the Pound has lost much value because of Brexit anxiety) and in violation of a clause promising "payment pursuant to accepted practices," it is hard to imagine the policyholder prevailing without expert testimony. The insurer has paid in the currency of a major industrial nation (something even Boris Johnson and Tory government have yet to completely destroy). In this hypothetical case and in many insurance cases, the parties themselves may qualify as expert witnesses. For example, a major commercial policyholder or a Lloyd's syndicate manager with years of experience would presumably qualify to discuss what constitutes "accepted" practice regarding payment.

The flip side of this question is whether a policyholder or insurer is permitted to proffer expert testimony even if this is not required to maintain the claim. The general rule is that expert opinion is not admissible regarding legal characterization of policy meaning or insurer conduct. However, expert testimony regarding the history and development of an insurance product, including particular policy language, is logically admissible if helpful to the adjudicator. Similarly, expert testimony regarding insurance axioms, principles, custom, practice, and risk management practices carries a presumption of admissibility. Because judges are accorded wide discretion in this area that is reviewed with an "abuse of discretion" standard, the practical reality is that a decision to admit or exclude expert testimony is unlikely to be reversed in an insurance dispute.

## [2] Scope of Discovery and Privileges

There can also be thorny issues regarding the scope of discovery and admissibility of evidence in bad faith litigation, as well as debates over the scope of attorney-client privilege, as discussed in the *Vanliner* case below. *See, e.g., Jacobsen v. Allstate Ins. Co.*, 215 P.3d 649 (Mont. 2009) (approving discovery of information regarding insurer's claims processing model); *Fortner v. Grange Mut. Ins. Co.*, 686 S.E.2d 93 (Ga. 2009) (ruling favorably on policyholder's proffer of evidence bearing on bad faith claim).

A recurring issue on which courts are divided is the degree to which an insurer enjoys the protections against discovery provided by the trial preparation materials or "work product" privilege. As "everyone" "knows" from first-year civil procedure, materials prepared in anticipation of litigation enjoy a qualified privilege from discovery provided by FED. R. CIV. P. 26(b)(3) and state analogs. Although the facts underlying attorney "work product" are not privileged, the documents themselves — particularly attorney mental impressions reflected in the documents — are not subject to discovery unless the requesting party can demonstrate that it has substantial need for the documents and cannot obtain the substantial equivalent of the documents or information without undue hardship.

Insurers sometimes take a very broad view of what constitutes "anticipation of litigation," essentially contending that, as insurers, they are always anticipating lawsuits and that every document produced regarding a claim is in anticipation of litigation and hence subject to work product protection. Policyholders counter, more persuasively in our view, that documents produced in the ordinary course of business cannot, without something more, be considered made in anticipation of litigation, because such an approach would allow the trial preparation privilege to unfairly swallow the general rule that business records are subject to production in litigation.

A majority of courts take positions closer to ours than to those of the more aggressive, non-disclosing insurers. *See, e.g., Anastasi v. Fidelity National Title Ins. Co.*, 366 P.3d 160, 170 (Haw. 2016) ("Most courts have recognized that an insurance carrier's investigation of a claim is generally performed in the ordinary course of business and *not* protected by work product doctrine.") (emphasis in original); *Harper v. Auto-Owners Ins. Co.*, 138 F.R.D. 655, 664 (S.D. Ind. 1991) ("It is presumed that a document or thing prepared before a final decision was reached on an insured's claim, and which constitutes part of the factual inquiry into or evaluation of that claim, was prepared in the ordinary and routine course of the insurer's business of claim determination and is not work product."); *Allstate Indem. Co. v. Ruiz*, 899 So. 2d 1121 (Fla. 2005) (discovery of work product permitted in first-party bad faith actions). But each case is fact-specific. *See United States v. Richey*, 632 F.3d 559, 567–68 (9th Cir. 2011) (test is whether document was created "because of" litigation and not for other reasons; under this test, "courts are instructed to consider whether given the totality of the circumstances it can be fairly said that a document was prepared or obtained because of the prospect of litigation").

Notwithstanding these groundrules, insurers have won more than a few work product battles and appear to have done even better when attorney-client privilege is the issue. This privilege applies to communications between an attorney and client (including their respective agents) for the purposes of facilitating legal representation and which are made in confidence and kept confidential. Thus, insurer communications with counsel (including in-house counsel) may be subject to the privilege even when made during the course of an ongoing claims investigation. *See, e.g., Genovese v. Provident Life & Accident Ins. Co.*, 74 So. 3d 1064 (Fla. 2011) (barring discovery of attorney-client communications related to denial of disability insurance benefits). *But see Dakota, Minn. & E. R.R. Corp. v. Acuity*, 771 N.W.2d 623 (S.D. 2009) (where insurer delegated initial claims function and relied upon outside counsel to conduct investigation and determine coverage, communications between insurer and counsel were not protected by attorney-client privilege).

If the insurer interposes an "advice of counsel" defense to a challenged coverage decision, this normally waives the privilege, at least to the advice-connected communications. In addition, the privilege may be waived through failure to maintain confidentiality. The privilege may also be overcome by a sufficient showing that counsel's services have been used in the service of criminal or fraudulent activity. Although it's rare, one might find institutional bad faith sufficiently egregious to make this exception applicable.

As with all litigation, there can be statute of limitations issues. *See, e.g., Noland v. Va. Ins. Reciprocal*, 686 S.E.2d 23 (W. Va. 2009) (one-year statute of limitations set forth in statute governs common law bad faith claim). There may also be issues regarding whether a policyholder or insurer has engaged in abuse of process or malicious prosecution. *See, e.g., Young v. Allstate Ins. Co.*, 198 P.3d 666 (Haw. 2008) (declining to recognize a tort of malicious defense of a claim on the part of an insurer).

## Boone v. Vanliner Insurance Company

Supreme Court of Ohio
91 Ohio St. 3d 209, 744 N.E.2d 154 (2001)

**Douglas, J.**

Appellant, Richard Boone, is an over-the-road truck driver and a resident of Ohio. Appellee, Vanliner Insurance Company ("Vanliner"), issued a commercial vehicle liability insurance policy to Boone, individually, and a separate policy to Boone's employer. Each policy of insurance provided $1,000,000 liability coverage. Boone's employer's policy also provided $1,000,000 uninsured/underinsured motorist coverage and Boone's policy listed uninsured/underinsured motorist coverage in the amount of $50,000.

On June 12, 1995, Boone was in Tampa, Florida, transporting goods for his employer when he was involved in a three-vehicle accident. Boone, driving a tractor-trailer, was travelling behind a dump truck driven by Robert Allison, when Brett Verona, the operator of the third vehicle, lost control while attempting to change lanes. Due to Verona's negligence, Allison was unable to prevent his vehicle from colliding with Verona's. Boone's attempt to avoid hitting Allison's truck was also unsuccessful.

As a result of the accident, Boone suffered serious injuries, including bilateral fractures of both knees. Verona's insurer paid $100,000, the limit of Verona's liability coverage, toward Boone's damages. Boone, alleging that his damages exceeded $100,000, subsequently sought underinsured motorist benefits from Vanliner through his employer's policy of insurance. Vanliner denied Boone's claim, asserting that an exclusion provision in the policy precluded underinsured motorist coverage with regard to Boone's accident.

On June 12, 1997, Boone brought a declaratory judgment action against Vanliner seeking a determination that his policy and his employer's policy of insurance with Vanliner each provided him with $1,000,000 in uninsured/underinsured motorist coverage. With regard to his individual policy, Boone alleged that he was entitled to $1,000,000 uninsured/underinsured coverage by operation of law because Vanliner had failed to obtain a written waiver of uninsured/underinsured coverage in an amount equal to his liability insurance as required by Ohio law. The complaint included a claim for bad faith, alleging that Vanliner lacked reasonable justification for denying underinsured motorist coverage. To support his bad faith claim, Boone sought access, through discovery, to Vanliner's claims file.

In its answer to Boone's complaint, Vanliner denied that Boone was entitled to uninsured/underinsured motorist benefits under either policy. However, Vanliner subsequently changed its position and admitted that each policy of insurance provided Boone with $1,000,000 of uninsured/underinsured motorist coverage. Vanliner subsequently moved the court for a protective order with regard to numerous documents in its claims file. In its motion, Vanliner contended that several documents were protected from discovery by the attorney-client privilege and/or work-product doctrine.

The trial court ordered Vanliner to submit its claims file to the court for an *in camera* inspection to determine which documents, if any, were protected from discovery. The claims file consists of 1,741 documents numbered "0" through "1741." The trial court found that one hundred seventy-five of the documents were protected from discovery and ordered Vanliner to release the unprotected documents to Boone. In determining which documents were protected, the trial court [followed Ohio precedent holding] that certain attorney-client communications and work-product materials in an insurer's claims file were not protected from discovery by the attorney-client privilege or work-product doctrine.

The issue before us is whether, in an action alleging bad faith denial of insurance coverage, the insured is entitled to obtain, through discovery, claims file documents containing attorney-client communications and work product that may cast light on whether the denial was made in bad faith.

We [have] stated that "documents and other things showing the lack of a good faith effort to settle by a party or the attorneys acting on his or her behalf are wholly unworthy of the protections afforded by any claimed privilege." [citation omitted]. Thus, we held that "in an R.C. 1343.03(C) proceeding for prejudgment interest, neither the attorney-client privilege nor the so-called work product exception precludes discovery of the contents of an insurer's claims file. The only privileged matters contained in the file are those that go directly to the theory of defense of the underlying case in which the decision or verdict has been rendered."

Boone argues that claims file materials showing an insurer's lack of good faith in determining coverage are equally unworthy of protection. Vanliner, on the other hand, asks us to affirm the court of appeals' decision.... Vanliner further contends that if insureds alleging bad faith are able to access certain attorney-client communications within the claims file, then insurers will be discouraged from seeking legal advice as to whether a certain claim is covered under a policy of insurance. This argument is not well taken because it assumes that insurers will violate their duty to conduct a thorough investigation by failing, when necessary, to seek legal counsel regarding whether an insured's claim is covered under the policy of insurance, in order to avoid the insured later having access to such communications, through discovery.

Vanliner further argues that the release of the documents at issue in this case will undermine its ability to defend on the underlying underinsured motorist claim that remains pending. We find this argument unpersuasive. If this were a legitimate concern, we believe that Vanliner would have moved the trial court to stay the bad faith claim, severing it from the underlying underinsured motorist claim. Our review of the record in this case reveals that Vanliner took no such action.

For the foregoing reasons, we hold that in an action alleging bad faith denial of insurance coverage, the insured is entitled to discover claims file materials containing attorney-client communications related to the issue of coverage that were created prior to the denial of coverage. At that stage of the claims handling, the claims file materials will not contain work product, *i.e.*, things prepared in anticipation of litigation, because at that point it has not yet been determined whether coverage exists. Of course, if the trial court finds that the release of this information will inhibit the insurer's ability to defend on the underlying claim, it may issue a stay of the bad faith claim and related production of discovery pending the outcome of the underlying claim.

**Cook, J.,** dissenting.

The majority today adopts a wholesale exception to the attorney-client privilege in actions alleging bad-faith denial of insurance coverage. The majority concludes that "claims file materials that show an insurer's lack of good faith in denying coverage are unworthy of protection." Because the majority's broad holding diminishes the attorney-client privilege without a reasoned basis for doing so, I dissent.

With its "unworthy of protection" rationale, the majority effectively equates an insurer's communications with its attorney prior to a denial of coverage, in any case alleging bad faith, with communications in furtherance of a civil fraud. But bad faith by an insurer is conceptually different from fraud. Bad-faith denial of insurance coverage means merely that the insurer lacked a "reasonable justification" for denying a claim. *Zoppo v. Homestead Ins. Co.* (1994), 71 Ohio St. 3d 552, 644 N.E.2d 397, paragraph one of the syllabus. In contrast, an actionable claim of fraud requires proof of a false statement made with intent to mislead.... Proof of an insurer's bad faith in denying coverage does not require proof of any false or misleading statements; an insurer could, for example, act in bad faith by denying coverage without explanation.... Because bad faith is not inherently similar to fraud, there is no reason why an allegation of bad faith should result in an exception to the attorney-client privilege akin to the crime-fraud exception.

The majority's holding is also startling for its practical effect. After today's decision, an insured need only *allege* the insurer's bad faith in the complaint in order to discover communications between the insurer and the insurer's attorney. Not even an allegation of the crime-fraud exception's applicability carries such an absolute entitlement to discovery of attorney-client communications. In order to overcome the attorney-client privilege based on the crime-fraud exception, a party must demonstrate "a factual basis for a showing of probable cause to believe that a crime or fraud has been committed and that the communications were in furtherance of the crime or fraud."...

The rule created today requires no similar prima facie showing of bad faith before an insured is entitled to discover attorney-client communications of the insurer. The result of the majority's decision is a categorical exception to the attorney-client privilege applicable in *any* case alleging a bad-faith denial of insurance coverage. This is a sweeping exception that a number of courts have refused to adopt. The majority has simply decided that insurance-bad-faith cases should be treated differently as far as the attorney-client privilege is concerned, ignoring that "the nature of the relationship, not the nature of the cause of action, controls whether communications between attorney and client can be discovered."...

### Notes and Questions

1. In *Vanliner*, did the insurer's status not only earn it a heightened contract-cum-tort duty but also give it less protection than other civil litigants? What are the merits of Justice Cook's dissent as opposed to the majority opinion?

2. In applying *Vanliner* as a trial judge, what showing should be required before an insurer's file of attorney communications becomes discoverable? At what juncture of litigation can this realistically be established? Under *Vanliner*, the mere allegation of bad faith does not make every communication with counsel discoverable, does it?

3. In response to the *Vanliner* decision, the Ohio legislature passed a law declaring that it was the public policy of Ohio to support the attorney-client privilege and that discovery of privileged materials required a prima facie showing of wavier by the insurer (which appears to include waiver by insurer misconduct such as the crime-

fraud exception) and that before attorney-insurer communications could be disclosed, the court must conduct an in camera inspection of the disputed documents in chambers. *See Nationwide Mut. Fire Ins. Co. v. Jones*, 2017 Ohio App. LEXIS 2300 (Ct. App. 4th App. Dist. May 31, 2017).

## *[3] Recovery of Counsel Fees*

As you learned in Civil Procedure, the U.S. follows (unsurprisingly) the "American Rule" regarding counsel fees. This is in contrast to the "English Rule" in which the losing litigant must pay the prevailing party's fees.[7] In the U.S., a litigant is ordinarily responsible for paying its own fees subject to a few exceptions: statutorily authorized (e.g., 42 U.S.C. § 1988) or rule authorized (e.g., FED. R. CIV. P. 11) fee shifting; creation of a common fund or benefit for others (who did not have to shell out for lawyers because of the litigant's efforts); or sanction for frivolous or vexatious litigation. As reflected in the sanctions exception, the basis for fee shifting may be a mixture of statutes, rules, and common law.

Recovery of counsel fees for insurance litigation is similar to and different from the norm. The similarity is that fee recovery can stem from a mixture of statutes, rules, regulations, and common law. The difference is that—good news for policyholders as compared with non-insurance claimants—fee shifting is more common for insurance disputes. "[M]ost states have carved out an exception of some type to the American Rule when it is judicially determined that an insurer is obligated to provide coverage to an insured." *See* RANDY MANILOFF & JEFFREY STEMPEL, GENERAL LIABILITY INSURANCE COVERAGE: KEY ISSUES IN EVERY STATE 290 (4th ed. 2018). But there are pronounced state-to-state differences. *See* MANILOFF & STEMPEL, Ch. 8 (surveying and summarizing state law on the topic). Consequently, counsel for both policyholders and insurers must be aware of controlling state law in their respective cases in order to maximize chances of fees recovery and minimize the chance that fees may be imposed.[8]

---

7. The fee shifting is not in practice as automatic and severe as often portrayed by commentators. In England, the prevailing party must present its proposed bill to a "Taxing Master" who typically winnows down the amount the losing litigant must pay to the prevailing party. In addition, a significant number of English cases qualify for "legal aid" status in which government-supported counsel prosecute the case. If the case is unsuccessful, there is no fee-shifting in these cases absent special circumstances (e.g., the losing litigant obtained legal aid status through fraud). Canada is also a fee-shifting country which applies the English rule. However, the fees the unsuccessful litigating party are expected to pay are tempered by having to be "fair" and "reasonable" and "what the opposing party would have expected to pay." How Canadian (says Knutsen). In actual fact, the legal bill the losing party must pay is typically about 60% of the winner's actual "real cost" legal fees. *See, e.g.,* ONTARIO R. CIV. P. 57; Erik S. Knutsen, *The Cost of Costs: The Unfortunate Deterrence of Everyday Civil Litigation in Canada*, 36 QUEEN's L.J. 113 (2010) (arguing that the pressures and uncertainty of fee-shifting have eclipsed the substantive concerns in Canadian civil litigation to a detrimental degree, such that fees and fear of fees—not justice—drive dispute resolution in many instances).

8. But, as with litigation generally, counsel must not let the fee concern "tail" wag the "dog" of the substantive legal dispute. For example, it would be a mistake for counsel to settle a strong case too cheaply solely because of fears of fee shifting. But that said, appreciating the likelihood of fee shifting in the event of defeat should be part of counsel's evaluation of the value of a claim and formulation of settlement strategy.

The rationale for providing some advantage to policyholders is that without fee shifting, an aggrieved policyholder that succeeds in obtaining benefits that should have been paid from the outset would be no better off financially than if it had simply self-insured. It would be paying premiums just for the opportunity to bring suit against the insurer. *See* Maniloff & Stempel at 290; *Olympic Steamship Co., Inc. v. Centennial Ins. Co.*, 811 P.2d 673, 681 (Wash. 1991) ("When an insured purchases a contract of insurance, it seeks protection from expenses arising from litigation, not vexatious, time-consuming, expensive litigation with its insurer") (citation and internal quotation marks omitted).

The most prominent dividing line between the states is whether a prevailing policyholder obtains fee-shifting automatically or whether the policyholder must prove blameworthy conduct by the insurer. Some states (e.g., Hawaii by statute; Maryland by judicial decision) provide for automatic fee-shifting. Others (e.g., Virginia by statute, Connecticut by judicial decision) require bad faith or similar misconduct by the insurer. That's why this discussion is in the bad faith chapter rather than another portion of this coursebook. There are a few states (e.g, Alabama, Kentucky) that appear not to depart from the American Rule at all for insurance cases.

In addition, where state courts have discretionary power to award fees based on concerns of fairness or litigation conduct or in contract matters, this may provide a basis for insurance litigation fee shifting. Where insurance disputes are in federal court (a frequent occurrence, because insurers prefer federal court when bringing declaratory judgment actions and prefer to remove actions to federal court if possible when sued by policyholders in state court), these state-conveyed judicial powers are often deemed sufficiently substantive to apply pursuant to *Erie R.R. v. Tompkins*. In addition, general rules regarding fee-shifting as a sanction for litigation misconduct (as opposed to claims misconduct) apply. For example, a policyholder that spoils evidence or makes unfounded defamatory statements about an adjuster may be subject to sanction (even if a separate spoliation tort or defamation claim might not be available, because of litigation privilege in the latter instance).

## [4] Forum Selection, Arbitration or Alternative Dispute Resolution: Some Cautions

Many insurance policies, most prominently the "Bermuda Form" used by excess and umbrella insurers, including some not headquartered in Bermuda, contain arbitration or other alternative dispute resolution clauses, as well as forum selection and choice of law clauses. Sometimes the provisions of an insurance policy are more than just "procedural" and have substantive implications. For example, the Bermuda Form arbitration provision routinely used in policies issued by ACE and XL insurance companies provides for arbitration in London, with arbitrators chosen pursuant to the English Arbitration Act and choice of New York substantive law, but without the reasonable expectations approach or use of the contra proferentem principle.

Thus, by purchasing insurance with this clause, the policyholder has done much more than agree to arbitrate (although that alone includes important matters such as eliminating jury trial, broad discovery and full appellate review) and has adopted a hybrid form of law that most view as favoring insurers. Further, in practice, the arbitration will be conducted by British arbitrators who will be inclined to see insurance contracts through the eyes of a British-trained attorney, which generally means extreme focus on policy text to the exclusion of contextual factors and rather literal application of the text. Although this is not necessarily a ticket to defeat for policyholders, it can be where the insurer is relying on a broad construction of exclusionary or limiting policy language. Further, in our experience, British lawyers and judges are less likely than their U.S. counterparts to construe exclusions narrowly and to insist that the burden of proof to prove linguistic meaning be placed on the party asserting the exclusion and which seeks to defeat otherwise available coverage.

# Chapter 13

# Insurance Layering, Excess and Umbrella Insurance, Self-Insurance and Reinsurance

## § 13.01. Excess Insurance: Duties of the Primary Insurer and the Excess Insurer

### [A] Introduction

There are two basic types of excess insurance: "true" excess insurance and overlapping insurance dealt with through "other insurance" clauses. "Other insurance," as discussed in previous chapters, occurs when two or more policies may be expected to respond to the same insurable risk. Adjudicating "other insurance" clauses happens with some frequency regarding auto insurance where, for example, a rental car may collide with a delivery truck that damages a city-owned meter reader. Because individual drivers, businesses, and government entities involved may all have insurance, a coordination problem can easily arise. Also, the "other insurance" clauses of most policies are designed to deal with problems of concurrent losses or losses that takes place essentially at the same time, or are at least confined to the same policy period.

"True" excess insurance, on the other hand, is provided by specifically denominated "excess" or "umbrella" policies. These excess insurance policies are sold at a comparatively modest cost to provide additional protection for the insured where the primary insurer's coverage ends. Excess insurance is considerably less expensive than primary insurance since most claims brought by the policyholder in theory will be small enough to be resolved by the primary insurer, and only comparatively large, and hopefully rare, claims will exceed the limits of the primary policy and pierce into the umbrella's layer of coverage. For very large risks, there may be second or third layer excess insurers, or more.

One example of an "umbrella" excess insurance policy would be where a hypothetical doctor or lawyer is insured by a primary insurer for up to $500,000 in a professional malpractice insurance policy, with an excess insurer's promise to insure any additional liability over $500,000 and up to $2 million. For larger risks, each layer of coverage may have several excess insurers issuing policies on the risk. For example, assume that a primary insurer insures a risk of loss for $5 million, and $20 million is contracted in excess insurance, which may be four $5 million excess policies underwritten by an American excess insurer, a Swiss excess insurer, a Japanese excess insurer, and a Lloyd's of London syndicate. If this hypothetical excess layer is partially tapped by an insurance claim in excess of the primary coverage, the four component excess policies would share proportionately in paying the excess portion of the claim. Alternately, excess insurance policies can be arranged where excess insurer A will pay the first $5 million over the primary insurance coverage, excess insurer B will then pay the next $10 million over what excess insurer A must pay, excess insurer C will pay the next $10 million over what excess insurer B must pay, and so on. *See, e.g.,* Stempel & Knutsen on Insurance Coverage § 16.01.

These "umbrella" insurance policies thus constitute "true" excess insurance coverage over the primary insurer's policy limit, since it is the express contractual intent of the insured, the primary insurer, and the excess insurer to provide this additional coverage. Moreover, the insured, who is in contractual privity with both the primary insurer and the excess insurer, has a legal cause of action against both the primary and excess insurers for any contractual nonperformance, while an insured normally does not have any contractual rights against a reinsurer.

Excess insurance sits atop primary insurance, with the excess insurer's responsibility to pay triggered when the underlying insurance is exhausted and the "attachment point" of the excess insurance has been reached. Commercial policyholders frequently have several layers of excess insurance coverage that attach and respond seriatim in the face of a large claim. Each layer may be "filled" by a single excess insurer writing one large policy or may be filled by a consortium of insurers signing on for a portion of that layer's risk. For example, the second level of excess insurance for a large manufacturer may begin at $25 million, provide an additional $25 million of coverage, and be filled by eight entities: four American excess insurers, two European excess insurers, and two London-based syndicates of insurer-investors.

Excess insurance policies typically require that the policyholder maintain underlying insurance, although if the underlying insurance is reduced by payment of other claims, this effectively lowers the attachment point of the excess insurer.

To a greater degree than primary insurance but a lesser degree than reinsurance, excess insurance policies may contain an arbitration clause, requiring that policyholder insurer disputes be settled by arbitration. These can become fairly exotic and involved. For example, Bermuda-based excess insurers XL and ACE frequently include in their policies a clause providing for arbitration in London pursuant to the procedure of the English Arbitration Act but providing for the application of New York law, but without the contra proferentem and reasonable expectations aspects of New York insurance law. If you think that's confusing to read about, imagine litigating a coverage dispute under those ground rules. There is a strong argument that this sort of "slice-and-dice" choice of law clause would be unenforceable under New York law and that it must be construed to import the whole of New York law into the proceeding.

*Query*: What are the duties of the primary insurer to the excess insurer and the insured?

## R.C. Wegman Constr. Co. v. Admiral Insurance Co.

Court of Appeals for the Seventh Circuit

629 F.3d 724 (2011)

**Posner, Circuit Judge.**

The defendant insurance company, Admiral, issued a liability insurance policy that provided a $1 million ceiling on coverage for a single occurrence (that is, an event that would trigger coverage). While the policy was in effect, Brian Budrik, a worker at a construction site managed by Wegman Construction Company, was injured in a fall and sued Wegman (an "additional insured" on the policy, which had been issued to Budrik's employer), along with other potentially liable entities, for negligence. The case went to trial, Budrik prevailed, and a judgment for a little more than $2 million was entered against Wegman. Wegman then filed the present suit in an Illinois state court against Admiral, claiming that Wegman would not have been liable for damages in excess of the $1 million policy limit had Admiral discharged the implied contractual duty of good faith that insurance companies owe their insureds.

As we explained in *Twin City Fire Ins. Co. v. Country Mutual Ins. Co.*, 23 F.3d 1175, 1179 (1994), applying Illinois law, a correlative to the standard provision that authorizes a liability insurer to control the defense of a claim against the insured is "the duty not to gamble with the insured's money by forgoing reasonable opportunities to settle a claim on terms that will protect the insured against an excess judgment. Were it not for this duty, a duty fairly implied in the insurance contract, in a case in which a claim could be settled at or near the policy limit, yet there was a good although not certain chance that it could be beaten at trial, the insurance company would be sorely tempted to take the case to trial. For that would place it in a 'Heads I win, tails you lose,' position. Suppose the claim was for $2 million, the policy limit was $1 million, the plaintiff was willing to settle for this amount, but the defendant's insurer believed that if the case was tried the plaintiff would have a 50 percent chance of winning $2 million and a 50 percent chance of losing. The insurer's incentive would be to refuse to settle, since if it lost the trial it would be no worse off than if it settled — in either case it would have to pay $1 million — but if it won it would have saved itself $1 million" (citations omitted)....

The complaint alleges the following facts, which we take as true for purposes of reviewing the district judge's grant of Admiral's motion to dismiss. Wegman had been sued by Budrik in 2003, two years after his injury. Admiral exercised the option granted it by the insurance policy to defend the Budrik suit at its expense; thus, the complaint explains, Admiral "accepted Wegman's defense" and "controlled" the defense. The complaint goes on to allege that "no later than May 2005 (at the time [that Budrik's] deposition [in his tort case] was conducted), [Admiral] knew" that Budrik had sustained serious injuries that had required a lumbar fusion, and that he had experienced "substantial pain and suffering for an extended period of time," had "sustained permanent physical disabilities," had been "unable to perform construction work" since the accident, had "sustained substantial loss of income and was likely to sustain substantial loss of income in the future," and "had incurred and would incur substantial medical expenses."

Admiral also knew, "as early as May 2005 and no later than April 2007," that Budrik was demanding "almost $6,000,000" to settle the suit; as a result Admiral "knew that the Budrik Lawsuit presented a realistic possibility of a potential loss to Wegman ... in excess of the Admiral Policy limits." Admiral failed to warn Wegman of this possibility. Had it done so, Wegman would have sought and obtained indemnity from its excess insurer—the policy limit in its excess policy was $10 million. A prudent insured notifies its excess insurer of any nontrivial claim.

Wegman, the complaint continues, "did not realize that the Lawsuit presented a realistic possibility of a loss in excess of the Admiral Policy limits until [September 2007,] a few days before the trial of the Budrik Lawsuit when a Wegman executive was casually discussing the Budrik Lawsuit with a relative who happened to be an attorney." Wegman promptly notified its excess insurer, but the excess insurer refused coverage on the ground that it had not received timely notice.

We learned at argument that Wegman has since hired a new attorney and sued the lawyer who had been retained by Admiral to handle Wegman's defense against Budrik's suit. But the present suit is only against Admiral, for failing to notify Wegman of the possibility of an excess judgment in time for Wegman to have invoked its excess coverage.

Neither the briefs nor the complaint, nor for that matter the insurance policy, judicial opinions, or treatises on insurance law, tell us much about how situations of the sort presented by this case are handled by insurance companies. We learned a little more at the oral argument and from our own research.... The situation in question is the emergence of a potential conflict of interest between insurer and insured in the midst of a suit in which the insured is represented by a lawyer procured and paid for by the insurer.

At the outset—and in fact in this case at the outset—usually neither insurance company nor insured has reason to believe that the insured's liability to the victim of the tort for which the insured is being sued will result in a judgment (if the case goes to trial) in excess of the policy limit. That means that as a practical matter the insured has no interest in the litigation; he is not paying for his attorney and will lose nothing if he loses the suit, if we set to one side possible concerns with loss of reputation or with the insurer's upping his premiums for future coverage.

If the insurance policy entitles the insurer to "defend the insured," the insurer will either designate an in-house lawyer to represent the insured or, as in this case, hire a lawyer from a defense firm to which the insurer refers such matters. Because only the insurer, on the defense side of the case, has (or at this stage is believed to have) a financial stake in the case, the lawyer will report to the insurer on the progress of the litigation, as well as (or possibly instead of) to his client. An insurance adjuster employed by the insurance company will be monitoring the lawyer carefully, both because the company is paying his fee (or salary, if he's in-house) and, more important, because it will be liable for any settlement or judgment up to the policy limit.

Thus "the insurer's duty to defend includes the right to assume control of the litigation … to allow insurers to protect their financial interest in the outcome of litigation and to minimize unwarranted liability claims. Giving the insurer exclusive control over litigation against the insured safeguards the orderly and proper disbursement of large sums of money involved in the insurance business." … By virtue of that control, however, the insurer's duty to the insured includes not only "the hiring of competent counsel" but also "keeping abreast of progress and status of litigation in order that it may act intelligently and in good faith on settlement offers." 4 *Couch on Insurance* § 202:17 (3d ed. 2007).

So it is likely that in May 2005, when Budrik was deposed, Admiral learned forthwith from the lawyer whom it had hired to represent Wegman of the extent of the injuries to which Budrik testified in his deposition, and thus knew that if the case went to trial, or was settled, the judgment or the settlement might well exceed $1 million. This likelihood created a conflict of interest by throwing the interests of Admiral and Wegman out of alignment. Suppose Admiral thought that if Budrik's case went to trial there was a 90 percent chance of a judgment no greater than $500,000 and a 10 percent chance of a judgment of $2 million (to simplify, we ignore other possibilities). Then the maximum expected cost to Admiral of trial would have been $550,000 (.90 × $500,000 + .10 × $1,000,000, the policy limit), and so (ignoring litigation expenses) Admiral would not want to settle for any higher figure. But Wegman would be facing an expected cost of $100,000 (.10 × ($2,000,000 – 1,000,000)), and no benefit, from a trial.

These numbers are hypothetical, but at the oral argument Admiral's lawyer confessed that his client had been gambling on minimizing its liability at the expense, if necessary, of Wegman. Under Illinois law Wegman would, if found to be no more than 25 percent responsible for Budrik's injury, be liable only for 25 percent of Budrik's damages, 735 ILCS 5/2-1117, and, since there were other defendants, the lawyer thought he had a good shot at such a result. But in the event, the jury found Wegman 27 percent responsible, which under Illinois law made it jointly liable for the entire damages. Thus, Admiral had hoped to get away with having to pay (in our numerical example) only half the policy limit (.25 × $2 million =.50 × $1 million), but at the risk that a judgment would be imposed on Wegman that far exceeded that limit.

Gambling with an insured's money is a breach of fiduciary duty. *Cramer v. Ins. Exchange Agency*, 174 Ill.2d 513, 221 Ill.Dec. 473, 675 N.E.2d 897, 903 (1996)…. Yet at oral argument Admiral's lawyer came close to denying the existence of the duty by saying that "simply by reason of the nature of the demand [the reference is to Budrik's demand for a $6 million settlement], an insurance company cannot be charged with knowledge of probability of an excess verdict, because routinely plaintiffs make excess demands."

When a potential conflict of interest between insured and insurer arises, the insurance company's duty of good faith requires it to notify the insured. The usual conflict of interest involves the insurance company's denying coverage, but the principle is the same when the conflict arises from the relation of the policy limit to the insured's potential liability. Once notified by the insurer of the conflict, the insured has the option of hiring a new lawyer, one whose loyalty will be exclusively to him.... If he exercises that option, the insurance company will be obligated to reimburse the reasonable expense of the new lawyer....

Had Wegman hired a new lawyer upon being promptly informed of the conflict back in May 2005, that lawyer would have tried to negotiate a settlement with Budrik that would not exceed the policy limit; and if the settlement was reasonable given the risk of an excess judgment, Admiral would be obligated to pay.... And since Wegman had excess insurance, notification to it of the risk of an excess judgment would have enabled it to notify its excess insurer promptly, in order to preserve the protection that the excess coverage provided....

The insurer's duty of good faith is not onerous. When the company is handling the defense of a suit against its insured at its own cost and initially believes there's no danger of an excess judgment against the insured, it has every incentive to monitor the progress of the litigation closely, for realistically it is the sole defendant. And monitoring the litigation places the insurer in a good position to learn about a conflict of interest if and when one arises. At that point, given the duty of good faith, it is strongly motivated to notify the insured of the conflict immediately lest it find itself liable not only for the excess judgment but also for punitive damages, which are awarded for egregious breaches of good faith....

Often notice proves costless to the insurance company. Rather than change lawyers in midstream and perhaps have a dispute with the insurer over whether the new lawyer's fee is "reasonable" and hence chargeable to the insurer, the insured is quite likely to take his chances on staying with his insurer-appointed lawyer and so decide to waive the conflict of interest, relying on the fact that the lawyer "remains bound, ... both ethically and legally, to protect the interests of the insured in the defense of the tort claim. The latter obligation is separate and distinct from the insurer's duty to inform the insured of its position, and is not waived, as defendant's argument suggests, by mere acquiescence to the conduct of the insurer." The insurance company can satisfy its duty of good faith at the price of a phone call.

Admiral's main argument is that an insurance company has no duty to notify the insured of a potential conflict of interest, only of an actual one, and that no conflict arises until settlement negotiations begin or the insured demands that the insurance company try to settle the case. Admiral attempts to bolster the argument by claiming that until then the insurer has no duty of notice to the insured because it would be unethical for it to interfere with the lawyer's representation of the insured because an insurance company isn't allowed to practice law.

Admiral misunderstands "conflict of interest." The term doesn't mean that the conflicted party is engaged in conduct harmful to another party. It means that their interests are divergent, which creates a potential for such harm. The conflict in this case arose when Admiral learned that an excess judgment (and therefore a settlement in excess of the policy limits, as judgment prospects guide settlement) was a nontrivial probability in Budrik's suit. Admiral's contention that it would have been practicing law had it notified Wegman of the risk of excess liability is ridiculous. What is true is that, had Admiral notified Wegman of the risk and as a result Wegman had hired its own lawyer, Admiral could not have interfered with Wegman's relation with that lawyer.... Controlling the defense, Admiral had a duty to warn Wegman when that control created a conflict of interest.

Wegman's complaint is less clear than it could be. It doesn't actually allege that it didn't learn until days before the trial that Budrik's injuries were so serious that a judgment in excess of $1 million was in the cards — only that it failed to "realize" until then that it faced such a danger. If it knew everything Admiral should have told it but didn't tell it, and knew all that in time to have triggered its excess coverage, and it just didn't put two and two together and get four, then Admiral's breach of duty did not harm it and the case should indeed have been dismissed. But there is no evidence of this; there is just Admiral's attempt to build a concession on the word "realize."

It's unlikely that had Wegman known it faced a judgment in excess of the limits of Admiral's policy, it would have failed to notify its excess insurer. Being only one of several defendants in Budrik's suit and relying on Admiral's duty of good faith notification of any conflict of interest, Wegman reasonably could assume that until told otherwise it had no skin in the game and therefore no need to follow the litigation closely.

Admiral suggests that the lawyer it appointed to represent Wegman had the duty to notify Wegman of the risk of an excess judgment, rather than Admiral. But as far as we know, the lawyer informed Admiral, knowing that Admiral would be duty-bound to inform Wegman. The lawyer may have fallen down on the job and notified no one; we've not been told what Wegman alleges in its suit against the lawyer. But the duty to notify of a conflict of interest is also the insurer's, and cannot be contracted away without the insured's consent. Admiral may have a right of contribution or indemnity by the lawyer if the latter failed to inform Admiral of the risk of excess liability, but that would not affect Admiral's liability to Wegman.

Ordinarily in a case such as this, the insured would have to prove that had it not been for the breach of duty by the insurance company, the case could have been settled within the policy limit, or at least for a lower amount than the judgment. Wegman will try to prove this and may succeed. But there is an additional wrinkle that may make such proof inessential. For remember that had Admiral warned Wegman of the likelihood of an excess judgment, Wegman would have sought and obtained coverage under its excess policy, and thus been freed from liability regardless of the outcome of Budrik's suit.

It could be argued ... that the loss of an opportunity to trigger excess coverage is not the kind of loss that the duty of good faith is intended to prevent, and so that duty was not breached by Admiral. But the argument would fail. For when a conflict of interest arises, so that the insured can no longer count on the insurance company and its lawyer to defend his interests but must (unless he wants to waive his rights) fend for himself, the hiring of his own lawyer is only one option that is opened up to him. Another is to seek additional coverage from another insurance policy; and that alternative was foreclosed by the failure of notice—assuming Wegman was indeed innocently ignorant of the substantial risk of an excess judgment until the eve of trial, as it alleges.

Allegation is not proof. The merits of Wegman's claim remain to be proved. But dismissal of the complaint was premature. The judgment is therefore reversed and the case remanded for further proceedings consistent with this opinion.

## Johnson Controls, Inc. v. London Market

Supreme Court of Wisconsin
325 Wis.2d 176, 784 N.W.2d 579 (2010)

**Ann Walsh Bradley, J.**

This case is before the court on certification from the court of appeals. We are asked to determine whether London Market had a duty to defend Johnson Controls. If it did, we then must determine when, if at all, that duty was triggered.

London Market contends that it had no duty to defend Johnson Controls because its insurance policy is an indemnity—only excess umbrella policy that does not promise a defense. Further, it asserts that the duty to defend set forth in the underlying Travelers insurance policies is not incorporated into the London Market excess policy.

In the alternative, London Market asserts that even if it had a duty to defend under the policy, that duty was never triggered because it is conditioned upon exhaustion of the underlying insurer's policy limits, and those limits were never exhausted. Further, London Market contends that Wisconsin law did not require it to drop down and defend Johnson Controls when the underlying insurer refused to defend.

Based on the language of the policies, we conclude that London Market had a duty to defend. Although its excess umbrella policy does not have a duty to defend provision, it does contain a follow form provision that incorporates the duty to defend found in the underlying Travelers policies.

We further determine that its duty to defend was not conditioned upon exhaustion of the underlying Travelers policies. Rather, under the terms of the "other insurance" provision, London Market's duty to defend was triggered when the underlying insurer "denie[d] primary liability under its policy." Accordingly, we affirm the circuit court and remand for further proceedings.

Johnson Controls is a manufacturing company based in Milwaukee, Wisconsin. During the 1970s, it contracted with various insurers for a layered program of primary, umbrella, and umbrella excess commercial general liability (CGL) policies. This appeal specifically involves the umbrella excess policy issued to Johnson Controls by London Market, effective from December 31, 1973, to December 31, 1976 (the 1973–1976 London Market policy). The London Market excess umbrella policy sat atop three successive policies issued by Travelers Indemnity Company (Travelers).

Before delving into the specific issues presented, it is helpful to provide some historical background about this case, which has been ongoing for over 21 years. In the mid-1980s, Johnson Controls started to receive notification that it had been identified as a potentially responsible party (PRP) in connection with environmental contamination at various sites across the country (some of the sites were lead smelting plants where Johnson Controls delivered lead acid batteries for recycling; others were contaminated landfills). As a PRP, Johnson Controls could be required to contribute to the environmental restoration and remediation costs at these sites.

Johnson Controls asserts that it notified its insurers, seeking defense and indemnification. The insurers refused to provide defense or indemnification, justifying their refusal on the ground that their CGL policies did not cover environmental restoration and remediation costs imposed under the Comprehensive Environmental Response, Compensation, and Liability Act (CERCLA).

In 1989, Johnson Controls filed suit against its various primary, umbrella, and excess insurers. It sought a declaratory judgment that its insurers were obligated to provide defense and indemnification under the terms of the insurance policies. London Market, like many of the other insurers, answered and filed a motion for partial summary judgment.

The court of appeals certified two questions to this court:

> First, should a duty to defend be imported from an underlying umbrella insurance policy into an excess umbrella liability policy by language in the excess policy stating that it is subject to the same terms, definitions, exclusions and conditions as the underlying policy "except as otherwise provided"? ...

> Second, is the excess liability carrier's duty to defend primary in nature, such that it may be triggered even if the excess policy expressly requires exhaustion of the underlying policy as a precondition to liability and the underlying policy has not been exhausted?

### III. Duty to Defend

We determine first whether London Market's policy contains a duty to defend. London Market asserts that its umbrella excess policy was an indemnity-only policy that did not promise a defense.

In support of its assertion that its policy does not provide a duty to defend, London Market advances that it is contrary to the role of an excess insurer and the purpose of excess insurance to provide a duty to defend. Such reliance on generalized statements about the role and purpose of excess coverage misses the mark.

Instead, "[t]he duty to defend an insured is based on the language in the insurance contract." ... In practice, most primary policies do contain a contractual duty to defend, and some umbrella and excess policies do as well. To determine whether an insurer has a duty to defend, we examine the language of the policy.

London Market asserts that it promised indemnification only, and that it did not promise to defend. It points to its insuring agreement, which states that London Market agrees, "subject to the limitations, terms and conditions hereinafter mentioned, to indemnify the Assured for all sums which the Assured shall be obligated to pay by reason of" certain liabilities:

> Underwriters hereby agree, subject to the limitations, terms and conditions hereinafter mentioned, to indemnify the Assured for all sums which the Assured shall be obligated to pay by reason of the liability ... for ... Property Damage ... arising out of the hazards covered by and as defined in the underlying [Travelers policies].

London Market's insuring agreement promises indemnification but is silent regarding defense.

London Market is correct that the language of the insuring agreement—read in isolation—does not impose an obligation to defend. However, this insuring agreement does not exist in isolation.

A. Follow Form Policy

Rather, the excess umbrella policy issued by London Market is a "follow form" policy, meaning that the policy is relatively brief and incorporates many of the provisions of an underlying policy—in this case, the excess umbrella policies issued by Travelers. [An excess policy may be written in two forms: as a stand-alone policy or as a policy that "'follows form.'... A stand-alone excess policy is an independent insuring agreement. In contrast, a follows form excess policy incorporates by reference the terms of the underlying policy and is designed to match the coverage provided by the underlying policy." [citation omitted]. One of the conditions "hereinafter mentioned" in the London Market policy is the follow form provision:

> This Policy is subject to the same terms, definitions, exclusions and conditions (except as regards the premium, the amount and Limits of Liability and except as otherwise provided herein) as are contained in or as may be added to the Underlying [Travelers policies] prior to the happening of an occurrence for which claim is made hereunder.

Thus, to determine the terms, definitions, exclusions, and conditions of the London Market policy, it is necessary to turn to the Travelers policies. [The dissent] is critical of our reliance on terms in the Travelers policies. This criticism ignores the fact that the London Market policy specifically directs the insured and the court to refer to the Travelers policies when determining the "terms, definitions, exclusions and conditions" of coverage. Due to the nature of the follow form provision, the scope of London Market's contractual obligations cannot be understood without reference to the Travelers policies.

Among other provisions, the underlying Travelers policies contain a duty to defend as well as a duty to indemnify:

> Liability. The company will pay on behalf of the insured all sums which the insured shall become legally obligated to pay as damages..., *and the company shall have the right and duty to defend any suit against the insured seeking damages on account of such injury or damage...*, but the company shall not be obligated to pay any claim or judgment or to defend any suit filed after the applicable limit of the company's liability has been exhausted by payments of judgments or settlements. (Emphasis added.)

To determine whether Travelers' duty to defend is incorporated into London Market's policy, we must examine the language of London Market's follow form provision. It states that the policy "is subject to the same terms, definitions, exclusions and conditions (except as regards the premium, the amount and Limits of Liability and except as otherwise provided herein) as are contained in" the underlying Travelers policies.

London Market's follow form provision does not expressly disclaim the duty to defend found in the Travelers policies. Rather, it explicitly sets forth three ways in which the London Market policy differs from the underlying Travelers policies: (1) the premium; (2) the amount and Limits of Liability; and (3) "except as otherwise provided herein."

No argument is made about the first two areas of difference. The parties focus on the third area of difference, "except as otherwise provided herein."

B. "Except as Otherwise Provided Herein"

London Market asserts that its policy does "otherwise provide" that there is no duty to defend. It contends that by omitting a promise to defend from the insuring agreement, it "otherwise provided" that there would be no duty to defend.

This argument is circular. As discussed above, the insuring agreement that London Market relies upon refers the insured to the follow form provision and to the terms of the underlying Travelers policies. Although London Market's insuring agreement does not promise a defense, the follow form provision incorporates the terms, definitions, exclusions, and conditions of the Travelers policies. One of those terms is Travelers' duty to defend, a duty that the London Market policy does not disclaim.

The phrase "except as otherwise provided herein" suggests that to "otherwise provide," there must be a provision. London Market can point to nothing except the void in its own agreement—an agreement which by its own terms is incomplete and incorporates those provisions in the Travelers policies that are not excepted. Due to the nature of the follow form provision, London Market cannot rely on the absence of a provision as "otherwise providing" that there would be no duty to defend.

Given that Travelers imposes a duty to defend and London Market's silence regarding that duty, a reasonable person in the position of the insured would interpret London Market's policy as incorporating the duty to defend found in the Travelers policies. Although it is not certain whether London Market intended to provide a duty to defend when it drafted the policy, we do not construe insurance policies based on what we believe the intentions of the insurer may have been. Accordingly, we refuse to rewrite insurance contracts by filling in gaps left in the draftsmanship.

An insurance company that uses a follow form policy must be cautious because it may inadvertently bind itself to unintended obligations. We have previously stated, "too often the insurance companies come to the courts asking that the courts supply the lacunae in their contract. Certainly, when the dispute concerns legal rights and obligations as between insurance companies, it is not too much to ask that they make specific provisions, either in their contracts or by treaties of understanding between themselves." *Loy v. Bunderson*, 320 N.W.2d 175 (Wis. 1982). Rather, we look to the policy language itself, as it would be understood by a reasonable insured.

Even if we were to determine that it was unclear whether the follow form's duty to defend was incorporated into the London Market policy, given London Market's silence regarding defense, we would conclude that the policy language should be construed to incorporate the duty to defend. It is axiomatic that policy language which is unclear and susceptible to more than one reasonable interpretation is ambiguous and is construed in favor of coverage. In interpreting the policy language, we conclude that London Market had a duty to defend.

Our interpretation is supported by case law. In another case addressing an excess insurer's contractual duty to defend, the Second Circuit Court of Appeals examined an excess policy containing a follow form provision. *See Home Ins. Co. v. Am. Home Prods. Corp.*, 902 F.2d 1111 (2d Cir.1990) [applying New York law]. Similar to London Market's policy, the policy in *Home* stated that it was "subject to the same warranties, terms and conditions [as the underlying policy] (except as otherwise provided herein)[.]"

In that case, the underlying policy covered payments for defense costs. However, Home's policy expressly excluded "all expenses and Costs" and further defined costs to include "legal expenses." *Id.* at 1113. Given Home's express exclusion of defense costs, the Second Circuit stated that the underlying policy "conflict[ed] with the subject Home policy which ... excludes from payment those expenses and costs" covered by the underlying policy. *Id.* at 1114.

Here, unlike in *Home*, there is no conflict between the Travelers policies and the London Market policy with respect to the duty to defend. As discussed above, the Travelers policies provide a duty to defend, and there is nothing in the London Market policy that "otherwise provides" that there will be no defense.

### IV. Parties' Arguments Extrinsic to the Policy Language

Having examined the language of the relevant policies and determined that London Market has a contractual duty to defend, we turn to address two additional arguments advanced by the parties in support of their respective positions regarding whether London Market's policy incorporates Travelers' duty to defend. Both arguments rely on evidence that is extrinsic to the language of the policy. We address each argument in turn.

## A. Subsequent Policies Expressly Exclude Any Duty to Defend

Johnson Controls asserts that evidence that London Market's 1973–1976 policy contains a duty to defend is found by the fact that four subsequent and otherwise identical policies issued by London Market expressly excluded any duty to defend. One policy stated that London Market "shall have the right but not the duty to assume ... the defense of any suit[.]" Another policy provided that London Market "shall not be called upon to assume charge of the settlement or defense of any claim[.]"

We do not find Johnson Controls' reliance on the subsequent policies to be helpful for two reasons. First, we do not believe that London Market's subsequent modification of its standard insuring agreement sheds light on the language of the 1973–1976 agreement. The question is what the language of the 1973–1976 contract does provide, not what the language could provide or what is provided for in a contract executed by the parties years later.

Second, even if subsequent policies were relevant in determining what the language of the 1973–1976 policy provides, it is unclear what conclusion we would reach. We could conclude, as Johnson Controls suggests, that the express disclaimer demonstrates that London Market knew how to disclaim the duty to defend but did not intend to do so in the 1973–1976 policy. We could also conclude, as suggested by London Market, that the fact that Johnson Controls continued to purchase excess coverage that expressly disclaimed the duty to defend indicates that Johnson Controls never expected defense from its excess insurer.

## B. Premium Charged

We turn next to London Market's arguments about the premium it charged for the umbrella excess policy. London Market contrasts the relatively small premium it charged with the larger premium Johnson Controls paid for the umbrella coverage provided by Travelers.[1] London Market asserts that the relatively low premium paid for its excess policy is evidence that the parties did not contract for London Market to provide a defense. It contends that this argument is borne out by [statements in case law to the effect that] "the intent of umbrella policies to serve a different function from primary policies with excess clauses is reflected in the rate structure of the two types of policies."

London Market's argument is unpersuasive for two reasons. First, contract interpretation should be based on the language of the policy rather than a court's conjecture about extrinsic information. Second, even if we considered the relative size of the two premiums in our analysis, we would not be persuaded that the lower premium evinces an absence of the duty to defend. There are additional reasons apart from defense costs that an umbrella excess policy might be less expensive than a primary policy or an umbrella policy.

---

1. [1] The premium for the London Market excess policy was $20,000, in comparison to $195,000 and $273,500 for two of the three underlying umbrella policies. The record does not reflect the premium for the third underlying policy.

In *Davis v. Allied Processors, Inc.*, the court of appeals explained that insurance companies calculate premiums based upon statistics. 571 N.W.2d 692 (Wis. Ct.App.1997). Excess policies may be less expensive because most judgments and settlements will be within the limits of the primary policy, leaving no exposure for the excess policy. *Id.* Excess coverage is normally not reached except in the case of a catastrophic loss:

> [I]t was far more likely that payment would be required for compensatory damages under the underlying policy than would be required for a compensatory loss of over [the limits of the underlying policy] through the umbrella policy. Because the risk was diminished for the umbrella policy, it could and did charge a smaller premium.

*Id.* We conclude that the extrinsic evidence offered by both parties is not helpful in our determination of whether the 1973–1976 London Market policy contains a duty to defend. Rather, for the reasons mentioned above, we conclude that London Market's policy incorporates the duty to defend provided in the underlying umbrella policies issued by Travelers.

### V. When the Duty to Defend Is Triggered

Having determined that London Market's policy incorporates the duty to defend found in the Travelers policies, we turn to address if and when that duty was triggered under these facts. Both London Market and the excess intervenors appear to assert that as a matter of law, an excess carrier's duty to defend may not be triggered until the limits of the underlying Travelers policies have been exhausted.

In its brief, London Market explains:

> Wisconsin law is clear. An excess insurer is just that. It is not a co-primary insurer, responsible for providing a defense from dollar one. That obligation falls solely on the primary insurer.... This court should reaffirm Wisconsin law, holding that an excess insurer is not required to provide a defense where the primary is required to do so.

London Market further asserts that the provisions of its policy are consistent with this general rule.

We agree that a primary insurer generally has the primary duty to defend a claim. "An excess insurer usually is not required to contribute to the defense of the insured so long as the primary insurer is required to defend." 2 Arnold P. Anderson, *Wisconsin Insurance Law* § 11.33 (5th ed. 2004). "True excess coverage attaches when a single insured has two policies that cover the same loss but only one policy is written with the expectation that the primary insurer will conduct all investigations, negotiations, and defense of claims until its limits are exhausted." *Id.* § 11.17.

However, this does not establish an immutable rule of law requiring exhaustion of all primary policies before an excess insurer's duty to defend can be triggered. Rather, it depends on the language of the policies.

Wisconsin case law instructs that the language of the policy should be our initial focus. After focusing on the policy language, we turn to examine Wisconsin cases that have held that an excess insurer's duty to defend may be triggered prior to the exhaustion of the primary policy.

## A. Policy Language

As stated above, the London Market policy incorporates the provisions of the Travelers policies unless otherwise provided. The Travelers policies explain when Travelers' duties to indemnify and to defend end-upon exhaustion of Travelers' limits of liability:

> [Travelers] shall not be obligated to pay any claim or judgment or to defend any suit filed after the applicable limit of the company's liability has been exhausted by payments of judgments or settlements.

According to the follow form provision, London Market's duty to defend would also be terminated upon the exhaustion of its limits of liability. Although the above language determines when Travelers and London Market's duties to indemnify and defend end, this language is silent regarding the question of when the duty to defend begins.

## B. Other Insurance Provision

However, a separate provision in the Travelers policies, the "other insurance" provision, sheds light on the inquiry. This provision explains that if another insurer denies primary liability, Travelers will respond as though the other insurance were not available. It provides:

> [I]f the insurer affording other insurance to the named insured denies primary *liability* under its policy, *[Travelers] will respond under this policy as though such other insurance were not available.*

(Emphasis added.) A reasonable person in the position of the insured would interpret this provision as promising that, where the excess insurer has a contractual duty to defend, it will step in and provide a defense in the event that the primary insurer refuses to do so.

Under the follow form provision, the language of the "other insurance" provision is incorporated into the London Market policy "unless otherwise provided herein." Thus, London Market would be required to "respond under [its] policy as though such other insurance were not available" in the event that the underlying insurer "denies primary liability under its policy"—unless the London Market policy otherwise provides.

We examine next whether the London Market policy does indeed otherwise provide. Our focus is directed to the meaning of the word "liability."

## C. Interpreting the Term "Liability"

London Market asserts that under the limits of liability provision in its policy, its duty to defend did not "attach" until the limits of the underlying Travelers policies were exhausted. The limits of liability provision states that "liability shall attach" to London Market only after Travelers has paid or has been held liable to pay its limits:

> It is expressly agreed that liability shall attach to the Underwriters only after the Underlying Umbrella Insurers have paid or have been held liable to pay the full amount of their respective net loss liability[.]

The limits of liability provision discusses when London Market's "liability" begins—after Traveler's has paid or has been held liable to pay the full amount of its net loss liability. However, it does not expressly state when the duty to defend begins. In isolation, it is unclear whether the term "liability" encompasses the duty to defend.

Although the London Market policy provides that "liability" does not attach until the underlying policies have been exhausted, it does not define the term "liability." An examination of the term "liability" as it is used in the context of the London Market policy indicates, however, that "liability" refers to indemnification for injuries or property for which Johnson Controls is held liable. It does not refer to the duty to defend....

Given a lack of definition and the disparate use of the term "liability" in the Travelers policies, it is not at all clear that the Travelers policies intend that "liability" be defined to include the duty to defend. Even if it were clear, however, such usage would conflict with the usage of the term "liability" in London Market's own policy. There, the term "liability" is consistently used to mean indemnification. As we previously explained, if there is a conflict between the London Market policy and the Travelers policies, the terms of the London Market policy control.

We conclude that although London Market's duty to indemnify is conditioned upon exhaustion of the underlying Travelers policies, its duty to defend is not so conditioned. Rather, under the "other insurance" provision, London Market was required to "respond under [its] policy as though such other insurance were not available" because Travelers "denie[d] primary liability under its policy." Thus, London Market was required to assume the defense.

D. Supportive Case Law

Contrary to the assertion of London Market, this conclusion does not fly in the face of an overarching rule of law requiring exhaustion of all primary policies before the duty to defend can be triggered. Quite the contrary. Wisconsin case law recognizes that an excess insurer's duty to defend may under certain circumstances be triggered prior to the exhaustion of the primary policy.

In *Teigen v. Jelco Wis., Inc.*, 367 N.W.2d 806 (Wis. 1985), for example, this court approved a settlement agreement between a primary insurer and the plaintiff who brought suit against the insured. The settlement agreement was for less than the limits of the primary policy. It released all claims against the primary and the insured, but it left the excess carrier potentially liable. Although the excess insurer argued that the primary wrongfully attempted to avoid its responsibility to defend the suit until it fully paid its policy limits, the court rejected that argument. *Id.* at 9–10, 367 N.W.2d 806. Thus, it concluded that the excess carrier was required to defend the suit, regardless of the fact that the underlying primary policy had not been fully exhausted.

*Teigen* is not alone....

... [I]n a recent decision of the Wisconsin court of appeals, *Southeast Wisconsin Professional Baseball Park District v. Mitsubishi Heavy Industries America*, 738 N.W.2d 87 (Wis. Ct. App. 2007), ... the primary insurer refused to defend despite the circuit court ordering it to defend on three separate occasions. *Id.*, ¶ 13. As a result, an excess carrier provided a defense. *Id.*, ¶ 8.

In a footnote, the court of appeals explained: "If the underlying insurer has refused to defend, asserting that there is no coverage under the substantive provisions of the underlying policy, the excess insurer will have a duty to defend, provided there is coverage under the excess policy and the claim falls within the policy limits of the excess insurer." *Id.*, ¶ 8, n. 4. Given that the primary had breached its primary duty to defend, however, the court required it to reimburse the excess insurer for the defense costs it incurred. *Id.*, ¶¶ 61–64.

The United States Court of Appeals for the Tenth Circuit [in] *Hocker v. New Hampshire Ins. Co.*, 922 F.2d 1476 (10th Cir.1991) ... explained that "as written," the umbrella policy "explicitly addresses the possibility that the primary insurer will wrongfully deny coverage for occurrences that it had warranted would be covered by its primary policy." *Id.* In those circumstances, "[t]he excess carrier must then drop down and provide a defense." *Id.* The court further clarified that had the umbrella insurer fulfilled this obligation, it would be able to maintain a subrogation claim against the primary insurer to recoup the legal expenses incurred. *Id.* at 1483, n. 6.

Some courts appear to have recognized a general rule that an insured that has purchased layers of coverage — including layers of a contractual duty to defend — should not be left without a "prompt and proper defense[.]" *New Hampshire Indem. Co., Inc. v. Budget Rent-A-Car Systems, Inc.*, 64 P.3d 1239 (Wash.2003). For example, the Washington Supreme Court stated: "[I]f a primary insurer fails to assume the defense, for any reason, the secondary insurer which has a duty to defend should provide the defense [.]" *Id.* at 1243. We need not and do not adopt a general rule to resolve this case, however, given that the language of the policies provides that London Market was required to assume the defense.

In sum, based on the language of the policies, we conclude that London Market had a duty to defend. Although its excess umbrella policy does not have a duty to defend provision, it does contain a follow form provision that incorporates the duty to defend found in the underlying Travelers policies.

We further determine that its duty to defend was not conditioned upon exhaustion of the underlying Travelers policies. Rather, under the terms of the "other insurance" provision, London Market's duty to defend was triggered when the underlying insurer "denie[d] primary liability under its policy." Accordingly, we affirm the circuit court and remand for further proceedings.

[Dissent omitted.]

## *Notes and Questions*

1. In a liability insurance claim, the duty to defend the insured initially rests upon the primary insurer, with the excess insurer as a third-party beneficiary. Thus, the primary insurer has a duty to act in good faith toward the excess insurer as well as the insured.

2. In an action for fraud arising out of alleged misrepresentations in the settlement of a medical malpractice suit, could the settlement be rescinded based on an attorney's and broker's stipulation that "to the best of his knowledge" there was no excess insurance coverage, when in fact there was? Must the plaintiff prove that this fraudulent misrepresentation was made by an agent of the excess insurer acting within the scope of his authority?

3. The issue of "drop down" liability normally arises when a primary insurer or lower level excess insurer becomes insolvent, and in the absence of insolvency, would have satisfied the claim without the excess insurer being "tapped." Some cases have held that the excess insurer would be responsible for providing "drop down" coverage. Most court decisions, however, protect excess insurers against "drop down" liability.

4. Where a guaranty fund covers the insolvency of liability insurers, this usually means that the policyholder remains liable to the third-party claimant for any amounts above the guaranty fund maximum up to the amount of the claimant's judgment or settlement.

## PROBLEM ONE

ConstructionCo depends on large trucks to haul its supplies, which means collisions involving Construction vehicles can lead to serious litigation. In Year One, a ConstructionCo truck is involved in a multi-vehicle intersection collision that causes substantial injury to a family of four in small sedan. Family sues ConstructionCo as well as a FreightCo, which also had a truck involved in the collision, and County, which had removed a stoplight for repair and replaced it with temporary four-way stop signs that were allegedly insufficiently visible.

ConstructionCo tenders defense of the claim to BrokerCo, the insurance intermediary from which it purchased coverage from Primary Insurer with $1 million per occurrence policy limits. Construction Co, also has a $10 million excess insurance policy from ExcessCo.

BrokerCo notifies Primary Insurer, which defends the case without reservation of rights through the assignment of panel counsel. The case moves slowly with discovery during Year 2 and Year 3. In Year 4, Family serves an Offer of Judgment in the amount of $1.5 million. BrokerCo then notifies ExcessCo of the litigation. ExcessCo argues that this is late notice but agrees to participate in an unsuccessful mediation. Trial takes place during Year 5, resulting in judgment against each of the three defendants (ConstructionCo, FreightCo, and County) in the amount of $2 million each.

ExcessCo commences a declaratory judgment action seeking a finding that it has no coverage responsibility because of the late notice it received.

- Is the notice late?

- When should notice have been given?

- Who should have given notice?
- BrokerCo?
- Construction Co?
- Primary Insurer?
- When should notice have been given to ExcessCo?
- What presumptive rule should be followed in determining the time for notice to an excess insurer?
- If ExcessCo avoids coverage, does ConstructionCo have a claim against BrokerCo?
- Does ExcessCo need to show prejudice from the late notice?
- Should it be required?
- How should the court rule?
- Does it make a difference that ConstructionCo counsel (provided by Primary Insurer) conducted a case assessment in which counsel concluded that it had a good chance of finding less than 25 percent fault by ConstructionCo which would, pursuant to controlling state law, mean that ConstructionCo was not liable at all?
- Why or why not?
- What if the Family's Offer of Judgment Had Been $999,000?
- Should Primary Insurer Have Accepted the Offer?

## PROBLEM TWO

American Hydrotherm had two multiperil liability insurance policies with Liberty Mutual Insurance Company and Great Atlantic Insurance Company. Under each policy, Liberty Mutual served as the primary insurer for coverage up to $500,000 and Great Atlantic as the excess insurer agreed to cover any loss over $500,000 and up to $2,000,000. A tragic explosion occurred in a Uniroyal Inc. plant in Missouri, killing two people and causing considerable property damage. American Hydrotherm was legally responsible for this explosion, and total damages were in excess of $750,000. Great Atlantic, the excess insurer, refused to make any payments under its excess insurance policy, contending that Liberty Mutual's two existing primary insurance policies provided combined coverage to American Hydrotherm totaling $1 million, and therefore no excess coverage was needed.

Subsequent to this explosion and loss, American Hydrotherm and Liberty Mutual agreed to reform their two primary insurance policies to provide that one $500,000 policy applied only to the insured's Canadian operations, and the other $500,000 policy applied only to the insured's American operations. Consequently, argued Liberty Mutual, Great Atlantic was now liable for excess coverage of $250,000 based upon the subsequent policy reformation between American Hydrotherm and Liberty Mutual. Great Atlantic, the excess insurer, argued that it should not be liable based on a policy reformation made subsequent to the loss by the insured and the primary insurer without the consent of the excess insurer.

• How should the court decide this case?

## PROBLEM THREE [A]

Plaintiff, the estate of a decedent who died from carbon monoxide (CO) poisoning due to a defective furnace installation, brings a wrongful death action. The decedent was a 38-year-old partner in a profitable investment banking firm. Investigation quickly confirms that the furnace was negligently installed.

The furnace installer, a small but not insignificant local business, has $1 million of primary general liability insurance for each occurrence, as well as an excess policy paying $5 million on top of the primary policy limits. The Excess Policy states that it has an "Attachment Point of $1 million in Policyholder liability by judgment or reasonable settlement."

Policyholder Defendant tenders the claim to Primary Insurer and notifies Excess Insurer. Primary Insurer is insolvent, and Excess Insurer refuses to assume the duty to defend, noting that its policy covers defense expenditures as part of the policyholder's "ultimate net loss" but does not require a defense.

Although the policy provides that Excess Insurer may become involved in defending the claim (something that would ordinarily be prudent for an excess insurer if the primary insurer were not defending), Excess Insurer declines.

Left without an insurer-provided defense, the furnace maker retains counsel at its own expense, incurring $150,000 in defense costs in the matter. Plaintiff's counsel builds a strong case during discovery. Trial ensues, resulting in a verdict of $10 million.

Policyholder demands that Excess Insurer contribute its policy limits toward satisfying the judgment.

• May Excess Insurer refuse to pay?

• On what grounds?

• Is Excess Insurer's anticipated defense persuasive?

• Is the language of the Excess Policy sufficient to resolve the claim?

• For which entity?

• In whose favor weigh considerations of

  ◦ Reasonable expectations?

  ◦ The purpose and function of excess insurance?

  ◦ Public policy?

## PROBLEM THREE [B]

Same facts as Problem 3 [A] except that Policyholder Defendant and Plaintiff settle for $6 million under an agreement whereby Policyholder Defendant Furnace Company pays Plaintiff using a $1 million loan that Policyholder will gradually pay off over 15 years and assigns its contract rights against Excess Insurer to Plaintiff along with any rights Policyholder may have against Excess Insurer for bad faith or unfair claims handling.

Plaintiff and Policyholder then call upon Excess Insurer to pay its $5 million policy limits to satisfy the remainder of the settlement. In a separate action, Policyholder seeks reimbursement of its counsel fees.

- May Excess Insurer refuse to pay?
- On what grounds?
- Is Excess Insurer's anticipated defense persuasive?
- Is the language of the Excess Policy sufficient to resolve the claim?
- For which entity?
- In whose favor weigh considerations of
    - Reasonable expectations?
    - The purpose and function of excess insurance?
    - Public policy?

## PROBLEM THREE [C]

Same facts as Problem 3 [A] except that the Excess Policy contains the following language:

The Insurance afforded under this Policy shall apply only after all applicable Underlying Insurance has been exhausted by actual payment under such Underlying Insurance, and shall only pay excess of any retention or deductible amounts provided in the Primary Policy and any other exhausted Underlying Insurance.

- May Excess Insurer refuse to pay?
- On what grounds?
- Is Excess Insurer's anticipated defense persuasive?
- Is the language of the Excess Policy sufficient to resolve the claim?
- For which entity?
- In whose favor weigh considerations of
    - Reasonable expectations?
    - The purpose and function of excess insurance?
    - Public policy?

## PROBLEM THREE [D]

Same facts as Problem 3 [C] except that Primary Insurer is not insolvent. The Primary Policy does, however, contain a broad "absolute" pollution exclusion of the type discussed in Ch. 11.[2] The claim is in a jurisdiction that has not yet decided the coverage issue, one on which the courts have differed. The excess policy follows form to the primary policy except that it has some additional language peculiar to excess insurance such as the payment clause outlined in Problem 3 [C].

Primary Insurer defends under reservation of rights,[3] taking the position that the pollution exclusion bars coverage for the claim because carbon monoxide is a "pollutant," the "discharge" or "release" of which by the leaky furnace caused the death of Investment Banker.

Policyholder and Primary Insurer are aware of the divergent lines of authority regarding the pollution exclusion and carbon monoxide poisoning. They compromise their coverage dispute 50-50, with each agreeing to pay half of any liability to Plaintiff on that basis up to $1 million.

Primary Insurer then, with Policyholder consent, settles Plaintiff's claim for $1 million. Policyholder contributes $500,000 toward the settlement, which effectively drains all of the surplus capital from the company. Primary Insurer pays its $500,000, and now everyone looks to Excess Insurer for payment of its $5 million policy limits.

- May Excess Insurer refuse to pay?
- On what grounds?
- Is Excess Insurer's anticipated defense persuasive?
- Is the language of the Excess Policy sufficient to resolve the claim?
- For which entity?

---

2. A typical pollution exclusion contained in a general liability states that any claim "arising out of the actual, alleged or threatened discharge, dispersal, seepage, migration, release or escape" of a pollutant falls outside coverage, with "pollutant" defined as "any solid, liquid, gaseous or thermal irritant or contaminant, including smoke, vapor, soot, fumes, acids, alkalis, chemicals, and waste," with waste including "materials to be recycled, reconditioned, or reclaimed." *See, e.g.,* Insurance Services Office, Commercial General Liability Policy CG 00 01 12 07 (2007).

3. Because the duty to defend is based on the facts as alleged by the claimant and is subject to the potential-for-coverage standard, it is our view that until the jurisdiction has controlling precedent on the application of the pollution exclusion that forecloses coverage for CO poisoning, there exists a potential for coverage. If the primary insurer refused to defend under these circumstances, it should be considered in breach of the duty to defend. Insurers often dispute this analysis, taking the position that until there is controlling precedent holding that CO poisoning claims are not barred by the pollution exclusion that the insurer is permitted to refuse a defense.

• In whose favor weigh considerations of

   ◦ Reasonable expectations?

   ◦ The purpose and function of excess insurance?

   ◦ Public policy?


## PROBLEM THREE [E]

Same facts as Problem 3 [D], but despite its reservation of rights, Primary Insurer (correctly) realizes that the claim presents a great potential for a verdict and judgment in excess of the $1 million policy limits.

Recognizing its duty to make reasonable settlement decisions, realizing that continued defense will be costly, and concerned that failure to at least attempt settlement will expose it to bad faith liability, Primary Insurer offers its policy limits in settlement to protect Policyholder Defendant from an excess judgment.

But Primary Insurer also files a declaratory judgment action seeking a finding of no coverage because of the pollution exclusion, reasoning that it may, depending on the law of the jurisdiction, be able to recoup the funds it pays in settlement and perhaps even defense expenditures. But claimant rejects a $1 million settlement offer by the Primary Insurer. Excess Insurer declines to contribute to the settlement offer or otherwise participate in settlement negotiations with the claimant.

Trial ensues and a verdict of $10 million is rendered. Primary Insurer and Policyholder Defendant resolve their coverage dispute regarding CO poisoning and the pollution exclusion on a 70/30 basis, with the primary insurer agreeing to provide $700,000 of liability coverage and Policyholder contributing $300,000 from its own funds.

Policyholder now seeks assurances of policy limits payment from Excess Insurer so that it can offer a $6 million settlement to Plaintiff.

• May Excess Insurer refuse to pay?

• On what grounds?

• Is Excess Insurer's anticipated defense persuasive?

• Is the language of the Excess Policy sufficient to resolve the claim?

• For which entity?

• In whose favor weigh considerations of

   ◦ Reasonable expectations?

   ◦ The purpose and function of excess insurance?

   ◦ Public policy?

# PROBLEM FOUR

Policyholder purchased $10 million of Directors & Officers insurance from Primary Insurer, $10 million of first-layer excess insurance from First Excess Insurer, and $10 million of second-layer excess insurance from Second Excess Insurer.

Plaintiffs filed a class action stock-dilution claim against Policyholder, which sought coverage from its insurers who disputed coverage, requiring Policyholder to defend the claim while simultaneously suing its insurers to obtain coverage.

Primary Insurer and Policyholder compromise their coverage dispute for $30 million, with Primary Insurer paying $6 million and Policyholder paying at least an additional $4 million. Policyholder then sought coverage from its excess insurers, arguing that their attachment points had been met by this $10 million in payments and additional $10 million in defense costs (a high but not unheard of figure for this type of litigation).[4]

Second Layer Excess Insurer (that has a $20 million attachment point) settles its coverage dispute with Policyholder on a 50-50 basis. But Second Layer Excess refuses to pay anything, taking the position that it does not attach because the underlying $10 million level of Primary Insurance has not been exhausted by payments of the Primary Insurer alone. First Layer Excess Insurer argues that Policyholder may not "fill the gap" between the amount paid by Primary Insurer and the attachment point of Second Layer Excess insurer.

> The Insurance afforded under this Policy shall apply only after all applicable Underlying Insurance has been exhausted by actual payment by the Insurer of such Underlying Insurance — and only by payment from the Underlying Insurer(s). Excess Insurer shall only pay excess of any retention or deductible amounts provided in the Primary Policy and other exhausted Underlying Insurance.

———————

These problems present a number of issues and may serve as useful review regarding insurer-policyholder duties and liability insurance generally. In the main, however, they are excess insurance attachment problems or perhaps more accurately labeled variants of the attachment problems that arise when the underlying insurer(s) does not provide all of the payment of the underlying limit, with the reasons varying from insolvency to exclusionary coverage language to issues of reasonable settlement and litigation behavior.

———————

4. Before crying too much for the excess insurers, remember that the typical excess policy gives the insurer the right (but not the duty) to participate in defense of the matter. Where the amount necessary to resolve the case by settlement or judgment clearly exceeds the limits of primary insurer, excess insurers frequently assume control of the defense, either formally or as a practical matter. First and/or Second Excess Insurer could therefore probably have taken over the defense and endeavored to spend less on defending the suit.

Resolution may turn not only upon the policy language of the excess insurance but also upon judicial attitudes toward the strict enforcement of clauses providing that only payment by the underlying insurer(s) can satisfy the attachment requirements.

For detailed discussion of the controversy, see Jeffrey W. Stempel, *An Analytic "Gap": The Perils of Robotic Enforcement of Payment-by-Underlying-Insurer-Only Language in Excess Insurance Policies*, 52 Tort, Trial & Ins. L.J. 807 (2017); Douglas R. Richmond, *The Tiresome Problem of Exhaustion in Excess Insurance*, in New Appleman on Insurance: Current Critical Issues in Insurance Law (Spring 2014).

Two commonly cited cases on opposite sides of the issue are *Zeig v. Massachusetts Bonding & Insurance Co.*, 23 F.2d 665 (2d Cir. 1928) (applying pre-*Erie* federal common law), and *Qualcomm, Inc. v. Certain Underwriters at Lloyd's, London*, 73 Cal. Rptr. 3d 770 (Cal. Ct. App. 2008).

The ALI *Restatement of the Law, Liability Insurance* (RLLI) position is as follows:

When an insured is covered by an insurance policy that provides coverage that is excess to an underlying insurance policy, the following rules apply, unless otherwise stated in the excess insurance policy:

(1) The excess insurer is not obligated to provide benefits under its policy until the underlying policy is exhausted;

(2) The underlying policy is exhausted when an amount equal to the limit of that policy has been paid to claimants for a covered loss, or for other covered benefits subject to that limit, by or on behalf of the underlying insurer or the insured; and

(3) If the underlying insurer is unable to perform, whether because of insolvency or otherwise, the excess insurer is not obligated to provide coverage in place of the underlying insurer.

RLLI § 39.

• How would § 39 apply to Problems 3 [A]–[E] and Problem 4?

• What is the key language on which resolution of these problems depends?

• Does RLLI § 39 permit consideration of factors other than policy language?

• Should it?

• What factors?

## ILLUSTRATION: HOW MEANINGFUL IS THE LABEL "UMBRELLA" INSURANCE?

Can you have a valid umbrella policy with holes? Can you have a skinny excess policy with coverage narrower than the underlying policy? At the risk of answering our own question, we think the answers are (a) "No" and (b) "Not unless there is an express and clear understanding to this effect by the parties."

(a) The very notion and nomenclature of an "umbrella" policy implies that it provides coverage beyond the contours of the underlying insurance.

Perhaps that is too timid a statement. Calling a policy an "umbrella" policy, in effect, promises that its scope of coverage will exceed that of the underlying insurance. There may also be combination or hybrid excess umbrella policies. This is the general view of insurance authorities and establishes an industry-wide understanding of what it means to provide "umbrella" coverage.

(b) Just as "umbrella" insurance suggests broader coverage, the term "excess" suggests that an excess policy provides more of the coverage contained in the underlying policy. Consequently, unless there is a specific agreement to the contrary, an excess policy should be congruent in scope to the underlying policy. In a particularly "hard" market where obtaining coverage is difficult, a policyholder may need to accept restrictions on normal, "follow-form" excess coverage as to some risks. In a very hard market, insurers may only be willing to write lower levels of coverage for some risks perceived as particularly difficult. This is not to say that all follow-form excess policies are carbon copies of the underlying insurance (although many excess policies consist only of a Declarations Sheet). An excess insurer writes coverage on its own form rather than simply signing on to the underlying form. However, the excess policy should not deviate in material respects from the followed form absent an express agreement to that effect. Frequently, an excess policy may have some insurer-specific language regarding the mechanics of notice, proof of loss, or other ministerial aspects of a claim. Rarely will an excess policy be substantively narrower in scope than the underlying policy.

(c) Because the terms "excess" and "umbrella" have such well-established meanings, the sentiments expressed above are the conventional wisdom of the insurance world. Where there is deviation from this norm, it should not be the result of mere differences in the text of the excess or umbrella insurance policy. Where the parties agreed to a normal and rational insurance program, this means excess insurance co-extensive with underlying insurance and umbrella insurance that is somewhat broader than the underlying insurance. This intent of the parties and this general understanding of policyholders, brokers, and insurers cannot be altered by an excess insurer simply providing a policy form weeks or months later with language at variance from the underlying or followed policy. At best, this is a nullity. At worst, it may indicate fraud and deceit by an excess or umbrella insurer.

(d) This is not to say that some policies titled "excess" or "umbrella" policies are not intentionally narrower than the underlying coverage. But when this takes place and is enforceable, it is because the scope of coverage reflected in the contract documents accurately captures the agreement of the parties, agreement that should be express and clear. However, even if there is an agreement to have a "skinny" excess policy or an "umbrella with holes," labeling these policies "excess" or "umbrella" is misleading. To properly reflect an understanding of this sort, the policies should be labeled "limited excess" or "restricted excess policies." As discussed previously, these sorts of policies are normally found only in a hard market. Where a market is even moderately soft, rational policyholders and brokers will insist upon excess or umbrella coverage at least as extensive as underlying coverage and will be able to obtain it at acceptable prices.

# § 13.02. Self-Insurance and Risk Retention Groups

## [A] Introduction

Up until the 1980s, self-insurance issues played a rather modest role in the field of insurance law. In property insurance, for example, self-insurance traditionally was found in the form of a "coinsurance deductible," or a division of risk between the insured and the insurer requiring the insured to be a partial self-insurer, and pay a stipulated amount of the loss, before the insurer became liable under its policy for the remaining amount of loss. Self-insurance issues also arise in automobile insurance controversies, especially relating to uninsured and underinsured motorists coverage.

Not until the so-called liability insurance "crisis" of the late 1980s, however, did self-insurance programs for a large number of American corporations, businesses, and medical and legal professionals become more than an insurance alternative, and often became a legal necessity.

Self-insurance and risk-retention programs generally fall into one of four subcategories: (1) an on-shore or off-shore "captive" insurance company; (2) a self-insurance trust; (3) a self-insurance reciprocal; or (4) an "in house" risk-retention program, collectively called a "self-insured retention" or SIR.

A risk retention group generally is defined as any limited liability association whose primary activity consists of assuming or spreading liability of its group members and which is chartered or licensed under the laws of a state, or was chartered or authorized to engage in the business of insurance under the laws of Bermuda or the Cayman Islands and has met the minimal capitalization requirements of each state. Such a risk retention group may not provide insurance coverage other than liability insurance or reinsurance for its members. *See* 15 U.S.C. § 3901(a)(4) (1986). Indeed, there are currently thousands of American "captive" insurance companies licensed to do business in Bermuda alone. *And see generally* 1986 amendments to the federal Risk Retention Act, 15 U.S.C. §§ 3901–3906 (1986).

Most liability self-insurance risk retention groups therefore were established because of the unavailability of traditional liability insurance coverage from many traditional insurance carriers. Under the federal Risk Retention Act of 1986, self-insurance risk retention groups have more limited capitalization requirements and more limited state regulation than traditional insurance companies.

More commonly, however, many corporate businesses and professional corporations choose to manage a portion of their liability risk toward third parties through the use of a self-insured retention program, or SIR, which places responsibility for losses up to a certain amount upon the self-insured, with a traditional excess insurance policy (or policies) covering losses above that initial amount.

*Query*: Exactly how, and when, must a self-insured's initial payment be made before an excess insurer's policy coverage comes into effect? A number of recent cases have dealt with this troubling issue, including the case below.

## Montgomery Ward & Co. Inc. v. Imperial Casualty and Indemnity Co. et al.

### California Court of Appeal, Second District
### 81 Cal. App. 4th 356, 97 Cal. Rptr. 2d 44 (2000)

**Johnson, J.**

Plaintiff and appellant Montgomery Ward filed this lawsuit against four insurance companies, seeking a declaration of coverage and compensatory damages for breach of contract under certain comprehensive general liability insurance policies issued from 1962 to 1976. Montgomery Ward sought coverage for defense and indemnity costs it had incurred because of alleged environmental contamination occurring over a number of years at three automotive service centers it operated in California. After disposing of certain issues by summary adjudication, the trial court dismissed all remaining causes of action in Montgomery Ward's suit.

The court ruled Montgomery Ward's "self-insured retentions" (SIRs)—the amounts of any loss for which Montgomery Ward retained responsibility under the terms of its policies, ranging from $50,000 to $250,000 for each policy—were the equivalent of primary insurance. The court then applied the principle that all primary insurance must be exhausted before any excess insurer has any obligation under and excess policy, thus requiring Montgomery Ward to exhaust its SIRs under as many as 20 potentially applicable policies before any of the [excess] insurers had any duty to indemnify Montgomery Ward.

After applying this principle, the court found Montgomery Ward had been fully compensated for its remaining losses by its settlements with other insurers. We reverse.

The principal issue raised by Montgomery Ward on appeal is whether the trial court erred in concluding SIRs may be treated as primary/underlying insurance to which the rule of horizontal exhaustion applies, requiring Montgomery Ward to exhaust its SIRs on all potentially applicable policies before any insurer has any duty to indemnify Montgomery Ward for its losses. We conclude SIRs are not primary insurance and the principle of horizontal exhaustion does not apply.…

The trial court's decision and the Insurers' arguments on appeal depend upon the conclusion that retained limits or SIRs in the insurance policies issued to Montgomery Ward are the same as primary or underlying insurance. There is no support for this conclusion in the language of the policies themselves, nor do we find any pertinent support in California precedent. Accordingly, we conclude the principle of horizontal exhaustion does not apply to SIRs in these circumstances.… .

The Insurers argue the SIRs or retained limits in the "excess" policies they issued to Montgomery Ward were themselves "primary policies" for purposes of the horizontal exhaustion rule. If that is so, then in this continuing loss case, Montgomery Ward must satisfy its SIR under every potentially applicable policy—to the tune of at least $2.9 million for each occurrence—before any insurer under any of the policies has any responsibility.

Such a result would require us to ignore completely the terms of the insurance contracts themselves, as well as overlook the general guidance given by the Supreme Court on the subject of self-insurance. This we decline to do, and we see nothing in the cases cited by the Insurers that would require, or indeed support, such a result.

We begin, as we must, be looking at the policy language. As the [California Supreme Court in *Montrose Chemical Corp. v. Admiral Ins. Co.*, 913 P.2d 878 (Cal. 1995),] explains:

> Insurance policies are contracts and, therefore, are governed in the first instance by the rules of construction applicable to contracts. Under statutory rules of contract interpretation, the mutual intention of the parties at the time the contract is formed governs its interpretation.... Such intent is to be inferred, if possible, solely from the written provisions of the contract.... The 'clear and explicit' meaning of these provisions, interpreted in their 'ordinary and popular sense', controls judicial interpretation unless 'used by the parties in a technical sense, or unless a special meaning is given to them by usage'. If the meaning a layperson would ascribe to the language of a contract of insurance is clear and unambiguous, a court will apply that meaning.

We see no ambiguity in the policies at issue here. While there are differences among the policies, in practical effect their terms, for these purposes, are essentially the same. In each of the Century policies, for example, Century agreed to: "indemnify the insured for ultimate net loss in excess of the retained limit...." The policy states:

> [Century's] limits of liability shall be only for the ultimate next loss in excess of ... Fifty Thousand Dollars ($50,000) as a result of any one occurrence or accident, *whether insurance shall be purchased by or in behalf of the insured or the insured shall retain such first loss for the insured's own account* (herein called the retained limit).... (Emphasis added.)

Century's (and Imperial's) policies also specifically say they are excess "[i]f other collectible insurance with any other insurer is available to the insured covering a loss also covered hereunder...." Home's policies say they are excess over "specific valid and Collectible Underlying Insurances whether scheduled hereunder or not".

We think this language is clear. In the event of a covered occurrence, Century contracted to indemnify Montgomery Ward for its ultimate net loss, as defined, in excess of $50,000 (up to the policy limits) *whether or not* Montgomery Ward chose to protect itself with primary insurance. Indeed, all of the policies make it clear that there is a difference between underlying insurance and retained limits, and the Insurers understood this difference when they entered into these contracts.

The Insurers now ask us to relieve them of this clear contractual obligation, and instead to deem retained limits in other potentially applicable policies to be primary insurance. To do so, we would have to find Montgomery Ward's SIRs in all of its policies constitute "other collectible insurance with any other insurer" (under the Imperial and Century policies) or "specific valid and Collectible Underlying Insurances" (under the Home policies) as to which the Insurers' policies are excess. This we will not do. We are offered no public policy or other compelling reason to engraft new meaning on plain language, and accordingly "we may not rewrite what they themselves wrote" [citation omitted].

The cases cited by the Insurers do not give us pause in our conclusions. It is a great leap from [those cases with their particular policy provisions] to the proposed principle that an SIR *is* a primary policy and should be treated as primary insurance, and it is a leap we will not take. The significant point is that these cases, like all other insurance cases, look first to the terms of the policy....

The Insurers also point to our decision in *Stonewall Ins. Co. v. City of Palos Verdes Estates*, (1996) 46 Cal. App. 4th 1810, 54 Cal. Rptr. 2d 176 as support for the proposition [that] excess do not attach until policies of primary insurance are exhausted. That was indeed our conclusion, but (a) it begs the question of what are policies of primary insurance, and (b) the Insurers omit reference to the first principle from which our conclusion flowed: namely "[t]he liability of excess insurers to the [insured] is a question of contract" [citation omitted]....

Finally, we note our conclusion [that] SIRs may not be deemed primary insurance coverage is consonant ... with the [California] Supreme Court's general statements about self-insurance in [*Aerojet-General Corp. v. Transport Indemnity Co.*]....

> In a strict sense, "self-insurance" is a "misnomer" ... "Insurance is a contract whereby one undertakes to indemnify another against loss, damage, or liability arising from a contingent or unknown event" (Insurance Code, Sec. 22) "Self-insurance ... is equivalent to no insurance ...' [citations omitted]. As such, it is 'repugnant to the [very] concept of insurance....' If insurance requires the undertaking by one to indemnify another, it cannot be satisfied by a self-contradictory undertaking by one to indemnify oneself." (*Aerojet*, 17 Cal. 4th 38, 72 ftn. 20, 70 Cal Rptr. 2d 118, 948 P.2d 909)....

In sum, we see no basis in the insurance contracts, or in applicable law, from which to conclude [that] Montgomery Ward's SIRs are the equivalent of policies of primary insurance.

[The court's duty to defend argument is omitted.]

## Notes and Questions

1. According to Professor Eric Mills Holmes, there is "an often repeated maxim that self-insurance is no insurance." Was this the underlying philosophy of the Cal-

ifornia appellate court in *Montgomery Ward & Co. v. Imperial Casualty and Indemnity Co.*? Can the parties still contractually agree to treat SIRs in the same manner as primary insurance, even though an SIR might *not* constitute insurance?

Some other courts have not followed this *Montgomery Ward* rationale. For example, in *Missouri Pac. R.R. v. International Ins. Co.*, 679 N.E.2d 801 (Ill. App. Ct. 1997), an Illinois appellate court found that, in an action involving noise-induced hearing loss and asbestos exposure claims spanning several policy years, the insured's SIR *did* constitute primary insurance coverage that the insured was required to exhaust each policy year before looking to its excess insurers for coverage. Can these cases be reconciled? Attorneys Mark Flory and Angela Walsh conclude:

> While an insured has virtually no control over how the courts decide these [SIR and excess insurance] issues, it is important to bear in mind that an insured does have the power to clarify matters through the negotiation and drafting of the policy language. Since courts will always look first to the language of the [insurance] contract, [these] uncertainties should be addressed through careful drafting.

Mark Flory & Angela Walsh, *Know Thy Self-Insurance*, 36 Tort & Ins. L.J. 1005, 1010 (2001).

> *Query*: How *should* you draft the policy as an attorney representing a self-insured corporation? How would you draft the policy as an attorney representing an excess insurance carrier?

2. Self-insurance issues are not solely limited to liability insurance coverage, since some companies have self-insured their employees for health insurance coverage and other employee benefits. Although traditional health insurers are heavily regulated by state insurance code statutes, there is a serious loophole in the federal Employee Retirement Income Security Act (ERISA, 29 U.S.C. § 1001 *et seq.*) which holds that, under federal preemption principles, ERISA supersedes "any and all State laws insofar as they relate to any employee benefit plan" described in 29 U.S.C. § 1003(a).

Consequently, ERISA imposes virtually no regulations or requirements for risk retention plans to provide standardized health care benefits, and this lack of federal regulation has created a regulatory vacuum. *See, e.g.*, Widiss & Gostin, *What's Wrong with the ERISA Vacuum? The Case Against Unrestricted Freedom for Employers to Terminate Employee Health Care Plans and to Decide What Coverage Is to Be Provided When Risk Retention Plans are Established for Health Care*, 41 Drake L. Rev. 635 (1992).

3. The popularity of risk retention groups tends to ebb and flow according to whether the market for conventional insurance is "soft" (where insurance is easy to obtain at relatively low rates) or "hard" (where insurance is difficult to obtain or available only at high rates or with more exclusions or sub-limitations than usual).

But just what is the distinction between a captive and a risk retention group? The two are so close, both in concept and in technicality, that observers tend to use the terms interchangeably. The distinction is that a true captive tends to operate as a separate insurance company while an RRG is more responsive to member wishes and direction (subject to the applicable bounds of regulation). Whatever the precise definitional nomenclature, there is no doubt that captives are big business. About half of all U.S. risk transfers are held by captives, and captives appear to be catching on in areas outside their traditional base of the Caribbean, North America, and Europe.

### PROBLEM FIVE

Under the federal Risk Retention Act amendments of 1986, a risk retention group—whether it is an on-shore or off-shore "captive," or self-insurance reciprocal or trust—must still be minimally regulated by the state. *See, e.g.,* 15 U.S.C. §§ 3902, 3903; Va. Code Ann. § 38.2-5100. But what is the impact of this "minimal" state regulation under the Risk Retention Act? Consider the following fact situation:

The National Association of Home Builders formed the Homeowners Warranty Corporation [HOW] under the laws of the District of Columbia, and HOW distributed its homeowner warranty liability policies to home-builders nationwide under the auspices of the INA Underwriters Insurance Company. However, in 1981, INA informed HOW that it would no longer continue to underwrite HOW's liability risks as its insurer.

In 1981, after passage of the federal Risk Retention Act, HOW formed its own HOW Insurance Company as a risk retention entity doing business as a Delaware insurer, and again distributing its policies nationwide. In 1983, the Delaware Insurance Commissioner issued an Order to Show Cause against the HOW Insurance Company, alleging that HOW had misrepresented approval by the Delaware Insurance Commissioner to do business as a Delaware insurer, but two court opinions found HOW Insurance Company was a risk retention group and exempt from all state regulations except those permitted by the Risk Retention Act. The Delaware Insurance Commissioner did not appeal these rulings.

Thereafter, the Georgia Insurance Commissioner attempted to enjoin HOW Insurance Company from selling its policies or doing business in Georgia under the Commissioner's statutory authority and regulatory powers over all insurance companies doing business in Georgia.

• How should the court rule in this case?

# § 13.03. Reinsurance

## [A] Introduction

Reinsurance is a contract in which a reinsurer agrees to assume in whole or in part a risk undertaken by the original insurer. Reinsurance commonly is used when the potential risk of loss is too great for only one insurance company to cover adequately.

Oil tanker fleets and refineries, space communication satellites, and immense sky-scrapers are three examples of risk assumption that would be all but impossible without reinsurance. For example, when the World Trade Center in New York was destroyed by a terrorist attack on September 11, 2001, it was insured by more than 20 excess insurance and reinsurance companies.

Lloyd's of London is just one of many well-known names among reinsurance underwriters. Other large reinsurance companies are in Germany and Switzerland, and American reinsurance markets are found in New York, Miami, and Chicago. Lloyd's of London is not an insurance company *per se*, but it is a market in which over 26,000 individual members form hundreds of syndicates to insure, reinsure, or provide excess insurance for everything from supertankers and skyscrapers to football quarterbacks' arms. Elvis Presley at one time insured his guitar-playing fingers with Lloyd's of London, and tenor Lucciano Pavarotti reportedly insured his voice with Lloyd's. Lloyd's reputedly has an unofficial motto: "There are no bad risks—just bad rates."

Reinsurance may be written on a particular risk ("facultative reinsurance") or written to cover an insurer's "book" of business, or at least a broader segment of the risks underwritten by the insurer ("treaty" reinsurance). The reinsurer's obligations, under either type of reinsurance, are generally administered according to one of three formulas:

> Under the "proportional" or "quota share" approach, the net profit or loss from underwriting (the sum of premiums, losses, and administrative expenses but not investment income) is pro-rated among the primary insurer and the reinsurer.
>
> In a variant of this arrangement, known as "surplus" reinsurance, the parties have a quota share agreement that is different for various premiums and layers of losses.
>
> With excess or "excess-of-loss" reinsurance, the reinsurer receives a set premium from the primary carrier in return for paying claims that exceed a certain threshold. Excess reinsurance for primary insurers operates essentially as does excess primary insurance for policyholders.

*See* Jeffrey W. Stempel & Erik S. Knutsen, Stempel & Knutsen on Insurance Coverage § 17.01 (4th ed. 2016).

Although descriptions of reinsurance, such as that quoted above, frequently refer to an arrangement between a "primary insurer" and a reinsurer, this is perhaps inartful description resulting from too much effort to differentiate the terms. Any "insurer," including of course excess or umbrella insurers, may purchase reinsurance. A company that essentially self-insures through a wholly owned "captive" or in-house insurer may also purchase reinsurance on that risk.

The insuring entity that buys reinsurance is known as the "cedant" or "ceding company" because it cedes some of its risk to the reinsurer. The arrangement allows the insurer to spread its risk. As "insurance among insurers," reinsurance has the same risk distribution qualities of ordinary insurance. The ceding company absorbs a small but certain loss (part of its premium dollar or profit given to the reinsurer) in return for protection against contingent but potentially larger losses (a wave of unexpected policyholder claims).

By spreading the risk in this manner, insurers not only obtain contingency protection but also usually are able to use the reinsurance to satisfy government regulations regarding mandatory insurer capacity or reserves, thereby freeing the insurer to underwrite more risk, take in more premium, and become a larger, at least potentially more profitable, insurer. Reinsurers often spread the risk still further by purchasing reinsurance of their obligations to insurers. Reinsurance among reinsurers is known as "retrocession."

As to coverage issues, reinsurance differs from regular insurance in another significant way: reinsurance contracts are much less standardized than the ISO-drafted policy forms that dominate home, auto, and liability insurance. To be sure, certain terms and phrases are staples of reinsurance. However, because reinsurance tends to involve larger sums and transactions among experts or insiders, the reinsurance contract is more frequently customized and is the product of more extensive negotiation than is the case for ordinary insurance (except for insurance for particularly large risks).

Reinsurance also differs from insurance in terms of its history, culture, and dispute resolution infrastructure. Historically, reinsurance has been an activity confined to specialists rather than a mass retailing operation in the manner of standardized automobile or homeowners insurance (or even liability insurance for small companies). If consumer insurance is something like retail or Sears, reinsurance is more like wholesale or commodity trading. Not as many people are involved in the activity, they tend to have more expertise, they are more likely to have personal relationships, and there is more of a self-identified fraternity of reinsurers than exists for insurers.

This has led to a somewhat different ethos about reinsurance, which is more like the floor of Lloyd's, where deals are made on a handshake among "repeat players." As a result, litigation was historically disfavored and rare in reinsurance matters, particularly among reinsurers but also where conflict arose between insurer and reinsurer. The historical and cultural norm was to simply "work things out" without suing. Subsequently, this has changed, reflecting larger social evolution. Businesses now appear dramatically less skittish about suing one another than was the case 30 to 50 years ago.

But, unlike other areas of the law, reinsurance controversies are still more commonly processed outside the courtroom. Most reinsurance treaties or facultative certificates contain arbitration agreements. Reinsurance and insurance arbitration tends to differ from consumer or commercial arbitration in the United States. The typical reinsurance arbitration clause provides for a three-person panel of arbitrators. Each disputant designates an arbitrator and the two arbitrators choose a third arbitrator or "umpire" that is not affiliated with either side.

Although the two-party selected arbitrators are of course well aware of who chose them (and, for the cynics among us, it should be noted that the rate of compensation typically paid to insurance arbitrators in London is quite handsome), the custom is that all three arbitrators will attempt to decide the issue based upon the contract language, applicable law, and insurance industry custom and practice despite the fact that only one arbitrator is the designated neutral. *See* Stempel & Knusten on Insurance Coverage § 17.06[a].

For additional background on reinsurance, see Barry R. Ostrager & Mary Kay Vyskocil, Modern Reinsurance Law and Practice (2d ed. 2000); Reinsurance (Robert Strain ed., 1980); Patrick L. Brockett, Robert C. Witt & Paul R. Aird, *An Overview of Reinsurance and the Reinsurance Markets*, 9 J. Ins. Reg. 432 (1991).

"Traditional" reinsurance has existed in some form since at least 1370. *See* Adam B. Leichtling & Laura M. Paredes, *Fundamental Concepts in Reinsurance in Latin American Countries*, 37 U. Miami Inter-Am. L. Rev. 1 (2005) (noting documented existence of maritime insurer's purchase of reinsurance against loss paid in connection with insurance of voyage). By traditional, we mean reinsurance in which the reinsurer takes on a true underwriting risk—the chance that the reinsurer could unexpectedly be called upon to pay fortuitous losses as well as the chance that the reinsurer could make more from the ceding insurer's premium payments than the reinsurer paid in connection with losses. When we spoke of risk transfer in Chapter 1, we were referring to underwriting risk.

However, in addition to underwriting risk, there is also investment risk and timing risk. Investment risk is the risk that an insurer's investment portfolio might underperform expectations. Timing risk is the risk that an insurance company might pay out for losses more quickly than was anticipated, which of course reduces the amount of investment income earned by the reinsurer and is thus a cousin to investment risk. Because insurers and reinsurers make much of their money due to the "float" or lag time between receipt of premiums and payment of claims, both insurers and reinsurers tend to want longer lag time. That way, insurers and reinsurers can make money even if their underwriters have "guessed wrong" about the number and severity of claims under their policies.

## ILLUSTRATIONS

To take a simple example: if a policyholder has two significant bodily injury claims during the policy year rather than the one predicted by the actuaries, the insurer may be in trouble because it assessed premiums based on the prediction of a single claim. However, if the claims are not paid until after several years of litigation, an insurer with a good investment portfolio may nonetheless make money on the account, although this is a little far-fetched in connection with a single policyholder and policy. Even the most efficient defense of a claim will cost significant sums that will probably outpace investment return on a single policy's premium. But where risks are pooled, the years of interest or other investment wealth created while a pool of claims is adjusted or litigated can be particularly significant. As a result, insurers have a strong incentive to delay paying claims as long as possible, so long as this does not create bad faith exposure (*see* Chapter 12).

To take a larger, more complex example: even though asbestos liability claims have been the largest "mass tort" in history, they are estimated to be only a 3–5 percent drag on liability insurer earnings. Why? Because liability insurers have in most cases not been required to pay these claims until years or even decades after the injuries took place. Furthermore, when it has come time to pay the piper, insurers pay with dollars that are worth less because of intervening inflation. Consequently, although long-tail claims bother insurers because of their potential to trigger more than one liability policy, the long-tail claims also enable insurers to have a greater float, larger investment returns, and to pay in inflation-diminished dollars.

## The Business of Reinsurance

Reinsurers face the same situation and hence have an interest in paying claims later rather than earlier. Consequently, reinsurers are happy to have insurers take their time in paying claims and seeking payment from the reinsurers. Because reinsurers are ordinarily held not to have a contractual relation with the underlying policyholder, the reinsurer often has little or no bad faith exposure unless the reinsurer has been involved in claims processing or is acting in concert with an insurer committing bad faith (more on this later in the chapter). A prudent reinsurer may even enjoy having the ceding insurer delay claims payments for years as this normally gives the reinsurer economic advantage while the risk of a bad faith punitive damages award is shouldered by the ceding insurer.

However, even with the advantages of the time value of money, insurers face investment and timing risk. For example, in one case involving bankruptcy of asbestos defendant policyholders, a federal appeals court ruled that confirmation of the bankrupt debtor's Chapter 11 Plan triggered the debtor's liability policies and required the insurers to immediately pay policy proceeds into the trust fund established to pay the policyholder-debtor's asbestos claims liability even though many of those claims would not actually be processed until years in the future. *See UNR Indus. v. Continental Casualty Co.*, 942 F.2d 1101 (7th Cir. 1991) (applying Illinois law).

As you might imagine, insurers were not too happy about that result. But, perhaps viewing the case as an apparition, the insurance industry made relatively little protest. But when a Los Angeles trial court followed the *UNR* approach, insurers vigorously objected in the trade press and legal periodicals and successfully challenged the result on appeal, obtaining a ruling that implementation of a bankruptcy reorganization did not operate to trigger or accelerate insurer payment obligations for asbestos claims. *See Fuller-Austin Insulation Co. v. Highlands Ins. Co.*, 135 Cal. App. 4th 958, 38 Cal. Rptr. 3d 716 (2006). Similar coverage battles remain active so it is too early to say which side will prevail.

Our point is simply that the investment and timing risk are significant. Even in relatively simple situations, timing and investment risk can matter. For example,

Acme Insurance may provide fire coverage on the home of Anthony Aardvark. Even if Anthony is well-known for smoking in bed (and has had three prior house fires because of it) and was charged a high premium, timing risk can matter. For example, if Anthony nods off while smoking on Day 2 of the policy period, this is much worse for the insurer than if he makes it to Day 364, lengthening the time before which the insurer will be called upon to pay the claim. The insurer's substantive investment decisions are also important. If the insurer invested substantially in poorly performing stock, it will have substantially less investment income than anticipated, no matter when misfortune strikes the Aardvark home.

All this becomes important for reinsurance purposes because insurers would prefer to smooth out the rough ups and downs of their risks, not only underwriting risks but investment and timing risks as well. "Financial" or "Finite" reinsurance can assist in this regarding the latter two risks even when there is no shift of underwriting risk. By purchasing finite reinsurance, the ceding insurer gains a commitment for future payments at specified times, effectively transferring investment risk and timing risk to the reinsurer. Without more, however, some timing risk remains with the ceding insurer in that the insurer may be called upon to pay claims sooner than it receives its scheduled payments from the reinsurer.

There is also at least some investment risk in that the insurer may have been able to earn more with the premium money than it received in return from the reinsurer. However, as discussed above, some finite reinsurance contracts provide limitations on timing risk, retroactively increase premiums, or return excess premium payments. Provisions of this type may effectively strip away even timing and investment risk transfer from the resulting "reinsurance" products. When this happens, the resulting transaction looks very much like a favorable loan (or a CEO's compensation package approved by a board of directors violating its fiduciary duty to shareholders): there is little or no risk transfer and the contract is simply a financing vehicle.

So what, you say? Although there is nothing illegal about entering a contract that addresses investment and timing risk alone or that is simply a loan, there is a problem if one treats such a contract as insurance with underwriting risk for tax purposes. This is because American tax law permits an insurer to deduct premium payments. When an insurer purchases traditional reinsurance, the amount of reinsurance is treated as a reserve and results in a considerable tax savings for the insurer in return for the insurer's payment of premium to the reinsurer.

But if there has been no transfer of underwriting risk because over time premiums equal reinsurance policy or treaty benefits, the insurer has improperly taken a tax deduction simply for lending money to itself through a third party. The transaction creates the impression of income, profit, or a balance sheet that does not exist. Of course, when insurers or reinsurers treat pure financial reinsurance as if it were risk-shifting traditional reinsurance, this can be tax fraud as well as fraud upon the investment community. Now you know regulators get upset if finite reinsurance is improperly treated as traditional reinsurance.

The Financial Accounting Standard Board (FASB) Statement No. 113 (1992) holds that a reinsurance contract can be considered an insurance contract rather than an investment contract based upon (1) the amount of underwriting risk to which the reinsurer is exposed and (2) the timing of the reinsurer's reimbursement claims.

> For short-duration reinsurance contracts to be considered [true] insurance contracts [for tax purposes], the reinsurer must assume significant insurance [i.e., underwriting] risk, and it must be "reasonably possible that the reinsurer may realize a significant loss from the transaction." For long-duration reinsurance contracts to be considered insurance contracts, they must satisfy the same criteria as for short-duration contracts, and in addition, the insurer must be subject to mortality or morbidity risks.

> If a reinsurance contract fails to meet the conditions stated above, then it is considered to be an investment contract. In accounting for an investment contract, the primary insurer would report the premium paid, less the premium retained by the reinsurer, as a deposit.

*See* Heather M. Hulburt, *Financial Reinsurance and the AIG/General Re Scandal*, CPCU EJOURNAL, Nov. 2005, at 1 (endnotes omitted). Because financial/finite reinsurance "seldom involves the transfer of underwriting risk," these reinsurance transactions generally should not have the same tax benefits accorded to traditional reinsurance. What has gotten insurers and certain individuals in trouble with regulators was not the use of financial reinsurance but treating it like traditional reinsurance. *See* Hulbert; *supra*, at 1, 5–6, Diana Reitz, *Why Do Finite-Risk Deals Raise Eyebrows?*, NATIONAL UNDERWRITER, Apr. 18, 2005 (Prop. & Cas. ed.), at 58; Ianthe Jeanne Dugan & Theo Francis, *How a Hot Insurance Product Burned AIG*, WALL ST. J., Mar. 15, 2005, at C1, col. 1.

## [B] An Emerging Roadmap: The Principles of Reinsurance Contract Law ("PRICL")

With the support of the International Institute for the Unification of Private Law ("UNIDROIT"), a Project Group sponsored by the science funds of Austria, Germany and Switzerland is in the process of drafting Principles of Reinsurance Law ("PRICL"). The PRICL serves as a combination Model Act and Restatement that the sponsors hope will become widely used in the choice of law clauses of reinsurance contracts.

Like model laws and restatements, the PRICL is "soft" law that itself is not enforceable until enacted into a sovereign's statute or adopted by a court as part of common law doctrine — or agreed to by the parties as part of a contract. Work on the project began in 2015. In 2019, the first installment of the project was presented to UNIDROIT. Continuing work on the second installment of the project remains ongoing with an estimated completion date of 2022.

The first installment of the PRICL contains an initial article (Article I) that provides for application by party choice (Art. 1.1.1), use of the UNIDROIT Principles of International Commercial Contracts ("PICC") as a set of default rules for matters not addressed in the PRICL (Art. 1.1.2), and permits customization by the parties (Art. 1.1.3). Article 1.1.4 provides for the application of trade usage in construing reinsurance contracts but does not override the mandatory contract rules of otherwise applicable jurisdictional law (Art. 1.1.5). Article 1.1.6 provides that "[i]n the interpretation of the PRICL, regard is to be had to ... purposes [of the PRICL] including the need to promote the observance of good faith and fair dealing in the reinsurance sector and uniformity."

Rather than use terms like "cedent" or "retrocessionaire," the PRICL identifies contract parties as either the "reinsured" (e.g., the front-line insurer or a reinsurer seeking retrocession) or the "reinsurer" (e.g., the reinsurer of the ceding insurance company or the retrocessionaire of that reinsurer).

Duties of reinsurer and reinsured are set forth in Chapter 2, where the duty of "utmost good faith" (discussed below) is adopted and defined as "honesty and transparency as well as fairly taking into account the interests of the other party" (Art. 2.1.2). Other duties include confidentiality (Art. 2.1.3), good faith in dispute resolution (Art. 2.1.4), adequate disclosure during the contracting process (Art. 2.2.1), reasonably prompt payment (2.3.1 as to premiums; Art. 2.4.5 as to claims), adequate contract documentation (2.3.2), notice of changed circumstances or increased risk (Art. 2.3.3), as well as rights to inspect files (Art. 2.3.4), adequate notice (Art. 2.4.2), cooperation (Art. 2.4.4), and reasonable and prudent claims handling (Art. 2.4.2).

Regarding remedies, PRICL Chapter 3 provides — in what is something of a departure from traditional rules — proportionality. For example, according to traditional doctrine, a failure to disclose material information might well support rescission of the entire reinsurance contract. Under the PRICL provisions, it is more likely that a failure to disclose may impact the amount owed (or not owed) on a claim but without exempting the entire claim from payment or vitiating the entire reinsurance contract, which would have the practical impact of destroying coverage for unrelated claims unaffected by the lack of disclosure for which coverage was purchased. In this sense, PRICL Chapter 3 can be seen as more consistent than traditional doctrine with the principle that "law abhors a forfeiture," or at least abhors a disproportionate forfeiture.

PRICL Chapter 4 address the allocation of losses, which can be an important aspect of the reinsurance claims process, because the amounts owed may vary greatly depending on how a claim is classified and matched to a particular contract period, which in turn impacts the degree to which policy limits may or may not constrain the amount of coverage owed. Chapter 5 concerns the aggregation of losses, which has similar importance. The manner in which claims are combined or "batched" affects the amount of coverage available during particular contract periods subject to particular limits or provisions. Reinsurance contracts in general either provide for "event-based" aggregation hinging on a the materialization of a particular peril (Art. 5.2) or "cause-based" allegation that batches losses according to a common cause (Art. 5.3).

A full discussion of these particularized aspects of reinsurance exceeds the scope (and page limit) of this coursebook. The PRICL provides not only black-letter principles but also extensive commentary and illustrations and can serve as a treatise of sorts on reinsurance. Other treatises include: CLYDE & CO, REINSURANCE PRACTICE AND THE LAW (supplemented annually); GRAYDON S. STARLING & DEAN HANSELL, LAW OF REINSURANCE § 10:6 (2013 edition), and for the German-speaking, KLAUS GERATHEWOHL, *Ruckversicherung* (1976). *See also* YONG QIANG HAN & GREG PYNT (EDS.), *CARTER V. BOEHM* AND PRE-CONTRACTUAL DUTIES IN INSURANCE LAW: A GLOBAL PERSPECTIVE AFTER 250 YEARS (2018) (collecting commentary on good faith duties in different jurisdictions as part of 350th anniversary of key duty case *Carter v Boehm*, 3 Burr 1905, 1909 (1766), authored by Lord Mansfield); YONG Q. HAN, *Disenchanting the Principles of Utmost Good Faith in Insurance Law*, 115 J. GANSU INST POL SCI & LAW 153 (2011); Deborah F Cohen, Timothy E DeMassi & Aaron Krauss, Uberrimae Fidei *and Reinsurance Rescission: Does a Gentlemen's Agreement Have a Place in Today's Commercial Market?*, 29 TORT & INS L.J. 602, 603 (1994).

## [C] Relationship between the Insurer/Reinsured and the Reinsurer

Reinsurance normally refers to a contract between two or more insurance companies, where the reinsurer agrees to indemnify the reinsured (ceding company) in whole or in part for a loss sustained by the original third party insured.

*Query*: Should such a contract be interpreted under contra proferentem and "common man or woman in the marketplace" principles, or are both insurance companies "sophisticated policyholders" in bargaining and contracting on an equal basis? The following case illustrates the contractual rights and obligations, and interpretive conundrum, between a self-insured entity, a primary excess insurer, and a secondary excess reinsurer.

### Christiana General Insurance Corporation of New York v. Great American Insurance Company

United States District Court, Southern District of New York
745 F. Supp. 150 (1990)

**Leisure, District Judge.**

.... The essential facts of this action are not in dispute. The disputed issues will be discussed below in the body of this opinion. This case arises out of reinsurance contracts between the parties. For four policy years stretching from 1980 to 1984, plaintiff Christiana General Insurance Company of New York ("Christiana") agreed by contract to reinsure certain risks insured by defendant Great American Insurance Company "GAIC"). In the instant action, Great American was an excess insurer on a policy issued to American Honda Motor Company, Inc. ("American Honda"), and to various American Honda subsidiaries and affiliates. For the 1980 and 1981 policy years, GAIC's contract with American Honda stated that GAIC would provide $10 million in coverage in excess of $15 million dollars in losses. Thus, should American Honda's insured losses for one of those years exceed $15 million, GAIC would be obligated to cover those losses, up to $10 million. For the 1982 policy year, GAIC provided $10 million in coverage in excess of $17 million, and for the 1983 policy year, GAIC provided $7 million in coverage in excess of $18 million.

In each of the policy years 1980 through 1983, Christiana reinsured a portion of GAIC's liability obligation to American Honda. Reinsurance is a contract between two insurance companies designed to spread the risks associated with insuring large accounts. Under a reinsurance contract, one insurer, known as the ceding insurer, transfers all or a portion of the risk it has underwritten to another insurer, known as the reinsurer, for a portion of the premium paid by the insured to the ceding insurer. As Judge Kevin Duffy of this Court has succinctly put it, "Reinsurance is simply an insurance policy issued to insurers." ...

In the instant case, GAIC, after entering into its insurance agreement with American Honda, utilized a licensed New York reinsurance intermediary, Willcox, Barringer & Co. ("Willcox"), who brokered GAIC's American Honda liability to a number of reinsurance companies, including Christiana. Provision 7 of each of the facultative reinsurance certificates provides:

> Prompt notice shall be given by the Company [GAIC] to the Reinsurer of any occurrence or accident which appears likely to involve this reinsurance and, while the Reinsurer does not undertake to investigate or defend claims or suits, the Reinsurer through its representative and/or counsel, shall nevertheless have the right and be given the opportunity to associate with the Company and its representatives at the Reinsurer's expense in the defense and control of any claim, suit or proceeding which may involve this reinsurance, with the full cooperation of the Company.

It is this provision that underlies much of plaintiff's allegations in this action. Plaintiff asserts that defendant failed to give adequate notice to its reinsurers that defendant's excess insurance layer was likely to be pierced for most or all of the policy years reinsured in part by defendant. Plaintiff further alleges that failure to provide prompt notice to plaintiff and other reinsurers constituted a breach of a fiduciary duty of good faith owed to the reinsurers by GAIC. Finally, plaintiff contends that GAIC misrepresented the products and risks being reinsured, thus misleading plaintiff and other reinsurers into accepting risks they otherwise would have rejected.

American Honda is the wholly-owned United States subsidiary of the well-known Japanese manufacturer of automobiles, motorcycles, power equipment and related products. American Honda is the exclusive distributor of Honda products in the United States.... Among the Honda products distributed by American Honda are all-terrain vehicles ("ATVs"). ATV's are three- or four-wheeled motorized vehicles capable of operating off-road. They come in a number of models designed for a variety of purposes. Some of the more powerful models, particularly in a four-wheel configuration, can be used as a small tractor. During the late 1970s and early 1980s, however, ATVs were principally marketed as recreational vehicles. Apparently, many users treated ATVs in a manner previously reserved for "dirt bikes"—racing them off-road or attempting to traverse difficult terrain at relatively high speeds. Most states did not require a driver's license or any other type of permit to operate an ATV, and only a few states required riders to wear a helmet or other protective gear. Accordingly, it was not uncommon for children under the age of sixteen to operate ATVs with little or no training or protective clothing.

ATVs, it turns out, were not well designed for the activities for which many Americans purchased them. The three-wheeled versions, which look similar to large, motorized tricycles with oversized, deep-tread tires, were particularly popular with off-road enthusiasts. The smaller, less-powerful three-wheel ATVs were popular amongst teenagers and children both as recreational vehicles and, in some cases, as a form of transportation. ATVs, particularly the three-wheeled models, turned out to be unstable and deceptively difficult to operate. In the early 1980s, as the popularity of ATVs began to increase, the number of accidents resulting from ATV use increased dramatically. The injuries suffered in ATV accidents were often severe. By mid-1985, there were 161 ATV-related deaths reported nationwide for the period from 1982 to 1985. Of those victims, 73 were under the age of sixteen, and 39 were under the age of twelve. There were also numerous reports of accident victims with severe brain and spinal cord injuries.

In the spring of 1985 the Federal Consumer Product Safety Commission ("CPSC") released a report, indicating that ATVs might pose an unreasonable risk of injury. Two months after its first announcement, the CPSC issued a proposed rule, designed to reduce the risks associated with ATVs, and initiated judicial action to ban the products as unduly hazardous. The CPSC action spurred journalistic interest in the ATVs. Between the two CPSC announcements in the spring of 1985, the ABC television news show 20/20 aired a segment which focused on the risks associated with ATVs, and on some of the accidents which had resulted from ATV use. Despite this publicity, American Honda continued to market and sell ATVs. Finally, in 1988, with injuries and deaths from ATV use continuing to mount, American Honda and its parent entered into a consent decree with the CPSC to reduce the harm associated with ATVs. Specifically, American Honda agreed to cease selling all three-wheel ATVs, to limit sales of the remaining models to buyers of an appropriate age, and to undertake an extensive program to promote safe ATV use. This consent decree has, apparently, resulted in a significant reduction in ATV-related injuries.

The legacy of the ATVs is obvious in the instant action. As early as 1985, it was clear to at least some of American Honda's primary and excess insurers that the ATVs posed a serious liability problem. The number of lawsuits arising from ATV accidents was rising rapidly, and many of those claims were for substantial injuries which would likely result in large awards or settlements. By the fall of 1987, led by the ATV cases, liability claims against American Honda had pierced, or were on the verge of piercing, GAIC's layer of excess insurance for the 1980 through 1983 policy years. By 1988, ATV losses exceeded those for all other Honda products combined. These losses have resulted in a significant drain on GAIC's layer of insurance, and thus has resulted in GAIC calling on its reinsurers, including Christiana, for indemnification under the facultative certificates.

Christiana has refused to indemnify GAIC for losses on the American Honda account. Christiana alleges that it was not notified of its potential liability in a timely fashion, and that GAIC misrepresented to Christiana at the time of the reinsurance contracts which products were being insured. Additionally, Christiana alleges that by not giving earlier notice of potential liability to it reinsurers, GAIC breached a duty of good faith to those reinsurers.

As noted above, the extent of the potential liability problems arising from ATV use began to surface in 1985, with the action by the CPSC and the resulting media attention. Just as the public awareness of the ATV problem was growing, there apparently was knowledge among American Honda's insurers that the ATV losses, along with the expected losses from other Honda products, could well result in major liability for the insurers. In April 1985, Johnson & Higgins, who acted as American Honda's insurance broker, informed GAIC that, given the current rate of loss for the 1979 and 1980 policy years, it was possible that GAIC's layer of insurance could become involved in covering the claimed losses. A month later, Johnson & Higgins notified GAIC that existing claims might also involve the 1982 policy year. Within GAIC, some concern was expressed during 1985 about the extent of GAIC's possible exposure on it American Honda policies. Johnson & Higgins forwarded at least some case files to GAIC for their review.

Throughout 1986, there was continuous activity within GAIC regarding the American Honda account. Officials within GAIC were aware of the company's potential exposure for one or more policy years. However, it is clear that no one at GAIC knew which policy year would definitely be affected, or when GAIC's insurance layer for any one of those policy years would actually be pierced and GAIC would be required to take over management of any claims.

In November 1986, GAIC was informed by INA that it was possible that INA's layer of insurance for the 1983 policy year would be expended during the following 12 months. That same month, American Honda indicated to GAIC that it was likely that GAIC's layer for at least some years would be penetrated within the next six months. This information apparently led Jerry Runnels ("Runnels"), a vice-president of GAIC in the claims department [to write] to a colleague, Robert Adams ("Adams"), a vice-president in the accounting department, that it appeared that GAIC's layer would be penetrated soon for at least two policy years. It is clear from this memo that GAIC did not have a complete picture of their potential liability, or the timeframe in which it would arise.

Plaintiff has made much of the fact that GAIC knew, through Runnels, that by early 1987 GAIC's layer of insurance had been penetrated on an incurred basis. There are two ways of calculating losses on an insurance policy: on an incurred basis, and on a paid basis. Incurred losses are losses actually paid plus reserves put in place to cover what are expected losses based on pending claims. Paid losses are just that: losses actually paid. An excess insurer, and thus its reinsurers, are not actually called upon to participate in claims handling and coverage until the underlying levels of insurance have been exceeded on a paid basis. Thus, the fact that INA's and American Honda's figures in 1986 and early 1987 indicated that GAIC's layer was penetrated on an incurred basis did not mean that GAIC at that point was required to participate in any existing claims. It simply indicated a strong possibility that, should INA's reserve figures prove to be correct, GAIC's layer would eventually be involved. However, it remained at least theoretically possible that GAIC's layer would never actually be called upon to make payments, and it was certainly true that there would be a gap in time between when GAIC's layer was penetrated on an incurred basis and when it would be penetrated on a paid basis.

### Governing Law

The parties agree that New York law applies to this action. The reinsurance contracts were negotiated, issued, and made in New York by a New York reinsurance company. Additionally, New York would be the place of performance under the contracts. These are sufficient contacts to justify the application of New York law under the New York choice of law doctrine.

### Notice to Reinsurers

New York law strongly supports prompt notice clauses in primary insurance contracts. Failure by an insured to meet a contractual notice requirement excuses an insurer's performance, regardless of whether the insurer was prejudiced by the late notice. An insured's late notice may be excused in certain limited cases. "The reasonableness of a particular insured's delay in providing notice is ordinarily a question of fact reserved for trial. In the absence of a reasonable excuse or mitigating factor for the delay, however, the timeliness of the insured's notice may be disposed of as a matter of law in advance of trial. It is noteworthy that even relatively short periods of delay repeatedly have been found to be unreasonable as a matter of law in the absence of a reasonable excuse or mitigating factor." *Travelers* [*Ins. Co. v. Buffalo Reinsurance Co.*], 735 F. Supp. at 500 [(S.D.N.Y. 1990)]. Thus, if plaintiff in the instant action were a primary insurer and defendant were an insured, the sole questions before the Court would be whether the notice provided to plaintiff was timely, and whether defendant had put forth a reasonable excuse or mitigating factor justifying and untimeliness.

However, this case is more complex than the normal late notice action. This action involves a contract between an insurer and a reinsurer, where the underlying insurance is an excess, rather than primary, policy, and the liability at issue arose from an unexpected liability crisis. Each of these factors has an impact on the Court's analysis of the "prompt notice" provision in the reinsurance contract and of GAIC's actions in relation to that provision.

There is a remarkable absence of case law in New York on the relationship between reinsurers and reinsured. In particular, it is far from clear how New York courts would apply the law of prompt notice in primary insurance cases to cases involving reinsurance. It is not clear whether "prompt notice" has the same meaning in the rein-surance context as it does in the primary insurance context. It is also not clear whether prejudice must be shown by the reinsurer, even though a primary insurer enforcing a notice provision is not required to show prejudice. It appears that only one court in this state has confronted the issue of notice in the reinsurance context. That court decided that the issues in reinsurance were sufficiently distinguishable from those in primary insurance to justify a different notice rule, which requires a showing of prej-udice by the reinsurer before that reinsurer is excused from its obligations.

In the instant case, Christiana asserts that notice should have been given as early as 1985 when the publicity regarding ATVs indicated that a major liability crisis was brewing for all Honda insurers. Christiana points to the 20/20 broadcast, the CPSC reports, and deposition testimony from GAIC employees to show that GAIC was aware by late 1985 that there was a possibility that its layer of insurance would become involved at some point due to the number of serious ATV accidents. If the Court were to find notice unnecessary in 1985, Christiana asserts that notice by late 1986 should be required, when GAIC received information from INA that its layer of in-surance had been exhausted on an incurred basis. Finally, Christiana claims that notice at the very latest should have been provided in April 1987 when, after com-pletion of the audit of the American Honda account, it became clear to GAIC that the piercing of its layer on a paid basis was imminent.

After reviewing the existing case law and applying it to the relationship between an excess insurer and its reinsurer, the Court finds that a reinsurer must show prejudice from late notice before it can be excused from its liability under the reinsurance con-tract. The policy considerations underlying New York's rule that a primary insurer need not demonstrate prejudice when an insured breaches a notice provision are not present in a reinsurance contract. Reinsurers have no duty to defend claims, nor is the potential staleness of a claim as significant a concern to a reinsurer as it is to a primary insurer. Thus, reinsurers must show prejudice from the allegedly late notice in order to avoid liability under a reinsurance contract.

Additionally, the Court does not find that notice to the reinsurers was required at any time prior to April 1987. Upon review of the record, the Court agrees with GAIC that, up to the time of the completion of the audit in April 1987, actual penetration of GAIC's layers, while likely, was far from certain, and the timing of such penetration was speculative. Only when it is sufficiently certain that the excess insurer's layer will be pierced on a paid basis, so that the excess insurer sets reserves for probable claims, should the excess insurer be required to inform its reinsurers that their liability is likely to be affected. Even absent this logical standard, the Court does not find that the notice provision in the case at bar would have required notice at a date earlier than May 1987. It is clear from the record before the Court that GAIC knew from at least the second half of 1986 that it was likely that its layer of insurance would be pierced for at least some policy years. However, until completion of the audit, it was uncertain when GAIC's layer would be pierced in which policy years, and which of the hundreds of ATV and other claims were likely to become GAIC's responsibility.

The Court thus finds that a reinsurer must show prejudice from late notice before the reinsurer may be relieved of liability. Further, the Court finds that the appropriate date for notice to the reinsurers in the instant case was April 1987. Finally, the Court finds there to be a genuine issue of material fact as to whether the actual notice given to the reinsurers in June 1987 was sufficient given the custom and practice in the reinsurance industry. Accordingly, the parties' cross-motions for summary judgment on this issue of late notice is denied.

### GAIC's Duty to Christiana

Christiana asserts that a reinsured has a fiduciary duty to act with the utmost good faith, and that that duty was breached by GAIC. Specifically, Christiana claims that GAIC took a number of actions prior to 1987 to avoid or prevent notice to its reinsurers, that GAIC failed to investigate adequately the extent of possible liability, despite indications of such liability; and, finally, that GAIC failed to provide sufficient information to its reinsurers at the August 1987 meeting.

The Court must first examine the nature of the relationship between reinsurers and ceding insurers. Plaintiff has not cited a single case that indicates clearly that a ceding insurer owes a fiduciary duty to it facultative reinsurer. There is law, however, that indicates that a ceding insurer owes a non-fiduciary duty of good faith to its reinsurer. However, nothing in the cases cited by the parties, or discovered by the Court, indicates that the duty between a ceding insurer and a facultative reinsurer rises to the level of being a fiduciary one.

### Misrepresentation

The parties agree that rescission may be granted where the reinsured makes a material misrepresentation to the reinsurer. The issues before the Court are whether any misrepresentations were made to plaintiff, and, if misrepresentations are found to exist, whether those misrepresentations are material so as to warrant rescission.

GAIC does not deny that Christiana was never explicitly informed that ATVs were a part of the risk it was reinsuring. GAIC does claim, however, that recision in this instance would be inappropriate because GAIC did not knowingly withhold any information within its possession from Christiana. GAIC further asserts that the failure to disclose ATVs as a separate risk was not material at the time Christiana entered into the reinsurance contracts at issue.

The Court has carefully reviewed the record, and finds that Christiana cannot now support its assertion that this information was material. The Court has no doubt that by late 1985, information that ATVs were included in the proposed coverage was material to any risk determination. By 1985, both CPSC and the national media had publicized what was then a growing risk posed by ATVs, and a then-increasing number of ATV-related injuries.

## Notes and Questions

1. The *Christiana* case was appealed to the Second Circuit Court of Appeals, which found that: (1) under New York law, an excess layer reinsured (Great American) may

have a duty to notify its reinsurer (Christiana) of a potential claim under its policy, even prior to setting reserves for the insured risk, but; (2) Great American had no duty to disclose a risk of loss that it did not itself consider material in deciding to issue its policy, absent a specific inquiry by its reinsurer, Christiana; and (3) the mere fact that the reinsured, Great American, may have been entitled to rescind its policy based on Honda's nondisclosures did not relieve the reinsurer, Christiana, of its obligation to indemnify the reinsured. 979 F.2d 268 (2d Cir. 1992) (affirmed in part, reversed in part, and remanded).

2. On the issue of the rules of notice for reinsurers as compared to insurers, the New York Court of Appeals (New York's highest court) weighed in shortly after the *Christiana* decision and disappointed the reinsurance community by holding that reinsurers were not entitled to the benefit of New York's strict notice law then in effect, which did not excuse late notice to an insurer even when the insurer is not prejudiced by the delay. Instead, reinsurers operating under New York law must demonstrate that they have been prejudiced by late notice (which is essentially the rule in almost all other states). *See Unigard Sec. Ins. Co. v. North River Ins. Co.*, 79 N.Y.2d 576, 584 N.Y.S.2d 290, 594 N.E.2d 571 (1992). Because insurance law is largely state law, the *Unigard* decision controls in federal court.

For a time, there was some uncertainty over whether excess insurers in New York were subject to the "no-prejudice-required" notice rule of insurance or the "prejudice-required" rule of reinsurance. The Court of Appeals eventually determined the excess insurers were more like primary insurers for purposes of state law and policy on notice and held that an excess insurer may prevail on a defense of late notice even in the absence of prejudice from the delay. *See American Home Assur. Co. v. International Ins. Co.*, 90 N.Y.2d 433, 661 N.Y.S.2d 584, 684 N.E.2d 14 (1997).

Subsequent to these cases distinguishing between primary insurers, excess insurers, and reinsurers regarding notice, New York enacted legislation relaxing its traditional strict rule that late notice to a primary insurer voids coverage even if the primary insurer was not prejudiced by the delay in notice. *See* Chapter 7. Thus, the distinctions that fomented the *Christiana* and *Unigard* litigation are now largely moot — but the cases nonetheless illustrate the distinctions between primary insurance and reinsurance.

3. Contract ambiguity and fraudulent non-disclosure of material facts are two commonly litigated reasons to rescind a contract between an insurance company and a reinsurance company. The problem with such alleged ambiguity in the insurance contract, however, is that experienced insurance executives, their underwriters, brokers, and attorneys normally negotiate and draft these reinsurance contracts; and these sophisticated negotiating parties are, therefore, not the normal "unversed layman" or "common man or woman in the marketplace" when it comes to insurance contract interpretation. How then should alleged contract ambiguity in reinsurance contracts between sophisticated insurers be interpreted? The courts are split on this issue. Some courts still apply the contra proferentem doctrine of ambiguities in favor of the non-drafting party, regardless of the parties' sophistication and knowledge of

insurance contract interpretation principles. Other courts, due to the parties' sophistication in insurance law matters, refuse to apply the contra proferentem ambiguities doctrine.

Still other courts arguably apply a "middle ground" position to ambiguous insurance contract provisions between sophisticated insurers and reinsurers. These courts apply the contra proferentem doctrine of ambiguities only when the intent of the parties cannot be determined by the use of extrinsic evidence, such as trade custom and usage in the insurance industry. *See* Jeffrey W. Stempel, *Reassessing the "Sophisticated" Policyholder Defense in Insurance Coverage Litigation*, 42 DRAKE L. REV. 807 (1993); Hazel G. Beh, *Reassessing the Sophisticated Insured Exception*, 39 TORT TRIAL & INS. PRAC. L.J. 85 (2004).

4. Because insurance contract interpretation disputes will often arise between the insurer and the reinsurer, the reinsurance contract may also provide for arbitration of disputes between the insurer and the reinsurer.

### PROBLEM SIX

American Insurance Company [AIC] was the primary insurer of Dow Chemical Corporation, and North American Company for Property and Casualty Insurance [NACPAC] was the reinsurer.

The original liability insurance contract between AIC and Dow provided coverage for both compensatory and punitive damages, but the reinsurance contract between AIC and NACPAC excluded coverage for punitive damages.

Dow was sued in an action for both compensatory and punitive damages based upon a fire in a building insulated by Styrofoam, a Dow Corporation product.

AIC settled this legal claim for both punitive and compensatory damages. It then sued NACPAC under a standard reinsurance "follow the fortunes" clause which provided that "All claims involving this reinsurance, when settled by the [insurer], shall be binding on the reinsurer."

• How should the court decide this case?

## [D] The Duty of Utmost Good Faith and the Follow-the-Fortunes Doctrine

Although reinsurance is not standardized to the degree found with front-line insurance, certain provisions are widespread and expected in the typical reinsurance contract. One such term is the "follow-the-fortunes" clause. It generally provides that the reinsurer shall be bound by the insurer's coverage obligations as imposed by judgment.

Relatedly, the "follow-the-settlements" doctrine binds reinsurers to the good faith settlements made by the insurer. American courts tend to label almost all aspects of a reinsurer's inability to re-litigate the reinsured's fate concerning a claim as a "follow the fortunes" matter. English and European attorneys and entities tend to draw a more pronounced line. They tend to use follow-the-fortunes as referring to only adjudicated (or otherwise imposed) outcomes and to use follow-the-settlements to refer solely to situations where the reinsured has settled a claim for an agreed payment rather than being on the receiving end of an adverse judgment. PRICL Article 2.4.3 provides that

> [t]he reinsurer shall follow the fortunes of the reinsured and follow the settlements of the reinsured by reimbursing the reinsured for payment of loss covered by the reinsurance contract and arguably covered by the primary insurance contract.

In other words, if the insurer/reinsured is hit with a verdict—even a "runaway" verdict awarding more than a reasonable amount in compensation—the reinsurer is as "stuck" with the outcome as is the insurer/reinsured. When the insurer/reinsured resolves a claim that "arguably" falls within coverage, the reinsurer is bound by the settlement so long as it was made in good faith, even if the reinsurer thinks the insurer/reinsured overpaid to resolve the claim. Absent unusual circumstances or misconduct by the insurer/reinsured, reinsurers are not permitted to relitigate good faith, reasonable, non-collusive settlements any more than they are permitted to relitigate judicial outcomes.

Although a collusive or fraudulent arrangement between claimant, policyholder, and insurer should not bind the reinsurer, the reinsurer normally is stuck with whatever transpires on the risk. Although the reinsurer may think that the insurer "blinked" too quickly by agreeing to arguably disputable coverage or paying too large a settlement to avoid a litigation threat, the purpose of the follow-the-fortunes/follow-the-settlements doctrine is to prevent another round of expensive litigation on these issues.

The doctrine thus provides a substantial measure of protection to the insurer in making judgment calls as to defense of a claim, accepting or disputing coverage, and settlement of the claim. This way, the insurer need not walk on eggshells or look constantly over its shoulder worrying about whether its reinsurers will disagree with the insurer's assessment of a matter.

But what are the practical limits of the follow-the-fortunes concept? What are the confines of this duty of utmost good faith duty and what are the consequences of breach?

## ReliaStar Life Insurance Company v. IOA Re, Inc.

United States Court of Appeals for the Eighth Circuit
303 F.3d 874 (2002)

**Bowman, Circuit Judge.**

ReliaStar Life Insurance Company sued IOA Re, Inc. and Swiss Re Life Canada (collectively, the retrocessionaires) for breach of contract arising out of an alleged failure to pay under reinsurance contracts. IOA Re and Swiss Re counterclaimed, alleging that they were entitled to rescind the reinsurance contracts, and that in any case ReliaStar committed a breach of contract by failing to remit premiums to the retrocessionaires. The parties filed cross-motions for summary judgment in the District Court, and the court denied the retrocessionaires' motion for partial summary judgment and granted ReliaStar's motion for summary judgment. The retrocessionaires appeal. We affirm, but remand for clarification of one issue related to the District Court's award of damages to ReliaStar.

ReliaStar is a reinsurance company based in Minnesota. For the 1996 to 1997 policy year, ReliaStar reinsured the risk of Canada Life Assurance Company on a product commonly called "snowbird" insurance. This type of insurance provides "short-term medical insurance for individual Canadians traveling out of their home provinces [including out of country], where Canadian provincial medical coverage did not extend." Br. of Plaintiff-Appellee at 3. Canada Life ceded to ReliaStar its risk for seventy-five percent of the first $100,000 (Canadian) of each claim under the program; in exchange, ReliaStar was to receive seventy-five percent of the net premium collected. This variety of risk sharing is known as a quota-share arrangement.

ReliaStar then sought to spread the risk ceded to it by Canada Life through quota-share reinsurance from IOA Re, a Delaware corporation, and Swiss Re, a Canadian company. Reinsurers of a reinsurer, such as IOA Re and Swiss Re in this case, are known in the industry as retrocessionaires, and the coverage they provide is known as retrocessional coverage. Swiss Re's participation was arranged through a company called Reinsurance Management Associates (RMA), a managing general underwriter which "accepted risk and performed various administrative and management functions for insurance carrier clients." Br. of Plaintiff-Appellee at 6. Swiss Re issued a retrocessional placement slip for this coverage sometime in December 1996, and ReliaStar ceded one-third of its exposure under the Canada Life reinsurance policy (amounting to twenty-five percent of the total insurance liability of Canada Life) to Swiss Re. In return, Swiss Re was to receive twenty-five percent of the net premium collected by Canada Life.

IOA Re is also a managing general underwriter, and it accepted the retrocessional coverage from ReliaStar on behalf of the pool of other companies for which IOA Re provided services. Answer and Counterclaim of Defendants at 3. IOA Re signed a retrocessional placement slip for this coverage in early 1997, also assuming one-third of ReliaStar's liability in exchange for twenty-five percent of the net premium collected.

The snowbird insurance program for the 1996 to 1997 policy period paid out more than expected on claims and ended in a loss position. Before the end of the policy period, Canada Life began to bill losses to ReliaStar that exceeded the net premiums paid to ReliaStar. On October 2, 1997, ReliaStar submitted the first bills to the retrocessionaires for their portion of the losses. ReliaStar submitted these losses for payment despite the fact that it had not forwarded any premium payments to either retrocessionaire. ReliaStar maintains that it deducted the net premium payments to which the retrocessionaires were entitled from the amount of losses billed to them.

In November 1998, IOA Re notified ReliaStar that it was "canceling the Certificate of Reinsurance" and "rescinding the retrocessional coverage therein," for reasons that included non-payment of premium and failure to provide requested documentation of claims. Swiss Re, although it had reconfirmed its intention to pay in a May 1998 fax to ReliaStar, similarly refused to make any payments to ReliaStar, and eventually claimed that they owed no payment to ReliaStar. Br. of Plaintiff-Appellee at 13.

ReliaStar filed this diversity action in December 1999, bringing breach of contract claims under Minnesota law against the retrocessionaires for failure to pay under the retrocessional contracts. The District Court, on cross-motions for summary judgment, held that ReliaStar was entitled to judgment as a matter of law on its breach of retrocession contract claims. The District Court awarded ReliaStar $2,606,684 (Canadian) from each defendant for the amounts ReliaStar paid to Canada Life, and awarded ReliaStar $541,779 from each defendant based on ReliaStar's evidence of lost investment income attributable to the retrocessionaires' refusal to pay. The court ordered the retrocessionaires to pay the judgment in U.S. dollars at the currency exchange rate as of the date the retrocessionaires first refused to pay the losses billed to them on October 2, 1997.

Reinsurance relationships are governed by the traditional principle of "utmost good faith." ... The duty of good faith is essential to the industry, inasmuch as "reinsurers depend on ceding insurers to provide information concerning potential liability on the underlying policies." ... Reinsurers must rely on this principle because they generally do not duplicate the functions of the ceding insurers, such as evaluating risks and processing claims. To arrange their business otherwise would result in greatly increased costs for both reinsurance and the underlying policies themselves.

Flowing from this duty of good faith is a doctrine, widely recognized in the insurance industry, known as the "follow-the-fortunes" doctrine. Essentially, this doctrine posits that if the cedent has acted in good faith in handling the claims presented to it and in providing coverage of the claims, "the reinsurer may not second guess the coverage decisions of the cedent." ...

The District Court, applying the follow-the-fortunes doctrine to the contracts at issue, held that ReliaStar had fulfilled its obligations under the contracts because it had not acted in bad faith, with gross negligence, or recklessly in paying the losses billed to it by Canada Life and in subsequently billing an appropriate portion of those losses to the retrocessionaires. The retrocessionaires take issue with the District Court's conclusion. They argue that their retrocessional contracts with ReliaStar expressly denied the application of the follow-the-fortunes doctrine. Moreover, they claim that the factual record contains "substantial material evidence of ReliaStar's gross negligence and recklessness in its claims handling processes, as well as significant evidence that ReliaStar had misrepresented the nature of the underlying insurance program."

In addition, they argue that the District Court erred in converting the damages award to U.S. dollars and in failing to clearly identify the applicable exchange rate for such a conversion. IOA Re and Swiss Re first find error in the District Court's rejection of their claim that they were entitled to rescind the retrocessional coverage they provided to ReliaStar because ReliaStar induced IOA Re and Swiss Re to enter the arrangements through misrepresentation. The District Court held that ReliaStar had not misrepresented any material fact and that IOA Re and Swiss Re therefore were not entitled to rescind their retrocessional coverage.

The usual rules of contract law apply to our examination of reinsurance contracts. Under Minnesota law, "one who has been induced to enter a contract by fraudulent misrepresentations may elect to rescind the contract." ... IOA Re and Swiss Re argue that ReliaStar failed to disclose or misrepresented to them various facts and thus they are permitted to rescind the retrocessional coverage they agreed to provide. They argue that the record contains "substantial evidence supporting their right to rescind the contract."

Upon careful examination of the record, we must disagree. The alleged "substantial evidence" cited by the retrocessionaires fails to adequately support their rescission claim. For example, IOA and Swiss argue that ReliaStar knew the snowbird program would be a "losing proposition" but failed to disclose this to either retrocessionaire. The portions of the record they cite to do not, however, support this assertion. In fact, in deposition testimony the retrocessionaires claim supports their argument, the witness admits that to his knowledge ReliaStar *did not know* the insurance was going to be in a loss position at the time that statements about the program's profitability were made to IOA Re and Swiss Re personnel.

The evidence cited in support of the other supposed misrepresentations, taken in the light most favorable to IOA Re and Swiss Re, also does not sustain the retrocessionaires' position. Their citations to the record do not point to any specific instances where ReliaStar, at the time it solicited reinsurance coverage from IOA Re and Swiss Re, misrepresented material facts regarding the snowbird insurance program.... We cannot see how this evidence could be construed, even in the most generous light, as constituting misrepresentations made by ReliaStar to either of the retrocessionaires.

The District Court rightly concluded that the retrocessionaires failed, as a matter of law, to put forth sufficient evidence in support of their claims to survive summary judgment on the question of whether the retrocessionaires had the right to rescind their contracts with ReliaStar on the basis of material misrepresentations.

IOA and Swiss Re next argue that the District Court erroneously applied the follow-the-fortunes doctrine to the facts of this case. The District Court held that the doctrine "requires a reinsurer to follow-the-fortunes [sic] of the ceding company and pay all reinsurance obligations." IOA and Swiss Re contend that the terms of their reinsurance contracts with ReliaStar "required strict proof of the claims paid by ReliaStar" and therefore the contracts did not incorporate the customary follow-the-fortunes doctrine.

They contend that their reinsurance contracts "incorporated the terms and conditions of the underlying reinsurance contract which required strict proof of coverage" and thus that under the terms of their contracts the follow-the-fortunes doctrine does not apply to their retrocessional coverage of ReliaStar's risk.

The District Court rejected the argument that the retrocessional agreements incorporate any limiting language that might be found in the Canada Life/ReliaStar reinsurance agreement. The court concluded that IOA Re and Swiss Re failed to introduce any evidence "indicating that ReliaStar consented to adopting the limitations included in the reinsurance contract between Canada Life and ReliaStar." The court explained that the retrocessional placement slips merely identify the "pertinent insurance contract."

Under Minnesota law, construction of a contract, including deciding whether it is ambiguous, is a legal determination.... If after examining the entire contract it is not subject to more than one reasonable interpretation, then there is no ambiguity.... We give the policy terms "their plain, ordinary, and popular meaning," ... without resort to parol evidence....

IOA Re and Swiss Re rely on affidavits from their employees that state they understood that the underlying Canada Life/ReliaStar agreement would "form a part of the retrocessional agreement." This "understanding" is not sufficient as a matter of law to create ambiguity in the contract and thus create a material issue of fact precluding summary judgment on this issue.

Looking to the plain language of the reinsurance agreements, we fail to see any ambiguity in the contract terms. The retrocessionaires seize upon language in the retrocessional placement slips that states, "Conditions: See attached ETFS Travel Health Medical Reinsurance Agreement," to argue that the retrocession contracts incorporated the loss notice and settlement procedures agreed to between Canada Life and ReliaStar. We disagree.

The plain purpose of these slips is to set out the parties to the retrocession agreement, the period of coverage, and the coverage that the retrocessionaire is to provide, among other details. These other details include identifying the portion of the insured risk that is being ceded to the retrocessionaire. Taken as a whole, the language of these slips, and in particular the conditions clause, cannot reasonably be interpreted as sweeping under its scope a set of specific procedures agreed to between Canada Life and ReliaStar in a separate agreement to which neither of the retrocessionaires were a party.

The language in question certainly does not make explicit that the retrocessional contract incorporates those specific terms. We conclude that the loss settlement procedures of the underlying insurance policy did not form part of the operative terms of the retrocessional contracts at issue. Thus, we reject the argument that the parties entered into any express contractual undertakings, as between the retrocessionaires and ReliaStar, to preempt application of the customary follow-the-fortunes doctrine.

The retrocessionaires further challenge the District Court's application of the follow-the-fortunes doctrine to this case because they claim that the existence of an industry custom is a question of fact that should be left to a jury. We note that the record does not reflect any dispute between the two sides as to the existence of this custom. To the contrary, the retrocessionaires' expert admits that "[a] reinsurer has the duty to 'follow the fortunes' of the cedent or retrocedent as long as the losses paid are covered under the underlying contract or policy and fall within the terms and conditions of the reinsurance treaty." ... He further agrees that the "follow-the-fortunes" obligation is "customary with reinsurance contracts." ... He explains that this custom applies unless "the reinsured has not dealt with the reinsurer or retrocessionaire in the 'utmost good faith' [or] ... the reinsured fails to prove reinsured losses." ...

ReliaStar's expert agrees that follow-the-fortunes is a "key principle[]" of the reinsurance business, and means "when the ceding company has paid claims in good faith, the reinsurer may not second guess such payment but must fulfill its own payment obligations." ... Thus, there does not appear to be a dispute between the parties as to the nature of the follow-the-fortunes doctrine and as to its customary application in the reinsurance business. The real dispute appears to be whether the language of the parties' contracts rendered this industry custom inapplicable to their insurance arrangement. Having concluded that the contracts did not contain "anti-follow-the-fortunes" provisions, the District Court, we believe, was correct to apply the customary follow-the-fortunes doctrine to the dispute at hand.

The retrocessionaires next argue that if the follow-the-fortunes doctrine applies to them, then the District Court erred in concluding that ReliaStar had not acted in bad faith, because ReliaStar had not shown it "acted in a reasonable, businesslike fashion, and that it submitted legitimate, reinsured losses." ... They contend that the District Court erred in interpreting "bad faith" to require proof of "deliberate deception, gross negligence, or recklessness," or even fraudulent behavior.

In *American Bankers Insurance v. Northwestern National Insurance*, [198 F.3d 1332 (11th Cir. 1999),] the Eleventh Circuit discussed the question of what constitutes good faith in the context of a ceding insurer's payment or settlement of claims.... In that case, the court concluded that "simple negligence cannot be enough to establish bad faith," because otherwise "every decision by the ceding insurance company could be second-guessed and litigated under a simple negligence standard." *Id.* The court therefore concluded "that the proper minimum standard for bad faith should be deliberate deception, gross negligence or recklessness." ... One court has even described this standard as requiring "an extraordinary showing of a disingenuous or dishonest failure to carry out a contract." *North River Ins. Co. v. CIGNA Reinsurance Co.*, 52 F.3d 1194, 1216 (3d Cir. 1995). We agree with the formulation of "bad faith" adopted by other circuits in the just-cited cases, and we adopt the same standard as our own. We therefore hold that the District Court did not err in applying this standard to the "bad faith" question in this case.

Moreover and despite IOA Re's and Swiss Re's arguments to the contrary, a thorough review of the record convinces us that the retrocessionaires have not presented evidence sufficient to make a submissible case on their allegations of bad faith. The record reflects problems with the snowbird insurance program and with the claims documentation (as noted in the IIAS audit report), among other issues. It also reflects efforts by ReliaStar to provide information to the retrocessionaires and to determine how it could change the snowbird program to prevent similar losses in future policy terms. We conclude that, as a matter of law, the evidence the retrocessionaires point to does not amount to evidence of "deliberate deception, gross negligence or reck-lessness." Summary judgment on this issue in favor of ReliaStar was appropriate.

Finally, the retrocessionaires argue that they are not obligated to pay ReliaStar's loss claims because ReliaStar failed to comply with the loss-notice and claims deadlines contained in the underlying insurance. Because we already have concluded that these terms were not incorporated into the retrocessional coverage contracts with IOA Re and Swiss Re, we conclude that summary judgment was appropriate on these disputed claims.

## Bellefonte Reinsurance Co. v. Aetna Casualty and Surety Co.

United States Court of Appeals for the Second Circuit
903 F.2d 910 (1990)

**Timbers, Circuit Judge.**

Appellant Aetna Casualty and Surety Co. ("Aetna") appeals from a summary judg-ment entered November 28, 1989, in the Southern District of New York, John F. Keenan, *District Judge*, in favor of appellees, six reinsurance companies ("the rein-surers"). The district court held that the reinsurers were not obligated to pay Aetna any additional sums for defense costs over and above the limits on liability stated in the reinsurance certificates.

The sole issue on appeal is whether the reinsurers are obligated to pay additional sums for defense costs over and above the limits stated in the reinsurance certificates.

For the reasons which follow, we affirm the judgment of the district court.

We summarize only those facts and prior proceedings believed necessary to an understanding of the issue raised on appeal.

This appeal arises out of the explosion of litigation over the Dalkon Shield in-trauterine device. Aetna was the primary insurer of A.H. Robins Co., manufacturer of the Dalkon Shield. Appellees are six reinsurance companies that agreed to reinsure a portion of Aetna's risk.

From 1968 through 1977, Aetna issued primary and excess insurance policies which insured Robins against liability for personal injuries arising from use of Robins' products. From 1971 through 1976, the reinsurers issued certificates of facultative reinsurance which would reinsure specified portions of the excess insurance policies issued by Aetna for Robins.

After a number of products liability actions were brought against Robins, Aetna and Robins had a dispute over the extent of Aetna's liability as insurer for expenses incurred in defending the actions. Robins commenced a declaratory judgment action against Aetna in the Chancery Court in Richmond, Virginia. It sought a decision that defense costs were to be paid by Aetna, regardless of whether those defense costs exceeded the limitations of liability stated in the excess insurance policies. In 1984, the parties settled their dispute. Aetna agreed to pay an amount substantially in excess of the cap stated in the policies ($72 million more, according to appellees). The reinsurers did not participate in these settlement negotiations. They did not sign the agreement.

After signing the settlement agreement, Aetna turned to the reinsurers for a portion of the excess. Aetna had signed separate reinsurance agreements with each of the six reinsurers, but all of the certificates contain relevant provisions which are substantially the same. The following excerpts are from the certificate of appellee Constitution Reinsurance Corp.:

> "[Provision 1] [Reinsurer] ... does hereby reinsure Aetna ... (herein called the Company) in respect of the Company's contract hereinafter described, in consideration of the payment of the premium and subject to the terms, conditions and amount of liability set forth herein, as follows.... [Provision 2] Reinsurance Accepted$500,000 part of $5,000,000 excess of $10,000,000 excess of underlying limits ... [Provision 3] The Company warrants to retain for its own account ... the amount of liability specified ... above, and the liability of the Reinsurer specified ... above [i.e., amount of reinsurance accepted] shall follow that of the Company.... [Provision 4] All claims involving this reinsurance, when settled by the Company, shall be binding on the Reinsurer, which shall be bound to pay its proportion of such settlements, and in addition thereto, in the ratio that the Reinsurer's loss payment bears to the Company's gross loss payment, its proportion of expenses ... incurred by the Company in the investigation and settlement of claims or suits...."

The reinsurers conceded that they were liable up to the amount of the limitation of liability provisions (Provisions 1 and 2) of each of the reinsurance certificates, but refused to pay any share of the excess amount. Aetna sought a sum totaling more than $5 million—from all of the reinsurers combined—in excess of the liability caps.

The reinsurers commenced the instant action in 1985, seeking a declaratory judgment limiting their liability to the amount stated in the reinsurance certificates. Aetna answered and counterclaimed for a declaratory judgment that the reinsurance certificates obligated the reinsurers to "follow the fortunes" of Aetna and indemnify Aetna for the excess defense costs owed to Robins. The reinsurers and Aetna both moved for summary judgment.

In an opinion dated September 5, 1989, the district court held that the dollar amount typed in the column entitled "Reinsurance Accepted" was an overall limitation, and that the reinsurance certificates were cost-inclusive and capped by that amount. In an opinion dated November 21, 1989, the court denied Aetna's motion for reconsideration. The order granting the reinsurers' motion for summary judgment was entered November 28. This appeal followed.

The sole issue presented on this appeal is whether the reinsurers are obligated to Aetna for an amount greater than the amounts stated in the reinsurance certificates.

We are mindful in interpreting the agreements that, as with all contracts, they should be construed, if possible, so as to give effect to all of their material provisions.

We turn first to Aetna's contention that the "follow the fortunes" doctrine of reinsurance law obligates a reinsurer to indemnify a reinsured for all of the reinsured's defense expenses and costs, even when those expenses and costs bring the total amount to more than the explicit limitation on liability contained in Provisions 1 and 2 of each reinsurance certificate. Aetna claims that the "follow the fortunes" doctrine applies whenever the reinsured makes a reasonable settlement with the underlying insured. We reject this claim. We hold that the doctrine of "follow the fortunes" does not render the reinsurers liable in this case.

Aetna asserts that the third provision of each of the certificates contains a general "follow the fortunes" clause, typical of most reinsurance contracts. The doctrine of "follow the fortunes" has been defined as meaning that "the reinsurer will follow the fortunes or be placed in the position of the [insurer]." ... Basically, the doctrine burdens the reinsurer with those risks which the direct insurer bears under the direct insurer's policy covering the original insured.... GERATHEWOHL, 1 REINSURANCE PRINCIPLES AND PRACTICE 466 (1980).

The reinsurers do not dispute that they must follow Aetna's fortunes with respect to the Robins settlement up to the liability cap. Aetna, however, contends that the reinsurers are liable beyond the stated limits where, as here, the excess was for "reasonable" defense costs expended on settlement in "good faith" of a dispute arising from the underlying policy.

According to Aetna, that result is required by our decision in [prior case] *AIC* [*American Ins. Co. v. North American Co. for Property and Casualty Ins.*, 697 F.2d 79, 81 (2 Cir. 1982)]. There, the reinsurer agreed to assume part of the risk of damage awards assessed against the underlying insured. In one action, a jury awarded punitive damages against the insured. The underlying policy was ambiguous as to whether punitive damages were included. Rather than appeal, however, the insurer decided to settle in an amount that included part of the punitive damage award. The insurer then demanded from the reinsurer an amount that included a proportional amount of the punitive damage award. We held that, despite the ambiguity, punitive damages were not covered by the underlying policy. We declined to apply the "follow the fortunes" doctrine to hold the reinsurer liable. *AIC, supra*, at 81.

Although the result in *AIC* was in favor of the reinsurer, Aetna seizes on the following language in that opinion to support its contention here:

> "In some cases in which there is a genuine ambiguity over what a settlement covers, a 'follow the fortunes' clause may oblige a reinsurer to contribute to a settlement even though it might encompass excluded claims."

Assuming arguendo that there was such ambiguity in the Aetna-Robins policies, the quoted dictum in *AIC* does not render appellees liable. In that case, there was no question of a cap on liability in the reinsurance agreement, only with respect to the scope of coverage in the underlying policy. The amount in question was less than the cap. There is nothing in *AIC* (nor in any other case cited by Aetna), which leads to the conclusion that a "follow the fortunes" clause can render a reinsurer liable for an amount in excess of the bargained-for coverage.

To read the reinsurance certificates in this case as Aetna suggests—allowing the "follow the fortunes" clause to override the limitation on liability—would strip the limitation clause and other conditions of all meaning; the reinsurer would be obliged merely to reimburse the insurer for any and all funds paid. Such a reading would be contrary to the parties' express agreement and to the settled law of contract interpretation.

The "follow the fortunes" clauses in the certificates are structured so that they coexist with, rather than supplant, the liability cap. To construe the certificates otherwise would effectively eliminate the limitation on the reinsurers' liability to the stated amounts. *Calvert Fire Ins. Co. v. Yosemite Ins. Co.*, 573 F. Supp. 27, 29 (E.D.N.C. 1983) (reinsurers' liability followed the fortunes of insurer only within limits specified in reinsurance certificate).

We agree with the district court that "the limitation is to be a cap on all payments by the reinsurer." We hold that the district court correctly read the first two provisions of the reinsurance certificates to cap the reinsurers' liability, and that the "follow the fortunes" doctrine does not allow Aetna to recover defense costs beyond the express cap stated in the certificates.

We turn next to Aetna's contention that the phrase "in addition thereto," set forth in the fourth provision of each of the reinsurance certificates, indicates that liability for defense costs is separate from liability for the underlying losses sustained by Robins (i.e., Robins' direct liability to the Dalkon Shield claimants). According to Aetna, that phrase indicates that the monetary limitation on liability set forth in the first two provisions of the certificates caps only the reinsurers' liability for the underlying losses, not the reinsurers' liability for defense expenses and costs. We disagree.

We read the phrase "in addition thereto" merely to differentiate the obligations for losses and for expenses. The phrase in no way exempts defense costs from the overall monetary limitation in the certificate. This monetary limitation is a cap on all payments under the certificate. In our view, the "in addition thereto" provision merely outlines the different components of potential liability under the certificate. It does not indicate that either component is not within the overall limitation.

Aetna contends that the reinsurer's duty to indemnify the insurer is different and separate from the reinsurer's duty to defend. In support of this contention, it points to the statement in *Federal Ins. Co. v. Cablevision Systems Devel. Co.*, 662 F. Supp. 1537, 1539 (E.D.N.Y.), aff'd, 836 F.2d 54 (2 Cir. 1987), that an insurer's duty to defend is, in theory, "essentially limitless." That statement has no application to the instant case. Here, the limitation on liability provision capped the reinsurers' liability under the certificates. All other contractual language must be construed in light of that cap.

Likewise, Aetna's reliance on *Peerless Ins. Co. v. Inland Mutual Ins. Co.*, 251 F.2d 696 (4 Cir. 1958), is misplaced. In *Peerless* the reinsurer was held liable for an amount, agreed to in a settlement, in excess of the stated limit. The court in that case, however, found that the reinsurer played such a substantial role in the settlement of the underlying claim that it acted as a co-insurer. *Id.* at 703–04. In the instant case, by contrast, the reinsurers took no part in negotiations and never agreed to the settlement between Aetna and Robins.

We reject Aetna's contentions that the "follow the fortunes" doctrine, or the "in addition thereto" language in each reinsurance certificate, exempts defense costs from the clauses limiting the reinsurers' overall liability under the certificates. We hold that these costs are "subject to" the express cap on liability set forth in each certificate.

## *Notes and Questions*

1. Is the court being too hard on the reinsurer in the *Reliastar Life v. IOA* case? State as succinctly as you can the rationale for the *uberrimae fidei* doctrine. Is it persuasive? Has the modern information age made the doctrine less necessary than at the time of Edward Lloyd's Coffeehouse? *See generally* Stephen W. Thomas, Note, *Utmost Good Faith in Reinsurance: A Tradition in Need of Adjustment,* 41 Duke L.J. 1548 (1992).

2. Although the duty of utmost good faith certainly has teeth, the reinsurer cannot sleep on its rights vis-à-vis an insurer. *See Old Reliable Fire Ins. Co. v. Castle Reinsurance Co.,* 665 F.2d 239 (8th Cir. 1981) (notwithstanding *uberrimae fidei,* reinsurer presented with essentially correct information must make inquiry of insurer for further information if in doubt or if expecting to rely on its perceived implications of the information in order to avoid coverage for larger losses than anticipated).

3. In addition to protecting the reinsurer, the doctrine of utmost good faith, like the doctrine of good faith between insurer and policyholder, also may be seen as something of a two-way street that can provide protection to the insurer as well. *See, e.g., Unigard Sec. Ins. Co. v. North River Ins. Co.,* 4 F.3d 1049 (2d Cir. 1993) (ceding company has significant duty of disclosure and candor to reinsurer); *United Fire & Cas. Co. v. Arkwright Mut. Ins. Co.,* 53 F. Supp. 2d 632, 640 (S.D.N.Y. 1999) ("the burden is on the reinsured to volunteer all material facts").

4. Did the *Bellefonte* court strike the right balance between the limitations of the reinsurance contract and the terms and spirit of the follow-the-fortunes clause?

5. Other prominent cases involving these issues include *North River Ins. Co. v. CIGNA Reinsurance Co.,* 52 F.3d 1194 (3d Cir. 1995) (applying Ohio law as to insurance questions and New York law on reinsurance issues) (largely requiring reinsurers to follow fortunes of insurer over protest by reinsurers); *Unigard Sec. Ins. Co. v. North River Ins. Co.,* 4 F.3d 1049 (2d Cir. 1993) (following *Bellefonte*); *American Ins. Co. v. North American Co. for Property & Cas. Ins.,* 697 F.2d 79, 80–81 (2d Cir. 1982) (reinsurer not responsible for punitive damages portion of settlement where this was clearly excluded by reinsurance certificate); *Michigan Millers Mut. Ins. Co. v. North American Reinsurance Corp.,* 182 Mich. App. 410, 452 N.W.2d 841 (1990) (reinsurer not liable for payments below attachment point of excess insurance where excess insurer was the ceding company). *See* Stempel & Knutsen on Insurance Contracts § 17.03 for further discussion of follow-the-fortunes issues.

## [E] Duties and Relationship between the Insured and the Reinsurer

Reinsurance contracts are solely between an insurer and a reinsurer. The reinsurer contractually agrees to assume in whole or in part a risk undertaken by the original insurer. Thus, a reinsurance contract creates no contractual rights between the insured and the reinsurance company. However, a reinsurer may voluntarily assume liability to the original insured through a "cut through" clause in the reinsurance policy.

*Query*: Can any other contractual, third-party beneficiary, or successor relationship exist between the reinsurer and the original insured party?

Under a standard reinsurance contract, the initial insurer (also called the reinsured or the ceding company) retains its contractual relationship with the insured party, and handles all matters with the insured, absent any contrary provisions in the reinsurance agreement. In this normal situation, there would be no contractual privity or third-party beneficiary relationship between the original insured and the reinsurer.

But what happens when the language in a reinsurance contract provides that the reinsurer agrees "to assume and carry out directly with the policyholder any of the policy obligations of the ceding insurer"? In such a case, an insured was found to have a legal cause of action against the reinsurer. *See, e.g., Arrow Trucking Co. v. Continental Ins. Co.*, 465 So. 2d 691 (La. 1985).

*Query*: Should an original insured have a direct cause of action against the reinsurer when the original insurer was insolvent and when the reinsurance agreement between the insurer and the reinsurer was replete with the word "coinsurance" to describe the duties undertaken by the reinsurer? *See Estate of Osborn v. Gerling Global Life Ins. Co.*, 529 So. 2d 169 (Miss. 1988).

### PROBLEM SEVEN

Driver was insured through an automobile liability insurance policy issued by InsureCo. InsureCo entered into a reinsurance contract with Reinsurer to assume a certain portion of InsureCo's risk regarding Driver's policy.

The reinsurance contract stated in part that "[s]ettlement of claims involving this reinsurance shall not be made without the consent of Reinsurer, except in those instances where an immediate decision is necessary and it is impracticable to obtain the consent of Reinsurer."

Driver, acting negligently, was involved in an automobile accident with Plaintiff, who sustained serious and permanent injuries. InsureCo refused an offer to settle within its $50,000 policy limits, and it failed to inform Reinsurer of Driver's settlement offer. A jury verdict of $96,687.75 resulted. Plaintiff settled with Driver for $125,000 (the judgment plus pre-judgment interest plus agreed counsel fees that are recoverable pursuant to controlling state law), an amount that is reasonable, in return for a covenant not to execute against Driver and assignment of Driver's rights against InsureCo.

InsureCo became insolvent. Driver brought suit against Reinsurer based upon the argument that InsureCo acted as Reinsurer's agent, since Reinsurer, by virtue of the contract language cited above, had assumed control over any settlement proceedings.

• How should the court rule in this case?

## Additional Potential Reinsurer Liability to Policyholders

Although reinsurers may not be in strict contractual privity with policyholders, they may face bad faith liability where they step into the shoes of an insurer and act in bad faith or where they work in concert with an insurer in a manner that exhibits bad faith toward the policyholder. Similarly, a reinsurer may be liable in damages to policyholders if the reinsurer tortiously interferes with the insurer-policyholder relationship or induces bad faith by the insurer where the reinsurer unreasonably attempts to convince an insurer to refuse coverage, undervalue a claim, attempt to intimidate a policyholder into a low settlement, or other misconduct.

Many reinsurers would perhaps dispute this analysis, arguing that under the traditional rules of privity of contract, they are beyond the reach of the policyholder. Some reinsurers may even expect consultation by insurers and expect to have a voice regarding claims. However frequent reinsurer participation in claims decisions may be, it remains inconsistent with the basic premises of the insurer-policyholder relationship and the insurer-reinsurer relationship. Although it is correct that there is no contractual relationship between reinsurer and policyholder, the need for a reinsurer to stay outside the circle of policyholder and insurer follows as a natural corollary of the nature of reinsurance in relation to insurance. Consequently, reinsurers that "meddle" in an insurer's coverage and claims decisions may be liable to the extent the insurer is or would be liable to the policyholder for bad faith conduct.

Recall a key operating premise of reinsurance, as essentially "codified" through the follow-the-fortunes doctrine and express follow-the-fortunes language in reinsurance treaties and contracts. The assumption is that the insurer will make reasonable determinations regarding coverage and claims handling, including settlement of claims and litigation. After the insurer has settled, the matter of coverage liability is essentially over. According to longstanding custom and practice (often reflected in express contract language), the reinsurer is bound by the insurer's decisions, so long as those decisions are made in good faith. If an insurer pays a suspicious claim, the reinsurer cannot second-guess the insurer. Conversely, if the insurer spurns an early settlement offer but the plaintiff then recovers a large verdict, the reinsurer is also bound by the decisions of the insurer and their consequences. If a reinsurer thinks an insurer makes poor claims or coverage decisions, the reinsurer's remedy is not to contest those decisions in subsequent litigation but to cease doing business with insurers in which the reinsurer lacks confidence.

These are well-established norms of reinsurance. Only if the insurer's payment is palpably unreasonable, in bad faith or is for a loss clearly outside the scope of the policy can the reinsurer avoid the force of the follow-the-fortunes principle. The rationale of the doctrine is to prevent a second round of coverage litigation between insurer and reinsurer and to prevent either reinsurer or insurer from raising issues in their intramural dispute that may adversely affect underlying tort or coverage litigation. An additional value of the doctrine is that it discourages reinsurers from meddling in the insurer-policyholder relationship. The expectation is that insurer and policyholder will work together in connection with claims and that, after the matter is finalized, the reinsurer will follow the insurer's fortunes.

If a reinsurer interjects itself into the insurer-policyholder relationship, the reinsurer has not only undermined the basic premises of reinsurance and the follow-the-fortunes doctrine but has also interfered with the fiduciary-like relationship between insurer and policyholder. Consider this scenario: a policyholder's home or business burns down. The insurer concludes that the fire was intentionally set and must determine whether it was the work of local juvenile delinquents or policyholder arson. Normally, the insurer alone must decide what it believes was the cause of the loss and pay or deny the claim accordingly.

Consider what happens if the reinsurer inserts itself into the claims decision. The reinsurer may view the evidence as tilting toward the policyholder arson explanation rather than the vandalism explanation and correspondingly urge the insurer to deny the claim. If the arson evidence is so weak as to make denial unreasonable, the insurer has committed bad faith toward the policyholder. Logically, the reinsurer has also committed bad faith because it has been part of this unreasonable coverage denial.

Alternatively, the reinsurer may not be completely immersed in the sifting of evidence as to the cause of the loss but may intercede and strongly criticize the underwriting decisions of the insurer, perhaps suggesting that the policy should never have been issued. The reinsurer may even express concern about continuing to work with an insurer that it regards as a poor underwriter. The effect of such conduct by the reinsurer will not be lost on even the dullest insurer. The insurer will likely take the hint and attempt to display its resistance to claims disliked by the reinsurer and deny coverage or seek to pay as little as possible, regardless of the strength of the claim.

To the extent anything like this hypothetical scenario takes place, the reinsurer has acted improperly by interfering in the insurer-policyholder relationship. Where the reinsurer's meddling induces the insurer to act in bad faith, the reinsurer is logically responsible as well. At a minimum, the insurer has acted in bad faith simply by willingly permitting a third party to intrude into its near-fiduciary relationship with the policyholder. Whether one views this as sounding more in tortious interference with the insurer-policyholder contract or as bad faith because the reinsurer has elected to act as an insurer in connection with the claim, the effect is the same. To the extent the policyholder is treated in bad faith (through unreasonable decisions or unreasonable claims conduct), the reinsurer is at least partially at fault.

Although insurers of course prefer to have good relations with reinsurers, the insurer cannot validly permit its claims or coverage decisions to be determined by the reinsurer. The policyholder is the one to whom an insurer owes a duty of good faith. The insurer must make coverage decisions with an eye toward the policyholder's interests and fair treatment of the policyholder. Within that framework of giving at least equal consideration to the interests of the policyholder, the insurer must "call it as it sees it" (not as its reinsurers see it) regarding claims. An insurer violates its duties to the policyholder if it gives reinsurers power over the policyholder's claim. The insurer is required to make a good faith decision on each claim, giving equal consideration to the interests of the policyholder.

In addition, a court may find the reinsurer and the insurer to be in a "joint venture" regarding a claim or their operations and thereby consider the reinsurer and the insurer essentially one entity regarding operations, including any bad faith treatment of policyholders. In *Albert H. Wohlers & Co. v. Bartgis*, 114 Nev. 1249, 969 P.2d 949 (1998), one court held that an insurance intermediary (a general agent in the case but its rationale would apply to other types of agents, brokers, and reinsurers as well) can be liable on a bad faith claim or other insurer responsibility to the same extent as would the insurer if the intermediary and the insurer are in a "joint venture." In determining whether a joint venture exists, the court considered whether the intermediary (1) developed promotional material for the insurer; (2) issued policies; (3) billed premiums; (4) collected premiums; (5) adjusted claims; (6) paid claims; (7) assisted the insurer with development of the policy or insurance product line; (8) shared in the profits of the insurer; or (9) otherwise had a pecuniary interest in keeping claim costs down. *See* 114 Nev. 1249, 969 P.2d 949, 959 (1998).

The *Wohlers v. Bartgis* court did not comment explicitly on the relative strength of these factors or whether a specific number of factors must be shown to establish a joint venture. The logical reading of the opinion suggests that there is no rigid formula but that the existence of a critical mass of these factors establishes a joint venture. It also appears that profit-sharing or an economic incentive to suppress claim costs is the most important factor in determining whether an intermediary acts in a joint venture with an insurer. *See also Farr v. Transamerica Occidental Life Ins. Co.*, 145 Ariz. 1, 699 P.2d 376 (Ct. App. 1984). Applied to reinsurers, this list of factors strongly suggests that insurers and reinsurers are always engaged in a joint venture and become more closely linked if the reinsurer is involved in an insurer's claims decisions. Consequently, reinsurers subject to *Wohlers* or similar precedent undoubtedly face bad faith exposure when they become part of the claims adjustment process or have a joint economic self-interest in suppressing claim costs, and a reinsurer may face bad faith exposure when it aids and abets bad faith conduct by a primary insurer.

Unfortunately, some reinsurers and insurers appear to have forgotten the basic ground rules of the follow-the-fortunes doctrine and insurer duties to the policyholder. Some reinsurance contracts contain "control clauses ... intended to give more power and involvement to the reinsurer" regarding claims, "traditionally an area left exclusively to the ceding insurer." *See* Adam B. Leichtling & Lara M. Paredes, *Fundamental Concepts in Reinsurance in Latin American Countries,* 37 U. MIAMI INTER-AM. L. REV. 1, 24 (2005). Control clauses may: (1) "[r]equire the ceding insurer to inform the reinsurer of modifications to the underlying insurance contract and materialization of the risk"; (2) "[r]equire the ceding insurer to consult with or give the reinsurer final decisions regarding the adjustment of catastrophes and losses and selection of the adjuster or attorney"; or (3) "[g]ive the reinsurer the final decision on acceptance or rejection of a claim or the amount of covered loss." *See* Leichtling & Paredes, *supra,* at 24–25. Where a reinsurance policy or treaty contains this type of "control" language, the reinsurer is obviously in a joint venture with the insurer under the *Wohlers v. Bartgis* analysis and has, in essence, codified a regime of bad faith toward the policyholder.

# Index

References are to sections.

**Grace Periods**

## H

**Health Insurance**

**History and Fundamental Concepts of Insurance**